European Marketing Data and Statistics

European Marketing Data and Statistics

2010

45th edition

Euromonitor International Plc, 60-61 Britton Street, London EC1M 5UX

European Marketing Data and Statistics 2010

First published 1964
Forty-fifth edition
ISBN 978-1-84264--511-6
Published by:

Western and Southern Europe
Euromonitor International - Head Office
60-61 Britton Street, London, EC1M 5UX, United Kingdom
Tel: +44 (0) 20 7251 8024
Fax: +44 (0) 20 7608 3149
email: info@euromonitor.com

North America
Euromonitor International
224 South Michigan Avenue
Suite 1500, Chicago, IL 60604, USA
Tel: + 1 312 922 1115
Fax: +1 312 922 1157
email: insight@euromonitorintl.com

Latin America
Euromonitor International
Avenida Apoquindo 3600, 5th Floor, Las Condes
Santiago C.P. 7550108, Chile
+56 02 7992426
+56 02 4332226

Asia Pacific and Australasia
Euromonitor International
3 Lim Teck Kim Road
#08-01 Singapore Technologies Building, Singapore 088934
Tel: +65 6429 0590
Fax: +65 6324 1855
email: info@euromonitor.com.sg

China
Euromonitor International
Level 21 Unit 06, Tian An Center
No. 338 Nanjing Road (West), Shanghai 200003, China
Tel: +86 21 6372 6288
Fax: +86 21 6372 6289
email: info@euromonitor.com.cn

Middle East and North Africa
Euromonitor International
Building 5E, Block A, office 321, Dubai Airport Free Zone
P.O. Box 54709, Dubai, U.A.E.
Tel: +971 4 609 1340
Fax: +971 4 609 1343
email: info-mena@euromonitor.com

Central and South Africa
Euromonitor International
The Forum, Unit GS04, 6473 Northbank Lane, Century City
Cape Town, 7441, Republic of South Africa
Tel: +27 21 552 0037
Fax: +27 21 552 7071
email: info-africa@euromonitor.com

Central and Eastern Europe
Euromonitor International
Jogailos Street 4, Vilnius, LT-01116, Lithuania
Tel: +370 5 243 1577
Fax: +370 5 243 1599
email: info@euromonitor.lt

Website
Website: http://www.euromonitor.com

Euromonitor International is a member of the Data Publishers Association and the European Association of Directory Publishers

Summary of contents

Table of contents

Section Twenty-two   Retailing 447

Section Twenty-three   Travel and Tourism 459

Section Twenty-four   Marketing Geography 473

Foreword and Guide

Foreword

European Marketing Data and Statistics 2010 is a compendium of statistical information on the countries of Western and Eastern Europe. Published annually, it provides a wealth of detailed and up-to-date statistical information relevant to pan-European market planning. The information is regularly updated and held on an international database of market information comprising 23 subject areas.

Published annually since the late 1960s, **European Marketing Data and Statistics**, or EMDAS, is now in its 45th edition. All data sections have been thoroughly revised for this new edition.

The data are presented in table form and a number of extrapolated tables have been included. The data coverage includes a considerable number of long-term time-series (dating back to 1980 as available) which permit the analysis of socio-economic trends over a longer time span as a basis for forecasting. The inclusion of figures from the most recent complete year (in this edition 2008) for key parameters ensures that up-to-date information is available for analysis. Quarterly datasets cover 2007, 2008 and the first half of 2009 where available, whilst monthly datasets cover the latest 12 months available.

In addition to reporting on major European countries, the country coverage also includes smaller European countries and principalities. Although the availability of statistical information on these countries is limited and they are minor markets, it assists in building up a more comprehensive picture of the total European market and will be of interest to academic users.

The handbook contains a full alphabetical index, and we have included a section summarising the major sources of pan-regional and international information which have been used in the compilation of data. Readers requiring detailed guidance on sources of information are referred to the World Directory of Business Information Web Sites (Euromonitor International, 2007), the World Directory of Trade and Business Journals (Euromonitor International, 2007), the World Directory of Trade and Business Associations (Euromonitor International, 2007), the World Directory of Non-Official Statistical Sources (Euromonitor International, 2007), and the World Directory of Business Information Libraries (Euromonitor International, 2007) for more comprehensive listings.

A companion volume of marketing data, International Marketing Data and Statistics (IMDAS) is also available. Country coverage in IMDAS 2010 provides a comprehensive worldwide context, and data are provided in the same format for ease of comparison with the European figures presented here. The data included in both volumes are also accessible as part of the Global Marketing Information Database (GMID) on the web.

User comments are welcomed concerning the databases in **European Marketing Data and Statistics**. Also, whilst the editors have made every effort to ensure accuracy Euromonitor International cannot accept responsibility for any errors which may have occurred.

Guide to Using the Handbook

Scope of the Handbook

European Marketing Data and Statistics (EMDAS) is a statistical yearbook of business and marketing information, featuring over 500 pages of up-to-date and detailed marketing statistics on 23 principal subject areas. These statistics are stored on a database of international marketing information and are regularly updated by Euromonitor International's research team.

The sections of EMDAS cover a wide variety of marketing topics, ranging from socio-economic trends and background information through to key consumer marketing parameters. Data covering international trade, transport, industrial output and agricultural resources are included, as well as sections on service industries such as tourism and retailing.

In EMDAS 2010, each statistical tabulation presents pan-European comparative information, either in the form of time-series from 1980 to 2008 or 2009, or with single-year data for the latest year available. All the countries are listed down the left-hand column, presented in two geographical entities (Western and Eastern Europe). Where appropriate, regional subtotals are included.

Where data is in value form, units have been generally left in national currencies. However the spreadsheets on which the data is stored facilitate calculations in US dollars. These are calculated only for the latest year available (usually 2008) as fluctuations in exchange rates and contrasts in rates of inflation render year-on-year conversions meaningless.

In addition, calculations have been made where deemed appropriate to show growth rates over a defined period, and per capita data. These permit easy cross-comparisons between countries, regions and markets.

Using EMDAS 2010 is easy. Whatever topic is of interest, you simply look up the tables (using the contents or index) and the table will show the relevant data for all countries. The heading shows the relevant section, title summary and title of the table, and unit. A guide to the sources used in the compilation of the data appears at the foot of the table, while any relevant notes are gathered together at the end of each section.

The aim of EMDAS is to locate in one handbook the essential statistical information relevant to European market planning. The handbook will save the busy marketeer or researcher hours of time trawling through statistics from many sources and provides a wealth of hard-to-get information drawn from the many reports and studies compiled by Euromonitor International over the last 2-3 years - many based on trade interviews and original extrapolations. Business users and librarians will find the handbook especially useful.

Subject Coverage

EMDAS 2010 is presented in 24 separate sections or "databases" which have all been specially compiled by Euromonitor International. The subjects have been selected as those most appropriate for strategic planning and European market analysis, covering both background marketing parameters and detailed consumer market information. The 24 databases are discussed below.

1 Advertising

This section includes a range of data on advertising expenditure trends, organised into seven tables.

2 Agricultural Resources and Output

This section presents key data on land use and output of various agricultural and forestry products. There are 11 tables on the database, mostly including figures for 2008.

3 Automotives and Transport

This 35-table database covers the circulation, manufacture and sales of cars, commercial vehicles and two-wheelers, including tables on automotive fuel prices; it also covers major movements in terms of the road, rail, air and shipping transport sectors. Five new tables have been added to this section for this edition. Quarterly and/or monthly datasets are included in this edition for three indicators.

4 Banking and Finance

This section features tabulations mainly showing data from 1980-2008 and covering bank assets, liabilities, claims and interest rates, as well as information on credit card holders and accepting outlets. Quarterly datasets are available for four indicators.

5 Consumer Expenditure

The presentation of this section comprises total consumer spending, a consolidated breakdown by product sector, and a series of tables analysing each major consumer sector. New 2008 data have been included and all the data are presented in 19-year trends with growth rates and 2008 dollar comparisons.

6 Consumer Market Sizes

Per capita consumption and retail market sizes are included in 19 tables for 2008. For the first time in this edition, data has been included for DIY, gardening, housewares and home furnishings. The information is drawn from Euromonitor International's market information database, which forms the basis for the publication Consumer Western Europe (25th edition, Euromonitor International, 2009), and its companion title Consumer Eastern Europe (17th edition, Euromonitor International, 2009).

7 Consumer Prices and Costs

Trends in consumer prices and selected European living costs are included in 16 tables of data. Quarterly and monthly consumer price indices are included in EMDAS 2010.

8 Economic Indicators

This database features tables of key economic data, again with the emphasis on time-series data. All the main economic indicators are covered, including GDP, GNP, inflation, money supply, public and private consumption, government finance and exchange rates. Eleven new tables are featured in this edition for the first time. Quarterly and/or monthly datasets are included for ten economic indicators.

9 Education

A range of educational statistics are included in this seven-table section, which features three brand new tables.

10 Energy Resources and Output

This section consists of 22 tables on energy supply and demand. Coverage extends to household energy consumption with several tables containing data for more than 20 years. Five new tables have been included in this edition for the first time. Quarterly and monthly datasets are available for two indicators.

11 Environmental Data

This section includes tables covering various environmental factors. Coverage includes pollution, recycling, waste generation, protected areas and threatened species.

12 External Trade

This section includes 17 tables which give a cohesive and structured trade overview covering total imports and exports and external trade breakdowns by origin, destination and commodity. Quarterly and monthly datasets feature for total imports, total exports and trade balance.

13 Health

This database comprises eleven tables covering major health indicators (including a table on the number of reported AIDS cases). For the first time in this edition new datasets have been added looking at trends in the obese population, and numbers of healthcare professionals.

14 Home Ownership

This section includes comparative data on housing stock and new dwellings completed, as well as brand new tables on numbers of households by tenure and type of dwelling.

15 Household Profiles

This section comprises 12 tables of comparative statistics on households. Data on household composition are included, as well as possession of household durables.

16 Income and Deductions

This section includes six tables covering gross and disposable income parameters. Two new tables covering savings have been added to this edition.

17 Industry

This section provides key industrial indices for a 29-year period and includes output tables covering major industrial materials. Quarterly and monthly datasets are now included for general industrial production, manufacturing production and mining production indices.

18 IT and Telecommunications

This section features information on a number of communications and information technology topics including Internet statistics. Four new tables have been included in this edition.

19 Labour

This database covers the key employment indicators including numbers employed, unemployed and hours of work. The structure of the economically active population by age group and status is included for latest years available, along with a breakdown of the total workforce into industry sectors. Quarterly and/or monthly datasets are included for seven indicators.

20 Media and Leisure

This section includes eight tables covering available data on cinema, newspapers, and TV households. For the first time in this edition, tables have been included covering cable TV, satellite TV, and digital satellite pay-TV.

21 Population

This database features statistical compilations covering population trends, vital statistics, urbanisation, demographic analysis by age and sex, and population forecasts. Much of the data included are from 1980 to the latest year, forming a basis for forecasting and projections. New parameters included for the first time are pensioners, and population by marital status and educational attainment. Quarterly and monthly datasets are available for birth rates and death rates.

22 Retailing

This section has drawn on Euromonitor International's extensive European retail research in recent years, with tables covering retail sales and channels and breakdowns for different retail sectors.

23 Travel and Tourism

This database consists of 13 tabulations covering tourism values and movements, tourist accommodation and its usage, reflecting holidaying habits across Europe.

24 Marketing Geography

This database includes a summary of data (population, area, currency, location, language, religion, main industries, economic and political structure, energy resources, heads of state and of government and last election results) for each country covered.

Data Coverage

Each of the statistical compilations is presented in one of five data periods:

(1) A 29-year trend table from 1980-2008, with data for each country drawn from the same consistent source. Some intermediary years have been excluded for reasons of space.

(2) A different period trend, eg 1990-2008 (19-year trend) or a recent period.

(3) Latest year available, with the years differing between countries. These are used where the information is drawn from occasional studies, eg a census, or where statistical offices vary in the speed of publishing statistics.

(4) A single year, eg 2008, where space does not permit trends or where an interactive range of information is provided (eg imports by origin, usage of GDP, etc).

(5) Quarterly datasets cover 2007, 2008 and the first half of 2009 where available, whilst monthly datasets are for the latest 12 months available.

The statistics in this volume are as available during the compilation period (June-October 2009). Figures for 2008 (in some cases provisional or estimated) have been included where possible. Various one-off surveys cover earlier years only.

Country Coverage

This edition of EMDAS includes a total of 44 countries in both Western and Eastern Europe. These are grouped into two geographic entities, as follows:

Western Europe

Austria	Belgium
Cyprus	Denmark
Finland	France
Germany	Gibraltar
Greece	Iceland
Ireland	Italy
Liechtenstein	Luxembourg
Malta	Monaco
Netherlands	Norway
Portugal	Spain
Sweden	Switzerland
Turkey	United Kingdom

Eastern Europe

Albania	Belarus
Bosnia-Herzegovina	Bulgaria
Croatia	Czech Republic
Estonia	Georgia
Hungary	Latvia
Lithuania	Macedonia
Moldova	Poland
Romania	Russia
Serbia and Montenegro	Slovakia
Slovenia	Ukraine

Country Note

Data for Germany prior to 1991 refer to the former East and West Germany, for the Czech Republic data prior to 1993 refer to the former Czechoslovakia, and for Serbia and Montenegro data prior to 1992 refer to the former Yugoslavia.

Sources

European Marketing Data and Statistics is based on an extensive and on-going programme of research into European markets and industries. A Europe-wide network of market analysts and researchers work to pull together available data on socio-economic patterns, market conditions and trends, living standards and background information relevant to business, export and market planning.

The principal sources used in the compilation of EMDAS are as follows:

— International and European organisations, such as the United Nations, OECD, and the International Monetary Fund.

— National statistical offices and central banks in each country.

— Pan-European and national trade and industry associations.

— Industry study groups and unofficial research publishers.

— Euromonitor International's own research publications, including one-off reports and statistical compilations.

— Original research specially commissioned for the handbook, including consumer research, trade interviews and retail surveys.

A guide to the main sources used in the compilation of each table is included at the foot of each table. For reasons of space the main sources are only briefly cited; in some cases, many different reports and publications are used in the preparation of just one table. For example, we may have extracted data from publications by the national statistical offices for all the countries covered in order to compile one table. In other cases, statistical compilations are from secondary sources, which have in turn used many different sources.

A brief guide to the main sources used in each of the databases follows.

1 Advertising

Drawn from data published by the World Association of Newspapers and various other media study groups, advertising associations and agents in various countries.

2 Agricultural Resources and Output

Mainly based on the publications and databases of the Food and Agricultural Organisation of the United Nations (FAO).

3 Automotives and Transport

Automotives data are drawn from national statistics, and the publications of various motor trades organisations. Transport statistics are based on national statistics and on various UN publications; the International Civil Aviation Organisation; the International Road Federation and Lloyd's Register of Shipping.

4 Banking and Finance

The major source of comparative financial data is the IMF's International Financial Statistics.

5 Consumer Expenditure

Drawn from the OECD and the national accounts of each country (generally published by the national statistical offices). Euromonitor International estimates have been used to reach levels of consolidation.

6 Consumer Market Sizes

Drawn from Euromonitor International's consumer market database; primary sources include trade associations and interviews with industry leaders in all countries.

7 Consumer Prices and Costs

Mainly from national statistics, the International Monetary Fund and the OECD; living costs from the International Labour Organisation.

8 Economic Indicators

The principal international sources are the OECD and the International Monetary Fund (IMF). National statistical offices (yearbooks, national accounts) and economic bulletins by leading banks are also used.

9 Education

The key international source is UNESCO with data from national statistical offices incorporated as available.

10 Energy Resources and Output

This compilation draws mainly on data from BP, the UN and the OECD/IEA, national statistics and various industry publications.

11 Environmental Data

Drawn largely from the OECD, United Nations, and the World Resources Institute, as well as national statistics.

12 External Trade

The IMF, UN and OECD track external trade flows in some detail. National statistical yearbooks are also utilised.

13 Health

Compiled from various publications from national statistical offices, OECD and UN publications and incorporating Euromonitor International estimates and calculations.

14 Home Ownership

Data are compiled from national statistical offices of each country.

15 Household Profiles

Compiled from various publications from national statistical offices, and from Eurostat and UN publications, and incorporating Euromonitor International estimates and calculations.

16 Income and Deductions

Data from national statistical offices of each country. Specific sources include Household Budget Surveys and National Accounts. Euromonitor International estimates have been used.

17 Industry

Mainly drawn from UN and OECD publications, and from national statistics. Various industry sectors are covered by associations as stated.

18 IT and Telecommunications

Mainly based on national statistics and UN data, particularly the publications of the International Telecommunications Union (ITU), and incorporating some data from the World Bank.

19 Labour

In addition to national statistics, the primary international source is the International Labour Organisation, which publishes both a statistical yearbook and quarterly bulletins.

20 Media and Leisure

Mainly drawn from the UN, UNESCO, the Council of Europe and national statistical offices.

21 *Population*
Drawn mainly from the statistical yearbooks of the national statistical offices supplemented with population data and forecasts from the UN, Eurostat and the Council of Europe.

22 *Retailing*
Drawn from a wide number of Euromonitor International's own surveys and market reports on European retailing, including Retail Trade International (Euromonitor International 2009), and also original research. Primary sources include retail trade censuses (various countries) by national statistical offices, retail trade associations, major retailers etc.

23 *Travel and Tourism*
A compilation sourced from the World Tourism Organisation and Euromonitor International's own research.

24 *Marketing Geography*
Information mainly drawn from the business press, data from the yearbooks of the national statistical offices and various informal studies on the countries covered.

List of Abbreviations

BLEU	Belgo-Luxembourg Economic Union
EFMA	European Financial Management and Marketing Association
EFTA	European Free Trade Association
EU	European Union
FAO	Food and Agriculture Organisation of the United Nations
FT	Financial Times
IAA	International Advertising Association
IATA	International Air Transport Association
IBRD	International Bank for Reconstruction and Development (World Bank)
ICAO	International Civil Aviation Organisation
IEA	International Energy Authority
ILO	International Labour Organisation
IMF	International Monetary Fund
IMMA	International Motorcycle Manufacturers' Association
IRF	International Road Federation
ITU	International Telecommunication Union (a UN agency)
OECD	Organisation for Economic Co-operation and Development
SMMT	Society of Motor Manufacturers and Traders
UN	United Nations
UN ECE	United Nations Economic Commission for Europe
UNESCO	United Nations Educational, Scientific and Cultural Organisation
WHO	World Health Organisation
WTO	World Tourism Organisation
EAP	Economically active population
GDP	Gross domestic product
GNP	Gross national product
LPG	Liquefied petroleum gases
NGL	Natural gas liquids
SITC	Standard International Trade Classification
'000	thousand
gWh	gigawatt-hours
ha	hectare
hl	hectolitre
kg	kilogramme
km	kilometre
km2	square kilometre
kWh	kilowatt-hours
m2	square metre
m3	cubic metre
mn	million
MTOE	million tonnes of oil equivalent
MW	megawatts
R/P	reserves/production
TJ	terajoules
0	denotes less than 0.5 where no fraction given

1 SLOVENIA
2 CROATIA
3 BOSNIA-HERZEGOVINA
4 SERBIA
4a Vojvodina
4b Kosovo
5 MONTENEGRO
6 MACEDONIA

Section One

Advertising

Advertising Statistics

Table 1.1

Advertising Expenditure by Medium 2008

US$ million

	Television	Radio	Print	Cinema	Outdoor	Online	Total
Western Europe							
Austria	876.7	249.6	2,098.5	24.5	284.4	77.3	3,611.2
Belgium	1,735.7	580.9	2,240.6	47.6	366.9	157.8	5,129.4
Cyprus	692.9	37.0	70.7				800.5
Denmark	553.8	57.7	1,522.1	10.8	87.8	541.7	2,773.9
Finland	390.7	69.7	1,349.8	0.7	52.3	98.6	1,961.9
France	6,519.4	1,396.9	6,489.8	215.3	2,133.5	1,281.4	18,036.3
Germany	6,384.5	1,033.5	16,376.1	133.8	1,210.4	1,019.4	26,157.7
Gibraltar							
Greece	1,071.1	149.5	2,176.0	26.3	515.9		3,938.8
Iceland	43.9		121.9	0.2	3.0		169.1
Ireland	575.3	216.1	1,995.4	15.8	233.1	54.5	3,090.2
Italy	6,862.3	910.8	4,436.3	97.1	460.0	400.9	13,167.5
Liechtenstein							
Luxembourg	15.4	31.5	148.2	1.8	5.5		202.4
Malta							
Monaco							
Netherlands	1,246.6	399.5	3,390.6	146.9	279.9	290.2	5,753.7
Norway	1,116.9	193.7	2,307.5	34.4	190.0	817.7	4,660.1
Portugal	746.4	73.2	318.4	7.9	172.0	12.7	1,330.6
Spain	5,217.8	1,010.5	3,865.7	58.5	883.8	652.3	11,688.6
Sweden	665.3	85.6	1,680.2	12.6	171.2	323.2	2,938.0
Switzerland	913.4	128.1	2,126.6	46.7	415.2	62.0	3,692.1
Turkey	1,487.6	98.7	958.8	33.1	174.2	34.5	2,787.0
United Kingdom	5,986.8	857.3	9,952.4	294.9	1,568.9	4,792.1	23,452.4
Eastern Europe							
Albania							
Belarus							
Bosnia-Herzegovina							
Bulgaria	470.9	16.1	154.0		80.9	12.4	734.3
Croatia	725.7	42.4	293.5		69.1	2.9	1,133.7
Czech Republic	1,653.5	171.7	1,319.2	14.4	176.9	172.6	3,508.2
Estonia	42.3	11.3	83.3		9.7	8.8	155.4
Georgia							
Hungary	2,108.9	250.8	683.8	7.4	279.5	90.8	3,421.1
Latvia	70.0	22.7	73.8	1.2	18.9	10.3	196.9
Lithuania	395.0	11.9	107.5	0.6	27.8	7.8	550.5
Macedonia							
Moldova							
Poland	1,403.0	219.9	709.3	28.5	225.1	132.3	2,718.0
Romania	385.2	46.0	113.4	4.5	55.6	9.9	614.6
Russia	4,775.8	478.4	2,220.1	96.4	1,724.5	169.0	9,464.2
Slovakia	1,740.1	92.9	228.7	1.1	73.0	18.1	2,154.0
Slovenia	298.6	31.8	224.5	1.5	61.3	16.4	634.1
Ukraine	544.7	50.9	254.5	20.4	224.0	22.4	1,116.9

Source: *Euromonitor International from World Association of Newspapers/Jupiter Research*

Advertising Statistics

Table 1.2

TV Adspend 1985-2008
Million units of national currency

	1985	1990	1995	2000	2003	2004	2005	2006	2007	2008	US$ million 2008
Western Europe											
Austria	152	240	270	479	463	497	508	545	570	596	876.7
Belgium	150	234	393	782	945	1,004	982	1,071	1,124	1,179	1,735.7
Cyprus	2	3	16	131	238	256	305	349	423	471	692.9
Denmark	240	612	1,510	1,823	1,927	2,125	2,254	2,471	2,636	2,823	553.8
Finland	75	127	161	213	207	227	231	243	254	266	390.7
France	1,773	1,958	2,111	3,046	3,744	3,998	4,028	4,209	4,306	4,430	6,519.4
Germany	814	1,642	3,420	4,709	3,811	3,860	3,930	4,114	4,240	4,338	6,384.5
Gibraltar											
Greece	53	200	837	676	638	684	693	705	716	728	1,071.1
Iceland				2,823	2,972	3,220	3,346	3,485	3,575	3,865	43.9
Ireland	33	51	112	200	195	236	287	326	357	391	575.3
Italy	2,360	2,864	2,595	4,134	4,224	4,647	4,808	4,736	4,646	4,663	6,862.3
Liechtenstein											
Luxembourg	3	4	6	8	9	11	11	11	10	10	15.4
Malta											
Monaco											
Netherlands	142	271	483	783	746	757	779	810	829	847	1,246.6
Norway	9	137	2,333	4,630	4,916	5,196	5,696	5,923	6,100	6,299	1,116.9
Portugal	45	100	216	519	464	504	517	512	504	507	746.4
Spain	1,833	1,696	1,323	2,311	2,317	2,675	2,951	3,181	3,373	3,545	5,217.8
Sweden	25	324	2,373	3,959	3,749	4,143	4,546	4,466	4,386	4,385	665.3
Switzerland	88	220	339	520	533	737	810	889	948	989	913.4
Turkey	0	1	12	285	693	957	1,140	1,442	1,669	1,936	1,487.6
United Kingdom	1,088	1,548	2,267	3,327	3,173	3,392	3,455	3,282	3,249	3,257	5,986.8
Eastern Europe											
Albania											
Belarus											
Bosnia-Herzegovina											
Bulgaria	2	2	2	108	261	325	413	477	542	630	470.9
Croatia					1,801	1,842	2,046	2,810	3,218	3,581	725.7
Czech Republic	876	1,382	3,772	14,516	16,869	18,153	21,350	23,681	25,745	28,228	1,653.5
Estonia	3	22	65	155	232	254	310	363	403	453	42.3
Georgia											
Hungary	557	3,719	18,826	129,605	242,570	286,106	331,203	347,080	355,789	362,962	2,108.9
Latvia	2	1	5	10	14	17	22	27	31	34	70.0
Lithuania		2	16	74	606	606	777	837	878	931	395.0
Macedonia											
Moldova											
Poland	32	150	808	4,452	6,600	6,861	2,603	3,010	3,209	3,380	1,403.0
Romania			8	165	341	428	554	749	872	970	385.2
Russia			938	7,595	38,068	48,994	65,900	85,900	100,395	118,691	4,775.8
Slovakia			58	136	286	444	583	739	954	1,182	1,740.1
Slovenia	3	9	29	144	159	191	193	195	197	203	298.6
Ukraine					679	851	1,279	1,827	2,271	2,869	544.7

Source: *Euromonitor International from World Association of Newspapers*

Table 1.3

Radio Adspend 1985-2008
Million units of national currency

	1985	1990	1995	2000	2003	2004	2005	2006	2007	2008	US$ million 2008
Western Europe											
Austria	94	126	136	158	154	171	172	170	169	170	249.6
Belgium	21	48	100	186	229	253	290	327	357	395	580.9
Cyprus	2	2	6	7	14	14	17	19	22	25	37.0
Denmark	34	81	165	213	216	211	280	283	287	294	57.7
Finland	55	43	28	38	48	48	47	47	47	47	69.7
France	304	422	579	715	921	971	986	1,001	951	949	1,396.9
Germany	295	425	608	733	579	619	664	680	691	702	1,033.5
Gibraltar											
Greece	5	20	70	71	76	91	94	96	99	102	149.5
Iceland											
Ireland	13	20	33	55	87	91	106	124	135	147	216.1
Italy	238	217	201	454	440	529	534	576	600	619	910.8
Liechtenstein											
Luxembourg	5	7	9	12	18	20	20	21	21	21	31.5
Malta											
Monaco											
Netherlands	16	45	111	235	245	250	253	262	267	271	399.5
Norway	177	177	403	604	698	941	1,141	1,124	1,096	1,092	193.7
Portugal	96	43	25	62	54	57	56	52	51	50	73.2
Spain	2,139	899	346	502	508	540	610	637	661	687	1,010.5
Sweden		3	234	592	491	515	606	576	567	564	85.6
Switzerland	38	59	100	139	127	129	135	136	137	139	128.1
Turkey	0	0	2	47	60	75	80	101	113	128	98.7
United Kingdom	26	78	230	455	447	463	443	458	461	466	857.3
Eastern Europe											
Albania											
Belarus											
Bosnia-Herzegovina											
Bulgaria	1	1	3	6	8	20	25	22	21	21	16.1
Croatia					183	185	187	194	202	209	42.4
Czech Republic	262	413	635	1,050	2,169	2,157	2,398	2,640	2,783	2,932	171.7
Estonia		2	22	76	81	87	90	105	112	121	11.3
Georgia											
Hungary	140	774	4,187	12,042	15,929	26,514	26,819	33,764	39,169	43,166	250.8
Latvia			1	5	5	6	7	9	10	11	22.7
Lithuania			4	10	20	20	24	26	27	28	11.9
Macedonia											
Moldova											
Poland	6	22	123	544	872	1,043	435	482	508	530	219.9
Romania			1	10	22	40	59	80	97	116	46.0
Russia			151	1,266	4,759	5,764	8,500	9,500	10,554	11,891	478.4
Slovakia			9	14	27	37	45	49	56	63	92.9
Slovenia	9	10	13	21	10	9	18	19	20	22	31.8
Ukraine					42	73	104	141	198	268	50.9

Source: *Euromonitor International from World Association of Newspapers*

Advertising Statistics

Table 1.4

Print Adspend 1985-2008

Million units of national currency

	1985	1990	1995	2000	2003	2004	2005	2006	2007	2008	US$ million 2008
Western Europe											
Austria	180	403	671	1,134	1,139	1,186	1,255	1,320	1,375	1,426	2,098.5
Belgium	319	399	479	652	743	813	872	1,163	1,338	1,522	2,240.6
Cyprus	2	3	6	23	27	30	33	37	44	48	70.7
Denmark	5,481	4,967	5,478	5,965	5,325	5,667	6,180	6,767	7,204	7,760	1,522.1
Finland	447	583	556	828	774	817	837	859	885	917	1,349.8
France	3,629	2,695	3,274	4,587	4,291	4,381	4,430	4,506	4,396	4,410	6,489.8
Germany	8,756	9,920	12,037	13,476	10,473	10,573	10,550	10,836	10,987	11,127	16,376.1
Gibraltar											
Greece	87	148	292	823	855	1,013	1,139	1,243	1,361	1,479	2,176.0
Iceland				5,395	7,006	8,080	8,696	9,229	9,724	10,722	121.9
Ireland	99	108	175	446	763	927	926	1,102	1,243	1,356	1,995.4
Italy	3,108	2,069	1,792	2,976	2,681	2,711	2,783	2,882	2,943	3,014	4,436.3
Liechtenstein											
Luxembourg	27	34	46	57	87	89	92	95	97	101	148.2
Malta											
Monaco											
Netherlands	1,313	1,475	1,793	2,721	2,293	2,211	2,212	2,273	2,279	2,304	3,390.6
Norway	2,777	2,777	4,757	7,105	8,705	9,962	11,104	11,922	12,486	13,014	2,307.5
Portugal	221	150	134	280	214	217	218	215	215	216	318.4
Spain	4,302	2,940	1,677	2,427	2,097	2,248	2,341	2,479	2,554	2,627	3,865.7
Sweden	9,040	8,788	9,751	11,952	10,008	10,556	11,263	11,199	11,067	11,074	1,680.2
Switzerland	2,653	2,600	2,569	3,033	2,302	1,901	1,952	2,136	2,215	2,303	2,126.6
Turkey	0	0	13	272	472	682	890	1,020	1,127	1,248	958.8
United Kingdom	2,595	3,163	4,103	5,987	5,692	5,957	5,778	5,547	5,450	5,414	9,952.4
Eastern Europe											
Albania											
Belarus											
Bosnia-Herzegovina											
Bulgaria		1	1	54	97	108	138	159	178	206	154.0
Croatia					810	779	930	1,031	1,315	1,449	293.5
Czech Republic	199	973	3,698	11,309	13,760	15,535	16,855	19,151	20,785	22,521	1,319.2
Estonia	2	17	180	400	510	556	638	737	806	891	83.3
Georgia											
Hungary	2,169	6,626	21,732	64,682	88,104	98,050	106,208	110,735	114,507	117,693	683.8
Latvia	1	1	8	13	20	22	25	30	33	35	73.8
Lithuania		2	22	87	211	210	222	235	242	253	107.5
Macedonia											
Moldova											
Poland	19	80	428	2,247	2,964	3,646	1,543	1,593	1,650	1,709	709.3
Romania			2	67	123	202	198	231	264	286	113.4
Russia			1,364	9,564	28,705	34,584	39,300	44,600	49,417	55,176	2,220.1
Slovakia			21	41	78	97	112	123	140	155	228.7
Slovenia	16	23	36	70	79	97	107	124	138	153	224.5
Ukraine					318	418	684	924	1,096	1,341	254.5

Source: *Euromonitor International from World Association of Newspapers*

Advertising Statistics

Table 1.5

Cinema Adspend 1985-2008
Million units of national currency

	1985	1990	1995	2000	2003	2004	2005	2006	2007	2008	US$ million 2008
Western Europe											
Austria	3	4	6	11	11	10	14	15	16	17	24.5
Belgium	10	10	17	25	25	25	29	30	31	32	47.6
Cyprus											
Denmark	4	23	57	46	55	51	57	55	55	55	10.8
Finland	2	1	1	2	2	2	2	1	1	0	0.7
France	67	58	46	81	100	103	120	126	138	146	215.3
Germany	65	102	160	175	161	147	132	117	104	91	133.8
Gibraltar											
Greece	2	2	2	13	14	14	15	16	17	18	26.3
Iceland				100	31	27	23	21	19	19	0.2
Ireland	1	1	4	6	9	10	9	10	10	11	15.8
Italy	12	16	17	50	70	76	76	70	67	66	97.1
Liechtenstein											
Luxembourg			1	1	1	1	1	1	1	1	1.8
Malta											
Monaco											
Netherlands	9	9	11	13	7	6	7	55	78	100	146.9
Norway	60	60	73	124	143	147	162	173	182	194	34.4
Portugal				6	7	7	7	6	6	5	7.9
Spain	91	57	29	55	48	41	43	41	40	40	58.5
Sweden	68	70	81	78	59	68	74	78	81	83	12.6
Switzerland	47	30	34	45	38	50	50	50	50	51	46.7
Turkey	0	0	1	8	18	23	28	33	38	43	33.1
United Kingdom	20	32	59	109	151	162	158	158	158	160	294.9
Eastern Europe											
Albania											
Belarus											
Bosnia-Herzegovina											
Bulgaria											
Croatia											
Czech Republic					111	167	154	199	226	245	14.4
Estonia											
Georgia											
Hungary	1	11	122	1,076	1,328	1,265	1,323	1,280	1,265	1,270	7.4
Latvia					0	0	0	1	1	1	1.2
Lithuania					0	0	1	1	1	1	0.6
Macedonia											
Moldova											
Poland	1	2	3	27	99	128	53	64	66	69	28.5
Romania			0	0	2	6	7	8	10	11	4.5
Russia			84	368	432	1,100	1,600	1,973	2,395	96.4	
Slovakia			0	0	0	0	1	1	1	1	1.1
Slovenia						1	1	1	1	1.5	
Ukraine					16	26	37	47	107	20.4	

Source: *Euromonitor International from World Association of Newspapers*

Advertising Statistics

Table 1.6

Outdoor Adspend 1985-2008

Million units of national currency

	1985	1990	1995	2000	2003	2004	2005	2006	2007	2008	US$ million 2008
Western Europe											
Austria	29	54	79	112	138	139	157	170	180	193	284.4
Belgium	183	138	129	162	198	205	215	227	236	249	366.9
Cyprus											
Denmark			153	338	345	359	370	405	423	448	87.8
Finland	14	21	24	35	31	33	37	36	35	36	52.3
France	1,036	1,009	1,060	1,383	1,379	1,414	1,411	1,414	1,428	1,450	2,133.5
Germany	288	377	540	746	710	720	769	787	804	822	1,210.4
Gibraltar											
Greece	4	13	67	240	290	248	265	306	333	351	515.9
Iceland				279	270	264	259	256	253	267	3.0
Ireland	4	13	20	70	101	106	117	134	148	158	233.1
Italy	596	296	171	318	306	312	315	312	310	313	460.0
Liechtenstein											
Luxembourg						3	4	4	4	4	5.5
Malta											
Monaco											
Netherlands	71	72	84	139	122	139	151	165	178	190	279.9
Norway	176	176	258	263	575	658	759	894	991	1,072	190.0
Portugal	38	35	48	99	105	117	114	114	116	117	172.0
Spain	876	400	160	308	422	442	494	529	561	601	883.8
Sweden	343	446	573	848	925	1,000	1,065	1,091	1,109	1,128	171.2
Switzerland	427	386	446	592	566	392	402	423	439	450	415.2
Turkey	0	0	2	57	76	95	110	160	195	227	174.2
United Kingdom	124	191	349	592	668	721	762	792	816	853	1,568.9
Eastern Europe											
Albania											
Belarus											
Bosnia-Herzegovina											
Bulgaria			17	46	24	49	78	91	108		80.9
Croatia				218	223	234	272	311	341		69.1
Czech Republic			1,190	1,674	1,938	1,943	2,502	2,753	3,019		176.9
Estonia			14	31	57	66	67	84	94	104	9.7
Georgia											
Hungary	1	85	3,307	16,680	22,382	28,327	31,797	38,484	43,363	48,101	279.5
Latvia			1	2	2	3	4	7	8	9	18.9
Lithuania	1	1	5	17	32	40	46	52	58	65	27.8
Macedonia											
Moldova											
Poland	3	15	101	685	566	678	474	523	536	542	225.1
Romania			4	35	34	67	81	102	122	140	55.6
Russia			447	4,641	16,271	20,462	25,700	32,100	36,897	42,859	1,724.5
Slovakia			3	9	12	15	23	30	39	50	73.0
Slovenia	0	1	3	11	14	15	24	30	35	42	61.3
Ukraine				313	454	606	731	940	1,180		224.0

Source: *Euromonitor International from World Association of Newspapers*

Advertising Statistics

Table 1.7

Online Adspend 1999-2008

Million units of national currency

	1999	2000	2001	2002	2003	2004	2005	2006	2007	2008	US$ million 2008
Western Europe											
Austria			10	22	10	22	28	37	45	52.5	77.3
Belgium	7	13	11	11	18	32	44	72	88	107.2	157.8
Cyprus											
Denmark			310	418	486	582	742	1,794	2,339	2,761.5	541.7
Finland	6	11	15	15	17	23	36	47	56	67.0	98.6
France	79	144	115	99	131	179	382	542	740	870.7	1,281.4
Germany	77	153	185	227	246	271	332	495	614	692.7	1,019.4
Gibraltar											
Greece			2	5							
Iceland			8								
Ireland		2	3	4	6	9	16	26	32	37.0	54.5
Italy	29	139	107	99	103	107	138	197	242	272.4	400.9
Liechtenstein											
Luxembourg											
Malta											
Monaco											
Netherlands	21	38	34	32	40	66	97	137	166	197.2	290.2
Norway		300	235	250	325	455	2,119	3,119	3,966	4,611.7	817.7
Portugal	4	5	5	5	4	4	5	7	8	8.7	12.7
Spain	15	53	52	72	75	94	162	310	381	443.2	652.3
Sweden	497	1,037	895	1,139	1,325	1,974	2,996	2,237	2,136	2,130.1	323.2
Switzerland	12	25	19	20	30	29	36	52	61	67.2	62.0
Turkey			1	2	4	8	18	30	38	44.9	34.5
United Kingdom	43	132	141	162	295	700	1,162	1,714	2,144	2,606.8	4,792.1
Eastern Europe											
Albania											
Belarus											
Bosnia-Herzegovina											
Bulgaria						3	5	10	13	16.6	12.4
Croatia								9	12	14.1	2.9
Czech Republic	55	100	200	240	348	664	830	2,028	2,537	2,946.3	172.6
Estonia	4	13	19	20	28	29	40	66	82	93.8	8.8
Georgia											
Hungary						2,460	5,637	9,610	12,522	15,630.1	90.8
Latvia		0	0	1	1	1	2	3	4	5.0	10.3
Lithuania	0	1	0	1	5	5	10	14	16	18.4	7.8
Macedonia											
Moldova											
Poland			24	33	50	87	148	215	265	318.6	132.3
Romania				2	5	8	16	20	24.8	9.9	
Russia	25	84	175	345	553	865	1,700	2,700	3,351	4,200.4	169.0
Slovakia			2	3	4	6	7	8	10	12.3	18.1
Slovenia						3	4	7	9	11.2	16.4
Ukraine				5	5	10	10	31	57	118.0	22.4

Source: *Euromonitor International from World Association of Newspapers / Jupiter research*

Agricultural Resources and Output

Agricultural Statistics

Table 2.1

Indices of Agricultural Output 1985-2008

1999-2001 = 100

	1985	1990	1995	2000	2003	2004	2005	2006	2007	2008
Western Europe										
Austria	86.0	89.0	93.0	97.0	93.0	96.0	94.0	92.0	95.0	95.5
Belgium	80.0	85.0	97.0	104.0	98.0	100.0	96.0	47.0	48.0	48.0
Cyprus	85.0	91.0	99.0	101.0	103.0	107.0	97.0	94.0	91.0	88.3
Denmark	92.0	100.0	99.0	99.0	100.0	101.0	102.0	102.0	102.0	102.5
Finland	108.0	113.0	99.0	102.0	101.0	101.0	106.0	103.0	102.0	102.3
France	95.0	96.0	95.0	101.0	94.0	101.0	97.0	94.0	93.0	92.8
Germany	100.0	102.0	90.0	99.0	92.0	100.0	96.0	93.0	95.0	95.9
Gibraltar										
Greece	89.0	81.0	98.0	100.0	87.0	94.0	96.0	85.0	82.0	81.0
Iceland	114.0	97.0	94.0	101.0	104.0	105.0	104.0	104.0	104.0	104.0
Ireland	90.0	94.0	94.0	99.0	96.0	97.0	95.0	94.0	92.0	91.0
Italy	96.0	91.0	95.0	99.0	91.0	101.0	99.0	95.0	94.0	94.9
Liechtenstein	105.0	109.0	100.0	100.0	100.0	100.0	100.0	100.0	96.0	95.0
Luxembourg				111.0	94.0	94.0	89.0	53.0	56.0	50.4
Malta	63.0	68.0	87.0	98.0	97.0	97.0	90.0	98.0	95.0	94.7
Monaco			64.4	57.3	59.4	59.7	60.3	60.9	61.5	62.1
Netherlands	96.0	102.0	103.0	100.0	90.0	95.0	92.0	91.0	92.0	92.6
Norway	106.0	112.0	102.0	98.0	97.0	101.0	98.0	97.0	98.0	98.3
Portugal	81.0	101.0	99.0	100.0	94.0	103.0	96.0	100.0	96.0	96.7
Spain	77.0	88.0	73.0	102.0	111.0	107.0	94.0	101.0	99.0	96.5
Sweden	110.0	110.0	96.0	101.0	99.0	102.0	100.0	98.0	99.0	99.0
Switzerland	103.0	104.0	101.0	102.0	97.0	101.0	100.0	99.0	102.0	103.3
Turkey	75.0	88.0	91.0	104.0	103.0	104.0	110.0	110.0	101.0	100.6
United Kingdom	103.0	105.0	106.0	102.0	97.0	98.0	98.0	96.0	92.0	90.8
Eastern Europe										
Albania	81.0	86.0	99.0	100.0	108.0	112.0	111.0	117.0	113.0	114.4
Belarus			105.0	97.0	106.0	121.0	127.0	135.0	139.0	148.9
Bosnia-Herzegovina			93.0	91.0	96.0	120.0	119.0	127.0	126.0	135.5
Bulgaria	150.0	153.0	117.0	97.0	79.0	95.0	77.0	90.0	73.0	72.9
Croatia			95.0	91.0	86.0	91.0	88.0	94.0	99.0	102.6
Czech Republic			100.0	97.0	87.0	106.0	96.0	95.0	96.0	99.0
Estonia			128.0	97.0	109.0	107.0	116.0	115.0	127.0	132.1
Georgia			114.0	91.0	104.0	97.0	109.0	69.0	81.0	78.2
Hungary	125.0	123.0	91.0	93.0	86.0	119.0	103.0	101.0	97.0	101.6
Latvia			129.0	98.0	109.0	111.0	126.0	116.0	128.0	133.7
Lithuania			106.0	109.0	117.0	120.0	124.0	113.0	128.0	131.3
Macedonia			90.0	103.0	93.0	104.0	105.0	104.0	109.0	113.5
Moldova			144.0	104.0	107.0	113.0	115.0	112.0	87.0	83.2
Poland	114.0	120.0	97.0	98.0	101.0	110.0	104.0	102.0	103.0	103.6
Romania	125.0	106.0	110.0	89.0	105.0	126.0	105.0	107.0	91.0	88.8
Russia			99.0	99.0	104.0	112.0	115.0	118.0	123.0	128.3
Slovakia			109.0	92.0	95.0	110.0	109.0	89.0	82.0	79.7
Slovenia			95.0	99.0	103.0	106.0	102.0	100.0	103.0	103.0
Ukraine			123.0	100.0	99.0	111.0	118.0	116.0	108.0	110.7

Source: *UN Food and Agriculture Organisation, FAOSTAT*

Table 2.2

Indices of Food Output 1985-2008
1999-2001 = 100

	1985	1990	1995	2000	2003	2004	2005	2006	2007	2008
Western Europe										
Austria	86.0	89.0	93.0	97.0	93.0	96.0	94.0	92.0	95.0	95.5
Belgium	80.0	85.0	97.0	104.0	98.0	100.0	96.0	47.0	48.0	48.0
Cyprus	85.0	91.0	99.0	101.0	103.0	107.0	97.0	94.0	91.0	88.3
Denmark	92.0	100.0	99.0	99.0	100.0	101.0	102.0	102.0	102.0	102.5
Finland	108.0	113.0	99.0	102.0	101.0	101.0	106.0	103.0	102.0	102.3
France	95.0	96.0	95.0	101.0	94.0	101.0	97.0	94.0	93.0	92.8
Germany	100.0	102.0	90.0	99.0	92.0	100.0	96.0	93.0	96.0	97.2
Gibraltar		90.7	107.4	96.4	94.0	93.6	93.1	92.9	92.7	92.5
Greece	94.0	84.0	98.0	100.0	87.0	94.0	96.0	89.0	87.0	87.1
Iceland	114.0	97.0	94.0	100.0	105.0	106.0	105.0	106.0	106.0	106.3
Ireland	90.0	94.0	94.0	99.0	96.0	97.0	95.0	94.0	92.0	91.0
Italy	95.0	90.0	95.0	99.0	91.0	101.0	99.0	95.0	94.0	94.9
Liechtenstein	105.0	109.0	100.0	100.0	100.0	100.0	100.0	100.0	96.0	95.0
Luxembourg				111.0	94.0	94.0	89.0	53.0	56.0	50.4
Malta	63.0	68.0	87.0	98.0	97.0	97.0	90.0	98.0	95.0	94.7
Monaco		95.6	79.7	95.1	102.1	104.2	105.9	107.1	108.6	109.9
Netherlands	96.0	102.0	103.0	100.0	90.0	95.0	92.0	91.0	92.0	92.6
Norway	106.0	112.0	102.0	98.0	97.0	101.0	98.0	97.0	98.0	98.3
Portugal	81.0	101.0	99.0	100.0	94.0	103.0	96.0	100.0	96.0	96.7
Spain	77.0	88.0	73.0	103.0	112.0	107.0	94.0	102.0	99.0	96.3
Sweden	110.0	110.0	96.0	101.0	99.0	102.0	100.0	98.0	100.0	100.3
Switzerland	103.0	104.0	101.0	102.0	97.0	101.0	100.0	99.0	103.0	104.6
Turkey	75.0	88.0	90.0	104.0	103.0	104.0	111.0	111.0	101.0	100.7
United Kingdom	104.0	105.0	106.0	102.0	97.0	98.0	98.0	96.0	93.0	92.0
Eastern Europe										
Albania	74.0	82.0	99.0	100.0	109.0	113.0	112.0	119.0	115.0	116.6
Belarus			105.0	97.0	106.0	121.0	126.0	135.0	139.0	148.9
Bosnia-Herzegovina			94.0	91.0	96.0	120.0	119.0	127.0	126.0	135.5
Bulgaria	143.0	151.0	120.0	98.0	76.0	93.0	75.0	89.0	72.0	72.5
Croatia			95.0	91.0	85.0	91.0	88.0	94.0	98.0	101.6
Czech Republic			100.0	97.0	87.0	106.0	96.0	95.0	96.0	99.0
Estonia			128.0	97.0	109.0	107.0	116.0	115.0	127.0	132.1
Georgia			114.0	92.0	106.0	98.0	111.0	72.0	85.0	82.6
Hungary	124.0	123.0	91.0	93.0	86.0	119.0	103.0	101.0	98.0	102.9
Latvia			129.0	98.0	109.0	111.0	126.0	117.0	128.0	133.6
Lithuania			105.0	109.0	117.0	120.0	124.0	113.0	129.0	132.6
Macedonia			92.0	105.0	93.0	105.0	105.0	105.0	111.0	116.2
Moldova			145.0	103.0	110.0	116.0	119.0	115.0	89.0	85.0
Poland	112.0	119.0	97.0	98.0	101.0	110.0	104.0	102.0	103.0	103.6
Romania	124.0	105.0	110.0	89.0	105.0	127.0	106.0	108.0	91.0	88.9
Russia			99.0	99.0	103.0	112.0	115.0	118.0	123.0	128.6
Slovakia			108.0	92.0	95.0	111.0	110.0	89.0	82.0	79.7
Slovenia			95.0	99.0	103.0	106.0	102.0	100.0	103.0	103.0
Ukraine			122.0	100.0	99.0	111.0	118.0	116.0	108.0	110.7

Source: UN *Food and Agriculture Organisation, FAOSTAT*

Agricultural Statistics

Table 2.3

Land Use and Irrigation 2008
'000 hectares

	Total Area	Land Area	Arable Land	Permanent Crops	Permanent Pasture	Irrigated Land	Irrigated as % of Land Area
Western Europe							
Austria	8,387	8,245	1,388	66	1,810	125	1.52
Belgium	3,053	3,023	847	23	509	20	0.66
Cyprus	925	924	131	40	4	46	4.98
Denmark	4,309	4,243	2,216	7	333	430	10.13
Finland	33,815	30,459	2,248	5	27	76	0.25
France	55,150	55,010	18,537	1,124	9,880	2,724	4.95
Germany	35,705	34,877	11,933	193	4,884	485	1.39
Gibraltar	1	1					
Greece	13,196	12,890	2,571	1,134	4,582	1,637	12.70
Iceland	10,300	10,025	7		2,274		
Ireland	7,027	6,889	1,227	2	2,914		
Italy	30,134	29,411	7,404	2,518	4,434	3,972	13.51
Liechtenstein	16	16	4		5		
Luxembourg	259	259	59	3	68	4	1.54
Malta	32	32	9	1		3	10.00
Monaco	0						
Netherlands	4,153	3,388	910	33	978	404	11.92
Norway	32,380	30,428	855		177	117	0.38
Portugal	9,212	9,150	870	617	1,942	588	6.43
Spain	50,549	49,944	13,945	4,910	9,934	3,840	7.69
Sweden	45,029	41,033	2,708	3	550	172	0.42
Switzerland	4,128	4,000	413	24	1,088	25	0.63
Turkey	78,356	76,963	23,799	2,834	14,617	5,215	6.78
United Kingdom	24,361	24,193	5,775	44	11,146	130	0.54
Eastern Europe							
Albania	2,875	2,740	578	122	423	368	13.43
Belarus	20,760	20,748	5,408	113	3,355	131	0.63
Bosnia-Herzegovina	5,121	5,120	994	97	1,053	3	0.06
Bulgaria	11,099	10,797	3,003	177	1,936	405	3.75
Croatia	5,654	5,592	980	109	1,419	17	0.30
Czech Republic	7,887	7,726	3,040	239	975	47	0.61
Estonia	4,523	4,239	632	9	324	4	0.09
Georgia	6,970	6,949	802	264	1,940	433	6.23
Hungary	9,303	8,961	4,602	208	1,054	137	1.53
Latvia	6,459	6,229	1,160	13	638	1	0.01
Lithuania	6,530	6,268	2,095	39	804	4	0.06
Macedonia	2,571	2,543	566	46	630	55	2.16
Moldova	3,384	3,287	1,846	295	370	228	6.94
Poland	31,269	30,697	11,609	403	3,134	128	0.42
Romania	23,839	23,009	9,245	576	4,567	3,155	13.71
Russia	1,709,824	1,638,151	121,420	1,787	92,695	4,360	0.27
Slovakia	4,903	4,810	1,366	25	424	180	3.74
Slovenia	2,027	2,014	177	25	310	10	0.50
Ukraine	60,355	57,939	32,425	895	7,932	2,171	3.75

Source: *UN Food and Agriculture Organisation, FAOSTAT*

Table 2.4

Number of Livestock 2008

'000 head

	Asses	Cattle	Goats	Horses	Pigs	Sheep
Western Europe						
Austria		1,995.0	52.3	87.6	3,257.0	306.8
Belgium	0.0	2,617.1	26.6	46.5	6,249.2	156.6
Cyprus	5.2	59.2	362.2	0.7	466.1	268.4
Denmark		1,586.0		49.7	13,869.9	212.9
Finland		914.7	6.7	65.6	1,446.8	114.1
France	18.6	19,338.0	1,260.5	416.7	14,709.9	8,271.7
Germany		12,495.7	184.0	510.0	26,538.7	2,410.3
Gibraltar						
Greece	41.0	629.1	5,600.9	27.1	956.9	8,810.0
Iceland		63.9	0.4	75.8	42.5	448.9
Ireland	5.0	6,675.8	7.2	80.1	1,560.1	5,191.8
Italy	26.0	6,012.5	963.3	302.9	9,338.9	8,363.5
Liechtenstein		6.0			3.0	3.0
Luxembourg		193.5	1.6	4.6	101.5	8.7
Malta	0.8	19.1	5.9	1.1	74.2	11.4
Monaco						
Netherlands		3,719.4	395.9	129.9	11,774.3	1,396.2
Norway		932.7	73.4	30.7	831.8	2,413.7
Portugal	123.2	1,398.3	544.6	19.6	2,282.7	3,535.9
Spain	142.1	6,607.6	2,884.5	252.8	26,513.2	21,511.2
Sweden		1,539.4		94.4	1,665.4	518.3
Switzerland	5.8	1,572.4	75.7	55.6	1,656.8	450.5
Turkey	305.0	11,158.8	6,487.5	201.5	1.2	25,463.8
United Kingdom		9,844.0	94.3	191.0	4,845.6	33,256.3
Eastern Europe						
Albania	72.6	651.7	962.8	54.4	152.5	1,823.1
Belarus	9.0	3,995.6	70.9	148.1	3,722.4	51.6
Bosnia-Herzegovina		528.8	73.5	24.4	731.6	1,032.4
Bulgaria	119.5	621.1	522.1	118.3	1,056.2	1,659.1
Croatia	4.0	483.1	112.4	10.1	1,488.9	662.2
Czech Republic		1,405.6	17.7	21.9	2,658.7	151.1
Estonia		241.2	3.5	5.0	345.2	70.0
Georgia	10.0	1,355.3	112.4	42.1	523.3	857.8
Hungary	3.5	696.0	68.3	58.6	4,061.4	1,299.4
Latvia		369.0	14.1	13.4	408.9	42.4
Lithuania		868.4	20.1	59.8	1,136.0	40.7
Macedonia		252.5	129.2	57.2	269.8	743.2
Moldova	2.0	290.4	109.3	65.3	579.2	844.4
Poland		5,814.5	150.7	312.5	18,140.0	
Romania	30.1	2,982.0	755.6	794.6		7,733.8
Russia	17.5	20,620.9	2,186.8	1,290.9	16,692.0	18,702.9
Slovakia		493.5	37.9	8.1	1,102.4	339.3
Slovenia		450.3	29.2	22.9	594.9	133.5
Ukraine	11.7	5,893.2	656.5	517.2	8,255.4	959.7

Source: *UN Food and Agriculture Organisation, FAOSTAT*

Agricultural Statistics

Table 2.5

Production of Selected Crops 2008

'000 tonnes

	Apples	Bananas	Grapes	Hops	Potatoes	Rapeseed	Sugar Beet	Tomatoes
Western Europe								
Austria	475.8		345.7	0.4	660.7	152.7	2,574.3	47.9
Belgium	345.3		0.6	0.4	3,176.5	43.7	5,568.7	184.7
Cyprus	7.9	7.1	32.6		163.5			28.0
Denmark	28.2				1,624.3	639.0	2,064.2	19.8
Finland	3.7				729.0	126.4	543.0	39.4
France	2,123.7		5,538.2	1.5	7,189.3	4,740.8	34,020.8	661.6
Germany	1,100.1		1,579.6	27.1	11,177.2	5,335.2	25,812.4	64.1
Gibraltar								
Greece	255.2	4.0	850.0		923.5	8.0	828.0	1,293.3
Iceland					13.3			1.7
Ireland	13.0			0.0	347.9	40.3	1,246.5	13.0
Italy	2,051.3	0.4	8,461.9		1,843.3	18.2	4,202.9	5,473.1
Liechtenstein			0.2					
Luxembourg	1.9		15.4		19.2	18.9		0.1
Malta	0.1		3.3		11.3			17.0
Monaco								
Netherlands	376.0		0.1		7,104.1	14.8	5,251.3	695.0
Norway	9.0				292.3	8.8		12.1
Portugal	171.8	35.3	762.8	0.1	595.3		217.8	933.0
Spain	660.0	339.6	5,639.0	0.9	2,433.1	40.4	4,694.9	3,424.4
Sweden	20.6				727.1	212.3	2,037.6	17.5
Switzerland	274.4		126.8	0.0	479.1	61.6	1,612.0	31.0
Turkey	2,577.1	208.8	3,650.4		4,061.6	36.8	12,047.3	10,113.4
United Kingdom	294.5		0.9	1.3	5,407.8	2,274.4	5,652.7	88.0
Eastern Europe								
Albania	38.3		163.0	1.0	153.3		40.0	162.7
Belarus	273.3				8,357.9	272.5	3,805.4	283.0
Bosnia-Herzegovina	63.5		21.1		367.3	5.1		31.2
Bulgaria	21.8		385.1	0.8	207.2	100.9	12.9	98.4
Croatia	87.6		164.0		295.1	43.8	1,710.1	54.1
Czech Republic	198.8		108.8	5.4	806.8	1,064.3	2,660.1	32.3
Estonia	4.7		1.4		200.2	155.3		7.7
Georgia	109.6		243.1		165.8			66.3
Hungary	483.9		457.2		489.6	567.4	1,570.5	213.7
Latvia	38.4				646.5	228.0	10.0	5.9
Lithuania	42.8				427.7	347.6	764.9	1.0
Macedonia	175.3		197.0		174.8	1.9	7.1	118.4
Moldova	187.6		568.8		159.4	45.2	512.6	37.4
Poland	546.1			3.6	11,055.2	2,295.5	12,665.3	725.5
Romania	267.9		754.2	0.5	3,539.8	449.1	774.2	411.0
Russia	2,436.3		329.6	0.2	37,074.2	750.5	31,332.3	2,402.0
Slovakia	16.9		46.7	0.3	256.3	340.6	595.7	53.0
Slovenia	118.7		118.5	2.5	117.6	17.8	275.6	4.1
Ukraine	767.6		354.9	0.7	18,551.1	1,147.2	17,103.5	1,310.9

Source: UN Food and Agriculture Organisation, FAOSTAT

Table 2.6

Production of Dairy Products and Eggs 2008

'000 tonnes

	Butter and Ghee	Cheese	Fresh Cows' Milk	Hens' Eggs
Western Europe				
Austria	30.6	187.0	3,161.0	97.9
Belgium	86.8	47.0	2,980.0	163.2
Cyprus		5.7	141.7	8.9
Denmark	43.6	361.6	4,610.3	76.3
Finland	53.6	94.9	2,324.5	56.6
France	411.0	1,802.9	24,348.5	856.1
Germany	445.2	2,045.8	28,455.8	777.0
Gibraltar				
Greece	4.2	235.1	791.3	92.3
Iceland	1.9	7.1	131.1	3.0
Ireland	145.0	122.8	5,159.7	33.4
Italy	126.3	1,136.6	11,090.8	689.7
Liechtenstein			11.3	
Luxembourg	0.2		276.1	1.3
Malta		0.2	40.4	8.1
Monaco				
Netherlands	99.3	668.3	10,698.3	624.3
Norway	14.4	80.5	1,602.7	53.0
Portugal	31.3	73.4	1,916.3	114.9
Spain	62.1	111.3	5,941.5	656.0
Sweden	42.7	122.1	3,175.0	101.3
Switzerland	37.9	188.0	4,006.7	39.1
Turkey	133.6	151.0	11,836.0	830.1
United Kingdom	132.7	401.7	13,845.7	565.4
Eastern Europe				
Albania	0.8	14.3	851.7	26.6
Belarus	87.7	136.1	6,124.9	184.0
Bosnia-Herzegovina	0.4	11.2	795.4	21.9
Bulgaria	2.3	77.9	1,082.9	97.4
Croatia	2.4	21.8	919.8	48.2
Czech Republic	49.9	130.3	2,781.1	91.3
Estonia	7.2	16.5	705.1	8.4
Georgia	0.6	0.0	562.7	23.2
Hungary	5.6	85.4	1,824.8	148.0
Latvia	5.9	23.6	856.5	45.6
Lithuania	11.7	83.7	1,961.1	56.1
Macedonia	8.8	7.0	442.8	17.7
Moldova	3.3	7.3	560.5	40.0
Poland	204.0	600.1	12,187.3	557.6
Romania	8.3	63.7	5,851.8	303.4
Russia	271.2	630.9	31,918.5	2,140.6
Slovakia	8.1	75.1	1,073.3	75.5
Slovenia	5.4	21.4	672.5	21.0
Ukraine	94.7	269.6	11,540.5	850.5

Source: UN Food and Agriculture Organisation, FAOSTAT

Agricultural Statistics

Table 2.7

Production of Meat 2008

'000 tonnes

	Beef and Veal	Goat Meat	Horse Meat	Mutton and Lamb	Pig Meat	Poultry	Total (including others)
Western Europe							
Austria	221.7	0.6	0.1	5.4	495.7	124.9	855.2
Belgium	270.2	0.0	3.0	1.2	1,066.4	446.3	1,786.5
Cyprus	4.0	4.2		3.2	54.9	28.8	95.9
Denmark	123.3		0.8	1.8	1,799.8		2,098.0
Finland	87.0		0.3	0.8	218.3	98.2	407.3
France	1,520.6	7.5	4.6	92.6	2,277.1	1,330.6	5,483.8
Germany	1,161.6	0.5	2.5	18.0	5,205.8	1,147.6	7,628.7
Gibraltar							
Greece	71.8	58.1	2.7	95.5	110.8	146.9	494.5
Iceland	3.5		1.0	8.6	6.3	8.3	29.9
Ireland	586.6		1.4	63.8	205.7	143.8	1,001.6
Italy	1,114.0	1.8	17.4	59.0	1,607.7	1,038.5	4,098.5
Liechtenstein							
Luxembourg	15.3		0.4	0.1	9.4	5.4	22.4
Malta	1.4	0.0	0.1	0.1	7.9	4.2	15.3
Monaco							
Netherlands	385.4	0.4	0.6	16.6	1,290.2	675.8	2,368.4
Norway	84.0	0.3	0.3	22.5	119.1	75.3	307.1
Portugal	102.0	1.0	0.2	23.7	380.4	249.1	760.7
Spain	588.9	10.0	5.2	193.9	3,700.0	1,166.4	5,748.6
Sweden	130.4		0.7	4.9	255.0	100.9	511.2
Switzerland	132.6	0.5	0.7	5.0	246.9	59.5	448.8
Turkey	456.3	45.0	2.0	271.7	0.1	1,146.4	1,921.0
United Kingdom	936.3		3.1	329.3	749.3	1,424.4	3,448.5
Eastern Europe							
Albania	53.2	7.1		12.8	10.0	10.3	93.5
Belarus	291.3		2.0	0.9	396.2	187.9	878.6
Bosnia-Herzegovina	25.3			1.8	9.3	20.8	57.2
Bulgaria	18.7	5.7		15.8	75.6	124.0	238.0
Croatia	62.5	0.2	3.0	2.6	67.0	52.4	187.8
Czech Republic	73.6	0.1	0.1	1.8	338.6	211.5	667.0
Estonia	15.5	0.0		0.6	43.5	10.4	70.1
Georgia	24.9	0.4	0.6	3.4	17.0	10.7	56.1
Hungary	30.6	0.1	0.0	0.2	486.1	346.6	877.4
Latvia	23.1		0.1	0.5	41.6	22.6	88.4
Lithuania	55.3	0.2	0.0	0.6	94.6	74.4	225.7
Macedonia	6.6			6.3	8.7	3.6	25.2
Moldova	14.9		0.1	2.2	64.8	34.6	117.5
Poland	402.5		13.0	1.4	2,215.6	954.4	3,603.6
Romania	165.7	3.8	0.5	44.9	502.3	315.2	1,033.4
Russia	1,602.4	16.6	43.6	153.2	1,949.1	2,161.4	6,009.0
Slovakia	22.1	0.3	0.0	0.9	96.8	84.0	209.3
Slovenia	35.4	0.4	0.3	1.8	52.7	61.7	152.5
Ukraine	522.1	7.2	12.7	7.7	660.0	794.0	2,015.7

Source: *UN Food and Agriculture Organisation, FAOSTAT*

Table 2.8

Production of Cereals 2008
'000 tonnes

	Barley	Maize	Millet	Oats	Rice	Rye	Sorghum	Wheat	Total (including others)
Western Europe									
Austria	745.7	1,613.7	8.8	85.7		180.3		1,292.8	4,486.7
Belgium	385.1	590.9		21.4		3.4		1,336.6	2,381.9
Cyprus	35.7			0.9				11.0	47.6
Denmark	2,942.6			312.2		131.7		4,439.4	7,972.5
Finland	2,071.0			1,292.5		94.8		801.6	4,307.5
France	8,956.3	13,913.3	44.0	351.5	78.6	99.1	299.0	30,462.2	55,877.1
Germany	9,514.6	3,674.8		575.3		2,321.1		19,295.0	37,139.4
Gibraltar									
Greece	297.7	2,376.7		85.5	182.9	36.3	0.0	1,503.6	4,509.2
Iceland									
Ireland	1,057.1			160.4		0.4		611.5	1,841.3
Italy	1,222.0	9,399.1		430.5	1,483.1	7.6	195.3	6,800.8	19,571.3
Liechtenstein									
Luxembourg	41.9	1.6		4.4		6.6		67.3	138.1
Malta	1.4							10.1	11.5
Monaco									
Netherlands	250.8	201.1		7.0		9.1		912.0	1,400.3
Norway	436.9			245.8		39.8		399.2	1,121.7
Portugal	89.8	598.9		43.4	156.4	22.6		83.4	1,015.7
Spain	11,917.1	3,081.0	0.6	1,388.9	689.1	289.8	26.5	6,100.4	23,681.6
Sweden	1,354.7			878.0		138.9		2,203.5	4,907.4
Switzerland	195.4	180.9		8.2		9.7		543.3	988.9
Turkey	6,742.4	3,713.3	7.1	162.1	700.7	230.7	0.2	15,978.7	27,651.7
United Kingdom	4,833.3			740.3		39.8		12,470.3	18,163.3
Eastern Europe									
Albania	3.4	215.8		20.8		3.6		248.2	491.9
Belarus	1,871.1	708.5		518.2		1,274.2		1,488.4	7,155.8
Bosnia-Herzegovina	60.2	517.0		32.4		8.5		236.5	854.5
Bulgaria	125.6	198.6	1.7	15.4	23.8	4.3	1.2	1,412.4	1,783.1
Croatia	247.0	1,166.1	0.2	61.5		3.8	0.5	799.8	2,295.5
Czech Republic	1,747.7	827.8	1.7	136.9		132.2		3,571.1	6,617.1
Estonia	385.9			89.4		75.3		395.4	969.9
Georgia	29.6	228.9		1.6		0.0		69.3	329.4
Hungary	917.5	8,422.5	6.7	90.4	9.7	61.3	9.7	3,315.3	13,130.8
Latvia	372.8			137.8		209.2		909.8	1,693.8
Lithuania	1,065.0	33.7		120.1		173.4		1,377.5	3,069.5
Macedonia	92.2	109.1	0.0	3.2	15.6	5.6	0.1	171.9	397.6
Moldova	64.2	322.9	0.1	1.0		0.6	0.1	393.9	852.9
Poland	4,153.9	1,515.1	13.3	1,473.0		2,740.7		7,792.2	26,312.0
Romania	507.1	3,675.8	2.4	186.5	35.0	16.8	1.1	2,912.0	7,355.0
Russia	15,157.6	4,099.1	188.8	5,557.7	787.8	4,256.4	35.6	50,715.6	81,923.7
Slovakia	574.2	544.4	0.9	31.3		31.0	0.8	1,251.2	2,458.4
Slovenia	70.6	291.9	1.0	5.6		2.2		128.8	519.5
Ukraine	4,252.2	6,894.9	77.6	387.7	116.5	445.2	82.1	12,662.1	24,918.2

Source: *UN Food and Agriculture Organisation, FAOSTAT*

Agricultural Statistics

Table 2.9

Production of Forestry and Paper Products 2008
as stated

	Fuelwood and Charcoal ('000 cu m)	Household and Sanitary Paper ('000 tonnes)	Paper and Paperboard ('000 tonnes)	Printing and Writing Paper ('000 tonnes)	Roundwood ('000 cu m)	Sawnwood and Sleepers ('000 cu m)	Wood Pulp ('000 tonnes)
Western Europe							
Austria	5,335	116	5,185	2,621	23,272	11,320	2,008
Belgium	695	101	1,877	1,119	4,978	1,599	502
Cyprus	2				23	11	
Denmark	1,183		423	155	2,916	318	65
Finland	5,239	214	14,528	9,130	57,859	12,157	13,069
France	33,628	766	10,183	3,116	72,463	10,334	2,185
Germany	10,018	1,411	23,995	8,759	86,202	26,109	3,194
Gibraltar							
Greece	699	51	406	18	1,767	92	5
Iceland							
Ireland	39		45		2,761	1,004	
Italy	4,928	1,476	10,153	3,314	7,944	1,744	563
Liechtenstein	4				22		
Luxembourg	23				297	133	
Malta							
Monaco							
Netherlands	290	109	3,275	914	1,023	270	119
Norway	2,807	19	1,915	905	11,101	2,463	2,152
Portugal	600	75	1,673	1,030	10,784	994	2,105
Spain	2,003	750	7,110	1,783	13,994	3,217	2,090
Sweden	5,900	321	12,141	3,502	85,229	19,205	12,754
Switzerland	1,401	68	1,480	491	5,893	1,557	351
Turkey	4,507	146	1,643	217	18,105	6,733	70
United Kingdom	586	863	5,284	1,176	9,278	3,217	242
Eastern Europe							
Albania	221		3	5	296	97	
Belarus	1,373	8	285	6	8,801	2,377	68
Bosnia-Herzegovina	1,352	36	118		3,685	1,371	20
Bulgaria	2,419	27	455	3	5,605	702	135
Croatia	708	1	520	276	4,350	747	94
Czech Republic	1,828	24	1,004	178	19,624	6,106	797
Estonia	1,247		71	0	5,670	1,668	216
Georgia	458				644	122	
Hungary	2,971	41	551	93	5,638	249	5
Latvia	1,049		67	1	11,990	3,390	2
Lithuania	1,339	12	130	5	5,777	1,358	0
Macedonia	548		25		725	12	
Moldova	94				188	31	
Poland	3,503	275	3,121	831	37,124	3,180	1,066
Romania	4,199	84	593	17	15,233	4,058	151
Russia	44,104	177	7,684	609	217,578	23,844	7,023
Slovakia	468	143	942	572	9,640	3,080	702
Slovenia	826	64	863	318	3,017	675	95
Ukraine	9,941	126	987	32	17,634	2,572	27

Source: *UN Food and Agriculture Organisation, FAOSTAT*

Agricultural Statistics

Table 2.10

Land Used in Organic Farming 1985-2008
Hectares

	1985	1990	1995	2000	2003	2004	2005	2006	2007	2008
Western Europe										
Austria			335,865	271,950	328,803	344,916	360,972	361,487	372,026	390,332
Belgium	500	1,300	3,385	20,263	24,163	23,728	22,996	29,308	32,628	34,992
Cyprus				52	393	960	1,698	1,979	2,322	2,483
Denmark	4,500	11,581	40,884	165,258	165,148	154,921	145,636	138,079	145,393	160,789
Finland	1,000	6,726	44,695	147,423	159,987	162,024	147,587	144,558	148,760	152,003
France	45,000	72,000	118,393	371,000	550,000	534,037	560,838	552,824	557,133	580,000
Germany	24,940	90,021	309,487	546,023	734,027	767,891	807,406	825,539	865,336	905,337
Gibraltar										
Greece		150	2,401	24,800	244,455	246,488	288,255	302,256	278,397	256,820
Iceland			717	3,400	6,000	4,910	4,684	5,512	6,229	6,481
Ireland	1,000	3,800	12,634	32,355	28,514	30,670	35,266	39,947	41,122	44,547
Italy	5,000	13,218	204,494	1,040,377	1,052,002	954,361	1,067,102	1,148,162	1,150,253	1,151,070
Liechtenstein			410	690	984	984	1,040	1,027	1,048	1,076
Luxembourg	350	600	571	1,030	3,002	3,158	3,243	3,630	3,380	3,307
Malta					14	13	14	20	30	46
Monaco										
Netherlands	2,450	7,469	12,909	27,820	41,865	48,152	48,765	48,424	47,019	50,435
Norway	90	1,578	5,768	20,523	38,176	41,035	43,033	44,624	48,863	49,325
Portugal	50	1,000	10,719	50,002	120,729	206,524	233,458	269,374	233,475	239,577
Spain	2,140	3,650	24,079	380,838	717,204	733,182	807,569	926,390	988,323	1,317,752
Sweden	1,500	28,500	83,490	171,682	207,488	219,423	200,010	225,385	248,104	255,483
Switzerland			31,815	95,000	110,000	121,387	117,117	125,596	116,641	121,000
Turkey		1,037	10,000	21,000	103,190	108,597	93,133	100,275	124,263	131,266
United Kingdom	6,000	31,000	48,448	527,323	695,619	657,736	619,852	604,571	660,200	697,330
Eastern Europe										
Albania					192	804	987	1,170	77	139
Belarus										
Bosnia-Herzegovina					712	310	363	416	691	721
Bulgaria				500	437	12,284	14,320	4,692	13,646	17,941
Croatia			120	120	3,530	3,357	3,184	6,204	7,647	8,100
Czech Republic		3,480	14,127	165,699	254,995	260,120	254,982	281,535	312,890	349,284
Estonia				9,872	40,890	46,016	59,862	72,886	79,530	84,005
Georgia			100	100	100	100	130	247	251	268
Hungary				47,221	113,816	128,690	123,569	122,765	122,270	122,854
Latvia			1,147	20,000	48,000	57,333	118,612	135,558	173,463	187,654
Lithuania			582	4,709	23,289	41,869	69,430	96,718	120,418	143,228
Macedonia							249	509	1,333	1,401
Moldova							11,075	11,405	11,695	11,930
Poland		550	6,855	22,000	49,928	82,730	167,740	228,009	285,878	301,234
Romania				20,500	75,500	75,000	87,916	107,582	131,401	142,330
Russia			20,000	5,276	6,900	31,003	40,000	3,192	6,123	13,922
Slovakia		15,140	18,813	48,120	54,478	73,335	92,191	121,461	117,906	120,435
Slovenia			200	5,200	23,280	23,032	23,499	26,831	29,322	32,002
Ukraine					239,771	240,000	241,980	260,034	249,872	253,946

Source: *Euromonitor International from Organic Centre Wales, University of Wales*

Agricultural Statistics

Table 2.11

Number of Organic Farms 1985-2008

Number

	1985	1990	1995	2000	2003	2004	2005	2006	2007	2008
Western Europe										
Austria	420	1,539	18,542	19,031	19,056	19,826	20,310	20,162	19,997	20,119
Belgium	50	160	193	628	688	712	693	783	821	894
Cyprus				15	48	103	305	305	305	305
Denmark	130	523	1,050	3,466	3,510	3,166	2,892	2,794	2,835	2,751
Finland	60	671	2,793	5,225	4,983	4,887	4,296	3,966	4,406	4,591
France	2,500	2,700	3,538	9,283	11,377	11,059	11,402	11,640	11,978	12,388
Germany	1,610	3,438	6,642	12,732	16,476	16,603	17,020	17,557	18,703	19,743
Gibraltar										
Greece		25	568	5,270	6,028	8,269	14,614	23,900	23,769	21,730
Iceland			12	30	20	25	23	27	36	41
Ireland	8	150	378	1,014	889	897	978	1,104	1,134	1,209
Italy	600	1,500	10,630	51,120	44,043	36,639	44,733	45,115	45,231	45,300
Liechtenstein			22	33	43	42	35	41	39	41
Luxembourg	10	10	19	51	59	66	72	72	81	80
Malta					20	20	6	10	12	14
Monaco										
Netherlands	215	399	561	1,391	1,522	1,469	1,377	1,448	1,374	1,473
Norway	15	263	728	1,823	2,466	2,484	2,496	2,583	2,611	2,699
Portugal	1	50	349	763	1,455	1,302	1,577	1,696	1,949	2,294
Spain	264	350	1,042	13,424	18,747	16,013	15,693	17,214	18,226	23,473
Sweden	150	1,588	2,473	3,329	3,363	3,374	2,951	2,380	3,028	3,274
Switzerland	322	803	2,121	5,852	6,445	6,373	6,420	6,563	6,199	6,111
Turkey		313	2,000	10,000	13,044	12,806	14,401	14,256	16,364	18,020
United Kingdom	300	700	828	3,563	4,017	4,151	4,285	4,485	5,506	6,203
Eastern Europe										
Albania					60	57	75	93	100	111
Belarus										
Bosnia-Herzegovina					107	122	74	26	304	310
Bulgaria				50	58	351	351	218	240	286
Croatia			18	18	130	200	269	368	483	564
Czech Republic		30	176	563	810	836	829	963	1,318	1,628
Estonia				231	746	810	1,013	1,173	1,220	1,463
Georgia			5	5	5	5	38	47	49	53
Hungary				471	1,255	1,583	1,553	1,553	1,242	1,394
Latvia			90	225	1,200	1,525	2,873	4,095	4,108	4,398
Lithuania				230	700	1,170	1,811	2,284	2,855	3,273
Macedonia						50	50	101	127	133
Moldova							121	121	121	122
Poland		49	236	1,419	2,304	3,760	7,183	9,187	11,887	13,870
Romania				650	1,200	1,200	2,920	3,033	2,238	2,400
Russia			15	19	15	15	40	8	17	24
Slovakia		36	34	100	100	148	196	279	280	295
Slovenia			40	620	1,429	1,568	1,718	1,953	2,000	2,094
Ukraine					70	70	72	80	92	101

Source: *Euromonitor International from Organic Centre Wales, University of Wales*

Automotives and Transport

Automotives and Transport Statistics

Table 3.1

Commercial Vehicles in Use 1980-2008
'000

	1980	1985	1990	1995	1996	1997	1998	1999	2000	2001
Western Europe										
Austria	208.2	237.3	295.0	347.8	353.4	362.9	374.4	386.0	395.9	402.2
Belgium	354.5	340.2	423.6	487.3	501.0	517.6	542.7	571.7	593.3	614.8
Cyprus	25.2	45.0	76.6	103.9	106.8	108.5	112.0	114.0	117.6	120.9
Denmark	259.2	267.4	300.8	342.3	348.6	354.7	366.6	382.3	393.7	401.5
Finland	166.9	200.5	294.2	280.4	286.5	294.2	307.9	320.7	327.8	335.2
France	2,570.5	3,980.0	4,910.0	5,195.0	5,255.0	5,380.0	5,500.0	5,610.0	5,753.0	5,897.0
Germany			1,989.4	3,061.9	3,121.6	3,174.1	3,279.5	3,370.0	3,533.9	3,592.1
Gibraltar	0.7	1.0	2.5	1.1	1.6	1.7	1.8	2.0	2.3	2.5
Greece	418.7	565.0	776.7	847.5	850.0	893.1	902.2	974.0	1,055.0	1,112.9
Iceland	9.0	12.7	14.5	16.1	16.6	17.5	18.1	19.4	21.1	21.7
Ireland	70.2	101.0	152.2	155.2	161.4	174.3	188.2	208.6	226.4	243.4
Italy	1,428.8	1,910.1	2,494.5	2,863.4	3,112.4	3,291.2	3,336.7	3,413.8	3,581.5	3,755.6
Liechtenstein	1.2	1.5	2.0	2.3	2.5	2.6	2.8	2.9	2.5	2.6
Luxembourg	15.5	14.0	18.1	27.1	28.0	28.3	29.7	30.8	31.4	33.3
Malta	14.2	17.5	21.2	50.9	55.7	42.8	45.3	44.9	44.3	44.7
Monaco				2.7	2.7	2.6	2.7	2.7	2.9	2.9
Netherlands	376.0	428.0	560.0	658.0	681.0	695.0	739.0	807.0	883.0	950.0
Norway	164.5	249.7	329.5	382.0	392.1	412.2	427.0	440.1	451.0	462.2
Portugal	264.0	356.0	568.0	824.0	867.0	923.0	997.0	1,066.0	1,157.0	1,211.0
Spain	1,380.9	1,570.9	2,378.7	3,071.6	3,200.3	3,360.1	3,561.6	3,788.7	3,977.9	4,161.1
Sweden	194.4	231.4	324.1	322.3	326.5	336.1	352.9	369.2	388.6	409.9
Switzerland	169.4	200.5	283.4	299.3	300.7	302.7	306.4	313.6	318.8	326.6
Turkey	428.2	553.1	709.9	982.4	1,053.7	1,182.4	1,317.0	1,405.8	1,543.1	1,588.4
United Kingdom	1,912.8	1,650.0	2,861.0	3,208.7	3,248.8	3,316.5	3,395.3	3,395.3	3,463.5	3,418.0
Eastern Europe										
Albania				48.4	41.7	45.8	50.3	53.7	67.6	79.6
Belarus			70.8	96.5	101.0	107.6	111.6	116.0	118.9	119.9
Bosnia-Herzegovina								75.2	77.5	82.1
Bulgaria			240.2	257.1	261.0	265.7	271.0	279.0	283.0	289.0
Croatia			52.4	77.4	99.5	114.5	120.6	123.4	127.2	134.3
Czech Republic			162.7	222.7	246.0	267.4	280.2	287.2	293.9	314.8
Estonia	57.5	66.4	75.6	72.6	78.0	83.1	86.9	87.2	88.2	86.0
Georgia										51.5
Hungary	190.0	216.0	272.5	324.6	334.4	342.6	355.4	363.4	384.3	398.3
Latvia			71.7	85.2	90.2	95.3	96.5	101.8	108.6	111.0
Lithuania			98.2	118.5	104.8	108.6	114.6	112.2	114.2	116.0
Macedonia			20.6	15.1	19.7	25.9	33.5	40.7	45.9	48.7
Moldova			83.4	67.4	68.6	71.4	82.6	76.7	68.5	69.4
Poland	1,373.4	1,722.0	2,329.0	2,651.0	2,744.0	2,816.0	2,937.1	1,676.6	1,865.4	1,958.4
Romania			287.0	385.1	416.3	430.1	446.1	458.4	467.9	478.8
Russia										
Slovakia				160.2	154.2	159.7	166.1	168.8	169.6	170.2
Slovenia			49.1	60.9	65.6	66.3	72.3	77.7	59.2	61.2
Ukraine			59.7	175.7	180.0	197.6	222.1	289.7	349.9	430.8

Source: *European Automobile Manufacturers' Association (ACEA) / International Road Federation (IRF)*
Notes: *There may be wide variations from year to year in SMMT estimates and in other figures due to interpretation of definitions*

Automotives and Transport Statistics

Commercial Vehicles in Use 1980-2008 *(continued)*
'000

	2002	2003	2004	2005	2006	2007	2008	Number in use /'000 persons 2008
Western Europe								
Austria	386.4	396.9	405.0	410.3	417.1	423.8	426.3	51.0
Belgium	627.8	644.6	668.4	691.4	706.3	715.7	723.3	68.1
Cyprus	120.8	122.9	121.0	121.6	118.9	119.5	120.8	140.1
Denmark	411.2	422.4	482.4	479.4	518.7	534.8	543.5	99.5
Finland	341.8	348.9	376.8	370.8	383.5	396.4	399.7	75.4
France	5,984.0	6,068.0	6,139.0	6,198.0	6,261.0	6,303.9	6,340.5	102.1
Germany	3,567.5	3,541.2	3,539.7	3,133.2	3,172.0	3,231.9	3,254.5	39.6
Gibraltar	1.4	2.0	2.6	2.1	2.3	2.3	2.4	80.9
Greece	1,136.4	1,158.2	1,185.9	1,213.3	1,246.8	1,283.0	1,299.2	115.9
Iceland	22.0	22.9	24.8	27.4	30.0	33.0	34.0	107.6
Ireland	258.7	278.7	296.7	316.1	349.9	359.4	367.7	84.0
Italy	3,976.0	4,166.0	4,250.9	4,274.1	4,579.6	4,765.9	4,834.5	82.0
Liechtenstein	2.7	2.6	2.6	2.6	2.5	2.5	2.5	70.1
Luxembourg	35.1	35.9	35.6	36.1	36.1	36.1	36.2	75.3
Malta	45.0	45.4	45.7	45.5	46.7	47.8	48.5	119.0
Monaco	3.0	3.1	3.2	3.2	3.3	3.4	3.4	104.9
Netherlands	996.0	1,039.0	1,069.0	1,070.0	1,063.0	1,069.4	1,072.7	65.5
Norway	464.8	470.3	480.1	493.9	514.5	521.9	528.9	111.6
Portugal	1,253.0	1,275.1	1,305.7	1,323.3	1,335.0	1,355.0	1,361.6	127.9
Spain	4,315.8	4,419.4	4,660.4	4,907.9	5,146.4	5,388.8	5,510.1	122.3
Sweden	423.0	435.3	453.3	474.6	493.4	503.1	511.4	55.8
Switzerland	332.5	336.0	343.0	352.9	360.5	372.2	377.0	50.1
Turkey	1,636.2	1,747.4	2,379.0	2,653.9	2,938.6	3,181.4	3,270.5	44.0
United Kingdom	3,501.3	3,694.2	3,819.4	3,943.2	4,144.7	4,294.8	4,358.2	71.2
Eastern Europe								
Albania	82.0	85.2	79.8	82.8	83.6	84.0	84.6	26.9
Belarus	122.5	131.9	134.6	141.6	147.7	150.1	152.2	15.7
Bosnia-Herzegovina	88.2	94.5	98.2	106.3	109.0	110.9	113.1	29.4
Bulgaria	293.0	297.7	303.2	307.2	312.3	314.8	317.1	41.9
Croatia	143.5	153.1	159.7	157.5	164.1	170.8	172.3	38.8
Czech Republic	344.8	360.7	391.4	435.2	488.6	517.0	545.0	52.8
Estonia	85.5	88.8	91.0	91.4	92.8	93.9	94.4	70.7
Georgia	45.5	42.9	68.6	68.6	71.8	74.4	74.9	17.1
Hungary	414.0	424.7	427.9	445.1	463.1	468.2	473.6	47.2
Latvia	113.9	115.6	118.3	123.8	131.7	140.2	143.9	63.5
Lithuania	121.4	126.5	130.5	137.8	142.5	147.7	150.0	44.5
Macedonia	50.1	50.1	50.1	50.2	50.2	50.3	50.3	24.7
Moldova	70.5	70.6	68.5	71.7	74.5	75.1	76.0	20.9
Poland	2,518.5	2,518.5	2,632.2	2,494.3	2,476.0	2,609.0	2,601.3	68.4
Romania	487.9	505.0	525.6	532.6	614.3	692.7	714.9	33.3
Russia		3,200.0	5,536.0	5,642.3	5,642.3	5,695.5	5,713.2	40.2
Slovakia	168.7	166.8	162.7	183.3	198.1	208.6	223.8	41.5
Slovenia	63.1	65.1	68.7	72.1	75.9	83.8	86.4	42.8
Ukraine	500.0	703.0	985.7	1,050.0	1,108.6	1,163.5	1,187.2	25.7

Source: *European Automobile Manufacturers' Association (ACEA) / International Road Federation (IRF)*
Notes: *There may be wide variations from year to year in SMMT estimates and in other figures due to interpretation of definitions*

Automotives and Transport Statistics   **Table 3.2**

Passenger Cars in Use 1980-2008
'000

	1980	1985	1990	1995	1996	1997	1998	1999	2000	2001
Western Europe										
Austria	2,247.0	2,530.8	2,991.3	3,593.6	3,690.7	3,782.5	3,887.2	4,009.6	4,097.1	4,182.0
Belgium	3,158.7	3,278.8	3,833.3	4,239.1	4,307.7	4,373.1	4,458.0	4,547.2	4,628.9	4,684.5
Cyprus	92.0	120.0	178.6	219.7	226.8	235.0	249.2	257.0	267.6	280.1
Denmark	1,389.5	1,500.9	1,590.6	1,684.8	1,744.3	1,787.8	1,821.7	1,846.9	1,842.9	1,875.3
Finland	1,225.9	1,546.1	1,938.9	1,900.9	1,942.8	1,948.1	2,021.1	2,082.6	2,120.7	2,146.2
France	19,150.0	21,090.0	23,550.0	25,100.0	25,500.0	26,090.0	26,810.0	27,480.0	28,060.0	28,700.0
Germany			30,695.1	40,499.4	41,045.2	41,326.9	41,716.7	42,423.3	43,772.3	44,383.3
Gibraltar	6.5	10.6	19.8	18.4	19.0	19.3	20.0	22.5	25.8	27.4
Greece	879.8	1,188.0	1,735.5	2,204.8	2,339.4	2,500.1	2,675.7	2,910.0	3,150.0	3,423.7
Iceland	80.0	100.0	119.7	119.2	124.9	132.5	140.4	151.4	158.9	160.6
Ireland	734.4	709.5	796.4	990.4	1,057.4	1,134.4	1,196.9	1,269.2	1,319.3	1,384.7
Italy	17,686.2	22,494.6	27,416.0	30,301.4	30,624.3	31,106.8	31,370.8	32,038.3	32,583.8	33,239.0
Liechtenstein	12.6	14.8	16.9	18.8	19.3	19.9	20.5	21.2	21.8	22.6
Luxembourg	147.4	152.0	183.4	229.0	231.7	236.8	244.1	253.4	257.8	268.2
Malta	66.2	75.0	104.7	147.6	157.1	169.8	175.0	183.4	189.1	196.9
Monaco				20.7	20.9	20.8	21.4	22.6	22.9	23.0
Netherlands	4,515.0	4,901.0	5,196.0	5,633.0	5,740.0	5,810.0	5,931.0	6,120.0	6,343.0	6,539.0
Norway	1,233.6	1,514.0	1,613.0	1,684.7	1,661.2	1,758.0	1,786.4	1,813.6	1,851.9	1,872.9
Portugal	941.0	1,185.0	1,630.0	2,611.0	2,809.0	3,021.0	3,239.0	3,469.0	3,593.0	3,746.0
Spain	7,556.5	9,273.7	11,995.6	14,212.3	14,753.8	15,297.4	16,050.1	16,847.4	17,449.2	18,150.9
Sweden	2,883.0	3,151.2	3,601.0	3,630.8	3,654.9	3,701.2	3,790.7	3,890.2	3,998.6	4,018.5
Switzerland	2,246.8	2,617.2	2,985.4	3,229.2	3,268.1	3,323.4	3,383.3	3,467.3	3,545.2	3,629.7
Turkey	742.3	983.4	1,649.9	3,058.5	3,274.2	3,570.1	3,838.3	4,072.3	4,422.2	4,534.8
United Kingdom	15,437.7	19,458.2	21,989.0	24,428.6	25,547.6	26,318.3	27,010.4	27,010.4	27,959.7	28,640.3
Eastern Europe										
Albania			5.3	58.7	67.3	76.8	90.8	92.3	114.5	133.5
Belarus			604.5	939.6	1,035.8	1,132.8	1,279.2	1,351.0	1,385.9	1,432.2
Bosnia-Herzegovina			450.3					272.6	289.2	308.6
Bulgaria	500.0	600.0	1,276.8	1,647.6	1,645.0	1,648.0	1,703.0	1,756.2	1,809.4	1,914.0
Croatia			795.4	710.9	835.7	932.3	1,000.1	1,063.5	1,124.8	1,195.5
Czech Republic			2,520.4	3,043.3	3,192.5	3,391.5	3,493.0	3,439.7	3,438.9	3,529.8
Estonia	126.5	177.0	240.9	383.4	406.6	427.7	450.9	458.7	463.9	407.3
Georgia			485.0	360.6	323.6	265.6	260.4	247.9	247.9	248.0
Hungary	925.0	1,435.9	1,856.7	2,044.9	2,100.9	2,166.0	2,218.0	2,255.5	2,364.7	2,482.8
Latvia				331.8	379.9	431.8	482.7	525.6	556.8	586.2
Lithuania			493.0	718.5	785.1	882.1	980.9	1,089.3	1,172.4	1,133.5
Macedonia			230.8	285.9	274.7	283.2	288.9	290.0	299.0	304.0
Moldova			209.0	165.9	177.3	206.0	214.7	224.4	231.0	248.8
Poland	2,269.9	3,450.0	5,261.0	7,517.0	8,054.0	8,533.0	9,033.9	9,282.8	9,991.3	10,503.1
Romania			1,292.3	2,197.5	2,326.1	2,447.1	2,594.6	2,703.1	2,777.6	2,881.2
Russia			8,986.3	14,195.3	15,815.0	17,631.6	17,758.5	17,296.8	17,050.0	19,120.1
Slovakia			860.0	1,015.8	1,058.4	1,135.9	1,196.1	1,236.4	1,247.0	1,290.8
Slovenia			578.3	698.2	727.6	764.8	797.9	829.7	866.1	881.5
Ukraine			3,272.0	4,468.7	4,736.0	4,801.9	4,877.8	5,210.8	5,372.0	5,463.0

Source: *European Automobile Manufacturers' Association (ACEA) / International Road Federation (IRF)*
Notes: *There may be wide variations from year to year in SMMT estimates and in other figures due to interpretation of definitions*

Automotives and Transport Statistics

Passenger Cars in Use 1980-2008 *(continued)*
'000

	2002	2003	2004	2005	2006	2007	2008	Number in use /'000 persons 2008
Western Europe								
Austria	3,987.1	4,054.3	4,109.1	4,156.7	4,205.0	4,245.6	4,265.0	510.7
Belgium	4,724.9	4,772.6	4,818.6	4,861.4	4,929.3	5,006.3	5,028.7	473.6
Cyprus	287.6	302.5	335.6	355.1	372.9	389.6	397.0	460.4
Denmark	1,890.0	1,894.2	1,914.4	1,961.2	2,013.9	2,058.9	2,079.0	380.7
Finland	2,180.0	2,259.4	2,331.2	2,414.5	2,489.3	2,553.6	2,582.5	487.2
France	29,160.0	29,560.0	29,900.0	30,100.0	30,400.0	30,700.0	30,827.5	496.4
Germany	44,657.3	45,022.9	45,375.5	46,090.3	46,569.7	41,183.6	40,394.8	491.3
Gibraltar	12.9	12.8	13.9	14.6	14.7	15.0	15.2	518.3
Greece	3,477.1	3,696.9	3,960.2	4,204.5	4,446.5	4,821.4	4,918.6	438.7
Iceland	161.7	166.9	175.4	187.4	197.3	207.5	211.1	669.1
Ireland	1,447.9	1,507.1	1,582.8	1,662.2	1,778.9	1,882.9	1,915.0	437.4
Italy	33,706.2	34,310.4	33,973.1	34,667.5	35,297.3	35,680.1	35,892.5	608.6
Liechtenstein	23.3	23.5	23.9	24.4	24.3	24.5	24.8	697.7
Luxembourg	282.4	287.2	293.4	299.8	304.5	314.3	318.9	663.6
Malta	201.9	208.8	211.4	212.6	218.2	223.7	227.9	559.2
Monaco	22.6	22.7	22.9	23.0	23.1	23.2	23.4	711.5
Netherlands	6,710.0	6,855.0	7,151.0	7,299.0	7,413.0	7,597.0	7,644.8	466.6
Norway	1,899.7	1,933.6	1,977.9	2,028.8	2,084.8	2,153.7	2,183.0	460.8
Portugal	3,885.0	3,966.0	4,100.0	4,200.0	4,290.0	4,379.0	4,414.3	414.8
Spain	18,732.6	18,688.3	19,541.9	20,250.4	21,052.6	21,760.2	22,113.1	490.8
Sweden	4,042.8	4,075.4	4,113.4	4,153.7	4,202.5	4,258.5	4,282.6	467.7
Switzerland	3,701.0	3,753.9	3,811.4	3,861.4	3,900.0	3,955.8	3,979.9	528.5
Turkey	4,600.1	4,700.3	5,400.4	5,772.7	6,141.0	6,472.2	6,591.2	88.6
United Kingdom	28,484.0	29,007.8	29,378.2	29,747.5	29,880.0	30,177.9	30,318.3	495.5
Eastern Europe								
Albania	148.5	174.8	190.0	209.6	228.6	247.6	255.3	81.2
Belarus	1,515.9	1,620.1	1,671.3	1,737.1	1,814.8	1,844.1	1,868.0	192.8
Bosnia-Herzegovina	321.7	335.0	348.0	357.2	361.9	366.7	369.4	96.1
Bulgaria	1,951.0	1,990.0	2,041.0	2,063.6	2,072.4	2,109.9	2,127.8	281.0
Croatia	1,244.3	1,293.4	1,337.5	1,384.7	1,435.8	1,491.1	1,511.6	340.8
Czech Republic	3,647.1	3,706.0	3,815.5	3,958.7	4,108.6	4,280.1	4,366.7	423.3
Estonia	400.7	434.0	471.2	493.8	554.0	523.8	517.7	387.8
Georgia	252.0	255.2	255.2	269.7	273.9	278.3	280.4	64.0
Hungary	2,629.5	2,777.2	2,828.4	2,888.7	2,953.7	3,012.2	3,036.7	302.5
Latvia	619.1	648.9	686.1	742.4	822.0	908.5	945.1	416.9
Lithuania	1,180.9	1,256.9	1,315.9	1,455.3	1,529.8	1,597.6	1,635.1	485.7
Macedonia	308.0	300.0	312.5	299.8	303.5	305.6	303.3	148.7
Moldova	260.8	257.1	270.6	279.8	287.6	291.7	294.5	81.0
Poland	11,243.8	11,243.8	11,975.2	12,339.4	13,384.2	14,588.7	14,937.2	392.6
Romania	2,973.4	3,087.6	3,225.4	3,363.8	3,225.4	3,518.4	3,557.5	165.5
Russia	21,152.0	23,383.0	24,208.0	25,569.7	25,569.7	27,092.5	27,413.0	193.0
Slovakia	1,326.9	1,356.0	1,388.2	1,303.7	1,333.7	1,433.9	1,450.1	268.8
Slovenia	894.5	910.4	933.9	960.2	980.3	1,014.1	1,027.5	509.5
Ukraine	5,529.0	5,585.0	5,603.8	5,800.0	5,986.0	6,071.0	6,133.3	132.8

Source: *European Automobile Manufacturers' Association (ACEA) / International Road Federation (IRF)*
Notes: *There may be wide variations from year to year in SMMT estimates and in other figures due to interpretation of definitions*

Automotives and Transport Statistics

Table 3.3

Two-Wheelers in Use 1980-2008

'000

	1980	1985	1990	1995	1996	1997	1998	1999	2000	2001
Western Europe										
Austria	574.1	648.4	548.0	546.4	560.2	575.7	600.6	622.9	628.0	641.4
Belgium	445.7	466.1	481.8	548.5	559.0	571.6	588.1	607.9	626.9	639.8
Cyprus		40.0	51.0	50.4	46.9	45.2	44.3	44.8	43.3	42.0
Denmark				50.0	58.0	73.9	93.9	112.1	126.9	138.3
Finland			169.0	159.0	162.3	166.1	172.5	182.4	192.6	205.4
France				2,289.0	2,278.0	2,298.0	2,321.0	2,373.0	2,410.0	2,440.0
Germany			2,362.0	3,995.0	4,137.0	4,351.0	4,673.0	4,920.1	5,062.8	5,135.0
Gibraltar		1.6	2.8	6.6	6.6	5.9	5.9	6.9	8.5	9.6
Greece		162.3	256.6	475.7	517.9	571.0	633.8	710.8	781.4	853.4
Iceland		0.9	1.5	1.9	2.0	2.0	1.9	2.1	2.3	2.2
Ireland		26.0	22.7	23.5	23.3	24.4	24.4	26.7	30.6	32.9
Italy				7,905.8	8,344.7	8,655.6	8,812.4	9,367.9	9,773.1	9,979.9
Liechtenstein	0.6	1.3	1.3	1.7	1.9	2.0	2.2	2.4	2.6	2.8
Luxembourg		24.7	25.4	28.5	28.9	29.7	30.6	31.8	32.8	33.6
Malta				8.0	9.9	11.1	11.0	11.7	12.2	12.6
Monaco		4.0	4.7	5.3	5.4	5.6	6.0	6.3	6.6	6.8
Netherlands		728.0	612.0	848.0	878.0	898.0	931.0	964.0	970.8	964.8
Norway		186.6	203.5	197.8	200.5	216.8	228.5	239.6	249.9	261.9
Portugal	1,069.1	1,091.2	968.6	838.5	782.2	792.8	749.0	735.0	734.0	709.0
Spain		2,015.5	3,073.6	3,402.0	3,446.5	3,500.3	3,593.1	3,672.1	3,648.2	3,596.0
Sweden				258.9	271.0	280.0	287.5	300.0	317.3	340.6
Switzerland	808.8	862.1	763.9	721.6	716.5	727.8	733.9	744.4	732.6	751.4
Turkey	137.9	289.1	531.9	819.9	854.2	905.1	940.9	975.7	1,011.3	1,031.2
United Kingdom	1,457.0	1,148.0	879.8	900.2	921.1	955.8	1,015.5	1,041.1	1,157.7	1,212.0
Eastern Europe										
Albania			8.6	6.9	5.5	3.6	4.1	3.2	3.8	3.4
Belarus			404.1	504.2	533.9	553.5	558.3	533.7	523.6	536.0
Bosnia-Herzegovina										
Bulgaria			481.7	519.3	521.7	525.0	515.7	519.2	522.4	526.0
Croatia						42.2	50.5	58.1	65.3	73.8
Czech Republic			926.3	915.2	918.2	929.6	927.1	799.6	748.1	755.5
Estonia			2.7	3.3	4.7	5.3	6.1	6.7	6.7	6.8
Georgia			29.7	27.9	12.2	7.4	7.6	4.0	4.6	4.0
Hungary			92.3	85.3	85.6	86.6	87.0	87.6	91.2	93.1
Latvia				15.7	18.4	19.3	19.4	20.1	20.7	21.4
Lithuania				19.4	20.9	20.3	22.3	22.1	21.7	25.2
Macedonia			1.9	1.6	1.8	2.0	2.2	2.4	2.6	2.8
Moldova			196.4	144.7	109.8	93.8	77.7	61.6	45.5	29.5
Poland		1,546.5	1,356.6	929.3	886.0	843.8	819.2	804.5	803.0	802.8
Romania		238.0	249.3	262.2	255.0	250.5	245.7	242.5	239.2	237.9
Russia						7,809.3	7,165.9	6,328.6	7,735.0	7,718.4
Slovakia			286.3	229.1	223.7	222.8	240.6	181.7	181.1	180.2
Slovenia			50.4	45.9	46.6	47.3	48.0	48.7	49.4	50.1
Ukraine			3,253.4	3,102.6	3,000.5	2,794.8	2,609.2	2,372.0	2,251.5	1,960.3

Source: Euromonitor International from SMMT/national statistics
Notes: Two-wheelers consist of motorcycles and mopeds

Automotives and Transport Statistics

Two-Wheelers in Use 1980-2008 *(continued)*
'000

	2002	2003	2004	2005	2006	2007	2008	Number in use /'000 persons 2008
Western Europe								
Austria	596.8	606.9	612.2	627.7	645.0	668.0	674.2	80.7
Belgium	651.2	665.4	670.0	672.0	678.9	683.4	680.0	64.0
Cyprus	40.3	41.5	41.4	40.4	40.4	41.2	41.6	48.3
Denmark	146.4	151.3	155.7	162.1	171.9	184.3	187.5	34.3
Finland	222.7	244.4	270.6	299.6	325.3	352.2	361.3	68.2
France	2,441.0	2,448.0	2,462.0	2,480.0	2,493.0	2,508.0	2,513.1	40.5
Germany	5,256.9	5,306.0	5,462.5	5,462.5	5,540.7	5,579.8	5,592.9	68.0
Gibraltar	5.7	5.6	6.2	6.6	7.1	7.2	7.4	251.5
Greece	910.6	969.9	1,042.6	1,124.2	1,205.8	1,298.7	1,327.1	118.4
Iceland	2.6	2.7	3.1	4.2	5.7	8.1	8.6	27.3
Ireland	33.1	35.1	35.8	36.5	37.1	37.5	37.6	8.6
Italy	10,149.5	10,295.4	10,224.6	10,263.4	10,311.5	10,354.9	10,369.4	175.8
Liechtenstein	2.9	3.0	3.0	3.1	3.2	3.3	3.3	93.8
Luxembourg	34.7	36.0	36.9	37.7	38.3	38.8	39.0	81.2
Malta	13.1	13.4	12.6	11.9	11.1	10.4	9.7	23.7
Monaco	6.9	7.0	7.2	7.3	7.5	7.6	7.7	234.8
Netherlands	1,002.5	1,015.6	1,038.9	1,112.9	1,220.0	1,310.5	1,340.7	81.8
Norway	277.0	292.3	302.9	313.3	318.1	323.8	326.1	68.8
Portugal	604.0	633.0	611.0	593.0	573.0	554.0	547.7	51.5
Spain	3,561.5	3,657.1	3,854.1	4,066.3	4,176.3	4,211.2	4,250.9	94.3
Sweden	370.8	397.1	433.7	471.9	509.4	547.2	559.8	61.1
Switzerland	745.1	762.9	770.6	770.3	783.5	789.9	792.1	105.2
Turkey	1,046.9	1,073.4	1,218.7	1,441.1	1,822.8	2,003.5	2,090.7	28.1
United Kingdom	1,256.4	1,314.0	1,338.3	1,367.1	1,393.7	1,421.4	1,430.7	23.4
Eastern Europe								
Albania	3.4	3.9	4.9	7.2	11.6	13.9	14.9	4.7
Belarus	525.0	506.4	454.6	444.5	427.9	414.5	399.5	41.2
Bosnia-Herzegovina								
Bulgaria	530.3	535.7	541.9	546.2	550.1	554.0	555.4	73.4
Croatia	85.3	99.2	113.0	127.9	143.5	153.7	158.2	35.7
Czech Republic	760.2	751.6	756.6	794.0	822.7	855.8	866.8	84.0
Estonia	7.3	8.1	9.1	10.2	12.6	14.8	15.4	11.6
Georgia	2.8	3.3	5.2	5.5	5.7	5.9	6.0	1.4
Hungary	97.6	103.5	114.0	122.7	130.2	135.9	138.3	13.8
Latvia	22.2	22.9	29.9	32.5	36.9	39.0	40.0	17.7
Lithuania	27.5	28.8	29.0	30.5	32.5	40.8	40.0	11.9
Macedonia	3.0	3.2	3.4	3.6	3.8	4.0	4.2	2.0
Moldova	13.4	14.4	15.7	16.9	18.2	19.5	19.9	5.5
Poland	824.1	845.5	835.8	753.6	784.0	825.0	823.8	21.7
Romania	238.5	235.9	234.7	228.0	215.8	209.7	206.9	9.6
Russia	7,841.2	8,177.4	8,275.7	8,399.5	8,523.6	8,600.5	8,636.6	60.8
Slovakia	179.5	178.5	180.1	182.5	183.1	185.5	186.1	34.5
Slovenia	50.6	42.4	40.2	48.7	53.2	57.5	59.4	29.5
Ukraine	1,744.4	1,369.0	1,145.4	982.6	885.9	821.1	785.0	17.0

Source: *Euromonitor International from SMMT/national statistics*
Notes: *Two-wheelers consist of motorcycles and mopeds*

Automotives and Transport Statistics

Table 3.4

Production of Commercial Vehicles 1980-2008
'000

	1980	1985	1990	1995	1996	1997	1998	1999	2000	2001
Western Europe										
Austria	8.5	11.2	11.0	9.2	8.7	10.2	11.9	15.7	25.0	24.3
Belgium	47.0	48.7	90.0	103.6	89.9	96.3	114.0	98.9	121.1	128.6
Cyprus			22.0	5.0	4.0	4.0	4.0			
Denmark										
Finland	1.1	0.8	0.9	0.4	0.4	0.4	0.4	0.4	0.4	0.4
France	439.9	383.7	474.2	423.8	303.1	312.4	351.1	395.7	468.6	446.9
Germany	357.6	279.2	315.9	307.1	303.3	344.9	378.7	378.2	394.7	390.5
Gibraltar										
Greece			1.4	0.4	0.3	0.2	0.2	0.1	0.1	0.1
Iceland										
Ireland	2.6									
Italy	165.1	183.8	246.2	244.9	227.4	253.6	290.4	290.8	316.0	307.9
Liechtenstein										
Luxembourg										
Malta										
Monaco										
Netherlands	32.1	14.3	17.3	17.6	18.5	20.4	27.5	25.1	30.5	49.7
Norway										
Portugal	58.4	26.5	77.5	85.7	80.5	81.4	76.2	65.3	68.2	62.4
Spain	152.8	187.5	374.0	375.0	470.6	551.8	609.7	643.7	666.5	638.7
Sweden	63.1	60.3	74.4	102.5	95.4	104.0	114.5	108.6	35.7	38.1
Switzerland	1.2									
Turkey	19.4	37.3	62.8	49.0	69.0	101.6	104.6	75.8	133.5	95.3
United Kingdom	389.2	266.0	270.3	233.0	238.3	223.8	214.9	173.6	172.4	192.9
Eastern Europe										
Albania										
Belarus			43.0	13.0	10.5	13.0	12.7	13.6	14.6	16.8
Bosnia-Herzegovina										
Bulgaria			8.9	0.5	0.2	0.2	0.2	0.2	0.2	0.2
Croatia			129.0	31.0	35.7	38.7	41.7			
Czech Republic					37.6	52.0	44.3	29.3	29.8	9.5
Estonia										
Georgia										
Hungary	15.2	14.0	8.1	1.2	1.7	2.0	1.2	2.6	3.4	3.9
Latvia			17.1	4.3	1.2	1.1	1.0			
Lithuania										
Macedonia			14.6	1.8						
Moldova										
Poland	116.0	57.1	42.8	10.6	72.5	62.1	68.7	73.3	42.6	11.9
Romania	49.1	19.8	17.6	21.2	24.5	20.5	23.0	18.6	14.0	12.0
Russia			716.9	214.9	188.5	209.7	204.5	236.4	244.6	229.0
Slovakia			0.9	0.2	0.2	0.2	0.8	0.3	0.4	359.0
Slovenia								343.0	367.0	0.0
Ukraine		45.2	40.3	8.7	5.2	5.1	7.3	4.3	2.5	6.8

Source: European Automobile Manufacturers' Association (ACEA)

Automotives and Transport Statistics

Production of Commercial Vehicles 1980-2008 *(continued)*
'000

	2002	2003	2004	2005	2006	2007	2008
Western Europe							
Austria	19.9	21.0	21.5	22.7	26.9	28.1	25.4
Belgium	120.3	112.7	43.2	33.2	36.1	44.7	44.4
Cyprus							
Denmark							
Finland	0.4	0.4	0.5	0.4	0.4	0.3	0.4
France	309.1	399.7	438.6	436.0	446.0	465.0	423.0
Germany	346.1	361.2	377.9	407.5	421.1	504.3	513.7
Gibraltar							
Greece	0.1	0.1	0.1	0.1	0.1	0.1	0.1
Iceland							
Ireland							
Italy	301.3	295.2	308.4	312.8	319.1	373.5	364.6
Liechtenstein							
Luxembourg							
Malta							
Monaco							
Netherlands	48.9	52.2	59.9	65.6	72.1	76.7	73.3
Norway							
Portugal	68.3	73.8	75.9	81.5	83.8	42.2	42.9
Spain	588.3	630.5	609.7	654.3	698.8	693.9	598.6
Sweden	38.2	42.6	49.9	49.9	44.6	49.2	56.1
Switzerland							
Turkey	142.4	239.2	376.3	425.4	442.1	464.5	474.3
United Kingdom	193.1	188.9	209.3	206.8	206.3	215.7	202.9
Eastern Europe							
Albania							
Belarus	16.9	18.4	21.7	23.0	25.3	26.4	27.0
Bosnia-Herzegovina							
Bulgaria	0.2	0.2	0.2	0.2	0.2	0.2	0.2
Croatia							
Czech Republic	7.2	6.9	6.9	8.0	8.2	12.6	12.5
Estonia							
Georgia							
Hungary	3.3	3.8	4.1	3.5	3.2	4.0	3.7
Latvia							
Lithuania							
Macedonia							
Moldova							
Poland	23.6	15.2	78.0	85.4	82.3	89.6	104.5
Romania	14.2	19.5	23.2	20.6	11.9	7.6	14.3
Russia	239.7	268.4	276.0	283.1	330.4	371.5	382.1
Slovakia	276.0	187.0	0.0	0.0	0.0	0.0	0.0
Slovenia	0.0	7.6	15.0	39.6	35.3	24.2	17.6
Ukraine	3.4	4.9	7.8	19.0	20.4	22.5	25.0

Source: *European Automobile Manufacturers' Association (ACEA)*

Production of Passenger Cars 1980-2008
'000

	1980	1985	1990	1995	1996	1997	1998	1999	2000	2001
Western Europe										
Austria	7.5	7.1	12.7	59.2	97.4	97.8	91.3	123.6	116.0	131.1
Belgium	281.7	248.5	311.8	385.9	367.5	355.8	950.5	917.5	912.2	1,058.7
Cyprus										
Denmark										
Finland	21.5	38.7	30.2	34.6	28.5	33.7	31.5	34.0	38.3	41.9
France	2,938.6	2,632.4	3,294.8	3,050.9	2,087.5	2,258.8	2,603.0	2,784.5	2,879.8	3,181.6
Germany	3,520.9	4,166.7	4,660.7	4,360.2	4,539.6	4,678.0	5,348.1	5,309.5	5,131.9	5,301.2
Gibraltar										
Greece			12.6	3.2	3.2	3.1	3.0	3.0	2.9	2.9
Iceland										
Ireland	44.6									
Italy	1,445.2	1,389.2	1,874.7	1,422.4	1,318.0	1,573.9	1,402.4	1,410.5	1,422.3	1,271.8
Liechtenstein										
Luxembourg										
Malta										
Monaco										
Netherlands	80.8	108.1	121.3	100.4	145.2	197.2	243.0	262.2	215.1	189.3
Norway										
Portugal	45.5	61.0	60.2	73.2	152.6	189.1	187.7	187.0	178.5	177.4
Spain	1,028.8	1,230.1	1,679.3	1,958.8	1,941.7	2,010.3	2,216.4	2,208.7	2,366.4	2,211.2
Sweden	235.3	400.7	335.9	387.7	367.8	375.7	368.3	385.0	279.0	251.0
Switzerland										
Turkey	31.5	60.4	167.6	233.4	207.8	242.8	239.9	222.0	297.5	175.3
United Kingdom	923.7	1,048.0	1,295.6	1,532.1	1,686.1	1,711.9	1,760.7	1,799.0	1,641.5	1,492.4
Eastern Europe										
Albania										
Belarus										
Bosnia-Herzegovina										
Bulgaria		15.0	14.6	1.1	1.4	1.8	2.1	1.9	1.8	1.9
Croatia					0.3	0.6	0.8			
Czech Republic				213.0	270.2	361.5	368.5	348.5	428.2	456.9
Estonia										
Georgia										
Hungary				36.5	51.8	63.5	65.8	68.0	77.3	140.4
Latvia										
Lithuania										
Macedonia										
Moldova										
Poland	364.5	283.0	266.4	391.9	433.6	520.2	640.0	572.9	532.0	336.0
Romania	79.3	114.4	99.9	71.0	97.9	109.2	103.9	88.3	64.2	56.8
Russia	1,166.0	1,165.0	1,103.0	893.6	874.2	985.1	860.7	955.5	969.2	1,021.7
Slovakia				22.3	24.4	26.4	125.1	126.5	181.3	181.6
Slovenia			74.7	63.5	72.3	74.8	111.5	118.1	122.9	116.1
Ukraine		167.5	103.4	58.7	46.9	32.0	25.7	17.8	11.7	25.0

Source: *European Automobile Manufacturers' Association (ACEA)*

Automotives and Transport Statistics

Production of Passenger Cars 1980-2008 *(continued)*
'000

	2002	2003	2004	2005	2006	2007	2008
Western Europe							
Austria	132.8	118.7	227.2	230.5	248.1	200.0	125.4
Belgium	936.9	791.7	852.4	895.1	881.9	789.7	680.1
Cyprus							
Denmark							
Finland	41.1	19.2	10.1	21.2	32.4	24.0	18.0
France	3,292.8	3,220.3	3,227.4	3,113.0	2,723.2	2,550.9	2,145.0
Germany	5,123.2	5,145.4	5,192.1	5,350.2	5,398.5	5,709.1	5,526.9
Gibraltar							
Greece	2.8	2.6	2.4	2.3	2.2	2.1	2.1
Iceland							
Ireland							
Italy	1,125.8	1,026.5	833.6	725.5	892.5	910.9	659.2
Liechtenstein							
Luxembourg							
Malta							
Monaco							
Netherlands	182.4	163.1	187.6	115.1	87.3	61.9	59.2
Norway							
Portugal	182.6	165.6	150.8	137.6	143.5	134.0	132.2
Spain	2,266.9	2,399.4	2,402.5	2,098.2	2,078.6	2,195.8	1,943.0
Sweden	238.0	280.4	290.4	288.7	288.6	316.9	252.3
Switzerland							
Turkey	204.2	294.1	447.2	453.7	545.7	634.9	655.7
United Kingdom	1,629.9	1,657.6	1,647.2	1,596.3	1,442.1	1,534.6	1,446.6
Eastern Europe							
Albania							
Belarus							
Bosnia-Herzegovina							
Bulgaria	2.0	2.1	2.2	2.3	2.3	2.3	2.4
Croatia							
Czech Republic	441.3	436.3	443.1	596.8	848.8	925.1	933.3
Estonia							
Georgia							
Hungary	138.2	122.3	118.6	148.5	187.6	288.0	342.4
Latvia							
Lithuania							
Macedonia							
Moldova							
Poland	287.5	306.8	523.0	540.0	632.3	695.0	840.0
Romania	65.3	75.7	99.0	174.5	201.7	234.1	231.1
Russia	980.1	1,010.4	1,110.1	1,068.1	1,177.9	1,288.7	1,308.5
Slovakia	225.4	281.2	223.5	218.3	295.4	571.1	575.8
Slovenia	126.7	110.6	116.6	138.4	115.0	174.2	180.2
Ukraine	50.4	103.0	179.1	196.7	274.9	380.1	413.6

Source: *European Automobile Manufacturers' Association (ACEA)*

Production of Two-Wheelers 1985-2008

'000

	1985	1990	1995	2000	2003	2004	2005	2006	2007	2008
Western Europe										
Austria	160.8	20.9	13.2	29.2	56.0	56.7	60.0	69.0	73.4	75.3
Belgium	58.3	61.3	8.2	6.4	5.4	4.9	4.6	4.4	4.2	3.9
Cyprus										
Denmark										
Finland	14.8	5.2	0.3	0.2	0.1	0.1	0.1	0.1	0.2	0.2
France			394.6	451.4	154.8	255.7	259.2	232.4	258.3	258.6
Germany	85.8	55.3	44.6	112.6	109.1	102.8	101.0	106.3	111.6	112.6
Gibraltar										
Greece										
Iceland										
Ireland										
Italy	808.3	894.9	1,101.1	1,048.2	697.0	685.5	695.0	708.6	720.1	723.9
Liechtenstein										
Luxembourg										
Malta										
Monaco										
Netherlands				9.3	8.3	8.0	8.0	8.0	8.0	8.0
Norway										
Portugal					0.0	0.0	0.1	0.1	0.1	0.1
Spain	173.5	384.6	279.9	284.8	209.0	230.9	249.5	253.7	265.1	268.9
Sweden		1.3	0.1	0.1	0.3	0.3	0.4	0.5	0.6	0.7
Switzerland	11.7	0.8								
Turkey				217.2	216.0	229.5	236.7	243.7	245.3	247.0
United Kingdom	2.0	1.9	11.2	25.6	31.5	26.2	34.6	42.1	50.0	52.7
Eastern Europe										
Albania										
Belarus				36.6	38.1	38.7	38.9	39.2	39.5	39.6
Bosnia-Herzegovina										
Bulgaria										
Croatia										
Czech Republic				3.9	2.2	1.8	1.6	1.0	0.9	0.8
Estonia										
Georgia										
Hungary				0.3	0.2	0.2	0.2	0.2	0.2	0.2
Latvia				1.0	1.0	1.0	1.0	1.0	1.0	1.0
Lithuania				0.0	0.0	0.0	0.0	0.0	0.0	0.0
Macedonia										
Moldova										
Poland				0.0	0.0	0.0	0.0	0.0	0.0	0.0
Romania	2.0	4.1	0.1	0.2	0.2	0.3	0.3	0.3	0.3	0.3
Russia	818.0			32.8	25.8	25.3	25.1	24.9	24.7	24.5
Slovakia			17.2							
Slovenia		57.5	56.2	59.9	64.0	60.8	59.5	58.2	56.9	56.0
Ukraine				0.2	0.3	0.2	0.2	0.2	0.2	0.2

Source: *Euromonitor International from SMMT/national statistics*

Automotives and Transport Statistics

Table 3.7

Price of Automotive Diesel 1980-2008

Units of national currency per 10 litres (inc. tax)

	1980	1985	1990	1995	1996	1997	1998	1999	2000	2001
Western Europe										
Austria	6.21	7.81	5.98	6.25	6.67	6.88	6.31	6.36	7.78	7.48
Belgium	3.46	4.51	5.28	6.07	6.53	6.68	6.21	6.40	8.10	7.81
Cyprus										
Denmark	20.00	28.14	22.79	43.82	48.03	51.83	51.58	56.15	70.91	69.49
Finland	3.29	4.70	5.19	5.91	6.30	6.39	6.38	6.82	8.50	8.19
France		5.82	4.94	5.87	6.53	6.76	6.43	6.88	8.45	7.99
Germany			4.89	5.73	6.22	6.34	5.82	6.38	8.01	8.22
Gibraltar										
Greece	0.43	1.04	1.94	4.10	4.61	4.76	4.44	5.03	6.65	6.34
Iceland										
Ireland	3.20	7.06	6.95	6.79	7.36	7.36	7.05	7.00	8.42	8.20
Italy	2.33	4.16	6.39	6.93	7.39	7.43	7.10	7.62	8.92	8.69
Liechtenstein										
Luxembourg	3.01	4.97	3.11	4.96	5.36	5.53	5.11	5.43	6.89	6.56
Malta										
Monaco										
Netherlands	4.38	5.70	4.74	7.02	7.67	6.82	6.53	6.97	8.45	8.20
Norway	18.42	23.50	27.46	67.58	75.60	78.11	78.13	83.17	98.98	86.45
Portugal	0.82	3.29	4.96	5.22	5.60	5.74	5.64	5.49	6.54	6.69
Spain	3.51	4.51	4.81	4.93	5.43	5.60	5.30	5.65	6.95	6.93
Sweden	14.65	30.73	49.22	63.46	65.89	66.75	63.02	66.52	84.46	86.48
Switzerland	12.72	14.18	11.23	11.94	12.36	12.88	12.12	12.35	14.36	14.00
Turkey				0.19	0.40	0.79	1.19	2.37	4.35	7.33
United Kingdom	2.78	3.65	3.98	5.43	5.77	6.25	6.55	7.25	8.13	7.79
Eastern Europe										
Albania										
Belarus										
Bosnia-Herzegovina										
Bulgaria										
Croatia										
Czech Republic		55.00	98.00	156.50	166.60	187.60	180.30	189.80	247.00	241.10
Estonia										
Georgia										
Hungary	65.50	93.00	300.00	834.10	1,073.60	1,277.00	1,387.60	1,663.00	2,150.80	2,086.31
Latvia										
Lithuania										
Macedonia										
Moldova										
Poland				10.01	11.90	13.98	14.61	18.35	25.55	25.52
Romania				0.42	0.59	2.25	3.19	5.32	8.48	13.22
Russia							23.21	34.98	57.83	74.11
Slovakia			4.29	4.54	5.11	6.73	6.54	6.12	7.47	7.07
Slovenia										
Ukraine										

Source: Institute of Petroleum, OECD Energy Prices and Taxes/Euromonitor International

Automotives and Transport Statistics

Price of Automotive Diesel 1980-2008 *(continued)*

Units of national currency per 10 litres (inc. tax)

	2002	2003	2004	2005	2006	2007	2008	US$ per litre 2008
Western Europe								
Austria	7.19	7.27	8.09	9.48	10.09	10.35	12.38	1.82
Belgium	7.26	7.56	8.81	10.40	10.79	10.94	12.52	1.84
Cyprus			7.22	8.24	8.84	9.00	10.85	1.60
Denmark	67.93	67.85	68.21	76.62	81.80	82.58	95.05	1.86
Finland	7.84	8.08	8.48	9.69	10.22	10.18	12.64	1.86
France	7.71	7.93	8.83	10.23	10.79	10.92	12.70	1.87
Germany	8.40	8.87	9.38	10.68	11.17	11.68	13.33	1.96
Gibraltar								
Greece	6.22	6.37	7.40	8.79	9.54	9.84	12.06	1.77
Iceland								
Ireland	7.74	8.04	8.82	10.36	10.95	10.80	12.72	1.87
Italy	8.56	8.77	9.38	11.08	11.65	11.62	13.42	1.98
Liechtenstein								
Luxembourg	6.32	6.38	6.90	8.43	9.17	9.35	11.64	1.71
Malta			7.17	8.78	9.83	9.48	11.19	1.65
Monaco								
Netherlands	7.90	7.95	8.89	10.23	10.87	10.98	12.87	1.89
Norway	81.98	83.88	86.80	98.30	106.48	103.46	122.75	2.18
Portugal	6.45	7.10	7.87	9.37	10.61	10.81	12.62	1.86
Spain	6.89	6.94	7.55	8.93	9.47	9.57	11.30	1.66
Sweden	83.38	81.14	85.47	103.53	111.33	109.60	133.87	2.03
Switzerland	13.35	13.58	14.46	16.38	17.40	17.68	20.25	1.87
Turkey	10.96	13.94	15.39	19.56	22.24	23.02	28.73	2.21
United Kingdom	7.55	7.79	8.19	9.09	9.52	9.69	11.75	2.16
Eastern Europe								
Albania								
Belarus								
Bosnia-Herzegovina								
Bulgaria							21.19	1.58
Croatia								
Czech Republic	217.30	218.95	248.68	278.73	289.58	287.15	317.50	1.86
Estonia			107.97	130.93	135.82	135.66	179.24	1.68
Georgia								
Hungary	2,013.35	2,098.85	2,185.63	2,500.93	2,709.10	2,630.44	3,081.01	1.79
Latvia		4.50	5.60	6.03	6.08	6.30	7.68	1.60
Lithuania			24.60	28.44	30.65	30.30	37.70	1.60
Macedonia								
Moldova								
Poland	25.80	28.36	31.69	36.82	38.18	37.66	42.19	1.75
Romania	15.90	18.87	24.67	30.32	32.85	31.53	40.30	1.60
Russia	90.62	107.13	123.64	140.16	167.83	172.54	226.59	0.91
Slovakia	6.59	7.21	8.44	9.76	10.68	12.54	13.82	2.03
Slovenia						9.73	11.28	1.66
Ukraine								

Source: *Institute of Petroleum, OECD Energy Prices and Taxes/Euromonitor International*

Automotives and Transport Statistics

Table 3.8

Price of Automotive Diesel by Quarter 2007-2009

Units of national currency per 10 litres (inc. tax)

	2007 1st Quarter	2007 2nd Quarter	2007 3rd Quarter	2007 4th Quarter	2008 1st Quarter	2008 2nd Quarter	2008 3rd Quarter	2008 4th Quarter	2009 1st Quarter	2009 2nd Quarter
Western Europe										
Austria	9.45	9.86	10.60	11.49	11.55	13.34	13.29	11.04	9.33	9.45
Belgium	10.17	10.73	11.00	11.85	12.02	13.64	13.40	11.02	9.74	
Cyprus	8.23	8.78	9.16	9.83	10.20	11.48	12.01	9.71	7.95	8.09
Denmark	76.71	80.98	83.23	89.40	92.17	104.53	101.42	82.09	73.60	
Finland	9.74	9.87	10.12	11.01	12.25	13.49	13.79	11.04	9.61	
France	10.25	10.70	10.98	11.73	12.26	13.63	13.61	11.30	9.64	9.73
Germany	10.83	11.48	11.72	12.70	12.94	14.34	14.28	11.74	10.47	
Gibraltar										
Greece	9.14	9.62	9.93	10.67	11.30	13.07	13.06	10.80	9.24	
Iceland										
Ireland	10.24	10.65	11.02	11.28	11.85	12.54	14.19	12.29	9.75	
Italy	10.96	11.32	11.71	12.48	12.94	14.33	14.46	11.95	10.44	
Liechtenstein										
Luxembourg	8.66	9.15	9.42	10.16	10.61	12.09	12.21			
Malta	9.05	9.09	9.73	10.05	10.19	11.03	12.07	11.48	9.78	9.48
Monaco										
Netherlands	10.28	10.77	11.06	11.79	12.24	13.81	13.97	11.44	9.59	
Norway	99.15	101.00	103.70	110.00	117.00	127.50	131.50	115.00	104.80	
Portugal	10.11	10.60	10.91	11.61	12.09	13.57	13.52	11.29	9.54	
Spain	8.89	9.43	9.69	10.27	10.81	12.15	12.28	9.95	8.56	8.68
Sweden	105.66	108.50	108.20	116.05	126.39	140.79	141.56	126.75	111.49	
Switzerland	16.87	17.33	17.63	18.87	19.37	21.10	22.00	18.53	15.50	
Turkey	21.79	22.70	22.95	24.65	26.14	30.58	30.66	27.52	24.54	
United Kingdom	9.13	9.61	9.65	10.36	11.02	12.39	12.70	10.90	9.97	
Eastern Europe										
Albania										
Belarus										
Bosnia-Herzegovina										
Bulgaria					20.07	23.00	22.95	18.74	15.50	16.00
Croatia										
Czech Republic	269.70	281.00	287.33	310.55	313.22	333.98	337.42	285.36	251.12	
Estonia	129.29	129.33	134.99	149.04	173.44	190.06	194.60	158.85	133.08	130.69
Georgia										
Hungary	2,478.57	2,574.10	2,648.33	2,820.77	3,030.03	3,237.87	3,208.17	2,847.97	2,516.97	2,570.95
Latvia	5.96	6.11	6.24	6.87	7.34	8.14	8.28	6.97	6.20	6.24
Lithuania	28.56	29.87	30.47	32.29	36.12	40.61	40.94	33.11	30.70	29.97
Macedonia										
Moldova										
Poland	35.68	36.77	37.55	40.63	40.78	44.51	44.99	38.79	34.86	
Romania	30.40	30.90	31.20	33.60	37.80	42.90	43.20	37.30	34.80	
Russia	170.63	169.84	170.75	178.93	202.02	224.50	250.88	228.95	193.73	
Slovakia	11.97	12.33	12.55	13.32	13.75	14.39	14.61	12.53	10.74	
Slovenia	9.09	9.57	9.90	10.34	10.60	12.02	12.35	10.15	9.43	9.81
Ukraine										

Source: Institute of Petroleum, OECD Energy Prices and Taxes/Euromonitor International

Automotives and Transport Statistics

Table 3.9

Price of Leaded/Lead Replacement Petrol 1980-2008

Units of national currency per 10 litres (inc. tax)

	1980	1985	1990	1995	1996	1997	1998	1999	2000	2001
Western Europe										
Austria	6.30	8.65	7.12	8.57	8.52	8.56	8.06	8.14	8.30	8.50
Belgium	5.73	8.38	7.18	8.41	9.24	9.94	9.44	9.68	11.02	10.75
Cyprus										
Denmark	45.30	61.35	62.82	60.89						
Finland	4.85	6.50	8.57							
France	5.15	8.52	7.71	8.94	9.45	9.80	9.58	10.01	11.67	11.22
Germany	5.96	7.37	6.25	8.65	9.00	9.32	9.75	10.05	10.43	10.82
Gibraltar										
Greece	1.02	2.01	3.37	5.99	6.44	6.69	6.49	6.69	8.11	7.89
Iceland										
Ireland	4.06	8.43	8.18	7.69	8.16	8.48	8.77	8.91	10.37	10.95
Italy	3.62	6.82	7.61	9.46	9.74	9.91	9.61	10.30	11.27	10.91
Liechtenstein										
Luxembourg	4.42	6.76	5.38	6.95	7.23	7.56	7.16	7.33	7.52	7.73
Malta										
Monaco										
Netherlands	6.51	8.77	7.76	9.35	9.71					
Norway	37.15	51.28	65.44	87.74	90.58	93.32	96.85	96.85	111.76	101.95
Portugal	2.17	5.44	6.82	7.77	8.07	8.38	8.38	8.38	8.61	8.99
Spain	3.25	5.59	4.97	6.78	7.06	7.24	7.02	7.37	8.75	8.64
Sweden	29.47	46.63	64.66	78.88	81.89	85.79	84.28	87.11	98.13	99.18
Switzerland	11.60	12.60	10.80	12.30	12.57	13.22	12.60	12.93	13.09	13.23
Turkey				0.29	0.56	1.17	1.95	3.65	5.82	9.93
United Kingdom	3.29	4.31	4.86	5.97	6.16	6.72	7.11	7.72	8.49	7.97
Eastern Europe										
Albania										
Belarus										
Bosnia-Herzegovina										
Bulgaria	250.00									
Croatia	45.00									
Czech Republic	65.00	80.00	123.80	200.80	209.10	225.80	227.60	239.80	296.30	301.00
Estonia										
Georgia										
Hungary	110.00	200.00	500.00	1,010.00						
Latvia										
Lithuania										
Macedonia										
Moldova										
Poland			2.78	12.25	14.45	16.94	18.53	23.34	31.48	43.20
Romania				0.59	0.87	2.76	4.17	8.15	11.41	15.22
Russia										
Slovakia			4.50	4.90	5.20	5.80	5.40	5.80	7.80	7.30
Slovenia										
Ukraine	806.20									

Source: *Institute of Petroleum, OECD Energy Prices and Taxes/Euromonitor International*

Automotives and Transport Statistics

Price of Leaded/Lead Replacement Petrol 1980-2008 *(continued)*
Units of national currency per 10 litres (inc. tax)

	2002	2003	2004	2005	2006	2007	2008	US$ per litre 2008
Western Europe								
Austria	8.71	8.76	9.07	9.93	10.44	10.12	10.92	1.61
Belgium	10.48	10.14	9.99	11.00	11.78	11.88	13.60	2.00
Cyprus								
Denmark								
Finland								
France	10.95	10.97	11.43	12.69	13.57	13.76	14.66	2.16
Germany	11.45	11.83	12.38	13.20	13.81	14.07	14.72	2.17
Gibraltar								
Greece	7.84	7.89	8.69	9.44	10.36	10.76	11.83	1.74
Iceland								
Ireland	11.75	12.60	13.42	13.97	14.40	13.97	15.33	2.26
Italy	11.53	11.67	12.07	12.98	13.55	13.20	14.02	2.06
Liechtenstein								
Luxembourg	7.88	8.15	8.39	9.34	10.00	10.12	10.64	1.57
Malta			9.41	9.91	11.63	10.95	11.92	1.75
Monaco								
Netherlands							16.28	2.40
Norway	95.70	99.83	106.70	114.02	120.01	122.50	130.48	2.31
Portugal	9.55	9.97	10.92	12.05	13.80	13.91	14.68	2.16
Spain	8.71	8.86	9.39	10.39	11.13	10.90	11.67	1.72
Sweden	106.45	112.23	119.18	126.30	129.50	127.20	138.03	2.09
Switzerland	13.37	13.48	13.65	14.46	15.44	15.50	16.43	1.52
Turkey	14.79	18.10	19.66	25.20	27.45	28.49	31.79	2.44
United Kingdom	7.70	7.99	8.45	9.10	9.40	9.38	10.66	1.96
Eastern Europe								
Albania								
Belarus								
Bosnia-Herzegovina								
Bulgaria								
Croatia								
Czech Republic	307.84	312.26	317.31	338.72	343.38	333.06	346.67	2.03
Estonia								
Georgia								
Hungary								
Latvia			4.85	5.81	6.36	6.48	7.30	1.52
Lithuania								
Macedonia							.	
Moldova								
Poland	45.00	48.00	52.00	55.55	55.41	58.60	59.82	2.48
Romania	20.70	25.15	28.36	32.70	34.50	37.08	41.61	1.65
Russia								
Slovakia	7.00	7.60	8.80	9.68	10.62	12.62	12.85	1.89
Slovenia								
Ukraine								

Source: Institute of Petroleum, OECD Energy Prices and Taxes/Euromonitor International

Automotives and Transport Statistics

Table 3.10

Price of Premium Unleaded Petrol 1980-2008
Units of national currency per 10 litres (inc. tax)

	1980	1985	1990	1995	1996	1997	1998	1999	2000	2001
Western Europe										
Austria			6.84	8.21	8.31	8.61	8.12	8.14	9.42	9.04
Belgium			6.74	7.78	8.72	9.42	9.02	9.16	11.08	10.81
Cyprus				5.50	5.50	5.75	5.77	6.05	6.46	6.65
Denmark				60.58	64.48	66.64	64.28	72.10	83.59	82.06
Finland	6.60	6.68	6.48	8.38	9.39	9.41	9.49	10.16	11.58	11.31
France			7.53	8.62	9.16	9.51	9.28	9.63	11.12	10.58
Germany			5.77	7.93	8.27	8.54	8.14	8.74	10.15	10.24
Gibraltar										
Greece			3.18	5.59	6.00	6.26	6.05	6.22	7.69	7.54
Iceland										
Ireland			7.70	7.10	7.40	7.70	7.50	7.50	8.90	8.89
Italy			7.62	8.89	9.24	9.44	9.10	9.60	10.81	10.53
Liechtenstein										
Luxembourg			5.14	6.15	6.43	6.73	6.34	6.92	8.28	7.95
Malta										
Monaco										
Netherlands		8.49	7.43	8.85	9.26	9.88	9.84	10.30	12.08	12.02
Norway			59.44	81.08	84.05	87.93	87.22	92.37	105.66	95.85
Portugal			6.53	7.82	8.12	8.43	8.43	8.38	9.02	9.52
Spain				6.42	6.67	6.99	6.65	7.00	8.19	8.07
Sweden			64.70	75.04	78.48	82.15	80.53	83.35	95.12	94.50
Switzerland			10.20	11.83	12.00	12.51	11.93	12.29	14.48	14.14
Turkey			0.02	0.29	0.56	1.16	1.92	3.63	5.83	9.92
United Kingdom			4.20	5.86	6.37	7.13	7.78	8.29	8.73	8.28
Eastern Europe										
Albania										
Belarus										
Bosnia-Herzegovina										
Bulgaria										
Croatia	43.00									
Czech Republic			124.00	192.90	204.20	220.10	219.00	231.20	287.10	273.30
Estonia										
Georgia										
Hungary				971.30	1,197.90	1,421.90	1,548.00	1,855.40	2,324.10	2,252.50
Latvia										
Lithuania										
Macedonia										
Moldova										
Poland				11.75	13.95	16.60	18.36	23.30	31.37	31.52
Romania				0.59	0.87	2.66	4.05	8.14	11.21	15.17
Russia						21.53	24.23	50.70	73.93	62.50
Slovakia			5.42	5.01	5.36	5.81	5.53	6.14	7.89	7.32
Slovenia										
Ukraine										

Source: *Institute of Petroleum, OECD Energy Prices and Taxes/Euromonitor International*

Automotives and Transport Statistics

Price of Premium Unleaded Petrol 1980-2008 *(continued)*

Units of national currency per 10 litres (inc. tax)

	2002	2003	2004	2005	2006	2007	2008	US$ per litre 2008
Western Europe								
Austria	8.74	8.80	9.50	10.30	10.91	11.21	12.09	1.78
Belgium	10.53	10.20	11.40	12.80	13.53	13.84	14.56	2.14
Cyprus	6.95	6.07	7.86	8.47	9.19	9.46	10.26	1.51
Denmark	83.82	82.15	83.94	90.29	95.84	97.43	102.65	2.01
Finland	11.00	10.90	11.40	12.10	12.88	12.98	14.23	2.09
France	10.37	10.20	10.60	11.60	12.37	12.73	13.56	2.00
Germany	10.48	10.92	11.40	12.20	12.89	13.41	14.03	2.06
Gibraltar								
Greece	7.35	7.40	8.12	8.82	9.68	10.13	11.10	1.63
Iceland								
Ireland	8.55	8.71	9.50	10.50	11.17	11.16	12.25	1.80
Italy	10.48	10.59	11.30	12.20	12.86	12.98	13.79	2.03
Liechtenstein								
Luxembourg	7.73	7.78	9.00	10.20	10.82	11.22	12.35	1.82
Malta			8.71	9.46	11.05	10.40	11.32	1.67
Monaco								
Netherlands	12.10	11.59	12.53	13.52	14.15	14.59	15.37	2.26
Norway	92.70	93.73	99.85	108.16	114.57	116.83	125.28	2.22
Portugal	9.20	9.65	10.33	11.47	13.10	13.22	13.88	2.04
Spain	8.14	8.17	8.70	9.50	10.21	10.35	11.08	1.63
Sweden	96.83	94.03	99.64	109.55	114.55	116.10	125.98	1.91
Switzerland	13.55	13.12	14.01	15.27	16.43	16.84	17.85	1.65
Turkey	14.76	18.04	19.59	25.35	27.77	28.79	32.09	2.47
United Kingdom	7.98	7.60	8.02	8.67	9.12	9.43	10.71	1.97
Eastern Europe								
Albania								
Belarus								
Bosnia-Herzegovina								
Bulgaria							19.82	1.48
Croatia								
Czech Republic	245.89	248.05	266.80	284.80	295.99	295.04	303.33	1.78
Estonia			113.20	124.60	135.46	137.46	163.02	1.52
Georgia								
Hungary	2,228.60	2,327.90	2,396.20	2,601.00	2,771.57	2,761.57	2,925.78	1.70
Latvia			4.74	5.70	6.11	6.38	7.19	1.49
Lithuania			26.90	28.60	31.12	31.06	35.51	1.51
Macedonia								
Moldova								
Poland	31.92	33.53	37.36	39.91	39.81	42.10	42.98	1.78
Romania	20.22	24.29	27.20	32.40	33.48	32.95	37.23	1.48
Russia	70.06	87.71	121.03	152.84	177.22	189.57	223.32	0.90
Slovakia	7.04	7.57	8.78	9.66	10.61	12.62	12.86	1.89
Slovenia			8.91	9.52	9.95	10.30	10.68	1.57
Ukraine								

Source: *Institute of Petroleum, OECD Energy Prices and Taxes/Euromonitor International*

Automotives and Transport Statistics　　　**Table 3.11**

Price of Premium Unleaded Petrol by Quarter 2007-2009

Units of national currency per 10 litres (inc. tax)

	2007 1st Quarter	2007 2nd Quarter	2007 3rd Quarter	2007 4th Quarter	2008 1st Quarter	2008 2nd Quarter	2008 3rd Quarter	2008 4th Quarter	2009 1st Quarter	2009 2nd Quarter
Western Europe										
Austria	10.10	11.09	11.62	12.03	12.09	12.94	12.79	10.56	9.44	10.11
Belgium	12.93	14.06	13.88	14.50	14.69	15.53	15.40	12.63	12.07	
Cyprus	8.55	9.68	9.75	9.84	10.09	10.79	11.23	8.92	7.84	8.55
Denmark	89.92	100.88	98.54	100.38	102.06	109.49	110.41	88.65	87.65	
Finland	12.11	13.31	13.32	13.18	14.16	14.94	15.26	12.56	11.75	
France	11.92	12.99	12.91	13.09	13.54	14.29	14.39	12.03	11.18	11.80
Germany	12.55	13.66	13.66	13.77	14.00	14.81	15.13	12.18	11.84	
Gibraltar										
Greece	9.27	10.38	10.31	10.55	11.03	11.99	12.02	9.35	8.64	
Iceland										
Ireland	10.28	11.06	11.75	11.57	11.83	12.11	13.19	11.88	9.86	
Italy	12.15	13.11	13.26	13.41	13.71	14.48	14.72	12.26	11.39	
Liechtenstein										
Luxembourg	10.40	11.58	11.36	11.53	11.75	12.63	12.66			
Malta	9.92	10.15	10.77	10.77	10.85	10.99	11.98	11.46	10.57	10.56
Monaco										
Netherlands	13.77	14.94	14.77	14.87	15.23	16.17	16.50	13.58	12.55	
Norway	110.00	119.40	119.20	118.70	123.20	129.30	133.80	114.80	108.70	
Portugal	12.46	13.53	13.41	13.49	13.81	14.60	14.74	12.36	11.33	
Spain	9.53	10.56	10.59	10.70	10.92	11.76	12.00	9.62	8.92	9.65
Sweden	109.11	119.90	116.45	118.93	124.61	133.30	134.41	111.60	112.31	
Switzerland	15.53	17.13	17.20	17.50	17.67	18.53	19.20	16.00	13.63	
Turkey	27.27	29.42	28.72	29.76	31.16	34.03	33.52	29.67	28.62	
United Kingdom	8.72	9.45	9.54	10.00	10.46	11.27	11.47	9.65	8.87	
Eastern Europe										
Albania										
Belarus										
Bosnia-Herzegovina										
Bulgaria					19.41	21.14	21.53	17.18	15.50	16.90
Croatia										
Czech Republic	270.04	297.20	305.87	307.05	308.08	318.53	317.77	268.93	246.82	
Estonia	126.25	141.44	141.02	141.11	159.29	172.30	177.78	142.71	123.94	136.00
Georgia										
Hungary	2,557.04	2,790.26	2,840.42	2,858.54	2,955.93	3,061.62	3,060.92	2,624.64	2,475.56	2,677.90
Latvia	5.83	6.49	6.54	6.65	7.09	7.49	7.75	6.41	5.98	6.62
Lithuania	28.29	32.14	32.01	31.81	35.02	37.80	38.52	30.69	31.95	34.06
Macedonia										
Moldova										
Poland	38.14	43.16	43.54	43.55	42.73	44.68	45.29	39.24	36.55	
Romania	31.00	33.20	33.40	34.20	36.30	39.30	39.70	33.60	32.60	
Russia	186.30	186.77	190.02	195.19	206.52	225.38	241.72	219.66	185.80	
Slovakia	11.91	12.79	12.89	12.91	13.10	13.46	13.57	11.31	10.02	
Slovenia	9.62	10.70	10.64	10.24	10.41	11.19	11.65	9.48	9.40	10.04
Ukraine										

Source: *Institute of Petroleum, OECD Energy Prices and Taxes/Euromonitor International*

Automotives and Transport Statistics

Table 3.12

New Registrations of Commercial Vehicles 1980-2008

'000

	1980	1985	1990	1995	1996	1997	1998	1999	2000	2001
Western Europe										
Austria	21.8	22.3	30.9	29.2	29.9	31.5	34.6	35.6	38.0	34.0
Belgium	32.5	31.9	49.5	45.8	48.2	57.1	63.4	72.7	68.7	73.1
Cyprus		5.4	10.6	9.2	9.5	6.1	7.2	6.5	6.2	7.8
Denmark	19.4	38.5	23.3	30.7	32.1	35.5	35.1	38.0	37.0	36.2
Finland	17.9	18.7	32.2	10.6	13.1	16.5	19.5	19.9	18.7	18.1
France	323.3	342.2	447.0	357.8	378.0	355.2	398.6	433.5	477.2	496.3
Germany	175.5	134.6	203.4	260.5	249.2	263.9	295.9	324.9	314.8	296.6
Gibraltar		0.1	0.3	0.2	0.3	0.2	0.2	0.2	0.3	0.2
Greece		19.0	44.6	11.6	13.4	15.8	17.7	23.8	25.0	22.8
Iceland		0.8	2.0	0.8	0.9	1.2	1.4	1.7	2.0	1.2
Ireland	12.2	16.2	28.4	16.4	19.3	23.1	31.4	30.1	33.6	30.6
Italy	122.3	100.7	159.5	148.1	152.9	157.6	180.0	196.3	226.4	220.2
Liechtenstein				0.2	0.2	0.2	0.2	0.2	0.2	0.2
Luxembourg		3.4	6.1	2.9	2.7	2.9	3.6	4.4	4.7	5.2
Malta		0.6	1.4			4.2	2.7	2.3	2.0	1.8
Monaco										
Netherlands	48.0	63.1	69.0	65.1	84.1	96.4	114.8	116.7	114.4	101.5
Norway	15.1	42.5	23.0	38.0	36.8	37.1	36.3	33.0	35.7	37.5
Portugal	47.0	23.1	75.8	63.0	77.2	108.8	126.2	134.8	161.0	112.9
Spain	104.5	122.0	267.7	191.4	209.6	252.2	288.8	344.7	336.8	325.6
Sweden	19.7	22.9	33.1	14.8	21.2	25.8	31.6	35.2	39.3	36.1
Switzerland	22.4	20.5	28.9	20.1	20.5	21.6	23.7	25.6	29.1	31.2
Turkey			62.1	54.7	76.2	133.9	138.1	141.2	144.3	60.7
United Kingdom	272.0	286.7	293.5	249.9	256.9	274.2	294.5	288.1	298.0	313.4
Eastern Europe										
Albania										
Belarus			12.9	5.3	6.3	7.2	8.1	7.7	8.1	7.9
Bosnia-Herzegovina										
Bulgaria			14.6	10.7	9.7	4.2	9.4	6.4	4.2	2.3
Croatia			3.0	17.0	15.3	16.9	8.4	6.4	7.2	10.4
Czech Republic						46.1	66.9	29.4	33.9	23.5
Estonia			1.3	0.7	1.1	2.2	2.2	1.5	1.8	2.2
Georgia										
Hungary		27.0	23.4	31.2	26.4	23.2	28.3	31.2	32.7	29.8
Latvia				4.1	3.9	6.4	6.6	7.5	6.0	4.3
Lithuania										1.5
Macedonia			1.8	0.9						
Moldova								4.2	4.7	5.0
Poland		39.0	65.2	56.3	64.2	55.2	51.1	50.8	41.3	29.4
Romania			9.0	37.9	21.4	20.9	27.1	21.3	17.9	19.4
Russia						505.0	365.5	294.2	262.7	265.3
Slovakia										
Slovenia			2.9	6.2	6.0	5.8	6.0	6.9	5.1	5.7
Ukraine										

Source: *European Automobile Manufacturers' Association (ACEA) / International Road Federation (IRF)*

Automotives and Transport Statistics

New Registrations of Commercial Vehicles 1980-2008 *(continued)*
'000

	2002	2003	2004	2005	2006	2007	2008
Western Europe							
Austria	31.3	35.6	40.9	39.0	38.8	41.5	42.3
Belgium	60.2	62.2	70.0	74.9	72.1	78.7	78.0
Cyprus	9.5	9.2	3.8	5.1	6.1	6.5	6.8
Denmark	36.2	36.7	50.0	62.4	69.5	63.5	41.0
Finland	19.4	18.8	22.1	20.0	20.9	22.2	21.3
France	460.9	431.4	459.9	480.1	498.4	519.5	523.4
Germany	270.6	264.7	283.4	272.8	304.4	334.1	335.0
Gibraltar	0.2	0.3	1.2	0.6	0.3	0.6	0.4
Greece	20.3	20.7	27.2	25.5	26.4	27.0	25.1
Iceland	0.9	1.4	2.0	2.8	3.1	3.4	1.6
Ireland	28.4	30.5	31.2	38.4	43.6	49.8	34.1
Italy	320.2	242.3	255.1	251.4	272.0	293.0	269.6
Liechtenstein	0.2	0.2	0.2	0.2	0.2	0.2	0.2
Luxembourg	5.0	4.8	3.9	4.6	4.7	5.3	6.0
Malta	0.4	0.6	0.4	0.7	0.6	0.9	1.1
Monaco							
Netherlands	95.5	91.0	109.4	80.8	84.7	97.3	104.2
Norway	28.5	31.3	38.4	42.7	49.2	53.0	42.6
Portugal	84.7	73.4	76.6	75.1	70.5	74.8	61.7
Spain	305.9	250.2	275.3	329.2	351.1	324.5	201.4
Sweden	35.7	36.0	39.5	44.6	48.3	51.9	47.5
Switzerland	26.6	23.7	25.3	25.6	28.9	30.7	32.8
Turkey	80.3	164.6	285.2	310.2	313.7	274.0	270.3
United Kingdom	322.3	363.7	389.9	386.0	389.5	400.7	357.2
Eastern Europe							
Albania							
Belarus	7.9	7.3	7.2	7.5	7.5	7.6	7.7
Bosnia-Herzegovina							
Bulgaria	4.3	4.9	6.5	9.0	10.0	11.8	12.8
Croatia	13.3	9.1	8.2	9.1	10.3	9.9	9.0
Czech Republic	21.7	25.7	35.5	48.5	60.7	74.6	71.8
Estonia	2.5	6.3	6.2	7.9	8.2	6.6	4.1
Georgia							
Hungary	35.1	31.1	30.1	26.5	21.6	21.9	21.6
Latvia	3.2	2.0	2.5	3.0	4.9	6.7	4.0
Lithuania	1.7	2.8	4.1	5.5	6.7	9.2	6.7
Macedonia							
Moldova	4.3		12.5				
Poland	20.2	40.1	50.0	36.2	41.0	78.0	80.9
Romania	23.2	28.5	35.8	40.9	40.8	45.0	45.7
Russia	247.3	273.0	281.0	286.3	331.1	374.1	384.4
Slovakia	8.2	12.7	13.3	18.1	24.4	29.4	32.3
Slovenia	6.0	6.4	7.7	8.0	10.4	10.7	11.4
Ukraine							

Source: *European Automobile Manufacturers' Association (ACEA) / International Road Federation (IRF)*

Table 3.13

New Registrations of Passenger Cars 1985-2008

'000

	1985	1990	1995	2000	2003	2004	2005	2006	2007	2008
Western Europe										
Austria	242.7	288.6	279.6	309.4	300.1	311.3	307.9	308.5	298.2	293.7
Belgium	378.2	473.5	358.9	515.2	458.8	484.8	480.1	526.1	524.8	535.9
Cyprus	12.2	19.5	13.1	19.9	30.0	43.8	38.7	37.2	36.1	35.4
Denmark	157.5	80.9	135.7	113.6	96.5	122.5	148.6	156.7	162.7	150.0
Finland	139.0	139.1	79.9	134.8	147.4	142.6	148.2	145.7	125.6	139.6
France	1,766.3	2,309.1	1,930.5	2,133.9	2,009.2	2,013.7	2,067.8	2,000.5	2,064.5	2,050.3
Germany	2,379.3	3,040.8	3,314.1	3,378.3	3,236.9	3,266.8	3,342.1	3,468.0	3,148.2	3,090.0
Gibraltar	2.0	2.1	1.7	1.7	1.8	1.4	1.2	1.3	1.3	1.3
Greece	109.4	132.5	125.4	290.2	257.3	289.8	269.7	267.7	279.8	267.2
Iceland	5.7	6.8	6.4	13.6	9.9	12.0	18.1	17.2	15.9	9.0
Ireland	60.4	81.2	86.9	225.3	143.0	149.6	166.3	173.3	186.5	151.6
Italy	1,745.9	2,348.2	1,720.0	2,412.0	2,254.3	2,272.4	2,244.4	2,329.9	2,493.1	2,160.1
Liechtenstein			1.7	1.8	1.8	1.8	1.9	1.9	2.0	2.0
Luxembourg	26.9	34.6	28.0	41.9	43.6	48.2	48.5	50.8	51.3	52.4
Malta	4.1	8.9		11.3	10.8	6.2	6.6	6.7	7.0	7.3
Monaco										
Netherlands	495.7	502.7	446.4	597.6	489.0	483.9	465.2	484.0	505.5	500.0
Norway	159.1	61.9	90.5	97.4	89.9	115.6	109.9	109.2	129.2	110.6
Portugal	104.2	212.7	229.9	257.8	189.8	197.6	206.5	194.7	201.8	213.4
Spain	575.1	1,007.0	870.5	1,381.4	1,466.0	1,616.2	1,649.3	1,634.6	1,614.8	1,161.2
Sweden	263.0	229.9	169.8	354.6	307.1	311.5	311.8	313.8	306.8	254.0
Switzerland	265.5	323.0	268.0	314.5	269.7	267.5	257.5	267.5	284.7	287.5
Turkey	63.9	267.8	196.9	256.9	289.0	451.3	406.8	396.5	353.5	320.9
United Kingdom	1,832.0	2,008.9	1,945.4	2,221.6	2,579.1	2,567.3	2,439.7	2,344.9	2,404.0	2,131.8
Eastern Europe										
Albania										
Belarus		45.3	82.4	65.2	89.8	86.8	84.8	83.8	83.1	81.6
Bosnia-Herzegovina										
Bulgaria	48.0	33.4	74.4	63.5	45.0	54.0	26.0	36.7	43.5	45.1
Croatia		66.2	67.6	92.4	75.0	69.6	70.5	78.8	76.2	69.3
Czech Republic				148.7	149.6	133.0	127.4	124.0	132.5	143.7
Estonia			3.1	10.2	15.8	16.5	19.6	21.3	30.9	24.3
Georgia										
Hungary	101.3	83.9	127.8	149.1	274.4	255.8	239.7	203.1	171.7	155.9
Latvia			49.3	35.7	8.7	11.3	16.7	25.6	32.5	19.2
Lithuania					7.5	9.4	10.7	14.6	21.0	21.5
Macedonia		13.8	9.0							
Moldova				12.1		32.3				
Poland	259.9	358.1	311.1	478.7	353.6	318.1	235.5	238.8	292.4	320.0
Romania		82.0	87.1	66.3	106.8	145.1	215.5	256.4	312.5	285.5
Russia				821.3	1,223.6	1,453.3	1,578.1	2,080.9	2,570.8	2,694.9
Slovakia					57.5	57.4	56.9	59.1	59.7	70.0
Slovenia		69.3	63.5	63.5	71.6	78.8	79.4	81.5	65.5	68.5
Ukraine										

Source: *European Automobile Manufacturers' Association (ACEA) / International Road Federation (IRF)*

Automotives and Transport Statistics

Table 3.14

New Registrations of Diesel Cars 1985-2008
'000

	1985	1990	1995	2000	2003	2004	2005	2006	2007	2008	Diesel car registrations as % of all passenger car regis- trations
Western Europe											
Austria	32.2	66.3	119.1	182.8	214.6	220.3	199.9	191.8	175.9	160.4	54.6
Belgium	95.0	155.4	168.0	290.3	312.9	339.3	348.6	392.3	404.1	423.4	79.0
Cyprus								1.1			
Denmark	10.4	3.6	3.9	14.9	21.8	29.2	34.9	40.2	61.2	68.9	46.0
Finland	14.4	7.2	5.5	26.3	22.4	22.1	25.1	29.5	35.6	69.2	49.6
France	264.8	762.1	897.7	1,046.5	1,354.2	1,392.9	1,429.0	1,427.7	1,525.7	1,584.9	77.3
Germany	530.7	337.6	483.5	1,026.0	1,291.5	1,437.3	1,425.6	1,535.9	1,504.8	1,362.7	44.1
Gibraltar											
Greece				2.0	3.9	8.4	4.0	5.9	8.1	9.6	3.6
Iceland	0.4		0.5	2.3	1.7	1.6	3.6	4.3	4.8	3.0	33.2
Ireland	8.6	12.2	13.1	23.4	25.0	29.5	38.0	49.0	50.5	50.8	33.5
Italy	438.7	171.0	178.8	805.2	1,093.9	1,318.2	1,300.8	1,350.9	1,391.2	1,096.0	50.7
Liechtenstein							0.6	0.7			
Luxembourg	3.5	6.4	8.0	21.1	30.4	35.0	36.6	39.3	39.6	40.3	77.0
Malta											
Monaco											
Netherlands	71.3	54.8	61.8	134.4	110.5	118.8	123.9	130.0	143.1	125.5	25.1
Norway	1.7	2.2	5.5	8.8	21.0	32.5	43.1	52.8	96.1	80.1	72.4
Portugal	2.3	10.3	21.3	62.4	85.2	111.7	127.8	126.4	139.9	146.0	68.4
Spain	125.2	136.2	274.2	735.4	842.3	1,068.9	1,036.8	1,022.3	1,144.9	804.7	69.3
Sweden	5.7	1.4	4.7	18.2	20.1	21.1	26.6	55.8	106.5	91.9	36.2
Switzerland	9.3	9.0	10.7	29.0	58.7	69.3	72.2	80.1	91.7	93.2	32.4
Turkey											
United Kingdom	66.2	128.6	405.1	313.2	704.1	835.3	897.9	898.5	967.0	929.5	43.6
Eastern Europe											
Albania											
Belarus											
Bosnia-Herzegovina											
Bulgaria											
Croatia											
Czech Republic							35.3	34.9	34.6	34.9	24.3
Estonia											
Georgia											
Hungary											
Latvia			4.2	22.0	30.8	32.7	34.7	35.7	36.3	34.3	178.7
Lithuania											
Macedonia											
Moldova											
Poland								86.3			
Romania							61.2	103.2			
Russia											
Slovakia											
Slovenia											
Ukraine											

Source: *European Automobile Manufacturers' Association (ACEA) / International Road Federation (IRF)*

Table 3.15

New Registrations of Two-Wheelers 1985-2008

'000

	1985	1990	1995	2000	2003	2004	2005	2006	2007	2008
Western Europe										
Austria	49.2	20.1	29.4	45.1	36.0	39.0	45.0	47.0	53.0	51.0
Belgium	47.1	54.5	42.1	58.5	58.9	59.2	61.4	63.6	70.7	69.1
Cyprus	4.3	8.3	5.7	5.4	4.5	4.7	4.5	4.7	5.5	5.5
Denmark	2.6	1.7	2.3	13.1	6.6	7.8	10.7	12.3	14.3	13.8
Finland			95.4	11.6	19.0	25.6	30.1	36.8	42.3	41.6
France			302.4	371.8	342.1	349.8	351.5	371.8	381.6	385.2
Germany	214.7	171.2	342.7	361.3	284.3	254.8	266.0	275.7	286.2	285.9
Gibraltar	0.2	0.6	0.7	1.1	0.8	0.7	0.8	0.9	1.0	1.2
Greece	14.6	41.5	40.7	73.7	65.0	78.6	89.4	91.7	110.2	109.4
Iceland		0.1	0.1	0.2	0.2	0.4	0.4	0.5	0.5	0.5
Ireland	4.1	3.1	2.3	6.9	5.0	3.8	3.2	3.2	3.5	3.7
Italy			655.3	836.5	570.5	553.9	548.8	554.8	557.3	557.7
Liechtenstein			0.1	0.2	0.2	0.2	0.3	0.3	0.3	0.3
Luxembourg	0.5		1.3	1.7	2.1	1.9	2.0	2.2	2.3	2.4
Malta				0.5	0.5	0.4	0.3	0.4	0.5	0.5
Monaco			1.1							
Netherlands	47.7	74.4	77.0	86.6	62.6	56.7	57.7	63.6	67.0	68.1
Norway	23.6	8.8	10.1	17.3	18.2	18.9	19.2	19.5	19.8	20.1
Portugal	1.4	7.3	54.1	32.7	11.2	11.6	11.2	13.4	14.3	13.9
Spain			189.9	320.7	187.9	241.3	321.2	390.8	465.6	466.1
Sweden	11.3	7.6	10.1	28.4	43.5	53.7	40.7	42.0	46.4	45.6
Switzerland	34.2	31.1	27.1	50.8	48.9	47.9	45.2	45.7	47.9	46.6
Turkey		65.2	35.7	35.7	29.2	145.3	222.4	234.3	240.3	236.4
United Kingdom	123.6	94.4	68.9	170.1	155.7	133.9	132.8	133.1	133.5	128.2
Eastern Europe										
Albania			13.9							
Belarus		5.3	9.9	5.1	3.4	3.3	3.3	3.1	3.1	3.0
Bosnia-Herzegovina										
Bulgaria	16.0	6.0	2.8	3.5	3.9	4.0	4.1	4.3	4.4	3.4
Croatia		9.5	8.6	9.0	16.1	16.0	14.3	14.2	13.9	13.7
Czech Republic				3.9	13.7	14.1	15.6	14.5	14.1	13.7
Estonia		0.3	0.2	0.2	0.9	1.1	1.5	2.5	3.7	3.1
Georgia										
Hungary				1.3	8.9	16.2	12.5	10.7	9.4	8.6
Latvia				0.5	1.0	1.0	1.1	1.2	1.2	1.3
Lithuania				0.4	0.9	1.0	1.6	1.7	1.8	2.0
Macedonia		0.2	0.1							
Moldova										
Poland	50.0	31.4	5.3	7.2	7.3	10.8	11.7	11.0	12.3	12.0
Romania		5.0	2.0	0.1	0.1	0.1	0.1	0.2	0.2	0.2
Russia				5,745.3	3,950.0	3,274.0	2,994.4	2,628.8	2,335.2	2,005.5
Slovakia				1.1	4.0	4.0	4.8	5.7	6.2	6.7
Slovenia		0.8	0.7	1.2	7.2	7.4	9.5	9.8	10.7	11.0
Ukraine		2.0	2.1	0.5						

Source: *Euromonitor International from SMMT/national statistics*

Automotives and Transport Statistics

Table 3.16

Airline Freight Traffic 1980-2008
Million tonne-kilometres

	1980	1985	1990	1995	1996	1997	1998	1999	2000	2001
Western Europe										
Austria	21.7	35.3	62.2	147.7	192.1	236.3	265.5	340.8	422.4	373.8
Belgium	436.1	574.7	700.9	546.6	590.9	677.6	473.0	535.4	1,041.7	870.8
Cyprus	24.4	24.3	30.1	38.8	35.4	35.7	38.2	40.7	46.0	42.9
Denmark	159.7	154.5	147.7	144.7	169.6	213.0	199.0	196.1	215.8	201.2
Finland				224.9	248.2	312.6	306.6	303.5	300.5	190.0
France	2,287.2	3,258.5	4,300.5	4,567.9	4,811.3	5,081.9	4,554.6	4,726.6	5,428.0	5,029.6
Germany	1,974.5	2,920.3	4,781.9	6,006.0	6,136.6	6,309.8	6,212.4	6,598.8	7,281.4	7,205.7
Gibraltar										
Greece	58.1	67.5	88.0	115.3	118.7	129.1	112.6	103.4	149.8	116.7
Iceland		58.6	67.8	95.7	104.0	109.3	106.1	108.9	104.8	105.7
Ireland	93.9	98.7	111.1	95.7	102.1	122.1	129.6	138.0	174.5	165.7
Italy	484.0	692.6	1,091.1	1,334.6	1,459.1	1,443.3	1,475.9	1,614.6	1,773.2	1,555.7
Liechtenstein										
Luxembourg						2,260.2	2,245.5	2,506.1	3,523.3	3,768.4
Malta	3.5	2.5	3.5	8.5	9.7	9.0	11.2	10.5	15.7	15.1
Monaco										
Netherlands	1,109.7	1,769.7	2,434.6	3,852.4	3,926.0	3,970.8	3,755.0	3,967.6	4,521.2	4,303.4
Norway	168.8	160.5	152.7	148.1	169.6	216.7	203.4	200.6	224.6	207.2
Portugal	124.8	127.8	163.1	206.9	210.9	248.5	247.5	225.1	242.9	227.8
Spain	470.7	601.4	851.9	675.4	759.8	742.4	766.9	815.9	923.2	924.4
Sweden	252.7	245.5	232.4	209.3	249.6	293.6	294.2	291.0	308.9	283.1
Switzerland	427.9	670.1	875.5	1,562.1	1,511.3	1,829.7	1,963.4	1,877.3	2,033.8	1,698.9
Turkey			73.3	177.3	207.3	255.4	246.6	312.9	393.6	358.4
United Kingdom	2,664.3	3,519.4	4,711.9	7,214.1	7,618.1	6,450.6	4,663.5	4,925.2	5,340.1	4,650.4
Eastern Europe										
Albania										
Belarus				5.9	5.2	2.6	3.5	1.8	1.9	1.7
Bosnia-Herzegovina									0.6	0.6
Bulgaria				24.4	23.9	31.6	30.4	12.4	6.7	2.7
Croatia				1.8	2.3	2.0	2.0	2.0	3.4	3.6
Czech Republic				26.8	22.2	23.1	24.7	26.2	35.0	29.1
Estonia				0.7	1.6	5.5	3.2	4.1	2.1	3.1
Georgia					1.8	1.1	2.0	2.9	2.5	2.5
Hungary	8.5	9.3	6.3	19.2	29.3	34.9	37.0	39.9	55.1	35.8
Latvia				0.7	1.1	1.1	0.9	0.4	1.5	0.9
Lithuania				1.7	1.8	2.8	2.6	1.8	2.0	2.1
Macedonia					0.7	0.8	1.0	1.5	1.6	0.7
Moldova									0.9	0.3
Poland	20.8	10.5	57.0	68.9	70.0	92.0	91.8	80.3	82.9	74.2
Romania	7.4	7.0	9.0	18.9	15.7	13.4	12.1	11.3	13.4	11.0
Russia				1,604.0	899.2	833.7	736.5	592.7	1,082.1	943.2
Slovakia				0.1	0.2	0.2	0.2	0.2	0.5	0.7
Slovenia				4.1	3.6	3.6	3.4	3.7	3.9	4.1
Ukraine				24.7	16.5	11.8	27.4	13.2	13.0	12.9

Source: *Euromonitor International from International Civil Aviation Authority/national statistics*

Automotives and Transport Statistics

Airline Freight Traffic 1980-2008 *(continued)*

Million tonne-kilometres

	2002	2003	2004	2005	2006	2007	2008
Western Europe							
Austria	424.1	467.2	539.8	580.3	621.6	654.8	688.0
Belgium	655.6	604.6	717.1	710.0	745.2	792.1	839.0
Cyprus	44.1	47.7	52.5	52.1	51.3	52.2	53.1
Denmark	199.4	184.6	189.0				
Finland	237.2	276.2	343.3	371.4	425.0	471.9	518.9
France	5,229.8	5,262.2	5,776.7	5,995.9	6,296.0	6,440.7	6,585.4
Germany	7,391.9	7,503.8	8,288.2	7,949.5	8,392.5	8,577.7	8,762.9
Gibraltar							
Greece	91.8	70.4	67.3	74.3	82.2	86.1	90.0
Iceland	96.7	79.8	122.3	125.9	143.3	149.7	156.1
Ireland	122.3	127.5	130.2	113.5	130.5	132.6	134.6
Italy	1,440.2	1,413.6	1,438.1	1,411.1	1,418.8	1,420.5	1,422.3
Liechtenstein							
Luxembourg	4,157.7	4,347.9	4,670.3	5,149.8	5,270.4	5,561.5	5,852.7
Malta	13.2	13.3	12.5	11.9	12.4	12.7	13.0
Monaco							
Netherlands	4,388.4	4,526.8	4,978.6	5,089.1	5,122.7	5,222.9	5,323.1
Norway	205.1	195.1	197.9	195.2	194.3	189.3	184.3
Portugal	212.7	224.2	262.2	261.2	320.8	347.8	374.9
Spain	856.2	918.8	1,092.6	1,078.0	1,158.3	1,197.4	1,236.6
Sweden	283.9	271.1	276.8	274.7	276.5	278.3	280.1
Switzerland	1,088.9	1,305.2	1,152.2	1,161.5	1,085.8	1,085.1	1,084.3
Turkey	396.8	390.0	383.3	394.5	474.9	488.5	502.0
United Kingdom	4,997.1	5,214.0	5,779.2	6,088.7	6,314.6	6,477.1	6,639.5
Eastern Europe							
Albania							
Belarus	1.4	1.3	1.3	1.3	1.4	1.4	1.4
Bosnia-Herzegovina	0.6	0.6					
Bulgaria	0.1	1.0	3.5	4.1	4.2	4.5	4.8
Croatia	3.4	3.2	2.9	2.9	2.7	2.6	2.5
Czech Republic	31.5	40.5	45.2	44.2	45.1	46.7	48.4
Estonia	1.8	2.0	1.8	1.8	1.5	1.4	1.3
Georgia	5.2	5.4	2.9	2.9	3.1	3.2	3.3
Hungary	28.7	33.1	28.1	25.5	24.0	22.8	21.6
Latvia	1.2	0.9	1.5	3.0	14.4	16.6	18.8
Lithuania	2.0	1.8	1.9	2.1	2.0	2.0	1.9
Macedonia	0.2	0.2	0.1	0.1	0.1	0.1	0.1
Moldova	0.4	0.8	0.9	0.9	1.1	1.1	1.2
Poland	73.5	78.5	86.3	82.2	91.0	92.4	93.7
Romania	10.1	7.8	5.6	5.9	5.9	6.1	6.2
Russia	1,089.9	1,167.3	1,482.7	1,597.3	1,986.8	2,137.5	2,288.3
Slovakia	0.9	0.9	0.7	0.5	0.5	0.5	0.5
Slovenia	4.5	3.6	3.2	2.6	2.3	2.1	1.8
Ukraine	12.8	20.4	27.2	42.6	47.5	53.3	59.0

Source: Euromonitor International from International Civil Aviation Authority/national statistics

Automotives and Transport Statistics

Table 3.17

Airline Passenger Traffic 1980-2008

Million passenger-kilometres

	1980	1985	1990	1995	1996	1997	1998	1999	2000	2001
Western Europe										
Austria	1,953.8	2,500.6	4,172.4	6,858.1	8,791.0	10,066.0	13,908.0	15,324.0	14,232.4	13,875.4
Belgium	4,966.2	5,818.6	6,960.3	7,716.9	9,011.0	11,277.0	15,338.0	17,953.1	19,378.7	15,319.8
Cyprus	660.5	1,089.3	1,606.9	2,713.6	2,561.0	2,657.0	2,711.0	2,941.7	2,785.1	3,011.9
Denmark	2,963.5	2,975.1	4,173.1	4,950.8	5,466.0	5,669.0	5,658.0	5,872.6	6,128.0	6,952.0
Finland	2,019.1	2,728.9	4,716.4	6,852.8	8,731.0	9,575.0	10,716.0	7,800.0	7,634.9	8,194.8
France	34,099.2	40,015.4	53,600.3	69,913.5	81,594.0	84,675.0	90,903.0	97,884.8	113,438.1	113,278.7
Germany	25,150.8	30,761.8	46,018.6	72,105.8	77,765.0	86,189.0	90,393.0	97,153.0	112,795.0	111,302.8
Gibraltar										
Greece	4,792.3	5,878.4	7,478.6	7,864.9	8,533.0	9,261.0	8,556.0	9,960.0	9,841.2	9,800.9
Iceland	2,292.1	2,761.5	1,876.7	2,643.0	2,872.0	3,216.0	3,774.0	3,944.6	3,937.2	3,713.7
Ireland	2,550.3	2,522.8	4,938.7	5,652.1	6,732.0	8,964.0	10,401.0	11,315.3	13,664.3	13,917.3
Italy	11,891.8	14,099.1	22,209.8	32,796.5	36,157.0	38,180.0	38,122.0	40,913.8	44,389.3	40,950.0
Liechtenstein										
Luxembourg		101.9	130.3	340.8	421.0	281.0	454.0	521.3	557.3	586.0
Malta	565.9	542.8	709.3	1,559.1	1,663.0	1,681.0	1,888.0	2,028.8	2,383.8	2,359.2
Monaco					1.0	1.0	1.0	1.0	2.5	2.3
Netherlands	23,490.6	28,498.5	43,401.4	57,333.8	62,397.0	66,666.0	69,084.0	70,236.0	74,425.9	69,317.1
Norway	4,261.8	4,078.7	6,440.6	8,348.1	8,688.0	9,158.0	9,480.0	9,945.5	10,366.7	10,460.9
Portugal	4,919.9	5,311.1	7,863.8	8,238.7	8,423.0	10,466.0	12,120.0	12,072.0	11,216.5	11,182.4
Spain	20,358.2	23,416.0	30,641.9	24,168.0	25,812.0	28,140.0	32,472.0	44,100.0	52,427.3	55,323.7
Sweden	4,368.5	5,137.0	7,006.3	8,580.0	8,424.0	8,748.0	9,852.0	10,140.0	11,192.2	11,277.4
Switzerland	10,390.8	13,157.5	17,420.6	20,813.8	21,324.0	25,404.0	28,032.0	31,920.0	36,624.8	33,469.6
Turkey			5,097.8	10,276.6	10,947.0	12,379.0	13,032.0	13,356.0	17,282.1	16,057.6
United Kingdom	83,589.4	80,111.0	133,847.8	161,337.0	167,577.0	157,895.0	182,352.0	192,420.0	170,686.7	159,020.8
Eastern Europe										
Albania					9.0	35.0	86.3	95.9	105.5	94.9
Belarus				2,651.0	2,342.0	399.0	397.0	282.8	316.5	339.2
Bosnia-Herzegovina									48.1	44.3
Bulgaria			1,349.9	2,084.4	1,812.0	1,796.0	2,026.0	2,311.9	834.5	361.7
Croatia				486.0	486.0	469.0	624.0	643.0	643.8	735.9
Czech Republic				2,188.6	2,368.0	2,442.0	3,168.0	3,444.0	3,313.1	3,575.7
Estonia				138.0	158.0	209.0	227.3	297.6	235.0	246.8
Georgia				301.9	288.0	206.0	340.0	376.2	230.1	234.9
Hungary	1,027.3	1,284.1	1,475.6	1,768.8	2,077.0	2,346.0	2,510.0	2,662.0	3,572.6	2,951.9
Latvia				131.1	260.0	217.0	174.0	164.5	236.4	180.4
Lithuania				202.9	304.0	301.0	307.0	324.0	321.6	347.0
Macedonia									740.3	377.4
Moldova									125.0	146.1
Poland	2,259.5	1,732.7	3,014.6	3,599.9	3,917.0	4,204.0	4,255.0	4,568.8	4,757.5	4,914.6
Romania	772.0	898.4	1,077.8	1,692.0	1,823.0	1,702.0	1,709.0	1,795.7	2,097.9	1,854.2
Russia				60,482.2	52,713.0	49,278.0	50,304.0	47,684.0	42,950.3	48,320.8
Slovakia				68.6	84.0	72.0	84.0	72.0	107.8	84.8
Slovenia				325.6	380.0	375.0	408.0	516.0	562.5	656.7
Ukraine				2,029.8	1,792.0	1,853.0	2,064.0	1,560.0	1,387.4	1,418.2

Source: Euromonitor International from International Civil Aviation Authority/national statistics

Automotives and Transport Statistics

Airline Passenger Traffic 1980-2008 *(continued)*

Million passenger-kilometres

	2002	2003	2004	2005	2006	2007	2008
Western Europe							
Austria	13,794.3	14,558.4	17,529.5	18,835.3	19,921.3	17,407.9	16,463.9
Belgium	2,606.1	3,958.3	4,737.9	4,918.3	5,311.8	7,858.9	8,346.5
Cyprus	3,436.3	3,934.5	4,229.6	4,183.9	4,293.1	4,478.3	4,480.9
Denmark	7,453.0	7,201.6	8,101.5	8,594.8	9,005.6	9,393.7	9,249.6
Finland	8,807.2	9,055.9	11,142.5	11,899.7	13,417.6	16,416.2	17,916.3
France	117,273.4	115,571.1	123,984.0	135,016.8	144,096.0	151,011.6	154,464.3
Germany	124,245.6	149,671.8	170,628.0	182,507.6	204,117.8	214,654.7	219,925.6
Gibraltar							
Greece	8,586.7	7,353.6	9,166.2	9,410.5	9,225.3	9,646.6	8,816.9
Iceland	3,187.6	2,997.5	3,634.9	4,307.7	4,253.4	4,280.1	4,280.1
Ireland	18,575.2	27,440.9	34,597.0	44,791.9	54,272.0	67,667.3	72,695.6
Italy	34,327.6	41,176.9	43,237.0	51,127.4	50,039.5	50,486.2	51,649.9
Liechtenstein							
Luxembourg	436.8	548.5	572.6	565.7	610.9	665.9	680.6
Malta	2,305.5	2,174.0	2,281.8	2,292.2	2,475.5	2,698.3	2,829.4
Monaco	6.9	6.0	3.8	4.9	4.9	5.1	5.3
Netherlands	69,492.9	69,236.4	76,310.7	82,268.9	86,833.4	90,914.5	93,963.8
Norway	10,546.3	10,506.4	10,321.1	10,309.7	10,298.3	10,286.9	10,803.9
Portugal	12,109.1	13,562.3	16,092.9	16,833.6	19,010.1	21,381.3	23,178.1
Spain	54,044.3	57,594.3	64,140.6	70,975.5	77,100.4	88,404.4	88,860.5
Sweden	11,662.5	11,411.1	11,976.2	12,330.2	12,695.2	12,945.7	13,469.6
Switzerland	26,712.0	23,294.8	20,602.2	20,476.5	22,139.8	25,150.1	28,189.4
Turkey	16,931.9	16,451.0	20,499.8	24,297.4	27,889.6	33,689.5	35,844.3
United Kingdom	156,594.4	164,208.4	182,736.1	200,332.8	213,335.5	227,501.7	232,272.7
Eastern Europe							
Albania	103.3	124.0	138.7	152.3	161.1	175.6	184.2
Belarus	308.1	337.8	398.8	383.3	414.0	451.2	479.6
Bosnia-Herzegovina	43.4	47.3					
Bulgaria	56.7	457.3	747.1	1,122.6	1,345.6	1,442.5	1,531.7
Croatia	783.3	869.2	940.5	973.5	1,004.5	1,084.0	1,215.9
Czech Republic	3,855.1	4,938.0	5,988.0	6,605.4	6,651.8	6,310.9	6,318.9
Estonia	282.6	415.3	547.3	660.1	682.1	754.2	759.3
Georgia	521.1	634.5	472.7	520.0	505.3	612.1	606.5
Hungary	3,076.1	3,316.3	3,509.7	3,806.4	4,139.9	4,435.3	4,575.2
Latvia	183.8	244.8	581.2	1,161.2	1,510.3	1,501.1	1,492.0
Lithuania	355.1	394.8	556.8	700.3	622.7	576.9	546.1
Macedonia	235.6	280.2	275.6	248.7	268.6	253.1	246.4
Moldova	161.1	222.8	257.3	325.0	363.2	434.3	460.7
Poland	5,111.4	5,433.8	5,860.7	6,222.9	6,719.7	7,288.0	6,711.0
Romania	1,593.0	1,696.1	1,532.2	1,967.1	2,430.3	3,695.2	3,980.2
Russia	49,889.9	53,893.9	62,010.1	63,192.3	69,499.3	82,331.6	81,477.7
Slovakia	93.8	220.4	847.9	949.4	2,289.9	2,202.4	2,115.0
Slovenia	675.1	700.3	711.0	706.8	772.9	863.3	1,003.5
Ukraine	1,578.1	2,580.3	3,826.1	4,086.9	4,928.8	2,622.7	7,040.3

Source: Euromonitor International from International Civil Aviation Authority/national statistics

Automotives and Transport Statistics

Table 3.18

Airline Passenger Traffic by Quarter 2007-2009
Million passenger-kilometres

	2007 1st Quarter	2007 2nd Quarter	2007 3rd Quarter	2007 4th Quarter	2008 1st Quarter	2008 2nd Quarter	2008 3rd Quarter	2008 4th Quarter	2009 1st Quarter	2009 2nd Quarter
Western Europe										
Austria	4,549.7	4,242.7	4,653.7	3,961.7	3,723.8	4,340.7	4,612.7	3,786.8	3,112.8	
Belgium										
Cyprus	819.3	1,148.1	1,467.6	1,043.3	786.2	1,221.0	1,466.3	1,007.6	733.1	
Denmark	2,057.1	2,524.2	2,652.5	2,160.0	2,084.0	2,597.0	2,573.3	1,995.3	1,680.2	2,315.3
Finland	3,591.9	3,972.7	4,817.7	4,033.9	4,136.2	4,245.9	5,113.1	4,421.1	3,932.6	3,685.1
France	35,278.9	37,733.3	41,959.1	36,040.3	36,323.1	39,044.9	42,184.3	36,912.0	33,927.4	
Germany	47,440.7	55,928.5	58,846.2	52,439.3	49,775.4	57,043.1	62,060.3	51,046.8	45,262.8	52,855.0
Gibraltar										
Greece	1,778.1	2,527.7	3,160.0	2,180.9	1,763.4	2,283.6	2,895.9	1,874.1	1,392.6	
Iceland			1,517.6	855.7	704.2	1,059.5	1,452.0	675.3		
Ireland										
Italy										
Liechtenstein										
Luxembourg										
Malta										
Monaco										
Netherlands	20,534.6	23,316.1	24,872.3	22,191.4	21,233.9	23,729.4	25,817.7	23,182.8	20,189.2	21,929.6
Norway	2,170.1	2,793.8	2,927.5	2,395.5	2,315.9	3,237.1	3,043.2	2,207.7	1,928.1	2,352.4
Portugal	4,399.7	5,170.3	6,458.2	5,353.1	4,678.0	5,759.2	7,168.6	5,572.3	4,807.8	5,497.5
Spain	20,281.1	22,455.6	25,319.8	20,348.0	21,331.6	22,611.3	25,209.0	19,708.7	18,333.6	
Sweden	2,952.7	3,405.1	3,254.3	3,333.7	3,156.4	3,891.9	3,286.0	3,135.2	2,584.9	3,356.6
Switzerland	5,694.0	6,195.9	6,759.9	6,500.4	6,328.1	7,044.4	7,781.6	7,035.3	6,232.9	6,699.4
Turkey										
United Kingdom	49,554.1	58,343.2	64,846.2	54,758.2	51,511.2	59,510.2	66,700.2	54,551.2	48,949.1	
Eastern Europe										
Albania										
Belarus										
Bosnia-Herzegovina										
Bulgaria		316.5	450.7	314.7	309.0	421.4	503.6	297.6	243.8	
Croatia	154.9	306.7	389.6	232.8	189.8	346.7	432.6	246.8	179.8	323.7
Czech Republic	1,228.4	1,643.0	1,985.2	1,454.3	1,205.4	1,713.2	2,054.4	1,345.9	1,008.7	1,517.1
Estonia	135.2	206.3	246.4	166.3	144.2	225.4	248.4	141.2		
Georgia										
Hungary										
Latvia										
Lithuania	149.2	144.8	145.9	137.1	115.3	143.8	189.2	97.8		
Macedonia										
Moldova										
Poland	1,305.0	1,988.0	2,470.0	1,525.0	1,311.0	1,843.0	2,277.0	1,280.0	1,005.0	
Romania	686.0	941.1	1,133.1	935.1	860.1	981.1	1,260.1	879.1	731.0	928.9
Russia	15,167.0	17,397.9	31,265.2	18,501.5	18,577.6	20,498.9	25,164.3	17,236.8	13,973.5	
Slovakia										
Slovenia	161.2	229.3	266.4	206.3	198.3	285.4	305.5	214.3	171.3	237.2
Ukraine	1,187.9	325.6	625.2	484.0	1,562.0	1,686.0	2,312.3	1,480.1	1,238.6	

Source: *Euromonitor International from International Civil Aviation Authority/national statistics*

Table 3.19

Airline Passenger Traffic by Month 2008

Million passenger-kilometres

	January	February	March	April	May	June	July	August	September	October	November	December
Western Europe												
Austria	1,207.9	1,165.9	1,349.9	1,363.9	1,500.9	1,475.9	1,567.9	1,559.9	1,484.9	1,442.9	1,217.9	1,125.9
Belgium												
Cyprus	249.2	233.3	303.6	400.4	420.3	400.4	479.9	530.3	456.0	440.1	278.4	289.0
Denmark	623.9	674.6	785.4	831.4	867.8	897.9	915.3	829.8	828.2	810.8	649.3	535.2
Finland	1,347.1	1,280.6	1,508.5	1,371.4	1,342.9	1,531.7	1,714.2	1,736.4	1,662.5	1,667.8	1,409.3	1,343.9
France	12,216.4	11,026.8	13,079.9	12,750.2	13,043.5	13,251.2	14,786.9	14,499.4	12,898.0	13,150.3	11,392.8	12,368.9
Germany	16,458.3	15,634.4	17,682.6	17,233.7	19,651.0	20,158.4	21,274.5	20,697.2	20,088.6	19,375.9	16,254.5	15,416.4
Gibraltar												
Greece	620.3	449.5	693.6	676.3	759.0	848.3	971.1	1,037.8	887.0	712.3	560.2	601.6
Iceland	225.8	206.1	272.4	262.0	335.6	461.9	551.0	548.9	352.1	293.1	194.7	187.5
Ireland												
Italy												
Liechtenstein												
Luxembourg												
Malta												
Monaco												
Netherlands	7,075.6	6,496.2	7,662.2	7,691.2	7,885.2	8,153.0	8,799.0	8,805.1	8,213.6	8,473.0	7,333.7	7,376.1
Norway	682.3	774.0	859.6	1,065.5	1,018.9	1,152.7	1,085.1	991.9	966.3	937.8	707.8	562.1
Portugal	1,772.9	1,312.8	1,592.2	1,784.4	1,999.4	1,975.5	2,430.4	2,508.3	2,229.9	2,060.6	1,661.8	1,849.8
Spain	6,913.9	6,792.2	7,625.5	7,156.2	7,624.5	7,830.6	8,693.6	8,851.5	7,663.9	7,166.1	6,300.9	6,241.7
Sweden	920.7	1,053.0	1,182.7	1,277.9	1,317.6	1,296.4	984.2	1,055.7	1,246.2	1,262.0	1,037.1	836.1
Switzerland	2,068.6	1,955.4	2,304.0	2,265.0	2,383.2	2,396.2	2,667.7	2,660.7	2,453.3	2,509.4	2,265.0	2,261.0
Turkey												
United Kingdom	16,159.0	16,154.0	19,198.1	18,422.1	19,977.1	21,111.1	22,349.1	23,069.1	21,282.1	20,401.1	16,818.1	17,332.1
Eastern Europe												
Albania												
Belarus												
Bosnia-Herzegovina												
Bulgaria	104.9	85.0	119.1	118.1	152.1	151.2	165.4	179.5	158.7	118.1	80.3	99.2
Croatia	59.9	54.9	74.9	87.9	122.9	135.9	145.9	148.9	137.9	105.9	71.9	68.9
Czech Republic	399.4	337.2	468.7	498.8	570.1	644.3	680.5	730.6	643.3	557.0	405.5	383.4
Estonia	42.1	44.1	58.1	68.1	75.1	82.1	87.1	85.1	76.1	66.1	42.1	33.1
Georgia												
Hungary												
Latvia												
Lithuania	37.6	34.3	43.4	38.9	45.3	59.6	66.7	66.7	55.7	40.2	28.5	29.2
Macedonia												
Moldova												
Poland	446.0	376.0	489.0	516.0	602.0	725.0	802.0	811.0	664.0	515.0	362.0	403.0
Romania	297.0	268.0	295.0	292.0	333.0	356.0	409.0	448.0	403.0	333.0	264.0	282.0
Russia	6,162.2	5,852.6	6,562.9	6,398.1	6,554.2	7,546.7	8,750.1	9,122.2	7,292.0	6,228.3	5,629.1	5,379.4
Slovakia												
Slovenia	66.1	62.1	70.1	86.1	97.1	102.2	105.2	103.2	97.1	87.1	65.1	62.1
Ukraine	488.3	431.2	642.5	522.8	576.7	586.4	834.4	844.1	633.9	580.0	456.0	444.1

Source: *Euromonitor International from International Civil Aviation Authority/national statistics*

Distance Flown on Scheduled Flights 1980-2008
Million kilometres

	1980	1985	1990	1995	1996	1997	1998	1999	2000	2001
Western Europe										
Austria	44.1	50.2	69.8	101.5	110.5	118.0	125.5	133.6	139.1	134.2
Belgium	71.8	65.6	91.4	141.9	152.5	159.2	197.4	209.7	215.7	186.2
Cyprus	6.6	8.2	9.6	16.8	18.9	19.5	19.8	21.2	20.9	22.0
Denmark	41.2	42.3	63.4	78.2	79.3	84.5	85.6	85.5	85.4	91.7
Finland	33.1	38.8	58.1	70.6	82.2	92.0	94.8	100.7	101.6	95.2
France	345.3	335.4	431.2	597.9	608.8	680.5	742.5	842.7	961.0	902.0
Germany	228.7	266.2	419.0	619.6	652.7	703.6	735.6	781.3	839.5	860.8
Gibraltar										
Greece	40.5	46.4	52.5	62.5	65.8	68.4	68.3	70.5	89.9	95.3
Iceland	17.9	20.2	19.0	25.3	26.2	27.8	32.7	34.0	34.0	31.7
Ireland	31.8	27.4	55.5	55.6	59.2	69.9	78.5	83.5	106.0	118.6
Italy	160.8	159.9	211.6	298.9	299.6	338.3	343.7	358.5	392.1	392.6
Liechtenstein										
Luxembourg									60.7	66.3
Malta	3.8	3.5	5.8	14.5	20.4	20.0	20.1	22.5	26.0	25.3
Monaco					0.4	0.4	0.4	0.4	0.6	0.5
Netherlands	139.2	158.3	210.9	351.1	386.3	370.6	397.5	420.5	463.9	434.2
Norway	64.2	64.3	89.3	115.3	121.2	129.8	134.0	139.8	148.9	148.8
Portugal	49.3	46.8	65.8	85.7	96.4	105.7	107.2	112.3	104.8	111.9
Spain	193.0	187.3	224.5	279.8	285.3	304.9	331.1	343.0	418.3	459.6
Sweden	63.0	72.9	105.4	115.3	119.8	131.8	143.1	153.1	166.8	166.9
Switzerland	113.1	124.8	161.7	210.1	211.4	230.2	263.5	275.8	317.0	303.6
Turkey	25.2	27.9	44.4	96.8	100.9	113.4	123.4	135.5	148.1	143.0
United Kingdom	575.4	535.9	672.1	917.7	940.8	917.8	939.7	1,013.2	1,016.2	1,052.7
Eastern Europe										
Albania					0.4	1.1	1.6	2.1	2.7	2.2
Belarus					36.0	8.5	8.6	5.4	7.1	7.3
Bosnia-Herzegovina									1.5	1.5
Bulgaria	10.7	22.0	27.3	22.0	21.4	20.4	22.2	23.6	13.9	6.3
Croatia				6.5	9.0	9.5	10.1	10.2	10.3	10.9
Czech Republic				29.1	28.2	29.6	32.2	32.3	39.4	42.1
Estonia				3.9	3.9	4.9	6.1	6.7	6.2	6.1
Georgia				4.4	4.5	3.1	5.4	6.2	3.7	3.8
Hungary	16.9	18.7	21.6	27.4	30.0	32.5	35.2	37.1	42.1	38.1
Latvia				8.5	9.1	6.4	6.3	9.4	6.7	5.7
Lithuania				5.7	8.1	8.9	10.1	11.4	9.9	10.2
Macedonia									9.6	5.3
Moldova									4.1	4.6
Poland	34.6	22.8	37.8	38.4	40.1	45.1	44.5	46.8	55.4	70.2
Romania	12.7	12.2	14.1	18.7	23.5	26.1	21.6	22.3	30.1	25.6
Russia				777.3	723.8	608.6	578.8	523.3	533.7	568.2
Slovakia				2.4	2.1	2.3	3.3	3.5	2.0	1.6
Slovenia				6.5	6.8	6.8	7.8	9.1	9.8	11.1
Ukraine				53.8	36.2	36.4	35.8	24.0	31.5	30.3

Source: Euromonitor International from International Civil Aviation Authority/national statistics

Automotives and Transport Statistics

Distance Flown on Scheduled Flights 1980-2008 *(continued)*
Million kilometres

	2002	2003	2004	2005	2006	2007	2008
Western Europe							
Austria	129.9	130.3	148.7	158.9	170.0	175.2	180.3
Belgium	114.6	103.0	125.3	124.1	131.6	141.1	150.6
Cyprus	25.0	29.5	32.4	31.7	32.0	33.8	35.6
Denmark	80.9	78.3	85.4				
Finland	90.9	96.9	107.8	108.6	118.7	121.5	124.4
France	880.4	856.5	911.3	925.1	960.1	980.0	999.9
Germany	927.3	1,069.3	1,198.4	1,285.2	1,369.1	1,457.4	1,545.6
Gibraltar							
Greece	81.7	75.8	95.7	88.0	88.9	91.5	94.2
Iceland	26.5	25.1	29.2	32.2	33.8	34.2	34.6
Ireland	138.1	196.9	235.7	292.3	349.6	390.2	430.8
Italy	350.7	404.3	406.6	448.0	450.2	459.9	469.6
Liechtenstein							
Luxembourg	70.3	73.7	78.3	90.7	93.5	98.9	104.4
Malta	22.5	22.2	22.5	23.8	25.2	25.9	26.6
Monaco	0.7	0.7	0.6	0.6	0.7	0.7	0.8
Netherlands	433.3	438.1	469.8	481.3	502.6	516.3	530.0
Norway	129.4	127.4	128.0	127.7	125.7	123.5	121.5
Portugal	116.8	128.4	148.8	158.1	171.3	182.4	193.5
Spain	442.3	473.4	520.3	561.1	575.2	601.3	627.5
Sweden	129.6	125.3	133.1	133.3	137.3	141.3	145.2
Switzerland	256.1	217.7	171.9	165.7	162.3	157.5	153.4
Turkey	140.5	141.5	161.2	186.4	227.1	240.2	253.4
United Kingdom	1,048.0	1,086.7	1,204.7	1,324.2	1,399.8	1,463.7	1,527.6
Eastern Europe							
Albania	2.1	2.5	2.8	2.9	3.1	3.2	3.4
Belarus	6.5	6.7	7.1	6.3	6.7	6.8	6.8
Bosnia-Herzegovina	1.4	1.5					
Bulgaria	1.4	7.3	10.7	14.0	19.3	23.3	27.3
Croatia	11.4	11.7	12.2	13.5	13.3	13.7	14.2
Czech Republic	44.4	53.0	66.5	75.3	73.9	79.7	85.4
Estonia	5.9	6.9	8.1	9.2	9.1	9.3	9.6
Georgia	8.2	9.8	7.3	7.8	8.3	9.0	9.8
Hungary	38.7	44.5	52.3	53.7	51.9	51.8	51.6
Latvia	5.8	6.9	12.8	21.2	26.1	29.3	32.5
Lithuania	9.8	10.3	12.5	14.4	13.2	13.5	13.9
Macedonia	2.8	3.1	3.1	2.9	3.1	3.1	3.2
Moldova	4.6	5.1	5.5	5.6	5.3	5.6	5.8
Poland	65.6	67.9	72.9	77.0	80.2	84.4	88.5
Romania	20.6	26.2	28.0	36.0	40.6	43.6	46.6
Russia	653.2	601.8	694.4	680.0	748.7	784.5	820.3
Slovakia	2.7	5.0	11.8	13.0	13.7	14.7	15.6
Slovenia	12.1	12.9	13.7	14.6	15.5	16.5	17.4
Ukraine	31.7	43.8	54.4	56.5	62.5	67.6	72.8

Source: *Euromonitor International from International Civil Aviation Authority/national statistics*

Automotives and Transport Statistics

Table 3.21

Scheduled Airlines: Aircraft Departures 2000-2008
'000

	2000	2001	2002	2003	2004	2005	2006	2007	2008	% change 2000-2008
Western Europe										
Austria	138.7	133.6	135.5	128.4	137.0	142.0	149.5	151.3	153.1	10.4
Belgium	225.9	178.3	133.7	132.8	154.2	151.9	158.0	164.1	170.2	-24.7
Cyprus	12.6	13.3	15.1	16.9	19.1	17.4	17.5	18.4	19.2	52.9
Denmark	109.4	110.5	97.7	90.6	99.6					
Finland	145.2	128.9	108.9	107.0	109.2	107.1	114.7	117.3	119.8	-17.5
France	811.8	777.8	734.7	695.9	682.3	728.1	805.7	867.5	929.2	14.5
Germany	738.3	762.2	796.1	844.9	937.1	1,023.9	1,084.8	1,142.6	1,200.3	62.6
Gibraltar										
Greece	108.6	125.3	113.2	114.1	137.7	130.5	133.2	137.3	141.4	30.3
Iceland	12.6	11.7	10.0	9.8	10.8	11.8	12.8	13.8	14.8	17.6
Ireland	145.5	156.3	177.0	231.3	261.3	303.7	350.2	384.3	418.5	187.7
Italy	367.6	393.5	350.6	385.9	382.3	446.0	447.7	461.1	474.5	29.1
Liechtenstein										
Luxembourg	34.0	38.2	25.1	40.8	42.4	42.3	43.8	45.4	47.0	38.3
Malta	15.4	15.1	14.6	14.4	14.4	14.8	15.4	15.6	15.7	2.3
Monaco	31.5	29.9	15.0	14.0	12.0	12.2	14.1	13.9	13.7	-56.6
Netherlands	229.4	222.5	250.1	248.2	254.6	241.1	250.8	256.5	262.1	14.3
Norway	320.8	306.5	270.0	248.4	254.0	247.3	232.7	218.1	203.4	-36.6
Portugal	112.5	96.0	112.3	117.4	127.0	148.6	119.7	124.4	129.1	14.8
Spain	485.9	517.5	493.0	518.8	550.0	586.4	603.0	622.5	642.0	32.1
Sweden	247.7	233.8	198.3	183.5	190.3	187.9	190.0	192.2	194.4	-21.5
Switzerland	289.0	284.9	242.8	189.1	144.7	134.8	125.1	115.3	105.5	-63.5
Turkey	119.9	111.3	106.0	104.4	121.8	146.0	177.1	186.6	196.1	63.5
United Kingdom	876.2	925.6	924.9	891.2	970.0	1,018.1	1,037.0	1,063.8	1,090.7	24.5
Eastern Europe										
Albania	4.0	4.0	4.0	3.9	4.1	4.3	4.5	4.6	4.7	17.6
Belarus	5.8	5.9	5.5	6.0	6.2	5.4	5.6	5.7	5.7	-1.3
Bosnia-Herzegovina	4.8	4.5	4.4	4.6						
Bulgaria	12.2	6.7	2.3	4.6	7.8	9.7	12.5	13.6	14.8	21.6
Croatia	17.0	18.3	19.3	19.8	20.5	22.0	21.6	22.4	23.2	36.9
Czech Republic	40.0	44.2	46.6	52.1	66.1	75.3	75.4	81.3	87.2	118.0
Estonia	9.2	9.1	8.3	8.5	7.8	8.4	8.2	8.0	7.8	-14.7
Georgia	1.9	1.9	4.2	5.5	4.5	4.7	4.9	5.4	5.8	206.7
Hungary	32.3	31.7	33.3	40.2	46.8	47.4	45.8	48.0	50.3	55.7
Latvia	9.8	9.5	9.4	10.4	16.2	23.1	29.1	32.3	35.5	261.5
Lithuania	10.2	10.4	9.6	9.8	11.2	11.9	11.1	11.2	11.3	11.3
Macedonia	8,047.0	4,673.0	1,964.0	2,263.0	2,398.0	2,277.0	2,368.0	2,469.0	2,570.0	-68.1
Moldova	3.7	3.9	3.9	4.3	4.7	4.4	4.2	4.3	4.4	20.5
Poland	52.4	71.8	69.8	73.1	77.7	79.0	83.5	88.6	93.8	79.1
Romania	23.3	20.8	17.7	26.8	30.5	39.0	42.8	46.0	49.2	111.3
Russia	314.6	329.9	345.3	351.0	399.0	390.8	421.2	438.9	456.7	45.2
Slovakia	2.4	1.8	4.2	6.8	12.7	13.9	14.5	15.5	16.4	576.5
Slovenia	12.1	13.2	14.9	16.4	17.3	18.1	19.5	20.7	22.0	81.9
Ukraine	28.0	32.9	26.9	39.8	42.4	41.9	48.6	52.0	55.4	98.1

Source: Euromonitor International from International Civil Aviation Authority/national statistics

Automotives and Transport Statistics

Table 3.22

Scheduled Airlines: Passengers Carried 2000-2008
'000

	2000	2001	2002	2003	2004	2005	2006	2007	2008	% change 2000-2008	Passenger load factor (%)
Western Europe											
Austria	6,641.9	6,550.4	7,070.3	6,902.8	7,619.4	8,037.9	8,785.1	9,142.3	9,499.5	43.02	76.82
Belgium	10,738.1	8,489.0	2,341.8	2,904.1	3,264.6	3,340.5	3,641.2	3,966.0	4,290.8	-60.04	69.10
Cyprus	1,396.1	1,503.4	1,704.8	1,883.0	2,013.3	1,920.5	1,944.1	2,035.5	2,126.8	52.34	74.74
Denmark	5,922.6	6,382.1	6,322.4	5,886.0	6,428.7						74.17
Finland	6,828.1	6,697.6	6,415.6	6,183.9	7,049.4	7,075.2	7,597.1	7,725.3	7,853.5	15.02	74.27
France	52,581.3	50,476.5	49,305.9	47,258.8	48,543.5	52,477.2	59,537.9	63,630.9	67,723.9	28.80	80.30
Germany	57,962.9	56,389.4	61,889.7	72,693.1	82,099.7	90,788.8	99,647.3	106,594.7	113,542.1	95.89	81.25
Gibraltar											
Greece	7,937.4	8,430.3	7,579.2	7,518.9	9,277.0	9,452.2	9,481.3	9,738.6	9,995.9	25.93	70.06
Iceland	1,431.8	1,357.9	1,198.9	1,133.8	1,332.8	1,528.9	1,536.2	1,553.5	1,570.9	9.72	77.23
Ireland	13,983.0	15,450.8	19,728.8	28,863.7	34,748.9	42,872.5	50,737.8	56,863.6	62,989.4	350.47	84.21
Italy	30,418.1	31,031.1	28,244.6	36,345.8	35,922.1	36,115.8	36,709.1	37,757.6	38,806.1	27.58	71.98
Liechtenstein											
Luxembourg	870.8	885.9	822.5	853.9	855.8	851.1	927.7	954.0	980.3	12.58	56.13
Malta	1,364.9	1,340.0	1,399.0	1,309.1	1,365.2	1,371.9	1,495.3	1,526.4	1,557.5	14.11	70.89
Monaco	82.8	77.8	104.3	94.6	83.9	87.5	95.7	97.9	100.0	20.87	96.56
Netherlands	20,898.7	20,073.0	22,931.2	23,454.9	25,595.7	26,132.7	27,454.5	28,547.1	29,639.7	41.83	81.17
Norway	15,182.3	14,556.2	13,699.2	12,805.8	12,277.2	12,065.5	11,574.8	10,973.5	10,372.3	-31.68	64.74
Portugal	6,721.4	6,650.5	6,795.6	7,590.3	9,052.5	10,139.7	9,440.9	9,894.2	10,347.5	53.95	73.79
Spain	39,711.8	41,469.8	40,380.6	42,506.8	45,540.0	49,855.0	53,122.5	55,357.6	57,592.7	45.03	79.09
Sweden	13,354.3	13,123.4	12,421.2	11,586.0	11,623.9	11,666.3	11,706.5	11,746.7	11,786.8	-11.74	69.25
Switzerland	17,268.1	16,914.8	13,295.5	10,118.1	9,287.3	9,662.6	10,647.1	11,327.1	12,007.0	-30.47	82.28
Turkey	12,187.9	10,603.9	10,686.9	10,745.4	14,275.8	16,943.8	19,361.4	20,557.0	21,752.6	78.48	71.27
United Kingdom	70,436.0	70,331.7	72,381.2	76,388.7	86,054.8	93,602.9	97,544.6	102,062.7	106,580.8	51.32	76.76
Eastern Europe											
Albania	140.3	148.7	145.8	160.5	180.9	197.1	214.7	227.1	240.1	71.14	56.64
Belarus	210.9	221.7	204.9	234.3	274.2	281.9	307.4	323.5	339.6	61.01	60.37
Bosnia-Herzegovina	69.1	65.0	65.6	72.9							
Bulgaria	535.2	234.0	62.8	311.0	476.3	653.7	808.5	854.0	899.5	68.06	65.11
Croatia	929.4	1,062.5	1,127.1	1,266.6	1,336.2	1,360.5	1,388.8	1,465.4	1,542.0	65.92	63.98
Czech Republic	2,229.2	2,565.8	2,808.8	3,391.5	4,219.5	4,706.2	4,921.6	5,370.3	5,819.1	161.04	69.27
Estonia	277.6	277.8	304.1	395.5	509.6	577.8	598.1	651.5	705.0	153.95	65.43
Georgia	117.5	110.8	246.6	303.8	228.6	249.1	271.6	297.2	322.9	174.76	69.50
Hungary	2,197.5	2,023.4	2,098.8	2,260.8	2,546.2	2,735.2	2,591.7	2,657.4	2,723.0	23.91	65.79
Latvia	278.4	255.4	265.0	339.7	593.7	1,032.1	1,409.6	1,598.2	1,786.7	541.78	62.30
Lithuania	283.8	304.1	303.9	329.3	447.9	505.4	429.7	454.0	478.3	68.50	59.63
Macedonia	599.0	315.5	165.7	201.0	210.9	192.0	209.3	220.1	231.0	-61.43	70.50
Moldova	117.5	120.1	129.4	179.1	200.6	232.0	273.8	299.9	325.9	177.29	57.13
Poland	2,340.9	2,670.3	2,845.9	3,252.2	3,493.1	3,553.7	3,626.0	3,840.2	4,054.3	73.19	76.24
Romania	1,218.1	1,137.3	959.5	1,255.3	1,337.8	1,707.7	2,047.5	2,185.7	2,323.9	90.78	64.81
Russia	17,687.9	20,301.2	20,892.2	22,723.1	25,948.9	26,522.3	28,836.9	30,695.1	32,553.3	84.04	71.28
Slovakia	57.1	43.1	82.8	190.2	636.3	711.9	779.8	851.5	923.2	1,517.03	69.07
Slovenia	627.9	689.6	720.5	758.4	765.0	757.7	860.7	899.5	938.3	49.44	66.10
Ukraine	950.7	986.0	1,119.9	1,652.6	2,200.1	2,512.9	2,802.0	3,110.5	3,419.1	259.64	66.29

Source: *Euromonitor International from International Civil Aviation Authority/national statistics*
Notes: *Data for scheduled airlines as available for each country. Some airlines' figures may be excluded.*

Size of Merchant Shipping Fleet 1980-2008
'000 gross tons

	1980	1985	1990	1995	1996	1997	1998	1999	2000	2001
Western Europe										
Austria	88.8	134.2	139.3	91.9	94.7	83.4	68.0	71.1	51.2	35.3
Belgium	1,809.8	2,400.3	1,954.5	72.0	277.9	168.6	127.0	132.1	137.2	151.0
Cyprus	2,091.1	8,196.1	18,335.9	24,652.5	23,798.9	23,652.6	23,301.5	23,641.0	23,206.4	22,761.8
Denmark	5,390.4	4,942.2	5,188.1	5,747.2	5,632.0	5,753.8	5,686.7	5,353.6	6,357.8	7,109.0
Finland	2,346.2	1,649.7	1,093.6	1,581.4	1,543.7	1,558.8	1,629.1	1,658.4	1,620.4	1,595.4
France	11,924.6	8,237.4	3,832.4	4,194.3	4,236.0	4,570.4	4,737.7	4,766.4	4,681.2	4,677.7
Germany	9,887.8	7,611.4	5,737.8	5,626.2	5,842.1	6,949.6	8,083.6	6,513.8	6,552.2	6,300.2
Gibraltar	2.3	583.3	2,008.5	307.1	306.0	421.0	530.0	628.0	722.0	816.3
Greece	39,471.7	31,031.5	20,521.6	29,434.7	29,070.0	25,288.5	25,224.5	24,833.3	26,401.7	28,678.2
Iceland	188.2	180.3	176.6	190.2	205.9	214.9	198.4	192.1	185.8	193.4
Ireland	209.0	194.0	180.8	213.4	190.8	235.0	183.8	218.9	254.0	300.3
Italy	11,095.7	8,843.2	7,991.4	6,905.0	6,246.0	6,193.7	6,818.6	8,048.5	9,048.7	9,655.0
Liechtenstein										
Luxembourg			3.3	880.8	878.5	820.4	931.8	1,343.0	1,754.2	1,469.2
Malta	132.9	1,855.8	4,518.7	17,678.3	19,479.4	22,984.2	24,074.7	28,205.5	28,170.0	27,052.6
Monaco										
Netherlands	5,723.8	4,301.3	3,784.8	2,903.0	2,795.0	3,879.5	4,263.3	4,813.8	5,167.7	5,605.0
Norway										22,590.8
Portugal										1,199.2
Spain	8,112.2	6,256.2	3,807.1	1,618.6	1,062.0	1,141.5	1,206.8	1,269.0	1,552.6	2,147.5
Sweden	4,234.0	2,620.0	2,782.0	2,880.0	2,945.0	2,754.1	2,552.4	2,946.9	2,887.0	2,957.9
Switzerland	310.8	342.0	287.5	381.0	381.0	433.9	383.3	439.1	495.0	502.0
Turkey	1,454.8	3,684.4	3,718.6	6,267.6	6,069.0	6,567.3	6,251.4	6,324.6	5,832.7	5,896.7
United Kingdom	27,135.2	14,343.5	9,836.0	8,935.0	8,100.0	8,247.5	8,289.8	9,061.5	9,702.5	12,143.1
Eastern Europe										
Albania	56.1	56.1	55.8	63.0	43.4	30.4	28.7	21.4	23.7	25.2
Belarus										
Bosnia-Herzegovina										
Bulgaria	1,233.3	1,322.2	1,360.5	1,166.1	1,149.7	1,128.2	1,091.2	1,035.8	989.6	955.3
Croatia						871.0	896.4	868.9	841.4	775.2
Czech Republic	155.3	184.3	325.8	140.3	78.1	16.4				
Estonia				597.7	545.3	602.0	521.9	452.6	383.4	346.6
Georgia				282.0	206.0	128.1	117.8	132.2	270.6	276.6
Hungary	75.0	77.2	98.3	45.1	50.2	26.7	15.3	11.9	8.4	
Latvia				798.1	723.4	318.8	118.0	118.1	118.2	68.3
Lithuania				610.2	571.5	510.3	481.1	424.3	401.6	393.3
Macedonia										
Moldova										
Poland	3,639.1	3,315.3	3,369.2	2,358.0	2,292.6	1,877.7	1,424.2	1,319.1	1,119.2	618.3
Romania	1,856.3	3,023.8	4,004.6	2,536.4	2,567.5	2,344.7	2,088.2	1,220.6	766.9	637.7
Russia				10,818.0	13,755.4	12,282.4	11,089.9	10,649.0	10,485.9	10,247.8
Slovakia				19.3	19.4	15.2	15.2	15.2	15.2	15.2
Slovenia				2.1	1.0	2.3	1.8	1.8	1.7	1.9
Ukraine				4,613.0	3,825.4	2,690.0	2,033.2	1,775.2	1,546.3	1,407.7

Source: *Euromonitor International from Lloyd's Register/national statistics*
Notes: *Ships of 100 gross tons or more. Gross tonnage (gt) is a measure of the total volume within the hull, and above deck, available for cargo, passengers, crew, fuel, stores etc. 1gt = 100 cu ft*

Automotives and Transport Statistics

Size of Merchant Shipping Fleet 1980-2008 *(continued)*
'000 gross tons

	2002	2003	2004	2005	2006	2007	2008
Western Europe							
Austria	29.9	32.0	34.1	34.1	34.1	14.0	14.0
Belgium	186.7	1,392.9	3,973.3	4,058.4	4,312.7	4,091.3	4,241.8
Cyprus	22,997.0	22,054.2	21,283.4	19,019.1	19,032.2	18,954.3	20,109.4
Denmark	7,602.9	7,726.7	7,763.1	8,290.4	8,799.6	9,476.3	10,570.0
Finland	1,545.2	1,452.1	1,428.9	1,475.2	1,422.6	1,570.1	1,564.9
France	4,731.5	4,859.2	4,974.9	5,611.1	6,164.8	6,350.2	6,323.5
Germany	6,545.8	6,111.8	8,246.4	11,497.2	11,364.3	12,934.2	15,282.8
Gibraltar	960.9	993.0	1,142.4	1,156.6	1,297.4	1,515.4	1,607.1
Greece	28,782.8	32,203.1	32,040.7	30,744.7	32,048.1	35,704.5	36,822.3
Iceland	187.3	187.4	194.1	188.5	184.2	180.0	168.7
Ireland	279.6	471.0	496.8	309.8	193.4	187.2	185.5
Italy	9,595.9	10,245.8	10,956.0	11,616.0	12,571.2	12,971.7	13,599.9
Liechtenstein							
Luxembourg	1,493.8	1,006.0	689.7	570.0	779.9	883.5	729.9
Malta	26,331.4	25,134.3	22,352.6	23,015.6	24,849.8	27,754.4	31,633.3
Monaco							
Netherlands	5,664.3	5,702.6	5,622.9	5,669.4	5,818.8	6,139.8	6,684.2
Norway	22,194.5	20,509.3	18,936.2	17,531.9	18,222.3	18,156.0	18,311.3
Portugal	1,099.7	1,156.3	1,136.5	1,239.6	1,223.6	1,070.1	1,095.7
Spain	2,371.2	2,651.0	2,869.1	2,901.7	3,004.6	3,061.8	3,054.9
Sweden	3,177.5	3,579.3	3,666.9	3,765.7	3,876.5	4,044.9	4,389.3
Switzerland	559.1	588.7	487.5	479.6	510.0	588.6	640.4
Turkey	5,658.8	4,950.6	4,678.9	5,044.7	4,848.8	4,995.1	5,181.0
United Kingdom	13,773.0	17,314.2	18,344.3	19,652.0	20,835.7	21,947.2	24,262.0
Eastern Europe							
Albania	48.7	70.0	72.8	74.8	74.7	67.5	65.7
Belarus							
Bosnia-Herzegovina							
Bulgaria	889.3	747.9	789.5	894.2	875.5	911.1	876.1
Croatia	834.7	847.7	1,016.1	1,135.2	1,157.2	1,373.5	1,444.7
Czech Republic							
Estonia	357.4	358.2	334.9	292.5	416.7	389.8	363.5
Georgia	569.3	814.9	974.3	1,091.9	1,129.3	1,048.4	678.4
Hungary	3.8	7.6					
Latvia	88.7	90.9	294.3	304.8	333.3	261.8	289.7
Lithuania	435.3	442.1	453.4	476.7	448.6	425.8	423.7
Macedonia							
Moldova			3.7	11.4	15.7	50.1	178.7
Poland	585.6	282.4	162.7	190.1	193.4	193.3	212.9
Romania	622.0	563.1	426.7	336.5	272.1	269.5	261.8
Russia	10,380.0	10,430.8	8,638.9	8,334.5	8,046.0	7,587.3	7,527.0
Slovakia	7.4	29.2	126.4	211.2	232.7	233.3	189.9
Slovenia	2.3	1.7	1.5	1.1	1.6	1.6	2.1
Ukraine	1,349.9	1,378.8	1,144.8	1,154.0	1,136.5	1,144.6	1,087.1

Source: *Euromonitor International from Lloyd's Register/national statistics*
Notes: *Ships of 100 gross tons or more. Gross tonnage (gt) is a measure of the total volume within the hull, and above deck, available for cargo, passengers, crew, fuel, stores etc. 1gt = 100 cu ft*

Length of Public Railway Network 1980-2008

Kilometres at end-year

	1980	1985	1990	1995	1996	1997	1998	1999	2000	2001
Western Europe										
Austria			5,624	5,672	5,672	5,672	5,643	5,618	5,563	5,980
Belgium	3,978	3,712	3,479	3,368	3,380	3,422	3,470	3,472	3,471	3,454
Cyprus										
Denmark	2,461	2,471	2,344	2,303	2,275	2,248	2,264	2,756	2,768	2,768
Finland			5,846	5,859	5,860	5,865	5,867	5,836	5,854	5,850
France	34,382	34,678	34,260	31,940	31,852	31,821	31,735	29,113	29,272	29,445
Germany	28,517	27,634	40,980	41,718	40,826	38,450	38,150	37,589	36,642	36,050
Gibraltar										
Greece	2,461	2,461	2,484	2,474	2,474	2,503	2,299	2,299	2,385	2,377
Iceland										
Ireland	1,987	1,944	1,944	1,945	1,954	1,908	1,909	1,919	1,919	1,919
Italy	16,133	16,183	16,016	16,005	16,014	16,030	16,080	16,092	16,295	16,357
Liechtenstein										
Luxembourg	270	270	271	275	275	274	274	271	271	274
Malta										
Monaco										
Netherlands	2,760	2,794	2,780	2,813	2,813	2,805	2,808	2,808	2,802	2,809
Norway			4,044	4,023	4,021	4,021	4,021	4,021	4,179	4,178
Portugal	3,588	3,607	3,126	3,065	3,071	3,038	2,794	2,814	2,814	2,814
Spain	13,542	12,710	12,560	12,280	12,284	12,303	12,303	12,319	12,310	12,310
Sweden			10,801	9,782	9,821	9,798	9,855	9,884	9,877	11,021
Switzerland			2,978	2,987	2,989	3,450	4,000	5,108	5,062	5,053
Turkey	8,193	8,169	8,429	8,549	8,607	8,607	8,607	8,682	8,671	8,671
United Kingdom	18,028	17,122	16,924	16,999	17,001	16,991	16,994	16,994	16,994	16,994
Eastern Europe										
Albania			674	674	447	447	447	440	440	447
Belarus	5,512	5,540	5,569	5,543	5,543	5,542	5,533	5,523	5,512	5,509
Bosnia-Herzegovina			944	1,032	539	539	607	607	519	608
Bulgaria	4,267	4,297	4,299	4,293	4,293	4,291	4,290	4,290	4,320	4,320
Croatia		2,441	2,573	2,296	2,726	2,726	2,726	2,726	2,726	2,726
Czech Republic			9,451	9,327	9,435	9,430	9,430	9,365	9,365	9,444
Estonia	993	1,009	1,026	1,021	1,020	966	966	968	968	967
Georgia		1,465	1,583	1,575	1,575	1,576	1,576	1,545	1,562	1,565
Hungary	7,826	7,406	7,838	7,988	7,988	7,988	7,988	7,988	8,005	7,736
Latvia	2,384	2,384	2,397	2,413	2,413	2,413	2,413	2,413	2,331	2,305
Lithuania	2,008	2,014	2,007	2,002	1,997	1,997	1,997	1,905	1,905	1,695
Macedonia			696	699	697	699	699	699	699	699
Moldova			1,150			1,312	1,240	1,185	1,139	1,121
Poland	27,181	25,848	26,228	23,986	23,420	23,424	23,210	22,891	22,560	21,119
Romania	11,110	11,269	11,348	11,376	11,385	11,380	11,010	10,981	11,015	11,015
Russia			87,000	87,000	87,000	87,000	86,700	86,200	86,075	85,835
Slovakia			3,660	3,665	3,673	3,673	3,665	3,665	3,662	3,662
Slovenia	1,229	1,228	1,196	1,201	1,201	1,201	1,201	1,201	1,201	1,229
Ukraine	22,553	22,698	22,799	22,756	22,757	22,702	22,600	22,472	22,301	22,218

Source: *Euromonitor International from national statistics*

Automotives and Transport Statistics

Length of Public Railway Network 1980-2008 *(continued)*
Kilometres at end-year

	2002	2003	2004	2005	2006	2007	2008
Western Europe							
Austria	5,642	5,656	5,675	5,691	5,702	5,712	5,726
Belgium	3,518	3,521	3,536	3,544	3,560	3,570	3,582
Cyprus							
Denmark	2,768	2,779	2,785	2,644	2,644	2,644	2,610
Finland	5,850	5,851	5,741	5,732	5,905	5,971	6,001
France	29,352	29,269	29,246	28,412	29,463	29,989	30,168
Germany	35,868	36,054	34,725	34,228	34,128	34,070	33,574
Gibraltar							
Greece	2,383	2,414	2,449	2,576	2,509	2,487	2,505
Iceland							
Ireland	1,919	1,919	1,919	1,919	1,919	1,919	1,919
Italy	16,307	16,288	16,236	16,543	16,627	16,655	16,747
Liechtenstein							
Luxembourg	274	275	275	275	275	275	275
Malta							
Monaco							
Netherlands	2,806	2,811	2,811	2,813	2,776	2,766	2,754
Norway	4,077	4,077	4,077	4,087	4,087	4,087	4,090
Portugal	2,881	2,818	2,849	2,839	2,839	2,839	2,844
Spain	12,298	12,298	13,117	12,824	12,991	13,075	13,269
Sweden	11,095	11,037	11,050	11,017	11,020	11,022	11,018
Switzerland	5,049	5,028	5,062	5,062	5,062	5,062	5,071
Turkey	8,671	8,697	8,697	8,697	8,697	8,697	8,697
United Kingdom	17,020	16,652	16,652	16,116	15,810	15,670	15,425
Eastern Europe							
Albania	447	447	447	423	423	423	417
Belarus	5,512	5,502	5,498	5,498	5,494	5,492	5,490
Bosnia-Herzegovina	608	608	608	608	608	608	608
Bulgaria	4,318	4,318	4,259	4,154	4,146	4,141	4,097
Croatia	2,726	2,726	2,726	2,726	2,722	2,721	2,720
Czech Republic	9,499	9,501	9,511	9,513	9,496	9,490	9,487
Estonia	967	967	959	959	962	963	962
Georgia	1,565	1,564	1,336	1,336	1,336	1,336	1,279
Hungary	7,950	7,950	7,950	7,950	7,960	7,964	7,968
Latvia	2,270	2,270	2,270	2,270	2,269	2,269	2,269
Lithuania	1,775	1,774	1,782	1,771	1,771	1,771	1,770
Macedonia	699	699	699	699	699	699	699
Moldova	1,121	1,111	1,075	1,115	1,154	1,182	1,200
Poland	21,073	20,665	20,250	20,253	19,980	19,751	19,523
Romania	11,002	11,077	11,053	10,948	10,896	10,877	10,827
Russia	85,542	85,394	85,000	85,000	92,217	95,104	97,531
Slovakia	3,657	3,657	3,660	3,658	3,658	3,658	3,658
Slovenia	1,229	1,229	1,229	1,228	1,228	1,228	1,228
Ukraine	22,078	22,051	21,990	21,980	21,870	21,822	21,765

Source: *Euromonitor International from national statistics*

Automotives and Transport Statistics

Table 3.25

Railway Statistics of Major National Carriers 2008
As stated

	Locomotives (number)	Rail motor vehicles (number)	Passengers carried (million)	Average journey length (km)	Total goods carried (million tonnes)
Western Europe					
Austria	1,363	262	215.7	42.8	96.7
Belgium	680	1,491	211.9	48.5	80.3
Cyprus					
Denmark	149	670	161.5	36.1	7.5
Finland	635		67.8	56.0	44.8
France	4,436		1,063.0	79.2	98.4
Germany	4,058	5,233	2,342.7	33.1	374.6
Gibraltar					
Greece	181		9.5	190.3	4.7
Iceland					
Ireland	93		49.7	40.2	1.5
Italy	3,347		568.9	82.9	80.7
Liechtenstein			0.2	8.3	
Luxembourg	100		15.7	20.6	12.7
Malta					
Monaco					
Netherlands	182		325.2	45.7	33.0
Norway	159	188	56.7	51.8	35.2
Portugal	131	227	147.7	24.4	11.6
Spain	798	1,984	524.4	38.3	24.4
Sweden	630		168.5	61.3	68.3
Switzerland	1,871		305.0	58.9	56.2
Turkey	598		77.8	68.3	21.5
United Kingdom	1,679		1,132.1	39.1	118.9
Eastern Europe					
Albania	58		1.7	46.3	0.5
Belarus	427		73.2	120.5	145.3
Bosnia-Herzegovina	169		0.5	79.0	6.9
Bulgaria	552	76	34.1	71.0	21.9
Croatia	268	195	53.5	27.8	18.6
Czech Republic	2,302		184.2	38.7	90.6
Estonia	352		5.4	52.3	45.7
Georgia	318		3.8	204.8	23.1
Hungary	1,010	262	156.3	58.9	59.1
Latvia	190	387	30.3	36.3	46.3
Lithuania	243	66	5.6	77.1	52.6
Macedonia	56		1.1	103.4	4.7
Moldova	158		5.4	104.9	9.9
Poland	4,408	990	274.8	67.4	317.5
Romania	1,781		103.3	82.1	67.0
Russia			1,359.6	131.8	1,395.3
Slovakia	1,002		46.8	46.4	53.9
Slovenia	167	109	16.7	48.7	17.8
Ukraine	4,220		443.1	121.6	411.8

Source: *Euromonitor International from International Road Federation/national statistics*

Automotives and Transport Statistics

Table 3.26

Railway Freight Traffic 1980-2008

Million net tonne-kilometres

	1980	1985	1990	1995	1996	1997	1998	1999	2000	2001
Western Europe										
Austria	11,200	11,292	12,158	13,714	13,909	14,791	15,358	15,566	17,095	17,357
Belgium	8,037	8,277	8,354	8,407	8,454	8,700	8,764	8,468	8,734	8,174
Cyprus										
Denmark	1,619	1,749	1,801	1,998	1,767	1,992	2,065	1,974	2,025	1,961
Finland	8,300	8,066	8,400	9,559	8,800	9,900	9,900	9,800	10,107	9,857
France	68,815	55,121	50,670	48,136	49,506	53,855	53,967	53,438	55,448	50,396
Germany				69,483	68,490	72,389	73,273	71,494	75,884	76,092
Gibraltar										
Greece	814	733	647	306	337	243	226	234	426	379
Iceland										
Ireland	624	601	589	602	570	522	466	526	491	516
Italy	18,384	16,853	13,259	24,050	23,314	25,228	24,707	23,781	25,017	24,655
Liechtenstein										
Luxembourg	660	648	615	564	570	609	622	660	678	628
Malta										
Monaco										
Netherlands	3,468	3,269	3,070	3,097	3,123	3,406	3,793	3,988	3,819	3,834
Norway	3,084	2,928	2,559	2,715	3,108	2,399	2,421	2,456	2,399	2,451
Portugal	1,001	1,196	1,444	2,343	2,177	2,632	2,340	2,562	2,569	2,498
Spain	10,528	11,415	10,142	10,074	9,790	11,030	11,325	11,470	11,620	11,752
Sweden	15,914	17,331	19,102	19,391	18,840	18,605	18,597	18,503	18,729	18,954
Switzerland	7,799	7,434	8,958	8,686	8,710	8,505	9,128	9,825	9,937	10,091
Turkey	5,029	7,747	8,031	8,632	9,018	9,717	8,466	8,446	9,895	7,562
United Kingdom	17,640	16,047	16,778	13,000	13,300	15,100	16,900	17,300	18,200	19,700
Eastern Europe										
Albania				53	42	23	25	27	28	19
Belarus	66,264	73,243	75,373	25,510	26,018	30,636	30,370	30,529	31,425	29,727
Bosnia-Herzegovina				16	18	47	73	120	140	159
Bulgaria	17,663	18,172	14,132	8,560	7,517	7,353	6,070	5,176	5,538	4,905
Croatia	7,561	8,674	6,535	1,971	1,712	1,876	2,001	1,685	1,928	2,249
Czech Republic			41,150	22,634	22,333	20,733	18,288	16,457	18,983	18,302
Estonia			6,977	3,851	4,177	5,143	6,058	7,277	7,788	8,222
Georgia	14,656	13,487	12,354		2,394	2,006	2,694	3,160	3,912	4,481
Hungary	24,041	21,929	16,593	8,132	7,409	7,873	7,852	6,642	8,093	7,730
Latvia		19,933	18,538	9,757	12,400	13,970	13,000	12,210	13,310	14,179
Lithuania			19,258	7,220	8,103	8,622	8,265	8,341	8,919	7,741
Macedonia	712	992	769	169	271	280	408	380	509	462
Moldova	15,200		15,007	3,134	2,785	2,818	2,652	1,232	1,538	2,049
Poland	132,576	118,863	83,530	69,116	68,332	68,651	61,760	55,471	54,448	47,913
Romania	78,390	64,090	57,253	27,179	26,877	24,789	19,708	15,927	16,354	16,102
Russia	2,316,000	2,506,000	2,523,000	1,214,000	1,131,251	1,100,000	1,020,000	1,205,000	1,373,178	1,433,617
Slovakia			23,176	13,764	12,017	12,373	11,753	9,859	11,234	10,929
Slovenia	3,851	4,292	4,209	3,076	2,551	2,852	2,859	2,784	2,857	2,837
Ukraine			488,243	195,762	163,364	160,433	158,693	156,336	172,840	177,465

Source: *Euromonitor International from national statistics*

Automotives and Transport Statistics

Railway Freight Traffic 1980-2008 *(continued)*
Million net tonne-kilometres

	2002	2003	2004	2005	2006	2007	2008
Western Europe							
Austria	17,633	17,864	19,040	18,025	19,059	19,576	20,004
Belgium	8,363	8,306	8,725	9,157	9,835	10,279	10,772
Cyprus							
Denmark	1,906	1,997	2,169	1,976	1,892	1,889	1,861
Finland	9,664	10,047	10,105	9,706	11,060	11,812	12,254
France	50,295	47,400	46,974	41,901	40,924	40,410	38,662
Germany	76,300	79,800	86,400	95,400	107,007	115,250	124,112
Gibraltar							
Greece	327	456	588	611	662	692	751
Iceland							
Ireland	426	398	399	303	166	108	35
Italy	23,299	22,932	23,803	22,928	23,734	24,137	24,439
Liechtenstein							
Luxembourg	612	560	593	414	455	477	456
Malta							
Monaco							
Netherlands	3,685	4,026	4,331	4,589	4,815	5,008	5,254
Norway	2,191	2,158	2,277	2,395	2,454	2,499	2,584
Portugal	2,585	2,442	2,675	2,826	2,763	2,730	2,802
Spain	11,673	11,867	11,460	11,071	10,842	10,558	10,230
Sweden	19,197	20,170	20,856	21,675	22,271	22,625	23,238
Switzerland	9,639	9,534	10,245	10,149	10,072	10,029	10,153
Turkey	7,224	8,669	9,417	9,077	9,544	9,836	10,128
United Kingdom	18,700	18,900	18,900	19,964	20,496	20,895	21,394
Eastern Europe							
Albania	21	31	32	26	36	38	39
Belarus	34,169	38,402	40,331	43,559	45,723	46,943	49,078
Bosnia-Herzegovina	177	212	445	762	682	629	733
Bulgaria	4,627	5,274	5,212	5,163	5,225	5,256	5,252
Croatia	2,420	2,745	2,733	3,106	3,603	3,951	4,253
Czech Republic	17,042	17,069	16,214	15,973	16,364	16,581	16,459
Estonia	9,330	9,283	9,567	10,311	10,152	10,068	10,265
Georgia	5,065	5,539	4,862	6,127	6,760	6,997	7,361
Hungary	7,751	8,028	8,749	9,090	10,167	10,734	11,411
Latvia	15,020	17,604	16,877	17,921	15,273	14,631	13,888
Lithuania	9,767	11,457	11,637	12,457	12,896	13,211	13,649
Macedonia	334	376	426	530	614	661	732
Moldova	2,715	3,000	2,968	2,980	3,655	3,930	4,162
Poland	47,756	49,595	52,332	49,972	53,623	55,448	56,911
Romania	15,218	15,039	17,022	16,582	16,289	16,166	16,448
Russia	1,510,203	1,668,921	1,802,000	1,858,000	1,950,000	2,009,200	2,094,270
Slovakia	10,383	10,113	9,702	9,463	9,988	10,251	10,285
Slovenia	3,078	3,018	3,149	3,245	3,373	3,462	3,573
Ukraine	193,141	225,288	233,961	223,980	240,810	243,550	248,115

Source: *Euromonitor International from national statistics*

Table 3.27

Railway Passenger Traffic 1985-2008

Million passenger-kilometres

	1985	1990	1995	2000	2003	2004	2005	2006	2007	2008
Western Europe										
Austria	7,290	8,575	9,628	8,318	8,266	8,375	8,586	8,854	9,046	9,241
Belgium	6,572	6,540	6,757	7,755	8,265	8,676	9,150	9,607	9,881	10,285
Cyprus										
Denmark	4,546	4,851	4,783	5,343	5,300	5,401	5,534	5,652	5,726	5,832
Finland	3,224	3,300	3,184	3,405	3,300	3,352	3,478	3,606	3,697	3,796
France	62,070	63,740	55,560	69,571	71,385	74,014	76,559	79,474	81,658	84,226
Germany			60,514	74,015	69,596	69,997	72,497	74,738	75,986	77,583
Gibraltar										
Greece	1,732	1,978	1,568	1,886	1,752	1,668	1,854	1,811	1,797	1,808
Iceland										
Ireland	1,023	1,226	1,291	1,389	1,601	1,582	1,781	1,872	1,920	2,000
Italy	37,401	45,512	43,859	43,752	45,221	45,566	46,144	46,439	46,788	47,179
Liechtenstein						1	1	1	1	1
Luxembourg	288	264	304	332	262	266	272	298	311	323
Malta										
Monaco										
Netherlands	9,007	11,060	13,977	14,666	13,848	14,097	14,730	14,678	14,652	14,853
Norway	2,232	2,430	2,676	2,635	2,681	2,683	2,718	2,827	2,885	2,936
Portugal	5,725	5,664	4,809	3,632	3,339	3,415	3,412	3,514	3,554	3,608
Spain	15,979	15,476	15,318	18,547	19,333	19,022	19,806	19,865	19,949	20,103
Sweden	6,586	6,353	6,345	8,301	8,834	8,658	8,936	9,642	10,036	10,336
Switzerland	10,163	12,678	13,408	12,620	14,509	14,914	16,144	16,798	17,269	17,959
Turkey	6,489	6,410	5,797	5,833	5,878	5,237	5,036	5,277	5,428	5,315
United Kingdom	30,400	33,200	30,000	38,200	40,900	42,400	42,981	43,272	43,620	44,300
Eastern Europe										
Albania			197	125	105	89	73	80	85	80
Belarus	13,761	16,852	12,505	17,722	13,308	13,893	10,351	9,968	9,721	8,824
Bosnia-Herzegovina			63	9	19	19	23	30	34	38
Bulgaria	7,785	7,793	4,693	3,472	2,517	2,628	2,389	2,422	2,443	2,424
Croatia	4,063	3,429	943	1,252	1,163	1,213	1,266	1,362	1,422	1,486
Czech Republic		13,313	8,023	7,300	6,518	6,589	6,667	6,887	7,006	7,128
Estonia		1,510	421	261	182	192	248	260	264	285
Georgia	4,214	2,497	371	378	1,039	615	720	790	836	785
Hungary	10,464	11,400	5,880	9,693	10,286	10,544	9,880	9,584	9,420	9,203
Latvia		5,364	1,373	715	778	811	894	992	1,037	1,102
Lithuania		3,640	1,130	611	432	443	428	430	432	432
Macedonia	417	354	65	170	98	94	94	105	109	112
Moldova		1,464	1,019	315	352	346	355	471	521	563
Poland	51,978	50,373	26,635	19,706	19,638	18,690	18,157	18,553	18,751	18,529
Romania	31,082	30,582	18,879	11,632	8,497	8,493	8,489	8,486	8,484	8,480
Russia		274,400	192,117	167,054	157,600	164,300	171,600	173,699	174,874	179,192
Slovakia		6,381	4,202	2,870	2,455	2,228	2,182	2,213	2,229	2,173
Slovenia	1,667	1,429	595	705	777	764	777	793	805	812
Ukraine		81,998	63,752	51,767	52,558	51,726	52,655	53,230	53,606	53,868

Source: *Euromonitor International from national statistics*

Automotives and Transport Statistics

Table 3.28

Car Traffic Volume 1980-2008

Million car-kilometres

	1980	1985	1990	1995	1996	1997	1998	1999	2000	2001
Western Europe										
Austria	25,840	27,500								
Belgium	40,861	42,101	50,467	85,200	92,416	94,033	95,659	92,189	88,719	85,250
Cyprus										
Denmark	26,847	29,803	34,993	37,860	38,649	39,551	40,304	41,501	41,547	41,460
Finland	22,180	25,970	33,430	35,760	36,000	36,790	38,080	39,190	39,815	40,680
France		110,280	143,890	169,095	173,157	178,924	185,767	193,701	197,777	204,241
Germany				514,900	519,000	524,800	528,000	541,900	555,800	569,700
Gibraltar										
Greece	9,392				37,271	39,683	42,317	47,457	48,573	50,909
Iceland	986									2,039
Ireland	14,798	20,540	24,800		23,200		23,775	25,212	26,204	27,505
Italy				329,000	335,000	341,000	342,000	348,000	362,000	380,000
Liechtenstein										
Luxembourg	1,382	2,191	2,971	2,954	3,074	3,192	3,269	3,339	3,408	3,478
Malta									1,507	
Monaco				1						
Netherlands	61,400	65,000	76,960	89,094	89,973	89,661	90,400	93,185	93,185	95,185
Norway	22,743	22,565			25,388	25,512	27,500	27,643	28,113	27,563
Portugal		22,500	30,300	44,250	41,250	44,250	47,250	49,463	52,339	53,192
Spain	52,780	56,300	81,344	107,994	112,895	149,412	158,562	169,000	180,908	189,167
Sweden		52,900		57,400	56,571	56,596	54,700	56,000	56,400	56,600
Switzerland	32,071	36,468	42,649	43,794	44,962	45,142	47,069	48,166	49,585	50,765
Turkey	7,444	9,415	14,755	28,837	25,157	28,837	30,683	30,791	36,224	34,047
United Kingdom	201,100	228,000	329,700	353,200	362,400	370,900	375,600	377,444	376,798	382,756
Eastern Europe										
Albania				2						
Belarus				935	942	1,036	1,083	1,114	966	889
Bosnia-Herzegovina										
Bulgaria			10,597	11,230	12,055	12,117	12,696	12,718	13,189	13,529
Croatia						9,282	10,436	11,454	11,158	12,337
Czech Republic				24,540	24,200	25,900	26,240	27,320	28,400	31,707
Estonia					4,339	4,690	4,763	5,094	5,116	5,238
Georgia				17						248
Hungary			17,155				15,620	15,840	16,000	16,300
Latvia			1,660							6,392
Lithuania										
Macedonia			2,400	2,621	2,659					
Moldova				180	188	179	170	141	143	157
Poland	20,494	20,193	34,194	75,150	80,500	85,350	88,900	92,800	94,600	94,600
Romania			19,681	24,019	26,048	26,919	27,918	28,895	27,545	29,029
Russia				14,711	13,882	15,319	14,833	16,317	17,099	17,495
Slovakia				8,251	8,627	9,003	9,378	9,754	9,754	9,817
Slovenia			4,749	5,640	7,089	7,581	7,577	8,021	8,130	8,515
Ukraine							3,383	3,362	3,347	3,636

Source: *Euromonitor International from International Road Federation/national statistics*

Automotives and Transport Statistics

Car Traffic Volume 1980-2008 *(continued)*

Million car-kilometres

	2002	2003	2004	2005	2006	2007	2008
Western Europe							
Austria				59,414	60,679	61,944	63,209
Belgium	81,780	78,310	79,550	78,416	80,334	81,009	81,495
Cyprus			6,384				
Denmark	41,806	42,482	43,796	44,575	45,498	46,503	47,405
Finland	41,675	42,565	43,530	44,220	44,610	45,560	45,628
France	209,928	213,284	217,576	218,395	220,990	225,336	227,060
Germany	583,600	577,800	590,400	578,200	586,300	589,133	590,400
Gibraltar							
Greece	54,465	59,241	65,236	67,939	71,787	75,969	79,547
Iceland	2,062	2,085	2,108	2,131	2,154	2,177	2,200
Ireland	28,463	29,342	29,776	29,955	30,287	30,497	30,737
Italy	397,000	411,000	422,000	426,000	430,000	433,000	436,667
Liechtenstein							
Luxembourg	3,548	3,532	3,623	3,729	3,841	3,944	4,051
Malta							
Monaco							
Netherlands	98,812	101,151	103,709	104,767	106,090	107,188	108,348
Norway	28,507	29,162	29,395	29,543	29,607	29,692	29,791
Portugal	55,072	56,278	57,066	57,392	57,907	58,269	58,671
Spain	197,597	204,211	209,389	213,883	217,503	220,456	224,145
Sweden	44,092	60,000	60,500	63,000	63,000	65,320	66,927
Switzerland	51,758	52,000	53,768	54,338	52,415	51,862	51,544
Turkey	33,204	33,802	38,403	40,490	43,188	46,317	48,955
United Kingdom	392,926	393,049	398,056	397,191	402,177	405,220	407,608
Eastern Europe							
Albania							
Belarus	760	861	731	744	1,111	1,194	1,349
Bosnia-Herzegovina							
Bulgaria	13,897	14,698	15,033	15,368	15,694	15,916	16,151
Croatia	13,432	14,600	15,556	16,450	17,289	18,185	19,061
Czech Republic	33,445	34,298	35,013	35,309	35,705	36,017	36,352
Estonia	5,431	5,898	6,263	6,373	6,420	6,446	6,481
Georgia	252						
Hungary	15,800	15,800	16,200	16,365	16,491	16,606	16,741
Latvia	6,268	6,809	7,486	7,979	9,505	10,403	11,376
Lithuania		6,472	7,051	6,753	7,206	7,451	7,584
Macedonia							
Moldova	191	198	202	204	206	208	210
Poland	95,000	95,120	95,320	95,658	95,893	96,098	96,305
Romania	30,593	31,159	32,364	33,475	34,436	35,528	36,583
Russia	18,086	18,479	18,786	19,073	19,292	19,473	19,656
Slovakia	9,854	9,862	9,891	9,911	9,926	9,943	9,960
Slovenia	8,762	8,918	9,334	9,490	9,768	10,051	10,290
Ukraine	3,786	4,241	4,697	4,788	4,861	4,919	4,993

Source: *Euromonitor International from International Road Federation/national statistics*

Goods Transported by Road 1980-2008

Million car-kilometres

	1980	1985	1990	1995	1996	1997	1998	1999	2000	2001
Western Europe										
Austria	7,931	9,099	15,317		11,500	15,700	16,100	25,200	26,300	29,833
Belgium	16,738	19,124	25,979	27,500	29,822	32,144	34,466	36,788	32,450	38,682
Cyprus										
Denmark	9,600	9,500	10,664	10,786	9,976	10,307	10,740	11,087	11,696	11,619
Finland	18,400	20,800	26,300	23,200	24,100	25,400	26,500	26,500	28,500	27,600
France		84,422	114,830	157,100	158,126	160,177	166,970	181,430	183,696	188,514
Germany				199,196	199,196	203,119	210,402	226,982	226,477	225,972
Gibraltar										
Greece			12,485	16,700	13,383	13,851	13,522	13,909	18,360	19,104
Iceland										
Ireland					5,700	5,700	5,900	6,100	6,500	12,405
Italy	119,629	144,129	177,945	174,432	175,450	181,687	191,482	173,578	184,756	186,510
Liechtenstein										
Luxembourg	278	431			412	431	400	3,517	6,797	8,699
Malta										
Monaco										
Netherlands	17,663	19,249	23,300	23,491	21,300	21,600	29,200	48,600	45,700	56,167
Norway	5,252	6,418	7,692	10,395	10,651	11,838	12,636	15,094	12,483	13,287
Portugal	11,800		11,712	11,457	11,917	13,500	14,200	14,714	20,470	23,085
Spain	94,800	108,100	102,544	101,874	102,167	109,841	125,268	134,259	148,715	161,042
Sweden	21,362	21,177	26,519	29,324	31,185	33,126	36,500	33,739	32,419	34,161
Switzerland	7,287	8,640	11,214	12,868	16,289	17,863	19,504	20,487	21,949	23,500
Turkey	39,233	62,480	97,843	152,210	135,781	139,789	152,210	150,974	161,552	151,421
United Kingdom	95,900	102,100	136,300	149,600	153,900	157,100	159,500	164,562	165,827	163,551
Eastern Europe										
Albania					1,120	1,340	1,830	2,015	2,200	2,200
Belarus			22,361	9,539	8,658	9,065	9,686	9,232	9,745	10,241
Bosnia-Herzegovina										
Bulgaria										5,423
Croatia			2,458	1,251	1,117	1,091	1,151	1,093	1,090	6,783
Czech Republic				31,267	30,052	40,640	33,911	36,964	39,036	40,260
Estonia			2,097	1,549	1,897	2,773	3,791	3,929	3,689	4,677
Georgia				98	131	303	385	420	475	520
Hungary					13,000	13,000	14,000	13,100	13,329	12,500
Latvia			5,853	1,100	1,019	3,352	4,108	4,161	4,789	5,359
Lithuania			7,336	5,160	4,191	8,622	5,611	7,740	7,769	8,274
Macedonia			3,510	1,178	1,210	1,719	1,812	2,076	2,436	3,131
Moldova			6,305	1,121	944	946	940	952	1,001	964
Poland	44,546	36,593	49,800	71,600	79,200	95,500	69,543	70,452	72,843	74,403
Romania			28,993	19,748	19,807	21,750	15,785	13,456	14,288	18,544
Russia							21,000	22,000	23,000	22,000
Slovakia				5,158	5,171	3,779	4,750	18,516	14,340	13,799
Slovenia					2,287	2,777	3,844	4,240	5,252	7,035
Ukraine			79,668	34,478	22,201	20,532	18,266	18,206	16,811	14,405

Source: *Euromonitor International from International Road Federation/national statistics*

Automotives and Transport Statistics

Goods Transported by Road 1980-2008 *(continued)*
Million car-kilometres

	2002	2003	2004	2005	2006	2007	2008
Western Europe							
Austria	34,411	39,556	39,186	37,043	39,186	37,437	36,854
Belgium	44,915	51,147	54,856	48,944	51,572	52,989	53,611
Cyprus			1,100	1,374	1,144	1,029	982
Denmark	11,810	11,174	10,538	11,058	11,318	11,448	11,549
Finland	29,000	27,800	28,100	27,800	26,400	26,900	27,300
France	188,093	188,871	197,031	192,879	198,546	206,731	209,964
Germany	225,467	227,197	232,296	237,609	251,372	263,460	273,847
Gibraltar							
Greece	19,241	19,362	19,452	19,489	19,544	19,585	19,629
Iceland	800	800					
Ireland	14,448	15,900	16,483	16,991	17,687	19,146	20,034
Italy	192,700	195,887	197,742	199,614	200,766	201,579	202,432
Liechtenstein							
Luxembourg	9,142	9,493	9,692	9,829	9,913	9,968	10,029
Malta							
Monaco							
Netherlands	66,634	77,100	82,333	86,694	90,037	92,193	94,384
Norway	13,614	14,115	14,966	15,414	15,894	16,191	16,518
Portugal	23,187	23,311	23,435	25,231	45,032	46,406	48,320
Spain	179,519	187,044	214,717	227,381	235,792	252,041	264,483
Sweden	36,620	36,603	36,926	38,556	39,899	40,525	41,325
Switzerland	24,500	14,582	15,000	15,753	16,337	16,922	17,563
Turkey	150,912	152,163	156,853	166,831	177,399	185,811	195,464
United Kingdom	161,276	159,000	160,000	163,000	164,600	165,533	166,455
Eastern Europe							
Albania	2,200	2,200	2,200	2,200	2,200	2,200	2,200
Belarus	11,400	12,710	13,969	15,045	15,779	19,200	20,944
Bosnia-Herzegovina	221	221	483	657	809	1,005	1,179
Bulgaria	6,603	6,840	9,015	11,843	12,760	13,250	13,721
Croatia	7,413	8,241	8,819	9,328	10,175	10,820	11,487
Czech Republic	45,059	46,564	46,010	43,447	50,369	51,637	53,513
Estonia	4,387	6,364	6,837	7,641	8,183	8,486	8,852
Georgia	543	562	570	581	590	596	602
Hungary	12,000	12,505	10,798	9,090	8,605	8,085	7,784
Latvia	1,930	2,324	2,330	2,767	2,729	2,864	3,042
Lithuania	10,709	11,462	12,279	15,908	18,134	20,358	23,051
Macedonia	4,291	5,451	5,341	5,577	8,299	5,938	6,071
Moldova	1,153	1,577	1,673	1,791	1,880	1,931	2,017
Poland	74,679	85,989	110,481	119,740	136,490	153,324	167,605
Romania	25,350	30,854	37,220	51,531	60,258	70,059	81,006
Russia	23,200	25,200	25,707	26,117	26,441	26,648	26,899
Slovakia	14,929	16,859	18,517	22,550	22,114	21,676	21,413
Slovenia	6,609	7,040	9,007	11,033	12,112	13,239	14,180
Ukraine	12,000	14,100	15,300	19,700	25,300	29,400	31,750

Source: Euromonitor International from International Road Federation/national statistics

Average Annual Distance Travelled by Car 1980-2008
Kilometres

	1980	1985	1990	1995	1996	1997	1998	1999	2000	2001
Western Europe										
Austria	11,500	10,866								
Belgium	12,936	12,840	13,165	20,099	21,454	21,502	21,458	20,274	19,166	18,198
Cyprus										
Denmark	19,321	19,856	22,000	22,472	22,157	22,123	22,124	22,470	22,544	22,109
Finland	18,093	16,797	17,242	18,813	18,530	18,885	18,841	18,818	18,774	18,954
France		5,229	6,110	6,737	6,790	6,858	6,929	7,049	7,048	7,116
Germany				12,714	12,645	12,699	12,657	12,774	12,698	12,836
Gibraltar										
Greece	10,675				15,932	15,873	15,815	16,308	15,420	14,870
Iceland	12,325									12,695
Ireland	20,151	28,948	31,140		21,941		19,864	19,864	19,863	19,863
Italy				10,858	10,939	10,962	10,902	10,862	11,110	11,432
Liechtenstein										
Luxembourg	9,376	14,414	16,199	12,897	13,268	13,478	13,390	13,176	13,218	12,968
Malta									7,968	
Monaco				48						
Netherlands	13,599	13,263	14,811	15,816	15,675	15,432	15,242	15,226	14,691	14,557
Norway	18,436	14,904			15,282	14,512	15,394	15,242	15,180	14,717
Portugal		18,987	18,589	16,948	14,685	14,647	14,588	14,259	14,567	14,200
Spain	6,985	6,071	6,781	7,599	7,652	9,767	9,879	10,031	10,368	10,422
Sweden		16,787		15,809	15,478	15,291	14,430	14,395	14,105	14,085
Switzerland	14,274	13,934	14,286	13,562	13,758	13,583	13,912	13,892	13,986	13,986
Turkey	10,029	9,573	8,943	9,428	7,684	8,077	7,994	7,561	8,191	7,508
United Kingdom	13,027	11,717	14,994	14,458	14,185	14,093	13,906	13,974	13,476	13,364
Eastern Europe										
Albania				34						
Belarus				995	909	915	847	824	697	621
Bosnia-Herzegovina										
Bulgaria			8,300	6,816	7,328	7,353	7,455	7,242	7,289	7,068
Croatia						9,956	10,435	10,769	9,920	10,320
Czech Republic				8,064	7,580	7,637	7,512	7,942	8,259	8,983
Estonia					10,672	10,966	10,562	11,105	11,028	12,860
Georgia				47						1,000
Hungary			9,239				7,042	7,023	6,766	6,565
Latvia										10,904
Lithuania										
Macedonia			10,400	9,167	9,680					
Moldova				1,085	1,060	869	792	628	619	631
Poland	9,029	5,853	6,500	9,997	9,995	10,002	9,841	9,997	9,468	9,007
Romania			15,230	10,930	11,198	11,000	10,760	10,690	9,917	10,075
Russia				1,036	878	869	835	943	1,003	915
Slovakia				8,123	8,151	7,926	7,840	7,889	7,822	7,605
Slovenia			8,212	8,078	9,744	9,912	9,497	9,668	9,387	9,660
Ukraine							694	645	623	666

Source: *Euromonitor International from national statistics*

Average Annual Distance Travelled by Car 1980-2008 *(continued)*
Kilometres

	2002	2003	2004	2005	2006	2007	2008
Western Europe							
Austria				14,293	14,430	14,590	14,820
Belgium	17,308	16,408	16,509	16,130	16,297	16,181	16,206
Cyprus			19,021				
Denmark	22,120	22,427	22,878	22,729	22,592	22,587	22,801
Finland	19,117	18,839	18,673	18,315	17,921	17,842	17,668
France	7,199	7,215	7,277	7,256	7,269	7,340	7,366
Germany	13,068	12,833	13,011	12,545	12,590	14,305	14,616
Gibraltar							
Greece	15,664	16,024	16,473	16,159	16,145	15,757	16,173
Iceland	12,750	12,495	12,016	11,369	10,917	10,491	10,423
Ireland	19,658	19,469	18,812	18,022	17,026	16,197	16,051
Italy	11,778	11,979	12,422	12,288	12,182	12,136	12,166
Liechtenstein							
Luxembourg	12,562	12,296	12,348	12,441	12,614	12,549	12,701
Malta							
Monaco							
Netherlands	14,726	14,756	14,503	14,354	14,311	14,109	14,173
Norway	15,006	15,082	14,862	14,561	14,201	13,786	13,647
Portugal	14,176	14,190	13,919	13,665	13,498	13,307	13,291
Spain	10,548	10,927	10,715	10,562	10,331	10,131	10,136
Sweden	10,906	14,722	14,708	15,167	14,991	15,339	15,627
Switzerland	13,985	13,852	14,107	14,072	13,440	13,110	12,951
Turkey	7,218	7,191	7,111	7,014	7,033	7,156	7,427
United Kingdom	13,795	13,550	13,549	13,352	13,460	13,428	13,444
Eastern Europe							
Albania							
Belarus	501	531	437	428	612	648	722
Bosnia-Herzegovina							
Bulgaria	7,123	7,386	7,366	7,447	7,573	7,543	7,591
Croatia	10,795	11,288	11,630	11,880	12,041	12,195	12,610
Czech Republic	9,170	9,255	9,176	8,919	8,690	8,415	8,325
Estonia	13,553	13,591	13,292	12,906	11,588	12,307	12,518
Georgia	1,000						
Hungary	6,009	5,689	5,728	5,665	5,583	5,513	5,513
Latvia	10,125	10,493	10,911	10,747	11,563	11,452	12,037
Lithuania		5,149	5,358	4,640	4,710	4,664	4,638
Macedonia							
Moldova	732	770	747	729	716	713	713
Poland	8,449	8,460	7,960	7,752	7,165	6,587	6,447
Romania	10,289	10,092	10,034	9,952	10,677	10,098	10,283
Russia	855	790	776	746	754	719	717
Slovakia	7,426	7,273	7,125	7,602	7,442	6,934	6,869
Slovenia	9,795	9,795	9,994	9,884	9,964	9,911	10,014
Ukraine	685	759	838	826	812	810	814

Source: Euromonitor International from national statistics

Automotives and Transport Statistics

Table 3.31

Road Network 2008
Kilometres

	Total	Motorway	National Highway	Secondary Regional	Other Local	% Paved	Density (km per sq km of land)	Motorway Intensity % of Total Road Network
Western Europe								
Austria	107,620	1,680	10,472	23,665	71,803	100.00	1.31	1.56
Belgium	153,890	1,789	12,623	1,349	138,129	78.43	5.09	1.16
Cyprus	12,595	275	5,723	2,724	3,874	66.67	1.36	2.18
Denmark	72,408	1,038	646	9,695	61,029	100.00	1.71	1.43
Finland	79,565	718	13,860	13,531	51,456	65.40	0.26	0.90
France	1,050,274	11,357	26,057	399,380	613,480	100.00	1.91	1.08
Germany	644,636	12,650	40,716	86,600	504,670	100.00	1.85	1.96
Gibraltar								
Greece	118,855	880	10,683	31,692	75,600	91.80	0.92	0.74
Iceland	13,066		4,526	4,014	4,526	37.08	0.13	
Ireland	97,560	253	5,310	11,665	80,332	100.00	1.42	0.26
Italy	487,868	6,621	46,009	123,089	312,149	100.00	1.66	1.36
Liechtenstein	401		139	262		100.00	2.51	
Luxembourg	5,248	174	843	1,881	2,350	100.00	2.03	3.32
Malta	2,236		185		2,051	87.53	6.99	
Monaco	50					100.00		
Netherlands	127,700	2,568	6,788	58,198	60,146	90.00	3.77	2.01
Norway	93,540	279	27,591	27,272	38,398	78.90	0.31	0.30
Portugal	85,835	2,533	14,798	4,500	64,004	86.00	0.94	2.95
Spain	667,989	12,359	25,073	140,084	490,473	99.00	1.34	1.85
Sweden	796,184	3,191	29,244	158,255	605,493	71.60	1.94	0.40
Switzerland	71,372	1,782	18,138	51,452		100.00	1.78	2.50
Turkey	427,142	1,979	31,286	30,677	363,200	40.00	0.55	0.46
United Kingdom	396,976	12,107	38,154	114,700	232,015	100.00	1.64	3.05
Eastern Europe								
Albania	18,000		3,220	4,300	10,480	39.00	0.66	
Belarus	96,518		15,439	69,240	11,839	90.00	0.47	
Bosnia-Herzegovina	21,846		3,722	4,104	14,020	52.30	0.43	
Bulgaria	42,955	333	2,957	4,172	35,493	98.80	0.40	0.78
Croatia	29,051	890	6,956	10,660	10,545	84.88	0.52	3.06
Czech Republic	128,848	693	6,203	48,716	73,235	100.00	1.67	0.54
Estonia	57,321	99	3,970	12,441	40,811	22.80	1.35	0.17
Georgia	20,329	13	1,482	5,449	13,385	38.63	0.29	0.06
Hungary	159,780	600	30,500	53,300	75,380	44.15	1.78	0.38
Latvia	69,702		6,942	13,231	49,529	100.00	1.12	
Lithuania	80,095	417	6,389	14,626	58,663	28.40	1.28	0.52
Macedonia	15,280	331	1,129	4,138	9,682	63.80	0.60	2.17
Moldova	12,894		3,335	6,150	3,409	85.50	0.39	
Poland	386,906	826	18,738	158,782	208,559	72.10	1.26	0.21
Romania	199,021	286	14,789	36,010	147,936	30.25	0.86	0.14
Russia	946,000		713,000	233,000		81.10	0.06	
Slovakia	44,050	324	3,376	3,752	36,598	87.04	0.92	0.74
Slovenia	38,661	625	917	4,949	32,170	100.00	1.92	1.62
Ukraine	169,404	25	16,461	113,967	38,951	97.40	0.29	0.01

Source: *Euromonitor International from International Road Federation/national statistics*

Table 3.32

Kilometres Travelled by Road 1985-2008

Km per capita

	1985	1990	1995	2000	2003	2004	2005	2006	2007	2008
Western Europe										
Austria	3,636.0						7,239.8	7,340.9	7,450.1	7,568.3
Belgium	4,270.9	5,073.2	8,410.2	8,664.7	7,561.9	7,651.7	7,506.9	7,642.6	7,663.7	7,674.9
Cyprus						7,722.4				
Denmark	5,831.0	6,814.1	7,258.8	7,794.9	7,891.1	8,113.9	8,237.2	8,382.8	8,537.4	8,679.8
Finland	5,306.8	6,720.4	7,013.5	7,699.2	8,175.7	8,339.5	8,444.4	8,488.1	8,633.8	8,608.2
France	1,999.4	2,543.3	2,927.9	3,360.7	3,550.8	3,598.6	3,590.5	3,612.9	3,661.7	3,656.0
Germany			6,314.8	6,764.6	7,000.5	7,153.6	7,008.4	7,112.0	7,157.1	7,180.9
Gibraltar										
Greece				4,454.7	5,382.4	5,908.7	6,130.2	6,452.7	6,801.7	7,095.1
Iceland				7,236.5	7,235.0	7,205.8	7,146.9	7,065.0	6,973.8
Ireland	5,795.2	7,071.6		6,936.4	7,402.7	7,392.7	7,289.8	7,195.7	7,094.4	7,020.3
Italy			5,787.6	6,358.7	7,170.1	7,289.9	7,286.7	7,318.9	7,353.0	7,404.2
Liechtenstein										
Luxembourg	5,974.7	7,780.3	7,230.2	7,800.0	7,792.9	7,899.8	8,036.5	8,180.3	8,301.7	8,428.1
Malta				3,875.0						
Monaco			31.6							
Netherlands	4,497.1	5,167.7	5,776.3	5,874.0	6,246.8	6,378.9	6,425.2	6,495.0	6,552.6	6,613.4
Norway	5,442.8			6,277.3	6,406.1	6,421.7	6,413.5	6,380.5	6,342.9	6,288.8
Portugal	2,246.3	3,031.2	4,417.2	5,133.8	5,407.5	5,448.0	5,450.7	5,478.7	5,492.5	5,512.8
Spain	1,467.9	2,095.1	2,744.9	4,517.1	4,901.4	4,944.8	4,969.6	4,970.5	4,955.8	4,974.8
Sweden	6,340.9		6,510.6	6,364.7	6,710.8	6,740.4	6,991.2	6,963.1	7,167.5	7,308.7
Switzerland	5,648.8	6,390.5	6,239.3	6,921.0	7,109.8	7,301.3	7,328.0	7,027.0	6,917.5	6,845.1
Turkey	189.6	265.9	471.2	541.6	484.5	543.2	565.4	595.5	630.6	658.4
United Kingdom	4,036.7	5,768.3	6,095.6	6,409.7	6,612.8	6,667.6	6,613.2	6,659.3	6,663.0	6,661.8
Eastern Europe										
Albania			0.6							
Belarus			91.6	96.4	86.9	74.2	75.9	113.9	122.9	139.2
Bosnia-Herzegovina										
Bulgaria		1,208.7	1,352.5	1,653.1	1,877.8	1,932.7	1,988.6	2,044.5	2,087.7	2,133.2
Croatia				2,512.1	3,286.7	3,502.2	3,701.8	3,891.4	4,095.8	4,297.9
Czech Republic			2,378.6	2,774.4	3,361.5	3,428.8	3,454.7	3,483.0	3,501.2	3,523.6
Estonia				3,728.7	4,349.7	4,635.6	4,729.5	4,774.4	4,811.0	4,854.1
Georgia			3.5							
Hungary		1,653.5		1,565.3	1,557.8	1,601.3	1,620.7	1,636.6	1,651.0	1,667.6
Latvia		622.2			2,920.5	3,227.8	3,459.5	4,142.3	4,562.0	5,018.6
Lithuania					1,869.1	2,046.2	1,971.5	2,117.3	2,201.2	2,252.8
Macedonia		1,257.0	1,334.9							
Moldova			41.5	34.9	50.9	52.9	54.3	55.5	56.7	57.8
Poland	544.8	900.1	1,963.9	2,472.4	2,488.8	2,495.9	2,505.9	2,513.1	2,522.1	2,531.3
Romania		847.9	1,077.8	1,256.1	1,431.1	1,490.6	1,545.6	1,593.5	1,648.2	1,701.8
Russia			99.1	116.4	127.5	130.3	132.9	135.1	136.9	138.4
Slovakia			1,542.6	1,813.5	1,833.4	1,838.5	1,840.5	1,841.8	1,844.2	1,846.7
Slovenia		2,378.8	2,834.9	4,090.0	4,470.1	4,675.3	4,750.9	4,875.6	4,999.7	5,102.7
Ukraine				68.1	88.7	99.0	101.7	104.0	105.9	108.1

Source: *Euromonitor International from national statistics*

Automotives and Transport Statistics

Table 3.33

Kilometres Travelled by Rail 1985-2008

Km per capita

	1985	1990	1995	2000	2003	2004	2005	2006	2007	2008
Western Europe										
Austria	963.9	1,121.7	1,212.1	1,039.5	1,020.2	1,028.9	1,046.2	1,071.1	1,087.9	1,106.4
Belgium	666.7	657.4	667.0	757.4	798.1	834.5	875.9	914.0	934.8	968.6
Cyprus										
Denmark	889.4	944.6	917.0	1,002.4	984.5	1,000.6	1,022.7	1,041.4	1,051.2	1,067.9
Finland	658.8	663.4	624.5	658.4	633.8	642.2	664.2	686.1	700.5	716.1
France	1,125.3	1,126.6	962.0	1,182.2	1,188.4	1,224.1	1,258.7	1,299.3	1,326.9	1,356.2
Germany			742.2	900.8	843.2	848.1	878.7	906.6	923.1	943.6
Gibraltar										
Greece	174.6	195.4	148.0	173.0	159.2	151.1	167.3	162.8	160.9	161.2
Iceland										
Ireland	288.7	349.6	358.9	367.7	403.9	392.8	433.4	444.8	446.7	456.8
Italy	660.9	802.8	771.5	768.5	788.9	787.1	789.3	790.4	794.5	800.0
Liechtenstein						29.2	28.9	28.6	28.4	35.2
Luxembourg	785.3	691.4	744.1	759.9	578.1	580.0	586.2	634.7	654.3	672.1
Malta										
Monaco										
Netherlands	623.2	742.7	906.2	924.5	855.2	867.1	903.4	898.6	895.7	906.6
Norway	538.4	574.0	615.4	588.4	588.9	586.1	590.1	609.2	616.2	619.7
Portugal	571.6	566.6	480.1	356.3	320.8	326.0	324.0	332.5	335.0	339.0
Spain	416.6	398.6	389.3	463.1	464.0	449.2	460.2	454.0	448.5	446.2
Sweden	789.4	745.0	719.7	936.8	988.1	964.6	991.6	1,065.7	1,101.2	1,128.7
Switzerland	1,574.2	1,899.7	1,910.3	1,761.5	1,983.8	2,025.2	2,177.2	2,252.0	2,303.4	2,385.0
Turkey	130.7	115.5	94.7	87.2	84.2	74.1	70.3	72.8	73.9	71.5
United Kingdom	538.2	580.9	517.7	649.8	688.1	710.2	715.6	716.5	717.2	724.0
Eastern Europe										
Albania		62.9	40.7	34.0	28.7	23.5	25.6	27.1	25.5	
Belarus	1,385.9	1,653.9	1,224.7	1,768.8	1,344.4	1,410.6	1,056.2	1,022.3	1,000.6	910.6
Bosnia-Herzegovina			17.9	2.4	4.9	5.1	6.0	7.8	8.9	9.9
Bulgaria	869.4	888.9	565.2	435.2	321.6	337.9	309.1	315.5	320.4	320.2
Croatia	864.2	717.7	202.0	281.9	261.8	273.1	284.9	306.6	320.2	335.1
Czech Republic		1,292.4	777.7	713.1	638.8	645.3	652.3	671.8	681.1	690.9
Estonia		961.4	290.7	190.2	134.2	142.1	184.0	193.4	197.0	213.1
Georgia	849.4	485.3	77.4	85.2	239.3	142.5	166.5	179.4	190.3	179.2
Hungary	981.9	1,098.8	568.8	948.3	1,014.2	1,042.2	978.5	951.1	936.5	916.7
Latvia		2,010.4	549.1	300.2	333.5	349.7	387.6	432.3	454.8	486.2
Lithuania		985.5	310.2	174.0	124.8	128.6	125.0	126.3	127.5	128.2
Macedonia	228.1	185.4	33.1	84.8	48.4	46.3	46.2	51.6	53.7	55.0
Moldova		335.5	234.9	76.8	90.5	90.6	94.4	127.0	142.1	155.0
Poland	1,402.4	1,326.0	696.1	515.0	513.8	489.4	475.6	486.2	492.1	487.0
Romania	1,370.0	1,317.5	847.1	530.4	390.3	391.2	392.0	392.7	393.6	394.5
Russia		1,858.3	1,294.1	1,137.3	1,087.2	1,139.6	1,196.0	1,216.8	1,229.6	1,261.8
Slovakia		1,210.9	785.6	533.6	456.4	414.1	405.2	410.6	413.5	402.9
Slovenia	860.7	715.8	299.1	354.7	389.5	382.7	389.0	395.9	400.4	402.6
Ukraine		1,590.4	1,242.7	1,054.0	1,099.0	1,090.3	1,117.9	1,138.6	1,153.7	1,166.2

Source: *Euromonitor International from national statistics*

Table 3.34

Kilometres Travelled by Air 1985-2008
Km per capita

	1985	1990	1995	2000	2003	2004	2005	2006	2007	2008
Western Europe										
Andorra										
Austria	330.6	545.8	863.4	1,778.6	1,796.9	2,153.5	2,295.2	2,410.0	2,510.0	2,612.3
Belgium	590.3	699.7	761.7	1,892.6	382.2	455.7	470.8	505.3	566.5	627.6
Cyprus	1,682.8	2,361.0	3,709.7	3,540.7	4,815.2	5,116.3	5,004.7	5,080.3	5,322.5	5,560.6
Denmark	582.1	812.6	949.2	1,149.7	1,337.7	1,500.9				
Finland	557.6	948.1	1,344.0	1,476.4	1,739.4	2,134.7	2,272.4	2,553.0	2,725.3	2,895.0
France	725.5	947.4	1,210.6	1,927.6	1,924.0	2,050.6	2,219.8	2,442.7	2,525.3	2,598.8
Germany	395.9	581.7	884.3	1,372.8	1,813.4	2,067.4	2,212.2	2,354.8	2,523.0	2,690.9
Gibraltar										
Greece	592.6	738.9	742.3	902.6	668.1	830.2	849.1	829.2	816.8	804.5
Iceland	11,439.6	7,365.6	9,881.2	14,007.3	10,403.6	12,475.6	14,566.2	14,112.5	13,974.5	13,816.8
Ireland	711.8	1,408.3	1,571.1	3,617.0	6,923.1	8,589.7	10,900.5	12,894.2	14,199.5	15,487.1
Italy	249.2	391.7	576.9	779.7	718.4	746.9	874.5	892.8	913.5	935.0
Liechtenstein										
Luxembourg	277.9	341.2	834.1	1,275.6	1,210.1	1,248.5	1,219.0	1,301.2	1,590.3	1,704.5
Malta	1,576.3	1,969.6	4,127.0	6,129.4	5,470.5	5,702.0	5,693.9	6,119.6	6,343.1	6,569.0
Monaco				77.4	184.6	117.2	149.8	149.2	160.9	172.5
Netherlands	1,971.7	2,914.3	3,717.2	4,691.5	4,275.8	4,693.7	5,045.5	5,316.0	5,522.5	5,727.8
Norway	983.8	1,521.5	1,919.8	2,314.8	2,308.0	2,254.8	2,238.1	2,219.4	2,197.5	2,169.1
Portugal	530.2	786.7	822.4	1,100.2	1,303.1	1,536.4	1,598.7	1,798.3	1,914.0	2,030.0
Spain	610.5	789.2	614.3	1,309.1	1,382.4	1,514.7	1,649.1	1,762.0	1,825.7	1,893.8
Sweden	615.8	821.7	973.2	1,263.0	1,276.3	1,334.3	1,368.3	1,403.1	1,420.5	1,441.1
Switzerland	2,038.1	2,610.3	2,965.3	5,112.0	3,185.0	2,797.6	2,761.5	2,960.1	3,043.6	3,128.4
Turkey		91.9	167.9	258.4	235.8	290.0	339.3	384.6	403.8	422.6
United Kingdom	1,418.4	2,341.8	2,784.4	2,903.6	2,762.7	3,060.9	3,335.6	3,532.4	3,624.7	3,719.0
Eastern Europe										
Albania				34.4	40.2	44.8	49.0	52.6	55.5	58.5
Belarus			259.6	31.6	34.1	40.5	39.1	42.5	44.3	46.1
Bosnia-Herzegovina				12.8	12.3					
Bulgaria		154.0	251.0	104.6	58.4	96.0	145.3	177.0	189.7	202.6
Croatia			104.1	144.9	195.7	211.7	219.1	226.1	239.8	253.6
Czech Republic			212.1	323.7	484.0	586.4	646.3	648.9	700.7	752.6
Estonia			95.3	171.3	306.3	405.1	489.9	507.2	540.0	570.9
Georgia			63.0	51.9	146.1	109.5	120.3	127.6	140.4	153.4
Hungary	120.5	142.2	171.1	349.5	327.0	346.9	377.0	357.9	359.1	360.4
Latvia			52.4	99.3	105.0	250.6	503.5	658.2	755.4	853.6
Lithuania			55.7	91.6	114.0	161.6	204.5	169.9	183.4	197.1
Macedonia				368.4	138.3	135.7	122.3	131.9	135.8	139.7
Moldova				30.5	57.3	67.4	86.4	99.6	111.8	124.0
Poland	46.7	79.4	94.1	124.3	142.2	153.5	163.0	172.2	180.3	188.5
Romania	39.6	46.4	75.9	95.7	77.9	70.6	90.8	112.5	122.5	132.5
Russia			407.4	292.4	371.8	430.1	440.4	486.8	519.8	551.7
Slovakia			12.8	20.1	41.0	157.6	176.3	190.9	207.6	224.3
Slovenia			163.7	283.0	351.0	356.1	353.8	394.6	412.2	429.7
Ukraine			39.6	28.2	54.0	80.6	86.8	106.6	120.1	133.8

Source: Euromonitor International from International Civil Aviation Authority/national statistics

Banking and Finance

Banking and Finance Statistics

Table 4.1

Bank Claims on the Private Sector 1980-2008

National currency billion / US$ billion

	1980	1985	1990	1995	1996	1997	1998	1999	2000	2001
Western Europe										
Austria	54.8	83.7	122.3	162.0	172.7	188.7	188.7	197.1	213.0	224.1
Belgium	25.2	31.6	60.0	151.2	158.7	167.3	177.1	192.3	196.6	197.3
Cyprus	0.5	0.9	2.5	5.1	5.8	6.5	7.2	8.4	9.4	10.3
Denmark	94.0	190.4	429.2	312.9	331.1	357.7	405.4	420.6	1,749.3	1,902.2
Finland	15.2	34.2	75.7	58.9	58.5	56.7	60.3	65.0	70.1	77.8
France	321.2	555.8	969.3	1,028.3	1,014.2	1,034.3	1,007.8	1,115.3	1,225.2	1,314.3
Germany	649.8	889.9	1,250.7	1,856.4	1,994.1	2,115.6	2,286.5	2,326.4	2,445.7	2,497.1
Gibraltar										
Greece	2.6	7.0	14.2	26.8	30.4	34.9	40.3	52.0	63.9	83.1
Iceland	4.3	46.9	157.1	209.0	236.7	348.9	376.3	461.0	663.6	772.5
Ireland	5.5	10.4	17.3	37.0	43.1	55.9	68.6	91.8	110.7	129.1
Italy	111.2	212.5	385.2	530.8	547.7	580.3	632.3	788.2	896.8	966.6
Liechtenstein										
Luxembourg	4.0	5.6	11.1	13.0	13.7	15.3	13.6	19.8	22.5	29.1
Malta	0.1	0.3	0.6	1.1	1.3	1.4	1.5	1.7	1.8	2.0
Monaco										
Netherlands	102.0	122.9	193.8	284.4	317.1	357.8	409.2	484.0	560.8	605.7
Norway	96.8	241.3	461.7	527.5	599.8	708.0	801.6	849.7	969.6	1,075.5
Portugal	5.4	14.3	24.9	55.6	65.3	78.7	98.3	129.3	160.5	179.2
Spain	71.5	118.8	250.3	323.1	346.7	394.2	459.3	519.6	615.9	688.5
Sweden	219.2	340.6	791.2	596.7	623.2	711.1	771.7	848.4	958.7	2,298.0
Switzerland	195.8	335.2	532.8	611.7	608.2	625.6	635.7	676.5	668.9	660.9
Turkey			0.1	1.4	3.4	7.6	12.1	17.4	29.6	36.9
United Kingdom	63.7	167.4	645.3	829.1	911.9	973.0	1,016.8	1,094.4	1,254.3	1,367.8
Eastern Europe										
Albania				8.3	10.9	13.0	14.9	18.2	24.4	34.9
Belarus				7.4	12.3	30.3	113.0	279.7	802.5	1,400.8
Bosnia-Herzegovina						3.8	4.2	4.1	4.4	3.3
Bulgaria				0.4	1.1	1.6	2.4	2.9	3.4	4.4
Croatia				30.7	31.6	46.1	56.7	52.7	56.8	69.7
Czech Republic				1,036.6	1,153.9	1,250.4	1,176.3	1,098.5	1,029.9	916.4
Estonia				7.0	12.4	22.4	25.1	26.7	34.8	42.5
Georgia				0.1	0.1	0.2	0.2	0.3	0.4	0.5
Hungary		208.6	971.3	1,263.2	1,520.7	2,076.9	2,440.4	2,968.0	4,247.6	5,025.9
Latvia				0.2	0.2	0.4	0.6	0.7	0.9	1.4
Lithuania				3.9	3.7	4.4	5.6	6.3	6.0	6.6
Macedonia				39.2	46.8	50.7	34.5	43.6	42.2	41.2
Moldova				0.4	0.6	0.6	1.3	1.5	2.0	2.8
Poland		0.6	11.8	56.9	81.2	107.3	135.5	169.8	197.8	212.6
Romania			0.1		1.3	2.1	4.3	4.4	5.8	10.2
Russia				133.8	166.5	250.1	410.7	631.1	969.4	1,473.1
Slovakia				5.5	7.2	10.5	10.7	10.4	11.3	8.8
Slovenia				4.1	4.4	4.7	5.8	7.0	7.8	8.7
Ukraine				0.8	1.1	2.3	7.9	11.0	18.8	26.6

Source: *International Monetary Fund (IMF), International Financial Statistics*

Banking and Finance Statistics

Table 4.2

Bank Claims on the Private Sector 1980-2008 (continued)

National currency billion / US$ billion

	2002	2003	2004	2005	2006	2007	2008	US$ billion 2008
Western Europe								
Austria	229.5	234.9	247.7	276.8	292.4	309.0	333.7	491.2
Belgium	198.9	203.8	207.4	223.8	261.5	305.2	325.3	478.7
Cyprus	10.6	11.2	12.1	13.0	14.9	18.7	20.6	30.3
Denmark	1,996.8	2,123.2	2,318.4	2,654.0	3,031.5	3,432.5	3,791.9	743.8
Finland	83.8	93.4	102.9	118.1	130.6	146.6	159.5	234.7
France	1,325.9	1,407.6	1,499.8	1,591.8	1,769.2	1,991.3	2,102.0	3,093.5
Germany	2,505.8	2,497.4	2,479.7	2,504.6	2,536.1	2,556.0	2,686.9	3,954.4
Gibraltar								
Greece	94.5	110.4	129.7	153.4	177.5	209.3	226.8	333.8
Iceland	858.9	1,097.2	1,531.3	2,542.8	3,733.2	5,205.1	5,941.0	67.6
Ireland	142.4	160.2	200.3	260.7	321.8	377.7	396.6	583.6
Italy	1,030.8	1,110.8	1,178.9	1,271.5	1,403.1	1,555.9	1,647.9	2,425.3
Liechtenstein								
Luxembourg	24.9	26.5	29.1	39.1	52.5	69.3	72.4	106.5
Malta	2.0	1.9	2.1	2.2	2.5	2.7	2.9	4.2
Monaco								
Netherlands	656.6	705.8	775.2	847.3	903.2	1,070.4	1,145.7	1,686.1
Norway	1,144.6	1,232.5	1,354.1	1,583.5	1,879.2	2,027.1		
Portugal	190.8	194.0	202.7	216.9	244.2	275.0	298.7	439.6
Spain	770.9	886.2	1,050.4	1,321.0	1,634.5	1,918.0	2,205.5	3,245.9
Sweden	2,421.7	2,540.3	2,696.3	2,986.9	3,321.5	3,797.3	4,090.1	620.5
Switzerland	662.9	687.0	716.8	762.3	831.6	904.8	896.2	827.4
Turkey	50.9	66.2	96.6	144.4	196.7	248.7	309.8	238.0
United Kingdom	1,479.4	1,624.6	1,807.6	1,994.9	2,256.2	2,625.9	3,030.3	5,570.7
Eastern Europe								
Albania	39.5	51.9	71.1	123.6	194.7	288.9	381.8	4.6
Belarus	2,364.1	4,283.5	6,928.0	10,063.7	15,437.8	22,988.5	35,331.2	16.5
Bosnia-Herzegovina	4.2	5.1	5.9	7.5	9.2	11.8	14.3	10.7
Bulgaria	6.3	9.4	14.0	18.6	23.2	37.7	49.6	37.1
Croatia	91.0	104.7	119.9	140.1	172.2	198.2	222.2	45.0
Czech Republic	720.6	782.5	886.8	1,076.9	1,312.9	1,686.4	1,937.9	113.5
Estonia	54.3	69.0	92.1	121.9	173.4	229.6	244.8	22.9
Georgia	0.6	0.7	1.0	1.7	2.7	4.8	6.3	4.3
Hungary	5,989.2	7,988.9	9,480.0	11,271.3	13,152.2	15,624.5	18,518.1	107.6
Latvia	1.9	2.6	3.8	6.2	9.8	13.1	14.7	30.5
Lithuania	8.4	13.0	18.0	29.5	41.4	59.2	69.9	29.7
Macedonia	43.1	47.2	58.6	70.9	92.7	129.0	173.1	4.1
Moldova	3.9	5.6	6.8	8.9	12.3	19.7	22.9	2.2
Poland	221.8	236.7	260.1	284.4	352.8	464.1	632.9	262.7
Romania	15.4	27.1	38.6	57.5	89.1	144.7	193.9	77.0
Russia	1,915.1	2,772.5	4,109.0	5,557.6	8,312.0	12,539.9	17,100.2	688.1
Slovakia	10.2	9.1	10.1	13.5	17.2	23.2	27.4	40.3
Slovenia	9.5	10.7	13.1	16.2	20.5	22.6		
Ukraine	39.8	65.6	86.7	142.0	241.2	419.0	700.0	132.9

Source: International Monetary Fund (IMF), International Financial Statistics

Banking and Finance Statistics

Table 4.3

Assets of Deposit Money Banks 1980-2008
US$ billion

	1980	1985	1990	1995	1996	1997	1998	1999	2000	2001
Western Europe										
Austria	21.71	36.75	65.99	92.04	89.54			62.99	69.68	74.78
Belgium	60.77	92.67	192.03	273.06	267.76	262.47	277.35	112.05	108.17	126.96
Cyprus	0.05	0.12	2.53	5.34	6.44	16.74	12.13	11.97	15.96	16.37
Denmark	4.83	14.16	45.55	56.59	62.39	65.68	76.75	68.43	70.56	60.06
Finland	2.76	7.67	27.00	24.17	26.99	21.36	21.84	15.72	19.91	35.26
France	160.21	184.38	455.78	705.08	684.06	736.80		430.98	435.49	447.01
Germany	85.17	112.93	395.49	578.20	606.02	650.29	828.89	513.97	579.53	641.34
Gibraltar										
Greece	1.19	1.98	3.46	8.96	12.66	15.99	15.55	13.85	12.63	16.39
Iceland	0.03	0.06	0.13	0.09	0.11	0.13	0.12	0.22	0.27	0.32
Ireland	8.78	3.21	13.45	46.68	70.32	101.45	142.09	78.11	135.34	173.20
Italy	35.09	50.44	102.73	145.84	193.22	177.15	193.74	90.84	85.89	75.04
Liechtenstein										
Luxembourg	104.83	130.95	355.12	504.84	496.51	471.90	498.62	178.65	174.95	207.51
Malta	0.16	0.21	0.96	2.24	2.88	3.42	5.85	6.81	8.60	6.89
Monaco										
Netherlands	62.63	72.88	185.92	234.14	238.73	263.59		155.62	163.90	211.40
Norway	0.63	3.64	7.82	7.47	9.09	9.78	12.32	12.42	15.28	15.09
Portugal	1.13	1.43	6.16	35.92	37.50	47.45	54.67	25.17	29.90	26.87
Spain	12.79	20.04	39.11	146.06	129.73	111.18	126.79	61.25	77.37	82.00
Sweden	8.04	8.94	34.92	36.16	44.71	44.94	50.85	53.09	67.36	62.01
Switzerland	66.45	85.24	153.25	212.37	263.36	314.44	369.71	463.67	465.83	446.49
Turkey	0.55	2.01	5.51	10.97	10.37	11.57	12.73	16.07	18.18	13.33
United Kingdom	356.32	590.07	1,068.96	1,350.86	1,460.35	1,685.14	1,868.89	1,802.43	2,059.96	2,168.52
Eastern Europe										
Albania										
Belarus				0.29	0.33	0.37	0.31	0.34	0.33	0.30
Bosnia-Herzegovina										
Bulgaria				1.06	0.97	1.36	1.47	1.49	1.94	2.10
Croatia				1.75	2.27	2.57	2.04	1.62	2.42	3.93
Czech Republic				3.78	5.77	8.58	11.79	13.30	13.26	15.61
Estonia				0.32	0.32	0.56	0.48	0.56	0.62	0.87
Georgia				0.03	0.03	0.04	0.05	0.05	0.05	0.08
Hungary		0.34	1.16	0.92	1.68	2.49	3.31	3.59	2.74	4.44
Latvia				0.60	1.02	1.55	1.26	1.49	2.11	2.27
Lithuania				0.12	0.29	0.37	0.30	0.42	0.69	0.75
Macedonia				0.25	0.23	0.29	0.34	0.40	0.43	0.64
Moldova				0.17	0.20	0.15				
Poland	1.48	2.30	6.09	7.15	6.13	7.28	5.41	7.87	11.32	15.31
Romania	0.26	1.00	0.68	0.07	0.07	0.08	0.09	0.09	0.10	1.61
Russia				9.95	13.11	12.51	11.25	14.28	17.44	18.15
Slovakia				1.82	2.51	3.62	3.79	1.62	2.35	2.39
Slovenia				2.40	2.58	1.87	2.00	1.81	2.01	3.27
Ukraine				1.04	0.94	0.96	0.91	0.85	0.92	0.77

Source: *International Monetary Fund (IMF), International Financial Statistics*

Banking and Finance Statistics

Table 4.4

Assets of Deposit Money Banks 1980-2008 *(continued)*

US$ billion

	2002	2003	2004	2005	2006	2007	2008
Western Europe							
Austria	91.22	122.77	157.55	167.08	228.71	296.68	303.34
Belgium	164.25	194.31	236.40	274.52	314.10	399.43	331.54
Cyprus	14.49	17.72	23.85	33.10	49.06	69.22	48.96
Denmark	71.59	103.13	128.50	134.38	178.48	252.74	247.49
Finland	41.88	51.76	66.70	61.33	82.53	98.95	101.31
France	538.48	635.90	829.48	1,003.06	1,268.93	1,478.58	1,288.90
Germany	774.43	1,018.88	1,223.06	1,172.69	1,544.88	1,972.33	1,780.81
Gibraltar							
Greece	21.77	32.37	39.51	41.06	62.81	94.20	117.10
Iceland	0.57	1.59	2.86	8.55	18.58	16.61	17.60
Ireland	236.53	324.81	433.63	509.69	747.61	991.46	957.94
Italy	94.26	117.86	122.63	110.30	140.81	156.31	128.90
Liechtenstein							
Luxembourg	237.00	301.44	332.05	355.16	471.20	594.55	548.11
Malta	9.42	12.94	16.75	20.74	27.95	40.34	35.45
Monaco							
Netherlands	256.24	308.25	376.87	413.18	576.25	760.71	582.69
Norway	17.64	28.59	25.18	34.06	63.11	77.63	
Portugal	28.93	34.88	37.67	36.83	46.10	49.10	44.23
Spain	95.10	101.13	153.24	167.65	226.89	293.58	276.02
Sweden	72.53	102.26	157.44	160.90	229.17	303.92	299.71
Switzerland	557.85	616.29	680.72	709.24	803.01	1,116.56	834.81
Turkey	13.59	14.55	21.01	23.47	37.47	43.99	52.41
United Kingdom	2,477.29	3,023.60	3,643.33	3,937.75	4,914.15	5,539.19	5,851.71
Eastern Europe							
Albania							
Belarus	0.26	0.33	0.46	0.69	0.43	1.24	1.28
Bosnia-Herzegovina							
Bulgaria	2.02	1.94	3.13	3.27	5.57	5.91	5.51
Croatia	3.64	5.78	7.78	5.77	7.19	9.41	9.80
Czech Republic	14.64	15.32	20.53	24.10	27.07	38.35	36.00
Estonia	1.10	1.38	2.49	3.47	3.66	5.93	5.51
Georgia	0.09	0.11	0.16	0.16	0.22	0.39	0.69
Hungary	4.36	5.94	7.20	6.97	12.43	17.04	19.86
Latvia	3.02	4.04	5.78	5.63	6.68	11.17	9.73
Lithuania	0.72	0.93	1.86	2.54	3.75	5.03	4.49
Macedonia	0.56	0.67	0.82	0.73	0.86	0.92	0.55
Moldova							
Poland	13.71	14.92	24.96	25.51	29.54	29.93	20.39
Romania	1.19	1.08	1.81	1.45	1.81	2.47	2.43
Russia	19.03	20.66	25.48	37.97	62.49	93.44	159.26
Slovakia	2.05	2.33	2.87	3.03	3.94	5.93	6.69
Slovenia	2.26	2.58	2.89	4.19	6.51	6.12	6.22
Ukraine	0.85	1.36	2.30	2.83	4.07	6.06	7.49

Source: International Monetary Fund (IMF), International Financial Statistics

Banking and Finance Statistics

Table 4.5

Assets of Deposit Money Banks by Quarter 2007-2009

US$ million

	2007 1st Quarter	2007 2nd Quarter	2007 3rd Quarter	2007 4th Quarter	2008 1st Quarter	2008 2nd Quarter	2008 3rd Quarter	2008 4th Quarter	2009 1st Quarter	2009 2nd Quarter
Western Europe										
Austria	244,830.0	264,668.0	275,301.0	296,675.0	321,716.0	346,168.0	317,221.0	303,335.0	273,607.0	
Belgium	331,434.0	371,131.0	383,256.0	399,425.0	419,595.0	429,199.0	401,365.0	331,543.0	305,026.0	
Cyprus	52,352.0	58,774.5	66,392.4	69,223.2	41,263.0	41,607.5	44,781.3	48,958.6	52,641.1	
Denmark	198,594.1	208,925.0	232,846.9	252,743.0	270,430.0	286,783.0	255,282.0	247,492.0	225,728.0	
Finland	89,231.9	78,608.6	90,189.8	98,951.6	119,294.0	130,408.0	122,005.0	101,309.0	100,819.0	
France	1,400,740.0	1,482,290.0	1,427,980.0	1,478,580.0	1,621,320.0	1,524,050.0	1,413,270.0	1,288,900.0	1,162,410.0	
Germany	1,637,790.0	1,732,850.0	1,892,370.0	1,972,330.0	2,098,900.0	2,055,560.0	2,004,660.0	1,780,810.0	1,557,480.0	
Gibraltar										
Greece	77,018.0	76,775.9	85,025.8	94,202.6	99,312.0	111,109.0	113,070.0	117,095.0	113,259.0	
Iceland	18,295.5	20,880.2	16,612.2							
Ireland	821,986.0	909,556.0	942,280.0	991,461.0	1,105,490.0	1,092,560.0	990,413.0	957,943.0	908,101.0	
Italy	154,281.0	155,553.0	157,302.0	156,306.0	163,170.0	153,284.0	153,843.0	128,901.0	121,471.0	
Liechtenstein										
Luxembourg	489,143.0	522,137.0	567,443.0	594,548.0	661,639.0	662,012.0	649,914.0	548,113.0	541,470.0	550,515.0
Malta	31,110.1	35,494.9	38,671.3	40,336.5	35,235.5	39,712.7	39,190.2	35,449.4	32,635.2	
Monaco										
Netherlands	676,490.0	702,333.0	765,680.0	760,711.0	815,754.0	757,126.0	715,207.0	582,688.0	549,583.0	
Norway										
Portugal	43,715.0	43,938.5	44,808.5	49,104.8	50,456.1	52,134.7	48,226.9	44,225.4	44,724.2	
Spain	258,927.0	254,360.0	288,846.0	293,578.0	323,849.0	334,960.0	312,129.0	276,017.0	275,606.0	
Sweden	273,311.0	268,491.0	284,829.0	303,915.0	333,852.0	345,255.0	326,755.0	299,709.0	294,722.0	
Switzerland	1,007,050.0	981,035.0	1,013,960.0	1,116,560.0	1,146,490.0	948,525.0	912,218.0	834,806.0	759,241.0	
Turkey	37,048.1	44,994.9	43,322.5	43,993.9	47,110.1					
United Kingdom	5,539,190.0									
Eastern Europe										
Albania										
Belarus	965.7	1,247.4	1,245.4	1,240.6	1,756.0	1,123.2				
Bosnia-Herzegovina										
Bulgaria	4,859.7	4,765.2	4,429.5	5,915.0	5,006.1	5,878.1	5,326.2	5,510.0	5,065.7	
Croatia	6,563.1	7,007.5	8,377.0	9,411.4	9,170.8	8,302.7				
Czech Republic	28,527.2	32,434.9	33,703.9	38,349.7	43,760.7	50,390.4	43,673.3	35,995.3	31,892.3	
Estonia	3,720.9	4,976.9	4,983.2	5,926.5	6,128.9	5,702.8	5,301.4	5,506.7	4,798.2	
Georgia	306.8	343.5	372.5	393.7	372.9	413.5				
Hungary	13,436.2	14,283.8	15,043.3	17,041.4	19,892.5	21,543.7	23,429.2	19,862.3	18,371.2	
Latvia	7,577.7	7,833.3	9,418.5	11,169.4	10,076.4	11,004.5	9,862.1	9,729.3	8,362.8	
Lithuania	3,760.9	3,667.4	4,238.6	5,025.0	5,393.5	5,021.9	5,279.1	4,490.2	4,554.0	
Macedonia	863.0	861.7	885.2	923.7	866.2	834.6				
Moldova										
Poland	30,001.7	27,215.0	29,389.0	29,932.2	34,011.7	32,498.8	27,740.0	20,388.3	14,011.7	
Romania	1,918.6	2,588.9	1,488.8	2,470.5	1,905.2	2,407.4	2,098.0	2,431.0	2,621.5	
Russia	79,296.3	65,586.7	87,188.8	93,440.1	111,645.0	110,085.0				
Slovakia	3,805.5	4,232.2	4,599.3	5,925.1	5,667.2	7,091.7	6,393.1	6,685.7	4,385.0	
Slovenia	3,689.1	4,451.3	5,271.8	6,116.6	6,720.1	6,975.6	6,251.8	6,220.9	5,703.8	
Ukraine	4,941.4	4,932.0	5,562.1	6,061.4	6,355.3	8,206.6				

Source: *International Monetary Fund (IMF), International Financial Statistics*

Banking and Finance Statistics   **Table 4.6**

Liabilities of Deposit Money Banks 1980-2008

US$ billion

	1980	1985	1990	1995	1996	1997	1998	1999	2000	2001
Western Europe										
Austria	24.95	38.03	74.31	99.15	102.74			49.42	49.93	58.52
Belgium	72.95	112.93	239.79	302.86	293.66	280.03	297.91	181.82	163.88	176.33
Cyprus	0.18	0.41	3.24	6.00	7.49	17.79	13.40	13.33	17.14	17.84
Denmark	4.88	14.85	44.80	33.25	40.17	50.35	61.48	63.34	62.55	58.81
Finland	4.57	12.81	59.91	29.27	25.88	17.92	19.99	9.37	15.47	28.04
France	146.68	197.18	519.81	662.47	671.76	694.58	723.56	337.03	384.58	399.22
Germany	72.09	75.77	226.37	482.24	490.21	561.59	760.83	491.34	559.07	571.75
Gibraltar										
Greece	5.15	7.59	16.46	34.29	38.54	42.28	46.85	41.73	39.65	9.64
Iceland	0.18	0.42	0.71	0.42	0.75	0.88	1.48	1.99	2.65	2.50
Ireland	10.72	6.32	17.74	49.10	70.17	99.23	142.77	77.73	141.51	191.25
Italy	51.41	72.83	205.38	216.81	237.87	223.25	236.90	136.37	146.78	150.86
Liechtenstein										
Luxembourg	98.45	117.21	308.09	434.11	415.57	389.82		164.24	159.29	163.50
Malta	0.02	0.07	0.49	1.58	2.33	2.97	5.24	6.34	7.91	6.16
Monaco										
Netherlands	64.35	65.68	153.43	220.96	245.75	290.78		194.07	206.13	250.06
Norway	2.74	9.16	22.17	9.62	19.89	25.62	29.85	31.82	37.02	39.76
Portugal	0.81	1.64	5.78	32.43	36.98	48.28	60.98	31.35	47.62	50.01
Spain	24.50	20.94	63.99	109.25	123.36	135.02	179.18	125.66	147.33	157.56
Sweden	12.52	17.20	99.36	55.10	56.67	60.38	86.85	76.77	102.35	78.87
Switzerland	47.95	63.40	133.57	184.87	223.84	268.97	300.78	395.02	440.01	415.25
Turkey	0.70	3.06	4.46	6.11	8.93	12.16	15.51	20.10	25.17	11.74
United Kingdom	377.71	625.74	1,201.03	1,429.20	1,533.44	1,748.76	1,893.68	1,871.71	2,160.04	2,305.83
Eastern Europe										
Albania										
Belarus				0.12	0.14	0.16	0.14	0.12	0.11	0.19
Bosnia-Herzegovina										
Bulgaria				0.58	0.40	0.10	0.13	0.17	0.26	0.31
Croatia				2.85	2.25	2.19	2.59	2.25	2.18	2.62
Czech Republic				6.43	9.05	9.12	10.80	9.68	8.42	7.71
Estonia				0.14	0.34	0.91	0.88	0.88	0.98	0.99
Georgia				0.05	0.00	0.01	0.04	0.05	0.06	0.07
Hungary		1.20	1.69	2.88	3.08	4.48	5.46	5.58	5.51	5.97
Latvia				0.45	0.85	1.30	1.34	1.77	2.14	2.65
Lithuania				0.09	0.20	0.30	0.45	0.54	0.52	0.62
Macedonia				0.08	0.14	0.19	0.25	0.26	0.23	0.20
Moldova				0.06	0.24	0.29				
Poland	25.32	26.68	1.92	2.07	2.75	4.28	5.21	6.75	6.61	7.77
Romania	8.38	6.05	1.72	0.82	1.24	1.15	0.93	0.61	0.51	0.66
Russia				6.46	10.59	18.03	10.73	9.41	10.11	11.36
Slovakia				0.98	2.16	2.85	2.63	0.64	0.64	0.84
Slovenia				1.48	1.46	1.22	1.33	1.44	1.57	1.76
Ukraine				0.30	0.33	0.95	0.51	0.34	0.46	0.65

Source: *International Monetary Fund (IMF), International Financial Statistics*

Table 4.7

Liabilities of Deposit Money Banks 1980-2008 *(continued)*
US$ billion

	2002	2003	2004	2005	2006	2007	2008
Western Europe							
Austria	56.53	70.38	81.78	85.74	103.95	114.25	106.65
Belgium	199.01	236.31	274.68	328.34	350.61	477.40	332.58
Cyprus	16.76	19.37	25.24	33.77	48.15	67.17	33.41
Denmark	75.60	110.79	129.87	128.69	165.90	239.00	213.75
Finland	26.34	25.27	34.95	39.52	48.61	69.02	82.23
France	464.83	547.13	701.86	899.66	1,237.77	1,611.18	1,380.99
Germany	629.90	719.20	787.91	740.01	842.36	974.61	928.19
Gibraltar							
Greece	18.56	27.72	44.53	53.22	76.86	115.46	103.53
Iceland	2.81	3.05	3.66	5.34	9.50	30.63	14.49
Ireland	255.23	338.47	428.83	487.80	696.75	918.17	871.00
Italy	153.43	201.52	214.47	212.37	253.35	310.24	270.40
Liechtenstein							
Luxembourg	173.27	198.97	221.67	235.53	284.00	332.35	292.49
Malta	8.36	10.92	14.27	18.40	24.70	35.82	24.55
Monaco							
Netherlands	305.75	328.22	392.49	427.83	564.21	711.34	615.55
Norway	52.76	69.46	76.04	93.24	140.23	163.73	
Portugal	62.15	84.36	93.12	86.53	120.58	135.03	111.25
Spain	176.27	231.74	244.31	241.05	257.68	311.49	375.78
Sweden	91.64	109.49	157.60	139.93	184.51	196.71	228.79
Switzerland	498.61	546.82	608.31	634.71	717.63	1,044.11	810.24
Turkey	11.17	15.58	21.34	36.19	46.13	55.82	57.48
United Kingdom	2,684.13	3,276.43	4,033.35	4,251.40	5,254.85	5,959.07	6,311.18
Eastern Europe							
Albania							
Belarus	0.27	0.40	0.62	0.85	1.38	2.48	3.08
Bosnia-Herzegovina							
Bulgaria	0.47	0.96	3.38	3.22	4.25	8.87	13.27
Croatia	4.90	8.16	10.99	10.88	13.74	13.21	14.98
Czech Republic	7.66	10.09	10.27	9.79	12.05	19.69	22.71
Estonia	1.58	2.81	3.07	4.50	7.08	12.72	13.65
Georgia	0.09	0.10	0.12	0.29	0.52	1.20	1.73
Hungary	7.43	12.50	16.39	19.00	25.80	34.60	47.66
Latvia	3.74	5.30	8.06	10.00	15.68	25.66	25.79
Lithuania	0.85	1.88	2.81	5.07	8.14	13.83	17.15
Macedonia	0.21	0.20	0.24	0.28	0.37	0.57	0.55
Moldova							
Poland	9.07	12.64	13.72	12.65	19.68	37.93	58.55
Romania	1.00	2.22	4.98	8.15	16.42	29.90	36.73
Russia	12.89	23.16	32.17	51.45	105.26	167.99	170.61
Slovakia	1.50	3.15	5.83	10.01	7.09	13.23	17.02
Slovenia	2.79	4.59	6.26	9.75	14.02	4.54	3.62
Ukraine	0.74	1.63	2.25	5.24	12.83	28.61	36.86

Source: *International Monetary Fund (IMF), International Financial Statistics*

Table 4.8

Liabilities of Deposit Money Banks by Quarter 2007-2009

US$ million

	2007 1st Quarter	2007 2nd Quarter	2007 3rd Quarter	2007 4th Quarter	2008 1st Quarter	2008 2nd Quarter	2008 3rd Quarter	2008 4th Quarter	2009 1st Quarter	2009 2nd Quarter
Western Europe										
Austria	101,953.0	109,565.0	114,952.0	114,247.0	128,914.0	139,876.0	129,765.0	106,647.0	107,935.0	
Belgium	376,899.0	439,632.0	453,434.0	477,404.0	496,979.0	531,751.0	446,657.0	332,579.0	285,181.0	
Cyprus	51,019.1	57,159.8	64,448.5	67,174.3	37,944.1	38,602.9	33,829.5	33,409.2	32,864.1	
Denmark	182,866.0	188,455.0	210,650.0	238,995.0	266,842.0	282,685.0	256,012.0	213,754.0	215,595.0	
Finland	60,491.7	46,430.2	53,593.8	69,016.5	80,378.7	88,081.4	84,482.1	82,230.0	84,311.5	
France	1,381,930.0	1,494,530.0	1,542,070.0	1,611,180.0	1,725,860.0	1,662,130.0	1,536,450.0	1,380,990.0	1,286,030.0	
Germany	908,804.0	927,800.0	999,190.0	974,610.0	1,113,320.0	1,072,130.0	1,062,000.0	928,189.0	885,287.0	
Gibraltar										
Greece	87,376.7	94,728.1	101,159.0	115,458.0	125,038.0	128,398.0	121,337.0	103,530.0	90,857.7	
Iceland	9,915.7	12,829.1	21,055.8	30,626.0	34,033.9	35,205.0	35,317.9			
Ireland	762,673.0	816,773.0	873,707.0	918,172.0	1,054,100.0	1,053,390.0	962,575.0	870,997.0	777,138.0	
Italy	268,707.0	280,634.0	292,551.0	310,242.0	340,559.0	349,587.0	328,722.0	270,403.0	271,011.0	
Liechtenstein										
Luxembourg	280,792.0	291,535.0	314,858.0	332,345.0	343,494.0	345,057.0	341,813.0	292,494.0	268,639.0	256,382.0
Malta	27,190.0	30,981.2	33,475.2	35,820.4	24,244.5	26,838.2	26,859.6	24,551.0	23,339.6	
Monaco										
Netherlands	601,662.0	614,810.0	699,630.0	711,344.0	828,663.0	812,289.0	750,433.0	615,550.0	608,684.0	
Norway										
Portugal	118,554.0	121,696.0	129,066.0	135,031.0	139,549.0	140,929.0	123,315.0	111,252.0	109,730.0	
Spain	273,169.0	274,481.0	294,529.0	311,490.0	417,095.0	422,165.0	388,442.0	375,784.0	382,767.0	
Sweden	197,777.0	188,405.0	194,468.0	196,713.0	270,422.0	258,260.0	257,845.0	228,788.0	220,937.0	
Switzerland	935,072.0	908,470.0	937,628.0	1,044,110.0	1,066,880.0	870,468.0	841,796.0	810,239.0	777,056.0	
Turkey	46,103.0	50,647.4	51,722.5	55,818.7	60,441.2					
United Kingdom	5,959,070.0									
Eastern Europe										
Albania										
Belarus	1,851.6	2,250.1	2,547.0	2,481.6	3,199.0	3,353.4				
Bosnia-Herzegovina										
Bulgaria	4,723.6	5,129.1	6,416.6	8,874.0	9,596.6	13,036.2	12,959.6	13,271.1	11,669.0	
Croatia	14,025.9	13,502.4	12,089.5	13,209.0	15,288.7	14,139.7				
Czech Republic	12,516.5	15,061.6	17,661.1	19,690.5	24,591.4	28,393.3	24,639.5	22,711.3	19,541.5	
Estonia	7,950.4	9,384.3	11,282.4	12,722.4	14,030.9	14,499.1	13,221.3	13,649.9	12,217.2	
Georgia	676.0	812.4	1,030.4	1,195.5	1,317.7	1,642.2				
Hungary	26,493.8	29,289.1	31,947.3	34,601.9	40,348.6	44,389.0	43,687.5	47,657.6	45,841.1	
Latvia	17,619.3	19,350.6	22,257.5	25,657.0	26,683.1	28,503.4	27,174.9	25,793.9	21,896.6	
Lithuania	8,976.9	9,629.5	11,615.8	13,826.6	15,354.7	16,465.9	16,528.7	17,153.5	15,654.1	
Macedonia	362.5	439.2	502.8	572.2	561.7	571.3				
Moldova										
Poland	22,165.7	27,194.6	33,551.6	37,928.1	45,228.4	53,353.3	55,276.7	58,548.2	53,994.5	
Romania	17,444.5	20,313.0	26,072.7	29,904.8	33,164.1	37,288.7	36,288.6	36,733.5	32,503.0	
Russia	113,927.0	134,017.0	150,850.0	167,993.0	176,087.0	198,139.0				
Slovakia	10,052.0	9,898.3	10,889.7	13,234.1	13,837.3	16,888.9	15,452.2	17,015.1	1,825.9	
Slovenia	2,431.9	3,754.4	4,248.0	4,537.0	4,653.5	4,817.5	4,145.0	3,617.0	3,369.6	
Ukraine	15,153.5	19,222.4	23,530.6	28,612.2	31,211.4	35,693.4				

Source: *International Monetary Fund (IMF), International Financial Statistics*

Banking and Finance Statistics

Table 4.9

Annual Lending Rates 1980-2008

% per annum

	1980	1985	1990	1995	1996	1997	1998	1999	2000	2001
Western Europe										
Austria							6.42	5.64	6.33	
Belgium		12.54	13.00	8.42	7.17	7.06	7.25	6.71	7.98	8.46
Cyprus	9.00	9.00	9.00	8.50	8.50	8.08	8.00	8.00	8.00	7.52
Denmark	17.20	14.65	14.10	10.33	8.70	7.73	7.90	7.13	8.08	8.20
Finland	9.77	10.41	11.62	7.75	6.16	5.29	5.35	4.71	5.61	5.79
France	12.54	11.09	10.57	8.12	6.77	6.34	6.55	6.36	6.70	6.98
Germany	12.04	9.53	11.59	10.94	10.02	9.13	9.02	8.81	9.63	10.01
Gibraltar										
Greece	21.25	20.50	27.62	23.05	20.96	18.92	18.56	15.00	12.32	8.59
Iceland	45.00	32.60	16.18	11.58	12.43	12.89	12.78	13.30	16.80	17.95
Ireland	15.96	12.44	11.29	6.56	5.85	6.57	6.22	3.34	4.77	4.84
Italy	19.03	18.06	14.85	13.24	12.82	10.51	8.64	6.35	7.02	7.29
Liechtenstein										
Luxembourg	9.25	8.75	8.23	6.50	5.50	5.50	5.27			
Malta	8.00	8.00	8.50	7.38	7.77	7.99	8.09	7.70	7.28	6.90
Monaco										
Netherlands	13.50	9.25	11.75	7.21	5.90	6.13	6.50	3.46	4.79	5.00
Norway	13.00	13.41	14.15	7.60	6.68	6.00	9.80	7.61	8.93	8.69
Portugal	18.75	27.29	21.78	13.80	11.73	9.15	7.24	5.19	5.45	
Spain	16.85	13.52	16.01	10.05	8.50	6.08	5.01	3.95	5.18	5.16
Sweden	15.18	16.89	16.69	11.11	7.38	7.01	5.94	5.53	5.83	5.55
Switzerland		5.49	7.42	5.48	4.97	4.47	4.07	3.90	4.29	4.30
Turkey	25.67	53.50		88.00	74.70			82.00	33.00	
United Kingdom	16.17	12.33	14.75	6.69	5.96	6.58	7.21	5.33	5.98	5.08
Eastern Europe										
Albania				19.65	23.96	29.28		21.62	22.10	19.65
Belarus				175.00	62.33	31.80	26.99	51.04	67.67	46.97
Bosnia-Herzegovina							73.50	24.29	30.50	30.99
Bulgaria				79.36	291.06	213.02	14.08	13.50	11.34	11.11
Croatia				20.24	22.52	15.47	15.75	14.94	12.07	9.55
Czech Republic				12.80	12.54	13.20	12.81	8.68	7.16	7.20
Estonia				19.01	14.87	11.76	15.06	11.09	7.43	7.78
Georgia				85.62	58.24	50.64	46.00	33.42	32.75	27.25
Hungary			28.78	32.61	27.31	21.77	19.28	16.34	12.60	12.12
Latvia				34.56	25.78	15.25	14.29	14.20	11.87	11.17
Lithuania				27.08	21.56	14.39	12.21	13.09	12.14	9.63
Macedonia				45.95	21.58	21.42	21.03	20.45	18.93	19.35
Moldova				39.60	36.67	33.33	30.83	35.54	33.78	28.69
Poland	10.23	15.34	644.50	33.45	26.08	25.21	24.48	16.94	20.01	18.36
Romania				41.30	35.10	45.00	55.40	65.50	53.80	
Russia				320.31	146.81	32.04	41.79	39.72	24.43	17.91
Slovakia				16.85	13.92	18.65	21.17	21.07	14.89	11.24
Slovenia				23.36	22.60	20.02	16.09	12.38	15.77	15.05
Ukraine				122.70	79.88	49.12	54.50	54.95	41.53	32.28

Source: *International Monetary Fund (IMF), International Financial Statistics*

Table 4.10

Annual Lending Rates 1980-2008 *(continued)*

% per annum

	2002	2003	2004	2005	2006	2007	2008
Western Europe							
Austria							
Belgium	7.71	6.89	6.70	6.72	7.49	8.57	9.15
Cyprus	7.15	6.95	7.57	7.09	6.69	6.74	6.42
Denmark	7.10						
Finland	4.82	4.13	3.69	3.56	3.39	3.35	
France	6.60	6.60	6.60				
Germany	9.70	9.62					
Gibraltar							
Greece	7.41	6.79					
Iceland	15.37	11.95	12.02	14.78	17.91	19.29	20.15
Ireland	3.83	2.85	2.57	2.65	2.97	3.20	
Italy	6.54	5.83	5.51	5.31	5.62	6.33	6.84
Liechtenstein							
Luxembourg							
Malta	6.04	5.85	5.32	5.51	5.65	6.24	5.89
Monaco							
Netherlands	3.96	3.00	2.75	2.77	3.54	4.60	4.60
Norway	8.71	4.73	4.04	4.04	4.23	6.65	7.27
Portugal							
Spain	4.31	3.88					
Sweden	5.64	4.79	4.00	3.31	3.72	4.00	
Switzerland	3.93	3.27	3.20	3.12	3.03	3.15	3.34
Turkey							
United Kingdom	4.00	3.69	4.40	4.65	4.65	5.52	4.63
Eastern Europe							
Albania	15.30	14.27	11.76	13.08	12.94	14.10	13.02
Belarus	36.88	23.98	16.91	11.36	8.84	8.58	8.55
Bosnia-Herzegovina	12.70	10.87	10.28	9.61	8.01	7.17	6.98
Bulgaria	9.21	8.54	8.87	8.66	8.89	10.00	10.86
Croatia	12.84	11.58	11.75	11.19	9.93	9.33	10.07
Czech Republic	6.72	5.95	6.03	5.78	5.59	5.79	6.25
Estonia	6.70	5.51	5.66	4.93	5.03	6.46	8.55
Georgia	31.83	32.27	31.23	21.63	18.75	20.41	21.24
Hungary	10.17	9.60	12.82	8.54	8.08	9.09	10.18
Latvia	7.97	5.38	7.45	6.11	7.29	10.91	11.85
Lithuania	6.84	5.84	5.74	5.27	5.11	6.86	8.41
Macedonia	18.36	16.00	12.44	12.13	11.29	10.23	9.68
Moldova	23.52	19.29	20.94	19.26	18.13	18.83	21.06
Poland	12.03	7.30	7.56	6.83	5.48	6.16	
Romania							
Russia	15.70	12.98	11.44	10.68	10.43	10.03	12.23
Slovakia	10.25	8.46	9.07	6.68	7.67	7.99	5.80
Slovenia	13.17	10.75	8.65	7.80	7.41	5.91	6.66
Ukraine	25.35	17.89	17.40	16.17	15.17	13.90	17.49

Source: *International Monetary Fund (IMF), International Financial Statistics*

Banking and Finance Statistics

Table 4.11

Lending Rates by Quarter 2007-2009
% per annum

	2007 1st Quarter	2007 2nd Quarter	2007 3rd Quarter	2007 4th Quarter	2008 1st Quarter	2008 2nd Quarter	2008 3rd Quarter	2008 4th Quarter	2009 1st Quarter	2009 2nd Quarter
Western Europe										
Austria										
Belgium	8.2	8.4	8.8	8.8	8.8		9.5	9.5		
Cyprus	6.8	6.8	6.8	6.6	6.4					
Denmark										
Finland										
France										
Germany										
Gibraltar										
Greece										
Iceland	19.3	19.2	19.3	19.4	19.5	20.3	20.6			
Ireland										
Italy	6.1	6.2	6.4	6.7	6.7	6.8	7.0	6.9	5.6	
Liechtenstein										
Luxembourg										
Malta	6.1	6.2	6.3	6.3	6.0	5.9	6.2	5.4	4.5	
Monaco										
Netherlands	4.3	4.6	4.8	4.8	4.8	4.8	5.0	3.9	2.6	1.8
Norway					6.9	7.3	7.7	7.2	5.2	
Portugal										
Spain										
Sweden										
Switzerland	3.0	3.1	3.2	3.2	3.3	3.4	3.5	3.2	2.8	
Turkey										
United Kingdom	5.2	5.4	5.7	5.7	5.3	5.0	5.0	3.2	1.0	0.5
Eastern Europe										
Albania	14.5	14.6	13.7	13.7	14.4	12.8	12.3	12.5	11.4	
Belarus	8.7	8.8	8.4	8.4	8.5	8.3	8.4	9.0	11.5	
Bosnia-Herzegovina	7.5	7.1	7.1	7.0	6.9	6.8	6.9	7.3	7.5	
Bulgaria	9.9	9.9	9.9	10.2	10.6	10.8	10.8	11.3	11.3	
Croatia	9.4	9.3	9.4	9.3	9.8	9.7	9.9	10.8	11.4	
Czech Republic	5.7	5.7	5.8	6.0	6.2	6.3	6.3	6.3	6.1	
Estonia	5.9	6.4	6.5	7.1	7.6	8.6	8.8	9.1	9.5	
Georgia	19.7	20.8	21.3	19.8	19.3	21.4	21.2	23.2	26.2	
Hungary	9.2	9.3	9.0	8.8	8.9	9.7	10.0	12.1	11.7	
Latvia	7.7	11.3	11.6	13.1	11.8	10.4	10.6	14.7	17.3	
Lithuania	5.7	6.4	7.2	8.1	8.1	7.9	8.0	9.6	8.3	
Macedonia	10.6	10.3	10.1	9.9	9.7	9.6	9.6	9.8	9.8	
Moldova	18.6	18.8	18.9	19.0	19.1	20.3	22.4	22.5	23.1	21.2
Poland										
Romania										
Russia	10.0	9.6	9.8	10.7	10.9	11.2	12.0	14.9	16.6	
Slovakia	7.8	7.8	8.6	7.8	5.7	5.8	5.9			
Slovenia	5.6	5.7	6.1	6.3	6.2	6.6	6.9	6.9	5.9	
Ukraine	14.0	13.9	13.7	14.0	14.6	17.2	17.1	21.1	27.0	19.1

Source: International Monetary Fund (IMF), International Financial Statistics

Banking and Finance Statistics

Table 4.12

Reserves of Deposit Money Banks 1980-2008

National currency million

	1980	1985	1990	1995	1996	1997	1998	1999	2000	2001
Western Europe										
Austria	3,151.82	4,023.47	4,494.33	5,374.78	5,821.66	5,629.14		3,305.00	3,878.00	7,975.00
Belgium	520.58	545.37	629.65	939.52	6,093.22	5,666.85	5,556.00	3,509.00	7,130.00	5,945.00
Cyprus	100.66	241.22	506.08	567.28	488.58	462.80	469.11	700.66	779.60	960.54
Denmark	1,138.00	25,797.00	8,704.00	39,573.40	51,617.10	70,630.50	54,196.80	96,258.00	23,816.00	17,368.00
Finland	667.84	2,044.96	3,767.45	7,732.63	4,306.34	3,651.58	3,493.95	4,884.00	2,475.00	4,111.00
France	7,149.83	17,104.70	13,933.78	7,149.83	7,759.62	7,256.54		24,371.00	28,083.00	29,467.00
Germany	36,010.84	40,009.20	60,169.75	44,503.53	45,322.12	45,779.22	47,082.52	45,641.00	51,003.00	56,439.00
Gibraltar										
Greece	393.50	2,087.07	4,354.78	14,674.81	14,908.73	16,386.44	21,904.89	24,053.50	20,645.14	11,521.00
Iceland	1,045.00	7,365.00	15,042.00	10,325.00	13,418.00	14,100.00	13,990.00	29,026.00	25,731.00	20,701.40
Ireland	977.26	1,049.73	1,445.21	1,823.18	1,711.53	2,140.68	3,435.75	2,486.00		4,324.00
Italy	20,176.42	43,240.35	67,125.45	40,958.13	42,195.05	45,350.60	12,214.72	9,896.00	8,158.00	25,732.00
Liechtenstein										
Luxembourg	27.52	46.85	79.82	91.72	473.48	337.14		4,182.73	4,911.69	5,981.17
Malta	227.20	351.21	138.54	209.91	204.42	275.77	311.42	405.07	380.16	430.47
Monaco										
Netherlands	467.40	953.40	1,304.17	1,401.73	1,533.33	1,524.71		7,138.00	9,242.00	9,676.00
Norway	2,652.00	4,314.00	3,000.00	5,153.00	28,058.00	17,275.00	14,066.00	38,362.00	27,815.00	29,747.00
Portugal	854.34	5,288.85	11,108.23	10,426.77	9,433.66	8,220.84	8,070.20	4,247.00	3,447.00	2,757.00
Spain	3,778.14	23,536.48	31,027.85	22,388.30	19,606.82	18,587.50	17,981.08	15,793.00	8,391.00	14,725.00
Sweden	5,646.00	7,708.00	24,908.00	9,415.00	11,133.00	10,167.00	13,515.00	30,668.00	9,803.00	16,010.00
Switzerland	16,500.00	15,775.00	8,274.00	8,270.00	9,608.00	9,829.00	10,954.00	17,169.00	12,511.00	12,741.00
Turkey	0.22	1.83	13.38	171.69	365.51	725.57	1,428.70	2,516.35	3,272.62	4,807.40
United Kingdom	2,385.00	2,884.00	5,972.00	7,558.00	7,714.00	8,261.00	8,393.00	11,536.00	9,752.00	8,556.00
Eastern Europe										
Albania				10,301.50	12,904.40	16,442.00	21,565.50	28,150.20	30,161.90	33,814.60
Belarus				2,841.79	5,693.16	11,889.00	35,688.20	92,002.20	158,118.00	312,321.00
Bosnia-Herzegovina						71.37	90.29	274.67	287.41	871.93
Bulgaria				67.64	118.64	800.25	643.84	745.27	598.06	864.44
Croatia				3,508.33	4,573.90	5,056.70	5,908.10	8,987.90	10,588.90	15,002.70
Czech Republic				160,933.00	158,503.00	214,936.00	288,853.00	296,541.00	310,927.00	333,319.00
Estonia				1,293.06	1,922.52	3,885.31	4,509.51	5,790.89	6,787.13	4,896.57
Georgia				38.00	30.39	39.62	45.01	56.37	76.65	82.45
Hungary		117,700.00	118,367.00	273,721.00	154,003.00	291,124.00	365,637.00	447,525.00	646,928.00	520,074.00
Latvia				64.15	71.69	107.23	129.93	144.46	135.11	153.25
Lithuania				522.70	583.60	742.10	1,447.50	1,342.30	1,282.40	1,343.10
Macedonia				1,836.00	1,125.00	2,158.00	2,379.00	3,861.00	6,192.00	6,195.00
Moldova				54.38	36.54	52.05	200.66	360.92	465.22	652.38
Poland	112.51	131.43	3,908.89	8,806.00	10,632.90	15,049.10	23,335.90	14,866.60	14,660.80	21,485.30
Romania	8.13	3.59	0.87	329.32	363.21	534.73	1,304.97	3,501.43	5,103.77	8,712.49
Russia				36,712.00	48,301.00	74,981.00	75,438.00	168,180.00	310,781.00	356,771.00
Slovakia				195.73	278.24	328.97	261.65	277.32	1,204.46	1,039.70
Slovenia				947.54	1,233.13	2,262.66	2,249.03	2,103.46	2,208.11	3,327.83
Ukraine				960.25	848.63	925.50	1,454.57	2,613.25	4,749.59	3,687.92

Source: *International Monetary Fund (IMF), International Financial Statistics*

Banking and Finance Statistics

Table 4.13

Reserves of Deposit Money Banks 1980-2008 *(continued)*
National currency million

	2002	2003	2004	2005	2006	2007	2008
Western Europe							
Austria	3,729.00	4,864.00	3,819.00	4,819.00	5,068.00	8,398.00	15,373.00
Belgium	4,482.00	8,325.00	5,416.00	6,786.00	7,928.00	17,789.00	10,804.00
Cyprus	1,481.27	1,128.55	1,178.57	1,422.24	1,983.33	1,531.23	1,757.28
Denmark	32,474.00	18,907.00	27,703.00	25,793.00	22,539.00	18,067.00	44,838.00
Finland	3,759.00	2,146.00	3,156.00	3,535.00	3,766.00	5,910.00	8,110.00
France	33,293.00	25,995.00	26,384.00	25,692.00	26,321.00	49,179.00	67,627.00
Germany	45,585.00	46,857.00	41,248.00	47,942.00	49,495.00	64,986.00	102,611.00
Gibraltar							
Greece	4,841.00	2,479.00	5,387.00	4,354.00	4,625.00	7,248.00	7,936.00
Iceland	25,293.80	13,293.50	29,412.50	36,906.50	47,358.80	100,509.00	127,084.10
Ireland	4,909.00	4,303.00	4,760.00	8,720.00	13,473.00	22,428.00	20,215.00
Italy	10,344.00	10,384.00	13,126.00	11,624.00	14,716.00	41,918.00	34,935.00
Liechtenstein							
Luxembourg	4,638.04	6,765.57	5,063.32	6,810.32	9,741.90	10,779.70	45,531.70
Malta	724.20	612.25	396.98	376.73	458.27	421.14	489.18
Monaco							
Netherlands	8,365.00	12,539.00	11,215.00	15,681.00	13,010.00	20,671.00	21,736.00
Norway	65,871.80	39,492.90	47,702.00	53,372.90	30,448.80	41,910.85	
Portugal	1,884.00	964.00					
Spain	9,291.00	14,409.00	13,091.00	16,531.00	20,559.00	52,321.00	54,315.00
Sweden	12,085.00	20,564.00	15,819.00	10,701.00	11,762.00	15,012.00	219,934.00
Switzerland	13,619.00	14,328.00	13,166.00	13,603.00	15,320.00	19,505.00	50,894.00
Turkey	19,548.40	21,772.50	23,104.90	35,188.40	38,653.70	43,938.20	64,879.10
United Kingdom	8,919.00	9,731.00	12,998.00	13,375.00	29,734.00	32,245.00	60,788.00
Eastern Europe							
Albania	32,175.90	35,245.20	40,626.60	49,967.80	60,303.10	72,660.00	76,560.60
Belarus	438,923.00	772,808.00	1,134,530.00	1,810,240.00	2,349,290.00	2,410,680.00	3,516,910.00
Bosnia-Herzegovina	595.25	1,004.55	1,566.58	2,233.86	3,061.92	4,022.28	3,392.60
Bulgaria	1,071.15	1,388.25	2,428.00	2,955.00	4,244.00	6,733.00	6,135.00
Croatia	20,373.50	26,783.70	33,743.40	41,789.30	48,402.70	50,201.50	40,721.50
Czech Republic	60,197.00	56,563.00	49,989.00	45,561.00	60,208.00	66,665.00	147,168.00
Estonia	4,677.98	6,243.01	8,876.00	13,328.00	18,782.00	19,411.00	27,646.00
Georgia	126.13	148.91	220.40	268.93	442.26	627.62	558.09
Hungary	464,058.00	406,811.00	677,319.00	599,145.00	595,805.00	723,774.00	467,387.00
Latvia	213.73	205.00	311.00	594.00	1,317.00	1,557.00	1,221.00
Lithuania	1,391.80	1,897.10	1,868.00	2,819.00	3,419.00	4,789.00	4,216.00
Macedonia	6,364.00	7,090.00	7,192.00	11,454.00	15,247.00	19,912.00	24,581.00
Moldova	979.20	1,155.98	2,842.09	3,526.31	2,411.82	4,673.69	7,020.37
Poland	19,857.00	16,902.70	18,398.00	13,579.00	18,302.00	25,765.00	36,373.00
Romania	14,395.60	16,912.80	26,853.50	34,068.30	55,519.20	68,545.60	77,650.00
Russia	471,563.00	768,914.00	837,433.00	873,086.00	1,236,500.00	1,717,000.00	2,580,600.00
Slovakia	1,139.63	899.92	755.88	1,053.08	1,336.62	2,338.91	2,999.88
Slovenia	4,643.78	4,954.32	4,416.22	4,944.09	3,732.37	4,338.23	
Ukraine	4,516.01	7,127.74	11,629.30	22,559.50	22,429.70	30,471.70	31,547.20

Source: *International Monetary Fund (IMF), International Financial Statistics*

Banking and Finance Statistics   **Table 4.14**

Reserves of Deposit Money Banks by Quarter 2007-2009

Million units of national currency

	2007 1st Quarter	2007 2nd Quarter	2007 3rd Quarter	2007 4th Quarter	2008 1st Quarter	2008 2nd Quarter	2008 3rd Quarter	2008 4th Quarter	2009 1st Quarter	2009 2nd Quarter
Western Europe										
Austria	4,779.0	5,017.0	7,730.0	8,398.0	6,329.0	6,781.0	10,404.0	15,373.0	4,442.0	
Belgium	9,893.0	8,774.0	9,357.0	17,789.0	13,534.0	6,834.0	14,457.0	10,804.0	7,991.0	
Cyprus	1,170.7	1,402.2	1,370.2	1,531.2						
Denmark	18,961.0	18,644.0	14,904.0	18,067.0	36,902.0	29,392.0	49,652.0	44,838.0	39,255.0	
Finland	3,439.0	3,755.0	2,049.0	5,910.0	2,760.0	2,263.0	8,004.0	8,110.0	4,332.0	
France	29,006.0	36,697.0	41,407.0	49,179.0	43,307.0	40,770.0	49,018.0	67,627.0	38,264.0	
Germany	49,424.0	41,314.0	42,330.0	64,986.0	69,763.0	54,802.0	68,479.0	102,611.0	54,113.0	
Gibraltar										
Greece	4,344.0	5,239.0	4,826.0	7,248.0	6,418.0	3,317.0	6,972.0	7,936.0	4,348.0	
Iceland	40,697.6	54,422.4	100,509.0							
Ireland	16,350.0	15,744.0	12,042.0	22,428.0	14,702.0	12,557.0	17,332.0	20,215.0	10,358.0	
Italy	13,611.0	14,198.0	14,878.0	41,918.0	24,355.0	19,638.0	32,167.0	34,935.0	19,701.0	
Liechtenstein										
Luxembourg	7,735.9	5,720.1	10,293.4	10,779.7	10,475.8	9,159.0	16,232.5	45,531.7	18,162.3	16,290.2
Malta	612.4	513.1	303.4	421.1						
Monaco										
Netherlands	16,834.0	15,043.0	12,572.0	20,671.0	15,476.0	42,216.0	43,518.0	21,736.0	10,550.0	
Norway										
Portugal										
Spain	19,789.0	24,161.0	24,948.0	52,321.0	21,751.0	21,009.0	42,394.0	54,315.0	28,205.0	
Sweden	12,349.0	13,926.0	13,098.0	15,012.0	10,517.0	11,720.0	12,197.0	219,934.0	85,743.0	
Switzerland	13,385.0	16,028.0	14,512.0	19,505.0	20,109.0	17,295.0	17,871.0	50,894.0	84,089.0	
Turkey	36,881.1	41,246.6	41,195.5	43,938.2	45,815.1	48,841.0	53,954.1	64,879.1	65,090.9	
United Kingdom	25,871.0	24,583.0	33,157.0	32,245.0	35,452.0	34,645.0	88,410.0	60,788.0	66,292.0	
Eastern Europe										
Albania	60,563.9	61,890.0	69,220.0	72,660.0	68,121.4	74,812.0	74,469.7	76,560.6	70,560.1	
Belarus	1,671,560.0	1,832,250.0	1,958,630.0	2,410,680.0	2,586,720.0	3,314,610.0	3,069,600.0	3,516,910.0	2,792,550.0	2,904,880.0
Bosnia-Herzegovina	3,214.1	3,469.0	3,923.7	4,022.3	3,906.1	3,953.1	4,119.0	3,392.6	3,295.0	
Bulgaria	4,419.0	3,697.0	5,741.0	6,733.0	6,392.0	6,654.0	6,941.0	6,135.0	4,885.0	
Croatia	52,817.1	51,062.6	49,990.3	50,201.5	51,660.4	51,121.4	46,551.0	40,721.5	41,469.9	
Czech Republic	54,315.0	58,229.0	68,596.0	66,665.0	62,049.0	44,259.0	67,104.0	147,168.0	75,557.0	
Estonia	17,356.0	16,055.0	20,605.0	19,411.0	21,373.0	25,511.0	23,296.0	27,646.0	26,269.0	
Georgia	391.0	551.0	613.0	627.6	596.4	660.2	630.4	558.1	481.7	633.6
Hungary	701,275.0	930,430.0	668,678.0	723,774.0	554,807.0	588,076.0	639,481.0	467,387.0	413,206.0	
Latvia	1,244.0	1,360.0	1,500.0	1,557.0	1,582.0	1,556.0	1,468.0	1,221.0	808.0	
Lithuania	3,269.0	3,571.0	3,213.0	4,789.0	3,887.0	4,272.0	4,067.0	4,216.0	3,527.0	
Macedonia	14,597.0	16,245.0	15,991.0	19,912.0	18,697.0	22,896.0	23,921.0	24,581.0	22,099.7	
Moldova	3,266.7	2,533.6	2,749.3	4,673.7	4,977.4	5,176.4	7,500.7	7,020.4	6,132.0	
Poland	19,732.0	21,123.0	19,134.0	25,765.0	24,770.0	32,261.0	27,618.0	36,373.0	33,870.0	
Romania	51,428.7	50,211.8	56,333.7	68,545.6	68,002.7	67,431.3	69,089.5	77,650.0	78,306.2	
Russia	1,175,200.0	1,761,500.0	1,217,000.0	1,717,000.0	1,378,900.0	1,676,600.0	1,297,100.0	2,580,600.0		
Slovakia	6,230.2	1,307.4	1,649.7	2,338.9	733.3	408.6	771.7	2,999.9		
Slovenia										
Ukraine	22,111.8	26,564.0	30,747.4	30,471.7	26,252.4	29,147.0	37,493.9	31,547.2	27,382.7	34,327.0

Source: *International Monetary Fund (IMF), International Financial Statistics*

Banking and Finance Statistics

Table 4.15

Number of Credit Cards in Circulation 1998-2008

'000

	1998	1999	2000	2001	2002	2003	2004	2005	2006	2007	2008
Western Europe											
Austria	711.6	762.7	820.6	875.0	946.5	961.8	948.2	978.9	1,183.1	1,238.0	1,277.0
Belgium	188.0	200.0	217.0	221.0	227.0	232.0	234.0	239.0	242.0	256.0	274.0
Cyprus											
Denmark	738.5	835.9	927.2	1,043.0	980.0	1,115.8	1,306.6	1,448.4	1,508.2	2,625.3	3,031.3
Finland											
France	16,817.5	18,179.7	19,779.5	21,025.6	21,456.7	25,269.5	27,973.3	31,159.5	31,896.9	32,719.8	33,374.2
Germany	170.0	222.0	315.0	444.0	495.0	952.0	1,285.0	2,186.0	3,517.0	3,605.0	3,767.2
Gibraltar											
Greece	1,513.0	2,014.0	3,030.1	4,144.1	5,157.1	5,579.9	5,641.9	6,045.5	6,284.8	6,707.3	7,826.3
Iceland											
Ireland											
Italy	1,456.8	1,542.0	1,696.9	1,999.6	3,265.0	5,500.0	8,500.0	10,559.1	12,899.7	13,900.3	14,882.3
Liechtenstein											
Luxembourg											
Malta											
Monaco											
Netherlands	3,740.8	4,136.2	4,630.1	4,636.8	4,626.7	5,331.9	5,416.8	5,653.8	5,839.2	5,635.9	5,334.9
Norway	849.0	1,102.0	1,161.0	1,543.0	1,811.0	2,130.0	2,351.0	2,729.0	3,340.0	3,913.0	4,434.0
Portugal	1,961.4	2,072.8	2,271.4	2,522.6	3,180.7	3,690.9	4,742.4	5,434.3	6,191.5	6,572.0	7,609.7
Spain	2,584.0	3,310.2	3,564.0	4,259.0	5,663.2	6,680.0	8,972.2	11,304.0	14,250.0	17,384.0	18,059.3
Sweden	3,130.0	3,175.0	3,215.0	3,247.0	3,300.0	3,325.0	4,202.0	3,912.0	4,580.0	4,964.0	5,152.6
Switzerland	2,470.0	2,844.0	2,945.7	3,109.2	3,158.2	3,179.4	3,202.8	3,249.9	3,661.8	4,102.7	4,303.6
Turkey	7,200.0	10,046.0	13,409.0	13,997.0	15,706.0	19,863.0	26,681.0	29,978.0	32,433.0	37,335.2	43,394.0
United Kingdom	38,302.5	41,430.9	47,089.7	51,718.1	58,818.9	66,856.2	69,924.1	69,927.4	69,437.8	67,231.1	66,014.0
Eastern Europe											
Albania											
Belarus											
Bosnia-Herzegovina											
Bulgaria											
Croatia											
Czech Republic	62.0	117.1	196.0	328.0	555.0	652.0	1,051.0	1,604.0	2,150.0	2,909.0	3,614.0
Estonia											
Georgia											
Hungary	22.8	96.0	245.8	407.7	598.4	880.7	972.4	1,217.7	1,477.0	1,617.7	1,689.4
Latvia											
Lithuania											
Macedonia											
Moldova											
Poland	90.9	179.8	371.7	600.1	806.4	1,172.6	1,996.3	3,386.8	5,124.0	6,996.2	9,010.0
Romania											
Russia						596.6	1,398.3	2,514.6	6,569.6	8,944.3	9,295.8
Slovakia											
Slovenia											
Ukraine											

Source: *Euromonitor International from trade sources*

Banking and Finance Statistics

Table 4.16

Number of Charge Cards in Circulation 1998-2008
'000

	1998	1999	2000	2001	2002	2003	2004	2005	2006	2007	2008
Western Europe											
Austria	799.2	832.1	932.0	1,019.1	1,049.1	1,062.6	1,051.6	1,065.2	1,121.0	1,172.4	1,218.4
Belgium	1,973.6	2,354.2	2,540.3	2,615.0	2,579.0	2,897.2	3,176.0	3,259.7	3,323.8	3,538.0	3,837.0
Cyprus											
Denmark	122.5	128.6	137.6	154.1	172.6	198.5	240.2	264.2	319.7	334.9	362.7
Finland											
France	10,180.4	10,906.4	11,753.5	12,835.9	13,628.3	14,718.9	17,661.3	19,726.7	25,277.8	27,556.9	30,282.3
Germany	16,037.0	17,198.0	19,061.0	20,212.9	21,811.1	22,214.2	22,443.3	23,347.7	23,746.7	24,100.1	24,667.5
Gibraltar											
Greece	275.0	315.0	342.0	305.6	306.3	297.9	76.5	69.5	60.5	60.4	60.0
Iceland											
Ireland											
Italy	13,111.2	13,878.0	16,969.0	19,996.0	21,757.0	25,645.0	27,020.0	28,892.0	31,274.3	34,505.0	36,862.9
Liechtenstein											
Luxembourg											
Malta											
Monaco											
Netherlands	359.2	363.8	369.9	367.2	363.3	378.1	377.2	394.3	401.6	391.2	387.5
Norway	422.0	450.0	480.0	505.0	526.0	552.0	597.0	708.0	832.0	987.0	1,083.0
Portugal	206.9	265.3	316.3	330.2	394.3	451.9	581.9	646.0	729.0	751.4	856.0
Spain	10,338.0	12,461.8	12,493.0	13,487.0	15,273.8	17,177.0	19,989.8	21,855.2	24,031.0	25,743.0	26,760.7
Sweden	657.0	706.0	756.0	711.0	771.0	839.0	1,703.0	1,900.0	2,340.0	2,604.0	2,660.9
Switzerland	184.0	197.0	185.3	172.0	174.8	179.6	188.2	204.1	210.6	207.7	197.1
Turkey											
United Kingdom	3,306.5	3,495.1	3,840.3	4,511.9	4,425.1	4,546.8	4,543.9	4,845.6	4,957.2	5,744.2	6,520.6
Eastern Europe											
Albania											
Belarus											
Bosnia-Herzegovina											
Bulgaria											
Croatia											
Czech Republic	20.0	22.0	24.0	33.0	76.0	252.0	327.0	357.0	376.0	436.0	480.0
Estonia											
Georgia											
Hungary	5.2	6.0	6.4	6.2	5.3	10.8	17.2	18.2	20.0	18.7	18.8
Latvia											
Lithuania											
Macedonia											
Moldova											
Poland	456.1	846.6	1,040.5	1,124.2	1,204.4	861.2	884.2	891.8	853.4	778.3	827.3
Romania											
Russia											
Slovakia											
Slovenia											
Ukraine											

Source: *Euromonitor International from trade sources*

Banking and Finance Statistics

Table 4.17

Expenditure by Credit Card Holders 1998-2008

US$ million

	1998	1999	2000	2001	2002	2003	2004	2005	2006	2007	2008
Western Europe											
Austria	1,790.8	1,739.2	1,646.3	1,889.8	2,141.3	2,617.6	3,372.3	3,707.8	4,027.3	4,742.4	5,510.2
Belgium	55.1	59.2	57.7	71.2	83.0	129.0	186.4	279.8	414.0	477.0	563.7
Cyprus											
Denmark	649.6	654.1	588.1	604.1	663.9	815.8	913.4	938.2	971.1	1,144.4	1,279.7
Finland											
France	18,776.9	21,673.7	22,174.9	25,418.4	30,797.2	42,005.1	52,098.7	57,722.4	63,795.5	75,514.3	85,184.6
Germany	3,629.2	3,560.2	3,242.1	3,703.4	4,210.7	5,423.6	6,311.3	6,689.5	7,054.1	8,091.8	8,970.8
Gibraltar											
Greece	982.4	1,590.4	2,051.5	1,899.3	2,063.7	4,845.5	6,746.6	7,946.7	8,386.2	10,085.9	11,774.7
Iceland											
Ireland											
Italy	2,464.1	2,696.4	2,743.7	3,299.6	3,760.3	5,828.8	7,273.1	8,924.2	10,907.4	14,224.9	16,329.8
Liechtenstein											
Luxembourg											
Malta											
Monaco											
Netherlands	4,620.5	5,362.5	4,721.0	4,772.7	5,091.0	6,073.2	7,121.8	7,682.6	8,768.6	10,524.5	12,655.5
Norway	796.5	1,012.5	1,141.3	1,472.2	2,103.2	3,070.9	4,101.5	5,124.5	6,000.2	8,307.2	9,522.7
Portugal	5,898.8	7,079.8	7,829.4	7,681.0	9,374.1	12,003.3	14,930.1	16,736.6	18,942.5	21,757.1	26,507.2
Spain	3,729.8	4,405.3	4,245.8	4,867.8	7,999.6	11,578.9	16,273.7	19,715.7	22,296.7	26,963.3	28,444.5
Sweden	6,541.0	6,656.6	7,421.8	7,261.0	6,983.6	9,522.3	12,246.7	10,705.1	12,740.1	18,790.4	19,855.3
Switzerland	8,268.7	9,059.0	8,441.3	9,071.4	10,030.1	11,428.4	12,897.5	13,725.7	14,939.8	18,179.0	21,290.9
Turkey	15,725.4	12,739.5	16,814.7	9,900.9	14,527.7	23,748.5	41,034.5	57,719.4	69,097.7	98,497.1	127,718.3
United Kingdom	90,886.6	103,429.7	108,464.1	111,910.3	131,851.8	160,981.0	196,096.7	194,408.7	193,163.0	219,574.2	207,931.9
Eastern Europe											
Albania											
Belarus											
Bosnia-Herzegovina											
Bulgaria											
Croatia											
Czech Republic	28.0	60.2	121.8	205.6	452.7	989.8	1,740.4	2,520.4	3,655.8	5,868.8	9,427.2
Estonia											
Georgia											
Hungary	12.8	19.0	42.2	75.8	142.6	236.9	349.9	485.2	698.2	1,025.0	1,245.5
Latvia											
Lithuania											
Macedonia											
Moldova											
Poland	230.8	332.7	425.7	545.7	1,065.0	1,417.8	1,961.4	3,064.5	3,689.1	5,567.7	8,118.1
Romania											
Russia						236.5	608.9	1,423.0	3,861.6	6,822.5	8,470.8
Slovakia											
Slovenia											
Ukraine											

Source: *Euromonitor International from trade sources*

Table 4.18

Expenditure by Charge Card Holders 1998-2008

US$ million

	1998	1999	2000	2001	2002	2003	2004	2005	2006	2007	2008
Western Europe											
Austria	1,589.6	1,594.6	1,549.6	1,865.1	2,144.5	2,546.3	3,312.5	3,484.0	3,814.1	4,660.2	5,472.7
Belgium	5,086.6	5,549.3	5,440.3	6,269.5	6,734.1	8,329.2	9,598.3	10,380.9	11,988.5	15,428.0	17,887.3
Cyprus											
Denmark	1,394.6	956.8	948.8	979.4	1,084.4	1,314.0	1,642.8	1,742.6	1,805.0	2,089.1	2,310.8
Finland											
France	25,432.8	30,254.7	30,748.5	34,959.7	42,574.5	58,688.1	72,491.3	80,447.7	90,812.4	109,186.4	120,524.6
Germany	28,653.4	21,274.6	20,845.9	23,473.4	27,618.3	36,524.5	44,586.5	47,295.0	49,651.4	56,559.2	61,868.1
Gibraltar											
Greece	361.7	553.7	708.3	490.2	528.4	683.7	230.2	202.8	242.5	270.0	298.6
Iceland											
Ireland											
Italy	23,101.2	25,050.2	25,546.3	28,438.2	33,343.3	40,931.4	52,964.3	55,784.1	60,361.8	69,591.2	78,127.4
Liechtenstein											
Luxembourg											
Malta											
Monaco											
Netherlands	2,388.8	2,327.1	2,016.7	2,005.5	2,174.5	2,633.9	2,993.3	2,975.4	2,829.2	2,859.8	3,334.7
Norway	2,312.8	2,295.1	2,073.4	2,079.7	2,385.5	2,642.3	3,021.9	3,314.7	3,783.8	5,786.4	6,175.2
Portugal	857.8	928.9	923.7	964.1	1,040.1	1,294.2	1,561.2	1,690.0	1,806.4	2,060.9	2,378.4
Spain	8,703.0	9,361.2	8,241.8	9,040.2	14,534.4	20,584.8	27,709.2	33,141.3	37,161.1	50,108.1	59,062.0
Sweden	5,085.0	5,083.3	5,580.0	5,034.3	5,072.6	7,304.8	9,691.9	10,247.8	12,138.7	15,817.8	16,591.2
Switzerland	1,939.6	2,124.9	1,980.1	2,127.9	2,352.7	2,680.7	3,025.3	3,219.6	3,324.1	3,397.7	3,640.3
Turkey											
United Kingdom	22,646.6	26,325.4	29,809.1	33,445.3	34,864.9	38,687.0	46,164.8	47,986.9	55,624.3	66,676.7	68,112.1
Eastern Europe											
Albania											
Belarus											
Bosnia-Herzegovina											
Bulgaria											
Croatia											
Czech Republic	133.5	160.0	203.2	245.7	322.1	433.0	514.5	594.1	684.8	848.3	1,118.3
Estonia											
Georgia											
Hungary	6.5	7.0	8.6	8.2	6.6	14.9	32.9	43.7	70.8	104.4	128.2
Latvia											
Lithuania											
Macedonia											
Moldova											
Poland	432.9	676.8	855.8	1,263.7	2,349.9	2,686.4	2,821.4	3,458.4	4,756.1	5,927.4	7,706.3
Romania											
Russia											
Slovakia											
Slovenia											
Ukraine											

Source: *Euromonitor International from trade sources*

Banking and Finance Statistics

Table 4.19

Number of Credit Card Transactions 1998-2008
Million

	1998	1999	2000	2001	2002	2003	2004	2005	2006	2007	2008
Western Europe											
Austria	13.7	13.6	14.2	17.5	19.3	19.0	26.8	28.5	30.2	31.8	33.8
Belgium	0.7	0.8	0.9	0.9	1.1	1.3	1.6	2.4	3.5	3.7	4.2
Cyprus											
Denmark	3.1	2.9	3.0	3.2	3.3	3.4	3.9	4.6	5.4	6.3	6.8
Finland											
France	88.7	150.2	180.0	255.5	299.3	356.1	386.1	505.3	642.5	797.3	911.6
Germany	24.2	26.4	28.9	31.8	36.3	40.3	44.1	47.9	52.5	56.1	58.9
Gibraltar											
Greece	24.9	37.6	50.4	41.9	39.3	50.5	59.9	60.7	64.4	69.3	73.4
Iceland											
Ireland											
Italy	23.3	24.6	25.6	34.3	42.5	54.8	68.7	74.9	83.6	95.2	101.7
Liechtenstein											
Luxembourg											
Malta											
Monaco											
Netherlands	43.0	45.0	46.8	49.1	51.8	55.1	57.7	65.0	69.1	75.4	80.6
Norway	5.8	7.6	9.3	12.7	16.5	21.6	27.0	31.8	39.0	42.9	55.6
Portugal	64.5	90.9	121.0	171.5	190.3	204.2	219.8	236.9	258.6	280.2	314.6
Spain	36.5	40.3	41.5	48.7	75.8	88.4	115.0	135.0	178.6	259.3	320.0
Sweden	53.0	57.0	67.0	76.0	80.0	89.0	177.0	184.0	195.0	190.0	177.3
Switzerland	63.1	77.0	80.1	87.1	90.1	88.8	90.7	94.8	100.8	117.8	129.0
Turkey	299.9	359.9	465.0	511.9	594.1	787.2	1,079.2	1,240.4	1,273.4	1,368.4	1,603.4
United Kingdom	1,127.7	1,247.8	1,345.1	1,434.4	1,571.2	1,702.0	1,850.9	1,675.2	1,669.2	1,681.2	1,810.5
Eastern Europe											
Albania											
Belarus											
Bosnia-Herzegovina											
Bulgaria											
Croatia											
Czech Republic	2.5	3.5	6.4	8.3	14.5	20.0	27.0	41.0	51.0	67.0	86.9
Estonia											
Georgia											
Hungary	0.4	0.4	1.2	2.0	3.2	4.7	6.9	9.4	15.1	19.8	23.1
Latvia											
Lithuania											
Macedonia											
Moldova											
Poland	2.0	5.5	9.6	12.9	27.3	34.1	45.1	67.5	81.5	107.9	138.1
Romania											
Russia						2.5	5.9	12.2	29.5	42.5	50.1
Slovakia											
Slovenia											
Ukraine											

Source: Euromonitor International from trade sources

Banking and Finance Statistics

Table 4.20

Number of Charge Card Transactions 1998-2008
Million

	1998	1999	2000	2001	2002	2003	2004	2005	2006	2007	2008
Western Europe											
Austria	13.2	13.1	13.7	16.9	18.7	18.4	25.9	27.5	29.2	31.5	34.1
Belgium	54.1	57.7	64.4	69.4	70.5	70.4	74.0	79.0	92.0	109.0	119.4
Cyprus											
Denmark	16.3	18.9	21.0	22.4	23.7	25.0	27.3	28.7	31.3	32.9	35.1
Finland											
France	165.7	260.1	309.4	426.4	496.5	584.4	632.5	812.9	1,077.0	1,328.1	1,528.2
Germany	252.8	278.6	271.3	289.0	299.0	346.0	366.4	369.5	377.0	382.5	386.3
Gibraltar											
Greece	3.6	5.7	8.4	5.9	6.0	6.4	1.8	1.5	1.9	1.9	1.9
Iceland											
Ireland											
Italy	196.7	219.3	264.5	306.2	317.6	374.0	439.2	509.7	580.8	635.6	686.9
Liechtenstein											
Luxembourg											
Malta											
Monaco											
Netherlands	11.2	11.0	11.2	11.6	12.3	12.8	13.3	14.7	14.2	13.1	13.6
Norway	15.4	16.0	16.6	17.3	16.8	17.4	18.9	19.9	22.4	30.7	32.0
Portugal	27.3	33.8	37.4	41.5	41.8	47.2	53.1	57.6	62.0	66.9	73.9
Spain	152.5	178.7	180.5	210.3	325.2	376.7	463.0	540.0	641.9	777.8	824.0
Sweden	36.5	40.0	47.0	50.0	56.6	63.1	93.1	99.1	112.4	110.1	109.5
Switzerland	6.6	9.4	10.0	11.2	11.6	11.6	11.9	12.6	12.4	12.0	11.4
Turkey											
United Kingdom	169.7	185.0	198.0	235.7	230.8	240.7	240.7	247.3	268.8	279.5	294.3
Eastern Europe											
Albania											
Belarus											
Bosnia-Herzegovina											
Bulgaria											
Croatia											
Czech Republic	3.0	3.9	4.8	6.0	6.8	7.9	8.4	9.1	10.0	11.0	12.2
Estonia											
Georgia											
Hungary	0.1	0.1	0.1	0.1	0.1	0.1	0.2	0.3	0.4	0.5	0.5
Latvia											
Lithuania											
Macedonia											
Moldova											
Poland	10.7	17.9	29.7	52.1	89.0	96.1	91.0	97.7	107.1	132.0	153.1
Romania											
Russia											
Slovakia											
Slovenia											
Ukraine											

Source: *Euromonitor International from trade sources*

Table 4.21

Average Expenditure per Credit Card 1998-2008
US$ per card

	1998	1999	2000	2001	2002	2003	2004	2005	2006	2007	2008
Western Europe											
Austria	2,516.6	2,280.4	2,006.3	2,159.8	2,262.2	2,721.4	3,556.5	3,787.9	3,404.1	3,830.6	4,315.1
Belgium	293.3	295.8	265.9	322.1	365.5	556.0	796.6	1,170.8	1,710.9	1,863.2	2,057.2
Cyprus											
Denmark	879.7	782.5	634.3	579.2	677.4	731.1	699.1	647.8	643.9	435.9	422.2
Finland											
France	1,116.5	1,192.2	1,121.1	1,208.9	1,435.3	1,662.3	1,862.4	1,852.5	2,000.1	2,307.9	2,552.4
Germany	21,348.2	16,036.9	10,292.5	8,341.0	8,506.6	5,697.1	4,911.5	3,060.1	2,005.7	2,244.6	2,381.3
Gibraltar											
Greece	649.3	789.7	677.0	458.3	400.2	868.4	1,195.8	1,314.5	1,334.4	1,503.7	1,504.5
Iceland											
Ireland											
Italy	1,691.4	1,748.6	1,616.9	1,650.1	1,151.7	1,059.8	855.7	845.2	845.6	1,023.4	1,097.3
Liechtenstein											
Luxembourg											
Malta											
Monaco											
Netherlands	1,235.2	1,296.5	1,019.6	1,029.3	1,100.3	1,139.0	1,314.8	1,358.8	1,501.7	1,867.4	2,372.2
Norway	938.2	918.8	983.0	954.1	1,161.3	1,441.7	1,744.6	1,877.8	1,796.5	2,123.0	2,147.7
Portugal	3,007.4	3,415.6	3,446.9	3,044.9	2,947.2	3,252.2	3,148.2	3,079.8	3,059.4	3,310.6	3,483.3
Spain	1,443.4	1,330.8	1,191.3	1,142.9	1,412.6	1,733.4	1,813.8	1,744.1	1,564.7	1,551.0	1,575.1
Sweden	2,089.8	2,096.6	2,308.5	2,236.2	2,116.2	2,863.8	2,914.5	2,736.5	2,781.7	3,785.3	3,853.5
Switzerland	3,347.6	3,185.3	2,865.6	2,917.6	3,175.9	3,594.4	4,027.0	4,223.5	4,079.9	4,431.0	4,947.2
Turkey	2,184.1	1,268.1	1,254.0	707.4	925.0	1,195.6	1,538.0	1,925.4	2,130.5	2,638.2	2,943.2
United Kingdom	2,372.9	2,496.4	2,303.4	2,163.9	2,241.7	2,407.9	2,804.4	2,780.2	2,781.8	3,266.0	3,149.8
Eastern Europe											
Albania											
Belarus											
Bosnia-Herzegovina											
Bulgaria											
Croatia											
Czech Republic	451.4	514.3	621.2	626.8	815.6	1,518.0	1,655.9	1,571.3	1,700.4	2,017.5	2,608.5
Estonia											
Georgia											
Hungary	559.6	197.9	171.8	185.9	238.4	268.9	359.8	398.5	472.7	633.6	737.2
Latvia											
Lithuania											
Macedonia											
Moldova											
Poland	2,538.7	1,850.6	1,145.3	909.4	1,320.7	1,209.1	982.5	904.8	720.0	795.8	901.0
Romania											
Russia							396.4	435.5	565.9	587.8	762.8	911.2
Slovakia											
Slovenia											
Ukraine											

Source: Euromonitor International from trade sources

Average Expenditure per Charge Card 1998-2008

US$ per card

	1998	1999	2000	2001	2002	2003	2004	2005	2006	2007	2008
Western Europe											
Austria	1,988.9	1,916.5	1,662.6	1,830.2	2,044.2	2,396.3	3,150.0	3,270.7	3,402.4	3,974.8	4,491.8
Belgium	2,577.3	2,357.2	2,141.6	2,397.5	2,611.1	2,874.9	3,022.1	3,184.6	3,606.9	4,360.7	4,661.8
Cyprus											
Denmark	11,384.2	7,439.8	6,895.5	6,355.3	6,282.6	6,619.8	6,839.2	6,595.8	5,645.9	6,237.9	6,371.9
Finland											
France	2,498.2	2,774.0	2,616.1	2,723.6	3,124.0	3,987.3	4,104.5	4,078.1	3,592.6	3,962.2	3,980.0
Germany	1,786.7	1,237.0	1,093.6	1,161.3	1,266.2	1,644.2	1,986.6	2,025.7	2,090.9	2,346.8	2,508.1
Gibraltar											
Greece	1,315.2	1,757.7	2,071.2	1,603.8	1,724.8	2,295.3	3,008.4	2,917.0	4,007.5	4,468.0	4,974.3
Iceland											
Ireland											
Italy	1,761.9	1,805.0	1,505.5	1,422.2	1,532.5	1,596.1	1,960.2	1,930.8	1,930.1	2,016.8	2,119.4
Liechtenstein											
Luxembourg											
Malta											
Monaco											
Netherlands	6,649.5	6,396.8	5,452.3	5,461.7	5,985.6	6,965.3	7,936.1	7,546.4	7,045.3	7,310.9	8,605.5
Norway	5,480.5	5,100.3	4,319.6	4,118.2	4,535.1	4,786.8	5,061.8	4,681.8	4,547.9	5,862.6	5,701.9
Portugal	4,145.5	3,501.4	2,920.9	2,919.6	2,637.8	2,864.1	2,683.0	2,616.2	2,478.0	2,742.8	2,778.4
Spain	841.8	751.2	659.7	670.3	951.6	1,198.4	1,386.2	1,516.4	1,546.4	1,946.5	2,207.0
Sweden	7,739.7	7,200.1	7,380.9	7,080.6	6,579.3	8,706.6	5,691.1	5,393.6	5,187.5	6,074.4	6,235.2
Switzerland	10,541.1	10,786.5	10,688.6	12,371.3	13,459.6	14,930.2	16,071.7	15,772.4	15,787.0	16,358.5	18,469.4
Turkey											
United Kingdom	6,849.2	7,532.1	7,762.2	7,412.6	7,878.9	8,508.6	10,159.6	9,903.2	11,220.9	11,607.6	10,445.6
Eastern Europe											
Albania											
Belarus											
Bosnia-Herzegovina											
Bulgaria											
Croatia											
Czech Republic	6,675.2	7,273.0	8,467.0	7,446.6	4,237.9	1,718.1	1,573.5	1,664.2	1,821.2	1,945.6	2,329.8
Estonia											
Georgia											
Hungary	1,246.8	1,162.5	1,333.0	1,311.7	1,254.3	1,381.0	1,909.9	2,404.2	3,539.6	5,588.3	6,803.8
Latvia											
Lithuania											
Macedonia											
Moldova											
Poland	949.1	799.4	822.5	1,124.1	1,951.1	3,119.3	3,190.9	3,878.0	5,572.8	7,615.9	9,315.0
Romania											
Russia											
Slovakia											
Slovenia											
Ukraine											

Source: *Euromonitor International from trade sources*

Table 4.23

Average Expenditure per Credit Card Transaction 1998-2008

US$ per transaction

	1998	1999	2000	2001	2002	2003	2004	2005	2006	2007	2008
Western Europe											
Austria	130.9	128.0	115.9	108.2	110.9	137.7	125.7	130.2	133.3	149.0	162.8
Belgium	78.5	74.0	67.9	74.9	77.0	101.9	118.6	115.7	118.3	127.5	134.5
Cyprus											
Denmark	209.6	222.5	194.1	187.8	203.6	238.5	235.4	205.8	181.2	180.8	187.4
Finland											
France	211.7	144.3	123.2	99.5	102.9	118.0	134.9	114.2	99.3	94.7	93.4
Germany	150.0	134.7	112.2	116.6	116.1	134.6	143.2	139.6	134.4	144.2	152.3
Gibraltar											
Greece	39.5	42.2	40.7	45.3	52.5	95.9	112.6	131.0	130.3	145.6	160.4
Iceland											
Ireland											
Italy	105.8	109.6	107.3	96.2	88.5	106.4	105.9	119.2	130.4	149.4	160.6
Liechtenstein											
Luxembourg											
Malta											
Monaco											
Netherlands	107.6	119.2	100.8	97.3	98.3	110.1	123.4	118.2	126.9	139.6	157.0
Norway	138.3	132.7	122.5	116.3	127.6	142.3	152.0	161.1	153.9	193.6	171.3
Portugal	91.5	77.9	64.7	44.8	49.3	58.8	67.9	70.6	73.3	77.7	84.3
Spain	102.2	109.3	102.3	100.0	105.5	131.1	141.5	146.0	124.8	104.0	88.9
Sweden	123.4	116.8	110.8	95.5	87.3	107.0	69.2	58.2	65.3	98.9	112.0
Switzerland	131.1	117.6	105.3	104.2	111.3	128.6	142.2	144.9	148.2	154.3	165.0
Turkey	52.4	35.4	36.2	19.3	24.5	30.2	38.0	46.5	54.3	72.0	79.7
United Kingdom	80.6	82.9	80.6	78.0	83.9	94.6	105.9	116.0	115.7	130.6	114.8
Eastern Europe											
Albania											
Belarus											
Bosnia-Herzegovina											
Bulgaria											
Croatia											
Czech Republic	11.2	17.2	19.0	24.8	31.2	49.5	64.5	61.5	71.7	87.6	108.5
Estonia											
Georgia											
Hungary	36.1	42.5	35.8	37.6	44.1	50.7	50.8	51.4	46.1	51.8	53.9
Latvia											
Lithuania											
Macedonia											
Moldova											
Poland	115.4	60.5	44.3	42.3	39.0	41.6	43.5	45.4	45.3	51.6	58.8
Romania											
Russia						94.6	103.2	116.6	130.9	160.5	169.1
Slovakia											
Slovenia											
Ukraine											

Source: *Euromonitor International from trade sources*

Banking and Finance Statistics

Table 4.24

Average Expenditure per Charge Card Transaction 1998-2008
US$ per transaction

	1998	1999	2000	2001	2002	2003	2004	2005	2006	2007	2008
Western Europe											
Austria	120.2	121.3	112.8	110.4	114.9	138.5	127.7	126.5	130.7	147.9	160.5
Belgium	94.0	96.2	84.5	90.3	95.5	118.3	129.7	131.4	130.3	141.5	149.8
Cyprus											
Denmark	85.6	50.7	45.2	43.7	45.7	52.7	60.2	60.7	57.7	63.6	65.9
Finland											
France	153.5	116.3	99.4	82.0	85.7	100.4	114.6	99.0	84.3	82.2	78.9
Germany	113.3	76.4	76.8	81.2	92.4	105.6	121.7	128.0	131.7	147.9	160.1
Gibraltar											
Greece	101.9	97.2	84.6	82.8	87.7	106.0	125.1	132.1	129.0	142.1	154.1
Iceland											
Ireland											
Italy	117.4	114.2	96.6	92.9	105.0	109.4	120.6	109.4	103.9	109.5	113.7
Liechtenstein											
Luxembourg											
Malta											
Monaco											
Netherlands	213.2	212.4	180.2	172.5	177.5	206.5	225.7	202.1	199.9	218.2	245.1
Norway	150.2	143.4	124.9	120.2	142.0	151.9	159.9	166.6	168.9	188.5	193.0
Portugal	31.4	27.5	24.7	23.3	24.9	27.4	29.4	29.3	29.2	30.8	32.2
Spain	57.1	52.4	45.7	43.0	44.7	54.7	59.8	61.4	57.9	64.4	71.7
Sweden	139.3	127.1	118.7	100.7	89.7	115.8	104.1	103.5	108.0	143.6	151.5
Switzerland	292.8	226.3	198.7	189.4	202.7	231.9	254.2	254.6	268.1	284.1	318.5
Turkey											
United Kingdom	133.4	142.3	150.5	141.9	151.0	160.7	191.8	194.1	207.0	238.6	231.4
Eastern Europe											
Albania											
Belarus											
Bosnia-Herzegovina											
Bulgaria											
Croatia											
Czech Republic	44.5	41.0	42.3	41.0	47.4	54.8	61.3	65.3	68.5	77.1	91.7
Estonia											
Georgia											
Hungary	106.6	101.0	103.2	99.5	77.9	174.7	193.3	174.8	194.6	226.1	246.2
Latvia											
Lithuania											
Macedonia											
Moldova											
Poland	40.6	37.8	28.8	24.3	26.4	28.0	31.0	35.4	44.4	44.9	50.3
Romania											
Russia											
Slovakia											
Slovenia											
Ukraine											

Source: *Euromonitor International from trade sources*

Consumer Expenditure

Consumer Expenditure Statistics

Table 5.1

Consumer Expenditure 1990-2008

Million units of national currency / as stated

	1990	1995	1996	1997	1998	1999	2000	2001
Western Europe								
Austria	81,194	97,278	101,199	102,514	105,768	108,423	114,176	117,785
Belgium	90,549	108,628	111,047	114,701	119,143	121,861	131,093	135,493
Cyprus	3,330	5,375	5,591	5,927	6,404	7,201	8,018	8,524
Denmark	419,184	515,752	535,160	560,603	580,505	589,504	608,142	624,005
Finland	43,386	48,025	50,229	53,046	56,472	57,977	61,941	65,307
France	584,671	668,678	689,718	700,253	728,863	751,860	797,959	831,025
Germany	790,448	1,013,340	1,039,580	1,062,500	1,081,860	1,113,840	1,149,690	1,194,030
Gibraltar	71	148	159	149	151	148	153	160
Greece	34,237	71,896	79,455	87,585	94,786	99,025	105,097	113,236
Iceland	202,035	241,065	257,937	286,139	320,711	354,499	386,592	407,746
Ireland	21,189	27,750	30,587	33,814	37,984	42,423	49,006	53,282
Italy	404,844	564,871	592,371	624,969	657,392	685,715	727,205	750,250
Liechtenstein	1,126	1,750	1,910	2,058	2,207	2,475	2,554	2,567
Luxembourg	4,943	6,541	6,825	7,477	7,785	8,150	8,883	9,410
Malta	1,322	2,012	2,122	2,376	2,523	2,876	3,161	3,240
Monaco								
Netherlands	121,604	150,920	160,242	169,088	181,430	194,600	209,020	222,408
Norway	343,344	446,191	480,563	507,070	533,151	564,422	604,646	631,581
Portugal	35,884	55,917	59,165	63,262	68,565	73,597	79,043	83,023
Spain	198,987	280,748	296,920	316,311	339,069	366,095	397,750	424,597
Sweden	692,917	874,597	894,755	930,179	961,686	1,016,262	1,064,368	1,100,597
Switzerland	182,480	216,079	221,345	226,470	231,277	237,606	245,264	252,132
Turkey	270	5,458	9,938	19,619	46,669	71,641	117,499	164,319
United Kingdom	342,613	448,267	481,702	511,577	544,519	576,993	609,617	638,254
Eastern Europe								
Albania	11,890	196,517	335,516	329,856	373,070	408,175	406,499	429,667
Belarus	2	70,254	114,185	207,159	403,784	1,773,389	5,211,536	9,917,949
Bosnia-Herzegovina			4,032	5,290	6,558	7,723	9,577	10,233
Bulgaria	30	638	1,340	12,929	15,866	17,623	19,533	21,929
Croatia	166	62,679	65,615	77,351	81,496	82,086	90,309	98,861
Czech Republic	309,121	759,693	896,017	1,002,251	1,092,484	1,137,893	1,193,313	1,270,498
Estonia		25,074	36,150	44,118	49,323	51,180	56,750	63,905
Georgia		3,304	4,007	4,689	4,362	4,617	5,430	5,184
Hungary	1,027,497	3,063,219	3,713,544	4,498,219	5,374,413	6,234,887	7,355,208	8,364,967
Latvia	49	1,640	2,038	2,335	2,466	2,601	2,884	3,176
Lithuania		17,057	21,804	25,038	28,156	29,225	30,000	32,095
Macedonia		118,692	126,323	134,791	140,164	142,815	172,523	161,493
Moldova	8	3,594	5,120	5,916	6,707	8,727	13,404	15,596
Poland	27,674	205,751	265,144	325,160	375,347	419,854	474,790	502,459
Romania	55	4,778	7,410	18,374	27,729	39,895	55,731	80,614
Russia	286	688,038	1,000,861	1,222,135	1,452,024	2,459,553	3,167,498	4,182,571
Slovakia		7,993	8,935	10,102	10,797	10,736	12,166	13,595
Slovenia	2,745	9,778	10,200	10,862	11,477	12,265	12,587	13,199
Ukraine	2	23,440	46,435	55,018	62,267	76,118	97,048	117,231

Source: *National statistical offices/OECD/Eurostat/Euromonitor International*

Consumer Expenditure Statistics

Consumer Expenditure 1990-2008 *(continued)*
Million units of national currency / as stated

	2002	2003	2004	2005	2006	2007	2008	Total US$ million 2008	US$ per capita 2008
Western Europe									
Austria	120,267	123,502	129,194	136,165	141,988	147,263	152,661	224,674.5	26,901.3
Belgium	138,043	141,354	146,812	152,833	160,268	168,161	176,981	260,465.8	24,529.6
Cyprus	8,502	8,644	9,077	9,745	10,373	11,669	12,822	18,870.2	21,880.1
Denmark	643,125	655,919	694,854	735,899	782,959	815,402	839,410	164,650.6	30,147.3
Finland	68,486	72,016	74,961	77,899	82,262	86,903	91,603	134,813.8	25,434.2
France	857,974	889,899	927,008	967,558	1,011,533	1,057,447	1,097,587	1,615,337.8	26,009.4
Germany	1,198,080	1,214,846	1,235,052	1,260,265	1,292,903	1,311,284	1,344,373	1,978,537.6	24,064.6
Gibraltar	160	158	154	154	159	160	166	306.0	10,450.0
Greece	123,615	130,925	138,183	148,100	160,537	170,113	180,399	265,497.0	23,680.8
Iceland	427,765	452,761	494,161	561,435	620,428	679,220	769,908	8,754.1	27,749.7
Ireland	57,494	61,204	64,493	69,941	76,277	83,331	85,120	125,273.1	28,611.9
Italy	771,278	798,455	826,718	853,522	886,456	916,119	936,712	1,378,575.6	23,375.3
Liechtenstein	2,546	2,534	2,620	2,777	2,859	2,945	2,951	2,724.8	76,796.4
Luxembourg	10,046	10,591	11,191	11,823	12,226	12,649	13,397	19,716.6	41,024.6
Malta	3,251	3,247	3,326	3,414	3,506	3,617	3,687	5,425.6	13,315.7
Monaco									
Netherlands	230,830	235,707	239,763	246,943	251,134	259,476	268,108	394,579.0	24,084.4
Norway	659,620	694,859	734,566	768,735	819,282	874,725	920,657	163,237.1	34,458.8
Portugal	86,555	88,768	93,402	97,444	102,469	107,002	111,658	164,328.8	15,440.6
Spain	446,068	473,257	508,494	546,739	585,739	624,023	646,697	951,754.5	21,123.6
Sweden	1,149,317	1,191,895	1,230,645	1,284,640	1,328,738	1,383,269	1,418,522	215,217.8	23,502.8
Switzerland	254,099	257,214	263,313	268,916	276,698	286,897	297,980	275,120.6	36,536.2
Turkey	238,897	324,692	399,390	452,847	523,207	584,210	647,214	497,267.8	6,687.5
United Kingdom	670,401	702,450	738,229	772,378	805,253	845,369	876,011	1,610,414.8	26,320.0
Eastern Europe									
Albania	473,513	511,939	584,035	617,864	687,492	737,428	800,950	9,547.1	3,037.3
Belarus	15,647,102	21,049,739	27,001,692	34,170,019	41,158,150	50,766,774	67,847,879	31,758.0	3,277.4
Bosnia-Herzegovina	11,395	13,030	14,331	15,766	17,338	19,391	21,006	15,732.4	4,092.9
Bulgaria	23,738	25,334	28,081	31,606	36,822	41,579	48,665	36,395.5	4,807.0
Croatia	108,975	116,162	124,323	133,072	141,829	155,285	166,266	33,690.9	7,596.7
Czech Republic	1,292,546	1,364,730	1,450,983	1,499,196	1,597,039	1,719,897	1,872,055	109,658.4	10,629.3
Estonia	71,082	77,797	87,965	99,542	118,043	137,315	141,824	13,261.5	9,932.7
Georgia	5,793	6,082	7,104	7,589	10,544	11,614	13,488	9,047.8	2,064.7
Hungary	9,497,068	10,555,229	11,234,430	11,988,512	12,594,582	13,432,724	14,079,621	81,804.5	8,148.7
Latvia	3,517	3,906	4,550	5,463	6,972	8,823	9,079	18,881.5	8,329.8
Lithuania	34,131	37,182	41,272	47,032	53,931	64,076	73,507	31,185.8	9,264.0
Macedonia	184,760	187,761	204,733	218,734	238,642	268,000	309,749	7,398.3	3,626.7
Moldova	17,738	23,765	27,432	33,134	39,542	46,196	54,871	5,280.1	1,453.2
Poland	536,052	549,894	592,705	617,291	657,474	706,719	774,176	321,336.0	8,446.1
Romania	102,525	128,641	167,944	197,810	233,834	273,707	325,549	129,244.4	6,012.3
Russia	5,224,184	6,334,737	8,104,309	10,262,259	12,601,039	15,529,878	19,564,592	787,215.7	5,543.4
Slovakia	14,509	16,235	18,788	22,301	25,733	31,126	37,252	54,824.5	10,164.7
Slovenia	14,101	14,793	15,385	16,061	16,908	18,468	20,082	29,554.8	14,656.5
Ukraine	128,394	149,710	184,236	255,628	322,282	426,311	584,458	110,961.4	2,402.2

Source: *National statistical offices/OECD/Eurostat/Euromonitor International*

Consumer Expenditure Statistics

Table 5.2

Consumer Expenditure by Object 2008

US$ million

	Food and Non-alcoholic Beverages	Alcoholic Beverages and Tobacco	Clothing and Footwear	Housing	Household Goods and Services	Health Goods and Medical Services
Western Europe						
Austria	22,805.2	5,411.9	14,050.8	48,942.3	15,248.7	7,092.5
Belgium	34,191.4	9,719.1	13,523.1	60,764.3	13,921.7	11,541.6
Denmark	17,421.4	5,656.0	7,534.5	43,120.8	9,968.7	4,202.2
Finland	16,287.6	6,538.9	6,507.5	34,213.9	7,793.3	5,924.8
France	219,821.1	49,005.6	75,092.8	399,285.5	91,565.1	57,263.6
Germany	225,583.6	70,300.7	100,867.7	489,871.9	131,244.4	94,150.8
Greece	37,828.9	12,806.0	24,990.5	39,903.2	16,793.1	16,716.2
Ireland	9,438.6	6,042.2	5,273.3	26,483.6	8,650.3	5,221.8
Italy	197,901.5	38,318.5	98,627.1	303,670.5	101,873.6	41,634.1
Netherlands	40,028.8	11,501.8	19,988.3	90,744.7	23,115.6	21,904.3
Norway	21,379.8	7,039.3	9,384.0	34,141.8	10,509.9	5,263.0
Portugal	25,807.2	5,934.0	10,916.6	23,544.3	10,536.1	9,501.0
Spain	127,571.6	29,791.3	45,774.7	160,741.8	46,821.7	35,611.3
Sweden	24,971.7	7,511.6	11,631.4	59,616.1	11,832.9	6,137.6
Switzerland	28,259.5	9,799.9	10,413.5	67,536.3	12,430.1	44,313.9
Turkey	122,037.6	20,350.7	29,027.0	133,715.7	30,184.4	10,728.4
United Kingdom	156,433.1	57,590.8	87,070.3	322,728.5	85,193.9	25,821.7
Eastern Europe						
Belarus	13,982.4	1,810.0	2,577.5	4,048.9	1,478.7	774.5
Bulgaria	6,924.7	1,450.6	1,070.6	6,551.0	1,672.7	1,480.8
Croatia	8,783.3	934.4	2,169.0	10,213.3	1,367.6	735.3
Czech Republic	17,449.3	8,212.9	5,109.5	24,668.2	5,227.6	2,303.8
Estonia	2,033.1	1,085.3	1,001.8	2,468.0	742.1	406.0
Hungary	13,590.8	6,497.5	3,003.8	15,961.9	6,276.9	3,340.1
Latvia	3,620.3	1,168.5	1,265.1	3,781.3	683.2	1,100.1
Lithuania	7,190.1	1,854.5	2,044.5	4,050.4	1,775.8	1,685.2
Poland	65,634.0	21,036.6	14,352.9	77,529.4	13,973.9	13,082.6
Romania	44,236.5	6,348.3	4,283.9	31,294.4	6,696.4	4,485.6
Russia	198,536.4	16,088.7	77,584.8	86,506.1	58,887.1	24,640.3
Slovakia	9,419.1	2,395.5	2,077.4	14,668.4	2,839.1	1,502.6
Slovenia	4,306.2	1,190.6	1,826.3	5,569.9	1,823.1	1,012.5
Ukraine	46,859.0	7,020.9	16,959.4	9,877.5	4,347.9	4,833.3

Source: *National statistical offices/OECD/Eurostat/Euromonitor International*

Consumer Expenditure by Object 2008 *(continued)*

US$ million

	Transport	Communi-cations	Leisure and Recreation	Education	Hotels and Catering	Miscellaneous Goods and Services	Total
Western Europe							
Austria	28,485.5	5,803.0	26,360.6	1,524.8	28,329.6	20,619.5	224,674.5
Belgium	39,479.9	6,483.7	24,358.6	1,525.8	13,003.8	31,952.6	260,465.8
Denmark	23,953.0	3,660.7	17,406.4	1,205.6	8,753.5	21,767.8	164,650.6
Finland	17,479.4	3,700.1	15,448.4	604.7	8,661.5	11,653.7	134,813.8
France	239,245.2	48,402.9	148,546.7	11,288.9	99,746.5	176,073.9	1,615,337.8
Germany	264,924.2	58,525.5	186,696.7	13,577.4	101,853.4	240,941.2	1,978,537.6
Greece	20,175.0	7,804.5	16,567.8	5,165.4	50,147.9	16,598.4	265,497.0
Ireland	13,917.3	5,622.7	9,478.5	1,856.3	16,266.9	17,021.6	125,273.1
Italy	187,893.5	39,790.9	96,435.3	10,438.8	136,581.4	125,410.2	1,378,575.6
Netherlands	44,718.7	18,978.8	41,422.4	2,070.4	19,149.2	60,955.9	394,579.0
Norway	24,020.5	5,456.3	22,155.3	919.3	9,419.8	13,548.4	163,237.1
Portugal	22,779.7	4,612.6	11,289.2	1,959.1	17,050.1	20,399.0	164,328.8
Spain	114,138.9	27,397.8	91,325.5	12,576.5	184,387.3	75,616.1	951,754.5
Sweden	28,671.7	6,854.5	25,701.9	655.2	11,156.9	20,476.3	215,217.8
Switzerland	22,369.6	6,796.9	22,449.0	1,573.0	19,928.5	29,250.4	275,120.6
Turkey	68,625.7	21,328.5	10,712.2	10,015.1	20,416.1	20,126.1	497,267.8
United Kingdom	239,830.5	33,970.4	183,968.2	24,765.5	168,277.5	224,764.4	1,610,414.8
Eastern Europe							
Belarus	2,336.1	1,253.1	1,088.4	434.3	771.4	1,202.7	31,758.0
Bulgaria	7,373.2	2,278.4	2,265.4	254.8	3,384.6	1,688.8	36,395.5
Croatia	3,110.2	1,409.1	1,692.0	181.5	946.0	2,149.2	33,690.9
Czech Republic	11,932.9	4,767.8	12,933.7	1,112.7	6,425.6	9,514.2	109,658.4
Estonia	1,657.6	445.8	1,130.2	145.0	1,098.9	1,047.6	13,261.5
Hungary	13,347.4	4,076.2	6,587.1	1,049.1	4,258.2	3,815.5	81,804.5
Latvia	2,183.0	997.2	1,888.6	708.6	815.7	669.8	18,881.5
Lithuania	5,442.0	1,061.2	2,493.4	272.3	917.3	2,399.2	31,185.8
Poland	26,826.4	11,055.8	23,327.7	4,130.0	9,020.5	41,366.3	321,336.0
Romania	14,425.7	2,911.9	5,508.1	1,699.0	4,263.8	3,090.8	129,244.4
Russia	157,037.8	28,253.5	54,044.8	13,287.8	28,055.5	44,292.7	787,215.7
Slovakia	4,965.3	2,274.5	5,155.3	943.1	3,353.7	5,230.5	54,824.5
Slovenia	4,261.9	1,166.2	3,112.4	338.6	2,148.6	2,798.5	29,554.8
Ukraine	5,269.1	3,355.8	4,275.3	2,333.7	2,956.6	2,872.9	110,961.4

Source: National statistical offices/OECD/Eurostat/Euromonitor International

Consumer Expenditure Statistics **Table 5.3**

Consumer Expenditure on Food and Non-alcoholic Beverages 1990-2008

Million units of national currency / as stated

	1990	1995	1996	1997	1998	1999	2000	2001
Western Europe								
Austria	11,517	12,367	12,447	12,526	12,608	12,619	12,628	12,945
Belgium	14,465	15,243	15,379	15,766	15,970	15,594	16,115	17,221
Cyprus								
Denmark	59,706	68,186	69,386	72,033	73,139	71,953	74,403	77,075
Finland	7,095	7,411	7,068	7,191	7,335	7,569	7,808	8,321
France	91,003	99,624	100,467	103,035	105,965	107,962	112,679	119,301
Germany	109,485	124,900	125,340	125,130	126,670	128,480	132,140	137,930
Gibraltar								
Greece	7,372	12,956	14,032	15,087	15,963	16,452	17,112	18,021
Iceland								
Ireland	3,876	4,248	4,523	4,561	4,757	4,914	5,393	5,695
Italy	76,483	94,327	98,268	100,888	103,451	104,927	109,549	112,272
Liechtenstein								
Luxembourg								
Malta								
Monaco								
Netherlands	17,225	19,667	20,262	21,043	21,994	22,699	23,298	24,830
Norway	59,277	72,466	74,197	77,714	82,188	86,560	90,821	92,796
Portugal	6,651	10,239	10,710	11,021	11,985	12,502	12,947	14,075
Spain	39,495	48,226	50,166	51,454	52,535	54,643	56,813	61,171
Sweden	104,423	122,377	116,748	118,979	121,213	124,579	127,531	133,575
Switzerland	22,089	24,161	24,240	24,559	24,972	25,516	26,028	27,349
Turkey	97	2,014	3,322	6,278	16,128	24,320	37,606	50,948
United Kingdom	42,285	49,700	53,025	53,787	55,162	57,040	58,628	59,804
Eastern Europe								
Albania								
Belarus	1	35,395	61,069	116,376	213,036	1,011,114	3,060,851	5,316,413
Bosnia-Herzegovina			1,345	1,755	2,163	2,534	3,124	3,320
Bulgaria	8	192	404	4,936	5,237	5,196	5,560	6,069
Croatia	59	20,104	20,587	23,737	24,507	23,601	22,600	26,289
Czech Republic	61,643	147,982	170,392	185,987	202,846	213,691	221,837	238,902
Estonia		8,606	10,678	12,674	12,760	12,286	11,681	12,810
Georgia		1,867	2,268	2,597	2,502	2,658	2,738	2,624
Hungary	222,434	741,138	839,162	1,000,353	1,169,660	1,246,813	1,403,228	1,594,071
Latvia	15	605	718	736	732	696	725	785
Lithuania		6,716	8,466	8,795	9,057	9,149	9,136	9,378
Macedonia		45,467	48,233	51,266	53,010	53,679	64,349	59,243
Moldova								
Poland	9,306	56,518	69,900	79,991	85,015	87,926	108,406	115,254
Romania	19	1,677	2,644	6,568	9,798	13,811	19,341	30,671
Russia	95	337,129	496,606	603,091	705,183	1,171,374	1,481,340	1,915,618
Slovakia		2,145	2,395	2,814	2,880	2,698	2,874	3,040
Slovenia	626	1,762	1,781	1,892	2,061	2,120	2,140	2,252
Ukraine	1	9,845	19,526	23,300	26,775	33,177	45,128	55,685

Source: *National statistical offices/OECD/Eurostat/Euromonitor International*

Consumer Expenditure Statistics

Consumer Expenditure on Food and Non-alcoholic Beverages 1990-2008 *(continued)*

Million units of national currency / as stated

	2002	2003	2004	2005	2006	2007	2008	Total US$ million 2008	US$ per capita 2008
Western Europe									
Austria	13,301	13,475	13,909	14,479	14,891	15,187	15,495.6	22,805.2	2,730.6
Belgium	18,351	19,413	20,129	20,519	21,581	22,342	23,232.3	34,191.4	3,220.0
Cyprus									
Denmark	78,437	78,740	79,979	82,227	84,804	87,229	88,816.8	17,421.4	3,189.8
Finland	8,596	9,116	9,382	9,687	10,164	10,617	11,067.1	16,287.6	3,072.9
France	123,769	128,306	130,986	133,526	139,572	144,853	149,363.6	219,821.1	3,539.5
Germany	138,180	137,935	139,796	144,136	148,395	149,991	153,279.2	225,583.6	2,743.7
Gibraltar									
Greece	19,494	20,173	20,905	22,023	23,742	24,690	25,703.9	37,828.9	3,374.1
Iceland									
Ireland	5,772	5,653	5,784	6,058	6,272	6,544	6,413.3	9,438.6	2,155.7
Italy	115,867	120,353	122,584	126,024	130,049	132,854	134,469.8	197,901.5	3,355.6
Liechtenstein									
Luxembourg									
Malta									
Monaco									
Netherlands	25,877	26,338	26,213	26,169	26,088	26,601	27,198.7	40,028.8	2,443.3
Norway	95,057	99,536	101,988	103,979	109,651	116,127	120,581.9	21,379.8	4,513.2
Portugal	14,562	15,123	15,595	15,772	16,428	16,994	17,535.4	25,807.2	2,424.9
Spain	65,928	69,040	72,112	77,092	81,260	84,955	86,682.1	127,571.6	2,831.4
Sweden	143,826	147,982	150,782	154,494	157,612	162,210	164,590.6	24,971.7	2,727.0
Switzerland	27,467	28,021	28,117	28,161	28,658	29,590	30,607.6	28,259.5	3,752.9
Turkey	63,715	89,241	105,531	112,666	129,709	144,634	158,836.9	122,037.6	1,641.2
United Kingdom	61,310	63,174	65,065	67,543	69,624	77,057	85,094.3	156,433.1	2,556.7
Eastern Europe									
Albania									
Belarus	7,906,477	9,751,699	12,284,901	15,546,259	18,725,634	22,644,790	29,872,083.8	13,982.4	1,443.0
Bosnia-Herzegovina	3,676	4,183	4,572	4,975	5,490	6,102	6,575.0	4,924.3	1,281.1
Bulgaria	6,014	6,023	6,579	6,890	7,664	8,310	9,259.1	6,924.7	914.6
Croatia	28,071	31,027	32,212	36,019	37,730	40,815	43,346.0	8,783.3	1,980.5
Czech Republic	234,454	231,873	247,081	250,583	262,785	278,637	297,889.6	17,449.3	1,691.4
Estonia	14,007	14,756	16,367	18,111	20,168	22,086	21,743.2	2,033.1	1,522.8
Georgia	2,847	2,964	3,468	3,467	4,806	5,024	5,675.6	3,807.1	868.8
Hungary	1,773,880	1,917,093	1,998,214	2,096,730	2,211,186	2,294,659	2,339,153.0	13,590.8	1,353.8
Latvia	880	921	1,010	1,143	1,354	1,698	1,740.7	3,620.3	1,597.2
Lithuania	9,572	10,402	11,659	12,275	13,258	15,223	16,947.7	7,190.1	2,135.9
Macedonia	67,124	67,158	67,801	75,157	78,391	86,247	98,923.9	2,362.8	1,158.2
Moldova									
Poland	116,675	115,974	125,780	129,952	137,310	145,535	158,128.0	65,634.0	1,725.1
Romania	36,779	45,452	58,580	68,369	80,468	93,901	111,425.6	44,236.5	2,057.8
Russia	2,178,485	2,388,196	2,917,551	3,407,070	3,981,928	4,410,485	4,934,206.0	198,536.4	1,398.1
Slovakia	3,252	3,456	3,700	4,249	4,785	5,569	6,400.1	9,419.1	1,746.4
Slovenia	2,375	2,461	2,424	2,484	2,563	2,752	2,925.9	4,306.2	2,135.5
Ukraine	59,061	67,199	80,850	109,624	136,275	180,261	246,816.6	46,859.0	1,014.4

Source: National statistical offices/OECD/Eurostat/Euromonitor International

Consumer Expenditure Statistics

Table 5.4

Consumer Expenditure on Alcoholic Beverages and Tobacco 1990-2008
Million units of national currency / as stated

	1990	1995	1996	1997	1998	1999	2000	2001
Western Europe								
Austria	2,559	2,719	2,695	2,902	3,104	3,219	3,312	3,301
Belgium	3,877	4,116	4,277	4,549	4,930	5,160	5,409	5,201
Cyprus								
Denmark	24,617	24,726	25,255	25,498	25,403	25,917	26,514	27,214
Finland	2,850	2,909	3,021	3,178	3,236	3,208	3,416	3,839
France	16,824	22,180	23,117	23,785	24,872	26,010	27,103	28,354
Germany	35,267	38,190	38,640	38,740	39,210	40,140	40,240	41,110
Gibraltar								
Greece	1,248	3,048	3,425	3,847	4,270	4,582	4,822	5,349
Iceland								
Ireland	1,296	1,890	2,004	2,176	2,385	2,705	3,152	3,320
Italy	10,404	13,943	15,001	15,494	16,368	17,317	18,228	18,898
Liechtenstein								
Luxembourg								
Malta								
Monaco								
Netherlands	4,423	5,040	5,224	5,424	5,525	5,827	5,994	6,701
Norway	17,584	21,169	22,622	25,103	25,975	27,987	29,206	29,892
Portugal	1,477	2,151	2,263	2,359	2,616	2,811	2,905	3,037
Spain	4,513	7,471	7,707	8,946	10,185	11,125	12,065	12,885
Sweden	35,160	38,636	38,352	38,201	37,519	40,064	41,562	43,957
Switzerland	8,098	8,397	8,492	8,624	8,816	9,052	9,363	9,363
Turkey	11	255	432	835	2,202	3,412	5,370	7,528
United Kingdom	14,753	18,776	20,439	21,553	22,459	24,458	24,617	25,158
Eastern Europe								
Albania								
Belarus	0	6,756	8,479	17,148	33,263	119,613	350,424	590,215
Bosnia-Herzegovina			266	346	427	499	614	651
Bulgaria	1	17	35	312	421	499	654	751
Croatia	6	2,340	2,426	2,830	2,959	2,846	2,726	3,175
Czech Republic	32,510	73,261	80,709	83,581	91,771	97,372	99,016	101,025
Estonia		1,879	2,738	3,240	3,769	4,174	4,342	4,617
Georgia		109	124	139	131	139	166	187
Hungary	104,617	252,462	301,249	365,160	457,858	513,526	597,342	685,278
Latvia	3	126	152	176	179	193	238	240
Lithuania		1,606	1,881	2,188	2,263	2,366	2,250	2,317
Macedonia		5,562	5,853	6,165	6,300	6,292	7,446	6,693
Moldova								
Poland	2,632	17,062	22,058	25,757	28,627	30,415	32,994	33,827
Romania	3	252	396	1,011	1,500	2,311	2,989	3,403
Russia	18	24,797	35,043	43,125	52,564	91,316	118,388	150,573
Slovakia		618	652	686	711	641	725	756
Slovenia	103	564	563	562	557	564	616	630
Ukraine	0	1,425	2,823	3,430	3,801	4,591	5,822	7,135

Source: *National statistical offices/OECD/Eurostat/Euromonitor International*

Consumer Expenditure Statistics

Consumer Expenditure on Alcoholic Beverages and Tobacco 1990-2008 *(continued)*

Million units of national currency / as stated

	2002	2003	2004	2005	2006	2007	2008	Total US$ million 2008	US$ per capita 2008
Western Europe									
Austria	3,605	3,658	3,612	3,551	3,533	3,615	3,677.3	5,411.9	648.0
Belgium	5,404	5,586	5,785	5,795	6,011	6,306	6,603.9	9,719.1	915.3
Cyprus									
Denmark	27,585	28,284	28,729	27,516	27,924	28,503	28,834.8	5,656.0	1,035.6
Finland	3,990	4,123	3,903	3,906	4,084	4,224	4,443.1	6,538.9	1,233.6
France	29,478	29,378	29,874	29,768	31,109	32,166	33,298.2	49,005.6	789.1
Germany	43,320	43,306	43,345	44,979	46,172	46,703	47,767.8	70,300.7	855.1
Gibraltar									
Greece	5,844	6,167	6,541	7,074	7,649	8,164	8,701.4	12,806.0	1,142.2
Iceland									
Ireland	3,695	3,707	3,598	3,744	3,830	4,097	4,105.6	6,042.2	1,380.0
Italy	19,827	20,780	21,826	22,938	24,161	25,210	26,036.6	38,318.5	649.7
Liechtenstein									
Luxembourg									
Malta									
Monaco									
Netherlands	6,867	6,986	7,221	7,360	7,480	7,643	7,815.2	11,501.8	702.0
Norway	30,624	31,016	33,243	34,340	36,365	38,246	39,701.4	7,039.3	1,486.0
Portugal	3,214	3,412	3,394	3,435	3,730	3,886	4,032.0	5,934.0	557.6
Spain	13,735	14,710	15,654	16,902	18,121	19,476	20,242.6	29,791.3	661.2
Sweden	46,481	46,737	45,892	46,939	47,025	48,492	49,509.6	7,511.6	820.3
Switzerland	9,448	10,018	9,905	9,760	9,963	10,278	10,614.1	9,799.9	1,301.4
Turkey	9,697	13,453	17,276	18,750	21,291	24,065	26,487.3	20,350.7	273.7
United Kingdom	25,966	27,297	28,203	28,588	30,154	31,058	31,327.4	57,590.8	941.2
Eastern Europe									
Albania									
Belarus	805,763	1,341,039	1,624,636	2,055,939	2,476,401	2,973,534	3,866,978.1	1,810.0	186.8
Bosnia-Herzegovina	718	814	884	991	1,074	1,195	1,288.6	965.1	251.1
Bulgaria	732	903	1,057	1,163	1,418	1,636	1,939.6	1,450.6	191.6
Croatia	3,472	3,993	4,152	4,338	4,241	4,477	4,611.5	934.4	210.7
Czech Republic	105,265	110,213	113,278	115,640	122,712	130,649	140,208.9	8,212.9	796.1
Estonia	5,382	5,716	7,092	8,005	9,474	11,106	11,606.7	1,085.3	812.9
Georgia	245	282	354	376	550	602	694.9	466.2	106.4
Hungary	791,470	878,784	914,285	967,118	1,010,811	1,075,520	1,118,307.9	6,497.5	647.2
Latvia	268	292	325	362	448	554	561.8	1,168.5	515.5
Lithuania	2,624	2,813	2,902	3,096	3,393	3,911	4,371.2	1,854.5	550.9
Macedonia	7,417	7,360	6,918	7,522	8,374	9,127	10,319.8	246.5	120.8
Moldova									
Poland	35,362	36,038	38,763	40,798	43,308	46,336	50,682.1	21,036.6	552.9
Romania	4,263	5,959	8,008	9,885	11,721	13,577	15,990.6	6,348.3	295.3
Russia	167,174	202,712	243,129	277,081	340,228	372,717	399,849.6	16,088.7	113.3
Slovakia	810	924	1,015	1,069	1,208	1,412	1,627.7	2,395.5	444.1
Slovenia	652	689	674	685	712	759	809.0	1,190.6	590.4
Ukraine	8,036	9,777	12,080	16,447	20,294	26,870	36,980.7	7,020.9	152.0

Source: National statistical offices/OECD/Eurostat/Euromonitor International

Consumer Expenditure Statistics

Table 5.5

Consumer Expenditure on Clothing and Footwear 1990-2008
Million units of national currency / as stated

	1990	1995	1996	1997	1998	1999	2000	2001
Western Europe								
Austria	7,822	7,584	7,682	7,741	7,855	7,807	8,024	8,321
Belgium	6,460	6,700	6,926	6,777	6,899	6,923	7,208	7,321
Cyprus								
Denmark	22,196	26,312	26,960	28,831	29,972	29,678	30,349	30,957
Finland	2,438	2,218	2,543	2,725	2,851	2,848	2,852	2,999
France	39,505	38,755	38,977	39,648	40,278	40,798	42,345	42,559
Germany	64,569	67,310	68,230	68,070	67,820	68,140	69,530	71,840
Gibraltar								
Greece	4,177	7,925	8,883	9,595	10,396	10,880	11,370	12,048
Iceland								
Ireland	1,493	2,006	2,185	2,407	2,704	2,905	3,377	3,535
Italy	40,269	51,453	52,939	55,979	60,168	62,001	64,471	66,331
Liechtenstein								
Luxembourg								
Malta								
Monaco								
Netherlands	9,252	9,748	10,000	10,468	11,407	12,050	12,659	13,334
Norway	23,440	27,830	28,665	30,488	31,701	33,511	34,834	37,013
Portugal	3,246	4,718	4,949	5,264	5,689	5,801	6,079	6,414
Spain	13,677	18,538	19,501	20,475	21,764	23,599	24,643	26,097
Sweden	42,098	45,874	45,776	46,849	49,212	53,181	56,325	59,283
Switzerland	11,344	10,403	10,183	10,382	10,474	10,677	10,691	10,968
Turkey	18	354	644	1,267	2,996	4,574	7,533	10,468
United Kingdom	21,259	28,000	29,535	30,901	31,947	33,375	35,479	36,822
Eastern Europe								
Albania								
Belarus	0	5,374	9,225	14,119	35,442	179,333	440,577	930,484
Bosnia-Herzegovina			304	390	471	536	639	651
Bulgaria	2	40	85	648	811	841	711	840
Croatia	4	2,397	2,747	3,528	4,028	4,656	7,085	7,132
Czech Republic	17,925	40,762	45,566	51,166	55,369	57,915	61,899	65,572
Estonia		1,544	2,072	2,578	2,879	2,737	3,751	4,266
Georgia		235	276	288	305	322	364	321
Hungary	85,483	157,941	183,083	222,732	261,111	298,878	330,680	376,745
Latvia	2	106	138	180	219	224	241	238
Lithuania		896	1,363	1,537	1,791	1,823	1,834	1,960
Macedonia		8,336	8,817	9,341	9,624	9,708	11,592	10,640
Moldova								
Poland	1,812	11,802	15,024	18,037	19,734	21,334	24,308	24,847
Romania	3	221	327	784	1,141	1,555	2,027	2,771
Russia	73	102,515	151,708	194,153	240,099	407,648	488,593	568,830
Slovakia		586	666	730	712	637	645	600
Slovenia	185	616	607	641	707	742	784	844
Ukraine	0	3,643	7,209	8,467	9,486	11,478	13,798	16,286

Source: National statistical offices/OECD/Eurostat/Euromonitor International

Consumer Expenditure Statistics

Consumer Expenditure on Clothing and Footwear 1990-2008 *(continued)*
Million units of national currency / as stated

	2002	2003	2004	2005	2006	2007	2008	Total US$ million 2008	US$ per capita 2008
Western Europe									
Austria	8,473	8,374	8,596	9,004	9,187	9,368	9,547.2	14,050.8	1,682.4
Belgium	7,544	7,630	7,855	8,196	8,537	8,798	9,188.6	13,523.1	1,273.5
Cyprus									
Denmark	31,559	32,360	33,795	35,048	36,845	37,864	38,412.0	7,534.5	1,379.6
Finland	3,172	3,386	3,575	3,760	4,012	4,210	4,421.7	6,507.5	1,227.7
France	44,195	45,472	46,228	46,607	48,714	50,013	51,023.9	75,092.8	1,209.1
Germany	68,260	66,487	66,888	67,674	68,762	68,280	68,537.4	100,867.7	1,226.8
Gibraltar									
Greece	12,810	13,308	13,782	14,491	15,605	16,288	16,980.5	24,990.5	2,229.0
Iceland									
Ireland	3,485	3,280	3,188	3,431	3,473	3,654	3,583.1	5,273.3	1,204.4
Italy	67,289	68,057	68,131	66,454	66,414	67,236	67,015.0	98,627.1	1,672.3
Liechtenstein									
Luxembourg									
Malta									
Monaco									
Netherlands	13,569	12,989	12,822	13,338	13,177	13,393	13,581.6	19,988.3	1,220.1
Norway	37,938	39,019	42,168	44,852	47,648	50,538	52,925.6	9,384.0	1,980.9
Portugal	6,815	6,703	6,798	6,906	7,073	7,252	7,417.6	10,916.6	1,025.7
Spain	26,555	26,781	27,974	28,973	29,846	30,926	31,102.9	45,774.7	1,015.9
Sweden	59,632	61,454	64,433	68,403	71,307	74,526	76,663.5	11,631.4	1,270.2
Switzerland	10,611	10,321	10,313	10,699	10,830	11,045	11,278.8	10,413.5	1,382.9
Turkey	14,981	20,285	26,032	28,108	30,725	34,490	37,779.8	29,027.0	390.4
United Kingdom	39,092	41,155	42,951	43,991	45,141	46,626	47,363.3	87,070.3	1,423.0
Eastern Europe									
Albania									
Belarus	1,460,374	1,737,666	2,133,872	2,700,365	3,252,619	4,120,414	5,506,620.5	2,577.5	266.0
Bosnia-Herzegovina	682	725	720	903	823	877	911.6	682.7	177.6
Bulgaria	853	873	916	1,015	1,143	1,252	1,431.5	1,070.6	141.4
Croatia	7,735	7,930	8,243	8,369	9,248	10,029	10,703.9	2,169.0	489.1
Czech Republic	67,492	68,392	70,834	72,306	76,012	81,032	87,228.4	5,109.5	495.3
Estonia	4,818	5,130	5,909	7,232	8,744	10,229	10,714.1	1,001.8	750.4
Georgia	334	371	422	427	550	551	610.1	409.3	93.4
Hungary	415,029	440,821	448,348	464,782	489,539	507,680	516,987.2	3,003.8	299.2
Latvia	266	278	312	386	487	608	608.3	1,265.1	558.1
Lithuania	2,044	2,186	2,695	3,062	3,473	4,173	4,819.1	2,044.5	607.3
Macedonia	12,009	11,976	12,291	13,367	13,958	15,351	17,520.8	418.5	205.1
Moldova									
Poland	25,851	26,231	28,226	28,446	30,157	31,950	34,579.5	14,352.9	377.3
Romania	3,659	4,685	6,024	7,061	8,303	9,390	10,790.4	4,283.9	199.3
Russia	705,265	798,177	940,100	1,098,062	1,373,513	1,615,107	1,928,206.4	77,584.8	546.3
Slovakia	633	605	632	910	1,071	1,235	1,411.5	2,077.4	385.2
Slovenia	887	936	953	994	1,043	1,143	1,241.0	1,826.3	905.7
Ukraine	18,347	21,044	27,138	38,507	49,253	65,105	89,329.1	16,959.4	367.1

Source: National statistical offices/OECD/Eurostat/Euromonitor International

Consumer Expenditure Statistics

Table 5.6

Consumer Expenditure on Housing 1990-2008
Million units of national currency / as stated

	1990	1995	1996	1997	1998	1999	2000	2001
Western Europe								
Austria	13,163	18,022	19,269	19,757	20,302	20,745	21,694	22,674
Belgium	19,578	24,667	26,120	26,944	27,229	27,543	29,633	30,981
Cyprus								
Denmark	109,404	135,538	142,029	145,944	151,319	155,216	162,042	170,925
Finland	7,870	11,839	12,504	13,486	14,127	14,655	15,319	16,221
France	116,929	153,127	160,758	164,368	170,987	176,488	183,170	190,772
Germany	144,046	227,650	239,330	248,030	251,550	257,270	266,460	279,250
Gibraltar								
Greece	5,549	12,661	14,212	15,360	16,526	15,892	16,730	17,809
Iceland								
Ireland	3,188	4,340	4,854	5,686	6,670	7,585	8,940	10,206
Italy	64,579	103,294	108,461	113,158	119,081	126,915	134,173	140,107
Liechtenstein								
Luxembourg								
Malta								
Monaco								
Netherlands	22,485	32,280	34,848	36,153	37,889	39,886	42,520	45,818
Norway	83,121	98,477	103,004	105,903	107,640	111,137	118,650	130,446
Portugal	5,051	7,542	8,005	8,516	8,992	9,524	10,096	10,752
Spain	27,919	40,084	42,952	45,567	48,263	51,273	60,945	65,590
Sweden	217,271	273,151	287,133	293,657	294,409	294,731	299,323	310,387
Switzerland	38,321	50,327	52,394	52,879	53,412	54,684	56,685	59,294
Turkey	59	1,261	2,461	5,063	11,594	17,843	31,087	42,448
United Kingdom	58,588	83,126	87,700	91,977	98,114	103,193	108,050	115,905
Eastern Europe								
Albania								
Belarus	0	6,373	11,620	17,393	32,844	89,003	290,529	713,836
Bosnia-Herzegovina			698	909	1,117	1,303	1,597	1,681
Bulgaria	9	172	361	3,117	4,131	4,745	4,611	5,085
Croatia	48	19,122	20,115	23,865	25,164	28,539	29,383	31,237
Czech Republic	64,563	157,156	177,601	196,198	217,733	228,315	247,479	261,819
Estonia		5,209	8,121	10,303	12,439	13,295	12,340	13,801
Georgia		219	289	362	334	341	455	450
Hungary	141,926	584,968	750,823	912,618	1,055,279	1,220,689	1,390,651	1,532,670
Latvia	19	337	418	473	516	560	619	707
Lithuania		3,612	4,204	4,730	4,889	4,912	5,090	5,071
Macedonia		26,436	28,061	29,839	30,916	31,347	37,558	34,979
Moldova								
Poland	4,935	42,500	53,703	70,544	82,430	94,535	97,182	110,440
Romania	8	837	1,351	3,504	5,389	8,401	12,508	17,624
Russia	16	43,345	60,199	69,355	79,130	135,340	189,836	296,963
Slovakia		1,495	1,684	1,923	2,085	2,276	2,790	3,058
Slovenia	617	1,836	1,953	2,097	2,242	2,394	2,515	2,659
Ukraine	0	2,579	5,105	5,995	6,717	8,128	9,770	11,532

Source: *National statistical offices/OECD/Eurostat/Euromonitor International*

Consumer Expenditure Statistics

Consumer Expenditure on Housing 1990-2008 *(continued)*

Million units of national currency / as stated

	2002	2003	2004	2005	2006	2007	2008	Total US$ million 2008	US$ per capita 2008
Western Europe									
Austria	23,078	23,960	25,224	28,229	30,193	31,667	33,255.2	48,942.3	5,860.1
Belgium	31,550	32,546	33,635	35,291	37,117	39,023	41,288.0	60,764.3	5,722.5
Cyprus									
Denmark	176,350	180,638	188,521	194,376	203,834	212,832	219,835.6	43,120.8	7,895.4
Finland	17,239	18,324	19,019	19,710	20,780	21,913	23,247.6	34,213.9	6,454.9
France	197,783	209,182	221,049	236,783	247,596	260,015	271,305.8	399,285.5	6,429.1
Germany	281,560	289,841	295,274	306,071	316,775	322,824	332,857.3	489,871.9	5,958.2
Gibraltar									
Greece	19,354	20,549	21,579	23,044	24,902	25,989	27,113.4	39,903.2	3,559.1
Iceland									
Ireland	11,489	12,675	13,288	14,332	15,718	17,409	17,995.1	26,483.6	6,048.8
Italy	147,176	156,071	166,637	176,709	188,456	198,081	206,337.5	303,670.5	5,149.1
Liechtenstein									
Luxembourg									
Malta									
Monaco									
Netherlands	47,359	49,927	51,696	54,764	57,085	59,201	61,659.1	90,744.7	5,538.9
Norway	139,632	149,237	153,377	161,324	171,437	182,584	192,559.6	34,141.8	7,207.2
Portugal	11,511	12,331	13,074	13,861	14,476	15,199	15,997.8	23,544.3	2,212.3
Spain	70,347	76,035	81,608	88,815	96,039	103,697	109,220.5	160,741.8	3,567.6
Sweden	325,605	343,223	352,263	362,630	374,870	386,168	392,935.6	59,616.1	6,510.4
Switzerland	60,027	60,659	62,234	64,815	67,109	69,940	73,147.9	67,536.3	8,968.9
Turkey	65,285	91,840	107,789	117,342	142,136	157,487	174,036.4	133,715.7	1,798.3
United Kingdom	121,238	129,051	138,544	148,103	160,188	169,492	175,553.3	322,728.5	5,274.5
Eastern Europe									
Albania									
Belarus	1,372,582	2,466,318	3,321,916	4,203,809	5,063,532	6,336,197	8,649,996.1	4,048.9	417.8
Bosnia-Herzegovina	1,843	2,059	2,224	2,324	2,541	2,778	2,939.1	2,201.3	572.7
Bulgaria	5,348	5,627	5,858	6,333	7,132	7,735	8,759.5	6,551.0	865.2
Croatia	33,643	34,095	35,370	39,306	42,014	46,293	50,402.9	10,213.3	2,302.9
Czech Republic	280,439	298,096	316,531	328,876	352,081	383,281	421,127.4	24,668.2	2,391.1
Estonia	14,959	15,976	17,409	19,064	22,037	26,212	26,394.2	2,468.0	1,848.5
Georgia	538	555	633	748	1,091	1,312	1,582.7	1,061.7	242.3
Hungary	1,728,537	1,967,814	2,185,355	2,351,107	2,472,975	2,624,976	2,747,257.0	15,961.9	1,590.0
Latvia	758	836	972	1,117	1,398	1,768	1,818.1	3,781.3	1,668.2
Lithuania	5,481	5,574	5,927	6,474	7,039	8,313	9,547.0	4,050.4	1,203.2
Macedonia	39,513	39,064	43,102	43,400	42,093	45,889	50,905.3	1,215.9	596.0
Moldova									
Poland	123,580	127,634	135,405	146,777	155,815	169,456	186,787.0	77,529.4	2,037.8
Romania	24,341	29,143	38,838	46,056	54,544	65,055	78,826.3	31,294.4	1,455.8
Russia	454,504	665,147	875,265	1,159,635	1,524,726	1,801,466	2,149,928.7	86,506.1	609.2
Slovakia	3,368	4,226	5,166	5,875	6,742	8,212	9,966.9	14,668.4	2,719.6
Slovenia	2,785	2,855	2,972	3,079	3,214	3,499	3,784.6	5,569.9	2,762.2
Ukraine	12,991	14,753	16,395	23,263	29,756	38,657	52,027.1	9,877.5	213.8

Source: National statistical offices/OECD/Eurostat/Euromonitor International

Consumer Expenditure Statistics

Table 5.7

Consumer Expenditure on Household Goods and Services 1990-2008

Million units of national currency / as stated

	1990	1995	1996	1997	1998	1999	2000	2001
Western Europe								
Austria	7,815	9,194	9,609	9,580	9,431	9,604	9,918	9,759
Belgium	5,667	6,524	6,315	6,700	6,641	6,715	6,736	7,131
Cyprus								
Denmark	24,534	29,896	30,357	32,413	33,703	34,570	35,138	36,040
Finland	2,335	2,132	2,289	2,500	2,769	2,772	3,006	3,214
France	39,037	41,034	42,119	43,002	44,660	46,193	48,418	49,609
Germany	66,001	83,960	84,210	85,800	87,600	86,750	90,530	91,030
Gibraltar								
Greece	2,437	4,611	5,026	5,423	5,931	6,297	6,859	7,201
Iceland								
Ireland	1,552	1,946	2,236	2,457	2,753	3,203	3,620	3,983
Italy	37,507	49,131	50,844	52,853	55,642	58,684	60,003	60,698
Liechtenstein								
Luxembourg								
Malta								
Monaco								
Netherlands	9,825	10,669	11,228	11,953	13,305	14,223	15,354	16,389
Norway	21,828	27,969	29,757	32,260	33,911	34,905	38,845	40,535
Portugal	2,628	3,951	4,321	4,684	5,211	5,509	5,902	6,015
Spain	12,480	16,956	17,588	18,580	20,253	22,000	23,013	23,958
Sweden	33,970	39,297	38,772	40,970	43,263	47,199	51,130	53,166
Switzerland	11,509	11,053	10,867	10,839	11,085	11,452	11,727	11,956
Turkey	33	506	927	1,770	3,797	5,551	8,681	11,436
United Kingdom	19,936	26,287	27,758	29,492	31,002	32,846	35,675	37,974
Eastern Europe								
Albania								
Belarus	0	2,524	4,174	7,237	15,982	69,014	168,869	388,968
Bosnia-Herzegovina			301	394	487	572	707	752
Bulgaria	1	16	35	272	402	513	678	759
Croatia	9	3,274	3,397	3,951	4,052	3,668	3,454	4,406
Czech Republic	19,513	46,526	55,049	59,485	64,686	66,433	70,998	70,653
Estonia		1,263	1,885	2,118	2,196	2,253	2,823	3,099
Georgia		129	144	147	148	142	213	197
Hungary	94,558	219,931	249,452	300,984	368,873	420,311	487,631	551,583
Latvia	1	44	55	64	66	81	91	98
Lithuania		603	825	1,204	1,302	1,313	1,279	1,612
Macedonia		3,928	4,225	4,573	4,825	5,004	6,233	5,926
Moldova								
Poland	1,221	9,391	12,606	15,825	18,106	19,976	20,757	21,561
Romania	4	260	381	897	1,323	1,706	2,305	3,090
Russia	17	24,769	31,727	35,493	43,033	86,338	149,379	255,137
Slovakia		412	448	507	571	541	576	704
Slovenia	144	565	563	599	637	704	748	805
Ukraine	0	665	1,317	1,546	1,732	2,096	2,520	2,974

Source: National statistical offices/OECD/Eurostat/Euromonitor International

Consumer Expenditure Statistics

Consumer Expenditure on Household Goods and Services 1990-2008 *(continued)*

Million units of national currency / as stated

	2002	2003	2004	2005	2006	2007	2008	Total US$ million 2008	US$ per capita 2008
Western Europe									
Austria	9,382	9,454	9,728	9,987	10,194	10,269	10,361.2	15,248.7	1,825.8
Belgium	7,359	7,661	7,910	8,253	8,688	9,076	9,459.5	13,921.7	1,311.1
Cyprus									
Denmark	37,711	38,889	41,590	44,167	47,265	49,289	50,822.0	9,968.7	1,825.3
Finland	3,341	3,617	3,938	4,253	4,648	5,005	5,295.4	7,793.3	1,470.3
France	51,525	53,331	54,999	55,689	58,212	60,409	62,216.5	91,565.1	1,474.3
Germany	87,450	86,281	86,970	87,750	89,126	88,778	89,177.7	131,244.4	1,596.3
Gibraltar									
Greece	7,920	8,307	8,768	9,343	10,154	10,766	11,410.6	16,793.1	1,497.9
Iceland									
Ireland	4,177	4,454	4,623	4,956	5,346	5,795	5,877.7	8,650.3	1,975.7
Italy	61,467	62,229	64,465	65,639	67,324	68,687	69,220.9	101,873.6	1,727.4
Liechtenstein									
Luxembourg									
Malta									
Monaco									
Netherlands	16,343	15,992	15,409	15,382	14,971	15,363	15,706.6	23,115.6	1,410.9
Norway	42,407	43,890	46,853	49,415	52,844	56,342	59,275.6	10,509.9	2,218.6
Portugal	6,293	6,311	6,443	6,659	6,742	6,964	7,159.0	10,536.1	990.0
Spain	24,453	26,084	26,996	28,428	29,909	31,335	31,814.4	46,821.7	1,039.2
Sweden	55,895	58,496	61,844	67,368	71,431	75,404	77,991.9	11,832.9	1,292.2
Switzerland	11,902	11,919	12,121	12,352	12,621	13,028	13,462.9	12,430.1	1,650.7
Turkey	17,411	18,591	26,455	30,695	32,435	35,798	39,286.2	30,184.4	405.9
United Kingdom	40,448	42,466	43,627	44,564	45,631	46,512	46,342.6	85,193.9	1,392.4
Eastern Europe									
Albania									
Belarus	732,465	888,400	1,184,118	1,498,474	1,804,928	2,303,846	3,159,013.9	1,478.7	152.6
Bosnia-Herzegovina	832	947	1,029	1,124	1,195	1,314	1,396.8	1,046.1	272.2
Bulgaria	764	846	1,044	1,250	1,533	1,829	2,236.6	1,672.7	220.9
Croatia	4,818	5,108	5,470	5,522	5,915	6,400	6,749.2	1,367.6	308.4
Czech Republic	69,077	73,938	75,919	76,211	79,681	83,994	89,243.4	5,227.6	506.7
Estonia	3,505	4,149	4,808	5,612	6,659	7,476	7,936.6	742.1	555.8
Georgia	203	210	265	280	377	444	527.8	354.0	80.8
Hungary	632,567	711,383	831,214	912,950	961,441	1,029,208	1,080,329.9	6,276.9	625.3
Latvia	108	132	157	186	239	310	328.5	683.2	301.4
Lithuania	1,723	1,875	2,144	2,493	2,933	3,557	4,185.6	1,775.8	527.5
Macedonia	6,990	7,696	8,028	9,396	13,045	15,235	18,415.6	439.9	215.6
Moldova									
Poland	23,653	23,742	25,406	26,892	28,618	30,811	33,666.5	13,973.9	367.3
Romania	3,831	5,950	7,980	9,771	12,174	14,202	16,867.4	6,696.4	311.5
Russia	344,796	462,436	559,197	738,883	919,876	1,133,681	1,463,515.4	58,887.1	414.7
Slovakia	772	744	923	1,125	1,314	1,606	1,929.1	2,839.1	526.4
Slovenia	863	898	927	971	1,025	1,129	1,238.8	1,823.1	904.1
Ukraine	3,351	4,560	6,502	9,225	11,800	16,107	22,901.2	4,347.9	94.1

Source: *National statistical offices/OECD/Eurostat/Euromonitor International*

Consumer Expenditure Statistics **Table 5.8**

Consumer Expenditure on Health Goods and Medical Services 1990-2008
Million units of national currency / as stated

	1990	1995	1996	1997	1998	1999	2000	2001
Western Europe								
Austria	2,231	3,231	3,295	3,302	3,535	3,608	3,691	3,820
Belgium	2,506	3,688	3,670	4,249	4,581	4,980	5,295	5,308
Cyprus								
Denmark	10,010	12,226	12,936	13,847	14,359	14,790	15,315	16,170
Finland	1,277	1,631	1,827	1,962	2,046	2,140	2,367	2,530
France	16,965	22,245	22,871	23,154	23,689	24,466	25,257	26,643
Germany	21,066	38,820	38,990	43,030	42,780	45,540	47,370	49,470
Gibraltar								
Greece	1,512	4,051	4,316	4,717	5,140	5,395	5,635	6,179
Iceland								
Ireland	600	837	893	968	1,041	1,155	1,302	1,571
Italy	9,553	18,960	20,384	21,956	23,280	23,735	24,373	23,622
Liechtenstein								
Luxembourg								
Malta								
Monaco								
Netherlands	5,553	6,237	7,374	7,453	7,916	8,497	8,852	9,897
Norway	8,405	11,521	12,548	13,445	14,418	15,396	16,822	18,090
Portugal	1,086	2,750	2,809	3,036	3,111	3,424	3,731	3,992
Spain	6,467	8,989	9,504	9,983	10,754	11,714	12,941	14,047
Sweden	13,659	18,607	18,773	21,064	22,629	23,838	25,888	28,294
Switzerland	19,451	27,260	28,825	29,788	31,379	32,416	33,962	35,733
Turkey	6	114	220	446	1,011	1,547	2,634	3,584
United Kingdom	4,432	7,000	7,432	7,757	8,306	8,775	9,208	9,976
Eastern Europe								
Albania								
Belarus	0	1,574	1,838	2,202	5,812	25,471	81,523	216,440
Bosnia-Herzegovina			131	175	221	266	337	370
Bulgaria	1	15	32	253	260	397	546	722
Croatia	2	779	824	986	1,074	1,139	1,473	1,573
Czech Republic	5,280	12,725	14,906	16,889	18,024	17,709	16,303	22,340
Estonia		323	495	579	651	831	1,658	1,928
Georgia		91	124	161	131	173	294	303
Hungary	19,142	86,301	106,089	133,307	160,400	204,740	243,834	297,630
Latvia	1	59	72	93	94	105	125	148
Lithuania		460	603	757	989	1,018	1,036	1,070
Macedonia		3,786	3,963	4,145	4,206	4,155	4,834	4,318
Moldova								
Poland	622	6,354	8,667	11,513	14,219	16,641	16,873	18,732
Romania	1	112	176	448	694	976	1,323	1,933
Russia	9	19,781	32,452	45,876	59,444	98,584	102,114	87,834
Slovakia		180	199	196	193	208	237	307
Slovenia	25	217	246	280	304	330	378	415
Ukraine	0	1,174	2,323	2,729	3,057	3,699	4,447	5,249

Source: National statistical offices/OECD/Eurostat/Euromonitor International

Consumer Expenditure Statistics

Consumer Expenditure on Health Goods and Medical Services 1990-2008 *(continued)*

Million units of national currency / as stated

	2002	2003	2004	2005	2006	2007	2008	Total US$ million 2008	US$ per capita 2008
Western Europe									
Austria	3,905	4,069	4,174	4,353	4,513	4,675	4,819.2	7,092.5	849.2
Belgium	5,891	6,124	6,092	6,520	6,837	7,318	7,842.3	11,541.6	1,086.9
Cyprus									
Denmark	16,768	17,086	18,036	18,900	19,968	20,798	21,423.2	4,202.2	769.4
Finland	2,757	2,898	3,076	3,282	3,508	3,761	4,025.8	5,924.8	1,117.8
France	27,928	29,154	31,429	33,787	35,331	37,160	38,909.4	57,263.6	922.0
Germany	52,780	53,889	55,876	57,350	59,586	61,285	63,973.4	94,150.8	1,145.1
Gibraltar									
Greece	6,980	7,652	8,225	9,059	9,849	10,570	11,358.3	16,716.2	1,491.0
Iceland									
Ireland	1,842	2,150	2,375	2,626	3,011	3,382	3,548.1	5,221.8	1,192.6
Italy	25,155	25,981	26,580	26,903	27,607	28,132	28,289.5	41,634.1	706.0
Liechtenstein									
Luxembourg									
Malta									
Monaco									
Netherlands	11,104	11,726	12,834	13,083	13,729	14,273	14,883.5	21,904.3	1,337.0
Norway	19,328	20,824	22,525	23,617	25,606	27,759	29,683.1	5,263.0	1,111.0
Portugal	4,229	4,725	5,084	5,390	5,745	6,076	6,455.7	9,501.0	892.7
Spain	14,969	16,433	17,792	19,479	21,277	22,994	24,197.1	35,611.3	790.4
Sweden	30,332	31,996	33,757	34,997	36,573	38,788	40,453.7	6,137.6	670.3
Switzerland	36,396	37,740	39,672	41,449	43,682	45,799	47,996.0	44,313.9	5,884.9
Turkey	5,557	7,232	8,942	10,136	11,411	12,632	13,963.5	10,728.4	144.3
United Kingdom	10,778	11,335	12,073	12,371	12,783	13,492	14,046.1	25,821.7	422.0
Eastern Europe									
Albania									
Belarus	358,727	454,398	587,254	743,156	895,140	1,185,057	1,654,716.2	774.5	79.9
Bosnia-Herzegovina	424	501	572	651	749	863	961.7	720.3	187.4
Bulgaria	914	1,004	1,113	1,259	1,482	1,681	1,980.0	1,480.8	195.6
Croatia	1,945	2,014	2,449	2,488	2,894	3,307	3,628.7	735.3	165.8
Czech Republic	21,209	22,706	26,049	29,105	31,950	35,187	39,330.2	2,303.8	223.3
Estonia	2,159	2,541	2,729	2,777	3,607	4,217	4,341.9	406.0	304.1
Georgia	363	383	445	559	855	998	1,210.3	811.9	185.3
Hungary	347,604	387,896	417,873	459,386	484,859	531,887	574,866.7	3,340.1	332.7
Latvia	162	179	224	302	398	506	529.0	1,100.1	485.3
Lithuania	1,541	1,618	1,720	2,338	2,835	3,409	3,972.2	1,685.2	500.6
Macedonia	4,622	4,371	4,306	3,798	3,754	3,787	3,914.7	93.5	45.8
Moldova									
Poland	20,746	21,477	24,858	24,731	26,295	28,574	31,519.1	13,082.6	343.9
Romania	2,907	3,910	5,300	6,434	7,776	9,391	11,298.6	4,485.6	208.7
Russia	120,156	139,364	194,503	256,556	378,031	481,426	612,384.0	24,640.3	173.5
Slovakia	309	341	516	534	643	810	1,021.0	1,502.6	278.6
Slovenia	452	480	489	518	551	617	688.0	1,012.5	502.1
Ukraine	5,913	6,384	7,915	11,231	14,365	18,782	25,458.1	4,833.3	104.6

Source: National statistical offices/OECD/Eurostat/Euromonitor International

Consumer Expenditure Statistics

Table 5.9

Consumer Expenditure on Transport 1990-2008

Million units of national currency / as stated

	1990	1995	1996	1997	1998	1999	2000	2001
Western Europe								
Austria	9,867	11,485	12,437	12,400	12,865	13,302	14,160	14,391
Belgium	12,993	14,120	14,790	15,227	16,331	17,326	18,833	19,011
Cyprus								
Denmark	48,453	68,181	72,710	76,220	77,892	78,062	73,916	71,524
Finland	6,294	5,895	6,463	6,888	7,464	7,558	8,046	7,881
France	89,625	97,908	103,038	100,219	106,273	113,592	120,484	123,849
Germany	125,841	137,050	145,740	146,330	150,050	156,210	157,680	162,580
Gibraltar								
Greece	3,642	6,437	6,933	7,636	8,227	9,066	8,754	9,289
Iceland								
Ireland	2,492	3,096	3,425	3,949	4,339	4,851	5,960	5,577
Italy	50,489	72,343	76,573	86,454	91,249	94,441	99,957	101,250
Liechtenstein								
Luxembourg								
Malta								
Monaco								
Netherlands	15,049	17,304	18,045	19,084	20,269	22,467	23,990	24,471
Norway	46,002	64,066	75,529	78,865	82,527	84,451	93,543	93,047
Portugal	4,883	7,924	8,557	9,314	10,379	11,645	12,592	12,441
Spain	18,753	31,569	34,467	38,277	42,137	47,414	49,471	51,346
Sweden	79,206	107,670	111,622	120,832	126,225	137,732	146,689	144,539
Switzerland	14,861	16,952	17,239	17,900	18,306	19,298	20,287	20,644
Turkey	2	147	345	779	1,964	3,615	6,568	11,941
United Kingdom	51,852	64,087	70,380	77,204	82,506	87,237	93,052	96,435
Eastern Europe								
Albania								
Belarus	0	4,351	6,456	12,920	25,693	101,886	318,085	619,768
Bosnia-Herzegovina			284	377	474	567	716	780
Bulgaria	4	74	156	1,411	1,584	1,953	2,613	3,154
Croatia	20	7,127	7,328	8,398	8,619	6,847	8,582	8,974
Czech Republic	33,094	81,985	99,621	107,817	114,686	118,326	129,855	132,652
Estonia		2,026	3,775	4,433	4,926	5,097	5,879	6,827
Georgia		151	206	266	222	262	360	334
Hungary	134,614	384,722	480,499	579,964	705,808	905,263	1,108,818	1,235,553
Latvia	2	129	173	244	264	256	265	294
Lithuania		1,351	1,861	2,428	3,249	3,647	4,244	4,615
Macedonia		8,837	9,463	10,184	10,743	11,126	13,753	13,471
Moldova								
Poland	1,588	15,673	23,188	28,026	34,691	42,064	43,477	45,835
Romania	9	656	988	2,388	3,506	4,688	6,367	9,083
Russia	14	47,473	70,018	85,630	101,482	172,116	230,552	322,058
Slovakia		682	740	824	923	958	1,080	1,316
Slovenia	446	1,701	1,765	1,841	1,858	2,004	1,984	2,010
Ukraine	0	1,174	2,323	2,729	3,057	3,699	4,447	5,249

Source: *National statistical offices/OECD/Eurostat/Euromonitor International*

Consumer Expenditure Statistics

Consumer Expenditure on Transport 1990-2008 *(continued)*

Million units of national currency / as stated

	2002	2003	2004	2005	2006	2007	2008	Total US$ million 2008	US$ per capita 2008
Western Europe									
Austria	14,821	15,265	16,554	17,035	17,845	18,590	19,355.3	28,485.5	3,410.7
Belgium	19,321	20,024	21,489	22,816	24,436	25,610	26,825.7	39,479.9	3,718.1
Cyprus									
Denmark	76,537	73,596	87,947	102,031	114,441	118,802	122,115.6	23,953.0	4,385.8
Finland	8,353	9,343	9,551	10,008	10,725	11,329	11,876.9	17,479.4	3,297.7
France	126,038	127,489	135,064	142,598	149,081	156,356	162,561.9	239,245.2	3,852.2
Germany	165,420	166,809	170,660	170,965	174,332	176,299	180,010.2	264,924.2	3,222.2
Gibraltar									
Greece	9,890	10,636	10,909	11,551	12,545	13,116	13,708.5	20,175.0	1,799.5
Iceland									
Ireland	5,886	6,245	6,821	7,737	8,634	9,332	9,456.5	13,917.3	3,178.7
Italy	103,266	107,208	111,506	116,298	121,408	125,210	127,669.6	187,893.5	3,186.0
Liechtenstein									
Luxembourg									
Malta									
Monaco									
Netherlands	26,096	26,379	27,113	28,010	28,482	29,413	30,385.4	44,718.7	2,729.6
Norway	96,009	98,087	108,926	113,587	120,165	128,397	135,475.5	24,020.5	5,070.6
Portugal	12,437	12,013	12,988	13,870	14,371	14,942	15,478.3	22,779.7	2,140.4
Spain	51,543	55,112	60,886	65,257	70,645	75,167	77,554.9	114,138.9	2,533.2
Sweden	149,035	153,434	158,599	169,936	176,886	184,266	188,978.2	28,671.7	3,131.1
Switzerland	20,330	20,107	20,696	21,666	22,340	23,242	24,228.3	22,369.6	2,970.7
Turkey	20,773	31,690	37,794	57,087	68,486	78,570	89,319.2	68,625.7	922.9
United Kingdom	100,147	104,569	108,849	114,773	118,862	124,052	130,459.6	239,830.5	3,919.7
Eastern Europe									
Albania									
Belarus	1,031,869	1,609,288	1,978,146	2,503,298	3,015,249	3,726,646	4,990,925.0	2,336.1	241.1
Bosnia-Herzegovina	890	1,044	1,186	1,334	1,532	1,758	1,950.0	1,460.4	379.9
Bulgaria	3,616	4,021	4,526	5,675	6,873	8,065	9,858.8	7,373.2	973.8
Croatia	9,665	10,896	12,121	11,789	13,191	14,465	15,348.8	3,110.2	701.3
Czech Republic	126,835	142,281	156,278	161,722	173,609	186,870	203,715.7	11,932.9	1,156.7
Estonia	7,566	9,043	10,434	12,046	14,384	16,869	17,726.8	1,657.6	1,241.5
Georgia	424	431	478	542	686	759	886.3	594.5	135.7
Hungary	1,411,024	1,620,329	1,743,154	1,875,134	1,970,780	2,145,874	2,297,260.3	13,347.4	1,329.6
Latvia	323	374	488	623	808	1,021	1,049.6	2,183.0	963.0
Lithuania	4,669	5,554	6,249	7,620	9,250	11,085	12,827.2	5,442.0	1,616.6
Macedonia	15,832	17,048	21,611	21,778	28,919	33,776	39,906.9	953.2	467.2
Moldova									
Poland	48,696	50,079	53,527	53,709	56,307	59,790	64,631.2	26,826.4	705.1
Romania	11,623	14,953	19,488	23,001	26,999	31,057	36,336.3	14,425.7	671.1
Russia	485,849	582,796	826,640	1,251,996	1,575,130	2,577,960	3,902,845.9	157,037.8	1,105.8
Slovakia	1,361	1,516	1,727	1,981	2,271	2,792	3,373.8	4,965.3	920.6
Slovenia	2,058	2,159	2,313	2,389	2,511	2,699	2,895.9	4,261.9	2,113.5
Ukraine	5,913	7,524	8,480	12,033	15,391	20,289	27,753.5	5,269.1	114.1

Source: *National statistical offices/OECD/Eurostat/Euromonitor International*

Consumer Expenditure Statistics   **Table 5.10**

Consumer Expenditure on Communications 1990-2008
Million units of national currency / as stated

	1990	1995	1996	1997	1998	1999	2000	2001
Western Europe								
Austria	1,482	1,850	1,972	2,237	2,473	2,652	2,957	2,979
Belgium	1,195	1,587	1,750	1,929	2,149	2,464	2,777	2,987
Cyprus								
Denmark	6,861	9,123	9,323	10,516	10,635	11,393	11,898	12,280
Finland	625	780	942	1,175	1,429	1,740	1,943	2,158
France	10,320	12,514	13,088	13,513	14,342	16,284	18,652	20,628
Germany	13,052	19,910	20,650	22,840	24,140	25,570	28,670	33,360
Gibraltar								
Greece	309	1,043	1,358	1,544	1,695	2,616	2,730	3,156
Iceland								
Ireland	333	511	603	691	732	846	1,130	1,330
Italy	6,315	10,443	11,697	13,239	15,163	17,223	19,281	20,597
Liechtenstein								
Luxembourg								
Malta								
Monaco								
Netherlands	1,975	3,356	4,157	4,792	5,836	6,889	8,103	9,223
Norway	7,247	8,329	9,247	9,626	11,451	14,645	16,279	17,637
Portugal	686	1,106	1,217	1,411	1,529	1,758	1,992	2,417
Spain	2,610	4,894	5,518	6,056	7,052	8,248	9,397	11,259
Sweden	12,172	19,624	22,549	25,030	28,337	30,796	31,021	35,302
Switzerland	3,528	4,664	4,781	4,905	5,039	5,145	5,288	5,639
Turkey	8	190	385	753	1,676	2,710	4,290	7,174
United Kingdom	6,510	9,067	9,359	9,984	10,902	12,005	13,356	14,157
Eastern Europe								
Albania								
Belarus	0	943	1,579	2,773	5,047	24,267	73,412	209,156
Bosnia-Herzegovina			84	115	148	181	233	259
Bulgaria	0	11	23	232	357	523	848	1,139
Croatia	0	480	632	929	1,206	1,325	1,942	2,716
Czech Republic	3,999	11,740	16,936	19,155	20,554	20,861	23,990	30,315
Estonia		401	660	813	979	1,188	1,719	2,013
Georgia		61	82	114	95	92	118	98
Hungary	6,340	61,867	95,676	133,953	183,975	252,603	312,089	389,307
Latvia	0	24	31	29	42	70	94	105
Lithuania		142	203	421	527	606	789	1,003
Macedonia		7,830	8,459	9,153	9,645	9,942	12,138	11,494
Moldova								
Poland	518	4,674	5,940	5,603	8,015	11,540	12,885	14,807
Romania	0	26	52	210	630	1,102	1,677	2,244
Russia	4	7,705	11,583	14,916	18,694	32,900	42,699	58,556
Slovakia		169	193	221	275	324	397	529
Slovenia	46	181	203	216	230	273	288	329
Ukraine	0	509	1,007	1,182	1,325	1,603	1,927	2,274

Source: *National statistical offices/OECD/Eurostat/Euromonitor International*

Consumer Expenditure Statistics

Consumer Expenditure on Communications 1990-2008 *(continued)*

Million units of national currency / as stated

	2002	2003	2004	2005	2006	2007	2008	Total US$ million 2008	US$ per capita 2008
Western Europe									
Austria	2,984	3,092	3,230	3,415	3,571	3,764	3,943.0	5,803.0	694.8
Belgium	3,106	3,181	3,465	3,505	3,699	4,038	4,405.6	6,483.7	610.6
Cyprus									
Denmark	12,283	12,810	14,065	15,428	16,902	17,823	18,662.7	3,660.7	670.3
Finland	2,267	2,331	2,452	2,192	2,190	2,368	2,514.1	3,700.1	698.1
France	22,706	24,380	25,393	26,798	28,020	30,505	32,888.7	48,402.9	779.4
Germany	33,310	34,306	34,654	35,327	36,104	37,706	39,766.8	58,525.5	711.8
Gibraltar									
Greece	3,523	3,442	3,636	3,920	4,238	4,729	5,303.0	7,804.5	696.1
Iceland									
Ireland	1,548	1,834	2,204	2,519	3,018	3,522	3,820.5	5,622.7	1,284.2
Italy	21,476	22,317	23,230	23,521	24,331	25,871	27,037.1	39,790.9	674.7
Liechtenstein									
Luxembourg									
Malta									
Monaco									
Netherlands	10,360	11,028	11,155	11,164	11,371	12,166	12,895.7	18,978.8	1,158.4
Norway	18,672	20,190	21,433	22,464	25,107	28,237	30,773.4	5,456.3	1,151.8
Portugal	2,550	2,600	2,748	2,766	2,783	2,952	3,134.2	4,612.6	433.4
Spain	12,160	12,233	13,642	14,731	15,727	17,394	18,616.2	27,397.8	608.1
Sweden	38,037	39,603	39,814	40,179	40,756	43,395	45,178.8	6,854.5	748.5
Switzerland	5,820	6,120	6,558	6,389	6,656	6,991	7,361.6	6,796.9	902.6
Turkey	10,816	13,946	17,883	19,555	21,873	24,616	27,759.9	21,328.5	286.8
United Kingdom	14,675	15,654	16,855	17,299	17,486	18,031	18,478.7	33,970.4	555.2
Eastern Europe									
Albania									
Belarus	443,309	696,764	989,951	1,252,760	1,508,963	1,939,821	2,677,092.3	1,253.1	129.3
Bosnia-Herzegovina	300	356	408	428	478	543	596.6	446.9	116.3
Bulgaria	1,387	1,546	1,695	1,929	2,276	2,581	3,046.5	2,278.4	300.9
Croatia	4,201	4,726	5,470	5,775	5,915	6,548	6,954.2	1,409.1	317.7
Czech Republic	38,167	46,199	49,790	54,606	59,312	68,801	81,394.2	4,767.8	462.1
Estonia	2,118	2,355	2,644	2,850	3,535	4,345	4,767.6	445.8	333.9
Georgia	149	185	205	232	294	325	379.8	254.8	58.1
Hungary	483,444	500,771	516,041	563,537	595,149	655,817	701,572.2	4,076.2	406.0
Latvia	129	165	205	253	365	464	479.5	997.2	439.9
Lithuania	1,106	1,170	1,206	1,232	1,593	2,037	2,501.3	1,061.2	315.2
Macedonia	13,241	13,538	14,972	15,937	17,278	19,475	22,467.3	536.6	263.1
Moldova									
Poland	15,958	16,927	18,411	20,780	21,780	23,841	26,636.1	11,055.8	290.6
Romania	2,736	3,105	3,933	4,345	5,009	6,013	7,334.8	2,911.9	135.5
Russia	94,035	152,034	235,025	379,704	504,042	590,135	702,182.6	28,253.5	199.0
Slovakia	567	641	732	830	962	1,234	1,545.5	2,274.5	421.7
Slovenia	388	411	471	529	588	682	792.4	1,166.2	578.3
Ukraine	2,562	3,420	5,088	7,220	9,235	12,643	17,675.8	3,355.8	72.6

Source: National statistical offices/OECD/Eurostat/Euromonitor International

Consumer Expenditure on Leisure and Recreation 1990-2008

Million units of national currency / as stated

	1990	1995	1996	1997	1998	1999	2000	2001
Western Europe								
Austria	8,715	10,763	11,251	11,450	12,287	13,147	13,727	14,117
Belgium	7,762	9,935	10,260	11,010	11,509	12,269	13,185	13,333
Cyprus								
Denmark	41,163	52,489	56,376	59,805	61,322	63,642	66,673	67,955
Finland	4,848	5,087	5,563	5,830	6,306	6,478	6,994	7,336
France	49,544	57,795	59,011	60,693	64,967	67,891	72,866	75,942
Germany	74,857	93,780	96,680	101,340	105,840	110,880	115,940	118,500
Gibraltar								
Greece	1,489	3,660	4,194	4,551	4,947	5,535	5,897	6,448
Iceland								
Ireland	1,776	2,145	2,417	2,510	2,732	2,827	3,607	4,037
Italy	30,696	40,101	43,100	45,395	47,902	50,260	53,397	54,379
Liechtenstein								
Luxembourg								
Malta								
Monaco								
Netherlands	14,142	16,722	17,821	19,134	20,812	22,804	24,576	26,043
Norway	29,590	51,714	57,403	61,885	66,897	73,416	78,541	83,416
Portugal	2,154	3,109	3,492	3,875	4,308	4,665	5,076	5,261
Spain	16,342	23,170	24,405	25,773	28,330	30,316	36,101	39,041
Sweden	70,609	90,816	93,370	99,960	108,064	118,305	126,972	132,713
Switzerland	17,079	19,642	19,768	20,023	20,314	20,798	21,292	21,657
Turkey	6	114	222	452	1,031	1,592	2,682	3,716
United Kingdom	35,494	49,274	53,575	58,012	63,246	67,481	70,154	73,452
Eastern Europe								
Albania								
Belarus	0	1,216	2,044	3,343	8,335	32,872	82,563	221,851
Bosnia-Herzegovina			107	148	192	239	313	355
Bulgaria	1	22	45	368	538	680	942	850
Croatia	5	2,265	2,455	2,999	3,300	3,564	4,714	4,567
Czech Republic	30,443	80,215	98,061	115,539	124,994	129,676	132,569	146,148
Estonia		1,247	2,225	2,887	3,368	3,503	4,646	5,309
Georgia		101	103	111	102	99	140	134
Hungary	95,107	244,761	292,213	345,941	402,421	464,576	555,127	637,834
Latvia	1	60	79	104	112	142	192	237
Lithuania		512	862	1,104	1,633	1,705	1,716	2,155
Macedonia		2,679	2,875	3,102	3,265	3,380	4,166	3,971
Moldova								
Poland	2,262	16,427	22,772	26,779	32,318	34,187	42,236	38,453
Romania	3	241	367	890	1,316	1,932	2,778	3,567
Russia	10	25,691	38,985	50,406	63,447	112,705	149,080	196,581
Slovakia		599	704	800	865	876	1,033	1,259
Slovenia	236	781	859	959	1,048	1,134	1,166	1,244
Ukraine	0	744	1,471	1,728	1,936	2,343	2,816	3,324

Source: *National statistical offices/OECD/Eurostat/Euromonitor International*

Consumer Expenditure Statistics

Consumer Expenditure on Leisure and Recreation 1990-2008 *(continued)*
Million units of national currency / as stated

	2002	2003	2004	2005	2006	2007	2008	Total US$ million 2008	US$ per capita 2008
Western Europe									
Austria	14,519	14,734	15,369	16,024	16,556	17,257	17,911.5	26,360.6	3,156.3
Belgium	12,892	13,099	13,614	14,281	14,973	15,722	16,551.2	24,358.6	2,294.0
Cyprus									
Denmark	69,640	72,394	75,664	78,179	82,487	86,179	88,740.0	17,406.4	3,187.1
Finland	7,566	7,929	8,426	8,855	9,408	9,972	10,496.9	15,448.4	2,914.5
France	80,075	82,862	86,401	88,758	92,787	97,114	100,934.3	148,546.7	2,391.8
Germany	116,430	115,846	117,724	119,766	122,644	124,251	126,856.4	186,696.7	2,270.8
Gibraltar									
Greece	7,183	7,654	8,174	8,887	9,708	10,445	11,257.5	16,567.8	1,477.8
Iceland									
Ireland	4,003	4,241	4,765	5,212	5,799	6,306	6,440.4	9,478.5	2,164.8
Italy	55,401	56,225	59,365	60,538	62,577	64,406	65,525.7	96,435.3	1,635.2
Liechtenstein									
Luxembourg									
Malta									
Monaco									
Netherlands	26,948	26,520	26,431	26,745	26,494	27,404	28,145.6	41,422.4	2,528.4
Norway	86,964	92,291	98,107	102,633	110,651	118,527	124,955.7	22,155.3	4,676.9
Portugal	5,607	5,685	6,117	6,485	6,930	7,298	7,670.7	11,289.2	1,060.7
Spain	40,931	43,979	47,181	50,854	54,698	59,106	62,053.7	91,325.5	2,026.9
Sweden	135,703	141,532	145,839	151,165	156,131	164,142	169,403.9	25,701.9	2,806.8
Switzerland	21,745	22,030	22,238	22,434	22,876	23,563	24,314.2	22,449.0	2,981.2
Turkey	5,890	7,135	9,838	11,521	11,380	12,609	13,942.4	10,712.2	144.1
United Kingdom	79,122	84,386	89,163	92,906	95,383	98,422	100,072.5	183,968.2	3,006.7
Eastern Europe									
Albania									
Belarus	355,931	620,358	904,596	1,144,746	1,378,858	1,723,411	2,325,309.1	1,088.4	112.3
Bosnia-Herzegovina	419	514	595	716	795	924	1,037.3	776.9	202.1
Bulgaria	1,058	1,171	1,450	1,710	2,092	2,489	3,029.1	2,265.4	299.2
Croatia	5,603	5,883	6,689	6,746	7,177	7,887	8,350.2	1,692.0	381.5
Czech Republic	148,410	159,258	167,585	175,369	188,270	202,778	220,800.6	12,933.7	1,253.7
Estonia	6,042	6,540	7,457	7,910	9,573	11,385	12,086.4	1,130.2	846.5
Georgia	133	121	134	158	241	324	397.4	266.5	60.8
Hungary	731,381	820,439	887,612	958,701	1,005,117	1,074,960	1,133,728.3	6,587.1	656.2
Latvia	259	303	379	493	679	870	908.1	1,888.6	833.2
Lithuania	2,227	2,468	2,778	3,486	4,237	5,075	5,877.1	2,493.4	740.7
Macedonia	4,687	4,941	5,431	6,315	7,260	8,400	10,009.4	239.1	117.2
Moldova									
Poland	39,056	42,121	46,519	46,770	48,183	51,352	56,201.9	23,327.7	613.2
Romania	4,428	5,859	7,553	8,671	10,079	11,723	13,874.1	5,508.1	256.2
Russia	250,761	380,084	510,571	728,620	806,467	993,912	1,343,169.6	54,044.8	380.6
Slovakia	1,343	1,378	1,580	1,994	2,319	2,867	3,502.9	5,155.3	955.8
Slovenia	1,330	1,404	1,520	1,613	1,733	1,921	2,114.8	3,112.4	1,543.4
Ukraine	3,745	5,244	6,784	9,627	12,313	16,340	22,519.1	4,275.3	92.6

Source: *National statistical offices/OECD/Eurostat/Euromonitor International*

Table 5.12

Consumer Expenditure on Education 1990-2008
Million units of national currency / as stated

	1990	1995	1996	1997	1998	1999	2000	2001
Western Europe								
Austria	296	412	436	560	480	507	531	639
Belgium	378	445	451	445	534	591	636	741
Cyprus								
Denmark	2,331	3,718	4,019	4,099	4,600	4,662	4,652	4,641
Finland	123	228	242	301	314	301	294	303
France	3,607	4,119	4,195	4,758	4,860	4,970	4,983	5,158
Germany	3,820	6,040	6,240	6,900	7,290	7,530	7,890	8,080
Gibraltar								
Greece	555	1,471	1,488	1,610	1,646	1,459	1,554	1,576
Iceland								
Ireland	183	365	441	371	331	364	456	517
Italy	4,022	5,702	5,976	6,177	6,311	6,602	6,804	6,994
Liechtenstein								
Luxembourg								
Malta								
Monaco								
Netherlands	979	968	973	1,013	1,068	1,125	1,176	1,233
Norway	2,058	1,962	2,288	2,438	2,508	2,806	3,049	3,733
Portugal	369	689	738	787	812	849	922	973
Spain	2,844	4,602	5,108	5,499	5,895	6,208	6,202	6,605
Sweden	678	1,229	1,438	1,611	1,706	2,312	2,431	2,544
Switzerland	696	892	950	976	1,023	1,048	1,079	1,192
Turkey	2	44	87	179	417	733	1,316	1,889
United Kingdom	3,222	6,197	6,565	7,440	7,814	8,943	9,534	9,409
Eastern Europe								
Albania								
Belarus	0	60	162	1,062	3,288	11,703	34,730	94,484
Bosnia-Herzegovina			41	55	68	81	101	109
Bulgaria	0	3	6	60	142	149	150	197
Croatia	1	264	286	356	395	438	517	645
Czech Republic	1,764	3,443	4,304	5,153	3,785	4,062	6,264	5,814
Estonia		195	343	418	539	521	623	706
Georgia		40	45	48	44	43	60	58
Hungary	7,582	42,429	52,167	57,263	64,719	71,353	79,162	91,896
Latvia	0	5	9	19	32	41	53	58
Lithuania		57	61	133	148	173	181	205
Macedonia		694	759	840	919	999	1,311	1,374
Moldova								
Poland	203	2,154	2,654	3,470	4,550	5,871	5,651	6,473
Romania	1	45	71	131	236	470	497	932
Russia	3	6,192	8,156	8,997	10,146	18,116	28,009	50,191
Slovakia		47	56	59	63	56	76	108
Slovenia	47	85	85	92	96	99	109	116
Ukraine	0	470	929	1,091	1,223	1,480	1,779	2,099

Source: National statistical offices/OECD/Eurostat/Euromonitor International

Consumer Expenditure Statistics

Consumer Expenditure on Education 1990-2008 *(continued)*
Million units of national currency / as stated

	2002	2003	2004	2005	2006	2007	2008	Total US$ million 2008	US$ per capita 2008
Western Europe									
Austria	754	789	823	864	904	958	1,036.0	1,524.8	182.6
Belgium	757	782	811	834	872	955	1,036.8	1,525.8	143.7
Cyprus									
Denmark	4,978	5,048	5,272	5,450	5,703	5,979	6,146.3	1,205.6	220.7
Finland	310	320	350	350	367	389	410.9	604.7	114.1
France	5,382	5,730	6,252	6,709	7,017	7,353	7,670.6	11,288.9	181.8
Germany	8,310	8,619	8,731	8,709	8,817	8,987	9,225.6	13,577.4	165.1
Gibraltar									
Greece	2,122	2,241	2,470	2,765	3,059	3,264	3,509.8	5,165.4	460.7
Iceland									
Ireland	687	805	806	947	1,071	1,187	1,261.3	1,856.3	424.0
Italy	7,058	7,441	7,844	7,011	7,042	7,104	7,093.0	10,438.8	177.0
Liechtenstein									
Luxembourg									
Malta									
Monaco									
Netherlands	1,316	1,427	1,527	1,336	1,340	1,371	1,406.8	2,070.4	126.4
Norway	3,880	3,775	3,939	4,136	4,473	4,838	5,184.9	919.3	194.1
Portugal	1,034	1,053	1,127	1,186	1,225	1,275	1,331.1	1,959.1	184.1
Spain	6,941	7,198	7,445	7,840	8,169	8,484	8,545.4	12,576.5	279.1
Sweden	1,660	2,844	3,188	3,345	3,611	3,971	4,318.4	655.2	71.6
Switzerland	1,240	1,303	1,402	1,420	1,500	1,597	1,703.7	1,573.0	208.9
Turkey	3,180	6,352	8,329	8,466	11,147	12,094	13,035.0	10,015.1	134.7
United Kingdom	9,381	9,610	11,134	11,824	12,470	13,249	13,471.6	24,765.5	404.8
Eastern Europe									
Albania									
Belarus	178,483	277,878	352,580	446,181	537,430	687,649	927,762.0	434.3	44.8
Bosnia-Herzegovina	124	142	161	173	207	237	262.9	196.9	51.2
Bulgaria	249	250	251	267	291	308	340.7	254.8	33.6
Croatia	592	637	758	825	780	858	895.5	181.5	40.9
Czech Republic	6,856	7,327	11,630	12,223	13,330	15,509	18,996.4	1,112.7	107.9
Estonia	806	881	936	1,065	1,269	1,495	1,550.5	145.0	108.6
Georgia	49	52	57	68	103	139	171.1	114.8	26.2
Hungary	110,132	134,896	136,014	149,800	160,511	171,195	180,564.4	1,049.1	104.5
Latvia	65	108	105	151	241	331	340.7	708.6	312.6
Lithuania	215	254	295	332	424	530	641.9	272.3	80.9
Macedonia	1,778	2,101	2,853	3,567	4,856	5,988	7,462.1	178.2	87.4
Moldova									
Poland	7,201	7,523	8,067	7,727	8,510	9,147	9,950.1	4,130.0	108.6
Romania	1,413	1,464	1,947	2,480	2,973	3,570	4,279.4	1,699.0	79.0
Russia	78,363	82,352	137,773	184,721	252,021	279,538	330,240.8	13,287.8	93.6
Slovakia	115	139	208	314	384	498	640.8	943.1	174.9
Slovenia	130	138	156	169	183	205	230.1	338.6	167.9
Ukraine	2,365	2,508	3,675	5,214	6,670	8,883	12,292.0	2,333.7	50.5

Source: *National statistical offices/OECD/Eurostat/Euromonitor International*

Table 5.13

Consumer Expenditure on Hotels and Catering 1990-2008

Million units of national currency / as stated

	1990	1995	1996	1997	1998	1999	2000	2001
Western Europe								
Austria	8,953	10,843	10,886	10,913	11,516	11,817	12,773	13,497
Belgium	5,617	5,947	6,004	6,054	6,141	6,455	7,004	7,247
Cyprus								
Denmark	22,077	25,798	25,946	27,514	29,569	29,728	31,118	31,575
Finland	3,320	3,383	3,588	3,648	3,729	3,766	3,963	4,202
France	34,191	39,403	39,146	40,650	43,427	45,944	49,559	51,560
Germany	45,045	57,420	57,650	58,890	59,930	61,890	65,700	66,810
Gibraltar								
Greece	4,267	10,541	11,827	14,068	15,312	15,444	17,643	19,579
Iceland								
Ireland	2,785	4,023	4,412	5,057	5,826	6,501	7,069	7,695
Italy	33,039	48,724	52,056	54,415	57,837	61,152	68,738	73,148
Liechtenstein								
Luxembourg								
Malta								
Monaco								
Netherlands	6,541	8,511	8,981	9,530	10,205	10,874	11,670	12,252
Norway	17,297	28,617	30,949	33,781	36,294	38,986	40,320	40,245
Portugal	3,846	5,917	6,137	6,527	7,213	7,488	8,181	8,753
Spain	36,794	51,418	53,788	57,587	61,839	67,425	71,984	75,660
Sweden	27,189	39,042	41,677	43,506	46,908	50,223	53,096	56,302
Switzerland	14,729	18,251	18,765	19,166	19,272	19,699	19,553	20,386
Turkey	10	204	398	813	1,859	2,870	4,890	6,781
United Kingdom	40,603	50,381	55,071	57,164	61,807	64,387	68,557	71,620
Eastern Europe								
Albania								
Belarus	0	3,388	4,034	7,394	12,732	55,934	149,944	250,571
Bosnia-Herzegovina			257	341	429	514	649	708
Bulgaria	3	57	119	997	1,540	1,651	1,683	1,849
Croatia	3	1,425	1,529	1,842	1,956	1,701	2,584	2,326
Czech Republic	22,272	55,987	65,599	76,622	83,248	80,709	88,664	92,576
Estonia		1,209	1,606	1,844	2,226	2,449	3,546	4,026
Georgia		99	139	179	181	200	243	237
Hungary	47,342	147,235	181,415	217,638	259,667	302,002	357,068	407,964
Latvia	2	66	79	101	96	133	143	161
Lithuania		514	672	901	961	1,014	962	1,032
Macedonia		1,626	1,838	2,098	2,358	2,622	3,473	3,625
Moldova								
Poland	912	6,634	8,268	9,661	11,773	12,641	14,736	15,076
Romania	4	346	498	1,151	1,602	2,032	2,714	3,671
Russia	14	21,466	24,682	22,540	20,667	33,589	58,258	108,747
Slovakia		591	654	718	809	811	934	1,063
Slovenia	167	691	709	766	814	815	820	867
Ukraine	0	430	852	1,001	1,121	1,356	1,630	1,925

Source: *National statistical offices/OECD/Eurostat/Euromonitor International*

Consumer Expenditure Statistics

Consumer Expenditure on Hotels and Catering 1990-2008 *(continued)*
Million units of national currency / as stated

	2002	2003	2004	2005	2006	2007	2008	Total US$ million 2008	US$ per capita 2008
Western Europe									
Austria	14,314	15,113	15,878	16,766	17,669	18,461	19,249.3	28,329.6	3,392.0
Belgium	7,467	7,584	7,675	7,800	8,018	8,394	8,835.8	13,003.8	1,224.6
Cyprus									
Denmark	31,767	31,759	32,767	38,185	41,309	43,249	44,626.3	8,753.5	1,602.7
Finland	4,246	4,502	4,804	5,024	5,357	5,620	5,885.3	8,661.5	1,634.1
France	53,945	56,086	57,124	59,194	61,878	65,061	67,775.6	99,746.5	1,606.1
Germany	65,770	65,385	65,958	66,510	67,559	68,037	69,207.1	101,853.4	1,238.8
Gibraltar									
Greece	21,383	23,189	25,034	27,106	29,496	31,678	34,074.4	50,147.9	4,472.9
Iceland									
Ireland	8,372	8,832	9,133	9,672	10,341	11,077	11,053.0	16,266.9	3,715.3
Italy	75,141	77,423	79,795	82,863	85,899	89,764	92,804.1	136,581.4	2,315.9
Liechtenstein									
Luxembourg									
Malta									
Monaco									
Netherlands	12,608	12,307	12,216	12,579	12,485	12,744	13,011.5	19,149.2	1,168.8
Norway	41,463	42,080	42,930	45,526	48,046	50,940	53,127.4	9,419.8	1,988.5
Portugal	9,183	9,173	9,750	10,131	10,635	11,113	11,585.2	17,050.1	1,602.1
Spain	80,702	86,562	94,807	103,432	112,414	120,307	125,287.2	184,387.3	4,092.4
Sweden	58,587	60,128	61,999	65,823	68,144	71,446	73,536.3	11,156.9	1,218.4
Switzerland	19,405	19,065	19,920	20,133	20,575	21,052	21,584.4	19,928.5	2,646.5
Turkey	10,596	13,457	17,919	19,842	21,719	23,940	26,572.4	20,416.1	274.6
United Kingdom	76,426	78,902	82,775	85,258	86,996	90,656	91,537.3	168,277.5	2,750.3
Eastern Europe									
Albania									
Belarus	381,710	440,835	688,212	870,917	1,049,029	1,255,552	1,647,918.7	771.4	79.6
Bosnia-Herzegovina	807	949	1,074	1,145	1,281	1,453	1,591.7	1,192.1	310.1
Bulgaria	2,007	2,193	2,507	2,826	3,345	3,830	4,525.7	3,384.6	447.0
Croatia	2,763	2,631	3,493	3,672	3,787	4,345	4,668.5	946.0	213.3
Czech Republic	86,361	87,087	94,394	94,684	98,711	103,665	109,695.9	6,425.6	622.8
Estonia	4,475	4,900	5,818	7,628	9,556	11,244	11,752.3	1,098.9	823.1
Georgia	267	281	329	352	491	542	630.6	423.0	96.5
Hungary	460,888	500,233	570,167	615,998	647,590	694,601	732,894.9	4,258.2	424.2
Latvia	166	160	189	233	297	375	392.2	815.7	359.9
Lithuania	1,106	1,178	1,269	1,440	1,627	1,906	2,162.1	917.3	272.5
Macedonia	4,663	5,262	6,709	8,251	9,570	11,455	13,873.2	331.4	162.4
Moldova									
Poland	15,515	15,994	17,169	17,640	18,736	19,937	21,732.6	9,020.5	237.1
Romania	4,476	5,236	6,469	7,172	8,284	9,336	10,739.9	4,263.8	198.3
Russia	130,605	196,377	283,651	297,606	327,627	465,896	697,260.3	28,055.5	197.6
Slovakia	1,100	1,234	1,356	1,442	1,612	1,936	2,278.8	3,353.7	621.8
Slovenia	924	1,011	1,085	1,156	1,226	1,341	1,459.9	2,148.6	1,065.5
Ukraine	2,168	3,192	4,523	6,418	8,209	11,085	15,572.9	2,956.6	64.0

Source: National statistical offices/OECD/Eurostat/Euromonitor International

Table 5.14

Consumer Expenditure on Miscellaneous Goods and Services 1990-2008
Million units of national currency / as stated

	1990	1995	1996	1997	1998	1999	2000	2001
Western Europe								
Austria	6,775	8,808	9,220	9,145	9,313	9,397	10,761	11,342
Belgium	10,050	15,659	15,104	15,052	16,229	15,841	18,260	19,010
Cyprus								
Denmark	47,832	59,560	59,864	63,885	68,594	69,894	76,125	77,646
Finland	4,311	4,512	4,179	4,162	4,866	4,944	5,933	6,303
France	77,120	79,973	82,930	83,428	84,544	81,264	92,443	96,650
Germany	87,400	118,310	117,880	117,400	118,980	125,440	127,540	134,070
Gibraltar								
Greece	1,681	3,492	3,761	4,146	4,732	5,405	5,991	6,579
Iceland								
Ireland	1,616	2,343	2,593	2,981	3,715	4,567	5,003	5,817
Italy	41,489	56,449	57,069	58,961	60,941	62,456	68,230	71,955
Liechtenstein								
Luxembourg								
Malta								
Monaco								
Netherlands	14,156	20,417	21,329	23,042	25,204	27,258	30,827	32,218
Norway	27,495	32,072	34,353	35,562	37,642	40,622	43,735	44,730
Portugal	3,807	5,821	5,966	6,468	6,721	7,621	8,620	8,893
Spain	17,094	24,831	26,215	28,115	30,062	32,129	34,175	36,939
Sweden	56,482	78,275	78,545	79,520	82,201	93,304	102,400	100,534
Switzerland	20,774	24,078	24,840	26,428	27,186	27,820	29,308	27,950
Turkey	18	253	496	983	1,995	2,875	4,843	6,405
United Kingdom	43,679	56,372	60,863	66,306	71,254	77,253	83,307	87,542
Eastern Europe								
Albania								
Belarus	0	2,299	3,504	5,192	12,311	53,180	160,030	365,763
Bosnia-Herzegovina			214	286	360	432	547	596
Bulgaria	1	19	40	322	442	475	535	515
Croatia	8	3,104	3,289	3,930	4,236	3,762	5,250	5,822
Czech Republic	16,115	47,911	67,273	84,659	94,788	102,824	94,439	102,684
Estonia		1,171	1,551	2,230	2,590	2,845	3,743	4,502
Georgia		202	206	277	167	147	278	242
Hungary	68,353	139,465	181,715	228,306	284,642	334,135	489,576	564,436
Latvia	1	77	113	117	115	100	99	105
Lithuania		588	802	840	1,347	1,499	1,484	1,677
Macedonia		3,510	3,777	4,085	4,354	4,561	5,672	5,760
Moldova								
Poland	1,662	16,561	20,364	29,954	35,869	42,724	55,284	57,153
Romania	1	105	160	393	593	911	1,206	1,626
Russia	11	27,177	39,703	48,553	58,136	99,528	129,251	171,485
Slovakia		470	544	624	710	709	799	853
Slovenia	103	780	866	916	923	1,085	1,039	1,029
Ukraine	0	783	1,549	1,819	2,038	2,466	2,965	3,499

Source: *National statistical offices/OECD/Eurostat/Euromonitor International*

Consumer Expenditure Statistics

Consumer Expenditure on Miscellaneous Goods and Services 1990-2008 *(continued)*

Million units of national currency / as stated

	2002	2003	2004	2005	2006	2007	2008	Total US$ million 2008	US$ per capita 2008
Western Europe									
Austria	11,131	11,518	12,098	12,458	12,933	13,452	14,010.5	20,619.5	2,468.9
Belgium	18,403	17,725	18,352	19,023	19,499	20,580	21,711.1	31,952.6	3,009.2
Cyprus									
Denmark	79,509	84,316	88,489	94,392	101,477	106,854	110,975.0	21,767.8	3,985.7
Finland	6,651	6,127	6,487	6,872	7,019	7,493	7,918.4	11,653.7	2,198.6
France	95,149	98,530	102,210	107,339	112,216	116,442	119,638.4	176,073.9	2,835.1
Germany	137,290	146,143	149,177	151,029	154,632	158,144	163,714.3	240,941.2	2,930.5
Gibraltar									
Greece	7,111	7,608	8,162	8,836	9,591	10,414	11,278.2	16,598.4	1,480.5
Iceland									
Ireland	6,540	7,328	7,908	8,708	9,762	11,026	11,565.8	17,021.6	3,887.7
Italy	72,155	74,370	74,756	78,623	81,189	83,565	85,213.5	125,410.2	2,126.5
Liechtenstein									
Luxembourg									
Malta									
Monaco									
Netherlands	32,385	34,089	35,126	37,014	38,434	39,904	41,418.2	60,955.9	3,720.6
Norway	47,646	54,914	59,076	62,862	67,289	72,189	76,413.0	13,548.4	2,860.0
Portugal	9,120	9,639	10,285	10,982	12,332	13,051	13,860.7	20,399.0	1,916.7
Spain	37,804	39,090	42,398	44,934	47,634	50,183	51,379.5	75,616.1	1,678.3
Sweden	104,524	104,467	112,235	119,361	124,392	130,461	134,961.6	20,476.3	2,236.1
Switzerland	29,709	29,911	30,137	29,639	29,888	30,770	31,680.8	29,250.4	3,884.5
Turkey	10,994	11,468	15,603	18,678	20,895	23,275	26,194.9	20,126.1	270.7
United Kingdom	91,818	94,851	98,990	105,158	110,537	116,722	122,264.2	224,764.4	3,673.5
Eastern Europe									
Albania									
Belarus	619,411	765,095	951,510	1,204,115	1,450,369	1,869,858	2,569,463.4	1,202.7	124.1
Bosnia-Herzegovina	681	795	906	1,003	1,172	1,346	1,494.5	1,119.3	291.2
Bulgaria	794	878	1,085	1,289	1,572	1,862	2,258.2	1,688.8	223.1
Croatia	6,466	7,222	7,895	8,223	8,936	9,861	10,606.6	2,149.2	484.6
Czech Republic	107,981	117,359	121,615	127,870	138,585	149,493	162,424.2	9,514.2	922.2
Estonia	5,245	5,810	6,362	7,243	9,036	10,652	11,203.4	1,047.6	784.6
Georgia	243	248	314	380	499	595	721.8	484.2	110.5
Hungary	611,111	674,769	586,152	573,269	584,625	626,347	656,699.6	3,815.5	380.1
Latvia	133	160	184	215	257	318	322.1	669.8	295.5
Lithuania	1,823	2,090	2,427	3,182	3,869	4,857	5,655.1	2,399.2	712.7
Macedonia	6,883	7,246	10,711	10,246	11,143	13,270	16,029.6	382.9	187.7
Moldova									
Poland	63,758	66,151	70,573	73,069	82,456	89,990	99,661.3	41,366.3	1,087.3
Romania	2,068	2,923	3,824	4,564	5,504	6,492	7,785.2	3,090.8	143.8
Russia	214,192	285,063	380,903	482,326	617,451	807,554	1,100,802.7	44,292.7	311.9
Slovakia	880	1,030	1,234	1,979	2,422	2,955	3,554.0	5,230.5	969.8
Slovenia	1,256	1,351	1,401	1,473	1,560	1,721	1,901.5	2,798.5	1,387.8
Ukraine	3,942	4,104	4,806	6,819	8,722	11,289	15,132.1	2,872.9	62.2

Source: *National statistical offices/OECD/Eurostat/Euromonitor International*

Consumer Market Sizes

Consumer Market Statistics

Table 6.1

Per Capita Retail Sales of Alcoholic Drinks 2008
Litres per capita

	Alcoholic Drinks	Beer	Wine	Spirits
Western Europe				
Austria	89.03	66.10	18.44	1.98
Belgium	66.31	42.73	20.49	2.65
Denmark	86.26	56.56	26.56	2.54
Finland	99.83	68.24	11.14	5.66
France	54.50	19.97	27.66	4.81
Germany	96.31	64.22	21.32	4.58
Greece	31.53	14.56	14.90	2.00
Ireland	66.58	42.89	13.29	3.29
Italy	48.68	19.80	27.14	1.36
Netherlands	78.34	54.63	20.27	2.52
Norway	58.93	41.76	12.67	2.68
Portugal	51.52	21.33	28.77	1.34
Spain	41.18	26.32	11.16	2.32
Sweden	66.26	41.49	18.08	2.11
Switzerland	60.05	28.23	28.35	2.17
Turkey	10.38	9.30	0.59	0.47
United Kingdom	65.06	35.93	18.03	3.71
Eastern Europe				
Bulgaria	61.35	51.33	5.12	4.89
Czech Republic	98.31	82.24	10.74	5.28
Hungary	75.53	51.89	19.95	3.63
Poland	85.69	71.47	6.52	7.58
Romania	79.51	67.77	9.68	2.06
Russia	97.17	73.01	8.25	12.76
Slovakia	81.99	67.21	10.26	4.30
Ukraine	72.95	58.07	5.44	7.85

Source: *Euromonitor International from industry sources/national statistics*
Notes: *Alcoholic drinks data are off-trade*

Table 6.2

Per Capita Retail Sales of Clothing and Footwear 2008

US$ per capita

	Total Clothing	Men's Outerwear	Women's Outerwear	Footwear
Western Europe				
Austria				
Belgium	815.71	208.58	342.03	172.80
Denmark				
Finland				
France	625.47	156.91	244.17	194.74
Germany	714.78	203.03	339.99	152.40
Greece	1,055.30	295.20	409.95	173.27
Ireland				
Italy	985.61	298.98	323.36	418.65
Netherlands	879.15	293.61	332.89	217.37
Norway				
Portugal	311.76	91.67	179.49	68.92
Spain	511.05	130.69	197.57	133.40
Sweden	927.84	247.03	416.05	171.93
Switzerland				
Turkey	66.01	27.17	20.33	12.72
United Kingdom	945.42	282.67	370.82	168.54
Eastern Europe				
Bulgaria				
Czech Republic				
Hungary	98.00	37.13	44.51	41.74
Poland	230.90	74.20	92.00	85.92
Romania				
Russia	266.46	75.64	105.17	43.23
Slovakia				
Ukraine				

Source: *Euromonitor International from industry sources/national statistics*

Consumer Market Statistics

Table 6.3

Per Capita Retail Sales of Consumer Electronics 2008

US$ per capita

	Digital Televisions	DVD Players	Home Audio & Cinema	Personal Computers	Cameras	Camcorders	Portable Media Players	Mobile Phone	In-Car Media Players
Western Europe									
Austria	81.73	7.58	20.76	63.52	39.40	13.68	11.62	75.15	9.01
Belgium	130.42	20.43	13.23	43.99	17.49	7.69	30.85	129.28	4.27
Denmark									
Finland									
France	133.60	18.33	30.97	97.27	28.37	5.54	23.37	146.11	2.24
Germany	103.28	3.72	20.21	42.31	39.91	5.20	19.95	61.89	4.81
Greece	67.29	10.87	13.80	44.51	14.37	6.84	6.04	117.46	1.01
Ireland									
Italy	124.15	12.80	24.16	24.62	18.54	5.13	9.18	66.24	3.83
Netherlands	157.03	18.77	38.16	105.97	44.60	9.19	21.17	39.30	7.93
Norway									
Portugal	113.10	6.81	20.11	41.15	18.65	5.48	13.80	84.93	5.14
Spain	100.09	12.76	8.58	49.89	24.42	6.15	13.71	105.65	4.20
Sweden	126.92	14.71	22.74	129.54	49.83	10.84	18.82	77.53	2.33
Switzerland									
Turkey	11.81	1.30	2.98	25.71	3.87	0.68	0.82	31.66	0.32
United Kingdom	140.76	22.90	29.59	96.85	50.95	9.20	31.69	33.76	7.14
Eastern Europe									
Bulgaria									
Czech Republic									
Hungary	72.54	4.19	8.61	73.51	17.62	15.61	3.46	49.66	5.84
Poland	39.22	3.52	7.42	88.82	20.58	3.76	4.83	36.74	2.70
Romania	12.08	7.15	5.95	33.51	5.40	2.30	0.92	35.84	0.58
Russia	14.76	3.72	18.06	15.05	12.53	6.76	7.96	53.17	2.02
Slovakia									
Ukraine									

Source: *Euromonitor International from industry sources/national statistics*

Table 6.4

Per Capita Retail Sales of Cosmetics and Toiletries 2008

US$ per capita

	Baby Care	Bath & Shower Products	Deodorants	Hair Care	Colour Cosmetics
Western Europe					
Austria	2.76	19.51	8.88	36.75	27.95
Belgium	3.32	18.86	13.80	33.99	26.33
Denmark	4.88	16.57	16.61	85.46	36.45
Finland	1.88	12.27	9.24	40.61	29.12
France	3.64	17.30	13.88	41.70	28.31
Germany	2.25	14.53	10.83	36.12	23.01
Greece	4.06	12.28	8.20	53.10	17.44
Ireland	6.70	22.35	18.03	46.05	30.69
Italy	3.85	19.50	11.16	30.01	22.59
Netherlands	3.79	21.21	14.36	42.90	28.89
Norway	5.20	36.29	18.10	87.96	63.43
Portugal	3.63	15.63	8.37	35.71	13.23
Spain	4.52	14.22	10.57	38.40	23.47
Sweden	2.03	15.88	10.05	50.75	43.04
Switzerland	4.03	26.72	10.89	41.28	38.04
Turkey	0.68	3.26	1.71	8.74	3.02
United Kingdom	3.80	21.66	24.63	36.98	40.20
Eastern Europe					
Bulgaria	0.95	6.64	3.77	9.47	5.47
Czech Republic	2.56	12.44	10.41	32.99	19.18
Hungary	1.21	15.09	10.81	20.35	9.59
Poland	1.88	9.04	8.86	22.20	11.83
Romania	0.51	6.55	5.41	9.22	8.36
Russia	1.70	7.29	3.33	15.32	11.85
Slovakia	1.31	14.02	7.77	21.27	18.15
Ukraine	1.05	2.56	3.48	9.54	7.10

Source: *Euromonitor International from industry sources/national statistics*

Consumer Market Statistics

Per Capita Retail Sales of Cosmetics and Toiletries 2008 *(continued)*

US$ per capita

	Men's Grooming	Oral Hygiene	Fragrances	Skin Care	Sun Care
Western Europe					
Austria	25.46	29.06	24.60	55.60	6.41
Belgium	20.60	18.64	44.98	51.65	6.25
Denmark	24.56	24.17	47.52	41.39	12.00
Finland	12.61	15.90	17.27	60.95	5.73
France	23.25	19.01	43.40	69.59	7.25
Germany	15.40	21.78	34.87	45.68	3.97
Greece	14.14	12.48	18.62	50.40	9.05
Ireland	34.80	28.09	29.75	30.47	7.37
Italy	17.35	25.53	25.79	46.48	8.63
Netherlands	27.19	25.72	46.00	44.55	6.71
Norway	30.20	31.25	23.90	86.36	14.81
Portugal	19.31	23.23	28.84	25.57	7.35
Spain	19.32	18.71	43.46	51.67	12.74
Sweden	16.32	19.53	19.60	39.87	7.11
Switzerland	24.18	30.17	57.59	36.94	11.56
Turkey	3.83	3.09	3.55	4.46	0.41
United Kingdom	24.93	25.63	24.34	53.55	10.61
Eastern Europe					
Bulgaria	2.75	4.42	5.68	9.81	1.27
Czech Republic	10.92	11.48	18.64	21.58	3.69
Hungary	12.26	10.57	12.44	22.69	1.41
Poland	10.42	8.00	18.04	19.65	1.29
Romania	2.47	3.26	14.83	13.63	0.74
Russia	8.09	7.64	15.82	17.79	0.84
Slovakia	9.74	8.71	20.71	24.67	0.80
Ukraine	4.51	3.51	8.63	11.89	0.59

Source: *Euromonitor International from industry sources/national statistics*

Consumer Market Statistics

Table 6.5

Per Capita Retail Sales of Disposable Paper Products 2008

US$ per capita

	Sanitary Protection	Nappies, Diapers & Pants	Toilet Paper	Tissues	Kitchen Towels
Western Europe					
Austria	10.83	14.23	23.78	9.21	7.89
Belgium	13.20	22.26	20.02	4.05	8.68
Denmark	19.59	20.83	21.10	1.86	11.39
Finland	14.06	20.75	24.74	2.04	10.13
France	11.03	16.97	18.66	5.26	7.53
Germany	9.20	9.79	15.46	5.31	5.97
Greece	11.63	8.39	17.92	3.04	9.24
Ireland	14.76	26.00	34.75	7.42	10.49
Italy	10.08	15.08	17.22	4.64	7.79
Netherlands	12.09	20.20	24.13	3.72	6.49
Norway	20.32	23.29	42.20	2.13	15.66
Portugal	9.55	12.70	19.12	1.96	5.28
Spain	14.74	13.97	17.80	2.84	5.68
Sweden	11.09	19.09	26.93	3.90	11.34
Switzerland	12.09	14.82	25.61	8.34	8.08
Turkey	3.07	6.77	3.71	0.43	1.75
United Kingdom	10.19	15.98	31.76	6.36	9.60
Eastern Europe					
Bulgaria	3.86	3.08	5.21	3.72	0.77
Czech Republic	9.93	7.44	12.08	4.43	1.57
Hungary	7.62	8.48	10.55	4.35	2.91
Poland	9.77	7.63	8.05	2.70	2.47
Romania	4.01	6.12	6.60	0.89	0.81
Russia	7.96	10.20	3.00	0.26	0.20
Slovakia	11.46	4.47	10.58	2.85	0.81
Ukraine	1.15	3.00	3.39	0.17	0.50

Source: *Euromonitor International from industry sources/national statistics*

Consumer Market Statistics

Table 6.6

Per Capita Retail Sales of DIY and Gardening 2008

US$ per capita

	DIY	Gardening
Western Europe		
Austria		
Belgium	335.82	212.69
Denmark		
Finland		
France	430.86	125.74
Germany	464.01	135.70
Greece	272.00	153.89
Ireland		
Italy	241.64	122.70
Netherlands	390.28	253.36
Norway		
Portugal	322.14	40.10
Spain	79.63	50.36
Sweden	289.95	230.30
Switzerland		
Turkey	60.26	9.36
United Kingdom	372.91	143.08
Eastern Europe		
Bulgaria		
Czech Republic		
Hungary	108.77	21.28
Poland	210.46	28.31
Romania		
Russia	87.18	2.25
Slovakia		
Ukraine		

Source: *Euromonitor International from industry sources/national statistics*

Consumer Market Statistics

Table 6.7

Per Capita Retail Sales of Large Electrical Appliances 2008

Units per '000 inhabitants

	Refrigeration Appliances	Fridge-freezers	Freezers	Large Cooking Appliances	Microwaves	Home Laundry Appliances	Dishwashers
Western Europe							
Austria	28.46	9.65	6.46	36.73	15.13	28.99	13.12
Belgium	52.07	25.03	18.12	48.47	30.03	46.71	16.65
Denmark	61.22	23.13	15.26	73.56	26.80	65.11	33.58
Finland	51.61	18.09	15.50	55.91	24.79	35.46	18.48
France	51.50	23.48	11.28	66.73	37.56	49.55	23.03
Germany	47.00	18.75	11.47	58.09	23.96	45.09	21.73
Greece	40.34	11.81	5.03	44.92	8.39	30.21	8.46
Ireland	69.87	31.48	19.05	100.49	61.14	105.34	19.80
Italy	50.97	37.99	9.11	49.11	18.19	39.76	16.76
Netherlands	53.53	35.03	13.92	58.63	28.40	62.51	22.65
Norway	80.73	40.46	19.70	94.71	41.10	72.73	41.75
Portugal	44.75	20.69	8.01	68.10	23.51	33.59	13.94
Spain	37.61	29.53	4.65	85.20	29.54	42.29	15.42
Sweden	73.64	23.98	22.06	74.73	36.98	49.70	27.43
Switzerland	37.39	12.73	8.51	48.37	19.94	38.20	17.28
Turkey	30.78	24.94	1.46	28.50	0.95	38.96	16.07
United Kingdom	64.01	31.03	17.52	67.06	50.61	79.97	15.45
Eastern Europe							
Bulgaria	26.27	19.08	4.67	13.30	0.06	23.58	0.01
Czech Republic	41.53	23.99	7.56	47.62	31.56	37.70	10.38
Hungary	41.59	29.98	7.16	28.94	24.42	37.71	7.59
Poland	36.41	31.46	1.64	51.17	14.88	31.09	9.22
Romania	19.24	13.97	3.42	9.74	0.04	17.27	0.01
Russia	32.01	26.56	1.40	18.90	27.06	39.24	1.15
Slovakia	49.45	23.65	6.35	44.87	26.27	34.75	4.12
Ukraine	1.29	0.86	0.03	2.00	0.01	1.13	0.00

Source: *Euromonitor International from industry sources/national statistics*

Consumer Market Statistics

Table 6.8

Per Capita Retail Sales of Small Electrical Appliances 2008

Units per '000 inhabitants

	Food Preparation Appliances	Small Cooking Appliances	Hair Care Appliances	Irons	Body Shavers	Vacuum Cleaners
Western Europe						
Austria	42.61	128.29	42.12	27.87	24.78	67.56
Belgium	19.94	182.29	59.42	46.89	40.73	79.69
Denmark	113.36	161.57	92.03	27.59	12.67	80.03
Finland	82.77	124.85	46.57	27.53	29.67	36.64
France	83.72	222.51	89.72	57.72	37.62	69.16
Germany	70.45	211.24	91.58	43.02	42.08	69.53
Greece	134.27	61.37	95.76	54.51	12.91	41.26
Ireland	72.69	190.18	205.64	74.27	42.54	100.65
Italy	67.02	80.81	84.28	65.30	26.80	59.87
Netherlands	16.18	129.15	62.35	57.28	24.11	83.42
Norway	81.29	144.88	108.75	28.47	16.70	84.22
Portugal	103.03	123.49	45.44	55.03	37.68	53.55
Spain	108.91	105.00	78.53	54.66	27.04	28.18
Sweden	128.81	161.92	106.11	33.69	22.56	86.25
Switzerland	56.17	169.04	55.51	36.72	32.66	89.03
Turkey	15.35	27.37	8.36	17.77	6.19	12.03
United Kingdom	64.68	161.56	195.63	88.02	40.46	132.68
Eastern Europe						
Bulgaria	4.42	18.32	53.99	32.70	9.67	14.58
Czech Republic	36.69	25.39	41.22	30.13	29.45	63.49
Hungary	13.00	33.33	83.07	44.87	14.27	20.19
Poland	55.05	17.92	58.52	29.81	40.23	36.75
Romania	3.24	13.41	39.54	23.95	7.08	10.68
Russia	30.73	17.70	40.94	43.65	22.61	29.85
Slovakia	39.86	24.52	21.14	7.33	7.12	11.91
Ukraine	3.87	1.67	4.96	5.29	2.12	3.22

Source: *Euromonitor International from industry sources/national statistics*

Table 6.9

Per Capita Retail Sales of Fresh Foods 2008

Kg per capita

	Meat	Fish and Seafood	Pulses	Vegetables	Starchy Roots	Fruits	Eggs	Sugar and Sweeteners
Western Europe								
Austria	101.83	14.55	0.30	75.25	64.16	75.32	10.61	53.23
Belgium	63.83	20.25	1.75	149.83	96.96	57.94	12.97	56.75
Denmark	74.04	9.07	0.69	81.13	71.17	97.85	14.17	51.65
Finland	37.59	22.61	1.23	60.76	53.73	53.65	8.04	33.42
France	54.61	6.19	0.92	32.18	31.55	39.13	14.73	6.93
Germany	60.48	4.53	0.21	71.23	30.85	63.69	12.69	43.29
Greece	99.55	23.54	3.49	257.04	57.44	138.34	7.95	32.79
Ireland	79.69	12.70	1.34	75.43	85.83	92.35	6.43	41.50
Italy	50.76	8.99	2.91	62.39	11.78	81.93	11.16	28.68
Netherlands	59.54	24.95	1.39	54.89	66.27	68.27	7.82	39.04
Norway	38.54	35.75	0.81	51.35	53.26	94.51	8.60	48.45
Portugal	103.48	80.44	2.41	203.10	97.21	131.50	11.50	34.31
Spain	50.21	20.44	4.65	54.76	32.82	99.39	12.18	7.50
Sweden	39.73	19.51	1.79	50.12	32.43	71.64	12.62	43.76
Switzerland	54.30	15.39	0.68	78.87	42.05	47.52	10.81	56.21
Turkey	19.41	8.34	11.08	237.94	65.00	86.12	6.22	27.17
United Kingdom	53.42	12.41	0.34	68.35	47.01	46.32	11.60	40.19
Eastern Europe								
Bulgaria	54.25	1.78	3.76	167.79	32.88	38.87	16.31	35.13
Czech Republic	57.04	10.15	1.05	80.92	58.01	42.74	18.02	32.90
Hungary	57.83	3.26	4.44	118.51	62.17	39.11	15.55	63.87
Poland	73.50	7.61	1.86	111.98	118.63	40.49	11.97	41.90
Romania	50.90	2.58	1.37	189.66	103.15	47.35	13.98	27.28
Russia	46.19	12.59	0.50	79.96	76.06	44.26	13.54	26.04
Slovakia	43.81	2.75	3.27	82.68	76.52	50.12	12.09	47.10
Ukraine	23.65	8.79	2.36	119.88	159.89	20.65	10.05	51.44

Source: *Euromonitor International from industry sources/national statistics*

Consumer Market Statistics

Table 6.10

Per Capita Retail Sales of Hot and Soft Drinks 2008
As stated

	Coffee (Grams)	Tea (Grams)	Bottled Water (Litres)	Carbonates (Litres)
Western Europe				
Austria	3,595.49	208.21	65.55	53.68
Belgium	4,130.97	113.20	107.62	84.59
Denmark	4,883.82	126.25	25.21	54.33
Finland	8,219.32	217.93	17.14	40.68
France	2,937.65	191.99	119.91	31.27
Germany	4,141.06	365.07	127.93	67.56
Greece	1,762.25	20.07	35.68	37.29
Ireland	695.41	2,308.20	39.69	73.57
Italy	2,407.46	103.03	145.14	29.24
Netherlands	4,939.90	574.91	18.90	56.66
Norway	6,647.90	206.07	21.11	114.57
Portugal	1,049.39	48.89	63.89	28.79
Spain	1,373.05	82.09	122.14	63.40
Sweden	6,324.00	346.20	23.29	55.99
Switzerland	4,758.18	361.57	84.33	52.08
Turkey	261.63	1,655.49	72.88	28.72
United Kingdom	888.84	1,967.47	37.51	60.15
Eastern Europe				
Bulgaria	1,570.71	76.94	65.75	46.48
Czech Republic	2,354.38	365.22	119.32	44.97
Hungary	3,403.07	201.40	77.00	49.58
Poland	2,832.33	1,002.82	53.12	48.30
Romania	1,402.55	47.86	58.39	52.13
Russia	756.09	1,214.08	22.45	24.50
Slovakia	2,372.51	342.04	78.39	58.44
Ukraine	716.75	427.45	35.12	36.53

Source: *Euromonitor International from industry sources/national statistics*

Per Capita Retail Sales of Household Care Products 2008

US$ per capita

	Laundry Care	Fabric Softeners	Hand Dishwashing	Automatic Dishwashing	Surface Care	Air Care
Western Europe						
Austria	43.28	5.95	3.84	7.12	12.38	7.54
Belgium	36.60	8.98	3.40	6.48	13.89	6.59
Denmark	33.54	6.97	5.45	6.07	13.06	1.11
Finland	25.10	5.65	4.71	5.75	10.65	1.49
France	41.09	4.32	4.94	6.09	12.49	9.35
Germany	36.37	4.88	3.36	5.92	14.40	3.62
Greece	45.59	6.49	5.33	3.73	13.46	2.80
Ireland	37.66	7.29	5.20	7.71	12.57	10.66
Italy	46.96	6.92	6.71	4.65	16.94	6.07
Netherlands	30.39	4.39	3.15	6.26	9.21	4.79
Norway	36.96	7.78	6.56	7.59	17.34	1.59
Portugal	31.87	4.17	4.75	4.74	13.96	6.71
Spain	45.30	8.48	4.79	5.37	13.92	9.13
Sweden	25.24	5.84	4.59	5.20	7.97	1.59
Switzerland	59.32	6.00	4.60	9.23	13.83	7.14
Turkey	14.44	1.78	3.25	2.27	1.92	0.30
United Kingdom	44.82	8.75	5.35	5.82	14.14	11.50
Eastern Europe						
Bulgaria	15.48	0.92	2.33	0.59	4.24	1.98
Czech Republic	27.46	2.95	4.85	1.49	5.53	2.33
Hungary	28.66	7.12	4.40	1.28	5.74	2.56
Poland	21.23	3.23	3.81	0.94	7.99	3.17
Romania	21.61	3.55	1.83	0.21	2.44	1.59
Russia	17.26	0.38	3.15	0.11	3.81	0.83
Slovakia	28.39	5.78	3.16	0.18	5.25	1.02
Ukraine	15.10	0.52	1.85	0.28	3.42	1.15

Source: *Euromonitor International from industry sources/national statistics*

Consumer Market Statistics

Table 6.12

Per Capita Retail Sales of Housewares and Home Furnishings 2008
US$ per capita

	Housewares	Home Furnishings
Western Europe		
Austria		
Belgium	82.27	653.82
Denmark		
Finland		
France	65.57	322.31
Germany	104.45	688.79
Greece	58.05	215.00
Ireland		
Italy	105.25	606.25
Netherlands	121.18	671.73
Norway		
Portugal	62.63	191.48
Spain	56.34	365.45
Sweden	130.82	595.43
Switzerland		
Turkey	14.96	92.10
United Kingdom	128.97	771.95
Eastern Europe		
Bulgaria		
Czech Republic		
Hungary	81.67	87.15
Poland	141.92	157.91
Romania		
Russia	43.90	113.67
Slovakia		
Ukraine		

Source: *Euromonitor International from industry sources/national statistics*

Consumer Market Statistics

Table 6.13

Per Capita Retail Sales of OTC Healthcare Products 2008
US$ per capita

	Analgesics	Cough,Cold and Allergy Remedies	Digestive Remedies	Medicated Skin Care	Vitamins & Dietary Supplements
Western Europe					
Austria	9.17	22.91	6.51	9.54	26.19
Belgium	19.31	21.52	12.65	7.63	32.32
Denmark	17.69	16.80	11.80	7.74	28.39
Finland	20.12	16.18	13.82	11.32	32.04
France	10.05	14.41	7.83	9.42	19.56
Germany	14.69	22.44	9.20	13.65	25.56
Greece	9.50	9.27	4.19	7.55	16.89
Ireland	25.46	22.41	10.34	12.86	18.85
Italy	13.32	14.12	8.98	10.28	35.86
Netherlands	8.18	16.94	6.06	5.30	20.47
Norway	16.73	23.71	11.88	10.82	115.58
Portugal	10.36	7.89	6.41	6.97	8.98
Spain	9.96	12.79	6.68	6.63	8.23
Sweden	22.32	33.57	8.50	10.43	28.77
Switzerland	19.13	35.46	13.14	22.12	23.32
Turkey	6.23	5.76	2.23	1.35	2.99
United Kingdom	16.75	18.55	10.43	15.73	22.61
Eastern Europe					
Bulgaria	9.39	5.36	1.27	1.65	7.68
Czech Republic	13.40	13.22	4.56	4.10	11.18
Hungary	7.26	9.79	4.92	5.32	15.80
Poland	9.66	8.03	6.29	2.94	9.07
Romania	4.20	3.39	2.14	1.11	5.14
Russia	3.52	6.08	3.47	2.12	9.59
Slovakia	8.55	13.08	4.87	3.81	8.86
Ukraine	1.43	5.86	2.64	0.96	4.96

Source: *Euromonitor International from industry sources/national statistics*

Consumer Market Statistics

Table 6.14

Per Capita Retail Sales of Dairy Products and Ice Cream 2008

US$ per capita

	Drinking Milk Products	Cheese	Yoghurt and Sour Milk Drinks	Other Dairy Products	Ice Cream
Western Europe					
Austria	73.06	92.10	46.90	55.86	48.21
Belgium	83.17	152.33	60.00	57.03	40.29
Denmark	152.67	194.63	66.64	63.69	124.75
Finland	151.01	189.42	110.50	84.21	109.47
France	57.66	175.72	58.10	70.53	39.82
Germany	63.79	132.08	52.05	65.31	45.54
Greece	73.50	49.46	50.71	39.23	40.40
Ireland	149.84	58.54	83.48	36.41	56.90
Italy	72.23	223.35	44.67	17.50	127.09
Netherlands	62.42	137.10	66.32	66.76	29.42
Norway	208.83	245.06	75.21	85.45	103.02
Portugal	94.09	121.99	58.40	18.42	55.48
Spain	130.35	72.22	66.06	29.84	47.07
Sweden	103.63	174.16	70.86	64.44	75.24
Switzerland	90.41	252.13	96.40	87.13	75.26
Turkey	10.78	14.36	35.43	1.00	16.86
United Kingdom	111.00	62.34	44.04	30.14	43.66
Eastern Europe					
Bulgaria	7.45	56.16	16.09	1.46	8.70
Czech Republic	44.30	93.25	40.47	55.54	34.35
Hungary	67.54	50.84	35.22	49.96	25.15
Poland	35.54	40.92	26.90	34.13	12.77
Romania	12.54	11.73	18.09	15.54	11.74
Russia	26.13	39.20	22.99	20.12	14.88
Slovakia	26.12	60.89	29.15	32.54	20.96
Ukraine	9.96	28.01	9.44	14.95	11.58

Source: Euromonitor International from industry sources/national statistics

Table 6.15

Per Capita Retail Sales of Bakery Products 2008

US$ per capita

	Bread	Pastries	Cakes	Biscuits	Breakfast Cereals
Western Europe					
Austria	309.67	38.93	68.19	44.32	10.46
Belgium	178.95	71.77	87.96	73.77	23.60
Denmark	248.75	16.85	39.82	29.23	30.04
Finland	249.72	31.86	49.86	36.47	27.75
France	161.02	64.18	82.08	46.15	15.25
Germany	165.64	20.64	47.56	26.10	12.37
Greece	153.62	128.70	23.69	19.04	10.36
Ireland	156.95	12.39	43.39	62.17	62.26
Italy	149.22	160.89	86.11	43.31	9.66
Netherlands	162.83	6.90	64.80	61.84	8.35
Norway	209.47	29.24	74.95	36.97	21.34
Portugal	79.66	11.95	12.21	49.84	17.57
Spain	155.92	29.46	12.53	27.23	9.83
Sweden	162.81	18.00	48.77	32.35	23.13
Switzerland	274.73	24.79	43.85	51.80	23.89
Turkey	259.47	3.78	16.24	13.93	1.10
United Kingdom	78.25	22.50	55.61	48.01	46.77
Eastern Europe					
Bulgaria	86.18	10.87	3.78	6.53	2.18
Czech Republic	97.17	10.17	10.35	33.25	5.12
Hungary	85.19	4.33	13.89	20.85	8.03
Poland	80.42	1.33	14.38	17.40	6.54
Romania	115.89	3.97	17.67	10.48	4.29
Russia	53.78	2.86	6.11	13.29	2.69
Slovakia	105.70	1.98	5.83	21.85	5.57
Ukraine	14.67	2.51	3.27	16.87	2.04

Source: *Euromonitor International from industry sources/national statistics*

Consumer Market Statistics

Table 6.16

Per Capita Retail Sales of Confectionery 2008

US$ per capita

	Total Confectionery	Chocolate Confectionery	Sugar Confectionery	Gum
Western Europe				
Austria	156.22	112.13	36.41	7.68
Belgium	142.34	92.94	35.56	13.84
Denmark	233.38	113.08	103.12	17.18
Finland	200.38	95.51	83.55	21.32
France	124.32	85.07	22.00	17.25
Germany	154.58	99.40	44.44	10.74
Greece	66.02	39.96	6.33	19.72
Ireland	253.65	183.69	51.24	18.72
Italy	102.44	58.83	26.09	17.52
Netherlands	129.34	59.97	52.57	16.81
Norway	315.31	190.22	92.83	32.26
Portugal	61.84	37.52	18.15	6.17
Spain	65.36	30.48	24.90	9.98
Sweden	207.67	99.41	88.46	19.79
Switzerland	230.43	156.69	50.11	23.62
Turkey	29.05	17.22	6.33	5.49
United Kingdom	214.31	153.02	49.17	12.12
Eastern Europe				
Bulgaria	37.05	25.62	4.57	6.86
Czech Republic	74.30	50.48	15.61	8.21
Hungary	74.54	50.21	14.03	10.30
Poland	70.56	48.16	13.61	8.78
Romania	29.82	19.28	3.48	7.07
Russia	75.02	52.88	15.21	6.93
Slovakia	63.32	51.78	5.15	6.38
Ukraine	47.21	32.39	9.29	5.52

Source: Euromonitor International from industry sources/national statistics

Consumer Market Statistics **Table 6.17**

Per Capita Retail Sales of Other Selected Packaged Foods 2008
US$ per capita

	Canned Preserved Food	Frozen Processed Food	Dried Processed Food	Chilled Processed Food	Oils and Fats	Sauces, Dressings & Condiments	Sweet and Savoury Snacks
Western Europe							
Austria	26.66	83.20	33.62	114.87	64.90	50.79	32.04
Belgium	85.93	94.22	45.78	216.81	66.07	52.36	33.56
Denmark	67.76	154.15	37.74	281.06	94.86	75.69	49.00
Finland	47.14	97.83	29.53	298.33	78.58	69.19	39.68
France	86.55	63.10	28.06	223.77	58.19	39.37	22.87
Germany	44.58	88.82	32.55	82.52	51.98	51.07	31.43
Greece	32.08	26.45	25.86	53.13	59.00	31.36	94.87
Ireland	41.25	136.71	43.98	150.77	61.17	59.01	126.55
Italy	40.83	47.27	55.25	291.98	57.11	50.02	15.52
Netherlands	38.38	57.09	32.59	166.77	46.61	49.23	44.91
Norway	97.84	200.18	60.26	303.29	87.78	112.79	139.80
Portugal	47.42	30.62	27.84	20.58	74.60	29.37	20.93
Spain	106.08	32.78	19.83	98.72	62.34	34.98	59.88
Sweden	75.01	127.09	35.49	225.43	71.91	84.68	55.46
Switzerland	90.56	94.08	49.04	233.42	76.30	47.06	46.89
Turkey	1.93	1.41	15.93	8.24	56.13	8.88	19.60
United Kingdom	68.59	130.88	30.15	300.29	41.94	67.65	111.47
Eastern Europe							
Bulgaria	11.93	19.02	16.48	58.63	34.63	12.90	5.20
Czech Republic	36.77	51.66	39.06	57.22	64.52	33.09	16.15
Hungary	40.61	29.64	38.99	101.64	42.43	32.23	18.53
Poland	20.20	16.23	23.59	19.59	51.78	36.30	24.06
Romania	10.02	0.90	19.64	44.59	31.89	3.67	13.45
Russia	32.16	45.10	20.73	38.85	40.85	23.51	23.59
Slovakia	39.75	24.53	26.25	70.38	46.26	30.92	22.77
Ukraine	18.73	16.05	8.45	50.23	25.42	18.15	26.82

Source: *Euromonitor International from industry sources/national statistics*

Table 6.18

Per Capita Retail Sales of Tobacco 2008

US$ per capita

	Total Tobacco	Cigarettes	Cigars	Smoking Tobacco
Western Europe				
Austria	420.50	392.32	22.95	5.23
Belgium	479.69	349.65	34.20	95.84
Denmark	474.44	419.27	22.70	30.54
Finland	319.57	279.78	16.19	23.60
France	357.04	317.67	11.91	27.46
Germany	409.24	354.61	13.85	40.78
Greece	611.53	589.75	18.96	2.82
Ireland	710.56	675.72	15.69	19.14
Italy	438.70	429.97	5.91	2.82
Netherlands	388.28	266.82	18.87	102.59
Norway	535.72	327.50	7.60	122.75
Portugal	387.15	364.59	17.12	5.44
Spain	380.66	354.74	17.24	8.69
Sweden	405.09	247.78	4.73	21.01
Switzerland	543.12	475.39	57.70	10.03
Turkey	193.64	193.47	0.02	0.15
United Kingdom	386.78	341.16	19.69	25.93
Eastern Europe				
Bulgaria	311.50	309.83	1.49	0.18
Czech Republic	429.64	405.56	7.12	16.95
Hungary	285.47	262.28	4.30	18.89
Poland	242.13	223.96	0.52	17.64
Romania	209.80	209.05	0.73	0.02
Russia	118.19	115.97	2.04	0.17
Slovakia	264.89	260.43	4.25	0.21
Ukraine	108.82	108.64	0.15	0.03

Source: *Euromonitor International from industry sources/national statistics*

Table 6.19

Per Capita Retail Sales of Toys and Games 2008
US$ per capita

	Toys and Games	Traditional Toys and Games	Video Games Hardware	Video Games Software
Western Europe				
Austria				
Belgium	112.50	53.29	24.97	34.23
Denmark				
Finland				
France	146.92	65.85	30.12	50.95
Germany	74.48	43.34	11.20	19.94
Greece	43.16	26.95	9.83	6.38
Ireland				
Italy	83.63	52.31	14.01	17.31
Netherlands	146.84	76.23	32.08	38.54
Norway				
Portugal	51.94	27.88	12.45	11.62
Spain	85.95	39.48	22.33	24.15
Sweden	122.81	56.03	16.57	50.21
Switzerland				
Turkey	5.75	4.80	0.47	0.48
United Kingdom	185.41	68.35	36.96	80.09
Eastern Europe				
Bulgaria				
Czech Republic				
Hungary	22.46	16.70	1.49	4.27
Poland	17.37	8.76	0.93	7.68
Romania	6.51	5.59	0.31	0.61
Russia	6.83	5.46	0.52	0.85
Slovakia				
Ukraine				

Source: *Euromonitor International from industry sources/national statistics*

Consumer Prices and Costs

Consumer Prices Statistics

Table 7.1

Index of Consumer Prices 1990-2008

1995 = 100

	1990	1995	2000	2003	2004	2005	2006	2007	2008
Western Europe									
Austria	85.3	100.0	107.2	113.5	115.9	118.5	120.3	122.9	126.8
Belgium	88.6	100.0	108.6	114.9	117.3	120.6	122.7	125.0	130.6
Cyprus	79.3	100.0	115.4	126.0	128.9	132.2	135.5	138.7	145.2
Denmark	90.7	100.0	112.1	120.0	121.4	123.6	125.9	128.1	132.4
Finland	89.8	100.0	108.0	113.4	113.7	114.6	116.4	119.4	124.2
France	89.6	100.0	106.2	112.3	114.7	116.8	118.6	120.4	123.8
Germany	84.3	100.0	106.4	111.2	113.1	114.8	116.6	119.3	122.4
Gibraltar	72.2	100.0	117.3	124.8	126.6	127.7	129.2	131.6	133.7
Greece	52.3	100.0	126.7	140.5	144.5	149.7	154.5	158.9	165.5
Iceland	83.8	100.0	114.9	131.2	134.9	140.5	149.9	157.5	177.5
Ireland	88.3	100.0	113.4	128.8	131.6	134.8	140.1	146.9	152.9
Italy	78.3	100.0	112.8	121.9	124.6	127.1	129.8	132.1	136.6
Liechtenstein									
Luxembourg	87.1	100.0	108.1	115.6	118.2	121.1	124.4	127.2	131.6
Malta	84.7	100.0	112.6	120.0	123.4	127.1	130.6	132.3	137.9
Monaco		100.0	107.5	110.6	111.6	112.6	113.4	114.5	115.7
Netherlands	87.4	100.0	111.2	122.1	123.6	125.7	127.2	129.2	132.4
Norway	88.9	100.0	112.0	119.8	120.4	122.2	125.0	126.0	130.7
Portugal	70.9	100.0	113.9	127.1	130.1	133.1	136.7	140.6	144.2
Spain	77.7	100.0	113.8	125.2	129.0	133.3	138.0	141.9	147.7
Sweden	81.4	100.0	102.3	109.1	109.5	110.0	111.5	114.0	117.9
Switzerland	85.6	100.0	103.8	106.1	107.0	108.3	109.4	110.2	112.9
Turkey	5.5	100.0	1,579.6	4,430.0	4,898.9	5,395.5	5,962.7	6,484.8	7,162.1
United Kingdom	83.1	100.0	108.2	112.5	114.0	116.3	119.0	121.8	126.2
Eastern Europe									
Albania	9.2	100.0	181.9	203.1	207.8	212.7	217.7	224.1	231.6
Belarus		100.0	4,576.7	13,496.7	15,940.7	17,588.8	18,825.8	20,411.2	23,439.8
Bosnia-Herzegovina		100.0	100.7	106.2	106.5	110.3	117.0	118.8	127.6
Bulgaria	2.2	100.0	3,447.1	4,000.3	4,254.2	4,468.6	4,793.1	5,195.8	5,837.4
Croatia		100.0	125.8	135.1	137.8	142.4	147.0	151.2	160.4
Czech Republic	39.6	100.0	138.6	147.9	152.1	154.9	158.8	163.4	173.8
Estonia		100.0	158.2	175.6	180.9	188.3	196.7	209.7	231.4
Georgia		100.0	191.7	221.9	234.6	253.9	277.3	302.9	333.1
Hungary	32.4	100.0	201.7	242.7	259.1	268.3	278.7	300.8	319.1
Latvia		100.0	140.3	150.8	160.2	171.0	182.2	200.5	231.4
Lithuania		100.0	145.1	145.8	147.5	151.4	157.1	166.1	184.2
Macedonia		100.0	109.8	119.5	120.6	120.8	124.8	129.3	138.6
Moldova		100.0	271.8	351.1	395.1	442.3	498.9	560.5	632.1
Poland	16.7	100.0	181.9	197.1	204.1	208.4	210.7	215.8	225.2
Romania	0.9	100.0	1,195.1	2,270.0	2,539.6	2,767.9	2,950.1	3,092.8	3,335.5
Russia		100.0	485.6	776.4	860.8	969.9	1,063.8	1,159.6	1,323.2
Slovakia		100.0	148.4	178.6	192.1	197.3	206.1	211.8	221.5
Slovenia		100.0	148.5	182.6	189.2	193.9	198.6	205.8	217.5
Ukraine		100.0	363.6	431.5	470.6	534.2	582.7	657.5	823.3

Source:*National statistical offices/OECD/Eurostat/Euromonitor International*

Consumer Prices Statistics

Table 7.2

Index of Consumer Prices by Quarter 2007-2009

1995 = 100

	2007 1st Quarter	2007 2nd Quarter	2007 3rd Quarter	2007 4th Quarter	2008 1st Quarter	2008 2nd Quarter	2008 3rd Quarter	2008 4th Quarter	2009 1st Quarter	2009 2nd Quarter
Western Europe										
Austria	121.4	122.8	123.0	124.5	125.4	127.2	127.5	127.3	126.8	127.5
Belgium	123.9	124.5	124.9	126.5	128.6	130.8	131.9	130.9	130.7	130.4
Cyprus	135.5	138.5	138.6	142.2	141.8	145.4	146.2	147.3	143.2	
Denmark	127.1	128.3	127.8	129.1	130.9	132.7	133.1	132.9	133.3	134.4
Finland	117.9	119.3	119.6	120.5	122.5	124.2	125.1	125.1	124.4	
France	119.0	120.3	120.5	121.7	122.6	124.3	124.5	123.9	123.4	124.0
Germany	118.1	119.0	119.6	120.5	121.5	122.4	123.3	122.6	122.5	122.7
Gibraltar	129.7	131.3	132.4	133.0	130.4	132.6	135.8	136.1	134.0	
Greece	156.2	159.2	158.3	162.1	162.9	166.7	165.7	166.8	165.4	167.8
Iceland	154.2	156.2	158.2	161.5	165.2	175.3	180.4	189.0	193.4	196.2
Ireland	143.9	146.6	148.0	149.3	150.7	153.4	154.4	153.1	148.4	146.5
Italy	130.9	131.7	132.5	133.5	134.9	136.5	137.7	137.1	136.8	137.5
Liechtenstein										
Luxembourg	125.7	127.1	127.1	128.9	129.9	132.1	132.6	131.6	130.7	132.0
Malta	129.8	131.5	132.6	135.1	134.6	136.5	138.5	142.0	140.0	141.2
Monaco										
Netherlands	128.1	129.7	129.2	129.8	130.8	132.7	133.3	132.8	133.4	134.9
Norway	124.9	125.5	125.5	128.0	129.3	129.6	131.3	132.6	132.4	133.6
Portugal	138.6	141.2	140.6	141.9	142.8	145.3	144.9	144.0	142.5	143.5
Spain	139.4	142.0	141.5	144.7	145.2	148.6	148.6	148.3	145.8	147.6
Sweden	112.4	113.7	113.9	115.8	116.1	118.0	118.8	118.7	117.0	117.5
Switzerland	108.9	110.5	110.0	111.4	111.6	113.5	113.2	113.2	111.6	112.6
Turkey	6,327.9	6,468.8	6,444.9	6,697.5	6,885.5	7,137.4	7,195.6	7,429.8	7,461.6	7,544.0
United Kingdom	119.7	121.6	122.1	123.7	124.0	126.5	127.7	126.6	123.9	124.9
Eastern Europe										
Albania	224.1	222.1	223.3	226.9	232.4	231.5	229.9	232.7	236.6	236.3
Belarus	19,925.1	20,073.2	20,352.5	21,294.2	22,510.7	23,189.0	23,665.3	24,394.2	25,978.4	
Bosnia-Herzegovina										
Bulgaria	5,009.7	5,036.1	5,264.7	5,472.7	5,674.9	5,790.1	5,906.2	5,978.5	6,014.6	
Croatia	148.8	151.0	150.4	154.7	157.4	160.7	162.0	161.4	163.5	
Czech Republic	160.6	162.8	164.1	166.2	172.5	173.8	175.0	174.0	176.2	176.3
Estonia	203.0	206.9	211.3	217.6	225.4	230.5	234.2	235.5	232.6	229.8
Georgia	295.3	297.8	301.9	316.7	328.6	332.2	335.2	336.4		
Hungary	294.0	299.9	302.0	307.3	314.5	320.2	321.1	320.5	324.0	
Latvia	191.4	196.7	202.2	211.8	222.8	231.5	234.1	237.3	243.4	242.4
Lithuania	161.2	164.0	166.7	172.4	178.3	183.8	186.3	188.5	193.8	193.4
Macedonia	127.1	128.4	129.1	132.6	137.5	139.4	138.3	139.3	138.8	138.8
Moldova	535.7	547.5	566.3	592.6	615.4	636.9	633.8	642.5	634.6	
Poland	213.0	215.8	215.5	218.7	222.1	225.4	225.9	227.2	230.2	234.5
Romania	3,023.4	3,055.3	3,102.4	3,190.1	3,263.8	3,316.8	3,353.9	3,407.4	3,484.7	3,518.6
Russia	1,120.4	1,143.7	1,167.2	1,207.2	1,264.5	1,313.7	1,341.4	1,373.3	1,438.0	
Slovakia	210.2	211.1	211.6	214.3	218.7	220.6	222.4	224.5	225.3	225.7
Slovenia	199.9	205.2	207.3	210.9	213.1	218.8	219.9	217.9	217.0	220.4
Ukraine	625.7	635.0	662.0	707.5	766.6	826.5	832.7	867.4	922.8	

Source:*National statistical offices/OECD/Eurostat/Euromonitor International*

Consumer Prices Statistics

Table 7.3

Index of Consumer Prices by Month 2008
1995 = 100

	January	February	March	April	May	June	July	August	September	October	November	December
Western Europe												
Austria	124.8	125.2	126.1	126.5	127.3	127.7	127.6	127.3	127.7	127.6	127.2	127.0
Belgium	127.7	128.6	129.5	129.8	131.0	131.7	132.4	131.6	131.8	131.6	130.8	130.5
Cyprus	140.9	141.6	143.0	144.5	145.7	146.1	145.2	145.7	147.6	148.8	147.3	145.9
Denmark	129.7	131.3	131.8	132.3	132.7	133.2	132.7	133.0	133.5	133.3	133.0	132.5
Finland	121.7	122.3	123.3	123.6	124.3	124.7	124.5	125.1	125.6	125.6	125.1	124.6
France	122.1	122.4	123.3	123.7	124.4	124.8	124.6	124.5	124.4	124.4	123.8	123.5
Germany	120.9	121.5	122.1	121.8	122.5	122.9	123.6	123.2	123.1	122.9	122.3	122.6
Gibraltar												
Greece	162.5	161.2	164.9	166.0	167.2	167.0	165.7	164.1	167.4	167.4	166.9	166.1
Iceland	162.9	165.1	167.6	173.2	175.6	177.2	178.9	180.4	182.0	185.9	189.1	192.1
Ireland	149.0	150.8	152.2	152.4	153.5	154.2	153.8	154.5	155.0	154.7	153.2	151.4
Italy	134.4	134.7	135.4	135.7	136.5	137.1	137.7	137.9	137.5	137.5	137.0	136.8
Liechtenstein												
Luxembourg	128.6	130.0	131.0	131.3	132.2	132.8	132.2	132.7	132.9	132.6	131.5	130.8
Malta	134.0	134.5	135.4	135.9	136.5	137.0	138.2	138.1	139.2	142.2	141.8	141.9
Monaco												
Netherlands	129.8	130.7	132.0	132.5	133.0	132.7	132.9	133.2	133.7	133.4	133.0	132.0
Norway	128.8	129.5	129.6	129.5	129.6	129.8	130.6	130.7	132.7	133.2	132.4	132.1
Portugal	142.0	142.0	144.2	144.6	145.2	146.1	145.1	144.4	145.1	144.9	143.9	143.1
Spain	144.6	144.8	146.1	147.7	148.7	149.5	148.8	148.5	148.4	149.0	148.3	147.6
Sweden	115.4	115.8	117.0	117.5	117.9	118.5	118.2	118.5	119.7	119.9	118.9	117.3
Switzerland	111.4	111.6	111.9	112.8	113.8	113.9	113.4	113.1	113.2	113.9	113.1	112.6
Turkey	6,804.7	6,892.7	6,958.9	7,075.6	7,181.2	7,155.3	7,196.5	7,178.9	7,211.3	7,398.9	7,460.5	7,429.9
United Kingdom	123.2	124.2	124.6	125.7	126.3	127.3	127.2	127.6	128.3	127.9	126.9	125.1
Eastern Europe												
Albania	230.2	232.5	234.6	233.6	231.4	229.5	228.1	229.5	231.9	232.1	231.9	234.1
Belarus	22,349.4	22,496.9	22,685.9	22,946.8	23,240.5	23,379.9	23,557.6	23,597.7	23,840.7	24,081.5	24,406.6	24,694.6
Bosnia-Herzegovina												
Bulgaria	5,617.8	5,680.2	5,726.7	5,775.5	5,802.0	5,792.8	5,879.5	5,886.7	5,952.5	5,984.5	5,981.2	5,969.8
Croatia	157.2	157.1	157.9	159.1	160.9	162.1	162.2	161.8	162.1	161.9	161.7	160.7
Czech Republic	172.3	172.7	172.6	173.1	173.9	174.2	175.2	175.1	174.8	174.8	173.8	173.4
Estonia	224.3	225.1	226.8	229.0	230.5	231.9	233.6	233.9	235.2	236.0	235.3	235.0
Georgia	326.5	329.5	329.9	330.7	333.2	332.8	328.8	339.7	337.0	335.5	337.6	336.3
Hungary	311.6	314.9	316.8	317.9	321.2	321.6	321.7	320.9	320.7	321.4	320.6	319.5
Latvia	219.8	222.7	225.9	229.4	231.7	233.2	233.9	233.0	235.5	238.3	237.4	236.3
Lithuania	176.4	178.4	180.2	182.4	183.9	185.0	185.8	186.1	187.0	188.9	188.4	188.3
Macedonia	136.4	137.5	138.5	139.1	139.4	139.8	138.5	138.3	138.0	139.0	139.2	139.7
Moldova	607.1	616.2	622.9	632.9	642.4	635.3	629.6	634.0	637.8	642.9	642.9	641.6
Poland	221.2	222.1	223.1	224.0	225.8	226.3	226.3	225.4	226.0	226.9	227.4	227.2
Romania	3,241.3	3,264.1	3,286.0	3,303.1	3,319.1	3,328.3	3,351.4	3,348.5	3,361.8	3,397.5	3,408.5	3,416.3
Russia	1,249.4	1,264.5	1,279.6	1,297.8	1,315.3	1,328.0	1,334.7	1,339.4	1,350.2	1,362.6	1,373.9	1,383.4
Slovakia	217.9	218.8	219.4	219.8	220.6	221.3	221.6	222.1	223.5	224.4	224.8	224.4
Slovenia	212.2	212.2	214.9	216.6	218.9	220.9	220.8	219.6	219.5	219.5	217.9	216.5
Ukraine	743.5	763.6	792.6	817.2	827.8	834.4	830.2	829.4	838.5	852.8	865.6	883.8

Source:National statistical offices/OECD/Eurostat/Euromonitor International

Consumer Prices Statistics | Table 7.4

Index of Food and Non-Alcoholic Beverage Prices 1990-2008
1995 = 100

	1990	1995	2000	2003	2004	2005	2006	2007	2008
Western Europe									
Austria	92.0	100.0	103.6	111.8	113.8	114.9	115.9	117.1	118.0
Belgium	87.2	100.0	107.0	117.0	117.6	120.6	122.1	123.6	125.4
Cyprus	78.2	100.0	83.2	94.0	96.9	100.2			
Denmark	93.8	100.0	107.6	115.9	114.4	114.8	113.4	112.7	112.1
Finland	109.7	100.0	98.9	107.2	107.6	107.9	109.7	111.4	112.6
France	93.8	100.0	108.7	122.0	122.6	122.6	125.5	126.5	127.7
Germany	92.7	100.0	103.4	108.8	108.5	109.1	108.3	108.5	108.7
Gibraltar	88.0	100.0	110.3	119.5	121.9	124.2			
Greece	60.2	100.0	122.9	143.2	144.4	145.8	149.3	151.0	152.9
Iceland	93.3	100.0	117.4	132.9	137.1	140.9			
Ireland	99.3	100.0	110.0	115.4	111.9	108.2	105.4	102.5	99.7
Italy	82.8	100.0	106.8	117.0	118.8	117.4	118.0	118.1	117.9
Liechtenstein									
Luxembourg	92.6	100.0	107.7	118.1	120.9	123.2			
Malta	87.3	100.0	110.0	118.6	120.9	122.8			
Monaco									
Netherlands	93.0	100.0	107.0	118.1	113.7	112.2	110.2	107.9	106.1
Norway	94.5	100.0	114.8	115.0	116.5	118.8	122.0	124.0	126.2
Portugal	80.6	100.0	111.6	132.2	134.7	132.8	136.5	138.2	139.3
Spain	76.4	100.0	111.4	126.2	130.2	136.1	140.4	144.5	148.8
Sweden	89.6	100.0	92.8	99.7	98.3	97.2	96.9	96.1	95.5
Switzerland	94.7	100.0	97.3	100.9	100.1	98.0	97.3	96.1	95.0
Turkey	5.5	100.0	1,455.5	4,024.8	4,468.1	4,460.7	4,914.6	5,170.4	5,383.5
United Kingdom	93.9	100.0	104.7	110.9	112.9	114.9	117.4	119.4	121.4
Eastern Europe									
Albania		100.0	213.7	235.9	241.9	246.7			
Belarus		100.0	5,442.0	11,756.0	13,345.4	15,471.0	16,535.5	17,924.4	19,284.7
Bosnia-Herzegovina									
Bulgaria	2.2	100.0	3,475.2	3,598.4	3,895.2	3,914.0	4,141.8	4,299.4	4,435.6
Croatia		100.0	115.1	119.5	121.2	126.9	132.8	136.7	141.1
Czech Republic	38.7	100.0	108.0	108.9	112.7	112.6	114.1	115.6	116.5
Estonia		100.0	126.8	138.2	146.9	153.9	157.4	163.0	167.9
Georgia		100.0	173.7	207.7	217.4	227.1			
Hungary	33.7	100.0	182.9	210.7	221.6	221.9	230.2	236.0	240.4
Latvia		100.0	115.9	129.1	137.8	145.2	151.8	158.4	164.7
Lithuania		100.0	98.5	102.0	103.7	103.1	103.9	104.5	104.6
Macedonia		100.0	101.5	111.3	114.0	116.2			
Moldova		100.0	240.8	311.4	332.4	356.4			
Poland	21.7	100.0	159.0	174.2	180.5	182.7	189.2	196.4	208.8
Romania	0.6	100.0	845.9	1,539.6	1,714.4	1,764.3	1,865.3	1,960.5	2,034.1
Russia		100.0	487.4	616.5	630.8	679.4	714.2	742.5	777.0
Slovakia		100.0	116.2	125.8	133.7	135.0	140.0	144.0	147.1
Slovenia		100.0	133.3	163.3	163.4	161.6	162.5	162.3	162.0
Ukraine		100.0	840.6	1,258.7	1,522.9	1,870.4	1,915.0	2,105.8	2,282.5

Source: *National statistical offices/OECD/Eurostat/Euromonitor International*

Consumer Prices Statistics

Table 7.5

Costs of Selected Food and Drink Items 2008

US$

	Apples (Kg)	Beer (33cl)	Butter (250g)	Flour (Kg)	Fresh Chicken (Kg)	Instant Coffee (250g)
Western Europe						
Austria	2.50	0.72	2.62	1.39	6.15	
Belgium	2.08	0.59	2.22	1.01	5.90	8.88
Cyprus	4.37	1.74	3.15	1.31	5.95	10.71
Denmark	2.84	1.02	2.71	1.17		12.89
Finland	2.75	1.79	1.71	0.62	2.60	11.62
France	3.13	0.71	2.32	1.27	13.01	
Germany						
Gibraltar	3.23	1.04	2.04	2.43	5.23	13.71
Greece	2.15	0.96	2.21	2.27	4.42	9.82
Iceland	1.58	1.75	1.13	0.75	5.62	13.86
Ireland		6.48	1.85	1.30	6.61	
Italy	3.63	0.73	3.12	0.96	7.11	
Liechtenstein						
Luxembourg	3.56	0.87	2.23	1.19	8.50	12.85
Malta	1.74	1.21	1.64	0.85	3.19	7.36
Monaco						
Netherlands	2.28	0.78	1.66	0.76	6.02	9.79
Norway	2.33	2.53	2.40	1.43	8.46	17.92
Portugal	1.86	0.67	2.37	1.25	3.68	11.48
Spain	2.60	0.70	2.80	1.04	4.70	8.07
Sweden	2.84	1.20	1.66	0.76	5.41	13.54
Switzerland	3.55	1.05	3.65	1.70	10.58	12.94
Turkey	1.32	1.07	2.86	1.15	4.52	10.14
United Kingdom	2.51	2.59	1.85	0.90	4.31	9.16
Eastern Europe						
Albania						
Belarus	1.35	0.36	1.07	0.64	3.47	7.92
Bosnia-Herzegovina						
Bulgaria	1.28	0.33	1.53	0.90	3.54	9.64
Croatia	1.41	0.65	2.11	1.01	4.82	13.59
Czech Republic	1.83	0.67	2.15	0.77	3.99	10.96
Estonia	1.76	0.55	3.07	1.08	4.55	8.20
Georgia	0.81	0.49	1.40	1.04	4.55	8.74
Hungary	1.64	0.50	2.88	0.88	4.12	12.10
Latvia	1.82	0.68	2.00	0.82	4.53	8.31
Lithuania	1.88	0.57	2.57	1.06	3.50	9.09
Macedonia	0.87	0.48	1.55	0.61	2.94	9.38
Moldova	0.99	0.69	1.85	1.08	4.32	8.73
Poland	1.68	0.72	2.26	0.81	2.70	12.72
Romania	1.49	0.90	1.82	0.71	3.50	11.15
Russia	1.90	0.48	1.65	0.73	3.69	8.80
Slovakia	1.64	0.49	2.49	0.65	3.47	13.28
Slovenia	1.71	0.68	2.82	1.54	5.03	12.80
Ukraine	1.24	0.32	1.35	0.56	2.89	6.76

Source: *Euromonitor International from International Labour Organisation*
Note: *'Cost' refers to national average retail prices paid by consumers, including related costs, such as sales or value-added, taxes.*

Costs of Selected Food and Drink Items 2008 *(continued)*
US$

	Milk (Litre)	Potatoes (Kg)	Red Table Wine (Litre)	Soft Drinks (Cola etc.) (33cl)	Sugar (Kg)	Tea (100g)
Western Europe						
Austria	1.64	1.56	8.56	0.38	1.59	5.82
Belgium	1.35	1.39	10.29	0.43	1.38	4.63
Cyprus	1.66	1.19	6.71	0.48	1.94	2.02
Denmark	1.76	2.17		1.20	1.96	2.94
Finland	1.10	1.04	12.84	0.63	1.48	4.70
France	1.60	2.02	2.49		1.99	
Germany						
Gibraltar	2.13	2.41	11.58	0.83	1.27	1.89
Greece	1.90	1.14	6.22		1.24	2.15
Iceland	0.84	1.55	19.99	1.42	1.55	4.39
Ireland	1.47	2.04	16.81		1.52	2.34
Italy	2.49	2.09	3.26	0.47	1.37	4.59
Liechtenstein						
Luxembourg	1.76	2.18	2.12	0.43	2.08	4.31
Malta	0.91	0.78	3.19	0.80	0.88	0.79
Monaco						
Netherlands	1.43	1.16	6.43	0.37	1.34	1.90
Norway	2.30	1.91	21.45	1.90	2.57	6.41
Portugal	1.16	0.88	2.16	0.69	1.47	5.03
Spain	1.42	1.23	1.46	0.35	1.34	4.67
Sweden	1.16	1.71	9.61	1.19	1.51	3.23
Switzerland	1.40	1.96	11.02	0.79	1.66	3.88
Turkey	1.49	0.56	11.30	0.88	1.65	0.83
United Kingdom	1.32	1.41	9.82	0.74	1.44	1.22
Eastern Europe						
Albania						
Belarus	0.49	0.29	5.54	0.21	0.91	1.32
Bosnia-Herzegovina						
Bulgaria	1.16	0.74	5.14	0.22	1.48	2.02
Croatia	1.10	0.79	4.84	0.45	1.28	1.77
Czech Republic	1.52	0.63	4.02	0.12	1.33	2.50
Estonia	1.24	0.71	7.73	0.64	1.43	1.29
Georgia	1.71	0.46	5.03	0.33	0.96	1.01
Hungary	1.21	1.05	1.97	0.77	1.34	1.78
Latvia	1.23	0.69		0.33	1.65	1.08
Lithuania	1.32	0.63	9.17	0.57	1.37	3.32
Macedonia	1.04	0.59	1.79	0.35	0.90	1.82
Moldova	0.89	0.57	4.92	0.60	1.08	1.36
Poland	0.44	0.33	8.80	0.61	1.25	1.03
Romania	0.97	0.63	2.63	0.48	1.39	
Russia	1.10	0.57	6.09	0.26	0.92	0.94
Slovakia	0.96	0.53	3.38	0.27	1.40	2.40
Slovenia	1.10	0.72	2.54	0.40	1.19	6.12
Ukraine	0.82	0.53	1.31	0.19	0.67	0.57

Source: *Euromonitor International from International Labour Organisation*
Note: *'Cost' refers to national average retail prices paid by consumers, including related costs, such as sales or value-added, taxes.*

Table 7.6

Index of Alcoholic Beverage and Tobacco Prices 1990-2008
1995 = 100

	1990	1995	2000	2003	2004	2005	2006	2007	2008
Western Europe									
Austria	86.7	100.0	107.4	120.8	123.3	130.1	133.8	137.6	141.8
Belgium	82.8	100.0	112.9	124.5	130.3	132.2	136.6	140.1	143.0
Cyprus									
Denmark	96.5	100.0	108.8	111.7	106.0	108.3	106.9	105.5	105.3
Finland	85.6	100.0	106.4	111.7	98.7	97.1	94.3	90.0	87.4
France	73.8	100.0	121.2	143.2	161.2	161.1	177.9	187.9	196.1
Germany	85.3	100.0	109.8	120.8	128.1	137.8	146.1	153.9	161.9
Gibraltar									
Greece	43.5	100.0	139.9	167.1	174.6	178.8	185.6	191.0	195.9
Iceland									
Ireland	82.2	100.0	132.2	160.5	166.7	169.0	177.4	182.3	187.1
Italy	67.4	100.0	119.3	132.8	141.9	148.9	157.4	164.3	171.1
Liechtenstein									
Luxembourg									
Malta									
Monaco									
Netherlands	82.1	100.0	114.4	130.4	139.7	143.5	149.2	154.6	159.1
Norway	75.5	100.0	133.5	140.9	151.0	154.9	161.3	167.1	172.0
Portugal	72.7	100.0	122.1	148.2	153.8	159.4	168.8	175.5	174.5
Spain	56.4	100.0	138.9	154.7	160.3	170.8	177.0	183.5	190.5
Sweden	76.4	100.0	110.5	115.3	115.0	115.3	116.7	117.1	117.7
Switzerland	92.6	100.0	105.8	108.6	111.0	114.4	116.9	119.2	121.6
Turkey	5.5	100.0	1,982.1	6,866.3	8,362.8	9,122.2	10,050.3	10,968.8	11,759.1
United Kingdom	74.9	100.0	127.2	138.3	141.4	144.3	149.0	152.2	155.5
Eastern Europe									
Albania									
Belarus		100.0	3,575.4	9,340.3	11,597.5	14,273.2	15,255.3	16,973.1	18,575.9
Bosnia-Herzegovina									
Bulgaria	2.5	100.0	3,762.2	4,902.0	6,304.9	6,544.9	6,925.9	7,512.7	7,903.2
Croatia		100.0	140.4	150.5	158.4	168.3	175.0	182.0	188.8
Czech Republic	38.7	100.0	150.4	159.7	164.5	166.9	171.3	174.7	177.8
Estonia		100.0	193.5	210.5	206.5	222.8	231.0	237.0	246.1
Georgia									
Hungary	41.1	100.0	227.9	293.6	326.0	330.1	343.3	357.8	367.6
Latvia		100.0	145.0	156.3	163.0	164.5	174.5	179.7	184.9
Lithuania		100.0	150.2	150.8	153.7	152.0	158.8	161.0	163.0
Macedonia									
Moldova									
Poland	18.5	100.0	180.9	179.5	179.3	178.2	177.1	176.3	175.6
Romania	1.7	100.0	1,008.3	1,867.7	2,209.8	2,403.4	2,541.1	2,737.2	2,895.6
Russia		100.0	596.7	842.2	897.0	906.0	918.4	940.6	954.4
Slovakia		100.0	129.2	162.4	178.5	180.3	194.4	203.6	211.2
Slovenia		100.0	142.1	193.1	203.0	211.2	224.6	233.8	243.1
Ukraine		100.0	353.3	583.4	714.6	911.5	947.4	1,053.2	1,155.8

Source: *National statistical offices/OECD/Eurostat/Euromonitor International*

Table 7.7

Index of Clothing and Footwear Prices 1990-2008
1995 = 100

	1990	1995	2000	2003	2004	2005	2006	2007	2008
Western Europe									
Austria	84.8	100.0	101.2	103.6	103.1	103.1	102.2	101.8	101.4
Belgium	90.6	100.0	104.6	108.5	108.8	108.8	108.8	108.9	109.0
Cyprus	81.2	100.0	113.8						
Denmark	94.4	100.0	105.1	107.4	107.1	106.1	106.3	106.0	105.7
Finland	89.1	100.0	97.2	97.0	96.8	96.7	97.6	98.7	99.3
France	91.5	100.0	102.9	105.0	105.3	105.4	107.5	108.3	109.3
Germany	89.8	100.0	104.5	105.0	104.4	102.7	100.3	99.3	97.9
Gibraltar	90.7	100.0	102.1						
Greece	60.3	100.0	131.8	143.2	149.0	156.2	162.1	167.5	173.1
Iceland	88.0	100.0	95.0						
Ireland	100.6	100.0	77.5	68.2	65.6	63.6	61.2	59.2	57.3
Italy	83.0	100.0	113.6	122.7	124.5	124.8	126.1	126.9	127.6
Liechtenstein									
Luxembourg	100.0								
Malta	89.7	100.0	95.2						
Monaco									
Netherlands	99.0	100.0	106.6	106.8	104.7	101.8	98.7	96.3	93.8
Norway	93.6	100.0	91.7	78.6	73.2	70.1	66.8	63.4	60.4
Portugal	94.7	100.0	95.7	107.9	107.6	105.4	106.9	107.0	106.9
Spain	74.7	100.0	113.7	121.8	123.2	126.6	128.8	130.8	133.1
Sweden	80.3	100.0	102.1	106.2	103.3	103.2	102.5	101.5	100.9
Switzerland	89.6	100.0	96.8	87.6	84.1	82.8	81.1	79.1	77.6
Turkey	5.5	100.0	1,315.7	3,626.2	3,988.0	4,001.0	4,408.0	4,632.8	4,828.4
United Kingdom	103.1	100.0	94.1	84.4	82.9	81.3	80.4	79.2	78.1
Eastern Europe									
Albania									
Belarus		100.0	5,523.0	16,442.5	19,424.2	23,165.0	24,758.9	27,174.8	29,481.8
Bosnia-Herzegovina									
Bulgaria	1.7	100.0	2,883.9	2,771.6	2,824.9	2,752.8	2,913.1	2,954.1	3,002.6
Croatia		100.0	128.1	136.2	135.5	136.3	136.1	136.1	136.0
Czech Republic	38.7	100.0	112.9	102.9	98.7	93.2	89.4	85.5	81.5
Estonia		100.0	157.8	174.7	175.9	181.4	189.5	193.7	199.0
Georgia									
Hungary	38.7	100.0	210.7	230.1	236.9	234.4	242.1	245.7	248.4
Latvia		100.0	180.7	186.8	191.6	214.1	230.3	242.9	258.6
Lithuania		100.0	140.5	119.3	122.9	138.8	143.5	150.5	158.6
Macedonia		100.0	99.4						
Moldova									
Poland	11.7	100.0	175.2	195.9	197.1	198.1	198.4	198.9	199.8
Romania	0.9	100.0	990.7	1,616.1	1,769.4	1,798.6	1,901.6	1,985.0	2,049.4
Russia		100.0	524.2	687.0	717.0	744.4	787.3	816.4	847.1
Slovakia		100.0	127.2	135.7	138.3	139.4	142.2	144.0	145.8
Slovenia		100.0	127.3	141.8	143.9	142.4	144.8	145.6	146.2
Ukraine		100.0	415.2	542.3	668.0	838.6	861.6	954.5	1,041.3

Source:National statistical offices/OECD/Eurostat/Euromonitor International

Consumer Prices Statistics

Table 7.8

Index of Housing Prices 1990-2008
1995 = 100

	1990	1995	2000	2003	2004	2005	2006	2007	2008
Western Europe									
Austria	78.5	100.0	115.8	126.1	130.8	138.0	143.0	147.9	153.1
Belgium	85.7	100.0	111.4	118.7	121.0	128.5	132.1	136.0	140.6
Cyprus									
Denmark	88.6	100.0	119.0	132.3	135.5	139.6	143.9	147.2	150.8
Finland	80.6	100.0	115.6	129.5	131.5	135.2	140.6	145.0	149.1
France	83.8	100.0	108.8	116.4	119.7	124.6	125.8	128.5	131.3
Germany	73.8	100.0	112.9	118.1	120.0	123.4	126.1	128.8	131.7
Gibraltar									
Greece	49.6	100.0	124.6	138.5	145.2	158.8	169.0	177.8	187.6
Iceland									
Ireland	87.3	100.0	172.2	226.9	228.7	234.1	242.2	246.6	252.1
Italy	68.6	100.0	123.6	139.5	145.8	150.1	155.2	159.4	163.6
Liechtenstein									
Luxembourg									
Malta									
Monaco									
Netherlands	80.7	100.0	121.4	138.2	142.3	150.5	156.3	161.6	167.3
Norway	86.9	100.0	114.9	139.8	138.3	140.6	145.3	146.8	149.3
Portugal	75.4	100.0	115.6	138.3	143.6	148.6	157.1	163.2	169.1
Spain	66.7	100.0	122.1	130.4	134.1	143.1	147.9	152.9	158.6
Sweden	78.7	100.0	103.9	115.9	117.6	119.5	123.3	125.4	127.8
Switzerland	81.3	100.0	101.2	101.9	102.2	103.8	104.4	104.9	105.8
Turkey	5.5	100.0	1,858.0	5,306.4	6,020.3	6,424.1	7,077.7	7,588.1	8,063.6
United Kingdom	74.8	100.0	123.0	143.0	152.0	162.9	174.2	183.3	192.9
Eastern Europe									
Albania									
Belarus		100.0	2,987.0	33,445.4	40,081.2	50,860.3	54,359.7	60,433.9	66,507.4
Bosnia-Herzegovina									
Bulgaria	2.2	100.0	4,495.6	6,070.4	6,628.7	6,752.7	7,145.7	7,457.5	7,732.7
Croatia		100.0	143.2	160.7	166.9	174.4	183.9	190.6	197.5
Czech Republic	38.7	100.0	167.3	199.1	203.8	213.4	220.8	227.1	234.3
Estonia		100.0	184.1	223.3	232.6	242.5	256.0	265.5	275.4
Georgia									
Hungary	31.8	100.0	239.5	292.4	328.5	347.0	360.4	380.2	396.0
Latvia		100.0	153.4	168.3	180.4	186.5	199.2	208.1	216.7
Lithuania		100.0	211.2	212.7	220.3	231.6	251.4	262.5	274.9
Macedonia									
Moldova									
Poland	12.5	100.0	194.1	214.4	219.7	224.1	226.8	230.1	233.7
Romania	0.9	100.0	1,729.5	3,742.1	4,626.5	5,344.6	5,650.8	6,206.3	6,681.7
Russia		100.0	786.5	2,102.7	2,494.6	2,844.2	3,371.0	3,738.9	4,118.9
Slovakia		100.0	204.6	298.5	350.6	385.7	413.7	446.9	476.0
Slovenia		100.0	179.6	222.7	237.3	259.0	275.9	291.4	307.8
Ukraine		100.0	308.9	518.7	578.1	736.8	782.6	859.3	944.5

Source:National statistical offices/OECD/Eurostat/Euromonitor International

Table 7.9

Index of Household Goods and Services Prices 1990-2008
1995 = 100

	1990	1995	2000	2003	2004	2005	2006	2007	2008
Western Europe									
Austria	87.1	100.0	102.6	105.1	105.2	105.9	106.0	106.2	106.5
Belgium	90.6	100.0	105.2	112.0	112.3	113.9	114.5	115.3	116.1
Cyprus									
Denmark	88.8	100.0	112.3	119.4	122.2	122.6	124.5	126.0	127.1
Finland	91.8	100.0	99.5	103.8	103.8	104.9	106.6	108.4	109.8
France	90.3	100.0	107.3	113.7	115.0	115.1	117.5	118.6	119.8
Germany	88.6	100.0	106.0	108.8	108.9	109.2	108.5	108.8	108.9
Gibraltar									
Greece	55.2	100.0	125.2	132.4	134.3	137.2	139.9	142.1	144.4
Iceland									
Ireland	99.2	100.0	114.8	120.5	119.1	118.2	117.4	116.4	115.7
Italy	81.4	100.0	111.0	117.2	118.5	119.0	119.8	120.4	120.9
Liechtenstein									
Luxembourg									
Malta									
Monaco									
Netherlands	92.9	100.0	107.1	117.3	116.1	115.6	115.1	114.5	114.0
Norway	93.6	100.0	105.8	108.4	107.1	107.3	107.5	107.1	107.1
Portugal	78.9	100.0	111.9	130.5	133.7	134.2	139.0	142.1	144.6
Spain	70.9	100.0	116.8	122.5	123.5	127.9	129.5	131.6	134.0
Sweden	82.4	100.0	99.9	105.8	103.6	101.1	100.3	98.7	97.2
Switzerland	90.8	100.0	96.7	96.2	95.2	93.8	93.1	92.0	91.0
Turkey	5.5	100.0	1,451.9	3,770.7	4,104.8	4,233.1	4,663.7	4,920.6	5,168.1
United Kingdom	94.8	100.0	105.8	107.8	110.4	111.4	113.3	114.9	116.4
Eastern Europe									
Albania									
Belarus		100.0	3,011.7	11,440.4	14,864.9	18,321.8	19,582.4	21,946.7	24,058.8
Bosnia-Herzegovina									
Bulgaria	2.2	100.0	2,474.5	2,464.8	2,471.2	2,423.3	2,564.3	2,593.3	2,638.4
Croatia		100.0	140.6	138.3	137.7	141.1	141.6	142.6	143.8
Czech Republic	38.7	100.0	131.3	129.4	126.4	123.7	122.2	120.2	118.3
Estonia		100.0	126.1	128.7	128.2	129.5	131.0	131.6	132.6
Georgia									
Hungary	33.0	100.0	185.2	194.2	195.1	191.9	195.1	195.4	195.5
Latvia		100.0	137.0	142.9	144.5	148.0	154.8	158.3	162.6
Lithuania		100.0	123.6	110.0	110.0	113.2	114.8	116.2	117.9
Macedonia									
Moldova									
Poland	19.4	100.0	220.6	224.8	218.7	209.0	201.9	195.1	188.3
Romania	0.9	100.0	839.1	1,381.7	1,512.1	1,549.4	1,638.1	1,713.1	1,773.1
Russia		100.0	533.3	978.0	1,063.4	1,267.2	1,463.2	1,603.9	1,769.0
Slovakia		100.0	123.2	121.8	120.8	118.9	118.5	117.5	116.5
Slovenia		100.0	115.6	138.4	141.7	146.7	151.1	154.8	158.7
Ukraine		100.0	326.9	472.1	638.2	775.1	775.7	863.9	932.4

Source:National statistical offices/OECD/Eurostat/Euromonitor International

Consumer Prices Statistics

Table 7.10

Index of Health Goods and Medical Services Prices 1990-2008
1995 = 100

	1990	1995	2000	2003	2004	2005	2006	2007	2008
Western Europe									
Austria	77.6	100.0	106.8	117.7	119.0	125.6	128.0	131.0	134.6
Belgium	82.4	100.0	112.6	122.6	126.1	123.3	124.9	125.7	125.5
Cyprus									
Denmark	94.4	100.0	106.5	108.4	108.3	109.5	110.1	110.6	111.3
Finland	80.1	100.0	110.7	121.5	123.6	126.6	130.8	134.7	138.0
France	92.3	100.0	104.7	107.5	108.2	108.5	106.8	106.6	106.1
Germany	86.3	100.0	109.0	109.0	125.5	128.3	138.4	147.4	154.2
Gibraltar									
Greece	41.8	100.0	95.4	107.4	113.1	118.2	124.1	128.9	133.6
Iceland									
Ireland	80.9	100.0	165.0	335.2	400.1	478.0	578.7	649.2	725.0
Italy	83.3	100.0	119.3	121.3	121.4	119.8	119.8	119.1	118.4
Liechtenstein									
Luxembourg									
Malta									
Monaco									
Netherlands	86.9	100.0	105.8	121.7	133.1	134.6	139.7	144.9	148.4
Norway	79.4	100.0	124.1	137.9	142.7	147.1	152.7	156.9	161.2
Portugal	71.1	100.0	120.9	143.9	147.5	147.5	152.6	155.8	158.3
Spain	73.5	100.0	117.0	123.3	122.9	125.6	126.3	127.2	128.5
Sweden	71.5	100.0	121.1	136.8	140.2	142.0	146.1	148.7	151.3
Switzerland	82.6	100.0	98.8	98.7	98.3	97.4	97.2	96.6	96.1
Turkey	5.5	100.0	2,197.8	5,542.4	6,304.6	6,357.0	7,003.7	7,424.3	7,764.0
United Kingdom	71.2	100.0	136.2	154.5	160.8	164.5	170.1	174.7	178.9
Eastern Europe									
Albania									
Belarus		100.0	4,457.9	24,639.3	29,487.6	37,121.7	39,675.9	44,043.1	48,385.5
Bosnia-Herzegovina									
Bulgaria	1.2	100.0	4,621.5	7,906.9	8,076.8	8,504.0	8,998.9	9,315.7	9,721.3
Croatia		100.0	123.9	159.1	164.7	170.1	178.5	184.0	189.6
Czech Republic	38.7	100.0	78.9	91.0	93.1	99.5	104.9	108.9	113.8
Estonia		100.0	164.5	222.6	229.6	235.5	251.0	259.2	268.1
Georgia									
Hungary	18.0	100.0	343.8	430.4	458.9	489.4	509.7	532.8	555.5
Latvia		100.0	119.9	137.4	154.8	182.0	196.0	213.0	230.8
Lithuania		100.0	119.6	122.3	135.2	142.3	148.6	156.2	162.3
Macedonia									
Moldova									
Poland	21.0	100.0	216.0	252.8	269.3	283.3	295.2	307.2	319.2
Romania	1.3	100.0	1,268.9	2,341.2	2,340.7	2,315.3	2,447.9	2,479.8	2,520.7
Russia		100.0	475.5	603.5	683.0	782.4	847.3	918.0	989.9
Slovakia		100.0	174.0	198.7	228.4	252.7	275.2	297.2	318.1
Slovenia		100.0	154.8	196.2	199.0	198.4	201.8	203.4	204.8
Ukraine		100.0	436.1	686.0	820.7	1,076.2	1,149.8	1,284.6	1,425.2

Source:*National statistical offices/OECD/Eurostat/Euromonitor International*

Table 7.11

Index of Transport Prices 1990-2008

1995 = 100

	1990	1995	2000	2003	2004	2005	2006	2007	2008
Western Europe									
Austria	85.1	100.0	110.6	115.6	119.6	124.9	127.9	131.5	135.0
Belgium	84.1	100.0	116.3	123.5	127.5	132.9	136.5	140.3	144.1
Cyprus									
Denmark	90.4	100.0	112.5	119.3	123.2	127.0	131.5	135.0	138.6
Finland	85.4	100.0	108.8	110.7	111.1	114.6	117.1	120.0	122.7
France	86.9	100.0	111.0	116.3	120.7	125.6	129.6	133.4	137.3
Germany	80.5	100.0	113.0	119.2	122.0	126.3	129.8	133.3	136.9
Gibraltar									
Greece	65.6	100.0	120.7	126.7	131.1	137.5	142.9	147.6	152.6
Iceland									
Ireland	98.5	100.0	119.9	128.5	134.6	139.1	144.5	149.1	153.6
Italy	78.1	100.0	113.5	117.4	120.0	123.4	125.8	128.1	130.5
Liechtenstein									
Luxembourg									
Malta									
Monaco									
Netherlands	86.0	100.0	112.6	119.1	123.2	128.3	132.1	135.9	139.6
Norway	81.0	100.0	116.3	123.6	125.7	131.5	135.9	139.3	143.4
Portugal	74.0	100.0	120.4	148.1	154.7	162.3	172.8	180.7	188.5
Spain	74.5	100.0	117.5	122.0	126.5	136.5	141.5	147.2	153.5
Sweden	83.4	100.0	104.7	109.7	112.6	116.5	120.2	123.2	126.5
Switzerland	84.2	100.0	100.2	98.3	98.4	100.2	101.0	101.6	102.6
Turkey	5.5	100.0	1,773.6	5,062.7	5,618.5	6,269.6	6,907.4	7,439.2	7,991.3
United Kingdom	85.6	100.0	118.5	122.8	127.4	131.4	135.9	139.7	143.5
Eastern Europe									
Albania									
Belarus		100.0	3,933.2	16,282.0	20,554.2	25,266.5	27,005.0	30,119.1	32,971.0
Bosnia-Herzegovina									
Bulgaria	2.2	100.0	3,587.0	3,886.6	4,128.5	4,450.7	4,709.8	4,948.5	5,213.1
Croatia		100.0	143.3	167.1	172.1	175.9	183.6	188.3	192.9
Czech Republic	38.7	100.0	125.4	125.5	128.9	131.6	134.9	137.7	140.4
Estonia		100.0	213.0	216.8	226.2	241.0	256.5	268.0	280.6
Georgia									
Hungary	33.0	100.0	224.3	234.0	246.1	255.9	265.4	274.5	283.2
Latvia		100.0	166.7	174.9	187.0	210.8	228.5	244.0	261.5
Lithuania		100.0	162.9	155.6	164.1	183.5	196.5	208.3	221.3
Macedonia									
Moldova									
Poland	12.9	100.0	189.0	202.2	205.2	207.6	209.0	210.7	212.7
Romania	0.9	100.0	1,143.6	2,427.1	2,790.0	3,084.6	3,261.3	3,504.3	3,719.0
Russia		100.0	468.7	892.2	1,041.9	1,353.3	1,537.2	1,724.2	1,932.4
Slovakia		100.0	139.0	148.1	161.7	166.5	172.6	179.7	185.1
Slovenia		100.0	161.3	199.4	210.6	216.6	224.7	232.1	238.6
Ukraine		100.0	291.4	393.4	430.0	524.5	542.1	585.4	632.5

Source:National statistical offices/OECD/Eurostat/Euromonitor International

Consumer Prices Statistics

Table 7.12

Index of Communication Prices 1990-2008

1995 = 100

	1990	1995	2000	2003	2004	2005	2006	2007	2008
Western Europe									
Austria	102.1	100.0	77.5	75.4	74.5	68.5	65.4	62.6	58.9
Belgium	76.1	100.0	102.4	97.3	99.5	100.3	101.3	102.4	103.3
Cyprus									
Denmark	101.5	100.0	93.3	81.8	79.7	78.5	77.1	75.8	74.6
Finland	102.3	100.0	84.4	80.2	72.4	61.8	56.5	50.0	43.2
France	101.7	100.0	73.5	68.6	67.8	66.9	65.1	64.0	62.9
Germany	93.0	100.0	78.8	75.8	75.0	73.9	73.3	72.8	72.3
Gibraltar									
Greece	50.9	100.0	95.7	85.4	81.7	81.6	79.2	77.4	76.0
Iceland									
Ireland	99.0	100.0	78.1	68.6	68.2	66.8	65.9	65.1	64.2
Italy	87.9	100.0	94.9	89.9	83.7	78.4	74.1	69.4	65.1
Liechtenstein									
Luxembourg									
Malta									
Monaco									
Netherlands	84.9	100.0	101.6	100.8	100.0	96.1	95.0	93.3	91.2
Norway	154.0	100.0	80.3	76.7	71.9	71.1	68.9	66.6	65.0
Portugal	90.1	100.0	90.2	94.1	93.9	92.9	93.9	94.2	94.3
Spain	80.2	100.0	101.8	94.3	92.7	92.5	90.3	89.2	88.1
Sweden	90.6	100.0	90.9	89.2	84.8	80.9	78.4	75.3	72.4
Switzerland	82.3	100.0	62.7	58.6	57.4	53.3	51.6	49.5	47.1
Turkey	5.5	100.0	1,967.9	5,728.7	6,219.7	6,122.3	6,745.2	7,037.0	7,285.0
United Kingdom	102.8	100.0	88.5	84.3	85.8	83.9	84.5	84.6	84.2
Eastern Europe									
Albania									
Belarus		100.0	6,917.2	45,195.4	60,493.3	71,955.8	76,906.8	86,115.5	93,747.5
Bosnia-Herzegovina									
Bulgaria	2.2	100.0	3,040.0	3,775.2	4,004.6	4,067.8	4,304.6	4,458.2	4,609.9
Croatia		100.0	183.2	258.9	258.1	257.6	256.2	255.3	254.0
Czech Republic	38.7	100.0	38.8	40.9	45.3	46.3	48.2	50.4	51.9
Estonia		100.0	199.4	205.8	204.5	199.9	210.4	211.7	213.8
Georgia									
Hungary	33.0	100.0	248.5	263.0	261.6	257.9	262.0	261.7	261.9
Latvia		100.0	209.6	182.0	177.5	176.4	188.8	190.7	194.9
Lithuania		100.0	314.9	366.0	331.5	314.0	355.3	352.2	357.9
Macedonia									
Moldova									
Poland	12.1	100.0	219.2	262.9	264.7	266.2	267.5	268.6	270.2
Romania	0.9	100.0	3,570.8	6,080.9	6,833.7	6,497.1	6,869.3	7,100.4	7,177.7
Russia		100.0	782.4	2,079.0	2,889.8	3,998.2	5,272.6	6,198.7	7,206.5
Slovakia		100.0	179.3	249.9	254.3	255.8	261.2	264.4	267.5
Slovenia		100.0	151.4	195.1	194.7	194.3	193.7	193.3	192.9
Ukraine		100.0	380.2	519.1	745.7	913.5	936.5	1,057.8	1,152.4

Source:*National statistical offices/OECD/Eurostat/Euromonitor International*

Table 7.13

Index of Leisure and Recreation Prices 1990-2008
1995 = 100

	1990	1995	2000	2003	2004	2005	2006	2007	2008
Western Europe									
Austria	86.8	100.0	98.9	103.7	103.9	104.3	104.0	104.1	104.1
Belgium	89.9	100.0	106.2	114.1	113.6	115.3	115.5	115.9	116.6
Cyprus									
Denmark	91.7	100.0	107.9	116.1	116.0	115.1	115.5	115.3	115.1
Finland	91.1	100.0	101.5	107.6	108.1	107.1	108.6	109.8	110.3
France	93.1	100.0	95.7	94.3	93.2	91.3	90.4	89.2	88.1
Germany	91.2	100.0	100.6	99.9	98.7	98.3	96.7	96.1	95.4
Gibraltar									
Greece	64.0	100.0	122.6	133.2	137.1	139.4	142.8	145.6	148.1
Iceland									
Ireland	97.0	100.0	110.7	121.9	121.1	119.7	119.9	119.3	118.8
Italy	81.6	100.0	105.9	111.8	112.3	111.6	111.3	111.0	110.6
Liechtenstein									
Luxembourg									
Malta									
Monaco									
Netherlands	93.5	100.0	102.2	110.2	108.9	108.0	107.1	106.3	105.4
Norway	91.4	100.0	103.7	105.2	104.7	105.3	105.8	105.9	106.2
Portugal	84.5	100.0	103.8	118.9	122.3	123.3	127.6	130.7	133.2
Spain	73.4	100.0	114.9	120.1	119.4	120.8	120.3	120.3	120.6
Sweden	86.7	100.0	95.8	97.5	95.0	92.2	90.8	88.9	87.0
Switzerland	88.0	100.0	95.9	94.0	92.4	90.5	89.3	87.7	86.3
Turkey	5.5	100.0	1,352.7	3,202.0	3,747.7	3,816.8	4,205.2	4,494.1	4,720.6
United Kingdom	93.1	100.0	97.8	95.0	94.4	92.2	91.2	90.2	88.9
Eastern Europe									
Albania									
Belarus		100.0	3,891.9	24,017.5	38,580.9	41,148.7	43,980.0	49,776.1	53,093.6
Bosnia-Herzegovina									
Bulgaria	2.2	100.0	4,003.9	4,455.5	4,604.3	4,549.3	4,814.1	4,918.1	5,028.8
Croatia		100.0	110.3	125.5	129.8	133.4	136.8	140.1	143.0
Czech Republic	38.7	100.0	166.5	177.0	178.6	181.3	184.1	186.2	188.6
Estonia		100.0	159.4	170.6	170.7	171.0	176.1	177.7	179.7
Georgia									
Hungary	33.0	100.0	200.9	227.6	237.2	238.6	244.3	249.2	253.0
Latvia		100.0	123.3	134.6	139.5	146.8	154.0	159.5	165.7
Lithuania		100.0	130.3	121.3	120.0	120.5	123.0	123.5	124.4
Macedonia									
Moldova									
Poland	15.8	100.0	203.4	217.7	217.2	216.4	215.5	214.7	214.2
Romania	0.9	100.0	1,157.8	1,763.7	1,970.1	2,048.7	2,166.1	2,283.5	2,377.4
Russia		100.0	334.8	731.0	1,022.4	1,181.8	1,340.5	1,517.2	1,668.4
Slovakia		100.0	131.8	142.2	151.9	157.3	161.9	167.5	172.2
Slovenia		100.0	144.3	174.1	180.1	182.2	187.1	190.8	194.1
Ukraine		100.0	339.8	571.6	696.1	859.3	901.3	997.2	1,088.4

Source:National statistical offices/OECD/Eurostat/Euromonitor International

Consumer Prices Statistics

Table 7.14

Index of Education Prices 1990-2008
1995 = 100

	1990	1995	2000	2003	2004	2005	2006	2007	2008
Western Europe									
Austria	73.5	100.0	115.9	165.4	168.7	172.6	175.9	179.0	182.0
Belgium	85.6	100.0	111.3	119.4	120.0	122.7	123.9	125.2	126.8
Cyprus									
Denmark	91.7	100.0	114.5	150.0	154.3	158.1	171.6	177.9	185.0
Finland	90.2	100.0	109.7	124.9	131.0	136.7	145.4	152.8	159.3
France	82.6	100.0	106.8	114.8	121.5	127.1	128.2	132.1	135.3
Germany	63.2	100.0	122.0	130.5	133.2	136.4	140.7	144.1	147.6
Gibraltar									
Greece	36.1	100.0	136.5	153.3	160.1	166.9	174.4	180.5	186.6
Iceland									
Ireland	93.8	100.0	129.1	159.7	171.8	183.9	197.6	208.6	219.8
Italy	78.3	100.0	111.6	120.0	122.9	125.5	128.1	130.2	132.4
Liechtenstein									
Luxembourg									
Malta									
Monaco									
Netherlands	79.2	100.0	114.8	126.3	129.6	124.7	125.2	124.9	123.4
Norway	86.9	100.0	121.8	145.9	151.8	154.7	161.6	166.0	170.3
Portugal	79.0	100.0	119.2	151.5	167.0	177.2	194.2	207.4	219.6
Spain	66.7	100.0	124.2	139.1	143.7	151.8	157.6	162.9	168.8
Sweden	88.0	100.0	123.0	67.1	72.7	73.9	60.2	58.2	53.8
Switzerland	77.4	100.0	107.4	110.0	110.2	109.8	110.4	110.3	110.3
Turkey	5.5	100.0	2,175.6	6,444.2	7,961.9	8,646.7	9,526.4	10,415.6	11,159.7
United Kingdom	72.6	100.0	130.5	157.6	167.1	175.9	188.1	197.0	206.1
Eastern Europe									
Albania									
Belarus		100.0	9,588.5	78,275.9	94,478.5	106,737.9	114,082.1	124,485.3	133,390.0
Bosnia-Herzegovina									
Bulgaria	1.7	100.0	6,332.9	8,843.8	9,406.5	9,652.6	10,214.4	10,611.9	11,011.3
Croatia		100.0	133.5	141.9	136.8	142.2	142.1	142.1	143.5
Czech Republic	38.7	100.0	169.0	186.5	193.1	199.0	207.4	213.5	219.8
Estonia		100.0	244.7	286.0	305.8	329.1	362.9	385.2	409.1
Georgia									
Hungary	28.7	100.0	229.5	298.1	333.8	356.2	397.8	426.9	455.3
Latvia		100.0	209.1	245.2	261.3	267.2	287.4	299.6	311.5
Lithuania		100.0	203.9	209.5	212.6	210.2	229.1	234.8	241.1
Macedonia									
Moldova									
Poland	14.8	100.0	194.0	222.4	227.5	231.8	234.3	237.5	241.0
Romania	1.7	100.0	3,796.3	7,170.4	8,171.3	8,410.2	8,891.9	9,394.3	9,760.2
Russia		100.0	616.1	1,269.5	1,669.5	1,891.8	2,250.3	2,534.8	2,799.0
Slovakia		100.0	122.3	140.0	158.1	209.2	245.7	276.2	304.3
Slovenia		100.0	157.4	198.5	214.1	226.2	238.5	250.1	261.0
Ukraine		100.0	443.6	675.8	971.9	1,223.4	1,216.3	1,373.4	1,495.0

Source: *National statistical offices/OECD/Eurostat/Euromonitor International*

Table 7.15

Index of Hotel and Catering Prices 1990-2008
1995 = 100

	1990	1995	2000	2003	2004	2005	2006	2007	2008
Western Europe									
Austria	82.2	100.0	109.7	120.0	123.3	126.8	129.5	132.3	135.0
Belgium	86.0	100.0	110.8	123.2	125.8	130.8	134.3	137.6	141.1
Cyprus									
Denmark	93.5	100.0	114.7	125.2	127.8	130.3	133.4	135.7	138.1
Finland	89.4	100.0	109.4	118.8	118.9	121.3	124.8	127.7	130.3
France	82.7	100.0	111.2	122.5	126.0	128.7	132.9	135.9	139.0
Germany	81.4	100.0	109.3	116.2	117.1	118.5	119.0	120.1	121.3
Gibraltar									
Greece	46.4	100.0	142.8	167.4	174.6	180.3	188.0	193.9	199.7
Iceland									
Ireland	87.2	100.0	124.9	150.0	155.4	160.2	167.1	172.0	177.2
Italy	75.8	100.0	116.3	130.2	133.3	134.7	137.4	139.2	141.0
Liechtenstein									
Luxembourg									
Malta									
Monaco									
Netherlands	85.2	100.0	114.5	130.3	132.6	134.8	136.5	138.4	140.0
Norway	87.2	100.0	117.8	131.1	133.3	135.9	139.6	142.0	144.5
Portugal	76.9	100.0	116.4	144.4	152.8	153.6	162.4	168.2	172.9
Spain	70.0	100.0	122.2	138.7	143.3	151.4	156.9	162.1	167.8
Sweden	81.9	100.0	106.0	117.5	118.8	120.9	123.6	125.4	127.4
Switzerland	76.5	100.0	100.3	104.7	104.4	104.0	104.2	103.8	103.6
Turkey	5.5	100.0	1,769.6	4,504.2	5,527.0	6,041.2	6,655.8	7,276.6	7,807.2
United Kingdom	81.5	100.0	121.7	135.6	140.4	145.8	151.4	156.1	160.8
Eastern Europe									
Albania									
Belarus		100.0	2,778.1	6,711.3	8,652.6	10,991.5	11,747.8	13,210.2	14,570.8
Bosnia-Herzegovina									
Bulgaria	2.2	100.0	4,279.5	4,913.5	5,191.8	5,251.2	5,556.8	5,743.4	5,929.0
Croatia		100.0	115.3	129.6	134.4	137.4	141.6	145.1	148.1
Czech Republic	38.7	100.0	141.8	155.3	163.1	169.4	177.2	183.5	189.8
Estonia		100.0	167.2	191.6	199.6	209.0	220.4	228.7	237.5
Georgia									
Hungary	33.0	100.0	218.5	287.1	315.0	328.1	338.2	353.2	364.9
Latvia		100.0	132.9	141.9	149.5	161.7	169.8	177.8	186.6
Lithuania		100.0	139.1	151.2	155.6	158.0	166.7	171.2	175.7
Macedonia									
Moldova									
Poland	18.5	100.0	164.5	162.6	165.0	166.9	168.0	169.4	171.0
Romania	0.9	100.0	1,961.1	4,131.9	4,797.7	5,264.7	5,566.2	5,984.2	6,340.6
Russia		100.0	221.6	388.2	441.7	458.3	532.5	574.3	615.0
Slovakia		100.0	129.8	158.8	177.5	190.1	199.4	211.1	221.3
Slovenia		100.0	138.5	176.0	186.6	195.1	206.4	215.2	223.9
Ukraine		100.0	355.6	541.2	697.9	861.6	890.7	992.2	1,081.5

Source: *National statistical offices/OECD/Eurostat/Euromonitor International*

Consumer Prices Statistics

Table 7.16

Index of Miscellaneous Goods and Services Prices 1990-2008

1995 = 100

	1990	1995	2000	2003	2004	2005	2006	2007	2008
Western Europe									
Austria	84.0	100.0	111.7	113.3	117.4	117.1	117.4	118.6	118.9
Belgium	104.2	100.0	100.5	98.0	103.1	104.1	105.5	107.7	109.1
Cyprus									
Denmark	85.8	100.0	105.2	111.5	114.5	117.8	121.3	124.1	127.1
Finland	94.5	100.0	118.8	108.0	114.9	114.7	111.9	114.0	113.8
France	101.1	100.0	101.2	104.3	106.6	109.4	111.3	113.4	115.5
Germany	86.0	100.0	93.1	103.8	106.8	107.5	111.1	113.5	115.7
Gibraltar									
Greece	38.0	100.0	135.5	147.1	150.0	154.9	158.9	162.3	166.0
Iceland									
Ireland	95.2	100.0	123.5	144.8	150.6	152.8	157.7	161.4	164.7
Italy	79.4	100.0	111.2	120.8	121.7	124.8	127.1	128.7	130.8
Liechtenstein									
Luxembourg									
Malta									
Monaco									
Netherlands	83.3	100.0	110.1	122.7	125.7	128.3	131.2	133.7	136.1
Norway	83.8	100.0	97.3	101.8	100.1	98.6	99.4	98.7	98.2
Portugal	73.6	100.0	120.8	149.5	154.6	156.5	164.0	168.9	173.2
Spain	67.5	100.0	121.7	132.0	134.6	140.3	143.6	146.9	150.6
Sweden	75.8	100.0	105.0	105.1	109.5	110.6	113.6	116.1	118.1
Switzerland	85.8	100.0	98.4	102.5	102.3	101.7	101.8	101.5	101.2
Turkey	5.5	100.0	1,670.6	4,926.4	5,482.0	5,648.4	6,223.1	6,596.3	6,934.4
United Kingdom	84.8	100.0	122.6	128.2	133.3	139.5	144.5	149.4	154.3
Eastern Europe									
Albania									
Belarus		100.0	4,647.0	25,047.4	22,313.1	7,598.7	8,121.6	3,216.2	1,940.3
Bosnia-Herzegovina									
Bulgaria	2.2	100.0	3,547.4	3,875.1	3,999.4	3,971.6	4,202.7	4,297.8	4,401.9
Croatia		100.0	142.3	146.7	149.6	152.6	154.8	157.1	159.1
Czech Republic	38.7	100.0	118.3	132.9	138.8	141.2	146.8	150.8	154.5
Estonia		100.0	160.7	174.3	178.4	183.3	191.1	195.9	201.1
Georgia									
Hungary	33.0	100.0	212.0	243.2	255.3	258.7	264.2	270.4	275.0
Latvia		100.0	171.4	168.3	182.7	193.0	202.7	212.6	221.9
Lithuania		100.0	147.5	154.6	150.1	150.9	157.1	157.8	159.9
Macedonia									
Moldova									
Poland	15.7	100.0	165.2	172.3	175.0	177.2	178.5	180.1	181.9
Romania	0.9	100.0	1,161.9	2,055.7	2,287.3	2,363.7	2,499.1	2,628.6	2,730.7
Russia		100.0	304.7	1,121.0	1,373.4	1,402.2	1,547.9	1,671.7	1,763.4
Slovakia		100.0	131.5	161.0	170.7	178.8	183.5	189.9	195.7
Slovenia		100.0	147.9	185.1	193.2	197.4	205.0	210.8	216.1
Ukraine		100.0	207.3	242.8	248.0	252.8	245.5	246.4	245.9

Source: *National statistical offices/OECD/Eurostat/Euromonitor International*

Economic Indicators

Economic Statistics

Table 8.1

Total Gross Domestic Product 1980-2008 (national currencies)
Billion units of national currency

	1980	1985	1990	1995	1996	1997	1998	1999	2000	2001
Western Europe										
Austria	76.32	103.07	136.33	174.61	180.15	183.48	190.85	197.98	207.53	212.50
Belgium	90.76	125.35	167.91	207.78	211.40	221.18	229.57	238.25	251.74	258.88
Cyprus	1.35	2.62	4.52	7.09	7.45	7.81	8.45	9.06	9.88	10.63
Denmark	392.88	648.54	840.65	1,019.55	1,069.49	1,125.64	1,163.62	1,213.47	1,293.96	1,335.61
Finland	33.32	57.50	89.75	95.91	99.26	107.58	117.06	122.69	132.20	139.79
France	445.23	743.89	1,033.03	1,194.60	1,227.25	1,267.43	1,323.65	1,367.97	1,441.37	1,497.17
Germany	766.60	955.30	1,274.90	1,848.45	1,876.18	1,915.58	1,965.38	2,012.00	2,062.50	2,113.16
Gibraltar				0.37	0.39	0.36	0.38	0.41	0.43	0.45
Greece	6.84	18.65	43.82	89.56	98.40	108.89	118.40	126.16	136.28	146.43
Iceland	16.14	122.42	365.05	445.11	477.69	526.32	588.37	632.40	683.75	771.89
Ireland	13.10	25.00	36.56	53.09	58.71	67.97	78.57	90.50	104.84	116.99
Italy	203.38	429.65	701.35	947.34	1,003.78	1,048.77	1,091.36	1,127.09	1,191.06	1,248.65
Liechtenstein	0.90	1.30	1.97	2.87	3.09	3.34	3.60	4.00	4.19	4.21
Luxembourg	3.76	5.84	9.18	15.11	15.80	16.42	17.41	19.89	22.00	22.57
Malta	1.01	1.22	1.89	2.94	3.08	3.27	3.45	3.63	3.97	4.04
Monaco	0.89	1.48	2.06	2.38	2.45	2.53	2.64	2.73	2.87	2.99
Netherlands	163.09	200.83	243.65	305.26	319.76	342.24	362.46	386.19	417.96	447.73
Norway	314.70	552.43	736.30	943.44	1,032.99	1,119.18	1,140.36	1,240.43	1,481.24	1,536.89
Portugal	7.78	22.10	53.89	85.14	90.51	97.90	106.50	114.19	122.27	129.31
Spain	96.50	180.15	318.04	447.21	473.86	503.92	539.49	579.94	630.26	680.68
Sweden	558.88	915.26	1,447.41	1,809.76	1,852.09	1,927.00	2,012.09	2,123.97	2,249.99	2,326.18
Switzerland	184.08	244.42	330.93	373.60	376.67	383.99	395.26	402.91	422.06	430.32
Turkey	0.01	0.04	0.39	7.76	14.77	28.84	70.20	104.60	166.66	240.22
United Kingdom	233.18	361.76	570.28	733.27	781.73	830.09	879.10	928.73	976.53	1,021.83
Eastern Europe										
Albania	15.53	16.86	16.81	229.79	346.40	346.20	409.21	471.58	523.04	583.37
Belarus			0.00	121.40	191.84	366.83	702.16	3,026.00	9,133.80	17,173.20
Bosnia-Herzegovina			0.00	2.86	4.12	6.56	7.44	8.60	9.61	10.48
Bulgaria	0.03	0.03	0.05	0.88	1.76	17.43	22.42	23.79	26.75	29.71
Croatia			0.33	115.53	126.80	145.39	160.60	164.05	176.69	190.80
Czech Republic	443.86	512.78	617.56	1,466.52	1,683.29	1,811.09	1,996.48	2,080.80	2,189.17	2,352.21
Estonia			0.80	43.28	56.89	70.12	78.74	83.84	96.38	109.07
Georgia			0.00	3.69	3.87	4.55	5.02	5.67	6.04	6.67
Hungary	819.00	1,174.10	2,322.37	5,765.90	7,080.41	8,771.69	10,360.30	11,701.70	13,512.28	15,238.37
Latvia			0.06	2.62	3.13	3.63	3.97	4.27	4.75	5.22
Lithuania			0.13	25.96	32.74	40.00	44.70	43.67	45.74	48.64
Macedonia			0.48	169.52	176.44	186.02	194.98	209.01	236.39	233.84
Moldova			0.01	6.48	7.80	8.92	9.12	12.32	16.02	19.05
Poland	0.25	1.04	56.03	337.22	422.44	515.35	600.90	665.69	744.38	779.56
Romania	0.06	0.08	0.09	7.21	10.89	25.29	37.38	54.57	80.38	116.77
Russia			0.64	1,428.50	2,007.80	2,342.50	2,629.60	4,823.20	7,305.60	8,943.60
Slovakia			12.16	14.97	16.65	18.85	19.93	19.19	22.04	23.54
Slovenia			5.84	15.93	16.55	17.89	19.29	20.71	21.43	22.71
Ukraine			0.00	54.52	81.52	93.37	102.59	130.44	170.07	204.19

Source:*Euromonitor International from International Monetary Fund (IMF), International Financial Statistics*

Economic Statistics

Total Gross Domestic Product 1980-2008 (national currencies) *(continued)*

Billion units of national currency

	2002	2003	2004	2005	2006	2007	2008	Total US$ billion 2008	US$ per capita 2008
Western Europe									
Austria	218.85	223.30	232.78	243.58	256.16	270.78	281.87	414.83	49,669.5
Belgium	267.65	274.73	289.63	302.11	318.22	334.92	344.21	506.57	47,707.1
Cyprus	10.98	11.76	12.65	13.46	14.44	15.60	16.95	24.94	28,922.1
Denmark	1,372.74	1,400.69	1,466.18	1,545.26	1,628.63	1,687.89	1,733.51	340.03	62,258.9
Finland	143.81	145.80	152.15	157.07	167.01	179.66	184.73	271.87	51,291.1
France	1,548.56	1,594.81	1,660.19	1,726.07	1,806.43	1,894.65	1,950.09	2,869.97	46,211.0
Germany	2,143.18	2,163.80	2,210.90	2,242.20	2,325.10	2,428.20	2,495.80	3,673.11	44,675.4
Gibraltar	0.47	0.51	0.56	0.57	0.57	0.58	0.60	1.11	37,972.3
Greece	156.61	171.41	185.85	197.65	213.21	228.18	242.95	357.55	31,891.4
Iceland	816.45	841.32	928.89	1,026.25	1,167.68	1,279.38	1,465.07	16.66	52,805.3
Ireland	130.19	139.44	148.97	162.17	177.29	190.60	185.71	273.31	62,423.8
Italy	1,295.23	1,335.35	1,391.53	1,429.48	1,485.38	1,544.92	1,572.24	2,313.90	39,234.8
Liechtenstein	4.19	4.14	4.30	4.56	5.00	5.26	5.45	5.03	141,705.3
Luxembourg	23.99	25.83	27.52	30.24	33.92	36.41	36.66	53.96	112,267.9
Malta	4.28	4.39	4.51	4.80	5.10	5.42	5.63	8.29	20,349.6
Monaco	3.09	3.18	3.31	3.44	3.72	4.37	4.72	6.95	211,822.2
Netherlands	465.21	476.95	491.18	513.41	540.22	568.66	595.88	876.97	53,528.8
Norway	1,532.31	1,593.83	1,743.04	1,945.72	2,159.57	2,277.11	2,548.32	451.83	95,379.7
Portugal	135.43	138.58	144.13	149.12	155.45	163.05	166.28	244.71	22,993.5
Spain	729.21	782.93	841.04	908.79	982.30	1,050.60	1,095.16	1,611.77	35,772.3
Sweden	2,420.76	2,515.15	2,624.96	2,735.22	2,900.79	3,063.87	3,156.88	478.96	52,304.8
Switzerland	434.26	437.73	451.38	463.80	490.54	521.07	541.83	500.26	66,434.9
Turkey	350.48	454.78	559.03	648.93	758.39	843.18	950.14	730.02	9,817.6
United Kingdom	1,075.56	1,139.75	1,202.96	1,254.06	1,325.80	1,398.88	1,446.11	2,658.46	43,448.9
Eastern Europe									
Albania	622.71	694.10	750.79	814.80	891.00	983.06	1,085.99	12.94	4,118.2
Belarus	26,138.30	36,564.80	49,445.20	65,067.10	79,267.00	96,087.20	128,829.00	60.30	6,223.1
Bosnia-Herzegovina	11.65	12.30	15.79	16.93	19.12	21.64	24.55	18.38	4,782.5
Bulgaria	32.40	34.63	38.82	42.80	49.36	56.52	66.73	49.90	6,591.2
Croatia	208.22	227.01	245.55	264.37	286.34	314.22	342.16	69.33	15,633.2
Czech Republic	2,464.43	2,577.11	2,814.76	2,983.86	3,222.37	3,535.46	3,693.53	216.35	20,971.3
Estonia	121.67	136.42	151.54	174.96	207.00	244.50	251.49	23.52	17,613.4
Georgia	7.46	8.56	9.82	11.62	13.79	17.00	19.07	12.79	2,919.1
Hungary	17,148.45	18,914.94	20,695.53	21,993.08	23,775.27	25,479.41	26,620.50	154.67	15,406.9
Latvia	5.76	6.39	7.43	9.06	11.17	14.78	16.24	33.78	14,903.6
Lithuania	52.07	56.96	62.70	72.06	82.79	98.14	111.50	47.30	14,052.1
Macedonia	243.97	251.49	265.26	286.62	310.92	354.32	398.64	9.52	4,667.5
Moldova	22.56	27.62	32.03	37.65	44.75	53.43	62.84	6.05	1,664.3
Poland	808.58	843.16	924.54	983.30	1,060.03	1,175.27	1,271.72	527.85	13,874.1
Romania	152.02	197.43	247.37	288.96	344.65	412.76	503.96	200.07	9,307.2
Russia	10,830.50	13,243.20	17,048.10	21,625.40	26,903.50	33,111.40	41,668.00	1,676.59	11,806.2
Slovakia	25.98	29.49	34.03	38.49	44.57	54.86	64.88	95.49	17,704.6
Slovenia	24.53	25.74	27.14	28.71	31.01	34.47	37.13	54.64	27,096.0
Ukraine	225.81	267.34	345.11	441.45	544.15	720.73	949.86	180.33	3,904.0

Source:Euromonitor International from International Monetary Fund (IMF), International Financial Statistics

Economic Statistics

Table 8.2

Total Gross Domestic Product 1980-2008 (US$)

US$ million

	1980	1985	1990	1995	1996	1997	1998	1999	2000	2001
Western Europe										
Austria	106,269.3	78,648.4	173,602.0	228,395.2	228,745.0	208,074.0	213,960.9	210,948.5	191,409.6	190,381.3
Belgium	126,362.3	95,649.3	213,820.4	271,780.9	268,424.4	250,831.8	257,370.5	253,856.6	232,187.8	231,938.4
Cyprus	1,872.8	1,998.8	5,757.6	9,270.2	9,458.7	8,857.1	9,467.9	9,656.3	9,115.5	9,521.7
Denmark	69,708.9	61,203.8	135,839.0	181,984.6	184,436.8	170,436.5	173,652.5	173,943.7	160,081.8	160,475.8
Finland	46,395.2	43,876.8	114,286.5	125,453.9	126,034.1	121,995.5	131,232.6	130,722.4	121,929.9	125,239.5
France	619,910.8	567,654.0	1,315,485.0	1,562,549.1	1,558,304.1	1,437,310.9	1,483,934.1	1,457,584.7	1,329,416.9	1,341,345.6
Germany	1,067,360.2	728,978.0	1,623,495.9	2,417,791.1	2,382,279.6	2,172,344.3	2,203,367.9	2,143,810.9	1,902,301.7	1,893,218.8
Gibraltar				590.4	606.9	592.6	634.8	655.4	648.7	645.3
Greece	9,524.9	14,232.4	55,804.2	117,138.8	124,939.6	123,481.1	132,734.8	134,419.7	125,695.8	131,187.3
Iceland	3,363.5	2,949.4	6,263.2	6,880.4	7,183.3	7,423.0	8,291.7	8,742.6	8,697.3	7,923.0
Ireland	18,234.0	19,074.9	46,556.6	69,446.0	74,551.7	77,082.7	88,087.9	96,429.8	96,701.1	104,813.6
Italy	283,176.3	327,860.0	893,122.7	1,239,128.9	1,274,547.1	1,189,343.7	1,223,515.0	1,200,929.4	1,098,545.3	1,118,686.6
Liechtenstein	534.7	529.1	1,421.5	2,428.5	2,504.0	2,298.4	2,479.7	2,664.1	2,483.9	2,491.8
Luxembourg	5,228.2	4,458.0	11,689.5	19,764.4	20,057.7	18,621.7	19,523.3	21,189.6	20,291.8	20,222.9
Malta	1,400.6	932.2	2,401.3	3,845.4	3,914.7	3,704.6	3,864.8	3,869.1	3,664.7	3,616.8
Monaco	1,236.1	1,131.9	2,623.0	3,115.6	3,107.2	2,865.9	2,958.9	2,906.4	2,650.8	2,674.6
Netherlands	227,076.5	153,248.7	310,273.8	399,284.4	406,008.9	388,110.4	406,354.8	411,493.4	385,496.2	401,130.4
Norway	63,714.1	64,257.0	117,623.9	148,920.8	160,158.2	158,223.8	151,139.1	159,046.4	168,287.7	170,923.8
Portugal	10,833.7	16,865.8	68,622.6	111,361.4	114,922.5	111,020.2	119,393.8	121,674.1	112,773.1	115,850.3
Spain	134,365.4	137,470.3	405,006.8	584,948.6	601,677.4	571,466.6	604,820.2	617,935.4	581,309.3	609,831.9
Sweden	132,135.9	106,376.6	244,545.3	253,706.4	276,186.0	252,394.1	253,097.3	257,063.7	245,571.7	225,206.1
Switzerland	109,852.0	99,474.1	238,219.6	315,947.9	304,749.1	264,582.2	272,630.6	268,218.7	249,912.8	254,988.2
Turkey	65,756.5	67,052.0	150,676.2	169,319.3	181,464.5	189,878.5	269,262.5	249,761.8	266,559.8	196,006.8
United Kingdom	541,916.6	464,241.1	1,012,617.7	1,157,176.9	1,219,621.3	1,358,947.4	1,455,891.1	1,502,660.8	1,478,307.5	1,471,756.1
Eastern Europe										
Albania	2,219.0	2,408.1	2,170.6	2,479.0	3,314.9	2,324.5	2,716.6	3,424.9	3,639.6	4,065.7
Belarus				10,537.5	14,500.4	14,097.7	15,222.1	12,138.2	10,417.8	12,354.8
Bosnia-Herzegovina					2,749.7	3,784.0	4,229.8	4,686.2	4,527.5	4,794.9
Bulgaria	18,620.1	31,645.6	20,726.0	13,105.7	9,900.4	10,364.9	12,736.7	12,955.1	12,599.8	13,598.7
Croatia				22,087.1	23,334.7	23,600.7	25,239.0	23,068.1	21,345.3	22,873.0
Czech Republic			34,398.1	55,255.6	62,011.2	57,135.2	61,846.6	60,192.2	56,716.6	61,842.9
Estonia				3,775.4	4,725.9	5,051.4	5,594.3	5,712.2	5,679.9	6,240.4
Georgia				2,926.2	3,063.4	3,510.5	3,613.5	2,800.0	3,058.0	3,219.5
Hungary	25,174.9	23,426.1	36,742.9	45,877.3	46,384.2	46,960.4	48,321.8	49,343.9	47,885.5	53,189.9
Latvia				4,956.7	5,681.8	6,252.0	6,732.8	7,288.5	7,833.1	8,313.0
Lithuania				6,489.1	8,184.9	9,999.4	11,174.7	10,916.7	11,434.2	12,159.2
Macedonia				4,475.0	4,413.2	3,720.1	3,580.1	3,673.2	3,586.9	3,437.0
Moldova				1,441.3	1,693.5	1,928.6	1,698.5	1,171.7	1,288.3	1,480.9
Poland	56,788.5	70,985.9	58,975.9	139,061.8	156,684.1	157,153.8	172,901.5	167,801.7	171,276.1	190,420.9
Romania	34,272.7	47,682.6	38,242.1	35,477.4	35,315.2	35,285.7	42,115.3	35,592.3	37,025.4	40,180.9
Russia				313,325.9	392,084.9	404,938.4	270,950.9	195,906.6	259,715.9	306,618.4
Slovakia			15,484.6	19,578.6	21,141.8	21,382.2	22,348.4	20,442.2	20,324.0	21,091.4
Slovenia			7,441.5	20,833.9	21,019.4	20,283.8	21,627.5	22,067.0	19,769.9	20,343.3
Ukraine				37,008.7	44,558.8	50,151.5	41,882.6	31,580.7	31,261.5	38,008.9

Source:*Euromonitor International from International Monetary Fund (IMF), International Financial Statistics*

Economic Statistics

Total Gross Domestic Product 1980-2008 (US$) *(continued)*
US$ million

	2002	2003	2004	2005	2006	2007	2008	US$ per capita 2008
Western Europe								
Austria	206,227.6	252,218.9	289,225.8	302,924.1	321,387.0	371,144.6	414,829.3	49,669.5
Belgium	252,217.9	310,301.8	359,856.6	375,709.1	399,251.2	459,050.3	506,574.0	47,707.1
Cyprus	10,346.5	13,284.2	15,721.8	16,741.8	18,110.8	21,376.9	24,943.4	28,922.1
Denmark	173,880.6	212,622.8	244,728.0	257,675.5	273,867.5	310,063.4	340,029.2	62,258.9
Finland	135,515.1	164,674.8	189,044.0	195,333.5	209,533.8	246,247.5	271,867.4	51,291.1
France	1,459,255.7	1,801,335.1	2,062,745.1	2,146,551.7	2,266,393.0	2,596,874.2	2,869,974.1	46,211.0
Germany	2,019,590.9	2,444,002.2	2,746,990.4	2,788,417.4	2,917,130.6	3,328,183.7	3,673,112.4	44,675.4
Gibraltar	710.7	830.2	1,030.3	1,029.4	1,051.2	1,164.6	1,112.1	37,972.3
Greece	147,583.4	193,606.6	230,915.9	245,792.9	267,494.6	312,752.6	357,549.3	31,891.4
Iceland	8,907.2	10,967.7	13,233.6	16,294.4	16,638.4	19,973.1	16,658.4	52,805.3
Ireland	122,682.4	157,499.0	185,097.6	201,673.4	222,428.1	261,247.1	273,313.5	62,423.8
Italy	1,220,535.2	1,508,276.3	1,728,942.7	1,777,711.3	1,863,592.4	2,117,519.5	2,313,897.4	39,234.8
Liechtenstein	2,688.6	3,070.8	3,454.4	3,658.3	3,988.8	4,381.2	5,027.8	141,705.3
Luxembourg	22,608.8	29,179.7	34,193.1	37,603.1	42,558.3	49,906.4	53,956.4	112,267.9
Malta	4,029.1	4,956.7	5,602.0	5,969.1	6,392.8	7,422.0	8,291.6	20,349.6
Monaco	2,909.7	3,591.8	4,113.0	4,280.1	4,664.0	5,983.0	6,951.8	211,822.2
Netherlands	438,386.9	538,707.2	610,284.4	638,477.0	677,769.0	779,432.6	876,971.4	53,528.8
Norway	191,927.5	225,109.7	258,579.6	302,012.6	336,731.9	388,474.8	451,830.1	95,379.7
Portugal	127,624.0	156,527.7	179,075.6	185,451.8	195,026.6	223,484.8	244,711.9	22,993.5
Spain	687,155.4	884,314.7	1,044,974.6	1,130,180.8	1,232,422.8	1,439,985.7	1,611,770.5	35,772.3
Sweden	248,611.6	311,038.4	357,191.9	366,009.0	393,154.2	453,318.1	478,961.2	52,304.8
Switzerland	278,619.0	325,051.9	362,990.6	372,475.8	391,233.7	434,089.2	500,260.1	66,434.9
Turkey	232,529.9	303,007.5	392,155.3	482,987.2	530,918.7	647,140.7	730,015.2	9,817.6
United Kingdom	1,613,628.4	1,861,468.3	2,204,191.7	2,279,621.9	2,439,851.5	2,799,210.3	2,658,462.1	43,448.9
Eastern Europe								
Albania	4,443.0	5,695.7	7,304.8	8,158.5	9,082.3	10,871.2	12,944.8	4,118.2
Belarus	14,594.9	17,825.4	22,888.5	30,210.1	36,961.9	44,773.4	60,301.9	6,223.1
Bosnia-Herzegovina	5,606.4	7,099.5	10,021.8	10,763.5	12,264.4	15,143.5	18,383.0	4,782.5
Bulgaria	15,600.3	19,984.7	24,647.5	27,188.0	31,656.4	39,550.7	49,904.3	6,591.2
Croatia	26,452.1	33,857.2	40,692.1	44,437.2	49,049.5	58,574.1	69,332.5	15,633.2
Czech Republic	75,276.3	91,357.7	109,524.7	124,548.7	142,610.5	174,214.7	216,353.9	20,971.3
Estonia	7,324.5	9,845.4	12,031.3	13,903.3	16,605.5	21,384.1	23,516.3	17,613.4
Georgia	3,395.8	3,991.4	5,125.8	6,410.9	7,745.3	10,176.1	12,791.9	2,919.1
Hungary	66,496.0	84,326.1	102,076.2	110,195.7	113,005.7	138,757.1	154,668.8	15,406.9
Latvia	9,314.8	11,186.5	13,761.6	16,041.8	19,934.9	28,766.1	33,782.5	14,903.6
Lithuania	14,161.2	18,608.9	22,548.4	25,976.8	30,082.1	38,886.4	47,303.9	14,052.1
Macedonia	3,791.3	4,629.5	5,368.5	5,815.7	6,371.0	7,921.4	9,521.4	4,667.5
Moldova	1,662.1	1,980.6	2,597.9	2,988.3	3,408.3	4,401.2	6,047.0	1,664.3
Poland	198,179.4	216,800.9	252,769.0	303,912.2	341,597.3	424,598.0	527,849.0	13,874.1
Romania	45,988.6	59,466.1	75,794.7	99,172.9	122,696.1	169,286.2	200,074.2	9,307.2
Russia	345,487.0	431,487.0	591,666.5	764,569.9	989,426.6	1,294,384.9	1,676,585.0	11,806.2
Slovakia	24,481.4	33,303.9	42,284.3	47,866.3	55,914.5	75,188.6	95,491.5	17,704.6
Slovenia	23,112.4	29,068.6	33,715.8	35,706.7	38,910.5	47,247.1	54,639.0	27,096.0
Ukraine	42,392.7	50,133.1	64,880.9	86,141.5	107,753.1	142,719.0	180,335.0	3,904.0

Source: *Euromonitor International from International Monetary Fund (IMF), International Financial Statistics*

Economic Statistics

Table 8.3

Total GDP by Quarter 2007-2009
Million units of national currency

	2007 1st Quarter	2007 2nd Quarter	2007 3rd Quarter	2007 4th Quarter	2008 1st Quarter	2008 2nd Quarter	2008 3rd Quarter	2008 4th Quarter	2009 1st Quarter
Western Europe									
Austria	65,448	66,979	68,280	70,075	68,957	70,669	71,368	70,873	67,066
Belgium	81,405	84,198	81,658	87,656	84,359	87,388	84,266	88,193	82,864
Cyprus	3,564	3,965	4,048	4,019	3,913	4,330	4,390	4,301	3,974
Denmark	401,696	420,236	421,494	444,467	416,863	441,694	434,671	440,285	398,803
Finland	42,009	44,717	44,742	48,191	43,816	47,002	46,257	47,653	41,283
France	466,093	470,793	476,610	481,150	487,710	488,498	489,781	484,097	478,872
Germany	600,283	604,726	610,090	613,102	626,764	626,795	625,059	617,182	593,453
Gibraltar									
Greece	51,890	56,979	60,303	59,009	55,489	60,982	64,387	62,089	56,629
Iceland	300,413	319,384	330,552	329,031	325,179	361,100	379,480	399,310	
Ireland	48,226	47,738	46,208	48,431	47,066	46,385	46,446	45,813	42,570
Italy	382,224	385,255	388,338	389,098	392,414	396,863	394,011	388,955	381,780
Liechtenstein									
Luxembourg	8,850	9,167	8,798	9,596	9,309	9,337	8,859	9,157	8,640
Malta	1,251	1,367	1,455	1,403	1,330	1,469	1,518	1,442	
Monaco									
Netherlands	139,262	140,840	143,060	145,502	147,590	148,162	149,772	150,359	144,278
Norway	550,410	546,658	553,900	626,143	615,190	645,082	630,897	657,153	615,917
Portugal	38,704	40,907	40,619	42,822	39,819	41,986	41,745	42,727	39,086
Spain	256,640	261,180	264,460	268,315	272,040	274,202	275,873	273,048	267,317
Sweden	733,633	778,059	738,493	813,688	764,403	820,356	768,106	804,016	738,209
Switzerland	127,128	129,126	131,278	133,535	135,049	135,744	135,882	135,151	133,785
Turkey	187,951	203,280	232,257	219,691	215,846	239,244	262,905	232,149	210,997
United Kingdom	344,238	348,010	351,635	354,999	362,184	363,353	362,179	358,397	347,718
Eastern Europe									
Albania									
Belarus	19,767,300	22,467,000	27,172,200	26,680,700	25,802,540	30,149,147	37,833,059	35,044,254	
Bosnia-Herzegovina									
Bulgaria	11,288	13,143	15,743	16,346	13,483	15,944	18,610	18,691	13,961
Croatia	71,357	78,931	85,475	78,460	79,068	86,875	93,462	82,753	77,867
Czech Republic	824,473	887,358	897,520	926,109	873,563	942,342	941,135	936,489	877,332
Estonia	55,710	61,076	62,220	65,498	59,897	65,827	63,974	61,795	52,933
Georgia	3,415	4,084	4,532	4,968	4,183	4,995	4,793	5,099	
Hungary	5,735,501	6,308,941	6,488,851	6,946,111	6,102,751	6,762,711	6,729,941	7,025,101	5,763,881
Latvia	3,091	3,631	3,840	4,217	3,742	4,147	4,154	4,200	3,287
Lithuania	20,223	24,385	26,195	27,336	24,461	28,604	29,855	28,579	20,653
Macedonia									
Moldova	9,730	11,801	15,498	16,401	12,156	15,223	18,008	17,454	12,855
Poland	269,794	282,568	290,695	332,208	298,016	310,507	314,211	348,981	314,512
Romania	70,211	88,796	113,244	140,510	88,580	111,325	141,250	162,803	
Russia	6,749,694	7,764,875	8,904,485	9,692,346	8,891,008	10,193,298	11,639,497	10,944,197	8,482,798
Slovakia	12,323	13,401	14,357	14,775	15,034	16,113	17,016	16,722	
Slovenia	7,838	8,754	8,958	8,920	8,726	9,636	9,647	9,117	8,250
Ukraine	137,938	165,066	197,379	212,562	187,767	233,763	275,851	252,738	183,266

Source:*Euromonitor International from International Monetary Fund (IMF), International Financial Statistics*

Economic Statistics

Table 8.4

Origin of Gross Domestic Product 2008

US$ million

	Agriculture, Forestry & Fishing	Mining & Quarrying	Manufacturing	Electricity, Gas & Water	Construction	Hotels and restaurants
Western Europe						
Austria	5,502.2	2,052.8	74,487.1	10,073.8	29,036.6	17,122.4
Belgium	3,627.3	486.0	72,838.5	9,014.7	22,495.4	6,737.3
Cyprus						
Denmark	1,906.0	14,878.8	37,343.5	4,860.8	17,385.6	4,425.4
Finland	5,045.3	813.3	54,899.7	5,741.1	15,628.7	3,625.2
France	43,619.1	2,693.8	282,418.0	51,745.2	173,953.6	55,210.7
Germany	24,047.8	7,463.6	752,882.4	93,599.2	123,085.3	53,461.0
Gibraltar						
Greece	10,458.0	1,333.0	33,257.7	8,624.8	19,470.8	21,521.8
Iceland						
Ireland	2,816.8	1,034.2	43,474.5	3,288.8	25,372.9	4,853.6
Italy	36,180.7	6,911.5	350,354.3	40,112.6	128,534.1	78,753.8
Liechtenstein						
Luxembourg						
Malta						
Monaco						
Netherlands	15,435.2	32,000.1	97,025.6	12,196.0	39,964.6	12,664.0
Norway	5,568.8	130,663.0	35,867.4	11,408.1	18,900.1	4,589.5
Portugal	4,802.8	714.4	27,723.2	5,605.6	13,048.5	9,801.6
Spain	34,688.2	3,739.4	190,965.6	26,490.9	193,601.4	109,849.0
Sweden	6,475.0	1,894.6	72,827.1	14,762.9	19,812.8	5,450.2
Switzerland	4,054.6	791.7	90,955.3	7,432.9	26,558.5	10,571.2
Turkey	45,001.6	9,399.1	123,922.1	14,469.5	7,487.7	20,430.0
United Kingdom	19,662.8	49,528.7	249,028.1	62,064.9	136,587.7	64,027.2
Eastern Europe						
Albania						
Belarus	4,488.1		15,888.5		5,393.3	
Bosnia-Herzegovina						
Bulgaria	2,599.6	1,491.0	7,584.5	1,252.7	2,638.8	1,117.1
Croatia	3,154.5	579.4	11,225.6	1,920.8	4,606.6	1,958.3
Czech Republic	4,472.0	2,800.5	54,589.0	7,137.0	12,808.3	3,775.7
Estonia	596.7	216.2	3,488.7	660.3	1,724.1	314.3
Georgia						
Hungary	5,360.3	292.7	31,103.3	3,152.2	6,185.7	2,006.8
Latvia	923.1	112.4	3,075.4	576.4	2,128.5	573.3
Lithuania	2,123.3	204.9	8,038.1	1,453.7	4,516.5	508.2
Macedonia						
Moldova						
Poland	18,950.4	12,311.0	91,300.6	14,890.3	30,475.5	5,474.2
Romania	10,702.2	1,469.8	37,509.1	3,091.3	15,665.6	4,092.2
Russia	74,532.8	182,787.6	144,676.3	65,445.7	93,339.6	21,110.2
Slovakia	2,957.3	416.9	19,405.9	5,787.1	6,082.4	1,064.8
Slovenia	920.4	244.7	10,798.9	1,424.7	3,139.9	1,101.4
Ukraine	9,776.6	7,218.5	36,406.0	5,191.2	6,641.7	2,080.0

Source: *Euromonitor International from national statistics*

Economic Statistics

Origin of Gross Domestic Product 2008 *(continued)*
US$ million

	Wholesale & Retail Trade, Repair of Motor Vehicles/goods	Transport, Storage & Communications	Financial Inter-mediation, Real Estate, Renting and Business	Public Admin and Defence, Compulsory Social Security	Education, Health, Social Work and Other Community Activities	Activities of Households	GDP by origin
Western Europe							
Austria	45,874.6	22,342.9	89,563.4	20,833.4	55,068.0	894.1	372,851.8
Belgium	59,094.9	38,648.9	127,067.8	31,480.3	70,568.4	1,172.1	443,231.7
Cyprus							
Denmark	31,010.0	29,599.3	71,344.8	18,046.0	60,575.2	453.5	291,828.8
Finland	25,243.4	23,564.0	50,740.5	11,175.9	41,180.2	240.5	237,898.0
France	241,799.3	155,674.3	852,674.0	190,378.4	451,379.9	14,611.7	2,516,157.6
Germany	345,745.2	192,740.2	985,963.9	181,191.4	531,422.8	11,031.2	3,302,634.0
Gibraltar							
Greece	50,371.7	33,541.8	63,202.9	27,476.8	45,948.5	2,612.5	317,820.3
Iceland							
Ireland	21,617.9	11,579.9	66,193.8	10,446.2	39,812.9	252.4	230,752.9
Italy	224,586.0	153,996.5	558,817.0	141,318.8	279,240.0	19,364.6	2,018,170.5
Liechtenstein							
Luxembourg							
Malta							
Monaco							
Netherlands	95,520.2	52,864.3	205,996.2	49,386.2	122,167.2	22,040.6	757,260.1
Norway	27,220.6	25,651.9	66,906.4	15,237.4	57,561.2	300.2	399,874.8
Portugal	26,560.5	14,595.8	46,744.5	21,322.9	37,324.9	1,667.6	209,912.5
Spain	146,457.9	96,004.6	305,563.8	83,274.9	203,585.7	11,530.4	1,405,751.9
Sweden	43,942.6	30,493.5	96,139.6	21,531.2	88,535.4	116.5	401,981.4
Switzerland	61,369.4	29,935.3	114,312.2	53,542.8	74,439.3		473,963.3
Turkey	97,174.1	92,836.7	40,318.3	56,563.0	67,202.3		574,804.3
United Kingdom	262,092.2	154,592.6	778,294.7	109,214.2	412,317.7	10,897.2	2,308,308.2
Eastern Europe							
Albania							
Belarus	6,279.8	4,840.1	4,802.2	2,860.4	6,064.3		50,616.6
Bosnia-Herzegovina							
Bulgaria	4,092.6	4,618.2	8,263.7	2,661.1	3,115.6		39,434.6
Croatia	8,326.2	6,431.7	10,241.6	2,014.1	5,917.7	85.5	56,462.1
Czech Republic	26,188.5	19,111.6	33,809.3	11,201.9	22,121.8	33.7	198,049.2
Estonia	2,912.6	2,113.6	6,372.2	1,336.5	2,496.5		20,895.3
Georgia							
Hungary	15,370.1	9,999.2	30,974.6	11,287.9	18,687.6		134,420.5
Latvia	6,383.9	3,310.4	6,257.4	1,686.6	3,183.0		28,210.6
Lithuania	7,229.9	5,473.1	6,482.7	1,934.7	4,202.8	38.7	42,206.5
Macedonia							
Moldova							
Poland	86,298.1	32,504.2	83,189.5	26,001.2	54,502.9	2,509.0	458,406.9
Romania	22,034.6	18,178.4	31,962.6	8,629.0	17,504.2		170,839.0
Russia	178,670.4	92,783.0	260,954.3	123,092.1	199,532.4		1,436,924.3
Slovakia	14,621.1	8,411.9	16,328.4	3,782.1	8,290.6		87,148.7
Slovenia	5,669.5	3,818.4	10,382.6	2,834.8	6,705.6	6.3	47,046.4
Ukraine	22,605.0	15,354.0	21,078.8	9,240.9	17,373.5	3.0	152,969.2

Source:*Euromonitor International from national statistics*

Economic Statistics

Table 8.5

Origin of Gross Domestic Product 2008 (% Analysis)

% of total GDP

	Agriculture, Forestry & Fishing	Mining & Quarrying	Manufacturing	Electricity, Gas & Water	Construction	Hotels and restaurants
Western Europe						
Austria	1.48	0.55	19.98	2.70	7.79	4.6
Belgium	0.82	0.11	16.43	2.03	5.08	1.5
Cyprus						
Denmark	0.65	5.10	12.80	1.67	5.96	1.5
Finland	2.12	0.34	23.08	2.41	6.57	1.5
France	1.73	0.11	11.22	2.06	6.91	2.2
Germany	0.73	0.23	22.80	2.83	3.73	1.6
Gibraltar						
Greece	3.29	0.42	10.46	2.71	6.13	6.8
Iceland						
Ireland	1.22	0.45	18.84	1.43	11.00	2.1
Italy	1.79	0.34	17.36	1.99	6.37	3.9
Liechtenstein						
Luxembourg						
Malta						
Monaco						
Netherlands	2.04	4.23	12.81	1.61	5.28	1.7
Norway	1.39	32.68	8.97	2.85	4.73	1.1
Portugal	2.29	0.34	13.21	2.67	6.22	4.7
Spain	2.47	0.27	13.58	1.88	13.77	7.8
Sweden	1.61	0.47	18.12	3.67	4.93	1.4
Switzerland	0.86	0.17	19.19	1.57	5.60	2.2
Turkey	7.83	1.64	21.56	2.52	1.30	3.6
United Kingdom	0.85	2.15	10.79	2.69	5.92	2.8
Eastern Europe						
Albania						
Belarus	8.87		31.39		10.66	
Bosnia-Herzegovina						
Bulgaria	6.59	3.78	19.23	3.18	6.69	2.8
Croatia	5.59	1.03	19.88	3.40	8.16	3.5
Czech Republic	2.26	1.41	27.56	3.60	6.47	1.9
Estonia	2.86	1.03	16.70	3.16	8.25	1.5
Georgia						
Hungary	3.99	0.22	23.14	2.35	4.60	1.5
Latvia	3.27	0.40	10.90	2.04	7.55	2.0
Lithuania	5.03	0.49	19.04	3.44	10.70	1.2
Macedonia						
Moldova						
Poland	4.13	2.69	19.92	3.25	6.65	1.2
Romania	6.26	0.86	21.96	1.81	9.17	2.4
Russia	5.19	12.72	10.07	4.55	6.50	1.5
Slovakia	3.39	0.48	22.27	6.64	6.98	1.2
Slovenia	1.96	0.52	22.95	3.03	6.67	2.3
Ukraine	6.39	4.72	23.80	3.39	4.34	1.4

Source: *Euromonitor International from national statistics*

Economic Statistics

Origin of Gross Domestic Product 2008 (% Analysis) *(continued)*
% of total GDP

	Wholesale & Retail Trade, Restaurants & Hotels	Transport, Storage & Commun- ications	Financial Inter- mediation, Real Estate, Renting and Business	Public Admin and Defence, Compulsory Social Security	Education, Health, Social Work and Other Community Activities	Activities of Households	GDP by origin
Western Europe							
Austria	12.30	5.99	24.02	5.59	3.82	0.24	100.0
Belgium	13.33	8.72	28.67	7.10	2.51	0.26	100.0
Cyprus							
Denmark	10.63	10.14	24.45	6.18	4.47	0.16	100.0
Finland	10.61	9.91	21.33	4.70	3.59	0.10	100.0
France	9.61	6.19	33.89	7.57	3.74	0.58	100.0
Germany	10.47	5.84	29.85	5.49	4.60	0.33	100.0
Gibraltar							
Greece	15.85	10.55	19.89	8.65	4.30	0.82	100.0
Iceland							
Ireland	9.37	5.02	28.69	4.53	3.11	0.11	100.0
Italy	11.13	7.63	27.69	7.00	2.94	0.96	100.0
Liechtenstein							
Luxembourg							
Malta							
Monaco							
Netherlands	12.61	6.98	27.20	6.52	2.91	2.91	100.0
Norway	6.81	6.41	16.73	3.81	2.78	0.08	100.0
Portugal	12.65	6.95	22.27	10.16	2.87	0.79	100.0
Spain	10.42	6.83	21.74	5.92	3.85	0.82	100.0
Sweden	10.93	7.59	23.92	5.36	4.36	0.03	100.0
Switzerland	12.95	6.32	24.12	11.30	9.38		100.0
Turkey	16.91	16.15	7.01	9.84	3.67		100.0
United Kingdom	11.35	6.70	33.72	4.73	4.90	0.47	100.0
Eastern Europe							
Albania							
Belarus	12.41	9.56	9.49	5.65	1.86		100.0
Bosnia-Herzegovina							
Bulgaria	10.38	11.71	20.96	6.75	2.44		100.0
Croatia	14.75	11.39	18.14	3.57	2.80	0.15	100.0
Czech Republic	13.22	9.65	17.07	5.66	3.30	0.02	100.0
Estonia	13.94	10.12	30.50	6.40	3.53		100.0
Georgia							
Hungary	11.43	7.44	23.04	8.40	4.21		100.0
Latvia	22.63	11.73	22.18	5.98	4.13		100.0
Lithuania	17.13	12.97	15.36	4.58	2.29	0.09	100.0
Macedonia							
Moldova							
Poland	18.83	7.09	18.15	5.67	3.49	0.55	100.0
Romania	12.90	10.64	18.71	5.05	3.01		100.0
Russia	12.43	6.46	18.16	8.57	3.26		100.0
Slovakia	16.78	9.65	18.74	4.34	2.31		100.0
Slovenia	12.05	8.12	22.07	6.03	3.72	0.01	100.0
Ukraine	14.78	10.04	13.78	6.04	2.32	0.00	100.0

Source:*Euromonitor International from national statistics*

Table 8.6

Usage of Gross Domestic Product 2008

US$ million

	Government Final Consumption	Private Final Consumption	Increases in Stocks	Gross Fixed Capital Formation	Exports of Goods & Services	Imports of Goods & Services	Total
Western Europe							
Austria	75,832.9	219,064.1	3,939.8	93,131.2	244,327.2	-222,229.3	414,829.3
Belgium	117,456.3	271,035.9	5,711.7	114,810.1	466,413.7	-468,680.2	506,574.0
Cyprus	4,660.6	17,062.1	239.7	5,816.5	11,741.8	-14,577.2	24,943.4
Denmark	90,074.4	166,960.0	2,530.7	74,279.8	186,593.3	-180,381.6	340,029.2
Finland	60,564.1	140,657.9	2,334.1	56,484.5	120,989.9	-110,347.9	271,867.4
France	665,245.7	1,639,694.6	26,362.9	623,360.6	750,458.2	-831,005.3	2,869,974.1
Germany	665,289.9	2,074,694.8	4,282.7	701,450.0	1,729,032.5	-1,499,135.5	3,673,112.4
Gibraltar		248.2					1,112.1
Greece	60,175.4	254,580.6	5,248.4	69,075.2	82,614.3	-114,146.8	357,549.3
Iceland	4,093.6	9,026.4	37.0	3,984.6	7,448.2	-7,931.5	16,658.4
Ireland	47,037.1	132,590.4	475.8	58,085.7	221,270.4	-188,619.9	273,313.5
Italy	464,081.1	1,366,869.4	4,002.6	478,102.1	669,780.1	-680,330.8	2,313,897.4
Liechtenstein	533.8	2,904.4	-6.5	1,089.0	2,818.7	-2,304.0	5,027.8
Luxembourg	8,619.4	18,435.5	627.8	10,872.0	96,727.2	-81,328.9	53,956.4
Malta	1,724.6	5,083.7	333.0	1,337.8	6,742.1	-7,060.5	8,291.6
Monaco	1,610.0	3,971.7	15.0	1,527.0	1,838.0	-2,009.9	6,951.8
Netherlands	219,302.1	400,979.7	1,459.9	179,331.7	672,573.4	-602,166.4	876,971.4
Norway	86,918.3	175,783.7	7,861.5	93,853.0	217,331.6	-129,918.1	451,830.1
Portugal	50,624.3	162,899.1	1,389.7	53,098.2	80,192.3	-103,856.7	244,711.9
Spain	307,986.3	921,274.5	2,987.6	473,157.2	425,782.6	-519,413.2	1,611,770.5
Sweden	126,621.0	222,560.9	768.8	93,383.4	259,663.8	-224,059.7	478,961.2
Switzerland	53,484.7	285,012.4	-491.6	106,332.3	282,114.7	-226,192.3	500,260.1
Turkey	93,591.4	508,747.7	13,003.1	148,156.0	174,680.0	-208,163.4	730,015.2
United Kingdom	580,209.1	1,704,882.3	2,614.1	443,660.1	766,650.9	-847,534.6	2,658,462.1
Eastern Europe							
Albania	1,309.9	10,172.3	-61.9	5,048.7	3,526.8	-6,996.8	12,944.8
Belarus	10,077.6	31,390.9	2,234.6	19,732.4	37,262.9	-41,716.2	60,301.9
Bosnia-Herzegovina	3,574.3	16,006.5	0.0	4,854.7	6,808.3	-12,861.1	18,383.0
Bulgaria	8,120.7	34,016.8	2,491.6	16,643.2	30,177.7	-41,545.7	49,904.3
Croatia	12,871.0	40,971.1	2,190.7	19,104.4	29,056.7	-34,861.1	69,332.5
Czech Republic	44,037.2	107,817.9	2,608.3	52,032.0	166,798.3	-155,949.3	216,353.9
Estonia	4,563.1	12,857.1	96.1	6,896.3	17,787.8	-18,768.0	23,516.3
Georgia	3,311.2	9,375.6	572.3	2,881.5	3,668.6	-7,382.9	12,791.9
Hungary	33,007.0	83,100.3	5,531.3	31,133.0	125,977.1	-124,080.1	154,668.8
Latvia	6,751.9	19,719.6	1,523.2	10,214.7	14,126.4	-18,553.3	33,782.5
Lithuania	9,053.1	30,942.3	894.8	11,709.7	28,280.7	-33,576.1	47,303.9
Macedonia	1,827.6	7,550.5	285.4	2,107.0	5,187.7	-7,692.7	9,521.4
Moldova	1,229.3	5,654.3	174.0	2,060.6	2,463.7	-5,534.9	6,047.0
Poland	90,410.7	323,523.6	14,335.0	114,642.0	207,746.4	-224,591.2	527,849.0
Romania	28,911.5	131,182.0	-4,273.4	66,278.8	61,867.3	-86,407.3	200,074.2
Russia	280,677.2	815,265.0	67,392.8	367,619.7	520,128.2	-367,584.6	1,676,585.0
Slovakia	16,402.9	53,935.6	2,724.3	24,769.9	78,864.8	-81,192.6	95,491.5
Slovenia	9,803.3	28,792.4	2,302.2	15,312.9	37,463.2	-39,034.8	54,639.0
Ukraine	31,949.7	110,913.0	3,002.3	49,083.4	84,458.0	-99,003.6	180,335.0

Source: *International Monetary Fund (IMF), International Financial Statistics*
Notes: *The difference between the sum of GDP by usage components and Total GDP (usually production approach measured GDP) appears due to the statistical discrepancies*

Economic Statistics

Table 8.7

Usage of Gross Domestic Product 2008 (% Analysis)

% of total GDP

	Government Final Consumption	Private Final Consumption	Increases in Stocks	Gross Fixed Capital Formation	Exports of Goods & Services	Imports of Goods & Services	Total
Western Europe							
Austria	18.28	52.81	0.95	22.45	58.90	-53.57	100.00
Belgium	23.19	53.50	1.13	22.66	92.07	-92.52	100.00
Cyprus	18.68	68.40	0.96	23.32	47.07	-58.44	100.00
Denmark	26.49	49.10	0.74	21.85	54.88	-53.05	100.00
Finland	22.28	51.74	0.86	20.78	44.50	-40.59	100.00
France	23.18	57.13	0.92	21.72	26.15	-28.96	100.00
Germany	18.11	56.48	0.12	19.10	47.07	-40.81	100.00
Gibraltar		22.32					100.00
Greece	16.83	71.20	1.47	19.32	23.11	-31.92	100.00
Iceland	24.57	54.19	0.22	23.92	44.71	-47.61	100.00
Ireland	17.21	48.51	0.17	21.25	80.96	-69.01	100.00
Italy	20.06	59.07	0.17	20.66	28.95	-29.40	100.00
Liechtenstein	10.62	57.77	-0.13	21.66	56.06	-45.83	100.00
Luxembourg	15.97	34.17	1.16	20.15	179.27	-150.73	100.00
Malta	20.80	61.31	4.02	16.13	81.31	-85.15	100.00
Monaco	23.16	57.13	0.22	21.97	26.44	-28.91	100.00
Netherlands	25.01	45.72	0.17	20.45	76.69	-68.66	100.00
Norway	19.24	38.90	1.74	20.77	48.10	-28.75	100.00
Portugal	20.69	66.57	0.57	21.70	32.77	-42.44	100.00
Spain	19.11	57.16	0.19	29.36	26.42	-32.23	100.00
Sweden	26.44	46.47	0.16	19.50	54.21	-46.78	100.00
Switzerland	10.69	56.97	-0.10	21.26	56.39	-45.21	100.00
Turkey	12.82	69.69	1.78	20.29	23.93	-28.51	100.00
United Kingdom	21.82	64.13	0.10	16.69	28.84	-31.88	100.00
Eastern Europe							
Albania	10.12	78.58	-0.48	39.00	27.24	-54.05	100.00
Belarus	16.71	52.06	3.71	32.72	61.79	-69.18	100.00
Bosnia-Herzegovina	19.44	87.07	0.00	26.41	37.04	-69.96	100.00
Bulgaria	16.27	68.16	4.99	33.35	60.47	-83.25	100.00
Croatia	18.56	59.09	3.16	27.55	41.91	-50.28	100.00
Czech Republic	20.35	49.83	1.21	24.05	77.10	-72.08	100.00
Estonia	19.40	54.67	0.41	29.33	75.64	-79.81	100.00
Georgia	25.89	73.29	4.47	22.53	28.68	-57.72	100.00
Hungary	21.34	53.73	3.58	20.13	81.45	-80.22	100.00
Latvia	19.99	58.37	4.51	30.24	41.82	-54.92	100.00
Lithuania	19.14	65.41	1.89	24.75	59.79	-70.98	100.00
Macedonia	19.19	79.30	3.00	22.13	54.48	-80.79	100.00
Moldova	20.33	93.51	2.88	34.08	40.74	-91.53	100.00
Poland	17.13	61.29	2.72	21.72	39.36	-42.55	100.00
Romania	14.45	65.57	-2.14	33.13	30.92	-43.19	100.00
Russia	16.74	48.63	4.02	21.93	31.02	-21.92	100.00
Slovakia	17.18	56.48	2.85	25.94	82.59	-85.03	100.00
Slovenia	17.94	52.70	4.21	28.03	68.56	-71.44	100.00
Ukraine	17.72	61.50	1.66	27.22	46.83	-54.90	100.00

Source:*International Monetary Fund (IMF), International Financial Statistics*
Notes: *The difference between the sum of GDP by usage components and Total GDP (usually production approach measured GDP) appears due to the statistical discrepancies*

Economic Statistics

Table 8.8

Increases in Stocks by Quarter 2007-2009

Million units of national currency

	2007 1st Quarter	2007 2nd Quarter	2007 3rd Quarter	2007 4th Quarter	2008 1st Quarter	2008 2nd Quarter	2008 3rd Quarter	2008 4th Quarter	2009 1st Quarter
Western Europe									
Austria	87.2	1,079.7	1,992.4	-1,607.5	-415.9	1,849.4	2,077.1	-833.6	15.4
Belgium	939.0	12.0	667.0	1,459.0	2,034.3	368.6	1,546.4	-68.3	-519.6
Cyprus	96.2	121.4	-261.2	127.1					
Denmark	5,183.0	4,755.0	4,615.0	-2,708.0	4,680.7	3,665.9	2,949.5	1,605.8	-835.1
Finland	1,882.0	326.0	794.0	463.0	1,061.0	149.0	1,039.0	-663.0	-73.0
France	3,059.2	2,764.5	3,188.5	2,004.9	7,860.1	6,121.3	5,735.2	-1,803.7	-14,361.3
Germany	405.2	-3,494.8	-1,367.5	-6,472.9	-696.9	-3,531.6	1,968.3	5,170.2	3,220.8
Gibraltar									
Greece	-1,516.2	-1,732.6	-814.9	4,295.1	-1,043.9	-888.6	648.8	4,849.8	-24.4
Iceland	1,546.0	1,100.0	4,089.0	-109.0	798.0	-6,749.0	14,860.0	-5,654.0	
Ireland	-113.3	-133.9	-344.8	497.0	-51.7	476.7	257.4	-359.1	-623.0
Italy	1,726.4	3,646.7	4,339.6	-916.7	891.9	-515.4	906.9	1,436.3	15.7
Liechtenstein									
Luxembourg	-11.5	-43.9	-2.2	251.1	82.7	25.9	310.5	7.5	-640.2
Malta	4.8	23.0	8.2	29.1					
Monaco									
Netherlands	-937.4	-238.5	177.3	-650.5	-633.5	-1,291.7	406.5	2,510.7	-1,211.7
Norway	18,649.0	4,504.0	1,164.0	16,314.0	14,551.0	13,164.0	9,350.0	7,274.0	23,716.0
Portugal	124.0	51.0	256.1	194.1	232.0	178.7	348.8	184.8	-171.8
Spain	360.0	314.0	384.0	523.0	532.0	531.0	505.0	462.1	308.4
Sweden	14,524.0	-4,215.0	12,149.0	-552.0	7,899.0	2,527.9	8,463.3	-13,823.2	-2,346.0
Switzerland	-654.3	-316.1	620.7	1,780.9	256.0	-986.5	-154.7	1,552.2	
Turkey	-4,555.8	-2,699.8	6,945.9	-2,654.5	-3,847.9	8,446.9	21,824.0	-9,498.9	-15,400.5
United Kingdom	948.0	383.0	3,466.0	2,563.0	-17,736.4	-21,175.7	-11,486.2	51,820.3	67,958.4
Eastern Europe									
Albania									
Belarus	-17,600.0	147,700.0	1,581,400.0	591,800.0	441,900.0	544,300.0	2,832,700.0	955,000.0	
Bosnia-Herzegovina									
Bulgaria	937.8	907.1	1,123.3	996.9	678.6	1,372.8	859.3	420.9	94.5
Croatia	8,368.6	6,272.0	-6,193.4	2,222.8	8,180.3	5,753.7	-3,367.6	244.6	5,155.8
Czech Republic	21,391.2	28,441.7	36,064.7	-7,138.6	16,189.0	14,692.0	12,799.0	848.0	-7,137.0
Estonia	3,138.9	3,631.5	4,884.5	1,314.4	2,084.2	2,190.1	893.5	-1,012.0	-1,454.1
Georgia	295.3	194.4	208.1	379.4	220.8	286.7	110.3	235.2	
Hungary	84,747.0	21,961.0	271,558.0	-4,040.0	214,041.0	104,399.0	353,236.0	-174,375.0	-218,194.0
Latvia	302.2	272.1	261.9	158.6	303.7	137.8	166.4	124.6	-78.4
Lithuania	672.6	1,086.6	1,014.9	-278.1	1,908.0	708.6	734.3	-1,241.8	-2,385.4
Macedonia									
Moldova	994.2	812.5	1,435.8	-638.3	432.6	1,075.7	735.0	-676.8	-479.1
Poland	7,333.6	6,796.6	8,145.3	9,675.5	13,478.6	9,102.9	13,369.6	-1,414.8	-5,852.7
Romania	661.5	346.0	-3,116.2	-1,437.0	-361.4	-6,093.9	-5,702.9	1,394.0	
Russia	239,467.1	233,998.2	649,765.9	-74,021.2	373,376.7	534,921.5	934,500.8	-164,729.1	-378,775.9
Slovakia	-22.9	381.0	526.4	71.6	656.6	375.8	653.9	164.7	
Slovenia									
Ukraine	1,877.0	-2,638.0	7,752.0	-2,306.0	267.0	5,274.0	17,123.0	-7,207.0	-13,353.0

Source:International Monetary Fund (IMF), International Financial Statistics

Economic Statistics

Table 8.9

Gross Fixed Capital Formation by Quarter 2007-2009
Million units of national currency

	2007 1st Quarter	2007 2nd Quarter	2007 3rd Quarter	2007 4th Quarter	2008 1st Quarter	2008 2nd Quarter	2008 3rd Quarter	2008 4th Quarter	2009 1st Quarter
Western Europe									
Austria	12,816.8	14,952.3	16,111.0	16,324.4	13,392.3	16,275.6	16,768.4	16,844.2	12,566.6
Belgium	16,358.0	17,725.0	17,135.0	21,300.0	17,878.0	19,695.3	18,268.6	22,169.1	17,582.2
Cyprus	754.3	801.0	798.5	798.4					
Denmark	87,226.0	93,465.0	92,132.0	101,490.0	90,865.0	97,708.7	94,100.5	96,013.9	83,749.5
Finland	7,337.0	9,228.0	9,597.0	10,404.0	8,372.0	9,228.0	10,239.0	10,541.0	7,773.0
France	99,311.3	101,323.2	102,851.4	105,290.1	106,827.9	107,157.3	106,937.0	102,637.7	99,793.0
Germany	112,702.6	112,025.1	113,280.4	115,492.0	120,462.6	119,202.5	120,182.6	116,772.3	106,761.2
Gibraltar									
Greece	11,669.1	13,269.0	13,083.2	13,325.2	10,726.8	11,854.1	11,351.2	13,003.0	9,962.4
Iceland	77,843.5	92,101.8	98,968.1	82,699.5	79,578.0	83,895.0	96,096.0	90,869.0	
Ireland	14,605.2	12,356.5	11,469.6	11,708.7	12,087.4	9,707.3	9,804.3	7,869.0	7,499.3
Italy	81,574.9	81,375.5	81,911.9	82,886.6	82,378.2	82,880.0	81,970.5	77,631.4	74,231.3
Liechtenstein									
Luxembourg	1,627.6	1,924.8	1,718.1	1,840.2	1,640.7	1,792.6	1,874.6	2,079.4	1,542.0
Malta	74.6	73.4	72.5	94.8					
Monaco									
Netherlands	28,031.8	27,766.7	28,418.3	28,956.2	30,609.3	31,027.4	30,707.5	29,508.8	28,367.5
Norway	108,197.0	117,477.0	123,056.0	135,838.0	123,631.0	129,430.0	133,523.0	142,747.0	122,839.0
Portugal	8,397.3	8,919.6	8,895.4	9,360.2	8,851.5	9,528.6	9,062.6	8,636.4	7,163.6
Spain	79,690.0	80,868.0	81,967.0	83,258.0	83,602.2	81,895.2	80,333.3	75,669.3	72,411.3
Sweden	131,241.0	155,011.0	132,621.0	162,837.0	141,660.0	168,695.0	140,147.0	164,997.0	126,362.0
Switzerland	27,574.2	28,562.1	27,965.6	28,324.1	28,909.8	28,708.7	28,042.8	27,358.8	27,674.8
Turkey	42,667.2	45,500.8	48,081.9	47,868.1	48,705.9	51,388.5	47,507.0	45,229.6	40,122.1
United Kingdom	61,279.0	61,395.0	62,363.0	63,729.0	62,897.6	60,973.6	59,377.7	58,087.1	54,775.7
Eastern Europe									
Albania									
Belarus	4,628,600.0	6,352,600.0	7,566,000.0	11,043,100.0	6,561,100.0	9,777,300.0	11,233,600.0	14,584,400.0	
Bosnia-Herzegovina									
Bulgaria	3,196.0	3,768.9	4,249.0	5,618.6	4,100.8	5,547.1	5,717.6	6,888.3	3,615.7
Croatia	19,530.7	21,272.1	21,170.9	20,412.8	22,410.4	25,121.1	24,237.4	22,512.1	19,643.7
Czech Republic	192,617.9	219,377.2	220,567.1	225,163.8	201,263.7	226,777.4	229,726.4	230,506.5	202,556.7
Estonia	16,900.9	19,742.4	19,807.6	21,104.7	17,268.3	18,978.4	18,275.1	15,941.4	12,410.1
Georgia	814.0	874.6	1,656.6	1,025.3	900.6	1,267.7	1,024.6	1,102.8	
Hungary	961,171.6	1,204,359.6	1,338,159.5	1,855,379.3	936,083.4	1,203,121.8	1,339,542.0	1,879,642.8	904,711.4
Latvia	911.0	1,210.2	1,355.3	1,498.7	1,000.8	1,265.6	1,296.2	1,348.8	662.9
Lithuania	5,106.7	6,929.0	7,562.1	7,856.1	5,728.2	7,352.5	7,859.0	6,661.1	3,510.8
Macedonia									
Moldova	1,913.3	4,045.2	4,737.6	7,525.6	2,320.3	4,801.4	5,628.0	8,663.6	2,198.6
Poland	38,510.8	53,336.0	60,045.7	101,899.5	44,583.2	62,534.9	63,044.3	106,037.6	46,256.2
Romania	14,322.8	24,910.2	39,475.4	44,590.7	21,042.3	36,845.7	58,452.1	50,606.9	
Russia	979,535.2	1,529,188.7	1,848,928.4	2,624,787.7	1,405,702.4	2,104,539.2	2,459,182.7	2,987,275.7	1,344,588.8
Slovakia	2,916.4	3,569.0	3,839.7	3,989.5	3,427.0	4,367.2	4,528.7	4,507.7	
Slovenia									
Ukraine	33,582.0	45,590.0	56,252.0	63,209.0	49,682.0	65,373.0	76,866.0	66,612.0	31,200.0

Source: International Monetary Fund (IMF), International Financial Statistics

Economic Statistics

Table 8.10

Total Gross National Income 1980-2008 (national currencies)
Million units of national currency

	1980	1985	1990	1995	1996	1997	1998	1999	2000	2001
Western Europe										
Austria	75,470	102,016	135,860	172,515	180,033	182,390	189,362	194,448	204,010	207,952
Belgium	88,226	121,930	163,654	211,403	215,571	225,777	230,049	242,912	257,435	262,806
Cyprus	1,514	3,086	4,232	6,612	6,894	7,288	8,645	8,850	9,419	10,209
Denmark	382,155	615,288	818,974	1,008,640	1,055,830	1,109,710	1,150,470	1,203,240	1,266,610	1,316,780
Finland	32,767	56,401	86,923	94,269	98,048	107,317	116,222	121,067	131,278	139,520
France	442,342	725,315	1,006,426	1,198,118	1,235,481	1,278,181	1,335,968	1,388,890	1,461,160	1,514,920
Germany	755,394	937,979	1,251,764	1,834,789	1,866,321	1,901,738	1,945,051	1,990,470	2,043,160	2,092,150
Gibraltar										
Greece	5,543	14,374	41,542	88,102	96,485	106,803	116,077	122,003	136,648	147,352
Iceland	15,675	117,211	359,053	441,303	476,310	514,338	575,682	620,011	664,837	747,638
Ireland	11,510	20,460	32,396	46,953	51,763	59,359	68,008	77,924	90,359	98,903
Italy	199,501	415,559	673,202	909,863	970,707	1,016,867	1,062,682	1,122,160	1,182,140	1,240,430
Liechtenstein										
Luxembourg	3,989	6,535	9,990	14,046	14,815	15,690	16,979	17,868	19,170	20,050
Malta	413	394	548	1,002	1,026	1,056	1,091	1,157	1,170	1,225
Monaco										
Netherlands	154,449	193,089	241,845	309,796	322,610	346,800	358,704	390,395	426,980	451,110
Norway	305,071	542,876	715,315	931,980	1,021,240	1,107,440	1,127,500	1,230,020	1,461,260	1,538,260
Portugal	16,629	24,478	51,002	75,812	80,676	84,503				
Spain	90,627	167,502	298,661	436,695	461,370	489,277	521,558	559,562	603,252	644,093
Sweden	549,779	883,312	1,396,300	1,767,370	1,810,800	1,884,950	1,983,610	2,103,000	2,230,660	2,303,500
Switzerland	177,345	241,355	327,585	377,560						
Turkey	4	28	287	7,855	15,064					
United Kingdom	228,084	352,581	560,449	727,497	776,504	827,707	887,495	924,587	974,732	1,027,910
Eastern Europe										
Albania										
Belarus			4	121,351	192,046	366,300	701,810	3,028,910	9,096,100	17,113,100
Bosnia-Herzegovina										
Bulgaria				852	1,692	16,844	21,911	23,464	26,082	29,045
Croatia										
Czech Republic				1,463,500	1,660,040	1,782,880	1,959,310	2,031,710	2,139,690	2,273,220
Estonia				43,204	56,962	68,076	77,485	82,320	92,340	103,772
Georgia										
Hungary	583,000	842,000	2,080,000							
Latvia				2,631	3,149	3,657	3,994	4,225	4,739	5,233
Lithuania				25,928	32,364	39,252	43,685	42,651	44,937	47,995
Macedonia										
Moldova				6,480	8,070	9,207	9,279	12,678	16,814	20,484
Poland	199	859	50,630							
Romania	62	82	86	7,214	10,839	24,975	38,145			
Russia										
Slovakia										
Slovenia			2,576	15,852	16,469	17,524	18,818	20,313	20,996	22,156
Ukraine				53,639	80,472	92,166	100,524	126,934	164,942	200,610

Source:International Monetary Fund (IMF), International Financial Statistics

Economic Statistics

Total Gross National Income 1980-2008 (national currencies) *(continued)*

Million units of national currency

	2002	2003	2004	2005	2006	2007	2008	Total US$ million 2008	US$ per capita 2008
Western Europe									
Austria	216,118	221,132	231,033	242,075	252,845	265,246	278,016	409,161.0	48,990.8
Belgium	271,036	278,530	292,244	303,533	320,318	336,744	345,402	508,334.1	47,872.9
Cyprus	10,780	11,487	12,182	13,174	14,081	15,606	16,107	23,705.2	27,486.4
Denmark	1,356,520	1,392,120	1,472,920	1,566,810	1,658,920	1,696,240	1,770,260	347,237.1	63,578.7
Finland	144,240	144,835	153,231	157,937	168,650	179,573	184,879	272,089.6	51,333.0
France	1,552,790	1,604,810	1,673,350	1,737,220	1,824,070	1,914,760	1,968,030	2,896,384.1	46,636.2
Germany	2,116,640	2,148,670	2,232,080	2,270,820	2,362,440	2,464,190	2,528,600	3,721,384.7	45,262.5
Gibraltar									
Greece	157,027	170,424	184,536	194,557	208,777	221,672	234,221	344,707.1	30,745.9
Iceland	815,123	828,135	891,145	989,675	1,084,300	1,236,330	1,004,590	11,422.6	36,208.3
Ireland	108,016	119,150	127,560	139,072	153,765	162,121	155,937	229,495.2	52,415.9
Italy	1,285,100	1,324,400	1,383,510	1,424,990	1,482,830	1,535,160	1,547,950	2,278,145.0	38,628.6
Liechtenstein									
Luxembourg	19,898	20,028	24,051	25,960	25,803	30,408	32,654	48,057.5	99,993.9
Malta	1,312	1,366	1,396	1,454	1,544	1,643	1,706	2,511.4	6,163.5
Monaco									
Netherlands	469,468	482,368	504,333	515,885	557,017	582,295	594,917	875,549.7	53,442.1
Norway	1,537,010	1,603,730	1,746,400	1,959,170	2,161,140	2,293,480	2,571,570	455,952.1	96,249.9
Portugal									
Spain	687,643	735,064	735,072	735,080	735,085	735,091			
Sweden	2,412,530	2,537,810	2,619,210	2,731,090	2,949,330	3,137,150	3,226,560	489,532.9	53,459.3
Switzerland									
Turkey									
United Kingdom	1,091,480	1,155,260	1,220,160	1,275,060	1,334,090	1,417,880	1,474,240	2,710,169.4	44,294.0
Eastern Europe									
Albania									
Belarus	26,084,300	36,616,300	49,951,600	65,186,600	79,020,900	85,938,050			
Bosnia-Herzegovina									
Bulgaria	33,154	35,125	39,317	43,189	48,130	55,639	65,741	49,166.2	6,493.7
Croatia									
Czech Republic	2,352,130	2,466,090	2,660,120	2,849,950	3,041,710	3,316,930	3,418,250	200,229.0	19,408.3
Estonia	116,369	128,941	143,693	166,831	194,130	220,245	232,340	21,725.4	16,272.0
Georgia									
Hungary									
Latvia	5,775	6,372	7,274	8,945	10,842	14,291	15,905	33,078.9	14,593.2
Lithuania	51,524	55,535	61,362	70,821	80,943	94,295	108,334	45,961.1	13,653.2
Macedonia									
Moldova	24,805	30,838	36,414	42,740	50,026	53,669			
Poland									
Romania									
Russia									
Slovakia									
Slovenia	23,537	24,676	25,941	27,371	30,644	31,502			
Ukraine	222,585	264,247	341,686	436,411	535,459	717,406	941,164	178,683.3	3,868.2

Source:*International Monetary Fund (IMF), International Financial Statistics*

Table 8.11

Total Gross National Income 1980-2008 (US$)

US$ million

	1980	1985	1990	1995	1996	1997	1998	1999	2000	2001
Western Europe										
Austria	105,079	77,847	173,009	225,652	228,597	206,837	212,292	207,187	188,164	186,308
Belgium	122,839	93,044	208,402	276,517	273,721	256,040	257,906	258,826	237,440	235,453
Cyprus	2,108	2,355	5,389	8,649	8,754	8,265	9,692	9,430	8,687	9,147
Denmark	67,807	58,066	132,337	180,038	182,081	168,024	171,691	172,477	156,698	158,213
Finland	45,623	43,039	110,690	123,304	124,497	121,702	130,295	128,998	121,081	124,999
France	615,885	553,479	1,281,613	1,567,151	1,568,752	1,449,508	1,497,740	1,479,879	1,347,669	1,357,245
Germany	1,051,758	715,761	1,594,034	2,399,922	2,369,761	2,156,647	2,180,577	2,120,870	1,884,464	1,874,396
Gibraltar										
Greece	7,717	10,968	52,900	115,238	122,512	121,119	130,133	129,996	126,034	132,015
Iceland	3,267	2,824	6,160	6,822	7,163	7,254	8,113	8,571	8,457	7,674
Ireland	16,026	15,613	41,254	61,415	65,726	67,315	76,243	83,029	83,341	88,609
Italy	277,771	317,108	857,275	1,190,110	1,232,555	1,153,168	1,191,363	1,195,675	1,090,321	1,111,324
Liechtenstein										
Luxembourg	5,554	4,987	12,721	18,372	18,811	17,793	19,035	19,039	17,681	17,963
Malta	576	301	698	1,311	1,303	1,197	1,223	1,232	1,079	1,098
Monaco										
Netherlands	215,044	147,344	307,973	405,216	409,634	393,285	402,139	415,971	393,816	404,158
Norway	61,765	63,145	114,272	147,112	158,336	156,564	149,435	157,712	166,018	171,076
Portugal	23,153	18,679	64,948	99,162	102,438	95,830				
Spain	126,183	127,819	380,324	571,202	585,824	554,860	584,713	596,220	556,396	577,055
Sweden	129,985	102,664	235,910	247,764	270,028	246,886	249,515	254,526	243,462	223,011
Switzerland	105,833	98,226	235,815	319,298						
Turkey	58,326	53,253	110,116	171,335	185,055					
United Kingdom	530,064	452,464	995,156	1,148,073	1,211,474	1,355,040	1,469,791	1,495,957	1,475,581	1,480,516
Eastern Europe										
Albania										
Belarus				10,533	14,516	14,077	15,215	12,150	10,375	12,312
Bosnia-Herzegovina										
Bulgaria				12,679	9,511	10,015	12,447	12,777	12,284	13,295
Croatia										
Czech Republic				55,142	61,155	56,245	60,695	58,772	55,435	59,766
Estonia				3,768	4,732	4,904	5,505	5,609	5,442	5,937
Georgia										
Hungary	17,921	16,800	32,908							
Latvia				4,988	5,718	6,295	6,771	7,220	7,814	8,333
Lithuania				6,482	8,091	9,813	10,921	10,663	11,234	11,999
Macedonia										
Moldova				1,441	1,753	1,991	1,728	1,206	1,352	1,592
Poland	45,051	58,352	53,295							
Romania	34,273	47,683	38,242	35,478	35,144	34,843	42,977			
Russia										
Slovakia										
Slovenia			3,281	20,734	20,912	19,873	21,097	21,644	19,365	19,850
Ukraine				36,413	43,987	49,507	41,038	30,731	30,319	37,343

Source:International Monetary Fund (IMF), International Financial Statistics

Economic Statistics

Total Gross National Income 1980-2008 (US$) *(continued)*

US$ million

	2002	2003	2004	2005	2006	2007	2008	US$ per capita 2008
Western Europe								
Austria	203,655	249,768	287,053	301,046	317,226	363,556	409,161	48,990.8
Belgium	255,406	314,598	363,106	377,476	401,879	461,554	508,334	47,872.9
Cyprus	10,158	12,974	15,136	16,383	17,666	21,390	23,705	27,486.4
Denmark	171,826	211,322	245,853	261,270	278,961	311,597	347,237	63,578.7
Finland	135,922	163,590	190,386	196,412	211,593	246,130	272,090	51,333.0
France	1,463,246	1,812,626	2,079,097	2,160,420	2,288,525	2,624,443	2,896,384	46,636.2
Germany	1,994,581	2,426,913	2,773,306	2,824,009	2,963,978	3,377,513	3,721,385	45,262.5
Gibraltar								
Greece	147,972	192,493	229,282	241,953	261,937	303,832	344,707	30,745.9
Iceland	8,893	10,796	12,696	15,714	15,450	19,301	11,423	36,208.3
Ireland	101,787	134,579	158,490	172,951	192,918	222,209	229,495	52,415.9
Italy	1,210,993	1,495,904	1,718,978	1,772,129	1,860,397	2,104,149	2,278,145	38,628.6
Liechtenstein								
Luxembourg	18,750	22,622	29,883	32,283	32,373	41,679	48,057	99,993.9
Malta	1,236	1,543	1,734	1,808	1,937	2,252	2,511	6,163.5
Monaco								
Netherlands	442,396	544,832	626,622	641,559	698,848	798,116	875,550	53,442.1
Norway	192,517	226,508	259,078	304,101	336,976	391,267	455,952	96,249.9
Portugal								
Spain	647,989	830,251	913,309	914,151	922,257	1,007,544		
Sweden	247,766	313,841	356,409	365,457	399,733	464,160	489,533	53,459.3
Switzerland								
Turkey								
United Kingdom	1,637,507	1,886,806	2,235,715	2,317,799	2,455,117	2,837,226	2,710,169	44,294.0
Eastern Europe								
Albania								
Belarus	14,565	17,851	23,123	30,266	36,847	40,044		
Bosnia-Herzegovina								
Bulgaria	15,962	20,272	24,961	27,437	30,867	38,934	49,166	6,493.7
Croatia								
Czech Republic	71,846	87,422	103,507	118,959	134,615	163,446	200,229	19,408.3
Estonia	7,005	9,306	11,408	13,258	15,573	19,262	21,725	16,272.0
Georgia								
Hungary								
Latvia	9,342	11,150	13,465	15,839	19,346	27,815	33,079	14,593.2
Lithuania	14,013	18,143	22,068	25,530	29,410	37,363	45,961	13,653.2
Macedonia								
Moldova	1,828	2,211	2,953	3,392	3,810	4,421		
Poland								
Romania								
Russia								
Slovakia								
Slovenia	22,179	27,871	32,231	34,039	38,447	43,177		
Ukraine	41,787	49,552	64,237	85,158	106,031	142,061	178,683	3,868.2

Source:*International Monetary Fund (IMF), International Financial Statistics*

Table 8.12

Total Gross National Income by Quarter 2007-2009

Million units of national currency

	2007 1st Quarter	2007 2nd Quarter	2007 3rd Quarter	2007 4th Quarter	2008 1st Quarter	2008 2nd Quarter	2008 3rd Quarter	2008 4th Quarter	2009 1st Quarter
Western Europe									
Austria	64,152	65,211	66,925	68,958	67,746	69,231	70,591	70,447	65,452
Belgium	80,953	87,851	80,380	87,560	83,772	90,851	82,915	87,864	82,357
Cyprus									
Denmark	399,024	426,038	423,521	447,656	417,081	454,761	445,714	452,704	406,110
Finland	42,466	42,668	45,597	48,842	44,671	44,639	47,210	48,359	41,420
France	471,423	476,120	481,638	485,579	492,490	492,803	494,019	488,717	484,284
Germany	612,930	609,920	619,420	621,920	632,185	637,138	636,030	623,247	598,180
Gibraltar									
Greece	50,597	53,376	59,620	58,080	53,879	57,683	62,888	59,770	54,936
Iceland									
Ireland	40,543	39,771	39,617	42,190	39,515	38,850	37,925	39,648	33,911
Italy	380,627	380,544	388,276	385,712	387,904	387,186	392,081	380,779	375,926
Liechtenstein									
Luxembourg									
Malta	367	407	436	433					
Monaco									
Netherlands	145,697	147,894	139,439	149,265	147,246	153,098	144,342	150,231	
Norway	541,199	534,610	572,373	645,299	593,781	643,196	642,845	691,747	581,775
Portugal									
Spain									
Sweden	760,642	774,769	762,676	839,064	790,573	812,562	792,078	831,347	774,382
Switzerland									
Turkey									
United Kingdom	344,794	350,828	354,798	367,460	372,860	372,065	368,970	360,344	
Eastern Europe									
Albania									
Belarus									
Bosnia-Herzegovina									
Bulgaria	11,227	12,934	15,141	16,337	13,545	15,614	18,376	18,206	13,629
Croatia									
Czech Republic	809,919	809,907	825,237	871,867	837,822	824,969	870,652	884,807	840,465
Estonia	49,270	55,823	55,948	59,203	53,897	59,644	59,223	59,576	50,811
Georgia									
Hungary									
Latvia	3,022	3,463	3,706	4,100	3,658	3,971	4,102	4,173	3,385
Lithuania	19,518	23,315	24,817	26,645	23,594	27,149	28,686	28,904	20,348
Macedonia									
Moldova									
Poland									
Romania									
Russia									
Slovakia									
Slovenia									
Ukraine	138,799	165,793	198,581	214,233	187,772	232,298	273,925	247,169	

Source: *International Monetary Fund (IMF), International Financial Statistics*

Economic Statistics

Table 8.13

Money Supply 1985-2008

Billion units of national currency

	1985	1990	1995	2000	2003	2004	2005	2006	2007	2008	Total US$ billion 2008
Western Europe											
Austria	6.9	9.1	12.3	14.5	12.3	14.1	14.9	15.4	15.9		
Belgium	10.1	11.1	11.5	13.5	14.9	17.2	18.2	18.9	19.6		
Cyprus	0.6	0.7	1.0	1.8	2.3	2.5	2.9	3.5	3.9	3.9	5.8
Denmark	156.5	244.5	292.0	386.0	469.1	536.6	643.6	699.5	755.2	755.2	148.1
Finland	1.4	2.4	2.6	3.3	7.2	8.6	9.2	9.6	10.2		
France	33.1	41.1	41.9	49.2	85.0	97.8	103.2	106.9	111.7		
Germany	58.7	91.9	134.7	142.2	125.9	141.3	147.7	152.2	156.9		
Gibraltar											
Greece	1.6	3.7	6.0	9.1	10.6	12.8	13.6	14.2	15.0		
Iceland	6.7	24.6	38.3	72.3	114.8	141.7	174.0	202.6	410.8	474.8	5.4
Ireland	1.4	2.0	2.7	5.4	4.7	6.4	7.2	7.7	8.2		
Italy	29.3	42.7	58.7	76.4	76.1	86.8	91.2	94.3	98.4		
Liechtenstein											
Luxembourg				0.7	0.8	1.1	1.2	1.3	1.4		
Malta	0.9	0.9	1.0	1.5	3.0	3.7	3.9	3.9	4.2	4.2	6.2
Monaco											
Netherlands	14.0	17.9	18.7	18.7	21.9	26.4	28.3	29.6	31.0		
Norway	98.6	237.6	358.7	565.1	748.0	801.0	842.0	879.1	917.2		
Portugal	1.6	3.1	4.2	6.5	9.9	11.8	12.6	13.2	13.8		
Spain	12.5	27.3	45.3	59.8	46.4	52.7	55.3	57.1	60.0		
Sweden	46.8			833.4	995.8	1,133.5	1,274.5	1,391.9	1,448.1	219.7
Switzerland	73.9	84.3	100.6	160.0	237.4	224.1	238.6	232.6	241.7	292.0	269.6
Turkey	0.0	0.0	0.4	7.3	23.0	28.6	63.0	67.2	74.7	81.5	62.6
United Kingdom	145.5	523.1	514.6	1,037.9	1,300.3	1,434.7	1,490.3	1,529.2	1,595.5		
Eastern Europe											
Albania			59.3	124.0	139.8	158.8	182.9	214.2	224.4	266.2	3.2
Belarus			10.0	508.4	2,002.6	3,111.4	4,945.8	7,023.2	8,739.9	10,718.5	5.0
Bosnia-Herzegovina			1.5	3.3	3.8	4.4	5.6	6.8	6.3	4.7
Bulgaria			0.2	4.8	8.0	10.3	12.4	16.1	20.7	19.9	14.9
Croatia			8.3	18.0	33.9	34.6	38.9	48.6	57.9	55.3	11.2
Czech Republic			431.1	499.0	964.2	1,026.3	1,162.8	1,325.6	1,526.6	1,674.8	98.1
Estonia			8.2	20.9	30.8	42.3	57.6	72.3	76.2	67.8	6.3
Georgia			0.2	0.4	0.5	0.8	1.0	1.3	1.8	1.6	1.1
Hungary	239.7	517.5	1,011.2	2,379.7	4,027.6	4,169.3	5,188.8	5,833.3	6,348.3	6,160.4	35.8
Latvia			0.4	0.8	1.6	2.0	2.9	4.1	3.9	3.3	7.0
Lithuania			3.5	5.7	10.5	15.1	20.9	24.8	27.9	23.3	9.9
Macedonia			11.5	21.4	28.3	28.8	31.4	36.8	48.9	56.9	1.4
Moldova			0.9	2.0	4.2	5.6	7.3	8.3	10.9	11.6	1.1
Poland	0.2	9.4	37.4	82.6	133.6	175.7	220.6	275.8	335.3	349.7	145.2
Romania	0.0	0.0	0.7	4.6	11.3	15.3	24.6	38.0	61.9	71.6	28.4
Russia			150.1	863.5	2,150.2	2,812.2	3,815.0	5,473.8	7,456.7	7,419.7	298.5
Slovakia			3.9	4.4	8.5	10.1	12.1	14.2	16.3	14.9	21.9
Slovenia			0.7	1.3	2.6	5.0	6.2	7.1	7.5		
Ukraine			4.7	20.8	53.3	67.1	98.6	123.3	181.7	225.1	42.7

Source: *International Monetary Fund (IMF), International Financial Statistics*
Notes: *The money supply refers to the total amount of money held by the nonbank public at a point in time in an economy. M1: Physical currency + demand deposits, which are checking accounts*

Economic Statistics

Table 8.14

Market Capitalisation 1990-2008

Million units of national currency

	1990	1995	2000	2003	2004	2005	2006	2007	2008
Western Europe									
Austria	8,583	23,784	32,456	48,277	69,068	101,578	152,476	166,862	128,565
Belgium	48,810	76,781	197,848	153,708	618,424	262,997	315,807	281,884	215,673
Cyprus		1,841	4,718	4,254	3,928	5,294	12,673	21,507	14,892
Denmark	241,973	314,982	870,279	801,168	906,701	1,067,680	1,373,793	1,511,968	1,126,399
Finland	16,942	32,288	318,363	150,760	147,903	168,465	211,598	269,340	192,965
France	234,348	381,895	1,568,459	1,200,220	1,494,785	1,375,055	1,935,694	2,024,352	1,631,897
Germany	264,947	422,357	1,377,214	955,317	961,400	982,022	1,305,430	1,538,055	1,330,878
Gibraltar									
Greece	11,344	12,480	120,173	94,595	100,800	116,606	166,012	193,298	136,257
Iceland		46,578	348,981	712,875	1,237,402	1,750,826	2,527,552	2,597,753	2,178,769
Ireland		19,752	88,778	75,317	91,821	91,777	130,204	105,080	89,767
Italy	117,007	160,184	833,070	544,350	635,475	641,816	818,283	783,749	683,292
Liechtenstein									
Luxembourg	7,836	22,270	36,881	33,053	40,358	41,214	63,385	121,255	76,415
Malta		113	2,218	1,620	2,287	3,295	3,590	4,112	3,396
Monaco									
Netherlands	89,560	260,775	694,391	432,625	500,842	585,003	623,716	698,222	532,044
Norway	163,379	282,466	572,422	670,348	953,355	1,230,211	1,800,755	2,094,479	1,800,760
Portugal	6,866	13,432	65,791	51,602	59,079	53,860	83,053	96,548	81,093
Spain	82,843	144,687	547,120	642,840	757,108	772,459	1,058,472	1,314,071	1,047,978
Sweden	579,450	1,270,072	3,008,322	2,344,033	2,768,923	3,018,740	4,223,073	4,140,479	3,917,228
Switzerland	222,266	512,744	1,338,095	978,946	1,026,943	1,168,755	1,519,353	1,529,419	1,281,561
Turkey	50	951	43,552	102,630	140,128	217,038	232,958	372,544	153,309
United Kingdom	478,137	892,038	1,703,214	1,506,720	1,538,004	1,681,994	2,059,182	1,929,253	1,846,241
Eastern Europe									
Albania									
Belarus									
Bosnia-Herzegovina									
Bulgaria	4	1,311	3,041	4,417	8,005	16,099	31,143	11,844
Croatia		3,039	22,701	41,072	66,128	76,852	169,329	353,936	132,210
Czech Republic		415,734	424,668	498,245	793,174	918,650	1,098,242	1,489,965	833,961
Estonia			31,324	52,521	78,125	43,981	74,335	69,030	20,860
Georgia			48	435	395	643	1,190	2,320	1,849
Hungary		301,509	3,391,983	3,752,477	5,821,117	6,501,515	8,822,606	8,736,998	3,197,751
Latvia		5	342	652	894	1,427	1,516	1,599	774
Lithuania		628	6,351	10,744	17,970	22,699	28,046	25,576	8,555
Macedonia			468	19,647	20,413	31,836	53,529	121,455	106,830
Moldova			4,875	7,077	7,076				
Poland		11,068	135,943	144,536	260,065	303,725	462,441	573,598	217,461
Romania		20	2,321	18,540	38,466	59,986	92,091	109,539	50,205
Russia		72,322	1,094,840	7,083,275	7,720,844	15,516,228	28,745,964	38,448,292	9,869,996
Slovakia		944	1,319	2,460	3,549	3,532	4,430	5,089	3,454
Slovenia		228	2,762	6,316	7,788	6,352	12,101	21,143	8,005
Ukraine			10,231	22,946	62,651	127,993	216,491	564,372	128,365

Source:World Bank

Economic Statistics

Table 8.15

Annual Rates of Inflation 1985-2008

% growth

	1985	1990	1995	2000	2003	2004	2005	2006	2007	2008
Western Europe										
Austria	3.19	3.26	2.25	2.35	1.36	2.06	2.30	1.45	2.22	3.18
Belgium	4.87	3.45	1.47	2.54	1.59	2.09	2.78	1.79	1.82	4.49
Cyprus	5.03	4.50	2.62	4.14	4.14	2.29	2.56	2.50	2.37	4.67
Denmark	4.65	2.65	2.10	2.92	2.09	1.16	1.81	1.89	1.71	3.40
Finland	5.87	6.10	0.99	3.37	0.88	0.19	0.86	1.57	2.51	4.06
France	5.83	3.38	1.78	1.69	2.08	2.13	1.81	1.60	1.49	2.85
Germany	2.10	2.70	1.72	1.45	1.04	1.67	1.56	1.58	2.29	2.63
Gibraltar	6.00	5.90	4.70	3.30	1.70	1.45	0.82	1.17	1.87	1.64
Greece	19.30	20.40	8.94	3.17	3.54	2.89	3.56	3.20	2.90	4.15
Iceland	31.69	15.51	1.65	5.16	2.06	2.80	4.16	6.69	5.06	12.69
Ireland	5.44	3.27	2.52	5.56	3.48	2.19	2.43	3.94	4.88	4.05
Italy	9.21	6.50	5.24	2.54	2.67	2.21	1.99	2.09	1.83	3.35
Liechtenstein	3.40	5.40		0.70	0.89	0.77	0.56	0.58	0.31	0.52
Luxembourg	4.09	3.70	1.92	3.15	2.05	2.23	2.49	2.68	2.30	3.40
Malta	-0.24	2.98	4.43	2.37	1.30	2.79	3.01	2.78	1.25	4.26
Monaco				1.07	0.93	0.90	0.87	0.75	0.94	1.08
Netherlands	2.22	2.45	1.92	2.32	2.11	1.24	1.67	1.17	1.61	2.47
Norway	5.67	4.11	2.46	3.09	2.48	0.47	1.52	2.33	0.73	3.77
Portugal	19.65	13.37	4.12	2.85	3.28	2.36	2.29	2.74	2.81	2.59
Spain	8.82	6.72	4.67	3.43	3.04	3.04	3.37	3.52	2.79	4.07
Sweden	7.36	10.38	2.46	0.90	1.93	0.37	0.45	1.36	2.21	3.44
Switzerland	3.43	5.38	1.80	1.54	0.64	0.80	1.17	1.06	0.73	2.42
Turkey	44.96	60.31	88.11	54.92	25.30	10.58	10.14	10.51	8.76	10.44
United Kingdom	5.20	7.00	2.60	0.79	1.36	1.34	2.04	2.30	2.35	3.63
Eastern Europe										
Albania		-0.20	7.79	0.05	0.48	2.28	2.37	2.37	2.93	3.36
Belarus			709.35	168.62	28.40	18.11	10.34	7.03	8.42	14.84
Bosnia-Herzegovina			12.90	5.03	0.55	0.28	3.58	6.10	1.50	7.40
Bulgaria	2.80	23.80	62.05	10.32	2.16	6.35	5.04	7.26	8.40	12.35
Croatia			4.04	4.63	1.77	2.03	3.34	3.21	2.87	6.07
Czech Republic	2.30	9.50	9.47	3.93	0.11	2.83	1.85	2.54	2.91	6.36
Estonia			28.78	4.03	1.34	3.05	4.09	4.43	6.59	10.37
Georgia			162.72	4.06	4.78	5.70	8.23	9.22	9.25	9.97
Hungary	7.01	28.97	28.30	9.80	4.64	6.78	3.55	3.88	7.93	6.07
Latvia			24.98	2.65	2.92	6.19	6.76	6.56	10.08	15.40
Lithuania			39.66	0.99	-1.13	1.14	2.66	3.75	5.75	10.93
Macedonia			16.37	6.61	1.10	0.93	0.16	3.27	3.61	7.22
Moldova			9.91	31.29	11.75	12.53	11.96	12.78	12.37	12.77
Poland	11.52	555.38	28.07	10.06	0.79	3.58	2.11	1.11	2.39	4.35
Romania	-0.20	127.90	32.24	45.67	15.27	11.88	8.99	6.58	4.84	7.85
Russia			197.47	20.78	13.68	10.86	12.68	9.68	9.01	14.11
Slovakia			9.92	12.04	8.55	7.55	2.71	4.48	2.76	4.60
Slovenia			13.41	8.88	5.58	3.59	2.48	2.46	3.61	5.65
Ukraine			376.75	28.20	5.20	9.05	13.51	9.09	12.84	25.20

Source:Euromonitor International from International Monetary Fund (IMF), International Financial Statistics and World Economic Outlook/UN/national statistics

Economic Statistics

Table 8.16

Rates of Inflation by Month 2008

% growth

	January	February	March	April	May	June	July	August	September	October	November	December
Western Europe												
Austria	3.20	3.19	3.46	3.25	3.63	3.81	3.72	3.63	3.71	3.02	2.26	1.31
Belgium	3.46	3.64	4.39	4.15	5.21	5.80	5.91	5.39	5.46	4.72	3.13	2.62
Cyprus	4.33	4.92	4.70	4.62	4.94	5.46	5.62	5.39	5.32	5.22	3.42	2.09
Denmark	2.94	3.08	3.07	3.24	3.40	3.84	3.95	4.31	4.20	3.66	2.68	2.42
Finland	3.85	3.72	3.86	3.51	4.17	4.40	4.35	4.66	4.71	4.37	3.61	3.47
France	2.85	2.88	3.21	3.07	3.35	3.62	3.68	3.19	3.01	2.70	1.65	1.02
Germany	2.83	2.81	3.10	2.41	2.99	3.28	3.26	3.07	2.88	2.39	1.42	1.13
Gibraltar												
Greece	3.87	4.39	4.45	4.42	4.86	4.90	4.87	4.67	4.59	3.89	2.85	2.02
Iceland	5.83	6.83	8.82	11.84	12.44	12.80	13.62	14.59	14.10	15.99	17.23	18.22
Ireland	4.30	4.76	5.02	4.30	4.67	4.95	4.35	4.33	4.32	4.02	2.48	1.14
Italy	2.99	2.90	3.28	3.35	3.57	3.78	4.08	4.07	3.77	3.46	2.69	2.24
Liechtenstein												
Luxembourg	3.33	3.06	3.49	3.48	3.98	4.29	4.86	3.99	3.99	3.24	2.00	1.08
Malta	3.54	3.71	3.90	3.56	3.76	4.04	4.81	4.42	4.13	5.43	4.85	4.94
Monaco												
Netherlands	2.02	2.25	2.14	2.04	2.36	2.58	3.17	3.18	3.07	2.75	2.23	1.88
Norway	3.67	3.74	3.21	3.13	3.13	3.38	4.33	4.50	5.31	5.44	3.22	2.13
Portugal	2.82	2.92	3.09	2.45	2.75	3.37	3.07	2.98	3.07	2.44	1.32	0.81
Spain	4.22	4.37	4.45	4.18	4.55	4.93	5.26	4.96	4.56	3.56	2.37	1.42
Sweden	3.19	3.10	3.41	3.34	3.85	4.18	4.13	4.34	4.37	3.97	2.46	0.90
Switzerland	2.41	2.35	2.62	2.28	2.86	2.91	3.07	2.92	2.92	2.58	1.45	0.70
Turkey	8.18	9.12	9.16	9.67	10.75	10.62	12.08	11.78	11.14	11.99	10.76	10.07
United Kingdom	3.69	3.71	3.42	3.80	3.92	4.16	4.58	4.33	4.54	3.82	2.72	0.86
Eastern Europe												
Albania	3.05	3.53	4.60	4.41	4.23	4.03	3.77	2.48	2.66	2.83	2.57	2.15
Belarus	12.92	12.73	13.25	14.77	15.80	16.00	16.33	16.22	16.33	15.70	14.71	13.30
Bosnia-Herzegovina												
Bulgaria	12.40	13.12	14.10	14.52	14.94	15.19	14.35	11.09	10.87	10.84	9.07	7.70
Croatia	6.14	5.74	5.71	5.67	6.39	7.55	8.35	7.46	6.34	5.94	4.69	2.81
Czech Republic	7.55	7.52	7.07	6.70	6.80	6.66	6.88	6.44	6.58	5.99	4.43	3.64
Estonia	10.97	11.23	10.91	11.38	11.29	11.41	10.99	11.01	10.47	9.79	7.99	6.95
Georgia	10.64	10.85	12.18	12.15	11.13	11.23	9.71	12.68	10.50	6.93	6.19	5.47
Hungary	7.17	6.86	6.66	6.66	6.97	6.67	6.67	6.56	5.76	5.06	4.28	3.49
Latvia	15.68	16.68	16.71	17.43	17.85	17.61	16.54	15.64	14.77	13.72	11.69	10.50
Lithuania	9.89	10.70	11.20	11.66	11.98	12.51	12.14	11.91	11.04	10.52	9.10	8.53
Macedonia	7.40	8.26	8.80	8.80	8.26	8.69	8.03	7.18	6.01	6.21	4.96	4.03
Moldova	13.89	14.90	15.47	16.15	16.84	15.56	13.27	11.62	10.53	9.67	8.28	7.11
Poland	4.21	4.34	4.25	4.15	4.49	4.70	5.00	5.02	4.48	4.32	3.79	3.43
Romania	7.25	7.96	8.61	8.62	8.44	8.59	9.03	8.00	7.28	7.38	6.73	6.29
Russia	12.56	12.69	13.34	14.34	15.14	15.17	14.74	15.02	15.07	14.21	13.75	13.28
Slovakia	3.82	4.03	4.24	4.23	4.59	4.65	4.87	5.01	5.35	5.17	4.87	4.36
Slovenia	6.36	6.51	6.82	6.48	6.37	6.92	6.85	5.95	5.52	4.82	3.13	2.05
Ukraine	19.35	21.79	26.16	30.11	31.02	29.24	26.79	25.88	24.52	23.10	22.25	22.25

Source:Euromonitor International from International Monetary Fund (IMF), International Financial Statistics and World Economic Outlook/UN/national statistics

Economic Statistics   **Table 8.17**

Public Consumption 1985-2008
Billion units of national currency

	1985	1990	1995	2000	2003	2004	2005	2006	2007	2008	Total US$ billion 2008
Western Europe											
Austria	19.8	25.5	35.3	39.7	42.1	43.4	45.1	47.3	49.4	51.5	75.8
Belgium	28.6	33.6	44.8	53.7	63.2	66.0	69.1	71.3	74.3	79.8	117.5
Cyprus	0.3	0.7	1.0	1.6	2.3	2.3	2.4	2.7	2.8	3.2	4.7
Denmark	164.2	211.2	257.2	325.1	371.2	389.0	402.5	422.5	438.8	459.2	90.1
Finland	11.8	19.5	21.9	26.9	31.7	33.4	35.1	36.6	38.4	41.2	60.6
France	168.6	224.2	282.3	330.1	378.4	393.8	408.6	422.2	436.9	452.0	665.2
Germany	220.6	272.3	361.8	391.9	416.9	415.9	420.0	425.4	435.6	452.1	665.3
Gibraltar											
Greece	3.1	6.6	13.8	24.3	29.4	31.7	33.0	34.2	38.1	40.9	60.2
Iceland	21.1	73.1	99.0	160.2	219.3	233.1	252.7	285.4	314.4	360.0	4.1
Ireland	4.8	6.0	8.7	14.5	21.1	23.0	24.9	27.3	30.2	32.0	47.0
Italy	80.3	141.2	170.2	219.7	262.9	276.2	290.8	299.3	304.4	315.3	464.1
Liechtenstein	0.1	0.2	0.3	0.5	0.5	0.5	0.5	0.6	0.6	0.6	0.5
Luxembourg	1.1	1.7	2.4	3.3	4.2	4.7	5.0	5.2	5.6	5.9	8.6
Malta	0.2	0.3	0.6	0.7	0.9	0.9	0.9	1.0	1.0	1.2	1.7
Monaco	0.3	0.4	0.6	0.7	0.8	0.8	0.8	0.9	1.0	1.1	1.6
Netherlands	47.7	56.1	72.7	91.9	116.8	118.9	121.7	135.5	142.5	149.0	219.3
Norway	102.1	155.9	203.7	286.1	358.7	373.3	387.2	413.0	447.1	490.2	86.9
Portugal	3.1	8.4	15.3	23.6	28.1	29.7	32.0	32.1	33.1	34.4	50.6
Spain	28.0	53.2	80.9	108.4	135.9	149.8	163.7	177.5	192.0	209.3	308.0
Sweden	251.2	389.6	481.7	585.1	691.7	702.5	722.7	762.5	792.8	834.6	126.6
Switzerland	25.2	37.0	44.2	46.8	52.3	53.0	54.2	55.2	56.5	57.9	53.5
Turkey	0.0	0.0	0.8	19.5	55.5	66.8	76.5	93.5	107.8	121.8	93.6
United Kingdom	75.7	112.5	143.0	182.0	232.8	251.1	268.1	285.2	294.7	315.6	580.2
Eastern Europe											
Albania	1.6	1.7	30.7	49.5	75.6	82.5	88.5	91.9	97.0	109.9	1.3
Belarus		0.0	24.9	1,779.1	7,817.3	10,299.9	13,524.4	15,225.1	17,830.9	21,529.8	10.1
Bosnia-Herzegovina		0.0	0.7	2.3	2.9	3.5	3.7	4.1	4.5	4.8	3.6
Bulgaria	0.0	0.0	0.1	4.8	6.6	7.2	7.7	8.2	9.1	10.9	8.1
Croatia		0.1	28.3	38.4	42.0	45.7	48.6	53.1	58.3	63.5	12.9
Czech Republic		143.5	306.3	460.9	603.2	621.6	658.5	684.7	718.5	751.8	44.0
Estonia		0.1	11.0	19.0	25.0	26.7	30.1	33.9	41.2	48.8	4.6
Georgia		0.0	0.3	0.5	0.8	1.4	2.0	2.1	3.7	4.9	3.3
Hungary	250.5	514.7	1,369.7	2,833.7	4,388.5	4,636.8	4,958.1	5,423.2	5,385.2	5,680.9	33.0
Latvia		0.0	0.6	1.0	1.4	1.5	1.6	1.9	2.6	3.2	6.8
Lithuania		0.0	5.6	10.4	11.3	12.2	13.5	16.0	17.9	21.3	9.1
Macedonia		0.1	31.5	43.0	52.0	53.1	54.0	57.6	62.0	76.5	1.8
Moldova		0.0	1.7	2.3	5.4	4.8	6.2	8.9	10.7	12.8	1.2
Poland	0.2	10.5	63.0	129.8	152.8	162.7	177.8	193.7	211.0	217.8	90.4
Romania	0.0	0.0	1.0	12.9	38.8	39.8	51.5	57.2	66.6	72.8	28.9
Russia		0.1	272.5	1,102.5	2,330.6	2,847.5	3,590.7	4,589.2	5,702.7	6,975.6	280.7
Slovakia		3.0	3.2	4.4	6.1	6.6	7.1	8.6	9.5	11.1	16.4
Slovenia		1.1	3.0	4.0	4.9	5.1	5.5	5.8	6.1	6.7	9.8
Ukraine		0.0	11.6	31.7	50.8	60.6	80.5	100.4	129.0	168.3	31.9

Source:*International Monetary Fund (IMF), International Financial Statistics*

Table 8.18

Public Consumption by Quarter 2007-2009

Million units of national currency

	2007 1st Quarter	2007 2nd Quarter	2007 3rd Quarter	2007 4th Quarter	2008 1st Quarter	2008 2nd Quarter	2008 3rd Quarter	2008 4th Quarter	2009 1st Quarter
Western Europe									
Austria	12,204.3	12,281.4	12,318.0	12,557.4	12,712.1	13,000.7	12,821.9	12,992.1	13,434.3
Belgium	18,736.0	18,767.0	17,760.0	19,047.0	19,858.6	20,164.1	19,017.0	20,769.3	21,050.8
Cyprus	623.9	608.7	653.1	888.2					
Denmark	106,669.0	108,800.0	109,068.0	114,278.0	109,418.0	113,511.8	115,543.8	120,737.4	117,032.4
Finland	9,119.0	9,634.0	9,211.0	10,474.0	9,645.0	10,463.0	9,821.0	11,223.0	10,069.0
France	107,878.7	108,787.6	109,756.4	110,504.3	111,437.6	112,421.1	113,677.0	114,484.2	114,811.7
Germany	108,530.0	108,460.0	108,980.0	109,670.0	111,874.0	113,355.3	113,365.3	113,455.4	115,877.4
Gibraltar									
Greece	9,431.4	9,413.4	9,550.3	9,671.2	10,086.0	10,129.0	10,422.5	10,250.4	10,890.0
Iceland	76,812.9	78,708.5	78,831.5	80,080.0	84,065.0	88,187.0	91,387.0	96,386.0	
Ireland	6,337.9	6,575.8	6,920.4	6,931.0	7,724.1	8,011.1	8,336.5	8,228.0	8,129.1
Italy	74,677.8	75,634.4	75,661.6	78,393.1	76,203.6	81,404.0	78,397.3	79,328.1	81,111.6
Liechtenstein									
Luxembourg	1,318.0	1,326.5	1,302.8	1,625.2	1,364.2	1,398.9	1,371.3	1,722.3	1,441.3
Malta	104.5	108.5	111.0	123.9					
Monaco									
Netherlands	35,093.1	35,414.5	35,811.3	36,162.0	36,486.2	36,853.2	37,477.2	38,194.3	38,584.7
Norway	111,575.0	108,926.0	110,867.0	115,723.0	116,906.0	123,516.0	122,134.0	127,663.0	133,408.0
Portugal	7,258.6	8,351.1	7,833.1	9,607.6	7,592.7	8,714.8	8,320.2	9,770.4	8,510.6
Spain	46,804.0	47,544.0	48,389.0	49,288.0	50,329.2	51,853.2	53,219.3	53,868.3	53,500.3
Sweden	185,955.0	200,824.0	190,225.0	215,759.0	195,795.5	210,687.3	203,501.5	224,587.8	205,327.9
Switzerland	13,739.9	13,883.7	13,762.3	13,720.0	13,892.3	14,100.4	14,356.4	14,458.5	14,596.6
Turkey	22,301.9	27,274.2	26,199.0	32,040.9	25,290.4	29,062.7	30,516.0	36,943.9	29,495.0
United Kingdom	72,808.0	73,228.0	74,433.0	74,244.0	78,182.8	78,342.1	78,708.1	80,380.9	80,704.6
Eastern Europe									
Albania									
Belarus	4,031,400.0	4,821,500.0	4,078,400.0	4,899,600.0	4,777,700.0	5,627,800.0	4,973,600.0	6,150,700.0	
Bosnia-Herzegovina									
Bulgaria	1,734.0	2,039.1	2,069.3	3,285.7	2,037.1	2,491.2	2,451.0	3,879.1	2,307.6
Croatia	13,556.3	14,392.3	14,841.1	15,460.7	14,683.7	15,754.0	16,075.4	17,005.9	16,200.5
Czech Republic	162,176.5	173,407.5	171,379.6	211,552.5	165,188.5	182,656.4	182,411.1	221,534.0	180,363.0
Estonia	9,071.0	10,723.0	9,058.0	12,302.3	11,055.2	12,952.6	10,308.2	14,728.9	11,137.0
Georgia	649.5	808.8	980.6	1,279.0	1,066.9	1,304.5	1,209.0	1,355.9	
Hungary	559,013.5	586,805.5	620,216.5	704,224.4	594,615.3	621,359.3	617,970.3	690,075.2	597,145.3
Latvia	553.6	614.6	626.7	780.0	705.3	803.1	806.0	932.0	728.6
Lithuania	3,513.5	4,653.1	4,096.6	5,621.4	4,189.5	5,609.6	4,941.4	6,598.4	4,521.4
Macedonia									
Moldova	2,586.4	2,966.3	2,502.5	3,222.4	2,785.8	3,360.7	2,752.7	3,875.4	3,131.9
Poland	51,905.9	54,204.9	51,894.9	53,021.4	52,232.1	53,323.1	52,689.4	59,576.5	57,152.2
Romania	10,310.7	13,644.7	17,279.4	25,392.5	12,579.2	16,755.2	17,968.7	25,520.9	
Russia	1,363,780.0	1,408,630.0	1,433,000.0	1,497,240.0	1,734,916.5	1,823,011.1	1,861,420.2	1,925,172.2	2,089,537.4
Slovakia	2,052.1	2,142.9	2,237.4	3,069.2	2,320.5	2,663.5	2,636.7	3,524.7	
Slovenia									
Ukraine	8,958.0	11,209.0	12,153.0	16,728.0	11,277.0	14,714.0	16,653.0	20,790.0	38,145.0

Source:*International Monetary Fund (IMF), International Financial Statistics*

Economic Statistics

Table 8.19

Private Consumption 1985-2008

Billion units of national currency

	1985	1990	1995	2000	2003	2004	2005	2006	2007	2008	Total US$ billion 2008
Western Europe											
Austria	60.1	77.5	96.9	113.8	122.5	127.7	133.8	139.1	143.9	148.8	219.1
Belgium	73.3	92.9	112.5	135.7	146.8	152.6	159.0	166.8	175.0	184.2	271.0
Cyprus	1.7	2.7	4.6	6.4	7.5	8.2	8.7	9.3	10.3	11.6	17.1
Denmark	346.0	423.2	521.8	616.7	666.9	707.2	745.1	792.8	826.7	851.2	167.0
Finland	30.3	45.5	49.8	64.4	74.9	78.1	81.2	85.9	90.7	95.6	140.7
France	436.2	589.8	676.3	803.3	900.0	940.0	981.5	1,026.1	1,073.3	1,114.1	1,639.7
Germany	639.1	817.5	1,067.2	1,214.2	1,284.6	1,303.1	1,325.4	1,356.3	1,375.4	1,409.7	2,074.7
Gibraltar	0.1	0.1	0.1	0.1	0.1	0.1	0.1	0.1	0.1	0.1	0.2
Greece	12.5	32.9	68.6	98.6	121.9	130.5	140.9	152.8	162.5	173.0	254.6
Iceland	77.2	218.1	258.2	414.5	481.5	530.3	610.4	685.4	746.6	793.9	9.0
Ireland	15.5	21.8	28.9	50.4	64.4	67.8	73.8	80.7	88.1	90.1	132.6
Italy	251.7	402.1	553.3	713.7	789.0	815.8	844.0	877.4	907.6	928.8	1,366.9
Liechtenstein	0.8	1.1	1.7	2.5	2.5	2.6	2.7	2.9	3.0	3.1	2.9
Luxembourg	3.5	4.8	6.5	9.0	9.7	10.2	10.7	11.3	11.7	12.5	18.4
Malta	0.9	1.2	1.8	2.6	2.8	3.0	3.1	3.2	3.3	3.5	5.1
Monaco	0.9	1.2	1.3	1.6	1.8	1.9	2.0	2.1	2.5	2.7	4.0
Netherlands	102.9	121.1	151.1	210.8	238.1	242.8	250.3	254.9	263.5	272.5	401.0
Norway	266.5	366.5	470.9	640.0	738.9	786.0	826.2	881.8	941.6	991.4	175.8
Portugal	15.1	34.7	55.5	78.1	87.8	92.3	96.7	101.6	106.1	110.7	162.9
Spain	111.7	192.8	268.4	376.0	451.2	487.1	525.1	564.3	602.4	626.0	921.3
Sweden	451.5	710.5	897.3	1,112.3	1,235.5	1,278.1	1,328.4	1,372.8	1,430.1	1,466.9	222.6
Switzerland	148.3	188.4	223.0	252.7	265.9	272.3	278.2	286.4	297.1	308.7	285.0
Turkey	0.0	0.3	5.5	117.5	324.0	398.6	465.4	534.8	597.7	662.2	508.7
United Kingdom	215.4	354.8	465.3	640.1	742.3	779.1	815.0	849.5	893.0	927.4	1,704.9
Eastern Europe											
Albania	9.9	12.2	203.1	400.4	521.9	585.7	635.7	697.9	785.0	853.4	10.2
Belarus		0.0	71.7	5,198.1	20,889.6	26,858.8	33,827.0	40,803.1	50,247.6	67,063.6	31.4
Bosnia-Herzegovina		0.0	3.1	10.0	12.7	15.1	16.7	18.2	20.0	21.4	16.0
Bulgaria	0.0	0.0	0.6	18.5	24.4	26.9	30.0	34.8	39.1	45.5	34.0
Croatia		0.2	78.1	111.0	142.9	151.7	163.4	172.7	189.0	202.2	41.0
Czech Republic		308.6	746.0	1,149.2	1,332.5	1,416.9	1,464.5	1,561.8	1,686.8	1,840.6	107.8
Estonia		0.5	23.1	52.4	74.6	83.4	95.0	113.0	132.3	137.5	12.9
Georgia		0.0	3.1	5.5	6.2	7.2	7.8	10.9	12.0	14.0	9.4
Hungary	591.2	1,128.8	3,109.1	7,054.6	10,515.3	11,294.5	12,124.8	12,748.1	13,615.1	14,302.6	83.1
Latvia		0.0	1.6	3.0	4.0	4.7	5.7	7.3	9.2	9.5	19.7
Lithuania		0.1	17.1	29.6	36.5	40.7	46.5	53.4	63.5	72.9	30.9
Macedonia		0.3	119.4	176.0	191.9	209.1	222.7	243.1	273.3	316.1	7.6
Moldova		0.0	3.7	14.2	25.0	28.5	35.2	42.0	50.0	58.8	5.7
Poland	0.6	27.2	203.8	477.4	555.0	598.1	623.4	662.3	711.8	779.4	323.5
Romania	0.0	0.1	4.9	56.3	130.5	170.4	200.9	237.5	277.8	330.4	131.2
Russia		0.3	744.1	3,374.3	6,694.1	8,554.0	10,728.2	13,040.5	16,083.2	20,261.7	815.3
Slovakia		7.0	7.7	12.4	16.7	19.4	22.0	25.3	30.6	36.6	53.9
Slovenia		2.8	9.5	12.3	14.4	14.9	15.6	16.4	18.0	19.6	28.8
Ukraine		0.0	30.1	96.3	150.8	184.9	257.4	324.6	429.6	584.2	110.9

Source: *International Monetary Fund (IMF), International Financial Statistics*

Economic Statistics

Table 8.20

Private Consumption by Quarter 2007-2009

Million units of national currency

	2007 1st Quarter	2007 2nd Quarter	2007 3rd Quarter	2007 4th Quarter	2008 1st Quarter	2008 2nd Quarter	2008 3rd Quarter	2008 4th Quarter	2009 1st Quarter
Western Europe									
Austria	34,536.0	35,312.2	35,733.1	38,314.9	35,969.6	36,639.6	37,324.4	38,915.7	35,945.1
Belgium	42,339.2	44,358.2	43,386.2	44,945.2	45,066.8	46,938.7	45,910.8	46,246.7	44,619.8
Cyprus	2,513.8	2,517.3	2,556.8	2,754.8					
Denmark	197,440.5	205,527.8	204,098.4	219,653.3	207,322.4	217,453.0	211,386.4	215,022.2	196,732.4
Finland	21,372.0	22,828.0	22,771.0	23,714.0	22,750.7	24,333.7	24,104.0	24,385.6	22,222.3
France	262,561.4	266,191.2	270,272.9	274,250.6	276,131.4	278,747.0	280,132.3	279,126.1	278,652.0
Germany	338,770.1	343,082.1	345,593.3	347,944.4	351,005.3	351,598.3	354,965.4	352,141.0	350,743.9
Gibraltar									
Greece	41,025.3	41,620.8	40,687.8	39,129.5	43,804.5	44,696.0	43,455.8	41,025.6	44,451.5
Iceland	168,729.8	189,801.9	187,955.7	200,094.5	198,450.0	209,679.0	200,198.0	185,523.0	
Ireland	21,413.9	21,425.3	21,459.9	23,806.2	22,943.1	21,937.5	21,765.2	23,446.5	20,547.2
Italy	224,413.4	225,963.3	227,902.2	229,316.1	230,957.2	232,549.0	234,654.7	230,597.2	225,837.9
Liechtenstein									
Luxembourg	2,827.4	2,876.8	2,906.3	3,117.5	2,975.9	3,134.2	3,147.9	3,268.5	2,978.0
Malta	763.7	812.6	855.7	901.5					
Monaco									
Netherlands	65,041.9	65,318.3	65,991.4	67,146.5	67,508.5	67,911.0	68,370.8	68,666.7	66,384.7
Norway	218,814.0	232,400.0	239,539.0	250,839.0	232,479.0	247,552.0	252,366.0	259,023.0	235,899.0
Portugal	25,859.6	26,539.5	25,978.0	27,682.6	27,280.3	27,640.0	27,410.5	28,355.6	26,511.8
Spain	146,987.0	149,432.0	151,253.0	154,744.0	156,193.0	157,057.0	157,800.0	154,936.0	151,002.0
Sweden	339,800.0	360,378.0	353,468.0	376,490.0	353,280.0	375,669.0	362,303.0	375,669.0	352,890.0
Switzerland	73,129.4	73,720.4	74,623.0	75,596.4	76,465.6	77,318.1	77,567.9	77,342.4	77,033.1
Turkey	138,359.0	145,053.0	158,428.9	155,880.9	158,488.9	167,145.9	171,477.9	165,042.9	156,271.9
United Kingdom	219,834.0	222,871.0	223,915.0	226,370.0	230,646.0	232,011.0	234,060.0	230,681.0	226,678.0
Eastern Europe									
Albania									
Belarus	11,339,600.0	11,811,700.0	14,218,000.0	12,878,300.0	14,102,300.0	15,482,000.0	20,210,500.0	17,268,800.0	
Bosnia-Herzegovina									
Bulgaria	8,681.7	9,067.9	10,188.8	11,142.4	10,406.7	10,800.5	11,859.6	12,417.7	10,325.2
Croatia	36,784.5	39,785.7	35,972.1	42,538.7	40,529.7	43,341.5	38,917.5	43,160.9	38,143.2
Czech Republic	387,526.0	418,265.0	431,481.0	449,565.0	429,149.7	460,975.5	473,063.3	477,445.4	447,150.4
Estonia	31,158.4	32,863.7	32,665.7	35,646.9	33,688.9	35,319.1	34,466.7	34,023.7	29,094.2
Georgia	2,897.8	2,852.6	2,797.9	3,465.8	3,260.4	3,380.4	3,429.7	3,906.4	
Hungary	3,246,839.4	3,333,035.6	3,433,382.2	3,601,853.8	3,455,364.4	3,570,837.0	3,642,032.5	3,634,414.1	3,377,238.5
Latvia	2,000.2	2,275.0	2,418.5	2,519.5	2,332.6	2,468.1	2,432.7	2,248.0	2,119.6
Lithuania	13,856.9	15,481.2	16,335.7	17,795.7	17,041.6	18,620.4	18,872.8	18,398.7	15,570.8
Macedonia									
Moldova	10,198.3	10,676.7	15,582.1	12,369.1	13,687.0	15,782.4	18,261.1	14,249.2	12,965.8
Poland	178,265.8	177,459.9	178,883.7	177,166.9	196,710.7	195,028.7	196,030.7	191,675.8	208,622.7
Romania	55,228.9	62,785.2	71,765.6	88,064.7	68,393.6	78,075.4	86,539.0	97,421.0	
Russia	3,421,350.6	3,807,271.8	4,170,233.0	4,684,344.6	4,307,545.7	4,882,245.2	5,351,924.7	5,719,984.4	4,828,655.2
Slovakia	7,290.0	7,431.8	7,801.6	8,123.2	8,880.8	8,894.3	9,352.5	9,520.5	
Slovenia									
Ukraine	87,106.8	100,147.3	108,346.8	133,079.1	126,972.7	142,962.7	151,405.2	165,974.4	114,103.9

Source:*International Monetary Fund (IMF), International Financial Statistics*

Economic Statistics

Table 8.21

Government Finance and International Liquidity 2008

US$ million / as stated

	Budget Expenditure	Budget Revenue	Budget Surplus/ Deficit	Foreign Debt	Foreign Exchange Reserves	Gold Reserves (million troy oz)
Western Europe						
Austria	180,382.0	121,652.1	-58,729.8	210,512.0	8,244.4	9.0
Belgium	104,050.3	63,652.5	-40,397.8	271,439.0	7,767.1	7.3
Cyprus	9,812.6	7,560.9	-2,251.7		585.5	0.4
Denmark				45,126.0	39,823.0	2.1
Finland	66,155.2	67,166.2	1,011.1	76,871.9	6,397.6	1.6
France	1,640,248.5	1,442,435.1	-197,813.4	1,090,993.0	30,382.2	80.1
Germany	550,532.6	494,493.3	-56,039.3	1,177,374.0	38,557.0	109.7
Gibraltar						
Greece	100,395.9	74,197.2	-26,198.7	267,186.0	158.7	3.6
Iceland	6,941.0	5,057.0	-1,884.0	6,051.9	3,486.2	0.1
Ireland	70,871.1	54,614.1	-16,257.0	80,348.0	609.2	0.2
Italy	1,128,065.5	1,057,886.7	-70,178.8	1,064,426.0	35,306.0	78.8
Liechtenstein						
Luxembourg	15,193.5	16,222.2	1,028.6	767.0	258.4	0.1
Malta	3,393.7	3,247.5	-146.2		288.3	0.0
Monaco						
Netherlands	254,941.7	253,735.9	-1,205.8	353,873.0	9,368.9	19.7
Norway	201,647.2	205,980.5	4,333.3	126,156.0	50,214.1	
Portugal	83,496.6	83,709.8	213.1	122,876.0	1,022.0	12.3
Spain	221,929.3	247,938.2	26,008.9	316,196.0	11,540.0	9.1
Sweden	117,589.5	134,860.0	17,270.5	55,680.0	25,127.0	4.4
Switzerland	50,326.4	46,252.9	-4,073.5	22,536.0	44,151.0	33.4
Turkey	141,655.7	82,859.9	-58,795.8	72,234.0	70,231.0	3.7
United Kingdom				350,990.0	41,550.3	10.0
Eastern Europe						
Albania	2,808.5	3,215.1	406.6		2,307.4	0.1
Belarus	12,837.5	14,199.8	1,362.3	3,597.0	2,686.0	0.4
Bosnia-Herzegovina					3,515.3	
Bulgaria	14,989.6	16,650.5	1,660.9	3,785.0	16,757.4	1.3
Croatia	23,361.9	23,459.4	97.5	5,796.0	12,956.8	
Czech Republic	57,497.2	57,631.8	134.6	15,251.0	36,459.2	0.4
Estonia				691.0	3,964.8	0.0
Georgia	3,628.7	3,926.8	298.2	2,261.0	1,467.8	
Hungary	50,980.9	43,439.8	-7,541.1	53,400.0	33,620.0	0.1
Latvia	10,620.3	9,727.0	-893.3	2,763.0	5,027.2	0.2
Lithuania	14,122.3	14,272.7	150.3	3,989.5	6,279.6	0.2
Macedonia					1,919.0	0.2
Moldova	1,280.0	1,484.4	204.5		1,672.3	
Poland	170,725.6	161,235.9	-9,489.7	67,708.0	58,931.0	3.3
Romania	41,152.7	43,932.6	2,779.9	14,270.0	36,746.9	3.3
Russia	260,432.4	372,270.4	111,838.1	29,477.0	411,494.0	16.7
Slovakia	29,205.4	28,879.8	-325.6	10,093.0	17,804.9	1.1
Slovenia	20,227.4	20,209.3	-18.1	5,182.0	809.9	0.1
Ukraine	34,595.2	33,420.9	-1,174.3	14,590.0	30,791.9	0.9

Source: *Euromonitor International from industry sources/national statistics*

Economic Statistics   **Table 8.22**

Foreign Exchange Reserves by Quarter 2007-2009

US$ million

	2007 1st Quarter	2007 2nd Quarter	2007 3rd Quarter	2007 4th Quarter	2008 1st Quarter	2008 2nd Quarter	2008 3rd Quarter	2008 4th Quarter	2009 1st Quarter	2009 2nd Quarter
Western Europe										
Austria	7,110.5	7,344.0	9,175.2	10,260.5	10,515.0	10,595.0	9,411.4	8,244.4	5,820.9	5,321.0
Belgium	7,627.2	7,664.1	8,644.9	9,297.8	9,585.2	8,613.5	7,602.0	7,767.1	7,859.7	8,021.0
Cyprus	4,465.5	5,160.2	5,439.5	6,100.1	926.2	830.2	943.0	585.5	520.4	557.0
Denmark	30,761.0	30,669.0	33,857.0	32,029.0	36,537.0	32,754.0	28,951.0	39,823.0	45,179.0	
Finland	6,006.4	5,822.0	6,598.9	6,689.2	7,075.9	6,732.8	6,547.9	6,397.6	6,206.9	6,835.0
France	41,730.6	40,897.2	47,271.4	43,587.4	47,488.2	43,494.5	39,288.9	30,382.2	21,741.3	24,548.0
Germany	38,189.4	39,664.2	40,968.8	40,768.3	43,707.5	43,817.6	40,769.3	38,557.0	38,087.5	38,505.0
Gibraltar										
Greece	463.5	355.2	575.7	518.2	270.4	249.1	190.2	158.7	105.1	126.0
Iceland	2,283.5	2,243.9	2,433.0	2,549.1	2,786.1	2,484.2	3,633.4	3,486.2	3,058.7	2,933.5
Ireland	568.7	529.1	595.8	590.8	570.8	571.3	564.0	609.2	540.8	602.0
Italy	25,940.8	28,395.6	28,599.0	27,319.2	28,491.6	31,457.1	33,456.1	35,306.0	33,757.1	35,098.0
Liechtenstein										
Luxembourg	158.2	159.7	193.1	93.8	609.0	453.6	603.1	258.4	275.7	284.0
Malta	2,704.0	2,635.0	2,874.0	3,662.0	548.8	473.3	369.9	288.3	304.7	416.0
Monaco										
Netherlands	8,897.8	8,502.8	8,860.5	8,748.7	10,239.9	9,534.1	10,023.5	9,368.9	8,787.3	9,174.0
Norway	56,342.1	56,084.7	58,951.7	60,294.1	55,033.4	49,806.9	43,643.8	50,214.1	45,743.8	
Portugal	1,878.0	1,626.9	932.4	1,044.4	1,349.6	1,368.8	1,189.2	1,022.0	921.3	770.0
Spain	9,989.8	10,285.4	10,345.0	10,792.0	11,400.5	10,946.5	11,057.6	11,540.0	11,566.0	11,833.0
Sweden	24,717.0	25,436.0	26,652.0	26,382.0	27,116.0	26,040.0	33,415.0	25,127.0	22,969.0	35,416.0
Switzerland	37,175.0	37,389.0	41,588.0	43,867.0	46,494.0	46,089.0	44,212.0	44,151.0	49,093.0	75,375.0
Turkey	67,242.0	68,176.0	71,578.0	73,155.8	76,321.0	75,702.4	76,427.7	70,231.0	67,237.0	65,911.0
United Kingdom	41,848.7	40,874.3	41,620.2	47,497.8	49,205.2	46,751.9	40,673.3	41,550.3	37,068.8	41,158.1
Eastern Europe										
Albania	1,787.2	1,829.3	2,082.9	2,097.0	2,146.7	2,159.2	2,201.9	2,307.4	2,037.9	2,333.3
Belarus	1,252.9	2,057.1	1,969.1	3,952.1	4,200.7	4,171.8	3,735.8	2,686.0	3,513.5	2,224.2
Bosnia-Herzegovina	3,492.6	3,753.0	4,345.5	4,524.5	4,546.0	4,026.7	3,843.4	3,515.3	3,379.3	
Bulgaria	11,060.1	12,037.5	15,600.6	16,424.2	17,894.1	19,618.9	19,906.7	16,757.4	14,489.1	15,545.4
Croatia	12,678.1	12,349.3	12,465.8	13,674.0	15,543.8	15,675.7	14,050.8	12,956.8	11,684.6	12,735.0
Czech Republic	31,334.6	30,910.8	32,449.4	34,445.2	37,461.6	37,570.6	35,825.1	36,459.2	36,304.8	37,744.2
Estonia	2,784.0	2,805.5	3,449.3	3,262.6	3,694.9	4,052.5	3,682.1	3,964.8	3,518.9	3,781.9
Georgia	1,008.1	1,220.1	1,469.8	1,346.3	1,419.8	1,525.8	1,369.8	1,467.8	1,490.7	1,504.5
Hungary	22,374.0	22,569.0	23,090.0	23,773.0	26,310.0	27,051.0	24,730.0	33,620.0	36,810.0	
Latvia	4,478.8	4,767.9	5,242.0	5,553.1	6,299.5	6,302.4	6,021.8	5,027.2	4,178.6	3,709.3
Lithuania	5,521.1	6,017.9	6,514.4	7,565.6	6,981.1	7,245.4	6,337.9	6,279.6	5,532.4	6,072.2
Macedonia	1,753.2	1,796.1	2,020.3	2,080.8	2,204.4	2,226.2	2,227.2	1,919.0	1,477.7	1,490.8
Moldova	785.8	878.5	1,043.3	1,333.5	1,423.1	1,525.8	1,803.7	1,672.3	1,132.3	
Poland	48,330.3	52,049.4	55,616.1	62,720.3	73,593.1	79,167.8	70,980.7	58,931.0	57,798.3	63,633.7
Romania	28,671.4	29,661.0	35,739.5	37,193.6	39,668.0	39,268.9	37,305.4	36,746.9	33,274.6	37,299.1
Russia	330,043.0	397,032.0	414,895.0	466,376.0	498,499.0	554,794.0	542,470.0	411,494.0	366,956.0	394,265.0
Slovakia	15,854.0	16,864.5	17,673.6	18,025.8	18,977.0	18,845.2	17,493.3	17,804.9	171.7	54.0
Slovenia	1,025.2	1,056.1	1,030.7	942.0	1,087.5	948.0	883.5	809.9	651.0	588.0
Ukraine	22,447.7	25,381.9	30,063.5	31,783.2	32,424.8	34,695.0	36,785.3	30,791.9	24,595.8	26,527.0

Source: International Monetary Fund (IMF), International Financial Statistics

Economic Statistics

Table 8.23

Foreign Exchange Reserves by Month 2008

US$ million

	January	February	March	April	May	June	July	August	September	October	November	December
Western Europe												
Austria	10,078.9	10,278.7	10,515.0	10,495.7	10,477.2	10,595.0	10,601.4	10,106.7	9,411.4	8,625.0	7,969.7	8,244.4
Belgium	8,859.6	9,206.4	9,585.2	9,600.6	8,990.0	8,613.5	9,076.2	8,354.8	7,602.0	7,538.1	7,589.1	7,767.1
Cyprus	1,003.7	1,030.7	926.2	813.1	898.7	830.2	856.7	674.9	943.0	599.3	634.3	585.5
Denmark	33,832.0	34,677.0	36,537.0	34,218.0	31,697.0	32,754.0	32,138.0	30,592.0	28,951.0	20,856.0	27,765.0	39,823.0
Finland	6,770.3	6,831.2	7,075.9	6,708.6	6,677.7	6,732.8	6,675.3	6,471.6	6,547.9	6,378.5	6,297.3	6,397.6
France	49,783.3	42,774.0	47,488.2	46,834.5	44,213.3	43,494.5	47,391.9	42,657.8	39,288.9	39,281.4	34,462.2	30,382.2
Germany	42,195.1	42,931.7	43,707.5	44,965.0	42,736.9	43,817.6	42,377.6	41,571.9	40,769.3	40,805.8	39,460.1	38,557.0
Gibraltar												
Greece	203.7	277.6	270.4	242.4	207.8	249.1	271.6	254.9	190.2	84.2	98.0	158.7
Iceland	2,604.7	2,700.0	2,786.1	2,694.0	2,474.9	2,484.2	2,788.0	3,647.9	3,633.4	3,349.0	3,510.6	3,486.2
Ireland	575.7	581.9	570.8	561.9	539.3	571.3	548.2	523.2	564.0	592.1	583.6	609.2
Italy	29,589.8	29,163.1	28,491.6	31,209.0	31,240.9	31,457.1	31,279.8	31,191.0	33,456.1	34,400.5	34,421.4	35,306.0
Liechtenstein												
Luxembourg	175.5	379.1	609.0	624.3	737.0	453.6	447.6	247.4	603.1	257.3	506.2	258.4
Malta	435.6	485.8	548.8	477.2	687.8	473.3	480.0	391.1	369.9	264.7	262.0	288.3
Monaco												
Netherlands	9,029.1	9,192.7	10,239.9	9,650.3	9,697.2	9,534.1	9,497.7	9,395.0	10,023.5	9,169.7	9,019.6	9,368.9
Norway	58,385.9	57,218.7	55,033.4	56,623.5	55,927.7	49,806.9	48,871.2	46,959.6	43,643.8	38,323.1	41,652.9	50,214.1
Portugal	953.2	1,284.6	1,349.6	1,407.7	1,373.3	1,368.8	1,501.0	1,454.0	1,189.2	1,267.3	1,113.3	1,022.0
Spain	10,925.0	11,106.8	11,400.5	11,039.6	10,872.7	10,946.5	11,190.0	11,007.0	11,057.6	10,729.9	11,118.3	11,540.0
Sweden	26,481.0	29,301.0	27,116.0	29,455.0	27,343.0	26,040.0	28,424.0	27,558.0	33,415.0	25,016.0	27,769.0	25,127.0
Switzerland	43,891.0	43,861.0	46,494.0	46,332.0	46,610.0	46,089.0	45,343.0	44,475.0	44,212.0	43,264.0	43,055.0	44,151.0
Turkey	74,262.5	74,896.0	76,321.0	74,233.9	73,643.1	75,702.4	75,487.1	75,590.5	76,427.7	70,681.9	70,482.7	70,231.0
United Kingdom	48,554.4	49,754.0	49,205.2	48,641.0	47,381.8	46,751.9	43,855.5	41,700.4	40,673.3	41,413.7	41,774.1	41,550.3
Eastern Europe												
Albania	2,084.9	2,119.3	2,146.7	2,106.3	2,074.8	2,159.2	2,194.3	2,204.5	2,201.9	2,043.6	2,242.4	2,307.4
Belarus	3,537.1	3,977.3	4,200.7	4,081.3	4,039.2	4,171.8	4,217.7	4,191.0	3,735.8	3,727.7	3,415.9	2,686.0
Bosnia-Herzegovina	4,296.9	4,330.3	4,546.0	4,133.3	4,071.0	4,026.7	4,108.4	3,950.2	3,843.4	3,192.8	3,177.3	3,515.3
Bulgaria	16,130.6	16,386.5	17,894.1	18,933.4	18,684.1	19,618.9	20,070.5	20,054.0	19,906.7	17,114.5	17,136.6	16,757.4
Croatia	13,817.3	14,600.3	15,543.8	15,456.7	15,577.9	15,675.7	15,255.1	14,501.7	14,050.8	12,330.6	12,457.5	12,956.8
Czech Republic	35,557.7	36,502.0	37,461.6	37,841.9	37,343.6	37,570.6	37,422.3	36,509.5	35,825.1	33,531.4	33,980.8	36,459.2
Estonia	3,774.1	3,530.4	3,694.9	3,724.8	4,014.1	4,052.5	4,230.3	4,175.7	3,682.1	4,183.0	3,696.9	3,964.8
Georgia	1,208.5	1,245.6	1,419.8	1,908.2	1,496.6	1,525.8	1,454.6	1,122.6	1,369.8	1,271.3	1,339.6	1,467.8
Hungary	23,872.0	24,200.0	26,310.0	25,888.0	25,837.0	27,051.0	26,594.0	25,188.0	24,730.0	22,419.0	29,189.0	33,620.0
Latvia	5,673.2	5,676.3	6,299.5	6,294.9	6,341.6	6,302.4	6,158.5	5,942.9	6,021.8	5,401.2	4,244.5	5,027.2
Lithuania	7,514.7	6,872.5	6,981.1	7,185.9	6,705.1	7,245.4	6,706.7	6,487.6	6,337.9	6,203.8	5,384.6	6,279.6
Macedonia	2,086.0	2,144.1	2,204.4	2,146.0	2,149.0	2,226.2	2,227.3	2,173.9	2,227.2	2,021.5	1,845.3	1,919.0
Moldova	1,350.7	1,364.7	1,423.1	1,436.7	1,445.6	1,525.8	1,699.1	1,775.4	1,803.7	1,633.4	1,598.4	1,672.3
Poland	65,251.2	69,039.4	73,593.1	75,949.1	75,704.6	79,167.8	81,654.9	78,552.4	70,980.7	61,179.2	60,328.3	58,931.0
Romania	37,973.1	38,403.3	39,668.0	39,284.9	38,801.1	39,268.9	39,288.3	38,076.6	37,305.4	34,661.5	34,901.3	36,746.9
Russia	474,694.0	480,629.0	498,499.0	519,372.0	532,725.0	554,794.0	582,294.0	568,750.0	542,470.0	471,652.0	441,373.0	411,494.0
Slovakia	18,213.2	18,459.6	18,977.0	18,851.5	18,686.3	18,845.2	18,724.2	17,882.5	17,493.3	16,216.5	16,127.6	17,804.9
Slovenia	952.1	910.7	1,087.5	945.7	913.9	948.0	1,059.2	868.8	883.5	805.4	806.4	809.9
Ukraine	31,062.8	31,740.1	32,424.8	32,701.4	33,469.4	34,695.0	37,139.1	37,339.7	36,785.3	31,228.6	32,044.1	30,791.9

Source: *International Monetary Fund (IMF), International Financial Statistics*

Table 8.24

Gold Reserves by Quarter 2007-2009

million troy oz

	2007 1st Quarter	2007 2nd Quarter	2007 3rd Quarter	2007 4th Quarter	2008 1st Quarter	2008 2nd Quarter	2008 3rd Quarter	2008 4th Quarter	2009 1st Quarter	2009 2nd Quarter
Western Europe										
Austria	9.28	9.16	9.00	9.00	9.00	9.00	9.00	9.00	9.00	9.00
Belgium	7.32	7.32	7.32	7.32	7.32	7.32	7.32	7.32	7.32	7.32
Cyprus	0.47	0.47	0.47	0.47	0.45	0.45	0.45	0.45	0.45	0.45
Denmark	2.14	2.14	2.14	2.14	2.14	2.14	2.14	2.14	2.14	2.14
Finland	1.58	1.58	1.58	1.58	1.58	1.58	1.58	1.58	1.58	1.58
France	86.45	85.75	84.96	83.69	82.58	81.96	81.26	80.13	78.86	78.63
Germany	110.04	109.98	109.87	109.87	109.87	109.74	109.72	109.72	109.72	109.58
Gibraltar										
Greece	3.60	3.60	3.61	3.62	3.63	3.63	3.63	3.62	3.61	3.61
Iceland	0.06	0.06	0.06	0.06	0.06	0.06	0.06	0.06	0.06	0.06
Ireland	0.18	0.18	0.18	0.18	0.18	0.18	0.18	0.18	0.18	0.18
Italy	78.83	78.83	78.83	78.83	78.83	78.83	78.83	78.83	78.83	78.83
Liechtenstein										
Luxembourg	0.07	0.07	0.07	0.07	0.07	0.07	0.07	0.07	0.07	0.07
Malta	0.01	0.01	0.01	0.02	0.01	0.01	0.01	0.01	0.02	0.02
Monaco										
Netherlands	20.61	20.61	20.61	19.98	19.98	19.98	19.98	19.69	19.69	19.69
Norway										
Portugal	12.30	12.30	12.30	12.30	12.30	12.30	12.30	12.30	12.30	12.30
Spain	12.12	9.85	9.05	9.05	9.05	9.05	9.05	9.05	9.05	9.05
Sweden	5.02	4.93	4.85	4.78	4.71	4.63	4.52	4.40	4.30	4.21
Switzerland	41.48	41.03	37.85	36.82	35.79	34.63	33.44	33.44	33.44	33.44
Turkey	3.73	3.73	3.73	3.73	3.73	3.73	3.73	3.73	3.73	3.73
United Kingdom	9.98	9.98	9.98	9.98	9.98	9.98	9.98	9.98	9.98	9.98
Eastern Europe										
Albania	0.07	0.07	0.07	0.07	0.07	0.07	0.07	0.05	0.05	0.05
Belarus	0.43	0.44	0.25	0.27	0.58	0.48	0.43	0.43	0.48	
Bosnia-Herzegovina										
Bulgaria	1.28	1.28	1.28	1.28	1.28	1.27	1.28	1.28	1.28	1.28
Croatia										
Czech Republic	0.43	0.43	0.43	0.43	0.43	0.43	0.42	0.42	0.42	0.42
Estonia	0.01	0.01	0.01	0.01	0.01	0.01	0.01	0.01	0.01	0.01
Georgia										
Hungary	0.10	0.10	0.10	0.10	0.10	0.10	0.10	0.10	0.10	
Latvia	0.25	0.25	0.25	0.25	0.25	0.25	0.25	0.25	0.25	0.25
Lithuania	0.19	0.19	0.19	0.19	0.19	0.19	0.19	0.19	0.19	0.19
Macedonia	0.22	0.22	0.22	0.22	0.22	0.22	0.22	0.22	0.22	0.22
Moldova										
Poland	3.31	3.31	3.31	3.31	3.31	3.31	3.31	3.31	3.31	3.31
Romania	3.37	3.37	3.37	3.33	3.33	3.33	3.33	3.33	3.33	3.33
Russia	12.87	13.08	13.78	14.48	14.69	14.89	15.94	16.71	17.10	17.69
Slovakia	1.13	1.13	1.13	1.13	1.13	1.13	1.13	1.13	1.02	1.02
Slovenia	0.10	0.10	0.10	0.10	0.10	0.10	0.10	0.10	0.10	0.10
Ukraine	0.81	0.82	0.82	0.84	0.84	0.84	0.85	0.85	0.86	0.86

Source:International Monetary Fund (IMF), International Financial Statistics

Economic Statistics

Table 8.25

Gold Reserves by Month 2008

million troy oz

	January	February	March	April	May	June	July	August	September	October	November	December
Western Europe												
Austria	9.00	9.00	9.00	9.00	9.00	9.00	9.00	9.00	9.00	9.00	9.00	9.00
Belgium	7.32	7.32	7.32	7.32	7.32	7.32	7.32	7.32	7.32	7.32	7.32	7.32
Cyprus	0.45	0.45	0.45	0.45	0.45	0.45	0.45	0.45	0.45	0.45	0.45	0.45
Denmark	2.14	2.14	2.14	2.14	2.14	2.14	2.14	2.14	2.14	2.14	2.14	2.14
Finland	1.58	1.58	1.58	1.58	1.58	1.58	1.58	1.58	1.58	1.58	1.58	1.58
France	83.17	82.80	82.58	82.38	82.21	81.96	81.69	81.53	81.26	80.66	80.62	80.13
Germany	109.87	109.87	109.87	109.87	109.87	109.74	109.74	109.74	109.72	109.72	109.72	109.72
Gibraltar												
Greece	3.62	3.63	3.63	3.63	3.63	3.63	3.63	3.63	3.63	3.62	3.62	3.62
Iceland	0.06	0.06	0.06	0.06	0.06	0.06	0.06	0.06	0.06	0.06	0.06	0.06
Ireland	0.18	0.18	0.18	0.18	0.18	0.18	0.18	0.18	0.18	0.18	0.18	0.18
Italy	78.83	78.83	78.83	78.83	78.83	78.83	78.83	78.83	78.83	78.83	78.83	78.83
Liechtenstein												
Luxembourg	0.07	0.07	0.07	0.07	0.07	0.07	0.07	0.07	0.07	0.07	0.07	0.07
Malta	0.01	0.01	0.01	0.01	0.01	0.01	0.01	0.01	0.01	0.01	0.01	0.01
Monaco												
Netherlands	19.98	19.98	19.98	19.98	19.98	19.98	19.98	19.98	19.98	19.98	19.72	19.69
Norway												
Portugal	12.30	12.30	12.30	12.30	12.30	12.30	12.30	12.30	12.30	12.30	12.30	12.30
Spain	9.05	9.05	9.05	9.05	9.05	9.05	9.05	9.05	9.05	9.05	9.05	9.05
Sweden	4.75	4.73	4.71	4.68	4.66	4.63	4.60	4.56	4.52	4.49	4.29	4.40
Switzerland	36.46	36.10	35.79	35.39	35.02	34.63	34.21	33.84	33.44	33.44	33.44	33.44
Turkey	3.73	3.73	3.73	3.73	3.73	3.73	3.73	3.73	3.73	3.73	3.73	3.73
United Kingdom	9.98	9.98	9.98	9.98	9.98	9.98	9.98	9.98	9.98	9.98	9.98	9.98
Eastern Europe												
Albania	0.07	0.07	0.07	0.07	0.07	0.07	0.07	0.07	0.07	0.07	0.07	0.05
Belarus	0.27	0.39	0.58	0.48	0.48	0.48	0.44	0.47	0.43	0.44	0.43	0.43
Bosnia-Herzegovina												
Bulgaria	1.28	1.28	1.28	1.28	1.28	1.27	1.28	1.28	1.28	1.28	1.28	1.28
Croatia												
Czech Republic	0.43	0.43	0.43	0.43	0.43	0.43	0.42	0.42	0.42	0.42	0.42	0.42
Estonia	0.01	0.01	0.01	0.01	0.01	0.01	0.01	0.01	0.01	0.01	0.01	0.01
Georgia												
Hungary	0.10	0.10	0.10	0.10	0.10	0.10	0.10	0.10	0.10	0.10	0.10	0.10
Latvia	0.25	0.25	0.25	0.25	0.25	0.25	0.25	0.25	0.25	0.25	0.25	0.25
Lithuania	0.19	0.19	0.19	0.19	0.19	0.19	0.19	0.19	0.19	0.19	0.19	0.19
Macedonia	0.22	0.22	0.22	0.22	0.22	0.22	0.22	0.22	0.22	0.22	0.22	0.22
Moldova												
Poland	3.31	3.31	3.31	3.31	3.31	3.31	3.31	3.31	3.31	3.31	3.31	3.31
Romania	3.33	3.33	3.33	3.33	3.33	3.33	3.33	3.33	3.33	3.33	3.33	3.33
Russia	14.50	14.51	14.69	14.72	14.77	14.89	15.19	15.65	15.94	16.30	16.40	16.71
Slovakia	1.13	1.13	1.13	1.13	1.13	1.13	1.13	1.13	1.13	1.13	1.13	1.13
Slovenia	0.10	0.10	0.10	0.10	0.10	0.10	0.10	0.10	0.10	0.10	0.10	0.10
Ukraine	0.84	0.84	0.84	0.84	0.84	0.84	0.85	0.85	0.85	0.85	0.85	0.85

Source:*International Monetary Fund (IMF), International Financial Statistics*

Economic Statistics

Table 8.26

Government Expenditure by Object 2008

US$ million

	General Public Services	Defence	Education	Health	Social Security & Welfare	Housing/ Amenities	Other Community/ Social	Economic Services	Other
Western Europe									
Austria	22,364	3,467	14,550	26,096	87,356	2,814	1,161	11,656	5,671
Belgium	73,001	5,214	5,999	37,051	94,515	0	379	11,570	5,508
Cyprus	2,798	427	1,800	704	2,340	484	253	1,015	522
Denmark	46,820	5,255	14,080	211	42,334	1,133	2,500	7,052	4,042
Finland	13,125	3,834	9,683	10,101	53,461	496	1,097	8,754	3,258
France	192,586	50,043	120,223	206,186	617,401	9,175	11,793	86,051	28,673
Germany	126,574	36,577	7,104	207,824	729,947	8,327	2,779	71,513	8,335
Gibraltar									
Greece	24,634	7,780	10,259	17,252	64,834	668	863	40,846	4,728
Iceland	802	10	529	1,239	1,044	20	209	668	278
Ireland	11,365	1,422	13,746	20,859	29,272	3,024	1,219	12,378	3,985
Italy	200,133	30,971	85,821	81,838	542,543	10,276	9,974	49,748	42,059
Liechtenstein									
Luxembourg	2,690	126	2,045	2,470	12,835	213	748	1,769	702
Malta	535	60	446	527	1,201	65	42	355	267
Monaco									
Netherlands	71,426	11,538	37,605	48,149	160,574	1,221	2,626	23,966	16,463
Norway	2,960	833	972	2,830	7,029	22	227	1,566	457
Portugal	28,706	2,683	12,702	15,718	44,200	201	991	6,225	3,976
Spain	150,735	16,023	2,237	6,337	184,118	530	5,435	34,243	17,809
Sweden	4,019	800	979	676	8,298	61	168	1,743	677
Switzerland	15,708	3,963	4,165	156	49,936	498	389	11,074	578
Turkey	129,895	8,516	7,433	5,272	7,680	4,499	801	3,102	4,668
United Kingdom	256,895	92,797	200,236	307,552	518,701	19,641	21,316	90,145	89,962
Eastern Europe									
Albania	306	150	389	180	579	135	31	344	67
Belarus	4,776	611	551	472	6,196	3	201	5,056	1,165
Bosnia-Herzegovina									
Bulgaria	4,110	328	377	408	2,965	95	93	896	816
Croatia	3,088	815	2,291	3,730	10,343	759	420	2,307	1,813
Czech Republic	343	93	278	544	912	49	34	356	163
Estonia	1,077	308	585	1,272	2,170	10	276	840	678
Georgia	180	1,319	262	179	546	2	71	63	549
Hungary	49	7	22	43	114	0	5	40	14
Latvia	1,277	773	1,843	1,613	3,462	205	610	2,448	1,592
Lithuania	775	251	264	805	1,439	3	88	460	216
Macedonia									
Moldova	537	32	157	318	654	12	33	314	118
Poland	6,615	2,331	6,726	6,404	25,111	262	468	4,544	2,500
Romania	1,617	1,396	1,126	3,178	4,779	327	291	2,741	1,448
Russia	109,412	52,526	20,937	40,880	102,252	9,636	4,769	14,381	44,555
Slovakia	2,704	1,315	1,956	5,593	8,289	337	310	4,075	1,901
Slovenia	2,635	704	2,296	4,228	9,291	110	305	1,716	1,021
Ukraine	13,683	2,097	3,338	1,793	25,081	419	563	6,743	4,012

Source: *Euromonitor International/International Monetary Fund (IMF), Government Finance Statistics/national statistics*

Economic Statistics

Table 8.27

Government Expenditure by Object 2008 (% Analysis)

% of total expenditure

	General Public Services	Defence	Education	Health	Social Security & Welfare	Housing/ Amenities	Other Community/ Social	Economic Services	Other
Western Europe									
Austria	12.77	1.98	8.31	14.90	49.88	1.61	0.66	6.66	3.24
Belgium	31.30	2.24	2.57	15.89	40.52	0.00	0.16	4.96	2.36
Cyprus	27.05	4.13	17.40	6.81	22.62	4.68	2.45	9.81	5.05
Denmark	37.93	4.26	11.41	0.17	34.30	0.92	2.03	5.71	3.28
Finland	12.64	3.69	9.33	9.73	51.50	0.48	1.06	8.43	3.14
France	14.57	3.79	9.09	15.60	46.70	0.69	0.89	6.51	2.17
Germany	10.56	3.05	0.59	17.33	60.88	0.69	0.23	5.96	0.70
Gibraltar									
Greece	14.33	4.53	5.97	10.04	37.72	0.39	0.50	23.77	2.75
Iceland	16.70	0.21	11.03	25.82	21.76	0.41	4.36	13.91	5.79
Ireland	11.68	1.46	14.13	21.44	30.09	3.11	1.25	12.73	4.10
Italy	19.00	2.94	8.15	7.77	51.51	0.98	0.95	4.72	3.99
Liechtenstein									
Luxembourg	11.40	0.53	8.67	10.47	54.39	0.90	3.17	7.50	2.97
Malta	15.28	1.72	12.75	15.07	34.34	1.85	1.21	10.15	7.62
Monaco									
Netherlands	19.12	3.09	10.07	12.89	42.98	0.33	0.70	6.42	4.41
Norway	17.52	4.93	5.75	16.75	41.60	0.13	1.35	9.27	2.71
Portugal	24.87	2.32	11.01	13.62	38.30	0.17	0.86	5.39	3.45
Spain	36.11	3.84	0.54	1.52	44.10	0.13	1.30	8.20	4.27
Sweden	23.07	4.59	5.62	3.88	47.63	0.35	0.97	10.01	3.88
Switzerland	18.17	4.58	4.82	0.18	57.75	0.58	0.45	12.81	0.67
Turkey	75.58	4.96	4.33	3.07	4.47	2.62	0.47	1.81	2.72
United Kingdom	16.08	5.81	12.54	19.26	32.47	1.23	1.33	5.64	5.63
Eastern Europe									
Albania	14.05	6.90	17.84	8.27	26.53	6.17	1.41	15.77	3.07
Belarus	25.09	3.21	2.90	2.48	32.56	0.02	1.06	26.57	6.12
Bosnia-Herzegovina									
Bulgaria	40.74	3.25	3.74	4.05	29.39	0.94	0.92	8.89	8.09
Croatia	12.08	3.19	8.96	14.59	40.46	2.97	1.64	9.02	7.09
Czech Republic	12.36	3.34	10.02	19.63	32.91	1.79	1.22	12.84	5.90
Estonia	14.93	4.27	8.10	17.63	30.07	0.14	3.83	11.64	9.40
Georgia	5.66	41.60	8.28	5.64	17.22	0.06	2.24	2.00	17.31
Hungary	16.60	2.48	7.47	14.59	38.72	0.07	1.80	13.60	4.66
Latvia	9.24	5.59	13.33	11.67	25.05	1.48	4.41	17.71	11.52
Lithuania	18.01	5.84	6.14	18.71	33.46	0.07	2.04	10.70	5.03
Macedonia									
Moldova	24.68	1.48	7.21	14.62	30.09	0.54	1.53	14.42	5.42
Poland	12.04	4.24	12.24	11.65	45.69	0.48	0.85	8.27	4.55
Romania	9.57	8.26	6.66	18.80	28.27	1.94	1.72	16.21	8.57
Russia	27.40	13.15	5.24	10.24	25.60	2.41	1.19	3.60	11.16
Slovakia	10.21	4.97	7.39	21.12	31.30	1.27	1.17	15.39	7.18
Slovenia	11.81	3.16	10.29	18.95	41.65	0.49	1.37	7.69	4.58
Ukraine	23.70	3.63	5.78	3.11	43.45	0.73	0.98	11.68	6.95

Source:*Euromonitor International/International Monetary Fund (IMF), Government Finance Statistics/national statistics*

Economic Statistics

Table 8.28

Current Account Balance 1998-2008

US$ million / as stated

	1998	1999	2000	2001	2002	2003	2004	2005	2006	2007	2008	Current account balance as % of total GDP
Western Europe												
Austria	-3,396.0	-3,451.0	-1,414.0	-1,569.0	5,545.0	4,279.0	6,024.0	6,120.0	9,111.0	11,530.0	14,451.0	3.5
Belgium	13,255.0	20,070.0	9,393.0	7,896.0	11,729.0	12,837.0	12,625.0	9,790.0	10,588.0	7,772.0	-12,891.0	-2.5
Cyprus	258.0	-158.0	-488.0	-315.0	-392.0	-297.0	-787.0	-994.0	-1,282.0	-2,515.0	-4,566.0	-18.3
Denmark	-1,485.0	3,328.0	2,252.0	5,025.0	4,321.0	7,332.0	7,467.0	11,195.0	7,902.0	2,203.0	3,356.0	1.0
Finland	7,292.0	7,763.0	9,907.0	10,733.0	11,987.0	8,495.0	12,392.0	7,097.0	9,484.0	10,215.0	6,451.0	2.4
France	39,866.0	45,328.0	21,366.0	24,599.0	17,945.0	14,740.0	12,482.0	-9,088.0	-11,558.0	-25,876.0	-64,776.0	-2.3
Germany	-16,330.0	-26,858.0	-32,557.0	380.0	40,585.0	46,286.0	127,923.0	143,811.0	178,837.0	250,263.0	235,257.0	6.4
Gibraltar												
Greece	-3,682.0	-7,295.0	-9,820.0	-9,400.0	-9,582.0	-12,804.0	-13,476.0	-17,874.0	-29,708.0	-44,400.0	-51,574.0	-14.4
Iceland	-561.0	-593.0	-883.0	-342.0	139.0	-523.0	-1,302.0	-2,625.0	-4,213.0	-4,043.0	-6,817.0	-40.9
Ireland	704.0	241.0	-350.0	-678.0	-1,223.0	-2.0	-1,078.0	-7,088.0	-7,916.0	-13,876.0	-13,886.0	-5.1
Italy	19,791.0	8,208.0	-5,863.0	-639.0	-9,483.0	-19,605.0	-16,208.0	-29,432.0	-48,350.0	-51,208.0	-78,812.0	-3.4
Liechtenstein												
Luxembourg	1,648.0	2,272.0	2,688.0	1,770.0	2,386.0	2,378.0	4,046.0	4,141.0	4,449.0	4,895.0	4,976.0	9.2
Malta	-229.0	-136.0	-488.0	-148.0	104.0	-156.0	-335.0	-523.0	-595.0	-523.0	-466.0	-5.5
Monaco												
Netherlands	12,970.0	15,643.0	7,251.0	9,770.0	10,939.0	29,568.0	45,898.0	46,433.0	63,275.0	59,598.0	65,746.0	7.5
Norway	-475.0	8,916.0	25,265.0	27,529.0	24,090.0	27,669.0	32,877.0	49,140.0	58,027.0	61,811.0	88,008.0	19.5
Portugal	-8,372.0	-10,311.0	-11,570.0	-11,465.0	-10,352.0	-9,563.0	-13,580.0	-17,613.0	-19,575.0	-21,073.0	-29,675.0	-12.1
Spain	-7,074.0	-18,100.0	-23,054.0	-24,023.0	-22,443.0	-31,071.0	-54,909.0	-83,291.0	-110,890.0	-144,435.0	-153,665.0	-9.5
Sweden	9,672.0	10,588.0	9,855.0	9,781.0	12,449.0	22,355.0	24,099.0	25,481.0	33,752.0	39,054.0	37,279.0	7.8
Switzerland	26,090.0	29,378.0	30,626.0	19,950.0	23,258.0	41,732.0	46,802.0	50,620.0	56,317.0	43,032.0	12,065.0	2.4
Turkey	2,152.0	-925.0	-9,920.0	3,760.0	-626.0	-7,515.0	-14,431.0	-22,136.0	-31,893.0	-37,684.0	-41,289.0	-5.7
United Kingdom	-5,266.0	-35,365.0	-39,096.0	-30,386.0	-28,009.0	-29,920.0	-45,643.0	-59,784.0	-80,785.0	-75,483.0	-46,457.0	-1.7
Eastern Europe												
Albania	-89.0	77.0	-134.0	-125.0	-318.0	-286.0	-292.0	-498.0	-508.0	-994.0	-1,823.0	-14.1
Belarus	-1,017.0	-194.0	-338.0	-411.0	-326.0	-434.0	-1,194.0	434.0	-1,448.0	-3,060.0	-5,049.0	-8.4
Bosnia-Herzegovina	-315.0	-481.0	-397.0	-746.0	-1,183.0	-1,627.0	-1,639.0	-1,938.0	-1,025.0	-1,920.0	-2,711.0	-14.7
Bulgaria	-62.0	-652.0	-704.0	-766.0	-380.0	-1,100.0	-1,625.0	-3,371.0	-5,842.0	-9,961.0	-12,707.0	-25.5
Croatia	-1,472.0	-1,536.0	-533.0	-729.0	-1,925.0	-1,835.0	-1,875.0	-2,555.0	-3,287.0	-4,443.0	-6,499.0	-9.4
Czech Republic	-1,308.0	-1,464.0	-2,688.0	-3,272.0	-4,264.0	-5,785.0	-5,751.0	-1,662.0	-3,640.0	-5,483.0	-6,669.0	-3.1
Estonia	-480.0	-246.0	-305.0	-323.0	-777.0	-1,113.0	-1,360.0	-1,388.0	-2,809.0	-3,808.0	-2,194.0	-9.3
Georgia	-462.0	-281.0	-239.0	-205.0	-216.0	-383.0	-354.0	-710.0	-1,175.0	-2,009.0	-2,915.0	-22.8
Hungary	-3,400.0	-3,762.0	-4,010.0	-3,204.0	-4,642.0	-6,702.0	-8,589.0	-8,290.0	-8,531.0	-9,049.0	-13,102.0	-8.5
Latvia	-595.0	-654.0	-371.0	-626.0	-624.0	-921.0	-1,762.0	-1,992.0	-4,522.0	-6,231.0	-4,295.0	-12.7
Lithuania	-1,298.0	-1,194.0	-675.0	-574.0	-734.0	-1,278.0	-1,724.0	-1,831.0	-3,218.0	-5,692.0	-5,475.0	-11.6
Macedonia	-311.0	-98.0	-68.0	-248.0	-356.0	-190.0	-451.0	-151.0	-56.0	-569.0	-1,253.0	-13.2
Moldova	-335.0	-68.0	-108.0	-37.0	-25.0	-130.0	-47.0	-248.0	-384.0	-747.0	-1,071.0	-17.7
Poland	-6,901.0	-12,487.0	-9,981.0	-5,376.0	-5,009.0	-4,599.0	-10,118.0	-3,705.0	-9,200.0	-20,100.0	-28,921.0	-5.5
Romania	-2,988.0	-1,465.0	-1,380.0	-2,228.0	-1,533.0	-3,460.0	-6,340.0	-8,811.0	-12,748.0	-22,899.0	-24,885.0	-12.4
Russia	219.0	24,616.0	46,839.0	33,935.0	29,116.0	35,410.0	59,514.0	84,443.0	94,340.0	77,012.0	102,400.0	6.1
Slovakia	-1,983.0	-983.0	-707.0	-1,747.0	-1,930.0	-1,976.0	-3,302.0	-4,072.0	-3,931.0	-4,007.0	-6,220.0	-6.5
Slovenia	-156.0	-878.0	-631.0	38.0	247.0	-227.0	-897.0	-620.0	-968.0	-1,994.0	-3,024.0	-5.5
Ukraine	-1,296.0	1,658.0	1,481.0	1,402.0	3,173.0	2,891.0	6,909.0	2,531.0	-1,617.0	-5,272.0	-12,933.0	-7.2

Source: *Euromonitor International from International Monetary Fund (IMF), International Financial Statistics*

Economic Statistics

Table 8.29

Remittances Inflows 1998-2008

US$ million

	1998	1999	2000	2001	2002	2003	2004	2005	2006	2007	2008
Western Europe											
Austria	1,417.0	1,526.0	1,441.0	1,519.0	1,711.0	2,308.9	2,480.2	2,941.1	2,639.3	2,965.0	3,237.0
Belgium	4,204.0	4,467.0	4,005.0	3,811.0	4,674.0	5,990.5	6,862.8	7,241.9	7,487.8	8,557.0	9,280.0
Cyprus	48.0	50.0	64.0	105.0	61.0	83.0	244.9	189.5	169.1	172.1	279.0
Denmark	765.0	803.0	667.0	699.0	785.0	941.0	1,075.4	866.0	983.0	1,028.0	1,087.0
Finland	375.0	444.0	473.0	491.0	477.0	526.0	666.4	692.6	698.2	771.9	772.0
France	10,021.0	9,301.0	8,631.0	9,194.0	10,353.0	11,311.0	12,277.1	11,945.4	12,303.6	13,745.7	15,133.0
Germany	4,264.0	4,329.0	3,644.0	3,933.0	4,685.0	5,783.5	6,580.8	6,933.0	7,585.0	9,839.0	11,064.0
Gibraltar											
Greece	2,284.0	2,284.0	2,194.0	2,014.0	1,659.0	1,564.0	1,241.9	1,220.1	1,542.6	2,483.7	2,687.0
Iceland	76.0	85.0	88.0	74.0	74.0	96.0	112.1	87.7	87.4	41.3	46.0
Ireland	274.0	295.0	252.0	244.0	316.0	337.0	413.9	512.6	531.5	579.9	643.0
Italy	2,115.0	1,999.0	1,937.0	2,266.0	2,263.0	2,140.0	2,172.7	2,395.4	2,625.3	3,165.0	3,136.0
Liechtenstein											
Luxembourg			578.5	576.5	826.0	1,033.4	1,130.0	1,268.7	1,371.5	1,565.2	1,737.0
Malta	21.0	21.0	14.0	14.0	23.0	27.0	32.9	33.5	35.0	43.0	50.0
Monaco											
Netherlands	1,464.0	1,978.0	1,157.0	1,357.0	1,215.0	2,024.0	2,164.3	2,196.8	2,475.5	2,547.8	3,006.0
Norway	301.0	262.0	246.0	254.0	302.0	392.0	465.0	505.3	524.5	612.7	684.0
Portugal	3,628.0	3,569.0	3,406.0	3,566.0	2,858.0	3,042.0	3,304.4	3,101.4	3,334.2	3,941.0	4,057.0
Spain	3,935.0	4,313.0	4,517.0	4,720.0	5,178.0	6,567.8	7,528.3	7,961.0	8,890.0	10,739.0	11,772.0
Sweden	393.0	472.0	510.0	543.0	540.0	578.0	419.9	611.5	594.6	774.7	822.0
Switzerland	1,227.0	1,222.0	1,119.0	1,301.0	1,372.0	1,706.0	1,889.5	1,828.0	1,903.4	2,034.7	2,358.0
Turkey	5,356.0	4,529.0	4,560.0	2,786.0	1,936.0	729.0	804.0	851.0	1,111.0	1,209.0	1,360.0
United Kingdom	2,995.0	3,400.0	3,614.0	4,825.0	4,485.0	5,029.0	6,350.5	6,302.1	6,974.9	8,234.1	8,234.0
Eastern Europe											
Albania	504.0	407.0	598.0	699.0	734.0	889.0	1,160.7	1,289.7	1,359.5	1,468.0	1,495.0
Belarus	315.0	193.0	139.0	149.0	141.0	222.0	256.7	254.6	339.8	354.2	448.0
Bosnia-Herzegovina	2,048.0	1,888.0	1,595.0	1,521.0	1,526.0	1,749.0	2,072.0	2,042.6	2,156.8	2,700.0	2,735.0
Bulgaria	51.0	43.0	58.0	71.0	1,177.0	1,718.0	1,722.8	1,612.9	1,716.0	2,132.0	2,634.0
Croatia	625.0	557.0	641.0	747.0	885.0	1,085.0	1,222.2	1,222.4	1,234.0	1,393.9	1,602.0
Czech Republic	350.0	318.0	297.0	257.0	335.0	499.0	814.5	1,026.1	1,189.9	1,332.4	1,415.0
Estonia	3.0	2.0	3.0	9.0	19.0	51.0	166.8	264.1	401.9	426.0	422.0
Georgia	373.0	361.0	274.0	181.0	231.0	235.0	303.2	346.1	485.3	695.7	732.0
Hungary	220.0	213.0	281.0	296.0	279.0	295.0	1,717.0	1,931.0	2,079.0	2,530.0	2,946.0
Latvia	49.0	49.0	72.0	112.0	138.0	173.0	229.4	381.0	482.1	551.9	601.0
Lithuania	3.0	3.0	50.0	79.0	109.0	115.0	324.5	534.3	994.1	1,433.0	1,537.0
Macedonia	63.0	77.0	81.0	73.0	106.0	174.0	213.0	226.6	266.6	345.0	408.0
Moldova	124.0	112.0	179.0	243.0	324.0	487.0	705.2	920.3	1,181.7	1,498.2	1,897.0
Poland	1,070.0	825.0	1,726.0	1,995.0	1,989.0	2,655.0	4,728.0	6,482.0	8,496.0	10,496.0	10,727.0
Romania	49.0	96.0	96.0	116.0	143.0	124.0	132.0	4,732.6	6,717.6	8,539.0	9,395.0
Russia	1,925.0	1,292.0	1,275.0	1,403.0	1,359.0	1,453.0	2,495.1	3,012.0	3,344.0	4,713.0	6,033.0
Slovakia	24.0	20.0	18.0	24.0	24.0	424.0	529.1	946.5	1,088.2	1,482.7	1,500.0
Slovenia	228.0	226.0	205.0	201.0	217.0	238.0	265.5	264.3	282.1	284.4	331.0
Ukraine	12.0	18.0	33.0	141.0	209.0	330.0	411.0	595.0	829.0	4,503.0	5,769.0

Source: *International Monetary Fund (IMF), International Financial Statistics*

Economic Statistics **Table 8.30**

Remittances Outflows 1998-2008

US$ million

	1998	1999	2000	2001	2002	2003	2004	2005	2006	2007	2008
Western Europe											
Austria	932.0	945.0	858.0	950.0	1,095.0	1,466.0	2,014.1	2,542.9	2,574.9	2,994.0	3,356.0
Belgium	3,347.0	3,653.0	3,588.0	3,958.0	1,845.5	2,329.3	2,617.0	2,753.9	2,698.1	3,161.0	3,689.0
Cyprus	52.0	52.0	63.0	100.0	117.0	202.0	255.4	273.3	279.0	370.0	577.0
Denmark	346.0	694.0	662.0	745.0	860.0	1,029.0	1,226.2	1,488.0	1,763.0	3,015.0	3,227.0
Finland	104.0	111.0	100.0	97.0	113.0	149.0	224.7	249.0	308.7	391.3	391.0
France	4,237.0	4,102.0	3,791.0	3,960.0	3,804.0	4,388.0	4,261.9	4,182.2	4,217.5	4,380.4	4,541.0
Germany	9,161.0	8,808.0	7,761.0	7,609.0	9,572.0	11,190.0	12,069.5	12,383.3	12,415.9	13,859.6	14,976.0
Gibraltar											
Greece		631.0	545.0	536.0	412.0	379.2	496.6	902.4	981.9	1,459.8	1,912.0
Iceland	18.0	23.0	31.0	17.0	23.0	26.0	46.6	65.2	79.9	100.1	100.0
Ireland	166.0	120.0	181.0	274.0	587.8	788.0	997.1	1,535.3	1,946.7	2,554.0	2,691.0
Italy	2,378.0	2,550.0	2,582.0	2,710.0	3,579.0	4,368.4	5,512.0	7,620.0	8,436.6	11,287.1	12,718.0
Liechtenstein											
Luxembourg			2,719.7	3,138.0	4,011.0	5,077.0	6,000.0	6,627.2	7,560.9	9,280.0	10,922.0
Malta	12.0	15.0	14.0	11.0	11.0	12.0	21.6	32.5	46.1	53.5	60.0
Monaco											
Netherlands	2,815.0	3,274.0	3,122.0	2,850.0	2,889.0	4,238.0	5,031.7	5,928.0	6,831.0	7,830.0	8,431.0
Norway	746.0	730.0	718.0	554.0	658.0	1,430.0	1,749.2	2,174.0	2,620.0	3,641.6	4,776.0
Portugal	300.0	355.0	454.0	706.0	792.0	935.3	1,163.3	1,306.2	1,377.1	1,284.0	1,410.0
Spain	1,244.0	1,612.0	2,059.0	2,470.0	2,914.1	5,140.0	6,976.8	8,135.8	11,326.0	15,183.0	14,656.0
Sweden	620.0	647.0	545.0	589.0	590.0	600.0	645.7	813.8	605.0	890.0	912.0
Switzerland	7,767.0	7,578.0	7,591.0	8,380.0	9,223.0	11,411.0	12,920.9	13,323.6	14,376.7	16,272.9	18,954.0
Turkey								96.0	107.0	106.0	111.0
United Kingdom	2,287.0	2,036.0	2,044.0	3,342.0	2,439.0	2,624.0	2,956.6	3,877.0	4,560.1	5,048.2	5,048.0
Eastern Europe											
Albania						4.0	4.9	6.5	26.5	10.0	10.0
Belarus	111.0	76.0	58.0	77.0	68.0	65.0	81.6	94.5	92.7	109.2	142.0
Bosnia-Herzegovina			2.0	11.0	14.0	21.0	62.1	40.0	54.5	65.3	70.0
Bulgaria	3.0	4.0	26.0	27.0	14.0	13.0	29.4	35.5	49.6	85.0	74.0
Croatia	41.0	47.0	44.0	46.0	51.0	67.0	68.7	61.8	274.5	85.5	110.0
Czech Republic	745.0	642.0	605.0	718.0	898.0	1,102.5	1,431.4	1,676.5	2,030.2	2,624.5	3,826.0
Estonia	3.0	3.0	3.0	2.0	5.0	18.5	26.5	50.4	75.4	95.7	113.0
Georgia	11.0	47.0	39.0	26.0	26.0	30.0	25.9	28.5	25.0	28.4	47.0
Hungary	75.0	98.0	86.0	101.0	107.0	114.0	127.6	915.0	986.0	1,220.0	1,407.0
Latvia	8.0	8.0	7.0	8.0	7.0	8.0	13.1	20.1	29.8	44.8	58.0
Lithuania	63.0	47.0	38.0	29.0	31.0	42.0	27.6	47.4	425.8	567.0	567.0
Macedonia	21.0	12.0	14.0	21.0	23.0	16.0	16.1	15.6	17.8	25.0	25.0
Moldova	24.0	25.0	46.0	59.0	56.0	67.4	67.3	68.4	85.7	86.7	115.0
Poland	176.0	191.0	311.0	345.0	353.0	325.0	460.0	602.0	800.0	1,278.0	1,716.0
Romania	6.0	8.0	6.0	5.0	7.0	8.0	8.0	33.4	56.8	351.0	436.0
Russia	2,552.0	1,409.0	1,101.0	1,823.0	2,226.0	3,233.0	5,188.0	7,008.0	11,467.0	17,763.0	26,145.0
Slovakia	9.0	8.0	8.0	8.0	11.0	16.0	21.9	39.0	47.7	73.2	73.0
Slovenia	31.0	28.0	29.0	29.0	46.0	66.0	80.2	94.4	128.7	206.8	371.0
Ukraine	3.0	3.0	10.0	5.0	15.0	29.0	20.0	34.0	30.0	42.0	54.0

Source: *International Monetary Fund (IMF), International Financial Statistics*

Economic Statistics   **Table 8.31**

Corruption Perception Index 1998-2008
Score

	1998	1999	2000	2001	2002	2003	2004	2005	2006	2007	2008
Western Europe											
Austria	7.5	7.6	7.7	7.8	7.8	8.0	8.4	8.7	8.6	8.1	8.1
Belgium	5.4	5.3	6.1	6.6	7.1	7.6	7.5	7.4	7.3	7.1	7.3
Cyprus						6.1	5.4	5.7	5.6	5.3	6.4
Denmark	10.0	10.0	9.8	9.5	9.5	9.5	9.5	9.5	9.5	9.4	9.3
Finland	9.6	9.8	10.0	9.9	9.7	9.7	9.7	9.6	9.6	9.4	9.0
France	6.7	6.6	6.7	6.7	6.3	6.9	7.1	7.5	7.4	7.3	6.9
Germany	7.9	8.0	7.6	7.4	7.3	7.7	8.2	8.2	8.0	7.8	7.9
Gibraltar											
Greece	4.9	4.9	4.9	4.2	4.2	4.3	4.3	4.3	4.4	4.6	4.7
Iceland	9.3	9.2	9.1	9.2	9.4	9.6	9.5	9.7	9.6	9.2	8.9
Ireland	8.2	7.7	7.2	7.5	6.9	7.5	7.5	7.4	7.4	7.5	7.7
Italy	4.6	4.7	4.6	5.5	5.2	5.3	4.8	5.0	4.9	5.2	4.8
Liechtenstein											
Luxembourg	8.7	8.8	8.6	8.7	9.0	8.7	8.4	8.5	8.6	8.4	8.3
Malta							6.8	6.6	6.4	5.8	5.8
Monaco											
Netherlands	9.0	9.0	8.9	8.8	9.0	8.9	8.7	8.6	8.7	9.0	8.9
Norway	9.0	8.9	9.1	8.6	8.5	8.8	8.9	8.9	8.8	8.7	7.9
Portugal	6.5	6.7	6.4	6.3	6.3	6.6	6.3	6.5	6.6	6.5	6.1
Spain	6.1	6.6	7.0	7.0	7.1	6.9	7.1	7.0	6.8	6.7	6.5
Sweden	9.5	9.4	9.4	9.0	9.3	9.3	9.2	9.2	9.2	9.3	9.3
Switzerland	8.9	8.9	8.6	8.4	8.5	8.8	9.1	9.1	9.1	9.0	9.0
Turkey	3.4	3.6	3.8	3.6	3.2	3.1	3.2	3.5	3.8	4.1	4.6
United Kingdom	8.7	8.6	8.7	8.3	8.7	8.7	8.6	8.6	8.6	8.4	7.7
Eastern Europe											
Albania		2.3			2.5	2.5	2.5	2.4	2.6	2.9	3.4
Belarus	3.9	3.4	4.1		4.8	4.2	3.3	2.6	2.1	2.1	2.0
Bosnia-Herzegovina						3.3	3.1	2.9	2.9	3.3	3.2
Bulgaria	2.9	3.3	3.5	3.9	4.0	3.9	4.1	4.0	4.0	4.1	3.6
Croatia		2.7	3.7	3.9	3.8	3.7	3.5	3.4	3.4	4.1	4.4
Czech Republic	4.8	4.6	4.3	3.9	3.7	3.9	4.2	4.3	4.8	5.2	5.2
Estonia	5.7	5.7	5.7	5.6	5.6	5.5	6.0	6.4	6.7	6.5	6.6
Georgia		2.3			2.4	1.8	2.0	2.3	2.8	3.4	3.9
Hungary	5.0	5.2	5.2	5.3	4.9	4.8	4.8	5.0	5.2	5.3	5.1
Latvia	2.7	3.4	3.4	3.4	3.7	3.8	4.0	4.2	4.7	4.8	5.0
Lithuania		3.8	4.1	4.8	4.8	4.7	4.6	4.8	4.8	4.8	4.6
Macedonia		3.3				2.3	2.7	2.7	2.7	3.3	3.6
Moldova		2.6	2.6	3.1	2.1	2.4	2.3	2.9	3.2	2.8	2.9
Poland	4.6	4.2	4.1	4.1	4.0	3.6	3.5	3.4	3.7	4.2	4.6
Romania	3.0	3.3	2.9	2.8	2.6	2.8	2.9	3.0	3.1	3.7	3.8
Russia	2.4	2.4	2.1	2.3	2.7	2.7	2.8	2.4	2.5	2.3	2.1
Slovakia	3.9	3.7	3.5	3.7	3.7	3.7	4.0	4.3	4.7	4.9	5.0
Slovenia		6.0	5.5	5.2	6.0	5.9	6.0	6.1	6.4	6.6	6.7
Ukraine	2.8	2.6	1.5	2.1	2.4	2.3	2.2	2.6	2.8	2.7	2.5

Source: *International Monetary Fund (IMF), International Financial Statistics*
Note: *Corruption perception index relates to perceptions of the degree of corruption as seen by business people and country analysts, and ranges between 10 (highly clean) and 0 (highly corrupt). It is a composite index, making use of surveys of business people and assessments by country analysts. It consists of credible sources using diverse sampling frames and different methodologies. These perceptions enhance our understanding of real levels of corruption from one country to another.*

Economic Statistics

Table 8.32

Monthly Minimum Wage 1998-2008

US$ per month

	1998	1999	2000	2001	2002	2003	2004	2005	2006	2007	2008
Western Europe											
Austria											
Belgium	1,204.1	1,167.8	1,031.2	1,021.3	1,095.9	1,339.6	1,473.6	1,504.8	1,548.2	1,758.5	1,965.9
Cyprus											
Denmark											
Finland											
France	1,150.3	1,117.7	996.9	971.5	1,030.5	1,257.4	1,446.2	1,514.6	1,573.7	1,754.4	1,944.1
Germany											
Gibraltar											
Greece	472.1	538.1	492.5	494.5	548.4	683.3	783.8	830.4	837.7	901.7	1,002.2
Iceland											
Ireland			871.6	904.0	950.8	1,211.9	1,469.8	1,608.0	1,622.2	2,003.9	2,151.7
Italy											
Liechtenstein											
Luxembourg	1,285.9	1,269.0	1,126.2	1,155.7	1,245.8	1,546.3	1,743.2	1,824.4	1,886.2	2,151.9	2,368.7
Malta		514.9	467.7	484.1	507.0	606.5	682.1	700.2	727.7	801.4	900.7
Monaco											
Netherlands	1,158.1	1,133.7	1,007.2	1,057.2	1,161.0	1,428.8	1,571.7	1,573.2	1,612.2	1,805.1	1,997.1
Norway											
Portugal	384.5	380.4	342.2	349.4	382.6	469.9	529.3	543.5	564.8	644.2	731.4
Spain	458.4	443.3	392.0	387.9	486.2	594.1	711.9	744.9	791.7	912.8	1,030.2
Sweden											
Switzerland											
Turkey	176.4	223.5	190.0	137.0	166.5	203.9	311.6	363.7	371.7	449.0	490.7
United Kingdom		983.7	946.1	998.1	1,039.7	1,159.6	1,394.4	1,512.4	1,586.3	1,832.9	1,671.1
Eastern Europe											
Albania											
Belarus		4.1	2.6	9.5	21.9	40.3	54.8	73.2	83.4	97.7
Bosnia-Herzegovina											
Bulgaria		34.9	35.3	39.8	48.1	63.5	76.2	95.3	102.6	126.0	164.5
Croatia	215.3	210.9	205.4	203.8	228.7	277.2	323.4	349.8	371.7	428.4	494.7
Czech Republic	82.1	104.1	110.1	131.5	174.1	219.8	260.7	299.9	352.1	394.2	468.6
Estonia		85.1	82.7	91.5	111.4	155.9	196.9	213.8	240.7	314.9	406.8
Georgia		9.9	10.1	9.6	9.1	9.3	10.4	11.0	11.2	12.0	13.4
Hungary	91.0	94.9	90.4	139.6	193.9	222.9	261.4	285.6	297.1	356.7	400.9
Latvia		85.4	82.4	95.6	97.1	122.5	148.1	141.7	160.6	233.6	332.8
Lithuania		107.5	107.5	107.5	116.9	140.5	179.8	198.3	218.0	277.4	339.4
Macedonia											
Moldova											
Poland	142.7	163.8	161.1	185.6	186.3	205.7	225.3	262.4	289.7	338.2	467.4
Romania		29.3	32.2	48.2	52.9	75.3	85.8	106.4	117.5	160.0	198.5
Russia		3.4	4.7	15.4	14.4	19.5	25.0	28.3	40.5	43.0	80.5
Slovakia	85.1	87.0	86.9	101.7	118.7	151.4	188.9	210.2	227.5	306.3	393.1
Slovenia	375.6	373.8	343.8	347.0	424.1	501.5	579.0	610.6	641.9	715.2	833.7
Ukraine		17.8	21.7	22.0	26.3	30.9	49.3	64.4	79.2	91.1	97.8

Source: *International Monetary Fund (IMF), International Financial Statistics*

Economic Statistics

Table 8.33

Foreign Direct Investment Inflows 1998-2008

National currency million / US$ million

	1998	1999	2000	2001	2002	2003	2004	2005	2006	2007	2008	US$ million 2008
Western Europe												
Austria	4,157	2,824	9,243	6,592	338	6,284	3,132	65,654	1,975	21,760	9,428	13,875
Belgium					19,187	30,583	35,747	27,372	45,228	82,653	39,856	58,656
Cyprus	308	763	927	1,054	1,171	804	900	934	1,491	1,634	1,439	2,118
Denmark	44,726	117,535	291,101	77,289	34,979	7,805	-52,746	76,966	14,391	64,550	58,075	11,392
Finland	10,729	4,363	9,894	4,174	8,782	3,074	2,311	3,820	6,099	9,011	-2,853	-4,199
France	26,332	43,162	45,949	56,188	52,603	38,123	26,423	68,350	62,361	116,340	82,156	120,910
Germany	21,087	52,472	227,782	29,210	56,891	27,384	-7,887	37,367	46,333	41,222	16,987	25,000
Gibraltar	-98	11	91	8	55	38	106	200	372			
Greece		532	1,175	1,769	56	1,179	1,694	529	4,305	1,429	3,604	5,304
Iceland	10,626	4,731	12,211	16,196	8,486	25,783	53,137	196,753	285,989	218,048	1,864	21
Ireland	9,843	17,196	27,649	10,685	31,281	19,841	-8,849	-24,392	-703	19,031	-8,004	-11,779
Italy	2,350	6,516	14,286	16,602	15,599	14,642	13,499	15,792	31,092	29,213	8,023	11,807
Liechtenstein												
Luxembourg					4,307	2,579	4,179	4,686	22,831	-26,617	2,047	3,012
Malta	253	805	652	268	-456	892	318	546	1,493	689	586	863
Monaco												
Netherlands	33,556	38,637	68,434	58,018	27,015	18,097	3,524	38,057	5,313	90,184	582	856
Norway	32,850	52,847	61,276	18,917	5,245	25,133	17,149	33,560	42,439	22,204	-8,704	-1,543
Portugal	2,680	1,096	7,244	6,891	1,862	6,423	1,337	3,264	8,743	2,167	2,429	3,575
Spain	12,740	17,385	42,106	31,435	42,441	22,671	19,953	19,759	24,845	52,164	48,384	71,207
Sweden	154,330	490,672	202,713	135,154	114,010	26,425	80,520	74,862	198,214	147,439	276,219	41,908
Switzerland	13,989	18,666	33,379	15,851	10,576	23,527	2,308	-654	40,060	59,694	20,173	18,626
Turkey	245	328	614	4,108	1,708	2,628	3,970	13,477	28,553	28,919	23,671	18,187
United Kingdom	45,075	55,217	80,696	37,381	17,017	16,905	31,288	97,596	83,748	98,834	53,058	97,540
Eastern Europe												
Albania	6,780	5,673	20,550	29,744	18,921	21,696	35,078	26,214	31,909	59,888	78,613	937
Belarus	9,373	110,687	104,158	133,162	442,536	352,408	353,851	656,915	759,174	3,831,182	4,597,319	2,152
Bosnia-Herzegovina	117	325	310	259	556	662	1,118	956	1,126	3,017	1,339	1,003
Bulgaria	946	1,504	2,126	1,776	1,879	3,633	4,193	6,788	12,096	16,729	12,308	9,205
Croatia	5,987	10,329	9,188	13,200	8,659	13,737	6,508	10,638	20,180	26,726	21,629	4,383
Czech Republic	119,446	218,222	192,493	214,546	278,166	57,018	127,928	277,954	124,767	215,237	185,472	10,864
Estonia	8,171	4,479	6,572	9,482	4,726	12,734	12,165	36,934	22,279	30,718	21,259	1,988
Georgia	369	167	259	228	352	718	944	821	2,083	2,924	1,909	1,280
Hungary	716,746	784,401	781,771	1,129,885	776,975	488,372	916,542	1,522,042	4,198,690	1,117,915	1,121,144	6,514
Latvia	211	203	250	83	157	173	344	403	933	1,155	686	1,426
Lithuania	3,702	1,946	1,516	1,783	2,620	548	2,150	2,862	5,065	5,090	4,543	1,927
Macedonia	8,195	5,031	14,174	30,422	6,794	6,397	15,961	4,781	20,700	14,300	25,057	598
Moldova	405	398	1,586	702	1,141	1,028	1,081	2,403	3,297	5,990	7,407	713
Poland	22,121	28,841	40,605	23,393	16,855	17,847	46,511	33,355	61,678	63,549	39,832	16,533
Romania	1,803	1,596	2,251	3,362	3,782	6,122	21,269	18,887	32,004	24,197	33,571	13,328
Russia	26,798	81,478	76,349	80,163	105,877	244,251	445,010	364,467	807,611	1,408,817	1,815,581	73,053
Slovakia	501	333	2,225		4,355	495	2,445	1,953	3,741	2,382	2,320	3,414
Slovenia	192	100	147	562	1,761	267	669	435	518	1,082	1,229	1,808
Ukraine	1,820	2,049	3,237	4,255	3,691	7,594	9,122	40,014	28,300	49,950	57,481	10,913

Source:UNCTAD

Economic Statistics

Table 8.34

Foreign Direct Investment Inward Stocks 1998-2008

National currency million / US$ million

	1998	1999	2000	2001	2002	2003	2004	2005	2006	2007	2008	US$ million 2008
Western Europe												
Austria	21,019	22,028	32,994	38,317	46,170	47,671	50,171	55,848	66,972	119,217	94,678	139,340
Belgium	-18,523	-19,110	-25,470	-29,408	243,558	311,200	375,499	384,513	425,064	432,625	352,608	518,940
Cyprus	1,108	1,929	3,155	4,302	5,213	5,957	6,916	6,986	11,619	12,915	14,069	20,706
Denmark	239,179	332,368	594,709	627,861	653,675	660,028	697,876	665,377	686,307	655,754	767,228	150,492
Finland	14,678	17,194	26,317	26,867	36,067	44,495	46,179	43,892	62,163	67,230	59,699	87,860
France	219,620	229,625	281,878	329,765	408,725	467,031	516,564	505,365	614,690	694,213	677,938	997,734
Germany	184,442	220,794	294,720	303,893	315,970	349,206	412,141	382,998	461,119	493,470	479,007	704,962
Gibraltar	226	312	425	455	492	489	536	607	675	703		
Greece	11,671	14,913	15,301	15,561	16,513	19,879	22,923	23,471	32,909	38,829	24,939	36,703
Iceland	33,066	34,557	39,109	66,860	73,134	91,534	146,553	296,559	536,384	817,726	309,026	3,514
Ireland	55,705	68,338	137,791	149,626	194,090	197,398	164,848	131,496	124,812	141,139	117,835	173,420
Italy	97,068	101,959	131,518	126,764	139,002	160,275	177,760	180,187	235,058	266,565	234,628	345,306
Liechtenstein												
Luxembourg	18,523	19,110	25,470	29,408	37,112	36,945	40,027	35,157	53,130	60,927	57,996	85,353
Malta	1,047	1,757	2,586	2,848	2,561	2,905	3,234	3,470	5,179	6,029	6,212	9,142
Monaco												
Netherlands	146,708	180,409	264,258	315,745	371,385	377,700	384,087	362,718	480,005	528,275	437,990	644,598
Norway	193,294	229,527	266,388	293,748	341,555	346,698	527,946	479,844	661,125	712,873	685,378	121,521
Portugal	26,838	25,256	34,742	40,208	47,368	53,639	53,901	50,932	70,107	84,132	67,826	99,820
Spain	112,444	117,653	169,651	197,926	272,806	300,646	318,711	298,470	351,375	442,048	434,090	638,858
Sweden	405,462	605,643	861,203	949,677	1,162,298	1,284,785	1,442,514	1,283,639	1,670,328	1,959,969	1,670,857	253,502
Switzerland	104,379	114,156	146,598	149,802	194,523	218,471	245,801	212,721	273,358	405,164	405,134	374,054
Turkey	4,548	7,633	11,993	24,169	28,424	50,391	54,932	95,630	126,279	204,931	90,784	69,751
United Kingdom	203,722	238,042	289,749	351,788	348,819	371,140	383,075	468,129	615,900	631,500	536,806	986,838
Eastern Europe												
Albania	59,300	59,880	35,467	46,916	50,490	68,215	86,669	100,011	136,072	186,191	220,011	2,622
Belarus	32,709	288,110	1,144,597	1,942,108	2,947,675	3,894,541	4,443,655	5,132,122	8,008,430	9,674,529	14,269,095	6,679
Bosnia-Herzegovina	1,302	1,683	2,257	2,583	3,008	3,168	4,353	4,570	6,810	9,674	10,387	7,779
Bulgaria	2,811	4,010	5,741	6,435	8,462	11,039	15,921	21,803	35,656	56,425	61,522	46,011
Croatia	12,290	18,225	23,074	32,475	47,475	57,055	74,847	86,810	159,744	241,667	153,287	31,061
Czech Republic	464,045	606,760	835,411	1,030,459	1,265,972	1,277,491	1,471,542	1,453,310	1,804,055	2,281,174	1,952,473	114,369
Estonia	25,638	36,216	44,877	55,231	70,208	97,020	126,763	142,067	157,857	192,261	170,704	15,962
Georgia	711	1,202	1,433	1,731	2,201	2,880	3,529	4,557	6,410	9,002	10,315	6,919
Hungary	4,445,163	5,516,063	6,453,403	7,851,806	9,341,662	10,843,076	12,688,947	12,368,116	17,164,848	18,424,115	10,958,607	63,671
Latvia	919	1,050	1,264	1,462	1,701	1,873	2,447	2,783	4,190	5,465	5,504	11,447
Lithuania	6,501	8,252	9,337	10,662	14,639	15,181	17,765	22,778	30,264	38,012	30,281	12,847
Macedonia	17,304	20,573	35,571	62,309	77,843	87,712	108,235	102,848	134,879	167,245	181,622	4,338
Moldova	1,362	3,358	5,581	7,065	8,675	9,992	10,714	13,310	17,073	22,532	26,739	2,573
Poland	78,061	103,442	148,739	168,997	197,224	225,049	316,249	293,362	448,546	486,276	388,916	161,427
Romania	4,018	8,696	15,090	24,233	25,936	40,512	66,859	75,220	127,675	153,515	181,015	71,864
Russia	125,311	450,611	905,872	1,543,569	2,222,106	2,968,809	3,523,777	5,100,053	7,384,792	12,566,128	5,311,904	213,734
Slovakia	2,604	2,992	5,146	6,230	9,052	12,905	16,829	19,022	30,555	33,015	31,210	45,933
Slovenia	2,477	2,518	3,136	2,895	4,364	5,585	6,109	6,641	8,946	10,249	10,724	15,782
Ukraine	6,861	13,416	21,081	25,792	31,555	40,347	51,096	88,191	116,781	192,198	247,522	46,993

Source:UNCTAD

Economic Statistics

Table 8.35

Foreign Direct Investment Outflows 1998-2008

National currency million / US$ million

	1998	1999	2000	2001	2002	2003	2004	2005	2006	2007	2008	US$ million 2008
Western Europe												
Austria	2,492	3,105	6,070	3,496	6,095	6,324	6,780	65,810	4,405	24,732	19,765	29,088
Belgium	25,730	114,784	93,634	112,338	9,447	34,567	27,914	24,472	39,579	70,606	46,858	68,962
Cyprus	63	171	187	278	582	522	573	440	714	891	1,024	1,507
Denmark	28,241	124,310	229,409	109,474	20,918	5,641	-59,491	97,188	48,443	108,887	145,525	28,545
Finland	16,678	6,325	25,911	9,441	7,983	-2,011	-922	3,396	3,830	5,585	1,107	1,629
France	40,764	117,709	188,989	97,074	53,707	47,260	45,820	91,532	97,447	165,682	152,787	224,860
Germany	80,217	101,988	64,771	43,810	20,831	4,560	16,065	61,884	101,839	132,260	107,446	158,130
Gibraltar												
Greece	-246	509	2,275	682	709	332	827	1,187	3,368	3,839	1,886	2,776
Iceland	5,337	9,007	29,445	32,363	31,379	29,470	181,620	448,059	373,411	853,892	-621,822	-7,070
Ireland	4,420	5,726	5,031	4,579	11,742	4,952	14,574	11,652	11,723	16,054	9,042	13,307
Italy	11,067	6,309	13,095	24,286	18,302	7,956	15,407	32,797	33,859	67,211	30,718	45,209
Liechtenstein												
Luxembourg					9,807	-36	5,582	7,270	2,907	37,683	13,954	20,536
Malta	19	55	23	11	-31	509	6	-20	24	24	189	279
Monaco												
Netherlands	32,948	53,637	80,785	56,662	33,701	39,523	23,219	104,474	51,194	19,527	37,267	54,847
Norway	24,142	45,292	83,024	7,590	42,994	42,851	35,391	140,593	135,769	73,270	151,240	26,816
Portugal	3,603	2,855	8,873	6,952	-223	5,821	5,937	1,811	5,719	3,987	1,490	2,193
Spain	18,171	41,344	62,246	36,710	35,713	25,461	49,501	33,710	82,481	103,003	54,275	79,878
Sweden	180,234	161,564	366,142	71,880	103,920	140,227	156,667	199,214	171,462	250,921	266,208	40,389
Switzerland	27,209	49,955	74,291	31,011	13,380	21,107	32,415	63,310	95,986	60,781	92,085	85,021
Turkey	96	270	544	610	265	749	1,112	1,430	1,320	2,744	3,364	2,585
United Kingdom	74,156	125,157	162,680	42,921	33,547	40,190	51,274	44,444	46,525	137,679	75,791	139,330
Eastern Europe												
Albania	151	964	862	1			1,398	405	1,042	1,341	7,833	93
Belarus	106	199	175	417	-369	3,077	2,808	5,385	6,434	32,620	18,159	9
Bosnia-Herzegovina							2	1	6	34		
Bulgaria	0	31	7	21	59	46	-342	484	273	391	979	732
Croatia	628	427	43	1,540	4,310	815	2,090	1,410	1,536	1,321	841	170
Czech Republic	4,046	3,111	1,647	6,264	6,921	5,867	26,664	-642	33,420	33,329	32,393	1,897
Estonia	89	1,217	1,076	3,497	2,192	2,163	3,378	8,651	13,890	17,962	10,664	997
Georgia		2	-1	0	9	8	18	-162	-28	126	62	42
Hungary	59,552	58,698	166,102	104,357	72,768	372,590	226,190	434,690	815,051	686,210	285,880	1,661
Latvia	32	10	7	11	2	29	59	72	97	172	111	231
Lithuania	17	34	15	28	65	114	730	951	797	1,535	935	397
Macedonia	1	17	-40	59	6	16	57	137	9	-47	-568	-14
Moldova	-4	1	1	2	6	2	40	-2	-10	146	347	33
Poland	1,098	123	70	-368	938	1,186	3,493	10,865	28,391	13,793	8,630	3,582
Romania	-8	25	-24	-49	53	129	228	-88	1,187	680	-685	-272
Russia	12,323	54,351	89,360	73,872	124,319	298,545	397,110	361,121	629,499	1,174,558	1,307,973	52,629
Slovakia	129	-353	23		3	21	-11	121	407	280	175	258
Slovenia	-5	45	71	148	160	421	443	506	722	1,149	995	1,465
Ukraine	-10	29	5	124	-27	69	21	1,409	-672	3,399	5,320	1,010

Source:UNCTAD

Economic Statistics

Table 8.36

Foreign Direct Investment Outflow Stocks 1998-2008

National currency million / US$ million

	1998	1999	2000	2001	2002	2003	2004	2005	2006	2007	2008	US$ million 2008
Western Europe												
Austria	15,581	17,951	26,911	31,823	45,085	49,545	54,557	52,625	66,342	113,847	103,663	152,562
Belgium	-7,121	-7,947	-8,595	-9,833	213,268	271,172	298,345	304,081	472,923	545,852	399,716	588,269
Cyprus	183	364	608	904	1,357	1,815	2,568	2,954	3,943	6,512	7,130	10,493
Denmark	260,507	358,109	590,879	651,317	684,330	675,950	756,607	777,102	827,917	779,881	981,507	192,523
Finland	26,231	31,768	56,497	58,292	67,846	67,331	68,426	65,664	75,390	84,496	77,818	114,526
France	256,955	313,555	482,961	568,207	622,135	641,249	680,468	698,843	840,392	943,486	955,315	1,405,954
Germany	332,259	387,977	587,964	689,807	738,254	735,318	744,571	746,257	851,320	945,587	992,183	1,460,213
Gibraltar												
Greece	2,490	3,693	6,607	7,836	9,552	10,923	11,100	10,937	17,868	23,091	22,043	32,441
Iceland	24,285	32,874	52,135	82,113	115,249	132,969	283,555	635,574	968,550	1,767,277	1,307,852	14,871
Ireland	18,119	23,680	30,277	45,561	62,486	65,950	85,348	83,750	98,273	106,418	108,284	159,363
Italy	157,849	170,671	195,671	203,806	206,662	211,662	225,890	235,989	302,062	379,993	353,466	520,202
Liechtenstein												
Luxembourg	7,121	7,947	8,595	9,833	19,250	18,906	22,441	26,866	35,574	65,252	42,579	62,664
Malta	152	174	220	289	289	818	893	799	913	904	1,031	1,517
Monaco												
Netherlands	204,266	244,835	331,185	370,742	420,796	463,221	472,647	493,310	572,942	639,788	573,301	843,737
Norway	238,461	331,061	407,596	498,023	579,584	584,936	620,284	634,773	783,106	838,518	965,365	171,164
Portugal	9,121	10,786	21,459	24,852	22,630	30,494	35,365	33,745	42,892	49,399	43,243	63,642
Spain	66,126	110,783	181,990	214,002	248,233	258,877	298,547	300,080	404,700	431,418	411,565	605,708
Sweden	743,891	877,882	1,129,295	1,273,324	1,426,563	1,501,891	1,577,435	1,560,302	1,934,743	2,212,368	2,104,604	319,310
Switzerland	267,102	292,297	392,082	425,677	455,432	459,710	498,133	532,986	649,556	789,729	784,901	724,687
Turkey	561	1,172	2,290	5,627	8,843	9,223	10,068	11,153	12,678	15,872	18,015	13,841
United Kingdom	294,891	424,247	593,094	603,826	662,642	726,808	680,664	668,661	782,515	920,033	825,023	1,516,681
Eastern Europe												
Albania	10,394	10,465	11,784	11,767	11,494	9,994	1,266	956	2,313	5,697	12,311	147
Belarus	1,333	6,058	20,867	27,383	6,626	12,718	17,714	29,938	39,674	98,720	106,821	50
Bosnia-Herzegovina	70	73	85	87	83	69	3	4	8	41	39	29
Bulgaria	131	126	142	74	83	91	-186	194	449	832	1,669	1,248
Croatia	6,371	6,243	6,832	7,416	13,173	13,631	12,839	12,176	14,096	18,256	17,939	3,635
Czech Republic	25,954	24,131	28,479	43,193	48,223	64,416	96,625	86,496	113,371	173,653	169,232	9,913
Estonia	2,792	4,127	4,397	7,722	11,230	14,249	17,870	24,407	45,038	70,593	71,503	6,686
Georgia					9	17	34	38	10	145	194	130
Hungary	168,159	219,179	361,147	445,815	558,706	787,115	1,220,211	1,563,936	2,561,824	3,231,083	2,440,390	14,179
Latvia	166	143	15	24	36	65	129	159	266	452	513	1,066
Lithuania	66	104	117	191	219	366	1,176	2,000	2,866	3,962	4,691	1,990
Macedonia	314	676	1,046	1,103	2,516	2,279	2,679	3,058	1,936	3,042	2,261	54
Moldova	122	241	285	297	319	330	354	377	383	498	779	75
Poland	4,049	4,062	4,424	4,736	5,931	8,348	11,785	20,306	50,559	53,561	52,562	21,817
Romania	120	220	296	338	479	692	889	622	2,471	3,023	2,297	912
Russia	86,041	235,182	566,550	1,289,803	1,954,578	2,789,076	3,091,455	4,148,734	5,698,110	9,469,030	5,041,083	202,837
Slovakia	364	325	406	501	515	729	672	480	920	1,101	1,292	1,901
Slovenia	567	588	832	1,103	1,597	2,081	2,435	3,788	4,259	5,251	5,877	8,650
Ukraine	240	409	925	838	767	885	1,053	2,398	1,687	30,689	36,894	7,004

Source:UNCTAD

Economic Statistics   **Table 8.37**

FDI intensity 1998-2008
% of total GDP

	1998	1999	2000	2001	2002	2003	2004	2005	2006	2007	2008
Western Europe											
Austria	2.2	1.4	4.5	3.1	0.2	2.8	1.3	27.0	0.8	8.0	3.3
Belgium					7.2	11.1	12.3	9.1	14.2	24.7	11.6
Cyprus	3.6	8.4	9.4	9.9	10.7	6.8	7.1	6.9	10.3	10.5	8.5
Denmark	3.8	9.7	22.5	5.8	2.5	0.6	-3.6	5.0	0.9	3.8	3.4
Finland	9.2	3.6	7.5	3.0	6.1	2.1	1.5	2.4	3.7	5.0	-1.5
France	2.0	3.2	3.2	3.8	3.4	2.4	1.6	4.0	3.5	6.1	4.2
Germany	1.1	2.6	11.0	1.4	2.7	1.3	-0.4	1.7	2.0	1.7	0.7
Gibraltar	-25.5	2.7	21.2	1.9	11.6	7.5	18.8	35.4	65.2		
Greece		0.4	0.9	1.2	0.0	0.7	0.9	0.3	2.0	0.6	1.5
Iceland	1.8	0.7	1.8	2.1	1.0	3.1	5.7	19.2	24.5	17.0	0.1
Ireland	12.5	19.0	26.4	9.1	24.0	14.2	-5.9	-15.0	-0.4	10.0	-4.3
Italy	0.2	0.6	1.2	1.3	1.2	1.1	1.0	1.1	2.1	1.9	0.5
Liechtenstein											
Luxembourg					18.0	10.0	15.2	15.5	67.3	-73.1	
Malta	7.8	22.0	15.4	6.2	-10.2	20.2	7.0	11.4	29.2	12.6	10.2
Monaco											
Netherlands	9.3	10.0	16.4	13.0	5.8	3.8	0.7	7.4	1.0	15.9	0.1
Norway	2.9	4.3	4.1	1.2	0.3	1.6	1.0	1.7	2.0	1.0	-0.3
Portugal	2.5	1.0	5.9	5.3	1.4	4.6	0.9	2.2	5.6	1.3	1.5
Spain	2.4	3.0	6.7	4.6	5.8	2.9	2.4	2.2	2.5	5.0	4.4
Sweden	7.7	23.1	9.0	5.8	4.7	1.1	3.1	2.7	6.8	4.8	8.7
Switzerland	3.5	4.6	7.9	3.7	2.4	5.4	0.5	-0.1	8.2	11.5	3.7
Turkey	0.3	0.3	0.4	1.7	0.5	0.6	0.7	2.1	3.8	3.4	2.5
United Kingdom	5.1	5.9	8.3	3.7	1.6	1.5	2.6	7.8	6.3	7.1	3.7
Eastern Europe											
Albania	1.7	1.2	3.9	5.1	3.0	3.1	4.7	3.2	3.6	6.1	7.2
Belarus	1.3	3.7	1.1	0.8	1.7	1.0	0.7	1.0	1.0	4.0	3.6
Bosnia-Herzegovina	1.2	3.0	2.6	2.0	4.0	4.6	7.1	5.6	5.9	13.9	5.5
Bulgaria	4.2	6.3	7.9	6.0	5.8	10.5	10.8	15.9	24.5	29.6	18.4
Croatia	3.7	6.3	5.2	6.9	4.2	6.1	2.7	4.0	7.0	8.5	6.3
Czech Republic	6.0	10.5	8.8	9.1	11.3	2.2	4.5	9.3	3.9	6.1	5.0
Estonia	10.4	5.3	6.8	8.7	3.9	9.3	8.0	21.1	10.8	12.6	8.5
Georgia	7.3	2.9	4.3	3.4	4.7	8.4	9.6	7.1	15.1	17.2	10.0
Hungary	7.1	6.9	5.8	7.4	4.5	2.6	4.4	6.9	17.7	4.4	4.2
Latvia	5.3	4.8	5.3	1.6	2.7	2.7	4.6	4.4	8.3	7.8	4.2
Lithuania	8.3	4.5	3.3	3.7	5.0	1.0	3.4	4.0	6.1	5.2	4.1
Macedonia	4.2	2.4	6.0	13.0	2.8	2.5	6.0	1.7	6.7	4.0	6.3
Moldova	4.4	3.2	9.9	3.7	5.1	3.7	3.4	6.4	7.4	11.2	11.8
Poland	3.7	4.3	5.5	3.0	2.1	2.1	5.0	3.4	5.8	5.4	3.1
Romania	4.8	2.9	2.8	2.9	2.5	3.1	8.6	6.5	9.3	5.9	6.7
Russia	1.0	1.7	1.0	0.9	1.0	1.8	2.6	1.7	3.0	4.3	4.4
Slovakia	2.5	1.7	10.1		16.8	1.7	7.2	5.1	8.4	4.3	3.6
Slovenia	1.0	0.5	0.7	2.5	7.2	1.0	2.5	1.5	1.7	3.1	3.3
Ukraine	1.8	1.6	1.9	2.1	1.6	2.8	2.6	9.1	5.2	7.0	6.0

Source:Euromonitor International from national statistics

Economic Statistics | **Table 8.38**

Exchange Rates Against the US$ 1985-2008

Units of national currency per US$

	1985	1990	1995	2000	2003	2004	2005	2006	2007	2008
Western Europe										
Austria	1.31	0.79	0.76	1.08	0.89	0.80	0.80	0.80	0.73	0.68
Belgium	1.31	0.79	0.76	1.08	0.89	0.80	0.80	0.80	0.73	0.68
Cyprus	1.31	0.79	0.76	1.08	0.89	0.80	0.80	0.80	0.73	0.68
Denmark	10.60	6.19	5.60	8.08	6.59	5.99	6.00	5.95	5.44	5.10
Finland	1.31	0.79	0.76	1.08	0.89	0.80	0.80	0.80	0.73	0.68
France	1.31	0.79	0.76	1.08	0.89	0.80	0.80	0.80	0.73	0.68
Germany	1.31	0.79	0.76	1.08	0.89	0.80	0.80	0.80	0.73	0.68
Gibraltar	0.78	0.56	0.63	0.66	0.61	0.55	0.55	0.54	0.50	0.54
Greece	1.31	0.79	0.76	1.08	0.89	0.80	0.80	0.80	0.73	0.68
Iceland	41.51	58.28	64.69	78.62	76.71	70.19	62.98	70.18	64.06	87.95
Ireland	1.31	0.79	0.76	1.08	0.89	0.80	0.80	0.80	0.73	0.68
Italy	1.31	0.79	0.76	1.08	0.89	0.80	0.80	0.80	0.73	0.68
Liechtenstein	2.46	1.39	1.18	1.69	1.35	1.24	1.25	1.25	1.20	1.08
Luxembourg	1.31	0.79	0.76	1.08	0.89	0.80	0.80	0.80	0.73	0.68
Malta	1.31	0.79	0.76	1.08	0.89	0.80	0.80	0.80	0.73	0.68
Monaco	1.31	0.79	0.76	1.08	0.89	0.80	0.80	0.80	0.73	0.68
Netherlands	1.31	0.79	0.76	1.08	0.89	0.80	0.80	0.80	0.73	0.68
Norway	8.60	6.26	6.34	8.80	7.08	6.74	6.44	6.41	5.86	5.64
Portugal	1.31	0.79	0.76	1.08	0.89	0.80	0.80	0.80	0.73	0.68
Spain	1.31	0.79	0.76	1.08	0.89	0.80	0.80	0.80	0.73	0.68
Sweden	8.60	5.92	7.13	9.16	8.09	7.35	7.47	7.38	6.76	6.59
Switzerland	2.46	1.39	1.18	1.69	1.35	1.24	1.25	1.25	1.20	1.08
Turkey	0.00	0.00	0.05	0.63	1.50	1.43	1.34	1.43	1.30	1.30
United Kingdom	0.78	0.56	0.63	0.66	0.61	0.55	0.55	0.54	0.50	0.54
Eastern Europe										
Albania	7.00	7.75	92.70	143.71	121.86	102.78	99.87	98.10	90.43	83.89
Belarus			11.52	876.75	2,051.27	2,160.26	2,153.82	2,144.56	2,146.08	2,136.40
Bosnia-Herzegovina				2.12	1.73	1.58	1.57	1.56	1.43	1.34
Bulgaria	0.00	0.00	0.07	2.12	1.73	1.58	1.57	1.56	1.43	1.34
Croatia			5.23	8.28	6.70	6.03	5.95	5.84	5.36	4.94
Czech Republic		17.95	26.54	38.60	28.21	25.70	23.96	22.60	20.29	17.07
Estonia			11.46	16.97	13.86	12.60	12.58	12.47	11.43	10.69
Georgia			1.26	1.98	2.15	1.92	1.81	1.78	1.67	1.49
Hungary	50.12	63.21	125.68	282.18	224.31	202.75	199.58	210.39	183.63	172.11
Latvia			0.53	0.61	0.57	0.54	0.56	0.56	0.51	0.48
Lithuania			4.00	4.00	3.06	2.78	2.77	2.75	2.52	2.36
Macedonia			37.88	65.90	54.32	49.41	49.28	48.80	44.73	41.87
Moldova			4.50	12.43	13.94	12.33	12.60	13.13	12.14	10.39
Poland	0.01	0.95	2.42	4.35	3.89	3.66	3.24	3.10	2.77	2.41
Romania	0.00	0.00	0.20	2.17	3.32	3.26	2.91	2.81	2.44	2.52
Russia			4.56	28.13	30.69	28.81	28.28	27.19	25.58	24.85
Slovakia	1.31	0.79	0.76	1.08	0.89	0.80	0.80	0.80	0.73	0.68
Slovenia	1.31	0.79	0.76	1.08	0.89	0.80	0.80	0.80	0.73	0.68
Ukraine			1.47	5.44	5.33	5.32	5.12	5.05	5.05	5.27

Source: *International Monetary Fund (IMF)/Euromonitor International research*
Notes: *Annual average market exchange rates*

Economic Statistics

Table 8.39

Exchange Rates Against the US$ by Month 2008

Units of national currency per US$

	January	February	March	April	May	June	July	August	September	October	November	December
Western Europe												
Austria	0.68	0.67	0.64	0.63	0.64	0.64	0.63	0.66	0.69	0.75	0.78	0.74
Belgium	0.68	0.67	0.64	0.63	0.64	0.64	0.63	0.66	0.69	0.75	0.78	0.74
Cyprus	0.68	0.67	0.64	0.63	0.64	0.64	0.63	0.66	0.69	0.75	0.78	0.74
Denmark	5.06	5.05	4.80	4.74	4.79	4.79	4.73	4.98	5.19	5.60	5.85	5.57
Finland	0.68	0.67	0.64	0.63	0.64	0.64	0.63	0.66	0.69	0.75	0.78	0.74
France	0.68	0.67	0.64	0.63	0.64	0.64	0.63	0.66	0.69	0.75	0.78	0.74
Germany	0.68	0.67	0.64	0.63	0.64	0.64	0.63	0.66	0.69	0.75	0.78	0.74
Gibraltar	0.51	0.51	0.50	0.50	0.51	0.51	0.50	0.51	0.56	0.59	0.65	0.67
Greece	0.68	0.67	0.64	0.63	0.64	0.64	0.63	0.66	0.69	0.75	0.78	0.74
Iceland	64.30	66.48	71.60	74.05	75.17	79.13	78.42	81.64	91.22	114.09	135.31	123.98
Ireland	0.68	0.67	0.64	0.63	0.64	0.64	0.63	0.66	0.69	0.75	0.78	0.74
Italy	0.68	0.67	0.64	0.63	0.64	0.64	0.63	0.66	0.69	0.75	0.78	0.74
Liechtenstein	1.10	1.09	1.01	1.01	1.04	1.04	1.03	1.09	1.11	1.14	1.19	1.15
Luxembourg	0.68	0.67	0.64	0.63	0.64	0.64	0.63	0.66	0.69	0.75	0.78	0.74
Malta	0.68	0.67	0.64	0.63	0.64	0.64	0.63	0.66	0.69	0.75	0.78	0.74
Monaco	0.68	0.67	0.64	0.63	0.64	0.64	0.63	0.66	0.69	0.75	0.78	0.74
Netherlands	0.68	0.67	0.64	0.63	0.64	0.64	0.63	0.66	0.69	0.75	0.78	0.74
Norway	5.41	5.39	5.13	5.06	5.05	5.14	5.10	5.33	5.68	6.46	6.92	7.01
Portugal	0.68	0.67	0.64	0.63	0.64	0.64	0.63	0.66	0.69	0.75	0.78	0.74
Spain	0.68	0.67	0.64	0.63	0.64	0.64	0.63	0.66	0.69	0.75	0.78	0.74
Sweden	6.41	6.35	6.06	5.95	5.99	6.03	6.00	6.28	6.66	7.41	7.96	8.02
Switzerland	1.10	1.09	1.01	1.01	1.04	1.04	1.03	1.09	1.11	1.14	1.19	1.15
Turkey	1.17	1.19	1.24	1.30	1.25	1.23	1.21	1.18	1.24	1.48	1.59	1.54
United Kingdom	0.51	0.51	0.50	0.50	0.51	0.51	0.50	0.51	0.56	0.59	0.65	0.67
Eastern Europe												
Albania	83.39	83.89	80.32	77.79	78.45	78.46	77.24	81.12	85.65	92.62	96.84	90.96
Belarus	2,150.01	2,148.01	2,145.91	2,143.64	2,136.53	2,128.77	2,119.15	2,111.44	2,112.06	2,114.26	2,137.23	2,189.82
Bosnia-Herzegovina	1.33	1.33	1.26	1.24	1.26	1.26	1.24	1.31	1.36	1.47	1.54	1.44
Bulgaria	1.33	1.33	1.26	1.24	1.26	1.26	1.24	1.31	1.36	1.47	1.54	1.46
Croatia	4.99	4.93	4.69	4.61	4.66	4.67	4.58	4.80	4.96	5.36	5.61	5.38
Czech Republic	17.70	17.21	16.25	15.92	16.12	15.63	14.92	16.23	17.05	18.58	19.77	19.48
Estonia	10.64	10.61	10.08	9.93	10.05	10.06	9.92	10.44	10.89	11.77	12.29	11.66
Georgia	1.59	1.57	1.51	1.45	1.45	1.43	1.41	1.41	1.40	1.41	1.59	1.66
Hungary	174.11	177.69	167.56	161.03	158.88	155.92	147.06	157.45	167.43	193.23	208.22	196.78
Latvia	0.48	0.48	0.45	0.45	0.45	0.45	0.45	0.48	0.49	0.52	0.55	0.52
Lithuania	2.35	2.35	2.23	2.19	2.22	2.22	2.19	2.29	2.40	2.58	2.71	2.57
Macedonia	41.69	41.63	39.54	38.90	39.37	39.33	38.79	40.79	42.59	45.79	48.27	45.73
Moldova	11.29	11.23	10.82	10.46	10.34	10.08	9.81	9.68	9.93	10.30	10.37	10.39
Poland	2.45	2.43	2.28	2.19	2.19	2.17	2.07	2.19	2.35	2.70	2.92	2.97
Romania	2.51	2.48	2.40	2.31	2.35	2.35	2.27	2.36	2.52	2.81	2.96	2.90
Russia	24.50	24.53	23.76	23.51	23.73	23.64	23.35	24.13	25.28	26.35	27.31	28.13
Slovakia	0.68	0.67	0.64	0.63	0.64	0.64	0.63	0.66	0.69	0.75	0.78	0.74
Slovenia	0.68	0.67	0.64	0.63	0.64	0.64	0.63	0.66	0.69	0.75	0.78	0.74
Ukraine	5.05	5.05	5.05	5.05	4.99	4.85	4.84	4.84	4.85	5.04	6.00	7.58

Source:*International Monetary Fund (IMF)/Euromonitor International research*

Table 8.40

Exchange Rates Against the EUR 1985-2008

Units of national currency per EUR

	1985	1990	1995	2000	2003	2004	2005	2006	2007	2008
Western Europe										
Austria	1.00	1.00	1.00	1.00	1.00	1.00	1.00	1.00	1.00	1.00
Belgium	1.00	1.00	1.00	1.00	1.00	1.00	1.00	1.00	1.00	1.00
Cyprus	1.00	1.00	1.00	1.00	1.00	1.00	1.00	1.00	1.00	1.00
Denmark	8.09	7.88	7.33	7.46	7.44	7.44	7.46	7.46	7.46	7.50
Finland	1.00	1.00	1.00	1.00	1.00	1.00	1.00	1.00	1.00	1.00
France	1.00	1.00	1.00	1.00	1.00	1.00	1.00	1.00	1.00	1.00
Germany	1.00	1.00	1.00	1.00	1.00	1.00	1.00	1.00	1.00	1.00
Gibraltar	0.59	0.72	0.83	0.61	0.69	0.68	0.68	0.68	0.68	0.80
Greece	1.00	1.00	1.00	1.00	1.00	1.00	1.00	1.00	1.00	1.00
Iceland	31.67	74.22	84.62	72.51	86.64	87.21	78.32	88.05	87.80	129.43
Ireland	1.00	1.00	1.00	1.00	1.00	1.00	1.00	1.00	1.00	1.00
Italy	1.00	1.00	1.00	1.00	1.00	1.00	1.00	1.00	1.00	1.00
Liechtenstein	1.88	1.77	1.55	1.56	1.52	1.55	1.55	1.57	1.65	1.59
Luxembourg	1.00	1.00	1.00	1.00	1.00	1.00	1.00	1.00	1.00	1.00
Malta	1.00	1.00	1.00	1.00	1.00	1.00	1.00	1.00	1.00	1.00
Monaco	1.00	1.00	1.00	1.00	1.00	1.00	1.00	1.00	1.00	1.00
Netherlands	1.00	1.00	1.00	1.00	1.00	1.00	1.00	1.00	1.00	1.00
Norway	6.56	7.97	8.29	8.12	8.00	8.38	8.01	8.05	8.03	8.30
Portugal	1.00	1.00	1.00	1.00	1.00	1.00	1.00	1.00	1.00	1.00
Spain	1.00	1.00	1.00	1.00	1.00	1.00	1.00	1.00	1.00	1.00
Sweden	6.57	7.54	9.33	8.45	9.13	9.13	9.29	9.26	9.26	9.70
Switzerland	1.88	1.77	1.55	1.56	1.52	1.55	1.55	1.57	1.65	1.59
Turkey	0.00	0.00	0.06	0.58	1.70	1.77	1.67	1.79	1.79	1.92
United Kingdom	0.59	0.72	0.83	0.61	0.69	0.68	0.68	0.68	0.68	0.80
Eastern Europe										
Albania	5.34	9.86	121.25	132.55	137.64	127.70	124.20	123.08	123.94	123.47
Belarus			15.07	808.65	2,316.90	2,684.07	2,678.51	2,690.62	2,941.50	3,144.18
Bosnia-Herzegovina			1.96	1.96	1.96	1.96	1.96	1.96	1.96	1.97
Bulgaria	0.00	0.00	0.09	1.96	1.96	1.96	1.96	1.96	1.96	1.97
Croatia			6.84	7.63	7.57	7.50	7.40	7.32	7.35	7.26
Czech Republic		22.86	34.72	35.60	31.86	31.93	29.79	28.35	27.82	25.12
Estonia			15.00	15.65	15.65	15.65	15.65	15.64	15.67	15.74
Georgia			1.65	1.82	2.42	2.38	2.25	2.23	2.29	2.19
Hungary	38.25	80.49	164.39	260.26	253.35	251.91	248.20	263.96	251.68	253.30
Latvia			0.69	0.56	0.65	0.67	0.70	0.70	0.70	0.71
Lithuania			5.23	3.69	3.46	3.45	3.45	3.45	3.46	3.47
Macedonia			49.55	60.79	61.36	61.39	61.29	61.23	61.31	61.62
Moldova			5.88	11.47	15.75	15.32	15.67	16.47	16.64	15.29
Poland	0.01	1.21	3.17	4.01	4.39	4.54	4.02	3.89	3.79	3.55
Romania	0.00	0.00	0.27	2.00	3.75	4.06	3.62	3.52	3.34	3.71
Russia			5.96	25.94	34.67	35.80	35.17	34.11	35.06	36.58
Slovakia	1.00	1.00	1.00	1.00	1.00	1.00	1.00	1.00	1.00	1.00
Slovenia	1.00	1.00	1.00	1.00	1.00	1.00	1.00	1.00	1.00	1.00
Ukraine			1.93	5.02	6.02	6.61	6.37	6.34	6.92	7.75

Source: *European Central Bank/Euromonitor International research*
Notes: *Annual average market exchange rates*

Economic Statistics

Table 8.41

Exchange Rates Against the EUR by Month 2007-2008

Units of national currency per EUR

	July 2007	August 2007	September 2007	October 2007	November 2007	December 2007	January 2008	February 2008	March 2008	April 2008	May 2008	June 2008
Western Europe												
Austria	1.00	1.00	1.00	1.00	1.00	1.00	1.00	1.00	1.00	1.00	1.00	1.00
Belgium	1.00	1.00	1.00	1.00	1.00	1.00	1.00	1.00	1.00	1.00	1.00	1.00
Cyprus	1.00	1.00	1.00	1.00	1.00	1.00	1.00	1.00	1.00	1.00	1.00	1.00
Denmark	7.46	7.47	7.36	7.48	7.47	7.48	7.44	7.44	7.43			
Finland	1.00	1.00	1.00	1.00	1.00	1.00	1.00	1.00	1.00	1.00	1.00	1.00
France	1.00	1.00	1.00	1.00	1.00	1.00	1.00	1.00	1.00	1.00	1.00	1.00
Germany	1.00	1.00	1.00	1.00	1.00	1.00	1.00	1.00	1.00	1.00	1.00	1.00
Gibraltar	0.91	0.91	0.91	0.63	0.64	0.65	0.75	0.75	0.77	0.80	0.79	0.79
Greece	1.00	1.00	1.00	1.00	1.00	1.00	1.00	1.00	1.00	1.00	1.00	1.00
Iceland	83.28	88.87	87.39	86.55	89.36	90.86	94.51	97.86	110.85			
Ireland	1.00	1.00	1.00	1.00	1.00	1.00	1.00	1.00	1.00	1.00	1.00	1.00
Italy	1.00	1.00	1.00	1.00	1.00	1.00	1.00	1.00	1.00	1.00	1.00	1.00
Liechtenstein	1.66	1.64	1.62	1.68	1.65	1.66	1.62	1.61	1.57			
Luxembourg	1.00	1.00	1.00	1.00	1.00	1.00	1.00	1.00	1.00	1.00	1.00	1.00
Malta	1.00	1.00	1.00	1.00	1.00	1.00	1.00	1.00	1.00	1.00	1.00	1.00
Monaco	1.00	1.00	1.00	1.00	1.00	1.00	1.00	1.00	1.00	1.00	1.00	1.00
Netherlands	1.00	1.00	1.00	1.00	1.00	1.00	1.00	1.00	1.00	1.00	1.00	1.00
Norway	7.96	8.00	7.74	7.72	7.97	8.03	7.95	7.93	7.94			
Portugal	1.00	1.00	1.00	1.00	1.00	1.00	1.00	1.00	1.00	1.00	1.00	1.00
Spain	1.00	1.00	1.00	1.00	1.00	1.00	1.00	1.00	1.00	1.00	1.00	1.00
Sweden	9.20	9.36	9.17	9.20	9.31	9.45	9.42	9.35	9.38			
Switzerland	1.66	1.64	1.62	1.68	1.65	1.66	1.62	1.61	1.57			
Turkey	1.76	1.80	1.73	1.70	1.75	1.72	1.72	1.75	1.92			
United Kingdom	0.68	0.68	0.68	0.70	0.71	0.72	0.75	0.75	0.77			
Eastern Europe												
Albania	122.60	122.62	122.36	122.79	122.13	121.25	122.57	123.49	124.35			
Belarus	2,948.73	2,934.34	2,947.34	3,067.84	3,165.87	3,144.56	3,160.24	3,161.88	3,322.17			
Bosnia-Herzegovina	1.96	1.96	1.93	1.96	1.96	1.96	1.95	1.95	1.95			
Bulgaria	1.96	1.96	1.93	1.96	1.96	1.96	1.95	1.95	1.95			
Croatia	7.32	7.34	7.24	7.35	7.36	7.33	7.33	7.26	7.26			
Czech Republic	28.38	27.96	27.25	27.42	26.78	26.34	26.02	25.33	25.16			
Estonia	15.68	15.70	15.45	15.69	15.68	15.68	15.64	15.62	15.61			
Georgia	2.29	2.28	2.28	2.34	2.39	2.34	2.34	2.30	2.33			
Hungary	247.39	256.13	250.29	251.56	254.72	253.88	255.92	261.56	259.41			
Latvia	0.71	0.71	0.70	0.71	0.70	0.70	0.70	0.70	0.70			
Lithuania	3.46	3.47	3.42	3.47	3.46	3.46	3.46	3.45	3.45			
Macedonia	61.39	61.42	60.47	61.42	61.40	61.37	61.27	61.27	61.21			
Moldova	16.72	16.42	16.17	16.39	16.67	16.48	16.60	16.54	16.76			
Poland	3.78	3.83	3.74	3.72	3.67	3.61	3.61	3.58	3.53			
Romania	3.14	3.24	3.30	3.36	3.48	3.54	3.69	3.65	3.71			
Russia	35.13	35.04	34.77	35.52	36.00	35.87	36.01	36.12	36.78			
Slovakia	33.42	33.70	33.44	33.78	33.30	33.41	33.51	33.11	32.48			
Slovenia	1.00	1.00	1.00	1.00	1.00	1.00	1.00	1.00	1.00	1.00	1.00	1.00
Ukraine	6.94	6.90	6.93	7.21	7.43	7.37	7.42	7.43	7.82			

Source:*European Central Bank/Euromonitor International research*

Education

Table 9.1

Education Statistcs 2008
As stated

	literacy rate (% of population aged 15+)	Compulsory education commencement (years)	School leaving age (years)
Western Europe			
Austria	99.9	6	14
Belgium	99.9	6	18
Cyprus	97.9	6	14
Denmark	99.2	7	16
Finland	99.0	7	16
France	99.0	6	16
Germany	99.9	6	18
Gibraltar	99.9	5	14
Greece	97.2	6	14
Iceland	99.9	6	16
Ireland	99.0	6	15
Italy	98.9	6	14
Liechtenstein	99.9	6	14
Luxembourg	99.9	6	15
Malta	91.8	5	15
Monaco	99.0	6	15
Netherlands	99.5	5	17
Norway	99.9	6	16
Portugal	95.2	6	14
Spain	97.5	6	16
Sweden	99.2	7	16
Switzerland	99.9	7	15
Turkey	89.2	6	14
United Kingdom	99.8	5	16
Eastern Europe			
Albania	99.1	6	13
Belarus	99.7	6	16
Bosnia-Herzegovina			
Bulgaria	98.3	7	14
Croatia	98.8	7	14
Czech Republic		6	15
Estonia	99.8	7	15
Georgia	99.0	6	15
Hungary	98.9	7	16
Latvia	99.8	7	15
Lithuania	99.7	7	15
Macedonia	97.1	7	14
Moldova	99.3	7	15
Poland	99.3	7	15
Romania	97.7	7	14
Russia	99.5	6	15
Slovakia		6	15
Slovenia	99.7	6	14
Ukraine	99.7	6	17

Source:*Euromonitor International from UNESCO/national statistics*

Table 9.2

Pre-primary Education: Schools, Staff and Pupils: 2008
As stated

	Pre-Primary Schools	Staff ('000)	Pupils ('000)	Pupil to Staff Ratio
Western Europe				
Austria	5,236	16.9	217.2	12.8
Belgium	4,969	30.2	414.3	13.7
Cyprus		1.2	21.4	18.0
Denmark	1,923	42.7	255.3	6.0
Finland	2,968	12.0	141.1	11.8
France	17,231	142.7	2,672.0	18.7
Germany	691	218.2	2,506.5	11.5
Gibraltar		0.0	0.5	24.1
Greece	5,712	12.0	144.0	12.0
Iceland		1.7	17.7	10.1
Ireland		5.1		
Italy	24,312	135.0	1,685.6	12.5
Liechtenstein		0.1	0.8	8.2
Luxembourg		1.3	15.1	11.4
Malta		1.6	7.5	4.7
Monaco		0.1	0.8	12.3
Netherlands	7,471		362.2	
Norway	6,690		165.4	
Portugal	7,159	19.9	271.2	13.7
Spain		124.4	1,627.2	13.1
Sweden	6,918	35.1	339.6	9.7
Switzerland		11.1	156.5	14.1
Turkey	24,115	20.1	686.5	34.2
United Kingdom	4,179	41.7	1,101.1	26.4
Eastern Europe				
Albania		3.7	77.1	20.6
Belarus	4,275	44.4	274.5	6.2
Bosnia-Herzegovina				
Bulgaria	3,386	18.5	207.7	11.2
Croatia	1,168	6.3	93.3	14.8
Czech Republic	4,406	26.4	278.4	10.5
Estonia	625	5.0	37.6	7.4
Georgia	1,151	5.9	78.7	13.4
Hungary	4,386	29.9	326.2	10.9
Latvia	570	6.7	68.6	10.2
Lithuania	664	11.0	90.5	8.3
Macedonia		2.8	35.9	12.8
Moldova	1,337	10.5	105.6	10.0
Poland	17,270	45.8	849.8	18.6
Romania	2,562	36.9	658.8	17.9
Russia	44,306	646.3	4,693.1	7.3
Slovakia	2,893	9.3	134.7	14.4
Slovenia	797	2.3	45.9	19.9
Ukraine	15,250	131.0	1,090.5	8.3

Source:Euromonitor International from UNESCO

Table 9.3

Primary Education: Schools, Staff and Pupils: 2008
As stated

	Primary Schools	Staff ('000)	Pupils ('000)	Pupil to Staff Ratio
Western Europe				
Austria	3,126	29.4	348.3	11.9
Belgium	4,338	65.4	724.8	11.1
Cyprus	983	3.8	58.0	15.2
Denmark	2,388	78.9	413.6	5.2
Finland	3,473	24.5	362.8	14.8
France	37,398	224.6	4,092.9	18.2
Germany	16,606	240.2	3,343.3	13.9
Gibraltar		0.1	2.4	16.6
Greece	5,672	65.2	641.6	9.8
Iceland		4.9	29.8	6.1
Ireland	3,286	29.9	471.5	15.8
Italy	17,499	269.0	2,827.9	10.5
Liechtenstein		0.3	2.3	8.0
Luxembourg		3.4	36.3	10.8
Malta		1.9	28.4	14.8
Monaco		0.1	1.7	14.9
Netherlands	6,950	139.2	1,269.8	9.1
Norway	1,839	46.4	428.1	9.2
Portugal	9,979	75.2	735.2	9.8
Spain		187.9	2,729.6	14.5
Sweden	4,847	58.3	635.0	10.9
Switzerland		40.2	506.2	12.6
Turkey	34,570	383.6	7,961.7	20.8
United Kingdom	22,054	241.3	4,349.5	18.0
Eastern Europe				
Albania		10.7	229.0	21.5
Belarus	536	20.2	334.7	16.6
Bosnia-Herzegovina				
Bulgaria	1,955	16.1	233.7	14.5
Croatia	2,133	11.8	194.5	16.4
Czech Republic	3,594	28.1	412.7	14.7
Estonia	300	7.5	72.0	9.7
Georgia	2,321	37.3	292.8	7.9
Hungary	3,418	38.7	385.4	10.0
Latvia	50	6.3	65.8	10.5
Lithuania	104	10.5	131.7	12.5
Macedonia		5.6	100.4	18.0
Moldova	370	9.8	158.2	16.1
Poland	13,838	233.6	2,350.9	10.1
Romania	6,279	53.9	871.4	16.2
Russia	19,519	278.2	4,944.3	17.8
Slovakia	2,229	13.0	217.2	16.6
Slovenia	444	6.2	93.3	15.2
Ukraine	26,455	103.8	1,584.9	15.3

Source: Euromonitor International from UNESCO

Education Statistics

Table 9.4

Secondary Education: Staff and Pupils: 2008

As stated

	Staff ('000)	Total Pupils ('000)	Pupils in Training Colleges ('000)	Pupils in Technical Colleges ('000)	Pupil to Staff Ratio
Western Europe					
Austria	71.9	786.0	138.9	346.6	10.9
Belgium	83.5	841.1	679.2	110.1	10.1
Cyprus	6.1	64.8		4.0	10.5
Denmark	71.3	461.9	125.2	130.7	6.5
Finland	20.9	439.2	137.4	271.4	21.0
France	531.8	5,962.2	728.4	1,514.4	11.2
Germany	592.0	8,049.8	2,800.6	1,807.5	13.6
Gibraltar	0.2	1.9			11.2
Greece	88.1	688.0	114.7	110.0	7.8
Iceland	3.4	35.1		7.8	10.4
Ireland	24.0	307.9	54.0	95.1	12.8
Italy	426.1	4,541.6	741.1	2,076.8	10.7
Liechtenstein	0.2	3.2		1.1	15.9
Luxembourg	3.9	38.6		10.9	9.9
Malta	4.2	40.3		20.9	9.7
Monaco	0.4	3.1		0.5	8.3
Netherlands	105.5	1,435.4	466.6	374.3	13.6
Norway	48.3	428.5	148.0	4.9	8.9
Portugal	99.2	658.3	188.6	104.4	6.6
Spain	286.7	3,057.5	443.6		10.7
Sweden	83.5	789.3	126.9	83.2	9.5
Switzerland	57.3	597.6	213.7	38.8	10.4
Turkey	142.3	5,615.5	1,470.8	1,277.0	39.5
United Kingdom	422.5	5,167.1	3,301.1	1,740.8	12.2
Eastern Europe					
Albania	24.0	418.6		35.6	17.4
Belarus	101.2	822.1	171.8	161.1	8.1
Bosnia-Herzegovina	7.9	105.5			13.3
Bulgaria	55.1	630.1	1.2	242.6	11.4
Croatia	45.0	390.6	158.4	149.2	8.7
Czech Republic	88.0	949.8	188.3	245.5	10.8
Estonia	7.1	117.1	19.2	9.9	16.5
Georgia	22.5	314.8		7.3	14.0
Hungary	88.9	932.4		135.2	10.5
Latvia	25.4	239.0	21.0	17.3	9.4
Lithuania	40.3	388.3	0.2	47.5	9.6
Macedonia	15.4	207.5		56.9	13.5
Moldova	30.3	75.0		23.9	2.5
Poland	270.3	3,130.6	245.0	643.3	11.6
Romania	153.8	1,868.4	327.2	134.8	12.1
Russia	1,245.0	9,598.0	1,531.1	2,535.6	7.7
Slovakia	47.9	591.9	46.7	69.3	12.4
Slovenia	14.6	160.7	17.4	97.7	11.0
Ukraine	339.1	3,410.7	487.4	2,205.0	10.1

Source: *Euromonitor International from UNESCO*

Education Statistics

Table 9.5

Higher and University Education: Establishments, Staff and Students: 2008
As stated

	Establish-ments	Teaching Staff ('000)	Students ('000)	Student to Staff Ratio	University Teachers ('000)	University Teachers (% of total)	University Students ('000)	University Students (% of total)	University Students to Staff Ratio
Western Europe									
Austria	194	47.2	268.3	5.7	17.3	36.8	245.9	91.6	14.2
Belgium		26.5	405.9	15.3	26.2	98.9	193.2	47.6	7.4
Cyprus		2.0	21.6	11.0	0.3	13.9	5.6	26.2	20.8
Denmark	172	20.4	236.2	11.5			200.9	85.1	
Finland	22	19.2	313.9	16.3	8.3	42.9	313.8	100.0	38.0
France	275	147.4	2,224.0	15.1	76.4	51.9	1,670.4	75.1	21.9
Germany	384	289.4	2,314.3	8.0	248.7	85.9	2,251.3	97.3	9.1
Gibraltar									
Greece	22	31.7	702.7	22.2	17.6	55.5	427.4	60.8	24.3
Iceland		2.0	16.4	8.0	1.2	58.1	16.4	99.7	13.8
Ireland	34	12.7	187.9	14.8	8.1	63.7	133.7	71.1	16.5
Italy		106.3	2,051.1	19.3	104.4	98.2	2,040.4	99.5	19.5
Liechtenstein			0.7				0.7	100.0	
Luxembourg		0.3	2.5	8.1			1.7	69.1	
Malta		0.8	9.2	11.7	0.6	74.7	8.0	86.2	13.5
Monaco									
Netherlands	63	44.1	615.1	14.0			221.4	36.0	
Norway	69	17.9	216.0	12.1	11.4	63.9	214.8	99.4	18.8
Portugal	339	38.3	347.5	9.1	31.0	80.8	339.8	97.8	11.0
Spain	3,156	152.4	1,757.2	11.5	112.9	74.1	1,518.2	86.4	13.4
Sweden		34.8	416.8	12.0	38.3	110.1	397.2	95.3	10.4
Switzerland		30.9	212.2	6.9	11.0	35.6	178.0	83.9	16.2
Turkey	1,294	88.5	2,514.6	28.4	81.2	91.8	1,798.6	71.5	22.1
United Kingdom	143	132.7	2,375.5	17.9	45.3	34.1	1,980.8	83.4	43.8
Eastern Europe									
Albania		2.5	91.9	36.5	1.3	51.2	63.4	69.0	49.2
Belarus	57	41.8	580.0	13.9	29.5	70.4	429.7	74.1	14.6
Bosnia-Herzegovina			71.6						
Bulgaria	53	23.9	257.5	10.8	25.1	104.7	225.8	87.7	9.0
Croatia	120	10.4	145.4	14.0	7.8	75.1	100.0	68.8	12.8
Czech Republic	255	20.2	351.9	17.4	20.5	101.8	322.4	91.6	15.7
Estonia	32	6.2	70.5	11.4	3.1	49.6	48.2	68.4	15.7
Georgia		10.9	129.5	11.9	15.6	143.4	129.5	100.0	8.3
Hungary	71	29.9	452.4	15.1	21.7	72.6	423.2	93.5	19.5
Latvia	62	6.5	133.9	20.6	6.3	96.5	113.4	84.7	18.1
Lithuania	50	13.5	212.8	15.8	10.3	76.7	152.4	71.6	14.8
Macedonia		3.5	49.2	14.2	3.4	97.2	48.6	98.8	14.4
Moldova	26	8.5	154.5	18.2	6.4	75.8	139.3	90.2	21.6
Poland	462	105.8	2,235.5	21.1	23.3	22.1	2,211.3	98.9	94.7
Romania	104	32.9	995.0	30.2	32.8	99.5	988.5	99.3	30.1
Russia	1,077	712.6	9,670.3	13.6			7,760.0	80.2	
Slovakia	32	13.6	231.2	16.9	13.5	98.7	231.1	100.0	17.2
Slovenia	45	5.0	123.9	25.0	4.1	82.5	73.8	59.6	18.1
Ukraine	351	198.3	3,014.5	15.2			2,596.5	86.1	

Source: Euromonitor International from UNESCO

Education Statistics

Table 9.6

Foreign Students in Higher Education in Host Countries 1985-2008
'000

	1985	1990	1995	2000	2003	2004	2005	2006	2007	2008
Western Europe										
Austria		17.9	26.3	30.4	31.1	33.7	34.7	36.1	37.3	38.6
Belgium		20.7	32.4	38.8	41.9	37.1	36.3	35.4	33.2	31.9
Cyprus				2.0	5.3	6.7	7.4	8.1	9.0	9.8
Denmark		7.7	11.1	16.5	22.1	24.0	25.9	27.4	28.6	29.6
Finland		1.6	3.4	5.6	7.4	7.9	8.5	9.2	9.7	10.0
France		136.0	138.2	137.1	221.6	237.6	249.7	258.9	267.6	277.6
Germany		107.0	159.9	187.0	240.6	246.1	246.3	248.4	250.1	251.4
Gibraltar										
Greece		1.5	2.5	3.2	12.5	14.4	16.3	17.6	18.7	19.5
Iceland				0.4	0.6	0.5	0.5	0.4	0.4	0.3
Ireland		3.3	5.8	7.4	10.2	12.7	13.9	14.6	15.4	16.0
Italy		21.4	22.4	24.9	36.1	40.6	44.1	47.9	51.6	54.6
Liechtenstein						0.4	0.5	0.5	0.5	0.6
Luxembourg				0.7	0.7	0.7	0.7	0.7	0.7	0.7
Malta				0.4	0.4	0.4	0.5	0.5	0.6	0.6
Monaco										
Netherlands		8.9	9.7	14.0	20.5	21.3	22.8	24.1	25.1	26.4
Norway		6.9	11.2	8.7	11.1	12.4	13.6	14.6	15.5	16.3
Portugal		3.8	7.2	11.2	15.5	16.2	17.1	17.9	18.5	19.2
Spain		10.3	19.1	40.7	53.6	41.7	38.8	36.7	35.0	32.8
Sweden		14.6	19.4	25.5	32.5	36.5	39.1	43.4	46.0	48.6
Switzerland		22.6	24.1	26.0	32.8	35.7	37.0	39.6	41.2	43.0
Turkey		7.7	14.1	17.7	15.7	15.3	16.4	17.1	17.4	17.9
United Kingdom		80.2	197.2	222.9	255.2	300.1	327.6	360.5	384.1	412.1
Eastern Europe										
Albania				0.7	0.5	0.5	0.4	0.4	0.4	0.3
Belarus			1.8	2.7	1.0	2.4	3.0	3.3	3.6	3.8
Bosnia-Herzegovina										
Bulgaria		7.3	8.2	8.1	8.0	8.3	8.4	8.5	8.5	8.6
Croatia			0.3	1.2	2.8	3.4	3.8	4.3	4.6	5.1
Czech Republic			3.3	5.7	12.5	14.9	18.4	22.9	25.6	29.3
Estonia			0.4	0.9	1.1	0.8	0.8	0.8	0.8	0.8
Georgia				0.2	0.9	1.1	1.2	1.3	1.4	1.5
Hungary		3.3	6.9	9.9	12.2	12.9	12.9	12.5	12.3	12.0
Latvia			0.6	6.0	2.4	1.3	1.2	1.0	0.9	0.8
Lithuania			0.3	0.6	0.7	0.8	0.9	0.9	0.9	1.0
Macedonia				0.2	0.1	0.1	0.2	0.2	0.2	0.2
Moldova					2.4	2.4	2.5	2.6	2.6	2.6
Poland		4.3	5.6	6.0	7.6	8.1	8.8	9.4	9.8	10.3
Romania		8.1	12.9	12.6	10.5	11.6	12.7	14.8	16.5	18.5
Russia			27.4	50.6	68.6	75.8	80.7	84.6	87.8	91.4
Slovakia			1.8	1.6	1.5	1.6	1.6	1.9	2.1	2.2
Slovenia			0.4	0.7	0.8	0.9	1.0	1.0	1.1	1.2
Ukraine			19.1	16.1	18.2	15.6	14.9	14.3	13.6	12.9

Source: *Euromonitor International from UNESCO*

Education Statistics

Table 9.7

Foreign students as % of All Higher Education Students 1985-2008
%

	1985	1990	1995	2000	2003	2004	2005	2006	2007	2008
Western Europe										
Austria		9.0	11.3	11.6	13.5	14.1	14.2	14.3	14.3	14.4
Belgium		7.9	9.2	10.9	11.2	9.6	9.3	9.0	8.3	7.9
Cyprus				19.5	28.9	32.1	36.6	39.3	42.3	45.6
Denmark		5.7	6.5	8.7	11.0	11.1	11.2	12.0	12.2	12.5
Finland		1.0	1.7	2.1	2.5	2.6	2.8	3.0	3.1	3.2
France		8.6	6.7	6.8	10.5	11.0	11.4	11.8	12.1	12.5
Germany			7.4	9.1	10.7	10.6	10.9	10.8	10.8	10.9
Gibraltar										
Greece		0.5	0.9	0.8	2.2	2.4	2.5	2.7	2.7	2.8
Iceland				4.2	4.4	3.3	3.0	2.6	2.3	2.1
Ireland		4.0	4.8	4.6	5.6	6.7	7.4	7.8	8.2	8.5
Italy		1.5	1.2	1.4	1.9	2.0	2.2	2.4	2.5	2.7
Liechtenstein						77.4	85.6	77.0	77.1	77.0
Luxembourg				27.8	22.8	24.0	26.0	27.2	28.9	30.0
Malta				5.6	4.6	5.6	5.1	5.8	6.2	6.4
Monaco										
Netherlands		1.9	1.9	2.9	3.9	3.9	4.0	4.2	4.2	4.3
Norway		5.2	6.5	4.6	5.2	5.8	6.4	6.8	7.2	7.5
Portugal		2.3	2.4	3.0	3.9	4.1	4.5	4.9	5.2	5.5
Spain		0.9	1.3	2.2	2.9	2.3	2.1	2.1	2.0	1.9
Sweden		8.1	7.9	7.4	7.8	8.5	9.2	10.3	11.0	11.7
Switzerland		16.9	16.3	16.6	17.7	18.2	18.5	19.3	19.7	20.3
Turkey		1.1	1.2	1.2	0.8	0.8	0.8	0.7	0.7	0.7
United Kingdom		7.0	10.9	11.0	11.2	13.4	14.3	15.4	16.3	17.4
Eastern Europe										
Albania				1.7	1.1	0.9	0.7	0.6	0.5	0.4
Belarus			0.6	0.7	0.2	0.5	0.6	0.6	0.6	0.7
Bosnia-Herzegovina										
Bulgaria		3.9	3.7	3.1	3.5	3.6	3.5	3.5	3.4	3.3
Croatia			0.4	1.2	2.3	2.7	2.8	3.1	3.3	3.5
Czech Republic			1.8	2.2	4.3	4.7	5.5	6.8	7.4	8.3
Estonia			1.6	1.6	1.7	1.3	1.2	1.2	1.2	1.1
Georgia				0.1	0.6	0.7	0.7	0.9	1.0	1.2
Hungary		3.3	4.1	3.2	3.1	3.1	3.0	2.8	2.8	2.7
Latvia			1.4	6.6	2.0	1.0	0.9	0.8	0.7	0.6
Lithuania			0.4	0.5	0.4	0.5	0.5	0.5	0.5	0.5
Macedonia				0.7	0.2	0.3	0.3	0.4	0.4	0.4
Moldova					2.1	2.0	1.9	1.8	1.7	1.7
Poland		0.9	0.8	0.4	0.4	0.4	0.4	0.4	0.4	0.5
Romania		4.6	5.1	2.8	1.6	1.7	1.7	1.8	1.8	1.9
Russia			0.6	0.8	0.8	0.9	0.9	0.9	0.9	0.9
Slovakia			2.2	1.1	1.0	1.0	0.9	1.0	1.0	1.0
Slovenia			0.8	0.8	0.8	0.8	0.9	0.9	0.9	0.9
Ukraine			1.2	0.9	0.8	0.6	0.6	0.5	0.5	0.4

Source: Euromonitor International from UNESCO

Energy Resources and Output

Energy Statistics   **Table 10.1**

Consumption of Refinery Products 2008

'000 metric tonnes

	Motor Gasoline	Liquefied Gases	Aviation Fuels	Diesel/ Gasoil	Biofuels
Western Europe					
Austria	1,977	166	762	8,918	61
Belgium	1,523	256	985	12,432	1
Cyprus	350	52	284	527	
Denmark	1,813	74	1,058	3,905	
Finland	1,892	361	596	3,949	
France	9,088	3,410	6,807	48,896	560
Germany	20,479	2,523	9,029	47,886	3,903
Gibraltar	26		4	72	
Greece	4,214	330	1,129	7,680	
Iceland	152	2	160	388	
Ireland	1,839	150	880	3,890	
Italy	12,216	3,344	4,082	32,474	176
Liechtenstein					
Luxembourg	436	8	453	2,597	1
Malta	85	19	92	88	
Monaco					
Netherlands	4,016	1,834	3,793	7,870	
Norway	1,526	1,324	717	3,653	
Portugal	1,655	798	946	5,633	
Spain	6,752	2,178	5,859	38,094	359
Sweden	3,757	1,148	911	4,486	335
Switzerland	3,482	189	1,140	7,059	9
Turkey	2,414	4,704	2,194	10,606	
United Kingdom	17,644	5,647	13,851	28,955	279
Eastern Europe					
Albania	212	75	74	768	
Belarus	1,115	230		2,400	
Bosnia-Herzegovina	481		103	496	
Bulgaria	495	411	225	1,911	
Croatia	666	203	113	1,957	
Czech Republic	2,007	279	365	4,476	0
Estonia	277	5	53	653	
Georgia	353	34	45	266	
Hungary	1,523	366	244	3,233	41
Latvia	337	63	75	746	
Lithuania	318	309	64	1,005	10
Macedonia	103	44	5	338	
Moldova	237	58	17	387	
Poland	3,763	2,880	350	10,645	102
Romania	1,716	798	115	3,100	
Russia	26,771	8,196	10,655	24,097	
Slovakia	688	93	43	1,288	34
Slovenia	584	87	26	1,645	
Ukraine	5,229	382	201	5,328	

Source:*Euromonitor International from OECD*

Table 10.2

Consumption of Motor Gasoline 1985-2008
'000 metric tonnes

	1985	1990	1995	2000	2003	2004	2005	2006	2007	2008
Western Europe										
Austria	2,430	2,552	2,394	1,981	2,192	2,133	2,071	2,050	2,011	1,977
Belgium	2,502	2,727	2,833	2,245	2,105	1,932	1,762	1,690	1,598	1,523
Cyprus	124	163	183	206	252	282	303	321	337	350
Denmark	1,530	1,581	1,893	1,966	1,949	1,925	1,868	1,852	1,832	1,813
Finland	1,521	1,986	1,897	1,785	1,841	1,878	1,876	1,886	1,889	1,892
France	18,006	18,231	15,613	13,803	12,042	11,447	10,721	10,131	9,601	9,088
Germany	26,212	31,274	30,134	28,806	25,850	24,993	23,171	22,213	21,347	20,479
Gibraltar	5	12	16	20	22	23	24	25	26	26
Greece	1,795	2,423	2,774	3,280	3,685	3,763	3,918	4,022	4,116	4,214
Iceland	99	134	136	143	145	149	149	150	151	152
Ireland	841	885	1,037	1,493	1,583	1,627	1,712	1,747	1,793	1,839
Italy	11,820	14,055	18,496	16,863	15,839	14,940	13,936	13,336	12,739	12,216
Liechtenstein										
Luxembourg	303	412	516	582	567	530	486	470	449	436
Malta	20	65	120	61	70	58	68	75	80	85
Monaco										
Netherlands	3,395	3,445	4,023	4,031	4,185	4,158	4,097	4,077	4,047	4,016
Norway	1,587	1,785	1,664	1,619	1,646	1,637	1,580	1,563	1,545	1,526
Portugal	855	1,369	1,890	2,123	2,005	1,927	1,808	1,754	1,702	1,655
Spain	5,894	8,145	8,534	8,524	7,886	7,534	7,260	7,075	6,894	6,752
Sweden	3,750	4,166	4,251	3,977	4,007	3,926	3,862	3,825	3,786	3,757
Switzerland	3,058	3,724	3,590	3,983	3,776	3,708	3,595	3,558	3,518	3,482
Turkey	1,916	3,196	4,330	3,619	2,715	2,415	2,673	2,539	2,490	2,414
United Kingdom	20,403	24,312	21,953	21,603	19,918	19,484	18,731	18,298	17,961	17,644
Eastern Europe										
Albania	121	60	133	101	145	175	181	192	204	212
Belarus		2,363	1,154	987	960	965	1,033	1,056	1,082	1,115
Bosnia-Herzegovina		349	118	240	274	320	377	409	446	481
Bulgaria	1,213	1,391	1,083	659	586	559	544	526	509	495
Croatia		764	575	784	756	723	709	695	679	666
Czech Republic	1,069	1,161	1,637	1,858	2,100	2,092	2,055	2,039	2,020	2,007
Estonia		523	247	282	306	287	290	285	279	277
Georgia		894	134	272	328	290	334	337	340	353
Hungary	1,336	1,790	1,427	1,336	1,424	1,442	1,477	1,491	1,505	1,523
Latvia		608	412	337	346	349	342	341	339	337
Lithuania		980	603	381	360	344	338	331	323	318
Macedonia		161	207	144	126	122	117	111	107	103
Moldova		774	223	117	192	210	212	224	232	237
Poland	2,944	3,079	4,372	5,001	4,042	4,095	3,955	3,880	3,835	3,763
Romania	1,405	2,083	1,022	1,326	1,660	1,715	1,695	1,704	1,716	1,716
Russia		30,436	24,836	23,259	25,662	26,451	26,260	26,475	26,701	26,771
Slovakia	408	438	504	592	668	614	643	661	675	688
Slovenia		565	821	807	749	666	655	628	600	584
Ukraine		10,960	4,355	3,825	4,069	4,183	4,756	4,799	5,001	5,229

Source: *Euromonitor International from OECD*

Energy Statistics

Table 10.3

Consumption of Aviation Fuels 1985-2008
'000 metric tonnes

	1985	1990	1995	2000	2003	2004	2005	2006	2007	2008
Western Europe										
Austria		302	449	571	494	582	657	689	727	762
Belgium		927	920	1,481	1,503	1,387	1,247	1,147	1,062	985
Cyprus		236	260	268	323	295	291	288	286	284
Denmark		662	694	823	740	863	919	967	1,021	1,058
Finland	245	447	397	492	493	534	550	567	584	596
France		3,735	4,565	6,507	6,319	6,606	6,615	6,682	6,768	6,807
Germany		5,417	5,804	7,142	6,950	7,512	8,085	8,394	8,738	9,029
Gibraltar		7	4	4	4	4	4	4	4	4
Greece		1,231	1,213	1,290	1,131	1,176	1,150	1,148	1,138	1,129
Iceland		80	73	137	106	121	136	144	153	160
Ireland		355	380	597	744	705	814	827	846	880
Italy		2,238	2,692	3,579	3,623	3,611	3,781	3,920	3,991	4,082
Liechtenstein										
Luxembourg		128	184	312	380	414	420	433	446	453
Malta		70	72	84	77	98	88	88	91	92
Monaco										
Netherlands		1,561	2,529	3,255	3,246	3,466	3,573	3,637	3,730	3,793
Norway		489	551	636	509	587	618	657	692	717
Portugal		565	604	769	759	818	858	890	922	946
Spain		2,391	3,023	4,368	4,387	4,864	5,183	5,422	5,668	5,859
Sweden		740	827	904	682	821	824	853	894	911
Switzerland		1,115	1,273	1,576	1,236	1,166	1,182	1,163	1,145	1,140
Turkey		467	1,120	1,228	1,694	1,812	1,957	2,039	2,121	2,194
United Kingdom		6,590	7,716	10,838	10,797	11,896	12,497	12,960	13,475	13,851
Eastern Europe										
Albania		27	31	40	47	57	62	66	71	74
Belarus										
Bosnia-Herzegovina		25	37	53	61	71	84	90	97	103
Bulgaria		269	322	98	177	167	195	207	214	225
Croatia		160	85	72	68	78	93	99	106	113
Czech Republic		169	180	192	251	322	337	348	357	365
Estonia		35	18	19	18	27	41	46	50	53
Georgia		197	4	15	26	37	37	40	44	45
Hungary		160	177	224	196	212	224	230	238	244
Latvia		71	27	26	39	48	57	64	70	75
Lithuania		131	40	26	32	38	49	54	59	64
Macedonia		5	31	28	7	5	6	6	5	5
Moldova		72	12	21	13	14	15	16	16	17
Poland		215	262	269	280	275	312	325	335	350
Romania		227	179	123	114	133	110	114	114	115
Russia		17,323	9,189	8,717	9,453	9,283	10,036	10,211	10,391	10,655
Slovakia		26	39	26	33	26	38	40	41	43
Slovenia		26	19	24	25	19	22	24	25	26
Ukraine		180	242	277	200	229	213	212	206	201

Source:*Euromonitor International from OECD*

Table 10.4

Consumption of Biofuels 1998-2008
'000 metric tonnes

	1998	1999	2000	2001	2002	2003	2004	2005	2006	2007	2008
Western Europe											
Austria	14	16	17	19	20	20	25	55	58	59	61
Belgium								1	1	1	1
Cyprus											
Denmark											
Finland											
France	283	301	357	351	368	338	369	423	466	515	560
Germany	89	116	222	311	489	712	934	1,775	2,440	3,194	3,903
Gibraltar											
Greece											
Iceland											
Ireland								1			
Italy							252	176	176	176	176
Liechtenstein											
Luxembourg								1	1	1	1
Malta											
Monaco											
Netherlands											
Norway											
Portugal											
Spain			72	72	139	191	228	259	293	326	359
Sweden				16	36	74	141	150	229	274	335
Switzerland							2	6	7	8	9
Turkey											
United Kingdom					3	14	16	81	147	213	279
Eastern Europe											
Albania											
Belarus											
Bosnia-Herzegovina											
Bulgaria											
Croatia											
Czech Republic	36	45	64	46	66	64	33	3	2	1	0
Estonia											
Georgia											
Hungary								5	23	32	41
Latvia								3			
Lithuania							1	3	5	8	10
Macedonia											
Moldova											
Poland						28	13	47	66	84	102
Romania											
Russia											
Slovakia				31	3	2	1	10	20	27	34
Slovenia											
Ukraine											

Source:International Energy Association

Energy Statistics

Table 10.5

Energy Intensity 1998-2008

US$ per tonne of energy consumed

	1998	1999	2000	2001	2002	2003	2004	2005	2006	2007	2008
Western Europe											
Austria	6,116	6,174	6,530	6,459	6,674	6,638	7,066	7,244	7,824	8,487	8,550
Belgium	3,671	3,741	3,820	4,072	4,155	4,035	4,109	4,212	4,351	4,609	4,802
Cyprus											
Denmark	56,602	61,142	68,830	71,735	74,676	71,547	80,142	88,834	83,421	93,237	100,881
Finland	4,578	4,780	5,080	5,290	5,380	5,052	5,325	5,995	6,068	6,534	6,903
France	5,374	5,461	5,678	5,816	6,060	6,165	6,332	6,594	6,960	7,435	7,562
Germany	5,892	6,141	6,260	6,304	6,513	6,538	6,717	6,932	7,082	7,834	8,008
Gibraltar											
Greece	4,131	4,173	4,271	4,595	4,772	5,282	5,458	5,842	6,157	6,588	7,021
Iceland	268,538	270,835	279,995	313,395	315,597	324,084	347,439	379,996	428,379	419,673	379,798
Ireland	6,416	6,893	7,672	8,029	9,024	9,941	10,278	10,938	11,713	12,403	12,274
Italy	6,531	6,544	6,810	7,110	7,437	7,428	7,611	7,809	8,165	8,656	8,901
Liechtenstein											
Luxembourg											
Malta											
Monaco											
Netherlands	4,251	4,609	4,846	5,025	5,201	5,290	5,286	5,430	5,837	6,353	6,507
Norway	28,234	29,860	32,291	37,484	35,700	41,587	44,668	43,135	52,078	50,526	55,222
Portugal	4,684	4,903	4,922	5,175	5,418	5,483	5,811	6,024	6,345	6,836	7,351
Spain	4,584	4,751	4,898	5,142	5,445	5,571	5,804	6,217	6,713	7,043	7,612
Sweden	38,980	41,149	46,324	44,644	49,919	54,443	54,293	53,820	60,789	63,889	67,565
Switzerland	13,696	13,511	14,527	13,824	14,933	15,166	15,815	16,867	17,010	18,137	18,127
Turkey	970	1,472	2,175	3,359	4,664	5,709	6,630	7,253	7,925	8,341	9,259
United Kingdom	3,960	4,210	4,382	4,534	4,882	5,094	5,341	5,568	5,962	6,514	6,833
Eastern Europe											
Albania											
Belarus	31,795	144,083	429,932	799,525	1,205,546	1,697,354	2,088,007	2,744,385	3,151,770	3,904,055	5,139,757
Bosnia-Herzegovina											
Bulgaria	1,083	1,321	1,501	1,611	1,742	1,729	2,014	2,155	2,391	2,819	3,316
Croatia											
Czech Republic	50,094	54,082	54,720	56,681	59,428	59,172	62,907	66,839	72,724	80,563	85,533
Estonia											
Georgia											
Hungary	424,466	480,434	588,494	634,746	734,313	785,763	861,804	864,114	945,129	1,025,412	1,078,971
Latvia											
Lithuania	4,852	5,603	6,579	6,009	6,049	6,261	6,841	8,566	10,226	11,261	12,863
Macedonia											
Moldova											
Poland	6,385	7,305	8,416	8,798	9,283	9,528	10,166	10,841	11,230	12,363	13,055
Romania	905	1,477	2,172	3,132	3,939	5,224	6,348	7,267	8,496	10,996	13,331
Russia	4,366	7,930	11,688	14,405	17,048	20,704	26,339	33,642	39,794	48,714	60,865
Slovakia	1,133	1,094	1,216	1,268	1,390	1,629	1,935	2,054	2,438	3,119	3,576
Slovenia											
Ukraine	778	969	1,262	1,524	1,708	2,022	2,477	3,197	3,981	5,351	7,226

Source: *Euromonitor International from national statistics*

Energy Statistics

Table 10.6

Production of Biofuels 1998-2008

Million tonnes of oil equivalent

	1998	1999	2000	2001	2002	2003	2004	2005	2006	2007	2008
Western Europe											
Austria	14	16	17	19	20	20	40	57	101	141	182
Belgium								17	17	17	17
Cyprus											
Denmark				22	36	40	58	64	64	69	74
Finland											
France	283	295	351	349	374	405	425	488	703	853	999
Germany	89	116	222	315	495	731	954	2,018	3,516	4,765	5,910
Gibraltar											
Greece											
Iceland											
Ireland								1	3	5	7
Italy							252	176	176	176	176
Liechtenstein											
Luxembourg							1	1	1	1	1
Malta											
Monaco											
Netherlands							2	53	61	70	78
Norway											
Portugal									70		
Spain			72	72	139	191	228	259	408	531	636
Sweden				16	36	74	141	150	229	274	335
Switzerland							2	6	7	8	9
Turkey									18		
United Kingdom								11	11	11	11
Eastern Europe											
Albania											
Belarus											
Bosnia-Herzegovina											
Bulgaria											
Croatia											
Czech Republic	14	27	61	63	94	103	77	113	97	101	107
Estonia											
Georgia											
Hungary								5	23	32	41
Latvia								2			
Lithuania							3	11	17	21	25
Macedonia											
Moldova											
Poland						28	13	108	151	199	244
Romania											
Russia											
Slovakia				36	3	2	11	33	41	47	53
Slovenia											
Ukraine											

Source:*International Energy Association*

Energy Statistics

Table 10.7

Production of Crude Oil 1998-2008

Million tonnes of oil equivalent

	1998	1999	2000	2001	2002	2003	2004	2005	2006	2007	2008
Western Europe											
Austria											
Belgium											
Cyprus											
Denmark	11.6	14.6	17.7	17.0	18.1	17.9	19.1	18.4	16.7	15.2	14.0
Finland											
France											
Germany											
Gibraltar											
Greece											
Iceland											
Ireland											
Italy	5.6	5.0	4.6	4.1	5.5	5.6	5.5	6.1	5.8	5.9	5.2
Liechtenstein											
Luxembourg											
Malta											
Monaco											
Netherlands											
Norway	149.6	149.7	160.2	162.0	157.3	153.0	149.9	138.2	128.7	118.8	114.2
Portugal											
Spain											
Sweden											
Switzerland											
Turkey											
United Kingdom	132.6	137.4	126.2	116.7	115.9	106.1	95.4	84.7	76.6	76.8	72.2
Eastern Europe											
Albania											
Belarus	1.7	1.7	2.0	2.0	2.3	2.4	2.8	3.0	3.2	3.4	3.5
Bosnia-Herzegovina											
Bulgaria											
Croatia											
Czech Republic											
Estonia											
Georgia											
Hungary											
Latvia											
Lithuania											
Macedonia											
Moldova											
Poland	0.4	0.4	0.4	0.4							
Romania	6.6	6.4	6.3	6.2	6.1	5.9	5.7	5.4	5.0	4.7	4.7
Russia	304.3	304.8	323.3	348.1	379.6	421.4	458.8	470.0	480.5	491.3	488.5
Slovakia											
Slovenia											
Ukraine											

Source: BP Amoco, BP Statistical Review of World Energy
Notes: Million tonnes of oil equivalent = the amount of oil required to fuel an oil-fired plant in order to generate the same amount of electricity

Table 10.8

Electricity Production 2008

GWh/% shares

	Net Total Production	% Fossil Fuels	% Combustible Renewables and Waste	% Geothermal	% Hydroelectric	% Nuclear	% Wind Powered
Western Europe							
Austria	66,841	31.63	8.14	0.00	56.98		3.22
Belgium	87,130	39.17	5.07		1.86	53.40	0.51
Cyprus	5,014	99.98					
Denmark	36,888	71.46	9.57		0.06		18.91
Finland	78,114	43.40	11.24		16.03	28.91	0.23
France	581,990	9.99	1.00		10.25	78.21	0.46
Germany	645,352	60.34	4.75		4.17	25.41	4.96
Gibraltar	159						
Greece	61,498	86.07	0.45		10.42		3.06
Iceland	10,156	0.03	0.01	28.16	71.79		
Ireland	30,011	88.76	0.44		3.82		6.98
Italy	326,474	80.59	2.21	1.73	14.04		1.14
Liechtenstein							
Luxembourg	3,622	74.39	2.35		21.03		1.60
Malta	2,357						
Monaco							
Netherlands	109,412	86.44	6.65		0.10	3.59	3.04
Norway	141,276	0.82	0.28		98.18		0.68
Portugal	42,422	62.54	4.18	0.15	26.23		6.88
Spain	328,578	61.89	1.28		10.12	17.80	8.78
Sweden	153,373	2.26	6.70		44.37	45.92	0.74
Switzerland	68,458	1.62	3.81		50.42	44.07	0.03
Turkey	201,991	75.86	0.10	0.05	23.92		0.07
United Kingdom	371,038	74.43	3.01		2.13	19.02	1.40
Eastern Europe							
Albania	5,157	1.72			98.28		
Belarus	34,280	99.80	0.08		0.11		0.00
Bosnia-Herzegovina	14,345	58.88			41.12		
Bulgaria	45,980	45.54	0.01		10.83	43.56	0.06
Croatia	11,698	48.39	0.18		51.26		0.17
Czech Republic	84,742	65.99	1.62		2.99	29.33	0.06
Estonia	9,443	98.67	0.35		0.16		0.83
Georgia	7,794	31.05			68.95		
Hungary	34,424	55.48	5.47		0.52	38.39	0.14
Latvia	5,102	43.23	0.84		55.03		0.90
Lithuania	12,252	24.28	0.41		5.23	69.97	0.11
Macedonia	7,340	77.12			22.88		
Moldova	4,447	98.14			1.86		
Poland	155,784	95.68	2.35		1.81		0.16
Romania	65,543	60.40	0.05		31.03	8.52	
Russia	1,041,708	67.04	0.20	0.04	17.12	15.59	0.00
Slovakia	30,591	24.82	1.60		16.21	57.20	0.02
Slovenia	16,392	38.98	0.73		23.35	36.94	
Ukraine	192,970	46.21			6.86	46.91	0.02

Source:*Euromonitor International from OECD*

Energy Statistics

Table 10.9

Electricity Production by Quarter 2007-2009
GWh

	2007 1st Quarter	2007 2nd Quarter	2007 3rd Quarter	2007 4th Quarter	2008 1st Quarter	2008 2nd Quarter	2008 3rd Quarter	2008 4th Quarter	2009 1st Quarter	2009 2nd Quarter
Western Europe										
Austria	14,958.0	14,513.7	16,579.3	17,740.3	16,201.0	16,839.5	17,624.2	16,176.0	16,004.9	19,272.2
Belgium	24,010.3	22,454.4	21,183.1	23,372.1	22,216.2	20,515.0	21,247.0	23,151.4	23,383.4	21,682.5
Cyprus	1,116.8	1,081.7	1,479.4	1,129.9	1,221.3	1,129.9	1,550.7	1,111.8	1,270.7	1,222.2
Denmark	12,359.9	7,603.0	7,881.6	12,150.2	11,016.5	7,276.2	6,716.9	11,878.6	11,808.0	7,220.6
Finland	23,363.4	17,794.9	16,971.1	23,830.7	21,466.8	17,570.3	17,474.3	21,602.9	22,488.9	15,735.4
France										
Germany	170,231.7	151,604.9	148,424.9	175,091.8	173,454.9	155,809.5	149,155.7	166,932.0	162,010.2	
Gibraltar										
Greece	15,877.2	16,144.4	16,932.9	15,970.6	14,559.7	14,799.7	17,386.9	14,751.9	15,125.6	13,860.8
Iceland										
Ireland	8,108.6	6,615.2	6,879.9	8,403.5	8,063.5	6,985.3	6,885.3	8,077.4	7,728.8	6,455.9
Italy	79,456.3	77,919.3	81,292.1	83,808.3	83,335.2	79,216.1	85,129.8	78,793.4	75,744.6	71,360.0
Liechtenstein										
Luxembourg	1,183.1	934.8	847.6	1,108.2	1,122.6	516.1	859.9	1,123.6	1,092.8	
Malta										
Monaco										
Netherlands	28,591.8	23,145.8	23,729.3	29,625.5	30,473.2	24,985.5	24,438.7	29,514.7	29,330.7	25,294.5
Norway	36,289.1	30,281.5	32,911.4	36,553.6	39,804.5	32,309.2	30,556.9	38,605.0	37,771.9	25,779.6
Portugal	12,951.4	10,829.4	10,724.5	11,565.5	11,028.6	9,529.6	11,113.3	10,750.0	12,187.1	
Spain	79,693.9	75,046.7	79,574.0	82,205.4	85,040.8	78,741.0	82,481.2	82,315.2	80,018.0	
Sweden	45,092.3	37,999.8	30,146.1	39,354.7	47,143.1	37,966.1	31,143.1	37,120.7	43,005.7	31,760.0
Switzerland	15,116.3	17,659.0	19,154.0	16,175.3	15,278.5	18,556.8	18,428.3	16,193.9	16,885.8	
Turkey	45,808.2			48,565.1	51,552.2	49,353.4	54,207.2	46,878.6	48,662.9	64,586.1
United Kingdom	100,636.6	86,257.1	83,328.2	102,590.0	103,220.5	85,679.4	82,722.6	99,415.7	100,428.8	78,616.0
Eastern Europe										
Albania										
Belarus										
Bosnia-Herzegovina										
Bulgaria	11,558.6	10,397.3	10,626.0	12,330.8	12,309.0	10,566.0	10,689.2	12,415.6	12,988.1	9,448.1
Croatia	2,820.9	2,658.3	2,966.3	3,194.6	2,963.5	2,848.9	2,818.1	3,067.9	3,705.3	2,834.0
Czech Republic	23,868.8	20,963.8	20,398.0	24,188.0	24,495.5	20,238.8	18,888.2	21,119.0	23,498.8	18,733.1
Estonia										
Georgia										
Hungary	8,614.7	7,602.1	7,868.6	9,480.8	9,103.6	8,114.6	8,188.3	9,017.5	8,234.5	7,088.6
Latvia	1,989.6	1,125.9	501.3	992.8	1,632.1	1,497.0	669.3	1,303.7	1,281.4	1,443.9
Lithuania	3,697.9	3,208.8	1,755.3	3,590.1	3,830.7	3,205.0	1,666.6	3,550.1	3,780.2	2,599.9
Macedonia										
Moldova	1,763.6	594.4	391.0	1,493.7					1,755.7	457.5
Poland	41,614.0	36,398.4	37,040.2	44,195.6	41,742.2	36,509.4	36,773.8	40,758.2	42,782.4	34,872.9
Romania	16,557.2	13,923.8	14,031.6	16,859.0	18,061.0	15,279.5	15,625.3	16,577.5	17,056.1	13,817.1
Russia	276,877.1	231,482.9	225,916.8	286,086.3	292,137.0	236,691.1	235,676.6	277,203.6	275,469.0	222,727.5
Slovakia	8,456.0	7,075.0	6,572.8	7,599.5	8,641.0	7,329.6	6,896.7	7,723.4	7,277.8	6,455.4
Slovenia	4,009.1	3,556.0	3,988.1	3,491.0	3,956.1	4,206.2	4,076.2	4,153.2	4,337.0	
Ukraine	52,419.2	45,362.0	45,202.0	53,450.5	54,541.2	45,790.6	45,958.6	46,680.0	47,033.2	

Source:*Euromonitor International from OECD*

Energy Statistics

Table 10.10

Electricity Production by Month 2008
GWh

	January	February	March	April	May	June	July	August	September	October	November	December
Western Europe												
Austria	5,535.4	5,101.1	5,564.5	5,326.3	5,683.6	5,829.7	6,239.0	6,004.8	5,380.3	5,439.4	5,139.1	5,597.5
Belgium	7,946.4	7,359.7	6,910.2	6,911.2	6,688.5	6,915.3	7,271.0	7,021.5	6,954.5	7,737.1	7,408.2	8,006.2
Cyprus	463.0	416.8	341.5	325.4	359.5	444.9	551.4	541.3	458.0	373.6	335.4	402.7
Denmark	4,130.7	3,583.0	3,302.8	2,631.1	2,362.7	2,282.4	2,022.5	2,080.3	2,614.0	3,621.5	4,198.0	4,059.0
Finland	7,575.8	6,830.0	7,061.0	6,382.8	5,671.8	5,515.7	5,472.4	5,804.7	6,197.1	6,866.9	7,469.2	7,266.7
France												
Germany	59,310.0	57,289.1	56,855.8	56,670.7	51,119.3	48,019.5	49,009.6	48,623.2	51,522.9	56,274.4	54,712.8	55,944.8
Gibraltar												
Greece	5,559.9	4,862.6	4,137.1	4,483.6	4,892.0	5,424.2	6,382.1	5,884.7	5,120.1	4,809.4	4,714.9	5,227.6
Iceland												
Ireland	2,854.6	2,607.1	2,601.7	2,395.2	2,318.8	2,271.4	2,297.2	2,281.1	2,306.9	2,643.7	2,724.4	2,709.3
Italy	28,573.8	27,335.8	27,425.5	25,686.5	25,787.6	27,742.0	30,498.3	26,174.1	28,457.3	28,002.8	25,558.7	25,232.0
Liechtenstein												
Luxembourg	391.0	350.9	380.7	287.3	116.0	112.9	152.9	354.0	353.0	387.9	371.5	364.3
Malta												
Monaco												
Netherlands	10,515.8	9,767.8	10,189.6	8,979.0	8,147.6	7,858.9	7,987.0	7,845.7	8,606.0	10,237.3	9,770.8	9,506.5
Norway	13,495.0	12,806.6	13,502.9	11,193.0	10,480.8	10,635.3	10,311.4	10,048.9	10,196.5	11,747.7	12,732.3	14,125.0
Portugal	4,385.3	3,576.6	3,066.6	2,833.8	3,298.1	3,397.7	3,944.0	3,429.9	3,739.4	3,459.5	3,502.6	3,787.9
Spain	29,724.5	28,170.5	27,145.8	26,500.0	26,159.2	26,081.8	28,672.8	27,105.4	26,702.9	26,411.4	27,162.6	28,741.2
Sweden	16,237.9	15,124.1	15,781.0	14,284.0	13,224.9	10,457.2	10,191.9	9,865.5	11,085.7	12,011.1	12,158.5	12,951.2
Switzerland	5,235.1	4,925.1	5,118.3	5,055.3	6,344.7	7,156.8		5,686.6	7,036.9	5,414.8	5,445.8	5,333.2
Turkey	18,147.5	16,760.4	16,644.3	15,998.6	16,513.9	16,840.9	18,612.9	18,761.6		15,102.4	15,610.6	16,165.6
United Kingdom	35,846.8	33,390.3	33,983.5	31,317.1	27,775.4	26,586.9	27,647.0	27,324.2	27,751.4	31,529.1	32,561.0	35,325.6
Eastern Europe												
Albania												
Belarus												
Bosnia-Herzegovina												
Bulgaria	4,589.5	3,807.0	3,912.6	3,683.8	3,499.6	3,382.6	3,631.0	3,605.1	3,453.0	3,734.5	4,266.6	4,414.6
Croatia	1,027.9	957.1	978.5	992.5	864.8	991.6	961.7	924.5	931.9	859.2	936.6	1,272.1
Czech Republic	8,617.7	7,939.4	7,938.4	7,493.2	6,482.3	6,263.3	6,441.8	6,237.9	6,208.5	6,770.3	6,892.0	7,456.7
Estonia												
Georgia												
Hungary	3,207.1	2,898.6	2,998.0	2,768.4	2,614.7	2,731.5	2,839.1	2,671.0	2,678.2	3,000.0	2,953.9	3,063.6
Latvia	451.7	453.7	726.7	750.9	410.0	336.1	217.6	154.5	297.3	396.4	413.8	493.5
Lithuania	1,307.5	1,246.7	1,276.6	1,078.3	1,079.3	1,047.5	978.3	263.7	424.6	1,131.6	1,170.0	1,248.5
Macedonia												
Moldova			606.6	335.4	221.9			138.1	138.1	404.4	749.7	
Poland	14,890.0	13,460.9	13,391.3	12,592.0	11,955.2	11,962.2	12,049.0	12,152.0	12,572.8	13,650.7	13,264.1	13,843.4
Romania	6,305.3	5,923.0	5,832.8	5,240.6	5,079.3	4,959.7	5,352.1	5,230.4	5,042.8	5,434.2	5,505.2	5,638.1
Russia	103,730.5	94,815.4	93,591.1	83,444.6	79,971.4	73,275.1	75,778.0	78,170.5	81,728.1	89,100.4	89,472.0	98,631.1
Slovakia	2,962.5	2,799.5	2,878.9	2,393.1	2,756.1	2,180.4	2,323.3	2,352.9	2,220.6	2,378.3	2,628.1	2,717.0
Slovenia	1,368.4	1,269.4	1,318.4	1,404.4	1,387.4	1,414.4	1,456.4	1,321.4	1,298.4	1,332.4	1,381.4	1,439.4
Ukraine	19,418.0	17,698.5	17,424.8	15,787.7	15,266.6	14,736.3	15,498.0	15,548.3	14,912.4	14,893.3	14,817.8	16,969.0

Source: Euromonitor International from OECD

Energy Statistics

Table 10.11

Production of Natural Gas 1985-2008

Million tonnes of oil equivalent

	1985	1990	1995	2000	2003	2004	2005	2006	2007	2008
Western Europe										
Austria										
Belgium										
Cyprus										
Denmark	1.01	2.82	4.76	7.34	7.17	8.49	9.40	9.37	8.30	9.08
Finland										
France			2.40	1.97	1.70	1.53	0.97	0.95	0.80	0.55
Germany	15.68	14.33	14.46	15.19	15.92	14.73	14.22	14.05	12.87	11.72
Gibraltar										
Greece			16.11							
Iceland										
Ireland			16.40							
Italy	11.54	14.03	16.35	13.72	11.46	10.69	9.96	9.06	8.01	7.54
Liechtenstein										
Luxembourg										
Malta										
Monaco										
Netherlands	61.60	54.93	61.01	52.28	52.25	61.61	56.29	55.41	54.49	60.77
Norway	23.57	22.93	25.03	44.77	65.81	70.62	76.47	78.85	80.70	89.31
Portugal										
Spain			0.43							
Sweden										
Switzerland										
Turkey			0.20							
United Kingdom	35.71	40.93	63.73	97.54	92.58	86.72	79.35	71.97	64.87	62.65
Eastern Europe										
Albania										
Belarus		0.25	0.25	0.24	0.23	0.24	0.24	0.24	0.24	0.24
Bosnia-Herzegovina										
Bulgaria										
Croatia			1.68	1.36	1.24	1.17	1.27	1.29	1.31	1.34
Czech Republic										
Estonia										
Georgia										
Hungary	5.80	3.80	3.70	2.40	2.46	2.42	2.38	2.30	2.25	2.19
Latvia										
Lithuania										
Macedonia										
Moldova										
Poland	4.13	2.38	3.14	3.31	3.61	3.93	3.88	3.88	3.90	3.65
Romania	31.34	25.50	16.24	12.38	11.73	11.51	11.16	10.75	10.37	10.37
Russia	376.31	522.08	484.93	475.82	505.22	515.97	522.09	534.45	532.78	541.51
Slovakia			2.99	2.75	3.50	3.30	3.10	2.90	2.70	2.50
Slovenia										
Ukraine	34.92	22.89	14.82	14.57	15.76	16.64	16.92	17.15	17.23	16.87

Source:BP Amoco, BP Statistical Review of World Energy
Notes: Million tonnes of oil equivalent = the amount of oil required to fuel an oil-fired plant in order to generate the same amount of electricity

Energy Statistics

Table 10.12

Production of Natural Gas by Quarter 2007-2009

Million tonnes of oil equivalent

	2007 1st Quarter	2007 2nd Quarter	2007 3rd Quarter	2007 4th Quarter	2008 1st Quarter	2008 2nd Quarter	2008 3rd Quarter	2008 4th Quarter	2009 1st Quarter	2009 2nd Quarter
Western Europe										
Austria										
Belgium										
Cyprus										
Denmark	2.18	1.52	2.05	2.54	2.53	2.19	2.07	2.29	2.42	2.09
Finland										
France	0.21	0.17	0.22	0.20	0.16	0.15	0.12	0.12	0.11	
Germany	3.53	3.01	2.84	3.49	3.28	2.88	2.55	3.01	2.85	
Gibraltar										
Greece										
Iceland										
Ireland										
Italy	2.09	2.03	1.94	1.94	1.90	1.93	1.90	1.81	1.74	1.70
Liechtenstein										
Luxembourg										
Malta										
Monaco										
Netherlands	17.28	8.33	8.20	20.68	21.66	10.93	8.95	19.23	20.19	8.31
Norway	20.24	18.60	19.01	22.86	24.97	21.31	17.81	25.21	24.90	20.75
Portugal										
Spain										
Sweden										
Switzerland										
Turkey										
United Kingdom	18.37	15.96	12.81	17.72	17.76	15.79	12.65	16.44	15.45	13.94
Eastern Europe										
Albania										
Belarus										
Bosnia-Herzegovina										
Bulgaria										
Croatia	0.34	0.32	0.33	0.33	0.34	0.34	0.33	0.33	0.33	0.35
Czech Republic										
Estonia										
Georgia										
Hungary	0.59	0.51	0.57	0.58	0.59	0.50	0.56	0.55	0.58	0.49
Latvia										
Lithuania										
Macedonia										
Moldova										
Poland	1.09	0.99	0.85	0.97	1.03	0.92	0.77	0.92	0.96	0.83
Romania	2.74	2.63	2.43	2.57	2.79	2.47	2.46	2.65	2.72	2.34
Russia	143.13	129.63	118.19	141.82	147.14	134.90	122.30	137.18	147.84	115.91
Slovakia										
Slovenia										
Ukraine	4.42	4.24	4.24	4.32	4.26	4.12	4.18	4.32	4.21	

Source: *BP Amoco, BP Statistical Review of World Energy*
Notes: *Million tonnes of oil equivalent = the amount of oil required to fuel an oil-fired plant in order to generate the same amount of electricity*

Energy Statistics

Table 10.13

Production of Natural Gas by Month 2008

Million tonnes of oil equivalent

	January	February	March	April	May	June	July	August	September	October	November	December
Western Europe												
Austria												
Belgium												
Cyprus												
Denmark	0.89	0.81	0.84	0.80	0.82	0.56	0.75	0.70	0.62	0.64	0.79	0.86
Finland												
France	0.05	0.05	0.06	0.05	0.05	0.05	0.05	0.04	0.03	0.02	0.04	0.05
Germany	1.15	1.03	1.10	0.91	0.98	1.00	0.83	0.85	0.87	1.00	1.01	1.00
Gibraltar												
Greece												
Iceland												
Ireland												
Italy	0.63	0.61	0.66	0.64	0.66	0.63	0.62	0.66	0.62	0.63	0.58	0.59
Liechtenstein												
Luxembourg												
Malta												
Monaco												
Netherlands	7.68	6.91	7.08	5.15	2.92	2.85	2.86	2.68	3.42	5.08	6.21	7.93
Norway	8.52	7.67	8.78	7.71	7.11	6.49	7.05	5.57	5.19	7.89	8.40	8.93
Portugal												
Spain												
Sweden												
Switzerland												
Turkey												
United Kingdom	6.16	5.56	6.04	5.42	5.42	4.95	3.72	4.20	4.74	5.25	5.47	5.72
Eastern Europe												
Albania												
Belarus												
Bosnia-Herzegovina												
Bulgaria												
Croatia	0.12	0.11	0.12	0.11	0.11	0.11	0.11	0.11	0.10	0.11	0.11	0.11
Czech Republic												
Estonia												
Georgia												
Hungary	0.18	0.16	0.25	0.18	0.16	0.16	0.18	0.19	0.18	0.19	0.18	0.18
Latvia												
Lithuania												
Macedonia												
Moldova												
Poland	0.35	0.35	0.34	0.34	0.30	0.28	0.26	0.26	0.26	0.28	0.31	0.32
Romania	0.99	0.89	0.91	0.86	0.83	0.78	0.81	0.81	0.84	0.87	0.87	0.90
Russia	50.34	47.34	49.47	47.23	45.51	42.16	40.29	39.60	42.41	45.73	44.51	46.93
Slovakia												
Slovenia												
Ukraine	1.45	1.35	1.46	1.35	1.39	1.37	1.41	1.40	1.37	1.46	1.40	1.46

Source: *BP Amoco, BP Statistical Review of World Energy*
Notes: *Million tonnes of oil equivalent = the amount of oil required to fuel an oil-fired plant in order to generate the same amount of electricity*

Table 10.14

Refinery Output 1990-2008

'000 tonnes per year

	1990	1995	2000	2003	2004	2005	2006	2007	2008
Western Europe									
Austria	8,779	9,271	8,770	9,157	8,846	9,182	8,988	8,997	9,248
Belgium	29,372	29,643	38,092	45,489	43,233	37,046	36,386	38,097	37,316
Cyprus	638	830	1,181	968	279				
Denmark	7,848	9,778	8,231	8,154	7,954	7,499	7,853	7,622	7,314
Finland	10,344	11,533	12,893	13,105	13,506	12,839	13,827	14,503	15,052
France	81,320	83,694	88,576	87,523	88,406	86,293	86,839	86,060	89,160
Germany	3,480	114,414	115,973	116,165	119,954	122,675	120,571	118,469	115,810
Gibraltar									
Greece	16,678	17,651	22,232	22,113	20,991	21,240	22,245	23,047	21,813
Iceland									
Ireland	1,526	2,273	3,286	3,130	2,895	3,120	3,231	3,255	3,093
Italy	91,020	91,171	94,771	97,840	98,140	100,598	99,199	100,704	94,536
Liechtenstein									
Luxembourg									
Malta									
Monaco									
Netherlands	67,905	80,123	80,185	82,275	83,486	84,900	80,881	66,121	65,447
Norway	13,018	13,109	15,196	14,645	14,093	15,424	16,403	16,216	14,676
Portugal	11,144	13,346	12,308	13,223	13,293	13,563	13,664	12,621	12,111
Spain	52,954	55,312	59,830	57,640	59,483	60,310	61,350	59,855	60,543
Sweden	17,239	19,105	22,712	19,384	20,308	19,800	19,861	17,903	20,857
Switzerland	3,047	4,638	4,647	4,614	5,214	4,855	5,500	4,740	5,095
Turkey	22,884	27,140	23,745	26,461	26,002	25,638	26,235	25,554	24,805
United Kingdom	88,120	92,617	86,341	84,529	89,826	85,763	82,841	81,210	79,827
Eastern Europe									
Albania	675	501	311	356	399	443	502	542	580
Belarus	855	12,147	11,490	12,754	15,646	17,582	18,492	18,788	18,400
Bosnia-Herzegovina			512	76	170	143	145	116	134
Bulgaria	6,974	7,255	5,181	5,174	5,779	6,297	7,136	6,929	7,121
Croatia		5,234	5,214	5,358	5,321	5,141	4,823	5,312	5,370
Czech Republic		7,260	6,131	6,710	6,999	8,132	8,179	7,753	8,662
Estonia		313							
Georgia		40	19	23	24	13	12	39	42
Hungary	8,316	7,837	7,483	7,287	7,149	8,234	8,512	8,639	8,485
Latvia									
Lithuania		3,269	4,903	7,106	8,629	9,206	8,257	5,776	5,301
Macedonia		111	936	972	991	1,147	1,026	1,050	1,018
Moldova									
Poland	12,686	13,860	18,480	18,000	18,564	18,465	20,947	21,570	22,254
Romania	22,709	14,559	10,990	12,040	13,077	14,867	14,407	13,835	13,746
Russia	267,723	178,148	176,803	190,284	193,929	205,702	216,548	223,731	229,668
Slovakia		4,954	5,810	6,156	6,575	6,191	6,276	6,628	6,508
Slovenia		593	184	8					
Ukraine		16,554	9,788	22,414	22,068	19,222	15,175	14,708	13,579

Source: *Euromonitor International from OECD*

Energy Statistics

Table 10.15

Primary Energy Consumption: Selected Materials 2008
Million tonnes of oil equivalent

	Crude Oil	Hydroelectricity	Natural Gas	Nuclear Energy	Coal	Total
Western Europe						
Austria	13.4	7.9	8.5		3.1	33.0
Belgium	41.3	0.1	15.3	10.4	4.6	71.7
Cyprus						
Denmark	8.9		4.1		4.1	17.2
Finland	10.5	3.9	3.6	5.4	3.4	26.8
France	92.2	14.3	39.8	99.6	11.9	257.9
Germany	118.3	4.4	73.8	33.7	80.9	311.1
Gibraltar						
Greece	21.4	0.8	3.8		8.6	34.6
Iceland	0.9	2.8			0.1	3.9
Ireland	9.0	0.2	4.5		1.4	15.1
Italy	80.9	8.8	69.9		17.0	176.6
Liechtenstein						
Luxembourg						
Malta						
Monaco						
Netherlands	46.5		34.7	0.9	9.2	91.4
Norway	9.8	31.8	4.0		0.5	46.0
Portugal	13.7	1.6	4.1		3.2	22.6
Spain	77.1	3.8	35.1	13.3	14.6	143.9
Sweden	14.5	14.8	0.9	14.5	2.0	46.7
Switzerland	12.1	8.1	2.8	6.2	0.1	29.4
Turkey	32.3	7.5	32.4		30.4	102.6
United Kingdom	78.7	1.1	84.5	11.9	35.4	211.6
Eastern Europe						
Albania						
Belarus	7.7		17.3		0.0	25.1
Bosnia-Herzegovina						
Bulgaria	5.4	0.8	2.9	3.6	7.5	20.1
Croatia						
Czech Republic	9.9	0.5	7.8	6.0	19.1	43.3
Estonia						
Georgia						
Hungary	7.7	0.1	10.8	3.4	2.8	24.7
Latvia						
Lithuania	3.1	0.2	2.9	2.2	0.2	8.7
Macedonia						
Moldova						
Poland	24.9	0.6	12.5		59.4	97.4
Romania	10.6	3.9	13.1	2.5	7.7	37.8
Russia	130.4	37.8	378.2	36.9	101.3	684.6
Slovakia	4.3	1.0	5.2	3.8	3.9	18.1
Slovenia						
Ukraine	15.5	2.6	53.8	20.3	39.3	131.5

Source:BP Amoco, BP Statistical Review of World Energy

Table 10.16

Consumption of Coal 1985-2008

Million tonnes of oil equivalent

	1985	1990	1995	2000	2003	2004	2005	2006	2007	2008
Western Europe										
Austria	3.5	3.6	2.4	3.2	2.9	2.9	2.8	2.8	3.1	3.1
Belgium	10.9	10.4	9.8	7.6	6.5	6.4	6.1	6.1	5.5	4.6
Cyprus										
Denmark	7.1	6.0	6.6	4.0	5.7	4.6	3.7	5.6	4.7	4.1
Finland	3.5	3.3	3.1	3.5	5.8	5.3	3.1	5.2	4.6	3.4
France	23.0	19.1	14.5	13.9	13.3	12.8	13.3	12.1	12.3	11.9
Germany	147.6	129.6	90.6	84.9	87.2	85.4	82.1	83.5	85.7	80.9
Gibraltar										
Greece	6.0	8.0	8.2	9.2	9.4	9.0	8.8	8.1	8.5	8.6
Iceland	0.1	0.1	0.1	0.1	0.1	0.1	0.1	0.1	0.1	0.1
Ireland	1.1	2.1	1.8	1.8	1.7	1.8	1.8	1.6	1.5	1.4
Italy	15.1	14.1	12.5	13.0	15.3	17.1	17.0	17.2	17.2	17.0
Liechtenstein										
Luxembourg										
Malta										
Monaco										
Netherlands	7.0	9.5	9.8	8.6	9.1	9.1	8.7	8.5	9.0	9.2
Norway	0.5	0.5	0.7	0.7	0.5	0.6	0.5	0.4	0.4	0.5
Portugal	0.8	2.8	4.2	4.5	3.8	3.7	3.8	3.8	3.3	3.2
Spain	19.2	19.0	18.5	21.6	20.5	21.0	21.2	18.5	20.2	14.6
Sweden	2.9	2.2	2.1	1.9	2.2	2.3	2.2	2.3	2.2	2.0
Switzerland	0.4	0.3	0.2	0.1	0.1	0.1	0.1	0.1	0.1	0.1
Turkey	10.6	16.8	17.5	25.5	21.8	23.0	26.1	28.8	31.0	30.4
United Kingdom	62.9	64.9	47.5	36.7	38.1	36.6	37.4	40.8	38.2	35.4
Eastern Europe										
Albania										
Belarus	1.1	1.2	0.3	0.1	0.1	0.1	0.1	0.1	0.1	0.0
Bosnia-Herzegovina										
Bulgaria	10.1	8.9	7.8	6.3	7.1	6.9	6.9	7.1	7.8	7.5
Croatia										
Czech Republic	38.2	33.5	23.5	21.0	20.8	20.5	19.8	19.4	20.0	19.1
Estonia										
Georgia										
Hungary	7.6	5.6	3.6	3.2	3.4	3.1	2.7	2.9	2.9	2.8
Latvia										
Lithuania	0.6	0.6	0.1	0.1	0.2	0.2	0.2	0.2	0.2	0.2
Macedonia										
Moldova										
Poland	99.9	80.2	71.7	57.6	57.7	57.3	55.7	58.0	57.9	59.4
Romania	16.9	11.7	9.7	7.0	7.8	7.4	7.6	8.5	7.4	7.7
Russia	195.6	180.6	119.4	105.2	104.0	99.5	94.2	96.7	93.5	101.3
Slovakia	7.2	6.9	5.1	4.0	4.2	4.1	3.9	3.8	3.8	3.9
Slovenia										
Ukraine	76.5	74.8	42.1	38.8	39.0	39.1	37.5	39.8	39.7	39.3

Source: *BP Amoco, BP Statistical Review of World Energy*
Notes: *Million tonnes of oil equivalent = the amount of oil required to fuel an oil-fired plant in order to generate the same amount of electricity*

Energy Statistics

Table 10.17

Consumption of Crude Oil 1985-2008

Million metric tonnes

	1985	1990	1995	2000	2003	2004	2005	2006	2007	2008
Western Europe										
Austria	9.8	10.8	11.3	11.8	14.1	13.8	14.2	14.2	13.4	13.4
Belgium	20.8	24.8	26.4	33.9	36.4	38.4	39.9	41.1	41.0	41.3
Cyprus										
Denmark	10.7	9.0	10.5	10.4	9.2	9.1	9.2	9.3	9.3	8.9
Finland	10.8	11.0	9.9	10.7	11.4	10.6	11.0	10.6	10.6	10.5
France	84.3	89.4	89.0	94.9	93.1	94.0	93.1	93.0	91.3	92.2
Germany	126.3	127.3	135.1	129.8	125.1	124.0	122.4	123.6	112.5	118.3
Gibraltar										
Greece	12.0	15.7	17.6	19.9	19.7	21.4	21.2	22.2	21.7	21.4
Iceland	0.5	0.6	0.8	0.9	0.9	1.0	1.0	1.0	1.0	0.9
Ireland	3.9	4.4	5.7	8.2	8.5	8.9	9.4	9.3	9.4	9.0
Italy	84.4	93.6	95.5	93.5	92.1	89.7	86.7	86.7	84.0	80.9
Liechtenstein										
Luxembourg										
Malta										
Monaco										
Netherlands	29.2	35.0	38.0	41.7	44.1	46.2	49.6	49.0	46.0	46.5
Norway	9.0	9.2	9.6	9.4	9.9	9.6	9.7	10.0	10.2	9.8
Portugal	8.8	11.1	13.0	15.5	15.2	15.4	16.0	14.4	14.4	13.7
Spain	42.9	48.7	56.3	70.0	75.5	77.6	78.8	78.1	78.8	77.1
Sweden	18.4	16.4	16.1	15.2	15.9	15.3	15.1	15.5	14.7	14.5
Switzerland	12.0	12.8	11.8	12.2	12.1	12.0	12.2	12.6	11.3	12.1
Turkey	16.8	22.1	28.4	31.1	31.0	31.0	30.2	29.5	30.5	32.3
United Kingdom	77.4	82.9	81.9	78.6	79.0	81.7	83.0	82.3	79.2	78.7
Eastern Europe										
Albania										
Belarus	25.2	24.8	10.4	7.0	7.2	7.4	7.1	8.0	7.6	7.7
Bosnia-Herzegovina										
Bulgaria	10.4	8.8	5.6	3.9	5.2	4.7	4.9	5.2	5.3	5.4
Croatia										
Czech Republic	10.6	8.4	8.0	7.9	8.7	9.5	9.9	9.8	9.7	9.9
Estonia										
Georgia										
Hungary	10.3	9.3	7.7	6.8	6.3	6.5	7.5	7.8	7.7	7.7
Latvia										
Lithuania	8.6	7.5	3.2	2.4	2.4	2.6	2.8	2.8	2.8	3.1
Macedonia										
Moldova										
Poland	16.4	15.8	14.9	20.0	19.9	21.1	21.9	23.3	24.2	24.9
Romania	15.0	18.7	13.5	10.0	9.4	10.9	10.5	10.3	10.3	10.6
Russia	244.5	249.7	146.1	123.5	123.4	123.3	121.9	127.1	126.2	130.4
Slovakia	6.2	5.0	3.2	3.4	3.3	3.2	3.8	4.0	4.1	4.3
Slovenia										
Ukraine	63.0	63.0	18.9	12.0	13.5	13.9	13.9	15.0	15.3	15.5

Source:BP Amoco, BP Statistical Review of World Energy

Table 10.18

Consumption of Natural Gas 1985-2008
Million tonnes of oil equivalent

	1985	1990	1995	2000	2003	2004	2005	2006	2007	2008
Western Europe										
Austria	5.0	5.8	7.1	7.3	8.5	8.5	9.0	8.5	8.0	8.5
Belgium	8.4	9.5	10.6	13.4	14.4	14.9	14.9	15.3	15.2	15.3
Cyprus										
Denmark	0.6	1.8	3.2	4.4	4.7	4.7	4.5	4.6	4.1	4.1
Finland	0.8	2.3	2.9	3.4	4.0	3.9	3.6	3.8	3.5	3.6
France	23.3	26.4	29.6	35.7	39.0	40.1	41.3	39.7	38.3	39.8
Germany	49.2	53.9	67.0	71.5	77.0	77.3	77.6	78.5	74.6	73.8
Gibraltar										
Greece	0.1	0.1		1.8	2.2	2.4	2.5	2.9	3.6	3.8
Iceland										
Ireland	2.0	1.9	2.3	3.4	3.7	3.7	3.5	4.0	4.3	4.5
Italy	27.2	39.1	44.9	58.4	64.1	66.5	71.2	69.7	70.0	69.9
Liechtenstein										
Luxembourg										
Malta										
Monaco										
Netherlands	32.9	31.1	34.6	35.1	36.0	36.8	35.3	34.3	33.3	34.7
Norway	1.1	1.9	2.7	3.6	3.9	4.1	4.0	4.0	3.8	4.0
Portugal				2.1	2.7	3.4	3.8	3.7	3.8	4.1
Spain	2.1	5.0	7.5	15.2	21.3	24.7	29.1	30.3	31.6	35.1
Sweden	0.1	0.6	0.7	0.7	0.7	0.7	0.7	0.8	0.9	0.9
Switzerland	1.3	1.6	2.2	2.4	2.6	2.7	2.8	2.7	2.6	2.8
Turkey		3.0	6.1	13.1	18.8	19.9	24.2	27.4	31.6	32.4
United Kingdom	46.6	47.2	63.5	87.2	85.8	87.7	85.2	81.1	81.8	84.5
Eastern Europe										
Albania										
Belarus	8.1	12.1	10.8	14.2	14.3	16.1	16.5	17.1	16.9	17.3
Bosnia-Herzegovina										
Bulgaria	4.6	5.3	4.5	2.9	2.5	2.5	2.8	2.9	2.9	2.9
Croatia										
Czech Republic	3.7	4.9	6.5	7.5	7.8	8.2	8.6	8.4	7.6	7.8
Estonia										
Georgia										
Hungary	8.6	8.7	9.2	9.7	11.9	11.7	12.1	11.5	10.8	10.8
Latvia										
Lithuania	3.8	5.0	2.1	2.5	2.8	2.8	2.9	2.9	3.3	2.9
Macedonia										
Moldova										
Poland	8.9	8.9	8.9	10.0	10.1	11.8	12.3	12.3	12.3	12.5
Romania	31.9	27.7	21.6	15.4	16.5	15.7	15.8	16.3	14.5	13.1
Russia	315.4	366.8	329.9	329.4	343.1	350.9	353.7	377.3	383.1	378.2
Slovakia	4.2	5.3	5.1	5.8	5.7	5.5	5.9	5.4	5.1	5.2
Slovenia										
Ukraine	78.4	111.6	66.5	63.9	59.2	63.9	63.8	58.6	56.4	53.8

Source: *BP Amoco, BP Statistical Review of World Energy*
Notes: *Million tonnes of oil equivalent = the amount of oil required to fuel an oil-fired plant in order to generate the same amount of electricity*

Table 10.19

Consumption of Nuclear Energy 1985-2008

Million tonnes of oil equivalent

	1985	1990	1995	2000	2003	2004	2005	2006	2007	2008
Western Europe										
Austria										
Belgium	7.8	9.7	9.4	10.9	10.7	10.7	10.8	10.5	10.9	10.4
Cyprus										
Denmark										
Finland	4.3	4.3	4.3	5.1	5.5	5.5	5.5	5.4	5.6	5.4
France	50.7	71.1	85.4	94.0	99.8	101.7	102.4	102.1	99.7	99.6
Germany	31.4	34.5	34.9	38.4	37.4	37.8	36.9	37.9	31.8	33.7
Gibraltar										
Greece										
Iceland										
Ireland										
Italy	1.6									
Liechtenstein										
Luxembourg										
Malta										
Monaco										
Netherlands	0.9	0.8	0.9	0.9	0.9	0.9	0.9	0.8	1.0	0.9
Norway										
Portugal										
Spain	6.3	12.3	12.5	14.1	14.0	14.4	13.0	13.6	12.5	13.3
Sweden	13.3	15.4	15.8	13.0	15.3	17.3	16.4	15.2	15.2	14.5
Switzerland	5.1	5.3	5.6	6.0	6.2	6.1	5.2	6.3	6.3	6.2
Turkey										
United Kingdom	13.8	14.9	20.1	19.3	20.1	18.1	18.5	17.1	14.3	11.9
Eastern Europe										
Albania										
Belarus										
Bosnia-Herzegovina										
Bulgaria	3.0	3.3	3.9	4.1	4.5	4.4	4.2	4.4	3.3	3.6
Croatia										
Czech Republic	0.5	2.8	2.8	3.1	5.9	6.0	5.6	5.9	5.9	6.0
Estonia										
Georgia										
Hungary	1.5	3.1	3.2	3.2	2.5	2.7	3.1	3.0	3.3	3.4
Latvia										
Lithuania	2.1	3.9	2.7	1.9	3.5	3.4	2.3	2.0	2.2	2.2
Macedonia										
Moldova										
Poland										
Romania				1.2	1.1	1.3	1.3	1.3	1.7	2.5
Russia	22.5	26.8	22.5	29.5	33.6	32.7	33.4	35.4	36.5	36.9
Slovakia	2.1	2.7	2.6	3.7	4.0	3.9	4.0	4.1	3.5	3.8
Slovenia										
Ukraine	12.1	17.2	16.0	17.5	18.4	19.7	20.1	20.4	20.9	20.3

Source: BP Amoco, BP Statistical Review of World Energy
Notes: Million tonnes of oil equivalent = the amount of oil required to fuel an oil-fired plant in order to generate the same amount of electricity

Table 10.20

Consumption of Hydroelectricity 1985-2008

Million tonnes of oil equivalent

	1985	1990	1995	2000	2003	2004	2005	2006	2007	2008
Western Europe										
Austria	7.0	7.1	8.4	9.5	8.1	7.7	7.7	7.3	7.5	7.9
Belgium	0.1	0.1	0.1	0.1	0.1	0.1	0.1	0.1	0.1	0.1
Cyprus										
Denmark										
Finland	2.8	2.5	2.9	3.3	2.1	3.4	3.1	2.6	3.2	3.9
France	14.1	12.2	16.5	15.3	13.5	13.5	11.8	12.7	13.3	14.3
Germany	3.9	3.9	4.5	4.9	4.3	4.7	4.6	4.4	4.7	4.4
Gibraltar										
Greece	0.6	0.5	0.9	0.9	1.2	1.2	1.3	1.5	0.8	0.8
Iceland	0.9	1.0	1.1	1.4	1.6	1.6	1.6	1.7	1.9	2.8
Ireland	0.2	0.2	0.2	0.2	0.1	0.1	0.1	0.2	0.2	0.2
Italy	9.3	7.2	8.6	10.0	8.3	9.6	8.2	8.4	7.3	8.8
Liechtenstein										
Luxembourg										
Malta										
Monaco										
Netherlands										
Norway	23.3	27.5	27.7	32.2	24.0	24.7	30.9	27.1	30.6	31.8
Portugal	2.4	2.1	1.9	2.7	3.6	2.3	1.2	2.7	2.3	1.6
Spain	7.1	5.8	5.2	7.7	9.3	7.2	4.0	5.8	6.0	3.8
Sweden	16.2	16.5	15.3	17.8	12.1	12.7	16.5	14.0	15.0	14.8
Switzerland	7.3	6.7	8.0	8.3	7.9	7.6	7.1	7.0	7.9	8.1
Turkey	2.7	5.2	8.0	7.0	8.0	10.4	9.0	10.0	8.0	7.5
United Kingdom	0.9	1.2	1.1	1.2	0.7	1.1	1.1	1.0	1.2	1.1
Eastern Europe										
Albania										
Belarus										
Bosnia-Herzegovina										
Bulgaria	0.5	0.4	0.5	0.6	0.7	0.7	1.1	1.0	0.7	0.8
Croatia										
Czech Republic	0.4	0.3	0.5	0.5	0.4	0.6	0.7	0.7	0.6	0.5
Estonia										
Georgia										
Hungary	0.1	0.1	0.1	0.1	0.1	0.1	0.1	0.1	0.1	0.1
Latvia										
Lithuania	0.1	0.1	0.2	0.1	0.2	0.2	0.2	0.2	0.2	0.2
Macedonia										
Moldova										
Poland	0.9	0.8	0.9	0.9	0.7	0.8	0.9	0.7	0.7	0.6
Romania	2.7	2.5	3.8	3.3	3.0	3.7	4.6	4.2	3.6	3.9
Russia	36.1	37.8	40.1	37.4	35.6	40.8	39.6	39.6	40.4	37.8
Slovakia	0.6	0.6	1.2	1.1	0.8	1.0	1.1	1.0	1.0	1.0
Slovenia										
Ukraine	2.4	2.4	2.3	2.6	2.1	2.7	2.8	2.9	2.3	2.6

Source: *BP Amoco, BP Statistical Review of World Energy*
Notes: *Million tonnes of oil equivalent = the amount of oil required to fuel an oil-fired plant in order to generate the same amount of electricity*

Residential Consumption of Electricity 1985-2008
'000 GWh

	1985	1990	1995	2000	2003	2004	2005	2006	2007	2008
Western Europe										
Austria	8.3	11.9	13.6	13.0	14.4	13.4	13.6	13.5	13.3	13.3
Belgium	15.5	18.4	22.1	23.7	26.0	26.5	26.0	26.0	26.0	25.9
Cyprus	0.3	0.4	0.8	1.1	1.3	1.3	1.4	1.5	1.5	1.6
Denmark	9.1	9.7	10.3	10.2	10.3	10.3	10.4	10.5	10.6	10.6
Finland	12.2	14.6	16.3	18.1	20.4	20.4	20.6	20.7	20.8	20.9
France	85.8	96.9	108.8	128.7	141.6	147.7	149.8	153.5	156.2	158.1
Germany	132.6	137.1	127.2	128.9	139.5	140.4	141.8	144.2	145.2	146.3
Gibraltar										
Greece	7.7	9.1	11.5	14.2	16.4	16.9	16.9	17.1	17.3	17.4
Iceland	0.5	0.6	0.6	0.6	0.6	0.7	0.7	0.7	0.7	0.7
Ireland	4.0	4.1	5.0	6.4	7.0	7.3	7.5	7.7	7.9	8.0
Italy	44.5	52.7	57.2	61.1	65.0	66.6	67.0	67.8	68.5	68.9
Liechtenstein										
Luxembourg	0.6	0.6	0.7	0.7	0.7	0.7	0.7	0.7	0.8	0.8
Malta	0.2	0.3	0.4	0.6	0.6	0.6	0.6	0.6	0.6	0.6
Monaco										
Netherlands	16.0	16.5	19.7	21.8	23.3	23.5	24.2	24.6	24.8	25.1
Norway	28.9	30.3	34.6	34.6	32.0	32.4	33.5	34.0	34.5	34.9
Portugal	4.5	5.9	7.9	10.1	11.8	12.4	13.2	13.7	14.1	14.4
Spain	23.3	30.2	36.0	43.6	54.2	58.0	62.6	65.2	67.7	69.8
Sweden	39.7	38.1	42.4	42.0	42.0	41.4	42.7	42.9	43.1	43.5
Switzerland	12.0	13.6	15.2	15.7	16.7	17.1	17.6	17.9	18.2	18.5
Turkey	5.0	9.1	14.5	23.9	25.2	27.6	30.9	32.2	33.3	34.3
United Kingdom	88.2	93.8	102.2	111.8	115.8	115.5	116.8	117.3	117.7	118.1
Eastern Europe										
Albania		0.7	0.9	2.5	3.0	2.8	2.7	2.7	2.6	2.5
Belarus		3.5	4.9	5.6	6.1	6.1	6.0	6.0	6.0	6.0
Bosnia-Herzegovina		3.0	2.5	3.7	3.8	3.8	4.1	4.2	4.2	4.3
Bulgaria	9.6	10.5	11.0	9.9	9.3	8.8	9.0	9.0	8.9	8.9
Croatia		4.5	4.6	5.7	5.7	6.1	6.3	6.4	6.6	6.7
Czech Republic	8.0	9.6	14.8	13.8	14.5	14.5	14.7	14.9	14.9	15.0
Estonia		0.9	1.1	1.5	1.6	1.6	1.6	1.6	1.6	1.6
Georgia		2.9	4.6	2.7	2.7	2.8	3.0	3.1	3.2	3.2
Hungary	7.4	9.2	9.8	9.8	11.1	11.0	11.1	11.3	11.3	11.4
Latvia		1.3	1.2	1.2	1.4	1.5	1.6	1.6	1.7	1.7
Lithuania		1.8	1.5	1.8	1.9	2.1	2.1	2.2	2.3	2.3
Macedonia		1.7	2.4	2.7	2.9	2.9	3.0	3.1	3.1	3.1
Moldova		1.7	1.9	1.2	1.4	1.6	1.7	1.8	1.9	1.9
Poland	14.9	20.2	18.1	21.0	24.9	25.5	25.1	25.8	26.0	26.2
Romania	4.8	5.4	7.1	7.7	8.2	8.0	9.2	9.5	9.7	10.0
Russia		106.9	126.1	140.7	142.3	143.3	108.9	106.1	103.1	99.8
Slovakia	2.9	3.7	5.0	5.4	5.0	4.8	4.7	4.6	4.5	4.4
Slovenia		2.2	2.6	2.6	3.0	3.0	3.0	3.0	3.0	3.0
Ukraine		17.2	36.0	30.1	23.1	24.2	26.1	27.0	27.9	28.7

Source:Euromonitor International from OECD

Table 10.22

Residential Consumption of Gas 1985-2008
'000 TJ

	1985	1990	1995	2000	2003	2004	2005	2006	2007	2008
Western Europe										
Austria		36.2	47.5	54.4	64.5	61.7	67.0	71.6	74.2	76.3
Belgium		115.5	145.5	153.2	167.4	175.2	173.3	177.3	180.7	182.6
Cyprus										
Denmark		19.3	29.9	30.6	33.4	33.2	32.8	33.1	33.7	34.0
Finland		1.3	0.8	1.0	1.2	1.3	1.4	1.5	1.6	1.6
France		306.5	365.0	589.0	611.9	686.8	672.3	677.3	693.2	702.1
Germany		671.9	978.4	1,090.5	1,251.5	1,320.4	1,350.4	1,376.2	1,420.0	1,454.9
Gibraltar										
Greece		0.1	0.1	0.2	0.9	1.6	3.4	4.9	6.6	7.7
Iceland										
Ireland		5.4	11.7	20.4	25.0	27.5	24.2	26.9	27.6	27.6
Italy		534.9	636.8	696.6	803.5	836.6	874.1	882.2	909.8	925.7
Liechtenstein										
Luxembourg		6.5	8.5	9.8	11.0	11.8	10.9	11.5	11.6	11.9
Malta										
Monaco										
Netherlands		365.8	400.9	370.7	372.8	367.5	349.9	346.1	340.9	338.9
Norway				0.0	0.1	0.1	0.2	0.3	0.3	0.3
Portugal		1.9	1.9	4.6	7.4	8.4	9.3	9.8	10.8	11.1
Spain		29.6	46.6	94.0	137.8	141.2	148.3	149.9	154.2	157.1
Sweden		2.4	4.1	4.8	3.2	3.2	3.3	3.4	3.5	3.6
Switzerland		28.3	37.5	40.2	44.6	46.1	47.4	48.4	49.8	50.5
Turkey		2.4	52.2	125.4	173.4	181.3	222.6	240.5	268.5	286.9
United Kingdom		1,081.4	1,173.6	1,331.7	1,391.4	1,427.1	1,374.8	1,397.7	1,399.9	1,404.8
Eastern Europe										
Albania		0.4	0.2							
Belarus		35.0	42.6	46.7	52.1	52.1	54.2	58.7	61.1	61.7
Bosnia-Herzegovina		1.4	1.1	3.8	4.3	5.1	6.0	6.4	6.5	6.7
Bulgaria				0.0	0.1	0.3	0.7	1.0	1.3	1.4
Croatia		8.4	14.7	19.1	24.3	24.2	26.4	29.4	31.4	32.3
Czech Republic		50.0	76.2	95.3	111.7	109.4	107.5	115.3	116.5	119.1
Estonia		2.6	2.2	2.0	1.7	1.8	2.1	2.1	2.2	2.2
Georgia		52.0	2.7	11.2	5.9	6.9	8.2	9.3	10.8	11.8
Hungary		76.4	134.5	140.7	183.6	166.0	182.7	186.8	187.9	189.6
Latvia		4.4	4.6	3.0	4.1	4.4	4.7	5.0	5.4	5.6
Lithuania		10.3	8.6	4.8	5.5	5.9	6.3	6.8	7.2	7.5
Macedonia										
Moldova		10.2	12.8	8.9	10.1	12.4	13.3	14.0	15.6	15.9
Poland		139.2	177.6	142.0	142.0	140.5	150.2	145.7	147.0	147.6
Romania		105.0	83.3	103.1	119.1	118.3	107.0	104.4	99.9	94.3
Russia		2,192.7	2,011.8	2,006.1	2,116.2	1,987.3	1,774.4	1,703.8	1,656.2	1,630.0
Slovakia		50.8	47.5	76.4	74.9	69.2	65.9	66.7	67.9	68.2
Slovenia		1.3	2.5	2.7	4.0	4.6	4.6	4.9	5.2	5.4
Ukraine		406.4	524.6	596.3	623.8	619.9	667.5	707.8	738.9	749.7

Source: Euromonitor International from OECD

Section Eleven

Environmental Data

Environmental Statistics

Table 11.1

Carbon Dioxide Emissions 2008

'000 metric tonnes / as stated

	Fossil Fuels	Natural Gases	Coal	Petroleum	CO2 emissions per unit of output (grams per US$)
Western Europe					
Austria	76,965.5	17,331.6	14,669.4	44,964.6	273.1
Belgium	143,926.0	35,307.7	15,251.4	93,366.9	418.1
Cyprus	9,376.6		131.4	9,245.1	553.3
Denmark	58,698.8	10,737.6	19,426.8	28,534.4	33.9
Finland	53,182.2	8,799.8	12,694.5	31,687.8	287.9
France	422,205.7	109,048.2	52,586.6	260,570.9	216.5
Germany	845,531.9	184,896.6	308,363.8	352,271.4	339.4
Gibraltar	4,689.7			4,689.7	7,752.6
Greece	108,135.8	7,565.6	30,813.4	69,756.8	445.1
Iceland	3,592.6		422.2	3,170.4	2.5
Ireland	50,579.5	10,019.3	8,368.9	32,191.3	272.3
Italy	464,551.5	170,206.2	65,096.2	229,249.1	295.5
Liechtenstein					
Luxembourg	13,161.0	3,089.5	495.7	9,575.8	352.1
Malta	3,243.4			3,243.4	563.2
Monaco					
Netherlands	256,669.8	76,649.9	33,565.8	146,454.1	431.7
Norway	46,961.1	14,921.0	2,413.4	29,626.7	18.5
Portugal	60,941.7	9,810.0	14,633.9	36,497.9	366.6
Spain	379,994.5	83,568.4	62,600.5	233,825.5	347.0
Sweden	54,771.1	2,125.5	7,757.0	44,888.7	17.3
Switzerland	45,812.2	6,406.7	504.4	38,901.1	86.1
Turkey	256,852.1	74,593.6	97,596.9	84,661.6	270.3
United Kingdom	591,536.5	175,507.8	167,948.2	248,080.4	409.1
Eastern Europe					
Albania	5,001.8	58.7	121.5	4,821.6	4.6
Belarus	72,900.7	46,304.4	407.9	26,188.4	0.6
Bosnia-Herzegovina	18,865.1	1,003.7	13,348.2	4,513.1	768.6
Bulgaria	46,905.1	10,790.1	18,250.5	17,864.6	702.9
Croatia	20,766.6	5,063.5	1,567.2	14,135.9	60.7
Czech Republic	118,742.9	17,248.2	72,862.0	28,632.7	32.0
Estonia	18,402.9	2,834.8	11,065.3	4,502.7	74.2
Georgia	5,216.8	3,215.1	20.5	1,981.3	273.4
Hungary	58,418.6	26,438.5	11,409.9	20,570.2	2.2
Latvia	9,331.3	3,644.3	436.9	5,250.0	574.5
Lithuania	17,452.9	5,340.9	1,167.5	10,944.4	156.5
Macedonia	6,465.2	275.5	3,572.2	2,617.4	16.2
Moldova	8,022.7	5,841.3	22.1	2,159.3	126.1
Poland	312,710.0	30,626.6	215,341.2	66,742.2	245.9
Romania	97,766.8	35,914.0	32,930.8	28,922.0	194.0
Russia	1,752,437.6	929,924.2	421,352.1	401,161.3	42.1
Slovakia	37,458.4	12,184.2	15,491.9	9,782.3	577.3
Slovenia	18,231.7	2,194.5	7,189.6	8,847.6	491.0
Ukraine	310,014.6	121,716.3	138,446.0	49,852.3	326.4

Source: *Energy Information Administration of the US Government, International Energy Annual*

Table 11.2

Emissions of Air and Water Pollutants 2008

'000 metric tonnes / as stated

	Carbon Monoxide	Nitrogen Oxide	Daily Organic Water Pollutants (kg)	Particulate Matter	Sulphur Oxide
Western Europe					
Austria	738	219	81,596	22	25
Belgium	834	271	101,577	27	136
Cyprus	30	18	7,822	1	40
Denmark	585	188	82,628	27	16
Finland	494	198	65,444	35	62
France	4,962	1,312	476,026	303	443
Germany	3,827	1,281	896,048	110	534
Gibraltar					
Greece	885	303	61,757	60	528
Iceland	18	26	9,238		8
Ireland	160	118	44,966	9	69
Italy	3,276	1,013	490,221	134	486
Liechtenstein	2	0		0	0
Luxembourg	0	0	5,759	2	3
Malta		12	4,656	1	3
Monaco					
Netherlands	495	297	135,922	20	59
Norway	388	189	42,830	47	22
Portugal	593	256	131,559	112	230
Spain	2,310	1,468	348,294	135	1,371
Sweden	558	165	119,510	35	38
Switzerland	291	78	95,146	8	18
Turkey	3,544	1,066	202,236	339	1,347
United Kingdom	2,137	1,556	555,399	96	593
Eastern Europe					
Albania			17,727		
Belarus	113	44		37	123
Bosnia-Herzegovina			25,828		480
Bulgaria	814	259	115,426	65	854
Croatia	310	67	41,759	8	58
Czech Republic	451	288	139,648	22	199
Estonia	139	28		13	70
Georgia					
Hungary	558	212	102,621	28	60
Latvia	331	46	29,235	16	2
Lithuania	205	65	43,472	9	44
Macedonia	98	26	13,417		40
Moldova			23,480		
Poland	2,558	936	259,722	135	1,169
Romania	1,366	334	32,046	203	695
Russia	15,947	2,641	1,595,115	1,157	2,968
Slovakia	282	81	37,055	32	81
Slovenia	104	46	41,430	10	23
Ukraine	1,188	222	600,800	794	865

Source: *Euromonitor International from national statistics/World Resources Institute/World Bank*

Consumption of Pesticides 2008
Tonnes

	Fungicides	Herbicides	Insecticides	Others	Total
Western Europe					
Austria	1,218	1,013	114	7	2,352
Belgium	3,064	5,636	619	114	9,433
Cyprus					
Denmark	243	1,622	118	589	2,573
Finland	229	1,505	13	94	1,842
France	61,242	40,199	662	16,856	118,960
Germany	6,434	12,290	945	4,371	24,040
Gibraltar					
Greece	6,094	3,289	2,914	46	12,344
Iceland					
Ireland	309	1,765	38	203	2,316
Italy	36,514	6,805	4,939	492	48,749
Liechtenstein					
Luxembourg					
Malta	32	27	12		71
Monaco					
Netherlands	2,897	2,540	151	175	5,763
Norway	51	144	4	2	202
Portugal	12,217	2,872	509	290	15,887
Spain	4,855	15,247	14,321	5,422	39,844
Sweden	368	1,712	7	60	2,148
Switzerland	624	602	28	29	1,283
Turkey	2,184	4,306	11,975	1,000	19,465
United Kingdom	4,343	20,488	1,494	3,329	29,655
Eastern Europe					
Albania					
Belarus					
Bosnia-Herzegovina					
Bulgaria	14	374	1	1	390
Croatia	1,894	506	36		2,436
Czech Republic	1,408	2,869	333	747	5,357
Estonia	8	374	4	13	398
Georgia					
Hungary	1,056	1,473	115	28	2,671
Latvia	28	379	3	55	465
Lithuania	82	308	13	67	469
Macedonia					
Moldova					
Poland	3,496	5,529	1,096		10,121
Romania	708	1,915	276		2,898
Russia	4,400	9,336	1,486	13	15,234
Slovakia	1,600	2,331	562	204	4,695
Slovenia	1,103	500	159	82	1,844
Ukraine	3,004	15,298	8,034		26,336

Source:*Euromonitor International from FAO*

Table 11.4

Amounts of Waste Generated 2008

'000 tonnes / Kg per capita

	Municipal Waste	Municipal Waste per capita	Nuclear Waste: Spent Fuel Arising	Nuclear Waste per capita	Hazardous Industrial Waste	Hazardous Industrial Waste per capita
Western Europe						
Austria	4,928	590			941	113
Belgium	5,292	498	0.13	0.01	3,487	328
Cyprus	605	702				
Denmark	4,547	832			391	72
Finland	2,735	516	0.06	0.01	2,823	533
France	35,498	572	1.15	0.02	9,634	155
Germany	46,808	569	0.41	0.00	22,848	278
Gibraltar						
Greece	5,057	451			241	22
Iceland	169	536			9	27
Ireland	3,366	769			700	160
Italy	32,975	559			8,510	144
Liechtenstein						
Luxembourg	341	709			287	596
Malta	281	690				
Monaco						
Netherlands	10,397	635	0.01	0.00	6,515	398
Norway	3,977	839			776	164
Portugal	5,153	484			181	17
Spain	25,271	561	0.20	0.00	4,183	93
Sweden	4,836	528	0.26	0.03	3,527	385
Switzerland	5,495	730	0.05	0.01	1,040	138
Turkey	31,621	425				
United Kingdom	34,548	565	0.20	0.00	8,615	141
Eastern Europe						
Albania						
Belarus						
Bosnia-Herzegovina						
Bulgaria	3,161	418			482	64
Croatia						
Czech Republic	3,012	292	0.08	0.01	1,217	118
Estonia	755	566			6,174	4,624
Georgia						
Hungary	4,569	455	0.04	0.00	1,240	124
Latvia	1,084	478			13	6
Lithuania	1,385	411			143	43
Macedonia						
Moldova						
Poland	13,105	344			2,877	76
Romania	8,816	410			3,102	144
Russia					140,848	992
Slovakia	1,687	313	0.06	0.01	557	103
Slovenia	904	449			119	59
Ukraine						

Source: *Euromonitor International from OECD/national statistics*

Environmental Statistics

Table 11.5

Levels of Recycling of Packaging Waste 2008
% of total consumption

	Aluminium	Glass	Paper and Cardboard
Western Europe			
Austria	55	81	75
Belgium	25	94	59
Cyprus			
Denmark		67	62
Finland	99	71	69
France	19	66	57
Germany	100	83	74
Gibraltar			
Greece	35	12	41
Iceland		85	15
Ireland	24	95	81
Italy	70	64	52
Liechtenstein			
Luxembourg			
Malta			
Monaco			
Netherlands	69	79	75
Norway		91	69
Portugal	17	43	52
Spain	31	51	63
Sweden	100	94	78
Switzerland	99	94	78
Turkey	57	31	43
United Kingdom	25	57	62
Eastern Europe			
Albania			
Belarus			
Bosnia-Herzegovina			
Bulgaria			
Croatia			
Czech Republic			49
Estonia			
Georgia			
Hungary			51
Latvia			
Lithuania			
Macedonia			
Moldova			
Poland		16	35
Romania			
Russia			
Slovakia		43	52
Slovenia			
Ukraine			

Source: *Euromonitor International from national statistics/World Resources Institute*

Environmental Statistics   **Table 11.6**

Landfill Sites 1998-2008
Number

	1998	1999	2000	2001	2002	2003	2004	2005	2006	2007	2008
Western Europe											
Austria	55.0	53.0	54.2	56.7	59.6	65.1	70.3	79.3	88.0	93.9	99.1
Belgium	81.0	90.0	89.0	85.2	78.2	69.0	64.5	59.9	55.9	53.0	50.4
Denmark	146.0	143.0	138.0	134.0	134.2	135.2	137.9	141.0	143.1	144.4	145.5
Finland	395.0	335.0	278.0	251.2	239.2	233.0	223.0	216.7	211.8	207.0	203.5
France	452.0	423.0	399.0	380.2	358.5	338.9	318.0	302.0	287.6	274.4	263.3
Germany	2,595.0	2,429.0	2,263.0	2,180.2	2,111.0	2,058.0	2,005.0	1,963.3	1,928.1	1,897.2	1,871.5
Greece	2,080.0	1,860.0	1,730.0	1,600.0	1,442.0	1,032.0	909.5	788.4	673.7	610.9	558.5
Ireland	126.0	126.0	126.0	126.0	114.5	95.5	61.5	32.0	18.2	13.1	10.4
Italy	750.0	715.0	687.0	653.0	619.0	592.0	566.0	543.0	523.0	505.0	486.5
Netherlands	42.0	38.0	35.0	32.0	29.8	28.1	27.0	25.8	24.9	24.1	23.4
Norway	131.0	125.0	119.0	112.0	99.3	89.0	81.3	73.4	66.8	61.1	55.9
Portugal	175.5	120.0	93.5	67.0	50.0	41.0	35.2	31.6	29.6	28.3	27.6
Spain	195.0	192.8	191.5	189.8	188.2	187.0	186.0	185.2	184.5	183.9	183.4
Sweden	280.0	260.0	243.0	227.6	214.1	200.2	179.9	165.0	154.1	143.8	135.8
Switzerland	56.0	56.0	55.3	54.4	52.6	51.6	51.0	50.3	49.8	49.4	49.1
Turkey	1,958.0	2,051.2	2,148.9	2,268.3	2,320.0	2,388.9	2,420.0	2,458.9	2,494.5	2,521.6	2,547.6
United Kingdom	3,435.0	2,870.0	1,691.0	1,497.2	1,281.9	1,105.5	907.0	808.6	721.0	649.8	606.9
Eastern Europe											
Belarus											
Bulgaria											
Croatia											
Czech Republic	341.0	347.0	357.0	363.0	375.0	363.3	321.1	264.0	235.5	208.9	189.2
Estonia	300.0	261.0	248.0	240.0	235.0	232.0	230.0	228.0	226.0	225.0	223.5
Hungary	731.0	729.0	701.0	665.0	591.7	439.1	321.0	244.6	204.0	188.3	181.0
Latvia	550.0	550.0	547.0	545.0	543.0	541.0	540.0	539.0	538.0	537.0	536.1
Lithuania											
Poland	1,428.0	1,401.0	1,390.0	1,408.0	1,401.9	1,381.2	1,359.0	1,348.1	1,336.1	1,326.1	1,318.8
Romania	697.0	765.0	747.1	693.0	626.4	534.0	449.0	421.9	410.0	396.2	390.4
Russia											
Slovakia	277.0	165.0	100.0	105.6	119.8	133.5	152.0	161.7	170.4	178.1	183.5
Slovenia											
Ukraine											

Source: *Euromonitor International from OECD/national statistics*

External Trade

External Trade Statistics

Table 12.1

Total Imports (cif) 1980-2008

US$ million

	1980	1985	1990	1995	1996	1997	1998	1999	2000	2001
Western Europe										
Austria	24,444	20,986	49,088	66,386	67,331	64,776	68,183	69,555	68,972	70,479
Belgium				159,683	163,604	157,260	164,669	164,607	176,957	178,683
Cyprus	1,202	1,247	2,568	3,694	3,983	3,698	3,685	3,618	3,846	3,923
Denmark	19,340	18,245	33,248	45,728	45,004	44,406	46,330	44,519	44,356	44,124
Finland	15,635	13,232	27,001	28,114	29,264	29,784	32,301	31,617	33,893	32,108
France	134,889	108,337	234,447	281,440	281,750	271,914	290,241	294,921	311,460	302,573
Germany	188,002	158,488	346,153	464,271	458,783	445,616	471,418	473,539	495,350	485,967
Gibraltar	146	145								
Greece	10,548	10,134	19,777	26,795	29,672	27,899	29,388	28,720	29,221	29,928
Iceland	999	905	1,680	1,756	2,032	1,993	2,489	2,503	2,591	2,252
Ireland	11,153	10,015	20,682	33,064	35,897	39,225	44,631	47,194	51,464	51,295
Italy	100,741	87,692	181,968	206,040	208,092	210,268	218,445	220,323	238,023	236,086
Liechtenstein										
Luxembourg	3,612	3,144	7,596	9,748	9,667	9,379	10,237	11,045	10,716	11,151
Malta	938	759	1,961	2,943	2,795	2,552	2,668	2,846	3,400	2,726
Monaco										
Netherlands	88,419	73,123	126,475	176,874	180,639	178,130	187,747	190,279	198,886	195,533
Norway	16,926	15,556	27,221	32,968	35,615	35,709	37,473	34,167	34,392	32,955
Portugal	9,309	7,652	25,264	33,306	35,177	35,064	38,536	39,825	38,185	39,415
Spain	34,078	29,963	87,554	113,319	121,782	122,711	133,149	144,436	152,870	153,607
Sweden	33,438	28,548	54,245	64,741	66,925	65,676	68,590	68,755	73,317	64,326
Switzerland	36,342	30,696	69,681	76,985	74,462	71,064	73,877	75,438	76,092	77,071
Turkey	7,910	11,343	22,303	35,710	43,628	48,560	45,921	40,226	54,503	41,399
United Kingdom	115,559	109,643	224,416	265,176	287,514	306,487	313,940	317,970	334,437	320,981
Eastern Europe										
Albania				714	937	646	842	1,154	1,090	1,327
Belarus				5,564	6,939	8,689	8,549	6,674	8,646	8,286
Bosnia-Herzegovina				524	1,204	1,555	2,120	2,431	2,290	2,340
Bulgaria		13,657	4,710	5,661	6,861	5,224	4,949	5,453	6,505	7,263
Croatia			5,188	7,352	7,784	9,101	8,276	7,799	7,887	9,147
Czech Republic				26,385	29,366	28,837	30,338	29,482	33,852	38,307
Estonia				2,400	2,896	3,518	3,925	3,427	4,236	4,300
Georgia				489	751	995	882	690	709	753
Hungary	9,245	8,224	8,671	15,380	18,058	21,115	25,679	27,923	31,955	33,725
Latvia				1,818	2,320	2,721	3,191	2,945	3,184	3,504
Lithuania				3,013	3,883	5,025	5,364	4,627	5,219	6,060
Macedonia				1,719	1,627	1,779	1,915	1,776	2,094	1,694
Moldova				841	1,072	1,171	1,024	586	776	893
Poland	16,690	11,855	8,413	29,050	37,137	42,308	46,495	45,903	48,940	50,275
Romania	13,843	11,267	9,843	10,278	11,435	11,280	11,821	10,392	13,055	15,561
Russia				68,863	74,879	79,076	63,817	43,588	49,125	59,140
Slovakia				9,225	11,432	10,774	13,725	11,888	13,412	15,501
Slovenia			4,727	9,492	9,423	9,357	10,110	10,083	10,116	10,148
Ukraine				15,484	17,603	17,128	14,676	11,846	13,956	15,775

Source: *Euromonitor International from International Monetary Fund (IMF), International Financial Statistics*
Notes: *US$ totals in this table may differ from the totals given for Imports (cif) by Origin and Imports (cif) by Commodity*

External Trade Statistics

Total Imports (cif) 1980-2008 *(continued)*
US$ million

	2002	2003	2004	2005	2006	2007	2008
Western Europe							
Austria	72,765	91,578	113,307	119,939	130,939	156,760	176,174
Belgium	198,036	234,902	285,506	318,738	351,893	413,583	470,829
Cyprus	3,863	4,288	5,659	6,282	6,951	8,687	10,618
Denmark	48,887	56,217	66,886	74,259	85,103	98,792	111,346
Finland	33,627	41,592	50,661	58,469	69,445	81,756	92,125
France	312,366	370,818	443,437	486,444	539,021	623,085	705,640
Germany	490,022	604,626	715,679	780,444	922,343	1,056,000	1,198,970
Gibraltar							
Greece	31,164	44,375	51,559	49,817	59,121	75,100	77,831
Iceland	2,274	2,789	3,553	4,557	5,084	6,105	5,645
Ireland	51,460	53,304	61,395	69,163	83,670	85,619	82,654
Italy	246,496	297,348	355,158	384,802	440,751	510,141	558,513
Liechtenstein							
Luxembourg	11,597	13,691	16,826	17,564	19,433	22,092	25,067
Malta	2,839	3,398	3,824	3,807	4,079	4,508	4,607
Monaco							
Netherlands	194,044	233,969	283,929	310,571	358,495	421,084	488,961
Norway	34,890	39,486	48,085	54,792	63,366	79,762	87,954
Portugal	38,308	40,835	49,210	53,443	65,592	76,367	89,910
Spain	163,501	208,512	257,591	287,617	326,033	384,955	417,049
Sweden	67,644	84,199	100,782	111,580	127,652	151,340	165,110
Switzerland	82,377	95,581	110,321	119,770	132,021	153,171	173,285
Turkey	51,554	69,340	97,540	116,774	139,576	169,792	201,823
United Kingdom	335,337	380,658	451,810	482,768	546,624	620,824	632,624
Eastern Europe							
Albania	1,503	1,864	2,309	2,618	3,058	4,188	5,251
Belarus	9,092	11,558	16,491	16,708	22,351	28,693	39,483
Bosnia-Herzegovina	2,781	3,276	3,957	4,660	4,908	5,800	
Bulgaria	7,987	10,902	14,467	18,163	23,270	30,086	37,369
Croatia	10,722	14,209	16,589	18,560	21,488	25,830	30,728
Czech Republic	42,773	53,801	71,619	76,340	93,433	118,467	141,593
Estonia	4,810	6,480	8,334	10,186	11,878	15,061	16,025
Georgia	796	1,141	1,846	2,490	3,678	5,217	6,066
Hungary	37,788	47,602	59,637	65,783	77,206	94,397	106,380
Latvia	4,053	5,242	7,048	8,592	11,430	15,177	15,768
Lithuania	7,526	9,668	12,386	15,511	19,413	24,445	31,121
Macedonia	1,995	2,306	2,932	3,228	3,752	5,177	6,844
Moldova	1,039	1,403	1,773	2,293	2,693	3,690	4,081
Poland	55,113	68,004	87,909	100,903	124,647	159,541	206,075
Romania	17,862	24,003	32,664	40,463	51,106	69,602	82,965
Russia	67,063	83,677	107,120	137,977	181,161	245,837	321,170
Slovakia	17,460	23,760	30,469	36,168	47,309	62,139	74,038
Slovenia	10,933	13,853	17,571	19,626	23,014	29,481	33,937
Ukraine	16,977	23,020	28,997	36,136	45,039	60,618	85,534

Source: *Euromonitor International from International Monetary Fund (IMF), International Financial Statistics*
Notes: *US$ totals in this table may differ from the totals given for Imports (cif) by Origin and Imports (cif) by Commodity*

External Trade Statistics **Table 12.2**

Total Imports by Quarter 2007-2009

US$ million

	2007 1st Quarter	2007 2nd Quarter	2007 3rd Quarter	2007 4th Quarter	2008 1st Quarter	2008 2nd Quarter	2008 3rd Quarter	2008 4th Quarter	2009 1st Quarter	2009 2nd Quarter
Western Europe										
Austria	36,683.5	37,628.9	39,199.8	43,247.8	44,586.2	49,197.1	45,285.5	37,105.2	30,998.0	
Belgium	97,572.0	99,443.0	101,013.0	115,555.0	118,537.0	130,598.0	122,812.0	98,882.0		
Cyprus	1,812.0	2,178.5	2,224.5	2,471.8						
Denmark	23,139.8	23,440.0	24,125.7	28,086.3	28,278.9	30,333.6	28,669.1	24,064.4	21,089.8	
Finland	19,198.0	20,306.6	19,915.6	22,335.9	23,560.6	25,812.3	24,039.0	18,713.3	14,112.2	
France	145,391.4	153,921.0	150,362.6	173,410.0	181,767.0	194,176.1	178,033.5	151,663.4		
Germany	248,576.9	256,578.0	260,841.0	290,004.1	300,955.0	319,456.1	314,796.1	263,762.9	224,522.7	
Gibraltar										
Greece	18,368.8	18,199.9	18,484.2	20,047.2	19,355.1	21,553.1	20,187.6	16,735.2	13,969.1	
Iceland	1,411.6	1,565.5	1,438.7	1,689.4	1,532.4	1,633.3	1,558.1	921.7	763.7	
Ireland	21,517.6	19,785.3	20,474.4	23,841.3	23,146.6	22,572.9	19,901.1	17,033.4	16,295.2	
Italy	122,781.2	127,464.7	121,693.8	138,201.3	142,103.4	155,990.6	142,547.3	117,871.7	94,548.5	
Liechtenstein										
Luxembourg	5,241.3	5,694.8	5,371.4	5,784.3	6,068.1	7,047.9	6,465.1	5,486.1		
Malta	991.2	1,089.8	1,148.5	1,278.2						
Monaco										
Netherlands	97,739.8	102,089.1	103,426.1	117,829.1	124,835.0	131,523.0	127,776.0	104,827.0	87,447.8	
Norway	18,177.9	19,092.9	19,164.3	23,326.4	22,192.0	24,517.6	22,929.3	18,315.2	15,561.5	16,097.4
Portugal	17,263.6	18,890.0	18,655.1	21,558.2	22,577.1	24,566.8	22,787.0	19,979.3	14,550.2	
Spain	88,418.3	94,937.5	92,454.0	109,145.1	111,415.7	116,731.7	104,773.7	84,128.0	66,645.1	
Sweden	34,795.1	36,200.8	37,280.6	43,063.5	42,496.9	47,787.8	41,728.1	33,097.3	26,681.7	
Switzerland	36,447.2	37,500.7	37,299.0	41,924.0	43,395.3	47,609.9	43,786.3	38,493.4	35,729.8	
Turkey	35,181.4	42,130.2	44,208.5	48,271.9	49,177.0	56,671.8	57,689.5	38,284.7	28,171.5	
United Kingdom	145,999.6	152,677.2	157,311.7	164,835.5	160,714.1	173,262.5	171,623.8	127,023.6	110,029.5	
Eastern Europe										
Albania	867.7	1,013.6	1,053.2	1,253.0	1,179.0	1,379.2	1,357.4	1,334.9	958.6	
Belarus	5,607.4	6,906.1	7,349.5	8,830.1	8,764.2	10,761.4	11,260.0	8,697.3	5,969.1	
Bosnia-Herzegovina										
Bulgaria	6,144.2	7,019.2	7,780.5	9,142.6	8,590.0	10,831.1	10,083.0	7,864.7	5,221.9	
Croatia	5,596.6	6,583.0	6,459.0	7,191.0	7,287.1	8,842.5	8,202.3	6,396.5	4,811.6	
Czech Republic	26,334.3	28,412.2	29,151.1	34,569.3	35,809.7	39,140.7	36,328.9	30,313.8	23,011.9	
Estonia	3,439.3	3,867.1	3,612.9	4,141.5	3,927.1	4,464.6	4,227.3	3,406.4	2,304.2	
Georgia	1,045.1	1,179.3	1,317.7	1,674.6	1,410.3	1,765.1	1,498.6	1,392.0	965.6	
Hungary	21,521.4	22,737.7	23,713.2	26,424.7	27,367.3	29,713.5	27,675.8	21,623.3	17,159.4	
Latvia	3,340.4	3,764.8	3,968.5	4,103.0	4,022.2	4,276.4	4,211.8	3,257.4	2,223.4	
Lithuania	5,209.0	6,194.1	6,349.4	6,692.7	7,797.1	8,804.1	8,525.1	5,994.2	3,980.9	
Macedonia	1,013.2	1,176.3	1,267.2	1,720.4	1,572.2	1,936.9	1,846.2	1,488.3	1,141.5	
Moldova	759.0	855.4	915.6	1,159.8	1,045.8	1,287.7	1,338.4	409.0	781.9	
Poland	35,738.3	38,417.9	39,599.0	45,785.7	49,220.6	57,474.9	55,882.6	43,497.0	32,744.5	
Romania	14,973.7	16,764.3	17,294.4	20,569.3	19,730.2	23,395.1	22,655.9	17,183.8	11,169.1	
Russia	47,053.6	58,038.2	64,179.6	76,565.6	66,205.6	82,694.6	92,320.7	79,949.0	41,941.9	
Slovakia	13,602.7	15,216.0	15,026.4	18,293.8	17,649.3	20,830.6	18,998.3	16,559.9		
Slovenia	6,614.8	7,270.2	7,305.1	8,290.5	8,412.2	9,557.7	8,857.2	7,110.2	5,387.8	
Ukraine	12,964.5	14,338.1	15,053.1	18,262.2	18,841.4	23,582.7	25,479.3	17,631.0	9,779.5	

Source: *Euromonitor International from International Monetary Fund (IMF), International Financial Statistics*
Notes: *US$ totals in this table may differ from the totals given for Imports (cif) by Origin and Imports (cif) by Commodity*

External Trade Statistics

Table 12.3

Total Imports by Month 2008
US$ million

	January	February	March	April	May	June	July	August	September	October	November	December
Western Europe												
Austria	13,984.0	14,920.2	15,682.0	17,039.7	15,374.1	16,783.3	16,775.6	13,151.5	15,358.4	14,198.0	11,660.6	11,246.6
Belgium	39,574.4	37,204.2	41,758.5	44,523.6	40,072.1	46,002.4	43,664.8	37,227.3	41,920.0	37,944.7	30,872.4	30,064.8
Cyprus												
Denmark	9,513.3	9,141.0	9,624.6	10,541.4	9,584.9	10,207.4	9,720.6	9,040.1	9,908.4	9,125.3	7,515.1	7,424.0
Finland	7,611.7	7,536.7	8,412.2	8,936.2	8,789.1	8,087.0	8,630.4	7,376.6	8,032.0	7,137.9	5,810.4	5,765.0
France	60,232.4	59,322.9	62,211.7	66,416.0	60,855.4	66,904.7	67,258.2	49,932.6	60,842.7	57,530.9	48,073.4	46,059.1
Germany	98,163.5	99,093.3	103,698.2	111,033.4	102,669.3	105,753.4	114,799.5	96,848.0	103,148.5	96,857.7	85,170.0	81,735.2
Gibraltar												
Greece	5,620.8	5,999.0	7,735.2	7,079.2	6,852.9	7,621.0	7,710.1	5,439.5	7,037.9	6,515.0	5,102.2	5,118.0
Iceland	527.9	485.7	518.8	528.3	633.2	471.8	696.3	409.7	452.2	339.4	322.7	259.6
Ireland	7,934.3	7,604.5	7,607.8	7,709.8	7,407.7	7,455.4	7,780.0	5,849.5	6,271.6	6,124.1	5,410.9	5,498.4
Italy	47,605.1	45,725.9	48,772.3	53,565.4	52,355.5	50,069.7	56,130.7	35,984.8	50,431.9	45,301.7	37,394.9	35,175.1
Liechtenstein												
Luxembourg	1,853.0	2,019.9	2,195.2	2,409.4	2,323.0	2,315.5	2,555.2	1,836.2	2,073.7	2,013.1	1,832.8	1,640.2
Malta												
Monaco												
Netherlands	40,959.4	40,685.8	43,189.9	43,926.7	43,027.7	44,568.5	44,904.2	40,107.2	42,764.6	39,147.4	33,258.2	32,421.5
Norway	7,270.3	7,823.4	7,098.3	8,370.0	7,855.6	8,292.1	7,874.4	6,871.1	8,183.9	6,991.0	5,776.9	5,547.3
Portugal	7,197.1	7,637.8	7,742.2	8,442.0	8,186.0	7,938.8	8,879.2	6,575.1	7,332.7	7,523.1	6,401.6	6,054.6
Spain	35,439.4	36,415.9	39,560.5	40,967.0	38,243.8	37,521.0	39,739.7	29,516.7	35,517.2	31,022.0	25,763.0	27,343.0
Sweden	13,967.2	13,895.4	14,634.2	16,729.2	15,435.1	15,623.5	13,992.4	13,380.7	14,355.0	13,174.7	10,767.7	9,154.9
Switzerland	13,829.8	14,484.0	15,081.5	16,956.2	15,017.9	15,635.8	16,605.1	12,571.4	14,609.8	14,400.4	12,183.3	11,909.7
Turkey	16,338.6	16,026.4	16,812.0	17,889.3	19,305.4	19,477.0	20,557.1	19,251.3	17,881.0	14,942.5	12,071.4	11,270.8
United Kingdom	53,165.1	53,443.0	54,106.0	57,200.6	57,084.3	58,977.7	61,513.6	57,327.7	52,782.5	47,195.5	41,236.9	38,591.2
Eastern Europe												
Albania	372.2	393.4	413.4	448.4	466.9	463.9	486.4	438.2	432.8	459.6	401.6	473.8
Belarus	2,624.5	2,883.1	3,256.6	3,474.9	3,461.6	3,824.9	4,069.4	3,650.1	3,540.5	3,317.4	2,542.3	2,837.6
Bosnia-Herzegovina												
Bulgaria	2,676.8	2,808.0	3,105.3	3,546.3	3,487.7	3,797.1	3,851.3	3,063.9	3,167.7	3,172.3	2,448.0	2,244.4
Croatia	2,237.1	2,412.9	2,637.2	3,088.8	2,799.5	2,954.2	3,024.5	2,403.0	2,774.8	2,431.1	1,995.4	1,970.0
Czech Republic	11,366.1	11,903.1	12,540.5	13,700.8	12,360.4	13,079.5	13,337.5	10,587.9	12,403.4	11,976.8	9,856.0	8,481.0
Estonia	1,264.5	1,272.5	1,390.1	1,610.2	1,444.3	1,410.1	1,526.6	1,299.3	1,401.4	1,338.3	1,057.2	1,010.9
Georgia	404.5	475.9	530.0	580.2	611.8	573.2	586.4	404.7	507.4	511.8	415.7	464.5
Hungary	8,972.3	8,972.7	9,422.3	10,249.6	9,522.8	9,941.2	10,243.1	8,016.4	9,416.3	8,420.6	7,256.4	5,946.3
Latvia	1,231.7	1,383.5	1,407.0	1,539.1	1,371.5	1,365.9	1,507.1	1,257.0	1,447.7	1,262.2	967.9	1,027.3
Lithuania	2,351.0	2,476.6	2,969.5	3,042.5	2,809.4	2,952.2	3,101.2	2,647.0	2,776.9	2,277.0	1,879.1	1,838.2
Macedonia	451.1	552.2	569.0	608.8	642.9	685.1	725.5	580.5	540.2	567.0	467.8	453.5
Moldova	261.4	370.8	413.6	448.4	395.9	443.5	446.2	454.4	437.9	142.8	130.7	135.5
Poland	15,496.0	16,515.3	17,209.2	19,521.0	18,474.4	19,479.4	18,999.2	17,713.0	19,170.4	18,756.8	13,696.6	11,043.5
Romania	5,827.7	6,519.0	7,383.5	7,814.0	7,516.0	8,065.1	8,178.6	6,708.4	7,768.9	7,175.2	5,436.5	4,572.1
Russia	17,205.9	23,269.6	25,730.2	27,850.6	26,849.8	27,994.2	31,889.4	30,127.7	30,303.6	29,951.2	23,837.9	26,160.0
Slovakia	5,514.2	5,939.1	6,196.0	7,236.9	6,453.1	7,140.7	6,850.9	5,601.7	6,545.7	6,458.5	5,453.2	4,648.2
Slovenia	2,678.1	2,748.1	2,985.9	3,233.7	3,176.4	3,147.6	3,301.7	2,507.0	3,048.5	2,892.0	2,209.9	2,008.3
Ukraine	4,638.6	6,483.3	7,719.4	7,950.1	7,712.1	7,920.5	8,827.4	8,229.5	8,422.5	7,582.8	5,268.2	4,780.0

Source: *Euromonitor International from International Monetary Fund (IMF), International Financial Statistics*
Notes: *US$ totals in this table may differ from the totals given for Imports (cif) by Origin and Imports (cif) by Commodity*

External Trade Statistics

Table 12.4

Imports (cif) by Origin 2008
US$ million

	France	Germany	Italy	Netherlands	Sweden	UK	Total EU	Norway	Switzerland	Russia	Poland
Western Europe											
Austria	5,606	81,633	12,997	7,582	2,231	2,974	143,440	678	9,541	3,322	2,731
Belgium	51,754	81,209	14,886	91,768	9,488	26,716	330,769	6,511	3,884	8,150	4,204
Cyprus	431	882	1,136	433	188	929	7,187	67	84	43	57
Denmark	4,166	23,575	4,359	7,574	15,817	5,775	80,617	6,964	1,007	1,643	3,061
Finland	3,062	15,171	2,620	6,383	13,247	4,564	57,106	1,829	633	16,455	1,374
France		137,162	64,480	50,023	10,859	38,861	476,327	10,752	17,744	19,936	11,150
Germany	100,318		68,192	150,178	20,824	64,565	775,858	29,774	44,610	51,192	40,250
Gibraltar											
Greece	4,772	11,128	10,741	4,172	798	3,046	48,647	265	1,334	3,493	691
Iceland	177	810	225	409	649	362	3,346	610	107	85	109
Ireland	3,532	8,830	2,093	4,803	732	33,902	57,029	1,823	705	236	585
Italy	52,045	95,633		31,615	6,923	18,745	300,664	4,702	18,122	24,892	11,029
Liechtenstein											
Luxembourg	3,291	7,840	519	1,575	208	506	23,633	7	345	25	342
Malta	408	385	1,333	208	11	643	3,364	4	62	1	25
Monaco											
Netherlands	27,253	102,927	12,848		9,574	35,955	280,541	13,283	3,657	32,491	6,286
Norway	3,597	13,029	3,248	3,950	14,273	5,745	60,749		953	2,419	2,305
Portugal	8,068	10,888	4,577	3,898	1,125	2,742	62,742	1,152	641	784	425
Spain	52,314	67,100	35,016	18,820	4,568	20,095	228,924	2,908	4,616	13,987	4,579
Sweden	9,458	33,360	6,313	10,070		11,911	115,566	15,645	1,437	7,738	5,794
Switzerland	19,275	63,466	23,542	8,408	1,860	9,200	160,076	1,133		10,007	1,381
Turkey	9,328	21,222	11,933	3,959	2,010	6,117	74,802	694	5,356	31,262	2,173
United Kingdom	47,543	91,433	28,100	50,906	14,070		330,960	42,204	8,316	12,055	8,538
Eastern Europe											
Albania	38	309	1,504	59	17	29	3,231	4	226	204	23
Belarus	563	2,792	873	364	166	271	8,548	97	266	23,604	1,155
Bosnia-Herzegovina	116	1,200	1,023	167	57	41	6,050	4	77	137	125
Bulgaria	1,242	4,411	2,945	924	282	505	21,099	11	327	5,462	785
Croatia	1,001	4,113	5,262	536	327	580	19,714	83	444	3,215	600
Czech Republic	5,313	42,942	5,866	7,905	1,351	3,896	108,445	273	1,255	8,726	9,099
Estonia	314	2,273	428	630	1,806	503	12,839	89	61	1,227	793
Georgia	101	478	257	107	42	77	2,075	4	36	702	61
Hungary	5,014	30,197	4,880	4,936	963	2,239	73,620	43	919	10,083	4,462
Latvia	357	2,250	545	583	789	236	12,177	115	178	1,688	1,122
Lithuania	941	3,842	1,102	1,127	1,031	688	17,798	118	122	9,918	3,215
Macedonia	87	786	356	162	21	53	4,121	5	45	60	264
Moldova	100	499	336	101	24	38	2,761	6	27	1,125	206
Poland	10,773	60,907	13,616	11,336	5,335	5,981	146,183	1,761	1,431	20,964	
Romania	5,061	14,058	10,212	3,165	697	1,659	57,451	155	604	5,380	2,892
Russia	9,624	42,141	13,677	8,113	4,619	7,468	124,324	1,054	1,758		8,412
Slovakia	3,175	16,137	2,979	1,685	498	947	53,549	69	419	8,544	3,676
Slovenia	1,939	6,872	6,589	1,177	295	496	26,410	9	330	730	642
Ukraine	1,941	10,826	3,950	2,347	796	1,163	40,914	299	524	22,019	7,367

Source: *International Monetary Fund (IMF), Direction of Trade Statistics*

External Trade Statistics

Imports (cif) by Origin 2008 *(continued)*

US$ million

	Africa & Middle East	Asia/ Pacific	of which: Japan	China	Australasia	Latin America	of which: Brazil	USA	Canada	Total, including Others
Western Europe										
Austria	4,599	11,114	1,536	4,688	144	1,247	267	3,315	473	182,363
Belgium	19,464	51,906	12,411	19,354	2,252	11,627	4,237	26,066	2,972	468,375
Cyprus	1,225	1,200	242	567	34	182	103	183	16	10,544
Denmark	972	10,429	677	6,273	345	1,885	438	3,368	484	109,356
Finland	771	9,697	1,154	4,573	925	1,773	610	1,982	799	92,682
France	54,873	63,539	9,515	26,747	1,931	11,891	4,992	32,053	3,693	700,198
Germany	33,962	156,357	25,596	74,977	2,383	26,075	10,151	50,399	4,093	1,193,669
Gibraltar										
Greece	4,990	11,219	1,280	4,800	111	1,176	349	2,050	182	78,006
Iceland	38	819	318	351	252	160	9	569	94	6,022
Ireland	761	7,154	1,651	2,340	187	671	254	10,533	498	79,291
Italy	78,007	72,914	8,396	33,247	2,092	15,844	6,320	17,922	2,839	555,058
Liechtenstein										
Luxembourg	78	6,319	109	5,827	3	84	8	563	91	31,515
Malta	65	766	101	150	18	37	48	104	11	4,482
Monaco										
Netherlands	38,191	116,559	18,031	54,070	2,408	28,678	11,014	47,352	3,639	569,469
Norway	1,338	11,309	2,064	5,361	291	2,313	966	4,943	2,932	87,823
Portugal	9,551	5,598	810	1,692	58	3,614	2,188	1,823	284	86,826
Spain	55,136	48,841	7,294	25,759	1,329	22,259	4,676	15,178	1,643	406,376
Sweden	1,819	15,329	3,416	6,962	623	2,633	914	5,707	566	168,371
Switzerland	6,014	18,384	4,795	4,431	471	2,381	875	24,258	1,329	227,639
Turkey	23,822	37,333	4,247	15,680	876	3,819	1,313	11,616	1,083	198,398
United Kingdom	27,615	104,282	15,650	43,470	5,500	14,916	4,902	57,395	11,207	622,577
Eastern Europe										
Albania	62	261	3	188	3	92	63	44	38	4,905
Belarus	184	2,579	315	1,415	12	371	155	485	36	38,711
Bosnia-Herzegovina	13	121	3	80	4	12		38	7	9,630
Bulgaria	490	1,897	208	1,102	85	1,181	265	415	64	36,959
Croatia	363	3,158	439	1,885	17	480	257	632	93	30,026
Czech Republic	529	16,284	3,020	6,889	38	417	183	1,709	313	139,936
Estonia	24	818	99	430	4	54	28	182	29	15,940
Georgia	442	1,398	135	241	36	117	65	607	13	6,937
Hungary	316	16,569	2,906	8,490	22	471	137	1,545	166	106,903
Latvia	43	748	51	377	5	44	15	176	27	16,072
Lithuania	153	1,472	83	750	9	110	38	563	20	31,534
Macedonia	35	215	7	65	2	84	38	44	21	5,691
Moldova	27	255	3	59	1	46	40	74	1	5,463
Poland	1,648	19,561	1,936	8,803	129	2,249	463	2,917	284	203,525
Romania	906	10,064	494	3,181	193	1,002	531	1,098	156	83,177
Russia	3,307	82,671	13,664	25,769	1,089	9,190	3,867	10,692	1,276	268,429
Slovakia	120	8,491	699	2,888	16	106	47	388	77	73,301
Slovenia	753	2,773	166	880	16	541	216	590	160	36,517
Ukraine	1,007	20,711	1,571	7,034	323	541	313	1,977	147	92,674

Source: *International Monetary Fund (IMF), Direction of Trade Statistics*
Notes: *US$ totals in this table may differ from the totals given for Imports (cif) by Commodity and Total Imports (cif)*

External Trade Statistics

Table 12.5

Imports (cif) by Origin 2008 (% Analysis)

% of total imports

	France	Germany	Italy	Netherlands	Sweden	UK	Total EU	Norway	Switzerland	Russia	Poland
Western Europe											
Austria	3.07	44.76	7.13	4.16	1.22	1.63	78.66	0.37	5.23	1.82	1.50
Belgium	11.05	17.34	3.18	19.59	2.03	5.70	70.62	1.39	0.83	1.74	0.90
Cyprus	4.08	8.36	10.77	4.10	1.78	8.81	68.16	0.64	0.79	0.40	0.54
Denmark	3.81	21.56	3.99	6.93	14.46	5.28	73.72	6.37	0.92	1.50	2.80
Finland	3.30	16.37	2.83	6.89	14.29	4.92	61.62	1.97	0.68	17.75	1.48
France		19.59	9.21	7.14	1.55	5.55	68.03	1.54	2.53	2.85	1.59
Germany	8.40		5.71	12.58	1.74	5.41	65.00	2.49	3.74	4.29	3.37
Gibraltar											
Greece	6.12	14.27	13.77	5.35	1.02	3.91	62.36	0.34	1.71	4.48	0.89
Iceland	2.93	13.46	3.73	6.80	10.78	6.01	55.56	10.14	1.77	1.41	1.81
Ireland	4.46	11.14	2.64	6.06	0.92	42.76	71.92	2.30	0.89	0.30	0.74
Italy	9.38	17.23		5.70	1.25	3.38	54.17	0.85	3.26	4.48	1.99
Liechtenstein											
Luxembourg	10.44	24.88	1.65	5.00	0.66	1.61	74.99	0.02	1.10	0.08	1.09
Malta	9.10	8.59	29.74	4.65	0.25	14.34	75.07	0.09	1.38	0.03	0.56
Monaco											
Netherlands	4.79	18.07	2.26		1.68	6.31	49.26	2.33	0.64	5.71	1.10
Norway	4.10	14.84	3.70	4.50	16.25	6.54	69.17		1.09	2.75	2.62
Portugal	9.29	12.54	5.27	4.49	1.30	3.16	72.26	1.33	0.74	0.90	0.49
Spain	12.87	16.51	8.62	4.63	1.12	4.94	56.33	0.72	1.14	3.44	1.13
Sweden	5.62	19.81	3.75	5.98		7.07	68.64	9.29	0.85	4.60	3.44
Switzerland	8.47	27.88	10.34	3.69	0.82	4.04	70.32	0.50		4.40	0.61
Turkey	4.70	10.70	6.01	2.00	1.01	3.08	37.70	0.35	2.70	15.76	1.10
United Kingdom	7.64	14.69	4.51	8.18	2.26		53.16	6.78	1.34	1.94	1.37
Eastern Europe											
Albania	0.77	6.29	30.66	1.20	0.34	0.58	65.86	0.08	4.60	4.17	0.48
Belarus	1.46	7.21	2.25	0.94	0.43	0.70	22.08	0.25	0.69	60.97	2.98
Bosnia-Herzegovina	1.21	12.46	10.62	1.73	0.59	0.43	62.82	0.04	0.80	1.43	1.29
Bulgaria	3.36	11.94	7.97	2.50	0.76	1.37	57.09	0.03	0.89	14.78	2.13
Croatia	3.33	13.70	17.52	1.78	1.09	1.93	65.66	0.28	1.48	10.71	2.00
Czech Republic	3.80	30.69	4.19	5.65	0.97	2.78	77.50	0.20	0.90	6.24	6.50
Estonia	1.97	14.26	2.68	3.95	11.33	3.16	80.55	0.56	0.38	7.70	4.97
Georgia	1.46	6.89	3.71	1.54	0.61	1.10	29.92	0.06	0.52	10.12	0.88
Hungary	4.69	28.25	4.56	4.62	0.90	2.09	68.87	0.04	0.86	9.43	4.17
Latvia	2.22	14.00	3.39	3.63	4.91	1.47	75.76	0.71	1.11	10.50	6.98
Lithuania	2.98	12.18	3.49	3.57	3.27	2.18	56.44	0.37	0.39	31.45	10.20
Macedonia	1.54	13.81	6.26	2.85	0.37	0.93	72.42	0.09	0.79	1.05	4.64
Moldova	1.83	9.14	6.16	1.85	0.45	0.70	50.55	0.12	0.49	20.59	3.78
Poland	5.29	29.93	6.69	5.57	2.62	2.94	71.83	0.87	0.70	10.30	
Romania	6.08	16.90	12.28	3.81	0.84	1.99	69.07	0.19	0.73	6.47	3.48
Russia	3.59	15.70	5.10	3.02	1.72	2.78	46.32	0.39	0.65		3.13
Slovakia	4.33	22.01	4.06	2.30	0.68	1.29	73.05	0.09	0.57	11.66	5.02
Slovenia	5.31	18.82	18.04	3.22	0.81	1.36	72.32	0.02	0.90	2.00	1.76
Ukraine	2.09	11.68	4.26	2.53	0.86	1.25	44.15	0.32	0.57	23.76	7.95

Source: *International Monetary Fund (IMF), Direction of Trade Statistics*

External Trade Statistics

Imports (cif) by Origin 2008 (% Analysis) *(continued)*
% of total imports

	Africa & Middle East	Asia/ Pacific	of which: Japan	China	Australasia	Latin America	of which: Brazil	USA	Canada	Total, including Others
Western Europe										
Austria	2.52	6.09	0.84	2.57	0.08	0.68	0.15	1.82	0.26	100.00
Belgium	4.16	11.08	2.65	4.13	0.48	2.48	0.90	5.57	0.63	100.00
Cyprus	11.62	11.38	2.29	5.37	0.32	1.72	0.98	1.74	0.15	100.00
Denmark	0.89	9.54	0.62	5.74	0.32	1.72	0.40	3.08	0.44	100.00
Finland	0.83	10.46	1.25	4.93	1.00	1.91	0.66	2.14	0.86	100.00
France	7.84	9.07	1.36	3.82	0.28	1.70	0.71	4.58	0.53	100.00
Germany	2.85	13.10	2.14	6.28	0.20	2.18	0.85	4.22	0.34	100.00
Gibraltar										
Greece	6.40	14.38	1.64	6.15	0.14	1.51	0.45	2.63	0.23	100.00
Iceland	0.63	13.60	5.28	5.83	4.19	2.66	0.15	9.45	1.56	100.00
Ireland	0.96	9.02	2.08	2.95	0.24	0.85	0.32	13.28	0.63	100.00
Italy	14.05	13.14	1.51	5.99	0.38	2.85	1.14	3.23	0.51	100.00
Liechtenstein										
Luxembourg	0.25	20.05	0.35	18.49	0.01	0.27	0.03	1.78	0.29	100.00
Malta	1.44	17.10	2.25	3.34	0.41	0.83	1.06	2.32	0.24	100.00
Monaco										
Netherlands	6.71	20.47	3.17	9.49	0.42	5.04	1.93	8.32	0.64	100.00
Norway	1.52	12.88	2.35	6.10	0.33	2.63	1.10	5.63	3.34	100.00
Portugal	11.00	6.45	0.93	1.95	0.07	4.16	2.52	2.10	0.33	100.00
Spain	13.57	12.02	1.79	6.34	0.33	5.48	1.15	3.73	0.40	100.00
Sweden	1.08	9.10	2.03	4.14	0.37	1.56	0.54	3.39	0.34	100.00
Switzerland	2.64	8.08	2.11	1.95	0.21	1.05	0.38	10.66	0.58	100.00
Turkey	12.01	18.82	2.14	7.90	0.44	1.92	0.66	5.85	0.55	100.00
United Kingdom	4.44	16.75	2.51	6.98	0.88	2.40	0.79	9.22	1.80	100.00
Eastern Europe										
Albania	1.26	5.32	0.06	3.84	0.06	1.88	1.29	0.90	0.77	100.00
Belarus	0.48	6.66	0.81	3.65	0.03	0.96	0.40	1.25	0.09	100.00
Bosnia-Herzegovina	0.14	1.25	0.03	0.83	0.04	0.13		0.39	0.07	100.00
Bulgaria	1.33	5.13	0.56	2.98	0.23	3.20	0.72	1.12	0.17	100.00
Croatia	1.21	10.52	1.46	6.28	0.06	1.60	0.85	2.11	0.31	100.00
Czech Republic	0.38	11.64	2.16	4.92	0.03	0.30	0.13	1.22	0.22	100.00
Estonia	0.15	5.13	0.62	2.70	0.03	0.34	0.18	1.14	0.18	100.00
Georgia	6.37	20.15	1.95	3.47	0.52	1.68	0.94	8.75	0.19	100.00
Hungary	0.30	15.50	2.72	7.94	0.02	0.44	0.13	1.45	0.15	100.00
Latvia	0.27	4.65	0.32	2.34	0.03	0.28	0.09	1.09	0.17	100.00
Lithuania	0.48	4.67	0.26	2.38	0.03	0.35	0.12	1.79	0.06	100.00
Macedonia	0.62	3.78	0.12	1.14	0.03	1.47	0.67	0.77	0.36	100.00
Moldova	0.49	4.66	0.06	1.07	0.02	0.85	0.73	1.36	0.02	100.00
Poland	0.81	9.61	0.95	4.33	0.06	1.11	0.23	1.43	0.14	100.00
Romania	1.09	12.10	0.59	3.82	0.23	1.20	0.64	1.32	0.19	100.00
Russia	1.23	30.80	5.09	9.60	0.41	3.42	1.44	3.98	0.48	100.00
Slovakia	0.16	11.58	0.95	3.94	0.02	0.14	0.06	0.53	0.11	100.00
Slovenia	2.06	7.59	0.45	2.41	0.04	1.48	0.59	1.61	0.44	100.00
Ukraine	1.09	22.35	1.70	7.59	0.35	0.58	0.34	2.13	0.16	100.00

Source: *International Monetary Fund (IMF), Direction of Trade Statistics*

External Trade Statistics

Table 12.6

Imports (cif) by Commodity: SITC Classification 2008
US$ million

	Food and live animals	Beverages and tobacco	Crude materials excluding fuels	Mineral fuels etc	Oils and fats
Western Europe					
Austria	9,836	933	7,319	20,937	610
Belgium	29,828	4,503	17,188	72,730	2,720
Cyprus	1,069	321	141	2,132	55
Denmark	11,010	1,291	3,096	8,901	826
Finland	3,629	759	11,088	13,781	127
France	45,165	6,068	16,924	117,429	3,543
Germany	64,174	8,117	42,439	163,734	4,819
Gibraltar					
Greece	6,996	990	2,332	12,504	334
Iceland	384	65	500	607	17
Ireland	6,696	1,290	1,596	9,047	264
Italy	35,964	4,967	23,006	78,823	4,168
Liechtenstein					
Luxembourg	1,175	418	1,438	1,519	14
Malta	562	72	36	676	12
Monaco					
Netherlands	35,630	3,952	19,592	73,617	4,017
Norway	5,083	856	7,209	4,516	766
Portugal	9,740	607	2,883	14,344	479
Spain	31,013	4,370	18,953	72,949	1,475
Sweden	10,907	1,352	5,039	24,265	811
Switzerland	8,026	1,980	3,005	16,395	368
Turkey	4,021	413	16,148	30,890	1,048
United Kingdom	47,390	8,817	18,422	81,722	2,689
Eastern Europe					
Albania	625	164	106	840	73
Belarus	2,329	335	1,460	13,982	204
Bosnia-Herzegovina	1,211	326	446	1,627	53
Bulgaria	1,779	367	3,077	2,158	124
Croatia	2,174	196	631	5,401	120
Czech Republic	6,441	998	3,229	12,119	169
Estonia	1,042	450	412	2,491	86
Georgia	739	126	129	1,091	60
Hungary	3,876	565	1,301	11,490	146
Latvia	1,423	354	555	2,314	82
Lithuania	2,399	403	907	4,831	121
Macedonia	621	51	350	1,418	68
Moldova	429	153	96	1,105	13
Poland	11,625	1,348	6,057	22,019	678
Romania	4,747	580	2,238	10,461	334
Russia	24,426	3,541	6,111	2,784	1,185
Slovakia	3,140	617	1,842	7,529	93
Slovenia	1,957	238	1,776	4,320	94
Ukraine	4,283	1,022	2,826	21,475	482

Source: United Nations, UN Trade Statistics

External Trade Statistics

Imports (cif) by Commodity: SITC Classification 2008 *(continued)*

US$ million

	Chemicals	Basic manufactures	Machinery and transport equipment	Miscellaneous manufactured goods	Others	Total
Western Europe						
Austria	19,076	29,563	60,068	23,405	3,280	175,026
Belgium	105,868	73,932	116,234	41,510	6,202	470,715
Cyprus	942	1,630	2,986	1,528	45	10,849
Denmark	11,962	18,558	37,556	16,596	1,021	110,817
Finland	9,244	12,571	34,847	7,857	2,752	96,654
France	88,998	96,881	229,105	90,196	695	695,004
Germany	142,654	163,881	385,501	119,363	109,527	1,204,209
Gibraltar						
Greece	11,002	11,516	22,031	9,977	769	78,450
Iceland	466	973	2,956	899	6	6,872
Ireland	10,978	8,762	34,707	10,528	5,194	89,062
Italy	67,538	89,321	147,051	55,260	47,865	553,962
Liechtenstein						
Luxembourg	1,566	3,120	5,416	1,564	8,288	24,519
Malta	501	483	1,965	605	60	4,974
Monaco						
Netherlands	63,311	53,387	153,164	45,046	62,590	514,306
Norway	8,365	15,448	38,064	13,630	550	94,487
Portugal	10,149	15,729	27,933	9,387	4,198	95,449
Spain	48,506	62,524	160,483	48,627	2,241	451,140
Sweden	18,068	24,576	58,680	17,825	5,830	167,354
Switzerland	37,449	30,924	49,932	34,735	656	183,470
Turkey	27,420	43,801	61,573	12,855	21,741	219,910
United Kingdom	68,218	78,319	201,990	94,491	29,746	631,804
Eastern Europe						
Albania	456	1,214	1,140	588	44	5,188
Belarus	3,554	6,370	8,319	1,539	1,391	39,483
Bosnia-Herzegovina	1,158	2,489	2,600	1,026	31	10,967
Bulgaria	3,178	7,812	11,202	2,458	7,183	39,338
Croatia	3,246	5,713	9,986	3,251	10	30,728
Czech Republic	14,701	30,485	63,748	14,192	79	146,162
Estonia	1,555	2,749	4,885	1,475	878	16,023
Georgia	553	970	1,771	581	35	6,056
Hungary	9,417	15,167	53,518	6,845	10,462	112,787
Latvia	1,719	2,499	4,191	1,529	972	15,638
Lithuania	3,940	4,753	10,455	2,405	455	30,670
Macedonia	611	1,845	1,442	440	6	6,852
Moldova	565	907	1,101	447	84	4,899
Poland	26,651	44,930	73,829	18,331	8,792	214,261
Romania	8,798	17,768	29,148	7,056	1,836	82,965
Russia	26,325	32,392	128,552	23,727	11,277	260,320
Slovakia	5,977	12,123	32,427	7,479	357	71,584
Slovenia	3,983	6,926	11,378	3,138	113	33,923
Ukraine	11,555	13,905	29,794	4,599	494	90,436

Source: *United Nations, UN Trade Statistics*
Notes: *US$ totals in this table may differ from the totals given for Imports (cif) by Origin and Total Imports (cif)*

External Trade Statistics

Table 12.7

Imports (cif) by Commodity: SITC Classification 2008 (% Analysis)
% of total imports

	Food and live animals	Beverages and tobacco	Crude materials excluding fuels	Mineral fuels etc	Oils and fats
Western Europe					
Austria	5.62	0.53	4.18	11.96	0.35
Belgium	6.34	0.96	3.65	15.45	0.58
Cyprus	9.85	2.96	1.30	19.65	0.51
Denmark	9.93	1.16	2.79	8.03	0.75
Finland	3.75	0.78	11.47	14.26	0.13
France	6.50	0.87	2.44	16.90	0.51
Germany	5.33	0.67	3.52	13.60	0.40
Gibraltar					
Greece	8.92	1.26	2.97	15.94	0.43
Iceland	5.59	0.94	7.28	8.83	0.24
Ireland	7.52	1.45	1.79	10.16	0.30
Italy	6.49	0.90	4.15	14.23	0.75
Liechtenstein					
Luxembourg	4.79	1.71	5.86	6.20	0.06
Malta	11.31	1.45	0.73	13.59	0.25
Monaco					
Netherlands	6.93	0.77	3.81	14.31	0.78
Norway	5.38	0.91	7.63	4.78	0.81
Portugal	10.20	0.64	3.02	15.03	0.50
Spain	6.87	0.97	4.20	16.17	0.33
Sweden	6.52	0.81	3.01	14.50	0.48
Switzerland	4.37	1.08	1.64	8.94	0.20
Turkey	1.83	0.19	7.34	14.05	0.48
United Kingdom	7.50	1.40	2.92	12.93	0.43
Eastern Europe					
Albania	12.04	3.17	2.05	16.20	1.41
Belarus	5.90	0.85	3.70	35.41	0.52
Bosnia-Herzegovina	11.04	2.98	4.07	14.83	0.48
Bulgaria	4.52	0.93	7.82	5.48	0.32
Croatia	7.08	0.64	2.05	17.58	0.39
Czech Republic	4.41	0.68	2.21	8.29	0.12
Estonia	6.50	2.81	2.57	15.54	0.54
Georgia	12.20	2.08	2.13	18.02	1.00
Hungary	3.44	0.50	1.15	10.19	0.13
Latvia	9.10	2.27	3.55	14.80	0.52
Lithuania	7.82	1.32	2.96	15.75	0.40
Macedonia	9.06	0.75	5.11	20.69	0.99
Moldova	8.76	3.12	1.97	22.55	0.27
Poland	5.43	0.63	2.83	10.28	0.32
Romania	5.72	0.70	2.70	12.61	0.40
Russia	9.38	1.36	2.35	1.07	0.46
Slovakia	4.39	0.86	2.57	10.52	0.13
Slovenia	5.77	0.70	5.23	12.74	0.28
Ukraine	4.74	1.13	3.13	23.75	0.53

Source: *United Nations, UN Trade Statistics*

External Trade Statistics

Imports (cif) by Commodity: SITC Classification 2008 (% Analysis) *(continued)*
% of total imports

	Chemicals	Basic manufactures	Machinery and transport equipment	Miscellaneous manufactured goods	Others	Total
Western Europe						
Austria	10.90	16.89	34.32	13.37	1.87	100.00
Belgium	22.49	15.71	24.69	8.82	1.32	100.00
Cyprus	8.69	15.02	27.52	14.08	0.42	100.00
Denmark	10.79	16.75	33.89	14.98	0.92	100.00
Finland	9.56	13.01	36.05	8.13	2.85	100.00
France	12.81	13.94	32.96	12.98	0.10	100.00
Germany	11.85	13.61	32.01	9.91	9.10	100.00
Gibraltar						
Greece	14.02	14.68	28.08	12.72	0.98	100.00
Iceland	6.78	14.16	43.01	13.07	0.08	100.00
Ireland	12.33	9.84	38.97	11.82	5.83	100.00
Italy	12.19	16.12	26.55	9.98	8.64	100.00
Liechtenstein						
Luxembourg	6.39	12.72	22.09	6.38	33.80	100.00
Malta	10.07	9.71	39.51	12.16	1.20	100.00
Monaco						
Netherlands	12.31	10.38	29.78	8.76	12.17	100.00
Norway	8.85	16.35	40.29	14.43	0.58	100.00
Portugal	10.63	16.48	29.27	9.83	4.40	100.00
Spain	10.75	13.86	35.57	10.78	0.50	100.00
Sweden	10.80	14.68	35.06	10.65	3.48	100.00
Switzerland	20.41	16.86	27.22	18.93	0.36	100.00
Turkey	12.47	19.92	28.00	5.85	9.89	100.00
United Kingdom	10.80	12.40	31.97	14.96	4.71	100.00
Eastern Europe						
Albania	8.78	23.40	21.98	11.33	0.84	100.00
Belarus	9.00	16.13	21.07	3.90	3.52	100.00
Bosnia-Herzegovina	10.56	22.70	23.71	9.36	0.28	100.00
Bulgaria	8.08	19.86	28.48	6.25	18.26	100.00
Croatia	10.56	18.59	32.50	10.58	0.03	100.00
Czech Republic	10.06	20.86	43.61	9.71	0.05	100.00
Estonia	9.70	17.16	30.49	9.21	5.48	100.00
Georgia	9.13	16.02	29.25	9.60	0.57	100.00
Hungary	8.35	13.45	47.45	6.07	9.28	100.00
Latvia	10.99	15.98	26.80	9.78	6.22	100.00
Lithuania	12.84	15.50	34.09	7.84	1.48	100.00
Macedonia	8.92	26.93	21.04	6.42	0.08	100.00
Moldova	11.53	18.51	22.47	9.12	1.71	100.00
Poland	12.44	20.97	34.46	8.56	4.10	100.00
Romania	10.60	21.42	35.13	8.50	2.21	100.00
Russia	10.11	12.44	49.38	9.11	4.33	100.00
Slovakia	8.35	16.94	45.30	10.45	0.50	100.00
Slovenia	11.74	20.42	33.54	9.25	0.33	100.00
Ukraine	12.78	15.38	32.94	5.09	0.55	100.00

Source: United Nations, UN Trade Statistics

Total Exports (fob) 1980-2008
US$ million

	1980	1985	1990	1995	1996	1997	1998	1999	2000	2001
Western Europe										
Austria	17,489	17,239	41,135	57,643	57,818	58,590	62,742	64,124	64,155	66,481
Belgium				175,849	175,356	171,881	179,078	178,972	187,838	190,327
Cyprus	532	476	957	1,229	1,395	1,101	1,061	995	951	976
Denmark	16,749	17,090	37,037	51,478	51,480	49,119	48,839	50,399	50,380	51,068
Finland	14,150	13,617	26,571	39,573	38,435	39,316	42,963	41,841	45,473	42,794
France	116,030	101,671	216,591	286,738	287,667	289,736	305,641	302,493	300,965	297,261
Germany	192,860	183,933	410,104	523,802	524,198	512,427	543,397	542,870	550,113	571,358
Gibraltar	40	62								
Greece	5,153	4,539	8,105	10,961	11,948	11,128	10,732	10,475	10,747	9,483
Iceland	918	815	1,592	1,804	1,639	1,852	2,045	2,005	1,892	2,022
Ireland	8,398	10,357	23,747	44,635	48,668	53,512	64,477	71,219	77,081	83,004
Italy	78,104	76,717	170,486	233,998	252,039	240,404	245,700	235,175	239,886	244,210
Liechtenstein										
Luxembourg	3,005	2,831	6,305	7,750	7,210	6,999	7,922	7,895	7,946	8,238
Malta	483	400	1,130	1,914	1,731	1,630	1,834	1,983	2,443	1,958
Monaco										
Netherlands	84,948	77,873	131,775	196,276	197,417	194,905	201,374	200,778	213,382	216,141
Norway	18,543	19,985	34,049	41,992	49,645	48,542	40,399	45,455	60,058	59,191
Portugal	4,640	5,685	16,422	23,207	24,605	23,973	24,814	25,227	23,274	24,445
Spain	20,720	24,247	55,521	91,046	101,996	104,359	109,228	109,964	113,325	115,155
Sweden	30,906	30,461	57,538	79,801	84,896	82,946	84,969	84,812	87,724	78,208
Switzerland	29,632	27,433	63,784	78,040	76,196	72,493	75,431	76,122	74,856	78,066
Turkey	2,910	7,957	12,959	21,599	23,245	26,260	26,881	26,587	27,775	31,334
United Kingdom	110,144	101,299	185,107	241,976	262,009	281,037	271,718	268,178	281,744	267,375
Eastern Europe										
Albania				202	211	139	208	351	258	307
Belarus				4,803	5,652	7,301	7,070	5,909	7,326	7,451
Bosnia-Herzegovina				24	58	193	352	518	675	799
Bulgaria		13,339	4,822	5,359	6,602	5,323	4,195	3,964	4,809	5,115
Croatia			4,020	4,517	4,643	3,981	4,517	4,303	4,432	4,666
Czech Republic				21,686	21,916	22,747	26,418	26,241	28,996	33,399
Estonia				1,663	1,766	2,127	2,509	2,381	3,166	3,314
Georgia				155	203	244	191	238	323	318
Hungary	8,671	8,538	9,598	12,801	15,631	18,990	22,992	24,950	28,016	30,530
Latvia				1,305	1,443	1,672	1,811	1,723	1,865	2,001
Lithuania				2,039	2,656	3,200	3,235	2,754	3,548	4,279
Macedonia				1,204	1,147	1,237	1,311	1,191	1,323	1,158
Moldova				739	823	890	644	474	472	568
Poland	14,191	11,489	13,627	22,895	24,440	25,751	27,191	27,397	31,651	36,092
Romania	11,209	12,167	5,775	7,910	8,085	8,431	8,300	8,505	10,367	11,391
Russia				82,913	90,563	89,008	74,884	75,665	105,565	101,884
Slovakia				8,595	8,823	8,254	10,721	10,226	11,889	12,641
Slovenia			4,118	8,316	8,312	8,372	9,048	8,546	8,732	9,252
Ukraine				13,128	14,401	14,232	12,637	11,582	14,573	16,265

Source: *Euromonitor International from International Monetary Fund (IMF), International Financial Statistics*
Notes: *US$ totals in this table may differ from the totals given for Exports (fob) by Destination and Exports (fob) by Commodity*

External Trade Statistics

Total Exports (fob) 1980-2008 *(continued)*

US$ million

	2002	2003	2004	2005	2006	2007	2008
Western Europe							
Austria	73,081	89,240	111,686	117,711	130,370	156,650	173,958
Belgium	215,769	255,549	306,721	335,837	366,923	432,288	477,398
Cyprus	770	834	1,081	1,303	1,153	1,254	1,606
Denmark	56,304	65,267	75,620	83,562	91,709	102,857	115,817
Finland	44,650	52,504	60,895	65,234	77,284	90,092	96,880
France	312,098	366,052	425,072	443,845	488,103	550,433	605,249
Germany	615,438	751,684	909,237	977,881	1,122,070	1,323,820	1,463,880
Gibraltar							
Greece	10,315	13,195	14,996	15,511	20,180	23,472	25,231
Iceland	2,227	2,385	2,896	2,942	3,239	4,350	5,214
Ireland	87,418	92,411	104,180	109,604	104,866	122,630	126,102
Italy	254,097	299,412	353,434	372,928	416,188	499,944	548,815
Liechtenstein							
Luxembourg	8,495	9,979	12,175	12,696	14,174	16,048	17,857
Malta	2,225	2,467	2,627	2,376	2,707	2,983	2,795
Monaco							
Netherlands	219,758	264,798	317,966	349,812	399,569	476,787	541,483
Norway	59,702	67,479	81,750	101,938	120,464	137,998	165,270
Portugal	25,523	30,591	33,014	32,203	42,881	50,241	57,225
Spain	123,507	155,995	182,107	190,982	213,341	248,917	277,696
Sweden	82,919	102,407	123,298	130,885	147,904	169,157	183,099
Switzerland	87,359	100,724	117,816	126,083	141,669	164,797	191,403
Turkey	36,059	47,253	63,167	73,476	85,535	107,136	132,003
United Kingdom	276,219	304,111	341,550	371,384	427,641	434,957	459,950
Eastern Europe							
Albania	340	448	605	658	798	1,078	1,355
Belarus	8,021	9,946	13,774	15,979	19,734	24,275	32,902
Bosnia-Herzegovina	887	1,230	1,769	3,173	4,227	4,686	
Bulgaria	5,749	7,540	9,931	11,739	15,102	18,575	22,587
Croatia	4,904	6,187	8,024	8,773	10,376	12,364	14,112
Czech Republic	38,486	48,709	67,194	77,985	95,140	122,760	146,089
Estonia	3,448	4,539	5,934	7,675	8,754	10,957	12,403
Georgia	346	461	647	865	993	1,240	1,507
Hungary	34,512	42,532	54,892	62,179	74,216	93,985	107,465
Latvia	2,284	2,893	3,982	5,108	5,896	7,890	9,270
Lithuania	5,232	6,970	9,307	11,782	14,153	17,162	23,755
Macedonia	1,116	1,367	1,676	2,041	2,398	3,302	3,920
Moldova	644	789	980	1,091	1,052	1,342	1,335
Poland	41,010	53,537	73,792	89,347	109,584	136,360	169,537
Romania	13,876	17,619	23,485	27,730	32,336	40,042	49,539
Russia	107,301	135,929	183,207	243,799	303,926	354,403	471,765
Slovakia	14,478	21,966	27,605	31,998	41,939	57,770	71,051
Slovenia	10,357	12,767	15,879	17,896	20,985	26,553	29,233
Ukraine	17,957	23,067	32,666	34,228	38,368	49,296	67,003

Source: *Euromonitor International from International Monetary Fund (IMF), International Financial Statistics*
Notes: *US$ totals in this table may differ from the totals given for Exports (fob) by Destination and Exports (fob) by Commodity*

External Trade Statistics   **Table 12.9**

Total Exports by Quarter 2007-2009
US$ million

	2007 1st Quarter	2007 2nd Quarter	2007 3rd Quarter	2007 4th Quarter	2008 1st Quarter	2008 2nd Quarter	2008 3rd Quarter	2008 4th Quarter	2009 1st Quarter	2009 2nd Quarter
Western Europe										
Austria	36,680.3	38,490.3	38,247.3	43,232.2	44,059.0	48,345.4	43,925.3	37,628.4	30,574.8	
Belgium	103,859.8	104,869.8	106,841.8	116,716.7	122,555.9	134,382.6	122,937.0	97,522.6	84,957.1	
Cyprus	333.5	343.0	256.1	321.8						
Denmark	24,052.0	24,500.8	25,400.8	28,903.3	29,329.9	31,868.2	30,076.5	24,542.3	21,253.6	
Finland	20,558.2	23,370.3	21,983.4	24,179.8	24,644.0	28,269.3	24,403.1	19,563.1	13,974.5	
France	131,501.7	136,651.5	131,596.6	150,683.2	159,501.7	167,070.5	150,187.7	128,489.0	109,294.2	
Germany	311,823.7	321,532.7	329,857.7	360,605.8	377,554.2	403,193.2	374,873.2	308,259.4	259,511.5	
Gibraltar										
Greece	5,764.1	5,549.4	5,796.5	6,361.7	5,914.1	7,084.2	6,625.7	5,606.9	4,323.3	
Iceland	1,166.8	937.1	856.1	1,389.6	1,153.5	1,508.9	1,375.8	1,175.5	862.4	
Ireland	29,782.9	30,560.5	30,829.2	31,457.4	32,031.1	34,324.3	31,300.6	28,446.0	28,354.7	
Italy	116,495.2	126,603.7	121,106.9	135,738.2	134,418.7	152,685.1	145,928.8	115,782.5	89,804.9	
Liechtenstein										
Luxembourg	3,914.0	4,102.6	3,818.4	4,213.0	4,649.8	5,059.3	4,698.7	3,449.4	2,949.4	
Malta	678.8	740.6	750.1	813.0						
Monaco										
Netherlands	110,784.4	113,923.2	116,600.1	135,479.3	140,107.8	146,429.3	138,723.7	116,222.2	97,730.1	
Norway	31,389.9	32,838.2	33,126.1	40,643.8	42,965.6	47,051.7	43,494.3	31,758.4	28,269.0	26,566.4
Portugal	12,168.0	12,517.0	12,148.1	13,407.7	14,920.4	15,536.1	14,276.3	12,492.1	9,429.8	
Spain	59,169.2	62,720.4	58,237.5	68,789.8	71,134.0	78,197.3	70,089.7	58,275.1	48,420.0	
Sweden	40,329.1	40,955.5	39,954.5	47,917.8	48,900.9	52,655.7	45,137.5	36,404.9	29,712.8	
Switzerland	39,104.4	40,283.7	40,599.6	44,809.4	46,995.2	53,362.7	48,760.3	42,284.8	38,174.9	
Turkey	23,182.7	26,410.6	26,677.9	30,864.9	33,128.4	35,612.6	36,456.3	26,805.8	24,363.1	
United Kingdom	102,711.2	107,841.0	107,090.0	117,314.8	114,621.2	126,740.6	125,297.4	93,290.7	79,867.1	
Eastern Europe										
Albania	238.3	282.7	270.8	285.8	309.9	407.2	363.5	274.2	224.0	
Belarus	4,748.1	5,927.6	6,446.7	7,152.9	8,010.3	9,242.8	9,328.1	6,320.9	4,116.9	
Bosnia-Herzegovina										
Bulgaria	3,802.4	4,505.7	4,932.9	5,334.1	5,481.0	6,386.5	6,363.8	4,355.7	3,476.3	
Croatia	2,633.4	3,053.4	3,164.0	3,513.5	3,260.4	3,816.8	4,007.2	3,027.3	2,453.0	
Czech Republic	28,108.1	29,333.9	29,792.1	35,525.8	37,861.6	41,106.4	37,599.1	29,521.9	24,719.6	
Estonia	2,459.4	2,811.6	2,636.0	3,049.4	2,993.0	3,446.4	3,292.9	2,670.7	1,951.6	
Georgia	223.7	320.3	330.5	365.7	330.6	473.3	446.1	257.2	219.0	
Hungary	21,325.5	22,744.5	23,584.2	26,330.7	28,167.6	30,106.3	27,410.3	21,780.7	17,988.4	
Latvia	1,696.6	1,951.7	2,000.0	2,241.5	2,298.4	2,531.1	2,511.9	1,928.2	1,479.0	
Lithuania	3,667.6	4,270.8	4,597.3	4,626.6	5,459.6	6,741.5	6,787.6	4,766.3	3,571.7	
Macedonia	680.3	865.9	832.7	923.2	919.1	1,151.5	1,069.0	780.8	521.2	
Moldova	274.4	325.7	322.4	419.3	346.9	391.3	465.1	131.4	180.0	
Poland	31,247.3	32,773.1	34,050.8	38,288.8	41,563.8	47,650.4	45,812.9	34,509.8	30,149.0	
Romania	9,160.6	9,618.6	10,044.3	11,218.2	12,117.6	13,863.0	13,372.1	10,186.2	8,529.8	
Russia	71,694.0	83,733.0	89,484.0	109,492.0	110,131.0	126,689.0	136,835.0	98,110.0	57,883.0	
Slovakia	12,839.1	13,988.7	14,100.2	16,841.8	17,334.0	19,653.1	18,195.6	15,868.1		
Slovenia	6,173.5	6,636.0	6,594.1	7,149.0	7,476.0	8,284.3	7,513.6	5,959.1	5,087.3	
Ukraine	10,732.7	12,398.4	12,560.0	13,605.0	13,812.7	18,774.3	21,002.9	13,412.6	8,337.4	

Source: *Euromonitor International from International Monetary Fund (IMF), International Financial Statistics*
Notes: *US$ totals in this table may differ from the totals given for Exports (fob) by Destination and Exports (fob) by Commodity*

External Trade Statistics **Table 12.10**

Total Exports by Month 2008

US$ million

	January	February	March	April	May	June	July	August	September	October	November	December
Western Europe												
Austria	14,081.2	14,745.9	15,231.9	16,991.2	15,027.5	16,326.6	16,451.9	12,321.2	15,152.2	14,773.3	12,000.1	10,855.1
Belgium	39,653.6	40,144.3	42,758.0	45,947.3	41,493.4	46,941.9	44,822.2	35,585.6	42,529.2	38,126.2	30,214.2	29,182.1
Cyprus												
Denmark	9,715.7	9,956.0	9,658.2	11,050.9	10,272.0	10,545.3	10,443.7	9,293.0	10,339.8	9,452.9	7,626.2	7,463.2
Finland	7,754.5	8,216.5	8,673.1	10,156.8	9,078.4	9,034.1	8,606.8	7,586.1	8,210.2	7,714.0	6,123.6	5,725.5
France	50,892.1	53,579.9	55,029.8	58,935.8	51,088.8	57,045.9	58,710.1	39,570.1	51,907.6	48,203.6	38,929.1	41,356.2
Germany	123,623.7	124,308.7	129,621.7	140,956.7	125,224.7	137,011.7	136,875.7	113,013.8	124,983.7	118,942.9	97,773.3	91,543.1
Gibraltar												
Greece	1,752.6	2,033.5	2,128.0	2,295.5	2,337.4	2,451.3	2,545.4	1,696.4	2,383.9	2,259.8	1,677.9	1,669.2
Iceland	378.2	294.6	480.8	479.4	563.9	465.6	437.5	385.3	553.0	417.5	320.6	437.5
Ireland	10,421.0	10,719.5	10,890.6	11,564.6	11,465.6	11,294.1	11,274.6	9,530.2	10,495.8	9,921.6	9,419.4	9,104.9
Italy	41,339.9	45,434.4	47,644.5	51,628.3	52,391.2	48,665.5	62,861.8	34,116.9	48,950.0	45,324.9	35,893.9	34,563.7
Liechtenstein												
Luxembourg	1,537.2	1,520.2	1,592.4	1,738.3	1,590.4	1,730.7	1,795.6	1,327.4	1,575.7	1,427.2	1,055.5	966.7
Malta												
Monaco												
Netherlands	45,550.1	45,686.5	48,871.2	49,936.4	47,119.4	49,373.6	48,917.7	42,771.5	47,034.5	43,977.7	36,532.1	35,712.3
Norway	14,033.8	14,154.3	14,777.5	16,024.7	15,739.3	15,287.7	15,863.5	14,663.8	12,967.0	11,981.0	10,454.2	9,323.2
Portugal	4,879.3	4,954.9	5,086.2	5,284.3	5,148.5	5,103.3	5,968.6	3,618.4	4,689.3	4,832.9	4,112.4	3,546.9
Spain	21,970.1	24,509.9	24,653.9	28,291.9	25,855.9	24,049.4	27,105.5	18,144.8	24,839.4	22,180.8	18,191.2	17,903.1
Sweden	15,797.8	16,617.2	16,485.9	18,520.5	17,094.3	17,040.9	15,637.9	13,593.3	15,906.2	14,569.9	11,474.2	10,360.7
Switzerland	14,826.5	15,894.9	16,273.8	18,478.2	16,851.8	18,032.7	18,857.3	13,864.1	16,038.9	16,141.0	14,048.0	12,095.9
Turkey	10,626.3	11,073.3	11,428.7	11,364.3	12,475.3	11,772.9	12,595.3	11,050.3	12,810.6	9,727.4	9,393.1	7,685.2
United Kingdom	37,738.2	38,098.3	38,784.7	41,831.9	41,837.9	43,070.8	44,942.0	41,266.0	39,089.5	35,148.6	29,735.1	28,407.0
Eastern Europe												
Albania	90.1	105.2	114.5	131.4	129.7	146.2	143.0	95.4	125.1	103.3	94.4	76.5
Belarus	2,419.3	2,651.3	2,939.7	2,852.0	3,083.1	3,307.7	3,238.9	3,069.5	3,019.7	2,662.1	1,921.7	1,737.1
Bosnia-Herzegovina												
Bulgaria	1,640.5	1,787.5	2,053.0	2,161.8	2,055.1	2,169.6	2,391.0	1,958.4	2,014.4	1,712.4	1,370.2	1,273.1
Croatia	1,031.1	1,122.8	1,106.6	1,267.9	1,309.9	1,239.1	1,601.1	1,134.8	1,271.2	1,072.6	1,017.5	937.2
Czech Republic	12,066.4	12,620.6	13,174.7	14,125.2	12,985.1	13,996.2	13,816.0	10,711.0	13,072.2	11,717.4	9,834.8	7,969.8
Estonia	952.9	985.3	1,054.8	1,234.3	1,141.5	1,070.6	1,097.0	1,066.4	1,129.6	1,125.0	805.0	740.7
Georgia	97.1	101.6	131.9	137.5	146.2	189.6	161.5	113.2	171.3	110.5	71.3	75.4
Hungary	8,961.7	9,338.4	9,867.5	10,435.4	9,567.8	10,103.2	9,745.1	7,967.1	9,698.2	8,419.9	7,461.7	5,899.1
Latvia	695.4	767.9	835.2	901.7	832.1	797.3	871.8	768.0	872.1	766.1	578.6	583.5
Lithuania	1,588.5	1,819.1	2,052.0	2,299.6	2,123.5	2,318.5	2,422.5	2,178.3	2,186.7	1,849.3	1,537.3	1,379.8
Macedonia	268.1	316.8	334.2	360.5	403.5	387.5	419.4	300.3	349.3	307.3	243.5	230.0
Moldova	88.6	123.8	134.5	135.2	126.5	129.5	156.1	154.5	154.4	50.1	41.2	40.0
Poland	13,322.7	14,161.8	14,079.2	16,622.4	15,231.0	15,796.9	15,485.8	14,302.5	16,024.5	15,458.0	10,838.1	8,213.6
Romania	3,699.8	4,214.7	4,203.1	4,373.5	4,688.7	4,800.8	5,102.3	4,019.8	4,250.0	4,366.2	3,251.7	2,568.3
Russia	34,520.9	35,686.0	39,924.1	40,249.0	42,587.4	43,852.6	47,351.8	45,689.0	43,794.2	39,117.5	30,354.9	28,637.6
Slovakia	5,476.5	5,849.3	6,008.2	6,581.2	6,343.4	6,728.5	6,407.7	5,483.5	6,304.5	6,567.1	5,184.4	4,116.5
Slovenia	2,339.4	2,485.4	2,651.2	2,901.2	2,655.6	2,727.5	2,798.7	2,008.1	2,706.8	2,470.9	1,921.9	1,566.3
Ukraine	3,663.2	4,699.7	5,449.8	5,579.9	6,304.5	6,890.0	7,663.0	6,665.5	6,674.3	5,634.2	3,715.6	4,062.8

Source: *Euromonitor International from International Monetary Fund (IMF), International Financial Statistics*
Notes: *US$ totals in this table may differ from the totals given for Exports (fob) by Destination and Exports (fob) by Commodity*

External Trade Statistics

Table 12.11

Exports (fob) by Destination 2008
US$ million

	France	Germany	Italy	Netherlands	Sweden	UK	Total EU	Norway	Switzerland	Russia	Poland
Western Europe											
Austria	6,713.1	53,411.2	15,567.7	3,214.5	1,976.7	5,763.4	130,974.7	893.4	7,576.7	5,046.8	5,116.0
Belgium	83,065.6	94,884.6	22,382.7	58,473.1	6,777.1	34,565.8	367,790.9	2,187.2	6,635.8	5,490.6	7,719.6
Cyprus	16.8	95.7	37.2	24.5	14.6	172.9	846.5	3.9	7.4	27.3	3.7
Denmark	5,630.6	20,888.4	3,776.0	5,413.2	17,049.1	9,780.8	81,585.0	6,640.9	960.5	2,041.8	2,816.7
Finland	3,604.6	10,677.2	3,577.2	5,494.3	10,587.1	5,799.8	54,054.9	3,525.8	871.1	11,465.4	2,815.6
France		94,105.6	59,486.0	27,511.9	8,996.8	51,899.6	380,745.9	2,711.4	18,151.7	9,502.6	11,189.9
Germany	142,575.0		94,312.7	96,465.4	30,470.0	98,530.3	932,277.2	11,207.0	57,696.4	47,543.7	59,170.9
Gibraltar											
Greece	1,071.9	2,954.9	3,296.7	613.8	258.3	1,260.9	16,185.9	57.6	174.3	525.3	356.5
Iceland	103.8	682.4	22.1	1,711.6	40.5	680.1	4,078.9	169.8	74.8	82.5	38.3
Ireland	7,758.9	9,264.3	4,620.8	4,853.8	1,449.0	23,909.2	78,660.0	825.7	4,102.1	538.9	1,063.2
Italy	67,028.2	74,123.2		13,630.4	6,357.1	30,710.6	315,147.6	2,709.3	22,651.3	15,612.3	14,683.8
Liechtenstein											
Luxembourg	4,883.8	5,726.0	1,904.9	1,539.5	818.1	1,713.5	22,491.9	67.2	256.0	187.1	547.4
Malta	368.3	412.1	164.2	25.4	8.6	264.5	1,253.5	13.2	13.7	3.5	22.2
Monaco											
Netherlands	55,194.2	163,427.2	32,371.8		11,389.5	59,935.0	497,875.1	5,342.9	7,532.8	10,594.9	12,562.1
Norway	17,392.6	22,214.3	5,171.0	19,178.8	11,839.6	49,814.0	140,098.2		1,430.9	983.0	2,097.6
Portugal	6,976.3	7,671.5	2,294.5	1,877.4	727.4	3,157.3	39,650.0	175.0	465.1	311.6	479.6
Spain	55,892.6	32,100.9	24,548.9	9,113.8	2,657.9	20,311.0	180,525.7	2,073.6	4,022.7	4,169.8	4,202.5
Sweden	10,634.6	21,363.9	6,916.8	10,527.0		15,457.1	110,088.7	19,102.3	1,885.9	4,582.4	5,197.7
Switzerland	15,575.6	40,554.3	15,167.0	3,284.2	1,260.5	7,340.7	108,608.2	900.9		2,305.2	1,223.5
Turkey	7,513.0	13,633.0	9,043.8	3,461.8	1,061.3	8,672.6	63,379.7	426.1	3,359.7	6,582.8	1,806.3
United Kingdom	37,538.4	56,833.0	19,489.9	38,308.1	10,505.9		260,498.0	5,229.6	9,115.6	7,226.9	5,530.8
Eastern Europe											
Albania	11.0	33.5	643.4	36.4	10.8	8.0	922.7	1.3	0.9	15.3	1.0
Belarus	85.2	812.4	320.5	5,559.3	95.9	1,451.3	14,428.3	178.1	9.3	10,585.1	1,808.4
Bosnia-Herzegovina	53.3	466.9	598.6	37.4	32.6	38.6	2,599.1	11.0	16.3	12.9	37.8
Bulgaria	919.3	2,074.4	1,923.5	312.3	104.9	479.4	13,578.7	52.5	120.7	671.8	428.5
Croatia	298.4	1,517.7	2,688.8	178.7	69.9	335.7	8,589.6	31.1	138.8	186.2	141.4
Czech Republic	7,823.5	44,892.6	6,815.7	5,665.9	2,587.1	7,001.6	124,402.8	640.3	2,147.3	4,256.1	9,485.2
Estonia	172.8	708.5	169.3	316.1	1,872.9	376.5	8,697.2	484.5	32.9	1,145.1	295.8
Georgia	62.9	78.4	38.4	14.1	0.1	139.1	1,056.4	0.5	1.0	38.1	8.0
Hungary	5,323.9	30,891.9	6,240.4	3,187.3	1,182.4	5,118.9	84,196.6	259.1	1,476.2	4,096.0	4,920.0
Latvia	189.5	872.0	166.2	238.8	710.0	404.9	6,925.1	261.6	70.0	1,383.5	379.2
Lithuania	1,239.8	1,836.7	401.6	850.0	818.7	1,149.8	14,318.0	513.6	225.9	3,664.7	1,483.2
Macedonia	24.0	692.3	342.6	72.0	8.3	49.0	2,376.8	4.4	12.8	42.1	10.6
Moldova	33.7	120.9	197.9	11.8	10.7	29.6	1,001.9	1.7	2.8	457.6	93.5
Poland	11,632.7	44,741.0	11,568.5	7,079.6	5,846.2	10,221.9	130,742.6	3,155.5	1,320.3	9,072.5	
Romania	3,808.1	8,102.1	8,176.0	1,182.1	317.8	1,740.5	34,967.8	369.8	482.4	929.8	1,066.9
Russia	15,022.6	41,285.7	31,947.5	42,703.9	5,525.7	12,558.4	254,323.4	1,772.5	10,553.8		19,702.9
Slovakia	5,230.2	15,440.2	4,395.1	2,450.6	1,130.2	3,278.3	60,619.6	162.4	566.8	2,551.0	4,838.5
Slovenia	2,163.1	7,006.5	4,313.5	574.9	281.6	808.5	23,302.1	77.0	271.4	1,638.8	1,435.1
Ukraine	612.1	1,910.3	3,412.0	519.4	83.3	210.5	19,269.5	114.5	91.8	13,069.6	2,160.5

Source: *International Monetary Fund (IMF), Direction of Trade Statistics*

External Trade Statistics

Exports (fob) by Destination 2008 *(continued)*

US$ million

	Africa & Middle East	Asia/ Pacific	of which: Japan	China	Australasia	Latin America	of which: Brazil	USA	Canada	Total, including Others
Western Europe										
Austria	5,657.1	10,063.4	1,507.9	2,842.3	1,253.9	2,641.8	1,052.9	7,796.8	1,273.0	179,684.3
Belgium	21,309.0	24,896.2	3,198.0	5,003.6	2,118.9	6,693.7	2,737.4	23,000.8	3,100.6	470,741.7
Cyprus	211.7	94.5	25.8	10.8	8.7	1.9	0.1	11.1	2.0	1,242.8
Denmark	3,216.4	8,387.0	2,246.9	2,189.9	996.5	1,708.5	517.7	6,226.8	1,206.0	115,110.3
Finland	5,645.7	9,254.5	1,996.4	3,448.8	937.8	2,320.0	997.5	7,663.1	673.3	97,181.8
France	54,648.2	51,936.5	9,076.6	13,413.7	5,345.0	15,799.7	4,379.1	36,914.7	4,206.2	590,846.8
Germany	66,951.9	129,889.4	18,813.3	50,131.9	10,773.4	34,545.6	12,734.1	104,728.0	9,187.1	1,447,573.2
Gibraltar										
Greece	1,826.8	609.4	57.9	158.9	121.4	243.2	58.0	988.6	119.3	23,814.5
Iceland	72.9	407.6	193.1	40.2	9.2	31.0	6.5	234.8	30.8	5,306.9
Ireland	2,775.7	10,100.5	2,478.9	2,338.1	1,158.5	1,496.4	260.5	24,280.6	577.7	123,759.3
Italy	52,698.3	39,361.7	6,400.9	9,993.0	4,786.3	17,443.4	4,839.3	35,429.7	3,899.0	533,567.9
Liechtenstein										
Luxembourg	340.3	514.3	47.0	254.7	49.3	158.3	34.4	438.9	92.4	24,936.0
Malta	250.6	863.3	136.1	26.2	7.1	38.3	7.1	303.9	19.2	2,764.4
Monaco										
Netherlands	26,263.1	26,726.8	4,520.4	6,534.0	2,378.9	9,349.8	1,774.5	25,841.1	2,409.7	625,701.6
Norway	2,026.0	8,347.1	1,407.0	1,834.4	288.5	1,536.7	488.5	8,735.0	4,834.7	167,540.4
Portugal	5,801.9	2,694.8	302.7	301.9	90.6	1,192.0	434.6	2,250.4	316.9	53,234.5
Spain	20,964.4	10,734.6	1,984.5	3,477.3	1,703.3	13,403.7	2,110.9	11,217.8	1,154.6	257,697.6
Sweden	9,987.2	14,017.1	2,163.4	4,188.7	2,289.0	4,265.2	1,436.3	13,635.3	1,967.4	183,981.2
Switzerland	12,604.2	29,898.5	5,858.6	6,483.9	2,154.5	5,209.9	1,724.9	16,636.8	2,617.3	187,577.2
Turkey	31,735.9	8,650.2	298.6	1,363.4	430.9	1,609.8	306.9	4,174.2	354.8	126,090.2
United Kingdom	34,304.4	46,732.7	7,369.1	9,616.8	6,112.8	8,496.8	2,527.2	66,250.6	6,747.1	456,128.9
Eastern Europe										
Albania	0.6	79.2	1.3	65.5	0.3	1.1	0.1	11.3	2.8	1,128.0
Belarus	487.4	2,148.6	7.0	614.7	26.0	1,477.6	1,073.8	143.8	15.9	32,782.9
Bosnia-Herzegovina	53.2	14.8	5.2	5.4	2.1	0.4		25.5	5.7	3,563.0
Bulgaria	1,612.4	974.7	26.4	156.8	24.8	249.3	57.7	356.4	60.8	21,443.9
Croatia	620.8	252.3	60.8	35.3	16.6	80.0	7.4	335.0	30.8	12,853.3
Czech Republic	2,818.2	3,753.0	564.6	807.5	350.3	865.5	322.8	2,579.7	203.8	145,835.0
Estonia	270.8	309.9	54.4	72.9	13.6	82.7	38.6	566.2	108.6	12,225.0
Georgia	62.8	324.0	1.7	6.9	5.9	40.0	21.2	286.5	62.9	2,395.5
Hungary	3,129.1	3,435.0	477.2	1,180.3	150.9	556.5	122.3	2,801.8	226.0	107,114.1
Latvia	236.9	250.4	32.5	30.9	7.0	182.7	2.9	144.7	21.4	9,936.2
Lithuania	361.8	1,022.0	17.5	33.5	50.4	197.1	78.2	980.7	317.6	23,532.0
Macedonia	20.0	32.0	7.8	6.4	3.8	0.8		71.6	10.3	3,688.5
Moldova	33.5	60.6	4.7	1.2	0.7	9.7	2.9	11.3	1.9	1,874.0
Poland	3,672.7	3,932.2	425.7	1,455.1	320.4	1,812.1	524.5	2,463.1	654.9	168,794.6
Romania	2,920.7	1,367.5	103.1	277.4	42.4	584.3	128.0	765.6	40.4	49,836.4
Russia	16,643.1	76,535.0	8,492.1	19,697.4	188.8	6,669.0	1,514.2	20,483.0	716.2	456,559.3
Slovakia	796.2	1,324.6	113.7	658.4	169.8	389.4	85.9	1,322.7	150.9	70,759.4
Slovenia	858.0	635.7	35.6	209.1	48.4	146.4	43.5	439.2	48.6	32,673.8
Ukraine	9,318.7	8,279.9	168.5	826.8	118.5	1,228.6	376.5	1,716.0	93.7	63,053.6

Source: *International Monetary Fund (IMF), Direction of Trade Statistics*
Notes: *US$ totals in this table may differ from the totals given for Exports (fob) by Commodity and Total Exports (fob)*

External Trade Statistics

Table 12.12

Exports (fob) by Destination 2008 (% Analysis)
% of total exports

	France	Germany	Italy	Netherlands	Sweden	UK	Total EU	Norway	Switzerland	Russia	Poland
Western Europe											
Austria	3.74	29.73	8.66	1.79	1.10	3.21	72.89	0.50	4.22	2.81	2.85
Belgium	17.65	20.16	4.75	12.42	1.44	7.34	78.13	0.46	1.41	1.17	1.64
Cyprus	1.35	7.70	2.99	1.97	1.17	13.92	68.11	0.32	0.60	2.20	0.30
Denmark	4.89	18.15	3.28	4.70	14.81	8.50	70.88	5.77	0.83	1.77	2.45
Finland	3.71	10.99	3.68	5.65	10.89	5.97	55.62	3.63	0.90	11.80	2.90
France		15.93	10.07	4.66	1.52	8.78	64.44	0.46	3.07	1.61	1.89
Germany	9.85		6.52	6.66	2.10	6.81	64.40	0.77	3.99	3.28	4.09
Gibraltar											
Greece	4.50	12.41	13.84	2.58	1.08	5.29	67.97	0.24	0.73	2.21	1.50
Iceland	1.96	12.86	0.42	32.25	0.76	12.82	76.86	3.20	1.41	1.55	0.72
Ireland	6.27	7.49	3.73	3.92	1.17	19.32	63.56	0.67	3.31	0.44	0.86
Italy	12.56	13.89		2.55	1.19	5.76	59.06	0.51	4.25	2.93	2.75
Liechtenstein											
Luxembourg	19.59	22.96	7.64	6.17	3.28	6.87	90.20	0.27	1.03	0.75	2.20
Malta	13.32	14.91	5.94	0.92	0.31	9.57	45.34	0.48	0.50	0.13	0.80
Monaco											
Netherlands	8.82	26.12	5.17		1.82	9.58	79.57	0.85	1.20	1.69	2.01
Norway	10.38	13.26	3.09	11.45	7.07	29.73	83.62		0.85	0.59	1.25
Portugal	13.10	14.41	4.31	3.53	1.37	5.93	74.48	0.33	0.87	0.59	0.90
Spain	21.69	12.46	9.53	3.54	1.03	7.88	70.05	0.80	1.56	1.62	1.63
Sweden	5.78	11.61	3.76	5.72		8.40	59.84	10.38	1.03	2.49	2.83
Switzerland	8.30	21.62	8.09	1.75	0.67	3.91	57.90	0.48		1.23	0.65
Turkey	5.96	10.81	7.17	2.75	0.84	6.88	50.27	0.34	2.66	5.22	1.43
United Kingdom	8.23	12.46	4.27	8.40	2.30		57.11	1.15	2.00	1.58	1.21
Eastern Europe											
Albania	0.98	2.97	57.04	3.22	0.96	0.71	81.80	0.11	0.08	1.36	0.09
Belarus	0.26	2.48	0.98	16.96	0.29	4.43	44.01	0.54	0.03	32.29	5.52
Bosnia-Herzegovina	1.50	13.11	16.80	1.05	0.91	1.08	72.95	0.31	0.46	0.36	1.06
Bulgaria	4.29	9.67	8.97	1.46	0.49	2.24	63.32	0.24	0.56	3.13	2.00
Croatia	2.32	11.81	20.92	1.39	0.54	2.61	66.83	0.24	1.08	1.45	1.10
Czech Republic	5.36	30.78	4.67	3.89	1.77	4.80	85.30	0.44	1.47	2.92	6.50
Estonia	1.41	5.80	1.38	2.59	15.32	3.08	71.14	3.96	0.27	9.37	2.42
Georgia	2.63	3.27	1.60	0.59	0.00	5.81	44.10	0.02	0.04	1.59	0.33
Hungary	4.97	28.84	5.83	2.98	1.10	4.78	78.60	0.24	1.38	3.82	4.59
Latvia	1.91	8.78	1.67	2.40	7.15	4.07	69.70	2.63	0.70	13.92	3.82
Lithuania	5.27	7.80	1.71	3.61	3.48	4.89	60.84	2.18	0.96	15.57	6.30
Macedonia	0.65	18.77	9.29	1.95	0.23	1.33	64.44	0.12	0.35	1.14	0.29
Moldova	1.80	6.45	10.56	0.63	0.57	1.58	53.46	0.09	0.15	24.42	4.99
Poland	6.89	26.51	6.85	4.19	3.46	6.06	77.46	1.87	0.78	5.37	
Romania	7.64	16.26	16.41	2.37	0.64	3.49	70.17	0.74	0.97	1.87	2.14
Russia	3.29	9.04	7.00	9.35	1.21	2.75	55.70	0.39	2.31		4.32
Slovakia	7.39	21.82	6.21	3.46	1.60	4.63	85.67	0.23	0.80	3.61	6.84
Slovenia	6.62	21.44	13.20	1.76	0.86	2.47	71.32	0.24	0.83	5.02	4.39
Ukraine	0.97	3.03	5.41	0.82	0.13	0.33	30.56	0.18	0.15	20.73	3.43

Source: *International Monetary Fund (IMF), Direction of Trade Statistics*

External Trade Statistics

Exports (fob) by Destination 2008 (% Analysis) *(continued)*
% of total exports

	Africa & Middle East	Asia/ Pacific	of which: Japan	China	Australasia	Latin America	of which: Brazil	USA	Canada	Total, including Others
Western Europe										
Austria	3.15	5.60	0.84	1.58	0.70	1.47	0.59	4.34	0.71	100.00
Belgium	4.53	5.29	0.68	1.06	0.45	1.42	0.58	4.89	0.66	100.00
Cyprus	17.04	7.61	2.08	0.87	0.70	0.16	0.00	0.90	0.16	100.00
Denmark	2.79	7.29	1.95	1.90	0.87	1.48	0.45	5.41	1.05	100.00
Finland	5.81	9.52	2.05	3.55	0.96	2.39	1.03	7.89	0.69	100.00
France	9.25	8.79	1.54	2.27	0.90	2.67	0.74	6.25	0.71	100.00
Germany	4.63	8.97	1.30	3.46	0.74	2.39	0.88	7.23	0.63	100.00
Gibraltar										
Greece	7.67	2.56	0.24	0.67	0.51	1.02	0.24	4.15	0.50	100.00
Iceland	1.37	7.68	3.64	0.76	0.17	0.58	0.12	4.43	0.58	100.00
Ireland	2.24	8.16	2.00	1.89	0.94	1.21	0.21	19.62	0.47	100.00
Italy	9.88	7.38	1.20	1.87	0.90	3.27	0.91	6.64	0.73	100.00
Liechtenstein										
Luxembourg	1.36	2.06	0.19	1.02	0.20	0.63	0.14	1.76	0.37	100.00
Malta	9.07	31.23	4.92	0.95	0.26	1.38	0.26	10.99	0.69	100.00
Monaco										
Netherlands	4.20	4.27	0.72	1.04	0.38	1.49	0.28	4.13	0.39	100.00
Norway	1.21	4.98	0.84	1.09	0.17	0.92	0.29	5.21	2.89	100.00
Portugal	10.90	5.06	0.57	0.57	0.17	2.24	0.82	4.23	0.60	100.00
Spain	8.14	4.17	0.77	1.35	0.66	5.20	0.82	4.35	0.45	100.00
Sweden	5.43	7.62	1.18	2.28	1.24	2.32	0.78	7.41	1.07	100.00
Switzerland	6.72	15.94	3.12	3.46	1.15	2.78	0.92	8.87	1.40	100.00
Turkey	25.17	6.86	0.24	1.08	0.34	1.28	0.24	3.31	0.28	100.00
United Kingdom	7.52	10.25	1.62	2.11	1.34	1.86	0.55	14.52	1.48	100.00
Eastern Europe										
Albania	0.06	7.02	0.11	5.80	0.03	0.10	0.01	1.00	0.25	100.00
Belarus	1.49	6.55	0.02	1.88	0.08	4.51	3.28	0.44	0.05	100.00
Bosnia-Herzegovina	1.49	0.41	0.15	0.15	0.06	0.01		0.71	0.16	100.00
Bulgaria	7.52	4.55	0.12	0.73	0.12	1.16	0.27	1.66	0.28	100.00
Croatia	4.83	1.96	0.47	0.27	0.13	0.62	0.06	2.61	0.24	100.00
Czech Republic	1.93	2.57	0.39	0.55	0.24	0.59	0.22	1.77	0.14	100.00
Estonia	2.22	2.53	0.44	0.60	0.11	0.68	0.32	4.63	0.89	100.00
Georgia	2.62	13.53	0.07	0.29	0.25	1.67	0.89	11.96	2.62	100.00
Hungary	2.92	3.21	0.45	1.10	0.14	0.52	0.11	2.62	0.21	100.00
Latvia	2.38	2.52	0.33	0.31	0.07	1.84	0.03	1.46	0.22	100.00
Lithuania	1.54	4.34	0.07	0.14	0.21	0.84	0.33	4.17	1.35	100.00
Macedonia	0.54	0.87	0.21	0.17	0.10	0.02		1.94	0.28	100.00
Moldova	1.79	3.24	0.25	0.07	0.04	0.52	0.15	0.60	0.10	100.00
Poland	2.18	2.33	0.25	0.86	0.19	1.07	0.31	1.46	0.39	100.00
Romania	5.86	2.74	0.21	0.56	0.09	1.17	0.26	1.54	0.08	100.00
Russia	3.65	16.76	1.86	4.31	0.04	1.46	0.33	4.49	0.16	100.00
Slovakia	1.13	1.87	0.16	0.93	0.24	0.55	0.12	1.87	0.21	100.00
Slovenia	2.63	1.95	0.11	0.64	0.15	0.45	0.13	1.34	0.15	100.00
Ukraine	14.78	13.13	0.27	1.31	0.19	1.95	0.60	2.72	0.15	100.00

Source: *International Monetary Fund (IMF), Direction of Trade Statistics*

External Trade Statistics

Table 12.13

Exports (fob) by Commodity: SITC Classification 2008

US$ million

	Food and live animals	Beverages and tobacco	Crude materials excluding fuels	Mineral fuels etc	Oils and fats
Western Europe					
Austria	8,273.0	2,496.4	4,558.4	5,780.9	255.8
Belgium	34,702.6	3,855.4	11,804.9	43,699.9	1,996.5
Cyprus	289.5	90.1	86.5	339.9	3.5
Denmark	18,264.4	1,186.9	4,051.2	13,276.8	674.9
Finland	1,788.2	203.5	5,806.9	5,849.2	128.0
France	48,470.4	16,916.2	13,603.4	30,139.0	1,756.5
Germany	56,137.1	10,387.3	26,070.0	37,525.5	2,987.5
Gibraltar					
Greece	3,481.3	613.0	968.5	3,264.5	539.1
Iceland	2,085.2	11.1	65.8	98.0	75.3
Ireland	11,421.4	2,184.5	2,469.7	1,122.3	41.2
Italy	26,444.6	7,322.7	5,752.3	24,605.3	2,326.9
Liechtenstein					
Luxembourg	762.9	280.1	367.5	153.5	1.0
Malta	157.6	5.7	23.2	65.1	0.0
Monaco					
Netherlands	54,581.1	9,608.9	25,217.2	51,350.2	4,506.8
Norway	7,695.8	118.7	1,666.7	120,300.5	254.7
Portugal	3,211.1	2,068.8	2,587.2	3,066.1	333.5
Spain	31,359.0	4,131.9	6,736.8	15,005.5	3,623.2
Sweden	5,741.6	1,088.2	10,817.8	13,512.6	361.7
Switzerland	4,720.3	2,111.7	2,220.8	6,369.0	36.5
Turkey	9,941.2	969.0	3,528.1	7,949.1	355.0
United Kingdom	15,872.8	9,177.3	10,736.6	60,306.2	658.0
Eastern Europe					
Albania	50.2	3.9	214.1	118.5	0.4
Belarus	2,146.9	33.1	528.4	12,336.9	28.7
Bosnia-Herzegovina	215.9	21.7	681.7	370.3	28.6
Bulgaria	1,250.5	395.2	1,685.4	3,509.4	64.2
Croatia	1,051.7	247.6	863.5	1,814.1	35.7
Czech Republic	4,565.2	938.0	3,830.8	3,951.1	170.0
Estonia	728.4	247.6	1,065.9	1,380.0	57.6
Georgia	104.4	138.3	329.3	44.2	2.0
Hungary	6,293.8	316.4	1,662.0	3,546.9	216.7
Latvia	973.6	337.3	1,310.5	316.4	17.6
Lithuania	3,066.2	383.4	1,099.0	2,321.2	55.5
Macedonia	312.8	242.1	247.0	212.7	3.7
Moldova	247.7	214.9	155.1	3.1	63.1
Poland	15,151.1	1,697.9	3,815.4	5,708.8	438.5
Romania	1,741.2	514.3	2,783.2	4,535.0	144.7
Russia	11,158.5	1,048.5	19,168.6	315,888.0	846.5
Slovakia	2,508.4	100.9	1,357.1	2,987.6	43.7
Slovenia	918.7	106.6	901.7	879.0	22.5
Ukraine	4,420.6	1,062.3	5,161.6	2,600.9	2,894.7

Source: *United Nations, UN Trade Statistics*

External Trade Statistics

Exports (fob) by Commodity: SITC Classification 2008 *(continued)*
US$ million

	Chemicals	Basic manufactures	Machinery and transport equipment	Miscellaneous manufactured goods	Others	Total
Western Europe						
Austria	16,618.9	40,000.9	68,421.2	18,966.8	6,855.8	172,228.0
Belgium	129,572.4	88,543.1	110,343.1	40,864.3	11,805.6	477,187.8
Cyprus	277.8	89.1	296.4	239.7	0.8	1,713.3
Denmark	15,258.6	12,941.2	31,187.6	17,324.8	1,665.7	115,832.1
Finland	7,663.0	30,631.5	44,054.6	4,719.3	1,384.8	102,229.2
France	99,984.2	79,674.7	227,846.1	61,746.8	14,367.6	594,505.0
Germany	214,293.3	202,056.8	677,257.4	139,317.7	100,104.8	1,466,137.4
Gibraltar						
Greece	3,264.0	5,074.6	3,191.6	2,436.3	856.3	23,689.2
Iceland	76.5	1,884.3	1,433.2	95.8	65.2	5,890.4
Ireland	63,937.7	2,593.4	30,603.1	11,232.4	3,475.2	129,080.7
Italy	53,254.2	108,986.1	201,488.2	90,618.2	16,276.9	537,075.5
Liechtenstein						
Luxembourg	1,012.8	8,288.2	4,319.1	1,561.1	1,084.2	17,830.4
Malta	352.5	160.4	1,940.7	476.2	27.4	3,208.7
Monaco						
Netherlands	85,601.9	49,073.0	176,955.8	36,227.8	80,943.3	574,065.9
Norway	4,416.9	15,442.4	16,546.7	4,221.0	6,905.0	177,568.4
Portugal	4,414.4	12,914.4	18,800.4	8,882.2	4,714.5	60,992.7
Spain	38,784.6	55,298.7	112,115.9	24,485.5	6,705.8	298,246.9
Sweden	18,748.5	35,738.2	71,180.9	14,852.5	11,814.7	183,856.7
Switzerland	68,906.7	22,750.8	48,712.8	44,825.1	271.1	200,924.8
Turkey	5,934.5	38,664.6	46,367.9	23,941.4	3,195.2	140,845.8
United Kingdom	74,664.0	59,164.3	148,315.4	51,336.3	25,365.1	455,595.8
Eastern Europe						
Albania	6.2	285.9	53.9	618.2	3.7	1,443.0
Belarus	5,013.3	4,706.5	5,774.2	1,770.8	563.4	32,902.2
Bosnia-Herzegovina	221.8	1,631.2	680.0	1,045.6	1.8	4,898.5
Bulgaria	1,906.7	7,128.9	3,827.3	3,705.2	836.8	24,309.6
Croatia	1,395.5	2,161.2	4,723.5	1,816.2	2.5	14,111.7
Czech Republic	8,710.6	29,866.1	85,000.9	15,673.0	115.0	152,820.8
Estonia	749.4	2,273.5	3,516.5	1,766.2	661.7	12,446.9
Georgia	157.8	391.0	193.6	34.3	102.7	1,497.5
Hungary	8,129.5	10,109.6	64,398.1	7,977.5	10,872.4	113,522.9
Latvia	821.8	2,309.9	1,689.3	886.4	541.9	9,204.6
Lithuania	3,320.8	2,500.9	4,852.3	3,230.8	238.1	21,068.3
Macedonia	155.9	2,079.6	169.4	830.4	1.4	4,254.9
Moldova	42.3	236.0	180.7	443.2	11.1	1,597.3
Poland	13,399.0	40,374.0	74,130.8	20,976.0	2,898.7	178,590.1
Romania	2,996.4	9,488.2	17,539.7	8,890.6	905.6	49,538.9
Russia	20,280.2	73,566.4	15,139.6	3,013.2	35,640.9	495,750.4
Slovakia	3,288.5	14,602.1	41,902.7	6,179.7	973.5	73,944.2
Slovenia	4,185.1	6,959.8	11,641.4	3,544.6	72.9	29,232.3
Ukraine	6,267.3	34,060.3	12,264.6	2,107.5	595.2	71,435.1

Source: *United Nations, UN Trade Statistics*
Notes: *US$ totals in this table may differ from the totals given for Exports (fob) by Destination and Total Exports (fob)*

External Trade Statistics

Table 12.14

Exports (fob) by Commodity: SITC Classification 2008 (% Analysis)

% of total exports

	Food and live animals	Beverages and tobacco	Crude materials excluding fuels	Mineral fuels etc	Oils and fats
Western Europe					
Austria	4.80	1.45	2.65	3.36	0.15
Belgium	7.27	0.81	2.47	9.16	0.42
Cyprus	16.90	5.26	5.05	19.84	0.20
Denmark	15.77	1.02	3.50	11.46	0.58
Finland	1.75	0.20	5.68	5.72	0.13
France	8.15	2.85	2.29	5.07	0.30
Germany	3.83	0.71	1.78	2.56	0.20
Gibraltar					
Greece	14.70	2.59	4.09	13.78	2.28
Iceland	35.40	0.19	1.12	1.66	1.28
Ireland	8.85	1.69	1.91	0.87	0.03
Italy	4.92	1.36	1.07	4.58	0.43
Liechtenstein					
Luxembourg	4.28	1.57	2.06	0.86	0.01
Malta	4.91	0.18	0.72	2.03	0.00
Monaco					
Netherlands	9.51	1.67	4.39	8.94	0.79
Norway	4.33	0.07	0.94	67.75	0.14
Portugal	5.26	3.39	4.24	5.03	0.55
Spain	10.51	1.39	2.26	5.03	1.21
Sweden	3.12	0.59	5.88	7.35	0.20
Switzerland	2.35	1.05	1.11	3.17	0.02
Turkey	7.06	0.69	2.50	5.64	0.25
United Kingdom	3.48	2.01	2.36	13.24	0.14
Eastern Europe					
Albania	3.48	0.27	14.84	8.21	0.02
Belarus	6.52	0.10	1.61	37.50	0.09
Bosnia-Herzegovina	4.41	0.44	13.92	7.56	0.58
Bulgaria	5.14	1.63	6.93	14.44	0.26
Croatia	7.45	1.75	6.12	12.86	0.25
Czech Republic	2.99	0.61	2.51	2.59	0.11
Estonia	5.85	1.99	8.56	11.09	0.46
Georgia	6.97	9.24	21.99	2.95	0.14
Hungary	5.54	0.28	1.46	3.12	0.19
Latvia	10.58	3.66	14.24	3.44	0.19
Lithuania	14.55	1.82	5.22	11.02	0.26
Macedonia	7.35	5.69	5.80	5.00	0.09
Moldova	15.51	13.45	9.71	0.19	3.95
Poland	8.48	0.95	2.14	3.20	0.25
Romania	3.51	1.04	5.62	9.15	0.29
Russia	2.25	0.21	3.87	63.72	0.17
Slovakia	3.39	0.14	1.84	4.04	0.06
Slovenia	3.14	0.36	3.08	3.01	0.08
Ukraine	6.19	1.49	7.23	3.64	4.05

Source: *United Nations, UN Trade Statistics*

External Trade Statistics

Exports (fob) by Commodity: SITC Classification 2008 (% Analysis) *(continued)*
% of total exports

	Chemicals	Basic manufactures	Machinery and transport equipment	Miscellaneous manufactured goods	Others	Total
Western Europe						
Austria	9.65	23.23	39.73	11.01	3.98	100.00
Belgium	27.15	18.56	23.12	8.56	2.47	100.00
Cyprus	16.21	5.20	17.30	13.99	0.04	100.00
Denmark	13.17	11.17	26.92	14.96	1.44	100.00
Finland	7.50	29.96	43.09	4.62	1.35	100.00
France	16.82	13.40	38.33	10.39	2.42	100.00
Germany	14.62	13.78	46.19	9.50	6.83	100.00
Gibraltar						
Greece	13.78	21.42	13.47	10.28	3.61	100.00
Iceland	1.30	31.99	24.33	1.63	1.11	100.00
Ireland	49.53	2.01	23.71	8.70	2.69	100.00
Italy	9.92	20.29	37.52	16.87	3.03	100.00
Liechtenstein						
Luxembourg	5.68	46.48	24.22	8.76	6.08	100.00
Malta	10.98	5.00	60.48	14.84	0.85	100.00
Monaco						
Netherlands	14.91	8.55	30.82	6.31	14.10	100.00
Norway	2.49	8.70	9.32	2.38	3.89	100.00
Portugal	7.24	21.17	30.82	14.56	7.73	100.00
Spain	13.00	18.54	37.59	8.21	2.25	100.00
Sweden	10.20	19.44	38.72	8.08	6.43	100.00
Switzerland	34.29	11.32	24.24	22.31	0.13	100.00
Turkey	4.21	27.45	32.92	17.00	2.27	100.00
United Kingdom	16.39	12.99	32.55	11.27	5.57	100.00
Eastern Europe						
Albania	0.43	19.81	3.74	42.84	0.26	100.00
Belarus	15.24	14.30	17.55	5.38	1.71	100.00
Bosnia-Herzegovina	4.53	33.30	13.88	21.35	0.04	100.00
Bulgaria	7.84	29.33	15.74	15.24	3.44	100.00
Croatia	9.89	15.32	33.47	12.87	0.02	100.00
Czech Republic	5.70	19.54	55.62	10.26	0.08	100.00
Estonia	6.02	18.27	28.25	14.19	5.32	100.00
Georgia	10.53	26.11	12.93	2.29	6.86	100.00
Hungary	7.16	8.91	56.73	7.03	9.58	100.00
Latvia	8.93	25.10	18.35	9.63	5.89	100.00
Lithuania	15.76	11.87	23.03	15.33	1.13	100.00
Macedonia	3.66	48.88	3.98	19.52	0.03	100.00
Moldova	2.65	14.77	11.31	27.75	0.70	100.00
Poland	7.50	22.61	41.51	11.75	1.62	100.00
Romania	6.05	19.15	35.41	17.95	1.83	100.00
Russia	4.09	14.84	3.05	0.61	7.19	100.00
Slovakia	4.45	19.75	56.67	8.36	1.32	100.00
Slovenia	14.32	23.81	39.82	12.13	0.25	100.00
Ukraine	8.77	47.68	17.17	2.95	0.83	100.00

Source: United Nations, UN Trade Statistics

External Trade Statistics

Table 12.15

Trade Balance 1980-2008
US$ million

	1980	1985	1990	1995	1996	1997	1998	1999	2000	2001
Western Europe										
Austria	-6,955	-3,747	-7,953	-8,743	-9,513	-6,186	-5,440	-5,431	-4,818	-3,998
Belgium				16,166	11,752	14,621	14,409	14,365	10,881	11,644
Cyprus	-671	-771	-1,611	-2,465	-2,587	-2,597	-2,624	-2,623	-2,895	-2,947
Denmark	-2,591	-1,155	3,789	5,750	6,476	4,712	2,509	5,880	6,024	6,944
Finland	-1,484	385	-430	11,459	9,170	9,532	10,662	10,224	11,580	10,686
France	-18,859	-6,666	-17,856	5,298	5,917	17,822	15,400	7,572	-10,495	-5,312
Germany	4,858	25,445	63,951	59,531	65,415	66,811	71,979	69,331	54,763	85,391
Gibraltar	-107	-83								
Greece	-5,395	-5,596	-11,672	-15,834	-17,724	-16,771	-18,656	-18,244	-18,474	-20,444
Iceland	-81	-90	-89	48	-393	-142	-443	-499	-699	-231
Ireland	-2,755	342	3,065	11,571	12,771	14,287	19,846	24,025	25,617	31,709
Italy	-22,637	-10,976	-11,482	27,958	43,947	30,136	27,255	14,852	1,863	8,124
Liechtenstein										
Luxembourg	-607	-314	-1,291	-1,998	-2,456	-2,379	-2,315	-3,150	-2,769	-2,913
Malta	-455	-359	-831	-1,029	-1,064	-922	-834	-863	-957	-768
Monaco										
Netherlands	-3,472	4,750	5,300	19,402	16,778	16,775	13,627	10,499	14,496	20,608
Norway	1,616	4,430	6,828	9,024	14,030	12,833	2,926	11,289	25,666	26,236
Portugal	-4,670	-1,967	-8,843	-10,100	-10,572	-11,091	-13,722	-14,598	-14,910	-14,970
Spain	-13,358	-5,716	-32,033	-22,273	-19,786	-18,352	-23,921	-34,472	-39,545	-38,452
Sweden	-2,533	1,913	3,293	15,061	17,972	17,271	16,379	16,057	14,407	13,882
Switzerland	-6,709	-3,264	-5,897	1,055	1,735	1,429	1,554	684	-1,236	996
Turkey	-4,999	-3,386	-9,344	-14,111	-20,383	-22,300	-19,040	-13,639	-26,728	-10,065
United Kingdom	-5,415	-8,344	-39,309	-23,200	-25,505	-25,450	-42,222	-49,792	-52,693	-53,606
Eastern Europe										
Albania				-511	-726	-507	-634	-803	-832	-1,020
Belarus				-760	-1,288	-1,388	-1,480	-765	-1,320	-836
Bosnia-Herzegovina				-500	-1,146	-1,362	-1,768	-1,913	-1,615	-1,541
Bulgaria		-318	112	-302	-259	100	-755	-1,490	-1,696	-2,148
Croatia			-1,168	-2,834	-3,140	-5,120	-3,758	-3,496	-3,455	-4,481
Czech Republic				-4,699	-7,451	-6,091	-3,919	-3,241	-4,857	-4,908
Estonia				-737	-1,130	-1,390	-1,415	-1,046	-1,069	-986
Georgia				-333	-548	-751	-691	-452	-387	-436
Hungary	-573	314	927	-2,578	-2,427	-2,126	-2,687	-2,973	-3,939	-3,195
Latvia				-513	-876	-1,049	-1,380	-1,222	-1,319	-1,504
Lithuania				-974	-1,228	-1,824	-2,129	-1,873	-1,671	-1,781
Macedonia				-515	-479	-542	-604	-585	-771	-536
Moldova				-102	-249	-282	-380	-112	-305	-325
Poland	-2,499	-366	5,214	-6,155	-12,697	-16,556	-19,303	-18,506	-17,289	-14,183
Romania	-2,634	900	-4,068	-2,368	-3,351	-2,849	-3,521	-1,887	-2,688	-4,170
Russia				14,050	15,684	9,932	11,068	32,078	56,440	42,744
Slovakia				-630	-2,609	-2,520	-3,004	-1,662	-1,523	-2,860
Slovenia			-609	-1,175	-1,111	-985	-1,062	-1,537	-1,384	-895
Ukraine				-2,356	-3,202	-2,896	-2,039	-264	617	490

Source: *Euromonitor International from International Monetary Fund (IMF), International Financial Statistics*

External Trade Statistics

Trade Balance 1980-2008 *(continued)*
US$ million

	2002	2003	2004	2005	2006	2007	2008
Western Europe							
Austria	316	-2,338	-1,621	-2,228	-569	-110	-2,216
Belgium	17,733	20,647	21,215	17,099	15,030	18,705	6,569
Cyprus	-3,094	-3,455	-4,577	-4,979	-5,798	-7,432	-9,012
Denmark	7,417	9,051	8,734	9,303	6,606	4,065	4,471
Finland	11,023	10,911	10,234	6,765	7,839	8,336	4,754
France	-268	-4,766	-18,365	-42,599	-50,918	-72,652	-100,391
Germany	125,416	147,058	193,558	197,437	199,727	267,820	264,910
Gibraltar							
Greece	-20,849	-31,180	-36,564	-34,306	-38,940	-51,628	-52,600
Iceland	-47	-404	-657	-1,614	-1,845	-1,756	-432
Ireland	35,958	39,107	42,785	40,441	21,196	37,011	43,448
Italy	7,601	2,064	-1,724	-11,874	-24,563	-10,197	-9,698
Liechtenstein							
Luxembourg	-3,102	-3,712	-4,651	-4,868	-5,259	-6,044	-7,210
Malta	-614	-931	-1,197	-1,432	-1,371	-1,525	-1,812
Monaco							
Netherlands	25,714	30,829	34,037	39,241	41,074	55,703	52,522
Norway	24,812	27,994	33,665	47,146	57,098	58,237	77,316
Portugal	-12,785	-10,244	-16,196	-21,240	-22,711	-26,126	-32,685
Spain	-39,994	-52,517	-75,484	-96,635	-112,692	-136,038	-139,353
Sweden	15,275	18,208	22,516	19,305	20,252	17,817	17,989
Switzerland	4,982	5,143	7,495	6,313	9,648	11,626	18,118
Turkey	-15,495	-22,087	-34,373	-43,298	-54,041	-62,656	-69,820
United Kingdom	-59,118	-76,547	-110,260	-111,384	-118,983	-185,867	-172,674
Eastern Europe							
Albania	-1,164	-1,416	-1,703	-1,960	-2,261	-3,110	-3,896
Belarus	-1,071	-1,612	-2,717	-729	-2,618	-4,418	-6,581
Bosnia-Herzegovina	-1,893	-2,046	-2,188	-1,487	-681	-1,114	
Bulgaria	-2,238	-3,361	-4,536	-6,423	-8,168	-11,511	-14,782
Croatia	-5,818	-8,022	-8,565	-9,788	-11,112	-13,465	-16,617
Czech Republic	-4,287	-5,092	-4,426	1,645	1,707	4,293	4,496
Estonia	-1,363	-1,942	-2,400	-2,512	-3,124	-4,104	-3,622
Georgia	-450	-680	-1,199	-1,624	-2,685	-3,977	-4,559
Hungary	-3,276	-5,070	-4,744	-3,605	-2,990	-412	1,085
Latvia	-1,769	-2,350	-3,066	-3,483	-5,535	-7,287	-6,498
Lithuania	-2,294	-2,698	-3,079	-3,729	-5,259	-7,283	-7,366
Macedonia	-880	-939	-1,256	-1,187	-1,355	-1,875	-2,923
Moldova	-395	-614	-793	-1,202	-1,642	-2,348	-2,746
Poland	-14,103	-14,467	-14,117	-11,556	-15,063	-23,181	-36,538
Romania	-3,986	-6,384	-9,179	-12,733	-18,770	-29,560	-33,426
Russia	40,238	52,252	76,087	105,822	122,765	108,566	150,595
Slovakia	-2,983	-1,794	-2,864	-4,171	-5,370	-4,369	-2,987
Slovenia	-576	-1,086	-1,692	-1,730	-2,029	-2,928	-4,704
Ukraine	980	47	3,669	-1,908	-6,671	-11,322	-18,532

Source: *Euromonitor International from International Monetary Fund (IMF), International Financial Statistics*

External Trade Statistics

Table 12.16

Trade Balance by Quarter 2007-2009

US$ million

	2007 1st Quarter	2007 2nd Quarter	2007 3rd Quarter	2007 4th Quarter	2008 1st Quarter	2008 2nd Quarter	2008 3rd Quarter	2008 4th Quarter	2009 1st Quarter	2009 2nd Quarter
Western Europe										
Austria	-30.5	-215.7	169.7	-33.5	-627.8	-154.3	1,007.3	-2,441.3	-323.4	
Belgium	6,287.8	5,426.8	5,828.8	1,161.7	4,042.6	3,804.2	109.1	-1,386.9		
Cyprus	-1,478.4	-1,835.5	-1,968.5	-2,150.1						
Denmark	912.2	1,060.8	1,275.1	817.1	1,055.7	1,541.3	1,416.0	481.9	169.5	
Finland	1,360.2	3,063.7	2,067.8	1,843.9	1,083.4	2,457.0	364.1	849.8	-137.7	
France	-13,887.4	-17,269.1	-18,766.9	-22,728.6	-22,259.4	-27,104.8	-27,849.8	-23,177.0		
Germany	63,246.8	64,954.8	69,016.8	70,601.7	76,599.2	83,737.1	60,077.2	44,496.5	35,001.7	
Gibraltar										
Greece	-12,604.7	-12,650.5	-12,687.7	-13,685.5	-13,441.0	-14,468.9	-13,561.9	-11,128.3	-9,645.8	
Iceland	-244.8	-628.4	-582.6	-299.9	-378.8	-124.3	-182.4	253.9	98.8	
Ireland	8,265.3	10,775.2	10,354.8	7,616.1	8,884.5	11,751.4	11,399.4	11,412.6	12,059.6	
Italy	-6,374.8	-822.0	-544.1	-2,456.2	-7,659.0	-3,302.6	3,352.7	-2,089.0	-4,728.4	
Liechtenstein										
Luxembourg	-1,327.3	-1,592.2	-1,553.1	-1,571.3	-1,418.2	-1,988.6	-1,766.4	-2,036.7		
Malta	-312.4	-349.2	-398.4	-465.2						
Monaco										
Netherlands	13,044.6	11,834.1	13,174.0	17,650.2	15,272.8	14,906.3	10,947.7	11,395.2	10,348.8	
Norway	13,212.0	13,745.3	13,961.8	17,317.4	20,773.6	22,534.1	20,565.0	13,443.2	12,707.5	10,469.1
Portugal	-5,095.6	-6,373.0	-6,507.0	-8,150.4	-7,656.7	-9,030.7	-8,510.7	-7,487.2	-5,120.4	
Spain	-29,249.1	-32,217.1	-34,216.5	-40,355.2	-40,281.7	-38,534.4	-34,684.0	-25,852.9	-18,225.1	
Sweden	5,534.0	4,754.7	2,674.0	4,854.3	6,404.0	4,868.0	3,409.4	3,307.6	3,031.0	
Switzerland	2,657.1	2,782.9	3,300.5	2,885.4	3,613.7	5,741.4	4,968.2	3,794.8	2,464.1	0.0
Turkey	-11,998.7	-15,719.6	-17,530.7	-17,407.0	-16,048.7	-21,059.2	-21,233.2	-11,479.0	-3,808.5	
United Kingdom	-43,288.4	-44,836.2	-50,221.7	-47,520.7	-46,091.0	-46,522.6	-46,326.8	-33,733.6	-30,162.3	0.0
Eastern Europe										
Albania	-629.4	-730.9	-782.4	-967.2	-869.1	-972.0	-993.9	-1,060.8	-735.2	
Belarus	-859.3	-978.5	-902.8	-1,677.2	-753.9	-1,518.6	-1,931.9	-2,376.4	-1,852.2	
Bosnia-Herzegovina										
Bulgaria	-2,341.7	-2,513.5	-2,847.5	-3,808.5	-3,109.1	-4,444.6	-3,719.2	-3,509.1	-1,745.6	
Croatia	-2,963.1	-3,529.6	-3,295.1	-3,677.4	-4,026.7	-5,025.6	-4,195.1	-3,369.2	-2,358.7	
Czech Republic	1,773.8	921.7	641.0	956.5	1,074.7	966.9	219.0	2,235.4		
Estonia	-979.8	-1,055.4	-976.9	-1,092.1	-934.1	-1,018.2	-934.4	-735.7	-352.7	
Georgia	-821.4	-859.0	-987.2	-1,308.9	-1,079.8	-1,291.8	-1,052.5	-1,134.8	-746.7	
Hungary	-195.9	6.8	-129.0	-94.0	800.3	392.8	-265.5	157.4	829.0	
Latvia	-1,643.8	-1,813.1	-1,968.5	-1,861.6	-1,723.8	-1,745.3	-1,699.9	-1,329.2	-744.4	
Lithuania	-1,541.4	-1,923.2	-1,752.1	-2,066.1	-2,336.5	-2,061.4	-1,736.2	-1,228.0	-408.7	
Macedonia	-332.9	-310.3	-434.5	-797.2	-653.1	-785.3	-777.2	-707.5	-620.2	
Moldova	-484.6	-529.7	-593.2	-740.5	-698.9	-896.4	-873.3	-277.6	-601.9	
Poland	-4,491.0	-5,644.9	-5,548.2	-7,497.0	-7,656.7	-9,824.4	-10,069.6	-8,987.2	-2,634.7	
Romania	-5,813.1	-7,145.7	-7,250.1	-9,351.1	-7,612.6	-9,532.1	-9,283.8	-6,997.6	-2,639.3	
Russia	24,640.4	25,694.8	25,304.4	32,926.4	43,925.4	43,994.4	44,514.3	18,161.0	15,941.1	
Slovakia	-763.5	-1,227.3	-926.2	-1,452.0	-315.4	-1,177.5	-802.7	-691.8		
Slovenia	-441.3	-634.2	-711.0	-1,141.5	-936.1	-1,273.5	-1,343.6	-1,151.2	-299.4	
Ukraine	-2,231.8	-1,939.7	-2,493.1	-4,657.2	-5,017.7	-4,794.9	-4,488.4	-4,231.0	-1,436.1	

Source: *Euromonitor International from International Monetary Fund (IMF), International Financial Statistics*

External Trade Statistics

Table 12.17

Trade Balance by Month 2008

US$ million

	January	February	March	April	May	June	July	August	September	October	November	December
Western Europe												
Austria	-720.5	-214.3	307.0	-545.2	112.1	278.8	13.7	1,160.7	-167.1	-1,682.1	-1,116.5	357.3
Belgium	74.5	2,964.3	1,003.8	1,431.7	1,429.9	942.5	1,162.9	-1,663.3	609.4	178.0	-669.1	-895.7
Cyprus												
Denmark	202.4	815.1	33.5	509.5	687.2	338.0	723.1	253.0	431.4	327.6	111.2	39.2
Finland	142.8	679.8	260.8	1,220.6	289.3	947.1	-23.6	209.6	178.1	576.1	313.2	-39.5
France	-9,341.5	-5,738.7	-7,179.2	-7,477.0	-9,768.4	-9,859.4	-8,546.5	-10,367.8	-8,935.5	-9,329.1	-9,148.0	-4,699.9
Germany	25,460.2	25,215.4	25,923.5	29,923.3	22,555.4	31,258.4	22,076.2	16,165.7	21,835.3	22,085.2	12,603.3	9,808.0
Gibraltar												
Greece	-3,868.2	-3,965.5	-5,607.2	-4,783.7	-4,515.5	-5,169.7	-5,164.7	-3,743.1	-4,654.0	-4,255.2	-3,424.3	-3,448.8
Iceland	-149.7	-191.1	-37.9	-48.9	-69.3	-6.2	-258.8	-24.4	100.8	78.1	-2.1	177.9
Ireland	2,486.7	3,115.0	3,282.9	3,854.8	4,057.8	3,838.8	3,494.6	3,680.7	4,224.2	3,797.5	4,008.5	3,606.5
Italy	-6,238.6	-294.0	-1,126.4	-1,932.2	31.1	-1,401.5	6,693.3	-1,861.8	-1,478.9	19.2	-1,496.9	-611.3
Liechtenstein												
Luxembourg	-315.8	-499.7	-602.8	-671.1	-732.6	-584.9	-759.6	-508.9	-497.9	-586.0	-777.3	-673.5
Malta												
Monaco												
Netherlands	4,590.7	5,000.8	5,681.3	6,009.6	4,091.6	4,805.0	4,013.5	2,664.3	4,269.9	4,830.4	3,273.9	3,290.8
Norway	6,763.5	6,330.9	7,679.3	7,654.7	7,883.7	6,995.6	7,989.1	7,792.7	4,783.2	4,990.0	4,677.3	3,775.9
Portugal	-2,317.8	-2,682.9	-2,656.0	-3,157.7	-3,037.6	-2,835.5	-2,910.6	-2,956.7	-2,643.4	-2,690.3	-2,289.2	-2,507.7
Spain	-13,469.2	-11,905.9	-14,906.5	-12,675.0	-12,387.8	-13,471.5	-12,634.2	-11,371.9	-10,677.8	-8,841.2	-7,571.8	-9,439.9
Sweden	1,830.5	2,721.8	1,851.7	1,791.3	1,659.2	1,417.4	1,645.5	212.6	1,551.3	1,395.3	706.5	1,205.8
Switzerland	1,003.3	1,412.4	1,198.0	1,525.7	1,830.0	2,385.7	2,244.6	1,293.0	1,430.6	1,737.1	1,856.0	201.7
Turkey	-5,712.3	-4,953.1	-5,383.3	-6,525.0	-6,830.1	-7,704.1	-7,961.8	-8,201.0	-5,070.4	-5,215.1	-2,678.3	-3,585.6
United Kingdom	-15,426.2	-15,344.0	-15,320.8	-15,368.8	-15,246.7	-15,907.1	-16,571.9	-16,061.3	-13,693.6	-12,047.6	-11,501.5	-10,184.5
Eastern Europe												
Albania	-282.1	-288.1	-298.9	-317.1	-337.2	-317.7	-343.4	-342.8	-307.7	-356.3	-307.2	-397.3
Belarus	-205.2	-231.8	-316.9	-622.9	-378.5	-517.2	-830.5	-580.6	-520.8	-655.3	-620.6	-1,100.5
Bosnia-Herzegovina												
Bulgaria	-1,036.3	-1,020.5	-1,052.2	-1,384.5	-1,432.6	-1,627.5	-1,460.3	-1,105.5	-1,153.3	-1,460.0	-1,077.8	-971.3
Croatia	-1,206.0	-1,290.1	-1,530.5	-1,820.9	-1,489.6	-1,715.1	-1,423.4	-1,268.2	-1,503.5	-1,358.5	-978.0	-1,032.8
Czech Republic	407.2	266.4	401.1	594.3	302.8	69.7	430.3	-186.0	-25.3	-349.4	1,322.9	1,261.8
Estonia	-311.5	-287.3	-335.3	-375.9	-302.8	-339.5	-429.6	-233.0	-271.8	-213.3	-252.2	-270.2
Georgia	-307.3	-374.3	-398.1	-442.7	-465.6	-383.5	-424.9	-291.5	-336.1	-401.3	-344.5	-389.0
Hungary	-10.6	365.7	445.2	185.7	45.0	162.0	-498.1	-49.3	281.9	-0.7	205.3	-47.2
Latvia	-536.3	-615.6	-571.8	-637.4	-539.4	-568.6	-635.3	-489.0	-575.6	-496.1	-389.3	-443.9
Lithuania	-762.5	-657.5	-917.6	-742.9	-685.9	-633.8	-678.7	-468.7	-590.2	-427.7	-341.8	-458.3
Macedonia	-183.0	-235.3	-234.8	-248.3	-239.4	-297.7	-306.1	-280.1	-190.9	-259.7	-224.3	-223.5
Moldova	-172.8	-247.0	-279.1	-313.1	-269.3	-313.9	-290.0	-299.8	-283.4	-92.7	-89.5	-95.5
Poland	-2,173.3	-2,353.5	-3,130.0	-2,898.6	-3,243.4	-3,682.5	-3,513.3	-3,410.5	-3,145.8	-3,298.8	-2,858.5	-2,829.9
Romania	-2,127.9	-2,304.3	-3,180.4	-3,440.5	-2,827.3	-3,264.3	-3,076.3	-2,688.6	-3,518.9	-2,809.0	-2,184.8	-2,003.8
Russia	17,315.1	12,416.4	14,193.9	12,398.4	15,737.6	15,858.4	15,462.4	15,561.4	13,490.5	9,166.3	6,517.0	2,477.6
Slovakia	-37.7	-89.9	-187.8	-655.6	-109.7	-412.2	-443.2	-118.2	-241.3	108.6	-268.8	-531.7
Slovenia	-338.7	-262.7	-334.7	-332.5	-520.8	-420.2	-503.0	-499.0	-341.7	-421.2	-288.0	-442.0
Ukraine	-975.4	-1,783.6	-2,269.7	-2,370.2	-1,407.6	-1,030.5	-1,164.3	-1,563.9	-1,748.1	-1,948.6	-1,552.7	-717.1

Source: *Euromonitor International from International Monetary Fund (IMF), International Financial Statistics*

Health

Health Statistics

Table 13.1

Hospitals and Beds 2008

As stated

	In-patient Beds ('000)	Hospitals and Clinics	Beds per '000 inhabitants
Western Europe			
Austria	61	272	7.4
Belgium	55	208	5.1
Cyprus	3	94	2.9
Denmark	20	49	3.7
Finland	36	331	6.9
France	435	2,643	7.0
Germany	658	3,251	8.0
Gibraltar			
Greece	53	312	4.8
Iceland	4	20	12.6
Ireland	24	175	5.5
Italy	230	1,264	3.9
Liechtenstein			
Luxembourg	3		5.3
Malta	4	9	9.8
Monaco			
Netherlands	69	187	4.2
Norway	19		4.0
Portugal	40	195	3.7
Spain	146	743	3.2
Sweden		79	
Switzerland	14	307	1.9
Turkey	207	1,353	2.8
United Kingdom	200		3.3
Eastern Europe			
Albania	9	45	2.9
Belarus	109	702	11.2
Bosnia-Herzegovina	12	40	3.1
Bulgaria	47	351	6.2
Croatia	24	79	5.4
Czech Republic	83	339	8.0
Estonia	7	59	5.5
Georgia	15	262	3.5
Hungary	80	176	8.0
Latvia	17	86	7.5
Lithuania	25	160	7.5
Macedonia	9	55	4.6
Moldova	22	72	5.9
Poland	278	761	7.3
Romania	140	419	6.5
Russia	1,303	4,363	9.2
Slovakia	35	147	6.5
Slovenia	9	30	4.7
Ukraine	399	2,567	8.6

Source: *Euromonitor International from OECD/World Health Organisation/National Statistics*

Table 13.2

Number of Doctors 1985-2008
Number

	1985	1990	1995	2000	2003	2004	2005	2006	2007	2008
Western Europe										
Austria	14,215	17,189	21,363	25,332	27,413	28,223	29,164	30,295	31,175	32,079
Belgium	27,989	32,547	35,917	39,519	41,465	41,734	42,176	42,426	42,839	43,169
Cyprus	846	1,199	1,607	1,800	1,879	1,965	1,976	1,950	1,973	1,974
Denmark	13,844	15,101	16,401	17,467	18,493	19,287	19,786	20,325	20,961	21,517
Finland	9,750	11,450	12,400	14,250	13,799	13,875	13,960	14,430	14,656	14,923
France	146,800	173,100	186,700	194,000	201,400	203,487	205,864	207,277	208,191	213,643
Germany	160,902	195,254	250,314	267,965	277,885	279,722	281,309	284,427	288,182	290,910
Gibraltar										
Greece	29,103	34,336	41,039	47,251	52,325	53,943	55,556	59,599	62,079	64,827
Iceland	626	726	809	968	1,047	1,056	1,104	1,120	1,144	1,173
Ireland	5,680	5,995	7,563	8,438	10,270	11,141	11,670	12,184	13,141	13,558
Italy	215,206	266,447	221,000	237,000	237,000	241,175	222,216	215,377	206,171	194,076
Liechtenstein										
Luxembourg	240	295	324	365	399	409	423	435	448	462
Malta	538	800	920	1,024	1,254	1,302	1,407	1,564	1,357	1,374
Monaco	68	81	186							
Netherlands	32,193	37,461	43,162	50,856	56,540	58,550	60,519	62,497	64,417	66,355
Norway	9,176	10,841	12,146	12,813	15,503	16,064	17,032	17,497	18,182	18,900
Portugal	24,390	28,016	29,353	32,498	34,440	35,213	36,138	36,857	37,623	38,397
Spain			97,000	127,100	135,300	144,000	163,500	159,900	163,800	176,597
Sweden	21,596	24,600	25,480	27,340	30,105	30,837	31,545	32,495	33,412	34,277
Switzerland	17,667	20,030	22,275	25,216	27,268	27,742	28,251	28,812	29,052	29,451
Turkey	36,427	50,639	69,349	85,106	97,763	104,226	106,698	106,029	108,894	110,457
United Kingdom	80,763	92,583	101,803	114,818	129,443	138,310	144,162	148,648	155,159	160,809
Eastern Europe										
Albania	4,159	4,516	4,244	4,325	3,699	3,699	3,652	3,626	3,626	3,605
Belarus	33,144	36,358	42,713	45,817	45,027	45,281	45,649	46,359	46,965	47,537
Bosnia-Herzegovina	5,829	7,032	5,322	5,368	5,576	5,458	5,540	5,559	5,551	5,576
Bulgaria	25,665	28,497	29,069	27,526	28,128	27,423	28,197	28,111	27,911	28,061
Croatia	9,139	10,152	9,723	10,439	10,820	11,093	11,100	11,250	11,799	12,022
Czech Republic	26,649	28,036	30,942	34,604	35,960	35,476	35,605	35,694	36,815	37,135
Estonia	5,089	5,498	4,585	4,240	4,292	4,330	4,310	4,414	4,451	4,487
Georgia	24,216	26,685	21,186	21,063	20,962	21,396	20,311	20,597	19,951	19,506
Hungary	26,716	29,077	30,538	31,996	32,877	33,727	28,055	30,575	27,957	26,050
Latvia	10,571	10,966	7,395	7,602	6,940	7,198	7,259	7,200	6,940	6,853
Lithuania	13,186	14,891	14,737	14,034	13,682	13,397	13,650	13,510	13,729	13,843
Macedonia	3,561	4,396	4,516	4,455	4,448	4,490	4,999	5,187	5,432	5,744
Moldova	13,893	15,485	15,242	13,580	11,246	11,116	11,083	11,153	11,167	11,207
Poland	73,199	81,641	89,421	85,031	87,617	85,623	76,046	77,479	74,039	70,141
Romania	40,050	41,813	40,112	42,374	42,538	42,960	42,333	41,455	41,096	40,466
Russia	553,673	602,059	566,873	608,736	609,043	607,052	607,699	614,183	615,957	618,970
Slovakia	14,528	15,580	16,196	17,453	17,172	16,868	16,262	16,262	16,197	15,948
Slovenia	3,712	3,980	4,206	4,317	4,518	4,617	4,723	4,766	4,927	4,944
Ukraine	203,756	221,494	225,959	147,957	143,202	142,415	141,526	143,728	144,096	144,777

Source: UNAIDS/World Health Organisation

Health Statistics

Table 13.3

Number of Dentists 1985-2008

Number

	1985	1990	1995	2000	2003	2004	2005	2006	2007	2008
Western Europe										
Austria	3,078	3,317	3,687	3,732	4,037	4,113	4,232	4,467	4,490	4,597
Belgium	6,214	7,135	7,852	8,465	8,597	8,660	8,655	8,714	8,643	8,783
Cyprus	301	428	543	619	671	697	728	715	730	740
Denmark	4,186	4,270	4,143	4,214	4,225	4,257	4,287	4,266	4,283	4,291
Finland	3,916	4,490	4,760	4,760	4,610	4,540	4,530	4,490	4,453	4,425
France	34,744	37,931	39,714	40,539	40,648	40,904	41,088	41,374	41,444	41,841
Germany	45,257	50,328	57,612	60,366	61,865	62,279	62,468	62,689	63,100	63,355
Gibraltar										
Greece	8,737	10,038	10,663	12,362	13,079	13,316	13,438	14,180	14,557	14,976
Iceland	197	230	270	283	288	287	289	286	285	284
Ireland	1,168	1,313	1,568	1,899	2,171	2,237	2,327	2,414	2,537	2,599
Italy		13,430	23,000	23,000	31,000	33,000	35,000	37,000	38,832	40,646
Liechtenstein										
Luxembourg	168	198	223	282	316	343	359	379	401	422
Malta	65	96	116	157	167	181	195	190	175	173
Monaco	32	33	34							
Netherlands	7,118	7,544	7,258	7,397	7,759	7,950	7,994	8,054	8,113	8,164
Norway	3,702	4,178	4,550	3,578	3,712	3,697	3,901	4,106	4,108	4,247
Portugal	1,265	1,687	2,532	4,370	5,510	5,788	6,149	6,472	6,789	7,121
Spain	5,137	10,347	14,012	17,538	20,005	21,055	22,150	23,300	24,515	25,568
Sweden		7,647	7,154	7,290	7,433	7,429	7,541	7,651	7,722	
Switzerland	3,117	3,268	3,474	3,468	3,598	3,679	3,764	3,847	3,926	4,004
Turkey	8,305	10,514	11,717	16,002	18,073	18,363	18,540	18,089	18,304	18,271
United Kingdom	20,413	21,654	22,536	26,393	27,790	28,552	29,882	29,819	30,504	31,152
Eastern Europe										
Albania	982	1,115	1,145	1,457	1,350	1,247	1,142	1,035	956	853
Belarus	2,426	3,239	3,695	4,485	4,315	4,456	4,555	4,647	4,784	4,894
Bosnia-Herzegovina	1,250	1,408	853	725	690	630	629	610	582	566
Bulgaria	5,745	6,109	5,481	6,778	6,475	6,491	6,493	6,512	6,432	6,411
Croatia	2,087	2,262	2,672	2,974	3,085	3,193	3,218	3,230	3,265	3,286
Czech Republic	5,406	5,626	6,247	6,658	6,737	6,843	6,906	6,933	6,948	6,986
Estonia	688	753	867	1,034	1,112	1,148	1,186	1,175	1,195	1,209
Georgia	2,321	2,467	1,893	1,650	1,532	1,341	1,320	1,269	1,219	1,181
Hungary	2,808	3,806	4,096	4,693	5,364	5,150	4,508	4,997	4,245	3,946
Latvia	1,483	1,539	931	1,278	1,287	1,390	1,450	1,561	1,552	1,604
Lithuania	2,156	2,236	1,742	2,446	2,372	2,272	2,453	2,249	2,395	2,436
Macedonia	778	1,112	1,086	1,129	1,132	1,134	1,375	1,175	1,189	1,206
Moldova	1,675	1,950	1,923	1,595	1,403	1,439	1,494	1,521	1,566	1,610
Poland	17,440	18,205	17,805	11,758	10,737	10,081	11,881	12,187	12,658	13,504
Romania	7,340	6,717	6,045	4,983	4,919	5,013	4,694	4,360	4,175	3,897
Russia		42,102	44,304	46,469	45,972	45,886	45,633	45,628	45,523	45,411
Slovakia	2,515	2,579	2,203	2,582	2,364	2,441	2,464	2,495	2,539	2,571
Slovenia	1,025	1,121	1,264	1,159	1,203	1,193	1,198	1,202	1,202	1,209
Ukraine	16,579	18,052	19,490	19,489	19,354	19,269	19,338	19,169	19,135	19,110

Source: UNAIDS/World Health Organisation

Table 13.4

Number of Nurses 1985-2008

Number

	1985	1990	1995	2000	2003	2004	2005	2006	2007	2008
Western Europe										
Austria	26,618	30,798	40,354	45,505	47,281	49,574	50,492	52,045	52,795	54,105
Belgium	75,474	92,701	110,957	123,847	135,589	139,577	155,488	163,908	173,639	185,050
Cyprus	2,155	2,478	2,821	2,931	3,069	3,247	3,328	3,361	3,459	3,530
Denmark	25,876	28,141	46,906	49,839	50,306	51,514	52,313	51,787	52,331	52,587
Finland		22,100	24,600	33,085	38,100	42,300	43,900	45,040	47,425	49,167
France	286,162	304,480	341,085	382,926	423,431	437,525	452,483	469,011	483,380	497,212
Germany	562,624	623,813	607,090	615,000	635,000	638,000	643,000	644,000	646,264	648,827
Gibraltar										
Greece	14,203	23,324	29,869	33,869	38,786	38,766	37,493	36,434	36,971	36,360
Iceland	1,754	1,995	2,233	2,443	2,674	2,760	2,833	2,930	3,015	3,100
Ireland		39,595	42,937	53,072	58,981	60,774	62,639	65,415	67,245	68,593
Italy	240,552	264,414	294,709	299,166	312,377	386,000	405,000	413,000	444,969	463,095
Liechtenstein										
Luxembourg			2,913	3,317	4,151	4,288	4,678	5,101	5,439	5,846
Malta	1,412	1,436	1,468	1,471	2,298	2,041	2,221	2,280	2,387	2,501
Monaco	245	344	454							
Netherlands	87,000	129,000	176,831	206,525	226,200	231,863	236,975	241,804	246,545	251,350
Norway	38,263	56,132	67,770	57,986	65,550	67,799	70,247	72,408	73,768	75,781
Portugal	24,677	27,652	33,549	37,477	43,978	45,906	48,296	50,955	53,250	55,678
Spain	143,508	158,497	227,500	263,600	315,200	317,500	321,800	322,600	325,091	326,419
Sweden	72,386	78,500	85,265	88,017	92,942	95,010	96,560	98,378	100,546	102,402
Switzerland				92,474	104,678	104,389	104,653	106,242	106,611	107,192
Turkey	59,366	96,866	138,136	159,730	173,951	182,988	185,438	186,864	219,384	231,997
United Kingdom	284,116	450,000	470,386	662,862	723,560	733,718	739,857	723,404	723,216	719,219
Eastern Europe										
Albania		14,785	14,318	12,570	11,238	11,136	11,136	12,746	12,746	13,127
Belarus	108,570	118,085	115,596	120,706	115,116	115,360	116,551	116,337	116,193	116,514
Bosnia-Herzegovina	18,875	20,939	16,188	16,943	17,170	16,899	17,082	17,109	17,082	17,125
Bulgaria	50,805	53,810	51,035	31,479	29,650	29,769	31,235	31,599	32,244	33,037
Croatia	20,910	24,153	19,272	22,157	22,372	22,799	22,974	23,355	23,852	24,179
Czech Republic	84,169	90,008	92,135	94,488	99,351	87,082	87,154	86,894	86,989	86,991
Estonia	10,464	11,636	9,682	8,517	8,815	8,676	8,845	8,803	8,792	8,823
Georgia	52,979	53,143	38,541	20,955	18,802	17,334	17,267	16,672	15,948	15,518
Hungary		76,966	79,786	78,941	84,819	84,685	88,814	91,058	90,889	92,946
Latvia	23,100	22,900	15,125	12,295	12,150	12,248	12,528	12,398	12,472	12,539
Lithuania	31,596	35,450	34,314	28,017	26,229	25,620	25,364	25,169	24,804	24,549
Macedonia	8,825	10,374	10,666	7,250	7,234	7,266	7,012	7,545	7,645	7,767
Moldova	37,531	42,676	40,788	32,834	25,848	25,370	25,397	25,192	27,002	27,580
Poland	179,727	207,767	211,603	189,632	181,291	177,501	178,790	178,781	177,784	177,753
Romania	84,937	94,036	97,999	90,177	86,802	86,833	80,804	85,785	85,445	84,957
Russia	1,176,553	3,835,110	1,199,775	1,153,668	1,153,683	1,148,752	1,141,359	1,148,755	1,147,323	1,147,047
Slovakia	34,878	38,800	37,974	40,380	36,569	35,746	34,038	32,612	31,285	29,783
Slovenia	10,378	11,225	12,705	13,765	14,748	14,863	15,057	15,361	15,565	15,858
Ukraine	566,576	607,200	595,054	384,629	369,755	367,519	367,163	365,138	364,145	363,391

Source: UNAIDS/World Health Organisation

Health Statistics

Table 13.5

Number of Active Pharmacists 1985-2008

Number

	1985	1990	1995	2000	2003	2004	2005	2006	2007	2008
Western Europe										
Austria	3,136	3,486	4,071	4,532	4,869	4,997	5,076	4,929	5,339	5,005
Belgium	10,792	12,335	9,499	10,724	11,379	11,618	11,882	12,109	12,364	12,605
Cyprus	93	96	118	120	107	145	160	160	178	190
Denmark	2,523	2,700	3,048	3,326	3,518	3,564	3,650	3,723	3,795	3,872
Finland	6,743	6,877	7,204	7,660	8,086	8,232	8,399	8,591	8,770	8,953
France	45,521	51,977	57,389	64,338	67,664	69,148	70,320	70,869	70,498	73,572
Germany	31,068	35,118	44,696	47,907	47,956	47,830	48,058	48,724	49,528	50,078
Gibraltar										
Greece	5,994	7,463	8,348	8,977	9,339	9,461	9,571	9,695	9,818	9,938
Iceland	84	134	207	230	279	287	299	312	323	335
Ireland	2,068	2,160	2,438	3,044	3,385	3,565	3,800	4,108	4,504	4,699
Italy	51,036	54,787	57,880	62,862	66,119	53,000	50,000	44,000	36,160	30,287
Liechtenstein										
Luxembourg	254	307	269	325	371	375	385	401	405	416
Malta	322	409	580	731	800	837	884	790	630	559
Monaco	60	63	61							
Netherlands	1,900	2,247	2,556	2,664	3,134	2,734	2,789	2,825	2,871	2,916
Norway	2,946	2,629	2,294	2,351	2,689	2,752	2,853	3,043	3,239	3,404
Portugal	4,807	5,438	6,549	8,056	8,932	9,395	10,320	10,912	11,568	12,291
Spain	30,569	23,000	24,900	32,600	35,800	36,700	41,100	39,900	41,342	42,814
Sweden	4,107	5,080	5,945	5,670	6,446	6,564	6,582	6,605	6,680	6,718
Switzerland	2,738	3,565	4,178	4,450	4,568	4,460	4,487	4,269	4,160	4,051
Turkey	12,202	15,792	19,090	23,266	23,632	24,615	24,618	24,280	25,541	24,446
United Kingdom	31,840	33,395	36,839	37,934	38,929	39,979	38,986	41,302	42,102	42,801
Eastern Europe										
Albania	1,000	1,195	1,241	1,074	1,100	1,124	1,149	1,173	1,237	1,272
Belarus	2,815	3,261	2,500	3,198	2,901	2,896	2,898	2,930	2,994	3,027
Bosnia-Herzegovina	625	815	578	380	363	370	308	290	270	237
Bulgaria	4,209	4,366	1,882	1,020	908	897	855	831	792	758
Croatia	1,767	1,857	1,773	2,142	2,348	2,414	2,480	2,549	2,607	2,669
Czech Republic	4,029	3,962	3,763	5,059	5,610	5,674	5,761	5,842	5,785	5,825
Estonia	742	926	724	815	776	845	851	869	899	916
Georgia	3,073	3,011	536	456	364	270	258	257	249	242
Hungary	3,500	3,390	3,422	4,905	5,125	5,156	5,313	5,364	5,483	5,591
Latvia										
Lithuania	1,780	2,000	2,235	2,195	2,390	2,300	2,398	2,184	2,743	2,888
Macedonia	277	372	349	311	319	322	878	908	1,105	1,366
Moldova	3,145	3,380	2,905	2,672	2,654	2,877	2,920	2,834	2,993	3,036
Poland	16,064	15,110	19,447	22,161	25,217	22,170	21,971	22,442	21,499	21,262
Romania	6,558	6,286	2,646	1,588	1,275	1,295	1,042	901	778	606
Russia		50,023	8,026	10,279	11,404	11,204	11,542	11,521	11,561	11,680
Slovakia	1,893	2,050	1,260	2,245	2,783	2,637	2,650	2,625	2,572	2,549
Slovenia	533	646	665	754	820	848	905	944	990	1,035
Ukraine	42,468	44,783	36,343	23,548	23,487	23,485	22,264	22,257	21,682	21,415

Source: UNAIDS/World Health Organisation

Table 13.6

Causes of Death: Male 2008
Per 100,000 inhabitants

	Tuberculosis	HIV	Cancer	Diabetes	Mental and Behaviour Disorders	Diseases of Circulatory System	Diseases of Respiratory System	Diseases of Digestive System
Western Europe								
Austria	0.8	1.8	248.4	36.4	12.2	334.5	61.8	45.6
Belgium	0.8	0.9	324.4	12.1	19.6	327.5	127.8	43.8
Cyprus								
Denmark	0.8	1.2	294.7	27.3	34.9	394.2	101.0	44.8
Finland	0.6	0.1	213.7	9.8	30.2	360.9	50.6	57.9
France	1.0	2.6	305.2	20.3	28.1	254.4	67.3	47.1
Germany	0.7	1.0	280.7	24.1	14.1	364.7	64.6	53.9
Gibraltar								
Greece	0.7	0.1	292.9	10.4	1.3	441.2	74.0	24.3
Iceland								
Ireland	0.4	0.0	184.8	12.0	11.9	232.1	83.1	23.1
Italy	1.0	2.5	319.7	26.2	12.3	378.0	77.4	43.5
Liechtenstein								
Luxembourg								
Malta								
Monaco								
Netherlands	0.5	0.8	264.9	19.4	23.7	242.0	91.0	28.3
Norway	0.5	1.0	242.6	11.6	16.6	286.8	62.7	28.8
Portugal	4.7	0.2	396.0	19.8	11.1	634.0	58.3	117.1
Spain	1.3	5.8	288.4	18.4	18.9	260.8	103.0	48.7
Sweden	0.2	0.5	267.2	22.0	28.3	419.6	67.0	32.3
Switzerland	0.2	1.4	236.2	16.6	26.5	253.6	55.0	27.6
Turkey								
United Kingdom	0.7	0.3	271.2	10.6	19.1	332.4	118.0	46.2
Eastern Europe								
Albania	0.8	0.0	118.5	5.8	3.8	292.3	33.2	13.0
Belarus	16.8		247.0	4.2	10.8	820.3	100.9	44.2
Bosnia-Herzegovina								
Bulgaria	5.2	0.0	263.0	22.6	3.6	991.2	52.1	55.1
Croatia	4.3	0.1	335.9	17.1	16.8	464.8	89.9	70.9
Czech Republic	0.6	0.0	323.8	10.8	3.4	483.6	51.8	51.2
Estonia	5.4	3.3	321.7	10.4	23.3	638.0	48.0	66.0
Georgia	8.3	0.0	92.6	13.9	0.6	579.8	23.6	36.4
Hungary	4.7	0.2	396.0	19.8	11.1	634.0	58.3	117.1
Latvia	17.3	0.8	294.9	7.4	2.5	742.7	59.1	55.0
Lithuania	19.9	0.3	283.6	10.0	2.8	704.9	81.2	74.9
Macedonia								
Moldova								
Poland	3.6	0.5	280.9	11.1	8.8	430.8	53.8	49.8
Romania	17.0	1.0	242.2	10.0	7.8	735.9	80.5	89.6
Russia	43.6	0.6	238.0	4.9	9.8	998.9	115.6	78.6
Slovakia	1.5	0.1	272.2	9.4	0.2	510.6	54.6	61.0
Slovenia	0.1	0.2	288.2	20.6	6.3	315.7	75.7	75.5
Ukraine	39.7		241.6	5.3	9.1	940.6	99.3	70.5

Source: *World Health Organisation/Euromonitor International*

Health Statistics

Table 13.7

Causes of Death: Female 2008
Per 100,000 inhabitants

	Tuberculosis	HIV	Cancer	Diabetes	Mental and Behaviour Disorders	Diseases of Circulatory System	Diseases of Respiratory System	Diseases of Digestive System
Western Europe								
Austria	0.6	0.2	214.5	48.8	3.6	486.5	58.5	33.7
Belgium	0.2	0.3	228.0	22.5	30.7	388.1	93.5	48.9
Cyprus								
Denmark	1.0	0.4	288.5	31.7	45.2	410.4	107.2	50.8
Finland	0.4	0.1	184.1	10.4	65.1	352.7	36.7	41.4
France	0.7	0.8	192.0	23.1	39.4	282.5	59.4	37.6
Germany	0.3	0.2	237.0	35.3	11.9	486.0	56.0	50.7
Gibraltar								
Greece	0.2	0.1	178.8	11.1	1.8	464.2	67.1	16.6
Iceland								
Ireland	0.5	0.3	175.6	10.9	14.3	220.4	96.8	26.0
Italy	0.5	0.7	221.5	36.2	22.1	442.2	54.3	41.2
Liechtenstein								
Luxembourg								
Malta								
Monaco								
Netherlands	0.1	0.2	223.4	24.8	53.8	258.2	86.7	34.7
Norway	0.2	0.4	207.7	12.3	33.7	345.0	60.1	33.2
Portugal	1.3	0.1	279.4	24.9	4.1	676.9	40.6	61.3
Spain	0.6	1.1	164.0	27.4	34.0	301.5	67.6	40.6
Sweden	0.1	0.2	228.1	22.1	53.3	448.7	65.2	34.4
Switzerland	0.3	0.3	186.0	21.9	45.1	312.3	44.4	29.0
Turkey								
United Kingdom	0.5	0.3	238.0	11.1	37.3	347.2	132.9	51.7
Eastern Europe								
Albania	0.5	0.0	71.8	5.9	4.2	259.1	23.3	8.0
Belarus	2.6		153.9	7.6	3.9	816.1	39.8	24.9
Bosnia-Herzegovina								
Bulgaria	1.5	0.0	167.9	27.5	1.5	896.8	27.0	23.5
Croatia	2.5	0.0	214.9	23.1	14.0	568.2	62.3	41.2
Czech Republic	0.5	0.0	245.0	14.4	1.0	549.2	35.8	36.6
Estonia	0.9	0.8	214.4	17.4	8.4	675.9	18.0	41.9
Georgia	1.9	0.0	85.0	13.6	0.1	607.7	16.5	15.2
Hungary	1.3	0.1	279.4	24.9	4.1	676.9	40.6	61.3
Latvia	6.0	0.4	218.0	16.7	1.1	844.2	20.7	42.1
Lithuania	3.6	0.0	203.2	11.7	0.9	747.2	28.6	48.4
Macedonia								
Moldova								
Poland	0.8	0.1	197.1	15.1	1.5	447.5	32.8	34.8
Romania	3.5	0.8	163.6	11.0	2.1	758.6	45.3	52.4
Russia	7.2	0.2	170.9	10.0	3.6	1,004.6	38.1	49.6
Slovakia	1.0	0.1	176.2	11.0	0.0	544.6	38.1	31.8
Slovenia	0.0	0.0	225.8	32.8	5.3	377.5	60.7	51.7
Ukraine	5.5		158.9	6.7	2.4	1,032.3	31.5	33.9

Source: World Health Organisation/Euromonitor International

Table 13.8

Reported AIDS Cases by Date of Report 1985-2008

Number

	1985	1990	1995	2000	2003	2004	2005	2006	2007	2008
Western Europe										
Austria	28	164	209	85	50	72	58	58	57	55
Belgium	69	206	254	145	126	122	150	100	91	81
Cyprus		6	6	11	5	2	3	3	3	3
Denmark	38	197	213	58	39	59	44	50	49	46
Finland	4	16	41	17	25	19	26	44	48	54
France	584	4,323	5,314	1,735	1,465	1,375	1,314	1,018	869	700
Germany	313	1,555	1,920	780	648	668	626	366	319	261
Gibraltar										
Greece	14	143	216	131	94	86	100	91	90	89
Iceland	1	3	4	1	1	3	1	3	2	2
Ireland	7	68	53	13	39	44	48	24	22	20
Italy	198	3,135	5,653	1,948	1,718	1,616	1,499	1,126	994	856
Liechtenstein										
Luxembourg	2	9	15	10	8	12	8	9	9	10
Malta		1	4	3	2	1	3	4	4	5
Monaco	1	2	3							
Netherlands	65	419	534	250	281	281	314	189	164	133
Norway	14	60	68	38	50	36	32	25	20	17
Portugal	29	261	821	1,011	894	788	761	695	629	576
Spain	176	3,945	7,179	2,849	2,226	2,029	1,752	1,518	1,361	1,213
Sweden	34	132	196	61	53	65	46	57	58	60
Switzerland	120	612	620	210	215	220	185	154	140	122
Turkey	2	14	27	48	44	55	30	31	29	26
United Kingdom	246	1,242	1,770	833	928	881	833	858	877	878
Eastern Europe										
Albania			3	3	5	6	9	15	18	21
Belarus			3		33	90	162	269	314	357
Bosnia-Herzegovina			7	4	6	5	6	4	3	2
Bulgaria		4	1	16	15	20	19	16	16	15
Croatia		9	15	19	10	13	17	20	23	26
Czech Republic		5	13	14	8	13	11	12	13	13
Estonia			4	3	10	29	29	32	37	39
Georgia		2	4	15	46	112	120	133	148	154
Hungary		19	31	27	26	23	33	22	21	20
Latvia		2	3	23	75	76	75	61	58	55
Lithuania		1	1	7	9	21	10	27	32	35
Macedonia		1	5	4		3	12	6	7	8
Moldova			2	4	46	58	60	103	118	134
Poland		21	115	124	143	175	149	114	104	80
Romania	5	1,202	767	662	363	308	306	211	191	175
Russia		50	46	157	314	396	548	842	959	1,084
Slovakia	1	1	2	5	2	2	3	4	5	6
Slovenia		3	15	7	6	10	10	5	5	4
Ukraine		1	42	650	1,865	2,683	4,025	4,535	4,891	5,185

Source: UNAIDS/World Health Organisation

Health Statistics

Table 13.9

Food Supply: Average Consumption of Calories, Protein and Fat 2008

Daily averages, calories / grams per inhabitant

	Calories (number)	Protein (grams)	Fat (grams)
Western Europe			
Austria	3,790	111.5	166.7
Belgium	3,561	119.1	134.1
Cyprus	3,365	105.5	131.6
Denmark	3,511	110.7	143.9
Finland	3,072	104.1	128.7
France	3,609	118.9	170.8
Germany	3,611	104.0	137.1
Gibraltar			
Greece	3,600	120.2	133.6
Iceland	3,377	124.0	136.6
Ireland	3,745	120.7	134.2
Italy	3,694	113.8	155.4
Liechtenstein			
Luxembourg			
Malta	3,598	126.5	108.8
Monaco			
Netherlands	3,562	103.6	136.2
Norway	3,890	110.4	132.0
Portugal	3,750	117.4	146.5
Spain	3,606	116.8	163.5
Sweden	3,300	126.2	119.6
Switzerland	3,578	103.1	166.9
Turkey	3,250	95.5	94.5
United Kingdom	3,543	112.0	123.9
Eastern Europe			
Albania	2,929	101.5	86.5
Belarus	2,699	84.2	87.5
Bosnia-Herzegovina	2,883	71.1	68.6
Bulgaria	3,100	92.8	101.5
Croatia	2,894	78.7	99.0
Czech Republic	3,625	98.2	116.9
Estonia	3,440	87.8	107.3
Georgia	3,128	79.3	68.7
Hungary	3,837	98.1	165.5
Latvia	3,081	87.6	126.3
Lithuania	3,623	118.8	104.4
Macedonia	3,215	75.0	85.7
Moldova	2,591	66.6	58.1
Poland	3,534	122.2	109.2
Romania	4,101	129.8	112.6
Russia	3,197	95.9	94.4
Slovakia	2,629	74.5	97.2
Slovenia	2,806	96.7	98.3
Ukraine	3,283	88.3	98.4

Source: *Euromonitor International from FAO/National Statistics*

Health Statistics

Table 13.10

Government Health Expenditure Statistics 2008
As stated

	Government Health Spend as a % of Total Central Government Spend	Per Capita Health Spend (US$)	Government Spend on Drugs (US$ million)
Western Europe			
Austria	10.1	5,219	3,511.5
Belgium	10.7	5,270	4,142.9
Cyprus	6.5	1,619	
Denmark	9.6	6,487	5,645.5
Finland	8.2	4,457	1,744.0
France	11.0	5,323	35,288.8
Germany	10.5	4,874	41,467.1
Gibraltar			
Greece	9.5	3,142	5,744.9
Iceland	8.9	5,568	118.6
Ireland	7.2	4,452	1,940.8
Italy	8.6	3,342	18,357.7
Liechtenstein			
Luxembourg	6.5	7,623	250.1
Malta	8.1	1,700	
Monaco	5.0	2,292	
Netherlands	9.5	5,042	4,857.3
Norway	7.7	7,859	1,521.3
Portugal	10.4	2,480	2,824.2
Spain	8.6	3,235	20,931.3
Sweden	9.1	5,091	3,267.8
Switzerland	11.2	7,303	3,803.5
Turkey	5.3	504	
United Kingdom	8.8	4,185	
Eastern Europe			
Albania	5.6	233	
Belarus	6.4	382	
Bosnia-Herzegovina	7.8	384	
Bulgaria	5.3	348	
Croatia	7.3	1,048	
Czech Republic	6.4	1,348	1,902.2
Estonia	4.8	800	
Georgia	8.2	248	
Hungary	7.1	1,166	2,940.7
Latvia	5.2	694	
Lithuania	6.0	865	
Macedonia	8.2	386	
Moldova	8.2	135	
Poland	6.2	919	3,147.1
Romania	5.9	587	
Russia	5.0	606	
Slovakia	7.6	1,417	1,366.1
Slovenia	8.2	2,272	
Ukraine	7.1	305	

Source: *Euromonitor International from IMF*

Health Statistics

Table 13.11

Obese Population (BMI 30kg/sq m or more) 1985-2008

% of population aged 15+

	1985	1990	1995	2000	2003	2004	2005	2006	2007	2008
Western Europe										
Austria	7	8	9	10	11	11	12	12	13	13
Belgium	9	10	11	11	12	13	13	13	14	14
Cyprus										
Denmark	5	7	8	10	10	11	11	11	11	12
Finland	7	8	10	11	13	14	14	14	15	15
France	5	6	7	9	9	10	10	11	11	11
Germany	8	9	10	12	13	13	14	14	14	15
Gibraltar										
Greece	7	8	9	10	11	11	11	11	11	11
Iceland		8	11	12	13	13	14	14	14	15
Ireland	5	6	7	9	9	9	10	10	10	11
Italy	4	5	8	9	9	9	10	10	11	11
Liechtenstein										
Luxembourg		11	14	16	18	19	19	19	20	20
Malta										
Monaco										
Netherlands	5	6	7	9	11	11	11	11	11	12
Norway	2	3	5	7	9	9	9	9	10	10
Portugal	4	6	8	11	13	14	15	15	16	16
Spain	6	7	10	12	13	14	14	15	15	15
Sweden	4	6	7	9	10	10	10	10	10	11
Switzerland	4	5	6	7	8	9	9	10	10	10
Turkey	15	19	22	22	21	21	22	22	22	22
United Kingdom	9	13	16	21	23	23	23	24	24	24
Eastern Europe										
Albania										
Belarus	19	20	22	23	24	24	24	24	25	25
Bosnia-Herzegovina	16	17	17	18	18	18	18	18	18	18
Bulgaria	10	11	11	12	15	16	17	18	18	19
Croatia	9	10	10	14	17	17	17	18	18	18
Czech Republic	10	11	11	15	15	15	16	16	16	17
Estonia	10	11	11	14	14	14	15	15	16	16
Georgia	6	6	7	8	9	10	10	10	11	11
Hungary	15	16	17	18	19	19	19	19	20	20
Latvia	15	15	14	12	15	16	17	17	18	18
Lithuania	10	13	16	20	15	16	17	20	20	20
Macedonia	5	6	8	11	14	14	15	16	17	17
Moldova										
Poland	6	8	11	14	16	17	17	18	19	19
Romania	8	8	8	9	9	9	9	9	9	9
Russia	15	17	18	20	21	21	21	21	22	22
Slovakia	11	11	11	13	15	17	18	19	20	21
Slovenia	11	11	12	14	16	17	17	17	18	18
Ukraine	12	12	12	13	13	13	13	13	14	14

Source: OECD/International Obesity Taskforce/Euromonitor International

Home Ownership

Home Ownership Statistics

Table 14.1

Total Housing Stock 1980-2008
'000 units

	1980	1985	1990	1995	1996	1997	1998	1999	2000	2001
Western Europe										
Austria	3,038	3,141	3,347	3,590	3,638	3,686	3,734	3,783	3,827	3,858
Belgium	3,811	3,997	3,882	3,931	3,974	4,025	4,076	4,127	4,186	4,249
Cyprus	151	187	222	251	257	262	266	268		
Denmark	2,152	2,239	2,366	2,442	2,455	2,465	2,480	2,496	2,510	2,527
Finland	1,838	2,015	2,210	2,374	2,391	2,416	2,449	2,478	2,512	2,544
France	23,432	25,132	26,792	28,283	28,565	28,844	29,121	29,391	29,699	30,005
Germany	30,956	32,645	33,856	35,954	36,492	37,050	37,532	37,958	38,384	38,682
Gibraltar										
Greece	3,940	4,262	4,588	4,946	5,029	5,107	5,204	5,293	5,387	5,476
Iceland										
Ireland	879	961	1,026	1,115	1,145	1,177	1,212	1,251	1,293	1,337
Italy	21,585	23,282	24,768	26,039	26,267	26,487	26,713	26,907	27,107	27,292
Liechtenstein										
Luxembourg										
Malta										
Monaco										
Netherlands	4,918	5,415	5,802	6,192	6,276	6,358	6,441	6,522	6,590	6,651
Norway	1,544	1,651	1,751	1,844	1,862	1,880	1,901	1,921	1,940	1,964
Portugal	3,756	3,906	4,130	4,508	4,600	4,682	4,771	4,885	5,002	5,106
Spain	13,356	15,062	16,854	18,707	19,080	19,449	19,827	20,197	20,572	21,034
Sweden	3,627	3,835	4,045	4,234	4,249	4,260	4,271	4,282	4,294	4,308
Switzerland	2,703	2,925	3,140	3,390	3,434	3,472	3,508	3,542	3,575	3,604
Turkey	10,359	11,306	12,331	13,651	13,974	14,301	14,664	15,029	15,405	15,784
United Kingdom	21,448	22,383	23,510	24,341	24,529	24,720	24,913	25,097	25,283	25,456
Eastern Europe										
Albania										
Belarus	2,665	2,936	3,285	3,621	3,666	3,709	3,752	3,800	3,819	3,847
Bosnia-Herzegovina										
Bulgaria	2,839	3,162	3,387	3,474	3,512	3,558	3,602	3,642	3,669	3,686
Croatia	1,356	1,502	1,589	1,607	1,615	1,624	1,633	1,645	1,653	1,661
Czech Republic	3,987	4,127	4,217	4,230	4,235	4,244	4,256	4,281	4,321	4,366
Estonia	465	533	596	617	618	619	619	620	621	622
Georgia										
Hungary	3,542	3,826	3,853	3,989	4,010	4,032	4,047	4,061	4,065	4,076
Latvia	854	902	953	952	950	954	955	943	941	942
Lithuania	999	1,077	1,159	1,247	1,270	1,278	1,306	1,324	1,309	1,292
Macedonia										
Moldova										
Poland	9,794	10,666	11,022	11,491	11,547	11,613	11,688	11,763	11,845	11,946
Romania	6,999	7,645	7,896	7,782	7,811	7,837	7,860	7,885	7,908	8,107
Russia	23,731	29,922	38,679	45,245	46,181	46,949	47,603	48,142	48,561	48,857
Slovakia	1,635	1,702	1,759	1,810	1,821	1,834	1,847	1,859	1,872	1,885
Slovenia	578	632	690	737	744	751	757	765	771	778
Ukraine	16,557	17,146	17,656	18,303	18,565	18,784	18,858	18,866	18,921	18,960

Source: *National statistical offices/Euromonitor International*

Home Ownership Statistics

Total Housing Stock 1980-2008 *(continued)*
'000 units

	2002	2003	2004	2005	2006	2007	2008
Western Europe							
Austria	3,896	3,921	3,940	3,956	3,988	4,016	4,042
Belgium	4,320	4,387	4,454	4,510	4,563	4,611	4,663
Cyprus							
Denmark	2,540	2,558	2,578	2,619	2,643	2,669	2,694
Finland	2,574	2,604	2,632	2,667	2,687	2,732	2,775
France	30,337	30,669	30,984	31,306	31,622	31,921	32,229
Germany	38,925	39,142	39,362	39,551	39,754	39,918	40,057
Gibraltar							
Greece	5,584	5,712	5,839	5,938	6,044	6,143	6,225
Iceland							
Ireland	1,387	1,390	1,416	1,460	1,509	1,558	1,607
Italy	27,487	27,664	27,843	28,011	28,188	28,348	28,507
Liechtenstein							
Luxembourg							
Malta							
Monaco							
Netherlands	6,710	6,764	6,810	6,859	6,912	6,967	7,028
Norway	1,985	2,047	2,112	2,184	2,215	2,243	2,274
Portugal	5,232	5,323	5,395	5,470	5,533	5,590	5,647
Spain	21,551	22,059	22,623	23,210	23,859	24,496	25,151
Sweden	4,329	4,351	4,380	4,404	4,436	4,470	4,510
Switzerland	3,638	3,672	3,710	3,749	3,792	3,821	3,851
Turkey	16,176	16,565	16,941	17,326	17,702	18,071	18,426
United Kingdom	25,617	25,787	25,964	26,153	26,348	26,546	26,737
Eastern Europe							
Albania							
Belarus	3,871	3,894	3,907	3,921	3,934	3,965	3,974
Bosnia-Herzegovina							
Bulgaria	3,692	3,697	3,705	3,716	3,729	3,747	3,772
Croatia	1,671	1,683	1,693	1,704	1,715	1,728	1,740
Czech Republic	4,419	4,480	4,556	4,640	4,730	4,842	4,981
Estonia	623	624	626	629	633	638	645
Georgia							
Hungary	4,104	4,119	4,134	4,173	4,209	4,238	4,270
Latvia	958	967	987	998	1,018	1,036	1,061
Lithuania	1,295	1,292	1,300	1,300	1,299	1,305	1,316
Macedonia							
Moldova							
Poland	12,438	12,596	12,683	12,776	12,877	12,994	13,109
Romania	8,129	8,152	8,176	8,201	8,231	8,267	8,311
Russia	49,073	49,265	49,462	49,669	49,796	49,988	50,178
Slovakia	1,898	1,911	1,925	1,941	1,956	1,970	1,986
Slovenia	785	791	798	805	812	820	828
Ukraine	19,023	19,049	19,075	19,132	19,107	19,183	19,257

Source: National statistical offices/Euromonitor International

Home Ownership Statistics

Table 14.2

New Dwellings Completed 1980-2008

'000 units

	1980	1985	1990	1995	1996	1997	1998	1999	2000	2001
Western Europe										
Austria	51.0	41.2	36.6	53.4	58.0	58.0	57.5	59.5	53.8	45.9
Belgium	48.6	30.3	43.1	41.6	46.3	44.5	43.0	41.4	39.7	38.0
Cyprus	9.0	7.5	8.1	8.8	9.0	9.6	9.9	10.2		
Denmark	30.3	22.7	27.2	13.5	14.2	17.7	18.4	17.5	16.5	17.3
Finland	49.6	50.3	65.4	25.0	20.8	26.9	29.8	28.9	32.7	30.6
France	341.6	327.7	317.7	288.1	281.4	280.1	271.3	297.6	316.7	310.0
Germany	379.3	280.9	256.5	602.8	559.5	578.2	500.7	473.0	423.1	326.2
Gibraltar										
Greece	136.0	88.5	120.2	70.9	86.7	89.6	97.3	88.5	89.3	108.0
Iceland										
Ireland	27.8	23.9	19.5	30.6	33.7	38.8	42.3	46.5	49.8	52.6
Italy	287.0	180.7	194.9	145.3	172.0	156.0	150.0	129.4	142.4	148.4
Liechtenstein										
Luxembourg										
Malta										
Monaco										
Netherlands	116.4	98.1	97.4	93.8	88.9	92.3	90.5	78.6	70.7	73.0
Norway	38.1	26.1	27.1	19.2	17.9	18.7	20.7	19.9	19.5	23.4
Portugal	40.9	39.1	46.8	68.8	69.7	74.2	90.8	108.1	112.4	114.8
Spain	262.9	188.7	281.2	221.3	274.3	299.1	298.8	356.8	416.2	505.3
Sweden	51.4	32.9	58.4	12.7	13.1	13.0	11.5	11.7	13.0	15.4
Switzerland	40.9	44.2	40.0	46.2	42.0	36.0	33.7	33.1	32.2	28.9
Turkey	139.2	121.0	232.0	248.9	267.3	277.1	239.0	215.6	245.2	243.5
United Kingdom	242.0	207.5	203.4	199.7	188.9	191.1	179.7	182.1	178.9	175.5
Eastern Europe										
Albania										
Belarus	80.4	88.5	86.1	52.8	38.2	46.1	47.7	46.1	39.4	32.5
Bosnia-Herzegovina										
Bulgaria	74.3	64.9	26.0	6.8	8.1	7.5	4.9	9.8	8.8	5.9
Croatia	31.0	22.8	18.6	7.4	12.6	12.5	12.6	12.2	16.0	12.9
Czech Republic	80.7	66.7	44.6	12.7	14.5	16.8	22.2	23.7	25.2	24.8
Estonia	14.4	13.5	7.6	1.1	0.9	1.0	0.9	0.8	0.7	0.6
Georgia										
Hungary	89.1	72.5	43.8	24.7	28.3	28.1	20.3	19.3	21.6	28.1
Latvia	19.9	19.9	13.3	1.8	1.5	1.5	1.4	1.1	0.9	0.8
Lithuania	28.3	28.8	22.1	5.6	5.6	5.6	4.2	4.4	4.5	3.8
Macedonia										
Moldova										
Poland	217.1	189.6	134.2	67.1	62.1	73.7	80.6	82.0	87.8	106.0
Romania	197.8	105.6	48.6	35.8	29.5	29.9	29.7	29.5	26.4	27.0
Russia	436.8	671.8	800.0	602.0	482.0	426.0	388.0	371.0	373.0	382.0
Slovakia	48.2	38.0	24.7	6.2	6.3	7.2	8.2	10.7	12.9	10.3
Slovenia	13.6	10.8	8.1	6.1	6.7	6.6	7.0	5.4	6.8	6.4
Ukraine	329.0	341.0	289.0	119.0	88.8	80.4	70.2	73.5	62.9	65.6

Source: National statistical offices/Euromonitor International

Home Ownership Statistics

New Dwellings Completed 1980-2008 *(continued)*
'000 units

	2002	2003	2004	2005	2006	2007	2008
Western Europe							
Austria	41.9	40.2	36.2	34.0	33.2	32.6	29.7
Belgium	36.5	34.9	33.5	32.4	31.2	30.5	29.3
Cyprus							
Denmark	18.9	24.5	27.3	28.3	28.6	30.4	33.7
Finland	27.2	28.1	29.3	31.2	33.7	35.9	32.9
France	334.0	320.0	317.4	305.2	303.0	299.0	300.9
Germany	289.6	268.1	278.0	242.3	249.4	210.7	189.3
Gibraltar							
Greece	128.2	127.0	122.2	195.2	125.4	103.9	130.2
Iceland							
Ireland	57.7	68.8	77.0	81.0	93.4	78.0	81.0
Italy	145.8	142.3	138.9	134.2	130.2	126.2	120.8
Liechtenstein							
Luxembourg							
Malta							
Monaco							
Netherlands	66.7	59.6	65.3	67.0	72.4	80.2	89.0
Norway	21.7	21.4	23.6	29.5	28.5	31.0	32.3
Portugal	125.1	91.2	73.3	74.6	65.6	59.8	57.3
Spain	519.3	508.3	565.3	590.6	658.0	694.2	709.9
Sweden	19.9	20.0	25.3	23.1	29.8	30.5	40.8
Switzerland	28.6	32.1	36.9	38.0	42.0	35.2	31.4
Turkey	161.5	183.5	205.2	249.8	295.4	326.5	325.1
United Kingdom	183.1	190.4	206.1	215.2	218.9	214.4	207.0
Eastern Europe							
Albania							
Belarus	28.8	32.0	40.4	43.3	45.6	53.1	47.9
Bosnia-Herzegovina							
Bulgaria	6.2	6.3	9.8	13.9	15.3	21.6	26.9
Croatia	18.0	18.5	18.8	20.0	22.1	22.8	23.2
Czech Republic	27.3	27.1	32.3	32.9	30.2	41.6	38.4
Estonia	1.1	2.4	3.1	3.9	5.1	7.1	7.2
Georgia							
Hungary	31.5	35.5	43.9	41.1	33.9	36.2	42.6
Latvia	0.8	0.8	2.8	3.8	5.9	9.3	12.9
Lithuania	4.6	4.6	6.8	5.9	7.3	9.3	9.2
Macedonia							
Moldova							
Poland	97.6	162.7	108.1	114.1	115.4	133.7	165.2
Romania	27.7	29.1	30.1	32.9	39.6	44.8	56.5
Russia	396.0	427.0	477.0	515.0	609.0	721.0	786.0
Slovakia	14.2	14.0	12.6	14.9	14.4	16.5	17.5
Slovenia	7.3	6.6	7.0	7.5	7.5	8.4	9.2
Ukraine	64.4	63.2	71.2	76.0	82.0	95.0	96.9

Source: National statistical offices/Euromonitor International

Home Ownership Statistics

Table 14.3

Number of Households by Tenure 2008

'000 / as stated

	Home Owner with mortgage	Home Owner without mortgage	Rented	Other	Home Owner with mortgage (% of total)	Home Owner without mortgage (% of total)	Rented (% of total)	Other (% of total)
Western Europe								
Austria	673	1,274	1,461	169	18.8	35.6	40.8	4.7
Belgium	1,276	1,748	1,427	122	27.9	38.2	31.2	2.7
Cyprus								
Denmark	838	464	1,173	73	32.9	18.2	46.1	2.9
Finland	573	814	840	280	22.9	32.5	33.5	11.2
France	5,401	9,811	10,480	901	20.3	36.9	39.4	3.4
Germany	9,489	6,304	24,093		23.8	15.8	60.4	
Gibraltar								
Greece	538	2,391	785	244	13.6	60.4	19.8	6.2
Iceland								
Ireland	636	548	364	22	40.5	34.9	23.2	1.4
Italy	4,889	12,629	4,236	2,372	20.3	52.3	17.6	9.8
Liechtenstein								
Luxembourg								
Malta								
Monaco								
Netherlands	3,532	511	2,973	216	48.8	7.1	41.1	3.0
Norway	1,070	530	504		50.9	25.2	24.0	
Portugal	888	2,138	721	343	21.7	52.3	17.6	8.4
Spain	7,176	7,150	1,670	1,085	42.0	41.9	9.8	6.4
Sweden	1,071	1,693	1,371	388	23.7	37.4	30.3	8.6
Switzerland	760	1,382	1,090	155	22.4	40.8	32.2	4.6
Turkey	1,269	12,752	2,609	1,205	7.1	71.5	14.6	6.8
United Kingdom	9,207	7,510	7,353	2,881	34.2	27.9	27.3	10.7
Eastern Europe								
Albania								
Belarus	242	3,114	369	357	5.9	76.3	9.0	8.7
Bosnia-Herzegovina								
Bulgaria	161	2,524	226	20	5.5	86.1	7.7	0.7
Croatia	105	1,254	111	36	7.0	83.2	7.4	2.4
Czech Republic	342	1,811	1,173	1,143	7.7	40.5	26.3	25.6
Estonia	81	422	71	14	13.8	71.7	12.1	2.4
Georgia								
Hungary	585	3,238	268	42	14.2	78.3	6.5	1.0
Latvia	115	449	244	2	14.1	55.4	30.1	0.3
Lithuania	106	1,087	77	121	7.6	78.1	5.6	8.7
Macedonia								
Moldova								
Poland	782	8,220	2,951	2,336	5.5	57.5	20.7	16.4
Romania	302	6,867	246	26	4.1	92.3	3.3	0.4
Russia	2,551	30,471	19,837		4.8	57.6	37.5	
Slovakia	125	1,638	186	291	5.6	73.1	8.3	13.0
Slovenia	32	595	40	62	4.3	81.7	5.5	8.5
Ukraine	498	15,932	3,187	381	2.5	79.7	15.9	1.9

Source: National statistical offices/Euromonitor International

Table 14.4

Number of Households by Type of Dwelling 2008
'000

	Detached House	Semi-Detached & Terraced House	Apartment	Other	Detached House (% of total)	Semi-Detached & Terraced House (% of total)	Apartment (% of total)	Other (% of total)
Western Europe								
Austria	1,137	650	1,720	70	31.8	18.2	48.1	2.0
Belgium	1,018	782	2,509	263	22.3	17.1	54.9	5.8
Cyprus								
Denmark	1,003	320	1,210	14	39.4	12.5	47.5	0.6
Finland	955	378	1,070	103	38.1	15.1	42.7	4.1
France	10,879	3,661	10,830	1,223	40.9	13.8	40.7	4.6
Germany	9,846	7,732	21,296	1,012	24.7	19.4	53.4	2.5
Gibraltar								
Greece	1,560	1,152	1,216	30	39.4	29.1	30.7	0.7
Iceland								
Ireland	641	749	102	79	40.8	47.7	6.5	5.0
Italy	3,386	2,887	17,853	0	14.0	12.0	74.0	0.0
Liechtenstein								
Luxembourg								
Malta								
Monaco								
Netherlands	1,230	3,830	1,999	175	17.0	52.9	27.6	2.4
Norway	1,291	350	464		61.3	16.6	22.0	
Portugal	1,923	1,109	1,005	53	47.0	27.1	24.6	1.3
Spain	3,887	3,593	9,601		22.8	21.0	56.2	
Sweden	1,837	1,232	1,196	259	40.6	27.2	26.4	5.7
Switzerland	782	725	1,424	457	23.1	21.4	42.0	13.5
Turkey			9,326	373			52.3	2.1
United Kingdom	6,295	16,069	3,812	776	23.4	59.6	14.1	2.9
Eastern Europe								
Albania								
Belarus			2,646	139			64.8	3.4
Bosnia-Herzegovina								
Bulgaria			1,331	16			45.4	0.5
Croatia			1,085	19			72.0	1.3
Czech Republic			2,425	119			54.3	2.7
Estonia	154	33	388	13	26.2	5.5	66.0	2.3
Georgia								
Hungary			2,338	19			56.6	0.5
Latvia	163	53	577	18	20.1	6.5	71.1	2.2
Lithuania	312	129	872	78	22.5	9.3	62.6	5.6
Macedonia								
Moldova								
Poland			6,809	355			47.7	2.5
Romania			2,777	134			37.3	1.8
Russia	7,438	3,145	40,539	1,737	14.1	5.9	76.7	3.3
Slovakia			1,294	44			57.8	2.0
Slovenia			350				48.1	
Ukraine	9,549	1,953	8,218	277	47.8	9.8	41.1	1.4

Source: *National statistical offices/Euromonitor International*

Household Profiles

Household Statistics

Table 15.1

Number of Households 1985-2008

'000

	1985	1990	1995	2000	2003	2004	2005	2006	2007	2008
Western Europe										
Austria	2,887	2,996	3,131	3,303	3,398	3,430	3,475	3,512	3,546	3,578
Belgium	3,766	3,959	4,095	4,238	4,362	4,402	4,440	4,488	4,533	4,572
Cyprus	212	229	249	264	266	267	267	268	269	270
Denmark	2,160	2,265	2,358	2,434	2,467	2,481	2,499	2,516	2,532	2,547
Finland	1,910	2,037	2,181	2,295	2,377	2,403	2,430	2,454	2,482	2,507
France	20,283	21,542	22,830	24,108	25,060	25,374	25,689	25,992	26,296	26,593
Germany	32,967	34,775	36,938	38,124	38,944	39,122	39,178	39,767	39,825	39,887
Gibraltar	7	7	8	8	8	9	9	9	9	9
Greece	3,062	3,168	3,403	3,627	3,745	3,785	3,827	3,870	3,914	3,958
Iceland	101	107	112	120	124	126	127	128	130	131
Ireland	966	1,012	1,104	1,220	1,326	1,366	1,413	1,470	1,522	1,571
Italy	18,916	19,688	20,822	21,645	22,359	22,813	23,268	23,612	23,886	24,126
Liechtenstein				13	14	14	14	14	15	15
Luxembourg	133	142	156	169	177	179	181	183	186	188
Malta	107	111	115	120	123	123	124	125	126	126
Monaco	12	12	14	15	16	16	16	16	17	17
Netherlands	5,613	6,061	6,516	6,819	6,996	7,049	7,091	7,146	7,191	7,233
Norway	1,635	1,751	1,859	1,948	1,986	1,998	2,011	2,051	2,065	2,105
Portugal	3,039	3,129	3,294	3,578	3,804	3,875	3,939	3,993	4,044	4,090
Spain	10,439	11,627	12,785	13,934	15,065	15,487	15,906	16,323	16,735	17,081
Sweden	3,670	3,830	4,234	4,363	4,407	4,426	4,445	4,465	4,500	4,523
Switzerland	2,602	2,860	3,098	3,182	3,264	3,292	3,320	3,345	3,368	3,388
Turkey	8,963	11,189	13,232	15,070	16,086	16,426	16,770	17,119	17,475	17,835
United Kingdom	21,960	23,207	24,282	25,193	25,778	25,991	26,246	26,488	26,722	26,952
Eastern Europe										
Albania	589	710	717	728	751	759	768	776	784	792
Belarus	3,292	3,535	3,734	3,899	3,987	4,011	4,033	4,052	4,068	4,082
Bosnia-Herzegovina	1,124	1,236	1,017	1,150	1,193	1,199	1,205	1,211	1,217	1,221
Bulgaria	3,030	3,000	2,914	2,914	2,932	2,935	2,937	2,937	2,935	2,932
Croatia	1,481	1,536	1,527	1,475	1,487	1,492	1,497	1,500	1,504	1,507
Czech Republic	3,962	4,032	4,147	4,251	4,316	4,342	4,366	4,401	4,437	4,469
Estonia	479	521	572	582	586	587	588	589	589	589
Georgia	1,364	1,421	1,323	1,253	1,219	1,209	1,199	1,190	1,182	1,174
Hungary	3,882	3,890	3,869	3,847	3,918	3,957	4,002	4,047	4,091	4,133
Latvia	779	834	810	802	805	807	808	810	810	810
Lithuania	1,184	1,292	1,336	1,353	1,375	1,381	1,385	1,387	1,390	1,391
Macedonia	430	470	510	549	571	578	585	591	598	604
Moldova			1,088	1,163	1,183	1,188	1,193	1,198	1,204	1,210
Poland	11,683	12,113	12,501	13,031	13,508	13,670	13,827	13,983	14,135	14,289
Romania	7,163	7,378	7,202	7,269	7,341	7,360	7,382	7,405	7,424	7,442
Russia	33,553	42,280	48,872	52,197	52,842	52,931	52,954	52,947	52,914	52,859
Slovakia	1,735	1,815	1,919	2,045	2,124	2,150	2,175	2,199	2,220	2,240
Slovenia	608	636	651	675	695	701	706	713	721	728
Ukraine	14,097	14,559	15,775	17,684	19,121	19,438	19,672	19,821	19,933	19,997

Source: *National statistical offices/Euromonitor International*

Household Statistics

Table 15.2

Average Number of Occupants per Household at Jan 1st 1985-2008
Persons

	1985	1990	1995	2000	2003	2004	2005	2006	2007	2008	Number of Children per Household 2008
Western Europe											
Austria	2.62	2.55	2.54	2.42	2.38	2.37	2.36	2.35	2.34	2.33	0.44
Belgium	2.62	2.51	2.47	2.42	2.37	2.36	2.35	2.34	2.33	2.32	0.48
Cyprus	3.05	2.97	2.94	2.98	3.07	3.10	3.13	3.15	3.17	3.19	0.73
Denmark	2.37	2.27	2.21	2.19	2.18	2.18	2.17	2.16	2.15	2.14	0.48
Finland	2.56	2.44	2.34	2.25	2.19	2.17	2.16	2.14	2.13	2.11	0.44
France	2.72	2.63	2.53	2.44	2.40	2.38	2.37	2.35	2.34	2.34	0.51
Germany	2.36	2.27	2.21	2.16	2.12	2.11	2.11	2.07	2.07	2.06	0.35
Gibraltar	3.80	3.83	3.61	3.43	3.35	3.32	3.30	3.28	3.26	3.24	0.58
Greece	3.24	3.19	3.11	3.01	2.94	2.92	2.90	2.87	2.85	2.83	0.49
Iceland	2.39	2.38	2.39	2.34	2.32	2.32	2.33	2.35	2.38	2.41	0.61
Ireland	3.67	3.47	3.26	3.10	2.99	2.95	2.91	2.86	2.82	2.79	0.68
Italy	2.99	2.88	2.73	2.63	2.56	2.54	2.51	2.49	2.47	2.44	0.41
Liechtenstein				2.52	2.48	2.46	2.45	2.43	2.41	2.40	0.40
Luxembourg	2.76	2.69	2.63	2.58	2.56	2.57	2.57	2.56	2.56	2.55	0.55
Malta	3.22	3.24	3.28	3.23	3.24	3.24	3.24	3.23	3.23	3.23	0.64
Monaco	2.36	2.51	2.26	2.10	2.04	2.02	2.01	1.99	1.98	1.97	0.27
Netherlands	2.58	2.46	2.37	2.33	2.31	2.31	2.30	2.29	2.27	2.26	0.49
Norway	2.54	2.42	2.34	2.30	2.29	2.29	2.29	2.26	2.27	2.25	0.52
Portugal	3.30	3.19	3.04	2.85	2.74	2.70	2.67	2.65	2.62	2.60	0.49
Spain	3.67	3.34	3.08	2.87	2.77	2.73	2.71	2.68	2.66	2.64	0.46
Sweden	2.27	2.23	2.08	2.03	2.03	2.03	2.03	2.03	2.03	2.02	0.42
Switzerland	2.48	2.33	2.27	2.25	2.24	2.24	2.23	2.23	2.23	2.22	0.42
Turkey	5.54	4.96	4.63	4.44	4.34	4.30	4.27	4.24	4.20	4.17	1.37
United Kingdom	2.57	2.46	2.39	2.33	2.31	2.30	2.29	2.28	2.28	2.27	0.49
Eastern Europe											
Albania	5.02	4.64	4.37	4.21	4.11	4.08	4.05	4.02	4.00	3.97	1.20
Belarus	3.02	2.88	2.73	2.57	2.48	2.46	2.43	2.41	2.39	2.37	0.45
Bosnia-Herzegovina	3.78	3.64	3.46	3.26	3.21	3.20	3.19	3.17	3.16	3.15	0.61
Bulgaria	2.95	2.92	2.85	2.74	2.67	2.65	2.63	2.61	2.60	2.58	0.43
Croatia	3.17	3.11	3.06	3.01	2.99	2.98	2.97	2.96	2.95	2.94	0.56
Czech Republic	2.60	2.55	2.49	2.41	2.36	2.35	2.34	2.33	2.32	2.31	0.41
Estonia	3.18	3.01	2.53	2.36	2.31	2.30	2.29	2.28	2.28	2.27	0.43
Georgia	3.64	3.62	3.62	3.54	3.56	3.57	3.60	3.70	3.72	3.73	0.83
Hungary	2.75	2.67	2.67	2.66	2.59	2.56	2.52	2.49	2.46	2.43	0.46
Latvia	3.30	3.20	3.09	2.97	2.90	2.88	2.85	2.83	2.82	2.80	0.50
Lithuania	2.98	2.86	2.73	2.60	2.52	2.49	2.47	2.45	2.44	2.42	0.48
Macedonia	4.25	4.06	3.85	3.66	3.55	3.51	3.48	3.44	3.41	3.38	0.77
Moldova			3.99	3.53	3.29	3.21	3.15	3.10	3.05	3.00	0.68
Poland	3.17	3.14	3.06	2.94	2.83	2.79	2.76	2.73	2.70	2.66	0.52
Romania	3.17	3.15	3.09	3.02	2.97	2.95	2.93	2.92	2.90	2.89	0.55
Russia	4.25	3.49	3.04	2.81	2.74	2.72	2.71	2.70	2.69	2.69	0.50
Slovakia	2.96	2.90	2.79	2.63	2.53	2.50	2.48	2.45	2.43	2.41	0.48
Slovenia	3.19	3.14	3.05	2.94	2.87	2.85	2.83	2.81	2.79	2.77	0.47
Ukraine	3.59	3.54	3.25	2.78	2.50	2.44	2.39	2.36	2.33	2.31	0.42

Source: National statistics/UN//Euromonitor International

Household Statistics

Table 15.3

Number of Households by Urban/Rural Split 2008
% of total

	Urban	Rural	Total
Western Europe			
Austria	72.5	27.5	100.0
Belgium	97.7	2.3	100.0
Cyprus			100.0
Denmark	85.1	14.9	100.0
Finland	65.3	34.7	100.0
France	78.9	21.1	100.0
Germany	85.3	14.7	100.0
Gibraltar			100.0
Greece	77.3	22.7	100.0
Iceland			100.0
Ireland	62.9	37.1	100.0
Italy	73.1	26.9	100.0
Liechtenstein			100.0
Luxembourg			100.0
Malta			100.0
Monaco			100.0
Netherlands	84.1	15.9	100.0
Norway	79.5	20.5	100.0
Portugal	72.4	27.6	100.0
Spain	83.5	16.5	100.0
Sweden	86.3	13.7	100.0
Switzerland	77.8	22.2	100.0
Turkey	63.5	36.5	100.0
United Kingdom	89.9	10.1	100.0
Eastern Europe			
Albania			100.0
Belarus	71.7	28.3	100.0
Bosnia-Herzegovina			100.0
Bulgaria	70.2	29.8	100.0
Croatia	60.7	39.3	100.0
Czech Republic	76.3	23.7	100.0
Estonia	70.1	29.9	100.0
Georgia			100.0
Hungary	69.6	30.4	100.0
Latvia	70.4	29.6	100.0
Lithuania	69.1	30.9	100.0
Macedonia			100.0
Moldova			100.0
Poland	67.6	32.4	100.0
Romania	54.1	45.9	100.0
Russia	75.0	25.0	100.0
Slovakia	55.0	45.0	100.0
Slovenia	54.3	45.7	100.0
Ukraine	69.5	30.5	100.0

Source: National statistical offices/Euromonitor International

Household Statistics

Table 15.4

Households by Number of Persons 2008

% of total households

	One Person	Two Persons	Three Persons	Four Persons	Five Persons	Six or More Persons
Western Europe						
Austria	35.4	28.5	16.0	13.3	4.6	2.2
Belgium	32.8	32.3	15.3	12.8	5.2	1.7
Cyprus						
Denmark	38.9	32.9	11.4	11.4	4.0	1.4
Finland	38.9	34.4	11.8	9.5	3.8	1.5
France	33.6	32.3	15.0	12.4	4.8	1.9
Germany	38.4	35.1	12.9	9.9	3.5	0.3
Gibraltar						
Greece	22.1	29.7	20.7	18.3	5.8	3.5
Iceland						
Ireland	23.1	29.6	17.8	16.0	8.8	4.7
Italy	28.2	29.2	20.1	17.1	4.4	1.0
Liechtenstein						
Luxembourg						
Malta						
Monaco						
Netherlands	35.6	32.6	12.4	13.5	4.3	1.6
Norway	39.5	28.5	12.4	11.8	5.8	2.0
Portugal	20.1	32.1	23.6	17.6	5.0	1.6
Spain	24.1	27.5	20.1	19.6	6.0	2.6
Sweden	46.9	26.0	11.2	11.1	3.4	1.4
Switzerland	37.4	31.6	12.0	12.5	4.6	1.9
Turkey	5.8	15.5	18.9	25.3	14.9	19.6
United Kingdom	33.8	32.0	16.2	13.1	3.8	1.1
Eastern Europe						
Albania						
Belarus	27.2	31.8	26.3	9.8	3.4	1.4
Bosnia-Herzegovina						
Bulgaria	24.9	29.9	20.9	16.1	5.3	2.9
Croatia	22.4	24.4	18.4	18.9	9.2	6.8
Czech Republic	32.8	29.5	17.9	15.4	3.5	0.9
Estonia	35.0	29.4	17.5	12.4	4.0	1.6
Georgia						
Hungary	31.2	30.5	17.8	13.4	4.8	2.3
Latvia	22.4	32.1	19.5	14.6	5.9	5.6
Lithuania	32.0	27.7	18.2	14.7	4.7	2.7
Macedonia						
Moldova						
Poland	28.4	25.5	17.5	15.8	7.2	5.6
Romania	20.0	27.5	23.1	16.9	7.1	5.4
Russia	24.3	26.8	23.2	16.5	6.2	2.9
Slovakia	35.4	23.6	16.8	17.0	4.9	2.3
Slovenia	23.9	24.4	20.0	21.7	6.6	3.4
Ukraine	32.6	32.9	16.8	10.9	3.8	3.0

Source: National statistical offices/Euromonitor International

Household Statistics

Table 15.5

Number of Households by Number of Rooms 2008
% of total

	1	2	3	4	5+	Total
Western Europe						
Austria	8.8	19.6	32.0	20.0	19.6	100.0
Belgium	6.3	14.4	19.3	22.2	37.9	100.0
Cyprus						100.0
Denmark	6.7	21.2	23.2	19.4	29.5	100.0
Finland	13.8	32.0	20.6	19.8	13.9	100.0
France	6.7	12.5	21.3	26.2	33.3	100.0
Germany	2.2	6.3	21.8	29.5	40.3	100.0
Gibraltar						100.0
Greece	3.3	15.8	27.7	38.2	15.0	100.0
Iceland						100.0
Ireland	0.4	2.5	6.3	15.3	75.4	100.0
Italy	0.7	8.9	25.3	34.8	30.3	100.0
Liechtenstein						100.0
Luxembourg						100.0
Malta						100.0
Monaco						100.0
Netherlands	2.8	7.1	21.6	33.7	34.8	100.0
Norway	4.5	11.5	18.9	16.7	48.5	100.0
Portugal	0.8	2.0	12.4	29.6	55.3	100.0
Spain	0.6	2.4	8.8	17.3	70.8	100.0
Sweden	8.1	22.4	25.5	21.4	22.7	100.0
Switzerland	3.9	11.3	26.2	29.4	29.2	100.0
Turkey	4.2	15.2	26.8	37.6	16.3	100.0
United Kingdom	0.2	2.2	7.6	18.1	71.9	100.0
Eastern Europe						
Albania						100.0
Belarus	17.8	38.9	32.6	8.7	2.1	100.0
Bosnia-Herzegovina						100.0
Bulgaria	9.3	37.4	38.6	10.4	4.3	100.0
Croatia	24.4	48.9	20.2	4.0	2.5	100.0
Czech Republic	13.5	38.7	26.8	10.3	10.7	100.0
Estonia	18.5	49.5	29.3	1.6	1.1	100.0
Georgia						100.0
Hungary	17.4	40.9	28.9	7.1	5.8	100.0
Latvia	17.5	48.6	23.1	6.2	4.6	100.0
Lithuania	14.6	45.4	31.4	6.2	2.3	100.0
Macedonia						100.0
Moldova						100.0
Poland	1.9	13.8	31.5	42.3	10.5	100.0
Romania	10.0	35.7	37.8	11.3	5.3	100.0
Russia	14.4	39.6	25.9	13.5	6.6	100.0
Slovakia	16.1	40.7	29.6	8.3	5.3	100.0
Slovenia	14.4	29.4	26.3	15.5	14.4	100.0
Ukraine	11.0	29.4	31.1	19.9	8.5	100.0

Source: *National statistical offices/Euromonitor International*

Table 15.6

Number of Households by Sex of Head of Household 2008
% of total

	Male	Female	Total
Western Europe			
Austria	61.6	38.4	100.0
Belgium	69.1	30.9	100.0
Cyprus			100.0
Denmark	56.0	44.0	100.0
Finland	61.4	38.6	100.0
France	72.3	27.7	100.0
Germany	67.5	32.5	100.0
Gibraltar			100.0
Greece	75.0	25.0	100.0
Iceland			100.0
Ireland	58.0	42.0	100.0
Italy	71.9	28.1	100.0
Liechtenstein			100.0
Luxembourg			100.0
Malta			100.0
Monaco			100.0
Netherlands	68.3	31.7	100.0
Norway	61.0	39.0	100.0
Portugal	75.6	24.4	100.0
Spain	76.8	23.2	100.0
Sweden	61.8	38.2	100.0
Switzerland	58.7	41.3	100.0
Turkey	87.3	12.7	100.0
United Kingdom	59.3	40.7	100.0
Eastern Europe			
Albania			100.0
Belarus	49.5	50.5	100.0
Bosnia-Herzegovina			100.0
Bulgaria	70.5	29.5	100.0
Croatia	59.0	41.0	100.0
Czech Republic	63.6	36.4	100.0
Estonia	49.0	51.0	100.0
Georgia			100.0
Hungary	65.6	34.4	100.0
Latvia	52.2	47.8	100.0
Lithuania	49.9	50.1	100.0
Macedonia			100.0
Moldova			100.0
Poland	61.1	38.9	100.0
Romania	71.4	28.6	100.0
Russia	51.2	48.8	100.0
Slovakia	68.0	32.0	100.0
Slovenia	50.1	49.9	100.0
Ukraine	50.2	49.8	100.0

Source: National statistical offices/Euromonitor International

Household Statistics

Table 15.7

Number of Households by Age of Head of Household: 2008
%

	< 29	30-39	40-49	50-59	60+	Total
Western Europe						
Austria	9.15	23.89	18.40	18.81	29.76	100.00
Belgium	9.60	21.55	23.87	13.13	31.85	100.00
Cyprus						
Denmark	10.33	20.88	20.27	19.21	29.32	100.00
Finland	11.19	16.88	19.69	19.87	32.37	100.00
France	11.80	18.30	19.89	18.21	31.80	100.00
Germany	12.83	17.92	17.71	16.70	34.83	100.00
Gibraltar						
Greece	12.70	23.34	22.52	17.24	24.20	100.00
Iceland						
Ireland	14.75	20.91	20.03	19.45	24.85	100.00
Italy	6.57	14.30	17.92	17.72	43.50	100.00
Liechtenstein						
Luxembourg						
Malta						
Monaco						
Netherlands	10.38	20.35	21.10	19.34	28.84	100.00
Norway	16.23	20.93	20.22	17.80	24.82	100.00
Portugal	14.04	20.97	21.38	16.42	27.19	100.00
Spain	4.82	14.91	21.27	20.24	38.76	100.00
Sweden	13.24	15.39	17.68	16.97	36.72	100.00
Switzerland	8.82	18.39	23.09	20.36	29.34	100.00
Turkey	20.80	14.03	21.17	21.40	22.59	100.00
United Kingdom	11.81	19.65	18.19	20.12	30.24	100.00
Eastern Europe						
Albania						
Belarus	8.64	19.39	19.50	19.67	32.79	100.00
Bosnia-Herzegovina						
Bulgaria	1.41	14.25	31.93	25.75	26.66	100.00
Croatia	7.29	14.58	14.49	21.95	41.68	100.00
Czech Republic	12.14	20.84	25.66	19.25	22.10	100.00
Estonia	8.06	23.42	20.22	23.57	24.72	100.00
Georgia						
Hungary	6.53	15.59	15.33	20.35	42.20	100.00
Latvia	10.03	18.63	18.56	17.84	34.94	100.00
Lithuania	7.87	18.88	16.99	18.88	37.39	100.00
Macedonia						
Moldova						
Poland	10.89	15.23	24.57	18.40	30.90	100.00
Romania	3.98	11.54	17.81	19.58	47.09	100.00
Russia	12.70	15.69	18.93	18.00	34.68	100.00
Slovakia	8.79	29.26	22.02	18.74	21.19	100.00
Slovenia	10.31	19.27	17.91	19.04	33.48	100.00
Ukraine	13.27	15.94	12.77	20.18	37.84	100.00

Source: National statistical offices/Euromonitor International

Table 15.8

Number of Households by Education of Head of Household 2008
% of total

	Primary & no education	Secondary	Higher	Total
Western Europe				
Austria	23.7	47.7	28.5	100.0
Belgium	19.5	65.5	15.1	100.0
Cyprus				100.0
Denmark	28.1	46.7	25.1	100.0
Finland	34.6	45.6	19.8	100.0
France	14.4	56.7	23.1	100.0
Germany	12.7	60.0	25.8	100.0
Gibraltar				100.0
Greece	47.5	40.0	12.5	100.0
Iceland				100.0
Ireland	21.4	45.8	32.8	100.0
Italy	19.4	70.2	10.4	100.0
Liechtenstein				100.0
Luxembourg				100.0
Malta				100.0
Monaco				100.0
Netherlands	19.2	54.6	26.2	100.0
Norway	24.5	53.7	21.8	100.0
Portugal	58.4	23.7	17.9	100.0
Spain	48.0	34.1	17.9	100.0
Sweden	29.2	46.2	24.6	100.0
Switzerland	20.5	49.8	29.6	100.0
Turkey	66.5	18.5	15.0	100.0
United Kingdom	13.9	56.8	29.3	100.0
Eastern Europe				
Albania				100.0
Belarus	22.5	58.7	18.9	100.0
Bosnia-Herzegovina				100.0
Bulgaria	43.7	39.2	17.1	100.0
Croatia	39.7	47.1	13.2	100.0
Czech Republic	26.7	57.5	15.9	100.0
Estonia	22.1	59.9	18.0	100.0
Georgia				100.0
Hungary	40.1	48.7	11.1	100.0
Latvia	38.4	41.2	20.4	100.0
Lithuania	16.7	67.3	16.0	100.0
Macedonia				100.0
Moldova				100.0
Poland	25.3	63.8	10.8	100.0
Romania	26.8	64.1	9.1	100.0
Russia	21.9	62.4	15.7	100.0
Slovakia	18.3	65.8	15.9	100.0
Slovenia	24.9	58.4	16.8	100.0
Ukraine	26.8	52.0	21.2	100.0

Source: *National statistical offices/Euromonitor International*

Household Statistics

Table 15.9

Number of Households by Status of Head of Household 2008
'000 / % of total

	Employee (%)	Employer/ Self-employed (%)	Un-employed (%)	Other (%)	Total (%)
Western Europe					
Austria	55.9	10.2	1.8	32.1	100.0
Belgium	50.9	9.3	5.5	34.3	100.0
Cyprus					
Denmark	50.4	3.6	0.8	45.3	100.0
Finland	58.2	9.5	3.2	29.1	100.0
France	54.1	5.1	10.2	30.7	100.0
Germany	43.8	7.6	9.1	39.5	100.0
Gibraltar					
Greece	42.6	15.1	5.3	37.0	100.0
Iceland					
Ireland	57.4	8.3	2.0	32.3	100.0
Italy	68.0	18.1	7.6	6.3	100.0
Liechtenstein					
Luxembourg					
Malta					
Monaco					
Netherlands	66.4	8.1	2.5	23.0	100.0
Norway	62.0	4.5	2.5	31.0	100.0
Portugal	46.6	17.0	3.1	33.3	100.0
Spain	46.2	9.6	2.7	41.5	100.0
Sweden	62.4	7.8	3.1	26.7	100.0
Switzerland	56.2	13.0	3.5	27.3	100.0
Turkey	37.1	36.1	3.9	22.9	100.0
United Kingdom	53.6	6.5	1.2	38.7	100.0
Eastern Europe					
Albania					
Belarus					
Bosnia-Herzegovina					
Bulgaria	38.0	12.9	12.5	36.5	100.0
Croatia	50.0	2.5	12.1	35.4	100.0
Czech Republic	56.5	13.9	7.3	22.4	100.0
Estonia	59.3	5.5	4.7	30.5	100.0
Georgia					
Hungary	55.0	2.7	1.9	40.5	100.0
Latvia	53.7	5.1	7.7	33.6	100.0
Lithuania	53.7	7.7	7.1	31.5	100.0
Macedonia					
Moldova					
Poland	48.1	10.9	8.9	32.2	100.0
Romania	25.7	3.5	7.7	63.1	100.0
Russia	56.4	10.5	4.5	28.6	100.0
Slovakia	48.5	4.8	7.2	39.6	100.0
Slovenia	53.9	12.0	4.3	29.8	100.0
Ukraine	38.1	12.8	7.6	41.5	100.0

Source: National statistical offices/Euromonitor International

Household Statistics

Table 15.10

Number of Households by Type 2008

% of total

	Single Person	Couple Without Children	Couple With Children	Single Parent Family	Other
Western Europe					
Austria	35.4	24.8	30.9	6.3	2.7
Belgium	32.8	23.2	26.9	11.7	5.4
Cyprus					
Denmark	38.9	31.8	17.7	4.4	7.3
Finland	38.9	30.2	21.4	6.4	3.1
France	33.6	26.6	30.8	7.2	1.8
Germany	38.4	26.8	27.8	5.1	1.9
Gibraltar					
Greece	22.1	30.6	21.5	16.6	9.2
Iceland					
Ireland	23.1	16.3	37.0	10.6	13.0
Italy	28.2	21.3	38.1	9.0	3.4
Liechtenstein					
Luxembourg					
Malta					
Monaco					
Netherlands	35.6	28.5	28.4	6.8	0.7
Norway	39.5	22.7	22.8	5.7	9.3
Portugal	20.1	25.1	37.5	13.3	4.1
Spain	24.1	17.4	33.5	8.8	16.2
Sweden	46.9	29.3	16.8	5.0	2.1
Switzerland	37.4	28.4	27.3	5.6	1.3
Turkey	5.8	14.8	63.3	3.6	12.4
United Kingdom	33.8	28.8	19.1	7.4	10.8
Eastern Europe					
Albania					
Belarus	27.2	24.7	25.4	6.0	16.7
Bosnia-Herzegovina					
Bulgaria	24.9	29.8	22.7	2.4	20.2
Croatia	22.4	15.1	26.6	3.8	32.1
Czech Republic	32.8	33.2	26.3	7.4	0.4
Estonia	35.0	21.2	11.0	6.6	26.1
Georgia					
Hungary	31.2	38.7	16.4	7.7	6.0
Latvia	22.4	25.2	16.1	5.8	30.6
Lithuania	32.0	21.2	18.6	3.7	24.6
Macedonia					
Moldova					
Poland	28.4	24.0	40.5	3.2	3.8
Romania	20.0	33.2	20.8	3.5	22.5
Russia	24.3	24.9	30.6	11.8	8.4
Slovakia	35.4	30.9	27.7	2.5	3.6
Slovenia	23.9	18.5	18.7	1.6	37.3
Ukraine	32.6	13.6	10.3	2.2	41.3

Source: *National statistical offices/Euromonitor International*

Household Statistics

Table 15.11

Number of Households by Annual Disposable Income Band 2008

% of total

	Over $500	Over $750	Over $1,000	Over $1,750	Over $2,500	Over $5,000	Over $7,500	Over $10,000	Over $15,000
Western Europe									
Austria	100.00	100.00	100.00	100.00	100.00	99.99	99.96	99.88	99.48
Belgium	100.00	100.00	100.00	99.99	99.97	99.84	99.56	99.11	97.56
Cyprus									
Denmark	99.99	99.98	99.97	99.91	99.81	99.30	98.48	97.38	94.41
Finland	100.00	100.00	100.00	100.00	99.99	99.94	99.78	99.45	97.99
France	100.00	100.00	100.00	99.99	99.97	99.85	99.59	99.17	97.79
Germany	100.00	99.99	99.99	99.95	99.90	99.52	98.82	97.78	94.67
Gibraltar									
Greece	100.00	99.99	99.98	99.95	99.88	99.46	98.69	97.55	94.14
Iceland									
Ireland	99.99	99.98	99.97	99.92	99.85	99.45	98.82	97.98	95.73
Italy	100.00	100.00	100.00	99.99	99.98	99.87	99.58	99.04	96.94
Liechtenstein									
Luxembourg									
Malta									
Monaco									
Netherlands	100.00	100.00	100.00	100.00	100.00	99.96	99.85	99.60	98.40
Norway	100.00	100.00	100.00	100.00	100.00	100.00	99.98	99.94	99.72
Portugal	100.00	100.00	99.99	99.97	99.92	99.47	98.36	96.39	89.56
Spain	100.00	100.00	100.00	99.99	99.97	99.80	99.44	98.82	96.71
Sweden	100.00	100.00	100.00	100.00	100.00	99.99	99.93	99.77	98.71
Switzerland	100.00	100.00	100.00	99.99	99.97	99.85	99.63	99.29	98.22
Turkey	99.99	99.98	99.96	99.86	99.66	98.13	95.07	90.44	77.48
United Kingdom	99.97	99.94	99.90	99.73	99.52	98.46	96.99	95.17	90.75
Eastern Europe									
Albania									
Belarus	99.99	99.94	99.82	98.66	95.37	64.89	33.88	18.36	7.48
Bosnia-Herzegovina									
Bulgaria	99.95	99.86	99.71	98.85	97.26	86.32	69.38	51.95	27.13
Croatia	100.00	100.00	100.00	99.99	99.95	99.35	97.25	92.63	74.72
Czech Republic	100.00	100.00	100.00	100.00	99.98	99.74	98.74	96.18	83.72
Estonia	100.00	100.00	99.99	99.93	99.79	98.12	93.57	85.50	62.69
Georgia									
Hungary	100.00	100.00	100.00	99.97	99.88	98.38	93.10	82.39	52.14
Latvia	99.94	99.87	99.77	99.33	98.65	94.90	89.22	82.18	66.31
Lithuania	100.00	100.00	100.00	99.99	99.97	99.33	96.03	87.42	59.21
Macedonia									
Moldova									
Poland	100.00	100.00	99.99	99.96	99.86	98.61	94.96	88.09	67.22
Romania	100.00	100.00	100.00	99.99	99.97	99.09	93.95	80.56	45.23
Russia	99.95	99.88	99.77	99.14	98.04	90.77	79.12	65.77	42.34
Slovakia	100.00	100.00	100.00	100.00	99.98	99.72	98.61	95.82	82.40
Slovenia	100.00	100.00	100.00	100.00	100.00	99.97	99.87	99.61	98.21
Ukraine	99.59	98.90	97.78	91.70	81.88	42.64	19.48	9.81	3.90

Source: *National statistical offices/OECD/Eurostat/Euromonitor International*

Household Statistics

Number of Households by Annual Disposable Income Band 2008 *(continued)*
% of total

	Over $25,000	Over $35,000	Over $45,000	Over $55,000	Over $65,000	Over $75,000	Over $100,000	Over $125,000	Over $150,000
Western Europe									
Austria	96.85	90.21	78.97	64.75	50.39	38.02	18.50	9.80	5.85
Belgium	91.63	82.02	69.86	56.82	44.48	33.87	16.30	8.25	4.85
Cyprus									
Denmark	86.05	75.68	64.66	54.02	44.40	36.08	20.98	12.20	7.24
Finland	90.36	75.89	58.13	41.91	29.54	20.95	9.94	5.76	3.98
France	92.62	84.27	73.48	61.47	49.54	38.70	19.20	9.45	5.23
Germany	84.75	71.63	57.74	44.99	34.34	25.97	13.07	7.07	4.25
Gibraltar									
Greece	83.48	69.84	55.93	43.57	33.48	25.63	13.45	7.51	4.50
Iceland									
Ireland	89.30	81.13	72.11	62.98	54.28	46.33	30.48	19.89	13.13
Italy	87.88	73.48	57.71	43.88	33.12	25.18	13.56	8.05	5.18
Liechtenstein									
Luxembourg									
Malta									
Monaco									
Netherlands	91.45	77.19	59.07	42.42	29.84	21.18	10.15	5.93	4.09
Norway	98.21	94.12	86.52	75.83	63.69	51.93	29.89	17.73	11.18
Portugal	67.56	45.52	30.05	20.39	14.42	10.64	5.81	3.76	2.74
Spain	88.60	76.01	61.33	47.18	35.23	25.97	12.44	6.77	4.34
Sweden	89.58	68.54	45.89	29.94	20.20	14.33	7.45	4.83	3.62
Switzerland	94.45	88.55	80.90	72.08	62.74	53.49	33.44	19.63	11.25
Turkey	48.39	28.06	16.79	10.73	7.37	5.40	3.12	2.26	1.80
United Kingdom	79.89	68.05	56.58	46.23	37.34	29.93	17.01	9.73	5.69
Eastern Europe									
Albania									
Belarus	2.94	1.92	1.39	1.08	0.87	0.73	0.51	0.38	0.30
Bosnia-Herzegovina									
Bulgaria	8.91	4.29	2.76	2.10	1.70	1.42	0.99	0.75	0.59
Croatia	33.76	14.99	8.09	5.25	3.93	3.27	2.26	1.70	1.34
Czech Republic	42.57	18.70	9.69	6.11	4.50	3.70	2.55	1.91	1.51
Estonia	26.90	12.70	7.20	4.75	3.51	2.84	1.97	1.49	1.18
Georgia									
Hungary	16.73	7.29	4.36	3.24	2.62	2.18	1.51	1.13	0.90
Latvia	38.21	21.06	12.07	7.47	5.04	3.71	2.35	1.77	1.41
Lithuania	24.22	12.58	7.80	5.42	4.08	3.24	2.13	1.61	1.28
Macedonia									
Moldova									
Poland	31.35	15.73	9.17	6.04	4.37	3.38	2.21	1.67	1.33
Romania	15.00	7.30	4.53	3.28	2.65	2.21	1.53	1.15	0.91
Russia	17.91	9.08	5.42	3.66	2.70	2.14	1.50	1.14	0.91
Slovakia	40.01	17.06	8.89	5.78	4.40	3.52	2.43	1.82	1.44
Slovenia	88.75	68.62	45.47	28.01	17.47	11.59	5.85	3.97	3.13
Ukraine	1.93	1.26	0.92	0.71	0.58	0.48	0.33	0.25	0.20

Source: National statistical offices/OECD/Eurostat/Euromonitor International

Table 15.12

Possession of Household Durables 2008

% of total households

	Air Cond-itioner	Bicycle	Black/White TV	Internet Enabled Computer	Cable TV	Camera	Cassette /Radio Player	CD Player
Western Europe								
Austria	5.7	68.4	0.9	54.5	35.6	97.8	68.3	68.3
Belgium	6.6	68.4	1.9	60.8	89.7	81.6	64.8	64.2
Cyprus								
Denmark	4.5	61.8	1.3	74.0	63.3	98.8	58.7	86.4
Finland	2.8	85.0	1.4	66.0	56.2	86.0	54.1	62.4
France	7.2	74.4	0.9	57.0	12.4	77.1	67.5	23.4
Germany	6.2	79.5	0.7	50.0	51.5	81.5	75.6	82.0
Gibraltar								
Greece	15.9	43.4	1.8	22.0	0.6	89.3	71.6	18.9
Iceland								
Ireland	7.3	61.4	0.1	43.0	35.3	87.0	52.0	39.8
Italy	28.6	51.0	1.8	31.0	0.9	63.9	55.4	12.2
Liechtenstein								
Luxembourg								
Malta								
Monaco								
Netherlands	6.2	91.8	3.4	76.0	81.5	90.4	67.2	86.0
Norway	2.8	80.8	1.6	73.0	45.8	89.6	61.3	86.8
Portugal	9.6	24.1	3.3	39.3	39.1	41.1	67.0	42.1
Spain	17.9	38.0	1.7	45.0	15.6	68.7	89.0	41.7
Sweden	3.0	84.7	1.4	71.0	59.0	90.3	61.5	81.4
Switzerland	9.2	86.5	1.8	70.0	87.7	98.9	62.1	58.1
Turkey	9.2	25.7	7.9	19.0	12.0	30.0	90.8	7.5
United Kingdom	7.6	63.7	0.3	56.0	13.0	83.1	53.7	87.2
Eastern Europe								
Albania								
Belarus	1.6	30.5	6.4		41.2	27.7	15.9	6.1
Bosnia-Herzegovina								
Bulgaria	2.1	40.6	8.0	21.0	43.5	42.0	35.9	7.1
Croatia	23.6	40.8	3.2	27.0	17.5	60.5	33.9	22.1
Czech Republic	4.4	46.9	3.1	33.1	21.9	57.7	69.0	24.5
Estonia	3.5	75.7	2.5	54.0	55.8	50.2	39.3	13.8
Georgia								
Hungary	3.2	76.2	1.8	43.6	60.1	71.6	70.6	28.1
Latvia	3.5	56.3	3.6	39.7	44.0	31.0	54.6	8.2
Lithuania	3.4	45.9	4.0	43.0	40.2	34.4	56.0	7.7
Macedonia								
Moldova								
Poland	3.8	63.1	0.6	38.0	35.4	58.7	52.5	16.4
Romania	2.2	24.8	2.4	13.0	53.8	41.1	27.3	3.0
Russia	3.2	36.4	8.4	24.0	41.5	43.6	49.7	11.1
Slovakia	3.6	66.9	2.4	35.0	38.0	46.4	53.4	10.8
Slovenia	14.1	61.0	2.5	49.7	61.0	67.0	89.6	26.1
Ukraine	1.1	34.1	8.0		19.1	22.3	18.0	9.1

Source: *National statistical offices/Euromonitor International*

Household Statistics

Possession of Household Durables 2008 *(continued)*
% of total households

	Colour TV Set	Cooker	Dish-Washer	DVD Player/ Recorder	Fax Machine	Freezer
Western Europe						
Austria	98.9	95.4	78.0	77.4		86.8
Belgium	99.0	96.2	53.6	73.7	5.8	64.0
Cyprus						
Denmark	98.1	97.2	65.0	84.0	14.7	98.5
Finland	95.1	98.8	54.7	72.3	5.7	89.5
France	97.3	97.0	45.5	83.1		54.0
Germany	98.0	95.8	62.5	69.1		75.0
Gibraltar						
Greece	99.7	95.1	33.1	51.3		23.1
Iceland						
Ireland	99.7	97.9	58.0	80.7		37.9
Italy	96.6	95.0	40.7	85.2	5.0	48.3
Liechtenstein						
Luxembourg						
Malta						
Monaco						
Netherlands	99.0	95.7	57.0	87.8		84.4
Norway	98.3	98.6	73.7	85.0		93.9
Portugal	99.1	99.9	49.4	78.4		68.9
Spain	99.4	97.3	42.1	73.4		38.8
Sweden	97.7	97.9	66.4	79.7		98.9
Switzerland	94.6	95.4	69.7	84.6		69.3
Turkey	92.8	60.8	26.7	21.2		2.6
United Kingdom	99.0	95.2	38.7	88.7		97.7
Eastern Europe						
Albania						
Belarus	95.5	90.6	4.2	17.3		16.9
Bosnia-Herzegovina						
Bulgaria	90.0	79.1	5.7	18.1		27.3
Croatia	96.7	95.4	22.7	42.2		70.0
Czech Republic	98.2	97.9	21.9	50.4		34.3
Estonia	96.9	97.8	7.2	36.8		41.1
Georgia						
Hungary	97.3	97.5	7.7	54.2		52.0
Latvia	95.8	97.3	1.9	28.4		16.1
Lithuania	97.4	97.3	2.8	28.5		19.8
Macedonia						
Moldova						
Poland	97.5	97.3	8.2	47.4		31.0
Romania	92.6	93.1	4.9	18.0		23.9
Russia	96.1	93.2	5.4	44.6		26.9
Slovakia	99.0	97.7	9.0	32.7		40.0
Slovenia	97.1	96.0	48.6	56.3	10.4	81.5
Ukraine	92.7	88.5	0.1	17.8		4.6

Source: National statistical offices/Euromonitor International

Household Statistics

Possession of Household Durables 2008 *(continued)*

% of total households

	Hi-Fi Stereo	Internet Enabled Comp- uter	Microwave Oven	Mobile Phone	Motor- cycle	Passenger Car	Personal Computer	Refrig- erator
Western Europe								
Austria	85.3	68.9	72.7	92.5	29.9	82.2	74.8	98.9
Belgium	75.8	65.1	89.1	93.1	14.9	88.9	72.8	99.1
Cyprus								
Denmark	90.6	83.0	75.0	95.0	21.8	73.0	88.0	99.2
Finland	90.4	72.0	91.5	92.1	13.0	73.3	72.5	97.4
France	65.3	62.0	80.3	78.0	18.6	83.6	67.1	96.7
Germany	74.6	69.1	69.6	86.3	24.1	77.1	75.4	98.6
Gibraltar								
Greece	61.7	31.0	39.6	83.4	11.6	73.9	43.0	95.5
Iceland								
Ireland	72.0	63.0	90.4	94.5	5.9	80.9	70.9	99.7
Italy	58.8	47.0	35.1	88.6	17.2	61.2	55.4	99.0
Liechtenstein								
Luxembourg								
Malta								
Monaco								
Netherlands	91.8	86.0	92.2	95.5	11.9	77.6	87.4	99.3
Norway	91.3	84.0	82.7	97.9	11.6	78.9	85.1	99.0
Portugal	47.9	46.0	83.0	89.8	19.4	67.2	51.3	99.5
Spain	68.6	51.0	83.3	89.1	21.6	78.1	58.4	100.0
Sweden	88.3	84.0	79.5	97.3	4.1	85.5	84.5	99.1
Switzerland	77.8	77.6	64.4	92.4	32.5	88.6	79.9	100.0
Turkey	42.8	23.3	6.4	87.2	12.1	28.4	36.3	98.2
United Kingdom	76.0	65.0	91.9	81.6	9.4	75.8	72.3	99.4
Eastern Europe								
Albania								
Belarus	27.4	14.2	21.6	68.6	4.3	56.6	27.4	97.5
Bosnia-Herzegovina								
Bulgaria	28.5	25.0	31.5	86.4	5.6	47.1	26.3	87.0
Croatia	35.5	31.5	31.0	92.8	20.9	59.9	38.0	94.4
Czech Republic	46.8	41.7	78.0	99.3	26.0	73.9	61.2	76.4
Estonia	54.1	58.1	59.5	90.0	2.5	49.6	57.7	95.2
Georgia								
Hungary	34.3	48.0	85.2	88.1	14.4	51.2	54.2	70.5
Latvia	51.8	52.8	36.1	82.8	0.7	50.1	56.7	99.2
Lithuania	44.3	47.1	54.9	81.9	2.4	54.0	48.0	96.2
Macedonia								
Moldova								
Poland	45.6	43.4	45.6	84.6	3.2	54.5	55.0	99.1
Romania	15.4	30.0	30.7	86.6	1.2	24.8	41.0	87.2
Russia	46.5	31.8	39.7	86.6	17.3	37.6	42.2	96.3
Slovakia	19.4	58.3	72.7	88.5	6.9	55.8	63.2	83.1
Slovenia	55.6	59.0	51.7	92.0	3.0	80.3	65.0	99.3
Ukraine	17.2	13.0	27.9	35.0	2.1	32.9	16.3	95.4

Source: *National statistical offices/Euromonitor International*

Household Statistics

Possession of Household Durables 2008 *(continued)*

% of total households

	Satell-ite TV	Shower	Telephone	Tumble Drier	Vacuum Cleaner	Video Camera	Game Console	Video Recorder	Washing Machine
Western Europe									
Austria	48.7	93.2	62.6	23.0	98.2	22.4	17.2	65.1	96.5
Belgium	10.3	89.1	73.9	50.8	97.0	31.1	17.2	76.1	89.5
Cyprus									
Denmark	34.7	99.4	74.3	52.3	96.4	22.3	16.7	84.7	80.0
Finland	23.8	99.8	37.9	56.1	97.0	23.2	18.5	75.2	88.6
France	26.6	90.5	98.0	43.3	90.2	8.6	20.0	61.1	94.9
Germany	41.8	99.0	89.7	44.9	95.5	11.9	18.6	47.1	95.8
Gibraltar									
Greece	14.7	97.2	93.6	12.7	83.2	6.1	10.2	46.4	92.7
Iceland									
Ireland	39.5	97.6	86.7	26.7	95.9	12.9	14.0	81.4	97.2
Italy	30.2	81.1	72.6	17.5	80.0	26.2	15.8	70.9	97.7
Liechtenstein									
Luxembourg									
Malta									
Monaco									
Netherlands	14.5	98.2	99.7	61.2	97.2	28.9	13.1	79.0	97.2
Norway	30.9	99.6	89.3	42.8	95.8	23.1	19.5	41.9	90.7
Portugal	17.9	95.5	56.5	13.2	84.9	15.6	15.6	47.7	92.3
Spain	19.9	98.1	82.8	16.4	83.5	9.6	10.9	66.7	99.1
Sweden	35.7	98.4	99.0	45.4	96.6	26.6	15.9	78.8	75.6
Switzerland	16.8	99.8	87.9	41.1	99.1	52.3	16.8	65.7	99.5
Turkey	39.7	79.2	70.2	1.5	82.7	3.6	16.5	14.6	91.1
United Kingdom	35.5	92.6	88.6	58.4	95.7	11.8	17.1	84.1	96.0
Eastern Europe									
Albania									
Belarus	10.0	72.7	55.5	1.5	58.0	0.8	5.3	25.0	76.8
Bosnia-Herzegovina									
Bulgaria	8.2	61.1	80.9	4.0	82.8	0.3	3.9	39.6	72.3
Croatia	43.3	77.9	80.4	8.6	82.0	6.8	9.5	39.5	88.2
Czech Republic	14.6	78.3	29.9	2.5	89.6	7.0	10.1	61.1	94.2
Estonia	21.3	76.9	50.9	5.9	84.3	8.7	6.4	35.1	86.5
Georgia									
Hungary	21.4	74.8	25.1	2.3	93.2	13.1	10.5	62.1	88.4
Latvia	17.7	66.3	46.5	3.5	79.9	6.3	6.8	34.1	87.3
Lithuania	10.6	69.5	36.2	3.8	76.4	8.5	6.8	24.4	87.6
Macedonia									
Moldova									
Poland	29.2	77.5	66.5	1.4	95.1	6.1	8.2	77.6	86.6
Romania	29.8	45.1	34.5	0.5	57.6	0.9	3.1	5.2	69.3
Russia	7.0	62.8	59.3	1.1	85.0	7.4	3.8	17.3	96.3
Slovakia	43.0	78.9	50.7	1.7	88.7	5.9	8.6	51.5	75.8
Slovenia	16.3	77.8	77.8	9.4	92.7	5.6	10.6	50.9	96.9
Ukraine	5.2	71.2	55.0	1.5	68.5	3.9	3.7	10.0	79.2

Source: National statistical offices/Euromonitor International

Income and Deductions

Income Statistics

Table 16.1

Annual Gross Income 1990-2008

National currency billion / US$ per capita

	1990	1995	2000	2003	2004	2005	2006	2007	2008	US$ per capita 2008
Western Europe										
Austria	129.4	171.0	201.6	217.4	225.1	234.4	243.3	254.1	263.1	46,355
Belgium	130.8	168.0	195.8	209.2	213.7	221.5	233.8	246.9	260.5	36,106
Denmark	720.6	884.6	1,106.6	1,195.0	1,247.5	1,296.4	1,367.6	1,412.1	1,439.9	51,715
Finland	76.1	84.3	105.8	119.8	124.7	129.0	133.9	140.3	150.4	41,746
France	992.3	1,176.3	1,391.8	1,563.6	1,625.5	1,679.5	1,738.4	1,806.9	1,876.3	44,464
Germany	1,262.0	1,844.2	2,058.5	2,158.0	2,196.4	2,237.5	2,297.3	2,335.1	2,390.0	42,782
Greece	41.1	83.6	120.6	146.2	156.7	168.6	183.4	195.5	207.8	27,282
Ireland	31.8	41.7	73.2	93.7	99.3	108.2	118.6	128.6	126.9	42,660
Italy	582.9	755.9	874.7	969.3	1,002.7	1,031.8	1,072.5	1,111.8	1,143.6	28,539
Netherlands	177.4	215.7	277.4	325.2	331.2	340.5	356.3	369.6	386.2	34,691
Norway	559.2	720.7	1,012.1	1,194.8	1,281.0	1,357.9	1,461.2	1,564.1	1,653.8	62,370
Portugal	49.9	80.1	110.3	126.3	131.3	137.7	145.0	152.2	159.4	22,037
Spain	305.0	425.9	567.3	681.1	759.1	818.0	880.0	949.2	991.3	32,380
Sweden	1,225.0	1,564.9	1,853.1	2,063.0	2,139.9	2,220.5	2,308.8	2,412.9	2,505.5	41,513
Switzerland	259.3	304.5	342.4	345.9	351.2	362.4	377.3	393.6	411.4	50,448
Turkey	0.4	7.5	141.9	412.4	508.3	581.4	676.5	757.5	838.1	8,660
United Kingdom	541.4	723.4	934.6	1,074.9	1,126.2	1,201.2	1,257.9	1,323.7	1,375.9	41,341
Eastern Europe										
Belarus	0.0	83.6	6,463.0	25,346.0	32,181.7	40,708.2	49,178.3	60,612.3	81,950.4	3,959
Bulgaria	0.0	0.7	23.5	30.8	34.2	38.2	44.1	50.0	58.8	5,812
Croatia	0.2	69.5	109.3	139.1	148.7	159.7	170.9	188.1	201.2	9,192
Czech Republic	595.1	1,189.4	1,732.1	2,038.1	2,172.1	2,268.0	2,426.4	2,632.6	2,907.7	16,509
Estonia	7.0	34.9	71.3	98.1	106.9	122.2	144.9	168.6	180.4	12,634
Hungary	1,332.8	3,974.0	9,068.8	12,378.9	13,680.3	14,676.5	15,637.0	16,759.3	17,677.6	10,231
Latvia	0.1	2.1	4.0	5.3	6.2	7.3	9.0	10.9	11.3	10,379
Lithuania	0.1	21.7	40.0	46.6	51.5	58.6	67.3	80.2	92.5	11,655
Poland	45.7	315.8	680.5	763.3	808.9	850.3	907.9	990.5	1,096.1	11,958
Romania	0.1	6.2	69.2	169.9	215.1	251.8	296.0	347.1	411.0	7,591
Russia	0.6	900.2	4,384.5	9,466.8	11,875.7	14,479.0	17,772.3	21,948.1	27,750.1	7,863
Slovakia	10.4	11.8	18.4	23.8	26.9	30.7	35.0	42.3	50.7	13,829
Slovenia	4.5	11.5	16.3	22.7	24.3	25.4	26.7	29.6	32.1	23,446
Ukraine	0.0	31.9	135.1	174.5	227.7	320.5	390.5	516.4	707.8	2,909

Source: *Euromonitor International from national statistics*

Income Statistics

Table 16.2

Gross Income by Source 2008
% of gross income

	Benefits	Employment	Investments	Other Sources	Total
Western Europe					
Austria	10.73	83.02	5.55	0.71	100.00
Belgium	26.18	57.63	15.58	0.62	100.00
Denmark	19.32	66.85	7.45	6.38	100.00
Finland	16.47	68.51	12.80	2.22	100.00
France	28.87	62.71	8.00	0.39	100.00
Germany	20.06	62.79	13.92	3.23	100.00
Greece	20.72	55.26	20.23	3.80	100.00
Ireland	13.32	65.76	15.69	5.23	100.00
Italy	19.61	59.98	18.00	2.41	100.00
Netherlands	23.12	62.94	13.21	0.73	100.00
Norway	22.18	71.71	5.85	0.26	100.00
Portugal	15.99	73.42	4.09	6.51	100.00
Spain	11.98	75.91	8.12	3.98	100.00
Sweden	19.49	69.98	7.20	3.34	100.00
Switzerland	23.15	72.87	2.49	1.49	100.00
Turkey	7.14	70.60	19.17	3.09	100.00
United Kingdom	18.91	68.17	7.90	5.02	100.00
Eastern Europe					
Belarus	24.07	69.62	0.84	5.47	100.00
Bulgaria	18.79	44.61	25.39	11.20	100.00
Croatia	23.94	65.83	6.06	4.17	100.00
Czech Republic	12.17	65.39	17.52	4.92	100.00
Estonia	30.34	62.38	1.28	6.00	100.00
Hungary	19.05	57.42	12.84	10.68	100.00
Latvia	17.22	62.65	19.48	0.65	100.00
Lithuania	20.72	64.46	6.59	8.23	100.00
Poland	25.93	59.76	2.18	12.12	100.00
Romania	12.19	72.78	10.60	4.42	100.00
Russia	14.44	77.83	6.12	1.62	100.00
Slovakia	18.43	77.99	0.96	2.62	100.00
Slovenia	23.11	62.96	4.29	9.64	100.00
Ukraine	13.21	83.40	0.94	2.46	100.00

Source: *Euromonitor International from national statistics*

Income Statistics

Table 16.3

Tax and Social Security Contributions 1990-2008

National currency billion / US$ per capita

	1990	1995	2000	2003	2004	2005	2006	2007	2008	US$ per capita 2008
Western Europe										
Austria	48.3	53.3	65.3	71.8	73.8	76.4	79.2	82.0	85.0	14,985
Belgium	23.0	30.7	39.4	41.8	42.9	44.2	47.3	50.8	53.0	7,350
Denmark	287.1	359.0	455.1	470.9	476.9	483.7	502.0	509.9	513.6	18,447
Finland	27.6	30.7	39.5	42.0	43.0	45.6	47.6	50.2	53.7	14,914
France	327.3	389.6	468.8	521.0	536.0	556.7	573.7	595.9	619.0	14,668
Germany	374.3	599.2	675.0	682.8	694.4	707.5	732.9	743.1	760.1	13,606
Greece	6.9	14.2	27.4	34.0	35.7	37.0	39.3	41.7	43.6	5,720
Ireland	8.0	10.8	18.5	23.8	25.7	28.0	31.4	34.0	33.7	11,327
Italy	47.6	54.6	55.0	41.8	43.6	46.1	56.6	69.7	76.6	1,910
Netherlands	37.9	50.5	69.5	78.3	79.8	85.1	93.3	96.7	100.3	9,011
Norway	192.9	240.1	356.9	408.1	438.8	465.5	502.0	536.7	577.3	21,771
Portugal	11.7	18.3	27.1	31.2	32.6	35.3	36.8	38.5	39.1	5,408
Spain	87.7	125.4	171.0	206.9	218.7	237.2	260.6	284.1	301.6	9,852
Sweden	459.6	629.1	773.6	839.3	862.6	888.6	924.2	965.9	1,010.8	16,748
Switzerland	55.2	59.8	66.0	61.8	59.0	64.6	70.8	76.0	80.9	9,923
Turkey	0.1	2.1	22.2	69.7	85.6	98.7	115.0	131.0	148.3	1,533
United Kingdom	175.7	219.3	285.7	327.5	349.5	384.4	405.5	428.4	451.9	13,579
Eastern Europe										
Belarus	0.0	15.3	1,401.1	4,697.3	5,678.0	7,325.0	8,881.3	10,723.7	14,161.1	684
Bulgaria	0.0	0.0	3.6	4.9	5.4	6.1	6.9	7.9	9.8	967
Croatia	0.0	3.7	15.3	19.4	20.7	22.7	24.5	27.6	29.0	1,325
Czech Republic	273.9	327.9	501.1	629.3	711.5	746.0	810.8	865.1	958.6	5,443
Estonia	1.8	9.5	17.7	26.4	28.9	33.6	39.8	45.8	49.7	3,483
Hungary	397.5	1,186.1	2,682.9	3,499.9	3,803.7	4,130.6	4,590.4	4,963.2	5,231.8	3,028
Latvia	0.0	0.5	0.9	1.2	1.5	1.7	1.8	2.0	2.1	1,932
Lithuania	0.0	3.9	8.0	8.8	10.1	11.9	14.2	16.9	19.7	2,487
Poland	7.2	74.4	156.4	174.4	181.1	198.7	219.0	244.4	270.3	2,949
Romania	0.0	1.2	12.8	40.6	46.8	53.3	62.4	74.5	87.1	1,609
Russia	0.1	141.2	854.4	1,809.7	2,260.7	2,511.1	3,040.5	3,754.6	4,707.1	1,334
Slovakia	2.5	3.3	4.5	6.1	6.6	7.7	8.9	10.8	13.1	3,563
Slovenia	0.9	2.3	4.4	6.2	6.7	6.9	7.5	8.5	9.2	6,688
Ukraine	0.0	6.9	29.7	46.1	60.4	83.2	100.0	130.7	177.0	727

Source: *Euromonitor International from national statistics*

Income Statistics   **Table 16.4**

Annual Disposable Income 1990-2008

National currency billion / US$ per capita

	1990	1995	2000	2003	2004	2005	2006	2007	2008	US$ per capita 2008
Western Europe										
Austria	81.2	117.7	136.3	145.6	151.3	158.0	164.4	172.1	178.7	31,483
Belgium	107.8	137.2	156.4	167.3	170.9	177.3	186.4	195.7	206.5	28,616
Denmark	433.5	525.7	651.5	724.0	770.6	812.6	865.6	902.2	928.6	33,352
Finland	48.6	53.6	66.3	77.8	81.7	83.4	86.4	90.1	96.3	26,744
France	630.9	790.9	923.0	1,042.7	1,089.4	1,126.2	1,179.5	1,240.6	1,283.2	30,407
Germany	887.7	1,245.1	1,383.5	1,475.2	1,502.0	1,529.6	1,563.7	1,591.1	1,628.3	29,147
Greece	34.3	69.4	93.3	112.2	121.1	131.7	143.9	153.7	164.3	21,567
Ireland	23.9	30.8	54.7	69.9	73.6	80.2	87.2	94.6	93.5	31,416
Italy	535.3	701.4	819.7	927.5	959.1	985.6	1,015.8	1,042.0	1,067.4	26,638
Netherlands	139.4	165.2	207.9	246.9	251.4	255.3	262.9	272.9	285.1	25,611
Norway	366.3	480.6	655.2	786.7	842.2	892.4	960.1	1,029.9	1,088.1	41,037
Portugal	38.2	61.7	83.2	95.1	98.7	102.4	107.9	113.4	119.2	16,489
Spain	217.3	300.6	396.3	474.3	540.4	580.9	619.4	665.0	694.4	22,682
Sweden	765.4	935.8	1,079.5	1,223.7	1,277.3	1,331.9	1,384.6	1,447.0	1,501.6	24,880
Switzerland	204.2	244.8	276.4	284.1	292.2	297.9	306.6	317.3	329.4	40,383
Turkey	0.3	5.5	119.7	342.7	422.7	482.7	561.5	628.0	693.8	7,168
United Kingdom	365.7	504.2	648.8	747.4	775.4	814.8	851.2	895.5	930.7	27,963
Eastern Europe										
Belarus	0.0	68.3	5,061.9	20,648.7	26,503.7	33,383.2	40,296.9	49,888.6	66,726.8	3,223
Bulgaria	0.0	0.7	19.9	25.9	28.7	32.1	37.2	42.1	49.2	4,864
Croatia	0.2	65.8	93.9	119.7	127.9	137.1	146.3	160.6	172.7	7,892
Czech Republic	321.2	861.5	1,231.1	1,408.8	1,460.6	1,522.0	1,618.6	1,772.9	1,956.8	11,110
Estonia	5.2	25.4	53.5	71.6	78.0	88.6	105.1	122.8	132.0	9,243
Hungary	935.3	2,787.8	6,385.9	8,879.0	9,876.6	10,545.9	11,046.7	11,807.0	12,569.5	7,275
Latvia	0.0	1.6	3.1	4.1	4.7	5.6	7.1	8.9	9.4	8,585
Lithuania	0.1	17.8	32.0	37.8	41.4	46.7	53.1	63.3	73.1	9,211
Poland	38.6	241.3	524.1	588.9	627.8	651.5	688.9	745.9	819.1	8,936
Romania	0.1	5.0	56.4	129.3	168.3	198.3	234.1	273.7	325.5	6,011
Russia	0.5	759.0	3,530.1	7,657.1	9,615.0	11,967.8	14,731.7	18,171.7	22,950.8	6,503
Slovakia	7.9	8.5	13.9	17.7	20.3	23.1	26.0	31.5	37.7	10,282
Slovenia	3.5	9.2	11.9	16.2	17.4	18.3	19.1	21.1	22.9	16,742
Ukraine	0.0	25.0	105.4	136.0	177.3	250.7	306.4	406.5	559.8	2,301

Source: *Euromonitor International from national statistics*

Income Statistics

Table 16.5

Net Savings 1990-2008

National currency billion / US$ per capita

	1990	1995	2000	2003	2004	2005	2006	2007	2008	US$ per capita 2008
Western Europe										
Austria	6.0	24.0	26.1	27.1	27.9	28.6	29.9	33.0	34.8	6,131
Belgium	16.1	26.5	22.8	23.1	21.0	21.3	22.7	24.0	25.8	3,581
Denmark	16.6	12.0	44.7	67.9	74.7	79.5	85.7	89.1	91.6	3,289
Finland	4.7	5.8	4.5	6.1	6.9	5.8	4.3	3.5	5.0	1,390
France	85.7	125.3	139.1	164.4	172.3	164.2	163.0	164.7	169.7	4,020
Germany	88.4	207.4	203.2	228.0	236.6	240.0	242.9	251.8	255.6	4,574
Greece	1.6	1.1	-5.0	-9.1	-8.8	-8.5	-8.2	-8.0	-7.8	-1,022
Ireland	3.1	3.5	6.3	8.3	8.9	9.6	10.1	10.4	7.3	2,462
Italy	135.9	151.3	109.9	143.2	148.3	147.0	144.1	140.5	145.1	3,620
Netherlands	18.9	16.0	0.7	13.1	13.0	9.4	12.4	13.3	15.4	1,381
Norway	19.1	31.4	42.0	78.2	89.3	102.7	116.9	129.3	139.5	5,260
Portugal	4.4	7.9	7.5	10.0	9.3	8.7	9.5	10.6	12.0	1,655
Spain	26.9	35.5	25.8	29.9	60.6	64.4	64.7	73.3	79.9	2,609
Sweden	72.6	61.9	3.6	30.8	42.9	49.0	58.8	67.3	88.1	1,460
Switzerland	24.8	31.2	34.6	29.3	30.8	31.2	32.0	32.6	33.6	4,121
Turkey	0.0	0.2	5.5	26.1	32.8	39.6	47.6	53.7	57.4	594
United Kingdom	22.6	55.5	32.3	32.8	25.2	30.4	34.0	37.1	39.9	1,199
Eastern Europe										
Belarus	0.0	0.3	50.0	317.0	373.5	504.7	706.2	1,079.0	1,514.3	73
Bulgaria	0.0	0.1	1.5	1.8	2.0	2.3	2.6	3.3	4.1	400
Croatia	0.0	3.3	4.3	4.6	4.8	5.3	5.9	6.8	8.1	369
Czech Republic	16.7	125.4	96.4	91.3	61.5	75.6	76.6	107.3	139.1	790
Estonia		2.3	2.0	-2.4	-4.7	-5.3	-4.8	-5.0	-3.4	-239
Hungary	-59.5	-179.2	-512.9	-1,381.7	-1,119.5	-1,249.9	-1,352.0	-1,423.5	-1,322.7	-766
Latvia	0.0	0.0	0.1	0.1	0.1	0.0	0.0	-0.1	0.1	66
Lithuania		0.7	2.6	1.5	0.8	0.4	-0.2	0.1	0.5	62
Poland	11.8	40.6	54.3	42.7	38.4	37.3	36.0	44.1	50.4	550
Romania	0.0	0.2	1.0	1.2	1.1	1.2	1.3	1.5	1.9	35
Russia	0.2	39.2	234.9	1,117.0	1,209.4	1,377.8	1,842.9	2,270.0	2,895.7	820
Slovakia		0.9	1.7	1.3	1.2	1.5	1.2	1.5	1.8	496
Slovenia	0.8	-0.1	-0.2	2.2	2.8	3.1	3.0	3.5	3.8	2,778
Ukraine	0.0	2.3	12.4	-10.3	-3.4	-0.8	-10.8	-13.4	-16.7	-69

Source: *Euromonitor International from national statistics*

Income Statistics

Table 16.6

Savings Ratio 1990-2008
% of personal disposable income

	1990	1995	2000	2003	2004	2005	2006	2007	2008
Western Europe									
Austria	7.4	20.4	19.2	18.6	18.4	18.1	18.2	19.2	19.5
Belgium	14.9	19.3	14.6	13.8	12.3	12.0	12.2	12.3	12.5
Denmark	3.8	2.3	6.9	9.4	9.7	9.8	9.9	9.9	9.9
Finland	9.8	10.8	6.8	7.8	8.5	6.9	5.0	3.8	5.2
France	12.9	15.9	15.1	15.8	15.8	14.6	14.0	13.6	13.5
Germany	10.0	16.7	14.7	15.5	15.8	15.7	15.5	15.8	15.7
Greece	4.5	1.6	-5.3	-8.1	-7.3	-6.5	-5.7	-5.2	-4.7
Ireland	12.8	11.4	11.5	11.9	12.1	12.0	11.6	11.0	7.8
Italy	25.4	21.6	13.4	15.4	15.5	14.9	14.2	13.5	13.6
Netherlands	13.6	9.7	0.3	5.3	5.2	3.7	4.7	4.9	5.4
Norway	5.2	6.5	6.4	9.9	10.6	11.5	12.2	12.5	12.8
Portugal	11.5	12.8	9.0	10.6	9.4	8.5	8.8	9.4	10.0
Spain	12.4	11.8	6.5	6.3	11.2	11.1	10.4	11.0	11.5
Sweden	9.5	6.6	0.3	2.5	3.4	3.7	4.2	4.7	5.9
Switzerland	12.1	12.7	12.5	10.3	10.5	10.5	10.4	10.3	10.2
Turkey	3.2	3.5	4.6	7.6	7.8	8.2	8.5	8.6	8.3
United Kingdom	6.2	11.0	5.0	4.4	3.3	3.7	4.0	4.1	4.3
Eastern Europe									
Belarus	13.5	0.4	1.0	1.5	1.4	1.5	1.8	2.2	2.3
Bulgaria	6.3	9.0	7.6	6.7	7.0	7.0	7.0	7.8	8.2
Croatia	5.6	5.1	4.6	3.9	3.8	3.9	4.0	4.2	4.7
Czech Republic	5.2	14.6	7.8	6.5	4.2	5.0	4.7	6.1	7.1
Estonia		9.0	3.7	-3.4	-6.1	-6.0	-4.6	-4.1	-2.6
Hungary	-6.4	-6.4	-8.0	-15.6	-11.3	-11.9	-12.2	-12.1	-10.5
Latvia	-0.1	-2.3	3.0	2.5	1.5	-0.3	0.0	-1.5	0.8
Lithuania		3.9	8.0	3.9	2.0	0.9	-0.3	0.1	0.7
Poland	30.6	16.8	10.4	7.2	6.1	5.7	5.2	5.9	6.1
Romania	2.9	3.4	1.7	0.9	0.6	0.6	0.5	0.5	0.6
Russia	37.4	5.2	6.7	14.6	12.6	11.5	12.5	12.5	12.6
Slovakia		10.3	12.0	7.1	6.0	6.3	4.5	4.7	4.8
Slovenia	21.6	-0.6	-1.3	13.3	16.0	16.7	15.6	16.7	16.6
Ukraine	8.2	9.4	11.8	-7.5	-1.9	-0.3	-3.5	-3.3	-3.0

Source: Euromonitor International from national statistics

Section Seventeen

Industry

Industry Statistics   **Table 17.1**

Indices of General Industrial Production 1980-2008
1995 = 100

	1980	1985	1990	1995	1996	1997	1998	1999	2000	2001
Western Europe										
Austria	68.1	74.2	89.0	100.0	101.0	107.4	116.2	123.2	134.1	138.1
Belgium	80.9	84.1	99.4	100.0	100.8	105.4	108.9	110.1	115.5	115.0
Cyprus	63.0	73.3	97.2	100.0	96.8	96.7	99.4	100.9	105.4	105.1
Denmark	66.3	80.2	86.2	100.0	101.7	106.2	109.4	109.6	115.5	117.3
Finland	65.7	76.2	87.3	100.0	102.9	111.8	122.3	129.3	144.5	144.6
France	87.9	86.1	100.4	100.0	100.9	104.0	107.7	110.2	114.4	115.9
Germany			100.0	100.0	100.7	103.4	107.2	108.4	114.5	114.6
Gibraltar										
Greece	91.9	98.4	101.8	100.0	100.9	102.8	112.0	114.2	122.5	120.3
Iceland										
Ireland	34.4	44.0	63.1	100.0	107.6	127.0	152.1	174.6	201.6	222.0
Italy	82.0	79.5	93.5	100.0	99.1	102.4	104.3	104.4	107.7	106.8
Liechtenstein										
Luxembourg	68.1	82.4	98.0	100.0	100.1	105.3	114.5	116.3	122.1	126.4
Malta										
Monaco										
Netherlands	79.1	83.9	92.2	100.0	102.4	102.6	104.8	106.5	110.0	111.1
Norway	49.7	60.1	78.6	100.0	105.4	109.0	107.8	107.5	110.7	109.2
Portugal	62.3	73.5	100.6	100.0	107.0	109.6	114.0	117.6	118.1	120.4
Spain	81.0	83.4	97.2	100.0	99.3	106.1	111.9	114.8	119.3	117.9
Sweden	73.6	81.0	89.2	100.0	100.9	104.6	110.3	113.4	119.9	118.7
Switzerland	79.9	82.3	97.0	100.0	100.0	104.6	108.4	112.2	121.7	120.8
Turkey		60.0	85.5	100.0	105.9	117.2	118.6	114.3	121.2	110.7
United Kingdom	76.5	82.6	94.1	100.0	101.3	102.8	103.9	105.3	107.2	105.7
Eastern Europe										
Albania				100.0	82.8	53.6	82.5	59.7	121.3	91.3
Belarus			169.2	100.0	103.5	123.0	138.2	152.4	164.3	174.0
Bosnia-Herzegovina										
Bulgaria	143.4	177.8	166.1	100.0	105.1	85.8	78.5	72.2	78.2	79.6
Croatia			178.3	100.0	103.1	110.2	114.2	112.6	114.5	121.4
Czech Republic			131.8	100.0	102.0	106.5	108.2	104.7	105.7	112.8
Estonia			207.0	100.0	102.9	117.9	122.7	118.6	135.9	148.0
Georgia										
Hungary	111.7	122.9	113.8	100.0	103.4	114.8	129.0	142.4	168.4	175.0
Latvia			260.4	100.0	105.5	120.1	123.8	101.7	104.9	112.1
Lithuania			197.2	100.0	104.1	108.9	117.8	104.6	110.1	127.7
Macedonia			207.5	100.0	103.2	104.7	109.5	106.7	110.4	99.3
Moldova										
Poland	99.9	98.9	80.8	100.0	109.4	121.7	127.4	133.5	143.5	144.1
Romania	148.6	183.5	152.7	100.0	105.7	98.7	81.9	77.7	83.2	90.3
Russia			202.4	100.0	92.4	93.3	88.8	96.7	105.2	108.3
Slovakia			125.3	100.0	102.5	103.8	108.6	106.3	115.2	123.0
Slovenia			124.7	100.0	101.0	102.0	105.8	105.2	111.8	115.0
Ukraine			190.8	100.0	94.9	93.1	91.6	95.9	109.0	123.1

Source: United Nations/Euromonitor International
Notes: Indices based on value of production (or contribution to GDP) at constant prices

Industry Statistics

Indices of General Industrial Production 1980-2008 *(continued)*
1995 = 100

	2002	2003	2004	2005	2006	2007	2008
Western Europe							
Austria	139.2	142.1	151.0	157.3	169.0	178.2	181.7
Belgium	116.7	117.5	121.5	121.0	127.1	130.5	129.8
Cyprus	105.2	113.6	115.7	116.8	117.8	121.5	124.7
Denmark	119.0	119.2	119.2	121.2	125.4	125.9	126.0
Finland	147.7	149.5	157.6	157.7	172.6	180.3	179.4
France	114.4	114.1	116.7	117.0	117.6	119.3	116.3
Germany	113.6	114.0	117.5	121.5	128.6	136.5	136.5
Gibraltar							
Greece	121.3	121.6	123.1	121.8	122.6	125.3	120.9
Iceland							
Ireland	237.9	249.0	249.8	257.3	270.4	290.0	286.9
Italy	105.4	104.3	105.3	103.4	105.4	105.9	101.4
Liechtenstein							
Luxembourg	129.4	134.1	139.3	140.2	143.1	143.5	137.5
Malta							
Monaco							
Netherlands	112.1	110.6	115.1	115.5	117.2	119.9	121.6
Norway	110.0	105.5	107.9	107.1	104.6	103.7	103.9
Portugal	121.0	119.6	114.8	110.4	113.8	114.2	109.5
Spain	118.0	119.9	122.1	122.2	126.7	129.6	121.2
Sweden	118.7	120.4	127.1	130.3	134.2	138.6	134.6
Switzerland	114.6	114.6	119.7	122.9	132.5	145.0	146.8
Turkey	121.1	131.8	144.5	152.4	164.3	175.7	174.2
United Kingdom	103.6	102.9	104.2	102.6	103.3	104.0	101.3
Eastern Europe							
Albania	75.6	70.5	67.2	60.2	55.1	53.4	51.8
Belarus	181.9	194.8	225.9	249.8	277.5	301.9	335.5
Bosnia-Herzegovina							
Bulgaria	83.3	94.2	106.3	113.6	120.5	132.0	132.9
Croatia	128.0	133.2	138.1	145.1	159.1	160.1	162.7
Czech Republic	114.9	121.2	132.9	141.6	157.5	171.7	172.3
Estonia	160.1	177.5	196.1	217.7	239.3	255.0	238.4
Georgia							
Hungary	180.7	192.7	207.0	222.3	244.4	264.4	261.1
Latvia	118.6	126.4	133.9	141.5	148.3	149.0	138.8
Lithuania	131.6	152.8	169.4	181.4	194.8	202.5	208.0
Macedonia	94.0	98.4	96.2	103.0	106.8	110.7	116.6
Moldova							
Poland	146.1	158.9	179.1	186.4	208.8	228.8	237.0
Romania	94.3	97.5	101.9	104.3	112.3	117.9	119.1
Russia	111.7	121.6	131.7	137.0	142.3	157.3	161.1
Slovakia	130.9	137.4	143.1	147.7	162.5	183.2	186.7
Slovenia	117.8	119.5	126.1	130.2	138.3	146.8	144.6
Ukraine	131.2	152.2	170.1	174.9	185.0	203.9	205.1

Source: United Nations/Euromonitor International
Notes: Indices based on value of production (or contribution to GDP) at constant prices

Industry Statistics

Table 17.2

Indices of General Industrial Production by Quarter 2007-2009

1995 = 100

	2007 1st Quarter	2007 2nd Quarter	2007 3rd Quarter	2007 4th Quarter	2008 1st Quarter	2008 2nd Quarter	2008 3rd Quarter	2008 4th Quarter	2009 1st Quarter	2009 2nd Quarter
Western Europe										
Austria	169.9	176.4	175.9	190.7	178.0	185.1	180.7	183.0	155.2	
Belgium	131.8	131.5	125.0	133.7	134.0	134.6	126.6	124.0	112.6	
Cyprus	112.4	121.8	124.3	127.6	116.5	129.2	129.0	124.2	106.4	
Denmark	128.8	121.6	119.6	133.6	127.3	128.9	119.9	128.0	113.7	
Finland	163.7	183.9	179.8	193.6	171.5	188.7	181.5	175.9	134.5	
France	120.5	117.7	108.6	130.5	123.1	119.1	109.1	114.2	103.6	
Germany	132.2	134.8	136.7	142.2	136.7	142.2	136.6	130.4	109.9	
Gibraltar										
Greece	121.6	127.7	127.5	124.5	110.3	119.6	122.1	131.7	99.9	
Iceland										
Ireland	293.7	292.1	274.0	300.0	301.9	294.7	274.8	276.3	294.0	
Italy	110.4	109.8	96.2	107.3	108.3	109.3	93.1	95.0	84.8	
Liechtenstein										
Luxembourg	151.6	146.4	129.1	146.9	146.7	145.7	139.1	118.5	109.4	
Malta										
Monaco										
Netherlands	120.3	113.5	111.4	134.4	132.7	118.5	109.3	125.7	120.2	
Norway	107.3	99.3	99.6	108.5	107.5	101.5	96.9	109.6	107.8	
Portugal	116.6	114.1	110.4	115.6	113.5	110.9	106.2	107.2	99.7	
Spain	133.3	133.6	120.8	130.7	128.9	130.1	114.5	111.5	101.8	
Sweden	143.5	141.1	123.7	146.1	142.6	144.0	123.1	128.9	113.9	
Switzerland	135.1	144.6	144.8	155.5	140.7	153.9	146.1	146.6	127.5	
Turkey	163.6	179.2	180.4	179.7	172.7	179.1	177.4	167.7	134.7	
United Kingdom	103.7	103.3	100.8	108.2	103.0	102.0	97.6	102.6	90.1	
Eastern Europe										
Albania										
Belarus	248.8	303.0	306.8	349.2						
Bosnia-Herzegovina										
Bulgaria	124.2	128.3	134.4	141.3	127.1	135.9	138.2	130.5	104.7	
Croatia			163.4				162.8			
Czech Republic	169.9	173.7	161.6	181.4	177.8	182.6	167.5	161.3	144.0	
Estonia	247.0	260.0	247.2	265.8	242.6	254.3	242.0	214.9	180.0	
Georgia										
Hungary	252.2	256.3	262.6	286.6	267.6	269.3	258.2	249.2	207.2	
Latvia	151.8	144.5	145.2	154.6	147.3	141.0	132.5	134.6	115.2	
Lithuania	194.3	202.3	205.9	207.4	206.3	218.0	210.1	197.4	177.9	
Macedonia	100.0	107.2	114.3	121.2						
Moldova										
Poland	219.6	223.6	227.6	244.4	241.0	241.9	233.9	230.9	215.6	
Romania	112.9	118.7	119.2	120.8	120.0	123.7	119.4	113.1	104.4	
Russia	150.3	153.9	157.4	167.6	158.9	161.7	164.1	159.5	136.3	
Slovakia	176.8	183.5	178.3	194.1	193.3	199.1	185.0	169.5	148.6	
Slovenia	142.8	148.3	144.5	151.7	146.2	153.5	143.3	135.3	118.3	
Ukraine	186.4	198.4	212.1	218.8						

Source: *United Nations/Euromonitor International*
Notes: *Indices based on value of production (or contribution to GDP) at constant prices*

Table 17.3

Indices of General Industrial Production by Month 2008
1995 = 100

	January	February	March	April	May	June	July	August	September	October	November	December
Western Europe												
Austria	168.7	178.0	187.3	188.9	176.7	189.7	185.1	159.1	198.0	198.0	179.4	171.7
Belgium	133.6	134.2	134.3	137.4	129.3	137.1	123.5	119.3	137.1	137.2	118.7	116.2
Cyprus	115.3	116.1	117.9	117.5	129.2	140.8	131.1	116.1	139.7	136.5	124.7	111.3
Denmark	131.5	125.1	125.2	129.0	128.7	128.9	108.1	120.3	131.4	135.7	126.7	121.6
Finland	172.2	168.3	174.0	188.5	195.1	182.5	174.3	177.6	192.6	199.9	175.9	151.8
France	123.2	122.2	123.8	124.4	110.0	122.9	119.4	84.6	123.2	125.7	109.0	107.9
Germany	135.1	138.3	136.6	149.5	133.0	144.0	140.9	123.3	145.6	142.7	132.2	116.4
Gibraltar												
Greece	111.7	108.8	110.3	113.9	118.6	126.2	135.7	109.3	121.5	148.6	138.8	107.6
Iceland												
Ireland	290.7	295.5	319.5	279.9	308.5	295.8	253.7	290.4	280.4	276.1	299.6	253.2
Italy	104.4	111.1	109.4	110.6	109.8	107.3	116.8	53.8	108.6	110.4	96.9	77.8
Liechtenstein												
Luxembourg	145.7	145.0	149.4	153.2	142.7	141.1	150.3	117.5	149.4	140.9	119.9	94.6
Malta												
Monaco												
Netherlands	134.2	131.1	132.8	126.6	112.6	116.3	108.5	100.6	118.7	128.4	123.0	125.7
Norway	111.1	104.3	107.2	104.5	103.5	96.6	99.0	95.4	96.3	110.1	109.1	109.5
Portugal	118.2	111.1	111.3	110.4	111.0	111.3	117.8	88.3	112.6	113.4	109.8	98.5
Spain	131.4	133.8	121.4	137.0	129.6	123.7	135.9	85.0	122.7	124.1	111.8	98.7
Sweden	143.2	141.3	143.3	147.6	144.6	139.8	105.9	121.0	142.3	140.3	127.6	118.9
Switzerland												
Turkey	169.1	166.9	182.1	179.5	171.7	186.1	182.8	182.4	167.0	171.1	166.4	165.7
United Kingdom	101.2	102.4	105.4	104.1	100.8	101.1	101.3	100.6	91.1	104.0	106.2	97.7
Eastern Europe												
Albania												
Belarus												
Bosnia-Herzegovina												
Bulgaria	120.4	126.0	134.8	133.5	135.4	138.8	142.3	136.5	135.8	134.8	127.7	128.8
Croatia	149.5	158.4	165.9	168.6	166.1	169.6	173.9	148.6	165.8	170.7	162.3	153.6
Czech Republic	175.0	178.9	179.5	187.4	177.5	182.9	170.3	150.8	181.4	177.3	161.9	144.5
Estonia	239.1	244.8	243.9	265.9	253.3	243.7	231.5	235.2	259.4	243.9	211.9	188.8
Georgia												
Hungary	255.9	274.1	272.8	277.0	260.0	270.8	261.1	231.9	281.6	281.2	262.7	203.7
Latvia	145.9	149.4	146.6	149.8	138.5	134.6	133.1	127.0	137.4	144.8	130.1	128.9
Lithuania	199.6	205.8	213.6	223.5	214.7	215.9	214.7	204.5	211.2	197.8	193.5	200.9
Macedonia												
Moldova												
Poland	238.0	241.7	243.4	253.2	230.2	242.3	235.9	215.2	250.8	255.5	222.1	215.2
Romania	112.6	122.3	125.0	119.4	127.3	124.6	125.3	106.8	126.1	129.8	115.0	94.5
Russia	149.9	154.4	172.4	164.6	161.4	159.2	164.4	162.8	165.1	169.8	151.4	157.3
Slovakia	190.7	195.9	193.4	202.1	197.0	198.2	195.5	167.1	192.5	197.3	174.4	136.9
Slovenia	140.5	147.0	151.0	157.1	148.3	155.0	149.1	121.3	159.4	160.5	135.7	109.8
Ukraine												

Source: *United Nations/Euromonitor International*
Notes: *Indices based on value of production (or contribution to GDP) at constant prices*

Industry Statistics

Table 17.4

Indices of Manufacturing Production 1980-2008

1995 = 100

	1980	1985	1990	1995	1996	1997	1998	1999	2000	2001
Western Europe										
Austria	66.5	72.5	88.7	100.0	100.7	108.0	117.8	124.9	137.3	139.9
Belgium	74.4	77.4	94.0	100.0	100.5	105.4	108.4	109.7	116.2	116.1
Cyprus		79.7	103.3	100.0	94.9	94.3	95.4	96.3	100.1	98.2
Denmark	64.8	79.1	86.2	100.0	101.7	106.4	109.5	109.7	115.6	117.9
Finland	66.1	76.7	87.0	100.0	102.5	111.8	123.5	130.9	147.9	147.2
France	93.7	91.9	102.2	100.0	100.6	104.4	108.4	111.5	116.3	117.6
Germany			100.0	100.0	100.5	103.6	108.0	109.4	116.3	116.8
Gibraltar										
Greece	99.4	100.3	102.2	100.0	99.6	101.9	110.2	109.2	114.8	111.9
Iceland										
Ireland	31.6	41.4	61.6	100.0	108.0	129.5	156.8	180.4	208.8	230.5
Italy	83.1	79.8	93.9	100.0	98.9	102.2	103.9	103.6	106.7	105.8
Liechtenstein										
Luxembourg	69.4	84.7	99.0	100.0	100.3	106.1	115.7	117.7	123.6	126.7
Malta										
Monaco										
Netherlands	73.3	79.9	92.9	100.0	100.6	103.2	106.7	109.2	113.8	113.6
Norway	80.8	88.9	89.7	100.0	102.8	106.2	108.8	106.2	103.0	101.9
Portugal	69.5	81.3	104.3	100.0	105.3	110.0	112.8	114.4	114.8	117.4
Spain	81.3	82.2	96.8	100.0	99.3	106.6	113.2	115.8	119.7	117.3
Sweden	73.7	81.0	89.1	100.0	101.0	105.0	111.2	114.6	121.8	120.6
Switzerland	79.2	81.6	97.0	100.0	100.3	104.9	109.1	112.8	123.2	121.8
Turkey		65.2	90.5	100.0	106.5	118.8	118.9	113.9	121.3	109.8
United Kingdom	80.7	83.9	97.7	100.0	100.6	102.7	103.3	104.1	106.6	105.2
Eastern Europe										
Albania				100.0	81.1	74.8	68.5	77.7	116.0	77.6
Belarus			170.9	100.0	103.8	123.6	139.3	154.2	167.0	176.4
Bosnia-Herzegovina										
Bulgaria				100.0	104.8	84.2	74.8	69.7	74.7	75.7
Croatia			188.0	100.0	101.2	105.2	108.6	105.4	108.5	115.4
Czech Republic			162.9	100.0	101.6	108.1	110.9	107.9	108.2	116.2
Estonia			215.5	100.0	102.2	121.1	127.9	124.7	145.3	160.1
Georgia										
Hungary	115.4	126.9	116.4	100.0	103.4	118.5	137.7	154.7	186.8	194.6
Latvia			261.8	100.0	107.3	125.6	130.2	103.6	108.4	116.5
Lithuania			216.0	100.0	100.9	106.6	115.4	102.8	111.9	129.6
Macedonia										
Moldova										
Poland	93.8	90.9	75.7	100.0	111.5	126.6	134.9	142.4	153.7	153.5
Romania			159.7	100.0	107.2	100.8	82.5	78.5	85.1	93.7
Russia			230.4	100.0	89.7	91.6	85.9	96.9	107.5	109.7
Slovakia			127.9	100.0	102.3	104.0	110.4	106.7	116.6	128.1
Slovenia			126.1	100.0	101.2	101.4	105.4	105.3	112.7	115.9
Ukraine			201.2	100.0	94.9	94.5	93.7	97.1	113.2	132.7

Source: *United Nations/Euromonitor International*
Notes: *Indices based on value of production (or contribution to GDP) at constant prices*

Indices of Manufacturing Production 1980-2008 *(continued)*

1995 = 100

	2002	2003	2004	2005	2006	2007	2008
Western Europe							
Austria	139.9	143.2	153.6	159.9	172.3	182.9	184.9
Belgium	117.1	117.7	122.7	120.3	126.0	129.8	129.2
Cyprus	95.8	103.8	105.5	104.9	104.6	107.8	111.2
Denmark	119.1	118.2	117.9	120.0	125.0	137.2	130.4
Finland	150.1	150.1	150.7	161.7	175.7	185.2	184.7
France	116.0	115.0	117.9	118.3	119.1	121.1	117.5
Germany	115.5	115.7	119.3	123.7	131.8	140.8	141.1
Gibraltar							
Greece	111.8	111.3	112.6	111.8	112.7	114.7	110.1
Iceland							
Ireland	247.8	259.1	259.5	267.7	281.9	302.9	299.2
Italy	103.8	102.0	102.8	100.2	102.2	102.9	98.1
Liechtenstein							
Luxembourg	128.9	134.2	140.3	142.8	145.5	146.8	139.2
Malta							
Monaco							
Netherlands	113.7	112.4	116.3	118.6	121.9	125.7	124.4
Norway	96.7	92.6	93.9	96.8	101.1	105.2	108.1
Portugal	117.9	117.3	116.4	114.5	117.2	121.0	117.3
Spain	117.8	119.6	121.0	120.7	125.6	128.6	119.1
Sweden	121.8	125.0	130.8	133.9	140.1	144.6	139.5
Switzerland	115.4	115.3	120.9	124.7	135.2	148.6	158.7
Turkey	121.8	133.1	146.9	153.9	165.8	176.7	173.5
United Kingdom	102.4	102.2	104.8	104.0	106.1	106.9	104.2
Eastern Europe							
Albania	53.6	54.7	51.4	44.5	42.1	38.7	35.3
Belarus	184.3	197.2	229.4	253.5	282.9	307.5	340.7
Bosnia-Herzegovina							
Bulgaria	81.3	96.5	117.0	126.5	135.7	146.9	148.9
Croatia	120.5	126.7	131.8	140.5	151.0	156.4	158.8
Czech Republic	118.6	125.0	138.4	148.9	166.8	183.2	184.5
Estonia	174.1	192.8	216.2	241.8	268.1	281.7	266.5
Georgia							
Hungary	201.6	215.8	234.1	252.6	279.3	303.7	298.1
Latvia	123.8	133.5	141.8	151.0	158.2	156.6	143.6
Lithuania	133.3	152.1	170.1	184.7	200.7	209.4	216.3
Macedonia							
Moldova							
Poland	156.3	172.8	198.0	207.0	235.3	260.7	271.3
Romania	99.7	103.7	109.4	112.6	122.3	129.4	130.4
Russia	110.8	122.2	135.0	142.6	148.9	172.7	179.1
Slovakia	138.8	149.0	156.1	163.1	183.8	211.7	216.9
Slovenia	118.1	120.0	125.8	130.4	139.3	149.2	146.7
Ukraine	144.5	171.2	194.5	199.6	211.1	235.8	237.1

Source: *United Nations/Euromonitor International*
Notes: *Indices based on value of production (or contribution to GDP) at constant prices*

Industry Statistics

Table 17.5

Indices of Manufacturing Production by Quarter 2007-2009
1995 = 100

	2007 1st Quarter	2007 2nd Quarter	2007 3rd Quarter	2007 4th Quarter	2008 1st Quarter	2008 2nd Quarter	2008 3rd Quarter	2008 4th Quarter	2009 1st Quarter	2009 2nd Quarter
Western Europe										
Austria	172.2	182.9	182.5	194.0	179.9	190.8	185.1	183.9	152.8	
Belgium	131.2	131.6	123.7	132.8	133.3	135.7	126.1	121.8	109.2	
Cyprus	98.4	110.6	104.9	117.3	104.3	117.8	107.5	115.2	93.8	
Denmark	138.4	135.0	131.0	144.4	128.4	136.5	126.3	130.3	113.0	
Finland	166.3	190.0	184.9	199.5	175.2	197.1	185.9	180.8	130.6	
France	122.1	122.8	112.4	127.0	106.0	120.5	126.0	117.4	81.9	
Germany	135.8	139.4	141.7	146.5	140.4	147.6	142.2	134.1	111.0	
Gibraltar										
Greece	111.3	118.7	114.3	114.3	106.5	117.1	113.3	103.4	92.1	
Iceland										
Ireland	306.0	306.3	286.4	313.1	314.1	308.9	288.6	285.2	306.2	
Italy	107.1	108.0	92.9	103.4	104.6	106.3	89.6	91.7	81.3	
Liechtenstein										
Luxembourg	151.0	154.4	135.8	146.1	147.3	150.2	141.7	117.5	107.2	
Malta										
Monaco										
Netherlands	125.8	126.8	121.3	129.1	126.5	128.4	120.1	122.5	110.1	
Norway	107.4	105.0	98.6	109.8	107.1	114.0	101.6	109.5	106.0	
Portugal	121.3	122.3	117.3	123.0	121.5	121.5	113.0	113.1	101.7	
Spain	132.3	133.9	119.0	129.0	126.6	129.3	112.0	108.4	98.5	
Sweden	146.8	147.9	130.7	152.9	145.9	150.2	128.9	132.8	111.5	
Switzerland	137.8	148.6	148.9	159.1	151.3	167.2	158.2	158.1	135.4	
Turkey	164.4	181.6	179.2	181.8	175.1	187.3	173.0	158.5	132.1	
United Kingdom	104.3	107.0	105.7	110.6	104.2	106.6	104.6	101.6	89.6	
Eastern Europe										
Albania										
Belarus										
Bosnia-Herzegovina										
Bulgaria	134.9	145.7	151.6	155.5	139.3	156.7	155.9	143.6	106.2	
Croatia	143.9	161.0	160.6	160.2	151.3	165.8	159.9	158.0	130.4	
Czech Republic	180.0	186.8	173.1	192.8	186.8	199.1	182.4	169.5	146.2	
Estonia	268.1	295.7	275.7	287.4	268.3	289.0	272.7	236.0	183.6	
Georgia										
Hungary	285.9	295.6	305.2	328.3	305.4	309.7	296.4	281.0	230.6	
Latvia	148.2	159.5	163.7	155.0	143.9	153.1	144.7	132.7	106.8	
Lithuania	191.1	215.8	221.6	208.9	206.8	233.6	223.6	201.2	174.7	
Macedonia										
Moldova										
Poland	248.2	256.7	261.8	276.0	271.3	280.4	271.4	262.0	243.4	
Romania	123.2	131.0	131.2	132.3	130.2	137.8	131.9	121.6	110.3	
Russia	154.4	172.8	179.3	184.2	167.2	186.0	190.0	173.2	132.3	
Slovakia	201.5	214.6	205.0	225.7	223.3	237.3	213.9	193.3	165.2	
Slovenia	144.1	151.2	147.4	154.1	147.9	156.8	146.3	136.0	117.2	
Ukraine										

Source: *United Nations/Euromonitor International*
Notes: *Indices based on value of production (or contribution to GDP) at constant prices*

Table 17.6

Indices of Manufacturing Production by Month 2008
1995 = 100

	January	February	March	April	May	June	July	August	September	October	November	December
Western Europe												
Austria	168.7	180.7	190.2	194.5	181.7	196.3	190.2	160.7	204.6	203.1	179.8	168.9
Belgium	132.3	133.6	134.1	138.8	129.7	138.6	123.0	117.5	137.7	137.1	115.8	112.6
Cyprus	99.9	103.6	109.4	111.3	122.0	120.2	131.4	73.1	118.0	117.7	113.7	114.3
Denmark	131.5	127.6	126.2	135.9	133.9	139.7	109.2	127.4	142.3	143.6	127.4	119.8
Finland	174.6	172.0	178.9	197.6	204.3	189.2	176.8	180.9	200.0	209.3	179.6	153.4
France	121.0	105.7	91.4	118.4	116.4	126.7	128.8	114.5	134.6	126.4	109.3	116.4
Germany	138.4	142.5	140.3	154.9	137.4	150.5	146.9	127.8	151.9	147.8	136.2	118.2
Gibraltar												
Greece	103.0	104.5	111.9	113.7	116.2	121.3	126.6	95.9	117.4	110.3	101.9	98.0
Iceland												
Ireland	300.6	307.1	334.6	291.3	325.1	310.2	264.9	306.8	294.2	286.6	310.7	258.2
Italy	100.2	107.5	106.0	107.6	107.1	104.2	113.7	49.6	105.6	107.5	93.8	74.0
Liechtenstein												
Luxembourg	145.8	146.0	150.1	156.4	147.8	146.5	155.7	117.7	151.8	141.4	119.4	91.5
Malta												
Monaco												
Netherlands	126.2	126.7	126.7	129.9	124.6	130.8	120.2	109.9	130.3	133.4	120.0	114.1
Norway	114.1	111.2	96.1	118.0	109.8	114.2	80.3	107.5	117.1	123.3	111.3	93.7
Portugal	123.5	119.4	121.7	122.1	121.5	121.0	127.3	91.1	120.6	122.7	117.2	99.4
Spain	128.9	132.1	118.9	136.2	129.0	122.6	134.6	80.0	121.6	122.7	109.0	93.7
Sweden	144.8	145.8	147.0	153.0	148.1	149.4	108.7	126.8	151.3	147.4	131.7	119.3
Switzerland												
Turkey	169.6	169.0	186.7	184.7	191.1	186.1	182.5	164.0	172.5	168.5	168.4	138.5
United Kingdom	101.0	104.2	107.4	107.6	104.8	107.3	106.8	96.4	110.7	111.7	99.4	93.7
Eastern Europe												
Albania												
Belarus												
Bosnia-Herzegovina												
Bulgaria	127.1	138.5	152.1	152.8	155.3	162.0	168.5	143.8	155.4	155.1	139.4	136.3
Croatia	139.3	153.1	161.6	165.7	164.1	167.7	172.7	143.3	163.8	169.3	159.1	145.7
Czech Republic	181.5	189.3	189.6	202.1	193.2	202.1	186.7	162.4	198.3	191.1	169.5	147.9
Estonia	260.5	270.6	273.8	303.2	286.3	277.4	262.9	263.9	291.2	272.1	232.7	203.0
Georgia												
Hungary	291.4	314.6	310.3	318.1	298.9	312.1	300.1	264.2	325.1	321.8	297.9	223.2
Latvia	137.9	148.1	145.8	158.4	152.2	148.8	147.1	139.9	147.1	151.0	127.3	119.7
Lithuania	195.3	207.1	218.0	235.3	231.4	234.0	231.8	215.8	223.3	207.1	195.5	201.0
Macedonia												
Moldova												
Poland	265.9	272.3	275.7	291.4	267.6	282.1	274.0	248.0	292.3	295.6	251.8	238.7
Romania	120.1	133.9	136.5	132.2	142.2	139.0	139.3	116.3	140.2	143.4	124.3	97.1
Russia	146.5	162.9	192.2	187.5	185.5	185.1	191.4	187.5	191.2	191.9	162.6	165.2
Slovakia	218.2	227.5	224.0	242.0	231.4	238.6	225.8	189.3	226.5	233.1	199.6	147.2
Slovenia	141.1	149.2	153.3	160.0	151.7	158.6	152.1	123.0	163.8	164.0	136.5	107.5
Ukraine												

Source: *United Nations/Euromonitor International*
Notes: *Indices based on value of production (or contribution to GDP) at constant prices*

Industry Statistics **Table 17.7**

Indices of Mining Production 1980-2008
1995 = 100

	1980	1985	1990	1995	1996	1997	1998	1999	2000	2001
Western Europe										
Austria	107.0	117.7	111.5	100.0	100.2	96.7	103.9	107.4	112.3	109.6
Belgium			69.0	100.0	106.7	113.4	116.6	125.2	138.1	139.5
Cyprus			82.2	100.0	97.6	101.4	121.1	130.2	135.3	128.9
Denmark			103.1	100.0	103.4	87.8	93.0	93.5	93.8	92.3
Finland			94.9	100.0	100.6	127.0	92.7	128.1	99.4	120.0
France			116.0	100.0	91.7	88.0	86.9	86.8	88.4	87.4
Germany	57.2	104.7	100.0	100.0	94.4	92.2	85.8	85.5	79.6	74.3
Gibraltar										
Greece	155.3	153.7	120.9	100.0	103.6	103.9	102.6	96.4	109.3	111.9
Iceland										
Ireland	65.6	65.6	85.7	100.0	98.4	84.2	78.0	92.9	114.7	114.6
Italy			87.6	100.0	102.4	108.5	107.9	107.8	98.4	90.8
Liechtenstein										
Luxembourg			103.4	100.0	89.9	89.4	100.2	107.8	108.8	109.9
Malta										
Monaco										
Netherlands			89.1	100.0	113.5	104.2	103.1	99.5	97.2	104.1
Norway			94.1	100.0	99.5	103.3	109.2	109.8	115.7	119.2
Portugal			114.3	100.0	103.3	103.3	105.2	102.2	103.8	105.8
Spain			101.9	100.0	94.3	91.9	92.0	90.1	91.1	88.2
Sweden			95.0	100.0	98.3	94.9	94.5	96.4	97.8	95.5
Switzerland				100.0	98.3	100.5	87.9	93.5	94.2	94.7
Turkey			95.5	100.0	103.3	109.4	121.7	109.6	106.6	98.0
United Kingdom			73.3	100.0	103.2	102.1	104.2	108.6	105.1	99.3
Eastern Europe										
Albania				100.0	87.7	54.5	56.2	41.4	36.4	32.1
Belarus				100.0	99.0	111.7	118.6	123.9	117.5	130.6
Bosnia-Herzegovina										
Bulgaria				100.0	115.5	93.3	90.9	78.6	80.7	73.7
Croatia			132.1	100.0	97.0	96.6	94.2	96.1	97.8	99.8
Czech Republic	125.0	137.5	144.7	100.0	101.4	98.5	92.8	81.6	88.2	88.9
Estonia	268.8	236.5	195.7	100.0	105.7	105.3	100.7	87.0	91.7	95.0
Georgia										
Hungary			192.3	100.0	102.5	93.9	74.7	75.3	68.2	79.4
Latvia	579.9	168.2	257.7	100.0	102.4	110.4	117.2	123.9	134.9	141.4
Lithuania				100.0	122.0	136.3	185.7	177.1	198.1	263.1
Macedonia										
Moldova										
Poland			108.8	100.0	101.3	99.7	86.6	83.2	82.1	77.9
Romania			120.5	100.0	100.7	95.0	81.6	76.1	79.8	84.4
Russia			141.2	100.0	97.0	97.2	94.9	98.7	105.0	111.3
Slovakia			233.6	100.0	105.6	118.0	104.7	103.8	101.4	88.1
Slovenia			132.3	100.0	100.5	102.3	102.0	97.8	95.2	87.7
Ukraine			201.2	100.0	94.8	97.9	95.3	98.3	104.6	108.0

Source: *United Nations/Euromonitor International*
Notes: *Indices based on value of production (or contribution to GDP) at constant prices*

Industry Statistics

Indices of Mining Production 1980-2008 *(continued)*
1995 = 100

	2002	2003	2004	2005	2006	2007	2008
Western Europe							
Austria	113.1	112.5	106.2	104.4	115.0	114.9	116.6
Belgium	182.2	190.1	186.3	195.3	201.0	258.5	277.3
Cyprus	143.6	149.0	156.0	162.1	160.2	159.7	179.7
Denmark	88.2	95.8	100.6	105.0	99.2	89.3	89.3
Finland	131.1	131.7	115.5	151.1	190.7	149.8	149.7
France	83.0	81.9	81.2	79.1	81.2	81.8	78.9
Germany	73.2	72.6	70.3	69.2	67.0	66.6	60.7
Gibraltar							
Greece	122.7	116.4	116.5	110.3	107.1	106.1	101.5
Iceland							
Ireland	109.0	132.7	129.8	129.4	141.1	147.0	133.6
Italy	106.2	108.2	106.0	114.1	110.7	111.6	101.3
Liechtenstein							
Luxembourg	100.0	88.7	87.0	85.6	67.1	68.2	66.9
Malta							
Monaco							
Netherlands	104.5	101.3	112.3	92.4	88.5	89.4	98.4
Norway	117.2	123.7	117.6	114.6	126.1	146.4	145.3
Portugal	100.2	90.7	94.6	92.5	83.4	92.0	94.0
Spain	87.7	87.7	83.5	80.2	82.2	81.1	70.7
Sweden	96.9	95.9	104.4	110.5	111.6	118.3	119.6
Switzerland	93.3	92.6	96.5	91.5	100.4	106.6	98.0
Turkey	90.0	86.9	90.4	102.9	111.4	120.7	129.6
United Kingdom	99.7	94.6	87.3	80.0	74.0	72.6	67.9
Eastern Europe							
Albania	31.8	28.7	26.4	24.3	23.1	22.1	20.2
Belarus	134.7	147.4	160.8	173.5	178.0	189.2	198.7
Bosnia-Herzegovina							
Bulgaria	73.3	78.4	94.7	95.1	96.7	89.3	86.3
Croatia	116.8	119.4	115.5	112.1	122.7	127.0	124.8
Czech Republic	89.7	90.0	89.4	89.9	92.2	90.6	88.3
Estonia	109.7	115.3	105.1	116.9	127.5	141.2	123.2
Georgia							
Hungary	71.9	69.4	76.3	73.7	85.7	71.1	98.1
Latvia	154.2	162.4	180.3	226.3	247.3	281.0	287.9
Lithuania	250.8	271.8	251.2	231.4	228.8	231.2	214.5
Macedonia							
Moldova							
Poland	75.5	74.1	76.4	74.2	75.3	73.2	73.6
Romania	80.0	79.4	81.2	80.6	82.8	82.5	82.3
Russia	118.8	129.2	137.9	139.8	142.8	145.6	145.8
Slovakia	113.3	107.0	95.3	91.9	83.1	84.4	83.8
Slovenia	94.4	99.9	92.9	99.2	109.5	113.5	111.7
Ukraine	110.5	116.5	121.3	125.5	132.9	136.4	139.8

Source: *United Nations/Euromonitor International*
Notes: *Indices based on value of production (or contribution to GDP) at constant prices*

Industry Statistics

Table 17.8

Indices of Mining Production by Quarter 2007-2009
1995 = 100

	2007 1st Quarter	2007 2nd Quarter	2007 3rd Quarter	2007 4th Quarter	2008 1st Quarter	2008 2nd Quarter	2008 3rd Quarter	2008 4th Quarter	2009 1st Quarter	2009 2nd Quarter
Western Europe										
Austria	100.2	113.8	118.1	127.4	103.0	118.8	122.3	122.1	84.3	
Belgium	240.5	284.7	258.8	249.9	269.6	315.0	272.7	252.0	223.0	
Cyprus	154.3	163.9	146.0	174.4	178.1	187.7	170.3	182.6	135.7	
Denmark	92.1	78.2	87.3	99.6	94.4	87.8	84.9	90.1	84.4	
Finland	84.9	172.5	214.5	127.3	94.8	163.6	248.7	91.6	74.2	
France	77.1	85.9	82.7	81.4	78.9	86.4	79.0	71.1	65.9	
Germany	61.6	66.4	70.8	67.7	61.9	63.8	59.6	57.6	61.1	
Gibraltar										
Greece	104.2	106.2	114.3	99.9	90.6	104.5	113.4	97.6	83.4	
Iceland										
Ireland	130.8	160.4	165.7	131.3	125.5	157.4	124.0	127.7	114.2	
Italy	111.7	116.7	111.9	106.0	104.8	112.7	101.3	86.2	84.9	
Liechtenstein										
Luxembourg	58.1	77.0	66.1	71.6	63.2	67.7	65.4	71.3	55.1	
Malta										
Monaco										
Netherlands	102.9	57.3	57.3	140.2	138.6	73.1	59.9	121.8	132.7	
Norway	152.2	138.5	142.3	152.8	151.4	139.0	136.1	154.7	164.8	
Portugal	91.4	94.5	87.7	94.3	95.1	94.2	100.6	86.2	74.5	
Spain	76.2	87.3	82.1	78.7	74.2	77.4	68.9	62.3	51.2	
Sweden	119.1	110.7	118.7	124.9	109.6	123.4	126.1	119.4	93.0	
Switzerland	78.8	118.1	117.5	111.9	70.5	114.0	109.8	97.7	60.4	
Turkey	101.6	121.8	144.5	114.8	114.2	130.5	149.1	124.8	102.5	
United Kingdom	75.7	73.8	66.0	75.0	71.8	69.8	61.5	68.5	66.1	
Eastern Europe										
Albania										
Belarus										
Bosnia-Herzegovina										
Bulgaria	88.3	84.4	89.3	95.3	90.1	94.3	87.0	74.0	68.6	
Croatia	124.1	128.6	128.9	126.6	120.3	129.3	127.5	122.0	104.5	
Czech Republic	87.7	90.0	89.0	95.7	89.6	87.6	85.0	90.9	80.2	
Estonia	114.6	121.1	178.2	150.9	114.3	133.8	130.2	114.6	100.6	
Georgia										
Hungary	57.5	81.1	74.8	70.8	63.2	96.0	102.4	130.7	71.3	
Latvia	218.4	337.0	313.5	255.3	254.0	325.7	317.0	255.0	254.3	
Lithuania	169.9	254.9	254.5	245.5	172.2	250.5	249.5	186.0	113.3	
Macedonia										
Moldova										
Poland	71.1	72.3	74.0	75.4	70.8	75.4	76.4	72.0	60.5	
Romania	78.3	83.8	84.7	83.3	76.2	81.0	86.8	85.1	74.8	
Russia	141.3	144.4	150.5	146.4	142.1	144.8	151.3	145.2	136.9	
Slovakia	75.0	87.6	89.2	85.8	74.0	89.2	88.1	83.8	72.4	
Slovenia	108.3	124.1	102.1	119.5	118.3	118.0	96.2	114.2	109.0	
Ukraine										

Source: *United Nations/Euromonitor International*
Notes: *Indices based on value of production (or contribution to GDP) at constant prices*

Table 17.9

Indices of Mining Production by Month 2008
1995 = 100

	January	February	March	April	May	June	July	August	September	October	November	December
Western Europe												
Austria	88.4	103.4	117.3	120.2	114.2	122.1	120.7	120.6	125.8	132.8	124.1	109.3
Belgium	259.9	267.6	281.2	327.6	307.4	309.9	238.8	273.2	306.0	319.6	232.7	203.8
Cyprus	173.7	182.4	178.2	165.0	198.9	199.2	225.7	84.0	201.3	209.8	186.7	151.4
Denmark	99.2	88.1	95.8	88.8	96.6	78.1	92.0	84.4	78.3	84.2	90.7	95.4
Finland	102.1	94.1	88.2	108.4	181.6	201.0	280.9	254.2	211.1	125.4	96.6	52.9
France	74.3	81.2	81.1	89.2	79.9	90.2	91.2	60.8	85.1	86.6	69.0	57.6
Germany	61.1	61.6	63.0	67.7	63.3	60.5	60.6	57.6	60.6	61.8	57.2	53.8
Gibraltar												
Greece	99.3	91.2	81.3	96.8	100.2	116.4	123.7	103.2	113.4	113.9	95.7	83.3
Iceland												
Ireland	119.6	128.1	128.6	136.0	166.8	169.4	125.3	114.1	132.5	127.9	139.5	115.7
Italy	103.5	105.4	105.4	113.0	113.8	111.2	109.4	89.8	104.8	100.6	84.8	73.2
Liechtenstein												
Luxembourg	59.5	62.0	68.1	67.4	68.8	67.0	70.4	40.5	85.2	86.3	70.4	57.3
Malta												
Monaco												
Netherlands	146.5	132.9	136.4	101.2	60.6	57.6	57.5	54.0	68.2	98.1	118.4	149.1
Norway	155.0	143.5	155.5	142.5	145.3	129.2	150.1	130.5	127.8	150.6	153.0	160.5
Portugal	100.5	89.6	95.3	88.8	87.9	106.1	97.8	102.4	101.6	85.2	87.7	85.7
Spain	72.5	77.9	72.4	86.9	74.2	70.9	81.6	53.8	71.1	73.4	62.2	51.3
Sweden	116.3	109.9	102.5	120.6	123.7	125.9	126.2	126.1	125.9	125.7	125.1	107.2
Switzerland												
Turkey	113.7	109.7	119.2	118.9	130.1	142.4	150.0	153.0	144.2	143.1	120.1	111.1
United Kingdom	73.4	68.3	73.8	71.5	72.3	65.4	63.0	56.1	65.5	68.2	67.5	69.8
Eastern Europe												
Albania												
Belarus												
Bosnia-Herzegovina												
Bulgaria	86.6	92.0	91.8	88.5	98.5	95.9	85.0	85.7	90.2	77.1	77.2	67.6
Croatia	114.5	118.7	127.8	128.3	130.0	129.8	133.7	127.7	121.0	131.1	124.4	110.6
Czech Republic	90.3	89.1	89.5	89.3	92.4	81.3	76.8	84.4	93.7	89.1	102.5	81.2
Estonia	120.1	116.3	106.6	113.6	143.2	144.7	130.9	127.3	132.3	125.5	113.6	104.7
Georgia												
Hungary	50.6	63.8	75.1	103.9	93.2	90.9	103.3	101.8	102.2	130.0	111.4	150.6
Latvia	248.9	276.0	237.1	265.8	366.8	344.4	341.5	287.7	321.8	332.0	226.3	206.7
Lithuania	171.7	165.3	179.8	276.9	254.8	219.8	273.8	229.8	244.8	247.4	161.7	148.8
Macedonia												
Moldova												
Poland	71.1	72.1	69.2	78.6	70.2	77.5	78.9	70.0	80.3	78.0	72.6	65.3
Romania	73.0	72.0	83.5	78.5	82.9	81.6	85.3	87.9	87.3	89.1	84.4	81.9
Russia	145.2	135.8	145.3	140.9	146.3	147.1	150.6	152.9	150.4	149.9	141.1	144.5
Slovakia	72.2	72.0	77.8	91.1	90.1	86.4	88.2	90.1	86.1	91.4	84.7	75.2
Slovenia	105.9	117.4	131.5	133.8	111.5	108.8	101.3	80.1	107.3	122.3	113.0	107.1
Ukraine												

Source: *United Nations/Euromonitor International*
Notes: *Indices based on value of production (or contribution to GDP) at constant prices*

Section Eighteen

IT and
Telecommunications

IT and Telecommunications Statistics

Table 18.1

Internet Users 1990-2008
'000

	1990	1995	2000	2003	2004	2005	2006	2007	2008
Western Europe									
Austria	10	150	2,700	3,341	4,249	4,504	5,005	5,602	4,950
Belgium	0	100	3,000	5,153	5,581	6,043	6,471	7,006	7,436
Cyprus		3	120	250	298	326	357	398	467
Denmark	5	200	2,090	3,832	4,115	4,182	4,520	4,408	4,630
Finland	20	710	1,927	3,446	3,665	3,832	4,052	4,169	4,357
France	30	950	8,460	21,765	23,732	26,154	30,100	31,571	33,848
Germany	100	1,500	24,800	44,595	50,414	53,748	57,074	59,472	62,500
Gibraltar			6	6	6	6	6	7	7
Greece	0	80	1,000	1,772	2,220	2,446	3,231	3,678	3,631
Iceland		30	125	166	168	183	194	210	227
Ireland	0	40	679	1,242	1,387	1,535	2,147	2,452	2,830
Italy	10	300	13,200	22,880	27,170	28,000	30,764	32,000	29,118
Liechtenstein			12	20	22	22	22	22	23
Luxembourg		7	100	170	271	315	339	367	389
Malta		1	51	96	112	127	149	176	211
Monaco									
Netherlands	50	1,000	7,000	10,335	11,602	12,876	13,231	13,792	14,273
Norway	30	280	1,200	3,432	3,448	3,696	3,760	3,993	4,088
Portugal	0	150	1,680	2,700	3,028	3,358	3,796	4,249	4,451
Spain	5	150	5,486	15,593	17,059	18,948	20,822	23,025	26,171
Sweden	50	450	4,048	6,907	7,386	7,323	7,800	7,295	7,524
Switzerland	40	250	3,440	4,697	4,923	5,077	5,301	5,433	5,739
Turkey	0	50	2,500	8,550	9,389	10,247	13,150	21,141	24,483
United Kingdom	50	1,100	15,800	36,162	37,472	39,381	39,499	43,754	48,755
Eastern Europe									
Albania		0	4	30	75	188	471	722	1,172
Belarus	0	0	187	1,607	2,461	2,577	2,694	2,810	2,934
Bosnia-Herzegovina	0	0	40	150	585	806	950	1,055	1,308
Bulgaria	0	10	430	944	1,245	1,545	1,841	2,368	2,246
Croatia	0	24	299	1,014	1,375	1,472	1,685	1,985	2,244
Czech Republic	0	150	1,000	2,867	3,273	3,270	4,492	4,991	5,433
Estonia	0	40	392	613	668	785	808	855	927
Georgia	0	1	23	117	176	271	332	360	388
Hungary	0	70	715	2,191	2,835	3,736	4,532	5,215	5,500
Latvia	0	0	150	626	765	969	1,148	1,252	1,358
Lithuania	0	0	225	829	999	1,167	1,435	1,661	1,777
Macedonia	0	0	30	269	428	482	513	605	847
Moldova		0	53	288	406	550	728	954	1,204
Poland	0	250	2,800	9,522	11,182	13,485	15,399	16,756	18,900
Romania	0	17	800	1,942	2,615	3,582	4,542	5,145	5,939
Russia	0	220	2,900	12,000	18,500	21,800	25,689	30,000	35,019
Slovakia	0	28	507	1,150	1,450	1,700	1,931	2,312	2,771
Slovenia	0	57	300	635	728	924	1,003	1,061	992
Ukraine	0	22	350	2,500	5,000	8,000	9,000	10,000	10,354

Source: International Telecommunications Union/World Bank/Trade Sources/Euromonitor International

IT and Telecommunications Statistics

Table 18.2

Dial-up Internet Subscribers 1998-2008
'000

	1998	1999	2000	2001	2002	2003	2004	2005	2006	2007	2008
Western Europe											
Austria	215	574	860	779	749	908	714	598	928	899	798
Belgium	196	536	1,006	965	879	666	416	273	203	146	92
Cyprus	25	40	52	63	73	66	64	59	43	33	26
Denmark	580	1,125	1,221	1,218	1,120	964	744	465	164	143	93
Finland	290	457	581	816	784	827	600	403	291	217	159
France	1,267	2,975	5,263	6,385	7,469	7,048	5,378	3,746	2,557	1,508	768
Germany	3,750	7,980	12,735	11,900	11,795	12,530	12,000	9,200	7,330	5,940	4,776
Gibraltar											
Greece	100	193	271	288	392	520	649	722	446	96	28
Iceland	9	13	45	40	27	10	10	9	11	8	7
Ireland	120	240	550	600	648	683	664	603	444	290	223
Italy	1,140	2,870	5,685	11,610	12,150	14,550	12,426	10,878	9,602	8,202	6,668
Liechtenstein											
Luxembourg	6	11	25	41	64	92	77	49	32	10	4
Malta											
Monaco											
Netherlands	992	2,667	3,408	4,034	3,329	3,012	2,094	1,500	778	629	515
Norway	370	702	1,153	1,147	1,198	889	747	429	268	166	105
Portugal	173	255	313	370	406	403	395	271	154	87	51
Spain	667	2,240	3,146	3,244	2,677	2,559	1,852	1,199	847	536	348
Sweden	1,450	1,873	1,993	2,232	2,192	2,148	1,883	767	665	774	379
Switzerland	425	992	1,609	2,060	1,882	1,947	1,023	961	839	434	316
Turkey	194	312	460	669	919	996	933	663	406	131	58
United Kingdom	3,750	7,400	8,368	11,029	10,929	11,328	9,377	6,422	4,320	2,672	1,657
Eastern Europe											
Albania											
Belarus	2	4	5	8	18	23	30	36	40	42	44
Bosnia-Herzegovina											
Bulgaria	1	2	6	7	9	32	39	41	82	18	2
Croatia	30	75	187	331	538	567	832	838	964	937	785
Czech Republic	18	200	416	1,250	1,629	2,114	1,893	1,643	1,275	1,119	953
Estonia	35	60	80	79	75	47	33	18	12	6	3
Georgia											
Hungary	73	136	217	298	334	391	370	325	93	63	44
Latvia	2	21	33	40	28	27	18	12	6	3	1
Lithuania	16	31	53	56	59	47	45	23	11	6	3
Macedonia											
Moldova											
Poland	421	750	930	1,128	1,484	2,532	1,699	1,741	333	560	522
Romania	27	50	100	300	350	449	824	413	337	205	126
Russia	260	400	492	1,027	1,880	2,957	4,725	6,811	8,500	11,633	12,762
Slovakia	35	47	68	100	130	160	152	113	78	61	48
Slovenia	43	72	139	172	184	186	232	201	127	73	44
Ukraine	28	45	67	120	229	457	904	1,614	2,288	2,860	2,822

Source: Euromonitor International from trade sources/national statistics

IT and Telecommunications Statistics

Table 18.3

Broadband Internet Subscribers 1998-2008

'000

	1998	1999	2000	2001	2002	2003	2004	2005	2006	2007	2008
Western Europe											
Austria		50.9	190.5	320.6	451.0	589.0	870.0	1,174.0	1,452.0	1,622.0	1,792.4
Belgium	10.9	23.0	144.0	460.0	815.4	1,242.9	1,619.9	2,010.6	2,356.5	2,715.3	2,962.5
Cyprus				2.5	5.9	10.0	17.1	31.9	62.8	97.0	129.9
Denmark		10.0	67.0	238.0	451.3	718.3	1,017.6	1,343.9	1,735.3	1,958.8	2,021.4
Finland		8.5	35.0	134.0	273.5	491.1	800.0	1,174.2	1,428.0	1,617.0	1,762.5
France	13.5	55.0	196.0	601.5	1,591.0	3,569.4	6,561.0	9,471.0	12,711.0	15,550.0	17,725.0
Germany		20.0	265.0	2,100.0	3,205.0	4,470.0	7,000.0	10,800.0	15,000.0	19,600.0	22,532.0
Gibraltar											
Greece					2.0	10.5	51.5	160.1	488.2	1,017.5	1,506.6
Iceland		0.1	2.4	10.4	24.3	41.6	55.8	78.0	87.7	97.9	99.9
Ireland					10.6	41.8	152.1	322.5	601.9	805.9	896.3
Italy		30.0	115.0	390.0	850.0	2,250.0	4,724.5	6,821.9	8,638.9	10,860.0	13,216.6
Liechtenstein											
Luxembourg				1.2	5.7	15.4	36.5	70.1	98.8	128.5	141.6
Malta											
Monaco											
Netherlands	75.5	167.8	260.0	466.2	1,171.0	1,988.0	3,206.0	4,100.0	5,192.2	5,507.0	5,855.0
Norway		2.3	22.4	88.4	205.3	398.8	671.7	991.3	1,244.5	1,439.7	1,607.8
Portugal		0.3	25.2	99.3	260.6	502.0	838.4	1,165.4	1,425.7	1,524.6	1,692.3
Spain		1.0	76.4	430.1	1,247.5	2,121.9	3,401.4	5,035.2	6,690.7	8,070.3	9,157.0
Sweden		7.0	249.0	587.0	840.0	1,095.0	1,410.0	2,522.0	2,930.0	3,280.0	3,883.5
Switzerland			56.4	140.0	455.2	783.9	1,227.4	1,624.2	1,988.1	2,379.5	2,533.6
Turkey				10.9	21.2	199.3	577.9	1,589.8	2,773.7	4,554.0	5,736.6
United Kingdom			52.9	331.0	1,356.5	3,113.7	6,123.9	9,898.7	13,013.2	15,605.2	17,275.7
Eastern Europe											
Albania											
Belarus	0.0	0.0	0.0	0.0	0.0	0.1	0.8	1.6	1.1	3.0	6.5
Bosnia-Herzegovina											
Bulgaria							74.1	165.5	384.7	629.1	880.7
Croatia						3.4	23.0	116.0	251.8	387.1	580.6
Czech Republic			2.5	6.2	15.3	34.7	236.0	709.1	1,112.5	1,314.1	1,769.7
Estonia			3.0	17.3	45.7	90.3	138.7	179.2	246.8	277.8	300.8
Georgia											
Hungary		1.2	3.4	24.0	111.5	264.3	411.1	651.7	1,198.7	1,428.7	1,696.7
Latvia			0.3	3.2	10.0	19.5	49.1	60.8	109.7	146.1	179.9
Lithuania		0.1	0.1	2.8	40.3	114.1	129.1	234.1	368.7	507.6	642.4
Macedonia											
Moldova											
Poland				12.0	121.7	195.8	811.8	945.2	2,911.2	3,427.6	3,995.5
Romania			1.0	6.0	15.8	196.1	104.3	377.1	1,088.2	1,949.1	2,592.3
Russia					11.0	343.0	675.0	1,589.0	2,900.0	4,000.0	6,398.0
Slovakia					4.1	22.5	78.8	181.5	317.0	472.0	618.9
Slovenia			1.5	5.5	24.0	58.0	115.1	196.7	274.5	344.8	406.2
Ukraine					0.5	20.5	63.6	130.0	520.0	800.0	1,378.4

Source: Euromonitor International from trade sources/national statistics

Table 18.4

Personal Computers in Use 1990-2008
'000

	1990	1995	2000	2003	2004	2005	2006	2007	2008
Western Europe									
Austria		1,300	2,900	4,500	4,729	4,996	5,209	5,405	5,583
Belgium		1,800	2,300	3,300	3,627	3,954	4,400	4,706	5,001
Cyprus		35	150	219	249	279	324	354	383
Denmark		1,400	2,700	3,314	3,543	3,772	3,962	4,142	4,305
Finland		1,200	2,050	2,405	2,515	2,625	2,717	2,805	2,888
France		8,500	17,920	25,000	30,000	35,000	40,000	44,140	48,047
Germany		14,600	27,640	40,000	45,000	50,000	54,000	57,658	60,994
Gibraltar									
Greece		350	750	942	986	1,020	1,045	1,077	1,106
Iceland		55	110	134	138	142	160	176	191
Ireland		660	1,360	1,824	2,011	2,198	2,480	2,720	2,922
Italy		4,800	10,300	15,480	18,150	21,486	23,770	25,937	27,972
Liechtenstein									
Luxembourg			200	280	285	290	318	342	362
Malta		30	80	110	118	126	132	138	144
Monaco									
Netherlands		3,100	6,300	8,277	11,110	13,943	14,900	15,734	16,465
Norway		1,193	2,200	2,515	2,630	2,745	2,931	3,084	3,212
Portugal		550	1,050	1,398	1,402	1,607	1,719	1,829	1,922
Spain		2,400	5,800	9,346	10,957	12,000	16,000	17,640	18,981
Sweden		2,200	4,500	6,174	6,861	7,548	8,000	8,529	8,988
Switzerland		2,000	4,700	5,430	6,105	6,430	6,630	6,930	7,133
Turkey		920	2,500	3,333	3,703	4,073	4,400	4,743	5,077
United Kingdom		11,800	20,190	26,121	35,890	45,659	48,600	51,294	53,665
Eastern Europe									
Albania			25	42	48	54	120	144	158
Belarus									
Bosnia-Herzegovina									
Bulgaria		140	361	432	461	525	604	681	744
Croatia		100	499	800	837	870	900	927	954
Czech Republic		550	1,250	2,100	2,450	2,800	3,075	3,344	3,588
Estonia			220	595	620	650	680	700	720
Georgia									
Hungary		400	870	1,274	1,476	1,456	1,845	2,572	3,150
Latvia		20	340	436	501	566	748	890	1,002
Lithuania		24	240	450	533	616	620	623	626
Macedonia									
Moldova		9	64	85	112	348	424	489	544
Poland		1,100	2,670	5,480	4,520	5,346	6,456	7,372	8,131
Romania		300	713	2,100	2,450	2,800	3,200	4,144	4,892
Russia		2,600	9,300	13,000	15,000	17,400	19,000	20,644	22,235
Slovakia		220	740	1,270	1,593	1,929	2,320	2,776	3,115
Slovenia		200	548	650	704	808	816	858	892
Ukraine		430	890	1,123	1,327	1,810	2,121	2,402	2,653

Source: International Telecommunications Union/World Bank/Trade Sources/Euromonitor International

IT and Telecommunications Statistics

Table 18.5

ISDN Subscribers 1990-2008

'000

	1990	1995	2000	2003	2004	2005	2006	2007	2008
Western Europe									
Austria		17	347	458	461	444	413	408	403
Belgium	0	28	430	424	416	407	399	392	385
Cyprus			7	24	28	27	26	28	30
Denmark		14	376	377	357	321	283	267	251
Finland		6	208	236	170	176	175	177	172
France	7	284	1,700	2,081	2,204	2,334	2,475	2,596	2,724
Germany	16	961	7,465	11,551	12,095	12,655	12,808	13,698	14,449
Gibraltar		0	0	1	1	1	1	1	1
Greece		1	101	455	533	586	604	688	772
Iceland			17	17	17	16	15	15	15
Ireland			43	55	51	51	53	54	55
Italy		49	1,954	2,594	2,687	2,824	2,936	3,050	3,137
Liechtenstein		1	6	8	8	8	8	8	9
Luxembourg		2	41	74	79	81	80	83	85
Malta			0	1	2	2	2	3	3
Monaco		1	16	20	21	21	22	22	23
Netherlands		24	1,185	1,525	1,515	1,424	1,297	1,316	1,299
Norway		12	704	791	733	622	514	483	451
Portugal		8	195	282	278	274	267	279	284
Spain		11	646	1,096	1,097	1,114	1,129	1,164	1,198
Sweden		13	126	90	64	46	32	24	17
Switzerland	0	69	726	927	929	907	864	886	909
Turkey			7	16	14	14	15	15	16
United Kingdom	2	117	860	1,007	962	891	872	875	877
Eastern Europe									
Albania				0	0	1	1	1	1
Belarus	0		1	2	2	3	3	3	4
Bosnia-Herzegovina			1	9	17	23	26	31	36
Bulgaria			4	13	16	21	23	26	29
Croatia			1	111	127	133	127	139	151
Czech Republic			26	185	192	171	161	183	199
Estonia	0		9	42	43	43	44	45	50
Georgia									
Hungary	0		104	217	218	206	200	206	207
Latvia			6	11	22	25	27	30	34
Lithuania			3	13	15	16	16	17	18
Macedonia			3	11	14	15	16	18	20
Moldova			1	2	2	3	5	6	7
Poland	0		57	760	985	1,195	1,311	1,418	1,612
Romania			0	13	18	19	17	19	22
Russia			64	131	162	187	209	229	252
Slovakia			12	60	67	57	47	53	57
Slovenia		1	55	120	150	170	160	170	179
Ukraine			0	0	0	0	0	0	0

Source: International Telecommunications Union/World Bank/Trade Sources/Euromonitor International

Table 18.6

Capital Investment in Telecommunications 1985-2008

National currency million / US$ million

	1985	1990	1995	2000	2003	2004	2005	2006	2007	2008	US$ million 2008
Western Europe											
Austria	756	1,163	1,170	918	772	684	759	750	724	700	1,030.7
Belgium		629	993	1,574	1,051	1,328	1,062	1,051	1,022	1,019	1,500.1
Cyprus		17	23	68	57	44	41	38	35	33	48.3
Denmark		3,254	3,078	9,015	5,607	5,722	6,874	7,357	7,081	6,811	1,336.0
Finland	384	499	616	888	762	726	675	658	639	605	890.3
France		3,987	4,772	7,841	5,226	5,495	6,342	7,010	6,871	6,732	9,907.8
Germany	0	9,832	7,921	9,650	5,500	5,700	5,800	6,500	6,833	7,225	10,633.1
Gibraltar		2	2	3	2	2	3	3	3	3	6.0
Greece		175	458	2,114	1,127	1,088	721	805	684	570	839.3
Iceland	400	838	1,958	5,459	3,139	3,897	5,689	5,494	5,500	5,506	62.6
Ireland	178	223	246	410	257	242	243	256	262	250	367.6
Italy	2,761	5,113	3,966	7,113	7,887	7,084	8,000	6,837	6,791	6,728	9,901.8
Liechtenstein	11	12	16	18	19	19	19	20	21	21	19.4
Luxembourg		51	57	63	129	92	82	81	84	86	126.9
Malta	2	9	6	11	25	21	21	22	24	25	37.2
Monaco		1	1	1	1	1	1	1	1	1	1.8
Netherlands	637	1,108	1,250	3,353	3,313	3,312	3,445	3,360	3,412	3,475	5,114.3
Norway		2,747	5,129	18,718	21,033	21,869	22,738	24,182	25,081	26,130	4,632.9
Portugal	29,675	101,700	185,827	1,249	574	679	733	784	754	718	1,057.3
Spain		4,335	2,334	7,332	4,542	4,715	5,515	5,686	5,718	5,767	8,487.3
Sweden		6,286	7,783	22,621	11,746	11,592	8,832	10,198	9,176	8,155	1,237.2
Switzerland		3,077	2,156	3,794	2,133	2,060	2,030	6,544	7,003	7,461	6,889.0
Turkey		2	20	393	345	1,447	1,862	1,650	1,860	2,069	1,590.0
United Kingdom		2,758	4,557	10,971	8,411	7,629	7,442	7,408	7,248	6,716	12,346.6
Eastern Europe											
Albania		30	476	2,640	7,849	6,277	5,733	5,448	5,288	5,351	63.8
Belarus			482	39,390	215,101	288,841	343,441	382,535	418,380	452,441	211.8
Bosnia-Herzegovina			20	111	194	404	474	524	571	652	488.4
Bulgaria			3	115	606	580	945	815	807	808	604.0
Croatia		2	2,079	2,718	1,313	1,718	1,884	2,056	2,212	2,361	478.4
Czech Republic			20,000	46,430	42,525	12,206	13,736	14,171	12,453	12,535	734.3
Estonia			554	863	860	699	782	1,261	1,327	1,404	131.3
Georgia		18	5	163	142	149	156	168	181	186	124.6
Hungary	4,715	13,334	85,651	152,784	109,020	91,405	93,107	86,801	80,692	74,970	435.6
Latvia			62	44	23	15	29	29	34	34	70.2
Lithuania		35	120	517	310	273	394	526	547	575	243.9
Macedonia			1,604	3,033	2,137	1,878	2,038	2,199	2,060	1,912	45.7
Moldova			64	425	618	847	1,141	1,184	1,311	1,437	138.3
Poland		160	2,149	5,953	5,863	5,959	5,966	7,586	7,858	8,130	3,374.7
Romania		0	48	12,733,791	17,028,240	24,082,999	2,525	2,794	3,062	3,331	1,322.4
Russia		3	4,491	16,698	55,701	82,285	103,930	113,680	156,052	202,025	8,128.8
Slovakia			144	193	306	342	338	353	392	432	635.1
Slovenia		29	48	319	147	167	182	249	243	237	348.3
Ukraine			270	1,458	4,121	5,609	8,486	9,808	11,200	12,591	2,390.5

Source: *Euromonitor International from International Telecommunications Union/national statistics*

IT and Telecommunications Statistics

Table 18.7

Mobile Telecommunications Revenues 1990-2008

% of telecom revenue

	1990	1995	2000	2003	2004	2005	2006	2007	2008
Western Europe									
Austria			47	60	64	60	58	59	59
Belgium	2	10	48	64	40	40	36	32	29
Cyprus			32	46	49	47	45	47	49
Denmark		14	24	32	34	36	39	41	43
Finland	9	20	36	50	50	50	50	51	54
France	3	7	26	35	38	40	41	44	46
Germany		10	31	33	34	34	35	32	32
Gibraltar									
Greece		11	34	47	52	51	54	56	58
Iceland		10	27	40	42	43	47	49	52
Ireland			42	45	46	46	45	45	45
Italy			38	49	43	38	36	36	36
Liechtenstein									
Luxembourg	1	5	18	42	47	51	52	55	58
Malta		5	44	49	42	44	47	47	48
Monaco									
Netherlands	3	10	26	37	41	43	44	47	49
Norway		15	35	40	41	44	46	48	50
Portugal		14	41	33	36	36	37	36	36
Spain	1	5	41	41	28	30	32	30	29
Sweden	14	25	21	22	22	22	21	21	21
Switzerland		6	23	29	30	30	29	30	31
Turkey	2	7	43	37	44	52	56	59	61
United Kingdom		13	18	24	27	29	30	31	32
Eastern Europe									
Albania			27	70	77	81	82	83	85
Belarus			0	0	0	0	0	0	0
Bosnia-Herzegovina			26	39	40	43	42	43	45
Bulgaria				45	49	55	59	64	68
Croatia		4	28	52	53	53	56	58	59
Czech Republic		7	45	52	67	67	73	75	77
Estonia		29	47	57	48	61	62	65	66
Georgia			51	58	59	59	65	67	69
Hungary		33	30	33	34	34	37	38	39
Latvia		6	53	58	60	62	64	66	68
Lithuania		0		49	51	47	46	47	46
Macedonia			32	32	35	34	54	57	61
Moldova				31	37	37	42	43	47
Poland		8	24	49	44	46	48	50	52
Romania				45	46	50	56	60	64
Russia			26	38	44	46	49	51	55
Slovakia		12	35	53	59	60	65	68	70
Slovenia			66	56	49	48	48	46	45
Ukraine			20	38	47	56	64	68	72

Source: *Euromonitor International from International Telecommunications Union*

Table 18.8

Mobile Telephone Calls 1990-2008
Million minutes

	1990	1995	2000	2003	2004	2005	2006	2007	2008
Western Europe									
Austria			6,000	9,147	9,261	9,367	9,475	9,585	9,692
Belgium									
Cyprus									
Denmark		564	2,695	3,748	3,996	4,192	4,345	4,463	4,551
Finland		316	5,294	7,655	7,945	8,162	8,327	8,455	8,559
France			35,524	54,929	56,283	57,191	57,913	58,560	59,175
Germany			24,347	33,607	34,678	35,269	35,643	35,921	36,157
Gibraltar			5	7	8	9	9	10	11
Greece			5,700	9,056	9,327	9,476	9,571	9,644	9,708
Iceland			194	243	248	252	255	259	262
Ireland									
Italy			58,000	75,839	76,661	77,279	77,821	78,320	78,793
Liechtenstein									
Luxembourg			170	271	275	279	284	288	292
Malta			33	66	68	69	70	71	72
Monaco									
Netherlands			6,200	9,178	9,438	9,606	9,731	9,838	9,936
Norway			2,994	4,540	4,773	4,957	5,105	5,220	5,309
Portugal		436	6,187	9,904	10,155	10,317	10,439	10,540	10,630
Spain			17,026	27,788	28,648	29,148	29,486	29,749	29,976
Sweden			4,742	6,446	6,771	7,026	7,222	7,367	7,468
Switzerland			4,148	5,229	5,364	5,450	5,511	5,562	5,606
Turkey				8,712	9,606	10,231	10,682	11,046	11,369
United Kingdom		5,059	38,206	57,519	58,791	59,616	60,261	60,835	61,384
Eastern Europe									
Albania									
Belarus		6		867	1,713	2,403	2,735	2,860	2,912
Bosnia-Herzegovina									
Bulgaria									
Croatia				1,665	1,867	1,973	2,027	2,058	2,076
Czech Republic				2,245	2,344	2,389	2,412	2,428	2,440
Estonia									
Georgia									
Hungary									
Latvia									
Lithuania			284	1,105	1,227	1,288	1,319	1,337	1,347
Macedonia									
Moldova									
Poland									
Romania				2,075	2,522	2,856	3,073	3,205	3,285
Russia									
Slovakia			1,133	3,512	3,802	3,957	4,050	4,115	4,166
Slovenia				1,869	1,894	1,913	1,929	1,944	1,957
Ukraine									

Source: *Euromonitor International from International Telecommunications Union*

IT and Telecommunications Statistics

Table 18.9

Mobile Telephone Calls per Mobile Telephone Subscriber 1990-2008
Minutes

	1990	1995	2000	2003	2004	2005	2006	2007	2008
Western Europe									
Austria			980.9	1,257.5	1,158.8	1,081.1	1,020.9	967.0	896.1
Belgium									
Cyprus									
Denmark		685.9	801.2	786.2	773.4	769.3	745.6	707.3	694.8
Finland		304.1	1,419.8	1,612.5	1,592.8	1,548.8	1,468.6	1,390.6	1,253.1
France			1,222.8	1,317.2	1,263.5	1,189.3	1,121.0	1,057.8	1,020.7
Germany			505.1	518.6	486.2	444.9	416.1	369.7	337.1
Gibraltar			899.2	460.6	435.6	419.8	417.3	420.4	428.5
Greece			960.8	1,013.4	1,000.3	923.5	871.7	784.4	703.5
Iceland			902.2	868.9	855.0	829.3	777.2	765.0	755.5
Ireland									
Italy			1,372.9	1,335.9	1,221.7	1,080.8	967.7	872.1	889.5
Liechtenstein									
Luxembourg			560.5	502.9	426.3	388.1	397.2	391.0	392.0
Malta			288.4	228.9	222.4	213.2	201.7	196.2	191.6
Monaco									
Netherlands			576.5	695.3	637.7	606.6	562.6	510.1	498.6
Norway			928.7	1,118.1	1,054.8	1,042.5	1,019.3	1,005.6	991.7
Portugal		1,279.2	928.3	990.1	960.6	901.3	853.8	783.6	713.0
Spain			701.7	746.6	741.7	682.7	638.9	614.4	603.4
Sweden			744.2	732.4	770.8	771.7	751.7	710.4	688.0
Switzerland			894.3	844.8	854.9	797.4	741.2	677.5	638.5
Turkey				312.4	276.8	234.6	202.8	178.2	172.7
United Kingdom		882.0	879.3	1,060.1	985.0	910.6	863.8	830.8	812.3
Eastern Europe									
Albania									
Belarus		1,017.5		775.4	765.0	586.2	458.8	411.0	387.3
Bosnia-Herzegovina									
Bulgaria									
Croatia				656.2	658.3	540.5	461.3	408.7	350.5
Czech Republic				231.2	217.4	202.8	194.4	183.5	177.1
Estonia									
Georgia									
Hungary									
Latvia									
Lithuania			542.2	525.5	402.1	295.9	279.7	271.6	268.2
Macedonia									
Moldova									
Poland									
Romania				294.7	246.9	213.8	192.1	157.0	134.3
Russia									
Slovakia			910.9	954.8	889.4	871.6	827.8	678.1	754.7
Slovenia				1,074.8	1,024.5	1,087.5	1,060.1	1,008.2	952.4
Ukraine									

Source: *Euromonitor International from national statistics*

  Table 18.10

Telephone Lines in Use 1990-2008
'000

	1990	1995	2000	2003	2004	2005	2006	2007	2008
Western Europe									
Austria	3,223	3,797	3,997	3,877	3,821	3,739	3,561	3,374	3,272
Belgium	3,913	4,682	5,036	4,875	4,801	4,767	4,728	4,668	4,615
Cyprus	246	347	440	424	418	420	408	376	367
Denmark	2,911	3,193	3,835	3,614	3,491	3,349	3,099	2,824	2,679
Finland	2,670	2,810	2,849	2,568	2,368	2,120	1,910	1,740	1,582
France	28,085	32,400	33,987	33,913	33,703	33,707	33,897	33,882	33,867
Germany	31,887	42,000	50,220	54,233	54,526	54,791	54,540	53,750	53,987
Gibraltar	11	17	24	25	25	25	24	24	24
Greece	3,949	5,163	5,659	6,300	6,352	6,310	6,170	6,227	6,308
Iceland	130	149	196	193	190	194	189	187	185
Ireland	983	1,310	1,832	1,955	2,015	2,052	2,102	2,112	2,154
Italy	22,350	24,845	27,153	26,596	25,957	25,049	26,890	26,847	26,803
Liechtenstein	17	20	20	20	20	20	20	20	20
Luxembourg	184	229	249	245	245	245	247	248	248
Malta	128	171	204	208	207	202	202	198	197
Monaco	24	31	30	30	31	31	31	31	32
Netherlands	6,940	8,124	9,889	7,846	7,861	7,600	7,450	7,334	7,197
Norway	2,132	2,444	2,401	2,236	2,180	2,129	2,055	1,988	1,929
Portugal	2,379	3,643	4,321	4,281	4,238	4,234	4,234	4,139	4,113
Spain	12,603	15,095	17,104	17,759	17,934	19,461	19,870	18,583	18,759
Sweden	5,849	6,013	5,751	5,535	5,688	5,635	5,399	5,340	5,281
Switzerland	3,943	4,480	5,236	5,323	5,253	5,150	5,022	5,000	4,966
Turkey	6,861	13,127	18,395	18,917	19,125	18,978	18,832	18,413	18,415
United Kingdom	25,368	29,411	35,228	34,550	34,576	34,068	33,603	33,682	33,461
Eastern Europe									
Albania	40	42	153	255	275	354	394	427	450
Belarus	1,574	1,968	2,752	3,071	3,176	3,284	3,368	3,672	3,750
Bosnia-Herzegovina		238	780	938	952	969	989	1,064	1,097
Bulgaria	2,175	2,563	2,882	2,818	2,727	2,490	2,399	2,300	2,186
Croatia	823	1,287	1,721	1,871	1,888	1,883	1,827	1,825	1,825
Czech Republic	1,624	2,444	3,872	3,626	3,428	3,217	2,888	2,724	2,534
Estonia	320	412	523	461	444	442	452	495	492
Georgia	540	554	509	667	683	570	553	560	568
Hungary	996	2,157	3,798	3,603	3,564	3,416	3,360	3,251	3,167
Latvia	620	705	735	654	650	731	657	644	631
Lithuania	781	941	1,188	824	820	801	792	799	772
Macedonia	286	351	507	525	537	533	491	464	457
Moldova	462	566	584	791	863	929	1,018	1,080	1,151
Poland	3,293	5,728	10,946	12,292	12,553	11,836	11,476	10,336	10,249
Romania	2,366	2,968	3,899	4,332	4,389	4,386	4,197	4,300	4,331
Russia	20,700	25,019	32,070	36,100	38,500	40,100	43,900	45,872	47,843
Slovakia	711	1,118	1,698	1,295	1,250	1,197	1,167	1,151	1,072
Slovenia	422	615	785	812	811	816	837	857	867
Ukraine	7,028	8,311	10,417	11,110	12,142	11,667	12,341	12,858	13,207

Source: *Euromonitor International from International Telecommunications Union/national statistics*

IT and Telecommunications Statistics

Table 18.11

Mobile Telephone Subscriptions 1990-2008
'000

	1990	1995	2000	2003	2004	2005	2006	2007	2008
Western Europe									
Austria	73.7	383.5	6,117.0	7,274.0	7,992.0	8,665.0	9,281.0	9,912.0	10,816.0
Belgium	42.9	235.3	5,629.0	8,605.8	9,131.7	9,604.7	9,847.4	10,738.1	11,822.2
Cyprus	3.2	44.5	218.3	551.8	640.5	718.8	777.5	806.5	824.0
Denmark	148.2	822.3	3,363.6	4,767.1	5,166.9	5,449.2	5,828.2	6,310.0	6,550.7
Finland	257.9	1,039.1	3,728.6	4,747.1	4,988.0	5,270.0	5,670.0	6,080.0	6,830.0
France	283.2	1,302.5	29,052.4	41,702.0	44,544.0	48,088.0	51,662.0	55,358.1	57,972.0
Germany	272.6	3,725.0	48,202.0	64,800.0	71,322.0	79,271.0	85,652.0	97,151.0	107,245.0
Gibraltar		0.7	5.6	15.9	18.4	20.7	22.4	23.8	24.8
Greece	0.0	273.0	5,932.4	8,936.2	9,324.3	10,260.4	10,979.8	12,294.9	13,799.3
Iceland	10.0	30.9	214.9	279.7	290.1	304.0	328.5	338.0	346.6
Ireland	25.0	158.0	2,461.0	3,500.0	3,860.0	4,270.0	4,740.7	4,982.7	5,048.1
Italy	266.0	3,923.0	42,246.0	56,770.0	62,750.0	71,500.0	80,418.0	89,801.0	88,580.0
Liechtenstein	0.6	9.5	14.7	25.0	25.5	27.5	28.8	30.1	31.2
Luxembourg	0.8	26.8	303.3	539.0	646.0	720.0	713.8	735.8	744.5
Malta	1.1	10.8	114.4	290.0	306.1	324.0	346.8	360.8	373.5
Monaco	0.4	3.0	18.7	24.4	24.8	24.9	24.8	24.6	24.3
Netherlands	79.0	539.0	10,755.0	13,200.0	14,800.0	15,834.0	17,296.0	19,285.0	19,927.0
Norway	196.8	981.3	3,224.0	4,060.8	4,524.8	4,754.5	5,007.7	5,191.6	5,353.7
Portugal	6.5	340.8	6,665.0	10,002.7	10,571.1	11,447.3	12,226.4	13,450.9	14,909.6
Spain	54.7	945.0	24,265.1	37,219.8	38,622.6	42,694.1	46,152.0	48,422.5	49,681.6
Sweden	461.2	2,008.0	6,372.3	8,801.0	8,785.0	9,104.0	9,607.0	10,371.0	10,854.3
Switzerland	125.0	447.2	4,638.5	6,189.0	6,274.8	6,834.2	7,436.2	8,208.9	8,780.0
Turkey	31.8	437.1	16,133.4	27,887.5	34,707.5	43,609.0	52,662.7	61,975.8	65,824.1
United Kingdom	1,114.0	5,735.8	43,452.0	54,256.2	59,687.9	65,471.7	69,764.9	73,224.2	75,565.4
Eastern Europe									
Albania		1.8	29.8	1,100.0	1,259.6	1,530.2	1,748.7	1,996.8	2,233.6
Belarus	0.0	5.9	49.4	1,118.0	2,239.3	4,099.5	5,960.0	6,960.0	7,517.7
Bosnia-Herzegovina	0.0	0.0	93.4	1,074.8	1,407.4	1,594.4	1,887.8	2,450.4	3,179.0
Bulgaria	0.0	20.9	738.0	3,500.9	4,729.7	6,244.9	8,253.4	9,897.5	10,633.3
Croatia	0.2	33.7	1,033.0	2,537.3	2,835.5	3,649.7	4,395.2	5,034.6	5,924.0
Czech Republic	0.0	48.9	4,346.0	9,708.7	10,782.6	11,775.9	12,406.2	13,228.6	13,780.2
Estonia	0.0	30.5	557.0	1,050.2	1,255.7	1,445.3	1,658.7	1,981.8	2,524.5
Georgia	0.0	0.2	194.7	711.2	840.6	1,174.3	1,703.9	2,599.7	3,239.5
Hungary	2.6	265.0	3,076.3	7,944.6	8,727.2	9,320.0	9,965.7	11,029.9	12,224.2
Latvia	0.0	15.0	401.3	1,219.6	1,536.7	1,871.6	2,183.7	2,217.0	2,325.6
Lithuania	0.0	14.8	524.0	2,102.2	3,051.2	4,353.4	4,718.2	4,921.1	5,022.6
Macedonia	0.0	0.0	401.9	1,010.9	1,106.5	1,207.7	1,293.1	1,380.1	1,605.5
Moldova		0.0	139.0	475.9	787.0	1,089.8	1,358.2	1,761.2	2,175.7
Poland	0.0	75.0	6,747.0	17,401.2	23,096.1	29,166.4	36,745.5	41,388.8	45,634.3
Romania	0.0	9.1	2,499.0	7,039.9	10,215.4	13,354.1	15,991.0	20,417.0	24,467.0
Russia	0.0	88.5	3,263.2	36,135.1	73,722.2	120,000.0	150,674.0	163,300.0	187,500.0
Slovakia	0.0	12.3	1,243.7	3,678.8	4,275.2	4,540.4	4,893.2	6,068.1	5,520.0
Slovenia	0.0	27.3	1,215.6	1,739.1	1,848.6	1,759.2	1,819.6	1,928.4	2,054.9
Ukraine	0.0	14.0	818.5	6,498.4	13,735.0	30,013.5	48,987.3	55,240.4	55,694.5

Source: International Telecommunications Union/World Bank/Trade Sources/Euromonitor International

IT and Telecommunications Statistics

Table 18.12

National Telephone Calls 1990-2008

Million minutes

	1990	1995	2000	2003	2004	2005	2006	2007	2008
Western Europe									
Austria		13,760	8,176	13,643	11,800	7,117	6,406	6,130	5,853
Belgium			22,000	18,351	17,630	16,213	14,987	13,660	12,334
Cyprus	1,393	1,783	1,658	1,367	1,606	1,844	2,083	2,153	2,224
Denmark	10,920	12,657	22,438	36,860	32,280	26,466	27,374	28,197	29,020
Finland		13,982	17,983	13,832	11,443	7,789	5,336	4,165	3,068
France	104,664	104,400	121,949	107,776	106,840	105,302	105,092	104,214	101,680
Germany		167,762	273,085	194,898	183,000	171,000	163,000	152,807	124,104
Gibraltar	91	144	151	169	178	186	183	195	201
Greece				18,972	18,804	18,408	17,649	16,110	14,685
Iceland			1,923	1,210	1,398	965	850	761	678
Ireland		6,779	9,480	5,805	5,798	5,995	5,613	6,279	6,612
Italy		99,464	125,510	91,288	95,850	96,367	54,400	48,474	42,972
Liechtenstein		57	71	64	58	56	51	48	45
Luxembourg		1,302	2,162	2,200	2,096	1,752	1,643	1,588	1,506
Malta	374	812	998	742	657	571	621	586	554
Monaco	1,045	1,256	1,214	1,235	1,243	1,251	1,259	1,267	1,276
Netherlands			34,400	31,150	30,143	29,752	29,099	29,015	28,468
Norway		11,625	24,758	12,682	11,086	9,637	8,112	7,357	6,618
Portugal			14,606	19,302	19,950	21,572	21,538	22,351	23,458
Spain	46,025	45,587	51,345	58,223	53,787	52,790	50,433	48,593	46,753
Sweden	25,703	32,600	55,421	48,535	45,769	43,671	43,280	43,333	41,607
Switzerland	14,076	14,831	17,213	14,639	13,968	13,607	12,796	12,060	11,324
Turkey		37,384	26,859	53,312	54,884	52,897	39,880	42,050	44,220
United Kingdom		116,632	135,911	120,328	116,422	110,359	105,663	100,622	95,580
Eastern Europe									
Albania		123	235	765	436	567	663	745	711
Belarus	1,064	1,287	2,046	5,559	5,837	6,129	6,435	6,757	6,919
Bosnia-Herzegovina									
Bulgaria			12,798	5,536	5,204	2,599	3,135	2,621	2,158
Croatia				4,887	4,854	4,670	3,982	3,746	3,509
Czech Republic			10,629	5,571	4,591	3,762	3,156	2,726	2,330
Estonia		114	2,304	1,121	1,001	972	1,163	973	878
Georgia			2,440	2,768	2,829	2,891	2,989	3,067	3,156
Hungary		6,450	11,650	7,387	6,994	7,423	7,193	6,313	5,847
Latvia			1,719	1,447	1,355	1,205	1,121	1,060	1,008
Lithuania			4,138	1,381	1,557	1,574	1,547	1,520	1,555
Macedonia		2,274	2,277	1,514	1,140	744	1,390	1,277	1,164
Moldova		229	2,049	2,189	2,816	3,261	3,534	3,781	4,028
Poland		23,110	36,352	24,345	25,474	26,162	22,273	19,927	17,580
Romania		7,173	5,460	7,960	7,735	7,162	7,069	7,037	7,348
Russia		32,952	42,239	48,723	52,177	54,824	57,605	59,691	62,184
Slovakia		2,295	3,193	1,819	1,588	1,543	1,464	1,594	1,724
Slovenia	3,155	3,392	3,690	4,299	4,421	4,495	4,563	4,655	4,793
Ukraine		20,670	25,908	30,727	33,095	35,645	36,702	38,172	39,923

Source: *Euromonitor International from International Telecommunications Union/national statistics*

International Outgoing Telephone Calls 1990-2008
Million minutes

	1990	1995	2000	2003	2004	2005	2006	2007	2008
Western Europe									
Austria	559	901	1,087	1,207	1,181	1,230	1,129	1,099	1,072
Belgium	731	1,106	1,543	1,558	1,728	1,776	1,599	1,661	1,723
Cyprus	57	117	193	344	406	467	253	263	273
Denmark	368	529	707	641	663	637	596	577	559
Finland	186	314	468	231	215	187	155	126	99
France	2,126	2,850	4,952	4,907	4,281	4,116	4,823	4,802	4,780
Germany	3,146	5,238	9,223	9,544	10,091	10,000	12,000	12,463	13,142
Gibraltar		12	18	18	19	19	20	20	21
Greece	213	463	793	798	936	968	1,019	1,057	1,095
Iceland	19	29	60	43	33	32	40	38	37
Ireland	261	407	1,250	862	1,176	1,149	1,278	1,226	1,175
Italy	1,043	1,839	4,138	5,986	3,633	3,596	3,739	3,812	3,766
Liechtenstein	11	16	55	42	37	35	33	31	28
Luxembourg	151	232	326	433	435	427	423	419	433
Malta	13	29	43	22	17	32	46	47	47
Monaco									
Netherlands	905	1,459	2,550	2,072	1,769	1,570	1,385	1,191	956
Norway	281	437	559	558	516	562	622	632	643
Portugal	156	300	505	485	508	591	550	557	564
Spain	611	1,063	2,956	3,256	3,689	4,705	5,441	5,993	6,544
Sweden	631	875	1,086	1,162	1,188	1,189	1,081	1,080	1,079
Switzerland	1,332	1,733	2,624	2,472	2,685	2,348	2,159	2,082	2,004
Turkey	159	374	732	939	715	721	515	479	443
United Kingdom	2,530	4,068	7,981	6,259	6,210	5,747	5,722	5,513	5,317
Eastern Europe									
Albania	20	23	72	62	60	61	61	62	62
Belarus		132	179	268	299	314	330	352	364
Bosnia-Herzegovina		10	93	191	204	247	276	303	336
Bulgaria	62	84	110	88	110	116	85	78	72
Croatia	69	211	222	343	320	377	310	303	296
Czech Republic	83	259	360	345	289	274	260	243	230
Estonia		53	78	88	76	73	69	67	66
Georgia	5	13	60	85	70	63	106	113	121
Hungary	122	247	211	168	161	212	207	184	160
Latvia		44	58	50	44	40	49	48	47
Lithuania	2	55	39	35	45	54	52	54	56
Macedonia		45	73	62	21	16	28	13	10
Moldova		66	43	62	81	89	109	115	121
Poland	81	381	676	863	445	451	399	353	307
Romania	25	88	169	184	252	246	318	345	373
Russia	72	898	944	1,290	1,258	1,171	1,130	1,114	1,138
Slovakia	4	59	162	140	133	168	250	264	279
Slovenia		101	102	107	103	106	108	109	110
Ukraine		422	383	462	478	550	692	744	795

Source: *Euromonitor International from International Telecommunications Union/national statistics*

Labour

Labour Statistics

Table 19.1

Total Employed Population 1980-2008
'000

	1980	1985	1990	1995	2000	2003	2004	2005	2006	2007	2008
Western Europe											
Austria		3,228	3,421	3,732	3,777	3,798	3,744	3,824	3,928	4,028	4,062
Belgium	3,699	3,505	3,623	3,794	4,092	4,070	4,075	4,153	4,264	4,366	4,454
Cyprus	230	244	267	290	296	329	339	348	357	378	381
Denmark	2,364	2,569	2,670	2,614	2,733	2,701	2,729	2,744	2,797	2,790	2,795
Finland	2,232	2,466	2,494	2,137	2,355	2,384	2,385	2,420	2,466	2,511	2,540
France	21,599	22,039	22,504	23,124	23,636	24,830	25,035	25,206	25,171	25,629	25,772
Germany		32,687	36,111	35,782	36,324	35,927	35,463	36,654	37,379	38,210	39,034
Gibraltar	12	12	14	11	12	12	13	13	13	13	13
Greece	3,504	3,588	3,453	3,827	3,964	4,065	4,208	4,382	4,453	4,520	4,552
Iceland				142	156	157	158	161	169	176	177
Ireland			1,133	1,265	1,660	1,793	1,836	1,928	2,015	2,102	2,090
Italy	20,626	20,740	21,275	20,099	21,232	22,134	22,381	22,561	22,992	23,222	23,053
Liechtenstein			20	22	27	29	30	30	31	31	31
Luxembourg				164	181	188	186	193	195	205	208
Malta	120	113	127	133	143	149	146	148	151	155	155
Monaco											
Netherlands	5,373	5,593	6,400	6,889	7,815	8,039	7,930	7,885	8,108	8,312	8,413
Norway	1,906	2,014	2,029	2,079	2,268	2,267	2,274	2,288	2,361	2,443	2,497
Portugal	3,995	4,314	4,720	4,437	4,918	5,122	5,235	5,116	5,153	5,163	5,192
Spain	11,557	10,641	12,579	12,512	15,505	17,296	17,971	18,973	19,748	20,356	20,014
Sweden	3,926	4,306	4,576	4,063	4,240	4,315	4,290	4,364	4,429	4,541	4,612
Switzerland				3,687	3,882	3,962	3,959	3,974	4,053	4,124	4,183
Turkey			19,453	21,191	21,736	21,708	22,359	22,618	22,907	21,744	20,709
United Kingdom				26,062	27,793	27,821	28,010	28,665	28,926	29,100	29,203
Eastern Europe											
Albania				1,077	989	1,051	1,060	1,063	1,069	1,071	1,073
Belarus					4,395	4,281	4,307	4,325	4,387	4,458	4,467
Bosnia-Herzegovina						859	836	812	811	849	890
Bulgaria				3,216	2,934	2,834	2,922	2,980	3,110	3,253	3,359
Croatia					1,574	1,538	1,563	1,573	1,586	1,613	1,622
Czech Republic			5,225	5,001	4,723	4,733	4,706	4,766	4,828	4,922	4,992
Estonia			790	662	615	594	596	608	646	655	647
Georgia					1,749	1,814	1,783	1,745	1,747	1,704	1,691
Hungary				3,679	3,849	3,922	3,900	3,902	3,930	3,926	3,874
Latvia			1,061	898	973	1,007	1,018	1,036	1,088	1,119	1,110
Lithuania			1,622	1,529	1,398	1,438	1,436	1,474	1,499	1,534	1,512
Macedonia		493	518	555	553	545	523	545	570	590	610
Moldova					1,515	1,357	1,316	1,319	1,257	1,247	1,231
Poland			17,149	14,727	14,526	13,616	13,795	14,115	14,595	15,240	15,610
Romania			11,113	11,152	10,764	9,223	9,158	9,147	9,313	9,357	9,328
Russia				62,757	62,845	66,496	67,134	67,824	68,836	70,571	70,642
Slovakia			2,430	2,157	2,109	2,170	2,178	2,216	2,301	2,357	2,405
Slovenia				882	894	896	946	949	961	985	992
Ukraine				24,079	20,472	20,606	20,296	20,680	20,730	20,746	20,696

Source: *International Labour Organisation/Euromonitor International*

Table 19.2

Employment by Activity 2008

% of total employed population

	Agriculture, Forestry & Fishing	Community, Social & Personal Services	Construction	Electricity, Gas & Water	Finance, Insurance, Real Estate & Business	Manufact- uring
Western Europe						
Austria	5.6	26.9	8.1	0.6	13.2	17.0
Belgium	2.0	35.2	7.2	0.9	13.2	16.2
Cyprus	3.8	27.3	10.9	0.9	13.4	9.5
Denmark	2.8	36.9	6.9	0.6	12.8	15.4
Finland	4.4	32.4	7.0	0.6	14.5	17.6
France	3.4	33.9	6.9	0.8	13.8	15.3
Germany	2.2	30.3	6.6	0.9	13.8	22.0
Gibraltar						
Greece	11.3	25.2	8.8	0.9	9.0	12.3
Iceland	2.7	35.5	9.5	1.0	15.4	10.5
Ireland	5.3	26.7	13.6	0.6	13.7	12.6
Italy	3.9	24.8	8.4	0.6	13.9	20.9
Liechtenstein						
Luxembourg	1.5	22.4	11.2	0.4	25.8	10.5
Malta	2.0	29.5	7.7	2.3	10.9	15.1
Monaco						
Netherlands	3.1	33.2	6.1	0.5	15.2	12.3
Norway	2.7	39.0	7.5	0.7	13.5	11.3
Portugal	11.6	22.0	11.1	0.7	8.3	18.2
Spain	4.4	21.6	13.5	0.5	12.6	14.9
Sweden	2.3	37.6	6.5	0.5	16.8	14.3
Switzerland	4.0	26.8	6.8	0.6	17.7	15.8
Turkey	24.9	12.2	6.1	0.4	4.9	19.2
United Kingdom	1.4	33.8	8.3	0.8	16.5	12.8
Eastern Europe						
Albania	57.9	18.3	5.5	0.9		6.8
Belarus	15.8	23.7	4.0	2.4	2.7	22.4
Bosnia-Herzegovina						
Bulgaria	23.6	19.4	6.2	1.0	3.1	21.2
Croatia	11.8	20.4	9.1	1.8	7.8	20.0
Czech Republic	3.5	23.1	8.9	1.5	9.5	28.9
Estonia	4.6	25.1	13.4	1.3	9.0	20.0
Georgia	53.2	17.0	4.6	1.0	3.3	4.8
Hungary	4.5	26.4	8.0	1.5	10.3	22.4
Latvia	7.9	25.7	11.2	1.9	8.7	15.2
Lithuania	9.5	24.5	12.4	1.7	7.0	17.3
Macedonia	18.1	22.3	6.7	2.7	4.1	21.3
Moldova	31.1	22.7	6.6	1.9	3.8	10.9
Poland	14.1	22.5	7.2	1.4	9.0	20.9
Romania	28.8	15.8	7.7	1.8	4.2	21.0
Russia	8.6	27.7	7.6	3.0	8.1	16.4
Slovakia	4.1	23.4	10.2	1.7	8.3	27.0
Slovenia	10.5	24.3	6.1	0.9	8.9	26.1
Ukraine	15.8	23.7	5.0		7.4	15.2

Source: International Labour Organisation/Euromonitor International

Labour Statistics

Employment by Activity 2008 *(continued)*

% of total employed population

	Mining & Quarrying	Transport, Storage & Commun- ications	Wholesale & Retail Trade, Restaurants & Hotels	Undefined Sectors	Total
Western Europe					
Austria	0.3	6.0	22.4		100.0
Belgium	0.3	7.4	16.0	1.6	100.0
Cyprus	0.2	6.0	23.8	4.2	100.0
Denmark	0.2	6.2	18.0	0.2	100.0
Finland	0.2	6.9	15.8	0.6	100.0
France	0.1	6.2	17.4	2.2	100.0
Germany	0.3	5.7	17.6	0.6	100.0
Gibraltar					
Greece	0.4	5.9	24.7	1.5	100.0
Iceland	0.1	6.3	18.6	0.5	100.0
Ireland	0.5	5.7	20.4	0.8	100.0
Italy	0.2	5.4	20.3	1.6	100.0
Liechtenstein					
Luxembourg	0.1	8.0	18.0	2.1	100.0
Malta	0.4	8.1	23.8	0.2	100.0
Monaco					
Netherlands	0.1	6.1	18.7	4.7	100.0
Norway	1.6	6.4	17.1	0.2	100.0
Portugal	0.4	4.3	20.0	3.4	100.0
Spain	0.3	5.8	22.6	3.8	100.0
Sweden	0.2	6.2	15.4	0.2	100.0
Switzerland	0.1	6.2	20.6	1.4	100.0
Turkey	0.6	5.3	21.9	4.4	100.0
United Kingdom	0.5	6.7	18.6	0.8	100.0
Eastern Europe					
Albania	0.5	1.3	8.8		100.0
Belarus	1.3	6.8	17.5	3.2	100.0
Bosnia-Herzegovina					
Bulgaria	1.2	6.3	18.1		100.0
Croatia	0.7	7.4	20.7	0.3	100.0
Czech Republic	1.1	7.4	16.0	0.1	100.0
Estonia	0.8	8.9	16.9		100.0
Georgia	0.3	4.3	10.8	0.8	100.0
Hungary	0.2	7.4	19.1	0.1	100.0
Latvia	0.3	9.4	19.3	0.4	100.0
Lithuania	0.4	7.5	19.6	0.2	100.0
Macedonia	0.8	6.7	16.7	0.5	100.0
Moldova	0.3	5.7	16.7	0.4	100.0
Poland	1.4	6.5	16.9	0.1	100.0
Romania	1.1	5.3	14.2		100.0
Russia	1.9	9.2	17.2	0.1	100.0
Slovakia	0.7	7.1	17.3	0.4	100.0
Slovenia	0.4	6.1	15.6	1.1	100.0
Ukraine	3.2	7.0	22.6		100.0

Source: International Labour Organisation/Euromonitor International

Labour Statistics

Table 19.3

Employed Population by Quarter 2007-2009
'000

	2007 1st Quarter	2007 2nd Quarter	2007 3rd Quarter	2007 4th Quarter	2008 1st Quarter	2008 2nd Quarter	2008 3rd Quarter	2008 4th Quarter	2009 1st Quarter	2009 2nd Quarter
Western Europe										
Austria	3,948.5	4,034.9	4,095.2	4,033.0	3,988.7	4,080.1	4,110.2	4,069.1	3,994.3	
Belgium	4,333.5	4,330.9	4,371.2	4,429.4	4,457.5	4,422.1	4,472.7	4,462.9	4,426.2	
Cyprus	369.3	377.9	379.7	384.7	378.4	382.6	380.5	384.3	375.4	
Denmark	2,775.0	2,803.2	2,793.1	2,788.2	2,759.7	2,811.1	2,808.2	2,800.2	2,738.0	
Finland	2,433.8	2,543.9	2,561.5	2,504.8	2,482.3	2,583.7	2,575.7	2,518.8	2,456.3	2,506.8
France	25,252.1	25,601.3	25,868.0	25,794.3	25,599.5	25,795.9	25,971.8	25,722.6	25,439.9	
Germany	37,688.6	38,084.6	38,301.0	38,763.8	38,596.6	38,936.3	39,125.9	39,478.2	38,615.0	38,768.4
Gibraltar										
Greece	4,471.1	4,530.1	4,549.6	4,529.4	4,504.5	4,575.1	4,582.3	4,546.1	4,478.0	
Iceland	172.1	178.3	180.0	175.5	172.1	179.6	181.8	173.2	162.6	
Ireland	2,064.2	2,084.5	2,129.9	2,127.8	2,124.0	2,097.3	2,104.9	2,033.9	1,940.2	
Italy	22,846.7	23,298.4	23,417.5	23,326.2	22,821.7	23,226.5	23,165.0	22,997.1	22,619.6	
Liechtenstein										
Luxembourg	200.5	200.8	204.0	213.2	203.5	214.2	208.9	204.4		
Malta	153.1	154.9	156.3	155.3	152.4	154.6	157.6	155.1	156.1	
Monaco										
Netherlands	8,211.9	8,317.0	8,360.1	8,359.0	8,323.4	8,400.0	8,443.4	8,483.6	8,467.4	
Norway	2,395.8	2,433.7	2,458.7	2,483.8	2,469.1	2,504.7	2,514.6	2,497.8	2,479.1	2,498.8
Portugal	5,129.2	5,148.1	5,193.7	5,181.7	5,185.7	5,222.6	5,190.3	5,170.8	5,093.7	5,070.8
Spain	20,069.1	20,367.1	20,510.4	20,476.7	20,160.6	20,180.7	20,100.9	19,612.8	18,853.9	18,708.3
Sweden	4,430.5	4,535.3	4,649.0	4,547.9	4,536.7	4,636.1	4,700.7	4,574.2	4,482.8	4,535.4
Switzerland	4,071.9	4,110.9	4,151.6	4,160.7	4,161.4	4,193.0	4,186.6	4,192.9	4,188.0	
Turkey	20,825.4	22,223.3	22,574.8	21,352.5	19,569.2	21,227.8	21,505.7	20,532.4	19,479.6	20,888.8
United Kingdom	28,838.7	28,964.2	29,245.1	29,351.6	29,174.1	29,203.9	29,260.5	29,172.9	28,861.8	
Eastern Europe										
Albania	1,068.5	1,068.8	1,072.0	1,075.7	1,047.5	1,077.2	1,081.6	1,086.2		
Belarus										
Bosnia-Herzegovina										
Bulgaria	3,135.2	3,253.0	3,315.4	3,306.4	3,287.7	3,370.0	3,415.2	3,361.5	3,260.8	
Croatia	1,561.8	1,608.3	1,660.0	1,623.5	1,578.1	1,624.5	1,666.1	1,619.5	1,594.7	
Czech Republic	4,865.2	4,914.1	4,942.0	4,967.4	4,947.7	4,992.5	5,003.9	5,022.6	4,936.1	
Estonia	646.9	658.4	661.9	653.6	646.7	647.0	651.2	643.3	604.0	584.9
Georgia										
Hungary	3,905.4	3,942.4	3,947.3	3,909.3	3,838.7	3,863.0	3,918.8	3,874.9	3,758.3	
Latvia	1,085.3	1,109.0	1,131.8	1,149.8	1,122.8	1,126.9	1,117.6	1,071.2	1,032.4	985.7
Lithuania	1,507.7	1,543.9	1,560.2	1,524.9	1,502.6	1,517.4	1,529.8	1,499.4	1,425.8	
Macedonia	579.2	589.2	598.3	594.0	602.2	608.6	621.2	609.9	619.5	
Moldova	1,185.8	1,325.2	1,294.0	1,183.0	1,135.0	1,334.8	1,288.8	1,164.8	1,072.5	
Poland	14,838.7	15,151.7	15,432.0	15,537.7	15,328.4	15,501.3	15,798.6	15,813.5	15,526.0	
Romania	9,109.2	9,446.2	9,694.1	9,177.2	9,079.0	9,451.7	9,584.7	9,197.0	8,999.3	
Russia	69,190.5	70,663.5	71,618.5	70,811.5	69,174.5	71,304.7	71,807.4	70,281.4	67,355.8	
Slovakia	2,327.3	2,337.5	2,366.3	2,398.1	2,363.5	2,376.7	2,444.1	2,437.3	2,360.4	
Slovenia	957.6	993.6	1,006.2	983.3	966.2	985.6	1,018.0	996.4	957.5	
Ukraine	20,448.8	20,738.8	20,982.0	20,814.7	20,413.5	20,763.5	20,941.2	20,666.8	19,713.7	

Source: International Labour Organisation/Euromonitor International

Labour Statistics

Table 19.4

Level of Paid Employment in Manufacturing 1980-2008
'000

	1980	1985	1990	1995	2000	2003	2004	2005	2006	2007	2008
Western Europe											
Austria	1,259	1,153	1,098	862	726	698	656	668	701	689	660
Belgium	1,008	873	856	747	714	672	677	682	667	683	697
Cyprus	30	34	37	34	27	29	29	31	30	30	30
Denmark	374	398	401	496	488	422	419	424	411	417	418
Finland	567	528	495	403	437	418	411	414	417	421	425
France	5,182	4,584	4,410	3,909	3,900	3,712	3,618	3,524	3,495	3,459	3,478
Germany	8,717	8,064	8,876	8,499	8,141	7,839	7,723	7,613	7,741	7,995	8,168
Gibraltar	3	3	1	1	1	1	1	0	1	1	1
Greece	496	462	457	398	409	413	419	413	409	408	411
Iceland	25	27	23	21	21	19	20	19	18	17	17
Ireland	243	201	210	229	270	263	258	252	247	247	245
Italy	4,745	4,101	4,081	4,027	4,060	4,126	4,067	4,086	4,075	4,114	4,084
Liechtenstein											
Luxembourg	38	35	34	32	33	32	32	32	33	35	35
Malta	40	34	36	31	31	27	27	26	25	24	24
Monaco											
Netherlands	1,121	1,042	1,143	1,029	1,043	978	970	968	955	972	984
Norway	371	337	301	300	284	268	255	256	262	268	274
Portugal	921	926	1,037	858	961	884	872	853	867	842	846
Spain	2,723	2,199	2,557	2,045	2,578	2,680	2,709	2,720	2,716	2,712	2,666
Sweden	1,002	935	903	716	721	656	641	616	614	618	628
Switzerland	692	665	728	738	698	667	654	656	668	680	690
Turkey	1,986	2,129	2,582	2,525	2,845	3,026	3,121	3,366	3,478	3,344	3,234
United Kingdom	6,935	5,567	4,756	4,072	3,941	3,446	3,253	3,131	3,160	3,178	3,190
Eastern Europe											
Albania					32	37	38	38	39	40	41
Belarus		1,430	1,437	1,216	1,208	1,123	1,121	1,111	1,101	1,095	1,088
Bosnia-Herzegovina							89	83	82	82	80
Bulgaria	1,308	1,512	1,588	787	562	598	607	607	627	628	631
Croatia		537	546	338	278	277	277	274	280	289	291
Czech Republic	1,540	1,646	1,543	1,332	1,192	1,189	1,175	1,197	1,254	1,295	1,313
Estonia		215	206	158	133	129	134	133	131	129	127
Georgia					86	68	65	65	65	63	63
Hungary	1,386	1,278	1,118	652	753	734	715	689	753	750	696
Latvia			236	165	149	157	163	158	160	160	151
Lithuania		670	652	318	243	254	246	255	255	255	249
Macedonia		178	187	120	99	89	84	82	78	75	73
Moldova		387	365	156	98	104	108	106	104	97	93
Poland	4,126	3,702	3,014	2,616	2,467	2,206	2,244	2,259	2,311	2,413	2,471
Romania	3,031	3,266	3,452	2,192	1,560	1,582	1,492	1,425	1,409	1,415	1,411
Russia	23,812	23,490	18,884	13,181	12,335	12,536	12,448	12,278	12,233	12,089	11,358
Slovakia				556	516	539	547	557	574	597	610
Slovenia		383	373	297	253	252	254	261	248	251	253
Ukraine			5,975	4,159	2,916	2,356	2,351	2,371	2,329	2,268	2,192

Source: *International Labour Organisation/Euromonitor International*

Labour Statistics | **Table 19.5**

Total Unemployed 1980-2008
'000

	1980	1985	1990	1995	2000	2003	2004	2005	2006	2007	2008
Western Europe											
Austria		121	115	144	139	169	194	208	196	186	161
Belgium	453	455	285	390	309	364	380	391	383	369	334
Cyprus	5	10	6	10	15	14	16	19	17	16	15
Denmark	245	184	242	196	130	158	163	143	118	113	97
Finland	106	130	82	383	254	235	229	220	204	184	173
France	1,381	1,996	2,049	2,899	2,590	2,299	2,412	2,430	2,436	2,214	2,164
Germany		2,602	2,007	3,179	3,123	3,894	4,261	4,573	4,248	3,602	3,070
Gibraltar	0	0	0	2	0	0	0	0	1	1	1
Greece	215	304	281	424	519	442	493	466	427	398	377
Iceland				7	4	6	5	5	5	5	6
Ireland			172	178	75	83	85	87	93	100	141
Italy	1,645	2,388	2,618	2,633	2,490	2,095	1,959	1,890	1,670	1,506	1,675
Liechtenstein			0	0	0	1	1	1	1	1	1
Luxembourg				5	4	7	10	9	10	9	10
Malta	4	10	5	5	10	12	12	12	12	11	10
Monaco											
Netherlands	382	621	513	524	245	332	410	424	353	300	238
Norway	31	53	113	107	81	106	107	111	85	63	65
Portugal	324	382	229	343	208	348	370	429	434	455	436
Spain	1,488	2,939	2,441	3,716	2,497	2,242	2,214	1,912	1,837	1,834	2,558
Sweden	87	118	75	391	253	260	296	349	336	296	303
Switzerland				129	106	170	178	185	166	153	114
Turkey			1,523	1,610	1,499	2,493	2,501	2,520	2,448	2,331	2,460
United Kingdom				2,351	1,619	1,414	1,359	1,397	1,649	1,621	1,749
Eastern Europe											
Albania				232	294	276	266	259	254	250	248
Belarus					142	199	122	101	79	68	74
Bosnia-Herzegovina						319	339	363	366	347	272
Bulgaria				565	559	449	400	334	306	240	203
Croatia					297	256	250	229	199	172	150
Czech Republic			227	207	457	399	427	409	372	276	230
Estonia			5	68	90	66	64	52	41	32	38
Georgia					212	236	258	279	275	261	259
Hungary				417	263	245	253	304	317	312	332
Latvia			321	258	159	119	119	99	80	72	89
Lithuania			273	266	274	204	184	133	89	69	94
Macedonia		136	159	229	260	316	309	324	321	317	312
Moldova					140	117	117	104	100	67	62
Poland				2,277	2,785	3,329	3,230	3,047	2,345	1,620	1,195
Romania			566	968	821	692	800	705	728	638	572
Russia				6,712	7,138	5,716	5,775	5,608	5,310	4,588	4,756
Slovakia			202	324	485	459	481	428	353	292	256
Slovenia				70	66	62	60	66	61	50	46
Ukraine				1,437	2,656	2,008	1,907	1,601	1,515	1,418	1,392

Source: International Labour Organisation/Euromonitor International

Labour Statistics

Table 19.6

Unemployed Population by Quarter 2007-2009
'000

	2007 1st Quarter	2007 2nd Quarter	2007 3rd Quarter	2007 4th Quarter	2008 1st Quarter	2008 2nd Quarter	2008 3rd Quarter	2008 4th Quarter	2009 1st Quarter	2009 2nd Quarter
Western Europe										
Austria	220.9	169.1	159.2	193.2	180.6	142.8	138.8	180.0	217.2	183.2
Belgium	379.8	355.2	383.7	358.8	334.1	316.5	347.5	336.0	352.6	352.6
Cyprus	18.4	14.2	14.6	14.9	17.0	13.2	14.4	15.8	21.4	20.9
Denmark	149.1	118.1	99.9	86.3	120.2	88.3	81.9	98.2	161.3	183.6
Finland	198.7	211.1	164.4	161.7	176.3	203.1	151.4	160.0	203.5	265.6
France	2,381.9	2,104.9	2,192.3	2,176.9	2,184.1	1,990.4	2,149.7	2,331.4	2,579.4	2,512.1
Germany	4,015.8	3,657.9	3,489.7	3,244.2	3,379.2	3,087.0	2,968.6	2,845.6	3,338.4	3,283.3
Gibraltar										
Greece	435.6	389.2	379.0	387.4	405.1	356.8	354.6	391.2	458.0	
Iceland	3.8	6.4	4.2	3.8	4.5	6.2	5.3	7.8	13.1	
Ireland	91.0	99.4	108.3	102.5	108.5	122.8	161.7	172.2	228.2	
Italy	1,555.6	1,412.0	1,400.2	1,654.8	1,744.3	1,687.6	1,512.7	1,756.7	1,961.3	
Liechtenstein										
Luxembourg	9.3	8.2	8.1	8.7	9.6	8.9	9.2	10.5	12.4	12.1
Malta	11.4	10.3	10.5	10.5	9.8	9.5	9.3	10.0	10.8	11.1
Monaco										
Netherlands	349.5	306.9	281.9	261.7	256.6	243.1	222.4	229.4	271.2	297.7
Norway	72.1	61.0	65.2	53.7	65.8	58.6	66.8	70.5	104.5	108.5
Portugal	500.0	446.5	435.5	438.1	437.5	423.8	429.0	452.5	520.0	546.6
Spain	1,862.0	1,783.2	1,804.3	1,886.9	2,299.0	2,372.2	2,547.4	3,014.1	3,520.1	3,659.8
Sweden	318.6	292.0	312.6	261.6	298.7	329.3	289.7	294.6	376.7	446.1
Switzerland	174.2	149.1	141.2	147.4	120.5	108.3	107.0	121.8	144.5	151.5
Turkey	2,516.6	2,201.4	2,226.8	2,379.2	2,461.4	2,149.0	2,363.5	2,865.1	3,544.7	3,224.0
United Kingdom	1,662.3	1,589.7	1,697.3	1,533.7	1,577.6	1,609.4	1,883.6	1,924.5	2,169.5	
Eastern Europe										
Albania	255.8	251.4	246.2	247.3	248.2	246.8	246.9	249.4		
Belarus										
Bosnia-Herzegovina										
Bulgaria	272.6	237.9	235.0	215.3	233.4	211.4	187.9	179.4	225.7	
Croatia	188.8	183.3	155.5	160.3	164.8	148.1	139.8	148.5	166.6	163.5
Czech Republic	319.5	273.6	263.6	247.3	249.3	216.4	221.2	232.4	301.2	331.9
Estonia	33.5	31.4	30.9	33.0	32.0	32.6	36.6	51.0	90.2	123.7
Georgia										
Hungary	329.4	304.3	303.1	311.2	351.3	320.5	317.5	336.8	403.4	419.9
Latvia	82.3	75.8	68.5	61.8	81.4	81.4	86.8	107.3	168.3	
Lithuania	83.6	66.4	60.9	65.1	96.6	86.7	87.6	103.8	202.8	264.4
Macedonia	323.3	316.9	311.1	316.2	321.1	311.5	306.7	307.3	302.1	
Moldova	71.8	57.8	70.2	67.1	80.6	50.5	57.9	57.8	109.6	
Poland	1,920.0	1,647.1	1,491.9	1,421.0	1,385.4	1,196.2	1,092.8	1,103.8	1,354.4	1,344.7
Romania	756.8	619.6	568.6	605.4	601.6	541.9	544.1	599.4	761.6	845.2
Russia	5,220.8	4,520.5	4,266.5	4,344.2	5,004.8	4,230.3	4,475.8	5,314.7	6,755.4	6,428.1
Slovakia	316.8	289.7	284.3	276.9	256.6	249.1	252.6	267.4	323.9	376.1
Slovenia	53.9	49.5	47.8	48.0	48.2	44.3	43.7	46.3	55.7	61.3
Ukraine	1,568.9	1,409.5	1,330.6	1,361.3	1,525.4	1,354.3	1,309.1	1,377.4	2,026.7	

Source: *International Labour Organisation/Euromonitor International*

Table 19.7

Unemployment Rate 1980-2008

% of economically active population

	1980	1985	1990	1995	2000	2003	2004	2005	2006	2007	2008
Western Europe											
Austria		3.6	3.2	3.7	3.5	4.3	4.9	5.2	4.7	4.4	3.8
Belgium	10.9	11.5	7.3	9.3	7.0	8.2	8.5	8.6	8.2	7.8	7.0
Cyprus	2.3	4.0	2.3	3.3	4.9	4.1	4.6	5.2	4.6	3.9	3.8
Denmark	9.4	6.7	8.3	7.0	4.5	5.5	5.6	5.0	4.0	3.9	3.4
Finland	4.6	5.0	3.2	15.2	9.7	9.0	8.8	8.3	7.6	6.8	6.4
France	6.0	8.3	8.3	11.1	9.9	8.5	8.8	8.8	8.8	8.0	7.7
Germany		7.4	5.3	8.2	7.9	9.8	10.7	11.1	10.2	8.6	7.3
Gibraltar	1.7	3.7	2.7	16.6	3.2	3.8	3.4	3.7	3.8	3.9	4.0
Greece	5.8	7.8	7.5	10.0	11.6	9.8	10.5	9.6	8.8	8.1	7.6
Iceland				4.9	2.4	3.6	3.0	2.7	3.0	2.5	3.3
Ireland			13.2	12.3	4.3	4.4	4.4	4.3	4.4	4.6	6.3
Italy	7.4	10.3	11.0	11.6	10.5	8.6	8.0	7.7	6.8	6.1	6.8
Liechtenstein			0.1	0.9	1.1	2.2	2.4	2.5	2.6	2.7	2.7
Luxembourg				3.0	2.4	3.7	5.2	4.5	4.7	4.0	4.4
Malta	3.3	8.1	3.9	3.8	6.3	7.4	7.4	7.3	7.5	6.5	5.8
Monaco											
Netherlands	6.6	10.0	7.4	7.1	3.0	4.0	4.9	5.1	4.2	3.5	2.8
Norway	1.6	2.6	5.3	4.9	3.4	4.5	4.5	4.6	3.5	2.5	2.6
Portugal	7.5	8.1	4.6	7.2	4.1	6.4	6.6	7.7	7.8	8.1	7.7
Spain	11.4	21.6	16.3	22.9	13.9	11.5	11.0	9.2	8.5	8.3	11.3
Sweden	2.2	2.7	1.6	8.8	5.6	5.7	6.4	7.4	7.0	6.1	6.2
Switzerland				3.4	2.7	4.1	4.3	4.4	3.9	3.6	2.7
Turkey			7.3	7.1	6.5	10.3	10.1	10.0	9.7	9.7	10.6
United Kingdom				8.3	5.5	4.8	4.6	4.6	5.4	5.3	5.7
Eastern Europe											
Albania				17.7	22.9	20.8	20.0	19.6	19.2	18.9	18.8
Belarus					3.1	4.4	2.7	2.3	1.8	1.5	1.6
Bosnia-Herzegovina					27.1	28.8	30.9	31.1	29.0	23.4
Bulgaria				14.9	16.0	13.7	12.0	10.1	8.9	6.9	5.7
Croatia					15.9	14.2	13.8	12.7	11.1	9.6	8.5
Czech Republic			4.2	4.0	8.8	7.8	8.3	7.9	7.2	5.3	4.4
Estonia			0.7	9.3	12.7	10.0	9.6	7.9	5.9	4.7	5.6
Georgia					10.8	11.5	12.6	13.8	13.6	13.3	13.3
Hungary				10.2	6.4	5.9	6.1	7.2	7.5	7.4	7.9
Latvia			23.2	22.3	14.0	10.6	10.4	8.7	6.8	6.1	7.4
Lithuania			14.4	14.8	16.4	12.4	11.4	8.3	5.6	4.3	5.8
Macedonia		21.6	23.5	29.2	31.9	36.7	37.2	37.3	36.0	34.9	33.8
Moldova					8.5	7.9	8.1	7.3	7.4	5.1	4.8
Poland				13.4	16.1	19.6	19.0	17.8	13.8	9.6	7.1
Romania			4.8	8.0	7.1	7.0	8.0	7.2	7.3	6.4	5.8
Russia				9.7	10.2	7.9	7.9	7.6	7.2	6.1	6.3
Slovakia			7.7	13.0	18.7	17.5	18.1	16.2	13.3	11.0	9.6
Slovenia				7.4	6.9	6.5	6.0	6.5	5.9	4.8	4.4
Ukraine				5.6	11.5	8.9	8.6	7.2	6.8	6.4	6.3

Source: International Labour Organisation/Euromonitor International

Unemployment Rate by Quarter 2007-2009

% of economically active population

	2007 1st Quarter	2007 2nd Quarter	2007 3rd Quarter	2007 4th Quarter	2008 1st Quarter	2008 2nd Quarter	2008 3rd Quarter	2008 4th Quarter	2009 1st Quarter	2009 2nd Quarter
Western Europe										
Austria	4.6	4.4	4.6	4.0	4.2	3.4	3.7	3.9	4.7	4.6
Belgium	8.3	8.0	7.6	7.4	7.1	6.3	7.7	6.8	7.9	7.5
Cyprus	4.7	3.6	3.7	3.7	4.5	3.4	3.5	3.8	5.2	5.1
Denmark	4.5	3.7	4.1	3.3	3.3	3.0	3.4	3.5	5.2	6.0
Finland	7.6	7.7	6.0	6.1	6.7	7.3	5.6	6.0	7.6	9.6
France	8.6	7.7	7.8	7.7	8.2	7.7	8.0	8.8	9.8	9.6
Germany	9.4	8.6	8.4	8.1	7.9	7.4	6.9	6.9	7.8	7.5
Gibraltar										
Greece	8.9	7.9	7.7	7.9	8.3	7.2	7.2	8.0	9.4	8.9
Iceland	2.2	3.5	2.3	2.1	2.5	3.4	2.7	4.4	7.6	
Ireland	4.3	4.5	4.8	4.5	4.9	5.5	7.1	7.9	10.7	12.6
Italy	6.4	5.7	5.7	6.6	7.1	6.8	6.1	7.1	8.0	7.4
Liechtenstein										
Luxembourg	4.4	3.8	3.7	4.1	4.2	4.0	4.3	5.0	5.4	5.1
Malta	7.0	6.3	6.4	6.4	6.0	5.6	5.6	6.0	6.6	6.8
Monaco										
Netherlands	4.2	3.5	3.2	3.1	3.1	2.8	2.5	2.6	3.2	3.3
Norway	2.7	2.7	2.5	2.2	2.4	2.6	2.5	2.5	3.0	3.2
Portugal	8.5	8.0	8.0	7.9	7.9	7.5	8.0	8.1	9.2	9.3
Spain	8.5	8.0	8.0	8.6	9.7	10.5	11.4	13.9	17.4	18.0
Sweden	6.7	6.8	5.4	5.5	6.3	6.7	5.6	6.1	7.9	9.0
Switzerland	4.1	3.5	3.3	3.5	2.8	2.5	2.5	2.8	3.5	3.6
Turkey	11.0	8.7	9.0	10.0	11.5	8.9	9.9	12.2	15.5	13.3
United Kingdom	5.5	5.2	5.4	5.0	5.1	5.2	6.0	6.1	7.0	7.6
Eastern Europe										
Albania	19.3	19.1	18.7	18.7	19.2	18.6	18.6	18.7		
Belarus										
Bosnia-Herzegovina										
Bulgaria	8.0	6.8	6.6	6.1	6.6	5.9	5.2	5.1	6.5	6.4
Croatia	11.3	9.2	8.4	9.7	10.1	8.0	7.1	8.8	9.6	9.0
Czech Republic	6.0	5.3	5.1	4.9	4.7	4.2	4.3	4.4	5.8	6.3
Estonia	5.3	5.0	4.2	4.1	4.2	4.0	6.3	7.7	11.5	13.6
Georgia										
Hungary	7.5	7.0	7.2	7.7	8.0	7.7	7.8	8.1	9.7	9.6
Latvia	6.9	6.0	5.9	5.4	6.5	6.2	7.1	9.8	13.8	16.6
Lithuania	5.0	4.1	3.9	4.2	4.9	4.5	6.0	7.9	12.0	13.7
Macedonia										
Moldova	5.7	4.2	5.1	5.4						
Poland	11.3	9.6	9.0	8.5	8.0	7.1	6.6	6.7	8.3	7.9
Romania	7.0	6.5	6.0	6.1	6.3	5.6	5.4	5.8	6.9	6.3
Russia	7.2	5.9	5.6	5.6	6.9	5.8	5.7	6.9	8.7	
Slovakia	11.5	11.1	11.2	10.3	10.6	10.2	9.0	8.7	10.5	11.5
Slovenia	5.6	4.5	4.4	4.7	5.1	4.1	4.1	4.3	5.3	5.6
Ukraine										

Source: *International Labour Organisation/Euromonitor International*

Labour Statistics

Table 19.9

Unemployment Rate by Month 2008

% of economically active population

	January	February	March	April	May	June	July	August	September	October	November	December
Western Europe												
Austria	4.5	4.3	3.8	3.7	3.4	3.3	3.6	3.8	3.7	3.7	3.8	4.4
Belgium	7.3	7.1	6.8	6.4	6.1	6.5	7.7	7.9	7.5	6.9	6.6	6.9
Cyprus	4.7	4.6	4.2	3.4	3.2	3.4	3.9	3.4	3.3	3.2	3.8	4.3
Denmark	3.5	3.3	3.2	3.1	3.0	3.0	3.3	3.5	3.4	3.3	3.4	3.8
Finland	6.8	6.4	6.8	6.2	8.8	6.8	5.2	5.6	5.9	5.8	6.0	6.1
France	8.4	8.2	8.0	7.9	7.8	7.6	7.7	8.2	8.2	8.5	8.8	9.0
Germany	7.9	7.9	7.8	7.7	7.1	7.5	7.3	7.0	6.5	6.5	6.9	7.4
Gibraltar												
Greece	8.3	8.3	8.3	7.2	7.2	7.2	7.2	7.2	7.2	8.0	8.0	8.0
Iceland												
Ireland	4.9	4.9	5.1	5.1	5.4	6.1	6.9	7.3	7.1	7.3	7.8	8.6
Italy	7.1	7.1	7.1	6.8	6.8	6.8	6.1	6.1	6.1	7.1	7.1	7.1
Liechtenstein												
Luxembourg	4.3	4.4	4.1	4.0	4.0	3.9	4.2	4.3	4.5	4.8	5.0	5.3
Malta	6.1	6.0	5.8	5.7	5.5	5.4	5.5	5.7	5.6	5.8	6.2	5.9
Monaco												
Netherlands	3.0	3.2	3.2	3.0	2.8	2.6	2.4	2.5	2.6	2.6	2.5	2.7
Norway	2.3	2.5	2.4	2.4	2.7	2.7	2.6	2.5	2.5	2.6	2.5	2.6
Portugal	8.0	7.9	7.7	7.5	7.4	7.6	7.8	8.0	8.0	8.0	8.0	8.3
Spain	9.4	9.7	9.8	10.2	10.4	10.7	10.8	11.3	11.9	12.9	13.9	14.9
Sweden	6.4	6.1	6.3	6.0	5.9	8.1	5.8	5.2	5.9	5.7	6.2	6.4
Switzerland	2.9	2.8	2.7	2.7	2.5	2.4	2.4	2.5	2.5	2.6	2.8	3.1
Turkey	11.5	11.5	11.5	8.9	8.9	8.9	9.9	9.9	9.9	12.2	12.2	12.2
United Kingdom	5.0	5.2	5.2	5.0	5.2	5.5	5.8	6.0	6.0	6.1	6.0	6.2
Eastern Europe												
Albania												
Belarus												
Bosnia-Herzegovina												
Bulgaria	6.7	6.7	6.4	6.2	5.9	5.5	5.4	5.1	4.9	4.8	4.9	5.4
Croatia	10.2	10.1	9.9	8.4	8.0	7.6	7.1	7.0	7.2	8.6	8.8	9.0
Czech Republic	4.9	4.7	4.5	4.3	4.2	4.1	4.3	4.3	4.3	4.2	4.3	4.7
Estonia	4.2	4.2	4.2	4.0	4.0	4.0	6.3	6.3	6.3	7.7	7.7	7.7
Georgia												
Hungary	8.1	8.1	7.9	7.8	7.7	7.6	7.8	7.9	7.8	7.7	8.0	8.6
Latvia	6.3	6.7	6.6	6.4	6.1	6.3	6.7	7.1	7.7	8.6	9.8	11.1
Lithuania	4.9	4.9	4.9	4.5	4.5	4.5	6.0	6.0	6.0	7.9	7.9	7.9
Macedonia												
Moldova												
Poland	8.4	8.1	7.7	7.4	7.1	6.8	6.7	6.6	6.5	6.4	6.7	7.1
Romania	6.3	6.3	6.3	5.6	5.6	5.6	5.4	5.4	5.4	5.8	5.8	5.8
Russia	6.7	7.2	6.6	6.1	5.5	5.7	5.8	5.9	5.4	6.2	6.7	7.8
Slovakia	10.7	10.6	10.5	10.3	10.2	9.9	9.4	8.8	8.8	8.5	8.6	9.1
Slovenia	5.3	5.1	4.8	4.3	4.1	4.0	4.2	4.1	4.0	4.2	4.2	4.4
Ukraine												

Source: International Labour Organisation/Euromonitor International

Average Working Week in Non-Agricultural Activities 1980-2008
Hours

	1980	1985	1990	1995	2000	2003	2004	2005	2006	2007	2008
Western Europe											
Austria			34.6	35.4	35.4	35.8	34.2	33.5	33.0	32.6	32.2
Belgium	33.8	33.3	33.7	36.2	33.0	32.9	32.8	32.7	32.7	32.6	32.6
Cyprus	42.0	41.0	42.0	40.0	40.0	39.7	39.8	39.9	39.9	40.0	40.0
Denmark	32.6	32.1	31.5	31.5	31.6	31.7	31.7	31.7	31.8	31.8	31.8
Finland		36.4	35.5	36.5	36.3	35.9	36.0	35.9	35.8	35.8	35.7
France	40.8	38.9	39.0	38.9	36.9	35.6	35.6	35.7	35.8	35.9	35.6
Germany	41.6	40.7	39.7	38.5	38.2	38.0	38.0	37.9	37.8	37.7	37.7
Gibraltar	43.2	44.5	45.1	43.6	43.0	42.0	41.7	41.6	41.2	41.0	40.8
Greece				41.0	41.0	41.0	42.9	41.1	41.1	41.2	40.7
Iceland	49.3	48.6	46.4	46.0	42.8	41.0	40.4	39.8	39.2	38.7	38.3
Ireland			35.4	38.6	37.1	36.5	36.3	36.2	36.0	35.9	35.8
Italy	39.0	38.7	38.8	39.4	39.1	38.1	39.1	39.0	38.9	38.9	38.9
Liechtenstein											
Luxembourg	40.2	40.6	40.3	40.8	40.7	40.6	40.6	40.6	40.5	40.5	40.5
Malta	40.0	40.0	39.3	38.8	38.0	38.2	38.4	38.5	38.6	38.7	38.7
Monaco											
Netherlands	40.6	40.3	40.1	39.3	38.4	38.3	38.4	38.4	38.4	38.4	38.4
Norway	35.5	35.5	35.3	34.9	34.7	34.3	34.3	34.2	34.1	34.0	34.0
Portugal	38.4	41.0	41.1	38.1	37.3	36.5	35.4	35.7	35.9	36.1	36.3
Spain	40.1	37.5	36.6	36.0	35.8	35.1	34.9	34.6	34.4	34.2	34.1
Sweden	35.6	36.3	37.5	36.6	36.9	36.0	35.9	36.4	36.4	36.5	36.7
Switzerland	44.3	43.4	42.2	41.9	36.4	35.6	36.1	36.0	36.1	36.2	36.3
Turkey			50.1	51.3	51.6	51.9	52.5	54.0	54.6	55.3	56.0
United Kingdom			40.5	40.3	39.8	39.6	39.6	39.5	39.5	39.4	39.4
Eastern Europe											
Albania											
Belarus				35.5	38.3	38.3	39.0	39.2	39.4	39.7	39.9
Bosnia-Herzegovina											
Bulgaria					33.0	33.0	34.0	34.4	35.0	35.3	35.7
Croatia		45.5	44.5	44.5	41.8	41.5	41.5	41.3	41.2	41.1	41.0
Czech Republic				40.4	40.5	40.6	40.5	40.5	40.5	40.5	40.5
Estonia				34.0	34.7	34.4	34.7	34.9	35.0	35.0	35.1
Georgia					38.6	39.2	39.4	39.7	39.9	40.1	40.2
Hungary				36.6	37.3	37.0	37.6	37.7	37.9	38.1	38.3
Latvia				40.8	41.3	39.8	39.4	39.8	40.0	40.1	37.0
Lithuania				37.2	37.9	37.8	38.2	38.1	38.1	38.2	38.3
Macedonia											
Moldova				28.8	29.7	32.2	32.4	32.2	32.3	32.4	32.4
Poland	37.5	39.8	37.0	40.4	40.0	39.8	39.8	39.6	39.6	39.5	39.4
Romania				39.0	37.4	37.0	37.0	37.0	37.0	37.0	37.0
Russia				32.6	32.9	33.3	33.5	33.6	33.7	33.8	33.9
Slovakia				37.0	36.5	34.5	35.3	35.0	34.6	34.6	34.5
Slovenia		37.4	37.7	40.7	40.5	36.7	36.0	36.3	36.3	36.2	36.2
Ukraine				32.0	34.3	34.8	34.8	35.0	35.2	35.3

Source: *International Labour Organisation/Euromonitor International*
Notes: *Hours actually worked by wage earners, unless otherwise stated*

Table 19.11

Average Working Week in Manufacturing 1980-2008
Hours

	1980	1985	1990	1995	2000	2003	2004	2005	2006	2007	2008
Western Europe											
Austria	36.5	36.2	34.9	34.7	35.1	34.8	35.1	34.8	34.7	34.7	34.6
Belgium	33.4	33.1	33.4	32.9	32.9	32.9	32.9	32.9	32.9	32.8	32.8
Cyprus	41.0	41.0	41.0	40.0	40.2	40.1	40.0	39.9	39.9	39.8	39.8
Denmark	32.6	32.1	31.5	31.5	31.6	31.7	31.7	31.7	31.8	31.8	31.8
Finland	33.2	32.3	38.2	38.0	38.0	37.5	37.5	37.4	37.3	37.2	37.1
France	40.6	38.6	38.7	38.7	36.6	36.2	36.7	36.9	37.3	37.6	37.8
Germany	41.6	40.7	37.8	38.6	37.9	37.7	37.6	37.5	37.5	37.4	37.3
Gibraltar	45.8	48.7	46.9	46.8	45.1	44.8	50.0	49.1	50.2	50.2	50.3
Greece	40.7	39.3	41.1	41.1	43.0	42.0	42.3	42.3	42.4	42.5	42.5
Iceland				42.9	43.5	42.5	42.5	42.3	42.0	41.8	41.6
Ireland	41.1	41.1	41.5	40.8	40.7	39.7	39.9	40.0	39.8	39.9	39.8
Italy	38.5	39.0	39.0	40.7	40.5	39.2	39.4	39.8	39.9	40.1	40.3
Liechtenstein											
Luxembourg	40.0	40.2	39.8	40.2	40.0	39.7	39.6	39.5	39.4	39.3	39.2
Malta	40.0	40.0	39.9	39.9	41.0	38.7	39.4	39.6	39.8	39.8	39.9
Monaco											
Netherlands	40.8	40.3	39.9	39.0	38.6	38.5	38.5	38.5	38.5	38.5	38.5
Norway	38.1	38.2	37.0	36.7	36.5	36.3	36.3	36.3	36.2	36.2	36.1
Portugal	39.0	40.8	40.7	38.2	39.5	37.9	39.5	39.9	40.1	40.3	40.5
Spain	38.8	36.5	36.7	36.8	36.1	36.0	35.8	36.2	36.2	36.3	36.4
Sweden	37.7	38.4	38.5	37.6	38.2	37.5	37.5	37.9	38.1	38.2	38.4
Switzerland	43.8	43.0	41.6	41.4	41.1	39.6	39.9	40.3	40.5	40.8	41.0
Turkey			48.8	50.9	51.3	52.2	52.1	53.7	54.2	54.7	55.4
United Kingdom		41.8	42.4	42.2	41.4	41.0	40.9	40.8	40.6	40.5	40.5
Eastern Europe											
Albania											
Belarus											
Bosnia-Herzegovina											
Bulgaria					33.0	33.0	34.0	34.4	35.0	35.3	35.7
Croatia		46.2	45.1	44.3	41.5	41.3	41.4	41.0	40.9	40.7	40.5
Czech Republic	43.5	43.1	40.1	40.4	40.7	40.7	40.6	40.6	40.5	40.5	40.5
Estonia				33.1	33.9	33.7	34.0	34.0	34.1	34.2	34.2
Georgia					38.0	40.1	40.7	41.4	42.1	42.6	43.1
Hungary	40.2	36.3	35.9	36.8	37.4	37.0	37.6	37.7	37.9	38.2	38.3
Latvia				38.8	41.0	40.4	40.6	40.9	41.0	41.2	36.2
Lithuania					38.6	38.8	38.9	38.9	39.0	39.1	39.1
Macedonia											
Moldova		34.9	34.5	22.3	24.4	29.7	30.3	30.4	31.1	31.5	31.8
Poland	39.8	38.3	35.8	41.7	41.3	41.1	41.2	41.2	41.2	41.3	41.3
Romania		39.5	39.0	38.2	39.5	40.9	40.8	40.6	41.0	41.0	41.1
Russia				28.9	29.1	28.8	28.6	28.5	28.4	28.3	28.2
Slovakia				35.3	35.5	34.3	35.5	35.5	35.5	35.5	35.5
Slovenia		37.1	37.5	40.7	40.3	36.7	36.1	37.1	37.4	37.6	37.9
Ukraine					29.5	34.0	35.5	35.5	36.2	36.7	37.1

Source: *International Labour Organisation/Euromonitor International*
Notes: *Hours actually worked by wage earners, unless otherwise stated*

Labour Statistics

Table 19.12

Economically Active Population by Age Group 2008
'000

	Under 15	15-19	20-24	25-29	30-34	35-39	40-44
Western Europe							
Austria		213.3	384.4	450.1	491.8	613.9	648.8
Belgium		66.5	392.4	582.9	600.7	662.4	722.6
Cyprus		11.9	34.1	56.5	53.1	46.7	49.0
Denmark		212.0	230.9	277.7	338.9	356.4	378.6
Finland		119.2	244.9	281.8	279.7	295.7	344.1
France		629.3	2,253.2	3,413.6	3,559.9	3,824.0	3,962.7
Germany		1,513.3	3,392.2	4,116.6	4,078.3	5,203.5	6,527.0
Gibraltar							
Greece		56.2	320.3	677.1	709.4	715.5	689.3
Iceland		14.6	17.0	19.6	19.1	19.6	20.2
Ireland		81.2	269.2	355.0	304.7	272.6	249.4
Italy		324.2	1,547.4	2,636.8	3,629.0	3,889.8	3,845.8
Liechtenstein							
Luxembourg		2.5	13.0	27.0	32.1	34.6	34.9
Malta		9.6	23.2	22.4	20.8	18.7	18.2
Monaco							
Netherlands		643.8	802.4	876.9	893.8	1,111.2	1,132.8
Norway		138.2	215.3	256.3	295.9	331.7	315.8
Portugal		98.8	431.8	700.3	784.3	712.8	709.9
Spain		553.7	1,840.8	3,069.8	3,524.9	3,271.1	3,038.6
Sweden		191.6	398.5	481.7	560.0	593.8	617.9
Switzerland		241.0	362.6	425.6	447.2	514.1	573.2
Turkey	521.8	1,557.9	2,627.0	3,809.0	3,695.5	3,143.7	2,614.4
United Kingdom		1,667.4	3,118.9	3,448.0	3,136.0	3,722.7	3,855.3
Eastern Europe							
Albania							
Belarus		72.9	534.7	592.4	563.4	568.4	601.4
Bosnia-Herzegovina		30.0	118.0	141.1	150.3	154.2	154.9
Bulgaria		38.3	263.4	340.3	451.7	500.2	493.2
Croatia		34.2	144.7	198.1	176.1	201.5	247.3
Czech Republic		46.3	383.5	651.3	766.9	654.3	664.2
Estonia		12.7	64.6	81.7	83.5	81.9	86.0
Georgia		43.7	138.1	164.1	186.0	183.7	216.6
Hungary		27.2	289.5	592.5	633.5	614.4	495.5
Latvia		27.6	122.3	136.6	141.8	143.5	152.7
Lithuania		12.7	137.8	178.0	202.7	213.1	219.2
Macedonia		29.4	89.6	122.8	127.0	119.8	120.4
Moldova		32.0	105.8	126.5	133.8	145.8	168.5
Poland		210.3	1,623.1	2,477.4	2,482.8	2,102.1	1,985.4
Romania		188.9	755.3	1,257.8	1,404.0	1,484.8	1,152.8
Russia		1,741.0	7,857.8	9,806.3	9,369.4	8,674.7	9,765.7
Slovakia		28.4	244.4	383.5	384.8	335.7	348.7
Slovenia		21.6	87.5	132.4	140.7	141.9	139.4
Ukraine		639.4	2,363.2	2,753.2	2,736.6	2,650.7	3,166.6

Source: *International Labour Organisation/Euromonitor International*

Labour Statistics

Economically Active Population by Age Group 2008 *(continued)*
'000

	45-49	50-54	55-59	60-64	Over 65	Total
Western Europe						
Austria	566.1	437.2	282.5	79.7	55.0	4,222.6
Belgium	685.4	555.2	376.5	99.0	43.7	4,787.3
Cyprus	47.3	40.6	30.7	16.6	10.0	396.6
Denmark	333.5	309.0	298.3	127.6	29.1	2,892.0
Finland	340.1	338.2	300.2	135.8	33.1	2,712.8
France	3,746.4	3,498.7	2,403.5	509.5	135.6	27,936.4
Germany	5,783.6	4,916.6	4,301.5	1,626.5	645.2	42,104.4
Gibraltar						
Greece	615.8	505.1	360.0	190.0	90.3	4,928.9
Iceland	20.5	18.8	15.9	11.3	6.1	182.6
Ireland	228.5	192.1	147.8	87.2	43.6	2,231.4
Italy	3,288.7	2,738.4	1,795.2	654.5	378.2	24,727.9
Liechtenstein						
Luxembourg	30.9	25.1	14.0	2.7	0.4	217.3
Malta	20.4	19.0	9.5	2.7		164.5
Monaco						
Netherlands	1,079.6	928.5	736.5	328.0	117.0	8,650.5
Norway	290.4	269.7	239.7	158.6	50.3	2,562.0
Portugal	645.2	551.3	405.5	253.7	334.4	5,628.1
Spain	2,671.6	2,126.2	1,498.3	823.5	153.5	22,571.9
Sweden	540.7	525.4	522.0	393.3	90.1	4,915.0
Switzerland	532.4	453.8	391.9	248.2	107.9	4,297.9
Turkey	2,011.9	1,376.1	814.3	484.7	512.3	23,168.5
United Kingdom	3,916.8	3,426.3	2,507.1	1,533.4	619.7	30,951.6
Eastern Europe						
Albania						
Belarus	688.5	564.3	276.6	53.9	24.8	4,541.3
Bosnia-Herzegovina	151.6	114.8	81.6	36.6	29.0	1,162.0
Bulgaria	565.0	374.6	337.4	139.8	57.7	3,561.6
Croatia	262.0	244.6	160.9	55.7	47.5	1,772.4
Czech Republic	609.2	681.3	521.2	176.1	67.2	5,221.5
Estonia	76.5	80.6	58.8	34.8	23.9	685.1
Georgia	214.8	222.1	185.2	107.3	287.4	1,949.3
Hungary	512.3	593.8	344.1	73.3	29.2	4,205.4
Latvia	153.0	129.7	100.0	50.6	41.1	1,198.8
Lithuania	232.9	176.8	135.8	64.7	32.4	1,606.0
Macedonia	116.2	103.2	63.2	22.6	8.1	922.1
Moldova	213.2	152.1	132.1	39.3	43.4	1,292.5
Poland	2,185.1	2,090.7	1,093.7	328.3	226.0	16,805.0
Romania	1,051.7	1,073.8	733.0	325.1	472.6	9,899.9
Russia	10,914.9	9,049.1	5,579.2	1,382.3	1,258.0	75,398.4
Slovakia	350.0	343.6	194.2	42.3	6.1	2,661.8
Slovenia	147.6	121.3	68.1	16.9	19.9	1,037.2
Ukraine	2,980.9	2,518.0	1,204.5	612.6	462.2	22,087.8

Source: International Labour Organisation/Euromonitor International

Labour Statistics

Table 19.13

Economically Active Population by Age Group 2008 (% Analysis)
% of total EAP

	Under 15	15-19	20-24	25-29	30-34	35-39	40-44
Western Europe							
Austria		5.1	9.1	10.7	11.6	14.5	15.4
Belgium		1.4	8.2	12.2	12.5	13.8	15.1
Cyprus		3.0	8.6	14.2	13.4	11.8	12.4
Denmark		7.3	8.0	9.6	11.7	12.3	13.1
Finland		4.4	9.0	10.4	10.3	10.9	12.7
France		2.3	8.1	12.2	12.7	13.7	14.2
Germany		3.6	8.1	9.8	9.7	12.4	15.5
Gibraltar							
Greece		1.1	6.5	13.7	14.4	14.5	14.0
Iceland		8.0	9.3	10.7	10.5	10.7	11.0
Ireland		3.6	12.1	15.9	13.7	12.2	11.2
Italy		1.3	6.3	10.7	14.7	15.7	15.6
Liechtenstein							
Luxembourg		1.1	6.0	12.4	14.8	15.9	16.1
Malta		5.9	14.1	13.6	12.6	11.3	11.1
Monaco							
Netherlands		7.4	9.3	10.1	10.3	12.8	13.1
Norway		5.4	8.4	10.0	11.5	12.9	12.3
Portugal		1.8	7.7	12.4	13.9	12.7	12.6
Spain		2.5	8.2	13.6	15.6	14.5	13.5
Sweden		3.9	8.1	9.8	11.4	12.1	12.6
Switzerland		5.6	8.4	9.9	10.4	12.0	13.3
Turkey	2.3	6.7	11.3	16.4	16.0	13.6	11.3
United Kingdom		5.4	10.1	11.1	10.1	12.0	12.5
Eastern Europe							
Albania							
Belarus		1.6	11.8	13.0	12.4	12.5	13.2
Bosnia-Herzegovina		2.6	10.2	12.1	12.9	13.3	13.3
Bulgaria		1.1	7.4	9.6	12.7	14.0	13.8
Croatia		1.9	8.2	11.2	9.9	11.4	14.0
Czech Republic		0.9	7.3	12.5	14.7	12.5	12.7
Estonia		1.9	9.4	11.9	12.2	12.0	12.6
Georgia		2.2	7.1	8.4	9.5	9.4	11.1
Hungary		0.6	6.9	14.1	15.1	14.6	11.8
Latvia		2.3	10.2	11.4	11.8	12.0	12.7
Lithuania		0.8	8.6	11.1	12.6	13.3	13.6
Macedonia		3.2	9.7	13.3	13.8	13.0	13.1
Moldova		2.5	8.2	9.8	10.3	11.3	13.0
Poland		1.3	9.7	14.7	14.8	12.5	11.8
Romania		1.9	7.6	12.7	14.2	15.0	11.6
Russia		2.3	10.4	13.0	12.4	11.5	13.0
Slovakia		1.1	9.2	14.4	14.5	12.6	13.1
Slovenia		2.1	8.4	12.8	13.6	13.7	13.4
Ukraine		2.9	10.7	12.5	12.4	12.0	14.3

Source: International Labour Organisation/Euromonitor International

Labour Statistics

Economically Active Population by Age Group 2008 (% Analysis) *(continued)*
% of total EAP

	45-49	50-54	55-59	60-64	Over 65	Total
Western Europe						
Austria	13.4	10.4	6.7	1.9	1.3	100.0
Belgium	14.3	11.6	7.9	2.1	0.9	100.0
Cyprus	11.9	10.2	7.7	4.2	2.5	100.0
Denmark	11.5	10.7	10.3	4.4	1.0	100.0
Finland	12.5	12.5	11.1	5.0	1.2	100.0
France	13.4	12.5	8.6	1.8	0.5	100.0
Germany	13.7	11.7	10.2	3.9	1.5	100.0
Gibraltar						
Greece	12.5	10.2	7.3	3.9	1.8	100.0
Iceland	11.2	10.3	8.7	6.2	3.3	100.0
Ireland	10.2	8.6	6.6	3.9	2.0	100.0
Italy	13.3	11.1	7.3	2.6	1.5	100.0
Liechtenstein						
Luxembourg	14.2	11.5	6.4	1.3	0.2	100.0
Malta	12.4	11.6	5.7	1.7		100.0
Monaco						
Netherlands	12.5	10.7	8.5	3.8	1.4	100.0
Norway	11.3	10.5	9.4	6.2	2.0	100.0
Portugal	11.5	9.8	7.2	4.5	5.9	100.0
Spain	11.8	9.4	6.6	3.6	0.7	100.0
Sweden	11.0	10.7	10.6	8.0	1.8	100.0
Switzerland	12.4	10.6	9.1	5.8	2.5	100.0
Turkey	8.7	5.9	3.5	2.1	2.2	100.0
United Kingdom	12.7	11.1	8.1	5.0	2.0	100.0
Eastern Europe						
Albania						
Belarus	15.2	12.4	6.1	1.2	0.5	100.0
Bosnia-Herzegovina	13.0	9.9	7.0	3.1	2.5	100.0
Bulgaria	15.9	10.5	9.5	3.9	1.6	100.0
Croatia	14.8	13.8	9.1	3.1	2.7	100.0
Czech Republic	11.7	13.0	10.0	3.4	1.3	100.0
Estonia	11.2	11.8	8.6	5.1	3.5	100.0
Georgia	11.0	11.4	9.5	5.5	14.7	100.0
Hungary	12.2	14.1	8.2	1.7	0.7	100.0
Latvia	12.8	10.8	8.3	4.2	3.4	100.0
Lithuania	14.5	11.0	8.5	4.0	2.0	100.0
Macedonia	12.6	11.2	6.9	2.4	0.9	100.0
Moldova	16.5	11.8	10.2	3.0	3.4	100.0
Poland	13.0	12.4	6.5	2.0	1.3	100.0
Romania	10.6	10.8	7.4	3.3	4.8	100.0
Russia	14.5	12.0	7.4	1.8	1.7	100.0
Slovakia	13.1	12.9	7.3	1.6	0.2	100.0
Slovenia	14.2	11.7	6.6	1.6	1.9	100.0
Ukraine	13.5	11.4	5.5	2.8	2.1	100.0

Source: International Labour Organisation/Euromonitor International

Labour Statistics | **Table 19.14**

Economically Active Population by Sex 2008
As stated

	Total ('000)	EAP as % Total Population	Males ('000)	Males as % Total EAP	Females ('000)	Females as % Total EAP
Western Europe						
Austria	4,223	50.6	2,290	54.2	1,933	45.8
Belgium	4,787	45.1	2,609	54.5	2,178	45.5
Cyprus	397	46.0	219	55.1	178	44.9
Denmark	2,892	53.0	1,527	52.8	1,365	47.2
Finland	2,713	51.2	1,406	51.8	1,307	48.2
France	27,936	45.0	14,740	52.8	13,196	47.2
Germany	42,104	51.2	22,770	54.1	19,335	45.9
Gibraltar	13	45.3	8	57.7	6	42.3
Greece	4,929	44.0	2,923	59.3	2,006	40.7
Iceland	183	57.9	99	54.3	83	45.7
Ireland	2,231	51.0	1,271	57.0	960	43.0
Italy	24,728	41.9	14,779	59.8	9,949	40.2
Liechtenstein	32	90.0				
Luxembourg	217	45.2	120	55.0	98	45.0
Malta	165	40.4	108	65.8	56	34.2
Monaco						
Netherlands	8,651	52.8	4,692	54.2	3,958	45.8
Norway	2,562	54.1	1,350	52.7	1,212	47.3
Portugal	5,628	52.9	2,996	53.2	2,632	46.8
Spain	22,572	50.1	12,979	57.5	9,593	42.5
Sweden	4,915	53.7	2,582	52.5	2,333	47.5
Switzerland	4,298	57.1	2,334	54.3	1,964	45.7
Turkey	23,169	31.2	17,208	74.3	5,960	25.7
United Kingdom	30,952	50.6	16,830	54.4	14,121	45.6
Eastern Europe						
Albania	1,321	42.0	656	49.6	665	50.4
Belarus	4,541	46.9	2,142	47.2	2,399	52.8
Bosnia-Herzegovina	1,162	30.2	729	62.7	433	37.3
Bulgaria	3,562	47.0	1,897	53.3	1,664	46.7
Croatia	1,772	40.0	970	54.7	802	45.3
Czech Republic	5,222	50.6	2,958	56.6	2,264	43.4
Estonia	685	51.3	338	49.3	347	50.7
Georgia	1,949	44.5	1,022	52.4	927	47.6
Hungary	4,205	41.9	2,287	54.4	1,918	45.6
Latvia	1,199	52.9	618	51.6	581	48.4
Lithuania	1,606	47.7	816	50.8	790	49.2
Macedonia	922	45.2	557	60.4	365	39.6
Moldova	1,293	35.6	655	50.7	637	49.3
Poland	16,805	44.2	9,230	54.9	7,575	45.1
Romania	9,900	46.1	5,510	55.7	4,390	44.3
Russia	75,398	53.1	38,151	50.6	37,247	49.4
Slovakia	2,662	49.4	1,469	55.2	1,193	44.8
Slovenia	1,037	51.4	565	54.5	472	45.5
Ukraine	22,088	47.8	10,397	47.1	11,691	52.9

Source: *International Labour Organisation/Euromonitor International*

Labour Statistics   **Table 19.15**

Employed Male Population by Quarter 2007-2009
'000

	2007 1st Quarter	2007 2nd Quarter	2007 3rd Quarter	2007 4th Quarter	2008 1st Quarter	2008 2nd Quarter	2008 3rd Quarter	2008 4th Quarter	2009 1st Quarter	2009 2nd Quarter
Western Europe										
Austria	2,153.7	2,221.8	2,247.7	2,211.2	2,157.9	2,225.4	2,239.1	2,204.8	2,125.3	
Belgium	2,416.2	2,396.4	2,419.3	2,426.6	2,440.5	2,426.0	2,442.5	2,451.3	2,413.7	
Cyprus	204.5	209.2	210.7	212.8	208.9	212.0	212.1	213.1	207.6	
Denmark	1,477.4	1,484.4	1,477.4	1,467.4	1,461.6	1,491.3	1,495.2	1,475.4	1,433.9	
Finland	1,256.0	1,331.2	1,348.4	1,304.4	1,283.8	1,346.3	1,343.0	1,302.9	1,250.7	1,279.4
France	13,424.9	13,609.4	13,758.2	13,660.7	13,554.3	13,674.8	13,769.7	13,638.3	13,368.5	
Germany										
Gibraltar										
Greece	2,740.1	2,763.1	2,778.5	2,765.3	2,775.2	2,806.0	2,807.7	2,780.8	2,727.4	
Iceland	92.8	96.3	98.4	96.1	93.8	98.7	99.0	92.6	85.4	
Ireland	1,185.3	1,193.3	1,215.5	1,211.5	1,216.0	1,194.1	1,194.4	1,147.0	1,072.8	
Italy	13,833.5	14,121.5	14,197.7	14,076.1	13,832.7	14,095.6	14,086.5	13,904.6	13,670.9	
Liechtenstein										
Luxembourg	112.7	114.7	115.3	114.0	113.3	118.8	117.1	111.8		
Malta	104.0	103.9	104.3	102.9	102.0	100.3	103.3	103.8	103.8	
Monaco										
Netherlands	4,505.3	4,551.2	4,579.0	4,560.4	4,527.5	4,582.0	4,580.0	4,605.2	4,569.8	
Norway	1,261.8	1,282.8	1,296.7	1,306.7	1,295.1	1,320.7	1,326.6	1,310.8	1,292.1	1,311.8
Portugal	2,769.6	2,776.4	2,794.7	2,795.7	2,803.3	2,809.0	2,793.6	2,785.0	2,719.2	2,703.5
Spain	11,854.5	12,007.6	12,089.5	11,997.0	11,946.4	11,881.8	11,781.1	11,362.0	10,851.4	10,721.1
Sweden	2,332.3	2,386.0	2,448.6	2,394.2	2,391.1	2,442.3	2,479.7	2,410.7	2,347.5	2,370.0
Switzerland	2,232.9	2,257.3	2,276.1	2,276.0	2,277.4	2,290.5	2,301.7	2,283.9	2,278.2	
Turkey	15,386.2	16,168.5	16,524.0	15,942.7	14,767.8	15,650.5	15,857.3	15,252.7	14,473.2	15,147.9
United Kingdom	15,588.6	15,679.3	15,853.7	15,867.7	15,821.1	15,840.0	15,880.8	15,804.1	15,567.9	
Eastern Europe										
Albania										
Belarus										
Bosnia-Herzegovina										
Bulgaria	1,667.4	1,723.8	1,765.1	1,769.8	1,754.3	1,799.7	1,831.1	1,807.7	1,743.9	
Croatia	869.8	896.2	924.6	899.9	879.8	907.2	923.1	895.2	876.3	
Czech Republic	2,767.9	2,793.0	2,824.7	2,841.1	2,827.7	2,847.5	2,867.9	2,879.2	2,824.8	
Estonia	325.5	329.6	333.5	331.4	320.5	317.1	315.1	309.9	282.4	272.3
Georgia										
Hungary	2,125.5	2,155.1	2,161.9	2,129.5	2,100.6	2,123.0	2,148.5	2,104.3	2,041.3	
Latvia	553.8	566.7	583.2	590.1	579.5	579.3	574.8	547.1	508.7	
Lithuania	760.5	780.3	794.1	776.0	762.4	777.7	771.6	749.9	691.9	
Macedonia	348.7	359.8	366.7	359.8	360.4	367.0	381.1	375.6	385.4	
Moldova	604.3	653.9	638.5	589.3	570.8	668.9	648.8	577.6	536.1	
Poland	8,225.1	8,360.1	8,473.7	8,553.1	8,490.0	8,587.7	8,747.8	8,734.4	8,559.6	
Romania	5,017.8	5,152.7	5,272.4	5,033.3	5,050.2	5,224.2	5,252.9	5,087.3	5,005.0	
Russia										
Slovakia	1,296.0	1,308.0	1,335.0	1,348.2	1,323.1	1,329.1	1,369.5	1,369.1	1,327.3	
Slovenia	524.2	542.2	551.5	540.9	529.1	539.1	557.6	543.0	515.3	
Ukraine										

Source: International Labour Organisation/Euromonitor International

Labour Statistics   **Table 19.16**

Employed Female Population by Quarter 2007-2009
'000

	2007 1st Quarter	2007 2nd Quarter	2007 3rd Quarter	2007 4th Quarter	2008 1st Quarter	2008 2nd Quarter	2008 3rd Quarter	2008 4th Quarter	2009 1st Quarter	2009 2nd Quarter
Western Europe										
Austria	1,794.9	1,813.1	1,847.5	1,821.8	1,830.8	1,854.7	1,871.1	1,864.4	1,869.0	
Belgium	1,917.3	1,934.4	1,951.9	2,002.8	2,017.0	1,996.1	2,030.2	2,011.6	2,012.4	
Cyprus	164.8	168.7	169.0	171.9	169.5	170.6	168.4	171.2	167.8	
Denmark	1,297.6	1,318.7	1,315.7	1,320.8	1,298.1	1,319.9	1,313.0	1,324.8	1,304.1	
Finland	1,177.8	1,212.7	1,213.1	1,200.4	1,198.5	1,237.4	1,232.7	1,215.9	1,205.6	1,227.3
France	11,827.2	11,992.0	12,109.8	12,133.6	12,045.1	12,121.1	12,202.1	12,084.3	12,071.4	
Germany										
Gibraltar										
Greece	1,731.0	1,767.0	1,771.1	1,764.1	1,729.4	1,769.1	1,774.6	1,765.3	1,750.7	
Iceland	79.3	82.0	81.7	79.4	78.4	80.8	82.8	80.6	77.2	
Ireland	878.9	891.2	914.4	916.3	908.0	903.2	910.6	886.9	867.3	
Italy	9,013.2	9,176.9	9,219.8	9,250.1	8,989.1	9,130.9	9,078.5	9,092.4	8,948.7	
Liechtenstein										
Luxembourg	87.8	86.1	88.7	99.2	90.2	95.4	91.7	92.7		
Malta	49.0	51.0	52.0	52.4	50.4	54.3	54.3	51.3	52.3	
Monaco										
Netherlands	3,706.6	3,765.8	3,781.1	3,798.6	3,796.0	3,818.0	3,863.4	3,878.5	3,897.7	
Norway	1,134.0	1,151.0	1,162.0	1,177.0	1,174.1	1,184.0	1,188.0	1,187.0	1,187.0	1,187.0
Portugal	2,359.7	2,371.8	2,398.9	2,385.9	2,382.4	2,413.6	2,396.7	2,385.9	2,374.5	2,367.3
Spain	8,214.5	8,359.4	8,420.8	8,479.6	8,214.2	8,298.9	8,319.8	8,250.8	8,002.5	7,987.2
Sweden	2,098.2	2,149.3	2,200.4	2,153.7	2,145.6	2,193.8	2,220.9	2,163.4	2,135.3	2,165.3
Switzerland	1,839.0	1,853.6	1,875.5	1,884.7	1,884.0	1,902.5	1,884.8	1,909.0	1,909.8	
Turkey	5,439.2	6,054.7	6,050.8	5,409.9	4,801.5	5,577.4	5,648.5	5,279.7	5,006.5	5,740.9
United Kingdom	13,250.2	13,285.0	13,391.4	13,484.0	13,353.0	13,363.9	13,379.7	13,368.8	13,293.8	
Eastern Europe										
Albania										
Belarus										
Bosnia-Herzegovina										
Bulgaria	1,467.8	1,529.2	1,550.3	1,536.6	1,533.4	1,570.3	1,584.1	1,553.8	1,516.9	
Croatia	692.1	712.1	735.4	723.6	698.3	717.4	743.0	724.3	718.4	
Czech Republic	2,097.3	2,121.1	2,117.3	2,126.3	2,120.0	2,144.9	2,136.1	2,143.5	2,111.3	
Estonia	321.3	328.8	328.5	322.2	326.2	329.9	336.1	333.4	321.6	312.6
Georgia										
Hungary	1,780.0	1,787.2	1,785.3	1,779.9	1,738.0	1,740.0	1,770.3	1,770.6	1,717.0	
Latvia	531.6	542.3	548.6	559.7	543.3	547.6	542.8	524.1	523.7	
Lithuania	747.1	763.6	766.1	748.9	740.2	739.7	758.2	749.6	733.9	
Macedonia	230.5	229.4	231.6	234.2	241.8	241.7	240.1	234.3	234.1	
Moldova	581.6	671.2	655.4	593.8	564.2	665.9	640.0	587.2	536.4	
Poland	6,613.6	6,791.6	6,958.3	6,984.6	6,838.4	6,913.6	7,050.8	7,079.1	6,966.4	
Romania	4,091.4	4,293.5	4,421.7	4,143.9	4,028.8	4,227.5	4,331.8	4,109.8	3,994.3	
Russia										
Slovakia	1,031.3	1,029.5	1,031.4	1,049.9	1,040.4	1,047.6	1,074.6	1,068.1	1,033.1	
Slovenia	433.4	451.4	454.7	442.4	437.1	446.5	460.3	453.4	442.2	
Ukraine										

Source: *International Labour Organisation/Euromonitor International*

Unemployed Male Population by Quarter 2007-2009

'000

	2007 1st Quarter	2007 2nd Quarter	2007 3rd Quarter	2007 4th Quarter	2008 1st Quarter	2008 2nd Quarter	2008 3rd Quarter	2008 4th Quarter	2009 1st Quarter	2009 2nd Quarter
Western Europe										
Austria	121.4	75.6	68.6	93.2	103.7	68.3	64.8	95.4	131.7	96.4
Belgium	196.2	182.8	192.6	184.4	169.6	160.0	172.5	173.4	187.0	188.8
Cyprus	8.8	7.4	6.5	7.0	8.5	5.9	6.7	7.7	10.5	
Denmark	73.2	56.3	46.4	41.9	56.1	40.9	37.0	50.6	95.2	110.1
Finland	100.3	103.9	76.1	79.7	89.3	103.6	71.0	82.2	115.8	152.8
France	1,197.6	1,043.2	1,058.7	1,076.6	1,091.7	988.6	1,048.5	1,195.7	1,380.0	1,350.2
Germany	2,232.8	1,966.1	1,834.2	1,723.3	1,827.7	1,630.9	1,535.7	1,505.2	1,899.8	1,862.2
Gibraltar										
Greece	158.8	137.1	135.5	144.2	142.6	120.4	120.8	137.5	173.9	
Iceland	2.1	3.8	1.8	2.3	2.3	3.1	2.6	4.8	8.1	
Ireland	54.9	58.6	63.6	63.3	63.6	73.0	89.7	107.0	145.5	
Italy	772.7	675.2	660.0	780.4	824.9	786.2	710.7	875.8	984.5	
Liechtenstein										
Luxembourg										
Malta	7.1	6.6	6.3	6.3	5.9	5.9	5.7	6.2	6.6	6.8
Monaco										
Netherlands	173.5	146.7	133.3	122.5	130.1	121.9	107.0	115.7	142.5	108.5
Norway	40.4	32.9	33.0	29.7	37.3	32.4	35.1	42.0	68.1	70.1
Portugal	228.3	200.2	188.8	190.6	197.3	190.8	191.5	212.6	257.7	276.3
Spain	818.4	773.2	804.0	865.6	1,030.5	1,102.2	1,245.6	1,566.5	1,886.3	1,957.5
Sweden	168.1	146.8	149.1	130.0	149.1	164.9	141.8	150.1	201.3	242.1
Switzerland	78.4	63.7	58.0	63.9	49.8	42.1	40.3	49.8	64.6	65.8
Turkey	1,889.5	1,604.4	1,562.3	1,743.7	1,878.1	1,581.6	1,707.6	2,137.6	2,708.3	2,398.7
United Kingdom	966.2	918.0	963.3	871.7	890.7	914.4	1,059.9	1,110.2	1,265.7	
Eastern Europe										
Albania										
Belarus										
Bosnia-Herzegovina										
Bulgaria	138.5	125.3	113.5	105.5	113.6	101.8	92.4	88.7	116.3	
Croatia	88.2	92.7	71.2	73.2	76.6	67.5	63.3	67.1	78.0	78.3
Czech Republic	142.6	125.1	118.0	106.4	111.3	100.2	95.6	102.3	147.7	
Estonia	21.6	18.2	17.8	18.1	15.8	20.0	22.2	30.6	43.8	
Georgia										
Hungary	179.8	160.4	154.1	162.4	183.6	162.3	156.1	169.9	214.3	220.6
Latvia	45.9	41.5	36.9	33.3	42.1	42.5	45.7	61.6	107.1	
Lithuania	42.8	33.4	29.7	32.5	50.4	45.4	46.0	60.7	122.2	
Macedonia	194.0	190.7	184.6	187.9	195.2	190.5	177.4	181.6	177.5	
Moldova	44.4	35.1	42.5	44.1	52.1	30.9	34.9	37.2	75.0	
Poland	1,022.7	848.0	740.7	712.6	697.2	588.4	525.5	549.7	737.2	743.9
Romania	488.0	390.5	342.9	362.2	383.8	341.1	332.4	366.2	491.6	546.5
Russia										
Slovakia	161.6	142.6	138.0	131.7	120.0	120.3	116.8	126.9	162.1	
Slovenia	24.3	21.8	21.0	21.7	24.0	22.0	21.8	23.9	29.6	33.0
Ukraine										

Source: International Labour Organisation/Euromonitor International

Labour Statistics
Table 19.18

Unemployed Female Population by Quarter 2007-2009
'000

	2007 1st Quarter	2007 2nd Quarter	2007 3rd Quarter	2007 4th Quarter	2008 1st Quarter	2008 2nd Quarter	2008 3rd Quarter	2008 4th Quarter	2009 1st Quarter	2009 2nd Quarter
Western Europe										
Austria	99.6	93.5	90.5	100.0	76.8	74.5	74.1	84.6	85.5	86.8
Belgium	183.6	172.4	191.1	174.4	164.5	156.4	175.1	162.6	165.6	163.8
Cyprus	9.7	6.7	8.1	7.8	8.5	7.3	7.7	8.1	10.8	
Denmark	75.9	61.9	53.5	44.4	64.1	47.4	45.0	47.6	66.1	73.5
Finland	98.5	107.2	88.4	82.0	87.0	99.6	80.4	77.8	87.7	112.7
France	1,184.3	1,061.7	1,133.6	1,100.3	1,092.4	1,001.9	1,101.2	1,135.7	1,199.4	1,161.9
Germany	1,783.0	1,691.8	1,655.5	1,520.9	1,551.5	1,456.1	1,432.9	1,340.5	1,438.6	1,421.1
Gibraltar										
Greece	276.7	252.1	243.5	243.3	262.5	236.4	233.8	253.7	284.1	
Iceland	1.7	2.6	2.4	1.5	2.2	3.1	2.7	3.1	5.0	
Ireland	36.1	40.8	44.7	39.2	44.9	49.8	72.1	65.3	82.7	
Italy	782.9	736.9	740.3	874.4	919.3	901.4	801.9	880.9	976.8	
Liechtenstein										
Luxembourg										
Malta	4.3	3.7	4.2	4.2	3.9	3.6	3.5	3.8	4.2	4.3
Monaco										
Netherlands	176.0	160.2	148.5	139.2	126.5	121.2	115.4	113.7	128.8	89.9
Norway	31.7	28.2	32.2	24.0	28.6	26.3	31.7	28.5	36.4	38.5
Portugal	271.7	246.3	246.7	247.4	240.3	233.0	237.5	239.8	262.2	270.3
Spain	1,043.6	1,010.1	1,000.3	1,021.3	1,268.5	1,270.0	1,301.8	1,447.6	1,633.8	1,702.3
Sweden	150.5	145.2	163.5	131.6	149.5	164.4	147.9	144.5	175.4	204.0
Switzerland	95.8	85.5	83.2	83.5	70.8	66.2	66.7	72.1	79.9	85.8
Turkey	627.1	596.9	664.5	635.5	583.2	567.4	655.9	727.5	836.3	825.3
United Kingdom	696.1	671.7	734.1	662.0	686.9	694.9	823.7	814.3	903.8	
Eastern Europe										
Albania										
Belarus										
Bosnia-Herzegovina										
Bulgaria	134.1	112.6	121.5	109.8	119.7	109.6	95.4	90.7	109.4	
Croatia	100.6	90.6	84.4	87.1	88.2	80.6	76.4	81.3	88.5	85.2
Czech Republic	177.0	148.5	145.6	140.9	138.0	116.1	125.6	130.1	153.5	
Estonia	11.8	13.2	13.1	14.9	16.1	12.6	14.4	20.4	22.8	
Georgia										
Hungary	149.6	143.8	149.0	148.8	167.8	158.3	161.4	166.9	189.1	199.3
Latvia	36.4	34.2	31.7	28.5	39.3	38.9	41.1	45.7	61.2	
Lithuania	40.8	33.0	31.2	32.6	46.2	41.3	41.6	43.2	63.9	
Macedonia	129.3	126.2	126.6	128.3	125.8	121.1	129.4	125.7	124.7	
Moldova	27.4	22.7	27.7	23.0	28.5	19.6	23.0	20.5	34.6	
Poland	897.2	799.1	751.3	708.4	688.2	607.8	567.3	554.1	617.1	600.8
Romania	268.8	229.1	225.6	243.3	217.9	200.8	211.7	233.3	270.0	298.7
Russia										
Slovakia	155.2	147.1	146.3	145.2	136.5	128.9	135.8	140.5	161.8	
Slovenia	29.6	27.7	26.8	26.3	24.3	22.3	21.9	22.5	26.2	28.3
Ukraine										

Source: International Labour Organisation/Euromonitor International

Media and Leisure

Media and Leisure Statistics

Table 20.1

Cinema Statistics 2008
As stated

	Seating Capacity of Fixed Cinemas ('000)	Number of Cinema Screens	Box Office Revenues (US$ million)	Annual cinema trips per capita
Western Europe				
Austria	102.3	573	159.7	2.0
Belgium	113.8	520	206.1	2.3
Cyprus		33	5.1	1.0
Denmark	59.6	387	167.4	2.3
Finland	53.2	309	76.3	1.2
France	1,077.1	5,412	1,573.7	3.1
Germany	831.9	4,831	1,082.3	1.4
Gibraltar				
Greece		539		1.1
Iceland				4.3
Ireland	79.2	436	192.5	4.2
Italy		3,490	1,020.1	1.8
Liechtenstein				1.3
Luxembourg	4.9	27	13.3	2.3
Malta	8.7	44	2.6	2.2
Monaco				
Netherlands	106.0	635	237.8	1.3
Norway	80.5	424	148.2	2.2
Portugal	116.0	576	105.1	1.4
Spain	926.4	4,290	948.0	2.4
Sweden	170.0	1,042	186.4	1.5
Switzerland	110.4	555	182.9	2.2
Turkey	226.4	1,590	215.3	0.6
United Kingdom	766.9	3,571	1,572.3	2.7
Eastern Europe				
Albania				
Belarus				0.0
Bosnia-Herzegovina				
Bulgaria	27.3	124	9.9	0.3
Croatia	37.0	114	8.3	0.4
Czech Republic	154.8	683	71.5	1.1
Estonia		61		1.4
Georgia				
Hungary	79.6	387	51.1	1.1
Latvia	6.6	42	14.7	1.3
Lithuania	20.2	79	18.9	0.6
Macedonia	6.5	26		0.0
Moldova				
Poland	247.0	1,054	201.0	1.0
Romania	40.0	95	14.8	0.1
Russia	222.5	1,666	681.7	0.8
Slovakia	89.0	259	13.4	0.8
Slovenia		126	17.3	1.3
Ukraine		2,800		0.4

Source: *Euromonitor International from EAO/national statistics*

Media and Leisure Statistics

Table 20.2

Cinema Attendances 1990-2008

Million

	1990	1995	2000	2003	2004	2005	2006	2007	2008
Western Europe									
Austria	10.2	11.5	16.3	17.7	19.4	15.7	17.3	15.7	16.8
Belgium	17.1	19.2	23.5	22.7	24.1	22.1	23.9	22.7	24.3
Cyprus			0.9	1.0	1.0	0.8	0.8	0.9	0.8
Denmark	9.6	8.8	10.7	12.3	12.8	12.2	12.6	12.1	12.7
Finland	6.2	5.3	7.1	7.7	6.9	6.1	6.7	6.5	6.4
France	121.8	130.2	165.8	173.5	195.5	175.5	188.8	177.5	195.4
Germany	91.0	123.9	152.5	149.0	156.7	127.3	136.7	125.4	117.6
Gibraltar									
Greece	13.0	8.2	13.5	15.0	12.0	12.7	12.8	12.2	12.3
Iceland			1.6	1.5	1.5	1.4	1.4	1.4	1.4
Ireland	7.5	9.8	14.9	17.4	17.3	16.4	17.9	18.4	18.3
Italy	90.7	90.7	104.2	110.5	116.3	105.6	106.1	116.4	116.4
Liechtenstein		0.0	0.0	0.0	0.0				
Luxembourg	0.6	0.7	1.4	1.3	1.4	1.2	1.3	1.2	1.1
Malta			1.0	1.1	1.0	1.0	0.9	0.9	0.9
Monaco									
Netherlands	14.6	17.2	21.5	25.0	23.0	20.6	23.4	23.1	23.1
Norway	10.8	11.0	11.6	13.0	12.0	11.3	12.0	10.8	10.5
Portugal	9.6	12.0	17.9	18.7	17.1	15.8	16.4	16.3	16.2
Spain	78.5	96.7	135.4	137.5	143.9	127.7	121.7	116.9	109.3
Sweden	15.7	15.2	17.0	18.2	16.6	14.6	15.3	14.9	14.5
Switzerland	13.6	15.0	15.6	16.5	17.2	15.0	16.4	13.8	16.3
Turkey	9.5	12.6	25.3	24.6	29.7	27.3	34.9	31.2	31.5
United Kingdom	97.4	114.9	142.5	167.3	171.3	164.7	156.6	162.4	166.2
Eastern Europe									
Albania	3.3								
Belarus	115.7	12.4	2.0	1.0	0.8	0.7	0.6	0.5	0.4
Bosnia-Herzegovina									
Bulgaria	48.2	5.1	2.2	3.0	3.1	2.4	2.4	2.5	2.0
Croatia	8.7	3.7	2.7	2.3	3.0	2.2	2.7	2.5	2.4
Czech Republic		9.3	8.7	12.1	12.0	9.5	11.5	12.8	13.0
Estonia	1.1	1.0	1.1	1.3	1.2	1.1	1.6	1.6	1.7
Georgia									
Hungary	14.1	14.0	14.3	13.7	13.7	12.1	11.7	10.1	11.2
Latvia	0.4	1.0	1.5	1.1	1.7	1.7	2.1	2.4	2.6
Lithuania		0.7	2.1	1.4	1.5	1.2	2.5	3.3	3.8
Macedonia			0.6	0.3	0.3	0.1	0.1	0.1	0.1
Moldova									
Poland	16.0	22.0	18.7	23.8	33.4	23.6	32.0	32.6	39.7
Romania	32.7	17.0	5.1	4.5	4.0	2.8	2.8	2.9	2.7
Russia	10.3	13.3	42.8	68.0	67.4	83.6	91.8	106.6	113.1
Slovakia	8.4	5.6	2.6	3.0	2.9	2.2	3.4	2.8	2.8
Slovenia	4.0	2.9	2.2	3.0	3.0	2.4	2.7	2.6	2.6
Ukraine	54.9	30.9	4.9	4.8	4.7	4.7	4.6	4.5	4.5

Source: *Euromonitor International from European Audiovisual Observatory/national statistics*

Media and Leisure Statistics

Table 20.3

Video and DVD Rental Statistics 2008

Number / as stated

	DVD rental transactions (million)	Video rental transactions (million)	DVD rental turnover (US$ million)	Video rental turnover (US$ million)	New DVD rental releases	New video rental releases	Video and DVD rental outlets
Western Europe							
Austria	4.5	0.1	18.75	0.87	425	400	350
Belgium	21.3	0.1	95.93	0.77	939	367	750
Cyprus							
Denmark	13.1	0.1	90.23	1.74	559	180	1,650
Finland	6.3	1.9	35.70	8.28	571	451	800
France	32.6	0.5	133.45	3.40	538	438	1,900
Germany	104.1	2.0	395.11	12.18	400	408	4,137
Gibraltar							
Greece	4.4	0.9	9.89	2.95	700	600	530
Iceland	2.9	0.4	14.31	2.74	360	349	190
Ireland	14.0	3.8	95.19	26.35	332	364	1,000
Italy	68.5	6.7	277.85	31.54	363	274	2,800
Liechtenstein							
Luxembourg				3.34			
Malta							
Monaco							
Netherlands	22.4	2.0	101.92	6.14	750	281	750
Norway	16.2	0.2	100.45	1.86	559	221	1,565
Portugal	9.8	0.1	28.97	0.14	800	116	600
Spain	74.2	9.4	255.36	40.02	496	399	5,250
Sweden	41.5	4.5	255.92	40.71	571	236	800
Switzerland	2.4	0.1	14.05	0.62	425	402	300
Turkey							
United Kingdom	90.0	10.6	505.00	81.12	359	373	2,355
Eastern Europe							
Albania							
Belarus							
Bosnia-Herzegovina							
Bulgaria							
Croatia	2.6	0.5	6.27	1.52	487	404	800
Czech Republic		2.8	12.08	4.23	487	386	769
Estonia							
Georgia							
Hungary	1.5	6.8	5.23	20.81	403	638	1,000
Latvia							
Lithuania							
Macedonia							
Moldova							
Poland	3.1	5.9	6.55	13.74	650	274	1,100
Romania							
Russia		13.3					
Slovakia							
Slovenia							
Ukraine							

Source: *Euromonitor International from EAO/national statistics*

Newspapers 2008

Number / as stated

Table 20.4

	Total Number	Dailies	Non-Dailies	Total Circulation ('000)	Daily Circulation ('000)	Non-daily Circulation ('000)
Western Europe						
Austria	284	24	260		3,407	
Belgium	42	29	13		1,605	
Cyprus	34	23	11	152	105	48
Denmark	298	46	252	14,696	4,271	10,425
Finland	338	55	283	3,322	2,410	912
France	129	93	36	14,486	10,213	4,273
Germany	1,791	376	1,415	110,216	20,585	89,631
Gibraltar		1			6	
Greece	62	44	18	1,933	1,528	405
Iceland	27	3	24	326	246	80
Ireland	200	15	185	2,251	1,090	1,161
Italy	530	108	422	13,178	12,658	520
Liechtenstein	2	2		21	21	
Luxembourg	18	6	12	300	113	188
Malta	9	4	5		108	
Monaco			2			
Netherlands	525	32	493	20,411	4,680	15,731
Norway	300	77	223	2,973	2,173	800
Portugal	67	20	47	5,837	1,130	4,708
Spain	386	197	189	17,565	10,912	6,653
Sweden	233	90	143	7,484	4,978	2,506
Switzerland	535	100	435	4,135	3,674	460
Turkey	5,049	89	4,960		5,562	
United Kingdom	1,393	120	1,273	47,425	19,271	28,154
Eastern Europe						
Albania	115	32	83	59		
Belarus	708	18	690	16,459	1,427	15,032
Bosnia-Herzegovina		7			100	
Bulgaria	216	63	153	1,782	379	1,402
Croatia	225	18	207	3,793	1,029	2,763
Czech Republic	311	100	211	7,013	3,559	3,453
Estonia	153	18	135	665	411	254
Georgia	64	10	54		24	
Hungary	311	29	282		1,742	
Latvia	129	22	107	1,727	397	1,330
Lithuania	300	22	278	1,976		
Macedonia	25	14	11	247	228	19
Moldova	131	7	124	1,081	114	967
Poland	75	49	26	6,978	6,539	440
Romania		78			1,823	
Russia	28,254	597	27,657	9,155,363		
Slovakia	12	11	1	465	459	6
Slovenia	256	8	248		505	
Ukraine						

Source: *Euromonitor International from World Association of Newspapers*

Media and Leisure Statistics

Table 20.5

Number of Colour TV Households 1998-2008
'000

	1998	1999	2000	2001	2002	2003	2004	2005	2006	2007	2008
Western Europe											
Austria	3,132.1	3,171.9	3,218.2	3,265.7	3,306.1	3,339.7	3,377.0	3,426.6	3,466.9	3,503.1	3,536.7
Belgium	4,024.1	4,078.2	4,125.9	4,183.6	4,238.7	4,290.8	4,339.8	4,383.2	4,436.6	4,484.9	4,526.7
Cyprus											
Denmark	2,334.9	2,355.8	2,370.8	2,384.5	2,398.8	2,411.7	2,427.7	2,446.9	2,465.9	2,482.8	2,499.3
Finland	2,157.3	2,182.0	2,203.6	2,236.1	2,258.9	2,278.6	2,299.2	2,317.6	2,331.1	2,359.4	2,385.2
France	21,672.8	21,905.2	22,420.2	22,957.4	23,257.2	23,806.8	24,054.5	24,455.9	25,212.0	25,544.8	25,870.2
Germany	35,865.6	36,283.2	36,713.4	37,133.1	37,496.4	37,802.9	38,050.7	38,198.6	38,855.9	38,978.9	39,094.5
Gibraltar											
Greece	3,374.6	3,465.9	3,511.8	3,546.5	3,603.1	3,675.8	3,737.7	3,793.0	3,846.4	3,897.2	3,946.3
Iceland	97.0	99.0									
Ireland	1,117.5	1,148.1	1,181.0	1,219.6	1,264.8	1,310.8	1,355.1	1,405.3	1,462.9	1,516.2	1,566.4
Italy	20,519.6	20,672.6	20,826.8	20,999.3	21,205.2	21,554.0	21,965.2	22,290.5	22,714.6	23,032.0	23,310.7
Liechtenstein											
Luxembourg											
Malta	149.0	149.0									
Monaco											
Netherlands	6,622.8	6,649.3	6,750.8	6,798.3	6,795.3	6,856.1	6,928.1	6,982.5	7,049.7	7,106.2	7,160.5
Norway	1,858.2	1,879.2	1,900.8	1,917.3	1,930.6	1,945.9	1,959.1	1,973.3	2,014.5	2,028.9	2,069.0
Portugal	3,254.5	3,355.1	3,449.0	3,544.9	3,634.4	3,722.6	3,805.9	3,878.7	3,940.4	3,999.3	4,051.6
Spain	13,298.5	13,552.9	13,817.1	14,160.8	14,528.7	14,993.9	15,348.0	15,794.5	16,241.6	16,635.0	16,979.0
Sweden	4,091.1	4,121.5	4,153.6	4,182.0	4,215.9	4,249.4	4,282.6	4,311.0	4,344.6	4,387.7	4,419.1
Switzerland	2,924.4	2,947.2	2,976.1	3,004.2	3,037.5	3,071.8	3,101.8	3,132.0	3,158.5	3,182.4	3,203.9
Turkey	12,132.1	12,669.8	13,175.8	13,647.4	14,069.0	14,490.1	14,914.9	15,326.3	15,742.7	16,139.5	16,550.7
United Kingdom	24,321.2	24,501.8	24,689.2	24,880.2	25,327.4	25,520.7	25,731.3	25,983.4	26,223.4	26,454.5	26,695.7
Eastern Europe											
Albania											
Belarus	2,654.3	2,806.5	2,970.8	3,143.1	3,317.1	3,518.7	3,653.3	3,750.5	3,808.9	3,856.8	3,896.7
Bosnia-Herzegovina											
Bulgaria	2,024.8	2,117.5	2,191.4	2,284.4	2,349.3	2,413.1	2,473.2	2,527.2	2,571.9	2,609.3	2,639.2
Croatia	1,307.6	1,313.1	1,318.3	1,332.6	1,359.2	1,380.3	1,397.6	1,426.2	1,424.0	1,446.7	1,457.1
Czech Republic	3,834.7	3,897.8	3,957.5	4,014.6	4,070.3	4,126.7	4,183.8	4,235.2	4,290.5	4,344.0	4,386.3
Estonia	480.7	498.4	534.9	538.7	550.9	550.3	555.2	560.2	559.4	565.3	570.2
Georgia											
Hungary	3,095.1	3,239.8	3,418.2	3,553.7	3,708.4	3,768.6	3,818.1	3,872.6	3,924.9	3,975.4	4,022.8
Latvia	609.7	641.2	671.4	698.5	720.5	734.7	748.5	759.5	767.5	772.2	776.6
Lithuania	1,022.1	1,092.3	1,203.9	1,194.0	1,215.7	1,237.1	1,270.8	1,301.6	1,331.3	1,347.8	1,355.1
Macedonia											
Moldova	1,724.0	1,986.0									
Poland	12,011.1	12,323.6	12,509.8	12,714.3	12,936.9	13,107.1	13,169.9	13,273.9	13,549.2	13,752.7	13,932.2
Romania	3,699.5	4,007.4	4,332.0	4,672.8	5,025.1	5,344.2	5,763.1	6,208.4	6,515.6	6,730.8	6,892.4
Russia	37,398.3	39,346.7	41,444.3	43,267.2	45,015.2	46,712.6	48,008.1	48,717.9	49,717.4	50,337.3	50,781.4
Slovakia	1,644.4	1,693.0	1,726.3	1,756.8	1,814.9	1,895.0	1,973.6	2,060.1	2,153.8	2,192.6	2,218.5
Slovenia	614.9	626.2	644.4	657.9	660.5	664.1	674.7	680.2	689.2	698.4	706.9
Ukraine	10,734.0	11,389.6	12,131.3	12,958.8	13,876.3	15,048.3	16,133.5	16,878.8	17,581.5	18,179.5	18,537.0

Source: *Euromonitor International from Council of Europe*

Table 20.6

Number of Cable TV Households 1998-2008

'000

	1998	1999	2000	2001	2002	2003	2004	2005	2006	2007	2008	Cable TV households as % of colour TV households
Western Europe												
Austria	967.0	991.0	1,013.1	1,035.7	1,076.8	1,267.0	1,258.0	1,268.0	1,332.0	1,300.0	1,272.3	39.4
Belgium	3,725.2	3,751.8	3,788.7	3,814.9	3,880.3	3,917.3	3,999.3	4,003.7	4,025.1	4,063.6	4,101.0	91.1
Cyprus												
Denmark	1,316.5	1,350.0	1,375.0	1,399.9	1,435.0	1,475.2	1,504.8	1,542.7	1,562.6	1,587.8	1,613.0	64.5
Finland	905.6	933.0	950.0	1,000.0	1,040.0	1,099.0	1,185.8	1,246.3	1,317.7	1,372.3	1,409.2	57.8
France	2,600.0	2,850.0	2,974.0	3,375.0	3,430.0	3,523.0	3,782.0	3,622.1	3,378.9	3,302.8	3,294.9	13.0
Germany	17,700.0	18,550.0	20,380.0	20,300.0	20,700.0	20,130.0	20,720.0	20,970.0	20,460.0	20,280.0	20,530.2	52.5
Gibraltar												
Greece	0.0	0.0	0.0	0.0	0.0	1.8	5.4	9.1	14.7	20.8	25.6	0.9
Iceland	30.0	30.0										
Ireland	600.0	620.0	670.0	615.0	562.0	533.0	552.0	570.0	571.0	558.3	555.3	42.3
Italy	60.0	65.0	70.0	70.0	113.0	180.0	200.0	200.0	200.0	208.3	218.5	1.2
Liechtenstein												
Luxembourg												
Malta												
Monaco												
Netherlands	6,000.0	6,120.0	6,200.0	6,320.0	6,180.0	6,390.0	6,392.1	6,329.4	6,108.6	5,956.0	5,897.8	83.0
Norway	774.6	788.7	823.3	838.7	840.1	852.8	871.1	895.6	923.3	938.0	963.8	46.6
Portugal	595.9	740.5	924.9	1,119.3	1,262.0	1,333.9	1,341.4	1,400.2	1,423.8	1,530.5	1,597.4	38.7
Spain	462.3	492.0	526.7	587.8	811.4	996.7	1,678.8	1,838.7	1,989.8	2,426.6	2,664.6	10.0
Sweden	1,960.0	2,200.0	2,200.0	2,300.0	2,413.0	2,472.0	2,494.2	2,549.4	2,589.3	2,634.2	2,669.3	60.4
Switzerland	2,510.0	2,585.8	2,628.6	2,684.0	2,717.0	2,761.0	2,791.0	2,873.3	2,916.4	2,945.8	2,970.7	88.2
Turkey	611.1	750.3	990.1	1,340.7	1,614.1	1,783.3	1,957.6	2,012.4	1,951.6	2,027.0	2,140.2	12.9
United Kingdom	2,700.2	3,240.7	3,559.1	3,618.0	3,319.0	3,325.0	3,288.0	3,300.0	3,362.0	3,438.6	3,497.1	13.0
Eastern Europe												
Albania												
Belarus	150.5	228.9	340.0	652.2	765.4	944.3	1,091.1	1,222.3	1,408.0	1,578.5	1,682.0	43.2
Bosnia-Herzegovina												
Bulgaria	240.0	655.0	1,070.0	750.6	729.4	1,002.4	634.0	1,067.6	1,184.2	1,218.7	1,275.7	81.5
Croatia	150.1	192.2	169.1	193.0	250.0	173.4	174.4	225.9	229.6	246.6	262.9	18.0
Czech Republic	815.5	892.5	1,079.6	1,153.2	1,163.1	1,169.6	1,072.5	1,039.2	937.5	958.4	976.4	19.7
Estonia	158.3	201.5	228.8	248.9	260.7	270.8	279.9	286.3	308.0	319.8	328.5	57.6
Georgia												
Hungary	1,710.9	1,752.0	1,779.2	1,868.7	2,018.8	2,111.3	2,213.1	2,283.4	2,361.1	2,427.3	2,484.3	61.3
Latvia	232.8	303.6	348.2	355.2	365.7	382.6	381.9	379.4	360.2	358.0	356.6	45.9
Lithuania	267.6	295.4	318.9	372.3	363.6	377.6	377.0	415.9	477.1	526.6	559.3	41.3
Macedonia												
Moldova												
Poland	3,133.8	3,316.9	3,529.9	3,492.0	3,529.4	3,636.8	3,683.5	4,529.6	4,704.3	4,888.8	5,060.9	34.4
Romania	2,680.0	2,900.0	3,520.0	2,700.0	3,300.0	2,736.9	3,111.9	3,636.0	3,787.0	3,908.6	4,004.2	59.8
Russia	16,605.3	17,981.0	19,056.8	19,884.5	20,507.1	20,974.6	21,326.3	21,576.2	21,755.4	21,879.7	21,961.0	40.1
Slovakia	616.0	648.0	659.3	728.3	698.2	730.0	766.3	704.0	733.7	790.0	850.6	41.2
Slovenia	300.0	310.0	320.0	320.0	320.0	450.0	376.8	369.9	378.1	389.3	444.1	40.7
Ukraine	855.4	980.7	1,202.5	1,500.0	1,936.0	2,271.6	2,643.6	2,921.3	3,237.1	3,540.2	3,820.0	19.7

Source: *Euromonitor International from Council of Europe*

Media and Leisure Statistics

Table 20.7

Number of Satellite TV Households 1998-2008
'000

	1998	1999	2000	2001	2002	2003	2004	2005	2006	2007	2008	Satellite TV house-holds as % of colour TV house-holds
Western Europe												
Austria	1,227.0	1,260.0	1,450.0	1,560.0	1,560.0	1,579.3	1,609.0	1,684.0	1,699.0	1,722.0	1,744.0	50.2
Belgium	140.0	142.0	142.0	150.0	158.0	237.0	316.3	350.5	399.5	438.5	471.4	10.2
Cyprus												
Denmark	550.0	621.0	614.0	671.0	727.0	769.6	806.3	834.5	855.5	872.3	885.0	35.4
Finland	284.5	313.0	343.0	361.0	383.0	406.0	445.0	489.8	532.5	567.5	596.0	24.5
France	3,260.0	3,920.0	4,300.0	4,740.0	5,010.0	5,620.0	6,210.0	6,514.7	6,698.1	6,900.1	7,075.5	28.0
Germany	10,450.0	11,456.0	11,387.0	13,300.0	13,902.0	14,460.0	15,470.0	16,370.0	16,720.0	16,700.0	16,681.8	42.1
Gibraltar												
Greece	180.0	181.0	221.0	260.0	419.0	431.8	444.9	457.9	495.0	537.4	580.6	14.7
Iceland												
Ireland	110.0	130.0	150.0	220.0	286.0	315.0	355.0	407.0	484.0	548.0	621.4	32.6
Italy	960.7	1,800.8	2,350.0	2,550.0	3,895.9	4,858.5	5,589.2	6,165.9	6,587.7	6,950.8	7,286.1	31.3
Liechtenstein												
Luxembourg												
Malta												
Monaco												
Netherlands	300.0	320.0	330.0	340.0	520.0	671.6	790.0	882.8	953.4	1,006.6	1,052.2	14.6
Norway	330.0	390.0	530.0	520.0	510.0	520.4	549.4	581.2	613.4	629.6	650.3	31.4
Portugal	370.0	395.0	418.0	425.0	453.2	492.2	546.8	601.8	654.8	695.5	732.0	18.1
Spain	1,066.9	1,253.6	1,684.6	2,036.4	1,995.7	2,463.1	2,561.6	2,837.6	2,874.5	3,330.3	3,399.1	19.7
Sweden	810.0	850.0	1,050.0	862.0	1,090.0	1,247.4	1,361.8	1,451.2	1,515.9	1,571.9	1,616.5	19.6
Switzerland	390.0	253.0	253.0	440.0	486.0	516.4	538.5	552.9	561.5	566.7	570.2	15.2
Turkey	700.0	1,098.0	2,932.0	3,140.0	3,284.0	3,635.4	4,270.8	4,997.5	5,820.5	6,488.0	7,077.3	40.4
United Kingdom	4,570.0	4,830.0	5,300.0	6,590.0	7,088.0	7,187.0	7,794.0	8,300.0	8,791.0	9,214.3	9,575.3	36.4
Eastern Europe												
Albania												
Belarus	21.1	37.0	60.0	89.2	123.9	165.9	211.8	270.2	324.2	367.8	406.6	10.4
Bosnia-Herzegovina												
Bulgaria	180.0	264.0	208.0	160.0	160.0	198.4	211.4	220.9	225.5	232.7	239.8	6.8
Croatia	420.5	470.0	506.3	542.1	572.4	595.8	614.1	628.5	639.1	646.7	652.1	39.1
Czech Republic	750.0	883.0	616.0	520.0	371.3	390.4	434.2	436.6	506.2	585.7	654.0	13.5
Estonia	55.0	60.0	65.0	90.0	90.0	98.0	105.3	111.9	117.3	121.8	125.5	21.5
Georgia												
Hungary	850.0	840.0	830.0	826.9	830.0	837.3	846.2	856.3	866.1	875.7	884.8	23.0
Latvia	52.9	66.1	90.0	101.0	110.0	110.0	128.6	131.0	136.0	140.2	143.7	17.4
Lithuania	53.8	65.9	79.6	94.4	105.0	110.7	121.6	131.5	127.6	140.3	148.0	10.9
Macedonia												
Moldova												
Poland	2,224.9	2,380.5	2,748.7	2,804.9	3,121.0	3,250.8	3,380.2	3,604.7	3,859.2	4,035.6	4,165.8	29.7
Romania	150.0	154.0	193.0	200.0	204.0	212.9	268.7	387.6	613.1	1,700.0	2,215.2	4.1
Russia	224.9	346.4	413.1	571.1	1,670.9	2,261.4	2,672.9	3,009.9	3,278.0	3,526.1	3,717.4	6.3
Slovakia	350.0	431.5	540.3	753.1	806.9	860.8	888.5	912.1	931.9	948.9	964.2	55.5
Slovenia	100.2	114.0	98.6	110.9	113.6	113.8	114.0	115.1	116.3	117.5	118.7	16.8
Ukraine	81.2	110.8	130.0	136.9	141.0	149.1	174.9	236.1	555.0	870.7	1,044.7	3.7

Source: *Euromonitor International from Council of Europe*

Media and Leisure Statistics

Table 20.8

Number of Digital Satellite Pay TV Subscribers 1998-2008
'000

	1998	1999	2000	2001	2002	2003	2004	2005	2006	2007	2008	Digital pay TV house-holds as % of colour TV house-holds
Western Europe												
Austria						1,380.0	1,705.0	1,971.3	1,929.5	1,987.8	2,058.6	58.2
Belgium	20.0	25.0	35.0	35.0	35.0	35.0	38.0	44.0	50.0	54.0	58.0	1.3
Cyprus					54.5	54.5	58.3					
Denmark				226.0	235.0	310.0	332.0	347.5	392.6	413.3	433.6	17.7
Finland		40.0	77.9	237.0	180.0	57.5	45.0	27.8	17.7	14.4	11.9	0.5
France	1,773.0	2,190.0	2,617.6	3,149.0	3,472.0	3,990.0	4,255.0	4,520.0	4,544.0	5,225.0	5,467.5	22.0
Germany	260.0	520.0	760.0	900.0	1,377.0	1,528.0	1,532.0	1,594.7	1,480.5	1,485.2	1,481.5	3.8
Gibraltar												
Greece		4.0	60.0	88.0	120.0	164.6	185.3	221.0	235.3	254.0	267.0	6.8
Iceland												
Ireland			100.0	156.0	272.0	315.0	364.0	393.0	421.0	497.0	530.3	36.7
Italy	613.0	1,200.0	2,003.0	2,076.0	2,454.0	2,400.0	2,800.0	3,596.0	3,820.0	4,240.0	4,600.0	20.8
Liechtenstein												
Luxembourg												
Malta												
Monaco												
Netherlands		14.0	30.3	39.0	48.5	54.0	56.0	600.0	700.0	753.8	812.0	11.4
Norway		53.0	63.7	183.0	364.0	455.7	489.0	525.7	593.4	627.8	662.5	32.3
Portugal	28.7	60.0	131.0	224.0	290.0	348.0	367.0	389.0	373.0	427.0	366.0	9.3
Spain	912.4	1,180.3	1,684.6	2,036.0	1,996.0	1,796.0	1,822.0	1,960.0	1,990.0	2,056.0	2,146.7	13.8
Sweden		125.0	134.5	432.0	537.0	565.0	584.0	608.0	676.3	704.1	734.1	17.5
Switzerland												
Turkey					966.8	1,107.0	1,015.0					
United Kingdom	225.0	2,065.0	4,459.0	5,560.0	6,290.0	6,893.0	7,240.0	7,666.0	7,720.0	8,085.0	8,060.0	30.4
Eastern Europe												
Albania												
Belarus												
Bosnia-Herzegovina												
Bulgaria								29.0				
Croatia												
Czech Republic			21.5	40.0	52.0	76.7	81.7	112.5	134.5	149.0	165.8	4.5
Estonia												
Georgia												
Hungary			29.1	55.0	79.1	103.0	127.0	171.0	176.8	158.9	166.9	4.6
Latvia												
Lithuania												
Macedonia												
Moldova												
Poland	160.0	435.0	849.7	819.4	1,120.0	1,256.0	1,265.0	1,200.0	1,500.0	1,602.9	1,745.7	12.8
Romania								185.0				
Russia			120.0	180.0	206.3	260.0	283.0	360.0	450.0	560.0	606.2	1.2
Slovakia				12.0	9.9	12.1	14.2	17.3	17.1	22.3	23.7	1.1
Slovenia												
Ukraine												

Source: *Euromonitor International from Council of Europe*

Population

Population Statistics

Table 21.1

Total Population 1980-2008: National Estimates at Mid-Year
'000 / % growth

	1980	1985	1990	1995	1996	1997	1998	1999	2000	2001
Western Europe										
Austria	7,549	7,565	7,678	7,948	7,959	7,968	7,977	7,992	8,012	8,043
Belgium	9,859	9,858	9,967	10,137	10,157	10,181	10,203	10,226	10,251	10,287
Cyprus	614	651	685	737	748	759	770	781	792	802
Denmark	5,123	5,114	5,141	5,233	5,263	5,285	5,304	5,322	5,340	5,359
Finland	4,780	4,902	4,986	5,108	5,125	5,140	5,153	5,165	5,176	5,188
France	53,880	55,284	56,709	57,844	58,026	58,207	58,398	58,673	59,049	59,454
Germany	78,289	77,685	79,433	81,678	81,915	82,035	82,047	82,100	82,212	82,350
Gibraltar	27	27	27	27	27	27	27	27	28	28
Greece	9,643	9,934	10,157	10,634	10,709	10,777	10,835	10,883	10,917	10,950
Iceland	229	243	256	269	272	274	277	280	282	285
Ireland	3,413	3,546	3,514	3,609	3,638	3,674	3,713	3,755	3,805	3,866
Italy	56,434	56,593	56,719	56,846	56,863	56,894	56,911	56,922	56,949	56,981
Liechtenstein	26	27	29	31	31	31	32	32	33	33
Luxembourg	364	368	384	411	417	423	429	434	440	445
Malta	326	346	362	379	381	384	386	388	390	393
Monaco	26	29	30	32	32	32	32	32	32	32
Netherlands	14,150	14,492	14,952	15,459	15,530	15,611	15,707	15,812	15,926	16,046
Norway	4,086	4,153	4,241	4,359	4,381	4,405	4,431	4,462	4,491	4,514
Portugal	9,766	10,024	9,983	10,030	10,058	10,091	10,129	10,172	10,226	10,293
Spain	37,439	38,419	38,850	39,387	39,478	39,582	39,721	39,926	40,263	40,720
Sweden	8,310	8,350	8,559	8,827	8,841	8,846	8,851	8,858	8,872	8,896
Switzerland	6,319	6,470	6,716	7,041	7,072	7,089	7,110	7,144	7,184	7,230
Turkey	44,585	50,230	56,104	61,771	62,911	64,063	65,214	66,338	67,393	68,367
United Kingdom	56,314	56,550	57,248	58,019	58,167	58,317	58,487	58,682	58,893	59,109
Eastern Europe										
Albania	2,698	2,995	3,290	3,120	3,096	3,081	3,073	3,069	3,068	3,073
Belarus	9,627	9,958	10,189	10,194	10,160	10,117	10,072	10,035	10,005	9,971
Bosnia-Herzegovina	4,059	4,279	4,444	3,482	3,451	3,504	3,619	3,721	3,771	3,801
Bulgaria	8,851	8,952	8,718	8,264	8,189	8,122	8,062	8,006	7,954	7,903
Croatia	4,600	4,712	4,781	4,581	4,533	4,537	4,527	4,498	4,440	4,441
Czech Republic	10,285	10,302	10,303	10,308	10,291	10,275	10,260	10,245	10,228	10,213
Estonia	1,477	1,529	1,569	1,437	1,416	1,400	1,386	1,376	1,370	1,364
Georgia	4,787	4,984	5,159	4,734	4,616	4,532	4,487	4,453	4,418	4,386
Hungary	10,713	10,628	10,374	10,329	10,311	10,290	10,267	10,238	10,211	10,188
Latvia	2,512	2,579	2,663	2,485	2,457	2,433	2,410	2,390	2,373	2,355
Lithuania	3,413	3,545	3,698	3,629	3,602	3,575	3,549	3,524	3,500	3,481
Macedonia	1,801	1,834	1,916	1,968	1,978	1,988	1,997	2,005	2,013	2,019
Moldova	4,029	4,234	4,370	4,323	4,286	4,242	4,190	4,131	4,067	3,997
Poland	35,574	37,202	38,031	38,275	38,289	38,292	38,284	38,270	38,258	38,248
Romania	22,207	22,733	23,202	22,239	22,146	22,063	22,001	21,953	21,908	21,860
Russia	138,483	143,033	147,969	148,376	148,160	147,915	147,671	147,215	146,597	145,976
Slovakia	4,980	5,156	5,278	5,353	5,362	5,370	5,374	5,377	5,379	5,379
Slovenia	1,901	1,942	1,998	1,990	1,989	1,986	1,982	1,983	1,989	1,992
Ukraine	49,866	50,752	51,590	51,087	50,637	50,187	49,759	49,330	48,889	48,452

Source: National statistical offices/UN/Euromonitor International

Population Statistics

Total Population 1980-2008: National Estimates at Mid-Year *(continued)*
'000 / % growth

	2002	2003	2004	2005	2006	2007	2008	% Growth 1980-2008
Western Europe								
Austria	8,084	8,121	8,173	8,236	8,290	8,333	8,367	10.8
Belgium	10,333	10,376	10,421	10,479	10,541	10,594	10,639	7.9
Cyprus	812	822	831	841	849	858	867	41.3
Denmark	5,376	5,391	5,405	5,419	5,437	5,454	5,468	6.7
Finland	5,201	5,213	5,228	5,246	5,266	5,289	5,313	11.2
France	59,863	60,264	60,643	60,996	61,353	61,822	62,277	15.6
Germany	82,488	82,534	82,516	82,469	82,376	82,266	82,110	4.9
Gibraltar	28	29	29	29	29	29	29	10.1
Greece	10,988	11,024	11,062	11,104	11,147	11,190	11,232	16.5
Iceland	287	290	294	299	305	312	319	39.1
Ireland	3,932	3,996	4,068	4,159	4,254	4,339	4,413	29.3
Italy	57,157	57,605	58,175	58,607	58,820	58,932	59,014	4.6
Liechtenstein	34	34	34	35	35	35	36	39.7
Luxembourg	451	456	461	467	472	478	483	32.7
Malta	396	399	401	404	405	407	408	25.1
Monaco	32	32	32	33	33	33	33	25.2
Netherlands	16,149	16,225	16,282	16,320	16,346	16,371	16,397	15.9
Norway	4,538	4,565	4,592	4,623	4,661	4,709	4,768	16.7
Portugal	10,368	10,441	10,502	10,549	10,589	10,626	10,656	9.1
Spain	41,314	42,005	42,692	43,398	44,121	44,770	45,289	21.0
Sweden	8,925	8,958	8,994	9,030	9,081	9,135	9,179	10.5
Switzerland	7,285	7,339	7,390	7,437	7,478	7,514	7,545	19.4
Turkey	69,304	70,231	71,151	72,067	72,984	73,900	74,810	67.8
United Kingdom	59,328	59,569	59,880	60,227	60,605	61,001	61,399	9.0
Eastern Europe								
Albania	3,082	3,093	3,105	3,116	3,127	3,138	3,149	16.7
Belarus	9,925	9,874	9,825	9,775	9,733	9,702	9,681	0.6
Bosnia-Herzegovina	3,822	3,834	3,840	3,843	3,843	3,844	3,844	-5.3
Bulgaria	7,852	7,803	7,753	7,702	7,650	7,598	7,545	-14.7
Croatia	4,443	4,442	4,443	4,443	4,441	4,437	4,432	-3.7
Czech Republic	10,205	10,207	10,216	10,236	10,269	10,302	10,327	0.4
Estonia	1,359	1,354	1,349	1,346	1,342	1,337	1,333	-9.8
Georgia	4,357	4,329	4,318	4,361	4,398	4,388	4,384	-8.4
Hungary	10,159	10,130	10,107	10,087	10,067	10,048	10,029	-6.4
Latvia	2,339	2,325	2,313	2,301	2,288	2,274	2,260	-10.0
Lithuania	3,469	3,454	3,436	3,414	3,394	3,376	3,357	-1.6
Macedonia	2,024	2,028	2,032	2,035	2,037	2,039	2,040	13.3
Moldova	3,924	3,854	3,789	3,734	3,688	3,650	3,618	-10.2
Poland	38,230	38,205	38,182	38,165	38,129	38,074	38,018	6.9
Romania	21,803	21,742	21,685	21,634	21,583	21,526	21,466	-3.3
Russia	145,306	144,566	143,821	143,114	142,487	142,115	141,956	2.5
Slovakia	5,379	5,380	5,382	5,387	5,390	5,393	5,394	8.3
Slovenia	1,995	1,996	1,997	2,000	2,007	2,013	2,020	6.2
Ukraine	48,032	47,633	47,271	46,925	46,607	46,329	46,056	-7.6

Source: National statistical offices/UN/Euromonitor International

Population Statistics | **Table 21.2**

Total Population 1980-2008: National Estimates at January 1st
'000

	1980	1985	1990	1995	1996	1997	1998	1999	2000	2001
Western Europe										
Austria	7,546	7,563	7,645	7,943	7,953	7,965	7,971	7,982	8,002	8,021
Belgium	9,855	9,858	9,948	10,131	10,143	10,170	10,192	10,214	10,239	10,263
Cyprus	611	647	681	731	743	754	765	776	787	797
Denmark	5,122	5,111	5,135	5,216	5,251	5,275	5,295	5,314	5,330	5,349
Finland	4,771	4,894	4,974	5,099	5,117	5,132	5,147	5,160	5,171	5,181
France	53,731	55,157	56,577	57,753	57,936	58,116	58,299	58,497	58,850	59,249
Germany	78,180	77,709	79,113	81,539	81,817	82,012	82,057	82,037	82,163	82,260
Gibraltar	27	27	27	27	27	27	27	27	27	28
Greece	9,584	9,919	10,121	10,595	10,674	10,745	10,808	10,861	10,904	10,931
Iceland	228	241	255	267	270	273	276	278	281	283
Ireland	3,393	3,544	3,507	3,598	3,620	3,655	3,694	3,732	3,778	3,833
Italy	56,388	56,588	56,694	56,846	56,846	56,879	56,908	56,914	56,929	56,968
Liechtenstein	26	27	28	31	31	31	31	32	32	33
Luxembourg	364	367	382	409	414	420	426	431	437	442
Malta	324	344	360	378	380	383	385	387	389	392
Monaco	26	28	30	32	32	32	32	32	32	32
Netherlands	14,091	14,454	14,893	15,424	15,494	15,567	15,654	15,760	15,864	15,987
Norway	4,079	4,146	4,233	4,348	4,370	4,393	4,418	4,445	4,478	4,503
Portugal	9,714	10,017	9,996	10,018	10,043	10,073	10,110	10,149	10,195	10,257
Spain	37,242	38,353	38,826	39,343	39,431	39,525	39,639	39,803	40,050	40,477
Sweden	8,303	8,343	8,527	8,816	8,837	8,844	8,848	8,854	8,861	8,883
Switzerland	6,304	6,456	6,674	7,019	7,062	7,081	7,096	7,124	7,164	7,204
Turkey	44,021	49,663	55,495	61,204	62,338	63,485	64,642	65,787	66,889	67,896
United Kingdom	56,285	56,482	57,157	57,943	58,095	58,239	58,395	58,580	58,785	59,000
Eastern Europe										
Albania	2,671	2,957	3,289	3,134	3,106	3,087	3,076	3,070	3,068	3,069
Belarus	9,592	9,929	10,189	10,210	10,177	10,142	10,093	10,051	10,019	9,990
Bosnia-Herzegovina	4,040	4,246	4,498	3,523	3,442	3,459	3,550	3,689	3,753	3,790
Bulgaria	8,835	8,954	8,767	8,303	8,224	8,154	8,091	8,033	7,978	7,929
Croatia	4,598	4,702	4,778	4,669	4,494	4,572	4,501	4,554	4,442	4,437
Czech Republic	10,277	10,302	10,301	10,317	10,300	10,283	10,268	10,253	10,236	10,220
Estonia	1,472	1,523	1,571	1,448	1,425	1,406	1,393	1,379	1,372	1,367
Georgia	4,770	4,961	5,145	4,794	4,674	4,558	4,505	4,470	4,435	4,401
Hungary	10,709	10,657	10,375	10,337	10,321	10,301	10,280	10,253	10,222	10,200
Latvia	2,509	2,570	2,668	2,501	2,470	2,445	2,421	2,399	2,382	2,364
Lithuania	3,404	3,529	3,694	3,643	3,615	3,588	3,562	3,536	3,512	3,487
Macedonia	1,795	1,828	1,909	1,963	1,973	1,983	1,993	2,002	2,009	2,016
Moldova	4,010	4,215	4,364	4,339	4,307	4,266	4,218	4,162	4,100	4,033
Poland	35,413	37,063	37,988	38,265	38,284	38,294	38,290	38,277	38,263	38,254
Romania	22,133	22,687	23,211	22,285	22,193	22,099	22,026	21,976	21,929	21,887
Russia	138,127	142,539	147,665	148,460	148,292	148,029	147,802	147,539	146,890	146,304
Slovakia	4,963	5,140	5,270	5,349	5,358	5,366	5,373	5,376	5,379	5,379
Slovenia	1,893	1,937	1,996	1,989	1,990	1,987	1,985	1,978	1,988	1,990
Ukraine	49,781	50,648	51,557	51,300	50,874	50,400	49,973	49,545	49,115	48,664

Source: *Euromonitor International from national statistics/UN*

Population Statistics

Total Population 1980-2008: National Estimates at January 1st *(continued)*

'000

	2002	2003	2004	2005	2006	2007	2008	% Growth 1980-2008
Western Europe								
Austria	8,065	8,102	8,140	8,207	8,266	8,314	8,352	10.7
Belgium	10,310	10,356	10,396	10,446	10,511	10,570	10,618	7.7
Cyprus	807	817	827	836	845	854	862	41.2
Denmark	5,368	5,384	5,398	5,411	5,427	5,447	5,462	6.6
Finland	5,195	5,206	5,220	5,237	5,256	5,277	5,300	11.1
France	59,660	60,067	60,462	60,825	61,167	61,538	62,106	15.6
Germany	82,440	82,537	82,532	82,501	82,438	82,315	82,218	5.2
Gibraltar	28	28	29	29	29	29	29	10.3
Greece	10,969	11,006	11,041	11,083	11,125	11,169	11,211	17.0
Iceland	286	288	291	296	301	308	315	38.3
Ireland	3,900	3,964	4,028	4,109	4,209	4,299	4,378	29.0
Italy	56,994	57,321	57,888	58,462	58,752	58,888	58,976	4.6
Liechtenstein	34	34	34	35	35	35	35	37.5
Luxembourg	448	453	459	464	470	475	481	32.0
Malta	394	397	400	403	405	406	407	25.7
Monaco	32	32	32	33	33	33	33	25.9
Netherlands	16,105	16,193	16,258	16,306	16,334	16,358	16,383	16.3
Norway	4,524	4,552	4,577	4,606	4,640	4,681	4,737	16.1
Portugal	10,329	10,407	10,475	10,529	10,570	10,609	10,643	9.6
Spain	40,964	41,664	42,345	43,038	43,758	44,484	45,056	21.0
Sweden	8,909	8,941	8,976	9,011	9,048	9,113	9,157	10.3
Switzerland	7,256	7,314	7,364	7,415	7,459	7,497	7,530	19.5
Turkey	68,838	69,770	70,692	71,610	72,524	73,443	74,358	68.9
United Kingdom	59,218	59,438	59,700	60,060	60,393	60,817	61,186	8.7
Eastern Europe								
Albania	3,076	3,087	3,099	3,111	3,122	3,132	3,143	17.7
Belarus	9,951	9,899	9,849	9,800	9,751	9,714	9,690	1.0
Bosnia-Herzegovina	3,813	3,830	3,837	3,843	3,843	3,844	3,844	-4.9
Bulgaria	7,877	7,827	7,778	7,728	7,676	7,624	7,571	-14.3
Croatia	4,444	4,442	4,442	4,444	4,443	4,440	4,435	-3.5
Czech Republic	10,206	10,203	10,211	10,221	10,251	10,287	10,317	0.4
Estonia	1,361	1,356	1,351	1,348	1,345	1,340	1,335	-9.3
Georgia	4,371	4,343	4,315	4,322	4,401	4,395	4,382	-8.1
Hungary	10,175	10,142	10,117	10,098	10,077	10,058	10,039	-6.3
Latvia	2,346	2,331	2,319	2,306	2,295	2,280	2,267	-9.6
Lithuania	3,476	3,463	3,446	3,425	3,403	3,385	3,366	-1.1
Macedonia	2,022	2,026	2,030	2,034	2,036	2,038	2,040	13.7
Moldova	3,961	3,888	3,820	3,759	3,709	3,667	3,633	-9.4
Poland	38,242	38,219	38,191	38,174	38,157	38,102	38,046	7.4
Romania	21,833	21,773	21,711	21,659	21,610	21,556	21,497	-2.9
Russia	145,649	144,964	144,168	143,474	142,754	142,221	142,009	2.8
Slovakia	5,379	5,379	5,380	5,385	5,389	5,392	5,394	8.7
Slovenia	1,994	1,995	1,996	1,998	2,003	2,010	2,016	6.5
Ukraine	48,241	47,823	47,442	47,100	46,749	46,466	46,192	-7.2

Source: *Euromonitor International from national statistics/UN*

Population Statistics

Table 21.3

Population by Sex and Age at January 1st 2008
'000

	Total	Male	Female	0-14	15-64	65+
Western Europe						
Austria	8,352	4,065	4,287	1,287	5,634	1,431
Belgium	10,618	5,199	5,419	1,795	7,006	1,817
Cyprus	862	420	443	157	595	110
Denmark	5,462	2,704	2,758	1,009	3,602	850
Finland	5,300	2,597	2,704	895	3,531	875
France	62,106	30,064	32,042	11,380	40,470	10,256
Germany	82,218	40,274	41,944	11,282	54,417	16,519
Gibraltar	29	15	15	5	19	5
Greece	11,211	5,549	5,663	1,596	7,531	2,084
Iceland	315	161	155	66	213	37
Ireland	4,378	2,187	2,191	893	2,994	492
Italy	58,976	28,657	30,318	8,246	38,867	11,863
Liechtenstein	35	17	18	6	25	4
Luxembourg	481	238	242	86	327	67
Malta	407	203	205	65	285	57
Monaco	33	16	17	5	21	7
Netherlands	16,383	8,103	8,281	2,934	11,042	2,406
Norway	4,737	2,360	2,377	907	3,136	693
Portugal	10,643	5,154	5,489	1,644	7,152	1,847
Spain	45,056	22,222	22,835	6,610	30,864	7,583
Sweden	9,157	4,544	4,613	1,529	6,017	1,611
Switzerland	7,530	3,683	3,848	1,167	5,125	1,239
Turkey	74,358	37,478	36,880	20,467	49,479	4,412
United Kingdom	61,186	30,003	31,183	10,740	40,599	9,847
Eastern Europe						
Albania	3,143	1,552	1,591	761	2,089	293
Belarus	9,690	4,522	5,168	1,422	6,867	1,400
Bosnia-Herzegovina	3,844	1,849	1,994	599	2,715	530
Bulgaria	7,571	3,669	3,903	1,000	5,253	1,318
Croatia	4,435	2,136	2,299	687	2,980	767
Czech Republic	10,317	5,037	5,280	1,470	7,338	1,509
Estonia	1,335	614	721	197	909	229
Georgia	4,382	2,078	2,304	753	2,998	631
Hungary	10,039	4,764	5,275	1,510	6,912	1,618
Latvia	2,267	1,044	1,222	310	1,566	391
Lithuania	3,366	1,567	1,799	516	2,317	534
Macedonia	2,040	1,017	1,023	373	1,431	237
Moldova	3,633	1,726	1,907	624	2,604	405
Poland	38,046	18,390	19,655	5,865	27,082	5,098
Romania	21,497	10,467	11,030	3,285	15,025	3,186
Russia	142,009	65,717	76,292	20,824	101,596	19,589
Slovakia	5,394	2,619	2,774	851	3,897	645
Slovenia	2,016	990	1,026	280	1,411	325
Ukraine	46,192	21,294	24,898	6,486	32,190	7,517

Source: *Euromonitor International from national statistics/UN*

Table 21.4

Population by Sex and Age (%) at January 1st 2008

% of total population

	Total	Male	Female	0-14	15-64	65+
Western Europe						
Austria	100.00	48.68	51.32	15.40	67.46	17.13
Belgium	100.00	48.96	51.04	16.91	65.98	17.11
Cyprus	100.00	48.66	51.34	18.24	69.01	12.76
Denmark	100.00	49.51	50.49	18.48	65.95	15.57
Finland	100.00	48.99	51.01	16.88	66.61	16.51
France	100.00	48.41	51.59	18.32	65.16	16.51
Germany	100.00	48.98	51.02	13.72	66.19	20.09
Gibraltar	100.00	50.12	49.88	17.80	65.45	16.75
Greece	100.00	49.49	50.51	14.24	67.17	18.59
Iceland	100.00	50.94	49.06	20.92	67.39	11.69
Ireland	100.00	49.96	50.04	20.39	68.38	11.23
Italy	100.00	48.59	51.41	13.98	65.90	20.12
Liechtenstein	100.00	49.32	50.68	16.86	71.04	12.10
Luxembourg	100.00	49.57	50.43	17.99	67.98	14.04
Malta	100.00	49.78	50.22	15.99	70.00	14.02
Monaco	100.00	47.48	52.52	13.73	63.72	22.55
Netherlands	100.00	49.46	50.54	17.91	67.40	14.69
Norway	100.00	49.81	50.19	19.15	66.21	14.64
Portugal	100.00	48.42	51.58	15.44	67.20	17.35
Spain	100.00	49.32	50.68	14.67	68.50	16.83
Sweden	100.00	49.63	50.37	16.70	65.70	17.60
Switzerland	100.00	48.90	51.10	15.49	68.06	16.45
Turkey	100.00	50.40	49.60	27.52	66.54	5.93
United Kingdom	100.00	49.04	50.96	17.55	66.35	16.09
Eastern Europe						
Albania	100.00	49.39	50.61	24.21	66.45	9.33
Belarus	100.00	46.66	53.34	14.68	70.87	14.45
Bosnia-Herzegovina	100.00	48.11	51.89	15.58	70.63	13.79
Bulgaria	100.00	48.45	51.55	13.21	69.38	17.41
Croatia	100.00	48.16	51.84	15.50	67.20	17.30
Czech Republic	100.00	48.82	51.18	14.25	71.13	14.62
Estonia	100.00	46.02	53.98	14.77	68.11	17.12
Georgia	100.00	47.43	52.57	17.18	68.42	14.41
Hungary	100.00	47.46	52.54	15.04	68.85	16.11
Latvia	100.00	46.07	53.93	13.66	69.08	17.26
Lithuania	100.00	46.56	53.44	15.33	68.82	15.85
Macedonia	100.00	49.87	50.13	18.27	70.14	11.60
Moldova	100.00	47.51	52.49	17.19	71.68	11.14
Poland	100.00	48.34	51.66	15.42	71.18	13.40
Romania	100.00	48.69	51.31	15.28	69.90	14.82
Russia	100.00	46.28	53.72	14.66	71.54	13.79
Slovakia	100.00	48.56	51.44	15.77	72.26	11.97
Slovenia	100.00	49.10	50.90	13.89	69.97	16.13
Ukraine	100.00	46.10	53.90	14.04	69.69	16.27

Source: *Euromonitor International from national statistics/UN*

Population Statistics

Table 21.5

Number of Live Births 1980-2008
'000

	1980	1985	1990	1995	2000	2003	2004	2005	2006	2007	2008
Western Europe											
Austria	90.9	87.4	90.5	88.7	78.3	76.9	79.0	78.2	77.6	77.2	77.0
Belgium	124.8	114.3	123.6	114.2	114.9	112.1	115.6	118.0	120.8	122.0	122.8
Cyprus	12.4	13.2	12.8	11.5	10.0	9.7	9.6	9.7	9.7	9.8	9.9
Denmark	57.3	53.7	63.4	69.8	67.1	64.7	64.6	64.3	65.0	63.9	62.9
Finland	63.1	62.8	65.5	63.1	56.7	56.6	57.8	57.7	58.8	58.7	59.3
France	800.4	768.4	762.4	729.6	774.8	761.5	767.8	774.4	796.9	786.0	801.0
Germany	865.8	813.8	905.7	765.2	767.0	706.7	705.6	685.8	672.7	684.9	682.5
Gibraltar			0.5	0.4	0.4	0.4	0.4	0.4	0.4	0.4	0.4
Greece	148.1	116.5	102.2	101.5	101.0	99.2	97.5	97.0	96.7	96.4	96.1
Iceland	4.3	4.3	4.5	4.4	4.2	4.2	4.3	4.4	4.4	4.5	4.6
Ireland	74.1	62.4	53.0	48.8	54.2	60.9	62.5	63.4	64.3	65.3	65.8
Italy	640.4	577.3	569.3	525.6	543.1	544.1	562.6	554.0	560.0	563.9	575.8
Liechtenstein			0.4	0.4	0.4	0.3	0.4	0.4	0.4	0.4	0.3
Luxembourg	4.1	4.3	4.8	5.4	5.5	5.4	5.4	5.4	5.4	5.4	5.5
Malta	5.7	5.6	5.4	5.0	4.3	3.9	3.8	3.7	3.7	3.7	3.7
Monaco			0.8	0.8	0.8	0.8	0.8	0.9	0.9	1.0	1.0
Netherlands	181.3	178.1	198.0	190.5	206.6	200.3	194.0	187.9	185.1	182.4	180.4
Norway	51.0	51.1	60.9	60.3	59.2	56.5	57.0	56.8	55.9	55.2	54.6
Portugal	158.4	130.5	116.4	107.1	120.0	116.7	118.3	118.9	119.4	119.5	119.0
Spain	571.0	456.3	401.4	363.5	397.6	441.9	454.6	465.6	471.1	476.6	480.4
Sweden	97.1	98.5	123.9	103.4	90.4	99.2	100.9	101.3	105.9	106.4	107.0
Switzerland	73.7	74.7	83.9	82.2	78.5	71.8	73.1	72.9	72.4	72.1	72.0
Turkey	1,448.1	1,437.4	1,395.0	1,468.0	1,494.0	1,410.0	1,360.0	1,361.0	1,360.0	1,360.1	1,361.4
United Kingdom	753.7	750.7	798.6	732.0	679.3	695.5	716.0	722.5	748.6	772.2	796.1
Eastern Europe											
Albania	73.3	78.1	77.8	67.1	51.9	46.2	45.3	45.0	45.1	45.5	46.1
Belarus	154.4	165.0	142.2	101.1	93.7	88.5	88.9	90.5	96.7	103.6	107.9
Bosnia-Herzegovina	70.9	72.7	67.0	47.9	39.6	35.2	35.2	34.6	34.0	33.8	34.6
Bulgaria	128.2	119.0	105.2	72.0	73.7	67.4	69.9	71.1	72.4	71.9	71.3
Croatia	68.2	62.7	55.4	50.2	43.7	39.7	40.3	42.5	42.4	42.6	42.8
Czech Republic	153.8	135.9	130.6	96.1	90.9	93.7	97.7	102.2	105.8	103.9	102.4
Estonia	22.2	23.6	22.3	13.5	13.1	13.0	14.0	14.4	14.7	14.8	15.0
Georgia	89.5	97.7	92.8	56.3	48.8	46.2	49.6	46.5	47.8	49.3	56.6
Hungary	148.7	130.2	125.7	112.1	97.6	94.6	95.1	97.5	99.4	99.0	98.5
Latvia	35.5	39.8	37.9	21.6	20.2	21.0	20.3	21.5	21.7	22.1	22.5
Lithuania	51.8	58.5	56.9	41.2	34.1	30.6	30.4	30.5	31.1	31.2	31.4
Macedonia	37.2	35.3	33.0	29.2	25.2	23.9	23.5	23.1	22.7	22.4	22.0
Moldova	83.4	92.6	80.4	59.3	48.3	45.1	44.7	44.6	44.6	44.8	44.9
Poland	695.8	680.1	547.7	433.1	378.3	351.1	356.1	364.4	368.3	369.2	371.5
Romania	398.9	358.8	314.7	236.6	234.5	212.5	216.3	221.0	221.7	221.7	221.0
Russia	2,202.8	2,375.1	1,988.9	1,363.8	1,266.8	1,477.3	1,502.5	1,457.4	1,479.6	1,610.1	1,713.9
Slovakia	95.1	90.2	80.0	61.4	55.2	51.7	53.7	54.4	52.6	52.4	52.3
Slovenia	29.9	25.9	22.4	19.0	18.2	17.3	18.0	18.2	18.2	18.4	18.6
Ukraine	742.5	762.8	657.2	492.9	385.1	408.6	427.3	426.1	460.4	472.7	474.2

Source: National statistical offices/UN/Euromonitor International

Population Statistics

Table 21.6

Number of Deaths 1980-2008
'000

	1980	1985	1990	1995	2000	2003	2004	2005	2006	2007	2008
Western Europe											
Austria	92.4	89.6	83.0	81.2	76.8	77.2	74.3	75.2	75.3	75.4	75.7
Belgium	114.4	112.7	104.5	104.6	104.9	107.0	101.9	103.3	102.4	103.6	104.4
Cyprus	5.3	5.7	5.7	5.3	5.5	5.7	5.8	5.9	6.0	6.1	6.2
Denmark	55.9	58.4	60.9	63.1	58.0	57.6	55.8	55.0	55.5	54.8	54.2
Finland	44.4	48.2	50.1	49.3	49.3	49.0	47.6	47.9	48.1	49.1	49.0
France	547.1	552.5	526.2	531.6	530.9	552.3	509.4	527.5	516.4	521.0	533.0
Germany	952.4	929.6	921.4	884.6	838.8	853.9	818.3	830.2	821.6	827.2	844.4
Gibraltar			0.3	0.2	0.3	0.2	0.2	0.2	0.3	0.3	0.3
Greece	87.3	92.9	94.2	100.2	103.0	99.3	97.3	96.6	96.2	95.9	95.7
Iceland	1.5	1.7	1.7	1.8	1.8	1.8	1.8	1.8	1.8	1.9	1.9
Ireland	33.5	33.2	31.4	32.3	31.1	33.9	34.3	33.9	33.7	33.7	33.7
Italy	554.5	547.4	541.8	554.3	555.5	588.9	545.1	588.9	557.9	573.0	579.5
Liechtenstein		0.2	0.2	0.2	0.2	0.2	0.2	0.2	0.2	0.2	0.2
Luxembourg	4.2	4.0	4.0	4.0	4.0	3.9	3.9	3.9	3.9	3.9	3.9
Malta	3.0	3.0	2.7	2.9	3.0	3.0	3.0	3.1	3.1	3.2	3.2
Monaco			0.6	0.6	0.5	0.6	0.5	0.6	0.6	0.6	0.6
Netherlands	114.3	122.7	128.8	135.7	140.5	141.9	136.6	136.4	135.8	137.4	139.2
Norway	41.3	44.4	46.0	45.2	44.0	42.5	41.2	41.2	41.2	41.2	41.2
Portugal	95.0	97.3	103.1	103.5	105.4	110.7	112.7	113.9	114.9	115.5	115.5
Spain	289.3	312.5	333.1	346.2	360.4	384.8	371.9	387.0	381.0	385.8	390.7
Sweden	91.8	94.0	95.2	94.0	93.5	93.0	90.5	91.7	91.2	91.1	91.0
Switzerland	59.1	59.6	63.7	63.4	62.5	63.1	60.2	61.1	61.4	61.8	62.3
Turkey	427.2	422.5	404.0	436.0	477.0	446.0	443.0	450.0	450.0	460.5	471.2
United Kingdom	659.9	670.7	641.8	645.5	608.4	611.2	583.1	582.7	572.2	574.7	573.7
Eastern Europe											
Albania	16.7	17.2	18.8	19.9	18.4	17.9	18.0	18.3	18.7	19.1	19.5
Belarus	95.5	105.7	109.6	133.8	134.9	143.2	140.1	141.9	138.4	133.0	133.9
Bosnia-Herzegovina	26.1	29.0	29.1	26.8	30.5	31.8	32.6	34.4	33.2	35.0	34.0
Bulgaria	98.0	107.5	108.6	114.7	115.1	111.9	110.1	113.4	113.2	112.6	111.9
Croatia	50.1	52.1	52.2	50.5	50.2	52.6	49.8	51.8	51.2	51.7	52.2
Czech Republic	135.5	131.6	129.2	117.9	109.0	111.3	107.2	107.9	104.4	105.1	105.9
Estonia	18.2	19.3	19.5	20.8	18.4	18.2	17.7	17.3	17.6	17.6	17.6
Georgia	43.3	46.2	50.7	49.1	47.4	46.1	48.8	40.7	42.3	41.2	43.0
Hungary	145.4	147.6	145.7	145.4	135.6	135.8	132.5	135.7	132.3	132.2	131.9
Latvia	32.1	34.2	34.8	38.9	32.2	32.4	32.0	32.8	33.4	33.4	33.4
Lithuania	35.9	39.2	39.8	45.3	38.9	41.0	41.3	43.8	44.7	44.9	45.0
Macedonia	12.2	13.7	15.1	15.9	16.8	17.5	17.7	18.0	18.3	18.5	18.8
Moldova	45.3	45.6	45.3	49.9	50.4	49.3	48.9	48.5	48.1	47.7	47.4
Poland	350.2	384.0	390.3	386.1	368.0	365.2	363.5	368.3	376.0	377.6	379.4
Romania	231.9	246.7	247.1	271.7	255.8	266.6	258.9	262.1	264.6	267.0	268.7
Russia	1,525.8	1,625.3	1,656.0	2,203.8	2,225.3	2,365.8	2,295.4	2,303.9	2,166.7	2,080.4	2,076.0
Slovakia	50.6	52.5	54.6	52.7	52.7	52.2	51.9	53.5	52.8	53.0	53.2
Slovenia	18.8	19.9	18.6	19.0	18.6	19.5	18.5	18.8	18.5	18.7	18.9
Ukraine	568.2	617.5	629.6	792.6	758.1	765.4	761.3	782.0	758.1	762.9	760.5

Source: National statistical offices/UN/Euromonitor International

Population Statistics
Table 21.7

Birth Rates 1980-2008

Per '000 inhabitants

	1980	1985	1990	1995	2000	2003	2004	2005	2006	2007	2008
Western Europe											
Austria	12.0	11.6	11.8	11.2	9.8	9.5	9.7	9.5	9.4	9.3	9.2
Belgium	12.7	11.6	12.4	11.3	11.2	10.8	11.1	11.3	11.5	11.5	11.6
Cyprus	20.4	20.4	18.8	15.8	12.7	11.8	11.7	11.6	11.5	11.5	11.5
Denmark	11.2	10.5	12.4	13.4	12.6	12.0	12.0	11.9	12.0	11.7	11.5
Finland	13.2	12.8	13.2	12.4	11.0	10.9	11.1	11.0	11.2	11.1	11.2
France	14.9	13.9	13.5	12.6	13.2	12.7	12.7	12.7	13.0	12.8	12.9
Germany	11.1	10.5	11.4	9.4	9.3	8.6	8.5	8.3	8.2	8.3	8.3
Gibraltar			19.8	15.9	14.9	13.1	14.6	14.5	14.7	15.1	15.3
Greece	15.5	11.7	10.1	9.6	9.3	9.0	8.8	8.8	8.7	8.6	8.6
Iceland	18.7	17.7	17.5	16.5	14.8	14.6	14.7	14.7	14.8	14.7	14.7
Ireland	21.8	17.6	15.1	13.6	14.4	15.4	15.5	15.4	15.3	15.2	15.0
Italy	11.4	10.2	10.0	9.2	9.5	9.5	9.7	9.5	9.5	9.6	9.8
Liechtenstein			13.3	13.9	13.0	10.2	10.8	11.0	10.3	10.0	9.6
Luxembourg	11.3	11.8	12.7	13.3	12.5	11.8	11.7	11.6	11.5	11.4	11.3
Malta	17.6	16.3	15.0	13.3	11.1	9.8	9.5	9.3	9.1	9.1	9.0
Monaco			26.3	26.3	23.7	26.1	25.5	27.5	28.4	29.4	30.1
Netherlands	12.9	12.3	13.3	12.4	13.0	12.4	11.9	11.5	11.3	11.1	11.0
Norway	12.5	12.3	14.4	13.9	13.2	12.4	12.4	12.3	12.1	11.8	11.5
Portugal	16.3	13.0	11.6	10.7	11.8	11.2	11.3	11.3	11.3	11.3	11.2
Spain	15.3	11.9	10.3	9.2	9.9	10.6	10.7	10.8	10.8	10.7	10.7
Sweden	11.7	11.8	14.5	11.7	10.2	11.1	11.2	11.2	11.7	11.7	11.7
Switzerland	11.7	11.6	12.6	11.7	11.0	9.8	9.9	9.8	9.7	9.6	9.6
Turkey	32.9	28.9	25.1	24.0	22.3	20.2	19.2	19.0	18.8	18.5	18.3
United Kingdom	13.4	13.3	14.0	12.6	11.6	11.7	12.0	12.0	12.4	12.7	13.0
Eastern Europe											
Albania	27.4	26.4	23.7	21.4	16.9	15.0	14.6	14.5	14.5	14.5	14.7
Belarus	16.1	16.6	14.0	9.9	9.4	8.9	9.0	9.2	9.9	10.7	11.1
Bosnia-Herzegovina	17.6	17.1	14.9	13.6	10.5	9.2	9.2	9.0	8.9	8.8	9.0
Bulgaria	14.5	13.3	12.0	8.7	9.2	8.6	9.0	9.2	9.4	9.4	9.4
Croatia	14.8	13.3	11.6	10.7	9.8	8.9	9.1	9.6	9.5	9.6	9.6
Czech Republic	15.0	13.2	12.7	9.3	8.9	9.2	9.6	10.0	10.3	10.1	9.9
Estonia	15.1	15.5	14.2	9.3	9.5	9.6	10.4	10.6	10.9	11.1	11.2
Georgia	18.8	19.7	18.0	11.8	11.0	10.6	11.5	10.8	10.9	11.2	12.9
Hungary	13.9	12.2	12.1	10.8	9.5	9.3	9.4	9.7	9.9	9.8	9.8
Latvia	14.2	15.5	14.2	8.6	8.5	9.0	8.8	9.3	9.5	9.7	9.9
Lithuania	15.2	16.6	15.4	11.3	9.7	8.8	8.8	8.9	9.1	9.2	9.3
Macedonia	20.7	19.3	17.3	14.9	12.5	11.8	11.6	11.4	11.2	11.0	10.8
Moldova	20.8	22.0	18.4	13.7	11.8	11.6	11.7	11.9	12.0	12.2	12.4
Poland	19.6	18.3	14.4	11.3	9.9	9.2	9.3	9.5	9.7	9.7	9.8
Romania	18.0	15.8	13.6	10.6	10.7	9.8	10.0	10.2	10.3	10.3	10.3
Russia	15.9	16.7	13.5	9.2	8.6	10.2	10.4	10.2	10.4	11.3	12.1
Slovakia	19.2	17.5	15.2	11.5	10.3	9.6	10.0	10.1	9.8	9.7	9.7
Slovenia	15.8	13.4	11.2	9.5	9.1	8.7	9.0	9.1	9.1	9.1	9.2
Ukraine	14.9	15.1	12.7	9.6	7.8	8.5	9.0	9.0	9.8	10.2	10.3

Source: *National statistical offices/UN/Euromonitor International*

Population Statistics

Table 21.8

Birth Rates by Quarter 2007-2009

Per '000 inhabitants

	2007 1st Quarter	2007 2nd Quarter	2007 3rd Quarter	2007 4th Quarter	2008 1st Quarter	2008 2nd Quarter	2008 3rd Quarter	2008 4th Quarter	2009 1st Quarter	2009 2nd Quarter
Western Europe										
Austria	8.7	9.4	9.9	9.3	8.6	9.2	9.9	9.1		
Belgium										
Cyprus			11.8	11.4						
Denmark			12.5	11.5						
Finland	11.0	11.3	11.5	10.6	11.3	11.3	11.6	10.6	11.1	11.5
France			12.9	12.6	12.6	13.0	13.3	12.7	12.6	
Germany	8.2	8.1	8.9	8.1	8.1	8.4	9.0	7.7	7.8	
Gibraltar										
Greece			8.9	8.3	7.0	7.7	10.2	9.4		
Iceland										
Ireland	15.3	14.7	15.9	14.9	15.6	15.2	15.0			
Italy	9.4	9.2	9.8	9.8	9.4	9.5	10.3	9.7	9.3	
Liechtenstein										
Luxembourg	11.2	11.1	11.7	11.6	10.9	11.4	12.0	11.0		
Malta										
Monaco										
Netherlands	11.0	10.8	11.8	10.9	10.5	11.0	11.8	10.7	10.7	10.8
Norway	11.8	12.4	12.3	10.8	11.4	12.2	12.2	10.7	11.4	
Portugal			10.3	9.8						
Spain			10.7	10.7						
Sweden	11.7	12.3	12.0	10.6	11.8	12.4	12.2	10.4	11.7	12.4
Switzerland	9.4	9.6	10.2	9.3	9.5	9.9	9.6	9.3	9.4	9.7
Turkey										
United Kingdom	12.2		13.2		12.7	13.3				
Eastern Europe										
Albania										
Belarus	10.1		11.2	10.5	11.2	11.0				
Bosnia-Herzegovina										
Bulgaria										
Croatia										
Czech Republic			11.7	10.9						
Estonia	10.6	11.3	11.7	10.7	11.1	11.4	11.9	10.4	10.6	11.3
Georgia										
Hungary	9.7	9.4	10.5	9.8	9.6	9.5	10.5	9.6	9.5	9.3
Latvia	9.5	9.5	10.4	9.4	10.1	9.9	10.5	9.3	9.1	9.4
Lithuania	8.7	8.9	10.3	9.1	8.5	9.2	10.6	9.2	8.9	9.8
Macedonia	10.8	10.9	11.4	10.9	11.2	10.4				
Moldova	11.9	11.8	12.9	12.2	12.0	11.2	13.2	13.0	13.0	13.0
Poland			10.4	9.0	9.4	9.7	10.6	9.3	10.5	
Romania	10.3	9.8	10.9	10.1	10.3	9.7	10.8	10.2	9.9	9.8
Russia	11.0	11.0	11.5	11.8	11.9	11.8	12.2	12.4	12.0	12.3
Slovakia	9.2	9.7	10.4	9.6	9.1	9.5	10.6	9.6	9.7	10.3
Slovenia	8.8	9.2	9.6	9.0	8.8	9.1	9.9	9.2		
Ukraine	9.8	9.6	11.1	10.2	10.3				11.2	

Source: *National statistical offices/UN/Euromonitor International*

Table 21.9

Birth Rates by Month 2008
Per '000 inhabitants

	January	February	March	April	May	June	July	August	September	October	November	December
Western Europe												
Austria	8.1	8.9	8.7	9.4	8.9	9.3	10.0	9.3	10.2	9.4	8.4	9.5
Belgium												
Cyprus												
Denmark												
Finland												
France	12.8	12.7	12.4	13.1	13.2	12.9	13.5	13.1	13.3	12.9	12.6	12.7
Germany	8.6	8.3	7.4	8.5	8.1	8.7	9.5	8.4	9.0	8.3	7.4	7.5
Gibraltar												
Greece	7.7	6.9	6.5	6.6	7.2	9.2	10.2	9.8	10.5	9.8	9.1	9.3
Iceland												
Ireland												
Italy	10.3	9.3	8.7	9.4	9.8	9.4	10.4	9.4	11.2	10.3	9.3	9.6
Liechtenstein												
Luxembourg	12.2	10.2	10.4	10.6	11.9	11.8	13.7	11.5	11.0	11.4	10.9	10.6
Malta												
Monaco												
Netherlands	10.6	10.7	10.4	10.8	11.0	11.3	11.9	11.5	11.9	11.1	10.6	10.5
Norway												
Portugal												
Spain												
Sweden	11.5	12.0	11.8	12.8	12.3	12.2	12.8	12.0	11.8	11.1	10.2	9.9
Switzerland	9.8	9.7	9.2	9.8	9.8	10.1	9.8	9.6	9.5	9.4	9.1	9.4
Turkey												
United Kingdom												
Eastern Europe												
Albania												
Belarus	11.3	11.2	11.1	10.9	11.1							
Bosnia-Herzegovina												
Bulgaria												
Croatia												
Czech Republic												
Estonia	12.4	10.3	10.7	11.4	11.3	11.6	12.5	11.4	11.9	10.8	9.4	11.1
Georgia												
Hungary	10.0	9.7	9.1	9.4	9.2	10.0	10.9	10.1	10.7	9.7	9.4	9.8
Latvia	11.2	9.5	9.6	9.9	9.9	9.7	11.1	10.1	10.1	9.8	8.5	9.5
Lithuania	9.7	7.9	7.8	9.4	9.4	8.8	11.9	10.0	9.7	9.7	8.3	9.4
Macedonia	11.9	11.3	10.4	10.1	10.6							
Moldova	12.3	13.0	10.8	10.9	11.8	11.0	13.4	12.3	13.8	14.0	12.3	12.7
Poland	10.4	9.0	8.9	10.0	9.5	9.7	11.0	9.9	10.9	10.3	8.4	9.2
Romania	11.0	10.4	9.6	9.5	9.7	10.0	11.6	10.4	10.5	11.2	9.6	9.9
Russia	12.0	12.1	11.8	12.0	11.8	11.8	12.1	12.2	12.3	12.4	12.4	12.4
Slovakia	9.2	9.1	9.1	9.5	9.1	9.8	11.0	9.7	11.2	9.7	8.4	10.7
Slovenia												
Ukraine												

Source: National statistical offices/UN/Euromonitor International

Table 21.10

Death Rates 1980-2008

Per '000 inhabitants

	1980	1985	1990	1995	2000	2003	2004	2005	2006	2007	2008
Western Europe											
Austria	12.3	11.8	10.9	10.2	9.6	9.5	9.1	9.2	9.1	9.1	9.1
Belgium	11.6	11.4	10.5	10.3	10.2	10.3	9.8	9.9	9.7	9.8	9.8
Cyprus	8.7	8.8	8.3	7.3	7.0	6.9	7.0	7.0	7.0	7.1	7.2
Denmark	10.9	11.4	11.9	12.1	10.9	10.7	10.3	10.2	10.2	10.1	9.9
Finland	9.3	9.8	10.1	9.7	9.5	9.4	9.1	9.2	9.1	9.3	9.2
France	10.2	10.0	9.3	9.2	9.0	9.2	8.4	8.7	8.4	8.5	8.6
Germany	12.2	12.0	11.6	10.8	10.2	10.3	9.9	10.1	10.0	10.0	10.3
Gibraltar			10.4	7.5	9.6	8.2	8.4	8.6	8.7	8.8	8.8
Greece	9.1	9.4	9.3	9.5	9.4	9.0	8.8	8.7	8.6	8.6	8.5
Iceland	6.6	6.9	6.8	6.8	6.4	6.2	6.1	6.1	6.1	6.1	6.0
Ireland	9.9	9.4	8.9	9.0	8.2	8.6	8.5	8.2	8.0	7.8	7.7
Italy	9.8	9.7	9.6	9.8	9.8	10.3	9.4	10.1	9.5	9.7	9.8
Liechtenstein			6.9	7.3	7.4	6.4	5.8	6.2	6.3	6.5	6.5
Luxembourg	11.4	11.0	10.5	9.8	9.1	8.7	8.6	8.5	8.3	8.2	8.1
Malta	9.1	8.6	7.6	7.6	7.7	7.6	7.6	7.6	7.7	7.8	7.9
Monaco			19.5	17.7	17.1	19.1	16.2	18.5	18.1	18.8	18.9
Netherlands	8.1	8.5	8.7	8.8	8.9	8.8	8.4	8.4	8.3	8.4	8.5
Norway	10.1	10.7	10.9	10.4	9.8	9.3	9.0	9.0	8.9	8.8	8.7
Portugal	9.8	9.7	10.3	10.3	10.3	10.6	10.8	10.8	10.9	10.9	10.9
Spain	7.8	8.1	8.6	8.8	9.0	9.2	8.8	9.0	8.7	8.7	8.7
Sweden	11.1	11.3	11.2	10.7	10.5	10.4	10.1	10.2	10.1	10.0	9.9
Switzerland	9.4	9.2	9.6	9.0	8.7	8.6	8.2	8.2	8.2	8.2	8.3
Turkey	9.7	8.5	7.3	7.1	7.1	6.4	6.3	6.3	6.2	6.3	6.3
United Kingdom	11.7	11.9	11.2	11.1	10.3	10.3	9.8	9.7	9.5	9.4	9.4
Eastern Europe											
Albania	6.2	5.8	5.7	6.4	6.0	5.8	5.8	5.9	6.0	6.1	6.2
Belarus	10.0	10.6	10.8	13.1	13.5	14.5	14.2	14.5	14.2	13.7	13.8
Bosnia-Herzegovina	6.5	6.8	6.5	7.6	8.1	8.3	8.5	9.0	8.6	9.1	8.8
Bulgaria	11.1	12.0	12.4	13.8	14.4	14.3	14.2	14.7	14.7	14.8	14.8
Croatia	10.9	11.1	10.9	10.8	11.3	11.8	11.2	11.7	11.5	11.6	11.8
Czech Republic	13.2	12.8	12.5	11.4	10.6	10.9	10.5	10.6	10.2	10.2	10.3
Estonia	12.4	12.7	12.4	14.4	13.4	13.4	13.1	12.9	13.1	13.1	13.2
Georgia	9.1	9.3	9.9	10.2	10.7	10.6	11.3	9.4	9.6	9.4	9.8
Hungary	13.6	13.9	14.0	14.1	13.3	13.4	13.1	13.4	13.1	13.1	13.1
Latvia	12.8	13.3	13.0	15.6	13.5	13.9	13.8	14.2	14.6	14.6	14.7
Lithuania	10.5	11.1	10.8	12.4	11.1	11.8	12.0	12.8	13.1	13.3	13.4
Macedonia	6.8	7.5	7.9	8.1	8.4	8.6	8.7	8.8	9.0	9.1	9.2
Moldova	11.3	10.8	10.4	11.5	12.3	12.7	12.8	12.9	13.0	13.0	13.1
Poland	9.9	10.4	10.3	10.1	9.6	9.6	9.5	9.6	9.9	9.9	10.0
Romania	10.5	10.9	10.6	12.2	11.7	12.2	11.9	12.1	12.2	12.4	12.5
Russia	11.0	11.4	11.2	14.8	15.1	16.3	15.9	16.1	15.2	14.6	14.6
Slovakia	10.2	10.2	10.4	9.9	9.8	9.7	9.6	9.9	9.8	9.8	9.9
Slovenia	9.9	10.3	9.3	9.5	9.4	9.7	9.3	9.4	9.2	9.3	9.3
Ukraine	11.4	12.2	12.2	15.4	15.4	16.0	16.0	16.6	16.2	16.4	16.5

Source: National statistical offices/UN/Euromonitor International

Population Statistics

Table 21.11

Death Rates by Quarter 2007-2009
Per '000 inhabitants

	2007 1st Quarter	2007 2nd Quarter	2007 3rd Quarter	2007 4th Quarter	2008 1st Quarter	2008 2nd Quarter	2008 3rd Quarter	2008 4th Quarter	2009 1st Quarter	2009 2nd Quarter
Western Europe										
Austria	9.5	8.9	8.6	9.4	9.5	8.9	8.6	9.3		
Belgium										
Cyprus			6.5	6.9						
Denmark			9.5	10.2						
Finland	10.3	9.1	8.8	8.9	9.8	9.2	8.8	9.0	10.2	9.1
France			8.0	8.9	9.3	8.3	8.0	8.7	10.3	
Germany	10.8	9.9	9.3	10.2	11.1	10.2	9.6	10.1	11.7	
Gibraltar										
Greece			8.6	8.5	7.8	7.9	9.0	9.3		
Iceland										
Ireland	9.0	7.7	7.2	7.5	8.3	8.1	7.4			
Italy	10.7	9.4	9.0	9.9	11.1	9.4	9.1	9.7	11.4	
Liechtenstein										
Luxembourg	8.8	8.1	7.6	8.4	8.8	7.9	7.7	8.3		
Malta										
Monaco										
Netherlands	9.0	8.2	7.7	8.7	9.2	8.4	7.8	8.6	9.6	8.1
Norway	9.8	8.4	8.2	8.8	9.3	8.5	8.3	9.0	9.7	
Portugal			8.5	10.0						
Spain			8.1	9.2						
Sweden	11.0	9.7	9.2	10.0	10.6	9.8	9.3	10.0	11.1	9.3
Switzerland	9.0	7.8	7.6	8.5	9.1	8.0	7.5	8.4	9.6	7.9
Turkey										
United Kingdom	10.5		8.4		9.5	9.3				
Eastern Europe										
Albania										
Belarus	14.8		12.4	13.5	15.3					
Bosnia-Herzegovina										
Bulgaria										
Croatia										
Czech Republic			9.6	10.4						
Estonia	14.4	12.6	12.4	13.2	14.5	13.0	12.6	12.7	13.5	12.4
Georgia										
Hungary	14.1	12.8	12.5	13.2	14.0	12.9	12.2	13.4	14.6	12.6
Latvia	16.5	14.1	13.4	14.6	15.6	14.4	14.0	14.8	15.1	14.3
Lithuania	14.6	12.9	11.9	13.6	14.5	13.1	12.5	13.4	14.1	12.8
Macedonia	10.5	8.7	8.2	8.9	9.8	8.7				
Moldova	14.5	12.5	11.3	13.7	14.9	12.7	11.2	13.4	14.9	12.9
Poland			9.4	10.4	10.6	9.9	9.3	10.1	11.4	
Romania	13.5	12.0	11.1	12.9	13.5	12.3	11.1	13.0	13.8	12.3
Russia	15.1	14.7	14.4	14.3	15.3	14.7	14.3	14.1	14.5	14.1
Slovakia	10.3	9.5	9.6	10.0	10.1	9.7	9.4	10.2	10.2	9.5
Slovenia	10.2	9.0	8.6	9.4	10.0	9.1	8.8	9.5		
Ukraine	17.6	15.8	15.1	17.2	18.0				17.0	

Source: National statistical offices/UN/Euromonitor International

Population Statistics

Table 21.12

Death Rates by Month 2008
Per '000 inhabitants

	January	February	March	April	May	June	July	August	September	October	November	December
Western Europe												
Austria	9.4	9.7	9.2	9.5	8.6	8.6	8.7	7.8	9.1	9.2	8.4	10.3
Belgium												
Cyprus												
Denmark												
Finland												
France	9.7	9.3	8.8	8.8	8.1	8.0	8.1	7.7	8.0	8.4	8.4	9.3
Germany	12.3	10.6	10.5	11.1	9.7	9.7	9.9	8.9	10.1	9.9	9.5	10.9
Gibraltar												
Greece	7.5	7.4	8.6	7.2	7.5	9.0	9.0	9.7	8.4	9.0	9.0	9.9
Iceland												
Ireland												
Italy	11.8	11.1	10.3	9.8	9.2	9.2	9.3	8.6	9.3	9.6	9.0	10.3
Liechtenstein												
Luxembourg	9.1	8.3	8.9	8.4	8.0	7.2	7.3	8.3	7.3	7.8	8.0	9.1
Malta												
Monaco												
Netherlands	9.6	9.1	9.0	8.7	8.4	8.1	8.1	7.7	7.7	8.2	8.4	9.2
Norway												
Portugal												
Spain												
Sweden	10.8	10.4	10.8	10.5	9.6	9.4	9.4	9.1	9.5	9.5	9.9	10.8
Switzerland	9.5	9.0	8.8	8.5	7.8	7.8	7.6	7.4	7.6	7.8	8.3	9.1
Turkey												
United Kingdom												
Eastern Europe												
Albania												
Belarus	15.4	15.3	15.1	13.6								
Bosnia-Herzegovina												
Bulgaria												
Croatia												
Czech Republic												
Estonia	14.9	14.4	14.2	13.3	13.1	12.7	12.7	11.5	13.5	12.7	11.5	13.7
Georgia												
Hungary	14.3	14.0	13.9	13.5	12.5	12.6	11.9	12.1	12.6	13.0	13.1	14.1
Latvia	17.1	14.4	15.2	15.0	14.2	14.1	14.4	12.8	14.9	15.4	13.5	15.6
Lithuania	16.9	13.4	13.1	13.3	13.3	12.8	12.9	11.9	12.7	14.2	12.3	13.5
Macedonia	10.6	9.5	9.2	8.7	8.9							
Moldova	17.2	14.7	12.9	12.7	13.9	11.5	11.4	10.5	11.6	12.6	13.4	14.3
Poland	11.0	10.0	10.7	10.3	9.7	9.5	9.4	8.7	9.7	10.1	9.0	11.2
Romania	14.2	13.6	12.8	12.8	12.1	12.0	11.0	10.9	11.5	12.5	12.6	13.9
Russia	16.0	15.2	14.9	14.9	14.7	14.6	14.5	14.2	14.2	14.2	14.1	14.1
Slovakia	10.2	10.3	9.9	10.0	9.8	9.3	9.3	9.1	9.7	10.0	9.8	10.9
Slovenia												
Ukraine												

Source: National statistical offices/UN/Euromonitor International

Population Statistics

Table 21.13

Infant Mortality Rates 1980-2008
Deaths per '000 live births

	1980	1985	1990	1995	2000	2003	2004	2005	2006	2007	2008
Western Europe											
Austria	14.3	11.2	7.8	5.4	4.8	4.5	4.0	3.9	3.8	3.7	3.6
Belgium	12.1	9.8	6.5	5.8	4.8	4.2	4.1	4.0	3.9	3.8	3.7
Cyprus	18.0	14.4	11.0	8.5	5.6	4.1	3.5	3.5	3.3	3.1	3.0
Denmark	8.4	7.9	7.5	5.1	5.3	4.4	4.4	4.3	4.2	4.1	4.0
Finland	7.6	6.3	5.6	3.9	3.6	3.2	3.0	2.9	2.7	2.7	2.7
France	10.0	8.3	7.3	4.9	4.4	4.1	4.0	4.0	3.8	3.7	3.7
Germany	12.4	9.1	7.0	5.3	4.4	4.1	4.0	3.9	3.9	3.7	3.7
Gibraltar											
Greece	17.9	14.1	9.7	8.1	6.0	4.8	4.6	4.4	4.1	4.0	3.9
Iceland	7.4	6.1	5.5	4.1	3.2	3.1	3.0	3.0	3.0	2.9	2.9
Ireland	11.1	8.8	8.2	6.4	6.2	5.1	5.0	4.9	4.8	4.7	4.6
Italy	14.6	10.5	8.2	6.2	4.5	4.3	4.1	4.0	3.9	3.8	3.7
Liechtenstein											
Luxembourg	12.0	9.1	7.0	6.0	5.0	5.0	5.0	4.0	2.5	1.8	1.6
Malta	13.9	10.9	9.1	8.5	7.3	6.9	6.8	6.7	6.6	6.5	6.4
Monaco	8.0	7.6	7.0	6.0	5.0	4.0	3.0	4.0	3.0	2.8	2.7
Netherlands	8.6	8.0	7.1	5.5	5.1	4.7	4.6	4.6	4.5	4.3	4.2
Norway [a]	8.1	8.5	6.9	4.0	3.8	3.4	3.3	3.2	3.1	2.9	2.9
Portugal [b]	24.2	17.8	11.0	7.5	5.5	3.9	3.7	3.4	3.2	3.1	2.9
Spain	12.3	8.9	7.6	5.5	3.9	3.4	3.1	3.0	2.9	2.8	2.7
Sweden	6.9	6.8	6.0	4.1	3.4	3.0	2.9	2.8	2.7	2.6	2.4
Switzerland	9.1	6.9	6.8	5.0	4.9	4.3	4.2	4.1	4.0	3.9	3.8
Turkey	93.4	93.6	54.0	44.6	40.2	38.3	37.5	36.6	36.5	35.6	34.8
United Kingdom	13.9	10.7	8.9	7.0	6.3	6.0	5.8	5.6	5.6	5.4	5.3
Eastern Europe											
Albania	47.0	43.8	37.0	29.0	22.0	19.2	18.6	18.3	18.1	17.8	17.6
Belarus	16.2	14.6	12.1	13.5	9.3	7.5	7.1	6.7	6.4	6.2	6.1
Bosnia-Herzegovina	31.0	24.3	18.0	16.0	15.0	14.0	13.0	13.0	12.8	12.2	11.9
Bulgaria [c]	20.2	15.4	14.8	14.8	13.3	13.0	12.6	12.2	12.1	11.8	11.6
Croatia	20.6	16.6	10.7	8.9	7.4	6.7	6.5	6.3	6.2	6.0	5.9
Czech Republic	16.9	12.5	10.8	7.7	4.1	4.0	3.8	3.6	3.5	3.5	3.4
Estonia	17.1	14.1	12.3	14.8	8.4	6.8	6.6	6.2	5.9	5.5	5.4
Georgia	25.4	23.9	20.5	28.4	22.5	24.8	23.8	19.7	15.8	13.3	12.1
Hungary	23.2	20.4	14.8	10.7	9.2	7.3	6.9	6.8	6.3	6.0	5.9
Latvia	15.3	13.0	13.7	18.8	10.4	10.0	9.3	9.0	8.7	8.3	8.1
Lithuania	14.5	14.2	10.2	12.5	8.6	7.0	6.7	6.5	6.1	5.9	5.6
Macedonia	53.0	44.1	34.0	24.0	22.0	20.7	18.3	15.0	11.5	10.3	9.9
Moldova	35.0	30.9	19.0	21.2	18.3	14.4	12.2	12.4	11.8	11.3	11.0
Poland	25.4	22.2	19.4	13.6	8.1	6.9	6.6	6.3	5.9	5.8	5.5
Romania	29.3	25.6	26.9	21.2	18.6	15.7	15.0	14.5	13.7	13.2	12.7
Russia	22.0	20.8	17.6	18.2	15.2	12.3	11.5	11.0	10.6	10.2	9.9
Slovakia	20.9	16.3	12.0	11.0	8.6	8.2	7.3	7.1	6.7	6.3	6.2
Slovenia	15.3	13.0	8.4	5.5	4.9	4.1	4.0	3.9	3.7	3.7	3.6
Ukraine	16.6	15.9	13.0	14.8	12.0	9.8	9.5	9.1	8.7	8.4	8.2

Source: *Euromonitor International from UN/national statistical offices/Eurostat*
Notes: *Rates refer to deaths of infants under one year*
(a) Rates from 1977 to 1990 are annual averages for five-year periods, (b) NUTS Nomenclature of Territorial Units of Statistics; Note: 1998 data new methodology, (c) The crude death rates are calculated per thousands of the average annual population

Table 21.14

Marriage Rates 1980-2008
Per '000 inhabitants

	1980	1985	1990	1995	2000	2003	2004	2005	2006	2007	2008
Western Europe											
Austria	6.2	5.9	5.9	5.4	4.9	4.6	4.7	4.8	4.8	4.9	4.9
Belgium	6.7	5.8	6.5	5.1	4.4	4.0	4.2	4.2	4.2	4.2	4.2
Cyprus	8.3	8.7	8.2	9.1	11.8	13.2	13.3	13.4	13.3	13.3	13.3
Denmark	5.2	5.7	6.1	6.7	7.2	6.5	7.0	7.1	7.1	7.1	7.2
Finland	6.2	5.3	5.0	4.7	5.1	5.0	5.6	5.7	5.7	5.7	5.8
France	6.2	4.9	5.1	4.4	5.1	4.6	4.3	4.2	4.1	4.0	3.9
Germany	6.4	6.4	6.5	5.3	5.1	4.6	4.8	4.8	4.8	4.9	4.9
Gibraltar					5.4	6.3	5.5	5.6	5.7	5.8	5.9
Greece	6.5	6.4	5.8	6.0	4.5	5.5	5.5	5.4	5.4	5.3	5.3
Iceland	5.7	5.2	4.5	4.6	6.3	5.1	5.2	5.4	5.4	5.4	5.3
Ireland	6.4	5.3	5.1	4.3	5.1	5.1	5.1	5.0	5.0	4.9	4.8
Italy	5.7	5.3	5.6	5.1	5.0	4.6	4.5	4.5	4.4	4.4	4.4
Liechtenstein	13.5	12.7	11.5	13.4	7.3	4.4	4.8	5.4	5.6	5.5	5.6
Luxembourg	5.9	5.4	6.1	5.1	4.9	4.4	4.4	4.4	4.4	4.4	4.5
Malta	8.9	7.4	6.9	6.1	6.5	5.9	6.0	5.9	6.0	6.1	6.1
Monaco	6.5			6.0	5.0	5.7	5.3	5.0	4.9	4.9	4.8
Netherlands	6.4	5.7	6.4	5.3	5.6	5.0	4.5	4.4	4.3	4.2	4.2
Norway	5.4	4.9	5.2	5.0	5.7	4.9	4.9	4.8	4.8	4.7	4.7
Portugal	7.4	6.8	7.2	6.6	6.3	5.2	5.0	5.0	5.0	4.9	4.9
Spain	5.9	5.2	5.7	5.1	5.4	5.1	5.1	5.0	5.0	4.9	4.8
Sweden	4.5	4.6	4.7	3.8	4.5	4.4	4.8	4.8	4.9	4.9	5.0
Switzerland	5.7	6.0	7.0	5.8	5.5	5.5	5.4	5.3	5.2	5.2	5.1
Turkey	8.3	7.4	8.3	7.6	6.9	6.8	6.7	6.7	6.6	6.5	6.4
United Kingdom	7.4	7.0	6.6	5.6	5.2	5.2	5.2	5.2	5.1	5.1	5.1
Eastern Europe											
Albania	8.1	8.5	8.8	8.0	8.4	8.9	6.8	7.0	7.0	7.1	7.1
Belarus	10.2	9.9	9.7	7.5	6.2	7.1	7.2	7.3	7.4	7.4	7.5
Bosnia-Herzegovina	7.8	7.8	6.7	6.2	5.8	5.4	5.8	5.6	5.6	5.6	5.6
Bulgaria	7.9	7.4	6.8	4.4	4.4	3.9	4.0	4.0	4.0	4.0	4.0
Croatia	7.2	6.6	5.8	5.2	5.0	5.0	5.1	5.1	5.1	5.2	5.2
Czech Republic	7.6	7.8	8.8	5.3	5.4	4.8	5.0	5.1	5.1	5.1	5.1
Estonia	8.8	8.4	7.5	4.8	4.0	4.2	4.5	4.5	4.6	4.6	4.7
Georgia	10.6	8.9	6.8	4.5	2.9	2.9	3.4	4.2	5.0	5.7	6.0
Hungary	7.5	6.9	6.4	5.2	4.7	4.5	4.3	4.3	4.3	4.3	4.3
Latvia	9.8	9.4	8.9	4.4	3.9	4.3	4.5	4.6	4.7	4.8	4.9
Lithuania	9.3	9.7	9.8	6.1	4.8	4.9	5.6	5.8	6.0	6.3	6.4
Macedonia	9.0	8.9	8.2	8.1	7.1	7.1	6.9	7.1	7.3	7.6	7.4
Moldova	11.5	9.7	9.4	7.6	5.3	6.4	6.6	6.7	6.6	6.7	6.8
Poland	8.7	7.2	6.7	5.4	5.5	5.1	5.1	5.2	5.2	5.2	5.2
Romania	8.3	7.1	8.3	6.9	6.2	6.2	6.2	6.3	6.3	6.4	6.4
Russia	10.6	9.7	8.9	7.2	6.1	7.5	6.8	7.4	7.6	7.7	7.9
Slovakia	8.0	7.6	7.7	5.1	4.8	4.8	4.9	4.9	5.0	5.0	5.1
Slovenia	6.5	5.5	4.3	4.1	3.6	3.4	3.3	3.3	3.2	3.2	3.2
Ukraine	9.3	9.7	9.4	8.4	5.6	7.8	5.9	5.8	5.8	5.8	5.7

Source: *National statistical offices/Council of Europe/UN/Euromonitor International*
Notes: *Rates refer to legal marriages (recognised marriages performed and registered)*

Table 21.15

Divorce Rates 1980-2008
Per '000 inhabitants

	1980	1985	1990	1995	2000	2003	2004	2005	2006	2007	2008
Western Europe											
Austria	1.8	2.0	2.1	2.3	2.4	2.3	2.3	2.3	2.2	2.2	2.2
Belgium	1.5	1.9	2.0	3.5	2.6	3.0	3.0	3.0	3.0	3.0	3.0
Cyprus	0.3	0.4	0.5	1.0	1.5	1.8	2.0	1.8	1.9	1.9	2.0
Denmark	2.7	2.8	2.7	2.5	2.7	2.9	2.9	3.0	3.0	3.0	3.1
Finland	2.0	1.9	2.6	2.8	2.7	2.6	2.5	2.5	2.5	2.5	2.4
France	1.5	1.9	1.9	2.1	1.9	2.1	2.1	2.2	2.2	2.2	2.2
Germany	1.8	2.3	2.0	2.1	2.4	2.6	2.7	2.7	2.8	2.8	2.9
Gibraltar					3.5	5.6	4.1	3.3	3.3	3.2	3.0
Greece	0.7	0.8	0.6	1.0	1.0	1.1	1.1	1.1	1.2	1.2	1.2
Iceland	1.9	2.2	1.9	1.8	1.9	1.8	1.9	1.9	1.9	1.9	1.8
Ireland					0.7	0.7	0.7	0.7	0.7	0.7	0.7
Italy	0.2	0.3	0.5	0.5	0.7	0.8	0.8	0.8	0.8	0.8	0.8
Liechtenstein			1.0	1.2	3.9	2.5	2.9	2.7	2.8	2.9	2.9
Luxembourg	1.6	1.8	2.0	1.8	2.4	2.3	2.3	2.3	2.3	2.3	2.3
Malta											
Monaco	1.8			2.5	2.6	2.3	2.5	2.1	2.1	2.2	2.3
Netherlands	1.8	2.4	1.9	2.2	2.2	1.9	1.9	1.8	1.8	1.8	1.7
Norway	1.6	2.0	2.4	2.4	2.2	2.4	2.4	2.4	2.5	2.5	2.5
Portugal	0.6	0.9	0.9	1.2	1.9	2.1	2.2	2.3	2.4	2.4	2.4
Spain		0.5	0.6	0.8	1.0	1.0	1.0	1.1	1.1	1.1	1.1
Sweden	2.4	2.4	2.3	2.6	2.4	2.4	2.2	2.2	2.2	2.2	2.1
Switzerland	1.7	1.8	2.0	2.2	1.5	2.3	2.4	2.5	2.6	2.6	2.7
Turkey	0.4	0.4	0.5	0.5	0.5	0.7	0.8	0.8	0.8	0.8	0.8
United Kingdom	2.8	3.1	2.9	2.9	2.6	2.8	2.8	2.9	2.9	2.9	2.9
Eastern Europe											
Albania	0.8	0.8	0.8	0.7	0.7	1.2	1.0	1.3	1.4	1.5	1.5
Belarus	3.3	3.1	3.4	4.1	4.3	3.2	3.1	2.9	2.8	2.7	2.6
Bosnia-Herzegovina	0.4	0.4	0.4	0.5	0.5	0.5	0.4	0.5	0.4	0.4	0.5
Bulgaria	1.5	1.6	1.3	1.3	1.3	1.5	1.9	2.0	2.2	2.4	2.5
Croatia	1.2	1.1	1.1	0.9	1.0	1.1	1.1	1.2	1.2	1.2	1.3
Czech Republic	2.6	3.0	3.1	3.0	2.9	3.2	3.2	3.3	3.3	3.3	3.4
Estonia	4.2	4.0	3.7	5.1	3.1	2.9	3.1	3.1	3.1	3.1	3.2
Georgia	1.4	1.3	1.3	0.6	0.4	0.4	0.4	0.4	0.5	0.5	0.5
Hungary	2.6	2.8	2.4	2.4	2.3	2.5	2.4	2.4	2.4	2.4	2.3
Latvia	5.0	4.5	4.0	3.1	2.6	2.1	2.3	2.3	2.3	2.4	2.4
Lithuania	3.2	3.2	3.5	2.8	3.1	3.1	3.2	3.2	3.3	3.4	3.5
Macedonia	0.5	0.4	0.4	0.4	0.7	0.7	0.8	0.8	0.7	0.7	0.7
Moldova	2.8	2.7	3.0	3.4	2.4	3.8	3.9	4.0	4.1	4.2	4.2
Poland	1.1	1.3	1.1	1.0	1.1	1.3	1.5	1.5	1.5	1.6	1.6
Romania	1.5	1.4	1.4	1.6	1.4	1.5	1.6	1.7	1.7	1.8	1.8
Russia	4.2	4.0	3.8	4.5	4.3	5.5	4.4	4.2	4.1	4.0	3.9
Slovakia	1.3	1.5	1.7	1.7	1.7	2.0	2.0	2.1	2.2	2.2	2.3
Slovenia	1.2	1.3	0.9	0.8	1.1	1.2	1.2	1.2	1.2	1.2	1.2
Ukraine	3.7	3.6	3.7	3.9	4.0	3.7	3.6	3.6	3.6	3.5	3.5

Source: *National statistical offices/Council of Europe/UN/Euromonitor International*
Notes: *Rates refer to final divorce decrees granted under civil law*

Table 21.16

Fertility Rates 1980-2008

Children born per female

	1980	1985	1990	1995	2000	2003	2004	2005	2006	2007	2008
Western Europe											
Austria	1.7	1.5	1.5	1.4	1.4	1.4	1.4	1.4	1.4	1.4	1.4
Belgium	1.7	1.5	1.6	1.6	1.6	1.6	1.7	1.7	1.7	1.7	1.8
Cyprus	2.4	2.5	2.4	2.2	1.7	1.6	1.6	1.5	1.5	1.5	1.5
Denmark	1.6	1.5	1.7	1.8	1.8	1.8	1.8	1.8	1.8	1.8	1.8
Finland	1.6	1.6	1.8	1.8	1.7	1.8	1.8	1.8	1.8	1.8	1.8
France	2.0	1.8	1.8	1.7	1.9	1.9	1.9	1.9	2.0	2.0	2.1
Germany	1.6	1.4	1.5	1.2	1.4	1.3	1.4	1.3	1.3	1.4	1.4
Gibraltar											
Greece	2.2	1.7	1.4	1.3	1.3	1.3	1.3	1.2	1.2	1.2	1.2
Iceland	2.2	2.2	2.2	2.1	2.0	2.0	2.0	2.0	2.1	2.1	2.1
Ireland	3.2	2.5	2.1	1.8	1.9	2.0	2.0	2.0	2.1	2.1	2.0
Italy	1.7	1.4	1.4	1.2	1.3	1.3	1.3	1.3	1.4	1.4	1.4
Liechtenstein											
Luxembourg	1.5	1.5	1.6	1.7	1.7	1.7	1.7	1.7	1.7	1.7	1.7
Malta	2.0	2.0	2.0	2.0	1.6	1.4	1.4	1.3	1.3	1.3	1.3
Monaco											
Netherlands	1.6	1.5	1.6	1.5	1.7	1.8	1.7	1.7	1.8	1.8	1.8
Norway	1.7	1.7	1.9	1.9	1.9	1.8	1.8	1.8	1.9	1.9	1.9
Portugal	2.3	1.7	1.6	1.4	1.6	1.5	1.5	1.5	1.5	1.5	1.5
Spain	2.2	1.6	1.4	1.2	1.3	1.3	1.3	1.3	1.3	1.4	1.4
Sweden	1.7	1.7	2.1	1.7	1.6	1.7	1.8	1.8	1.8	1.8	1.8
Switzerland	1.6	1.5	1.6	1.5	1.5	1.4	1.4	1.4	1.4	1.4	1.4
Turkey	4.4	3.6	3.1	2.8	2.3	2.2	2.2	2.2	2.2	2.2	2.1
United Kingdom	1.9	1.8	1.8	1.7	1.6	1.7	1.8	1.8	1.9	1.9	1.9
Eastern Europe											
Albania	3.8	3.2	2.9	2.6	2.2	2.0	1.9	1.9	1.9	1.9	1.9
Belarus	2.0	2.1	1.9	1.4	1.3	1.2	1.2	1.2	1.3	1.4	1.4
Bosnia-Herzegovina	2.1	2.0	1.7	1.6	1.3	1.2	1.2	1.2	1.2	1.2	1.2
Bulgaria	2.1	2.0	1.8	1.2	1.3	1.2	1.3	1.3	1.3	1.3	1.3
Croatia	1.9	1.8	1.7	1.6	1.4	1.3	1.4	1.4	1.4	1.4	1.4
Czech Republic	2.1	2.0	1.9	1.3	1.1	1.2	1.2	1.3	1.3	1.3	1.3
Estonia	2.0	2.1	2.0	1.3	1.4	1.4	1.5	1.5	1.5	1.5	1.5
Georgia	2.3	2.3	2.2	1.5	1.5	1.4	1.5	1.4	1.4	1.5	1.7
Hungary	1.9	1.9	1.9	1.6	1.3	1.3	1.3	1.3	1.3	1.3	1.4
Latvia	1.9	2.1	2.0	1.3	1.2	1.3	1.2	1.3	1.3	1.3	1.4
Lithuania	2.0	2.1	2.0	1.6	1.4	1.3	1.3	1.3	1.3	1.3	1.3
Macedonia	2.5	2.3	2.1	2.0	1.8	1.8	1.7	1.6	1.6	1.5	1.5
Moldova	2.5	2.6	2.4	1.9	1.6	1.5	1.5	1.5	1.5	1.5	1.5
Poland	2.3	2.3	2.0	1.6	1.4	1.2	1.2	1.2	1.3	1.3	1.3
Romania	2.4	2.3	1.8	1.3	1.3	1.3	1.3	1.3	1.3	1.3	1.3
Russia	1.9	2.1	1.9	1.3	1.2	1.3	1.3	1.3	1.3	1.4	1.4
Slovakia	2.3	2.3	2.1	1.5	1.3	1.2	1.2	1.3	1.3	1.3	1.3
Slovenia	2.1	1.7	1.5	1.3	1.3	1.2	1.3	1.3	1.3	1.3	1.3
Ukraine	2.0	2.0	1.8	1.4	1.1	1.2	1.2	1.2	1.3	1.3	1.3

Source: National statistical offices/UN/Euromonitor International

Life Expectancy at Birth: Males and Females 2008

Years

	Male	Female
Western Europe		
Austria	77.4	82.9
Belgium	77.6	83.5
Cyprus	77.1	81.9
Denmark	76.4	80.8
Finland	76.0	83.1
France	77.7	84.6
Germany	77.3	82.6
Gibraltar	74.4	79.5
Greece	77.5	82.3
Iceland	79.6	83.1
Ireland	77.3	82.2
Italy	78.5	84.2
Liechtenstein	77.1	83.5
Luxembourg	76.4	82.5
Malta	77.6	82.0
Monaco	78.4	85.2
Netherlands	78.4	82.7
Norway	78.4	82.9
Portugal	75.6	82.2
Spain	77.9	84.5
Sweden	79.1	83.3
Switzerland	79.5	84.2
Turkey	69.3	74.4
United Kingdom	77.2	81.7
Eastern Europe		
Albania	73.6	79.8
Belarus	64.0	74.8
Bosnia-Herzegovina	72.2	77.5
Bulgaria	69.4	76.5
Croatia	72.8	79.6
Czech Republic	73.9	80.0
Estonia	67.6	79.0
Georgia	67.2	74.9
Hungary	69.7	77.8
Latvia	66.1	76.7
Lithuania	65.2	77.3
Macedonia	72.1	76.6
Moldova	65.2	72.5
Poland	71.4	79.9
Romania	69.1	76.2
Russia	59.0	72.8
Slovakia	70.8	78.4
Slovenia	74.5	81.6
Ukraine	62.5	74.2

Source: *Euromonitor International from World Bank*

Population Statistics

Table 21.18

Population Density 1980-2008

Persons per sq km

	1980	1985	1990	1995	2000	2003	2004	2005	2006	2007	2008
Western Europe											
Austria	91.5	91.7	92.7	96.3	97.1	98.3	98.7	99.5	100.3	100.8	101.3
Belgium	326.0	326.0	329.0	335.1	338.7	342.6	343.9	345.5	347.7	349.7	351.3
Cyprus	66.1	70.1	73.7	79.2	85.1	88.4	89.5	90.5	91.5	92.4	93.3
Denmark	120.9	120.6	121.1	122.9	125.6	126.9	127.2	127.5	127.9	128.4	128.7
Finland	15.7	16.1	16.3	16.7	17.0	17.1	17.1	17.2	17.3	17.3	17.4
France	97.7	100.3	102.8	105.0	107.0	109.2	109.9	110.6	111.2	111.9	112.9
Germany	224.2	222.8	226.8	233.8	235.6	236.7	236.6	236.5	236.4	236.0	235.7
Gibraltar	2,654.8	2,660.1	2,684.4	2,730.6	2,737.9	2,844.2	2,882.2	2,910.0	2,925.4	2,930.6	2,928.6
Greece	74.4	77.0	78.5	82.2	84.6	85.4	85.7	86.0	86.3	86.6	87.0
Iceland	2.3	2.4	2.5	2.7	2.8	2.9	2.9	2.9	3.0	3.1	3.1
Ireland	49.2	51.4	50.9	52.2	54.8	57.5	58.5	59.6	61.1	62.4	63.6
Italy	191.7	192.4	192.8	193.3	193.6	194.9	196.8	198.8	199.8	200.2	200.5
Liechtenstein	161.3	166.8	177.8	191.4	202.7	211.6	214.3	216.3	218.2	219.8	221.8
Luxembourg	140.9	141.9	147.7	158.1	168.7	175.0	177.1	179.2	181.3	183.4	185.6
Malta	1,012.9	1,076.1	1,125.4	1,180.6	1,215.3	1,241.9	1,250.5	1,258.0	1,264.1	1,269.1	1,273.3
Monaco											
Netherlands	415.9	426.6	439.6	455.3	468.2	477.9	479.9	481.3	482.1	482.8	483.6
Norway	13.4	13.6	13.9	14.3	14.7	15.0	15.0	15.1	15.2	15.4	15.6
Portugal	106.2	109.5	109.2	109.5	111.4	113.7	114.5	115.1	115.5	115.9	116.3
Spain	74.6	76.8	77.7	78.8	80.3	83.5	84.8	86.2	87.6	89.1	90.2
Sweden	20.2	20.3	20.8	21.5	21.6	21.8	21.9	22.0	22.0	22.2	22.3
Switzerland	157.6	161.4	166.8	175.5	179.1	182.8	184.1	185.4	186.5	187.4	188.3
Turkey	57.2	64.5	72.1	79.5	86.9	90.7	91.9	93.0	94.2	95.4	96.6
United Kingdom	232.6	233.5	236.3	239.5	243.0	245.7	246.8	248.3	249.6	251.4	252.9
Eastern Europe											
Albania	97.5	107.9	120.1	114.4	112.0	112.7	113.1	113.5	113.9	114.3	114.7
Belarus	46.2	47.9	49.1	49.2	48.3	47.7	47.5	47.2	47.0	46.8	46.7
Bosnia-Herzegovina				68.8	73.3	74.8	74.9	75.0	75.1	75.1	75.1
Bulgaria	79.9	80.9	79.2	75.1	72.1	70.8	71.5	71.1	71.0	70.6	70.1
Croatia	82.2	84.1	85.4	83.5	79.4	79.4	79.4	79.5	79.4	79.4	79.3
Czech Republic	133.0	133.3	133.3	133.5	132.5	132.0	132.2	132.3	132.7	133.2	133.5
Estonia	34.8	36.0	37.2	34.2	32.4	32.0	31.9	31.8	31.7	31.6	31.5
Georgia				69.0	63.8	62.5	62.1	62.2	63.3	63.2	63.1
Hungary	119.1	118.6	115.4	115.0	114.1	113.2	112.9	112.7	112.5	112.2	112.0
Latvia	40.4	41.4	43.0	40.3	38.4	37.4	37.2	37.0	36.8	36.6	36.4
Lithuania	52.5	54.5	57.0	58.1	56.0	55.2	55.0	54.6	54.3	54.0	53.7
Macedonia				77.2	79.0	79.7	79.8	80.0	80.1	80.2	80.2
Moldova				131.8	124.7	118.3	116.2	114.4	112.8	111.6	110.5
Poland	116.3	121.7	124.8	125.7	125.7	124.8	125.5	124.6	124.4	124.1	123.9
Romania	96.1	98.5	101.2	97.1	95.5	94.7	94.4	94.2	93.9	93.7	93.4
Russia	8.2	8.4	8.7	9.1	9.0	8.8	8.8	8.8	8.7	8.7	8.7
Slovakia	103.2	106.9	109.6	111.2	111.8	111.8	111.9	112.0	112.0	112.1	112.1
Slovenia	94.1	96.3	99.2	98.8	98.7	99.1	99.1	99.2	99.5	99.8	100.1
Ukraine	85.9	87.4	89.0	88.5	84.8	82.5	81.9	81.3	80.7	80.2	79.7

Source: National statistical offices/UN/Euromonitor International

Population Statistics

Table 21.19

Urban Population 1980-2008
% of total population

	1980	1985	1990	1995	2000	2003	2004	2005	2006	2007	2008
Western Europe											
Austria	54.4	58.8	63.5	65.7	66.5	66.8	66.9	67.0	67.1	67.2	67.3
Belgium	95.4	95.9	96.4	96.8	97.1	97.2	97.3	97.3	97.3	97.3	97.4
Cyprus	58.6	64.7	66.8	68.0	68.6	69.0	69.2	69.3	69.5	69.7	69.9
Denmark	83.9	84.3	84.8	85.1	85.1	85.3	85.4	85.5	85.6	85.7	85.8
Finland	56.5	56.6	56.8	57.8	60.4	62.0	62.1	62.2	62.3	62.4	62.6
France	73.3	73.7	74.1	74.9	75.7	76.3	76.5	76.7	76.9	77.1	77.4
Germany	82.6	84.0	85.3	86.5	87.5	88.1	88.3	88.5	88.7	88.8	89.0
Gibraltar	100.0	100.0	100.0	100.0	100.0	100.0	100.0	100.0	100.0	100.0	100.0
Greece	57.7	58.4	58.8	59.3	60.1	60.9	61.1	61.5	61.8	62.1	62.4
Iceland	88.3	89.6	90.8	91.6	92.2	92.2	92.2	92.2	92.2	92.3	92.3
Ireland	55.3	56.3	56.9	57.9	59.1	59.9	60.1	60.4	60.7	61.0	61.3
Italy	66.6	66.8	66.7	66.9	67.2	67.4	67.5	67.6	67.7	67.8	67.9
Liechtenstein	18.3	17.6	16.9	16.5	15.1	14.7	14.6	14.6	14.5	14.5	14.5
Luxembourg	80.0	80.7	80.9	82.9	83.8	83.2	83.0	82.8	82.7	82.5	82.4
Malta	89.8	89.8	90.4	90.9	92.4	93.2	93.4	93.6	93.9	94.1	94.3
Monaco	100.0	100.0	100.0	100.0	100.0	100.0	100.0	100.0	100.0	100.0	100.0
Netherlands	58.3	59.2	60.0	60.9	63.0	64.3	64.8	65.3	65.7	66.2	66.7
Norway	70.5	71.3	72.1	73.4	76.1	78.6	79.5	80.4	81.1	81.9	82.6
Portugal	29.4	37.5	46.3	50.3	53.1	54.6	55.1	55.7	56.2	56.8	57.3
Spain	72.8	74.2	75.3	75.9	76.3	76.5	76.6	76.7	76.8	76.9	77.0
Sweden	83.1	83.1	83.1	83.2	83.3	83.4	83.4	83.4	83.5	83.5	83.6
Switzerland	62.1	66.4	68.0	67.7	67.6	67.9	67.9	68.0	68.1	68.2	68.3
Turkey	49.4	55.9	59.6	62.1	64.8	66.4	66.9	67.4	67.9	68.4	68.8
United Kingdom	87.9	88.5	88.7	88.7	88.9	89.1	89.1	89.2	89.3	89.4	89.5
Eastern Europe											
Albania	33.8	35.1	36.4	38.9	41.7	43.6	44.2	44.8	45.4	46.1	46.7
Belarus	58.4	64.2	66.8	68.1	70.2	71.5	71.9	72.3	72.7	73.0	73.3
Bosnia-Herzegovina	35.5	37.6	39.2	41.1	43.2	44.7	45.2	45.7	46.3	46.9	47.4
Bulgaria	63.7	65.8	67.1	67.8	68.4	69.9	70.3	70.7	71.1	71.5	71.8
Croatia	50.1	52.2	54.0	55.8	57.7	59.0	59.5	59.9	60.3	60.8	61.3
Czech Republic	74.6	75.2	75.0	74.5	74.1	74.1	74.3	74.5	74.7	74.8	74.9
Estonia	69.8	71.0	71.5	70.0	69.2	69.2	69.3	69.3	69.3	69.4	69.4
Georgia	51.6	53.9	55.2	54.0	52.7	52.2	52.2	52.2	52.3	52.3	52.4
Hungary	57.6	62.8	65.4	65.2	64.5	65.6	66.0	66.2	66.5	66.8	67.1
Latvia	66.9	68.5	69.0	68.7	68.1	67.8	67.9	68.0	68.1	68.2	68.3
Lithuania	60.9	65.1	68.1	67.5	67.1	66.9	67.0	67.1	67.1	67.2	67.2
Macedonia	53.5	55.7	57.8	60.7	64.9	67.3	68.1	68.9	69.6	70.3	71.0
Moldova	40.4	44.2	46.8	46.3	44.6	43.4	43.0	42.6	42.2	41.9	41.7
Poland	59.7	61.2	61.8	61.8	61.8	61.7	61.8	61.8	61.8	61.8	61.9
Romania	49.2	53.0	54.3	54.9	54.6	54.8	54.8	54.9	54.9	54.9	55.0
Russia	70.6	72.6	73.7	72.9	72.9	73.4	73.5	73.6	73.7	73.9	74.0
Slovakia	51.9	55.6	56.9	56.3	55.5	55.6	55.8	55.9	56.2	56.3	56.5
Slovenia	49.3	50.4	50.8	50.8	50.8	50.8	50.8	50.8	50.9	51.0	51.1
Ukraine	64.6	66.4	67.5	67.8	67.4	67.4	67.5	67.6	67.7	67.8	67.9

Source: National statistical offices/UN/Euromonitor International

Table 21.20

Rural Population 1980-2008
% of total population

	1980	1985	1990	1995	2000	2003	2004	2005	2006	2007	2008
Western Europe											
Austria	45.6	41.2	36.5	34.3	33.5	33.2	33.1	33.0	32.9	32.8	32.7
Belgium	4.6	4.1	3.6	3.2	2.9	2.8	2.7	2.7	2.7	2.7	2.6
Cyprus	41.4	35.3	33.2	32.0	31.4	31.0	30.8	30.7	30.5	30.3	30.1
Denmark	16.1	15.7	15.2	14.9	14.9	14.7	14.6	14.5	14.4	14.3	14.2
Finland	43.5	43.4	43.2	42.2	39.6	38.0	37.9	37.8	37.7	37.6	37.4
France	26.7	26.3	25.9	25.1	24.3	23.7	23.5	23.3	23.1	22.9	22.6
Germany	17.4	16.0	14.7	13.5	12.5	11.9	11.7	11.5	11.3	11.2	11.0
Gibraltar											
Greece	42.3	41.6	41.2	40.7	39.9	39.1	38.9	38.5	38.2	37.9	37.6
Iceland	11.7	10.4	9.2	8.4	7.8	7.8	7.8	7.8	7.8	7.7	7.7
Ireland	44.7	43.7	43.1	42.1	40.9	40.1	39.9	39.6	39.3	39.0	38.7
Italy	33.4	33.2	33.3	33.1	32.8	32.6	32.5	32.4	32.3	32.2	32.1
Liechtenstein	81.7	82.4	83.1	83.5	84.9	85.3	85.4	85.4	85.5	85.5	85.5
Luxembourg	20.0	19.3	19.1	17.1	16.2	16.8	17.0	17.2	17.3	17.5	17.6
Malta	10.2	10.2	9.6	9.1	7.6	6.8	6.6	6.4	6.1	5.9	5.7
Monaco											
Netherlands	41.7	40.8	40.0	39.1	37.0	35.7	35.2	34.7	34.3	33.8	33.3
Norway	29.5	28.7	27.9	26.6	23.9	21.4	20.5	19.6	18.9	18.1	17.4
Portugal	70.6	62.5	53.7	49.7	46.9	45.4	44.9	44.3	43.8	43.2	42.7
Spain	27.2	25.8	24.7	24.1	23.7	23.5	23.4	23.3	23.2	23.1	23.0
Sweden	16.9	16.9	16.9	16.8	16.7	16.6	16.6	16.6	16.5	16.5	16.4
Switzerland	37.9	33.6	32.0	32.3	32.4	32.1	32.1	32.0	31.9	31.8	31.7
Turkey	50.6	44.1	40.4	37.9	35.2	33.6	33.1	32.6	32.1	31.6	31.2
United Kingdom	12.1	11.5	11.3	11.3	11.1	10.9	10.9	10.8	10.7	10.6	10.5
Eastern Europe											
Albania	66.2	64.9	63.6	61.1	58.3	56.4	55.8	55.2	54.6	53.9	53.3
Belarus	41.6	35.8	33.2	31.9	29.8	28.5	28.1	27.7	27.3	27.0	26.7
Bosnia-Herzegovina	64.5	62.4	60.8	58.9	56.8	55.3	54.8	54.3	53.7	53.1	52.6
Bulgaria	36.3	34.2	32.9	32.2	31.6	30.1	29.7	29.3	28.9	28.5	28.2
Croatia	49.9	47.8	46.0	44.2	42.3	41.0	40.5	40.1	39.7	39.2	38.7
Czech Republic	25.4	24.8	25.0	25.5	25.9	25.9	25.7	25.5	25.3	25.2	25.1
Estonia	30.2	29.0	28.5	30.0	30.8	30.8	30.7	30.7	30.7	30.6	30.6
Georgia	48.4	46.1	44.8	46.0	47.3	47.8	47.8	47.8	47.7	47.7	47.6
Hungary	42.4	37.2	34.6	34.8	35.5	34.4	34.0	33.8	33.5	33.2	32.9
Latvia	33.1	31.5	31.0	31.3	31.9	32.2	32.1	32.0	31.9	31.8	31.7
Lithuania	39.1	34.9	31.9	32.5	32.9	33.1	33.0	32.9	32.9	32.8	32.8
Macedonia	46.5	44.3	42.2	39.3	35.1	32.7	31.9	31.1	30.4	29.7	29.0
Moldova	59.6	55.8	53.2	53.7	55.4	56.6	57.0	57.4	57.8	58.1	58.3
Poland	40.3	38.8	38.2	38.2	38.2	38.3	38.2	38.2	38.2	38.2	38.1
Romania	50.8	47.0	45.7	45.1	45.4	45.2	45.2	45.1	45.1	45.1	45.0
Russia	29.4	27.4	26.3	27.1	27.1	26.6	26.5	26.4	26.3	26.1	26.0
Slovakia	48.1	44.4	43.1	43.7	44.5	44.4	44.2	44.1	43.8	43.7	43.5
Slovenia	50.7	49.6	49.2	49.2	49.2	49.2	49.2	49.2	49.1	49.0	48.9
Ukraine	35.4	33.6	32.5	32.2	32.6	32.6	32.5	32.4	32.3	32.2	32.1

Source: National statistical offices/UN/Euromonitor International

Population Statistics

Table 21.21

Number of Pensioners 1990-2008
'000

	1990	1995	2000	2003	2004	2005	2006	2007	2008
Western Europe									
Austria	1,364	1,395	1,452	1,507	1,525	1,547	1,566	1,588	1,611
Belgium	1,649	1,776	1,875	1,884	1,858	1,826	1,787	1,752	1,724
Cyprus	103	114	126	135	139	142	146	149	153
Denmark	701	707	700	698	701	704	708	713	721
Finland	673	732	777	811	825	831	855	859	873
France	10,764	11,599	12,121	12,217	12,252	12,297	12,338	12,567	12,832
Germany [a]	11,794	12,542	13,351	14,294	14,601	14,992	15,385	15,663	15,720
Gibraltar									
Greece	2,069	2,319	2,502	2,584	2,604	2,621	2,633	2,644	2,657
Iceland	34	38	40	42	42	43	44	45	46
Ireland	372	385	397	407	407	407	409	410	411
Italy	10,066	11,172	12,152	12,519	12,601	12,666	12,715	12,813	12,895
Liechtenstein									
Luxembourg	52	59	65	67	67	67	66	66	66
Malta	37	42	47	50	51	52	53	55	56
Monaco									
Netherlands	1,906	2,034	2,152	2,209	2,227	2,245	2,270	2,291	2,318
Norway	606	622	618	607	604	602	603	604	607
Portugal	1,311	1,457	1,645	1,726	1,742	1,753	1,756	1,750	1,750
Spain [b]	5,215	5,935	6,668	6,917	6,922	6,900	6,864	6,841	6,840
Sweden	1,864	1,865	1,870	1,904	1,930	1,966	2,009	2,054	2,099
Switzerland	1,042	1,101	1,165	1,188	1,183	1,177	1,186	1,199	1,215
Turkey	6,865	7,911	8,916	9,654	9,948	10,272	10,556	10,880	11,244
United Kingdom [c]	10,513	10,620	10,774	11,007	11,124	11,249	11,372	11,595	11,821
Eastern Europe									
Albania	305	312	335	358	366	375	383	392	401
Belarus	2,000	2,143	2,145	2,099	2,089	2,091	2,084	2,087	2,095
Bosnia-Herzegovina	435	419	560	624	638	652	665	679	693
Bulgaria [b]	1,806	1,887	1,858	1,858	1,812	1,775	1,734	1,673	1,614
Croatia	876	907	1,010	990	971	955	939	921	901
Czech Republic [d]	1,990	2,006	2,067	2,095	2,086	2,088	2,009	2,016	2,054
Estonia	266	268	286	285	281	276	271	264	258
Georgia	810	894	979	974	965	956	949	944	942
Hungary	2,287	2,294	2,011	1,983	1,991	2,002	2,023	2,022	2,028
Latvia	470	485	506	504	498	490	481	470	458
Lithuania	602	647	680	695	701	704	705	706	710
Macedonia	211	250	281	296	301	306	311	316	322
Moldova	667	686	686	688	691	696	703	713	726
Poland	4,799	5,222	5,616	5,774	5,782	5,789	5,798	5,837	5,899
Romania	3,024	3,353	3,632	3,748	3,758	3,778	3,768	3,768	3,759
Russia	27,622	29,931	30,175	29,612	29,275	29,163	29,089	29,281	29,556
Slovakia	674	707	736	738	739	742	746	753	762
Slovenia	296	330	360	370	367	363	358	352	345
Ukraine	10,986	11,523	11,569	11,461	11,355	11,318	11,211	11,164	11,125

Source: *Euromonitor International from national statistics/UN*
Notes: *(a) Data refer to number of pensions paid, (b) Data refer to all kinds of pensions, (c) Data refer to population of retirement age only, (d) Data refer to post-working age economically inactive population*

Table 21.22

Population by Marital Status 2008

'000 / % analysis

	Married	Divorced	Widowed	Single	Married (% analysis)	Divorced (% analysis)	Widowed (% analysis)	Single (% analysis)
Western Europe								
Austria	3,607	602	557	3,585	43.19	7.21	6.67	42.92
Belgium	4,540	821	723	4,534	42.75	7.73	6.81	42.70
Cyprus								
Denmark	2,187	416	324	2,534	40.05	7.61	5.94	46.39
Finland	1,986	500	303	2,511	37.47	9.43	5.72	47.38
France	24,767	3,775	3,956	29,608	39.88	6.08	6.37	47.67
Germany	35,908	6,134	5,923	34,253	43.67	7.46	7.20	41.66
Gibraltar								
Greece	5,622	333	828	4,429	50.14	2.97	7.38	39.51
Iceland								
Ireland	1,614	189	196	2,379	36.87	4.32	4.49	54.33
Italy	30,076	900	4,710	23,290	51.00	1.53	7.99	39.49
Liechtenstein								
Luxembourg								
Malta								
Monaco								
Netherlands	6,907	1,032	860	7,583	42.16	6.30	5.25	46.29
Norway	1,696	423	260	2,358	35.80	8.92	5.48	49.79
Portugal	5,802	302	661	3,878	54.51	2.84	6.21	36.43
Spain	22,879	1,446	2,857	17,875	50.78	3.21	6.34	39.67
Sweden	3,071	881	501	4,704	33.54	9.62	5.47	51.37
Switzerland	3,423	411	489	3,207	45.46	5.45	6.50	42.59
Turkey	35,469	768	2,615	35,485	47.71	1.03	3.52	47.74
United Kingdom	24,247	4,770	3,687	28,481	39.63	7.80	6.03	46.55
Eastern Europe								
Albania								
Belarus	4,449	784	885	3,571	45.91	8.09	9.14	36.86
Bosnia-Herzegovina								
Bulgaria	4,034	310	748	2,478	53.29	4.10	9.89	32.73
Croatia	2,083	136	439	1,765	47.10	3.08	9.92	39.90
Czech Republic	4,634	981	758	3,944	44.91	9.51	7.35	38.23
Estonia	440	153	125	617	32.96	11.45	9.37	46.23
Georgia	2,603	132	491	1,155	59.43	3.01	11.20	26.36
Hungary	4,077	863	991	4,108	40.61	8.59	9.88	40.92
Latvia	825	281	202	958	36.40	12.40	8.92	42.28
Lithuania	1,397	339	269	1,362	41.49	10.06	8.00	40.45
Macedonia	987	23	107	923	48.36	1.14	5.26	45.24
Moldova								
Poland	17,354	1,566	2,991	16,134	45.61	4.11	7.86	42.41
Romania	9,993	872	2,085	8,547	46.49	4.06	9.70	39.76
Russia	65,722	12,424	14,032	49,831	46.28	8.75	9.88	35.09
Slovakia	2,370	288	402	2,333	43.95	5.34	7.45	43.26
Slovenia	823	99	140	955	40.81	4.89	6.96	47.34
Ukraine	22,176	4,071	5,085	14,815	48.06	8.82	11.02	32.10

Source: Euromonitor International from national statistics/UN

Population Statistics

Table 21.23

Population by Educational Attainment 2008
'000 / % analysis

	Primary	Secondary	Higher	No Education	Other/ Unknown	Primary (% analysis)	Secondary (% analysis)	Higher (% analysis)	No Education (% analysis)	Other/ Unknown (% analysis)
Western Europe										
Austria	1,273	4,211	1,581	0	0	18.02	59.61	22.38	0.00	0.00
Belgium	1,461	5,153	2,150	59	0	16.56	58.40	24.37	0.67	0.00
Cyprus										
Denmark	690	2,567	1,041	0	154	15.50	57.65	23.38	0.00	3.46
Finland	732	2,510	1,163	0	0	16.62	56.98	26.40	0.00	0.00
France	7,619	29,038	10,917	283	2,870	15.02	57.24	21.52	0.56	5.66
Germany	9,232	42,813	17,698	0	1,192	13.02	60.35	24.95	0.00	1.68
Gibraltar										
Greece	2,257	5,510	1,710	139	0	23.47	57.31	17.78	1.44	0.00
Iceland										
Ireland	562	2,017	724	14	169	16.13	57.85	20.77	0.40	4.84
Italy	9,284	33,387	5,460	2,599						
Liechtenstein										
Luxembourg										
Malta										
Monaco										
Netherlands	1,514	8,390	3,545	0	0	11.25	62.38	26.36	0.00	0.00
Norway	377	2,466	890	0	97	9.85	64.40	23.23	0.00	2.52
Portugal	2,197	4,715	1,620	467	0	24.41	52.40	18.01	5.18	0.00
Spain	7,076	21,312	7,304	569	2,186	18.40	55.43	19.00	1.48	5.69
Sweden	724	4,517	2,272	0	115	9.50	59.21	29.78	0.00	1.51
Switzerland	836	3,854	1,673	0	0	13.15	60.57	26.29	0.00	0.00
Turkey	26,134	18,215	4,466	5,066	10	48.49	33.80	8.29	9.40	0.02
United Kingdom	6,619	29,086	14,419	322	0	13.12	57.66	28.58	0.64	0.00
Eastern Europe										
Albania										
Belarus	1,557	5,094	1,217	401	0	18.83	61.61	14.71	4.85	0.00
Bosnia-Herzegovina										
Bulgaria	1,530	4,230	741	70	0	23.28	64.37	11.28	1.07	0.00
Croatia	614	2,562	493	60	19	16.38	68.36	13.15	1.61	0.50
Czech Republic	1,377	6,057	1,253	41	119	15.56	68.46	14.17	0.46	1.35
Estonia	140	814	178	5	0	12.29	71.57	15.67	0.46	0.00
Georgia	844	1,552	863		371					
Hungary	1,481	5,813	1,180	56	0	17.36	68.15	13.84	0.66	0.00
Latvia	309	1,332	294	22	0	15.77	68.09	15.03	1.11	0.01
Lithuania	379	2,007	438	25	0	13.31	70.42	15.38	0.89	0.00
Macedonia	587	636	189	255						
Moldova										
Poland	5,563	21,575	4,408	216	418	17.29	67.04	13.70	0.67	1.30
Romania	4,107	11,861	1,840	394	9	22.55	65.13	10.10	2.16	0.05
Russia	22,199	74,683	17,949	6,355	0	18.32	61.63	14.81	5.24	0.00
Slovakia	747	3,113	606	19	58	16.45	68.52	13.34	0.42	1.27
Slovenia	215	1,240	270	12	0	12.37	71.41	15.55	0.67	0.00
Ukraine	9,438	23,292	4,903	2,073	0	23.77	58.66	12.35	5.22	0.00

Source: *Euromonitor International from national statistics/UN*

Table 21.24

Males and Females by Age at January 1st 2008
'000

	Males 0-14	Males 15-64	Males 65+	Females 0-14	Females 15-64	Females 65+
Western Europe						
Austria	659	2,822	584	628	2,812	847
Belgium	919	3,523	757	877	3,483	1,059
Cyprus	81	290	49	77	305	61
Denmark	516	1,817	370	493	1,785	480
Finland	457	1,785	356	438	1,746	520
France	5,800	20,047	4,218	5,580	20,423	6,038
Germany	5,789	27,541	6,945	5,493	26,877	9,574
Gibraltar						
Greece	822	3,807	920	774	3,725	1,164
Iceland	34	110	17	32	102	20
Ireland	458	1,511	219	435	1,483	273
Italy	4,239	19,463	4,955	4,007	19,403	6,908
Liechtenstein						
Luxembourg	44	166	28	42	161	39
Malta	34	145	24	32	140	33
Monaco						
Netherlands	1,502	5,565	1,036	1,433	5,478	1,370
Norway	465	1,598	297	443	1,538	396
Portugal	845	3,537	772	799	3,615	1,075
Spain	3,397	15,610	3,214	3,212	15,254	4,368
Sweden	784	3,054	707	746	2,963	904
Switzerland	598	2,563	521	568	2,562	718
Turkey	10,433	25,056	1,989	10,034	24,423	2,423
United Kingdom	5,492	20,239	4,272	5,248	20,360	5,575
Eastern Europe						
Albania	393	1,029	130	368	1,060	163
Belarus	731	3,338	452	691	3,529	948
Bosnia-Herzegovina	309	1,313	227	289	1,402	303
Bulgaria	514	2,614	541	487	2,639	777
Croatia	352	1,486	298	335	1,495	469
Czech Republic	755	3,686	596	715	3,652	912
Estonia	101	437	76	96	472	153
Georgia	398	1,431	249	355	1,567	382
Hungary	774	3,399	591	735	3,512	1,027
Latvia	158	758	128	151	808	263
Lithuania	265	1,120	183	251	1,197	351
Macedonia	193	723	102	179	708	135
Moldova	317	1,261	148	308	1,343	256
Poland	3,009	13,453	1,928	2,856	13,628	3,171
Romania	1,685	7,484	1,298	1,600	7,541	1,889
Russia	10,666	48,801	6,250	10,158	52,795	13,339
Slovakia	436	1,942	241	414	1,955	405
Slovenia	144	720	126	136	691	199
Ukraine	3,328	15,436	2,530	3,158	16,754	4,987

Source: *Euromonitor International from national statistics/UN*

Population Statistics

Table 21.25

Number of Males at January 1st 1990-2008

'000

	1990	1995	2000	2003	2004	2005	2006	2007	2008
Western Europe									
Austria	3,655	3,831	3,868	3,929	3,950	3,986	4,019	4,045	4,065
Belgium	4,860	4,955	5,006	5,067	5,087	5,111	5,144	5,174	5,199
Cyprus	339	365	387	399	403	407	411	415	420
Denmark	2,531	2,573	2,634	2,662	2,670	2,677	2,686	2,696	2,704
Finland	2,413	2,482	2,523	2,545	2,553	2,562	2,572	2,584	2,597
France	27,544	28,078	28,579	29,180	29,379	29,555	29,722	29,907	30,064
Germany	38,110	39,645	40,091	40,345	40,356	40,354	40,340	40,301	40,274
Gibraltar	14	14	14	14	14	15	15	15	15
Greece	4,982	5,243	5,400	5,449	5,464	5,487	5,508	5,529	5,549
Iceland	128	134	141	144	146	148	152	156	161
Ireland	1,743	1,787	1,877	1,970	2,003	2,047	2,102	2,147	2,187
Italy	27,528	27,570	27,566	27,766	28,069	28,377	28,527	28,604	28,657
Liechtenstein	14	15	16	17	17	17	17	17	17
Luxembourg	187	200	215	224	227	230	232	235	238
Malta	178	187	193	197	199	200	201	202	203
Monaco	14	15	15	15	15	15	15	16	16
Netherlands	7,358	7,627	7,846	8,015	8,046	8,066	8,077	8,089	8,103
Norway	2,093	2,150	2,217	2,256	2,269	2,284	2,302	2,326	2,360
Portugal	4,819	4,827	4,918	5,030	5,066	5,094	5,116	5,136	5,154
Spain	19,025	19,269	19,607	20,450	20,802	21,173	21,561	21,930	22,222
Sweden	4,212	4,356	4,380	4,427	4,447	4,466	4,487	4,521	4,544
Switzerland	3,258	3,428	3,501	3,575	3,602	3,629	3,653	3,669	3,683
Turkey	28,113	30,962	33,789	35,211	35,667	36,124	36,575	37,027	37,478
United Kingdom	27,774	28,156	28,634	29,036	29,193	29,395	29,578	29,818	30,003
Eastern Europe									
Albania	1,687	1,579	1,525	1,529	1,534	1,539	1,544	1,548	1,552
Belarus	4,777	4,780	4,703	4,638	4,610	4,583	4,555	4,535	4,522
Bosnia-Herzegovina	2,223	1,708	1,809	1,844	1,847	1,849	1,849	1,849	1,849
Bulgaria	4,324	4,069	3,888	3,807	3,780	3,752	3,723	3,695	3,669
Croatia	2,315	2,244	2,138	2,138	2,138	2,139	2,139	2,138	2,136
Czech Republic	4,998	5,013	4,981	4,967	4,975	4,981	5,003	5,021	5,037
Estonia	735	671	633	625	622	621	619	617	614
Georgia	2,440	2,268	2,093	2,047	2,032	2,037	2,084	2,079	2,078
Hungary	4,985	4,942	4,865	4,818	4,804	4,793	4,785	4,774	4,764
Latvia	1,241	1,154	1,097	1,073	1,068	1,063	1,057	1,051	1,044
Lithuania	1,747	1,717	1,644	1,617	1,609	1,598	1,587	1,577	1,567
Macedonia	958	983	1,004	1,012	1,014	1,015	1,016	1,017	1,017
Moldova	2,080	2,073	1,959	1,853	1,819	1,789	1,764	1,743	1,726
Poland	18,516	18,602	18,550	18,507	18,486	18,470	18,454	18,422	18,390
Romania	11,451	10,938	10,724	10,628	10,592	10,562	10,535	10,499	10,467
Russia	69,115	69,659	68,698	67,491	67,024	66,603	66,164	65,849	65,717
Slovakia	2,578	2,605	2,614	2,611	2,611	2,613	2,616	2,618	2,619
Slovenia	968	964	971	976	977	977	981	986	990
Ukraine	23,826	23,792	22,755	22,113	21,927	21,754	21,575	21,435	21,294

Source: Euromonitor International from national statistics/UN

Population Statistics

Table 21.26

Number of Females at January 1st 1990-2008
'000

	1990	1995	2000	2003	2004	2005	2006	2007	2008
Western Europe									
Austria	3,990	4,112	4,134	4,173	4,190	4,220	4,247	4,269	4,287
Belgium	5,088	5,176	5,233	5,289	5,309	5,335	5,368	5,396	5,419
Cyprus	341	366	399	418	424	429	434	439	443
Denmark	2,605	2,642	2,696	2,721	2,728	2,734	2,742	2,751	2,758
Finland	2,562	2,617	2,648	2,661	2,667	2,675	2,683	2,693	2,704
France	29,033	29,674	30,270	30,886	31,083	31,270	31,444	31,631	32,042
Germany	41,003	41,894	42,073	42,192	42,176	42,147	42,098	42,014	41,944
Gibraltar	13	14	14	14	14	15	15	15	15
Greece	5,139	5,352	5,504	5,558	5,576	5,596	5,617	5,640	5,663
Iceland	127	133	140	144	145	147	149	152	155
Ireland	1,764	1,810	1,901	1,994	2,025	2,062	2,107	2,152	2,191
Italy	29,167	29,276	29,363	29,555	29,820	30,086	30,225	30,284	30,318
Liechtenstein	15	16	17	17	17	18	18	18	18
Luxembourg	195	208	222	229	232	235	237	240	242
Malta	182	191	196	200	201	203	203	204	205
Monaco	16	17	17	17	17	17	17	17	17
Netherlands	7,534	7,797	8,018	8,177	8,212	8,240	8,257	8,269	8,281
Norway	2,140	2,198	2,261	2,296	2,308	2,322	2,338	2,355	2,377
Portugal	5,177	5,191	5,277	5,377	5,408	5,435	5,454	5,473	5,489
Spain	19,802	20,075	20,443	21,213	21,543	21,865	22,197	22,555	22,835
Sweden	4,315	4,460	4,481	4,514	4,529	4,545	4,561	4,592	4,613
Switzerland	3,416	3,591	3,664	3,739	3,763	3,786	3,807	3,828	3,848
Turkey	27,382	30,242	33,100	34,559	35,025	35,486	35,950	36,416	36,880
United Kingdom	29,383	29,787	30,151	30,402	30,507	30,665	30,815	30,999	31,183
Eastern Europe									
Albania	1,602	1,555	1,543	1,557	1,564	1,571	1,578	1,584	1,591
Belarus	5,411	5,431	5,316	5,261	5,239	5,217	5,195	5,179	5,168
Bosnia-Herzegovina	2,276	1,815	1,944	1,986	1,991	1,994	1,994	1,995	1,994
Bulgaria	4,444	4,234	4,091	4,020	3,999	3,976	3,953	3,928	3,903
Croatia	2,463	2,425	2,304	2,304	2,304	2,305	2,303	2,302	2,299
Czech Republic	5,302	5,304	5,256	5,237	5,237	5,240	5,248	5,266	5,280
Estonia	836	777	739	731	729	727	725	723	721
Georgia	2,706	2,527	2,342	2,296	2,283	2,285	2,317	2,315	2,304
Hungary	5,390	5,395	5,356	5,324	5,313	5,304	5,292	5,284	5,275
Latvia	1,428	1,346	1,285	1,258	1,251	1,244	1,237	1,230	1,222
Lithuania	1,946	1,926	1,868	1,845	1,837	1,827	1,817	1,808	1,799
Macedonia	951	981	1,005	1,015	1,017	1,019	1,020	1,022	1,023
Moldova	2,284	2,266	2,142	2,035	2,001	1,971	1,945	1,924	1,907
Poland	19,472	19,663	19,713	19,712	19,704	19,704	19,703	19,680	19,655
Romania	11,761	11,347	11,205	11,145	11,119	11,097	11,075	11,056	11,030
Russia	78,550	78,801	78,192	77,473	77,144	76,871	76,590	76,372	76,292
Slovakia	2,692	2,743	2,764	2,768	2,769	2,771	2,773	2,774	2,774
Slovenia	1,028	1,025	1,017	1,019	1,020	1,021	1,022	1,024	1,026
Ukraine	27,730	27,508	26,360	25,711	25,515	25,346	25,175	25,031	24,898

Source: *Euromonitor International from national statistics/UN*

Population Statistics

Table 21.27

Number of Children Aged 0-14 Years at January 1st 1990-2008
'000

	1990	1995	2000	2003	2004	2005	2006	2007	2008
Western Europe									
Austria	1,340	1,417	1,372	1,339	1,329	1,323	1,313	1,300	1,287
Belgium	1,801	1,827	1,805	1,803	1,797	1,795	1,796	1,795	1,795
Cyprus	176	184	178	171	168	166	163	160	157
Denmark	881	901	981	1,013	1,018	1,018	1,016	1,015	1,009
Finland	962	972	943	927	920	915	907	901	895
France	11,389	11,330	11,101	11,186	11,210	11,223	11,246	11,295	11,380
Germany	12,639	13,294	12,897	12,416	12,162	11,925	11,650	11,441	11,282
Gibraltar	5	5	5	5	5	5	5	5	5
Greece	1,984	1,850	1,682	1,610	1,599	1,598	1,594	1,594	1,596
Iceland	64	65	65	65	65	65	65	66	66
Ireland	959	883	829	832	841	851	862	878	893
Italy	9,522	8,402	8,151	8,147	8,190	8,256	8,284	8,272	8,246
Liechtenstein	6	6	6	6	6	6	6	6	6
Luxembourg	66	74	82	85	85	86	86	86	86
Malta	85	83	78	73	72	70	68	67	65
Monaco	4	4	4	4	4	4	4	4	5
Netherlands	2,715	2,838	2,946	3,010	3,016	3,009	2,985	2,959	2,934
Norway	801	845	895	910	911	909	907	906	907
Portugal	2,081	1,796	1,655	1,646	1,649	1,647	1,644	1,643	1,644
Spain	7,856	6,657	5,965	6,049	6,151	6,241	6,342	6,481	6,610
Sweden	1,522	1,663	1,640	1,612	1,599	1,584	1,561	1,546	1,529
Switzerland	1,137	1,237	1,249	1,222	1,214	1,205	1,194	1,181	1,167
Turkey	19,417	19,664	20,131	20,447	20,492	20,503	20,530	20,515	20,467
United Kingdom	10,833	11,292	11,244	10,970	10,892	10,848	10,806	10,716	10,740
Eastern Europe									
Albania	1,078	997	932	869	846	823	801	781	761
Belarus	2,351	2,252	1,898	1,670	1,595	1,530	1,478	1,444	1,422
Bosnia-Herzegovina	1,090	777	743	685	661	639	621	608	599
Bulgaria	1,801	1,506	1,267	1,141	1,102	1,069	1,041	1,018	1,000
Croatia	952	858	760	736	723	712	703	693	687
Czech Republic	2,239	1,945	1,700	1,590	1,554	1,527	1,501	1,483	1,470
Estonia	350	302	251	225	216	208	202	199	197
Georgia	1,267	1,157	972	861	826	801	792	771	753
Hungary	2,131	1,892	1,729	1,634	1,606	1,580	1,553	1,529	1,510
Latvia	572	522	428	373	357	341	329	318	310
Lithuania	834	798	710	633	609	585	560	538	516
Macedonia	499	483	444	419	410	401	392	382	373
Moldova	1,218	1,154	974	812	760	715	677	647	624
Poland	9,600	8,849	7,480	6,804	6,580	6,377	6,189	6,012	5,865
Romania	5,508	4,694	4,126	3,708	3,566	3,437	3,360	3,319	3,285
Russia	34,031	32,050	27,066	23,554	22,613	21,871	21,244	20,881	20,824
Slovakia	1,341	1,224	1,065	975	944	919	894	871	851
Slovenia	418	369	320	299	292	287	283	281	280
Ukraine	11,084	10,529	8,781	7,569	7,246	6,990	6,765	6,606	6,486

Source: *Euromonitor International from national statistics/UN*

Population Statistics

Table 21.28

Number of Persons of Working Age (15-64 Years) at January 1st 1990-2008
'000

	1990	1995	2000	2003	2004	2005	2006	2007	2008
Western Europe									
Austria	5,165	5,330	5,397	5,510	5,547	5,572	5,591	5,610	5,634
Belgium	6,673	6,707	6,719	6,791	6,819	6,851	6,906	6,965	7,006
Cyprus	431	468	519	550	559	569	578	587	595
Denmark	3,454	3,516	3,558	3,572	3,575	3,581	3,589	3,598	3,602
Finland	3,350	3,407	3,461	3,481	3,486	3,491	3,508	3,507	3,531
France	37,317	37,736	38,327	39,101	39,380	39,611	39,862	40,132	40,470
Germany	54,680	55,702	55,915	55,682	55,510	55,209	54,918	54,574	54,417
Gibraltar	18	18	18	19	19	19	19	19	19
Greece	6,781	7,197	7,432	7,468	7,471	7,478	7,472	7,506	7,531
Iceland	164	172	183	189	192	196	201	206	213
Ireland	2,148	2,304	2,525	2,690	2,738	2,800	2,880	2,942	2,994
Italy	38,820	39,073	38,466	38,273	38,569	38,827	38,875	38,878	38,867
Liechtenstein	20	21	23	24	24	25	25	25	25
Luxembourg	264	277	293	304	308	313	317	322	327
Malta	238	251	263	273	276	279	282	284	285
Monaco	20	20	21	21	21	21	21	21	21
Netherlands	10,272	10,552	10,766	10,962	10,991	11,008	11,019	11,031	11,042
Norway	2,741	2,809	2,901	2,968	2,993	3,019	3,051	3,090	3,136
Portugal	6,593	6,747	6,905	7,026	7,064	7,091	7,115	7,140	7,152
Spain	25,755	26,740	27,379	28,571	29,050	29,569	30,108	30,558	30,864
Sweden	5,488	5,614	5,689	5,795	5,835	5,873	5,922	5,984	6,017
Switzerland	4,565	4,750	4,821	4,950	4,994	5,035	5,073	5,103	5,125
Turkey	33,565	38,532	43,177	45,445	46,189	46,940	47,746	48,603	49,479
United Kingdom	37,340	37,477	38,248	38,993	39,280	39,595	39,917	40,381	40,599
Eastern Europe									
Albania	2,036	1,938	1,908	1,964	1,991	2,017	2,042	2,066	2,089
Belarus	6,764	6,712	6,790	6,840	6,846	6,850	6,851	6,851	6,867
Bosnia-Herzegovina	3,135	2,459	2,595	2,661	2,675	2,689	2,699	2,708	2,715
Bulgaria	5,830	5,564	5,421	5,353	5,346	5,334	5,314	5,287	5,253
Croatia	3,276	3,175	2,984	2,984	2,986	2,988	2,987	2,988	2,980
Czech Republic	6,777	7,018	7,124	7,196	7,234	7,259	7,293	7,323	7,338
Estonia	1,039	953	916	916	917	917	917	912	909
Georgia	3,396	3,101	2,907	2,885	2,881	2,903	2,975	2,990	2,998
Hungary	6,870	6,987	6,961	6,949	6,944	6,940	6,932	6,928	6,912
Latvia	1,781	1,642	1,600	1,589	1,587	1,584	1,580	1,573	1,566
Lithuania	2,461	2,402	2,319	2,320	2,319	2,323	2,321	2,319	2,317
Macedonia	1,268	1,309	1,363	1,390	1,399	1,407	1,415	1,423	1,431
Moldova	2,784	2,794	2,723	2,662	2,644	2,629	2,618	2,611	2,604
Poland	24,607	25,230	26,164	26,527	26,659	26,778	26,892	26,992	27,082
Romania	15,319	14,912	14,873	14,975	15,012	15,047	15,053	15,038	15,025
Russia	99,056	99,008	101,761	102,532	102,264	101,916	101,637	101,386	101,596
Slovakia	3,387	3,547	3,700	3,788	3,815	3,840	3,862	3,882	3,897
Slovenia	1,367	1,381	1,392	1,401	1,405	1,404	1,407	1,411	1,411
Ukraine	34,298	33,811	33,515	33,060	32,826	32,603	32,417	32,256	32,190

Source: Euromonitor International from national statistics/UN

Table 21.29

Number of Persons Aged 65 Years and Over at January 1st 1990-2008
'000

	1990	1995	2000	2003	2004	2005	2006	2007	2008
Western Europe									
Austria	1,140	1,197	1,234	1,253	1,264	1,312	1,362	1,404	1,431
Belgium	1,474	1,597	1,715	1,762	1,780	1,800	1,809	1,810	1,817
Cyprus	74	79	89	97	99	102	104	107	110
Denmark	800	799	790	798	805	813	823	834	850
Finland	662	720	767	799	813	831	841	869	875
France	7,872	8,686	9,422	9,779	9,871	9,991	10,059	10,111	10,256
Germany	11,794	12,542	13,351	14,439	14,860	15,367	15,870	16,299	16,519
Gibraltar	3	4	4	5	5	5	5	5	5
Greece	1,356	1,548	1,790	1,929	1,971	2,007	2,060	2,069	2,084
Iceland	27	30	33	34	34	35	35	36	37
Ireland	399	411	424	441	449	458	467	479	492
Italy	8,352	9,371	10,313	10,901	11,128	11,379	11,592	11,737	11,863
Liechtenstein	3	3	3	4	4	4	4	4	4
Luxembourg	51	57	62	64	65	66	66	67	67
Malta	38	43	48	51	52	53	55	56	57
Monaco	7	7	7	7	7	7	7	7	7
Netherlands	1,906	2,034	2,152	2,220	2,251	2,289	2,330	2,368	2,406
Norway	691	695	683	674	674	678	682	686	693
Portugal	1,322	1,475	1,635	1,736	1,761	1,791	1,810	1,826	1,847
Spain	5,215	5,946	6,706	7,044	7,144	7,228	7,308	7,445	7,583
Sweden	1,518	1,540	1,533	1,534	1,541	1,554	1,565	1,583	1,611
Switzerland	972	1,032	1,094	1,142	1,157	1,174	1,192	1,213	1,239
Turkey	2,513	3,008	3,581	3,878	4,011	4,167	4,248	4,325	4,412
United Kingdom	8,984	9,175	9,293	9,475	9,528	9,617	9,670	9,720	9,847
Eastern Europe									
Albania	175	199	228	253	262	271	279	286	293
Belarus	1,074	1,247	1,332	1,388	1,407	1,420	1,422	1,420	1,400
Bosnia-Herzegovina	274	287	415	484	501	514	523	528	530
Bulgaria	1,136	1,233	1,290	1,333	1,330	1,325	1,321	1,318	1,318
Croatia	550	636	697	722	733	745	753	759	767
Czech Republic	1,285	1,354	1,412	1,418	1,423	1,435	1,456	1,481	1,509
Estonia	182	193	205	215	219	222	225	228	229
Georgia	482	537	557	597	607	618	634	634	631
Hungary	1,374	1,458	1,531	1,559	1,567	1,578	1,591	1,601	1,618
Latvia	315	336	353	370	375	381	386	390	391
Lithuania	399	443	483	510	518	517	522	528	534
Macedonia	142	171	202	217	222	226	229	233	237
Moldova	362	391	403	413	415	415	413	409	405
Poland	3,781	4,186	4,619	4,888	4,951	5,018	5,076	5,099	5,098
Romania	2,383	2,679	2,930	3,090	3,133	3,175	3,197	3,198	3,186
Russia	14,578	17,402	18,063	18,878	19,291	19,687	19,873	19,954	19,589
Slovakia	541	578	613	616	620	626	633	639	645
Slovenia	212	240	275	295	300	306	313	319	325
Ukraine	6,175	6,961	6,819	7,193	7,369	7,507	7,567	7,603	7,517

Source: *Euromonitor International from national statistics/UN*

Table 21.30

Population by Age Group at January 1st 2008
'000

	0-4	5-9	10-14	15-19	20-24	25-29	30-34	35-39
Western Europe								
Austria	400.4	414.3	471.9	503.1	519.0	542.6	544.8	656.4
Belgium	598.9	588.9	607.4	650.2	634.4	676.3	677.3	754.6
Cyprus	48.7	50.3	58.3	65.7	67.1	67.0	61.7	59.4
Denmark	322.2	334.1	353.1	334.3	295.7	316.2	366.4	386.4
Finland	291.6	286.2	316.7	331.9	327.3	334.7	324.0	324.1
France	3,881.7	3,837.3	3,661.0	3,892.8	3,901.5	3,998.2	3,993.9	4,388.0
Germany	3,469.0	3,802.3	4,010.4	4,643.0	4,855.5	4,976.7	4,703.4	6,039.9
Gibraltar								
Greece	537.6	514.5	544.0	585.6	669.9	822.0	870.7	881.8
Iceland	22.2	21.2	22.6	23.2	22.8	23.7	23.3	22.2
Ireland	315.5	298.4	278.8	287.5	327.8	400.4	361.9	335.4
Italy	2,746.9	2,747.6	2,751.4	2,944.4	3,029.2	3,546.2	4,395.9	4,762.9
Liechtenstein								
Luxembourg	27.3	28.8	30.3	29.4	28.8	30.7	34.4	39.1
Malta	18.6	21.5	25.0	27.6	30.1	31.7	31.0	26.6
Monaco								
Netherlands	945.6	1,010.6	978.2	1,003.5	974.8	986.0	1,022.1	1,273.0
Norway	293.8	299.0	314.6	315.6	284.6	296.4	321.6	362.3
Portugal	547.2	555.4	540.9	580.0	650.3	776.0	853.4	803.2
Spain	2,371.0	2,163.8	2,074.7	2,259.3	2,708.0	3,568.9	3,990.0	3,794.6
Sweden	514.4	475.0	539.8	635.7	551.0	547.0	590.0	624.6
Switzerland	364.8	381.6	420.2	452.6	447.1	474.7	503.9	580.0
Turkey	6,463.1	6,963.7	7,040.2	6,465.1	6,385.1	6,768.9	6,592.8	5,723.4
United Kingdom	3,645.9	3,409.8	3,684.2	4,005.7	4,196.0	4,029.0	3,844.7	4,492.5
Eastern Europe								
Albania	216.6	242.8	301.8	312.2	290.3	235.5	192.6	194.7
Belarus	465.4	454.5	502.5	712.8	840.5	756.3	687.8	673.6
Bosnia-Herzegovina	171.2	203.1	224.4	258.0	304.8	288.1	274.9	277.6
Bulgaria	334.6	325.4	340.3	466.0	518.3	549.3	580.6	549.4
Croatia	208.5	223.6	255.3	264.7	295.5	315.0	302.6	293.8
Czech Republic	503.6	457.3	508.9	646.4	681.1	793.1	924.1	736.4
Estonia	70.2	62.0	65.0	97.2	106.0	97.2	92.0	92.5
Georgia	250.0	222.1	280.8	371.3	361.1	311.8	293.3	278.6
Hungary	484.8	481.9	542.8	619.1	654.6	759.3	847.2	722.7
Latvia	107.0	96.1	106.5	167.3	185.3	162.9	158.0	159.2
Lithuania	151.4	164.6	199.9	261.4	272.1	230.1	223.1	246.1
Macedonia	112.6	121.6	138.5	156.7	161.2	163.6	156.0	148.6
Moldova	199.9	182.2	242.4	335.0	349.1	279.8	237.5	219.5
Poland	1,788.6	1,860.0	2,216.8	2,710.4	3,204.0	3,167.2	2,914.8	2,476.9
Romania	1,074.9	1,085.8	1,124.5	1,485.0	1,660.7	1,710.3	1,731.6	1,811.9
Russia	7,449.0	6,481.5	6,893.7	10,206.9	12,764.0	11,475.3	10,492.9	9,702.5
Slovakia	266.6	267.3	317.0	390.7	434.4	463.6	458.8	376.1
Slovenia	91.5	91.1	97.5	114.3	133.3	152.5	151.7	145.1
Ukraine	2,156.8	1,931.3	2,397.8	3,217.5	3,883.5	3,513.1	3,326.6	3,183.2

Source: Euromonitor International from national statistics/UN

Population Statistics

Population by Age Group at January 1st 2008 *(continued)*
'000

	40-44	45-49	50-54	55-59	60-64	65-69	70-74	75-79	80+
Western Europe									
Austria	718.4	661.3	552.7	495.2	441.0	471.1	298.6	278.4	382.6
Belgium	807.4	799.7	738.6	677.2	590.7	462.0	450.5	406.0	498.5
Cyprus	62.0	62.1	57.6	49.1	43.4	35.3	28.0	21.9	24.9
Denmark	428.8	379.2	363.3	356.0	375.3	266.2	203.3	156.9	224.0
Finland	373.6	374.4	387.2	403.8	349.9	253.2	209.4	183.6	229.0
France	4,411.9	4,282.4	4,152.3	4,143.0	3,306.0	2,479.0	2,430.2	2,223.7	3,123.0
Germany	7,176.6	6,707.5	5,792.8	5,271.0	4,250.9	5,324.0	4,218.7	3,048.9	3,927.1
Gibraltar									
Greece	843.5	797.8	745.4	679.9	634.4	566.1	584.5	480.7	452.9
Iceland	22.2	22.7	20.8	17.7	14.2	10.4	8.6	7.8	10.1
Ireland	307.7	284.5	256.0	232.7	200.1	151.9	123.8	96.1	119.8
Italy	4,869.7	4,305.2	3,854.0	3,747.6	3,411.4	3,295.0	2,878.7	2,460.8	3,228.6
Liechtenstein									
Luxembourg	41.6	38.4	33.0	28.2	23.1	18.9	17.0	14.5	17.1
Malta	25.0	28.9	29.3	28.9	26.3	17.9	14.8	11.4	13.1
Monaco									
Netherlands	1,302.2	1,252.7	1,141.7	1,089.8	996.7	725.8	588.5	484.6	607.5
Norway	351.0	323.8	311.4	292.5	277.4	188.5	148.9	137.3	218.6
Portugal	789.6	758.6	695.8	662.2	583.2	515.8	490.9	398.0	442.2
Spain	3,596.6	3,275.6	2,824.6	2,525.4	2,321.2	1,902.8	1,887.1	1,672.0	2,120.8
Sweden	671.1	588.3	584.0	599.9	625.0	456.0	354.6	310.0	490.8
Switzerland	641.3	588.8	516.6	475.2	444.6	349.9	291.6	246.0	351.1
Turkey	4,825.0	4,239.9	3,613.8	2,790.7	2,073.8	1,670.8	1,330.9	749.9	660.7
United Kingdom	4,719.6	4,297.9	3,766.0	3,694.3	3,553.6	2,725.5	2,379.9	1,979.1	2,762.5
Eastern Europe									
Albania	206.9	210.0	185.8	141.5	119.2	103.3	83.0	55.1	52.1
Belarus	707.9	819.4	713.2	601.7	354.2	428.4	381.8	320.0	269.9
Bosnia-Herzegovina	294.8	305.0	289.2	245.2	177.6	165.6	167.3	114.2	82.9
Bulgaria	498.8	527.0	539.3	548.5	475.9	385.8	369.1	291.6	271.6
Croatia	316.5	328.7	335.4	302.7	225.5	232.9	218.1	169.1	147.1
Czech Republic	708.5	638.4	750.5	772.2	687.5	475.0	363.0	326.1	344.5
Estonia	86.9	95.9	91.5	85.9	64.4	71.4	59.2	49.5	48.5
Georgia	306.1	342.2	303.5	251.9	178.3	186.4	196.4	130.8	117.7
Hungary	626.9	629.7	790.5	691.9	570.0	498.5	407.0	340.4	371.5
Latvia	156.8	172.4	152.9	139.2	111.7	127.4	100.7	82.4	80.7
Lithuania	251.0	267.1	214.7	192.7	158.3	164.8	142.8	116.4	109.8
Macedonia	146.3	143.1	138.9	121.6	94.8	80.3	68.4	48.5	39.3
Moldova	241.9	281.6	276.2	229.8	153.9	131.7	120.3	83.9	68.7
Poland	2,382.2	2,761.9	3,024.2	2,693.5	1,746.8	1,449.7	1,369.7	1,148.5	1,130.5
Romania	1,354.1	1,352.5	1,542.0	1,388.7	988.6	981.9	913.6	695.4	595.4
Russia	9,804.1	11,954.7	10,947.7	9,349.6	4,898.1	6,601.8	5,198.4	4,213.5	3,575.3
Slovakia	374.4	382.1	404.0	357.9	255.3	205.7	162.8	137.5	139.5
Slovenia	157.1	154.4	158.1	141.4	103.1	98.6	85.1	70.4	71.2
Ukraine	3,182.7	3,653.7	3,293.4	3,058.3	1,877.6	2,586.9	1,979.1	1,535.0	1,415.8

Source: *Euromonitor International from national statistics/UN*

Table 21.31

Population by Age Group (%) at January 1st 2008

% of total

	0-4	5-9	10-14	15-19	20-24	25-29	30-34	35-39
Western Europe								
Austria	4.79	4.96	5.65	6.02	6.21	6.50	6.52	7.86
Belgium	5.64	5.55	5.72	6.12	5.97	6.37	6.38	7.11
Cyprus	5.65	5.83	6.75	7.62	7.79	7.77	7.16	6.89
Denmark	5.90	6.12	6.47	6.12	5.41	5.79	6.71	7.08
Finland	5.50	5.40	5.98	6.26	6.17	6.31	6.11	6.11
France	6.25	6.18	5.89	6.27	6.28	6.44	6.43	7.07
Germany	4.22	4.62	4.88	5.65	5.91	6.05	5.72	7.35
Gibraltar								
Greece	4.80	4.59	4.85	5.22	5.98	7.33	7.77	7.87
Iceland	7.05	6.71	7.16	7.35	7.22	7.50	7.38	7.04
Ireland	7.21	6.82	6.37	6.57	7.49	9.14	8.27	7.66
Italy	4.66	4.66	4.67	4.99	5.14	6.01	7.45	8.08
Liechtenstein								
Luxembourg	5.68	5.99	6.31	6.12	6.00	6.39	7.16	8.13
Malta	4.58	5.27	6.14	6.76	7.38	7.77	7.60	6.53
Monaco								
Netherlands	5.77	6.17	5.97	6.13	5.95	6.02	6.24	7.77
Norway	6.20	6.31	6.64	6.66	6.01	6.26	6.79	7.65
Portugal	5.14	5.22	5.08	5.45	6.11	7.29	8.02	7.55
Spain	5.26	4.80	4.60	5.01	6.01	7.92	8.86	8.42
Sweden	5.62	5.19	5.89	6.94	6.02	5.97	6.44	6.82
Switzerland	4.84	5.07	5.58	6.01	5.94	6.30	6.69	7.70
Turkey	8.69	9.37	9.47	8.69	8.59	9.10	8.87	7.70
United Kingdom	5.96	5.57	6.02	6.55	6.86	6.58	6.28	7.34
Eastern Europe								
Albania	6.89	7.72	9.60	9.93	9.24	7.49	6.13	6.19
Belarus	4.80	4.69	5.19	7.36	8.67	7.80	7.10	6.95
Bosnia-Herzegovina	4.45	5.28	5.84	6.71	7.93	7.49	7.15	7.22
Bulgaria	4.42	4.30	4.49	6.15	6.85	7.25	7.67	7.26
Croatia	4.70	5.04	5.76	5.97	6.66	7.10	6.82	6.63
Czech Republic	4.88	4.43	4.93	6.27	6.60	7.69	8.96	7.14
Estonia	5.26	4.65	4.87	7.28	7.94	7.28	6.89	6.93
Georgia	5.70	5.07	6.41	8.47	8.24	7.11	6.69	6.36
Hungary	4.83	4.80	5.41	6.17	6.52	7.56	8.44	7.20
Latvia	4.72	4.24	4.70	7.38	8.18	7.18	6.97	7.03
Lithuania	4.50	4.89	5.94	7.76	8.08	6.83	6.63	7.31
Macedonia	5.52	5.96	6.79	7.68	7.90	8.02	7.65	7.29
Moldova	5.50	5.01	6.67	9.22	9.61	7.70	6.54	6.04
Poland	4.70	4.89	5.83	7.12	8.42	8.32	7.66	6.51
Romania	5.00	5.05	5.23	6.91	7.73	7.96	8.06	8.43
Russia	5.25	4.56	4.85	7.19	8.99	8.08	7.39	6.83
Slovakia	4.94	4.96	5.88	7.24	8.05	8.60	8.51	6.97
Slovenia	4.54	4.52	4.84	5.67	6.61	7.56	7.52	7.20
Ukraine	4.67	4.18	5.19	6.97	8.41	7.61	7.20	6.89

Source: Euromonitor International from national statistics/UN

Population by Age Group (%) at January 1st 2008 *(continued)*
% of total

	40-44	45-49	50-54	55-59	60-64	65-69	70-74	75-79	80+
Western Europe									
Austria	8.60	7.92	6.62	5.93	5.28	5.64	3.58	3.33	4.58
Belgium	7.60	7.53	6.96	6.38	5.56	4.35	4.24	3.82	4.69
Cyprus	7.18	7.20	6.68	5.70	5.03	4.10	3.24	2.53	2.88
Denmark	7.85	6.94	6.65	6.52	6.87	4.87	3.72	2.87	4.10
Finland	7.05	7.06	7.30	7.62	6.60	4.78	3.95	3.46	4.32
France	7.10	6.90	6.69	6.67	5.32	3.99	3.91	3.58	5.03
Germany	8.73	8.16	7.05	6.41	5.17	6.48	5.13	3.71	4.78
Gibraltar									
Greece	7.52	7.12	6.65	6.06	5.66	5.05	5.21	4.29	4.04
Iceland	7.03	7.20	6.58	5.60	4.49	3.30	2.71	2.46	3.21
Ireland	7.03	6.50	5.85	5.32	4.57	3.47	2.83	2.20	2.74
Italy	8.26	7.30	6.53	6.35	5.78	5.59	4.88	4.17	5.47
Liechtenstein									
Luxembourg	8.65	7.99	6.86	5.87	4.80	3.93	3.53	3.02	3.55
Malta	6.12	7.09	7.18	7.09	6.46	4.39	3.62	2.79	3.22
Monaco									
Netherlands	7.95	7.65	6.97	6.65	6.08	4.43	3.59	2.96	3.71
Norway	7.41	6.84	6.57	6.18	5.85	3.98	3.14	2.90	4.61
Portugal	7.42	7.13	6.54	6.22	5.48	4.85	4.61	3.74	4.15
Spain	7.98	7.27	6.27	5.61	5.15	4.22	4.19	3.71	4.71
Sweden	7.33	6.42	6.38	6.55	6.83	4.98	3.87	3.39	5.36
Switzerland	8.52	7.82	6.86	6.31	5.90	4.65	3.87	3.27	4.66
Turkey	6.49	5.70	4.86	3.75	2.79	2.25	1.79	1.01	0.89
United Kingdom	7.71	7.02	6.16	6.04	5.81	4.45	3.89	3.23	4.51
Eastern Europe									
Albania	6.58	6.68	5.91	4.50	3.79	3.29	2.64	1.75	1.66
Belarus	7.31	8.46	7.36	6.21	3.66	4.42	3.94	3.30	2.79
Bosnia-Herzegovina	7.67	7.93	7.52	6.38	4.62	4.31	4.35	2.97	2.16
Bulgaria	6.59	6.96	7.12	7.24	6.29	5.10	4.87	3.85	3.59
Croatia	7.14	7.41	7.56	6.83	5.08	5.25	4.92	3.81	3.32
Czech Republic	6.87	6.19	7.27	7.48	6.66	4.60	3.52	3.16	3.34
Estonia	6.51	7.19	6.85	6.43	4.82	5.35	4.43	3.71	3.63
Georgia	6.98	7.81	6.93	5.75	4.07	4.25	4.48	2.98	2.68
Hungary	6.24	6.27	7.87	6.89	5.68	4.97	4.05	3.39	3.70
Latvia	6.92	7.61	6.75	6.14	4.93	5.62	4.44	3.63	3.56
Lithuania	7.46	7.93	6.38	5.73	4.70	4.90	4.24	3.46	3.26
Macedonia	7.17	7.01	6.81	5.96	4.65	3.94	3.35	2.38	1.93
Moldova	6.66	7.75	7.60	6.33	4.23	3.63	3.31	2.31	1.89
Poland	6.26	7.26	7.95	7.08	4.59	3.81	3.60	3.02	2.97
Romania	6.30	6.29	7.17	6.46	4.60	4.57	4.25	3.23	2.77
Russia	6.90	8.42	7.71	6.58	3.45	4.65	3.66	2.97	2.52
Slovakia	6.94	7.08	7.49	6.64	4.73	3.81	3.02	2.55	2.59
Slovenia	7.79	7.66	7.84	7.01	5.11	4.89	4.22	3.49	3.53
Ukraine	6.89	7.91	7.13	6.62	4.06	5.60	4.28	3.32	3.07

Source: Euromonitor International from national statistics/UN

Population Statistics

Table 21.32

Total Population 2010-2020 at January 1st
'000

	2010	2011	2012	2013	2014	2015	2016	2017	2018	2019	2020
Western Europe											
Austria	8,409	8,434	8,459	8,484	8,507	8,530	8,553	8,574	8,595	8,615	8,634
Belgium	10,699	10,736	10,773	10,809	10,844	10,879	10,913	10,947	10,980	11,012	11,044
Cyprus	880	889	897	906	916	925	934	943	952	961	970
Denmark	5,488	5,501	5,512	5,523	5,534	5,545	5,555	5,566	5,577	5,588	5,599
Finland	5,348	5,369	5,388	5,408	5,426	5,444	5,461	5,477	5,492	5,507	5,520
France	62,772	63,056	63,340	63,618	63,889	64,153	64,411	64,662	64,907	65,146	65,379
Germany	81,722	81,421	81,148	80,884	80,631	80,374	80,110	79,841	79,568	79,288	79,003
Gibraltar	29	29	29	29	29	29	29	29	29	29	29
Greece	11,290	11,325	11,357	11,387	11,414	11,437	11,457	11,473	11,486	11,495	11,501
Iceland	329	335	340	345	349	353	357	361	364	367	370
Ireland	4,507	4,560	4,613	4,665	4,716	4,766	4,815	4,862	4,908	4,953	4,996
Italy	59,115	59,164	59,198	59,219	59,224	59,216	59,195	59,160	59,114	59,056	58,989
Liechtenstein	36	36	37	37	37	38	38	38	38	39	39
Luxembourg	492	497	503	509	514	520	526	532	538	544	550
Malta	410	411	413	414	415	417	418	419	420	421	422
Monaco	33	33	33	33	34	34	34	34	34	34	34
Netherlands	16,439	16,470	16,501	16,531	16,561	16,590	16,619	16,646	16,673	16,700	16,726
Norway	4,858	4,913	4,964	5,013	5,061	5,108	5,156	5,205	5,254	5,303	5,352
Portugal	10,694	10,716	10,736	10,752	10,767	10,779	10,788	10,794	10,798	10,800	10,799
Spain	45,928	46,305	46,673	47,035	47,388	47,732	48,067	48,391	48,700	48,992	49,268
Sweden	9,244	9,288	9,332	9,376	9,421	9,466	9,513	9,561	9,609	9,657	9,706
Switzerland	7,589	7,618	7,647	7,675	7,704	7,732	7,761	7,790	7,819	7,849	7,879
Turkey	76,157	77,039	77,910	78,766	79,607	80,432	81,239	82,030	82,804	83,561	84,303
United Kingdom	61,966	62,260	62,582	62,938	63,325	63,717	64,114	64,514	64,918	65,324	65,730
Eastern Europe											
Albania	3,169	3,185	3,202	3,220	3,238	3,256	3,274	3,291	3,307	3,323	3,338
Belarus	9,653	9,626	9,599	9,572	9,544	9,515	9,486	9,457	9,426	9,395	9,362
Bosnia-Herzegovina	3,844	3,844	3,843	3,841	3,840	3,837	3,833	3,828	3,823	3,816	3,809
Bulgaria	7,467	7,415	7,362	7,306	7,250	7,191	7,131	7,070	7,009	6,947	6,885
Croatia	4,421	4,413	4,404	4,394	4,384	4,374	4,363	4,351	4,340	4,327	4,315
Czech Republic	10,353	10,365	10,368	10,367	10,364	10,361	10,358	10,357	10,357	10,356	10,354
Estonia	1,326	1,322	1,317	1,312	1,307	1,302	1,298	1,293	1,289	1,285	1,282
Georgia	4,389	4,393	4,398	4,403	4,409	4,414	4,418	4,422	4,425	4,428	4,429
Hungary	10,000	9,980	9,954	9,926	9,898	9,871	9,844	9,818	9,793	9,770	9,748
Latvia	2,240	2,228	2,214	2,199	2,185	2,172	2,159	2,146	2,133	2,121	2,110
Lithuania	3,329	3,311	3,292	3,272	3,253	3,234	3,216	3,198	3,181	3,165	3,150
Macedonia	2,041	2,041	2,041	2,040	2,039	2,037	2,035	2,033	2,031	2,028	2,025
Moldova	3,576	3,549	3,525	3,502	3,482	3,462	3,444	3,427	3,411	3,395	3,378
Poland	37,929	37,871	37,813	37,751	37,689	37,631	37,575	37,522	37,473	37,427	37,385
Romania	21,370	21,302	21,232	21,145	21,056	20,953	20,844	20,733	20,621	20,506	20,389
Russia	141,786	141,467	141,173	140,935	140,724	140,507	140,275	140,026	139,761	139,477	139,170
Slovakia	5,397	5,398	5,398	5,398	5,398	5,398	5,397	5,396	5,395	5,393	5,390
Slovenia	2,029	2,035	2,039	2,042	2,045	2,048	2,051	2,053	2,056	2,059	2,061
Ukraine	45,641	45,356	45,067	44,774	44,481	44,187	43,892	43,596	43,298	42,997	42,693

Source: *Euromonitor International from national statistics/UN*

Population Statistics

Table 21.33

Forecast Number of Children Aged 0-14 Years at January 1st 2010-2020
'000

	2010	2011	2012	2013	2014	2015	2016	2017	2018	2019	2020
Western Europe											
Austria	1,259	1,249	1,238	1,232	1,228	1,228	1,227	1,228	1,227	1,227	1,224
Belgium	1,808	1,818	1,826	1,834	1,843	1,852	1,860	1,868	1,878	1,886	1,890
Cyprus	153	153	152	153	153	154	156	157	159	161	163
Denmark	993	983	974	965	957	949	940	933	928	923	918
Finland	887	885	885	887	891	895	900	905	911	915	918
France	11,561	11,616	11,665	11,723	11,769	11,795	11,793	11,794	11,804	11,812	11,819
Germany	10,995	10,833	10,636	10,424	10,239	10,072	9,908	9,778	9,665	9,565	9,466
Gibraltar	5	5	5	5	5	5	5	5	5	5	5
Greece	1,606	1,609	1,615	1,621	1,630	1,637	1,640	1,640	1,638	1,633	1,625
Iceland	67	67	68	68	69	69	70	71	71	72	72
Ireland	918	928	935	940	943	945	946	947	942	934	926
Italy	8,223	8,209	8,184	8,150	8,104	8,046	7,968	7,888	7,800	7,698	7,582
Liechtenstein	6	6	6	6	6	6	6	6	6	6	6
Luxembourg	87	87	87	87	87	87	88	89	90	91	92
Malta	62	61	60	59	58	58	58	57	57	58	58
Monaco	5	5	5	5	5	5	5	5	5	5	5
Netherlands	2,886	2,867	2,847	2,826	2,799	2,771	2,738	2,711	2,686	2,664	2,651
Norway	918	923	926	929	934	939	944	952	962	971	980
Portugal	1,649	1,650	1,650	1,650	1,647	1,636	1,626	1,613	1,596	1,579	1,564
Spain	6,851	6,972	7,091	7,207	7,313	7,401	7,468	7,515	7,550	7,553	7,541
Sweden	1,513	1,516	1,527	1,542	1,559	1,577	1,594	1,611	1,624	1,635	1,645
Switzerland	1,145	1,137	1,128	1,122	1,117	1,115	1,118	1,122	1,128	1,135	1,143
Turkey	20,265	20,145	20,009	19,861	19,704	19,555	19,414	19,342	19,292	19,251	19,223
United Kingdom	10,831	10,867	10,912	10,977	11,071	11,188	11,332	11,491	11,649	11,791	11,919
Eastern Europe											
Albania	726	712	698	688	680	677	677	681	687	693	699
Belarus	1,420	1,428	1,440	1,458	1,470	1,480	1,489	1,498	1,509	1,519	1,526
Bosnia-Herzegovina	582	573	563	552	542	533	526	521	517	514	511
Bulgaria	977	973	970	971	970	961	951	939	927	914	897
Croatia	674	668	659	652	647	644	642	644	646	649	651
Czech Republic	1,456	1,466	1,481	1,494	1,507	1,522	1,534	1,544	1,552	1,557	1,557
Estonia	199	202	204	207	211	214	216	219	221	223	223
Georgia	735	733	735	740	747	754	761	767	771	774	774
Hungary	1,481	1,469	1,462	1,460	1,459	1,461	1,458	1,457	1,455	1,454	1,453
Latvia	306	308	312	317	322	326	329	332	335	336	338
Lithuania	491	482	475	470	465	462	460	461	463	464	465
Macedonia	356	349	343	338	334	329	325	322	318	315	312
Moldova	595	587	584	584	587	591	597	603	609	612	614
Poland	5,645	5,576	5,526	5,499	5,489	5,493	5,501	5,524	5,556	5,590	5,616
Romania	3,250	3,241	3,234	3,223	3,204	3,183	3,160	3,143	3,128	3,105	3,073
Russia	21,487	21,785	22,175	22,644	23,103	23,598	24,058	24,483	24,788	24,979	25,107
Slovakia	820	813	807	803	801	799	799	801	804	806	805
Slovenia	280	281	282	283	285	287	289	291	292	294	295
Ukraine	6,340	6,289	6,241	6,212	6,183	6,169	6,155	6,148	6,131	6,094	6,037

Source: Euromonitor International from national statistics/UN

Population Statistics

Table 21.34

Forecast Number of Persons of Working Age (15-64 Years) at January 1st 2010-2020

'000

	2010	2011	2012	2013	2014	2015	2016	2017	2018	2019	2020
Western Europe											
Austria	5,669	5,700	5,718	5,716	5,713	5,711	5,709	5,708	5,706	5,701	5,696
Belgium	7,035	7,042	7,030	7,019	7,007	6,996	6,986	6,976	6,960	6,944	6,930
Cyprus	610	616	622	627	632	636	640	644	648	651	653
Denmark	3,598	3,592	3,581	3,573	3,568	3,568	3,568	3,568	3,567	3,565	3,564
Finland	3,549	3,540	3,521	3,499	3,475	3,453	3,434	3,416	3,397	3,381	3,365
France	40,701	40,808	40,751	40,653	40,560	40,489	40,443	40,424	40,388	40,367	40,336
Germany	53,889	53,843	53,772	53,630	53,429	53,142	52,826	52,491	52,128	51,760	51,367
Gibraltar	19	19	19	19	19	19	19	19	19	19	19
Greece	7,562	7,559	7,541	7,527	7,519	7,518	7,497	7,484	7,471	7,463	7,447
Iceland	224	228	231	234	236	238	240	241	242	243	244
Ireland	3,071	3,100	3,128	3,158	3,187	3,217	3,246	3,274	3,305	3,337	3,368
Italy	38,807	38,794	38,617	38,449	38,274	38,141	38,025	37,934	37,847	37,762	37,654
Liechtenstein	26	26	26	26	26	27	27	27	27	27	28
Luxembourg	336	341	345	349	354	358	361	365	368	372	375
Malta	287	287	287	286	285	284	283	282	282	281	280
Monaco	21	21	21	21	21	21	21	22	22	22	22
Netherlands	11,039	11,040	10,974	10,919	10,882	10,854	10,836	10,816	10,786	10,758	10,720
Norway	3,218	3,250	3,273	3,296	3,318	3,342	3,365	3,388	3,407	3,426	3,446
Portugal	7,148	7,139	7,135	7,125	7,106	7,097	7,081	7,067	7,053	7,040	7,020
Spain	31,234	31,344	31,440	31,530	31,626	31,730	31,841	31,965	32,086	32,212	32,330
Sweden	6,040	6,036	6,023	6,008	5,993	5,981	5,976	5,977	5,980	5,987	6,001
Switzerland	5,149	5,158	5,163	5,167	5,167	5,169	5,167	5,167	5,163	5,157	5,150
Turkey	51,241	52,133	53,030	53,923	54,800	55,643	56,419	57,093	57,714	58,294	58,823
United Kingdom	41,008	41,127	41,180	41,194	41,256	41,339	41,426	41,518	41,618	41,733	41,862
Eastern Europe											
Albania	2,135	2,158	2,180	2,201	2,218	2,231	2,240	2,244	2,245	2,244	2,240
Belarus	6,906	6,916	6,893	6,855	6,809	6,746	6,695	6,643	6,587	6,537	6,478
Bosnia-Herzegovina	2,727	2,731	2,734	2,735	2,733	2,728	2,717	2,702	2,683	2,661	2,638
Bulgaria	5,171	5,115	5,048	4,976	4,903	4,832	4,757	4,696	4,632	4,569	4,510
Croatia	2,982	2,991	2,990	2,983	2,972	2,955	2,935	2,915	2,890	2,863	2,835
Czech Republic	7,308	7,276	7,205	7,128	7,057	6,992	6,925	6,862	6,804	6,752	6,706
Estonia	902	898	890	881	871	860	852	843	835	828	821
Georgia	3,024	3,030	3,031	3,028	3,023	3,014	3,003	2,990	2,975	2,960	2,944
Hungary	6,870	6,858	6,834	6,789	6,736	6,680	6,623	6,569	6,519	6,453	6,375
Latvia	1,547	1,536	1,522	1,505	1,486	1,467	1,451	1,435	1,419	1,407	1,393
Lithuania	2,305	2,294	2,284	2,271	2,256	2,238	2,218	2,197	2,175	2,156	2,137
Macedonia	1,442	1,445	1,446	1,446	1,445	1,442	1,438	1,432	1,426	1,418	1,410
Moldova	2,583	2,566	2,545	2,520	2,492	2,462	2,429	2,395	2,360	2,327	2,296
Poland	27,179	27,181	27,060	26,878	26,653	26,412	26,149	25,862	25,565	25,270	24,989
Romania	14,963	14,938	14,871	14,797	14,710	14,570	14,429	14,291	14,143	14,006	13,857
Russia	102,144	102,007	101,374	100,546	99,789	98,689	97,684	96,695	95,732	94,975	94,093
Slovakia	3,916	3,919	3,916	3,903	3,885	3,865	3,837	3,802	3,765	3,730	3,696
Slovenia	1,414	1,419	1,417	1,412	1,405	1,398	1,389	1,380	1,369	1,358	1,349
Ukraine	32,126	32,122	31,926	31,685	31,335	30,875	30,465	30,062	29,719	29,415	29,084

Source: *Euromonitor International from national statistics/UN*

Population Statistics

Table 21.35

Forecast Number of Persons Aged 65 Years and Over at January 1st 2010-2020
'000

	2010	2011	2012	2013	2014	2015	2016	2017	2018	2019	2020
Western Europe											
Austria	1,481	1,485	1,502	1,535	1,566	1,592	1,616	1,637	1,662	1,687	1,714
Belgium	1,856	1,877	1,917	1,955	1,994	2,031	2,067	2,102	2,142	2,182	2,224
Cyprus	116	119	123	126	130	134	137	141	145	149	153
Denmark	897	926	957	986	1,009	1,028	1,048	1,064	1,082	1,100	1,116
Finland	912	944	982	1,022	1,060	1,095	1,127	1,155	1,185	1,211	1,236
France	10,510	10,631	10,924	11,242	11,560	11,869	12,175	12,444	12,715	12,966	13,224
Germany	16,837	16,745	16,739	16,830	16,963	17,159	17,376	17,572	17,775	17,963	18,169
Gibraltar	5	5	5	5	5	5	5	5	5	5	5
Greece	2,122	2,156	2,201	2,239	2,265	2,282	2,320	2,349	2,377	2,400	2,430
Iceland	39	40	41	43	44	46	47	49	50	52	54
Ireland	518	533	550	567	586	605	623	642	662	682	702
Italy	12,085	12,161	12,397	12,619	12,847	13,030	13,201	13,338	13,467	13,596	13,753
Liechtenstein	5	5	5	5	5	5	5	5	5	5	5
Luxembourg	69	70	71	72	74	75	77	78	80	82	83
Malta	61	63	66	69	72	75	77	79	81	83	85
Monaco	7	7	8	8	8	8	8	8	8	8	8
Netherlands	2,514	2,563	2,679	2,787	2,881	2,965	3,045	3,120	3,201	3,278	3,355
Norway	722	740	765	787	808	827	847	865	885	906	927
Portugal	1,897	1,927	1,950	1,977	2,014	2,046	2,081	2,115	2,150	2,181	2,216
Spain	7,843	7,989	8,142	8,298	8,449	8,601	8,758	8,911	9,065	9,227	9,397
Sweden	1,691	1,736	1,782	1,825	1,868	1,908	1,943	1,973	2,004	2,036	2,061
Switzerland	1,294	1,323	1,355	1,387	1,419	1,448	1,476	1,501	1,529	1,556	1,586
Turkey	4,651	4,762	4,871	4,981	5,103	5,234	5,406	5,595	5,798	6,017	6,258
United Kingdom	10,126	10,267	10,489	10,767	10,999	11,190	11,356	11,505	11,652	11,801	11,949
Eastern Europe											
Albania	308	316	323	331	340	348	357	366	375	386	399
Belarus	1,326	1,282	1,266	1,259	1,265	1,289	1,303	1,315	1,330	1,339	1,358
Bosnia-Herzegovina	535	540	546	554	564	576	590	605	623	641	659
Bulgaria	1,319	1,327	1,345	1,358	1,376	1,398	1,423	1,435	1,449	1,465	1,479
Croatia	765	754	755	760	765	775	785	792	803	816	828
Czech Republic	1,589	1,623	1,682	1,745	1,800	1,848	1,899	1,951	2,001	2,047	2,091
Estonia	224	222	223	224	225	228	230	232	234	235	238
Georgia	629	630	632	635	639	645	654	665	679	694	711
Hungary	1,649	1,653	1,658	1,678	1,703	1,729	1,763	1,792	1,820	1,862	1,919
Latvia	387	383	379	378	378	379	378	379	379	378	379
Lithuania	534	535	533	531	532	535	538	541	544	546	548
Macedonia	244	247	251	255	260	266	272	279	287	295	303
Moldova	397	396	397	399	403	409	418	429	442	456	469
Poland	5,105	5,113	5,227	5,375	5,547	5,726	5,924	6,136	6,351	6,566	6,780
Romania	3,156	3,123	3,127	3,125	3,142	3,200	3,255	3,299	3,350	3,395	3,459
Russia	18,155	17,674	17,624	17,745	17,832	18,220	18,533	18,847	19,241	19,523	19,969
Slovakia	660	666	675	692	712	734	761	792	825	857	889
Slovenia	335	335	340	347	355	363	373	383	394	406	417
Ukraine	7,175	6,945	6,900	6,877	6,963	7,143	7,272	7,385	7,448	7,487	7,572

Source: Euromonitor International from national statistics/UN

Retailing

Retailing Statistics

Table 22.1

Total Retail Sales 2003-2008

US$ billion

	2003	2004	2005	2006	2007	2008
Western Europe						
Austria	56.4	63.6	64.4	65.9	73.7	80.2
Belgium	67.2	76.8	79.0	81.9	91.6	100.1
Denmark	36.2	41.3	43.4	46.4	53.3	55.5
Finland	29.8	34.2	36.2	38.3	44.6	50.5
France	391.3	437.3	443.6	457.4	510.6	561.8
Germany	431.7	477.0	478.0	492.2	551.5	598.2
Greece	40.8	48.5	54.7	58.8	67.6	75.2
Ireland	31.5	36.1	37.7	39.7	45.3	49.7
Italy	283.1	318.5	325.3	332.4	370.8	407.5
Netherlands	88.3	96.0	94.6	99.3	113.0	125.8
Norway	35.8	38.9	42.5	45.0	51.8	57.6
Portugal	34.7	38.4	40.2	42.0	46.3	51.3
Spain	204.6	234.4	244.5	255.2	283.9	310.9
Sweden	51.0	57.5	58.4	62.5	71.4	77.1
Switzerland	69.0	74.5	75.2	75.9	81.8	89.1
Turkey	89.5	99.0	109.0	111.1	135.8	152.9
United Kingdom	407.9	486.1	492.5	513.9	578.1	583.7
Eastern Europe						
Bulgaria	6.5	7.7	8.2	8.8	10.1	11.3
Czech Republic	19.7	22.3	24.8	27.5	32.0	34.7
Hungary	21.0	25.3	26.9	27.2	32.6	35.0
Poland	58.8	63.7	74.1	79.0	93.6	97.2
Romania	10.9	12.9	16.8	20.2	27.0	30.6
Russia	98.7	127.7	158.3	202.1	261.2	330.3
Slovakia	8.2	9.7	11.1	12.9	16.5	19.4
Ukraine	20.2	22.9	26.8	30.1	34.6	43.1

Source: *Euromonitor International from national sources*

Table 22.2

Store-based Retailer Sales by Type 2008
US$ billion

	Grocery Retailers	Non-Grocery Retailers	Total
Western Europe			
Austria	32.6	44.9	77.5
Belgium	47.7	49.9	97.6
Denmark	27.5	25.9	53.4
Finland	20.3	27.5	47.7
France	289.6	243.6	533.2
Germany	246.5	297.0	543.6
Greece	32.0	42.2	74.2
Ireland	23.3	25.4	48.6
Italy	163.7	234.1	397.8
Netherlands	50.3	70.4	120.7
Norway	27.9	27.2	55.1
Portugal	26.5	23.6	50.1
Spain	142.4	161.9	304.3
Sweden	37.6	36.9	74.5
Switzerland	43.0	42.5	85.5
Turkey	72.0	77.4	149.4
United Kingdom	267.1	268.2	535.3
Eastern Europe			
Bulgaria	4.5	6.7	11.1
Czech Republic	16.2	16.9	33.1
Hungary	19.4	14.7	34.1
Poland	52.9	42.1	95.0
Romania	15.9	13.8	29.7
Russia	173.9	144.2	318.1
Slovakia	9.6	9.4	19.0
Ukraine	20.7	20.6	41.4

Source: Euromonitor International from national sources

Retailing Statistics

Table 22.3

Number of Store-based Retailers by Type 2008

No of outlets

	Grocery Retailers	Non-Grocery Retailers	Total
Western Europe			
Austria	16,445	34,800	51,245
Belgium	25,073	49,527	74,600
Denmark	10,258	15,374	25,632
Finland	5,727	22,133	27,860
France	140,457	228,694	369,151
Germany	108,562	188,697	297,259
Greece	67,181	107,354	174,535
Ireland	9,094	14,799	23,893
Italy	263,592	668,275	931,867
Netherlands	33,924	71,360	105,284
Norway	9,774	22,210	31,984
Portugal	40,921	45,755	86,676
Spain	158,695	415,482	574,177
Sweden	13,366	34,878	48,244
Switzerland	17,054	31,927	48,980
Turkey	240,789	260,465	501,254
United Kingdom	94,080	194,774	288,854
Eastern Europe			
Bulgaria	36,580	46,234	82,814
Czech Republic	20,852	66,681	87,533
Hungary	44,079	101,327	145,406
Poland	166,848	155,930	322,778
Romania	74,891	63,004	137,895
Russia	324,356	167,772	492,128
Slovakia	27,419	20,593	48,012
Ukraine	79,516	55,290	134,806

Source: *Euromonitor International from national sources*

Table 22.4

Retail Sales through Grocery Retailers by Type 2008

% of total

	Hypermarkets	Supermarkets	Discounters	Small grocery retailers	Food/drink tobacco specialists	Other grocery retailers	Total
Western Europe							
Austria	8.53	38.48	20.30	14.00	10.46	8.23	100.00
Belgium	9.15	49.26	11.19	15.70	13.58	1.12	100.00
Denmark	22.04	32.50	22.63	16.22	6.21	0.40	100.00
Finland	30.20	32.63	4.48	26.89	5.38	0.42	100.00
France	43.85	23.88	6.63	7.82	16.86	0.95	100.00
Germany	19.51	23.88	36.30	12.17	6.87	1.26	100.00
Greece	3.97	43.12	7.69	12.21	15.86	17.15	100.00
Ireland	0.77	42.82	4.09	44.70	7.15	0.47	100.00
Italy	19.53	33.52	8.31	22.78	15.49	0.37	100.00
Netherlands	2.62	63.40	11.39	9.91	8.59	4.10	100.00
Norway	7.55	32.29	37.37	13.41	8.36	1.03	100.00
Portugal	22.68	35.97	11.02	8.02	18.03	4.28	100.00
Spain	17.18	47.32	6.25	4.60	22.18	2.46	100.00
Sweden	17.61	44.78	11.03	11.05	14.67	0.88	100.00
Switzerland	14.08	52.48	7.71	10.49	15.11	0.14	100.00
Turkey	5.79	27.39	9.70	37.08	20.04		100.00
United Kingdom	36.15	32.04	3.28	19.27	7.77	1.49	100.00
Eastern Europe							
Bulgaria	6.31	21.23		50.02	18.21	4.23	100.00
Czech Republic	38.71	12.02	15.23	3.99	9.27	20.78	100.00
Hungary	28.72	9.41	12.10	39.15	10.17	0.45	100.00
Poland	16.79	13.54	12.98	45.28	6.37	5.04	100.00
Romania	15.44	11.07	6.13	24.28	9.17	33.91	100.00
Russia	7.80	31.38	10.05	31.14	2.21	17.43	100.00
Slovakia	26.02	24.93	3.42	22.39	3.23	20.01	100.00
Ukraine	13.83	39.03	2.31	5.74	3.46	35.63	100.00

Source: *Euromonitor International from national sources*

Retail Sales through Non-Grocery Retailers by Type 2008

% of total

	Department stores	Variety stores	Mass merchandisers	Health and beauty retailers
Western Europe				
Austria		0.78		15.18
Belgium	2.23	1.46		20.21
Denmark	2.48	2.07	0.81	12.89
Finland	7.50	5.27	1.45	14.43
France	2.70	2.36		26.03
Germany	4.86	1.84		23.12
Greece	2.28	0.47		14.55
Ireland	9.57	20.41		13.49
Italy	1.42	1.03		17.18
Netherlands	5.87	3.48		19.08
Norway	0.33	2.63		12.22
Portugal	2.09			24.08
Spain	8.80	1.82		17.73
Sweden	2.87	0.12	3.81	16.60
Switzerland	11.58	1.35		15.59
Turkey	2.09	0.01		10.03
United Kingdom	12.16	5.39	1.42	9.81
Eastern Europe				
Bulgaria		0.11		16.14
Czech Republic	4.08	8.50		16.38
Hungary	1.23	8.75		15.80
Poland	5.80	1.05		19.85
Romania	1.55			16.95
Russia	6.77			13.48
Slovakia	2.94	5.78		32.39
Ukraine		1.40		21.32

Source: *Euromonitor International from national sources*

Retail Sales through Non-Grocery Retailers by Type 2008 *(continued)*
% of total

	Clothing and footwear retailers	Home and garden retailers	Electronics and appliance retailers	Leisure and personal goods retailers	Other non-grocery retailers	Total
Western Europe						
Austria	15.94	25.77	13.22	15.16	13.96	100.00
Belgium	17.89	24.61	11.69	16.59	5.33	100.00
Denmark	19.15	28.27	10.20	22.33	1.82	100.00
Finland	8.83	30.47	15.91	9.12	7.01	100.00
France	14.63	22.42	11.49	18.44	1.94	100.00
Germany	14.79	22.51	9.43	23.03	0.41	100.00
Greece	21.23	32.74	13.82	10.60	4.30	100.00
Ireland	17.79	19.21	2.91	14.20	2.42	100.00
Italy	26.49	17.67	6.72	11.30	18.19	100.00
Netherlands	18.60	24.11	8.41	15.75	4.70	100.00
Norway	20.27	33.28	14.23	15.86	1.18	100.00
Portugal	21.37	21.38	11.40	18.69	1.00	100.00
Spain	17.27	18.12	6.23	26.93	3.10	100.00
Sweden	18.88	26.50	10.85	14.76	5.60	100.00
Switzerland	18.87	12.97	8.38	15.25	16.01	100.00
Turkey	22.00	19.43	20.29	26.15		100.00
United Kingdom	22.98	17.53	8.75	18.19	3.78	100.00
Eastern Europe						
Bulgaria	25.48	29.84	11.97	12.87	3.59	100.00
Czech Republic	17.16	19.16	11.40	12.53	10.79	100.00
Hungary	11.50	22.09	10.33	20.16	10.14	100.00
Poland	14.89	20.03	15.18	17.85	5.34	100.00
Romania	4.95	23.67	22.60	16.74	13.56	100.00
Russia	12.90	16.56	29.38	13.52	7.38	100.00
Slovakia	17.64	18.72	5.22	16.05	1.26	100.00
Ukraine	34.65	11.68	13.89	14.07	2.98	100.00

Source: Euromonitor International from national sources

Table 22.6

Number of Grocery Retailers by Type 2008
Number of outlets

	Hypermarkets	Supermarkets	Discounters	Small grocery retailers	Food/drink tobacco specialists	Other grocery retailers	Total
Western Europe							
Austria	99	2,657	1,230	5,807	3,387	3,265	16,445
Belgium	63	1,513	766	8,377	12,759	1,595	25,073
Denmark	181	1,199	1,298	4,265	3,131	184	10,258
Finland	147	762	126	3,617	935	140	5,727
France	1,524	6,114	4,361	28,359	96,079	4,020	140,457
Germany	1,688	13,736	15,471	37,236	36,340	4,091	108,562
Greece	22	4,706	758	15,818	26,358	19,519	67,181
Ireland	4	380	151	6,609	1,780	170	9,094
Italy	765	9,132	4,351	75,114	128,920	45,310	263,592
Netherlands	24	4,959	779	6,213	12,559	9,390	33,924
Norway	69	2,274	1,666	4,263	1,027	475	9,774
Portugal	89	845	701	5,538	22,125	11,623	40,921
Spain	446	12,974	3,536	24,465	103,962	13,312	158,695
Sweden	160	2,440	370	4,244	4,860	1,292	13,366
Switzerland	90	2,529	869	6,646	6,754	166	17,054
Turkey	257	7,361	5,877	120,658	106,636		240,789
United Kingdom	902	4,013	1,118	52,456	31,015	4,576	94,080
Eastern Europe							
Bulgaria	34	459		27,704	6,195	2,188	36,580
Czech Republic	242	526	594	4,443	9,205	5,842	20,852
Hungary	137	600	555	18,713	12,102	11,972	44,079
Poland	350	1,916	1,892	134,286	22,244	6,160	166,848
Romania	72	353	214	14,864	11,352	48,036	74,891
Russia	307	16,218	5,849	162,338	12,750	126,894	324,356
Slovakia	97	575	150	14,091	8,025	4,481	27,419
Ukraine	106	1,792	176	35,592	3,953	37,897	79,516

Source: *Euromonitor International from national sources*

Table 22.7

Number of Non-Grocery Retailers by Type 2008

Number of outlets

	Department stores	Variety stores	Mass merchandisers	Health and beauty retailers
Western Europe				
Austria		244		4,367
Belgium	142	393		6,868
Denmark	9	228	3	1,743
Finland	60	236	3	2,514
France	100	382		41,292
Germany	532	2,868		42,495
Greece	57	121		11,983
Ireland	71	287		2,078
Italy	398	827		56,575
Netherlands	433	1,283		7,645
Norway	1	515		1,779
Portugal	2			8,853
Spain	145	16,053		34,602
Sweden	82	50	178	3,438
Switzerland	139	174		3,817
Turkey	240	30		28,605
United Kingdom	864	12,959	45	15,528
Eastern Europe				
Bulgaria		14		8,680
Czech Republic	55	750		6,462
Hungary	35	5,850		7,742
Poland	387	185		15,997
Romania	141			11,156
Russia	2,295			38,043
Slovakia	14	272		4,434
Ukraine		98		26,324

Source: *Euromonitor International from national sources*

Retailing Statistics

Number of Non-Grocery Retailers by Type 2008 *(continued)*
Number of outlets

	Clothing and footwear retailers	Home and garden retailers	Electronics and appliance retailers	Leisure and personal goods retailers	Other non-grocery retailers	Total
Western Europe						
Austria	4,398	6,642	2,691	6,970	9,489	34,800
Belgium	9,690	6,765	6,540	12,436	6,693	49,527
Denmark	3,892	1,606	1,360	4,824	1,709	15,374
Finland	3,495	3,296	2,428	4,904	5,197	22,133
France	50,015	32,870	19,767	51,694	32,574	228,694
Germany	32,208	23,927	23,566	54,061	9,040	188,697
Greece	29,648	32,541	9,906	14,224	8,874	107,354
Ireland	3,601	3,399	315	4,158	890	14,799
Italy	161,893	91,900	17,157	160,465	179,060	668,275
Netherlands	16,721	13,102	4,016	15,141	13,019	71,360
Norway	6,257	5,509	1,568	4,616	1,965	22,210
Portugal	6,595	8,440	6,323	10,471	5,071	45,755
Spain	75,798	78,170	12,957	139,032	58,725	415,482
Sweden	7,840	5,030	2,100	7,060	9,100	34,878
Switzerland	4,897	2,188	945	9,666	10,102	31,927
Turkey	54,717	78,151	16,348	82,375		260,465
United Kingdom	41,015	30,221	9,990	50,651	33,501	194,774
Eastern Europe						
Bulgaria	12,135	6,502	1,951	8,493	8,459	46,234
Czech Republic	13,300	8,564	1,550	11,361	24,639	66,681
Hungary	25,280	16,360	3,510	23,462	19,089	101,327
Poland	56,729	6,186	8,125	26,718	41,603	155,930
Romania	6,987	6,627	3,021	15,344	19,728	63,004
Russia	22,798	12,462	19,530	32,194	40,450	167,772
Slovakia	4,600	1,151	320	4,970	4,832	20,593
Ukraine	15,372	1,591	1,502	1,807	8,596	55,290

Source: *Euromonitor International from national sources*

Table 22.8

Non-Store Retail Sales by Type 2008
US$ billion

	Vending	Home shopping	Internet retailing	Direct selling	Total
Western Europe					
Austria	0.47	1.11	0.86	0.30	2.73
Belgium	0.72	0.32	1.31	0.18	2.53
Denmark	0.09	0.17	1.70	0.08	2.04
Finland	0.16	0.44	1.87	0.27	2.73
France	0.82	7.63	16.53	3.55	28.53
Germany	5.69	25.60	19.12	4.20	54.61
Greece	0.01	0.30	0.51	0.26	1.08
Ireland	0.22	0.19	0.61	0.06	1.07
Italy	2.26	1.18	2.75	3.43	9.62
Netherlands	0.61	1.08	3.16	0.21	5.06
Norway	0.06	1.26	0.98	0.14	2.45
Portugal	0.42	0.34	0.19	0.21	1.16
Spain	2.79	0.61	2.38	0.80	6.58
Sweden	0.14	0.74	1.50	0.20	2.58
Switzerland	0.56	1.33	1.41	0.25	3.55
Turkey			1.05	2.47	3.52
United Kingdom	1.01	12.76	32.82	1.80	48.39
Eastern Europe					
Bulgaria	0.01	0.00	0.03	0.09	0.13
Czech Republic	0.07	0.30	0.92	0.27	1.56
Hungary	0.05	0.27	0.32	0.26	0.91
Poland	0.07	0.15	1.34	0.70	2.25
Romania	0.00	0.22	0.19	0.45	0.86
Russia	0.54	3.25	4.13	4.26	12.17
Slovakia	0.04	0.18	0.06	0.14	0.43
Ukraine	0.01	0.04	1.05	0.61	1.70

Source: *Euromonitor International from national sources*

Retailing Statistics

Table 22.9

Non-Store Retail Sales by Type (% Analysis) 2008
% of total

	Vending	Home shopping	Internet retailing	Direct selling	Total
Western Europe					
Austria	17.4	40.5	31.4	10.8	100.0
Belgium	28.5	12.5	51.9	7.2	100.0
Denmark	4.2	8.5	83.5	3.8	100.0
Finland	5.7	16.1	68.3	9.9	100.0
France	2.9	26.8	57.9	12.4	100.0
Germany	10.4	46.9	35.0	7.7	100.0
Greece	1.1	27.8	46.7	24.3	100.0
Ireland	20.3	17.6	57.0	5.1	100.0
Italy	23.5	12.3	28.6	35.6	100.0
Netherlands	12.1	21.3	62.4	4.2	100.0
Norway	2.4	51.6	40.2	5.8	100.0
Portugal	36.0	29.4	16.0	18.5	100.0
Spain	42.5	9.2	36.2	12.1	100.0
Sweden	5.5	28.5	58.3	7.6	100.0
Switzerland	15.7	37.4	39.8	7.1	100.0
Turkey			29.8	70.2	100.0
United Kingdom	2.1	26.4	67.8	3.7	100.0
Eastern Europe					
Bulgaria	10.0	1.1	20.4	68.5	100.0
Czech Republic	4.2	19.4	59.0	17.3	100.0
Hungary	5.3	30.3	35.3	29.1	100.0
Poland	3.1	6.8	59.2	30.9	100.0
Romania	0.1	26.1	21.9	51.8	100.0
Russia	4.4	26.7	33.9	35.0	100.0
Slovakia	10.5	41.0	14.9	33.7	100.0
Ukraine	0.6	2.1	61.6	35.7	100.0

Source: *Euromonitor International from national sources*

Travel and Tourism

Travel and Tourism Statistics

Table 23.1

Average Tourist Stay in Accommodation Establishments 1990-2008
Nights

	1990	1995	2000	2003	2004	2005	2006	2007	2008
Western Europe									
Austria	4.90	4.80	4.00	3.81	3.72	3.69	3.60	3.40	3.41
Belgium									
Cyprus	12.80	11.02	11.00	6.48	6.73	6.79	6.32	6.19	6.37
Denmark									
Finland		1.84	1.90	1.89	1.83	1.84	1.82	1.82	1.84
France			1.88	1.87	1.82	1.81	1.82	2.18	2.29
Germany	2.20	2.39	2.32	2.29	2.25	2.22	2.19	2.18	2.16
Gibraltar									
Greece									
Iceland			1.86	1.80	1.80	1.80	1.80	1.80	1.80
Ireland									
Italy	4.27	4.29	4.23	3.40	3.31	3.33	3.27	3.26	3.34
Liechtenstein			2.12	2.10	2.10	2.20	2.10	2.20	2.20
Luxembourg		3.29	3.00	2.00	2.00	2.00	1.90	1.90	1.90
Malta			8.30	9.00	9.50	8.40	8.40	8.12	7.99
Monaco	2.96	2.84	2.87	2.87	2.78	2.81	2.92	2.88	2.92
Netherlands	3.72	3.00	3.19	1.90	1.80	1.80	1.80	1.78	1.81
Norway	1.73	1.61	1.67	1.66	1.66	1.65	1.62	1.63	1.60
Portugal	4.60	4.09	3.60	3.30	3.10	3.10	3.00	3.00	3.02
Spain	5.57	4.26	3.83	3.65	3.51	3.48	3.25	3.22	3.32
Sweden									
Switzerland	3.50	3.01	2.50	2.50	2.45	2.40	2.40	2.33	2.37
Turkey	3.43	4.00	4.20	3.28	3.29	3.20	2.90	2.94	2.83
United Kingdom									
Eastern Europe									
Albania		2.20	1.70	2.10	2.70	2.70	3.00	2.70	2.79
Belarus				2.70	2.77	2.93	3.00	3.04	3.02
Bosnia-Herzegovina			2.30	2.19	2.14	2.11	2.09	2.07	2.06
Bulgaria		3.50	3.90	4.21	4.23	4.20	4.07	3.80	3.75
Croatia		5.29	5.49	5.25	5.08	4.48	4.33	4.17	4.19
Czech Republic	2.40	3.10	3.30	3.70	3.40	2.80	2.80	2.70	2.77
Estonia		1.81	1.53	2.04	1.95	1.98	2.01	2.00	2.01
Georgia									
Hungary	3.70	3.18	2.86	2.79	2.71	2.66	2.63	5.58	5.43
Latvia		2.85	2.90	2.48	2.32	2.23	2.23	2.11	2.49
Lithuania		6.40	4.70	1.98	2.10	2.15	2.06	1.94	2.03
Macedonia	3.20	3.60	3.90	4.20	4.00	3.90	3.80	3.80	3.83
Moldova					2.40	2.60	2.90	2.70	2.86
Poland	2.30	2.40	3.35	1.89	1.91	1.93	1.93	1.95	2.17
Romania	2.96	3.40	3.20	3.50	3.25	3.20	3.18	2.94	2.70
Russia					5.00	4.81	5.30	5.30	5.36
Slovakia	3.20	3.40	3.10	3.20	2.90	2.80	2.80	3.10	3.03
Slovenia		3.73	3.31	3.23	3.12	3.01	2.97	2.96	3.24
Ukraine			2.70	2.60	2.60	2.60	2.68	2.72	2.67

Source: *Euromonitor International from World Tourism Organisation*

Table 23.2

Average Tourist Stay in the Country 1990-2008
Nights

	1990	1995	2000	2003	2004	2005	2006	2007	2008
Western Europe									
Austria			4.60	4.53	4.40	4.40	4.30	4.30	4.31
Belgium				2.32	2.31	2.29	2.31	2.30
Cyprus	14.80	11.51	11.00	7.42	7.91	7.94	7.52	7.39	7.60
Denmark						5.00	5.04	5.11	5.23
Finland			2.06	2.12	2.10	2.16	2.16	2.16	2.19
France	6.90	8.17	7.48	7.56	7.47	6.34	5.87	6.10	6.41
Germany				2.30	2.30	2.20	2.20	2.20	2.18
Gibraltar	3.00	4.00	4.30	4.40	4.50	4.55	4.59	4.63	4.63
Greece				5.97	6.00	5.54	5.56	5.37	5.73
Iceland			1.80	1.80	1.80	1.80	1.80	1.80	1.80
Ireland	11.00	8.42	7.40	7.71	7.42	7.49	7.60	7.30	7.47
Italy				3.99	3.84	3.89	3.81	3.81	3.91
Liechtenstein	1.91	2.10	2.10	2.10	2.10	2.20	2.10	2.20	2.20
Luxembourg		3.00	2.80	2.90	2.80	2.70	2.70	2.60	2.60
Malta	9.26	9.80	8.40	10.20	9.70	9.50	9.50	8.90	8.76
Monaco									
Netherlands			2.70	2.80	2.60	2.50	2.50	2.54	2.58
Norway									
Portugal	7.40	7.00	6.70	4.60	4.34	4.39	3.85	3.80	3.82
Spain	11.41	12.30	13.41	5.02	4.88	4.78	5.20	4.33	4.47
Sweden				2.28	2.08	2.06	2.33	2.14	1.96
Switzerland							2.50	2.48	2.52
Turkey	8.33	9.00	4.19	4.54	4.53	4.33	3.92	3.82	3.67
United Kingdom	10.90	9.40	8.08	8.20	8.20	8.30	8.40	7.70	8.02
Eastern Europe									
Albania			3.10	3.34	2.70	2.30	2.20	2.40	2.48
Belarus									
Bosnia-Herzegovina								2.30	2.30
Bulgaria	6.00	6.60	8.35	8.60	6.08	6.01	5.82	5.39	5.33
Croatia				5.58	5.39	5.43	5.43	5.33	5.35
Czech Republic	3.32	3.13	3.50	3.30	3.10	3.10	3.10	3.09	3.17
Estonia		1.90	1.90	2.04	2.00	2.05	2.12	2.11	2.12
Georgia			7.10	7.90	7.90	8.12	8.25	8.32	8.29
Hungary	6.58	6.39	3.51	3.41	3.21	3.13	3.04	2.95	2.87
Latvia			2.60	2.37	2.20	2.21	2.29	2.29	2.70
Lithuania		8.80	6.00	2.70	2.59	2.59	2.52	2.41	2.53
Macedonia				2.20	2.20	2.30	2.20	2.30	2.32
Moldova					2.50	2.80	3.40	2.90	3.07
Poland		4.70	4.80	4.10	4.60	4.40	3.40	2.90	3.22
Romania			2.48	2.50	2.50	2.40	2.30	2.30	2.11
Russia					4.38	4.63	5.20	5.20	5.26
Slovakia			3.90	3.60	3.30	3.20	3.20	3.10	3.03
Slovenia	3.10	3.12	3.12	3.04	2.91	2.80	2.78	2.78	3.04
Ukraine			5.30	4.80	4.00	3.80	3.91	3.97	3.90

Source: *Euromonitor International from World Tourism Organisation*

Travel and Tourism Statistics

Table 23.3

Domestic Tourist Nights 1990-2008
'000 nights

	1990	1995	2000	2003	2004	2005	2006	2007	2008
Western Europe									
Austria	15,620	16,302	18,897	19,634	19,800	20,329	21,184	22,219	22,802
Belgium		3,054	4,045	4,061	4,090	4,313	4,737	5,220	5,446
Cyprus	178	374	597	957	1,069	1,040	1,114	1,169	1,229
Denmark	16,835	18,727	19,602	21,678	21,534	21,914	23,203	24,518	25,231
Finland		8,464	9,786	9,671	10,032	10,388	10,676	11,182	11,508
France	72,556	90,349	114,059	115,536	118,134	122,222	123,105	126,536	128,952
Germany	234,579	149,628	170,947	163,554	165,655	168,843	172,428	177,586	180,227
Gibraltar									
Greece	11,346	12,523	14,628	13,716	13,280	13,942	14,249	16,675	17,384
Iceland		246	296	299	323	361	387	437	466
Ireland		6,698	6,786	7,829	7,799	8,174	7,978	8,791	9,070
Italy	123,975	123,467	136,392	135,217	136,845	138,123	140,397	141,311	142,914
Liechtenstein		1	3	3	3	3	3	3	3
Luxembourg		81	68	80	85	85	77	78	78
Malta									
Monaco									
Netherlands	7,102	8,799	14,027	13,384	13,761	14,375	15,783	17,831	18,679
Norway	8,665	9,862	11,398	11,262	11,764	12,349	12,859	13,458	13,853
Portugal	7,295	7,580	9,693	10,404	10,901	11,370	12,350	12,965	13,491
Spain	50,869	58,281	83,382	91,295	100,044	106,875	115,088	116,597	122,573
Sweden	12,528	14,771	16,586	16,235	16,465	17,517	18,606	19,574	20,260
Switzerland	13,152	12,316	14,013	14,236	13,837	14,622	15,204	15,447	15,697
Turkey	6,878	9,624	16,351	16,199	18,341	18,807	21,476	22,223	23,637
United Kingdom		450,000	576,370	490,540	408,950	442,300	400,100	394,400	366,892
Eastern Europe									
Albania		122	228	410	175	244	370	384	383
Belarus				2,753	2,926	3,306	3,649	3,739	3,989
Bosnia-Herzegovina			248	494	511	533	583	642	671
Bulgaria		3,648	3,024	3,058	3,423	3,957	4,342	4,867	5,244
Croatia		4,370	2,949	2,839	2,900	2,862	2,886	2,951	3,003
Czech Republic	25,390	10,142	12,358	9,779	9,051	8,601	8,854	9,206	8,952
Estonia		293	459	558	691	751	989	1,175	1,320
Georgia			2,115	2,398	2,476	2,576	2,647	2,715	2,803
Hungary	8,768	6,342	7,855	8,571	8,391	8,958	9,606	9,958	10,332
Latvia		735	669	669	717	796	855	979	1,040
Lithuania		326	293	342	511	728	934	1,082	1,232
Macedonia	738	464	443	347	289	275	267	283	266
Moldova			212	400	1,313	1,432	1,539	1,544	1,790
Poland	5,744	3,903	9,352	8,813	11,572	12,464	13,910	15,898	17,401
Romania		17,957	13,862	13,867	13,980	14,094	14,929	16,259	16,837
Russia				35,499	35,549	40,730	42,630	44,334	46,132
Slovakia	8,320	2,179	3,768	4,789	4,148	3,978	3,936	4,082	3,915
Slovenia	1,986	2,066	1,860	1,725	1,707	1,653	1,746	1,839	1,864
Ukraine			7,986	8,411	8,486	8,554	8,611	8,658	8,710

Source: *Euromonitor International from World Tourism Organisation*

Travel and Tourism Statistics

Table 23.4

International Tourist Nights 1990-2008

'000 nights

	1990	1995	2000	2003	2004	2005	2006	2007	2008
Western Europe									
Austria	94,788	56,198	58,029	60,622	60,746	62,396	62,789	63,953	64,097
Belgium	7,032	7,895	10,184	10,280	10,315	10,297	10,634	10,976	10,913
Cyprus	9,426	14,222	16,790	13,424	13,554	13,899	13,227	13,129	13,511
Denmark	24,330	28,113	26,280	26,152	24,925	23,012	23,429	23,928	24,483
Finland	2,830	2,926	3,562	3,758	3,758	3,887	4,339	4,635	4,698
France	38,720	54,339	77,014	69,323	70,391	72,054	68,821	72,391	76,121
Germany	39,146	28,659	36,354	35,172	38,491	40,839	44,921	46,508	46,004
Gibraltar		144	138	136	135	134	134	133	133
Greece	35,012	38,772	46,212	39,760	38,310	40,075	42,459	47,410	50,580
Iceland		598	890	1,070	1,146	1,208	1,341	1,480	1,480
Ireland	8,208	12,452	16,903	18,039	17,934	17,446	19,080	19,737	20,185
Italy	60,301	84,566	97,221	93,935	97,175	102,312	107,859	113,017	115,885
Liechtenstein		127	131	105	101	108	115	126	126
Luxembourg		1,051	1,169	1,144	1,195	1,273	1,284	1,360	1,360
Malta	9,604	7,632	6,978	7,712	7,725	7,603	7,377	7,976	7,851
Monaco		626	861	674	695	803	916	944	958
Netherlands	6,613	9,581	15,695	13,798	14,616	15,143	15,976	16,328	16,578
Norway	3,802	4,985	4,967	4,375	4,596	4,761	4,914	5,068	4,973
Portugal	19,349	20,357	24,102	23,215	23,002	23,873	25,216	26,773	26,912
Spain	68,630	101,182	143,762	136,865	134,654	138,762	151,940	155,093	160,060
Sweden	3,053	3,696	4,679	4,833	5,061	5,382	5,606	5,842	5,356
Switzerland	19,957	18,386	19,914	16,964	17,247	18,321	19,644	20,918	21,258
Turkey	13,271	18,438	28,377	40,819	49,614	55,996	46,588	56,491	54,303
United Kingdom	196,100	220,300	203,759	203,432	227,406	247,587	273,417	251,520	262,045
Eastern Europe									
Albania		89	98	137	85	110	129	141	146
Belarus				538	575	597	688	791	785
Bosnia-Herzegovina			263	419	460	485	594	695	694
Bulgaria		5,279	5,101	8,987	10,139	11,471	11,776	11,868	11,727
Croatia		4,574	15,125	16,830	17,072	18,415	17,807	17,988	18,065
Czech Republic	9,350	9,768	12,811	13,688	15,881	16,607	17,035	17,838	18,299
Estonia		615	1,253	2,086	2,602	2,791	2,772	2,668	2,686
Georgia			2,730	2,314	2,275	2,176	2,135	2,096	2,089
Hungary	13,618	9,998	10,514	10,040	10,508	10,779	10,046	10,171	9,891
Latvia		668	691	963	1,158	1,507	1,745	1,780	2,101
Lithuania		415	570	766	1,131	1,334	1,451	1,509	1,582
Macedonia	474	243	439	321	329	391	392	457	460
Moldova		99	85	84	153	170	202	194	206
Poland	5,350	3,064	4,944	5,450	6,876	7,869	7,911	8,409	9,339
Romania	4,238	2,208	2,085	2,688	3,211	3,377	3,169	3,497	3,207
Russia				10,036	10,687	10,696	10,637	10,616	10,751
Slovakia	1,936	2,340	3,138	3,989	3,820	4,055	4,362	4,406	4,313
Slovenia	1,573	2,059	2,758	3,166	3,258	3,322	3,401	3,707	4,058
Ukraine			948	1,420	1,380	1,395	1,437	1,459	1,431

Source: *Euromonitor International from World Tourism Organisation*

Travel and Tourism Statistics | **Table 23.5**

Tourist Expenditure 1980-2008
US$ million

	1980	1985	1990	1995	2000	2003	2004	2005	2006	2007	2008
Western Europe											
Austria	2,847	2,723	7,723	11,657	8,463	11,757	11,834	10,994	9,626	10,566	10,755
Belgium	3,272	2,050	5,471	9,215	9,429	12,210	13,956	14,948	15,574	17,268	17,444
Cyprus	56	78	111	293	413	611	810	932	967	1,479	1,550
Denmark	1,560	1,410	3,676	4,280	4,669	6,658	7,269	6,850	7,428	8,791	8,712
Finland	544	777	2,740	2,319	1,852	2,433	2,821	3,057	3,424	3,986	4,145
France	6,027	4,557	12,424	16,328	17,906	23,392	28,703	30,458	31,264	36,743	37,523
Germany			29,509	52,194	52,824	65,234	71,187	74,189	74,123	82,966	83,240
Gibraltar											
Greece	190	368	1,090	1,322	4,558	2,431	2,872	3,039	2,997	3,423	3,546
Iceland	42	94	278	282	471	521	693	980	1,076	1,341	1,341
Ireland	535	429	1,159	2,030	2,600	4,736	5,177	6,074	6,862	8,682	8,675
Italy	1,907	1,880	14,045	12,420	15,685	20,589	20,460	22,370	23,152	27,329	27,956
Liechtenstein	3										
Luxembourg					1,318	2,423	2,911	2,976	3,136	3,552	3,619
Malta	41	50	134	200	200	215	256	268	321	376	386
Monaco	6										
Netherlands	4,664	3,416	7,376	11,455	12,191	14,593	16,346	16,082	17,087	19,110	19,521
Norway	1,310	1,722	3,679	4,221	4,558	6,716	8,489	10,111	11,586	14,032	13,487
Portugal	290	235	867	2,141	2,228	2,409	2,763	3,050	3,298	3,922	3,985
Spain	1,229	1,010	4,254	4,461	5,572	9,071	12,153	15,046	16,697	19,724	19,662
Sweden	2,235	1,967	6,134	5,621	8,048	8,296	10,130	10,771	11,543	13,972	13,600
Switzerland	2,357	2,399	5,817	7,346	6,335	6,883	8,104	8,837	9,919	10,265	10,651
Turkey	115	324	520	912	1,713	2,113	2,524	2,872	2,743	3,260	3,447
United Kingdom	6,410	6,369	19,063	24,268	38,262	47,853	56,444	59,532	63,319	72,436	76,760
Eastern Europe											
Albania				5	272	489	642	786	965	923	1,026
Belarus				87	243	399	450	448	586	606	631
Bosnia-Herzegovina					78	106	117	122	156	186	198
Bulgaria	37	74	257	195	538	1,033	1,363	1,309	1,474	1,829	1,956
Croatia				421	568	672	848	754	737	985	993
Czech Republic				1,633	1,276	1,934	2,280	2,405	2,765	3,647	3,858
Estonia				91	204	319	400	448	592	670	694
Georgia					110	130	147	169	167	176	188
Hungary	196	208	477	1,070	1,651	2,594	2,848	2,382	2,126	2,949	2,894
Latvia				24	247	328	378	584	704	927	1,059
Lithuania				108	253	471	636	744	909	1,143	1,256
Macedonia				27	34	48	54	60	71	102	114
Moldova				56	73	99	113	141	187	213	233
Poland	380	184	423	5,500	3,313	3,085	4,776	5,548	7,224	7,753	8,072
Romania			103	697	425	479	539	925	1,310	1,535	1,689
Russia				11,599	8,848	12,880	15,285	17,434	18,235	22,258	22,038
Slovakia				330	296	573	745	846	1,055	1,533	1,637
Slovenia				524	511	753	868	950	974	1,103	1,238
Ukraine					576	789	2,463	2,805	2,834	3,293	3,468

Source: *Euromonitor International from World Tourism Organisation*

Travel and Tourism Statistics

Table 23.6

Tourism Receipts 1980-2008

US$ million

	1980	1985	1990	1995	2000	2003	2004	2005	2006	2007	2008
Western Europe											
Austria	6,442	5,084	13,410	14,593	9,998	13,842	15,290	15,589	16,510	18,754	21,454
Belgium	1,810	1,663	3,718	5,719	6,592	8,193	9,208	9,845	10,311	10,898	11,844
Cyprus	203	380	1,258	1,783	1,941	2,097	2,239	2,318	2,381	2,687	3,026
Denmark	1,337	1,326	3,322	3,672	3,671	5,271	5,652	5,293	5,587	6,218	6,501
Finland	677	501	1,170	1,676	1,406	1,870	2,067	2,180	2,380	2,822	3,151
France	8,197	7,942	20,185	27,527	30,981	36,619	44,895	43,942	46,512	54,165	59,321
Germany	6,715	5,018	10,493	18,028	18,611	23,125	27,613	29,121	32,846	36,092	38,909
Gibraltar	6	15	112	87	76	122	157	159	169	218	180
Greece	1,734	1,428	2,587	4,136	9,219	10,766	12,715	13,578	14,402	15,550	18,187
Iceland	23	41	139	167	227	319	370	408	439	640	466
Ireland	574	531	1,447	2,688	3,387	3,862	4,375	4,782	5,369	6,140	6,648
Italy	8,213	8,758	20,016	27,723	27,493	31,247	35,378	35,319	38,257	42,660	47,814
Liechtenstein	16	20									
Luxembourg					1,686	2,994	3,653	3,614	3,626	4,009	4,385
Malta	329	149	496	660	610	722	770	754	770	913	1,005
Monaco	260	300									
Netherlands	1,662	1,661	3,636	5,762	7,197	9,164	10,311	10,383	11,381	13,339	14,673
Norway	751	755	1,570	2,386	2,050	2,500	2,980	3,332	3,613	4,222	4,233
Portugal	1,147	1,137	3,555	4,339	5,243	6,622	7,672	7,676	8,416	10,162	11,089
Spain	6,968	8,151	18,593	25,388	31,454	39,634	45,067	47,681	51,292	57,883	62,218
Sweden	962	1,190	2,916	3,462	4,064	5,304	6,163	7,361	9,133	12,004	11,410
Switzerland	3,149	3,145	6,789	9,365	7,576	8,617	9,600	10,095	10,640	12,185	14,177
Turkey	327	1,482	3,308	4,957	7,636	13,203	15,888	18,152	16,853	18,487	19,800
United Kingdom	6,922	7,120	14,003	18,554	21,769	22,668	28,202	30,577	33,888	37,690	35,750
Eastern Europe											
Albania				7	398	522	735	854	1,012	1,002	1,199
Belarus				23	93	267	270	253	286	324	345
Bosnia-Herzegovina				7	233	377	481	519	607	729	832
Bulgaria	260	343	320	473	1,074	1,621	2,202	2,412	2,610	2,753	3,262
Croatia				1,351	2,758	6,310	6,727	7,370	7,990	9,233	10,140
Czech Republic	338	307	470	2,875	2,973	3,566	4,187	4,676	5,541	6,637	8,385
Estonia				353	505	671	887	948	1,035	1,036	1,143
Georgia					97	147	177	241	313	385	462
Hungary	504	512	1,000	1,723	3,733	4,061	4,034	4,120	4,254	4,739	4,715
Latvia				20	131	222	267	341	480	671	893
Lithuania				124	391	638	776	921	1,038	1,153	1,360
Macedonia			45	19	38	57	72	84	129	186	221
Moldova				57	39	54	91	103	112	164	211
Poland	282	118	358	6,600	5,677	4,069	5,833	6,274	7,239	10,599	11,670
Romania	136	182	106	590	359	449	503	1,052	1,308	1,467	1,590
Russia	325	163	410	4,312	3,430	4,502	5,530	5,870	7,628	9,607	9,714
Slovakia				620	433	865	901	1,210	1,513	2,026	2,308
Slovenia				1,082	961	1,342	1,625	1,795	1,797	2,218	2,659
Ukraine					736	935	2,560	3,125	3,485	4,597	4,672

Source: *Euromonitor International from World Tourism Organisation*

Travel and Tourism Statistics

Table 23.7

Total Number of Rooms in Tourist Accommodation 1990-2008
'000

	1990	1995	2000	2003	2004	2005	2006	2007	2008
Western Europe									
Austria	317.8	309.7	286.8	282.6	290.5	289.9	282.0	285.6	291.0
Belgium		59.7	61.9	63.2	64.0	66.6	67.8	67.7	68.1
Cyprus	24.5	35.0	43.4	44.9	45.5	45.2	44.4	43.8	44.3
Denmark	35.6	38.3	39.5	41.7	43.2	42.8	43.4	44.1	41.9
Finland	46.5	54.0	54.9	55.8	53.5	53.3	54.9	54.7	56.4
France	547.0	596.7	589.2	603.3	615.4	613.8	612.4	614.5	660.0
Germany		819.0	877.1	892.3	889.3	890.2	897.0	899.1	919.7
Gibraltar									
Greece	232.8	283.4	313.0	339.5	351.9	358.7	364.2	368.0	376.1
Iceland	3.3	4.9	6.0	7.3	7.5	8.0	8.0	8.7	8.8
Ireland	22.8	36.8	60.4	63.1	62.4	64.2	63.4	67.6	66.6
Italy	938.1	944.1	966.1	999.7	1,011.8	1,020.5	1,034.7	1,058.9	1,060.0
Liechtenstein			0.6	0.6	0.6	0.6	0.6	0.6	0.7
Luxembourg	7.9	8.2	7.7	7.5	7.4	7.5	7.5	7.6	8.0
Malta	34.2								
Monaco			2.2	2.2	2.2	2.6	2.6	2.8	2.9
Netherlands	60.7	71.3	82.0	88.1	93.0	94.4	94.5	99.0	102.0
Norway	54.0	60.0	65.2	67.1	66.4	67.5	69.5	71.0	75.0
Portugal	79.4	90.0	97.7	106.0	106.4	112.9	117.6	118.0	120.3
Spain	603.0	564.6	677.1	740.9	767.0	797.4	810.6	821.1	808.8
Sweden	82.0	100.0	96.1	96.4	98.9	100.2	101.7	103.8	101.6
Switzerland	146.9	143.5	140.8	140.0	133.6	127.4	127.5	127.7	133.6
Turkey	82.1	133.2	155.4	201.5	217.1	230.6	241.7	251.5	277.6
United Kingdom		440.0	463.0	599.9	606.9	518.0	616.8	616.0	632.0
Eastern Europe									
Albania		3.0	3.0	4.2	3.4	3.9	4.3	4.6	4.9
Belarus			2.0	12.7	12.9	12.9	13.3	13.7	14.9
Bosnia-Herzegovina		1.1	4.4	7.7	8.4	8.7	9.0	10.8	11.4
Bulgaria		57.0							
Croatia		85.4	81.3	77.1	79.2	80.7	76.0	76.1	76.6
Czech Republic	63.1	53.7	96.4	98.1	98.8	99.9	101.6	106.9	108.8
Estonia		4.4	7.6	12.4	15.0	16.6	17.8	19.3	20.0
Georgia			8.7	9.6	9.7	6.8	10.0	8.3	8.9
Hungary	34.0	47.8	57.9	64.1	64.3	66.1	66.9	65.6	65.5
Latvia		5.4	6.4	7.6	8.8	9.2	9.7	10.0	10.8
Lithuania		5.3	5.9	7.4	9.5	10.1	10.8	11.0	11.6
Macedonia	6.0	6.0	6.6	6.8	6.9	6.9	7.0	7.2	7.8
Moldova		2.6	3.0	2.6	2.6	2.5	2.5	2.3	2.4
Poland	43.4	48.2	60.9	68.6	83.0	84.9	88.4	93.9	96.7
Romania	87.1	95.5	95.4	97.3	101.6	105.8	111.8	112.2	118.7
Russia		214.1	183.4	177.2	178.6	199.0	208.3	219.4	231.7
Slovakia	14.5	23.4	28.4	35.9	35.5	35.7	35.9	41.6	45.4
Slovenia		16.2	16.3	15.5	15.8	15.8	16.4	17.3	20.8
Ukraine			44.8	32.6	32.6	33.4	44.8	60.4	74.3

Source: *Euromonitor International from World Tourism Organisation*

Travel and Tourism Statistics

Table 23.8

Total Number of Bed Places in Tourist Accommodation 1990-2008

'000

	1990	1995	2000	2003	2004	2005	2006	2007	2008
Western Europe									
Austria	650.6	646.1	642.6	631.1	637.1	639.4	643.7	646.9	659.2
Belgium		154.7	158.6	163.7	169.6	168.4	172.9	172.0	173.1
Cyprus	51.8	73.1	84.5	91.1	92.2	91.3	89.5	87.8	88.9
Denmark	88.5	99.0	102.1	106.1	109.1	108.1	108.9	109.8	104.4
Finland	97.4	113.0	117.3	120.1	120.1	115.2	118.2	118.9	122.6
France	1,082.1	1,193.3	1,178.3	1,206.6	1,230.8	1,227.6	1,224.8	1,229.1	1,320.0
Germany	1,110.0	1,490.9	1,649.2	1,672.2	1,667.9	1,678.3	1,690.9	1,703.3	1,742.5
Gibraltar									
Greece	438.4	535.8	594.0	644.9	668.3	682.1	693.3	700.9	716.4
Iceland	6.3	8.8	12.5	14.9	15.5	16.6	16.8	18.4	18.6
Ireland	45.2	79.8	140.2	146.9	145.3	149.6	148.8	157.4	155.0
Italy	1,703.5	1,738.0	1,854.1	1,969.5	1,999.7	2,028.5	2,087.0	2,142.8	2,144.9
Liechtenstein	1.2	1.2	1.2	1.2	1.2	1.2	1.3	1.3	1.3
Luxembourg			14.7	14.6	14.2	14.2	14.5	15.0	15.6
Malta	37.9	37.3	40.6	41.4	39.8	39.4	39.4	38.1	39.1
Monaco				3.2	3.7	5.3	5.3	4.4	4.6
Netherlands	111.3	142.5	173.0	180.2	189.8	192.2	192.1	200.3	206.5
Norway	112.7	131.2	140.6	143.8	141.1	143.6	151.3	154.3	163.1
Portugal	179.3	204.1	223.0	245.8	253.9	263.8	264.0	264.7	270.0
Spain	1,102.3	1,074.0	1,315.7	1,451.9	1,511.6	1,578.6	1,615.3	1,642.4	1,617.8
Sweden	161.9	222.5	188.3	184.8	190.0	197.5	201.3	207.4	203.1
Switzerland	269.8	265.0	259.7	258.7	251.3	239.2	240.4	241.0	252.1
Turkey	165.0	274.1	332.3	418.2	452.4	481.7	507.2	530.8	586.0
United Kingdom	993.5	879.7	1,111.0	1,203.7	1,223.0	1,062.3	1,255.7	1,250.5	1,283.0
Eastern Europe									
Albania		5.8	5.9	8.4	6.6	7.6	8.4	7.8	8.3
Belarus		1.0	14.4	23.6	23.6	23.5	24.1	24.6	26.8
Bosnia-Herzegovina		1.9	9.1	15.9	17.3	18.2	20.0	22.4	23.6
Bulgaria	114.3	114.2	120.2	144.0	171.0	221.1	252.3	273.3	278.5
Croatia		205.2	199.5	193.5	199.0	203.5	163.2	163.2	164.3
Czech Republic		131.2	236.5	226.8	229.7	232.2	236.1	248.0	252.5
Estonia		8.5	18.6	27.5	32.9	38.1	40.9	44.6	46.2
Georgia			17.2	17.7	18.1	14.0	20.5	16.7	18.0
Hungary	85.3	119.1	143.6	158.6	158.0	162.2	158.8	154.1	153.8
Latvia		14.0	11.9	15.0	17.9	19.2	19.7	20.7	22.3
Lithuania		10.5	11.1	14.3	18.6	19.9	21.5	21.9	23.1
Macedonia	15.1	15.0	16.1	16.3	16.5	16.4	16.8	17.1	18.4
Moldova		5.3	5.6	4.7	4.9	4.9	4.5	4.3	4.5
Poland	90.4	93.3	120.3	134.3	165.3	169.6	178.1	190.4	195.9
Romania	168.0	205.7	199.3	201.6	207.8	216.5	228.1	228.1	241.4
Russia		426.1	346.1	364.0	344.4	414.1	431.0	447.1	472.2
Slovakia	33.6	53.9	73.0	90.8	90.0	90.1	91.0	105.7	115.3
Slovenia		33.9	33.5	32.0	32.7	33.2	34.4	36.2	43.7
Ukraine			102.9	86.2	84.3	86.8	116.4	157.1	193.3

Source: *Euromonitor International from World Tourism Organisation*

Travel and Tourism Statistics

Table 23.9

Hotel Bed Occupancy Rates 1990-2008
% of beds occupied

	1990	1995	2000	2003	2004	2005	2006	2007	2008
Western Europe									
Austria	31.8	33.3	34.9	36.1	34.6	35.8	35.6	39.2	40.9
Belgium		31.3	30.5	30.5	30.6	30.6	30.6	30.7	31.0
Cyprus	62.3	58.6	65.1	57.5	57.6	61.6	59.9	61.8	62.2
Denmark	34.7	35.5	37.4	35.7	35.6	36.2	38.0	39.0	39.2
Finland	48.6	45.0	47.8	46.8	46.3	47.8	49.9	51.6	51.3
France	52.4	49.5	60.3	58.4	58.6	59.1	60.4	62.0	56.0
Germany	42.8	33.9	35.0	33.5	34.2	35.0	35.9	36.7	36.4
Gibraltar	40.8	39.2	37.8	38.2	38.4	38.6	38.7	38.8	38.8
Greece		56.6	65.0	60.7	55.6	58.6	59.8	57.0	56.9
Iceland	41.0	44.8	46.0	42.3	43.3	45.0	47.0	46.7	46.4
Ireland			65.0	60.0	60.0	62.0	64.0	64.0	64.1
Italy	41.5	40.0	42.7	39.6	39.8	40.1	40.8	41.8	42.5
Liechtenstein	33.4	28.4	30.9	25.3	24.2	25.6	25.6	27.9	27.8
Luxembourg		37.9	51.1	25.1	28.2	29.5	29.9	31.6	30.8
Malta	56.4	55.5	47.0	53.7	52.8	52.8	51.8	57.4	58.2
Monaco	55.7	49.5	71.5	59.0	58.0	58.4	58.8	63.6	63.3
Netherlands	38.5	35.3	48.5	42.8	42.1	42.1	45.3	46.7	45.7
Norway	35.4	36.7	37.5	35.5	37.0	38.1	37.3	39.5	37.7
Portugal	29.9	38.0	42.2	38.0	38.6	46.6	40.8	43.0	42.6
Spain	52.3	60.7	58.9	54.5	53.5	54.2	56.4	56.0	55.2
Sweden	31.0	32.0	35.0	34.3	34.3	35.0	36.1	37.2	38.4
Switzerland	44.0	38.5	42.3	38.7	39.2	39.7	41.7	43.6	43.1
Turkey	48.2	47.0	36.8	46.9	50.1	52.4	47.3	54.7	55.1
United Kingdom	57.0	44.0	43.0	44.0	45.0	44.0	47.0	48.0	46.4
Eastern Europe									
Albania		32.4	20.0	42.0	39.0	46.0	60.0	67.0	67.9
Belarus				38.2	40.5	45.5	49.3	50.4	49.5
Bosnia-Herzegovina			15.0	11.1	11.0	10.6	10.3	10.1	10.2
Bulgaria		36.5	28.3	34.8	35.9	37.6	35.8	33.2	36.6
Croatia	16.6	11.1	24.8	27.8	27.5	28.7	34.8	35.2	35.2
Czech Republic	46.0	28.8	46.0	35.4	37.0	35.8	35.8	35.8	36.4
Estonia		35.0	48.0	47.0	47.0	47.0	47.0	44.0	43.5
Georgia			34.0	72.0	72.0	72.3	73.4	74.7	74.6
Hungary	55.4	45.4	46.7	38.6	41.0	42.1	42.4	45.0	43.2
Latvia			32.0	31.7	31.5	36.4	35.6	36.5	35.8
Lithuania		23.0	28.4	32.5	36.7	40.8	42.1	46.3	46.2
Macedonia	10.9	10.6	15.0	11.2	10.3	11.1	10.8	11.8	12.2
Moldova		17.9	19.8	22.1	25.2	26.6	30.9	28.3	28.0
Poland	39.5	42.7	39.6	35.7	32.2	40.5	42.2	46.1	38.7
Romania		52.1	35.2	34.6	36.7	33.4	33.6	37.2	42.9
Russia		38.0	37.0	34.0	37.0	34.0	35.0	36.0	33.1
Slovakia	48.7	31.9	29.2	38.7	34.7	35.0	35.7	33.7	33.5
Slovenia		33.4	39.4	47.6	48.0	47.6	47.6	47.4	40.1
Ukraine			24.0	30.0	31.0	33.0	26.4	22.0	19.3

Source: *Euromonitor International from World Tourism Organisation*

Travel and Tourism Statistics | **Table 23.10**

International Tourist Arrivals 1990-2008
'000

	1990	1995	2000	2003	2004	2005	2006	2007	2008
Western Europe									
Austria		17,173	17,982	19,078	19,373	19,952	20,261	20,570	20,879
Belgium		5,523	6,403	6,690	6,710	6,747	6,995	7,141	7,274
Cyprus	1,576	2,100	2,686	2,303	2,349	2,470	2,401	2,446	2,492
Denmark	4,180	3,417	3,445	3,474	4,421	4,699	4,716	4,733	4,750
Finland			2,714	2,601	2,840	3,140	3,375	3,571	3,734
France	52,497	60,033	77,190	75,048	75,121	75,908	79,083	80,671	81,993
Germany		14,847	18,983	18,399	20,137	21,500	23,569	25,293	26,730
Gibraltar									
Greece	9,310	10,130	13,095	13,969	13,313	14,765	16,039	17,018	17,835
Iceland	354	473	634	771	836	871	971	1,042	1,114
Ireland	3,666	4,821	6,646	6,764	6,953	7,333	8,001	8,446	8,817
Italy		31,052	41,181	39,604	37,071	36,512	41,053	41,810	42,441
Liechtenstein	72	59	62	49	49	50	55	58	59
Luxembourg	694	768	852	867	878	913	908	917	924
Malta	872	1,116	1,216	1,127	1,156	1,171	1,124	1,133	1,140
Monaco	246	233	300	235	250	286	313	330	344
Netherlands		6,574	10,003	9,181	9,646	10,012	10,739	11,143	11,479
Norway	1,955	2,880	3,104	3,269	3,629	3,824	3,945	4,038	4,110
Portugal		9,511	12,097	11,707	10,639	10,612	11,282	11,657	11,969
Spain		38,803	47,897	50,854	52,430	55,914	58,190	59,816	61,170
Sweden	5,227	7,378	7,351	7,627	7,720	7,815	7,937	8,031	8,109
Switzerland	8,015	6,946	7,821	6,530	6,397	7,229	7,863	8,259	8,589
Turkey		7,083	9,586	13,341	16,826	20,273	18,916	19,662	20,409
United Kingdom				22,787	25,678	28,039	30,654	32,666	34,213
Eastern Europe									
Albania		40	32	41	32	48	60	64	68
Belarus		161	60	64	67	91	89	91	93
Bosnia-Herzegovina		36	106	165	190	217	256	289	316
Bulgaria		3,466	2,785	4,048	4,630	4,837	5,158	5,405	5,629
Croatia		1,324	5,831	7,409	7,912	8,467	8,659	8,834	8,992
Czech Republic			4,667	5,075	6,061	6,336	6,435	6,518	6,586
Estonia		530	1,220	1,462	1,750	1,917	1,940	2,017	2,086
Georgia		85	387	313	368	560	983	1,265	1,500
Hungary		14,121	11,207	11,304	12,212	9,979	9,259	8,859	8,526
Latvia			509	971	1,079	1,116	1,535	1,703	1,814
Lithuania		609	1,240	1,492	1,801	2,000	2,180	2,309	2,400
Macedonia		147	224	158	165	197	202	209	216
Moldova		32	19	21	24	23	13	12	12
Poland		19,215	17,400	13,720	14,290	15,200	15,670	16,062	16,388
Romania	6,533	5,445	5,264	5,594	6,599	5,839	6,037	6,178	6,279
Russia				20,443	19,892	19,940	19,999	20,049	20,090
Slovakia		903	1,090	1,387	1,401	1,515	1,612	1,673	1,723
Slovenia		732	1,090	1,373	1,499	1,555	1,617	1,661	1,698
Ukraine			6,425	12,514	15,629	17,630	18,900	19,958	20,840

Source: *Euromonitor International from World Tourism Organisation*

Travel and Tourism Statistics

Table 23.11

Tourist Arrivals by Method 2008
'000

	Air	Rail	Road	Sea
Western Europe				
Austria				
Belgium	6,039			975
Denmark				
Finland	2,396	79	1,662	1,677
France	20,090	5,163	48,525	8,216
Germany	71,274			
Greece	12,797	88	3,826	1,123
Ireland	6,947		808	1,062
Italy	22,226	1,962	42,378	1,963
Netherlands				
Norway	1,793	86	1,507	723
Portugal	7,163		16,863	
Spain	44,619	295	14,527	1,730
Sweden				
Switzerland				
Turkey	14,503	74	4,331	1,500
United Kingdom	25,876	3,438		5,112
Eastern Europe				
Belarus				
Bulgaria	2,528	197	4,975	193
Croatia	2,343	321	47,232	1,123
Czech Republic	6,237	2,658	83,459	
Estonia	224	35	1,096	2,392
Hungary	2,124	1,664	37,200	251
Latvia	761	184	4,301	274
Lithuania	440	495	1,277	187
Poland	3,014	1,755	60,590	319
Romania	1,167	329	4,566	217
Russia	4,483	7,281	9,891	1,121
Slovakia	18	64	14,951	3
Slovenia	329	49	1,318	2
Ukraine	1,167	7,392	12,010	271

Source: *Euromonitor International from World Tourism Organisation*

Table 23.12

Tourist Arrivals by Region 2008

'000

	Africa	Americas	East Asia /Pacific	Europe	Middle East	South Asia
Western Europe						
Austria	46	823	823	20,223	109	51
Belgium	64	439	303	6,298	21	48
Denmark		141	107	4,232		
Finland	10	105	164	3,323	3	5
France	1,415	5,814	3,056	68,591	606	
Germany	169	2,822	2,208	19,347	241	
Greece	29	642	329	16,812	69	5
Ireland	39	1,081	244	6,851		
Italy	282	3,729	1,316	38,636	280	196
Netherlands	75	1,288	727	9,018		
Norway		188	38	3,991		
Portugal		672	43	11,449		293
Spain	103	2,276	354	54,068	33	73
Sweden	21	213	174	3,064		
Switzerland	87	966	952	6,463	116	142
Turkey	179	592	664	21,128	908	1,292
United Kingdom	1,942	14,340	6,949	4,456	1,476	1,429
Eastern Europe						
Belarus		7	2	101	1	1
Bulgaria	2	72	31	5,652	11	11
Croatia		238	191	8,934		
Czech Republic	21	471	545	5,883		
Estonia	1	41	25	1,881		
Hungary	4	114	67	8,311		
Latvia	1	6	7	1,731	1	
Lithuania	2	54	29	1,477		
Poland	4	92	49	12,772	2	5
Romania	14	234	99	9,027	33	20
Russia	29	470	1,368	19,392	22	104
Slovakia	2	50	86	1,684	4	1
Slovenia	2	70	72	1,629	5	9
Ukraine	11	186	53	24,699	27	19

Source: *Euromonitor International from World Tourism Organisation*

Travel and Tourism Statistics

Table 23.13

Number of Airline Passengers Carried by Low-Cost Carriers 1999-2008

'000 / number of passengers carried by low-cost carriers as a % of all airline passengers

	1999	2000	2001	2002	2003	2004	2005	2006	2007	2008	Number of passengers carried by low-cost carriers as a % of all airline passengers
Western Europe											
Austria	1,000	1,100	1,200	1,470	1,634	1,980	2,228	2,851	3,669	3,912	16.48
Belgium	1,336	1,675	1,064	1,227	1,412	1,533	1,656	1,833	2,126	2,583	23.20
Cyprus											
Denmark	300	676	845	1,056	1,320	1,900	2,698	3,141	3,674	3,879	26.74
Finland	5	5	1	0	353	387	434	573	634	659	4.16
France	1,100	1,600	1,700	2,000	12,000	13,800	16,704	18,750	22,500	24,098	16.49
Germany	4,260	4,597	5,572	7,425	14,183	23,286	31,980	41,790	51,341	50,003	27.00
Gibraltar											
Greece	7,083	8,281	9,150	8,224	8,538	8,835	10,767	11,910	12,515	12,640	31.36
Iceland											
Ireland	3,030	3,885	5,115	7,276	8,487	10,996	12,953	15,573	17,827	17,399	62.28
Italy	862	1,373	2,721	4,032	5,450	6,953	7,642	10,952	15,491	18,531	13.17
Liechtenstein											
Luxembourg											
Malta											
Monaco											
Netherlands	6,130	8,240	9,275	10,220	10,590	11,100	11,988	13,050	13,610	13,893	28.02
Norway	796	2,661	3,303	3,816	4,215	5,370	6,895	7,623	8,392	7,973	26.42
Portugal	1,244	1,518	1,688	1,603	1,972	2,544	3,460	5,052	6,648	8,124	29.62
Spain	2,800	5,752	10,782	13,254	17,019	24,063	26,277	30,036	35,439	38,692	32.20
Sweden	987	1,031	1,242	1,456	1,856	2,143	2,547	2,846	3,093	2,996	9.84
Switzerland	496	984	1,238	1,832	2,963	4,018	5,235	6,994	7,557	8,157	21.13
Turkey						4,500	8,200	10,262	14,032	19,044	30.45
United Kingdom	10,000	23,000	30,360	36,432	43,718	52,462	59,000	67,260	75,950	78,220	37.96
Eastern Europe											
Albania											
Belarus											
Bosnia-Herzegovina											
Bulgaria							235	384	387	426	6.79
Croatia					213	2,031	3,346	3,739	3,802	3,846	41.76
Czech Republic	224	232	253	407	533	889	1,355	1,753	1,817	1,943	25.90
Estonia											
Georgia											
Hungary					89	982	1,905	2,238	2,587	2,825	32.78
Latvia											
Lithuania											
Macedonia											
Moldova											
Poland					16	1,066	3,199	5,803	8,619	10,073	48.50
Romania						3	332	633	1,400	1,829	25.00
Russia							301	997	1,013	1,150	3.51
Slovakia	25	27	31	52	155	400	691	1,100	1,313	1,480	71.53
Slovenia						68	165	130	174	182	10.50
Ukraine											

Source: Euromonitor International from World Tourism Organisation

Marketing Geography

Albania

Capital city	Tiranë
Capital population	406,000 *(2007)*
Population ('000)	3,155.27 *(2009)*
Urban population (%)	47.33 *(2009)*
Land area (sq km)	28,750
Languages	Albanian (dialects: Gheg, Tosk)
Religion	Religious activities were banned until 1990
Currency	Lek (ALL)
Head of state	Bamir Topi (2007)
Head of government	Sali Berisha (2005)
Ruling party	The Democratic Party of Albania leads the government.

Main urban areas	Population *(Year)*
Tiranë (capital)	406,000 *(2007)*
Dürres	99,546 *(2001)*

Location Albania is situated on the eastern Adriatic coast, with the former Yugoslavian provinces of Montenegro, Serbia and Macedonia marking its northern and eastern boundaries and with Greece to the south. Southern Albania faces the Greek island of Corfu across the Straits of Corfu. The climate is temperate and warm in summer with little rainfall. The capital is Tirana.

Political structure Albania is run under an executive Presidency answerable to a 140-member People's Assembly elected by popular vote. The president is elected for a five-year term by parliament. The president appoints the prime minister. The Assembly of the Republic of Albania has 140 members, elected for a four-year term, with 100 members in single-seat constituencies and 40 members elected through proportional representation.

Last elections Parliamentary elections were held in June 2009. The right-of-centre Democratic Party claimed 68 seats in the 140-member parliament while the Socialist Party won 65 seats. The Socialist Movement for Integration took 4 seats and the remainder were distributed among minor parties. In 2005, ex-Prime Minister, Sali Berisha, was returned to the office. Bamir Topi was elected President for a 5-year term following the July 2007 Presidential elections. He was finally sworn in after opposition lawmakers ended their coalition's boycott and supported his appointment.

Economy Albania was Europe's poorest country for many years, but levels of per capita income have more than doubled over the past ten years. Despite these achievements, the economy remains vulnerable on several fronts because of a culture of tax evasion, significant amounts of long and short-term domestic public debt, and weak anti-money laundering laws. Investment is badly needed to broaden the export base. The incidence of poverty has been reduced from 25% in 2002 to around 18.5% today. Poverty is worst in rural areas because family farms have such low levels of productivity.

Main industries Agriculture is geared to meet domestic needs, with wheat, maize, potatoes and fruit being the main crops. Farm land has been almost completely privatised. Farm output has recovered from a drought but a recovery after the return of normal rainfall. With about one million Albanians working outside the country (mostly in Greece and Italy), the flow of remittances underpins consumer spending, purchases of new homes and cars, and investment in small businesses. The share of the underground "black" economy in GDP is falling as the administration of tax revenues is improved. Albania's infrastructure is inadequate and there is little money for improvements. The country also inherited a very poor highway system from the Communist period. However, a major road-building project costing more than €70 million is underway. The tourist industry offers much potential but is yet to be developed. Albania possesses significant mineral resources, which include some of the world's richest deposits of chrome, molybdenum and copper, as well as nickel and limestone. Start-up operations have been recently launched for both copper and chrome.

Energy Albania has the second largest amount of oil reserves in the Balkans after Romania (approximately 198 million barrels). The country also produces about one billion cubic feet of natural gas to fulfil its domestic demand. Exploration is active, but has yielded no positive results so far. Albania presently imports more than half its modest energy needs.

Austria

Capital city	Vienna
Capital population	1,633,420 *(2009)*
Population ('000)	8,383.09 *(2009)*
Urban population (%)	67.36 *(2009)*
Land area (sq km)	83,855
Languages	German (minorities speak Slovene and Croat)
Religion	Roman Catholic
Currency	Euro (€)
Head of state	President Heinz Fischer (2004)
Head of government	Werner Faymann (2008)
Ruling party	A coalition of the Social Democrats and the Peoples' Party leads the government.

Main urban areas	Population *(Year)*
Vienna (capital)	1,633,420 *(2009)*
Graz	233,590 *(2009)*
Linz	178,109 *(2009)*
Salzburg	146,807 *(2009)*
Innsbruck	114,649 *(2009)*
Klagenfurt	103,098 *(2009)*
Villach	61,729 *(2009)*
Wels	60,495 *(2009)*
Sankt Poelten	50,613 *(2009)*
Dornbirn	44,615 *(2009)*

Location Austria occupies a strategic position in the centre of Western Europe, bordering on Germany and the Czech and Slovak Republics in the north, Hungary in the east, Italy and Slovenia in the south, and Switzerland in the west. The climate is temperate, but becomes very cold in winter because of the high altitude. The capital is Vienna.

Political structure The Republic of Austria was formed in 1955 following the end of the post-war administration by the Western allies. It consists of nine provinces, which have little autonomy. The country has a non-executive president who is elected every six years by popular vote, and a bicameral Federal Assembly with a 183-member Nationalrat and a 64-member Bundesrat, or Upper House. Both bodies are elected for four years at a time.

Last elections Parliamentary elections were held in September 2008. The Austrian People's Party (ÖVP) won 51 seats while the Social-Democratic Party took 57 seats and the Freedom Party received 34 seats. The Green Party won 20 seats and the Alliance for the Future of Austria (the Jorg Haider List) won 21 seats. Heinz Fischer of the Social Democratic Party won election as president in April 2004. He defeated Benita Ferrero-Waldner with 52.4% of the vote.

Economy The Austrian economy consistently performed better than the EU average over the past ten years. Growth was broadly based, driven by both consumer spending and investment. The country's export-oriented manufacturing sector was a major economic driver. However, Austria's openness and dependence on exports began to hurt in 2009 and little or no growth is expected through 2010. The opening up of the economies of Central and Eastern Europe has been a boost to Austrian business but most of that region is now in recession. Wage moderation as a result of a close social partnership helps to maintain competitiveness. Fundamental long-term challenges must still be addressed. The ageing population will depress potential growth over the longer term and put increasing pressure on the country's pension system. Greater competition within the enlarged EU will likely make Austria's high tax rates unsustainable. Continued success in the global knowledge-economy will also require more flexible institutions and attitudes.

Main industries Agriculture makes up just 1.5% of GDP. Farms are relatively inefficient and fragmented. Austria has been a food importer for many years but farm exports have been slowly rising and the trade deficit of this sector is now much reduced. Industrial growth weakened abruptly in late 2008 and the downturn worsened in 2009. The problem is that many manufacturers depend heavily on orders from the automobile industry in Germany and elsewhere in Europe. The country has few multinationals and only a handful of internationally recognised corporations, but many highly specialised and successful small and medium-sized companies. Most of these companies are family-owned; they make high-quality products and export them around the world. Exporters and manufacturers are now expected to see a prolonged period of slower growth as a result of the weakening global environment. Tourism remains the country's largest single industry and biggest foreign-exchange earner. However, the sector has been in decline for several years as Western European tourists sought out more exotic locations. Now, the recession in Germany and other Western European countries has reduced the number of visitors further. Austria's financial sector has close ties with Central and Eastern Europe, a market many times bigger than the domestic one, and faster growing. This region presently accounts for just 10% of the assets of Austrian banks but one-third of their profits. The financial sector's expansion in Eastern Europe has created additional risks as the economies in that region weaken. At home, the service sector remains relatively inefficient and sheltered from foreign competition.

Energy Austria's liberalisation of the electricity and gas markets is virtually complete. Utilities, however, will face enormous challenges if they are to fend off the interest of competitors. Both the oil and gas and the electricity sectors are too small to survive on their own in an open European market. The fear in Austria is that the local energy sector will be taken over by powerful German neighbours.

Belarus

Capital city	Minsk
Capital population	1,760,050 *(2009)*
Population ('000)	9,672.00 *(2009)*
Urban population (%)	73.67 *(2009)*
Land area (sq km)	207,595
Languages	Belarussian
Religion	Belarussian Orthodox, Roman Catholic
Currency	Belarus rouble (BYR)
Head of state	President Aleksandr Lukashenko (1994)
Head of government	Sjarhej Sidorski (2003)
Ruling party	The government is formed by non-partisans, loyal to the president.

Main urban areas	Population *(Year)*
Minsk (capital)	1,760,050 *(2009)*
Gomel	480,461 *(2009)*
Mogilev.	372,654 *(2009)*
Vitebsk	341,331 *(2009)*
Grodno	323,895 *(2009)*
Brest	306,530 *(2009)*
Bobrujsk	217,755 *(2009)*
Baranovichi	167,636 *(2009)*
Borisov.	148,920 *(2009)*

Location Belarus (Byelorussia, or White Russia), borders Poland in the west, Lithuania and Latvia in the north, and Ukraine in the south. The country is a large and swampy plain that is served by several major rivers. The capital is Minsk.

Political structure Belarus declared its independence from the old USSR in August 1990. The National Assembly has two chambers. The House of Representatives has 110 members chosen in single-seat constituencies and elected for four-year terms. The Council of the Republic has 64 members, 56 members indirectly elected and eight members appointed by the president.

Last elections Parliamentary elections were held in September 2008. Supporters of the president won all 110 seats. The result was controversial and poses problems for western countries which had hoped to maintain a dialogue with Belarus. In October 2004, voters approved a referendum allowing Lukashenko to run for a third term. Lukashenko was re-elected as president in March 2006 with 80% of the vote. Charges of voter fraud were widespread.

Economy Belarus's state-dominated economy performed well between 2004 and 2008. Growth averaged more than 8% during this period. A new energy agreement with Russia has now slowed the pace abruptly. Adverse movements in the terms of trade, falling exports and problems in securing finance all pose problems. The economy is also suffering from the effects of the global slowdown. Extensive state controls over the economy – notably on prices – complicate economic developments and reduce the efficacy of policy actions. Income distribution is much more equitable than in most countries. Fiscal policy is tight, due mainly to a decline in sources of available financing, such as privatisation proceeds. Structural reforms have progressed very little and the private sector controls only about 20% of GDP.

Main industries The agriculture sector is in difficulty with about 60% of agricultural enterprises being unprofitable. Forestry and agriculture, notably potatoes, grain, peat and cattle, are important sources of income and employment. Most of the country's industries are dependent on imports for their raw materials and intermediate supplies. Industrial output fell by 4.5% in the first quarter of 2009. Engineering, machine tools, agricultural equipment, chemicals, motor vehicles and some consumer durables such as watches, televisions and radios are all prominent state-run industries. Many of the products they produce are out of date and inferior to Western versions. These firms still export to Russia but few of their products could be sold in the EU. The financial situation of the industrial sector continues to be difficult, as indicated by high inventory levels and the fact that one-third of all industrial enterprises report losses. The construction industry is one bright spot in an otherwise discouraging situation. Construction activity continues to grow at a double-digit pace. The country's banking system is dominated by the state and is rather weak. Lending practices are extensively influenced by government decisions with loans going for designated purposes, mostly at controlled and subsidised interest rates. Over 80% of domestic assets in the banking system are controlled by just four state-owned banks. To help strengthen the banking system, the government provided a US$1.5 billion injection in 2009 and will abandon the programme of directed lending. An overwhelming portion of the republic's raw materials are imported from Russia, a situation which has given rise to frequent difficulties.

Energy Belarus has a small oil industry which produces around 37,000 barrels per day (bbl/d) of oil each year. The country has 198 million barrels of oil in proven reserves, but the absence of any legitimate reform programme discourages foreign investors from entering the industry. The state-owned oil production monopoly estimates that active oil deposits may last for another 17 years. The country must import nearly 75% of its oil from Russia. Belarus serves as a transit country for Russian oil exports. Although it does not transit nearly as much Russian natural gas as does Ukraine, its importance as a transit state is growing. In 2007, the country agreed to a new 5-year deal that doubles the price of gas during the year and will bring gas prices in line with European countries by 2011.

Belgium

Capital city	Brussels
Capital population	150,276 *(2009)*
Population ('000)	10,660.56 *(2009)*
Urban population (%)	97.38 *(2009)*
Land area (sq km)	30,520
Languages	Dutch (Flemish) and French (Walloon), with German minority
Religion	Mainly Roman Catholic
Currency	Euro (€)
Head of state	HM King Albert II (1993)
Head of government	Herman van Rompuy (2008)
Ruling party	The Christian Democrats lead a multiparty coalition.

Main urban areas	Population *(Year)*
Anvers	475,168 *(2009)*
Gand	238,552 *(2009)*
Charleroi	201,419 *(2009)*
Liege	190,857 *(2009)*
Brussels (capital)	150,276 *(2009)*
Schaerbeek	117,246 *(2009)*
Bruges	116,851 *(2009)*
Namur	108,104 *(2009)*
Anderlecht	100,256 *(2009)*
Mons	90,976 *(2009)*

Location Belgium lies on the north-western coast of continental Europe, facing the North Sea some distance north of the English Channel. Belgium's excellent road and rail communications make it an obvious choice for the administrative centre of the EU. The climate is moderate with mild winters. The capital is Brussels.

Political structure Belgium is a constitutional monarchy in which the monarch has often been required to mediate and to propose governments. There is a 150-seat Chamber of Representatives, normally elected for four years, and a Senate of 71 members. In the Senate, 40 members are directly elected, 21 are appointed and 10 are co-opted from already-elected officials. Four reforms since the 1970s have transformed Belgium from a unitary into a federal state. The result is a federation of three "regions": Flanders, Wallonia and Brussels-Capital, overlaid with three languages – Flemish, French and German. Each has its own parliament.

Last elections General elections were held in June 2007. In the Chamber of Representatives the Socialist party received 20 seats and the Reformist Movement won 23 seats, while the Christian Democrats and Flemish Alliance took 30 seats. The Flemish Interest Party received 17 seats and the Open VLD Party gained 18 seats. Smaller parties received the remaining seats. In the Senate, the Christian Democrats and Flemish Alliance won 9 seats, the Open Flemish Liberals took 5 seats as did the Flemish Interest Party, while the Reformist Movement gained 6 seats. Seven additional parties divided the remaining Senate seats. In July 2008, Yves Leterme resigned as prime minister and was replaced by Herman van Rompuy.

Economy The economy performed well in 2004-2007, growing at an average rate of more than 2.5% per year. The government managed to balance the budget throughout most of this period, leading to a steady fall in public debt. However, the economy began contract in the fourth quarter of 2008 and the downturn has continued in 2009. The recession is attributed to a slump in domestic demand. Exporters have been losing market share for more than a decade owing to a rise in labour costs and a lack of differentiated products. Belgium's heavy dependence on the financial sector means the recession will be a severe one and the recovery will be slow. Unemployment is expected to exceed 8%. The jump in inflation experienced during the first half of 2008 has already dissipated but the country's system of indexation will still generate higher wage growth through 2009.

Main industries Belgium's manufacturing sector accounts for 16.5% of GDP. Growth of output slowed in 2008 and a contraction began in 2009. Food processing industries are especially important with some of the world's largest producers including Kraft, Nestlé, Danone and Campina operating in the country. The pharmaceuticals sector employs nearly 30,000 workers and accounts for around 10% of total exports.

Long the country's industrial powerhouse, French-speaking Wallonia is now struggling with large pockets of unemployment and many obsolete industries. The global liquidity crisis hit the financial sector hard, forcing the government to intervene with major banking institutions. So far, the government's moves have been ad hoc but a broader framework to address the problem is needed. Previously, a wave of mergers and takeovers had left about four-fifths of the Belgian market in the hands of just a few banks.

Energy Competition among energy suppliers is gathering pace. The country's consumption of nuclear energy is among the highest in Europe, accounting for almost a tenth of all primary use. Nevertheless, the government has decided to phase out its seven reactors by 2025. There is strong opposition from industry, which argues that closure leaves no clear alternative. Crude oil accounts for almost half of the total energy consumption.

Bosnia-Herzegovina

Capital city	Sarajevo
Capital population	380,633 *(2009)*
Population ('000)	3,844.48 *(2009)*
Urban population (%)	48.02 *(2009)*
Land area (sq km)	51,129
Languages	Serbo-Croat
Religion	Mainly Islam
Currency	Bosnia and Herzegovina konvertib (BAM)
Head of state	Haris Silajdžic, Nebojša Radmanovic and Željko Komšic (2006)
Head of government	Nikola Spiric (2007)
Ruling party	The government is formed by a coalition of several parties.

Main urban areas	Population *(Year)*
Sarajevo (capital)	380,633 *(2009)*
Banja Luka	171,065 *(2009)*
Tuzla	85,631 *(2009)*
Zenica	83,695 *(2009)*
Mostar	62,517 *(2009)*
Brcko	50,868 *(2009)*
Bijeljina	43,676 *(2009)*
Bihac	38,414 *(2009)*
Prijedor	30,310 *(2009)*
Trebinje	24,640 *(2009)*

Location Bosnia-Herzegovina lies in the centre of the former territory of Yugoslavia, with its eastern borders alongside Serbia and Montenegro and the western edge against Croatia. The mountainous interior gives way to a stretch of coastline in the southwest running down to the city of Dubrovnik. The capital is Sarajevo.

Political structure The country has a rotating collective presidency of three. The candidate with the most votes in an ethnic group is elected. Together, they serve one four-year term, rotating the presidency every eight months. There is a bicameral parliament consisting of the House of Representatives (42 members) and the House of Peoples (15 members), two thirds of whose members are elected from the Muslim-Croat Federation and one third from the Serbian Republic. A valid majority requires at least one third of the members representing each entity. The Federation and the Serbian Republic have their own parliaments. Western governments have a "high representative" who can dismiss officials he deems to be impeding the peace process.

Last elections Presidential elections were held in October 2006. Haris Silajdžic took the Bosnjak office with 62.1% of the vote. Nebojša Radmanovic won the Serbian office with 54.8% of the vote while Željko Komšic won the Croatian presidency with 40.8% of the vote. Elections to the House of Representatives of the Federation were held in October 2006. The Party of Democratic Action won 8 seats, the Party for Bosnia and Herzegovina took 7, the Alliance of Independent Social Democrats also took 7, the Social Democratic Party received 5 and the Serb Democratic Party captured 3. Seven other parties are represented in the House.

Economy After the collapse of a socialist-built economy wracked by war and the deterioration of heavy industry, a remarkable recovery took place. Real GDP has tripled since 1995, but at the current rate of recovery, it will take more than 15 years before the level of economic activity reaches pre-war levels. Bosnia is still the poorest country in Europe. Around 18% of the population live in poverty and another 30% (including many state employees) are only slightly better off. The private sector accounts for just 5% of GDP. Steady growth in recent years has created various macroeconomic imbalances at a time when the economy has begun to slow. Until 2008, credit to the private sector was rising by about 25% per year, pushing up the current account deficit. Industrial output began to fall in late 2008 and the decline has accelerated during the first four months of 2009. Much economic activity takes place in the informal economy. Growth in the formal economy remains partially dependent on the international aid going to the country but these funds are now being supplied in smaller amounts and with conditions. Macroeconomic policies are sometimes chaotic and often poorly designed.

Main industries Bosnia-Herzegovina's economy relied almost exclusively on agriculture before the war and this sector is even more dominant today. The sector is dominated by crop production; livestock represents less than one-third of farm output. Arable land amounts to only about 45% of the country. Land mines and unexploded ordinance mean nearly 4% of land remains inaccessible. The industrial sector expanded briskly in recent years but growth began to slow in 2009. Industrial output in the Federation has fallen by 10.9% in the first half of 2009. Construction activity has collapsed as credit has disappeared. Many industrial workers have been laid off in 2009. In the Republika Srpska, however, industrial output continues to grow. The most important industries are chemicals, furniture, rubber and plastics. Bosnia's main exports are wood, paper, metals and metal products. Steps have been taken to improve bank supervision, including more comprehensive deposit insurance. Foreign banks dominate the banking industry.

Energy The country has no energy resources of its own and relies on imports.

Bulgaria

Capital city	Sofia
Capital population	1,189,602 *(2009)*
Population ('000)	7,519.18 *(2009)*
Urban population (%)	72.11 *(2009)*
Land area (sq km)	110,910
Languages	Bulgarian
Religion	Bulgarian Orthodox
Currency	Bulgarian lev (BGN)
Head of state	Georgi Parvanov (2002)
Head of government	Boyko Borisov (2009)
Ruling party	A Centre-Right coalition led by the newly created party known as The Citizens for European Development of Bulgaria (GERB) leads the government.

Main urban areas	Population *(Year)*
Sofia (capital)	1,189,602 *(2009)*
Plovdiv	347,600 *(2009)*
Varna	318,313 *(2009)*
Bourgas	188,861 *(2009)*
Ruse	156,959 *(2009)*
Stara Zagora	140,710 *(2009)*
Pleven	112,372 *(2009)*
Sliven	94,456 *(2009)*
Dobrich	93,163 *(2009)*
Shumen	86,978 *(2009)*

Location With its southern borders meeting Turkey, Greece, Macedonia and Serbia, and its northern border meeting Romania, Bulgaria has been exposed to a wide range of cultures. The climate is equable, with low rainfall especially along the popular Black Sea coast. The capital is Sofia.

Political structure The constitution provides for a unicameral 240-seat parliament which is elected according to a proportional system for a four-year term. The president is directly elected for a five-year term but most power rests with the Prime Minister who is generally leader of the dominant party.

Last elections Presidential elections were held in October 2006. Georgi Parvanov of the Bulgarian Socialist Party was re-elected in the second round of voting. He received 75.9% of the vote. Parliamentary elections were held in July 2009. The newly created party known as The Citizens for European Development of Bulgaria (GERB) took 116 seats while the Coalition for Bulgaria received 40 seats, The Movement for Rights and Freedoms captured 38 seat, the National Union Attack took 21 seats and the Blue Coalition gained 15 seats. Another ten seats went to the Order, Lawfulness and Justice Party.

Economy Bulgaria became a member of the EU in 2007. The economy performed well following an agreement on EU accession with GDP growth averaging 6.1% in 2004-2007. There was a surge in capital inflows and a credit boom during this period. By 2008, capital inflows were up to about 30% of GDP and the credit-to-GDP ratio was around 67%. Capital inflows have dried up however and per capita income remains about a third of the EU average. Bulgaria will probably still be the poorest member-state for years to come. Recent projections suggest that it will take more than 20 years to realise a per capita income that is two-thirds of the EU average. Low wage levels together with the prospect of EU membership pulled in investment over the past three years but productivity growth was slow. As a result, Bulgarian firms began to loose ground just at the time when EU membership exposed them to greater competition. Following many years of decline, the gross external debt ratio has started to rise again, and remains at a high level.

Main industries Agriculture presently accounts for 6.6% of GDP. Bulgaria has the potential to become a major agricultural supplier for all of Central Europe, but its farms are inefficient and underfinanced. The country's grain harvest is expected to fall by around 20% in 2009. EU subsidies equivalent to 1.7% of GDP will go to agriculture in the first three years of membership. Foreign-owned banks have sharply reduced their financing and provision of credit. Even prior to this move, Bulgaria lagged well behind the Central European lending average. The country's real estate market has weakened after a prolonged boom driven by Russians and other Eastern European buyers. The manufacturing sector is struggling as exports fall. Particularly hard hit are industries producing metal products. Local subsidiaries of foreign companies are running short of cash because of dwindling credit. Manufacturing output fell by more than 20% in the first quarter of 2009. Retail turnover is also shrinking. Tourism holds promise, especially sites along the Black Sea coast. However, the number of visitors began to fall in 2008 and the downturn continues in 2009. The country's roadway system is in very poor condition. Few repairs have been made over the past two decades owing to a shortage of funds. The EU Regional Development Fund will provide €300 million, most of it for this purpose, between 2007 and 2013. The EU has also earmarked €25 million for the technological modernisation of small and medium-sized enterprises.

Energy Bulgaria had 15 million barrels of proven oil reserves. It produces around 3,000 barrels per day (bbl/d) and consumes about 106,000 bbl/d. There is one oil refinery with a capacity of 115,000 bbl/d. The country also has a small amount of natural gas. A pipeline connecting the Bulgarian Black Sea port of Burgas with the Albanian Adriatic port of Vlore is under construction and should be finished by 2008. The project is estimated to cost US$1.2 billion. Bulgaria is also increasing its natural gas transit capacity. Presently, Russian gas passes through the country but the country could become a transit base for Iranian gas in the future. The government is pressing ahead with plans for a €6 billion nuclear power plant on the Danube to replace capacity lost by EU-ordered closures of reactors from the communist era.

Croatia

Capital city	Zagreb
Capital population	721,172 *(2009)*
Population ('000)	4,428.55 *(2009)*
Urban population (%)	61.72 *(2009)*
Land area (sq km)	56,538
Languages	Serbo-Croat
Religion	Mainly Roman Catholic
Currency	Kuna (HRK)
Head of state	President Stipe Mesic (2000)
Head of government	Jadranka Kosor (2009)
Ruling party	Croatian Democratic Union (HDZ)

Main urban areas	Population *(Year)*
Zagreb (capital)	721,172 *(2009)*
Split	199,099 *(2009)*
Rijeka	135,356 *(2009)*
Osijek	85,682 *(2009)*
Zadar	68,843 *(2009)*
Slavonski Brod.	64,050 *(2009)*
Pula	59,331 *(2009)*
Sesvete.	54,016 *(2009)*
Karlovac.	44,328 *(2009)*
Varaždin.	43,536 *(2009)*

Location Croatia lies in the north of the old Yugoslavia, with its western edge straddling the Adriatic coast and sharing an eastern border with Hungary. To the north is Slovenia, with Bosnia-Herzegovina and Serbia to the east. The capital is Zagreb.

Political structure The president is elected for a five-year term by the people. Legislative authority is vested in the House of Representatives with up to 160 members, directly elected for a four-year term. Since 1999, the constitution has been changed to shift power away from the president to the parliament.

Last elections Parliamentary elections were held in November 2007. The HDZ took 66 seats in the 153-member parliament while the Social Democratic Party won 56 seats. The remainder were scattered among eight other parties and independents. In January 2005, Mesic won a second five-year term as president. In July 2009, Ivo Sanader unexpectedly resigned as prime minister and was replaced by Kosor.

Economy Based on most economic indicators, Croatia performed better than Romania or Bulgaria throughout most of this decade. The economy is open to trade and capital flows, and privatisation is well advanced, although uneven. Croatia's openness has left the country especially vulnerable to recession in West Europe and a recession began in 2009. Rapid growth in credit led to a significant increase in debt. The public sector is still very large and imposes a drag on growth. Public agencies and enterprises are not subject to strict financial discipline, and state aid in various forms exceeds that in other Central and Eastern European countries. Rapid growth of commercial credit has created problems for the government. Unemployment is high and the incomes of many workers have yet to reach the levels they enjoyed in 1990. Savings rates are lower than in neighbouring countries and have fallen further in the past few years.

Main industries Agriculture is very inefficient and untouched by any reforms. Despite a mild climate and fertile land, the country is a net importer of food. Up to a fifth of the work force in the central and eastern regions is employed in agriculture but only 4-5% in the rest of the country. Farming output has contracted in recent years. The share of manufacturing in GDP has declined sharply since 1990. Private industry is the main source of job creation and enjoys a healthy rate of investment along with buoyant exports. Industrial output has contracted in 2009 but the pace appears to be decelerating. The service sector is the backbone of the economy, accounting for around 65% of GDP. In a normal year, tourism contributes almost half of all foreign exchange earnings and generates more than a quarter of GDP. However, the number of visitors has fallen sharply as West European economies have weakened. The country has thousands of kilometres of coastline but poor infrastructure. The financial system is adequate but faces some risks owing to rapid credit expansion. More than 90% of the banking system is controlled by foreign banks.

Energy Croatia has proven oil reserves of only 74 million barrels and produces about 23,000 barrels per day. The country also contains 1.05 trillion cubic feet of natural gas. Croatia is the largest consumer of natural gas in the Balkans and imports most of this from Russia. The country hopes to assume more importance as a transit centre for energy supplies moving to the West.

Cyprus

Capital city	Nicosia (Greek sector only)
Capital population	47,832 *(2001)*
Population ('000)	871.04 *(2009)*
Urban population (%)	70.06 *(2009)*
Land area (sq km)	9,250
Languages	Greek (78%), Turkish (18%), Armenian
Religion	Greek Orthodox (78%); Islamic (18%)
Currency	Euro (€)
Head of state	President Demetris Christofias (2008) (Northern Cyprus: Mehmet Ali Talat – 2005)
Head of government	President Demetris Christofias (2008) (Northern Cyprus: Ferdi Sabit Soyer – 2005)
Ruling party	The Democratic Rally leads a coalition with the Democratic Party. In Northern Cyprus, the Party of National Unity leads the government.

Main urban areas	Population *(Year)*
Limassol.	94,250 *(2001)*
Nicosia (Greek sector only) (capital).	47,832 *(2001)*

Location Cyprus is located in the eastern Mediterranean, barely 150km south of Turkey and much closer to Syria than to Greece, whose descendants represent by far the largest percentage of the population. The climate is warm and dry. The capital is Nicosia.

Political structure For international purposes, Cyprus is represented by the south of the island, where a Greek majority elects an executive president and a 56-seat House of Representatives. A further 24 unoccupied seats and the vice-presidency are reserved for Turkish-Cypriots but have not been filled since 1963. There are eight observer seats reserved for the Armenian, Maronite and Roman Catholic minorities. The so-called "Turkish Republic of Northern Cyprus", which was declared after the Turkish invasion of 1974, has an executive president and a 50-seat parliament. The two sides have long discussed UN proposals for a federal union, where each group would live in separate self-governing areas with separate parliaments.

Last elections In February 2008, Christofias became president of Greek-controlled Cyprus, defeating Yiannakis Kassoulides. Christofias won 53.5% of the vote. Elections to the House of Representatives took place in May 2006. The Progressive Party of the Working People took 18 seats, the Democratic Rally also received 18 seats and the Democratic Party claimed 11 seats. The remaining seats were dispersed among three smaller parties. Parliamentary elections in northern Cyprus were held in April 2009. The Party of National Unity took 26 seats, the Republican Turkish Party won 15 seats, the Democratic Party took five seats, the Communal Democratic Party received two seats and the Freedom and Reform Party won two seats. Presidential elections were held in the Turkish sector in April 2005. Talat was elected president with nearly 55.8% of the vote.

Economy The Cypriot economy has grown in recent years but is now struggling. Modest economic growth continues despite shocks to the tourism sector. Real per capita income now exceeds 80% of the average for the EU-25 (adjusted for purchasing power). The tax system is being modernised and a uniform corporate tax rate of 10% has been introduced, which implies a reduction in the taxation of profits. There is still a large income gap between the Greek and Turkish sectors of the country. Per capita income in the Greek zone is around US$20,000 but it is about half of that in the Turkish area. Many of the Turkish-Cypriots have left for a better life in Britain. In their place, Turks from the mainland have flooded in, mostly poor and uneducated. In the Turkish north, unemployment is high. Foreign remittances from the 200,000

Turkish-Cypriots abroad help to keep the Turkish part of the economy afloat. In recent years, gains in productivity have lagged behind real wage increases, undermining the island's competitiveness in many of its manufacturing industries.

Main industries Agriculture (along with mining) accounts for only 3% of GDP. The manufacturing sector accounts for 9% and its share has been falling over time. The most important sectors in terms of value added are food and beverages, clothing, furniture and metal products. Other industrial sectors, which continue to expand, include printing and publishing, plastics, chemical and pharmaceutical products. The manufacturing sector has been going through difficult times, experiencing a fall in the growth of production, exports and employment as a result of an erosion in competitiveness. However, Cyprus is rich in human capital, with large numbers of Greek-Cypriots having advanced degrees from foreign universities. The country also has the fourth largest ship register in the world. Within the service sector, the most important areas are tourism, finance, insurance and real estate. The larger Greek Cypriot banks have been little affected by the global financial turmoil. Tourism accounted for about 20% of GDP in recent years though its share has been falling. Tourism revenues in the Greek zone fell in 2008 even though the number of visitors rose. Both revenues and the number of visitors continue to fall in 2009. In the north, tourism suffers from the international boycott but several large investments have been made in the past two years. Cyprus' thriving offshore sector is a valuable source of foreign exchange. The island has more than 32,000 registered offshore companies and approximately half of them are active. Initiatives are underway to strengthen financial sector regulation and supervision, and align them to EU standards – including for insurance and the stock market. While structural reform has proceeded, competition continues to be limited and inefficiency prevalent in sectors such as air travel, electricity and telecommunications. In northern Cyprus the economy is dominated by the service sector with limited activity in agriculture and manufacturing. Investment is scarce, there is a lack of skilled labour and transport costs are high.

Energy Crude oil, all of which has to be imported, is the primary source of energy in Cyprus. Thermal plants are used to meet the island's electricity requirements.

Czech Republic

Capital city	Prague
Capital population	1,233,211 *(2009)*
Population ('000)	10,337.91 *(2009)*
Urban population (%)	75.07 *(2009)*
Land area (sq km)	78,864
Languages	Czech
Religion	Catholic (70%); Protestant (15%)
Currency	Czech koruna (CZK)
Head of state	Vaclav Klaus (2003)
Head of government	Jan Fischer (2009)
Ruling party	The Civic Democratic party leads a three-party coalition.

Main urban areas	Population *(Year)*
Prague (capital)	1,233,211 *(2009)*
Brno	370,592 *(2009)*
Ostrava	307,767 *(2009)*
Plzen	165,866 *(2009)*
Liberec	100,914 *(2009)*
Olomouc	100,373 *(2009)*
Usti nad Labem	95,289 *(2009)*
Ceske Budejovice	94,936 *(2009)*
Hradec Kralove	94,497 *(2009)*
Pardubice	89,892 *(2009)*

Location The Czech Republic formed part of a federation with Slovakia until January 1993, when the two parted. The country is located in central Europe, southeast of Germany, with Poland to the north, Austria to the south and Slovakia to the east. The climate is temperate with harsh winters. The capital is Prague.

Political structure Until the end of 1992, Czechoslovakia was a federation of two ethnically distinct states, the Czech and Slovak republics, which had been forged in 1919. In 1993, the two states declared their independence. The Czech parliament has two chambers. The Chamber of Deputies has 200 members, elected for a four-year term by proportional representation with a 5% barrier. The Senate has 81 members, elected for a six-year term in single-seat constituencies, in which one third is renewed every two years. The president is elected for a five-year term by the parliament.

Last elections Elections to the Senate were held in October 2008 with a third of the seats available, The Civic Democratic Party now holds 35 seats, the Czech Social Democratic Party has 29 seats, the Christian-Democratic Union controls 7 seats, and the remainder were divided up among smaller parties. Elections to the Chamber of Deputies took place in June 2006. The Civic Democratic Party claimed 81 seats. The Czech Social Democratic Party won 74 seats, the Communist Party of Bohemia and Moravia received 26 seats, the Christian Democratic Union won 13 seats and the Green Party took 6 seats. Although Topolanek emerged as the prime minister, the coalition cabinet was toppled in March 2009 and Fischer replaced him as prime minister in April 2009. Vaclav Klaus of the Civic Democratic Alliance won re-election as president in February 2008. He defeated Jan Švejnar.

Economy Economic growth was strong in 2005-2007, but performed poorly throughout 2008. Both exports and imports declined while industrial output hit record lows. In 2009, the country slipped into recession. The government deficit was just 1.5% of GDP in 2008 but the gap will widen substantially in 2009. Unemployment also began to rise. Meanwhile, business confidence has fallen as inventories have accumulated. The government still hopes to gain entry to the eurozone by 2012.

Main industries The Czech Republic's agricultural sector is not large but productivity is high by Eastern European standards. Farmers have taken advantage of membership of the EU to sell pork and milk to Germany for higher prices than they can fetch in the domestic market. Food processors, however, have suffered, cutting jobs and production. Czech farmers also face increased competition from Poland, where the agricultural sector is larger and costs are lower. The country is self-sufficient in wheat, barley, vegetables, potatoes and fruit. There are extensive forests offering substantial scope for timber development. Foreign-owned companies account for roughly half of industrial output and 70% of exports. Industrial output during 2009 has been dropping at a double-digit rate as demand for exports plummets. High-value manufacturers (such as automobile makers) are being the brunt of the downturn. In the longer run, services and research are seen as vital because some manufacturing investors are bound to move further east as Czech wages rise. The banking industry is suffering as financial turbulence in world markets continues. Household debt has been rising and more stringent forms of risk assessment are being enforced. Foreign banks control over 90% of assets. The tourist industry is competitive but revenues are expected to fall by 1.7% in 2009 as the recession spreads through Western Europe.

Energy The Czech Republic has proven oil reserves of only 15 million barrels and produces just 13,530 barrels per day (bbl/d). Exploration is taking place in the Western Carpathians, an area bordering Austria and Slovakia. There are two refineries having a combined capacity of 178,000 bbl/d. Reserves of natural gas are also minimal – only 140 billion cubic feet. With nearly 32,000 miles of natural gas pipelines, the Czech Republic is a major transit centre for Russian gas.

Denmark

Capital city	Copenhagen
Capital population	510,688 *(2009)*
Population ('000)	5,475.36 *(2009)*
Urban population (%)	85.91 *(2009)*
Land area (sq km)	43,075
Languages	Danish
Religion	Mainly Protestant
Currency	Danish krone (DKr)
Head of state	HM Queen Margrethe II (1972)
Head of government	Lars Lokke Rasmussen (2009)
Ruling party	The government is led by a liberal-conservative coalition.

Main urban areas	Population *(Year)*
Copenhagen (capital)	510,688 *(2009)*
Arhus	298,785 *(2009)*
Odense	186,740 *(2009)*
Aalborg	165,263 *(2009)*
Frederiksberg	93,649 *(2009)*
Esbjerg	83,296 *(2009)*
Gentofte	69,157 *(2009)*
Kolding	63,523 *(2009)*
Randers	62,973 *(2009)*
Gladsaxe	62,540 *(2009)*

Location Denmark is an archipelago of low-lying islands which control the straits between the Baltic Sea and the North Sea. The country borders Germany to the south, but is close to Sweden (no more than 50km across the Oresund strait). Denmark controls the Faroe Islands in the North Sea and Greenland, which lies off the coast of Canada. The capital is Copenhagen.

Political structure The Kingdom of Denmark is a constitutional monarchy in which executive authority lies with a Prime Minister who answers to a 179-member unicameral Parliament, with 175 members elected for a four-year term (135 of them by proportional representation in 17 districts and 40 others allotted in proportion to their total vote). There are two representatives each from the Faroe Islands and Greenland.

Last elections Parliamentary elections were held in November 2007. The Liberal Party won 46 seats while the Social Democratic party gained 45 seats, the Danish People's Party took 25 seats, the Socialist People's Party received 23 seats and the Conservative People's Party gained 18 seats. The remainder were scattered amongst minor parties. Anders Rasmussen resigned as prime minister in April and was replaced by Lars Lokke Rasmussen.

Economy Denmark's economy performed well throughout most of this decade but entered a cyclical slowdown in 2007 when the country's housing boom ended. The effects were accentuated later when the global slowdown spread. GDP contracted slightly in 2008 by about 1.1%) and the recession worsened in 2009. Denmark nevertheless enjoys some of the highest living standards of all West European countries and has one of the most equal distributions of income, thanks in large part to its comprehensive welfare system. Owing to a fall in profits, investment has turned sharply negative and private consumption has weakened. Unemployment began to rise in the last quarter of 2008.

Main industries Agriculture accounts for just 1.2% of GDP but the sector is important in terms of its net foreign currency earning capacity, its effect on employment in related industries and its importance in supplying foodstuffs domestically. Agriculture consists of thousands of mainly small farms supplying pig meat products, dairy goods and cereals such as wheat and barley. In general, farming is so intensive that it has recurrently threatened serious environmental consequences in Denmark's low-lying and often marshy landscape. Farmers are bound by special legislation requiring safe storage and treatment of wastes. In the manufacturing sector, engineering, food processing, pharmaceuticals and brewing are among Denmark's most successful industries. Biotechnology is also making strides but even more important is the country's elaborate infrastructure for information technology. Improvements in the subway systems in major cities during 2008-2012 are expected to cost US$2.4 billion. Private

construction has slumped badly but government incentives have been introduced to support the industry. Services account for the bulk of GDP. Housing prices are weakening but the housing bubble is not as severe as in other West European countries. The government plans to boost spending on infrastructure. In the financial sector, the liquidity crisis and the global slowdown has put most banks under severe pressure. The government has offered banks and mortgage companies loans totalling 100 billion krone.

Energy Denmark's total oil production is about 313,000 barrels per day. New fields have helped bolster output. The country maintains an "open door" policy towards oil companies. Under this policy, oil companies are invited to bid for licences in specified acreage and are not required to commit to drilling wells before seismic work has been completed. As part of EU efforts to create a single market for energy, Denmark has completely liberalised its market for electricity.

Estonia

Capital city	Tallinn
Capital population	397,987 *(2009)*
Population ('000)	1,330.60 *(2009)*
Urban population (%)	69.51 *(2009)*
Land area (sq km)	45,226
Languages	Estonian
Religion	Mainly Christian
Currency	Estonian Kroon (EEK)
Head of state	Toomas Hendrik Ilves (2006)
Head of government	Andrus Ansip (2005)
Ruling party	The government is formed by the Reform Party and the Centre Party.

Main urban areas	Population *(Year)*
Tallinn (capital)	397,987 *(2009)*
Tartu	102,659 *(2009)*
Narva	66,214 *(2009)*
Kohtla-Järve	44,810 *(2009)*
Pärnu	43,895 *(2009)*
Viljandi	20,043 *(2009)*
Rakvere	16,558 *(2009)*
Maardu	16,530 *(2009)*
Sillamae	16,305 *(2009)*
Kuressaare	14,969 *(2009)*

Location Estonia, the smallest of the three Baltic republics, faces Finland across the Gulf of Finland, with Latvia to the south and Russia dominating its entire eastern frontier. Like Latvia, its land is mainly low-lying and marshy, and its territory includes some 800 islands in the Baltic. The capital is Tallinn.

Political structure Estonia was one of the first Soviet states to declare its formal secession from the USSR, in the summer of 1991. It was recognised in September 1991. The Riigikogu (Parliament) has 101 members. The president is elected for a five-year term by parliament (1st-3rd round) or an electoral college (4th and further rounds).

Last elections In parliamentary elections held in March 2007, the Reform Party won 31 seats, the Centre Party took 29 seats and the Res Publica Party received 19 seats. The Social Democrats gained 10 seats, while the Green Party and the Peoples' Party both received 6 seats. Presidential elections were held in 2006 when Ilves came to office. Adrus Ansip was chosen by the President and took his office on 12 April 2005.

Economy Estonia's economy grew at around 7% per year in 2000-2007 but weakened perceptibly in 2008. The country has now entered a recession which is the worst since the early 1990s. No recovery is anticipated before 2010. Incomes are about half the average in Western Europe but the real living standard surpasses that in most new member states of the EU. Euro adoption remains a key objective but the authorities have limited tools to meet the Maastricht criteria. Foreign liabilities had reached 120% of GDP by 2008 with almost all of this being owed by the private sector. A large potion of this debt was used to finance rapid growth of credit.

Main industries Agriculture accounts for just over 2.9% of GDP and employs 4.6% of the work force. The sector is based mainly on livestock rearing, although dairy farming is also important. Manufacturing contributes more than a quarter of GDP. It depends on well-established engineering, machine-building and textile industries, along with consumer goods and food-processing industries. Estonia's close ties with Scandinavian countries provide ready-made markets for some of its products, as well as a source of capital and technological know-how. However, industrial output began to fall in 2008 and the downward trend continued in 2009. Export-oriented manufacturing is suffering the most. Services accounts for more than two-thirds of GDP and employs almost 60% of the work force. Retail sales fell by about 8% in 2008 and have continued to contract during 2009. Estonia's banking system is financially sound but profitability is falling as households struggle to reduce indebtedness. Foreign-owned banks have curtailed lending sharply. More than three million tourists visit the country each year, a majority of them from Finland. Estonia has substantial deposits of minerals (including phosphate and oil shale) as well as extensive forest resources. The latter benefit greatly from Scandinavian investment and should soon provide a substantial resource base for development of competitive industries in the fields of timber, paper and paper products.

Energy Estonia produces about 7,000 barrels per day, most of it from oil shale, which is abundant in the north-eastern part of the country. There are no domestic natural gas reserves. A substantial amount of electricity is produced by Estonia's oil shale-fired power plants and the country is a net exporter. Oil shale production is heavily polluting, however, and Estonia is under heavy pressure from the EU to cut back its output significantly. The government expects the oil shale industry to continue for another 40 years, but no new mines are scheduled to be built. There are no refineries, so the country must import all petroleum products, either by rail or by pipeline. Meanwhile, Estonia is positioning itself as a major transit centre for oil exports from Russia and the newly independent states to Europe. The country's ports at Tallinn and Muuga have become major terminals for the export of petroleum products from the former Soviet Union.

Finland

Capital city	Helsinki
Capital population	567,902 *(2009)*
Population ('000)	5,325.12 *(2009)*
Urban population (%)	62.64 *(2009)*
Land area (sq km)	337,030
Languages	Finnish (93%), Swedish (6.3%), Lapp (0.2%)
Religion	Lutheran (90%); Greek Orthodox
Currency	Euro (€)
Head of state	Tarja Halonen (2000)
Head of government	Matti Vanhanen (2003)
Ruling party	The Centre Party leads a coalition with the Social Democrats and the Swedish People's Party in Finland.

Main urban areas	Population *(Year)*
Helsinki (capital)	567,902 *(2009)*
Espoo	245,188 *(2009)*
Tampere	210,409 *(2009)*
Vantaa	195,881 *(2009)*
Turku	175,768 *(2009)*
Oulu	134,077 *(2009)*
Lahti	99,532 *(2009)*
Kuopio	91,409 *(2009)*
Jyvaskyla	86,812 *(2009)*
Pori	76,279 *(2009)*

Location Finland lies on the Baltic coast with its western border bridging Sweden, with Norway to the north, and the entire eastern flank meeting Russia. Most of the territory is forested, with the main habitation centres to the south. The climate ranges from sub-Arctic in the north to temperate in the south. The capital is Helsinki.

Political structure Finland has a semi-executive president who exercises extensive political powers even though the main executive functions are vested in the prime minister. Elected by universal suffrage for a six-year term, the president may appoint any prime minister and cabinet which can secure the approval of the 200-member Eduskunta (Parliament). Members of parliament are also elected for four-year terms. In January 1995, Finland became a full member of the EU.

Last elections In January 2006, Tarja Halonen was re-elected as president, defeating Sauli Niinisto. Parliamentary elections were held in March 2007. The Centre Party won 51 seats, while the National Coalition Party received 50 seats. The Social Democrats took 45 seats, the Left Alliance secured 17 seats and the Green League won 15 seats. The remaining seats were divided among several smaller parties. Anneli Jaatteenmaki of the Centre Party assumed the office of prime minister after the election but was forced to resign only two months later, being succeeded by Vanhanen.

Economy Finland enjoyed an economic boom in recent years but the economy began to slow in 2008. The country also ranks high in innovation performance and educational attainment, both of which are key drivers of productivity. However, the contribution of high-tech industries has waned and gains in employment have been meagre. Cuts in labour taxes are welcome, but an increase in public spending is risky, making it difficult to cope with the economic slowdown and the future fiscal implications of ageing. Population ageing in Finland will occur sooner and more rapidly than in most other OECD countries. Fiscal policy will therefore need to be stringent to ensure the long-run sustainability of public finances. The government's target of raising the employment rate to 70% by 2007 was met in 2006. But it will be difficult to meet the 75% goal for 2011 in present circumstances.

Main industries Agriculture accounts for 2.8% of GDP. Farm production, however, is on the increase as many farms are being consolidated and reorganised. These changes are driven by greater investment in agriculture, and are being encouraged by public aid. In manufacturing, forestry accounts for almost 30% of exports and a sizeable portion of GDP. Finland claims around a third of Western Europe's total capacity in the forestry industry and is the world's second largest exporter of paper products behind Canada. The electronics industry is dominated by Nokia which contributes more than a quarter of all exports and a significant portion of GDP. The metal and engineering industries are both growing strongly. The country is a major producer of luxury liners, oil-drilling platforms and a variety of metal products. Tourism is an underdeveloped part of the service sector. The government, however, plans to channel resources into this industry over the next several years with the goal of developing a year-around appeal. Officials hope to boost the sector's share of GDP by about by 3% by 2013.

Energy Finland relies totally on imports of oil and gas, which it once obtained from the Soviet Union. Plans for a substantial expansion of Finnish gas drilling projects in Russia have been considered but never implemented. Nuclear energy accounts for about a sixth of the country's total energy needs. Finland is currently the only EU member that is expanding its nuclear capacity. It hopes to bring a new 1,600-MW reactor online by 2009 but the project is behind schedule. The Nordic area has a common power market, and any shortage in one country may push up prices throughout the region.

France

Capital city	Paris
Capital population	2,186,633 *(2009)*
Population ('000)	62,448.98 *(2009)*
Urban population (%)	77.59 *(2009)*
Land area (sq km)	543,965
Languages	French
Religion	Roman Catholic
Currency	Euro (€)
Head of state	President Nicolas Sarkozy (2007)
Head of government	François Fillon (2007)
Ruling party	The Union for a Popular Movement (UMP) leads a coalition.

Main urban areas	Population *(Year)*
Paris (capital)	2,186,633 *(2009)*
Marseille	852,139 *(2009)*
Lyon	482,851 *(2009)*
Toulouse	467,357 *(2009)*
Nice	351,810 *(2009)*
Nantes	287,873 *(2009)*
Strasbourg	276,544 *(2009)*
Montpellier	262,904 *(2009)*
Bordeaux	240,577 *(2009)*
Lille	233,554 *(2009)*

Location France, the largest country in Western Europe, also lies at the heart of the continent. It meets Spain and Andorra in the south across the Pyrenees, and Italy in the southeast. Switzerland and Germany lie to the east and Belgium and Luxembourg in the north. The capital is Paris.

Political structure France has a semi-executive presidency in which the head of state, elected by universal suffrage for a five-year term, appoints a prime minister in accordance with the bicameral Parliament. The 577-seat National Assembly is elected every five years, and one third of the Senate's 321 members come up for re-election every three years, for a nine-year term. France has an unusually centralised decision-making process.

Last elections Presidential elections were held in May 2007. Sarkozy received 53% of the vote, defeating Ségolene Royal of the Socialist Party. Parliamentary elections were held in June 2007. The UMP and its allies took 345 seats. The Socialist Party and its allies (including the Green Party and the French Communist Party) won 227 seats. The remaining seats were scattered among several minor parties. In May 2005, French voters rejected the proposed EU constitution by 54.7%.

Economy Disposable income rose at a brisk rate throughout much of this decade but too much of the additional demand spilled over into imports. Economic performance collapsed in the fourth quarter of 2008 with the worst performance on record. Consumption plays a more important role than in other large Eurozone countries. The lacklustre performance has strained public finances. Over the medium-term a comprehensive reform of the healthcare system should help contain overall government spending. With the retirement age at only 60 years (compared to 65 years for most EU member states), reforms in the pension system are needed. Further fiscal consolidation and policies to lower structural unemployment are expected to absorb the remaining costs, while five-yearly reviews of the pension system will allow for further modifications. To strengthen labour market performance, subsidies are now offered to employers who hire people on protracted income support. Unemployment is rising nonetheless as the economy weakens.

Main industries Together, agriculture and the agro-food industries account for a larger share of economic activity than in many other Western European countries – about 6% of total value added in the economy and around 10% of total exports. France is the EU's largest producer of cereals. Farms are small, and even though the soil quality is usually excellent, they remain inefficient and require massive financial support. France grows soft fruits, cereals, maize, root vegetables, sugar beet, cattle and poultry, and is famed for its wine production. The manufacturing sector's greatest strengths are in motor vehicles, pharmaceuticals, transport equipment and aerospace (civil and military). The country's two major carmakers, Peugeot and

Renault, face growing competition, slumping demand and ageing product lines. Manufacturing contributes about three-quarters of total exports of goods and services but the sector's share in world markets is falling. A sharp drop in labour productivity is the main culprit. Manufacturing output is expected to contract throughout much of 2009 but should stabilise by the end of the year. There are fears that the slowdown could eventually lead to a flood of low-cost imports. France's services sector is large even by EU standards, accounting for the bulk of GDP. A significant portion of this sector consists of government services. The country's various financial industries are under severe strain. Paris has responded quickly by supporting its banks with cheap capital and state guarantees.

Energy France has 122 million barrels of proven oil reserves. Despite the lack of significant resources, France is the tenth-largest consumer of oil in the world, consuming 1.93 million bbl/d. The country's crude oil refining capacity is 1.96 million bbl/d. Strict EU environmental regulations have been forcing refineries in France, as well as in all EU member states, to upgrade their facilities not only to reduce their emissions but also to meet new fuel specifications. France has about 341 billion cubic feet (Bcf) of proven natural gas reserves. The country is also the world's largest nuclear power generator on a per capita basis, and ranks second in total installed nuclear capacity (behind the USA). Due to the lack of domestic oil sources, the French government has encouraged the use of nuclear power as an alternative energy source to oil where possible.

Georgia

Capital city	Tblisi
Capital population	1,036,399 *(2009)*
Population ('000)	4,385.40 *(2009)*
Urban population (%)	52.56 *(2009)*
Land area (sq km)	70,000
Languages	Georgian
Religion	Mainly Christian (Georgian Orthodox)
Currency	Georgian lari (GEL)
Head of state	Mikheil Saakashvili (2004)
Head of government	Nikoloz Gilauri (2009)
Ruling party	United National Movement (UNM)

Main urban areas	Population *(Year)*
Tblisi (capital)	1,036,399 *(2009)*
Kutaisi	175,752 *(2009)*
Batumi	118,536 *(2009)*
Rustavi	106,987 *(2009)*
Zugdidi	70,414 *(2009)*
Poti	46,425 *(2009)*
Gori	45,488 *(2009)*
Samtredia	28,784 *(2009)*
Senaki	27,914 *(2009)*
Khashuri	27,880 *(2009)*

Location Georgia is one of the smallest but most influential states to have emerged from the former USSR. Located on the Black Sea, it borders on Turkey in the south, Armenia and Azerbaijan in the east and the Russian Federation in the north. Its mainly mountainous terrain includes the Greater Caucasus in the north and the Lesser Caucasus in the south. The capital is Tbilisi.

Political structure Georgia's independent stance is underlined by the fact that it was the last of the former Soviet states (apart from the Baltic States) to join the Confederation of Independent States. Georgia has an executive president who is elected for a five-year term by the people. The unicameral Parliament has 150 members who serve four-year terms.

Last elections Parliamentary elections held in May 2008. The UNM took 119 seats and the Joint Opposition Bloc received 17 seats. The remaining seats were divided among several smaller parties. Saakashvili, the leader of the UNM, was re-elected as president in January 2008. He received 52.8% of the vote, defeating his nearest rival, Levan Gachechiladze who took 25% of the vote. In 2009, Gilauri was appointed as prime minister replacing Grigori Mgaloblishvili.

Economy Prior to the Russian invasion, the economy was growing at a double-digit pace, driven by construction, communications and the financial sector. The transport infrastructure was badly damaged and inflows of private capital dried up following the attack. As a result, there was little or no growth in the second half of 2008. Government efforts to stabilise the situation were largely successful although financial conditions continue to deteriorate. Private capital inflows dropped by 75% during 2008. Corruption remains a problem. According to the EBRD, Georgian enterprises are reported to pay the highest proportion of revenue in bribes in Central Asia. The government has made progress, however, launching several initiatives to combat the problem.

Main industries Georgia has a fertile agricultural sector. Output has fallen, however, after farmers in disputed areas were displaced and water supplies were cut off. Only a minority of farmers have made the transition from subsistence to commercial agriculture. A wide range of crops are produced, including tea, tobacco, citrus fruits and flowers. Wine production (and quality) has increased and presently amounts to around 50 million bottles per year. The industrial sector is expected to see only moderate growth in 2009 owing to a slump in domestic demand. Some firms have migrated from the informal to the formal sector as continued reforms make operations in the informal sector less attractive. The more important industries are based mainly on mineral resources. Metallurgy, construction materials and machine building represent the core of the sector, though many of these enterprises are badly in need of modernisation and additional capital investment. The Supsa oil pipeline brings in US$8 million a year in transit fees. As the Caspian oil and gas industry moves into the production phase, the volume of equipment and other imports into the region will grow. Georgia also has deposits of manganese and coal, and a number of oil refineries. In the service sector, some conflict-affected industries such as transport and tourism have contracted but services as a whole continues to grow. Financial services are being hurt not just by the conflict but also the turmoil in world financial markets. Banking liquidity and solvency has deteriorated dramatically during 2009. The percentage of non-performing loans has risen to about 13%.

Energy Georgia's proven reserves are estimated at 0.35 billion barrels, from which the country produces less than 1,000 barrels per day (bbl/d) of crude oil. Foreign oil companies are involved in oil exploration both on and offshore. Natural gas represents 50% of domestic consumption. Roughly 150 miles of the pipeline corridor extending from Baku, Azerbaijan, to Turkey will pass through Georgia. This corridor will include both the Baku-Tbilisi-Ceyhan oil pipeline and the Baku-Tbilisi-Erzurum natural gas pipeline, which was completed in July 2007. Analysts expect these pipelines to become two of the primary conduits for Caspian Sea region oil and natural gas exports over the next decade. Georgia will be paid transit tariffs by the pipeline's operators and will receive a small percentage of fuel passing through the Republic.

Germany

Capital city	Berlin
Capital population	3,427,074 *(2009)*
Population ('000)	82,002.36 *(2009)*
Urban population (%)	89.13 *(2009)*
Land area (sq km)	356,840
Languages	German
Religion	Roman Catholic (35%); Protestant (40%)
Currency	Euro (€)
Head of state	Horst Kohler (2004)
Head of government	Angela Merkel (2005)
Ruling party	The Christian Democratic Union leads a coalition with the Free Democratic Party.

Main urban areas	Population *(Year)*
Berlin (capital)	3,427,074 *(2009)*
Hamburg	1,784,240 *(2009)*
Munich	1,335,890 *(2009)*
Koln	1,004,457 *(2009)*
Frankfurt	663,981 *(2009)*
Stuttgart	599,951 *(2009)*
Dortmund	586,159 *(2009)*
Duesseldorf	584,405 *(2009)*
Essen	579,972 *(2009)*
Bremen	548,695 *(2009)*

Location Germany occupies a central position in Western Europe bordering no less than six other Western European countries. The country's terrain ranges from the marshes of the Danish border in the north, to the Bavarian Alps in the south. The five eastern Länder, together with the eastern sector of Berlin, formed the German Democratic Republic until unification in 1990. The capital is Berlin.

Political structure The Federal Republic consists of 16 states, of which 11 are in western Germany and five in the east. Germany has an extensively devolved political structure. At the federal level the non-executive president appoints a Chancellor as leader. Members of Parliament are elected for four years. There are circumstances in which some candidates win so-called "overhang mandates", resulting in a larger parliament. The Federal Council is indirectly elected. The Council has 69 members representing the governments of the states. Each state has its own Parliament and Premier.

Last elections Elections to the Bundestag were held in September 2009. The Christian Democratic Union received 194 seats while the Christian Social Union of Bavaria took 45 seats. The Social Democrats won 142 seats and the Free Democratic Party gained 93 seats. The Left Party now holds 76 seats and the Alliance90/Greens have 68 seats, bringing the size of the 17th German Bundestag to 622 members. Presidential elections were held in May 2009. Kohler was re-elected with 50.9% of the vote, defeating three other candidates.

Economy Germany's economy struggled in the first half of this decade and even experienced a brief recession (the first decline since 1993). A recovery was driven by improvements in external competitiveness and gains in consumer and business confidence. However, growth fell sharply in 2008 when exports fell at an unprecedented pace. The economy entered a sharp recession in 2009. Several large corporate failures and the turbulence in the world's financial system have revealed glaring vulnerabilities in the German economy. Accelerated savings caused a fall in consumption in the fourth quarter of 2008 and business confidence deteriorated. With tighter credit conditions and drop in capacity utilisation, business investment has waned.

Main industries Agriculture makes up less than 1% of GDP. Farms are small (although larger in the east), and crops include wheat, barley, potatoes, apples and grapes for wine making. Germany's manufacturing sector is dominated by many large companies producing motor vehicles, precision engineering, brewing, chemicals, pharmaceuticals and heavy metal products. Automotive producers employ one in every seven workers but are shedding workers as their export markets contract. Their situation became grave in late 2008 as markets collapsed. Small and medium-sized companies are the heart of the economy but are credit-starved. The manufacturing work force declined by 2.3% in the 12 months through May 2009. Many firms are concerned over possible falls in domestic demand and the threat of higher energy prices. A failure to implement structural reforms has forced some firms to move abroad. Another problem is corporate tax reform which has been a stop-start process, leaving companies uncertain about future tax bills and benefits. Productivity growth in the service sector is nil. The financial sector faces tighter regulatory and supervisory rules in the future. A new law passed in August 2008 gives the government the ability to more tightly regulate investment vehicles such as hedge funds. Rescue operations were launched for several banks in 2009, costing an estimated 0.7% of GDP.

Energy Germany has 367 million barrels of proven oil reserves, most of it in northern and north-eastern Germany. Over one-half of all crude oil production comes from a single field. Germany is the fifth-largest consumer of oil in the world, with consumption reaching 2.7 million barrels per day. The country relies on imports to meet most of its energy needs. Germany is a world leader in developing renewable energy. In 2000, the government set a goal to double the proportion of renewable energy sources by 2010. By 2050, half of Germany's entire energy demand should be met by solar, wind, biomass, hydro, and geothermic sources, according the German government. The country also has 9.0 trillion cubic feet of proven natural gas reserves, the third largest in the EU, after the Netherlands and the UK. Germany is the EU's second largest consumer of natural gas after the UK, and consumption is expected to rise in the future.

Gibraltar

Capital city	Gibraltar
Capital population	29,257 *(2008)*
Population ('000)	29.25 *(2009)*
Urban population (%)	100 *(2009)*
Land area (sq km)	5
Languages	English
Religion	Mainly Roman Catholic
Currency	Gibraltar pound (Gib£)
Head of state	HM Queen Elizabeth II (1952)
Head of government	Peter Caruana (1996)
Ruling party	Gibraltar Social Democrats (GSD)

Main urban areas	Population *(Year)*
Gibraltar (capital)	29,257 *(2008)*

Location Located on the southern tip of Spain, Gibraltar faces the coast of North Africa across a narrow strip of water that controls western access to the Mediterranean Sea. Hence the immense strategic importance attached over the centuries to its ownership, both as a defensive position and as a centre for the trans-shipment of sea cargoes. The capital is Gibraltar.

Political structure Gibraltar, a British dependent territory, is technically ruled from London, though in practice most decisions are taken not by the UK-appointed governor, but by the locally elected chief minister and his cabinet. They are answerable to a House of Assembly (parliament) comprising 17 elected members, an independent Speaker, the Attorney-General and the Financial & Development Secretary. Spain controls the border, which was reopened in 1985.

Last elections Parliamentary elections were held in October 2007. The GSD received 10 seats while a coalition of the Socialist Labour Party and the Gibraltar Liberal Party won the remaining seven seats.

Economy Favourable shifts in the exchange rate between the British pound and the euro have brought in many more shoppers and consumers in the past couple of years. Financial services, low taxes and a niche in online gambling have transformed an economy that, a quarter of a century ago, was more than 60% dependent on the Ministry of Defence. Gibraltar, however, still has a narrowly-based economy which is driven mainly by tourism, financial services and shipping. Tourism contributes up to half of all economic activity in one form or another. Unemployment is only about 3%. Foreign investment in Gibraltar is actively promoted by the government, largely to create job opportunities. More than 8,000 companies are incorporated in Gibraltar and pay no tax on capital income. Tax concessions are also available to light manufacturers who intend to export from Gibraltar. Corporate tax rates are expected to fall in the future, attracting more

businesses to Gibraltar. Many businessmen believe that further accommodation with Spain is essential if the economy is to show further progress. This goal would receive a substantial boost if Gibraltar's status could one day be renegotiated to resemble that of Andorra.

Main industries The economy used to be substantially dominated by the British naval dockyard and military presence, but major cuts over the last 20 years have reduced the share of these expenditures to a small fraction of the local economy. In recent years, Gibraltar has seen significant structural change from a public to a private sector economy, but changes in government spending still have a major impact on the level of employment. In 2004, the European Commission ruled that companies in Gibraltar must pay the same rate of corporate taxation as in Britain. Impressive port facilities exist, so that shipping and tourism are the mainstays of the economy. The colony's proximity to the North African coast is only one reason for the 3,000-4,000 merchant vessels that dock every year. There are also numerous bunkering and support services. About eight million people visit Gibraltar in a typical year, many of them arriving via cruise liners. Spanish visitors often arrive for shopping or for short breaks, though others may be motivated more by tax evasion than duty-free shopping. A number of large betting and gaming companies have taking advantage of the country's low-tax regime and good telecommunications facilities. In recent years, Gibraltar has built up a respectable finance centre that now accounts for one-fifth of the economy. The government pins its hopes for the future on the financial services sector, which has been growing rapidly. Growth in the technology sector is also promising, with a number of large betting and gaming companies taking advantage of the low-tax regime and good telecommunications facilities.

Energy Gibraltar depends completely on imports for all its fuel needs – primarily from Spain. Thermal power stations provide all domestic electricity.

Greece

Capital city	Athens
Capital population	717,146 *(2009)*
Population ('000)	11,251.89 *(2009)*
Urban population (%)	62.74 *(2009)*
Land area (sq km)	131,985
Languages	Greek
Religion	Mainly Roman Catholic
Currency	Euro (€)
Head of state	President Karolos Papoulias (2005)
Head of government	Costas Karamanlis (2004)
Ruling party	The New Democracy Party (ND) leads the government.

Main urban areas	Population *(Year)*
Athens (capital)	717,146 *(2009)*
Thessaloniki	346,168 *(2009)*
Piraeus	170,040 *(2009)*
Patras	166,660 *(2009)*
Heraklion	143,606 *(2009)*
Peristeri	137,930 *(2009)*
Larissa	133,343 *(2009)*
Kallithea	106,409 *(2009)*
Kalamaria	95,760 *(2009)*
Nikaia	94,786 *(2009)*

Location Greece comprises the mainland and the archipelago, which lies in the Mediterranean between the Adriatic and the Aegean and includes the larger islands of Corfu and Crete to the southeast. The capital is Athens.

Political structure Greece's modern political system dates back to 1975. The country has a non-executive president elected by parliament for a five-year term. The president's main function is to guarantee its political system and supervise its proper functioning. The president appoints his own cabinet, and is answerable to a 300-member Parliament which is also elected for a five-year term. Members are elected for a four-year term by a system of reinforced proportional representation in 51 multi-seat constituencies and five single-seat constituencies.

Last elections Parliamentary elections were held in September 2007. New Democracy received 152 seats in the 300-seat parliament with 102 seats going to the Panhellenic Socialist Movement. The Communist Party gained 22 seats, the Coalition of the Radical Left won 14 seats and the Popular Orthodox Rally took 10 seats. Karamanlis, the leader of New Democracy, will retain his position as prime minister. In February 2005, parliament elected Karolos Papoulias as president.

Economy The Greek economy outperformed that of most other industrialised countries during most of this decade. Per capita income is now around 90% of the EU-15 average. Spending for the Athens Olympics was a major factor behind this strong performance but has now run its course. Grants from the EU also helped; structural aid has amounted to more than 1.5% of GDP in every year since 2001. Finally, economists calculate that Greece's ties with southeastern Europe provided a growth impetus throughout most of this decade. The pace of growth began to fall in the early months of 2008. Weaker private consumption and declining investment were the main reasons for the slowdown. The economy entered recession in 2009 – the first since 1993. In the long-term, population ageing threatens fiscal sustainability. On current estimates, pension and health-care costs will rise by more than in any other EU country between now and 2040, while high public debt and the weak budget position leave little room for fiscal manoeuvre.

Main industries Agriculture employs a quarter of the population but accounts for only a small portion of GDP. The main products are tree fruits, vegetables, olives, tobacco, sugar, rice and wheat. Nursery products, frozen fish, tree nuts and wood products are among the fastest growing industries in this sector. The country's main agricultural exports are fresh and processed fruits and vegetables, especially canned peaches and tomato products, olive oil, durum wheat and tobacco. The manufacturing sector has performed poorly in the past couple of years. Greek companies have substantially increased their investments in Bulgaria and Romania as a result of these countries' accession to the EU but many of these new ventures are in trouble. Industrial output has been steadily falling in 2009. Tourism employs a fifth of the work force. Tourist bookings reached a ten-year high in 2007, but growth slowed in 2008 and bookings are expected to fall by 15-20% in 2009. The growth of imports and transit trade with new EU members has prompted Athens to begin expanding the ports of Piraeus and Thessaloniki. Total investment will be about €759 million, much of it from Chinese firms. Funds from the EU will help upgrade the highway network. Greece maintains one of the largest commercial shipping fleets in the world but shipping income has fallen sharply in 2009. The banking industry had hoped to increase the share of its profits coming from outside Greece but financial turbulence and the global recession has undermined this goal. The percentage of non-performing loans is rising as the economy stalls. Deposit insurance has been increased and liquidity assistance has been offered by the government.

Energy Greece presently has oil reserves of just 10 million barrels and produces around 1,250 barrels per day. This makes the country highly reliant on imports. Oil's market share is slowly declining, as natural gas becomes more important in the Greek energy market.

Hungary

Capital city	Budapest
Capital population	1,703,938 *(2009)*
Population ('000)	10,019.75 *(2009)*
Urban population (%)	67.32 *(2009)*
Land area (sq km)	93,030
Languages	Magyar
Religion	Mainly Roman Catholic
Currency	Forint (HUF)
Head of state	László Sólyom (2005)
Head of government	Gordon Bajnai (2009)
Ruling party	The governing coalition between the Hungarian Socialist Party (MSzP) and the Alliance of Free Democrats (SzDSz) parted ways in April 2008. The MSzP now leads a minority government.

Main urban areas	Population *(Year)*
Budapest (capital)	1,703,938 *(2009)*
Debrecen	205,345 *(2009)*
Miskolc	169,706 *(2009)*
Szeged	168,003 *(2009)*
Pecs	156,702 *(2009)*
Gyor	129,184 *(2009)*
Nyíregyháza	117,044 *(2009)*
Kecskemet	110,939 *(2009)*
Szekesfehervar	101,851 *(2009)*
Szombathely	79,131 *(2009)*

Location Hungary has long-standing ties with Austria to the west. Bordering on Serbia, Croatia and Slovenia to the south, Romania and Ukraine to the east and the Slovak Republic to the north, it is an important gateway to western Europe. The capital is Budapest.

Political structure Hungary has a non-executive president and a prime minister who is elected by popular mandate for a term of five years. The National Assembly has 386 members, elected for a four-year term: 176 members in single-seat constituencies, 152 by proportional representation in multi-seat constituencies and 58 members elected to realise proportional representation. Since 1995, the country's Romany have had their own 53-seat parliament.

Last elections Parliamentary elections to the unicameral National Assembly were held in April 2006. The MSzP won 186 seats while their coalition partners, the SzDSz, took 18 seats. Another 6 seats were taken by joint candidates of the two parties. The Hungarian Citizens' Party (Fidesz) took 164 seats while the Hungarian Democratic Forum captured 11 seats. The Association for Somogy County won the remaining seat. In 2004, voters approved a controversial plan to extend citizenship to 2.5 million ethnic Hungarians living abroad. However, not enough voters turned out for the referendum to pass. In June 2005, parliament elected Sólyom as president. Bajnai replaced Ferenc Gyursany as prime minister in March 2009.

Economy Growth rates fell much more rapidly than expected in 2008 and private consumption contracted. The financial and manufacturing sectors have been especially hard hit. Reforms have been terribly slow and sometimes marred by political considerations. The result has been budget problems driven by populist spending on everything from family benefits to energy subsidies. Public debt is very high, meaning that Hungary's refinancing needs are substantial. Hungary's fiscal deficit soared to more than 9% of GDP in 2006, forcing sharp cuts in public spending. A host of different policies are now being implemented in an effort to rein in the budget deficit. The initiative comes at a particularly difficult time, however, in view of the country's worsening recession. The economy has gradually been shifting from low- to medium-skilled export products over the course of the decade. Exports, however, represent 80% of GDP meaning that Hungary is extremely vulnerable to the economic downturn in Western Europe.

Main industries Agricultural output is rising after a particularly poor performance in 2008. The government subsidises low-quality food products but has devoted little to modernisation. The wine industry, with the help of foreign investors, has made real progress and gained market share in Western Europe. Agricultural exports have been rising and presently amount to well over €3 billion. However, sectors such as vegetable and fruit production as well as pork have been negatively affected by competition from other EU member states. Industrial output began to decline in the fourth quarter of 2008 and the slide accelerated in the first four months of 2009. Layoffs are on the rise as construction and electronic manufacturers expect further cuts in output. More than 70% of the country's manufactured exports come from foreign-owned plants set up by IBM, Philips and others. All these companies have seen their exports fall sharply. In the automotive industry, major companies including Ford, General Motors, Audi, and Suzuki have established multi-million dollar plants but are struggling as the global downturn continues. About two-fifths of small-and medium-sized enterprises are reported to be unprofitable. The country's system of urban transport remains very rudimentary, hindering labour mobility and development of the retail sector. High levels of home ownership and regional disparities in purchasing power also discourage labour mobility. The bulk of the banking system is foreign-owned (85% by market share). Bank lending has virtually dried up and banks' profits are meagre. Bankruptcies and liquidations are on the rise, putting major parts of the banking system under strain. . Officials are trying to convert Hungary into a regional hub for transportation, informatics and finance. Services, including financial services, advertising and retailing, are all becoming more competitive and customer friendly.

Energy Hungary is the largest producer of crude oil in Central Europe, though still a small producer by international standards. Presently, the country is producing about 45,000 barrels per day (bbl/d). Most of this comes from small fields in amounts less than 2,000 bbl/d. Oil reserves are approximately 127 million barrels. Oil companies have increased domestic exploration, estimating that only 60% of the country has been thoroughly explored. The government intends to invest US$40-US$50 million annually on exploration activities. Hungarian natural gas production has been declining for many years, though domestic production still accounts for a significant share of consumption. Hungary has several Soviet-designed nuclear power plants, although the EU regards these as unsafe by Western standards. The government intends to liberalise the energy sector and adjust prices of electricity and natural gas prices to cost-recovery levels.

Iceland

Capital city	Reykjavik
Capital population	118,665 *(2009)*
Population ('000)	322.69 *(2009)*
Urban population (%)	92.28 *(2009)*
Land area (sq km)	102,820
Languages	Icelandic
Religion	Mainly Evangelical Lutheran Church (93%)
Currency	Icelandic kröna (ISK)
Head of state	Ólafur Ragnar Grímsson (1996)
Head of government	Johanna Sigurdardottir (2009)
Ruling party	The Social Democratic Alliance leads a coalition.

Main urban areas	Population *(Year)*
Reykjavik (capital)	118,665 *(2009)*

Location Located in the North Atlantic, Iceland is a large volcanic island and enjoys generally clear summers. Recurrent volcanic eruptions in the 13th-17th centuries almost depopulated the island, but they have not been serious in recent times. Rich fishing grounds and geothermal energy are important to the economy. The capital is Reykjavik.

Political structure The president is elected for a four-year term by the people. A cabinet is appointed by the 63-member parliament (Althing) elected for a four-year term by proportional representation.

Last elections Grímsson was re-elected as president in June 2004 with 86% of the vote. Parliamentary elections were held in April 2009. The Social Democratic Alliance won 20 seats while the Independence Party received 16 seats. The Left-Green Movement won 14 seats and the Progressive Party gained 9 seats. The Citizens' Movement took 4 seats. In January 2009, Geir Haarde resigned as prime minister for health reasons and Sigurdardottir was appointed. Presidential elections scheduled for June 2008 were cancelled after no one had registered by the 24th May deadline to challenge incumbent President Grimsson.

Economy Being one of Europe's most wealthy economies, Iceland's economy grew strongly for more than a decade but problems began to emerge in 2007 and worsened in 2008. In November 2008, Iceland became the first western European country to be rescued by the IMF since 1976 when it received a US$2.1 billion loan. Thousands of Icelanders lost their savings and jobs after the country's once-booming financial sector crumbled. Unemployment could reach double digits by 2010 and GDP will contract drastically. In the longer term, the government will face pressure to consider some form of linkage with the euro. This is particularly important for the tourist industry which has suffered from the relatively high level of the krona in recent years.

Main industries Rapid growth changed the structure of the economy. Before the latest boom, the fishing industry accounted for 17% of GDP but that share has now fallen to less than 13%. Fishing still accounts for more than 80% of export earnings. The agricultural sector (including fishing) presently accounts for around 19% of GDP. Sheep are reared in large numbers, but otherwise agricultural activity tends to be restrained by the poor weather conditions. Industry contributes 21% of GDP and is dominated by a few industries such as aluminium and computer software. The sector has been mainly driven by investments in aluminium-related projects. With the downturn, much of this investment has dried up. To finance the country's growing current account deficit, major banks borrowed aggressively abroad. This left stretched them far in excess of their depositor base. The increased debt level of the mining industry also contributed to the problem. The government was forced to seize control over the country's largest banks in October 2008.

Energy Iceland has vast geothermal potential in its volcanic rock structure, of which only a small part is currently exploited. With sufficient capital investment, it could easily become a major exporter of electricity.

Ireland

Capital city	Dublin
Capital population	513,022 *(2009)*
Population ('000)	4,447.69 *(2009)*
Urban population (%)	61.61 *(2009)*
Land area (sq km)	68,895
Languages	Irish, English
Religion	Catholic (93%); Church of Ireland (3%); Presbyterian (0.4%)
Currency	Euro (€)
Head of state	President Mary Patricia McAleese (1997)
Head of government	Brian Cowen (2008)
Ruling party	The government is formed by the Fianna Fáil (FF), the Green Party and the Progressive Democrats (PD).

Main urban areas	Population *(Year)*
Dublin (capital)	513,022 *(2009)*
Cork	116,490 *(2009)*
Galway	76,288 *(2009)*
Limerick	51,144 *(2009)*
Waterford	46,574 *(2009)*
Swords	37,545 *(2009)*
Dundalk	30,195 *(2009)*
Drogheda	29,036 *(2009)*
Bray	27,482 *(2009)*
Tralee	20,074 *(2009)*

Location The Republic of Ireland (Eire) comprises the greater part of an island off the western coast of Great Britain, the remaining northern part of the island forming part of the UK. With little mountainous terrain but considerable areas of hills and down, Ireland's mild climate contributes to good agricultural conditions. The capital is Dublin.

Political structure In September 2009, voters approved a referendum on the EU's Lisbon Treaty by a substantial margin. Ireland's president is elected for a seven-year term by universal suffrage, but most executive powers are exercised by a prime minister and cabinet appointed from among the National Parliament (Oireachtas). The House of Representatives (Dail Eireann), or Lower House, has 166 members elected by universal suffrage for five years, and the Senate (Seanad Eireann), or Upper House, has 60. Eleven senators are appointed by the prime minister while the remainder are elected by several different methods.

Last elections McAleese was re-elected as president in November 2004. Elections to the House of Representatives took place in May 2007. The conservative Fianna Fáil Party won 78 seats. The Christian-Democratic Fine Gael took 51 seats and the Labour Party received 20 seats. The remainder were scattered amongst smaller parties. Elections to the Senate were held in July 2007 when the Fianna Fáil won 27 seats and the Fine Gael won 15 seats. The remainder was spread among several smaller parties. Bertie Ahern resigned as prime minister in April 2008 and was replaced by Cowen.

Economy The economy performed better than any other OECD country in 2000-2007. Government spending rose steadily with a 40% increase in public sector employment. However, the economy entered a recession in 2008. After years of rising prices, a weakening property market and turbulence in international financial markets began to cause problems. The economy shrank by 3.0% in 2008 (the first contraction since 1983) and the downturn accelerated in 2009. The effects of the financial crisis and global slowdown are compounded by a 20% drop in construction activity. The number of new houses to be constructed in 2009 will be less than a quarter of that in 2006 while a lack of government funding slows public construction.

Main industries The structure of Ireland's economy is different from that of other EU countries. The industrial sector is much larger than in other member states. The construction industry is in the midst of a deep slump with housing construction falling by 35% in 2009. Growth in industry has also recorded a sharp fall. Several companies have closed their operations or moved elsewhere. The financial industry is in also in trouble. In late 2008, the government decided to ignore the complaints of other EU members and guaranteed the entire €440 billion in liabilities of its six domestic financial institutions. Agriculture has contracted in both relative and absolute terms in recent years. Farming, however, is still relatively more important than in other economies in Western Europe. Retail sales account for half of all personal consumption but are down by more than 7% in 2009. In the past, economic growth led to bottlenecks in infrastructure which prompted the government to launch an expensive, seven-year programme to improve facilities. Although the economy is slowing today, the government plans large-scale investment in infrastructure throughout the remainder of this decade.

Energy Ireland has large reserves of coal and peat, but its oil and gas requirements are met through imports. Some oil reserves have been located in the Irish Sea.

Italy

Capital city	Rome
Capital population	2,529,561 *(2009)*
Population ('000)	59,051.65 *(2009)*
Urban population (%)	68.07 *(2009)*
Land area (sq km)	301,245
Languages	Italian
Religion	Roman Catholic (90%)
Currency	Euro (€)
Head of state	President Giorgio Napolitano (2006)
Head of government	Silvio Berlusconi (2008)
Ruling party	The government is led by a centre-right coalition.

Main urban areas	Population *(Year)*
Rome (capital)	2,529,561 *(2009)*
Milano	1,331,555 *(2009)*
Napoli	961,908 *(2009)*
Torino	916,451 *(2009)*
Palermo	653,636 *(2009)*
Genova	622,236 *(2009)*
Bologna	372,262 *(2009)*
Firenze	371,498 *(2009)*
Bari	330,891 *(2009)*
Catania	295,503 *(2009)*

Location In the north, Italy meets with France, Switzerland, Austria and Slovenia. In the south, it divides into two peninsulas, the lower of which almost connects with the island of Sicily. The capital is Rome.

Political structure Italy has been a republic since 1946, when it abolished the monarchy. The president is elected by parliament and 58 regional representatives for a seven-year term and exercises only semi-executive functions. The prime minister is appointed by the president. The 630-member Chamber of Deputies (Lower House) is elected for five years by universal suffrage through a system of proportional representation, as are all but seven of the 315-member Senate.

Last elections Napolitano was elected president by Parliament in May 2006. Parliamentary elections were held in April 2008. Berlusconi's centre-right coalition claimed a majority in both houses. In the Chamber of Deputies (lower house) the coalition won 344 seats. These consist of the People of Freedom Party (275 seats), the Northern League (61) and Movement for Autonomy (8). The centre-left coalition has 246 seats of which the Democratic Party has 217 and Italy of Values has 29. Other opposition parties include the Catholic Union of Christian and Centre Democrats (UDC) which took 36 seats. The remainder were scattered among several smaller parties. In the Senate, the centre-right coalition holds 171 seats. Included are the People of Freedom (144 seats), the Northern League (25 seats) and the MPA (2 seats). The centre-left coalition has 133 seats in the Senate made up of the Democratic Party (119 seats) and Italy of Values (14 seats). The Catholic UDC received 3 seats and the remainder were scattered among smaller parties and independents. In June 2009, three referendums were held with the intention of reforming electoral law. None of them reached the necessary quota of 50% voters. If they had been approved, they would have had the effect of turning Italian politics into something akin to a two-party system.

Economy Italy's economic performance has lagged behind that of other EU members for most of this decade. There has also been a decline in potential economic growth while costs are rising as productivity growth stagnates. These problems are rooted in country-specific factors such as the vulnerability of small, family-owned Italian firms and their patterns of product specialisation. Italy also faces increasing competition (in both domestic and international markets) from eastern European and Asian suppliers. The country's share of world exports (in volume terms) has fallen steadily. Hardest hit have been traditional exporters such as textiles, leather and apparel. Growth of overseas demand in these markets has been weak but the gains recorded by Italy's exports have been even lower.

Main industries The agricultural sector is small but well diversified, producing soft fruits and vegetables, as well as wheat, olives and citrus products for export. The most fertile areas are in the north. In the south, agriculture is mainly for subsistence purposes. More than 70% of the country's farms are small and inefficient. Agriculture accounts for 2.1% of GDP. Manufacturing output was contracting during 2008 and the downturn continued in 2009. There are relatively few large private companies, but those that exist play a major role in the economy. Examples are Fiat, which is controlled by the Agnelli family; Pirelli, controlled by the Pirelli family; and Fininvest, controlled by the former Prime Minister, Berlusconi. More than 90% of the industrial sector is made up of small and medium-sized firms. They are mainly found in so-called "industrial districts", mostly in the north-east and the centre of the country. In order to compete, these companies require a low-cost base that has proved difficult to maintain. Problems are compounded by a failure to invest in product innovation and research, leaving many small firms exposed to competition from China, Indonesia, Turkey and Eastern Europe. The service industry is also contracting. Retail sales have been falling for more than two years. Italy's tourist industry remains important but has lost much ground relative to other destinations. The global recession adds to the industry's problems. Thirty years ago, the country was the world's leading tourist destination but it presently ranks fifth.

Energy Italy has proven crude oil reserves of 600 million barrels, the third largest in the EU. The country produces an estimated 151,000 barrels of oil per day, sufficient to meet less than 10% of consumption. Italy is Europe's third largest oil importer. There are three main oil-producing fields in southern Italy and other fields located offshore in the Adriatic and in Sicily (both onshore and offshore). Within the EU, Italy has the greatest crude oil refining capacity, at 2.3 million barrels per day. There are large oil refining facilities along the Mediterranean coast and on Mediterranean islands, capable of processing a wide range of crude oils from North Africa and the Persian Gulf.

Latvia

Capital city	Riga
Capital population	710,520 *(2009)*
Population ('000)	2,253.46 *(2009)*
Urban population (%)	68.41 *(2009)*
Land area (sq km)	64,589
Languages	Latvian
Religion	Mainly Christian
Currency	Latvian lats (LVL)
Head of state	President Valdis Zatlers (2007)
Head of government	Valdis Dombrovskis(2009)
Ruling party	The New Era Party leads a coalition of five parties.

Main urban areas	Population *(Year)*
Riga (capital)	710,520 *(2009)*
Daugavpils	111,997 *(2009)*
Liepaja	79,548 *(2009)*
Jelgava	59,853 *(2009)*
Jurmala	54,166 *(2009)*
Ventspils	41,550 *(2009)*
Rezekne	38,098 *(2009)*
Valmiera	27,304 *(2009)*
Jekabpils	26,791 *(2009)*
Ogre	25,469 *(2009)*

Location Latvia, the second smallest of the three Baltic republics, lies between Lithuania in the south and Estonia in the north, with Russia dominating its eastern border, and with the Baltic Sea and the Gulf of Finland extending to the west. The land is mainly flat and low-lying, although chains of hills run through it. The capital is Riga.

Political structure Latvia's independence was officially recognised in September 1991, some six months after its original declaration. The country has a semi-executive president, who is the de facto Chairman of the Supreme Council (or Parliament). He is elected for a four-year term by the parliament. The Diet has 100 members, elected for a four-year term by proportional representation.

Last elections Parliamentary elections were held in October 2006. The New Era, a centrist party, obtained 18 seats, the Union of Greens and Farmers also won 18 seats, the Harmony Centre Party took 17 seats and

the Peoples' Party won 23 seats. Other representation was scattered among smaller parties. Valdis Zatlers won the May 2007 presidential election, defeating Aivars Endzins with 58% of the votes versus 39%. Ivars Godmanis resigned as prime minister in February 2009 and was replace by Dombrovskis.

Economy Throughout most of this decade, the Latvian economy has performed better than that of other accession countries. Real per capita income (in purchasing power parities) rose by 16% between 1995 and 2007. The gains were driven by strong growth in productivity, supplemented by rapid investment and solid growth in employment. However, per capita income in terms of purchasing power parities remains the lowest in the EU. Government data shows the economy contracted during 2008 while private consumption fell by more than 5%. The government was also forced to abandon its goal of adopting the euro for the time being. The target for euro adoption has been pushed back to 2011-2013. Unemployment rates in some eastern districts are more than five times higher than in Riga. The standard of living around Riga is high but in some rural inland areas per capita incomes are much lower. Roughly 69% of GDP is produced in the private sector today, up from 62% in 1997. In terms of employment, the percentage is slightly higher.

Main industries Agriculture accounts for only a tiny portion of GDP but 15% of total employment. Agriculture is centred on the cultivation of crops such as potatoes, cereals and fodder crops, along with dairy farming. The share of manufacturing makes up 12.8% of GDP, down from 30.9% in 1990. The bulk of industrial activity is in heavy industries such as chemicals and petrochemicals, metalworking and machine building. Growth of output has contracted markedly owing to weaker export demand. In the financial sector, real estate accounts for nearly half of total loans. This leaves banks dangerously exposed to the real property market. Furthermore, with half of all loans extended in foreign currency, banks face large indirect exchange rate risks. The percentage of non-performing loans has increased more than fourfold since mid 2008. The European Bank for Reconstruction and Development has bailed out one Latvian bank. The government has strengthened supervision of banks and implemented a other number of measures to improve the health of the banking system. Latvia has a good resource base and transport system but investors are hesitant as a result of the global slowdown. In the longer term, the government believes that banking, information technology, tourism and other services will provide plenty of opportunities for growth.

Energy Latvia produces no oil domestically and is entirely dependent on imports. Until 2002, Latvia's port, Ventspils, was Russia's primary northern crude oil export terminal. Russia stopped deliveries following the completion of its own port of Primorsk. Having been left starved of oil, authorities at Ventspils undertook an effort to increase shipments of crude oil and petroleum products delivered by rail. Ventspils has, however, lost significant market share, and has exposed its balance sheet to greater risk as petroleum products and rail-borne crude oil are more expensive than crude delivered via pipeline, and carry slimmer profits. The future of the port is uncertain.

Liechtenstein

Capital city	Vaduz
Capital population	5,104 *(2008)*
Population ('000)	35.79 *(2009)*
Urban population (%)	14.42 *(2009)*
Land area (sq km)	160
Languages	German
Religion	Mainly Roman Catholic
Currency	Swiss franc (CHF)
Head of state	Prince Hans-Adam II (1989)
Head of government	Klaus Tschütscher (Prime Minister Designate 2009)
Ruling party	The government is formed by the Patriotic Union Party.

Main urban areas	Population *(Year)*
Schaan	5,691 *(2008)*
Vaduz (capital)	5,104 *(2008)*

Location   Liechtenstein lies in Alpine territory to the east of Switzerland, bordering on the Austrian province of Vorarlberg. Thanks in part to an excellent communications system, the country's prominence is mainly to due to its activities as a tax haven and banking centre. Swiss authorities represent the country abroad. The capital is Vaduz.

Political structure   Liechtenstein is a constitutional monarchy in which executive power is exercised by the prime minister – though the constitution gives the monarchy considerable powers. The Landtag (Parliament) is elected by popular mandate for a four-year term and has 25 members. Only a few of the residents are eligible to vote, since the great majority of the population comprises foreign nationals. Prince Hans-Adam persuaded the conservative legislators to join the European Economic Area in 1995.

Last elections   Elections to the 25-seat Landtag were held in February 2009. The Patriotic Union won 13 seats, the Progressive Citizens' Party took 11 seats and the Free Voters' List received 1 seat. In March 2003, voters approved a referendum on constitutional changes that gives the Prince the right to sack the government, veto legislation and nominate judges.

Economy   Growth has not been impressive in recent years but it is more than 20 years since there was a recession in Liechtenstein. GDP per head is very high, while inflation is low and unemployment remains low at 2.6%. The country has substantial financial reserves and there is no national debt. Despite its small size and limited natural resources, Liechtenstein has developed into a prosperous, free-enterprise economy with a vital financial service sector and living standards on a par with the urban areas of its larger European neighbours. Low business taxes – the maximum tax rate is 18% – and easy incorporation rules have induced at least 75,000 holding or so-called "letter box companies" to establish nominal offices in Liechtenstein, providing 30% of state revenues. Altogether, Liechtenstein has around twice as many registered companies as inhabitants. Per capita exports are roughly four times greater than Switzerland's. The country participates in a customs union with Switzerland and is a member of the European Economic Area. Liechtenstein's main challenge is to balance the need for integration in a European framework with the implementation of steps to safeguard its independence.

Main industries   Liechtenstein's principal activity is the provision of financial services. The financial sector accounts for 30% of GDP, but only about 14% of employment. Services offered include, in particular, private asset management, international asset structuring, investment funds and insurance solutions. Approximately 90% of Liechtenstein's financial services business is provided to non-residents. The country is under pressure to agree to EU rules on interest payments taxation. Industry is limited in scale but of a specialist nature and the largest source of employment in the country. The sector accounts for about 47% of GDP. Industry is heavily export oriented. The most important activities are mechanical engineering, plant construction, manufacturing of precision instruments, dental technology and food-processing. Many firms operate in highly specialised market niches. The emphasis is less on the production of mass and inexpensive goods, and more on the development of high quality, high-tech products. The average business in Liechtenstein has less than ten employees. Liechtenstein is also one of the world's biggest producers of false teeth. Farming is important despite the relative lack of available land, with wheat, barley, corn, potatoes, livestock and dairy products being grown mainly on small plots of land. The labour force numbers about 31,000, of which 19,000 are foreigners. Most of these workers commute from Austria, Germany or Switzerland on a daily basis. In addition to feed production for animal husbandry, the cultivation of vegetables has gained importance in recent years.

Energy   Liechtenstein imports more than 90% of its energy requirements.

Lithuania

Capital city	Vilnius
Capital population	545,518 *(2009)*
Population ('000)	3,347.94 *(2009)*
Urban population (%)	67.31 *(2009)*
Land area (sq km)	65,300
Languages	Lithuanian
Religion	Mainly Roman Catholic
Currency	Lithuanian litas (LTL)
Head of state	President Dalia Grybauskaite (2009)
Head of government	Andrius Kubilius (2008)
Ruling party	The Homeland Union leads a coalition.

Main urban areas	Population *(Year)*
Vilnius (capital)	545,518 *(2009)*
Kaunas	353,654 *(2009)*
Klaipeda	183,703 *(2009)*
Siauliai	126,326 *(2009)*
Panevezys	113,075 *(2009)*
Alytus	67,960 *(2009)*
Marijampole	46,880 *(2009)*
Mazeikiai	40,390 *(2009)*
Jonava	34,381 *(2009)*
Utena	32,463 *(2009)*

Location   Lithuania, the most southerly of the three Baltic republics, lies on the Baltic coast with Latvia to its north, Poland to the south, and Belarus to the east. There is also a small Russian enclave on the Baltic coast, around Zelenogradsk. The capital is Vilnius.

Political structure   The country has an executive president who is elected directly for a five-year term and appoints the prime minister. The 141-seat Seimas (parliament) has 71 members elected in single-seat constituencies and 70 members elected by proportional representation. All members serve a four-year term.

Last elections   In presidential elections in May 2009, Grybauskaite, an independent, was elected with 68% of the vote. Parliamentary elections were held in October 2008. The Homeland Union won 45 seats, the Social Democratic Party took 25 seats, the National Resurrection Party gained 16 seats, the Order and Justice Party received 15 seats, the Liberals' Movement of the Republic of Lithuania won 11 seats, the Coalition Labour Party took 10 seats and the Liberal and Centre Union captured 8 seats. The remainder were divided among several smaller parties. Parliament elected Kubilius as prime minister in November 2008.

Economy   The fiscal deficit widened substantially during the present decade, driven by spending related to EU membership. The country's direction of trade has shifted drastically away from the market of the Commonwealth of Independent States towards the EU and North America but foreign demand is contracting as the global economy has weakened. The country enjoyed strong growth over the past decade but entered a severe recession in 2009. Capital inflows dried up in 2008 and were reversed in 2009. The potential for sustained economic growth exists if macroeconomic policies and structural reforms can be continued but these moves are unlikely so long as the economy is in recession. In the longer term, problems such as skills mismatches, a lack of labour mobility and insufficient job creation in the private sector limit productivity gains and slow the growth of domestic demand.

Main industries   Lithuania inherited the disproportionate weight of several enormous Soviet-era industrial projects. These included the Ignalina nuclear power complex and the Mazeikiu Nafta oil refinery, both geared to the needs of the integrated Soviet economy. The EU has spent millions of euros upgrading Ignalina, which generates four-fifths of the country's electricity, but the returns from these investments have been marginal. Now, the EU must spend more to close it. The agricultural sector accounts for only a small portion of GDP. Meat, dairy and fish products are the major farm exports. EU funds are expected to provide resources to help restructure the agricultural sector. Traditional Lithuanian exporters of textiles, furniture and foodstuffs made a rapid transition to Western markets but exports plummeted during 2009 and no recovery is expected in the medium term. Other important manufacturing industries are machine-building and metal-working which concentrate on the production of agricultural machinery, food processing equipment, shipbuilding and maintenance equipment. In the financial sector, banks are short of funding and the supply of credit has rapidly contracted. Non-performing loans reached 8.7% of the total during 2009 – more than double the percentage in the previous year. The government has increased deposit insurance in an effort to stabilise the banking system.

Energy Lithuania has 12 million barrels of proven reserves and produces about 9,000 barrels per day. Several onshore drilling projects are under way in western Lithuania. Russia is the main supplier of crude oil. The country recently completed a US$120 million upgrade of the port at Klaipeda, expanding petroleum product export capacity to 160,000 bbl/d. Lithuania's 263,000-bbl/d Mazeikiai refinery is the only refinery in the Baltic region, and the country's largest revenue generator.

Luxembourg

Capital city	Luxembourg-Ville
Capital population	88,586 *(2009)*
Population ('000)	486.18 *(2009)*
Urban population (%)	82.32 *(2009)*
Land area (sq km)	2,585
Languages	French (official); Letzeburgesch is the local French dialect, and German is also widely spoken as a first language
Religion	Mainly Roman Catholic (95%)
Currency	Euro (€)
Head of state	Grand Duke Henri (2000)
Head of government	Jean-Claude Juncker (1995)
Ruling party	The government is formed by the Christian Social Peoples' Party (CSV) and the Democratic Party (DP).

Main urban areas	Population *(Year)*
Luxembourg-Ville (capital)	88,586 *(2009)*

Location The Duchy of Luxembourg is situated in northwestern Europe, on the coalfields which extend from Lille in northern France through Belgium and into the Ruhr valley. With Germany to its east, Belgium to the northwest and France to the south, its excellent communications have helped to make it one of the most important trade and transport centres in the EU. Its climate is temperate, with generally mild winters. The capital is Luxembourg-Ville.

Political structure As a constitutional monarchy, Luxembourg vests all legislative authority in the unicameral Chamber of Deputies and in the cabinet. The Chamber of Deputies has 60 seats and its members are elected by popular mandate for a term of five years.

Last elections Elections to the Chamber of Deputies were held in June 2009. The CSV received 26 seats, the Socialist Workers' Party took 13 seats and the DP won 9 seats. Minor parties, including the Green Alternative, received the remaining seats. Juncker was re-elected as prime minister. In July 2005, the country voted in favour of the EU constitution with 56.5% of the votes. The vote went ahead despite rejections in France and the Netherlands.

Economy Luxembourg's economy grew steadily between 2004 and mid 2008 with impressive gains in employment. External demand for financial services strengthened, underpinning a large increase in the net exports' contribution to growth. Growth came to an abrupt halt in the second half of 2008, as the global financial crisis took its toll. Relatively generous wage settlements and falling productivity have led to a significant increase in labour costs that reduced corporate profitability and competitiveness. Upward pressures on the general government deficit persist. Luxembourg is in the unique position of being able to draw on a reservoir of well-educated labour from neighbouring regions in Germany, France and Belgium. As a consequence, the country's pace of growth can change for prolonged periods of time without triggering wage and price pressures.

Main industries The agricultural sector is very small, accounting for just 1% of GDP. However, production is adequate to allow for self-sufficiency in food products, mainly wheat, potatoes and other

vegetables. The tourist sector attracts about one million visitors per year. The country refrains from encouraging mass tourism but earns substantial income from the visitors it receives. The industrial sector, initially dominated by steel, has become increasingly diversified to include chemicals, rubber and other products. Several multinationals including Goodyear, Dupont and Delphi Automotive Systems maintain manufacturing operations and distribution centres in the country. Manufacturing output began to contract in late 2008 and the decline continued through 2009. The service sector is the biggest part of the economy, accounting for 65% of GDP. Services are led by the country's financial institutions. The financial sector, which itself accounts for about 28% of GDP, consists mostly of more than 150 foreign-owned subsidiary banks. Included is Europe's largest investment fund industry and the second largest money market industry. The financial industry, however, is seriously exposed to the global turmoil in international financial markets.

Energy Luxembourg has large coal stocks, but it relies on oil and gas imports from abroad for the majority of its energy needs.

Macedonia

Capital city	Skopje
Capital population	485,710 *(2009)*
Population ('000)	2,040.91 *(2009)*
Urban population (%)	71.63 *(2009)*
Land area (sq km)	25,713
Languages	Macedonian
Religion	Mainly Christian
Currency	Denar (MKD)
Head of state	Gjorge Ivanov (2009) - President Elect
Head of government	Nikola Gruevski (2006)
Ruling party	The Coalition for a Better Macedonia (VMRO-DPMNE) leads the government.

Main urban areas	Population *(Year)*
Skopje (capital)	485,710 *(2009)*
Kumanovo	82,844 *(2009)*
Bitola	81,205 *(2009)*
Prilep	72,730 *(2009)*
Tetovo	57,967 *(2009)*
Veles	48,420 *(2009)*
Gostivar	46,507 *(2009)*
Stip	44,132 *(2009)*
Ohrid	43,829 *(2009)*
Strumica	36,610 *(2009)*

Location Macedonia is south of Serbia and borders Bulgaria in the east, Albania in the west and Greece to the south. The geography is mainly mountainous with a river valley running north to south through the centre of the country. The capital is Skopje.

Political structure The country has a non-executive president and an elected cabinet that answers to a unicameral parliament. The president is elected for a five-year term by popular vote. Parliament has 120 members elected for four-year terms by proportional representation.

Last elections Presidential elections were called in April 2009. Ivanov was elected president, receiving 63% of the vote. His main rival was Ljubomir Frckoski who took 37% of the vote. Early parliamentary elections were held in June 2008. The VMRO-DPMNE won 63 seats, the Coalition for a Better Europe took 27 seats and the Democratic Union for Integration secured 18 seats. Minor parties and Albanians representatives took the remainder.

Economy Driven by domestic demand, remittances and higher levels of investment, the economy grew steadily between 2004 and 2008. Nonetheless, compared with other countries in the region, Macedonia's economic performance was tepid. The pace of growth declined sharply in 2009 with negative implication s for the incidence of poverty and standards of living. Weaker export demand and tighter conditions on foreign lending were the main culprits. The government has made progress in macroeconomic management, but these improvements have been offset by disappointments in the area of structural reforms. Ambitious programmes to improve roads, power, water and other infrastructure (mainly through internationally-funded projects) could lay the basis for more sustainable growth in the future. Inflation has been rising but wage hikes have prevented a drop in consumer income.

Main industries Agriculture accounts for about 11% of GDP. Macedonia's 180,000 private farmers produce about three-quarters of agricultural output on fragmented holdings with an average size of only 2.8 hectares. Important agricultural products include wheat, corn, maize, barley, tobacco, fruits and vegetables. Dairy farming is also significant. Farming is expected to grow in importance as the transition to a market economy gains momentum. Growth suffered in 2007 as a result of droughts. Industry makes up 28% of GDP. Industrial output fell by 10.8% in the first quarter of 2009 compared with the same period in 2008. The deterioration is mainly due to falling exports. The government plans to increase spending on infrastructure to improve roads, electricity and irrigation networks. Rail transport was privatised in 2008.

Energy Macedonia has only small amounts of oil and natural gas. The country experiences perennial fuel shortages. In 2008, large electricity users will be required to make their purchases at market prices thus eliminating the need for government subsidy.

Malta

Capital city	Valletta
Capital population	6,319 *(2008)*
Population ('000)	408.71 *(2009)*
Urban population (%)	94.49 *(2009)*
Land area (sq km)	316
Languages	Maltese, English
Religion	Roman Catholic
Currency	Euro (€)
Head of state	Eddie Fenech Adami (2004)
Head of government	Lawrence Gonzi (2004)
Ruling party	Nationalist Party (PN)

Main urban areas	Population *(Year)*
Birkirkara	22,241 *(2008)*
Valletta (capital)	6,319 *(2008)*

Location Malta lies in the southern half of the central Mediterranean, some 100km south of Sicily. Its close proximity to North Africa (Algeria, Tunisia and Libya) has left its mark on the country's character, as has its traditional activity in the world of shipping. The climate is warm and generally dry. The capital is Valletta.

Political structure Malta, an independent member of the Commonwealth, has a House of Representatives whose minimum 65 members are elected for a five-year term through the Single Transferable Vote (STV) system of proportional representation. Additional seats are given to the party with the largest popular vote to ensure a legislative majority. The House in turn appoints the president for five years, and he then appoints the prime minister and his cabinet.

Last elections In parliamentary elections held in March 2008, the Nationalist Party narrowly won a majority of votes – though not of seats – and accordingly was granted four extra seats in parliament, retaining its majority in the House of Representatives with 35 seats. The Labour Party holds the other 34 seats.

Economy Malta's economy has been growing slowly throughout most of this decade. However, the pace began to pick up in the second half of this decade as a result of a boom in public investment financed mainly by EU grants. The economy has enjoyed productivity gains, a rise in foreign investment and some measure of export diversification. Domestically, low rates of employment and a lack of skills have held back output and restricted employment growth. Malta's main hopes for a healthier economy are strong growth in Western Europe (which boosts tourism) and realisation of its goal of converting the island into a centre for trans-shipment throughout the Mediterranean.

Main industries The Maltese economy is primarily based on services, which accounts for almost 70% of GDP. Manufacturing makes up another quarter, while agriculture accounts for less than 5% of GDP. The semi-conductor industry is the most important part of manufacturing, typically accounting for about three-quarters of the

sector's exports. Exports of semi-conductors should rise in 2008 while some expansion of the pharmaceutical industry is planned. The island has lost much of its textile industry to Asia but other manufacturers are moving up-market. The production and export of high-quality wooden furniture, for example, is thriving. The country's main earner of foreign exchange is tourism. In most years the sector accounts for 20-30% of GDP. About one million people visit the island each year and an estimated 35,000 people – one-tenth of the island's total population – are directly or indirectly employed in tourism. The entry of now low-cost airlines is helping to boost tourism. Agriculture is the second most important foreign exchange earner with exports of fruits, vegetables, wheat, grapes and horticultural products (especially cut flowers). Malta has high hopes for its financial sector. Authorities hope to attract more international business and have offered tax relief for foreign investors. By 2008, more than 150 hedge funds had located on the island (up from none in 2000). With this success comes more pressure to combat money laundering and eliminate the financing of terrorism.

Energy Malta has no domestic energy sources and relies entirely on imports for its fuel requirements.

Moldova

Capital city	Kishinev
Capital population	630,260 *(2008)*
Population ('000)	3,603.51 *(2009)*
Urban population (%)	41.43 *(2009)*
Land area (sq km)	33,700
Languages	Romanian
Religion	Mainly Christian (Eastern Orthodox, Russian Orthodox)
Currency	Moldovan Lei (MDL)
Head of state	President Vladimir Voronin (2001)
Head of government	Zinaida Greceanîi (2008)
Ruling party	Under negotiation

Main urban areas	Population *(Year)*
Kishinev (capital)	630,260 *(2008)*
Tiraspol	155,000 *(2008)*
Balti	122,210 *(2008)*
Tighina	95,000 *(2008)*

Location Located in the western part of the former Soviet Union, Moldova is sandwiched between Romania and Ukraine. It includes a substantial part of the territory to the east of the Pruth River, once known as Bessarabia, and also a predominantly Russian area to the east. The climate is warm and pleasant, and agriculture flourishes. The capital is Chisinau.

Political structure Moldova comprises the bulk of the former Moldavian SSR within the former Soviet Union. The president is elected by parliament for a four-year term. Parliament has 101 members, elected for four-year terms by proportional representation. At least 50% of registered voters must participate in the election for the poll to be deemed valid.

Last elections Parliamentary elections were held in July 2009, just three months after the last election. The Communist Party took 48 seats while the Liberal Party won 15 seats and the Liberal Democratic Party gained 17 seats. The Party Alliance Our Moldova took the remaining 8 seats. Greceanîi was approved as prime minister in March 2008 with 56 votes out of the 101-seat parliament, and is the country's first female prime minister.

Economy Moldova has become the poorest country in Europe (replacing Albania for that dubious distinction). In recent years, the economy has been growing but disputes with Moscow have slowed progress. Growth has been driven by consumer spending, which in turn has been supported by gains in real wages and workers' remittances. Remittances have traditionally been several times greater than FDI, are among the highest of any country in central Europe. Private sector investment has risen but remains too low to support strong medium-term growth. As the Russian economy slows, Moldova's exports and remittances are falling rapidly. Moldovans continue to emigrate at a rapid pace. The government estimates that more than

500,000 have left the country to work abroad, either in Western Europe or Russia.

Main industries The economy depends heavily on agriculture. Crops include fruits, vegetables, wine and tobacco. Farm output is rising in 2009. Half the country's population depends on subsistence farming. The agricultural sector is still largely in government hands. Wine exports are recovering after a dispute with Moscow resulted in a temporary embargo by Russia. Light industry consists mainly of textiles and consumer goods. Low labour costs give these firms a competitive advantage. In addition, there is a modest chemical industry. There is some evidence of a shift of resources and employment into manufacturing (mainly textiles) where low labour costs offer a competitive advantage.

Energy Moldova's reserves are estimated at just 15 million barrels. It has no natural gas resources, and is entirely dependent on Russia to meet its consumption. In January 2006, Russia's Gazprom stopped natural gas supplies due to a lack of agreement over prices. An agreement was later reached whereby Moldova would pay US$170 per thousand cubic metres with the price rising to near-European levels over the next five years.

Monaco

Capital city	Monaco-Ville
Capital population	975 *(2008)*
Population ('000)	32.93 *(2009)*
Urban population (%)	100 *(2009)*
Land area (sq km)	2
Languages	French
Religion	Mainly Roman Catholic (90%)
Currency	Euro (€)
Head of state	HSH Prince Albert II (2005)
Head of government	Jean-Paul Proust (2005)
Ruling party	Union for Monaco (UPM)

Main urban areas	Population *(Year)*
Monte-Carlo	14,586 *(2008)*
Monaco-Ville (capital)	975 *(2008)*

Location Monaco, one of the smallest states in Europe, is a Mediterranean principality that is surrounded on all its land borders by France, though the Italian coastline is within easy reach. The country is entirely urban, having no undeveloped land whatever, apart from parks and gardens. The capital is Monte Carlo.

Political structure The Principality of Monaco is a hereditary monarchy, which has enjoyed French protection since 1861. Legislative power is vested jointly in the Prince and in the 24-member unicameral National Council, which is elected for a five-year term by universal suffrage. Executive power is exercised by the Prince in collaboration with a four-member Council of Government. The judicial code of France applies. Prince Rainier III died in April 2005. He was automatically succeeded by Albert in accordance with long-standing tradition.

Last elections National Council elections took place in February 2008. The distribution of seats remained unchanged from the previous election. The UPM won 21 seats and the National and Democratic Union, also known as the Rally for Monaco, took three seats. Although the principality has 30,000 residents, only the 5,000 Monegasques are eligible to vote.

Economy In an area of less than 200 hectares Monaco manages to generate billions of dollars in business. Growth is expected to slow in 2009 as the effects of the global recession cut into the profits of Monaco's financial sector. Unemployment is estimated to be around 3%. Plans to develop a huge artificial peninsular have been scrapped in part owing to the global recession. Unemployment is estimated to be around 3%. The principality's special protected status, under the control of France, gives it a high degree of security. Authorities are reluctant to admit it, but one of the reasons for the principality's success is its privileged fiscal status. Residents pay no personal income tax. Nor are they subject to a capital gains tax when they sell assets such as shares or property. In theory, corporate profits are taxed at the same rate as in France, but in practice professional firms pay no taxes.

Nor do local firms that conduct 75% of their operations within the principality. Some Monaco-based companies conduct business between themselves, in order to raise the proportion of activity in their country and therefore obtain eligibility for tax exemption.

Main industries The government has presided over a successful transformation of Monaco's economy into services and small, non-polluting industries producing high value products. The country has no income tax, low business taxes and thrives as a tax haven both for individuals who have established residence and for foreign companies that have set up businesses and offices. More than half of Monaco's annual revenue is generated from VAT levied on hotels, banks and the industrial sector. Industry employs about a quarter of the work force. Producers of chemicals, pharmaceuticals and cosmetics are prominent. The state retains monopolies in a number of sectors, including tobacco, the telephone network and the postal service. Another quarter of all revenue is derived from tourism. Approximately 40% of all tourism is business related. Tourism revenues are expected to decline slightly in 2009. Monaco is also a popular location for international companies that employ close to 20% of the workforce. The principality has invested heavily in telecommunications in an effort to carve out a role as a carrier of transit traffic. Monaco also plays host to over 40 financial institutions. The financial industry employs almost a quarter of the work force.

Energy The country depends on imports for all its energy needs.

Montenegro

Capital city	Podgorica
Capital population	145,192 *(2009)*
Population ('000)	628.02 *(2009)*
Urban population (%)	59.85 *(2009)*
Land area (sq km)	13,812
Languages	French
Religion	Mainly Roman Catholic (90%)
Currency	Euro (€)
Head of state	Filip Vujanovic (2002)
Head of government	Milo Djukanovic (2008)
Ruling party	The government is led by the Coalition for a European Montenegro.

Main urban areas	Population *(Year)*
Podgorica (capital)	145,192 *(2009)*
Niksic	58,712 *(2009)*
Pljevlja	21,354 *(2009)*
Bijelo Polje	15,357 *(2009)*
Bar	15,112 *(2009)*
Cetinje	14,569 *(2009)*
Herceg Novi	13,361 *(2009)*
Budva	13,093 *(2009)*
Berane	11,498 *(2009)*
Ulcinj	11,056 *(2009)*

Location In addition to its shared border with Serbia, Montenegro borders on Bosnia-Herzegovina to the north and Albania to the south. Podgorica is the capital of Montenegro.

Political structure The constitution was ratified and adopted in October 2007. Montenegro's Assembly of the Republic has 82 members who serve four-year terms. The president of Montenegro is elected for a period of five years. Montenegro voted for independence from Serbia by a narrow margin in 2006.

Last elections Presidential elections were held in April 2008. Filip Vujanovic was returned to office with 52% of the vote. Parliamentary elections were held in March 2009. The Coalition for European Montenegro won 47 seats, the Socialist Peoples' Party took 15 seats, the New Serb Democracy received 8 seats and the Movement for Changes won 5 seats. The remaining seats went to several minor parties. Željko Šturanovic resigned as prime minister due to health reasons in January 2008. He was replaced by Milo Djukanovic, who had previously served as prime minister.

Economy Montenegro's economy grew steadily between 2003 and 2008 and inflation slowed after adoption of the euro. Demand was supported by large increases in credit. Employment and wages rose and unemployment fell sharply from 20% in 2005 to less than 11% at the end of 2008. The economy slipped into recession in 2009 however with property prices falling by more than 50%. The country experienced a property boom in 2006 and 2007 with wealthy Russians and Europeans buying property along the coast. In 2008, foreign investment per capita was the highest of any European country.

Main industries Agriculture is the largest sector, with fruits, vegetables and tobacco being of particular importance. The most dynamic industries are machinery and chemicals. Aluminium processing is the dominant industry, accounting for 40% of GDP. Aluminium prices fell drastically in 2008, leading to substantial losses. Steelmaking and food processing are other significant industries. Tourism accounts for nearly 25% of GDP and employs almost 30,000. Investment of €60 million is underway and revenues are expected to triple in the next decade. Arrivals have risen in recent years but growth came to a near standstill in 2009 as West European economies have weakened. Montenegro's banking industry has been radically restructured but depends heavily on foreign financing which leaves it vulnerable to downturn in global markets. Non-performing loans are rising at an accelerating pace. In 2009, the European Investment Bank provided a loan of €150 million to support liquidity in the financial sector.

Energy Montenegro has only modest amounts of proven oil reserves. It produces around 5,000 barrels per day and must import most of its needs. The country also has a small amount of natural gas. Imports come mainly from Russia. Energy shortages slow economic growth.

Netherlands

Capital city	Amsterdam
Capital population	748,190 *(2009)*
Population ('000)	16,410.23 *(2009)*
Urban population (%)	67.21 *(2009)*
Land area (sq km)	41,160
Languages	Dutch
Religion	Roman Catholic (38%); Protestant (30%)
Currency	Euro (€)
Head of state	HM Queen Beatrix (1980)
Head of government	Jan Peter Balkenende (2002)
Ruling party	The Christian Democratic Appeal Party (CDA) leads a coalition.

Main urban areas	Population *(Year)*
Amsterdam (capital)	748,190 *(2009)*
Rotterdam	578,747 *(2009)*
The Hague	479,930 *(2009)*
Utrecht	299,174 *(2009)*
Eindhoven	211,230 *(2009)*
Tilburg	202,678 *(2009)*
Breda	185,632 *(2009)*
Groningen	183,904 *(2009)*
Nijmegen	172,937 *(2009)*

Location The Netherlands occupies some 250km of the North Sea coast between Belgium in the south and Germany in the north and east. About a third of the country is below water level, having been reclaimed from the sea by an extensive reclamation programme. The capital is Amsterdam.

Political structure The Netherlands is a constitutional monarchy in which the monarch rules through a Council of Ministers. Parliament consists of a 150-member Lower House, whose members are elected through a system of proportional representation for four-year terms, and a 75-seat First Chamber which is appointed by the provincial legislatures for a term of four years. The Netherlands rules over the Netherlands Antilles and Aruba, but wide autonomy prevails.

Last elections Elections to the Lower House were held in November 2006. The CDA took 41 seats while the Socialist Party received 25 seats. The opposition Labour Party won 33 seats while the Peoples' Party for Freedom and Democracy gained 22 seats and Democrats 66 received 3 seats. The Party for Freedom took 9 seats and the remaining seats were spread amongst several smaller parties including some new parties. In

June 2005, Dutch voters rejected the proposed EU constitution, with 62% opposing it.

Economy The country enjoyed strong growth between 2004 and 2007 but negative growth was recorded in three of the four quarters in 2008. The current recession is the first since 1982. The Netherlands's economy is very open and its heavy dependence on exports leaves it especially vulnerable to the downturn in world trade. Consumer and business confidence have fallen significantly. Retail sales began to contract in the fourth quarter of 2008. The government has announced a series of measures intended to restore confidence. Most of the funds will be used to aid the financial sector. Two failing banks have already had to be nationalised.

Main industries The manufacturing sector makes up 13.9% of GDP. Manufacturing is dominated by industries such as engineering, vehicle manufacture, electrical and electronic products, chemicals, aerospace and petrochemicals, all of international importance. Investment initiatives have attracted a wide variety of foreign firms in recent years, including Polaroid, Esso, Dow Chemical, Fuji, Nissan, Engelhardt, Amsco, Thorn EMI and Rank Xerox. The manufacturing sector makes up 13.9% of GDP. Manufacturing is dominated by industries such as engineering, vehicle manufacture, electrical and electronic products, chemicals, aerospace and petrochemicals, all of international importance. Investment initiatives have attracted a wide variety of foreign firms in recent years, including Polaroid, Esso, Dow Chemical, Fuji, Nissan, Engelhardt, Amsco, Thorn EMI and Rank Xerox. Manufacturing output declined during 2008. The services sector is comparatively large, providing over 70% of GDP. Commercial services account for nearly half of GDP (48%), with public-sector and personal services making up almost a quarter. In the financial sector credit quality has deteriorated with the continued expansion of mortgages. The ratio of mortgage debt-to-GDP is high. Several banks have been nationalised in order to avoid their collapse. A €20 billion stimulus package was approved in late 2008 to support troubled financial companies. As exports and imports of goods and services each account for well over 65% of nominal GDP, the Dutch economy depends crucially on foreign trade. Rotterdam is Europe's largest port, handling more than twice as much cargo as its nearest European rival, Antwerp. The port's industrial and distribution activities generate annual added value equivalent to around 10% of Dutch GDP. There are also a large number of coastal and international vessels providing cargo services, and an important ship servicing and repair industry exists around Rotterdam. All these activities are suffering as exports fall.

Energy The Netherlands has experienced a decline in offshore oil production. Proven reserves are 100 million barrels. Many oil fields are nearing the decommissioning stage. The Dutch gas sector is much larger than its oil sector. For years, the Netherlands, along with Russia, has been one of the top natural gas suppliers for Western Europe. Proved reserves are 62 trillion cubic feet. Most of the country's natural gas reserves are located onshore. By law, natural gas production is limited to an estimated 2.68 trillion cubic feet (Tcf) per year, with this ceiling dropping to 2.47 Tcf between 2008 and 2013. The law is intended to maintain reserves for future use.

Norway

Capital city	Oslo
Capital population	867,722 *(2009)*
Population ('000)	4,799.25 *(2009)*
Urban population (%)	83.18 *(2009)*
Land area (sq km)	323,895
Languages	Norwegian
Religion	Evangelical Lutheran church (92%)
Currency	Norwegian krone ISO (NOK)
Head of state	HM King Harald V (1991)
Head of government	Jens Stoltenberg (2005)
Ruling party	The Labour Party leads a three-party coalition.

Main urban areas	Population *(Year)*
Oslo (capital)	867,722 *(2009)*
Bergen	225,931 *(2009)*
Stavanger/Sandnes	188,491 *(2009)*
Trondheim	159,056 *(2009)*
Fredrikstad/Skarpsborg	101,520 *(2009)*
Drammen	95,615 *(2009)*
Porsgrunn/Skien	86,158 *(2009)*
Kristiansand	67,158 *(2009)*
Tromso	54,618 *(2009)*
Tonsberg	47,275 *(2009)*

Location Norway occupies almost the entire western half of the peninsula which it shares with Sweden, running southwest from the Arctic Circle to meet up with Denmark across the Skagerrak straits which form the entry from the North Sea to the Baltic Sea. With an almost entirely mountainous geography, and with most of its western coastline characterised by deep-sea inlets (fjords), most of its population live in the southern coastal lowlands. The capital is Oslo.

Political structure The Kingdom of Norway is a constitutional monarchy with executive power vested in a prime minister and cabinet, and legislative authority in a unicameral parliament (the Storting). Parliament's 169 members are elected by proportional representation for a four-year term. For legislative purposes they divide themselves into an Upper and Lower Chamber.

Last elections Parliamentary elections were held in September 2009. The Norwegian Labour Party won 64 seats. Its coalition allies, the Socialists and the Centre Party, both took 11 seats. The opposition Progressive Party captured 41 seats. The remaining seats were divided among several parties including the Christian Democrats, the Conservatives and the Liberal Party. Stoltenberg of the Labour Party is the prime minister.

Economy The Norwegian economy was one of the world's best performers during the past two decades. A slowdown began in 2008, however, with household demand and mainland business investment weakening significantly. Mainland GDP is expected to contract in 2009. Growth in employment has slowed though unemployment has not risen significantly. The country also enjoys a strong work ethic, as reflected in unusually high participation rates for men and women. Public spending is on the rise and has become a more important economic stimulus as demand in the private sector has slumped. Most economists expect the recession to be a mild one with a recovery taking place in 2010. The rapid rise in oil prices since 2007 enabled officials to increase the assets of the sovereign wealth fund. However, the authorities have acknowledged that even at the present level assets will not be sufficient to cover future pension obligations.

Main industries Oil has transformed the Norwegian economy, moving ahead of fishing, timber and agriculture as the country's leading industry. Norway's oil and natural gas extraction sector represents about 20% of the country's GDP and employs a similar proportion of the workforce, either directly or indirectly. The agricultural sector is very small and contracting. Farming provides employment for 4% of the work force. Farms tend to be small in size, and have required consistent government aid to survive. Norway is under pressure to reduce the amount of financial aid it provides to its farmers. Agriculture and food processing also enjoy extensive protection from foreign competition. A wave of acquisitions and mergers in the past has led to economies of scale but also a highly concentrated and vertically-integrated retail sector, notably in food. Fishing provides 10% of total exports and is an integral part of the country's political and social culture. Norway brings in around 2.5 million tonnes of fish each year and is the largest supplier in Europe. Manufacturing makes up a small portion of GDP and accounts for about a third of all exports in a typical year. Manufacturing exports have slumped while other parts of the sector depend heavily on the oil industry and are suffering. The construction industry has slowed as housing starts plummet.

Energy Norway has 7.5 billion barrels of proven oil reserves, the largest in Western Europe. All of Norway's oil reserves are located offshore. Oil production is expected to rise until 2011 and then fall gradually, while gas production should grow rapidly until 2013 before stabilising. The country consumes little of the oil it produces and is the world's sixth largest exporter. The Norwegian oil fields are in a region that is not readily accessible for smaller independent companies. Project development requires large upfront costs, and high tax rates favour larger fields which produce more. Investment levels reflect expectations that Norway's oil production will remain roughly constant for several years, and then begin a gradual decline. As fields mature, the government has become involved in finding new resources for its companies to develop outside the North Sea region. The country also has 102.7 trillion cubic feet (Tcf) of proven natural gas reserves. The North Sea holds the majority of these reserves, but there are also significant quantities in the Norwegian and Barents Seas. Norway is the eighth-largest natural gas producer in the world.

Poland

Capital city	Warsaw
Capital population	1,708,824 *(2009)*
Population ('000)	37,989.88 *(2009)*
Urban population (%)	61.98 *(2009)*
Land area (sq km)	312,685
Languages	Polish
Religion	Mainly Roman Catholic
Currency	New zloty (PLN)
Head of state	Lech Kaczynski (2005)
Head of government	Donald Tusk (2007)
Ruling party	The Civic Platform Party leads a coalition.

Main urban areas	Population *(Year)*
Warsaw (capital)	1,708,824 *(2009)*
Kraków	765,074 *(2009)*
Lódz	744,278 *(2009)*
Wroclaw	631,409 *(2009)*
Poznan	576,899 *(2009)*
Gdansk	460,780 *(2009)*
Szczecin	414,604 *(2009)*
Bydgoszcz	368,813 *(2009)*
Lublin	359,534 *(2009)*
Katowice	309,006 *(2009)*

Location Poland, one of the largest states in central Europe, extends from the 400-km Baltic coast, bordering Russia and Lithuania in the north, to the Czech and Slovak borders, some 1,200km to the south, and from Germany in the west to Russia, Belarus and Ukraine in the east. The country's terrain is of mixed and mainly agricultural quality. The capital is Warsaw.

Political structure The 1997 constitution provides for executive powers to be shared between the prime minister and the president. The president is elected by popular vote for a five-year term. The National Assembly has two chambers. The Diet (or Sejm) has 460 members, elected for a four-year term. Of these, 391 members are elected by proportional representation in multi-seat constituencies and 69 are selected in a national constituency by proportional representation among parties obtaining more than 7% of the popular vote. The Senate has 100 members elected for a four-year term in 40 multiple-seat constituencies.

Last elections Parliamentary elections were held in October 2007. In the Sejm, the Civic Platform Party took 209 seats, Law and Justice received 166 seats, the Democratic Left Alliance won 53 seats and the

Polish Peoples' Party received 31 seats. One seat went to the German Minority. In the Senate, Civic Platform won 60 seats, Law and Justice took 39 seats and one went to an independent. Elections for president were held in October 2005. Lech Kaczynski received 54% of the vote, defeating Donald Tusk.

Economy In recent years, Poland has enjoyed a pattern of balanced growth of 5-7%, rising employment and a small current account deficit. Large transfers from the EU and greater integration with EU trading partners helped boost investment while rising wages boosted private consumption. The economy entered a recession in 2009 but it should be a mild one. Poland's economy will fare much better than most other countries in the region during this recession. One reason is that exports make up a relatively small portion of total economic activity. Large internal and external imbalances have also been avoided. The country's lax fiscal policies have been tightened in order to qualify for eventual membership in the Eurozone. Severe labour shortages have abated as more Polish emigrants return from Western Europe as the global economy weakens.

Main industries Agriculture employs 15.6% of the work force. Many farms are uneconomically small but the structure of the sector is changing. Today, there are more large farms capable of competing on a continental-wide scale while the traditional peasant farms are disappearing. A small number of large farms produce up to 90% of the sector's output. Farmers still receive a variety of subsidies and other forms of assistance. They are exempt from income taxes; EU funds provide finance amounting to about PLN20 billion per year and pension payments are far lower than for urban workers. Industrial output has been falling at a double-digit pace during 2009. The country produces about 20% of Europe's flat-screen monitors and the government expects that the bulk of Europe's television sets will soon be Polish-made. In 2007, the first cars produced by a joint venture between General Motors and a Ukrainian industrial group rolled off the line. The company had planned to expand both its output and workforce through 2010 but those goals are being scaled back sharply as European demand plummets. Steel producers and car makers both cut production levels in 2009. Several large firms – including both steel makers and appliance manufacturers – have recently been forced to file for bankruptcy. Poland's location in the centre of Europe gives it ready access to the rest of the continent. Multinational companies dominate exports, but foreign markets are weakening rapidly. Car makers export more than 95% of their output, making them especially vulnerable to the downturn. The country's financial markets are also showing the strain of the downturn with equities falling by 50% over the year in 2008 and property prices down by about 10%. Three-quarters of Poland's banks are foreign-owned and they are rapidly cutting back on their lending. The country's financial markets are showing the strain of the downturn with equities falling by 50% over the year in 2008 and property prices down by about 10%. Three-quarters of Poland's banks are foreign-owned and they are rapidly cutting back on their lending. Retail sales are slipping but continue to grow slowly. Poland's transportation system is abysmal with just 3% of all roads meeting EU standards. The number of cars on the road more than doubled between 1991 and 2007 but the country has only 340 kilometres of expressway. With EU aid set to rise from 2% of GDP to 4%, the government has ambitious plans for improvements in transportation. The energy sector is equally obsolete. Up to 60% of all power generating facilities are more than 30 years old and badly in need of replacement.

Energy With proven oil reserves of only 96 million barrels, Poland produces about 37,600 barrels per day (bbl/d). The country's oil demand is expected to increase by as much as 50% by 2020. Poland has 350,000-bbl/d in refining capacity, the largest in Central Europe. Several of these refineries, however, were built in the 1960s and 1970s and are badly in need of modernisation. There is an estimated 3.9 trillion cubic feet of natural gas reserves and more exploration is actively being conducted. Natural gas, however, is uneconomical for power generation in Poland compared with coal. Poland has the largest coal reserves in the EU. The EU accession treaty requires Poland to liberalise its natural gas market. Along with divesting and unbundling state-owned natural gas companies, the government is required to open the natural gas market to outside competition, thus allowing customers to choose their own supplier.

Portugal

Capital city	Lisbon
Capital population	584,811 *(2009)*
Population ('000)	10,670.22 *(2009)*
Urban population (%)	57.84 *(2009)*
Land area (sq km)	91,630
Languages	Portuguese
Religion	Mainly Roman Catholic
Currency	Euro (€)
Head of state	Anibal Cavaco Silva (2006)
Head of government	José Socrates (2005)
Ruling party	The government is formed by the Socialist Party.

Main urban areas	Population *(Year)*
Lisbon (capital)	584,811 *(2009)*
Vila Nova de Gaia	324,084 *(2009)*
Porto	267,591 *(2009)*
Amadora	184,896 *(2009)*
Matosinhos	184,366 *(2009)*
Braga	172,340 *(2009)*
Coimbra	151,224 *(2009)*
Maia	141,370 *(2009)*
Feira	128,887 *(2009)*
Funchal	100,884 *(2009)*

Location Portugal occupies about half of the Atlantic coast on the Iberian peninsula, and more than three quarters of the west-facing section, with Spain, its only immediate neighbour, accounting for the rest. The country extends only a maximum of 200km inland but about 600km from north to south. The Atlantic archipelagos of the Azores and Madeira also belong to Portugal. The terrain is largely mountainous inland, but there are innumerable fertile valleys. The climate is Mediterranean. The capital is Lisbon.

Political structure The Republic of Portugal has an executive president who is elected by universal suffrage for a renewable term of five years and appoints the prime minister. Legislative authority is vested in the unicameral Assembly of the Republic, whose 230 members are elected by universal suffrage to serve four-year terms.

Last elections Presidential elections took place in January 2006. Cavaco Silva, a former prime minister, received 51% of the vote, defeating two other contenders. Elections to the Assembly of the Republic were held in February 2005. The Socialist Party won a majority, taking 120 seats. The Social Democrats received 72 seats, the Portuguese Communists won 14 seats and the Peoples' Party gained 12 seats. The remaining seats were scattered amongst smaller parties.

Economy The economy grew steadily from mid 2005 through 2007 but a sharp slowdown occurred in 2008 and the economy slipped into recession in 2009. Portugal depends on other EU countries for 85% of its export sales and its traditional low-cost, cheap-labour industries have seen their exports fall substantially. Their place has been taken by higher value-added, more technologically sophisticated sectors such as car components, electronics and chemicals but foreign demand for these products has slumped. Portuguese exporters also face growing competition from other economies – including new members of the EU – which are following a similar path. Potential output growth is believed to be about half what it was in the second half of the 1990s. Some of the economy's problems include: low levels of labour productivity in most sectors; a misallocation of capital equipment in the business sector and a reluctance to adopt new technologies.

Main industries The share of agriculture in GDP has been falling for several decades. However, farming still provides for a sizeable portion of national employment owing to the low level of labour productivity in the sector. The main agricultural products include citrus fruits, olives, wines and vegetables. Cork is grown for export, and the country has an important fishery industry. Yet Portugal's farmers are the poorest in the EU. They benefit least from the Common Agricultural Policy because these funds are channelled mainly to meat, dairy and cereal production, which is limited in the country. Tourism is an especially important sector, accounting for 10% of employment. Tourism receipts reached a record high in 2008 despite the slump in the international economy. Receipts are expected to fall in 2009 but experts still predict that Portugal could become the world's 10th largest market by 2020, pulling in 44 million visitors a year. To achieve this goal, the industry is planning to diversify into new regions and create new attractions. Tourism in Portugal is somewhat cheaper than I most of West Europe, a fact that should help it thrive in the medium term. In the past, the country's manufacturing sector has survived on account of low wages. Since 2005, many traditional industries such as clothing and footwear have been hurt by increased competition from Asian competitors where wages are even lower. A number of industries are also suffering from the global downturn with exports to Spain and Germany falling especially rapidly. In December 2008, the government announced a new €300 million credit line for automotive firms and suppliers of parts to help the industry through the crisis. The industry expects job losses of at least 12,000 during 2009.

Energy Portugal has extremely limited domestic energy resources, and must import about 90% of its energy needs, much of which is oil. The government has been working with Spain towards integrating the two countries' electricity markets in order to create a regional market. Despite decades of exploration activity, Portugal has yet to discover a commercially viable oil deposit. Portugal has two refineries with a combined capacity of 304,000 barrels per day. The natural gas sector has grown considerably in the last few years, although there are no commercially viable reserves. Privatisation in the Portuguese oil sector (nationalised in 1975) began in 1992, but the state retains a controlling share in the country's oil company.

Romania

Capital city	Bucharest
Capital population	1,879,120 *(2009)*
Population ('000)	21,435.18 *(2009)*
Urban population (%)	55.01 *(2009)*
Land area (sq km)	237,500
Languages	Romanian
Religion	Romanian Orthodox, Roman Catholic
Currency	Romanian New Leu (RON)
Head of state	Traian Basescu (2004)
Head of government	Emil Boc (2008)
Ruling party	A coalition is under negotiation following the latest parliamentary election.

Main urban areas	Population *(Year)*
Bucharest (capital)	1,879,120 *(2009)*
Cluj-Napoca	313,716 *(2009)*
Iasi	313,483 *(2009)*
Timisoara	311,610 *(2009)*
Constanta	302,388 *(2009)*
Craiova	302,128 *(2009)*
Galati	288,067 *(2009)*
Brasov	276,135 *(2009)*
Ploiesti	223,919 *(2009)*
Braila	209,459 *(2009)*

Location Romania borders on the Black Sea in the east and Ukraine and Moldova in the north, with Bulgaria in the south and Hungary and Serbia in the west. The capital is Bucharest.

Political structure The country's president is non-executive and answerable to a parliament. Nevertheless, he exercises considerable influence. The president is elected for a five-year term by the people. Parliament has two chambers. The Chamber of Deputies has 332 members, elected for four-year terms on the basis of a list system and independent candidatures by the principle of proportional representation. The Senate has 137 members, elected for four-year terms by proportional representation.

Last elections Presidential elections were held in November 2004 when Traian Basescu defeated Adrian Nastase, the prime minister. Basescu received 51.2% of the vote. Parliamentary elections took place in November 2008. In the Chamber of Deputies, the Democratic Liberal Party won 115 seats, the Social Democracy Party took 114 seats, the Liberal Party captured 65 seats and the Union of Democratic

Hungarians in Romania gained 22 seats. The remaining seats were scattered amongst smaller parties. Elections to the Senate were held at the same time. The Democratic Liberal Party received 51 seats, the Social Democracy Party was awarded 49 seats, the Liberal Party took 28 seats and the Union of Democratic Hungarians in Romania gained 9 seats. Parliament approved the appointment of Boc as prime minister after the elections in 2008.

Economy Romania made considerable progress in recent years, culminating in EU membership in 2007. Growth averaged better than 6% per year in 2003-2008. Foreign and domestic investment surged after entry in the EU. A boom in consumer spending and investment was driven by a rapid rise in borrowing which left Romania highly vulnerable when the global financial crisis hit. The economy began to weaken dramatically by the end of 2008 and entered a recession in 2009. The economy faces other problems once it gets back on track. Romania has the lowest income per capita in central Europe, the worst environmental standards, the largest tax arrears, the most pervasive corruption and the lowest education spending. Unreported, untaxed economic activity is estimated to represent nearly half of real GDP.

Main industries The share of the agricultural sector has contracted significantly since the end of the Cold War but the sector still provides employment for a third of the workforce. Private ownership of farmland makes up almost three quarters of the total. There are several million subsistence and semi-subsistence farms. Most will disappear as funds from the EU begin to modernise the sector. In the manufacturing sector, the share of traditional industries such as textiles and shoes is declining while that of automakers, car parts and engineering products has risen. Dacia, owned by Renault, has experienced success in recent years, though its fortunes have deteriorated in 2009 as the world market for automobiles has collapsed. Industrial output began to fall in 2009 and problems could continue through much of 2010. The mining sector is of special concern because it is the source of most resistance to economic reform. Mines producing copper, lead, zinc, gold, silver and coal require substantial subsidies. Tourism accounts for just 1% of GDP (compared to 5% in Hungary) but the number of visitors has risen over the past several years. At present, Romania is not ready for the influx, though many new, up-market facilities are being planned. The transportation infrastructure (particularly roadways) remains in poor shape. Foreign banks dominate the financial sector with three of the country's four largest banks being based in Austria. Consumers readily took out loans in foreign currencies but this credit has become much more expensive as the leu weakens.

Energy With proven reserves of 600 million barrels, Romania is largest oil producer in Central and Eastern Europe. However, production has fallen precipitously over the past two decades. Romania dominates South-eastern Europe's downstream petroleum industry. Several of its refineries were privatised in 2005 and 2006. Capacity far exceeds domestic demand for refined petroleum products, allowing the country to export a wide range of oil products and petrochemicals. However, years of low investment have left the country's refining industry in poor health, requiring massive amounts of capital to modernise and improve efficiency. Romania is central and eastern Europe's largest producer of natural gas. The country has natural gas reserves of 2.2 trillion cubic feet and a sizeable domestic market. A number of pipeline projects are planned to increase natural gas transport capacity.

Russia

Capital city	Moscow
Capital population	10,483,403 *(2009)*
Population ('000)	141,903.98 *(2009)*
Urban population (%)	74.11 *(2009)*
Land area (sq km)	17,075,400
Languages	Russian
Religion	Mainly Christian (Russian Orthodox)
Currency	Russian ruble (RUB)
Head of state	Dmitry Medvedev (2008)
Head of government	Vladimir Putin (2008)
Ruling party	The government is formed by the United Russia Party and non-partisan technocrats.

Main urban areas	Population *(Year)*
Moscow (capital)	10,483,403 *(2009)*
St Petersburg	4,441,817 *(2009)*
Novosibirsk	1,393,887 *(2009)*
Nizhniy Novgorod	1,270,780 *(2009)*
Yekaterinburg	1,245,335 *(2009)*
Omsk	1,137,487 *(2009)*
Samara	1,109,684 *(2009)*
Kazan	1,087,571 *(2009)*
Chelyabinsk	1,070,556 *(2009)*
Rostov-na-Donu	1,064,011 *(2009)*

Location Russia, the largest state in Asia, extends nearly 9,000km from the Finnish border in the west to the Bering Straits in the east. The vast terrain ranges from the Arctic wastes of the north to the Caspian Sea in the south. The capital is Moscow.

Political structure The executive president is elected by universal suffrage to a four year term, and answers to a Federal Assembly comprising two chambers: the 168-member Federation Council which includes two members from each administrative unit within the federation, and the 450-member State Duma, elected for a four-year terms. There is also a prime minister, who is appointed by the president on the Duma's recommendations.

Last elections In March 2008, Medvedev was elected president with 70.2% of the vote. His nearest rival was Gennady Zyuganov who received 17.7%. There were charges of vote rigging. Elections to the Duma took place in December 2007. The United Russia Party won 315 of the 450 seats, while the Communist Party took 57 seats. The Liberal Democratic Party won 40 seats and the Fair Russia Party gained 38 seats. Vladimir Putin, the previous president, was appointed as prime minister in May 2008.

Economy The long period of stellar growth came to an end in the fourth quarter of 2008 and GDP has contracted in 2009. This will be the first recession in a decade. As the economy slumps, unemployment is soaring. Russia has huge amounts of natural resources – including the world's fifth largest gold reserves – but the state has reasserted control over these and driven off foreign investors. The number living below the official poverty line is still high at 22 million but fell significantly during the period of high oil prices. Although the middle-income class has grown substantially, the number is still matched by those living in poverty. The economy remains heavily dependent on oil and natural gas exports, which account for two-thirds of export revenues. The huge drop in oil prices since mid 2008 created severe financial pressure. Large budget deficits are expected to replace the surpluses of recent years.

Main industries Agricultural output has been rising for the past several years and grew by about 10% in 2008. The sector's share in GDP is still small compared to other Eastern European countries owing in part to the fact that it receives only modest support from the state. Moscow has promised to provide more generous subsidies in the future. Manufacturing output began to contract in the second half of 2008 and the downturn has continued in 2009. The pace of the contraction has slowed, however. Moscow had expected car makers to invest substantial sums over the next few years but is now promising the industry more than RUB45 billion in financial assistance. Large wage increases have undermined the competitive position of many other manufacturers. There are massive mineral and forest resources

with iron ore, copper, aluminium, manganese, salt and precious metals all being produced, though facilities are in need of modernisation. Oil and gas account for 25% of GDP and 65% of exports but employ less than 1% of the population. Raw materials, such as oil, natural gas, and metals, make up more than two-thirds of all export revenues. However, the state has gained direct control over most natural resources (and especially energy) and will only allow foreign minority partners in on a selective basis. The banking system remains tumultuous and murky. Many banks have virtually stopped lending. Their reluctance meant that the money supply contracted by more than 11% in the first quarter of 2009. For those that can obtain credit, interest rates have soared. Infrastructure is in a terrible state. The rail network is deteriorating rapidly. Meanwhile, Russia's road capacity per capita is only about one-seventh of that of Canada's.

Energy Russia is the world's 8th largest exporter of oil. It has proven oil reserves of 79 billion barrels. New fields will produce almost all of Russia's annual oil growth in the next five years and will likely produce more than half of the country's oil in 2020. Russia holds the world's largest natural gas reserves, with 1,529 trillion cubic feet. The country is the world's largest natural gas producer, as well as the world's largest exporter. But unlike the Russian oil industry, the natural gas industry is not growing. Both production and consumption have remained relatively flat since independence. Output of natural gas is projected to grow slowly through 2009 and then begin a steep decline.

Serbia

Capital city	Belgrade
Capital population	1,099,042 *(2009)*
Population ('000)	7,367.22 *(2009)*
Urban population (%)	52.16 *(2009)*
Land area (sq km)	88,361
Languages	Russian
Religion	Mainly Christian (Russian Orthodox)
Currency	Serbian dinar (RSD)
Head of state	Boris Tadic (2008)
Head of government	Mirko Cvetkovic (2008)
Ruling party	The Democratic Party for a European Serbia leads a coalition with the Socialist Party and several ethnic minority representatives.

Main urban areas	Population *(Year)*
Belgrade (capital)	1,099,042 *(2009)*
Novi Sad	196,357 *(2009)*
Niš	173,775 *(2009)*
Kragujevac	146,659 *(2009)*
Subotica	100,318 *(2009)*
Zrenjanin	79,612 *(2009)*
Pancevo	79,108 *(2009)*
Cacak	74,130 *(2009)*
Leskovac	63,706 *(2009)*
Smederevo	63,004 *(2009)*

Location Serbia's northern border is with Hungary. On its eastern side are Romania and Bulgaria while Croatia is to its northwest. In the centre of the region is Belgrade, the capital.

Political structure Serbia's National Assembly has 250 members, elected to four-year terms. The Prime Minister is chosen by the National Assembly on the recommendation of the president.

Last elections Voters elected Boris Tadic as president of Serbia in February 2008. He defeated Tomislav Nikolic, receiving 50.3% of the vote. Elections to the Serbian parliament were held in May 2008. The Democratic Party for a European Serbia won 102 seats, the Serbian Radical Party won 78 seats, the Democratic Party took 30 seats, the Socialist Party received 20 seats, and the Liberal Democratic Party took 13 seats. The remainder were scattered among several smaller parties.

Economy Serbia's economy enjoyed growth of 6% or more in 2003-2007. The Belgrade area attracted some of the largest greenfield investments by foreign companies in south-eastern Europe. Activity in the private sector rose significantly during this period. By the fourth quarter of 2008, the pace of growth had fallen sharply and the economy is expected to be in recession in 2009. Exports, imports and industrial production were all falling at a double-digit pace in the first quarter of the year. The growth of credit markets has also dried up and fixed investment plummeted.

Main industries Agriculture is the largest sector of both economies, with fruits, vegetables and tobacco of particular importance. Serbia's farmers enjoyed a much better harvest in 2008 than in recent years. Industrial output in Serbia has been expanding by 4-5% per year but the pace had slowed by 2008. Fiat announced a large investment in the country and other carmakers have been considering the same but their plans may be curtailed as European demand for automobiles weakens. Serbia's textile industry – without an association agreement – is doing poorly. The Serbian government intends to increase its investments in the railway and road system significantly beginning in 2009. The entry of foreign banks is transforming Serbia's financial sector. Major foreign banks have agreed to rollover their exposure in Serbia to keep all branches well capitalised.

Energy Serbia has 78 million barrels of oil reserves and produces small amounts each year. The country's oil company was privatised in 2003. The Serbian region near Pozarevac is believed to contain hydrocarbons. However, most oil is imported, primarily via the Adria pipeline. These facilities were all damaged during the war.

Slovakia

Capital city	Bratislava
Capital population	434,626 *(2009)*
Population ('000)	5,395.32 *(2009)*
Urban population (%)	56.7 *(2009)*
Land area (sq km)	49,035
Languages	Czech, Slovak
Religion	Predominately Catholic
Currency	Euro (€)
Head of state	Ivan Gašparovic (2004)
Head of government	Robert Fico (2006)
Ruling party	The Direction – Social Democracy Party (Smer) leads a three-party coalition.

Main urban areas	Population *(Year)*
Bratislava (capital)	434,626 *(2009)*
Kosice	243,491 *(2009)*
Presov	97,758 *(2009)*
Nitra	90,488 *(2009)*
Zilina	88,640 *(2009)*
Banska Bystrica	85,186 *(2009)*
Trnava	73,522 *(2009)*
Martin	62,676 *(2009)*
Trencin	60,345 *(2009)*
Poprad	58,922 *(2009)*

Location Slovakia, which was linked until January 1993 in a federation with the Czech Republic, is located in central Europe, south east of Germany and south of Poland, but to the north of Austria and Hungary. The Czech Republic lies to the west. The climate is temperate, with occasionally harsh winters. The capital is Bratislava.

Political structure From 1919 until the end of 1992 Slovakia was part of a federation with the Czech Republic. At the start of 1993 the two countries began an independent existence. The president is elected for a five-year term by the people. The National Council of the Slovak Republic has 150 members, elected for four-year terms by proportional representation.

Last elections Presidential elections were held in April 2009. Gašparovic was re-elected, defeating Iveta Radicova with 55.5% of the vote. Parliamentary elections were held in June 2006. The Direction – Social Democracy Party won 50 seats, the Slovak Democratic and Christian Union took 31 seats, the Slovak National Party received 20 seats as did the Party of the Hungarian Coalition, the Peoples Party gained 15 seats and the Christian Democratic Movement took 14 seats.

Economy Over the past few years, Slovakia has been one of central Europe's strongest economic performers. GDP grew at an average rate

of 7.4% in 2004-2008 and unemployment fell. In January 2009, Slovakia became the sixteenth member of the eurozone. A decline in the pubic debt and the current account deficit during the period of rapid growth helped to make the transition to the euro much easier. However, as in many other countries, the pace of growth deteriorated significantly in 2009. There is an obvious need to push for smaller and more effective government, against a strong constituency in favour of maintaining the status quo which includes a large share of general government jobs in total employment. The Slovak economy suffers one of the lowest employment rates in the OECD area. Unemployment is concentrated among the low-skilled, the young and the elderly in the eastern part of the country. The number of jobless remains high but is falling. However, the long-term unemployment rate is the highest of all OECD countries.

Main industries The country's agricultural sector is comparatively small. Major crops are grains (wheat, barley and corn), oilseeds, potatoes, sugar beets, fruits and vegetables. Growth of industrial output has fallen to only 1%, the slowest rate in three years. Slovakia depends heavily on the automobile industry with Volkswagen alone accounting for one-fifth of all exports. With foreign demand for automobiles falling sharply, Slovakia's exports have plummeted. The electronics and constructing industries are also suffering. FDI in manufacturing is also declining but the country remains a favourite thanks to its combination of low wage rates and guaranteed access to the EU. Slovakian wages are just a fifth of those in Western Europe. Tourism receipts presently contribute around 2% to GDP but lack the necessary infrastructure. There is no tourism ministry and transportation links are poor. Banks continue to lend vigorously, showing no effects from the credit crunch in many countries. More than 90% of the banking industry is foreign-owned.

Energy Slovakia's oil reserves amount to only 9 million barrels. Production is equally miniscule, only about 8,850 barrels per day. Slovakia has limited amounts of natural gas but is very important as a transit country. It is estimated that about 25% of the natural gas consumed in West Europe transits through the country. This represents about 70% of the Russian natural gas exported to Western Europe. Slovakia's natural gas market is being liberalised in stages. The country has two nuclear power plants, which generate about 60% of its electricity. The two oldest reactors are due to be decommissioned as part of the energy chapter of Slovakia's accession agreement with the EU. However, some government officials oppose that decision. A reversal of the agreement would be strongly opposed by neighbouring Austria. Slovakia is self-sufficient in coal and lignite. These two fuels account for two-thirds of the country's total energy requirements.

Slovenia

Capital city	Ljubljana
Capital population	258,199 *(2009)*
Population ('000)	2,022.79 *(2009)*
Urban population (%)	51.11 *(2009)*
Land area (sq km)	20,254
Languages	Slovenian
Religion	Mainly Roman Catholic
Currency	Euro (€)
Head of state	Danilo Turk (2007)
Head of government	Borut Pahor (2008)
Ruling party	The Social Democrats lead a coalition.

Main urban areas	Population *(Year)*
Ljubljana (capital)	258,199 *(2009)*
Maribor	91,841 *(2009)*
Celje	37,320 *(2009)*
Kranj	35,452 *(2009)*
Velenje	26,996 *(2009)*
Koper-Capodistria	23,669 *(2009)*
Novo Mesto	22,805 *(2009)*
Ptuj	21,630 *(2009)*
Trbovlje	16,249 *(2009)*
Nova Gorica	13,596 *(2009)*

Location Slovenia lies in the far north of the former Yugoslav Federation. Austria lies to the north of the country, Italy to the west, Hungary to the east and Croatia to the south. The capital is Ljubljana.

Political structure Slovenia declared its independence in June 1991. The president, who has a mainly ceremonial function, is elected by universal suffrage for a five-year once-renewable period. He proposes a prime minister. The State Chamber has 90 members, elected for a four year term; 40 seats are directly elected, and 50 selected by proportional representation. Two seats of the 90 seats are set aside for ethnic minorities. The State Council has 40 members: 18 members representing local councillors and 22 members representing commercial and non-commercial interests.

Last elections Elections to the National Assembly were held in September 2008. The Social Democrats gained 29 seats, the Slovenian Democratic Party took 28 seats, the New Politics Party won 9 and the Democratic Party of Pensioners received 7 seats. Smaller parties accounted for the remainder. Turk was elected as president in November 2007 with 68% of the vote.

Economy Before accession, Slovenia's per capita GDP (at purchasing power parities) was about 50% of the EU average. But in the 25-country group that includes so many poorer countries, that figure has risen to about 90% by 2008. At this level, Slovenia is not eligible for structural funds given to the EU's poorest regions. The economy grew at a rate above economic potential from 2005 until mid-2007. However, the pace slowed markedly in 2008 and a recession began before the end of the year. The economy grew at a rate above economic potential from 2005 until mid-2007, but the pace slowed markedly in 2008. The relatively slow growth in productivity suggests that Slovenia is not moving up the technology ladder fast enough. While there is evidence of increasing specialisation into high-tech sectors, the pace of export-quality upgrading lags behind other countries in the region. Although wages are high, the quality of production and firms' export successes attest to Slovenia's competitiveness. Labour costs are estimated to be 53% of the EU average, the highest among the accession countries.

Main industries Slovenia's economic profile resembles those of Western countries to a much greater extent than is true in other parts of Eastern Europe. Agriculture accounts for only 2.5% of GDP, the smallest share among the central European countries. The country's farmers are very productive, with large surpluses of maize, wheat, sugar beet and potatoes being produced. Manufacturing makes up 24.6% of GDP, down from 33.0% in 1990. Slovenia's manufacturers have an impressive record in exploiting niche markets abroad and their exports are very important to the overall health of the economy. The country has not done well in attracting FDI relative to its neighbours. Industrial output began to fall in 2008 and the decline continues in 2009. Rates of capital utilisation have fallen sharply. The banking system is sound, but still largely state-owned and comparatively inefficient. Profits are under pressure in an increasingly competitive environment. The rapid growth of credit to enterprises is increasing risk.

Energy Slovenia has some coal, but must import most of its primary energy. It is for this reason that the country usually runs a trade deficit.

Spain

Capital city	Madrid
Capital population	3,245,003 *(2009)*
Population ('000)	45,520.70 *(2009)*
Urban population (%)	77.21 *(2009)*
Land area (sq km)	504,880
Languages	Spanish (Castilian, Catalan, Galician), Basque
Religion	Mainly Roman Catholic
Currency	Euro (€)
Head of state	HM King Juan Carlos (1975)
Head of government	José Luis Rodriguez Zapatero (2004)
Ruling party	Spanish Socialist Workers Party (PSOE)

Main urban areas	Population *(Year)*
Madrid (capital)	3,245,003 *(2009)*
Barcelona	1,629,602 *(2009)*
Valencia	815,082 *(2009)*
Sevilla	699,650 *(2009)*
Zaragoza	671,279 *(2009)*
Malaga	570,839 *(2009)*
Murcia	437,459 *(2009)*
Palma de Mallorca	404,107 *(2009)*
Palmas de las Gran Canaria	383,798 *(2009)*
Bilbao	352,973 *(2009)*

Location Spain occupies the greater part of the Iberian Peninsula with coastal orientations in all four directions. The mainland's neighbours are Portugal, which it surrounds on both its land borders, and France. It is a co-administrator of Andorra. The territory also includes the Balearic Islands (in the Mediterranean), the Canary Islands and the Moroccan enclaves of Ceuta and Melilla. The capital is Madrid.

Political structure Spain is a constitutional monarchy in which the King plays a relatively modest political role. There is a 350-member Congress of Deputies (Lower House) elected for four years, and a Senate with 248 members. In the Senate, 208 members are elected for a four year term in four-member constituencies, with 40 members designated by the regional legislatures. The administrative regions have been extensively reorganised to create 17 autonomous regions, including Andalusia, Catalonia and the Basque country.

Last elections Parliamentary elections were held in March 2008. In the Senate, the People's Party won 100 seats, the Spanish Socialist Workers Party took 88 seats and the remainder was divided among small parties and regional interests. In the Congress of Deputies the Spanish Socialist Workers Party received 169 seats whilst the People's Party and its allies won 153 seats. Catalan nationalists took 11 seats, Basque nationalists received 6 seats and the reformed communists won 2 seats. Remaining seats were divided among minor parties. The PSOE rules without the aid of a coalition, but often requires the cooperation of smaller parties to pass legislation.

Economy Prior to the global meltdown, the Spanish economy grew steadily for ten consecutive years, making it one of the best-performing economies in the EU. Per capita GDP rose to more than 90% of the average for the EU's 15 western member states. During this period of prolonged growth, the Spanish economy generated more than half of all new jobs in the Eurozone. Economic performance began to deteriorate dramatically in 2008 when the country's housing bubble collapsed, swelling the ranks of the unemployed. The downturn worsened in 2009 when Spain's open economy was hit by the global crisis. More than €100 billion in FDI poured into Spain in 2000-2007. Meanwhile, consumers borrowed freely to build or improve new homes. All this pushed private sector debt to more than 120% of GDP. More than 1 million newly-built homes lie empty.

Main industries Agriculture continues to be a very important sector, but water shortages plague many farmers. Fruits, nuts, olives, tomatoes and peppers are the main export products. Growth of industrial output stagnated in 2008 and is falling sharply during 2009. Employment in manufacturing continues to decline. Major industries include electronics, steel, chemicals, fertilisers, food, wine and tobacco products, leather goods and timber products. Most important, however, is the car industry – Spanish carmakers have made up one-fifth of all exports and 6% of GDP in recent years but are now struggling with a collapse in demand at home and abroad. Spain's construction and real estate groups were among the largest in Europe following a 10-year building boom but both industries are contracting dramatically now. Approximately 300,000 construction workers lost their jobs during 2008. Tourism, which accounts for 5% of GDP, is a key economic sector. The industry employs roughly one in 10 of the workforce. Arrivals fell in 2008 for the first time since 1997 and the downturn has worsened in 2009. The banking sector has been hurt by the international credit crisis and growing uncertainty at home. Madrid has had to bail out several regional banks. The government has also extended deposit insurance and provided more funding guarantees. Retail sales contracted by nearly 10% in the first half of 2009.

Energy Spain has approximately 150 million barrels of proven domestic crude oil reserves. Its crude oil production is also marginal, averaging just 3,000 barrels per day. Exploration is underway for oil and natural gas in two offshore regions, though preliminary results are disappointing. The government's 10-year energy plan depends heavily on natural gas and renewable energy. These two sources are projected to account for 22.5% and 12.0%, respectively, of Spain's primary energy consumption by 2011. Spain has only 90 billion cubic feet of proven natural gas reserves and natural gas production is insignificant.

Sweden

Capital city	Stockholm
Capital population	801,786 *(2009)*
Population ('000)	9,201.48 *(2009)*
Urban population (%)	83.73 *(2009)*
Land area (sq km)	449,790
Languages	Swedish
Religion	Evangelical Lutheran Church (95%)
Currency	Swedish krona (SEK)
Head of state	HM King Carl Gustaf XVI (1973)
Head of government	Fredrik Reinfeldt (2006)
Ruling party	A four-party coalition, the Alliance for Sweden, leads the government.

Main urban areas	Population *(Year)*
Stockholm (capital)	801,786 *(2009)*
Gothenburg	497,534 *(2009)*
Malmo	283,835 *(2009)*
Uppsala	187,230 *(2009)*
Linkoping	141,438 *(2009)*
Vasteras	134,870 *(2009)*
Orebro	128,754 *(2009)*
Helsingborg	126,076 *(2009)*
Norrkoping	125,911 *(2009)*
Jonkoping	124,750 *(2009)*

Location Sweden occupies the eastern and southern section of the Scandinavian Peninsula which runs southwest from the Arctic Circle to meet with Denmark across the narrow sea channel which gives access to the Baltic from the North Sea. The terrain is predominantly hilly and mountainous. The main population centres are in the south and east. The capital is Stockholm.

Political structure Sweden is a constitutional monarchy in which the King appoints the prime minister on the basis of parliamentary advice. Legislative authority is vested in a unicameral 349-seat Parliament (Riksdag), which is elected by universal suffrage for a term of four years. Sweden became a full member of the EU in January 1995 after having been in the European Monetary System for many years.

Last elections General elections were held in September 2006. The Workers' Party-Social Democrats won 130 seats, the Moderate Coalition Party received 97 seats and the Liberal People's Party took 28 seats. The remainder were scattered amongst several other parties. Altogether, the centre-right coalition known as the Alliance for Sweden will have a majority of seats. In September 2003, voters rejected the government's plan to adopt the euro.

Economy A strong economic upswing took place 2004-2007, outpacing the eurozone by a wide margin. Since then, the pace of growth has slowed markedly owing to global uncertainties and capacity constraints at home. In 2008, growth fell to its lowest level in 30 years. The country entered a recession in 2009. The share of household consumption in GDP has been steadily falling for the past several decades while the share of trade (both exports and imports) has been rising. These secular trends are a reflection of the increasing globalisation of the economy. By some measures, the degree of Sweden's globalisation is second only to that of the USA. Economists estimate that more than a fifth of the working-age population is economically inactive. It is this problem that has prompted the current government's ambitious reform of labour market policies.

Main industries Agriculture accounts for only a tiny portion of GDP, while manufacturing makes up about one fifth. The public sector dominates the economy, representing around 30% of economic activity in the country. Farming is the main livelihood in the north, though elsewhere forestry and related products are the mainstays of the local economy. Sweden is a leader in mobile phone usage and development of the mobile internet. Biotechnology is another important emerging industry. The country's automotive trio (Volvo, Saab and Scania) have reorganised, consolidated and sold off but are still struggling. In 2009, the government will provide aid worth US$3.5 billion in loans, loan guarantees and funding for research. A weakening of foreign demand in pharmaceuticals and telecoms has put pressure on these industries. Industrial output has been in decline for some time but signs of a turnaround appeared at the end of the second quarter of 2009. The service sector is the largest in the economy but retail sales are slumping. Household debt has been rising in recent years and, at around 120% of disposable income, is relatively high. Swedish banks have little exposure to the sub-prime crisis but are highly vulnerable to the problems in the Baltic States. The government has undertaken bank recapitalisation.

Energy Sweden has no indigenous fuels except for its hydroelectric energy. The government originally proclaimed its intention to phase out its nuclear plants by the year 2010. In 2009, however, a ban imposed after a 1980 referendum was scrapped. Sweden is one of seven EU countries to have completely opened its electricity market to competition in compliance with EU rules. In a normal year, about half of the country's electric power is produced by 12 commercial nuclear reactors.

Switzerland

Capital city	Bern
Capital population	123,098 *(2009)*
Population ('000)	7,559.86 *(2009)*
Urban population (%)	68.33 *(2009)*
Land area (sq km)	41,285
Languages	German, French, Italian, Romansch
Religion	Roman Catholic (47.6%); Protestant (44.3%)
Currency	Swiss franc (CHF)
Head of state	Hans-Rudolf Merz (2009)
Head of government	Doris Leuthard (2009)
Ruling party	A four-party coalition agreed by formula leads the government.

Main urban areas	Population *(Year)*
Zurich	364,639 *(2009)*
Geneva	181,233 *(2009)*
Basel	162,954 *(2009)*
Bern (capital)	123,098 *(2009)*
Lausanne	120,652 *(2009)*
Winterthur	92,936 *(2009)*
St Gallen	71,597 *(2009)*
Luzern	58,902 *(2009)*
Lugano	51,283 *(2009)*
Biel	49,619 *(2009)*

Location Centrally located in Europe, three of Switzerland's four official languages (French, German and Italian) reflect its three most important neighbours. Switzerland represents Liechtenstein at diplomatic level. The capital is Bern.

Political structure Switzerland is a federation of 20 cantons and six half-cantons which include German, French, Italian and Romansch speakers. The first three of these are official languages, while Romansch is a "semi-official" language. There is a high degree of political devolution. There is a 200-member National Council elected by a system of proportional representation and a 46-member Council of States elected by simple majority in the cantons. Members of both bodies serve four-year terms. At the federal level, the executive president is elected every year by the National Council from among the seven-member Cabinet.

Last elections Elections to the National Council took place in October 2007. The Swiss People's Party received 62 seats, the SPS took 43 seats and the Radical Free Democratic Party gained 31 seats as did the Christian Democratic People's Party. The Green Party won 20 seats and the remainder were scattered amongst several minor parties. Elections to the Council of States were held at the same time. The Christian Democratic People's Party received 14 seats, the Radical Free Democratic Party won 11 seats, the Social Democratic Party gained 9 seats and the Swiss People's Party took 7 seats. The remainder went to the Green Party. Members of both the National Council and the Council of States elected Merz as president in January 2009.

Economy Between 2004 and 2007 the rate of growth was above economic potential. Unemployment was low and falling while the government maintained a budget surplus. However, the economy entered a recession in the second half of 2008. Economists expect the downturn to be the worst since 1991. GDP per capita is one of the highest in the western world. The financial sector accounts for almost half of all growth but is suffering in the global downturn. Analysts see the country's slow gains in productivity as the main source of problems. Unemployment is on the rise but varies widely among regions. It is highest in French and Italian-speaking areas. In the longer term, the main challenge is to increase the economy's potential rate of growth, mainly by raising productivity. Substantial efforts are needed to deal with the serious shortcomings in the functioning of the product markets, which are reflected in the very high level of prices compared with other countries. Government spending accounts for more than 35% of GDP in most years.

Main industries Switzerland's agricultural sector is small and relatively inefficient. Since the mid-1990s, the level of support to agriculture has been one of the highest among industrialised countries. The country's farmers derive 75% of their farming income from subsidies. A lack of foreign competition leads to higher food prices than abroad. Productivity is low but rising. Farmers are able to meet only around 60% of the country's food needs. The service sector employs nearly three-quarters of the work force. Financial services, alone, accounts for about 13% of GDP. Banks are well capitalised but problems at UBS and Credit Suisse have hurt the industry. The number of banks in Switzerland could fall as pressures increase. The large insurance sector has a good track record, but strains are emerging there as well. The importance of the financial-services industry makes the economy especially vulnerable to the turmoil in global markets. Tourism, especially winter sports, is one of the most important parts of the economy but faces intense competition from other tourist-based countries. Several Swiss multinationals (particularly in pharmaceutical and precision engineering) are among the world's leaders but generate the bulk of their profits outside the country. The overseas investments of these huge companies exceed the size of the domestic economy and are an important reason for the country's high standard of living. Manufacturing output began to contract in the second half of 2008 and the slowdown has continued in 2009.

Energy Switzerland has no indigenous fuel sources apart from its hydroelectric potential and is forced to rely on nuclear power to an unusual degree. All other fuels are imported.

Turkey

Capital city	Ankara
Capital population	3,831,697 *(2009)*
Population ('000)	75,262.63 *(2009)*
Urban population (%)	69.24 *(2009)*
Land area (sq km)	779,450
Languages	Turkish
Religion	Islam (99%)
Currency	Turkish lira (TL)
Head of state	Abdullah Gul (2007)
Head of government	Recep Tayyip Erdogan (2002)
Ruling party	The Justice and Development Party (AKP) leads the government.

Main urban areas	Population *(Year)*
Istanbul	10,997,819 *(2009)*
Ankara (capital)	3,831,697 *(2009)*
Izmir	2,652,080 *(2009)*
Bursa	1,459,050 *(2009)*
Adana	1,394,377 *(2009)*
Gaziantep	1,216,074 *(2009)*
Konya	993,814 *(2009)*
Antalya	795,398 *(2009)*
Kayseri	718,010 *(2009)*
Icel	634,220 *(2009)*

Location With control over both banks of the Bosporus, Turkey controls access to the Black Sea. The country has a land border with Greece and Bulgaria to the west. In the southeast it meets with Syria and Iraq, while the eastern border meets with Iran and in the northeast it borders Georgia and Armenia. The capital is Ankara.

Political structure Turkey's president is elected by popular vote for seven years by parliament. The country has a unicameral Grand National Assembly with 550 members, elected for a five-year term by mitigated proportional representation with a barrier of 10%. Although Islam is dominant, the country has been secular since 1919. The Kurdish Democracy Party was banned in 1994 after a series of terrorist attacks.

Last elections Parliamentary elections were held in July 2007. The AKP, led by Erdogan won 341 seats while the Republican Peoples Party took 112 seats and the Nationalist Movement Party received 71 seats. The remaining seats are held by independents.

Main industries Agriculture accounts for about 10.6% of GDP. Much of the population works in agriculture, cultivating grapes, fruit, barley, cotton and other products. Farm output slumped in 2008 owing to the effects of a drought. Manufacturing makes up more than 22% of GDP. Output began to contract in the first months of 2009 and the decline is continuing today. The textile industry is often referred to as the country's "economic engine". The industry is dominated by clothes manufactures and accounts for nearly 40% of total exports (most of it to the EU). Turkey has become a production hub for the automobile industry with investments by Renault, Fiat, Hyundai and Toyota. Both textile and automobile exports have slumped as global demand has fallen. There is also a threat from cheaper competitors based in India and China. Measures of industrial growth and capacity utilisation have plummeted. The tourist industry thrived in recent years but the number of visitors stagnated in 2008 and began to decline in 2009. Tourist officials expect a recovery in 2010. The growth of credit has slowed but still remains high. Reforms to the banking system, introduced after the financial crisis in 2001, have strengthened the banking system. Ankara continues to push its privatisation programme. Turkey is building a seabed tunnel which will eventually be a key part of a railway link from the Middle East to Europe. The tunnel, which will cost US$3.5 billion, is expected to open in 2013

Energy Turkey has 300 million barrels of proven oil reserves and is currently producing around 43,000 barrels per day (bbl/d), down from 90,000 in the 1990s. Many oil fields are old and inefficient. However, there are oil prospects in Turkey's European provinces, in the Black Sea shelf region, and in other oil basins in southern and south-eastern Turkey. Turkey also has 300 billion cubic feet of proven natural gas reserves. The country is in the midst of a large-scale exploration for oil and gas in the Black Sea and Mediterranean. Oil provides over 40% of Turkey's total energy requirements, but its share is declining as the usage of natural gas rises. Oil and gas transportation is a crucial and contentious issue in the Caspian Sea/Central Asia region. Turkey and the United States have pushed for a "Western route" pipeline, carrying oil from Baku across Turkey to Ceyhan. In 2006, construction of a 1-million-bbl/d capacity, US$4 billion pipeline was completed.

Ukraine

Capital city	Kiev
Capital population	2,758,789 *(2009)*
Population ('000)	45,919.01 *(2009)*
Urban population (%)	68.03 *(2009)*
Land area (sq km)	603,700
Languages	Ukrainian
Religion	Mainly Christian
Currency	Ukrainian hryvnia (UAH)
Head of state	Viktor Yushchenko (2005)
Head of government	Yulia Tymoshenko (2007)
Ruling party	A coalition of Yuliya Tymoshenko Bloc and Our Ukraine-People's Self Defence lead the government.

Main urban areas	Population *(Year)*
Kiev (capital)	2,758,789 *(2009)*
Kharkov	1,365,927 *(2009)*
Dnepropetrovsk	1,009,909 *(2009)*
Odessa	974,755 *(2009)*
Doneck	958,855 *(2009)*
Zaporozhye	770,814 *(2009)*
Lvov	694,561 *(2009)*
Krivoy Rog	637,366 *(2009)*
Nikolajev	505,610 *(2009)*
Zdanov	472,995 *(2009)*

Location Ukraine borders on Poland, Slovakia, Hungary, Moldova and northern Romania in the west, on Belarus in the north and on Russia in the east and south, where it meets the Black Sea. There are innumerable rivers, including the Dnepr and its tributaries. The capital is Kiev.

Political structure The country has an executive president who is elected by universal suffrage for a five-year term. Parliament has 450 members elected for five-year terms by proportional representation.

Last elections Parliamentary elections were held in September 2007. The Party of Regions won 175 seats, the coalition led by Yulia Tymoshenko took 156 seats, Our Ukraine-People's Self-Defence Bloc received 72 seats, the Communist Party gained 27 seats and the Lytvyn Bloc took 20 seats. Presidential elections were held in November 2004. Viktor Yanukovich, the prime minister, won a narrow victory over Viktor Yushchenko but the Supreme Court later threw out the results. The election was rerun in December 2004 and Yushchenko emerged as victor with 54.1% of the vote. In December 2007, parliament elected Tymoshenko as prime minister (for the second time). Tymoshenko replaces Viktor Yanukovych, the Orange Revolution antagonist, as prime minister.

Economy In 2005-2007, growth was driven by strengthening domestic demand. Once an agricultural leader, Ukraine's economy has come to depend greatly on steel and other heavy industries. All these industries reported double-digit declines in output during the first quarter of 2009. The reorientation of trade towards Europe and Asia has been going on for several years and is generally regarded as a favourable development. However, it leaves the economy increasingly vulnerable during the current global downturn. Unofficial estimates suggest that the number of unemployed has doubled since the beginning of the global crisis. Up to one million are jobless now. Many have left the country to seek work. Approximately 500,000 are thought to be working in Poland alone.

Main industries The agricultural sector has strengthened in recent years. Ukraine is the world's sixth largest grain exporter and the prospects for a good harvest in 2009 are good. Large foreign investors have spent nearly US$1 billion in Ukraine grain production. A complication is the country's unorthodox policies. Industries such as food processing (where the government has minimised its intervention) are the backbone of the economy. Many manufacturers, however, are struggling in the present crisis. Industrial output began to contract steadily in the second half of 2008. Output has fallen at a double-digit pace during 2009. The country's all-important steel industry has been especially hard hit. The consequences are devastating since steel accounts for 40% of total exports. Many other heavy industries are reporting output declines of up to one-third in the last 12 months. Meanwhile, construction activity has contracted by more than half during the year. The banking industry is under stress. Confidence in the banking system has been quickly eroded and deposits are falling. Several banks will be restructured and recapitalised during 2009. A key element is deposit protection. Minerals are as important to Ukraine as oil is to Russia. The country has the world's largest supply of titanium, the third largest deposit of iron ore and 30% of the world's manganese ore. The metals industry accounts for two-fifth of all exports and output had doubled prior to the global crisis.

Energy Energy is Ukraine's greatest challenge. Most industries are very energy-inefficient, making the country one of the largest energy consumers in Europe. The country has 395 million barrels of proven oil reserves and has had no success in its exploration efforts. Ukraine remains highly dependent on imported oil, most of which comes from Russia. The price of gas imported from Russia has risen dramatically. Ukraine's geographic location provides a useful corridor for oil and natural gas to transit from Russia and the Caspian Sea to European markets. More than a fifth of Russia's oil exports go through the Ukraine or are consumed there. Up to 1.6 million bbl/d could eventually be exported through the country after a 15-year intergovernmental oil transit improvement agreement comes to fruition. The country has 39.6 trillion cubic feet of natural gas but imports large amounts from Russia. In March 2009, the government signed an agreement with the EU to modernise the gas transport system. The EU will provide US$5.5 billion for this purpose. In return, the Ukraine must create an independent gas operator.

United Kingdom

Capital city	London
Capital population	7,695,730 *(2009)*
Population ('000)	61,612.26 *(2009)*
Urban population (%)	89.57 *(2009)*
Land area (sq km)	244,755
Languages	English
Religion	Protestant
Currency	Pound sterling (£)
Head of state	HM Queen Elizabeth II (1952)
Head of government	Gordon Brown (2007)
Ruling party	Labour Party

Main urban areas	Population *(Year)*
London (capital)	7,695,730 *(2009)*
Birmingham	1,018,795 *(2009)*
Glasgow	639,610 *(2009)*
Leeds	483,417 *(2009)*
Manchester	477,916 *(2009)*
Bristol	473,251 *(2009)*
Liverpool	464,633 *(2009)*
Sheffield	461,536 *(2009)*
Edinburgh	455,788 *(2009)*
Leicester	351,357 *(2009)*

Location Lying off the coast of western continental Europe between the Atlantic Ocean and the North Sea, the UK consists mainly of two distinct land masses. The larger incorporates England, Scotland and the Principality of Wales, and the smaller consists of Northern Ireland – actually, the northeastern part of the island of Ireland. The capital is London.

Political structure The UK is considered to be a constitutional monarchy even though it has no written constitution. The non-executive monarch rules through an elected House of Commons (the lower House of Parliament), and this is supplemented in an advisory capacity by a House of Lords (Upper House). Devolved power returned to Northern Ireland in 2007, bringing an end to direct rule from London. In 1997, Scotland voted in favour of a referendum creating a Scottish parliament of 129 members. England and Scotland have shared the same monarch since 1603.

Last elections Elections to the House of Commons took place in May 2005. Labour took 356 seats while the Conservatives captured 197 seats. The Liberal Democrats claimed 62 seats with minor parties taking the remainder. Elections to the Scottish parliament were held in May 2007. The Labour Party won 46 seats while the Scottish National Party took 46 seats. The Scottish Conservatives received 17 seats while the Liberal Democrats won 16 seats. The remainder were divided amongst smaller parties. Tony Blair resigned as prime minister in June 2007 and was replaced by Gordon Brown.

Economy The economy was growing faster than the average for the Eurozone throughout most of this decade. The pace picked up in 2006 but an abrupt slowdown occurred in 2008 when the economy entered a recession in the third quarter. GDP fell by 1.6% in the fourth quarter of 2008. This was the worst result since the second quarter of 2008. Unemployment has also edged upward. Consumer spending has weakened as a result of problems in the housing market and the financial crisis. The savings ratio has soared as consumer confidence slumped. The fiscal position has deteriorated over the past several years. The deficit will rise further in the future as a result of the bailout of large banks. Labour productivity per hour worked remains lower than in other advanced countries. On average, workers in the UK must work nine hours to produce the same output that Germans achieve in eight and workers in France in seven. Growth of productivity has also slowed, reflecting a low capital-labour ratio, low efficiency in the use of capital and labour inputs, and a lack of innovation. The country's infrastructure is also regarded as decrepit and hinders gains in productivity.

Main industries Agriculture is of limited importance, despite the fact that the country is fully self-sufficient in most basic products. Farms tend to be larger than the European average. Growth of manufacturing output is slowing sharply. Car makers and other heavy industries are severely impacted. The government has introduced a £2.3 billion package to support automobile makers. The services sector accounts for two-thirds of GDP. Financial services – the most dynamic part of the sector in recent years – are suffering most. The downsizing of financial services will result in an immense decline in British asset prices. Bank liquidity has been boosted by the government. London's efforts to recapitalise banks have yet to bear results in terms of sustained credit provision. The UK is by far the largest petroleum producer and exporter in the EU (which does not include Norway). It also is the largest producer and an important exporter of natural gas in the EU. The government hopes to have 5% of all transport running on biofuels by 2010.

Energy The UK has 3.4 billion barrels of proven crude oil reserves, the most of any EU member country. The importance of oil has declined slightly over the past two decades. Total oil production was 1.5 million bbl/d in 2008. Analysts predict that the country will become a net importer of these fuels by the end of the decade. Unlike non-EU member Norway, the UK has some onshore oil production and is one of the world's largest oil consumers, ranking in the top 15. Waters in the central North Sea off the east coast of Scotland contain nearly half of the UK's remaining oil reserves, with about a quarter of reserves located in the northern North Sea near the Shetland Islands. There is still some unexplored territory west of the Shetlands. The UK has ambitious plans to develop its nuclear industry. The government is committed to building several nuclear plants and has attracted interest from most of Europe's leading energy companies.

Key European Marketing Information Sources

Sources introduction

This section identifies the major European sources for researching the European market. The listings are not intended to be exhaustive: rather we aim to list some of the main international and national organisations publishing statistics.

Readers are referred to several other currently available and forthcoming Euromonitor International publications for further information on European sources:

Source: Euromonitor
(1st edition, Euromonitor International 2008)

The directory has full contact details for more than 7,000 market information providers, together with details of their activities and publications. These include: official organisations; trade development bodies; business information libraries; leading market research companies; private research publishers; trade associations; major trade and business journals; and on-line database sources.

World Directory of Trade and Business Associations
(5th edition, Euromonitor International 2007)

This directory lists some 5,000 trade associations throughout the world from a broad range of sectors, with details of membership, key personnel, structure, aims and objectives, activities and publications.

World Directory of Business Information Web Sites
(7th edition, Euromonitor International 2007)

Comprehensive coverage of over 2,500 web sites from all over the world. Web sites included offer access to the following types of information: socio-economic statistics; consumer market statistics; industrial market statistics; market research surveys and reports; company information; and business news sources.

World Directory of Business Information Libraries
(6th edition, Euromonitor International, 2007)

This directory details around 1,500 of the world's major libraries that provide public access to business information, including libraries belonging to national statistical offices, chambers of commerce, academic bodies, private companies, etc.

World Directory of Non-Official Statistical Sources
(5th edition, Euromonitor International, 2007)

This directory provides details of over 7,000 regularly produced statistical information publications from non-official organisations throughout the world, with special emphasis on the major industrialised nations including the USA, Canada, and Japan.

Consumer Western Europe 2009/2010
(25th edition, Euromonitor International, 2009)

Primarily a handbook of consumer market data, this annual publication includes a sources section listing the major trade associations and trade journals publishing information on consumer markets across Western Europe.

Consumer Eastern Europe 2009/2010
(17th edition, Euromonitor International, 2009)

As for Consumer Western Europe, this annual publication includes a sources section listing the major trade associations and trade journals publishing information on consumer markets across Eastern Europe.

International Official Sources

Agence Internationale de l'Energie (AIE)

International Energy Agency (IEA)

Address: 9 rue de la Fédération, Paris Cédex 15, 75739, France
Telephone: +33 1 4057 6500
Fax: +33 1 4057 6559
E-mail: info@iea.org
Website: www.iea.org

Guides: web catalogue and online bookshop. The Studies and Country Reviews are available in paper and in PDF format and most statistical publications in paper, PDF or on CD-Rom

Activity: acts as energy policy advisor for its 26 member countries, conducts a broad programme of energy research, data compilation, publications and public dissemination of the latest energy policy analysis and recommendations on good practices.

Website(s) information:

International Energy Agency — **url:** www.iea.org **Description:** compilation of news and articles on the latest developments and issues affecting the world's energy resources sector. Access to oil market reports, and samples of country studies; environmental briefings and essays; and various statistics on world energy resources **Coverage:** by entering the "Statistics Section", online access is provided to a series of annually and monthly updated publications: Key World Statistics; Monthly Electricity Survey; Monthly Price Statistics; Monthly Natural Gas Survey; and Monthly Oil Survey. Access is also provided to IEA Energy Technology R&D Statistics database, 1974-1998, and to Energy Indicators per country

Publication(s):

CO2 Emissions from Fuel Combustion — **Language:** English/French **Frequency:** irregular **Content:** study of emissions of CO2 from 1971 to 2004 for more than 140 countries and regions by sector and by fuel. Emissions were calculated using IEA energy databases and the default methods and emission factors from the Revised 1996 IPCC Guidelines for National Greenhouse Gas Inventories

Coal Information — **Language:** English/French **Frequency:** annual **Content:** Part I provides a statistical overview of developments in the world coal market. It covers world coal production and coal reserves, coal demand by type (hard, steam, coking), hard coal trade and hard coal prices.
Part II provides, in tabular and graphic form, a more detailed and comprehensive statistical picture of historical and current coal developments in the 30 OECD Member countries, by region and individually

Electricity Information — **Language:** English/Russian **Frequency:** monthly **Content:** Part I provides a statistical overview of developments in the electricity and heat market.
Part II provides, in tabular form, detailed and comprehensive statistical coverage of the power and heat industry developments for each of the 30 OECD Member countries and for OECD and IEA regional aggregates

Energy Balances of Non-OECD Countries — **Content:** Contains data on the supply and consumption of coal, oil, gas, electricity, heat, renewables and waste presented as comprehensive energy balances, expressed in tonnes of oil equivalent for over 100 non-OECD countries. Historical tables summarise production, trade and final consumption data as well as key energy and economic indicators **Edition:** 2007

Energy Balances of OECD Countries — **Language:** English/French **Frequency:** annual **Content:** Contains data on the supply and consumption of coal, oil, gas, electricity, heat, renewables and waste presented as comprehensive energy balances expressed in million tonnes of oil equivalent. Historical tables summarise production, trade and final consumption data as well as key energy and economic indicators

Energy Prices and Taxes — **Language:** English **Frequency:** quarterly **Content:** International compilation of energy prices at all market levels: import prices, industry prices and consumer prices. The statistics cover main petroleum products, gas, coal and electricity, giving for imported products an average price both for importing country and country of origin

Energy Statistics of Non-OECD Countries — **Language:** English/French **Frequency:** annual **Content:** contains data on energy supply and consumption in original units for coal, oil, gas, electricity, heat, renewables and waste for over 100 non-OECD countries. Historical tables summarise data on production, trade and final consumption. The book includes definition of products and flows and explanatory notes on the individual country data **Edition:** 2007

Key World Energy Statistics — **Frequency:** annual **Content:** contains statistics on the supply, transformation and consumption of all major energy sources

Natural Gas Information — **Language:** English **Frequency:** annual **Content:** information on LNG and pipeline trade, gas reserves, storage capacity and prices. The main part of the book, concentrates on OECD countries, showing a detailed supply and demand balance for each country and for the three OECD regions: North America, Europe and Pacific, as well as a breakdown of gas consumption by end-user. Import and export data are reported by source and destination

Oil Information — **Frequency:** annual **Content:** Gives current developments in oil supply and demand. The first part of this publication contains key data on world production, trade, prices and consumption of major oil product groups, with time series back to the early 1970s. The second part gives a more detailed and comprehensive picture of oil supply, demand, trade, production and consumption by end-user for each OECD country individually and for the OECD regions

Renewables Information — **Language:** English/Spanish **Content:** Part I provides a statistical overview of developments in the markets for renewables and waste in the OECD Member countries. It also provides selected renewables indicators for non-OECD countries.
Part II provides, in tabular form, a more detailed and comprehensive picture, including preliminary data, of developments for renewable and waste energy sources for each of the 30 OECD Member countries. It encompasses economic and energy indicators, generating capacity, electricity and heat production **Edition:** 2007

World Energy Outlook — **Language:** English **Frequency:** monthly **Content:** Covers energy market reform, energy policy and projections. Projects the impact that targeted policies and more robust deployment of energy technologies could have on sustainability through to 2030

World Energy Statistics — **Language:** English **Frequency:** annual **Content:** Provides annual historical energy data extracted from four IEA/OECD data bases: energy statistics and energy balances, which contain data for most of the OECD countries from 1960 and energy statistics and balances for more than 100 non-OECD countries from 1971

Bank for International Settlements

Address: Centralbahnplatz 2, Basel, 4002, Switzerland
Telephone: +41 61 280 8080
Fax: +41 61 280 9100
E-mail: email@bis.org
Website: www.bis.org

Guides: annual and quarterly reports on financial markets, reports on current issues regarding business

Activity: fosters international monetary and financial cooperation and serves as a bank for central banks

Website(s) information:

Bank for International Settlements — **url:** www.bis.org **Description:** contains a series of detailed reports covering economic, banking and financial markets **Coverage:** statistics on the world banking industry and regulations: international banking statistics; consolidated banking statistics; securities statistics; derivatives statistics; triennial foreign exchange and derivatives survey; joint BIS-IMF-OECD-World Bank Statistics on External Debt; guide to the international banking statistics; the BIS statistics on international banking and financial market activity

Publication(s):

Annual Report — **Language:** English/German/Spanish/French/Italian **Frequency:** annual **Content:** annual survey of the global economy, monetary policy in the advanced industrial economies, foreign exchange markets, financial markets, etc

BIS Quarterly Review — **Language:** English/German/Spanish/French/Italian **Frequency:** quarterly **Content:** overview of the international banking market, the international debt securities market, the derivatives market, and special features

Common Fund for Commodities

Address: PO Box 74656, Amsterdam, 1070 BR, Netherlands
Telephone: +31 20 575 4949
Fax: +31 20 676 0231
Website: www.common-fund.org

Guides: reports based on project and country can be downloaded free

Activity: intergovernmental financial institution established within the framework of the UN. The Fund's specific mandate is to support developing countries that are commodity dependent to improve and diversify commodities production and trade

Website(s) information:

Common Fund for Commodities — **url:** www.common-fund.org **Description:** Common Fund for Commodities is a partnership of 106 Member States. The European Community (EC), the African Union (AU), the Common Market for Eastern and Southern Africa (COMESA) are institutional members. Membership is also open to Members States of the United Nations, its specialised agencies; and the International Atomic Energy Agency, in addition to intergovernmental and regional economic integration organisations. Projects can be selected by country and commodity and downloaded from the website

Food and Agricultural Organisation of the United Nations (FAO)

Address: Viale delle Terme di Caracalla, Rome, 00100, Italy
Telephone: +39 06 57051
Fax: +39 06 5705 3152
E-mail: FAO-HQ@fao.org
Website: www.fao.org

Guides: FAO Books in Print (annual catalogue of FAO publications in English, free of charge); list of documents (listing of publications in all languages)

Activity: the FAO leads international efforts to defeat hunger; helps developing countries and countries in transition to modernise and improve agriculture, forestry and fisheries practices and ensure good nutrition for all

Website(s) information:

FAOSTAT — **url:** www.fao.org **Description:** FAOSTAT is a statistical database of FAO that currently contains more than 3 million time-series records. FAOSTAT-ON LINE can be accessed on the FAO Web site at http://faostat.fao.org. Incorporates statistical information as available on-line at the end of May 2005, covering more than 300 countries and territories and 3000 items in many areas of agriculture, fisheries, forestry and nutrition **Coverage:** access to worldwide databases on food related sectors: agriculture; nutrition; fisheries; forestry; food quality control; innternational statistics cover production; trade; fertiliser and pesticides; land use and irrigation; forest products; fishery products; population; agricultural machinery; and food aid shipments

Publication(s):

FAO Statistical Yearbook — **Language:** English/French/Spanish/Arabic/Chinese **Frequency:** annual **Content:** indicators by topic for all countries of the world

Key Statistics of Food and Agriculture External Trade — **Content:** statistics on commodities imported and exported by country

Major Food and Agricultural Commodities and Producers — **Language:** English **Content:** agricultural production statistics for the 20 most important food and agricultural commodities (ranked by value) in a given country for the year indicated

State of Agricultural Commodity Markets — **Language:** English **Frequency:** irregular **Content:** coverage of the development and food security needs of developing countries

State of Food and Agricultural — **Language:** English/French/Spanish/Arabic/Chinese **Frequency:** annual **Content:** provides a set of indicators for the food and agricultural sector for the various countries in the world

State of the World's Forests — **Language:** English **Frequency:** biennial **Content:** offers a global perspective on the forest sector, including its environmental, economic and social dimensions. Part I reviews progress region by region. Each regional report is structured according to the seven thematic elements of sustainable forest management. Part II presents selected issues in the forest sector, probing the state of knowledge or recent activities in 18 topics of interest to forestry. Climate change, forest landscape restoration, forest tenure, invasive species, wildlife management

State of World Fisheries and Aquaculture — **Language:** English **Frequency:** annual **Content:** recognition of the many failures in management have now led FAO member countries and other relevant stakeholders to broaden the approach and governance used to manage fisheries and aquaculture in a sustainable manner

Summary of World Food and Agricultural Statistics — **Language:** English **Content:** broad range of statistics pertaining to world food and agriculture; presents the differences between developed and developing countries, continents and regions. The figures given refer to the most recent period for which data are available and, where relevant, for selected benchmark periods to allow analysis of trends over time

Yearbook of Forest Products — **Language:** English/French.Spanish.Arabic/Chinese **Content:** compilation of statistical data on basic forest products for all countries and territories of the world. Contains annual data on the production and trade of forest products and also contains historic information

International Atomic Energy Agency

Address: PO Box 100, Wagramer Strasse 5, Vienna, A-1400, Austria
Telephone: +43 1 2600-0
Fax: +43 1 2600-7
E-mail: info@iaea.org
Website: www.iaea.org

Activity: works for the safe, secure and peaceful uses of nuclear science and technology. Its key roles contribute to international peace and security, and to the World's Millennium Goals for social, economic and environmental development

Publication(s):

IAEA Annual Report — **Language:** English/Arabic/Chinese/French/Spanish/Russian **Content:** summarises and highlights developments over the past year in major areas of the Agency's work. It includes a summary of major issues, activities, and achievements, and status tables and graphs related to safeguards, safety, and science and technology

International Civil Aviation Organisation (ICAO)

Address: 999 University Street, Montreal, H3C 5H7, QUE, Canada
Telephone: +1 514 954 8219
Fax: +1 514 954 6077
E-mail: sta@icao.int
Website: www.icao.int

Activity: ICAO works in close co-operation with other members of the United Nations family such as the World Meteorological Organisation, the International Telecommunication Union, the Universal Postal Union, the World Health Organization and the International Maritime Organization. Non-governmental organizations which also participate in ICAO's work include the International Air Transport Association, the Airports Council International, the International Federation of Air Line Pilots' Associations, and the International Council of Aircraft Owner and Pilot Associations.

Website(s) information:

ICAOData — **url:** www.icaodata.com/ **Description:** The database contains detailed financial, traffic, personnel and fleet information for commercial air carriers. It also holds Traffic by Flight Stage (TFS) information and On-flight Origin/Destination statistics for air carriers. Financial and traffic data for airports and air navigation service providers also available **Coverage:** Coverage includes commercial air carriers (traffic, on-flight origin and destination, traffic by flight stage, fleet-personnel and financial data), airports (airport traffic and financial data), air navigation service providers (financial and traffic data), as well as data on civil aircraft on register

International Coffee Organisation

Address: 22 Berners Street, London, W1T 3DD, United Kingdom
Telephone: +44 20 7612 0600
Fax: +44 20 7612 0630
E-mail: info@ico.org
Website: www.ico.org

Guides: unrestricted free access is provided to Coffee Prices and Trade Statistics on this site. For the users who require more detailed information the ICO offers a subscription service to its statistical and economic data, including monthly exports, quarterly and annual statistics with comprehensive data which include statistics supply, exports/imports, indicator prices, prices paid to growers and retail prices.

Activity: intergovernmental organisation for coffee, bringing together producing and consuming countries to tackle the challenges facing the world coffee sector through international cooperation

Website(s) information:

***International Coffee Organisation* — url:** www.ico.org **Description:** Unrestricted free access is provided to coffee prices and trade statistics on this site. For the users who require more detailed information the ICO offers a subscription service to its statistical and economic data, including monthly exports, quarterly and annual statistics with comprehensive data which include statistics supply, exports/imports, indicator prices, prices paid to growers and retail prices **Coverage:** exports, imports, market prices, prices to growers, production, stocks and inventories

International Copper Study Group (ICSG)

Address:	6th Floor, Rue Almirante Barroso, Lisbon, 1000-013, Portugal
Telephone:	+351 21 351 3870
Fax:	+351 21 352 4035
E-mail:	mail@icsg.org
Website:	www.icsg.org

Activity: intergovernmental organisation that serves to increase copper market transparency and promote international discussions and cooperation on issues related to copper

Website(s) information:

***International Copper Study Group (ICSG)* — url:** www.icsg.org **Coverage:** trends in world refined copper stocks and prices; world refined copper production and usage trends; copper mine, smelter, refinery production, and refined copper usage by geographical area

Publication(s):

Copper Bulletin — **Frequency:** monthly **Content:** Includes statistics on copper and copper products, their production, consumption and trade by country, providing a global view of supply and demand

Copper Bulletin Yearbook — **Frequency:** annual **Content:** Includes annual statistics on copper and copper products, their production, usage and trade by country, as well as stocks and exchange prices, providing a global view of supply and demand for the past 10 years. Subscribers to the Copper Bulletin receive the Yearbook as part of their annual subscription

Directory of Copper and Copper Alloy Fabricators (First Use) — **Frequency:** annual **Content:** covers wire rod plants, ingot makers (for castings), master alloy plants, brass mills, and electrodeposited copper foil mills. Powder and chemical plants are not included. Encompasses data to the end of the year for over 75 countries and over 1200 existing, developing and planned first use plants, with anticipated changes in the coming year

Directory of Copper Mines and Plants — **Frequency:** quarterly **Content:** Highlights current capacity and provides a five year outlook of forecasted capacity for over 700 existing and planned copper mines, plants and refineries on a country by country basis

International Cotton Advisory Committee (ICAC)

Address:	1629 - K Street NW, Suite 702, Washington, DC 20006-1636, USA
Telephone:	+1 202 463 6660
Fax:	+1 202 463 6950
E-mail:	secretariat@icac.org
Website:	www.icac.org

Guides: online publications catalogue

Activity: provides statistics on world cotton production, consumption, trade and stocks and to identify emerging changes in the structure of the world cotton market

Website(s) information:

***International Cotton Advisory Committee (ICAC)* — url:** www.icac.org **Coverage:** Cotton supply and demand, production, prices, forecasts

Publication(s):

Cotton This Month — **Language:** English/French/Russian/Spanish **Frequency:** monthly **Content:** Supply, demand and price projections.

Cotton: Review of the World Situation — **Language:** English/French/Spanish **Frequency:** bi-monthly **Content:** Examination of the world cotton market. Provides projections of world supply and demand by country and international cotton prices

Cotton: World Statistics — **Language:** English/French/Spanish **Content:** World cotton supply/demand statistics since 1940/41 Data by country since 1980/81 with 5-year projections. Tables updated twice a year

World Cotton Trade — **Frequency:** annual **Content:** Trade developments in raw cotton since 1980

International Fund for Agricultural Development (IFAD)

Address:	Via del Serafico 107, Rome, 00142, Italy
Telephone:	+39 6 545 91
Fax:	+39 6 504 3463
E-mail:	ifad@ifad.org
Website:	www.ifad.org

Guides: publications available in English, Spanish, Arabic and French

Activity: specialist agency of the United Nations dedicated to eradicating rural poverty in developing countries

Website(s) information:

***International Fund for Agricultural Development* — url:** www.ifad.org **Coverage:** statistical information on rural poverty, rural finance, food security and nutrition, livestock and agricultural land areas

Publication(s):

IFAD Annual Report — **Language:** English/French/German **Frequency:** annual **Content:** provides statistical information on countries' performance in the areas of science, technology, globalisation and industry

International Grains Council

Address:	1 Canada Square, Canary Wharf, London, E14 5AE, United Kingdom
Telephone:	+44 20 7513 1122
Fax:	+44 20 7513 0630
E-mail:	igc-fac@igc.org.uk
Website:	www.igc.org.uk

Activity: intergovernmental organisation concerned with the grain trade. It administers the Grains Trade Convention 1995

Website(s) information:

***International Grains Council* — url:** www.igc.org.uk **Coverage:** Grain Market Report subscribers can take advantage of a weekly electronic service designed to provide updates on the latest grain market developments. In addition to the current monthly report GMRPlus will have two elements. Grain Market Indicators, to be issued each Wednesday, will provide the latest export price and US futures quotations and carry short market commentaries on wheat, maize (corn), other grains (barley, sorghum, oats, rye and soyabeans) and ocean freight rates. GMR Statistics Update will allow subscribers to access weekly updates of some key GMR statistical tables, as well as a weekly diary of main grain market events

Publication(s):

Grain Market Report — **Language:** English/French/Russian/Spanish **Frequency:** monthly **Content:** review of the current situation and outlook for wheat (including durum) and coarse grains (including maize (corn), barley, sorghum, oats and rye). Separate chapters cover production, trade, consumption, stocks, prices, ocean freight rates and national policy developments. The analysis is supported by some 30 statistical tables with periodic features on trade in wheat flour and barley malt. Subscribers can take advantage of a weekly electronic service designed to provide updates on the latest grain market

Wheat and Coarse Grain Shipments — **Content:** Provides 50 pages of tables, detailed statistics on commercial and non-commercial world trade in wheat (including wheat flour, durum and semolina) and coarse grains (including maize (corn), barley, sorghum, oats and rye) in the crop year **Edition:** 2004/2005

World Grain Statistics — **Frequency:** annual **Content:** tables on production, trade, consumption, stocks and prices for wheat (including durum and wheat flour) and coarse grains. Additional tables deal with ocean freight rates. Most tables cover a 10-year period **Edition:** 2005

International Jute Study Group (IJSG)

Address:	145 Monipuripara, Near Farmgate Tejgaon, Dhaka, 1215, Bangladesh
Telephone:	+880 2 912 4887
Fax:	+880 2 912 5248
E-mail:	info@jute.org
Website:	www.jute.org

Activity: intergovernmental body set up under the aegis of UNCTAD to function as the International Commodity Body (ICB) for jute, kenaf and other allied fibres

Website(s) information:

International Jute Study Group (IJSG) — **url:** www.jute.org **Description:** Online statistical search by country and by year **Coverage:** production, imports, exports and consumption of jute and jute products

---

International Labour Organisation (ILO)

Address: 4 route des Morillons, Geneva 22, 1211, Switzerland
Telephone: +41 22 799 7912
Fax: +41 22 799 8577
E-mail: communication@ilo.org
Website: www.ilo.org

Guides: online catalogue in PDF format
Labordoc, the ILO Library catalogue, contains over 350,000 references

Activity: UN specialised agency which seeks the promotion of social justice and internationally recognised human and labour rights

Website(s) information:

International Labour Migration Database (ILM) — **url:** www.ilo.org **Coverage:** contains basic data on stocks and flows of migrant labour

LABORDOC — **url:** www.ilo.org **Description:** Labordoc, the ILO Library's database, contains references and full text access to the world's literature on the world of work. It covers all aspects of work and sustainable livelihoods and the work-related aspects of economic and social development, human rights and technological change **Coverage:** databases covering a wide variety of topics and areas within the labour market sector: CISDOC; ILOLEX; LABORDOC; LABORSTA; NATLEX, etc.

LABORSTA — **url:** http//laborsta.ilo.org **Description:** LABORSTA is the main ILO database on labour statistics covering economically active population, employment, unemployment, employment by sex for detailed occupational group, public sector employment, statistical sources and methods, hours of work, wages, etc **Coverage:** yearly and periodical data of total and economically active population, employment, unemployment, hours of work, wages, labour costs, consumer price indices, occupational injuries, strikes and lockouts

Publication(s):

Bulletin of Labour Statistics — **Language:** English/French/Spanish **Frequency:** bi-annual **Content:** statistics on general level of employment; employment in non-agricultural activities and employment in manufacturing; data on unemployment rates; average number of hours worked; average earnings or wage rates; consumer prices; general indices and food indices **Readership:** international organisation; labour statisticians

Decent Working Time. New trends, new issues — **Language:** English **Frequency:** irregular **Content:** covers the problems relating to increasing employment insecurity and instability, time-related social inequalities, particularly in relation to gender, workers' ability to balance their paid work with their personal lives, and even the synchronisation of working hours with social times, such as community activities. In addition, the book offers valuable insights on how policy-makers, academics, and the social partners can together help further develop and refine an effective policy framework for advancing

Occupational Wages and Hours of Work and Retail Food Prices, Statistics from the ILO October Inquiry — **Edition:** 2005

Yearbook of Labour Statistics — **Language:** English/French/Spanish **Frequency:** annual **Content:** development of labour, living and working conditions throughout the world; includes statistical information on more than 190 countries, areas and territories, from the last ten years; information is on total and economically active population, employment, unemployment, hours of work, wages, labour costs, consumer prices, occupational injuries, and strikes and lockouts **Edition:** 65th Edition

---

International Lead and Zinc Study Group

Address: 5th Floor, Rua Almirante Barroso 38, Lisbon, 1000-013, Portugal
Telephone: +351 21 359 2420
Fax: +351 21 359 2429
E-mail: root@ilzsg.org
Website: www.ilzsg.org/ilzsgframe.htm

Activity: works to ensure transparency in the markets for lead and zinc worldwide; tracks world developments in the market

Website(s) information:

International Lead and Zinc Study Group — **url:** www.ilzsg.org **Description:** Includes subscription to electronic statistical database with data back to 1960. Statistical overview is free
Coverage: Detailed figures on mine production, metal production, metal consumption, principal imports and exports of concentrates and refined metal, secondary recovery, prices and stocks

Publication(s):

Lead & Zinc: End Use Industry Statistical Supplement — **Language:** English **Content:** This report covers the ten-year period 1994-2003, with information from 79 countries. Included are data on the world automotive industry, battery shipments in major markets, the construction sector, the galvanizing of steel sheet worldwide, general galvanizing in Europe, the production of kitchen appliances and brass production. Economic and social data by country and industrial production indices, for both total and metal products industries and historic oil price levels are also presented

Monthly Bulletin — **Language:** English **Content:** Detailed figures on mine production, metal production, metal consumption, principal imports and exports of concentrates and refined metal, secondary recovery, prices and stocks. Includes subscription to electronic statistical database with data back to 1960.

World Directory 2006: Primary and Secondary Lead Plants — **Language:** English **Content:** An overview and full detailed listing of primary and secondary lead smelters and refineries in 55 countries showing addresses, telephone and fax numbers, e-mail, web addresses types of plant operated and current capacities. Also includes summary tables and graphs. 92 pages

---

International Monetary Fund (IMF)

Address: 700 19th Street NW, Washington, DC 20431, , USA
Telephone: +1 202 623 7000
Fax: +1 202 623 4661
E-mail: publicaffairs@imf.org
Website: www.imf.org

Guides: publications catalogue available online

Activity: fosters global monetary cooperation among 184 member countries, secures financial stability, facilitates international trade, promotes high employment and sustainable economic growth

Website(s) information:

International Monetary Fund — **url:** www.imf.org **Description:** global view of international monetary and economic affairs. Access to a series of news, fact sheets, briefings and databases on world economic growth, international capital markets and various online publications, including IMF's Annual Report **Coverage:** statistics on different economic, financial and monetary issues can be found in various online publications and fact sheets. The Country Reports section includes individual country statistical appendixes for most IMF member nations

Publication(s):

Balance of Payments Statistics Yearbook — **Language:** English **Frequency:** annual **Content:** balance of payments statistics covering most countries in the world

Direction of Trade Statistics — **Language:** English/French/Spanish **Frequency:** quarterly **Content:** provides data on the country and area distribution of countries' exports and imports. Quarterly issues cover data for the most recent six quarters and the latest year for about 156 countries and ten quarters and five years for the world and area tables

Direction of Trade Statistics Yearbook — **Language:** English/French/Spanish/Arabic **Frequency:** annual **Content:** contains annual data covering 12 years for countries appearing in the monthly issues of IFS

Global Financial Stability Report — **Language:** English/French/German **Frequency:** Semi-annual **Content:** semi-annual publication provides comprehensive coverage of mature and emerging financial markets and seeks to identify potential fault lines in the global financial system that could lead to crises. It is designed to deepen understanding of global capital flows, which play a critical role as an engine of world economic growth

Government Finance Statistics Yearbook — **Language:** English **Frequency:** annual **Content:** contains statistical data on government financial operations for 133 IMF member countries

IMF Survey — **Language:** English **Frequency:** 22 per annum **Content:** macroeconomic research and policy analyses, country analyses, issues in international finance, as well as the latest development in IMF policies and activities

International Financial Statistics — **Language:** English **Frequency:** monthly **Content:** statistics covering international reserves, interest rates, exchange rates, prices, unit values and commodity prices, trade, national accounts

International Financial Statistics Yearbook — **Language:** English **Frequency:** annual **Content:** contains some additional series to the monthly edition

World Economic Outlook — **Language:** English/French/Spanish/Arabic **Frequency:** 2 per annum **Content:** global outlook on the world's economy, analysing latest economic and financial developments in developed and developing countries, as well as emerging markets

International Network for Bamboo and Rattan (INBAR)

Address: PO Box 100102-86, Beijing, 100102, China
Telephone: +86 10 6470 6161
Fax: +86 10 6470 2166
E-mail: info@inbar.int
Website: www.inbar.int

Activity: international organisation dedicated to improving the social, economic, and environmental benefits of bamboo and rattan. INBAR connects a global network of partners from the government, private, and not-for-profit sectors in over 50 countries to define and implement a global agenda for sustainable development through bamboo and rattan

Publication(s):

Journal of Bamboo and Rattan — **Language:** English **Frequency:** irregular **Content:** journal on research and development of bamboo and rattan, including technical properties, socio-economical aspects, environmental aspects and bio-energetics

International Nickel Study Group (INSG)

Address: Scheveningseweg 62, The Hague, 2517 KX, Netherlands
Telephone: +31 70 354 3326
Fax: +31 70 358 4612
E-mail: insg@insg.org
Website: www.insg.org

Activity: autonomous, intergovernmental organisation engaged in publishing statistics on nickel markets, facilities and environmental regulations and provides a forum for discussion on nickel issues

Website(s) information:

International Nickel Study Group (INSG) — **url:** www.insg.org/curstats.htm **Coverage:** world nickel statistics in thousands of tonnes

Publication(s):

World Nickel Statistics — **Frequency:** monthly **Content:** special Issues are published once a year in the November issue and contain annual data for the latest available 11-year period; the other eleven monthly issues focus on the latest available monthly data covering about 22 months plus annual data for the most recent two to three years

International Olive Oil Council (IOOC)

Address: Príncipe de Vergara 154, , Madrid, 28002, Spain
Telephone: +34 91 590 3638
Fax: +34 91 563 1263
E-mail: iooc@internationaloliveoil.org
Website: www.internationaloliveoil.org

Activity: intergovernmental organisation in charge of administering the International Olive Oil Agreement, groups 98% of world olive production, located primarily in the Mediterranean region

Website(s) information:

International Olive Council — **url:** www.internationaloliveoil.org **Description:** provides series of world statistics on production, imports, exports and consumption; access to publications and lists of importers and exporters

    Coverage: olive production, import, export and consumption statistics

Publication(s):

EU Producer Prices — **Language:** English **Frequency:** annual **Content:** data on producer prices of virgin olive oil, refined olive oil and refined olive-pomace oil on representative markets inside the European Union

World Olive Oil Figures — **Language:** English/French **Frequency:** annual **Content:** world statistics on production, imports, exports and consumption

World Table Olive Figures — **Language:** English/French **Frequency:** annual **Content:** world statistics on production, imports, exports and consumption

International Rubber Study Group

Address: 1st Floor, Heron House, 109/115 Wembley Hill Road, Wembley, HA9 8DA, Middlesex, United Kingdom
Telephone: +44 20 8900 5400
Fax: +44 20 8903 2848
E-mail: irsg@rubberstudy.com
Website: www.rubberstudy.com

Activity: provides a forum for the discussion of matters affecting the supply and demand for both synthetic and natural rubber. It covers all aspects of the world rubber industry, including marketing, shipping, distribution and trade in raw materials and the manufacture and sale of rubber products

Publication(s):

Outlook for Elastomers — **Frequency:** annual **Content:** Provides the Study Group's latest authoritative, in-depth analysis of production and consumption of elastomers for the previous year with estimates and forecasts for the current year, and the following year

Rubber Statistical Bulletin — **Frequency:** bi-monthly **Content:** reports authoritative rubber statistics. Data is reported in monthly format and is available by country

Summary of World Rubber Statistics — **Content:** Provides information on rubber production, consumption, trade and prices in a vastly simplified format, without the wealth of detail in the Group's flagship document, the Rubber Statistical Bulletin, on which it is based. Data is limited to two years - latest year versus last year - with trends over the past five years indicated in graphical format

World Rubber Statistics Handbook 1975-2001 — **Frequency:** irregular **Content:** Covers all aspects of the world elastomer economy and associated rubber products such as tyres, cars and commercial vehicles. It contains authoritative statistics on the production, consumption and trade in natural and synthetic rubber as reported in the bimonthly Rubber Statistical Bulletin, including revisions to data series back to 1975 **Edition:** Volume 6

International Statistical Institute (ISI)

Address: PO Box 950, Prinses Beatrixlaan 428, Voorburg, 2270 AZ, Netherlands
Telephone: +31 70 337 5737
Fax: +31 70 386 0025
E-mail: isi@cbs.nl
Website: www.cbs.nl/isi/

Activity: an autonomous society, which seeks to develop and improve statistical methods and their application through the promotion of international activity and co-operation

Website(s) information:

International Statistical Institute — **url:** www.cbs.nl/isi/ **Coverage:** contains addresses of publishers of statistics, mathematics and probability; a listing of statistical publications, books and statistics online; annual report, economic data

Publication(s):
Directory of Official Statistical Agencies & Societies — **Language:** English **Frequency:** annual **Content:** contact details of official statistical agencies throughout the world

International Telecommunication Union (ITU)

Address: Place des Nations, Geneva 20, 1211, Switzerland
Telephone: +41 22 730 5111
Fax: +41 22 733 7256
E-mail: itumail@itu.int
Website: www.itu.int

Activity: covers all aspects of telecommunication, from setting standards; adopting operational procedures; designing programmes to improve telecommunication infrastructure in the developing world

Website(s) information:
International Telecommunications Union (ITU) — **url:** www.itu.int **Coverage:** overview of the telecommunications industry worldwide; access to several industry related databases and to online publications as well as online statistical documents

Publication(s):
African Telecommunication Indicators — **Language:** English/French/Spanish **Frequency:** annual **Content:** 20 regional tables covering key telecommunication indicators, 55 individual country pages with a five-year profile from 1998-2002, and a directory with names of telecommunication ministries, regulators and operators in the region **Edition:** 7th Edition

Americas Telecommunication Indicators — **Language:** English/Spanish **Frequency:** annual **Content:** comprises an analytical overview, regional and country statistics and a directory of telecommunication organisations **Edition:** 2005

Asia-Pacific Telecommunication Indicators — **Language:** English/Russian **Content:** The publication consists of three parts: an analytical overview, regional statistics and a directory of telecommunication organizations **Edition:** 6th Edition

World Telecommunication Indicators — **Language:** English **Content:** contains time series data for the years 1960, 1965, 1970 and annually from 1975-2004 for around 80 communications statistics covering telephone network size and dimension, other services, quality of service, traffic, staff, tariffs, revenue and investment **Readership:** Telecommunication academics and libraries **Edition:** 9th

World Telecommunication/ICT Development Report — **Language:** English/French/Spanish **Frequency:** annual **Content:** reviews the progress made in measuring the impact of ICT on social and economic development; the report provides the latest telecommunication/ICT indicators for some 180 economies worldwide **Readership:** Telecommunication academics and libraries

Yearbook of Statistics - Telecommunications Services — **Language:** English **Frequency:** annual **Content:** compilation of annual statistical data relating to the development of the telecommunications industry worldwide **Readership:** Telecommunication academics and libraries **Edition:** 33rd Edition

International Trade Centre UNCTAD/WTO (ITC)

Address: Palais des Nations, Geneva 10, 1211, Switzerland
Telephone: +41 22 730 0111
Fax: +41 22 733 4439
E-mail: itcreg@intracen.org
Website: www.intracen.org

Guides: publishes directories and bibliographies, market survey and commodities handbooks, and trade promotion handbooks

Activity: technical cooperation agency of the United Nations Conference on Trade and Development (UNCTAD) and the World Trade Organization (WTO) for operational, enterprise-oriented aspects of trade development.
ITC supports developing and transition economies, and particularly their business sector, in their efforts to realize their full potential for developing exports and improving import operations

Website(s) information:
International Trade Centre (UNCTAD/WTO) — **url:** www.intracen.org **Description:** development and promotion of trade activities between developed and developing countries, as well as emerging economies. Information provided on: product-specific trade, from handicraft products to coffee, leather products, textiles, etc; trade in services; and access to ITC databases on Trade Information Index and Periodicals **Coverage:** country-specific business information, including trade statistics for UN individual member nations: trade performance index; national export performance; national import profile; trade and employment, etc

Publication(s):
International Trade Forum — **Language:** Spanish/French/English **Frequency:** quarterly **Content:** covers trade promotion and development of exporting and importing activities in developing countries and economies in transition

World Directory of Trade Promotion Organisations and Other Foreign Trade Bodies —

International Tropical Timber Organization (ITTO)

Address: International Organizations Center, 5th Floor, Pacifico-Yokohama 1-1-1, Minato-Mirai, Nishi-ku, Yokohama, 220-0012, Japan
Telephone: +81 45 223 1110
Fax: +81 45 223 1111
E-mail: itto@itto.or.jp
Website: www.itto.or.jp

Activity: intergovernmental organisation promoting the conservation and sustainable management, use and trade of tropical forest resources

Website(s) information:
International Tropical Timber Organization (ITTO) — **url:** www.itto.or.jp
Description: Registered users get free access to the ITTO MIS report, which is updated every two weeks, and access to the MIS archive, which contains reports dating back to 1998 **Coverage:** MIS delivers a twice-monthly report on the international tropical timber market. Provides market trends and trade news from around the world, as well as indicative prices for over 400 tropical timber and added-value products

Publication(s):
Annual Review and Assessment of the World Timber Situation — **Language:** English/French/Spanish **Content:** International statistics available on global production and trade of timber, with an emphasis on the tropics. Includes chapters on the Production and Trade of Timber, over 5 years and Trade in Secondary Processed Wood Products. It also provides information on trends in forest area, forest management and the economies of ITTO member countries. Data tables are available as Excel files

Organisation for Economic Co-operation and Development (OECD)

Address: 2 rue André Pascal, Paris Cédex 16, 75775, France
Telephone: +33 1 4524 8200
Fax: +33 1 4524 8500
E-mail: sales@oecd.org
Website: www.oecd.org

Guides: OECD Statistics Catalogue available online
Activity: discussion, development and fine-tuning of economic and social policies

Website(s) information:
SourceOECD — **url:** www.oecd.org **Description:** Online library of all OECD books, periodicals, working papers and statistical databases from January 1998 to date. Includes 100 indicators for the world's leading economies. **Coverage:** statistical section includes a wide range of data on different socio-economic indicators for OECD member countries. Statistics are sold as hard-copy publications, on CD-ROM format, or online. Some of the data available online (subject to charge) covers: general OECD statistics (from demographic trends to environment and health); economic statistics; agricultural and food statistics (agricultural databases); energy statistics; development co-operation and public management; education, labour and social affairs; science, technology and industry statistics; health statistics; and transport statistics

Publication(s):

Education Trends In Perspective: Analysis of the World Education Indicators — **Language:** English **Frequency:** irregular **Content:** Data on educational attainment, education expectancy, enrolment rates of different age groups, age ranges of universal primary and secondary education, female participation, upper secondary enrolment patterns, entry rates into upper secondary and tertiary education, graduation rates, grade repetition, population and GDP, expenditure on education, teaching staff, class size, teachers salaries, and expenditure per student

Health at a Glance — **Language:** English **Content:** provides the latest comparable data and trends on different aspects of the performance of health systems in OECD countries **Readership:** Health researchers, policy advisors in Governments, private sector and academic communities

Insurance Statistics Yearbook — **Language:** English/French **Frequency:** annual **Content:** Provides annual information on insurance activities including: number of companies, number of employees, premiums by type of insurance, market share by foreign companies in each country, business written abroad, premiums in terms of risk destination (foreign or domestic risks), foreign and domestic investments, gross claims payments, gross operating expenses and commissions, OECD market share, penetration, density, and premiums per employee

International Migration Outlook — **Language:** English/French **Frequency:** annual **Content:** international migration statistics and legislation

International Trade by Commodity Statistics — **Language:** English/French **Frequency:** 5 p.a. **Content:** Provides import and export data in US dollars broken down by commodity and by partner country. Each of the first four volumes of ITCS contains the tables for 7 or 8 OECD countries. The data are published in the volumes as they come in from reporting countries.
The fifth volume includes the OECD main country groupings (OECD-Total, NAFTA, OECD-Asia Pacific, OECD-Europe, EU-15, etc). For each country, this publication shows detailed tables relating to the SITC

Labour Force Statistics — **Language:** English/French **Content:** provides detailed statistics on population, labour force, employment and unemployment over the past 10 years

Main Economic Indicators — **Language:** English/French **Frequency:** monthly **Content:** provides a comprehensive picture of the most recent economic statistics in the 30 OECD countries and a number of non-member countries including Brazil, China, India, Indonesia, the Russian Federation, and South Africa

Monthly Statistics of International Trade — **Language:** English/French **Frequency:** monthly **Content:** source of data on trade flows between OECD countries and their trading partners. Provides detailed insight into the most recent trends in world trading patterns. Available in other formats (Pdf, CD-ROM, Online)

OECD Agricultural Outlook 2006-2015 — **Language:** English/French **Content:** Provides an assessment of agricultural market prospects based on medium-term projections that extend to 2015 for production, consumption, trade and prices of major agricultural commodities **Edition:** 12th Edition

OECD Communications Outlook — **Language:** English/French **Frequency:** irregular **Content:** provides an extensive range of indicators for different types of communications networks and compares performance indicators such as revenue, investment, employment and prices for service throughout the OECD area

OECD Economic Outlook — **Language:** English/French/German **Frequency:** 2 p.a. **Content:** analyses major trends and examines the economic policies required to foster high and sustainable growth in member countries. Developments in major non-OECD economies are also evaluated

OECD Economic Surveys — **Language:** English/French **Frequency:** regular **Content:** national economic survey and prospects for each OECD member country. Most reports are for 2006 and 2007

OECD Employment Outlook — **Language:** English/French **Frequency:** irregular **Content:** overview of labour markets in OECD countries and its comprehensive statistical annex, this edition also includes articles covering trade adjustment costs in OECD labour markets, regional disparities in labour markets, the role of in-work benefits in increasing employment, and evaluating the impact of labour market programmes and public employment services

OECD Factbook 2007 - Economic, Environmental, and Social Statistics — **Language:** English/French **Content:** statistical annual covering all OECD countries and most topics addressed by the OECD. Includes more than 100 indicators with definitions, time-series tables, and graphics showing key messages **Edition:** 3rd Edition

OECD Health Data — **Language:** English/French **Frequency:** annual **Content:** statistics and health indicators for 30 countries

OECD Journal on Development — **Language:** English **Frequency:** 4 per annum **Content:** annual reference document for statistics and analysis on the latest trends in international aid

OECD Science, Technology and Industry Scoreboard — **Language:** English **Frequency:** bi-annual **Content:** explores the growing interaction between knowledge and globalisation. As innovation becomes a key determinant for long-run economic growth and social well-being, the STI Scoreboard provides a comprehensive picture of countries' performance in the areas of science, technology, globalisation and industry **Edition:** 8th Edition

Oil, Gas, Coal and Electricity -Quarterly Statistics — **Language:** English/French **Frequency:** quarterly **Content:** detailed data on production of crude oil, natural gas, liquids and refinery stocks, crude oil and product trades, refinery intake and output, final consumption, stock levels and changes

Review of Fisheries in OECD Countries — **Language:** English/French **Frequency:** annual **Content:** volume 1 covers Policy and Summary Statistics (major developments affecting fisheries in OECD countries, including changes in government policies, trade, and fisheries and aquaculture production. Summary statistics are included for each country); Volume 2 covers Country Statistics (fishing fleet, employment in fisheries, government financial transfers, total allowable catches, landings, aquaculture production, recreational fisheries, and imports and exports)

Trends in the Transport Sector 1970-2006 — **Language:** English/French **Content:** Internationally comparable figures on key transport trends. Analysis of the transport situation in the western and eastern European countries, as well as the Baltic States and the CIS

Organisation Internationale de la Vigne et du Vin (OIV)
International Organisation for Vine and Wine

Address: 18 rue D'Aguesseau, Paris, 75008, France
Telephone: +33 1 4494 8080
Fax: +33 1 4266 9063
E-mail: contact@oiv.int
Website: www.oiv.int

Activity: intergovernmental organisation working with vines, wine, wine-based beverages, table grapes, raisins and other vine-based products

Website(s) information:
Organisation Internationale de la Vigne et du Vin (OIV) *(International Organisation of Vine & Wine)* — **url:** www.oiv.int **Coverage:** statistical figures for raisins, vinegar and wine

Publication(s):
State of the Vitiviniculture World Market — **Frequency:** annual **Content:** Data published in these reports was harmonised with data provided by the Statistics Department of the Food and Agriculture Organisation of the United Nations (FAO)

Organisation of Petroleum Exporting Countries (OPEC)
Address: Obere Donaustraße 93, Vienna, 1020, Austria
Telephone: +43 21 112 279
Fax: +43 21 498 27
E-mail: info@opec.org
Website: www.opec.org

Guides: OPEC produces a variety of publications, including research about the oil and gas industry with a special focus on its Member Countries

Activity: OPEC is made up of 11 developing nations whose economies rely on oil export revenues. The OPEC member countries coordinate their oil production policies in order to help stabilise the oil market and to help oil producers achieve a reasonable rate of return on their investments

Website(s) information:
Organisation of Petroleum Exporting Countries (OPEC) — **url:** www.opec.org **Description:** access to Annual Report, including overview of OPEC in the world economy; macroeconomic figures for member countries; crude production by member country; world supply/demand balance; prices for selected crudes **Coverage:** market indicators

Publication(s):
Annual Report — **Language:** English **Frequency:** Annual **Content:** reviews of OPEC Member Countries' economic performances and the world oil market, activities of the OPEC Secretariat and listings of OPEC officials

Annual Statistical Bulletin — **Language:** English **Frequency:** Annual **Content:** tables, charts and graphs detailing the world's oil and gas reserves, production and refining activities, plus economic and other data. archive available

OPEC Bulletin — **Language:** English **Frequency:** monthly **Content:** organization's monthly flagship magazine, featuring news from Member Countries, incisive forum articles, a review of the oil market

Organización Mundial del Turismo
World Tourism Organisation (WTO)

Address: Capitán Haya, 42, Madrid, 28020, Spain
Telephone: +34 91 567 8100
Fax: +34 91 571 3733
E-mail: ceu@world-tourism.org
Website: www.unwto.org

Guides: all the publications are available for purchase in electronic format in the UNWTOelibrary and in hardcopy format in the UNWTO Infoshop

Activity: agency of the United Nations specialised in the tourism industry

Website(s) information:
World Tourism Organisation — url: www.unwto.org **Description:** provides access to global tourism data and trends; news and articles on developments within specific market sectors; information on trade in tourism services, quality of tourism development and sustainable development of tourism **Coverage:** statistics for all the countries around the world. All statistical tables available are displayed and can be accessed individually; available for free as part of any subscription to the WTOelibrary; non-subscribers may purchase the complete set of statistical tables

Publication(s):
City Tourism and Culture — **Language:** English/Spanish/French **Frequency:** annual **Content:** information on cultural city trips, marketing and product development

Compendium of Tourism Statistics — **Language:** English/French/Spanish **Content:** condensed and quick-reference guide on the major tourism statistical indicators in each country. Provides statistical information on tourism in 209 countries and territories around the world over a five year period

Marketing Activities — **Language:** Spanish/English/French **Frequency:** annual **Content:** information on the promotional effectiveness of tourism destinations

Measuring the Importance of the Meetings Industry: Developing and Tourism Satellite Account Extension — **Language:** English **Frequency:** irregular **Content:** Examines the contribution to national economies of the meetings industry. Provides a summary of the demand and supply and examines the use of these data in development a model for evaluating the economic contribution of the industry in macroeconomic terms

Spanish Ecotourism — **Language:** English/Spanish/French **Frequency:** irregular **Content:** information and analysis on nature tourism and ecotourism markets, with data on market volume; characteristics; major trends; development profiles; consumer profiles; the role of the different marketing tactics; product typologies and the main marketing tools used

Tourism 2020 Vision: Global Forecast and Profile of Market Segments — **Language:** English/French/Spanish **Frequency:** irregular **Content:** Examines the development of tourism in the world in the 1990s and the global tourism prospects for the period to the year 2020. Analysis of the ten most dynamic market segments during the next decades

Tourism Highlights — **Language:** English **Frequency:** annual **Content:** statistics and analysis on international tourist arrivals, international tourism receipts, results by region, major regional destinations by arrivals and receipts, and outbound tourism

Tourism Indicators — **Language:** English/French/Spanish **Frequency:** irregular **Content:** international tourist arrivals and receipts; international tourism expenditure and outbound tourism by region of origin

Tourism Market Trends — **Language:** Spanish/English/French **Frequency:** annual **Content:** analysis of tourism flows and earnings in Europe; including data on global and regional trends with special emphasis on the countries of each region; arrivals, receipts, hotel capacity, and major source markets

World Tourism Barometer — **Language:** English/French/Spanish **Frequency:** 3 per annum **Content:** a short-term evolution of tourism; contains three permanent elements: an overview of short-term tourism data from destination countries and air transport, a retrospective and prospective evaluation of tourism performance by the UNWTO Panel of Tourism Experts and selected economic data relevant for tourism

Yearbook of Tourism Statistics — **Language:** English/French/Spanish **Frequency:** annual **Content:** provides data for 206 countries and territories data on total arrivals and overnight stays associates to inbound tourism with breakdown by country of origin

United Nations (UN)
Address: United Nations Publications, Room DC2-853, 2 UN Plaza, New York, NY 10017, USA
Telephone: +1 212 963 8302
Fax: +1 212 963 3489
E-mail: publications@un.org
Website: www.un.org

Guides: catalogue of UN Publications (annual, free); lists all publications currently in print from UN bodies and affiliated agencies whose publications are sold by UN Sales Sections; UNDOC Current Index (United Nations Document Index) is issued 10 times a year, on a subscription basis, and gives a comprehensive coverage of UN documentation

Activity: maintains international peace and security; develops friendly relations among nations; cooperates in solving international economic, social, cultural and humanitarian problems and in promotes respect for human rights and fundamental freedoms

Website(s) information:
United Nations — url: www.un.org **Description:** official site of the United Nations. Access to information in the form of online publications, reports and briefings, news, surveys and press releases, covering a wide range of issues in the areas of human rights, socio-economic and human development, environment and poverty reduction. Provides links to UN official bodies and institutions and is available in all UN official languages: English, French, Spanish, Russian, Arabic and Chinese. (For more information on UN Statistics see UN Statistical Division site)

United Nations Statistics Division — url: unstats.un.org/unsd/ **Description:** database of statistical data for member states of the United Nations, covering a total of 188 countries. Available in Spanish, French and English **Coverage:** data provided for each country covers: geography, economy, population and social indicators. 1) Geography: area, capital and largest city; official language; urban population; energy consumption; forest area; etc; 2) Economy: currency; GDP (US$); GDP per capita (US$); major export industries; unemployment; tourist arrivals; 3) Population: total population; density; years; female/male ratio; infant mortality; growth; total fertility rate; 4) Social indicators: life expectancy; literacy rate; parliamentary seats (women/men); spending on education; school enrolment; homicides; motor vehicles; telephones; refugees; etc

Publication(s):
Africa Renewal — **Language:** English/French **Frequency:** quarterly **Content:** development of African countries

Demographic Yearbook — **Language:** English **Content:** demographic statistics provided for some 200 countries, covering size, distribution and trends in population, fertility, mortality, marriage and divorce, international migration and population census data

Economic and Social Survey of Asia and the Pacific — **Language:** English **Frequency:** annual **Content:** analyses recent economic and social developments in the region with particular emphasis on economic and social policy issues and broad development strategies

Economic and Social Survey of Latin America and the Caribbean — **Language:** English **Frequency:** irregular **Content:** analyses the economic situation in the region

Economic Survey of Europe — **Language:** English **Frequency:** irregular **Content:** update on the current economic situation in Europe, North America and the Commonwealth of Independent States (CIS), focusing on regional disparities and economic convergence

Industrial Commodity Statistics Yearbook — **Language:** English **Frequency:** annual **Content:** Yearbook consists of two parts. Part one contains annual quantity data on production of industrial commodities by country, geographical region, economic grouping and for the world. For some 200 countries, information has been presented for about 230 commodities over a ten-year period . Part two presents data by country on apparent consumption of about 530 industrial commodities over the same period

International Trade Statistics Yearbook — **Language:** English **Frequency:** annual **Content:** presents the basic information for individual countries' external trade performance in terms of the overall trends in current value, as well as in volume and price; the importance of trading partners and the significance of individual commodities imported and exported

Monthly Bulletin of Statistics — **Language:** English **Frequency:** monthly **Content:** economic and social statistics from more that 200 countries and territories, as well as quarterly statistics on industrial production

Population and Vital Statistics Report — **Language:** English **Frequency:** quarterly **Content:** estimates of world and regional populations as well as estimates for 218 countries. Data is compiled and collected by national statistical offices and related official organisations, based on latest national population census

Statistical Yearbook for Asia and the Pacific — **Language:** English/French **Frequency:** annual **Content:** statistics covering a total of 56 countries, covering a wide range of topics including: population, manpower, national accounts, agriculture, forestry and fishing, industry, energy production and consumption, transportation and communication, internal and external trade, wages, banking, finance and social statistics

Statistical Yearbook for Latin America and the Caribbean — **Language:** English/French **Frequency:** annual **Content:** annual compilation of a wide range of socio-economic statistics for a total of 33 Latin American countries. Data covers topics including: population, national accounts, employment, social conditions, agriculture, industry, import-export goods and services, balance of payments and infrastructure services

UN Statistical Yearbook — **Language:** English **Frequency:** annual **Content:** presents an overall comprehensive description of the world economy, its structure, major trends and recent performance

World Economic and Social Survey — **Language:** English **Frequency:** annual **Content:** assesses the current global economic situation, including a forecast of output, international trade and other key economic variables

World Population Prospects — **Language:** English **Frequency:** irregular **Content:** presents population estimates and projections for the world, the more developed and less developed regions, the least developed countries, 5 major areas, 21 regions and 184 countries or areas

World Statistics Pocketbook — **Language:** English **Frequency:** annual **Content:** international compilation of basic economic, social and environmental indicators for 208 countries and areas worldwide. It covers 57 key indicators in the areas of population, economic activity, agriculture, industry, energy, international trade, transport, communications, gender, education and environment

United Nations Conference on Trade and Development (UNCTAD)

Address: Palais des Nations, 8-14 Avenue de la Paix, Geneva 10, 1211, Switzerland
Telephone: +41 22 917 5634
Fax: +41 22 917 0042
E-mail: sgo@unctad.org
Website: www.unctad.org

Guides: reference service holds a collection of 20,000 items; books, periodicals, CD-ROMs, on international economic relations, trade and development issues. Themes and documentation of UNCSTAD include: World Investment Report (annual), Trade and Development Report (annual), Handbook on Trade and Development Statistics, Least Developed Countries (reports), International trade in goods, services and commodities, investment, technology and enterprise development, services infrastructure for development and trade efficiency

Activity: promotes the development-friendly integration of developing countries into the world economy

Website(s) information:

UNCTAD GlobStat — **url:** globstat.unctad.org **Coverage:** statistics covering the world on countries, population and economic trends; external finance, debt, and foreign direct investment; transnational corporations and foreign affiliates; international trade in merchandise and service; production and international trade of commodities; production and international trade of manufacturers; information and communication technology

Publication(s):

Development and Globalisation: Facts and Figures — **Language:** English **Frequency:** annual **Content:** statistics on countries, population and economic trends; external finance, debt, and foreign direct investment; transnational corporations and foreign affiliates; international trade in merchandise and services; production and international trade of commodities and manufacturers; information and communication technology

Economic Development in Africa Report — **Language:** English **Frequency:** annual **Content:** analyses selected aspects of Africa's development problems and major policy issues confronting African countries. It makes policy recommendations for action by African countries themselves and by the international community to overcome the development challenges that the continent faces **Edition:** 6th

Information Economy Report (IER) and E-commerce and Development Report (ECDR) —

Review of Maritime Transport (RMT) — **Language:** English **Frequency:** annual **Content:** reports on the worldwide evolution of shipping, ports and multimodal transport related to the major traffic of liquid bulk, dry bulk and containers

Trade and Development Report — **Language:** English **Frequency:** annual **Content:** collection of statistical data relevant to the analysis of international trade, investment and development, for individual countries and for economic and trade groupings

UNCTAD Handbook of Statistics —

World Investment Report (WIR) — **Language:** English **Frequency:** annual **Content:** analyses current trends and major international policy issues regarding information and communication technologies and their use for, and effect on, trade and development

United Nations Educational, Scientific and Cultural Organisation (UNESCO)

Address: 7 place de Fontenoy, Paris Cédex 07, 75352, France
Telephone: +33 1 4568 0359
Fax: +33 1 4568 5642
E-mail: publishing.promotion@unesco.org
Website: www.unesco.org

Guides: UNESCO Publishing is the publishing arm. Their website presents titles currently for sale in English, French, Spanish, Russian and Arabic published or co-published by UNESCO. These include books, multimedia (DVDs, CD-Roms, VHS videos), periodicals, and scientific maps for professionals

Activity: specialised agency of the United Nations. Its purpose is to contribute to peace and security by promoting international collaboration through education, science, and culture

Website(s) information:

Unesco Institute for Statistics — **url:** www.uis.unesco.org **Description:** wide range of online documents and databases providing data and statistics on world education, science and technology, and culture. Includes access to the UNESCO database searchable by subject, region, country and year; wide range of country education indicators covering schooling, participation in education, internal efficiency, primary education, indicators on resources, and literacy; and selected tables from the UNESCO yearbook **Coverage:** provides statistical information, fast facts and regional profiles in the following fields: Education, Literacy, Science and Technology, Culture and Communication

United Nations Industrial Development Organisation (UNIDO)

Address: PO Box 300, Vienna International Centre, Wagramerstr. 5, Vienna, 1400, Austria
Telephone: +43 26026 0
Fax: +43 26926 69
E-mail: unido@unido.org
Website: www.unido.org

Guides: publications can be purchased through UNIDO or downloaded for free

Activity: working to improve the living conditions of people and promote global prosperity through offering tailor-made solutions for the sustainable industrial development of developing countries and countries with economies in transition

Website(s) information:

IDSB - Industrial Demand-Supply Database — **url:** www.unido.org **Description:** In addition to offering sets of production-related industrial statistics (i.e. INDSTAT3 and INDSTAT4 Databases), UNIDO is making its Industrial Demand-Supply Balance Databases (IDSB) available to external users **Coverage:** Database covers industrial output, trade and apparent consumption

INDSTAT — **url:** www.unido.org **Description:** INDSTAT data are compiled in collaboration with the Organisation for Economic Cooperation and Development (OECD): Data for non-OECD countries are collected by UNIDO while those for OECD member countries are collected and provided to UNIDO by OECD for inclusion in the database. UNIDO maintains and updates the data annually **Coverage:** Industrial statistics database containing time series data on selected data items for the period 1990 onwards. Information is presented by country, year and industry, covering number of establishments; employment; female employment; wages and salaries; output; value added; gross fixed capital formation

UNIDO — **url:** www.unido.org **Description:** free access to PDF documents, reports, economic research papers and publications **Coverage:** Globalisation and its implications; industrial growth, trade and finance; investment, productivity and export in African manufacturing; competitiveness; environmental resources and their management; enterprise and business development; industrial policy

Publication(s):

International Yearbook of Industrial Statistics — **Language:** English **Frequency:** annual **Content:** worldwide statistics on current performance and trends in the manufacturing sector. Analyses patterns of growth, structural change and industrial performance in individual industries in over 120 countries **Readership:** economists, planners, business people, policy makers

World Directory of Industrial Information Sources — **Language:** English **Content:** Industrial information sources for technology and equipment. Contains profiles of information providers such as information and documentation centres, banks, training institutes, development agencies, manufacturers associations etc

United Nations Population Fund (UNFPA)

Address: 220 East 42nd Street, New York, NY 10017, , USA
Telephone: +1 212 297 5028
Fax: +1 212 297 4908
E-mail: gharzeddine@unfpa.org
Website: www.unfpa.org

Activity: supports countries in using population data for policies and programmes to reduce poverty

Website(s) information:

United Nations Population Fund (UNFPA) — **url:** www.unfpa.org/worldwide/ **Description:** reports on every country and up-to-date demographic, health and economic indicators **Coverage:** provides indicators and policy developments by country; country/territory profiles

Publication(s):

Country Profiles for Population and Reproductive Health — **Frequency:** Every 2 years **Content:** covers the areas of socioeconomic health, adolescent reproductive health, gender equality and reproductive health commodity security. Indicators for ICPD Goals as well as MDGs are identified

Gender, Health and Development in the Americas: Basic Indicators — **Language:** English/Spanish **Frequency:** irregular **Content:** profiles gender differences in health and development in the 48 states and territories in Latin America and the Caribbean, focusing on women's reproductive health, access to key health services, and major causes of death

Maternal Mortality — **Language:** English **Frequency:** annual **Content:** Reports the global, regional, and country estimates of maternal mortality in the past year and the findings of the separate assessments of trends of maternal mortality levels since 1990.

State of World Population 2007 — **Language:** English/Spanish/French/Arabic/Russian **Content:** The 2007 State of World Population report outlines the challenges and opportunities presented by the coming, inevitable urban growth. It also dispels many misconceptions about urbanization and calls on policymakers to take concerted, proactive steps to harness the potential of cities to improve the lives of all

United Nations Statistics Division

Address: Statistics Division, United Nations, New York, NY 10017, USA
Fax: +1 212 963 4116
E-mail: statistics@un.org
Website: www.un.org/Depts/unsd

Guides: publishes data updates, including the Statistical Yearbook and World Statistics Pocketbook, and books and reports on statistics and statistical methods. Many of the Division's databases are also available on their website, as electronic publications and data files in the form of CD-ROMs, diskettes and magnetic tapes, or as printed publications

Activity: global centre for data on international trade, national accounts, energy, industry, environment, transport and demographic and social statistics gathered from many national and international sources

Website(s) information:

UN Statistical Division — **url:** www.un.org/Depts/unsd **Description:** wide range of world statistics, including: world economic statistics; environment statistics; demographic and social data **Coverage:** UNSD statistical databases on-line provide different world socio-economic data including population size and composition, birth, deaths, marriages, disability, education, oil data, national accounts, social indicators family, health, work, politics and human rights

Publication(s):

Bulletin of Statistics — **Language:** English **Frequency:** monthly **Content:** current economic and social statistics for more than 200 countries and territories of the world; contains over 50 tables of monthly and/or annual and quarterly data on a variety of subjects illustrating important economic trends and developments, including population, prices, employment and earnings, energy, manufacturing, transport, construction, international merchandise trade and finance

Energy Statistics Yearbook — **Language:** English/French **Frequency:** annual **Content:** annual compilation of a wide range of economic, social and environmental statistics on over 200 countries and areas of the world, compiled from more than 35 sources including UN agencies and other international, national and specialised organisations. This issue contains the most recent data available to the Statistics Division and presents them in 76 tables on topics such as: agriculture; balance of payments; culture and communication; development assistance; education; energy; environment

International Trade Statistics Yearbook Vols 1 & 2 — **Language:** English/French **Content:** provides information relevant to the external trade performance of approximately 180 countries or areas and highlights world trade of selected commodities

National Accounts Statistics: Analysis of Main Aggregates — **Language:** English **Frequency:** annual **Content:** Contains detailed national accounts estimates for 169 countries and areas. The national data for each country and area are presented in separate chapters using uniform table headings and classifications recommended in the United Nations System of National Accounts 1993 (SNA 1993). The yearbook publishes integrated accounts for institutional sectors, as well as the cross-classification of value added by institutional sector and economic activity

Population and Vital Statistics Report — **Language:** English **Content:** presents data for countries or areas on population size (total, male, and female) from the latest available census, estimated total population size for latest available year, and the number and rate of vital events (live births, deaths, and infant deaths) for the latest available year since 1980

Statistical Yearbook — **Language:** English/French **Frequency:** annual **Content:** contains data available to the Statistics Division and presents them in 76 tables on topics such as: agriculture; balance of payments; culture and communication; development assistance; education; energy; environment; finance; nutrition; industrial production; international merchandise trade; international tourism; labour force; manufacturing; national accounts; population; prices; research and development; transport; and wages

World's Women: Progress in Statistics — **Language:** English **Frequency:** irregular **Content:** reviews and analyses the current availability of data and assesses progress made in the reporting of national statistics, as opposed to internationally prepared estimates, relevant to gender concerns. Analysing statistics reported by 204 countries during the past 30 years, The World's Women sets out a blueprint for improving the availability of data in the areas of demographics, health, education, work, violence against women, poverty, decision-making and human rights

Universal Postal Union

Address: International Bureau, Case Postale 13, Berne 15, 3000, Switzerland
Telephone: +41 31 350 3111
Fax: +41 31 350 3110
E-mail: info@upu.int
Website: www.upu.int

Activity: 190 member countries; the UPU is the primary forum for cooperation between postal services and helps to ensure a truly universal network of up-to-date products and services. In this way, the organisation fulfils an advisory, mediating and liaison role, and renders technical assistance where needed. It sets the rules for international mail exchanges and makes recommendations to stimulate growth in mail volumes and to improve the quality of service

Website(s) information:

Universal Postal Union — **url:** www.upu.int **Description:** The UPU's statistical database provides a dynamic overview of postal development in each country. It contains data from over 200 countries or territories and includes approximately 100 indicators of postal development, grouped in 12 chapters. The data is collected annually by the International Bureau from all UPU member postal administrations

Coverage: postal statistics and trends

Publication(s):

Postal Statistics — **Language:** English **Frequency:** annual **Content:** It contains data from over 200 countries or territories and includes approximately 100 indicators of postal development, grouped in 12 chapters. The data is collected annually by the International Bureau from all UPU member postal administrations.

World Bank

Address:	1818 H Street NW, Washington, DC 20433, , USA
Telephone:	+1 202 473 1000
Fax:	+1 202 477 6391
E-mail:	pic@worldbank.org
Website:	www.worldbank.org

Guides: available online under: http://publications.worldbank.org/ecommerce

Activity: provides financial and technical assistance to developing countries

Website(s) information:

World Bank — **url:** www.worldbank.org **Description:** provides information about the World Bank and its activities; provides access to the World Bank's formal publications, including World Development Report and a range of books that cover the full spectrum of economic and social development; it is also the gateway to the World Development Indicators Online, the premier source for data on the global economy, and to the World Bank e-Library, the comprehensive and fully searchable collection of the Bank's books; holds over 15,000 free, downloadable documents, including operational documents (project documents, analytical and advisory work, and evaluations), formal and informal research papers, and most Bank publications **Coverage:** general economic indicators; vital statistics of world countries

World Development Indicators — **url:** http://publications.worldbank.org/WDI/ **Coverage:** contains statistical data for over 600 development indicators and time series data from 1960-2003 (selected data for 2004) for over 200 countries and 18 country groups; data includes social, economic, financial, natural resources, and environmental indicators

Publication(s):

Africa Development Indicators — **Language:** English **Frequency:** annual **Content:** general socio-economic indicators of African countries

Atlas of Global Development: A Visual Guide to the World's Greatest Challenges — **Language:** English **Frequency:** annual **Content:** Social, economic, and environmental issues that are facing the planet are presented in world maps, tables, graphs, text and photographs. Drawing on data from the World Bank's authoritative World Development Indicators, the book brings to life country comparisons of social indicators like life expectancy, infant mortality, safe water, population, growth, poverty and energy efficiency. Issues such as AIDS, population living below $1 a day, drinking water, and trade are presented

Global Economic Prospects 2007: Managing the Next Wave of Globalization — **Language:** English **Content:** Over the next 25 years developing countries will move to center stage in the global economy. analyses the opportunities and stresses this will create. While rich and poor countries alike stand to benefit, the integration process will make more acute stresses already apparent today - in income inequality, in labour markets, and in the environment

Global Monitoring Report 2007 — **Content:** Millennium Development Goals: assesses the contributions of developing countries, developed countries, and international financial institutions toward meeting universally agreed development commitments. Fourth in a series of annual reports leading up to 2015, this year's report reviews key developments of the past year, emerging priorities, and provides a detailed region-by-region picture of performance in the developing regions of the world, drawing on indicators for poverty, education, gender equality,

Sustainable Energy in China: The Closing Window of Opportunity — **Content:** This title uses historical data from 1980 and alternative scenarios through 2020 to assess China's future energy requirements and the resources to meet them. It calls for a high-level commitment to develop and implement an integrated, coordinated, and comprehensive energy policy

World Bank Annual Report — **Language:** English/French/Russian/Spanish/Arabic/Chinese/Portuguese/Hindi/German/Japanese **Frequency:** annual **Content:** provides an annual overview of World Bank activities

World Development Indicators — **Language:** English **Frequency:** annual **Content:** compilation of data about development. This statistical reference allows you to consult over 900 indicators for some 150 economies and 14 country groups in more than 80 tables. It provides a current overview of the most recent data available as well as important regional data and income group analysis.The CD-ROM editions contain 45 years of time series data, covering periods since 1960, and offer mapping, charting, and data export formats

World Development Report: Development and the Next Generation — **Language:** English/French **Frequency:** annual **Content:** analysis of world development policies, world disparities and inequalities, poverty and sustainable growth, and policies for future global progress **Edition:** 2007

World Conservation Union (IUCN)

Address:	Rue Mauverney 28, Gland, 1196, Switzerland
Telephone:	+41 22 999 0000
Fax:	+41 22 999 0002
E-mail:	webmaster@iucn.org
Website:	www.iucn.org

Guides: publications produced by the WCU from 1948 to the present. Includes publications of CITES - Convention on International Trade in Endangered Species of Wild Fauna and Flora, the Ramsar Convention on Wetlands, TRAFFIC - the joint wildlife trade monitoring programme of IUCN and WWF, UNEP-World Conservation Monitoring Centre, and a selection of titles from IUCN members or other publishers

Activity: the world's largest environmental network with over 1,000 members including states, government agencies, and non-governmental organisations in 140 countries

World Customs Organisation (WCO)

Address:	Rue du Marché 30, Brussels, B-1210, Belgium
Telephone:	+32 2 209 9503
Fax:	+32 2 209 9490
E-mail:	publications@wcoomd.org
Website:	www.wcoomd.org

Guides: online publications catalogue WCO News magazine available for free download

Activity: intergovernmental body that works to enhance the effectiveness and efficiency of Customs administrations

Publication(s):

Customs and Tobacco Report 2007 — **Language:** English/French **Content:** Global review of legitimate tobacco trading and smuggling. Includes statistical analyses of trends

World Health Organisation (WHO)/Organisation Mondiale de la Santé

Address:	Avenue Appia 20, Geneva 27, 1211, Switzerland
Telephone:	+41 22 791 2111
Fax:	+41 22 791 3111
E-mail:	info@who.int
Website:	www.who.ch

Guides: access to the online library database WHOLIS on their website

Activity: The WHO is the UN specialised agency for health; its objective is the attainment by all peoples of the highest possible level of health; the WHO is governed by 192 Member States

Website(s) information:

WHO Statistical Information System (WHOSIS) — **url:** www.who.int/whosis
Coverage: statistics cover basic health indicators; diseases; numbers of doctors, dentists and nurses; HIV/AIDS data; population estimates and projections; data can be accessed in respect of each member State

World Health Organisation (WHO) — **url:** www.who.ch **Coverage:** information on WHO and the present state of health services worldwide; includes information on child immunisation; health expenditures; infant mortality; maternal mortality; deaths by type of condition; etc.

Publication(s):

Bulletin of the World Health Organisation — **Language:** English/French/Spanish **Frequency:** monthly **Content:** aims to give public health policy and practice guidance, also encourages closer links between scientific investigation and the art of helping populations to lead healthier lives

World Health Report — **Language:** English **Frequency:** annual **Content:** the report reveals an estimated shortage of almost 4.3 million doctors, midwives, nurses and support workers worldwide. The shortage is most severe in the poorest countries, especially in sub-Saharan Africa, where health workers are most needed **Readership:** donor agencies, international organisations

World Intellectual Property Organisation (WIPO)

Address: 34 Chemin des Colombettes, Geneva, Switzerland
Telephone: +41 22 338 8186
Fax: +41 22 338 8210
E-mail: information.center@wipo.int
Website: www.wipo.int

Activity: WIPO is one of the 16 specialised agencies of the United Nations system of organisations. It administers 23 international treaties dealing with different aspects of intellectual property protection

Website(s) information:

World Intellectual Property Organisation (WIPO) — **url:**
http://www.wipo.int/ipstats/en/resources/ **Description:** Access to an online database with statistical information on patent filings, patent grants and patents in force and other free information products such as the WIPO Magazine **Coverage:** WIPO collects and publishes annual statistics on industrial property, by country and in accordance with the relevant international industrial property classification systems administered by WIPO. The statistics relate to patents, utility models, marks, industrial designs, plant varieties and microorganisms and are published in a unique collection of statistical tables which bring together data supplied by Industrial Property Offices in respect of filings under national, regional and international legislations

Publication(s):

World Patent Report - A Statistical Review — **Language:** English **Content:** The report, based on 2006 figures (the last year for which complete worldwide statistics are available) also shows that patents granted worldwide increased by 18% with some 727,000 patents granted in 2006 alone. The substantial increase in patents granted is due, in part, to efforts by patent offices to reduce backlogs as well as the substantial increase in the number of patents granted by China and Republic of Korea. According to these statistics, the total number of patents in force worldwide at the end

WPO Industrial Property Statistics — **Frequency:** regular updates **Content:** provides statistical information on the number of applications and registrations regarding patents, utility models, trademarks, industrial designs, as well as related information concerning plant varieties and microorganisms

World Meteorological Organization (WMO)

Address: Case Postale No 2300, 7bis avenue de la Paix, Geneva, CH-1211, Switzerland
Telephone: +41 22 730 8111
Fax: +41 22 730 8181
E-mail: wmo@wmo.int
Website: www.wmo.int

Activity: intergovernmental organisation with a membership of 187 Member States and Territories. It originated from the International Meteorological Organization (IMO), which was founded in 1873. WMO became the specialized agency of the United Nations for meteorology (weather and climate), operational hydrology and related geophysical sciences in 1951

Publication(s):

World Climate News — **Language:** English/Spanish/French **Frequency:** 6 monthly **Content:** official magazine of the WMO. Also produces a quarterly journal - The Bulletin

World Trade Organisation (WTO)

Address: Centre William Rappard, 154 rue de Lausanne, Geneva 21, CH-1211, Switzerland
Telephone: +41 22 739 5111
Fax: +41 22 731 4206
E-mail: enquiries@wto.org or publications@wto.org
Website: www.wto.org

Guides: online bookshop at www.onlinebookshop.wto.org

Activity: deals with the rules of trade between nations

Website(s) information:

World Trade Organisation (WTO) — **url:** www.wto.org **Description:** offers information on global trade and rules defining international commercial activities around the world; a compilation of news on the WTO and international trade; articles and briefings on various trade topics; access to free online publications on trade policies reviews, agreements and statistics **Coverage:** statistics compiled by the WTO, including International Trade Statistics (annual), an Annual Report, and a Historical Series; data covers the main features of trade activities around the world: global trade figures; merchandise trade by product; commercial services trade; trade by world region; trade by economic sector

Publication(s):

International Trade Statistics — **Language:** English/French/Spanish **Frequency:** annual **Content:** provides comprehensive, comparable and up-to-date statistics on trade in merchandise and commercial services for an assessment of world trade flows by country, region and main product groups or service categories

Pan-regional Official Sources

Eastern Europe

Interstate Statistical Committee of the Commonwealth of Independent States

Address: 39 Myasnitskaya Street, Building 1, Moscow, 107450, Russia
Telephone: +7 495 207 4237/207 4802
Fax: +7 495 207 4592
E-mail: statpro@sovam.com
Website: www.cisstat.com/eng/index.htm

Guides: full catalogue is available online
Activity: coordinates the activities of national statistical services, promotes the organisation of information exchange, carries out analysis of socio-economic development of the states and elaborating common recommendations in the field of statistics

Website(s) information:
Web Database Statistics of the CIS — url: www.cisstat.com/0base/index-en.htm **Description:** an online portal, which contains data drawn directly from the statistical services of all the CIS states; provides statistical information about society, economics, business, trade, environmental and demographic developments **Coverage:** statistical database covering all the CIS countries and providing data on basic economic indicators, movements of labour and people, environmental, trade, demographic data

Publication(s):
Commonwealth of Independent States — **Language:** Russian/English **Frequency:** annual **Content:** contains generalised comparable statistical materials on the basis of official data of the national statistical services of the countries of the CIS (Armenia, Azerbaijan, Belarus, Georgia, Kazakhstan, Kyrgyzstan, Moldova, Russia, Tajikistan, Ukraine, and Uzbekistan), characterising socio-economic situation in the Commonwealth countries by main indicators of macroeconomics, branch economy, external trade, social sphere. International comparisons are given for some indicators

Ministry of Foreign Affairs of Russia

Address: , 32/34 Smolenskaya-Sennaya pl., Moscow, 119200, Russia
Telephone: +7 95 244 3096
Fax: +7 95 244 1797
E-mail: ac-chair@mid.ru
Website: http://www.arctic-council.org

Guides: Links to publications and reports available on their website
Activity: government ministry

Publication(s):
Economic and Social Development of the Small Indigenous Peoples of the North up to the Year 2011 — **Language:** English **Content:** social development of indigenous populations report

Western Europe

Commonwealth Secretariat

Address: Marlborough House, Pall Mall, London, SW1Y 5HX, United Kingdom
Telephone: +44 20 7747 6500
Fax: +44 20 7930 0827
E-mail: info@thecommonwealth.org
Website: www.thecommonwealth.org

Guides: titles cover policy issues, case studies and best practices in areas of Commonwealth expertise, including globalisation and multilateral trade issues, export and enterprise development, education, gender, public service management and reform, human rights and corporate governance
Activity: active in a number of areas including development, democracy, debt management and trade

Website(s) information:
Commonwealth Network — url: www.thecommonwealth.org **Description:** news and articles on the Commonwealth and its 54 member countries, including information on regional and country level programmes on: health; debt management; education; finance; trade; gender equality; etc

Council of Europe

Address: Palais de l'Europe, Avenue de l'Europe, Strasbourg Cédex, 67075, France
Telephone: +33 3 8841 2000
Fax: +33 3 8841 2781
E-mail: infodoc@coe.int
Website: www.coe.int

Activity: acts as a political anchor and human rights watchdog for Europe's post-communist democracies, assists the countries of central and eastern Europe in carrying out and consolidating political, legal and constitutional reform in parallel with economic reform, provides know-how in areas such as human rights, local democracy, education, culture and the environment

Website(s) information:
Council of Europe/Conseil de L'Europe — url: www.coe.int **Description:** official web site of the Council of Europe, providing general information on the Council's structure, activities and services: the Committee of Ministers; Parliamentary Assembly; Human Rights Court; Commissioner for Human Rights; Congress of Local and Regional Authorities; and the Secretary General. Online access to different documents on Human Rights Case Law, European Treaties and publications and reports of the Library and Archive Division. A series of different theme files provide information on: human rights; social topics (e.g. population; demographic trends and migrations; health; development; etc); legal matters; and links to other European and international organisations

Publication(s):
Current Trends in International Migration in Europe — **Language:** English **Content:** migration statistics, stocks of foreign population, flows of foreign population, labour migration, the problem of asylum, migration of expertise, irregular migration and recent initiatives in international co-operation

Recent Demographic Development in Europe — **Frequency:** annual **Content:** information on population developments in forty-six European states: the size of the population and its rate of increase, rates of migration, marriage and divorce, fertility and mortality, and the size of foreign population

European Bank for Reconstruction and Development (EBRD)

Address: One Exchange Square, London, EC2A 2JN, United Kingdom
Telephone: +44 20 7338 6000
Fax: +44 20 7338 6100
E-mail: pubsdesk@ebrd.com
Website: www.ebrd.com

Activity: EBRD is the largest single investor in the region and mobilises significant foreign direct investment beyond its own financing. It is owned by 60 countries and two intergovernmental institutions. It provides project financing for banks, industries and businesses, both new ventures and investments in existing companies. It also works with publicly owned companies, to support privatisation, restructuring state-owned firms and improvement of municipal services. The Bank uses its close relationship with governments in the region to promote policies that will bolster the business environment

Website(s) information:
European Bank for Reconstruction and Development (EBRD) — url: www.ebrd.com **Description:** offers descriptions of all projects in the region, information on policies and online working papers. The papers are downloadable online and cover major issues of the European financial system and economic development: European financial structure; competition and enterprise performance; taxation; social changes; monetary transaction; legal changes

Publication(s):
EBRD Investments 1991-2004 — **Language:** English/French/German/Russian **Frequency:** annual **Content:** provides a complete list of every project the Bank has signed on a country-by-country basis

Economics of Transition — **Language:** English/French/German/Russian **Frequency:** quarterly **Content:** Publishes articles on the economics of structural transformation, institutional development, and growth in Central and Eastern Europe and the CIS, China and Vietnam, as well as studies of reform and institutional change in other emerging market environments, including India and Latin America

Environments in Transition — **Language:** English/French/German/Russian **Content:** information on the Bank's environmental programme. Includes updates on environmental aspects of newly approved projects in Central and Eastern Europe

Transition Report — **Language:** English/French/German/Russian **Frequency:** annual **Content:** analysis of the global process of transition to a market economy in central and eastern Europe, the Baltic states and the Commonwealth of Independent States. Includes statistical analysis of major macro-economic indicators, covering market liberalisation and competition matters, macroeconomic stabilisation, enterprise restructuring and privatisation, reform of finance and infrastructure and legal reform

European Central Bank

Address: Postfach 160319, Kaiserstrasse 29, Frankfurt am Main, 60066, Germany
Telephone: +49 69 1344 0
Fax: +49 69 1344 6000
E-mail: info@ecb.int
Website: www.ecb.int

Activity: central bank for Europe's single currency

Website(s) information:
European Central Bank — **url:** www.ecb.int **Coverage:** provides key information on the latest financial and monetary developments in Europe, including access to ECB monthly bulletins in all EU official languages; financial statement of the Euro-system; ECB interest rates; monetary policy operations; minimum reserve statistics; banking system's liquidity position; and general economic and financial developments in the Euro area

Publication(s):
Annual Report — **Language:** All official EU languages **Frequency:** annual **Content:** publication which describes the activities of the bank and reports on monetary policy of both the previous and the current year

Convergence Report — **Language:** All official EU languages **Frequency:** every two years **Content:** report on the progress made in the fulfilment by the Member States of their obligations regarding the achievement of economic and monetary union

ECB Statistics: An Overview — **Language:** English **Frequency:** irregular **Content:** statistics relating to monetary financial institutions, interest rates, balance of payments, international role of the Euro, exchange rates, statistical aspects of enlargement

Economic Research Publications — **Language:** English **Frequency:** irregular **Content:** publications of the Working Paper Series" which disseminate findings within the field of monetary and general economic research and "Occasional Paper Series" which deal with economic research topics

Monthly Bulletin — **Language:** all EU official languages **Frequency:** monthly **Content:** news and features on European Union monetary policies, financial and banking systems. Latest on the Euro, providing financial and economic statistical data for the Euro zone

Statistics Pocket Book — **Language:** English **Content:** population and the labour market, macroeconomic indicators, Euro area balance of payments, income, monetary policy, financial market developments, levels of GDP

European Commission Directorate General for Education and Culture

Address: Directorate-General for Education and Culture, Unit B1, Brussels, B-1049, Belgium
Telephone: +32 2299 9335
Fax: +32 2299 4577
E-mail: eac-info@ec.europa.eu
Website: www.europa.eu.int

Guides: a general overview of EU policy on education and training can be found on the SCADplus database

Activity: opportunities by the EU for living, studying and working in other countries; promotes cross-cultural understanding, personal development and the realisation of the EU's full economic potential

Website(s) information:
European Continuous Tracking Survey (Europinion) — **url:** www.europa.eu.int/comm/dg10/epo/ **Description:** series of consumer attitude surveys conducted across the countries of the European Union. Covers issues relating to the European Union and numerous economic and social issues

Information Network on Education in Europe (EURYDICE) — **url:** www.eurydice.org **Coverage:** EURYBASE database of education systems and on national policies in the field of education in Europe; includes information on legislation; educational structure for each European country; political and economic backgrounds of the various educational systems

Market Access Database — **url:** www.mkaccdb.eu.int **Description:** series of international trade information databases searchable by country. The Sectorial and Trade Barriers Database covers the following: general features of trade policy; tariff barriers; non-tariff barriers; investment related measures. Also includes Applied Tariffs Database; WTO Bound Tariffs Database; Exporters' Guide to Import Formalities; GATS Info-Point (some areas are only accessible from European Union member states) **Coverage:** statistics on EU trade flows by partner country

Publication(s):
Defining a Strategy for the direct Assessment of Skills — **Content:** potential and limits of a European initiative; focus of a European skills assessment initiative; methodological issues; data-collection process

Exploring Sources on Funding for Lifelong Learning — **Content:** statistical information; development of statistical indicators; assessment of existing international data sources; inventory and assessment of existing national data source; general review of the key variables; situation report on the key variables; scenarios and methodological basis for possible future data collection

Indicators for Monitoring Active Citizenship — **Content:** active citizenship and citizenship education; identification of indicators; the role of education in political socialisation and active citizenship; input and output indicators

Study on Access to Education and Training — **Content:** relationship between skills and competitiveness at micro and macro-level; analytical framework; data analysis and qualitative reviews

Study on Basic Skills — Explaining Student Performance — **Content:** overall performance; student background and basic skills; student attitudes and behaviour and basic skills; educational environment and basic skills; data collection activities

Study on Early School Leavers — **Content:** analytical framework; key study areas; overview of trends of the rate of early school leavers in each country studied; the influence of wider external factors; influence of socio-economic characteristics on early school leaving

Study on Private Household Spending on Education and Training — **Content:** factors affecting household expenditure on education; overview of expenditure in the European Union; recent trends in household spending education; indirect and opportunity cost in education

European Environment Agency

Address: Kongens Nytorv 6, Copenhagen K, 1050, Denmark
Telephone: +45 33 367 100
Fax: +45 33 367 199
E-mail: webmaster@eea-europa.eu
Website: www.eea.eu.int

Website(s) information:
European Environment Agency — **url:** www.eea.eu.int **Description:** provides reports and indicators on acidification, air quality, biodiversity, climate change, natural resources, ozone depletion and waste. Also contains sector sub-categories on agriculture, fishery, energy, population, economy, tourism and transport and areas sub-categories on coastal, seas and urban issues **Coverage:** contains data on environmental factors, such as pollution, waste and environmental management in agricultural and fishery industry

European Free Trade Association (EFTA)

Address: 9-11 rue de Varembé, Geneva 20, 1211, Switzerland
Telephone: +41 22 332 2626
Fax: +41 22 332 2677
E-mail: mail.gva@efta.int
Website: www.efta.int

Activity: EFTA was founded on the premise of free trade as a means of achieving growth and prosperity amongst its Member States as well as promoting closer economic co-operation between the Western European countries. EFTA members are Iceland, Liechtenstein, Norway and Switzerland

Website(s) information:
European Free Trade Association — url: www.efta.int **Coverage:** trade statistics by country, merchandise and commodities

Publication(s):
Annual Report — **Language:** English **Frequency:** annual **Content:** statistics published annually on EFTAs trade activities among itself, and among third countries; data includes products of trade and customs matters

European Investment Bank (EIB)

Address: Information and Communications Department, 100 boulevard Konrad Adenauer, L-2950, Luxembourg
Telephone: +352 43 791
Fax: +352 43 77041
E-mail: info@eib.org
Website: www.eib.org

Activity: European Union's financing institution, its purpose is to contribute towards the integration, balanced development and economic and social cohesion of the Member Countries

Website(s) information:
European Investment Bank — url: www.eib.org **Description:** provides information on latest developments on European financial and banking activities. Research reports including statistical data and analysis on: EIB financial resources; loans and borrowing operations; and evolution of the single monetary system

Publication(s):
EIB Information — **Language:** English/French/German/Italian **Frequency:** quarterly **Content:** Journal of the EIB with articles on recent operations and articles

General Fisheries Commission for the Mediterranean

Address: Viale delle Terme di Caracalla, Rome, 00100, Italy
Telephone: +39 6 5705 6441
Fax: +39 6 5705 6500
E-mail: alain.bonzon@fao.org
Website: www.faogfcm.org

Guides: online catalogue

Activity: to promote the development, conservation and management of living marine resources; formulate and recommend conservation measures

Website(s) information:
General Fisheries Commission for the Mediterranean — url: www.faogfcm.org **Description:** downloadable PDF format publications covering the Commission's policies governing the marine environment. Analysis of fish stocks **Coverage:** fish stocks, environmental impact data, socio-economic indicators, case studies

General Secretariat of the Benelux Economic Union

Address: Rue de la Regence 39, Brussels, 1000, Belgium
Telephone: +32 2 519 3811
Fax: +32 2 513 4206
E-mail: info@benelux.be

Activity: internal markets, cross-border cooperation; being responsible for justice, police and immigration; developing political cooperation; cooperating in the fields of culture, research, education and training

Publication(s):
Almanac Benelux — **Language:** French / Dutch **Frequency:** annual **Content:** gives an outline of the authorities and the persons who exercise activities in the frontier region or who work with people on the other side of the border

Rapports annuels (Annual Report) — **Language:** French / Dutch **Frequency:** annual **Content:** security policy, transborder workers, regional development, economic cooperation, international relations

Helsinki Commission - Baltic Marine Environment Protection Commission

Address: Katajanokanlaituri 6 B, , Helsinki, 00160, , Finland
Telephone: +358 207 412 649
Fax: +358 207 412 639
Website: www.helcom.fi

Activity: works to protect the marine environment of the Baltic Sea from all sources of pollution through intergovernmental co-operation between Denmark, Estonia, the European Community, Finland, Germany, Latvia, Lithuania, Poland, Russia and Sweden

Website(s) information:
HELCOM — url: www.helcom.fi **Description:** website's shipping pages are designed to provide information on: ships' traffic and navigational safety; ship-generated waste, accidental pollution and response; air pollution; releases of alien species in ballast water; annually updated factsheets available on the marine environment in the region

HM Revenue & Customs

Address: Thomas Paine House, Angel Square, Torrens Street, London, EC1V 1TA, United Kingdom
Telephone: +44 20 8929 0152
E-mail: enquiries.lon@hmce.gsi.gov.uk
Website: www.hmce.gov.uk

Activity: HM Revenue & Customs (HMRC) was formed following the merger of Inland Revenue and HM Customs and Excise Departments - it collects and administers direct and indirect taxes and pays and administers child and working benefits

Website(s) information:
HM Customs & Excise — url: www.hmce.gov.uk **Coverage:** quarterly regional and national UK trade statistics including exports and imports; and summary of trade with EU and non-EU countries

International Council for the Exploration of the Sea (ICES), The

Address: H C Andersens Blvd 44-46, Copenhagen V, 1553, Denmark
Telephone: +45 33 386 700
Fax: +45 33 934 215
E-mail: info@ices.dk
Website: www.ices.dk

Website(s) information:
The International Council for the Exploration of the Sea (ICES) — url: www.ices.dk **Description:** provides bulletins and magazines on the fishing industry, fisheries statistics, co-operative research reports on chemicals used in the fishing industry, study of the ecosystem, measuring of fish stocks and statistics on the annual catch for fisheries. Also provides a listing of ICES member countries **Coverage:** contains data on yearly nominal catches of fish and shellfish officially submitted by 19 ICES member countries in the Northeast Atlantic including over 200 species

Publication(s):
ICES Fisheries Statistics — **Language:** English **Frequency:** annual **Content:** contains data on nominal catch

Nordic Council of Ministers and Nordic Council

Address: Store Strandstræde 18, Copenhagen K, DK-1255, Denmark
Telephone: +45 33 960400
Fax: +45 33 111870
E-mail: nordisk-rad@norden.org
Website: www.norden.org

Guides: online catalogue. Publications are organised by policy area

Activity: forum for Nordic parliamentary co-operation. The Council has 87 elected members, representing the five countries and three autonomous territories

Website(s) information:

Nordic Council of Ministers and Nordic Council — **url:** www.norden.org
Description: downloadable PDF files in Swedish and English
Coverage: economic indicators, socio-economic indicators

Publication(s):

Indicators for the Information Society in the Baltic Region — **Language:** English **Content:** eIndicators: statistics about the information societies in the Baltic Region

Nordic Countries in Figures — **Language:** English **Content:** key figures on environment, population, health and causes of death, consumption, education, labour market, culture, national accounts, prices, foreign trade, research and development **Edition:** 2005

Nordic Statistical Yearbook — **Language:** English/Swedish **Content:** statistics of various aspects of social life in the five Nordic countries, Denmark, Finland, Iceland, Norway and Sweden. In addition data are also presented on the self-governing regions, the Faroe Islands, Greenland and the Åland Islands **Edition:** 43rd Edition

Nordic Social-Statistical Committee (NOSOSCO)

Address: Islands Brygge 67, Copenhagen S, 2300, Denmark
Telephone: +45 72 227 625
Fax: +45 32 955470
E-mail: mail@nom-nos.dk
Website: www.nom-nos.dk/nososco.htm

Guides: statistical data is available to download free of charge on website. Printed publications is available to order

Activity: coordinates Nordic socio-economic statistics, collaborating with adjacent areas (e.g. the Baltic countries), and following other international collaboration, mainly the social statistical collaboration in EU/EUROSTAT

Website(s) information:

Nordic Social-Statistical Committee (NOSOSCO) — **url:**
www.nom-nos.dk/nososco.htm **Description:** provides a compilation of social statistics for Denmark, Finland, Iceland, Norway, and Sweden **Coverage:** contains data on demographic trends, unemployment, illness, housing, social benefits, social security expenditure and financing in the Nordic countries

Publication(s):

Social Protection in the Nordic Countries — **Language:** English/Danish **Frequency:** irregular **Content:** contains data on population, family, children, employment and health

Press and Communication Service of the European Commission

Address: BERLAYMONT 4/363, 200 rue de la Loi, Brussels, 1049, Belgium
Telephone: +32 2296 6491
Fax: +32 2296 2695
E-mail: press-web@cec.eu.int
Website: www.europa.eu.int

Guides: list of all the publications available on the website, all free to download

Activity: press and communication service for the European Commission

Website(s) information:

Europa — **url:** www.europa.eu.int **Description:** available in all EU official languages, it is the official portal website of the European Union. It combines all information provided by most institutions and bodies of the EU including the European Parliament, the Council of the Union, the Commission, the Court of Justice, the Court of Auditors, the Economic and Social Committee, the Committee of the Regions, the European Central Bank and the European Investment Bank

Statistical Office of the European Commission (EUROSTAT)

Address: Batiment Joseph Monnet, Rue Alphonse Weicker, Luxembourg, L-2721, Luxembourg
Telephone: +352 430 134 567
Fax: +352 430 132 594
E-mail: estat-infodesk@cec.eu.int
Website: www.europa.eu.int/comm/eurostat

Guides: more than 300 million data, from many different domains, are available online, varying from consumer prices, through poverty and environmental indicators, to detailed external trade data by product

Activity: statistical office of the European Communities; its task is to provide the European Union with statistics at European level that enable comparisons between countries and regions; to supply statistics to other Directorates and supply the Commission and other European Institutions with data so they can define, implement and analyse Community policies. Themes are: General and regional statistics; Economy and finance; Population and social conditions; Industry, trade and services; Agriculture and fisheries; External trade; Transport; Environment and energy; Science and technology

Website(s) information:

Statistical Office of the European Commission (EUROSTAT) — **url:**
europa.eu.int/comm/eurostat **Coverage:** each section/sector covered by EUROSTAT includes data for a wide range of socio-economic indicators: general Statistics: exports and imports of goods; harmonised indices of consumer prices; GDP growth rate; total industrial production; unemployment rate; economy and Finance; population and social conditions; industry, trade and services; agriculture, forestry and fisheries; foreign trade; transport; energy and the environment

Publication(s):

Agricultural Statistics — **Language:** English **Frequency:** annual **Content:** chapters include general statistics, crop and animal production, farm structure, and agricultural prices and accounts; presents selected tables and graphs providing an overview on developments and the situation in the agricultural sector of the European Union. The most recent data are presented here (reference years 2006 and 2007, mostly) showing the situation in the 27 Member States and at the European level (EU-27).

Cultural Statistics — **Language:** English **Content:** main cultural statistics comparable at European level. Selected tables and graphs describe different areas of the cultural field for the 27 EU Member States, the candidate countries and the EFTA countries: cultural heritage, cultural employment, enterprises in certain cultural sectors - publishing, architectural activities and cinema, external trade in cultural goods, households cultural expenditure, cultural participation and time spent on cultural activities

EC Economic Data Pocketbook — **Language:** English **Frequency:** quarterly **Content:** collection of economic data from different domains, covering the European Aggregates, EU Member States and its main economic partners. The publication focuses on the structural aspects of the EU economy; consequently, most of the data given are annual, complemented by selected monthly and quarterly indicators

Energy - Yearly Statistics — **Language:** English/German/French **Frequency:** annual **Content:** overall view of the trends for the principal aggregates, taken from the "energy supplied" balance-sheets of the European Union in tonnes of oil equivalent. Also historical series for each energy source for the principal aggregates characterising the structure of energy economics

Energy, Transport and Environment Indicators Pocketbook — **Language:** English/French/German **Content:** comprises a broad set of data collected by Eurostat and the European Environment Agency. Provides an overview of the most relevant indicators on energy, transport and environment

European Business - Facts and Figures — **Language:** English **Frequency:** annual **Content:** structure, development and characteristics of European business and its different activities: from energy and the extractive industries to communications, information services and media. It presents the latest available statistics from a wide selection of statistical sources describing for each activity: production and employment; country specialisation and regional distribution; productivity and profitability; the importance of small and medium sized enterprises (SMEs); work-force characteristics; extern

European Union Foreign Direct Investment Yearbook — **Language:** English **Frequency:** annual **Content:** provides detailed data on EU - Foreign Direct Investment (FDI) for recent years (1999-2006), for both EU FDI abroad and FDI into the EU. It provides an overview of the position of the EU in World FDI and a comparison with the US

Eurostat Yearbook 2008 - A Portal to European Statistics — **Language:** English, German, French **Frequency:** annual **Content:** annual data on a wide range of social, economic, financial and political EU topics, covering: population and demography; education; labour market structure, earnings and working hours; social protection; consumption and spending patterns; housing, culture and leisure; crime; land and environment. Also includes trade and industry statistics covering: agriculture, forestry and fishing; industry and manufacturing activities; energy resources; service industries; transport; and tourism **Edition:** 12th Edition

Eurostatistics - Data for Short-Term Economic Analysis — **Content:** short-term economic analysis designed to monitor the evolution of the economic activity in the European Union, Euro-zone and Member States

Everything on Transport Statistics — **Language:** English/French/German **Frequency:** Annual **Content:** contains all public documents and data related to transport statistics in Europe and main partner countries. It contains about 27 million items of statistical data and more than 900 documents, mostly produced by Eurostat's transport unit. Historic data from 1972 available.

External and intra-European Union Trade - Statistical Yearbook — **Language:** English **Content:** provides data on long-term trends in the trade of the European Union and its Member States, annual statistics on the trade flows of the EU with its main trading partners, and between the Member States. Data from 1958.

External and intra-European Union trade - Statistical Yearbook — **Language:** English **Frequency:** annual **Content:** contains annual time series on trade of the European Union, the Euro-zone and the 25 Member States. In particular, it provides statistics on trade flows between the EU and its main trading partners with a breakdown by major product groups. Data from 1958.

Fishery Statistics - Data 1990-2006 — **Language:** English **Frequency:** annual **Content:** summary tables for EEA and EU-candidate countries on catches by fishing region, aquaculture production, total production, landings in EEA ports, trade in fishery products, supply balance sheets, EEA fishing fleets and the number of fishermen

Food: From Farm to Fork Statistics — **Language:** English/French/German **Frequency:** monthly **Content:** statistical information on how the food chain evolves in Europe; it gives different indicators for each step of the production-consumption chain, including food and feed

Gas and Electricity Market Statistics — **Language:** English **Frequency:** annual **Content:** provides basic quantitative information on gas and electricity prices, as well as on structures for gas and electricity existing in each country. It also includes statistical information on selected indicators. Data from 1990.

Health in Europe — **Language:** English **Frequency:** annual **Content:** provides a selection of figures on health and health determinants over a five-year period.

Science and Technology in Europe — **Language:** English/French/German **Content:** statistical data and indicators based on a number of data sources available at Eurostat (mainly related to science, technology, innovation and regions

Statistics in Focus — **Language:** English/French/German **Frequency:** irregular **Content:** provides summaries of the main results of statistical surveys, studies and analysis

The EU-15's New Economy: A Statistical Portrait — **Language:** English **Content:** statistical portrait of the EU-15 which makes it possible to benchmark the countries involved in terms of how they are managing to achieve the goals set in the Lisbon strategy

Tourism - Statistical Pocketbook — **Language:** English/French/German **Frequency:** annual **Content:** The data covers a five-year period. The figures presented in this publication cover on the one hand the supply of collective tourist accommodation in Europe, giving information on the available capacity in hotels and other types of collective accommodation and the tourist flows they receive.

Statistical, Economic and Social Research and Training Centre for Islamic Countries - SESRTCIC

Address: Attar Sokak 4, Gaziosmanpasa, Ankara, 06700, Turkey
Telephone: +90 312 468 6172
Fax: +90 312 467 3458
E-mail: oicankara@sesrtcic.org
Website: www.sesrtcic.org

Activity: collating socio-economic statistics

Website(s) information:
SESRTCIC Statistical Database — **url:** www.sesrtcic.org **Description:** various statistics and information covering 56 different Islamic countries in Africa and the Middle East, plus Albania and Turkey **Coverage:** data provided for each nation includes: demographic trends; labour force; health and education; economic sectors; communications and tourism; external trade; money and finances; and national accounts

Publication(s):
Statistical Yearbook of the OIC Countries — **Language:** Arabic/English/French **Content:** Presents data collected from various national and international statistical sources. This source provides, indicator wise and countrywise, information on 172 socio-economic indicators in the 57 OIC member countries for the last ten years **Edition:** 2005

UN Economic Commission for Europe (UNECE)

Address: Palais des Nations, Geneva 10, 1211, Switzerland
Telephone: +41 22 917 1234
Fax: +41 22 917 0505
E-mail: info.ece@unece.org
Website: www.unece.org

Guides: provides a list of publications on the website; topics include environment, human settlements, population, information and communications technologies, sustainable energy, and trade development

Activity: The UNECE strives to foster sustainable economic growth among its 56 member states; to that end UNECE provides a forum for communication among States; brokers international legal instruments addressing trade, transport and the environment; and supplies statistics and economic and environmental analysis

Website(s) information:
UN Economic Commission for Europe — **url:** www.unece.org **Description:** information on economic co-operation and development in Europe, environment and human settlement, sustainable energy, trade, industry and enterprise development, timber and transport; access to a series of press releases, articles and online documents, many of these supported by socio-economic statistical data on the region **Coverage:** includes socio-economic statistics for the member countries of Western, Central and Eastern Europe, as well as North America; data is provided on total population; percentage of population in capital city; country's total area; density of population per km2; GDP per capita; life expectancy at birth; and infant mortality rates. Additionally, it also includes statistics on gross industrial output; trade (exports/imports/ranking of major trade partners); unemployment and education; and final energy consumption

Publication(s):
Annual Bulletin of Housing and Building Statistics for Europe and North America — **Language:** English **Frequency:** annual **Content:** data refers to dwelling stock and structure of dwelling construction, dwellings completed by type of investor and by type of material used, energy consumption by household, consumer price and rent indices, etc.

Annual Bulletin of Transport Statistics for Europe and North America — **Language:** English **Frequency:** annual **Content:** covers: rail, road and inland waterway sectors, container transport, goods loaded and unloaded at sea ports, transport by oil pipeline and various international goods transport, sorted by transport and commodity group

Statistical Journal of the United Nations Economic Commission for Europe — **Language:** English **Frequency:** quarterly **Content:** information on new work going on within official statistics, international organisations, government departments, universities and research institutions **Readership:** statisticians, applied economists, social scientists and policy analysts

Trends in Europe and North America - The Statistical Yearbook of the Economic Commission for Europe — **Language:** English **Frequency:** annual **Content:** contains socio-economic data covering the members states

National Official Sources

Albania

Banka e Shqipërisë
Bank of Albania

Address: Scanderbeg Square, Nr 1, Tirana,
Telephone: +355 4 222 152
Fax: +355 4 223 558
E-mail: public@bankofalbania.org
Website: www.bankofalbania.org

Website(s) information:
Bank of Albania — **url:** www.bankofalbania.org

Publication(s):
Balance of Payments Bulletin — **Language:** English/Albanian **Frequency:** quarterly **Content:** provides detailed statistical information on Balance of Payments of the Republic of Albania

Economic Bulletin — **Language:** Albanian/English **Frequency:** quarterly **Content:** covers official statements of the Bank of Albania, financial, economic and legal articles, results of statistical surveys which are carried out by the Bank of Albania, list of commercial banks exercising economic activity in Albania, and a list of foreign exchange bureaux operating within the Republic of Albania

Official Bulletin — **Language:** Albanian/English **Frequency:** monthly **Content:** decisions approved by Bank of Albania Supervisory Council, which are not subject to any restrictions, all regulations approved by the Bank of Albania Supervisory Council which are obligatory for all commercial banks as well as for other operators, as required by the law

Trade Balance Bulletin — **Language:** English/Albanian **Frequency:** quarterly **Content:** provides a detailed information on foreign trade and main trading partners

Instituti i Statistikës (INSTAT)
Albanian Institute of Statistics (INSTAT)

Address: Rr Leke Dukagjini Nr 5, Tirana
Telephone: +355 4 222 411 ext 159
Fax: +355 4 228 300
E-mail: botim_difuzion@instat.gov.al
Website: www.instat.gov.al

Guides: publications cover economic development related production, foreign trade investments, prices, income, employment

Activity: compiles socio-economic statistics on Albania

Website(s) information:
Instituti Statistikes (INSTAT) *(Albanian Institute of Statistics)* — **url:** www.instat.gov.al **Coverage:** social and economic indicators (agriculture, energy, sales, construction, population, tourism, etc)

Publication(s):
Albania in figures — **Language:** Albanian/English **Frequency:** annual **Content:** statistical data on economic and social development of Albania

Conjuctura — **Language:** Albanian/English **Frequency:** quarterly **Content:** main economic indicators; provides statistical information on developing trends of the economy

Construction Cost Index — **Language:** Albanian/English **Frequency:** quarterly **Content:** statistical information on construction cost changes

Consumer Price Index — **Language:** Albanian/English **Frequency:** monthly **Content:** provides statistical information on consumer price changes

Retail Trade Indices — **Language:** Albanian **Frequency:** quarterly **Content:** information on development of volume indices in retail trade

Situation of Foreign Trade — **Language:** Albanian/English **Frequency:** monthly **Content:** provides statistical information on export, import and trade balance

Social Indicator Yearbooks — **Language:** Albanian/English **Frequency:** annual **Content:** provides statistical information on demography, labour, education, health, household indicators, investment, crimes etc

Statistika — **Language:** Albanian/English **Frequency:** quarterly **Content:** information on social and economic indicators, also included is data on demography, education, health, the labour market, production, foreign trade, transport, construction, tourism and businesses

Austria

Österreichische Nationalbank (OeNB)
National Bank of Austria

Address: Postfach 61, 1011 Vienna, Otto-Wagner Platz 3, Vienna, 1090
Telephone: +43 404 20
Fax: +43 404 20 2398
E-mail: oenb.info@oenb.co.at
Website: www.oenb.at

Guides: publications on the national bank, the economy and financial market, statistics, and European legislation

Activity: central bank of Austria. Cooperates in the forming of the economic development in Austria and other Euro countries, with a focus on a stability orientated monetary policy

Website(s) information:
Österreichische Nationalbank *(National Bank of Austria)* — **url:** www.oenb.at **Coverage:** online access to series of different financial publications covering the overall business environment and economic & banking system in Austria and other European countries

Publication(s):
Finanzmarktstabilitätsbericht *(Financial Market Stability Report)* — **Language:** German **Frequency:** 2 per annum **Content:** market report on financial stability and the factors that have and impact on the same

Geldpolitik & Wirtschaft *(Money Policy & Economy)* — **Language:** German/English **Frequency:** quarterly **Content:** quarterly analysis of the economic cycle, medium term macro economic forecasts, sums up results of economic policy workshops and conferences

Statistiken - Daten & Analysen *(Statistics - Data & Analyses)* — **Language:** German **Frequency:** quarterly **Content:** reports on the Austrian financial institutions, cash flow, and foreign trade

STATISTIK AUSTRIA - Bundesanstalt Statistik Österreich
Federal Austrian Statistical Agency

Address: Guglgasse 13, Vienna, 1110
Telephone: +43 71128 7070
Fax: +43 715 68 28
E-mail: info@statistik.gv.at
Website: www.statistik.at

Guides: offers a search machine for publications; statistics can either be downloaded from the website or ordered online; publications are categorised into population, business, spatial economics, economics, and general information

Activity: surveys and edits statistical data on politics, the economy, and society in Austria and other EU countries

Website(s) information:
Statistische Übersichten *(Statistical Overlook)* — **url:** www.statistik.at **Coverage:** statistical overviews in charts. The information is on indicators of the development of the Austrian economy. This includes prices, income, transport, tourism, energy, environment, and agriculture in Austria. Additional information on the economies of EU and OECD (developed) countries

Publication(s):
Der Tourismus in Österreich *(Tourism in Austria)* — **Language:** German **Frequency:** annual **Content:** tourism statistics containing information on arrivals and departures, and accommodation statistics. Includes regional breakdowns

Einkommen, Armut und Lebensbedingungen Ergebnisse aus EU-SILC *(Income, Poverty, and Living Conditions)* — **Language:** German **Frequency:** annual **Content:** statistics on Austrian wages, salaries, incomes, and general information on the living conditions

Jahrbuch der Gesundheitsstatistik *(Yearbook of Health Statistics)* — **Language:** German **Frequency:** annual **Content:** information and statistics on the Austrian health service system; includes the most common diseases and cause of deaths

Österreichischer Zahlenspiegel (Austrian Data Index) — **Language:** German **Frequency:** monthly **Content:** a collection of current issues in form of statistics and an overview chart of the most important economic indicators

Schnellbericht Der Außenhandel Österreichs (Report of Foreign Trade in Austria) — **Language:** German **Frequency:** monthly **Content:** overview of developments in foreign trade

Statistik der Kraftfahrzeuge (Austrian Automotive Industry Statistics) — **Language:** German **Frequency:** annual **Content:** statistics on motor vehicles in Austria: registrations by makes and types of vehicle; statistics on stock and new registrations are separated; publication includes a CD-Rom

Statistik der Landwirtschaft (Agriculture Statistics) — **Language:** German **Frequency:** annual **Content:** statistics on agriculture and forestry, including field crops, wine, cattle, milk and meat production. Includes regional data

Statistische Nachrichten (Statistical News) — **Language:** German **Frequency:** monthly **Content:** monthly figures covering main time series: population, employment, production, retail sales, wages and prices, etc

Statistisches Jahrbuch für die Republik Österreich (Austrian Statistical Yearbook) — **Language:** German/English **Frequency:** annual **Content:** general statistical yearbook - includes a wide range of annual socio-economic, demographic, cultural, and other statistics on the Austrian republic

Wiener Boerse

Vienna Stock Exchange

Address: PO Box 192, Wallnerstraße 8, Vienna, 1014
Telephone: +43 431 531 650
Fax: +43 431 532 97 40
E-mail: webmaster@wienerborse.at
Website: www.wienerborse.at

Guides: publishes brochures on various aspects of the financial market

Activity: the stock exchange comprises an equity market, a bond market, a derivatives market, and a segment for structured products; offers online real-time market prices

Website(s) information:
Wiener Boerse (Vienna Stock Exchange) — url: www.wienerborse.at **Coverage:** daily, monthly and yearly statistics on cash markets, capital market, derivatives, mutual funds and exchange rates

Publication(s):
Vienna Stock Exchange and its Issuers — **Language:** English **Frequency:** annual **Content:** the focus of this brochure is on the group of major players in the capital market: the companies whose stocks are traded on Wiener Börse. Facts and figures on the issuers for an overview of the companies listed on the exchange

Belarus

Council of Ministers of Republic of Belarus

Address: 11 Sovetskaya Street, Minsk, 220010
Telephone: +375 17 222 4173
Fax: +375 17 222 6665
E-mail: contact@government.by
Website: www.government.by

Activity: official government website concerning ministries and the government committee

Website(s) information:
Council of Ministers of Republic of Belarus — url: www.government.by **Description:** list and contacts of ministries and official governmental bodies

Ministry of Economy of the Belarus Republic

Address: 14 Bersona Street, Minsk, 220086
Telephone: +375 17 222 6048
Fax: +375 17 200 3777
E-mail: gen@plan.minsk.by
Website: www.economy.gov.by

Activity: carry out state policy and accomplish regulation and control of state assets and privatisation, support of enterprise, development of competition

Website(s) information:
Ministry of Economy of the Belarus Republic — url: www.economy.gov.by **Description:** provides information about the Ministry, its structure; reviews of the economic and social situation, long term-development strategies and programmes; provides new legal releases requirements and other related information **Coverage:** data on economic development

Ministry of Foreign Affairs of The Republic of Belarus

Address: 29 Myasnikova Street, Minsk, 220050
Telephone: +375 17 220 2635
Fax: +375 17 220 1964
E-mail: mail@mfabelar.gov.by
Website: www.mfa.gov.by

Activity: body of state administration of the Republic of Belarus implementing national policy in the field of foreign relations

Website(s) information:
Ministry of Foreign Affairs of the Republic of Belarus — url: www.mfa.gov.by **Description:** information on the ministry and its activities; provides general information about the country; gives access to statistical data and publications **Coverage:** economy and trade; investment climate and foreign trade and foreign policy; statistics on major economic indicators

Publication(s):
Advantages of Trade-Economic Cooperation with the Republic of Belarus — **Language:** English/Russian

Foreigh Trade — **Language:** Russian/English **Content:** tariff and Non-tariff Regulations; Customs Regulations; Foreign Trade Structures

Results of Economic Development of Belarus — **Language:** Russian/English **Frequency:** irregular **Content:** main macro-economic indicators of Belarus Republic

Ministry of Statistics and Analysis of the Republic of Belarus

Address: 12 Partizansky Avenue, Minsk, 220070
Telephone: +375 17 249 4278
Fax: +375 17 249 2204
E-mail: minstat@mail.belpak.by
Website: www.belstat.gov.by

Guides: releases more than 100 publications, of which biggest are annual, bi-annual, quarterly, which are available in Russian and English

Activity: national statistics office

Website(s) information:
Ministry of Statistics and Analysis — url: http://belstat.gov.by **Description:** provides information on the ministry and its activities; most of the data is accessible online in English language; site also contains links to other national statistics offices in CIS countries **Coverage:** data covers: population, unemployment, living standards, national accounts, finance, prices and tariffs, domestic and foreign trade, industry, agriculture, construction and transport; information broken down into territories as well as national statistics

Publication(s):
Basic Socio-Demographic Characteristics of Households of the Republic of Belarus — **Language:** English/Russian **Content:** covers indicators characterising the distribution of families by their size and composition, housing conditions, type of dwelling and number of rooms, and availability of land plots **Edition:** 2006

Belarus in Numbers - Statistical Reference Book — **Language:** Russian/English **Frequency:** annual **Content:** brief characteristics of the social and economic position with comparative figures for previous years. Also demographic measures, information about the standard of living of the population and the social sphere; development of key industries of the economy, investment and external economic activity, price behaviour

Industry of the Republic of Belarus — **Language:** English/Russian **Frequency:** annual **Content:** industrial production in the republic; technical and economic characteristics of industrial enterprises; indices on labour **Edition:** 2006

Investments and Building in the Belarus Republic — **Language:** Russian/Ukraine **Frequency:** annual **Content:** dynamics and structure of investments into fixed asset formation; information about foreign investments is given in branches of the economy; production capacities, apartment houses and objects of social sphere

National Accounts of the Republic of Belarus — **Language:** Russian/English **Frequency:** annual **Content:** contains information on production of goods and services, generation and distribution of income, consumption of goods and services, capital accumulation

Retail Trade of the Republic of Belarus — **Language:** English/Russian **Frequency:** annual **Content:** contains data on the development of the retail trade and catering industry; retail commodity turnover in the distribution over the forms of property and channels; commodity structure, volumes of sale of food and non-food items; commodity reserves in the retail outlet network **Edition:** 2006

Statistical Bulletin — **Language:** Russian/English **Frequency:** quarterly **Content:** comprises data on population, employment, wages and salaries, finance, industry, agriculture, capital investments, transport and communications, foreign trade, retail turnover, prices and tariffs, offences

National Academy of Science of Belarus Republic

Address: 66 Nezavisimost Avenue, Minsk, 220072
Telephone: +375 17 284 1801
Fax: +375 17 284 2816
E-mail: academy@mserv.bas-net.by
Website: www.ac.by

Activity: union of scientific institute and communities

National Bank of the Republic of Belarus

Address: 20 Nezavisimost Avenue, Minsk, 220008
Telephone: +375 17 219 2303/74
Fax: +375 17 219 2242
E-mail: email@nbrb.by
Website: www.nbrb.by

Guides: the publications of the Bank of Belarus provide information related to the activities of the Bank of Belarus, monetary and banking policies, balance of payments and financial statistics

Activity: is the central bank of the Republic of Belarus; its principal objective is to maintain price stability

Website(s) information:
National Bank of the Republic of Belarus — url: www.nbrb.by **Description:** provides full information about its activities, information on the basic tasks of monetary policy and its implementation, monetary policy operations, credit institutions supervision activities and other responsibilities established by the legislation as well as information on the national macroeconomic situation, such as analysis of the developments in the national economy and financial markets, and on the financial position of the Bank **Coverage:** basic indicators of the Belarussian financial market

Publication(s):
Annual Report of the National Bank of Republic Belarus — **Language:** Russian/English **Frequency:** annual **Content:** macro-economic indicators for the year

Bulletin of Banking Statistics — **Language:** English/Russian **Frequency:** quarterly **Content:** major macroeconomic and monetary indicators; financial markets **Edition:** 2006

Payment Systems in the Republic of Belarus — **Language:** Russian/English **Content:** data on governmental finances **Edition:** 2001

United Nations Information Centre

Address: 6/F 17 Kirov Street, Minsk, 220050
Telephone: +375 17 227 4876/8149
Fax: +375 17 226 0340
E-mail: dpi_unit@undp.org
Website: www.un.by

Website(s) information:
United Nations Information Centre - Belarus — url: http://un.by **Coverage:** general information about Belarus, including population and economic indicators

Publication(s):
Status of Achieving Millennium Development Goals — **Language:** English/Russian **Content:** report determines goals and targets in the spheres of poverty eradication, gender equality promotion, improvement of child and maternal health

Belgium

Agentschap voor buitenlandse handel / agence pour le commerce exterieur
Belgian Foreign Trade Agency

Address: 3 Rue Montoyer, Brussels, 1000
Telephone: +32 2206 3511
Fax: +32 2 203 1812
E-mail: info@abh-ace.org
Website: www.abh-ace.org

Guides: covers foreign trade and world economy; material in French, Dutch, English, German, Spanish; books, journals, company and trade directories, Belgian and international statistics

Activity: economic missions; export, statistics, foreign trade, Belgian markets, projects

Website(s) information:
ABH-ACE-FTA — url: www.abh-ace.org **Coverage:** Belgian and Luxembourg exporters directory available online; exports and imports statistics, monthly figures; status in world trade markets

Publication(s):
CD-ROM BLUE — **Language:** French / Dutch / English **Content:** extracts from the database updated by the Belgian Agency for Foreign Trade in cooperation with the Belgian Regional Authorities for Foreign trade; contains information on over 14,400 Belgian and Luxembourg companies **Edition:** 11th edition

Banque Nationale de Belgique
National Bank of Belgium

Address: 3 boulevard de Berlaimont, Brussels, 1000
Telephone: +32 2221 2111
Fax: +32 2221 3100
E-mail: info@nbb.be
Website: http://www.nbb.be/pub/index.htm

Guides: a Statistical Bulletin is published on an annual basis in French, Dutch, German and English explaining the methodology of the statistical reports published by the National Bank of Belgium

Activity: Belgium's central bank

Website(s) information:
Banque Nationale de Belgique (National Bank of Belgium) — url: www.bnb.be/sg/index.htm **Description:** information provided on NBB's interest rates, exchange rates, allocation of credits and annual accounts. Access to a wide range of publications including key statistics on major economic indicators and latest developments in the national and EU banking and financial sectors **Coverage:** belgostat.be provides a wide range of statistical information available, free to download

Publication(s):
Balance of Payments — **Frequency:** monthly/quarterly and annually **Content:** the National Bank is responsible for balance of payments statistics and international investment position statistics. In this context, it also draws up statistics relating to international trade in services and statistics for direct foreign investment

Belgian Prime News — **Frequency:** quarterly **Content:** each number contains a "Consensus forecast" concerning the anticipated movement of the main macroeconomic figures for Belgium, as well as a description of the most striking recent economic developments

Business Survey — **Frequency:** monthly and bi-annual **Content:** presents the results of company surveys. Gathering opinions of business people on the state of the economy and on developments which can be forecast over the short-term, these surveys provide a general and concise overview. Twice yearly surveys on investment in the manufacturing industry

Consumer Survey — **Frequency:** monthly **Content:** presents the results of household surveys. Gathers the opinions of consumers on the state of the economy and on developments which can be forecast over the short-term, these surveys provide an additional general overview

Economic Indicators — **Language:** French/Dutch/English **Frequency:** weekly **Content:** the National Bank releases an updated collection (the most recent past estimates and the latest available forecasts for the future) of the main Belgian economic and financial variables (gross domestic product and economic activity, prices, employment, public finance, foreign trade, interest rates and exchange rates

Economic Review — **Frequency:** 3 per annum **Content:** publishes articles on macroeconomic developments and the financial markets, transactions with foreign countries and the situation of enterprises. More specific analyses are also published in the Review

Financial Stability Review — **Content:** general overview of recent economic, financial and structural trends which are likely to have an effect on the stability of the financial system. This overview is complemented by thematic articles. The overview and the articles focus on three areas: monitoring of financial stability and prevention and resolution of systemic risks

Foreign Trade — **Language:** French/Dutch **Frequency:** monthly and quarterly **Content:** monthly bulletin published 10 weeks after the month under review which provides some overall macro-economic totals (foreign trade, price and volume growth, totals per partner country and per large product category). Together with this monthly bulletin a press release with the major figures is published online. Four months after the quarter under review a quarterly bulletin is published with additional information on a more detailed level (such as regional figures)

Money and Banking Statistics — **Frequency:** annual **Content:** the statistics on financial institutions and financial markets provides sector-related information and details on market developments. The statistics on the MFIs are complemented with information about interest rates, exchange rates, stock exchanges and payment systems and tools

National Accounts — **Frequency:** annual; and quarterly **Content:** national accounts are published in a number of series. A first estimate of the annual aggregates, based on the quarterly accounts, is published in April (end of March in electronic form). The detailed accounts and tables, with data per branch of industry and institutional sector (the government accounts can be consulted in June in electronic form), are available at the end of October (in electronic form at the end of September), followed by the supply and consumption tables. The annual accounts cycle is closed with the satellite account of non-profit institutions.
The quarterly accounts are published 70 days after the end of the quarter the estimates relate to. A flash estimate of the GDP, based on revised accounts of the previous quarters, is distributed 30 days after the end of each quarter via a press release

Rapport annuel de la Banque nationale (Annual Report of the National Bank) — **Language:** French/Dutch **Frequency:** annual **Content:** national bank's major publication. This document provides useful information on the recent economic and financial developments, both in Belgium and abroad. The synthesis presented by the Governor on behalf of the Council of Regency highlights the previous year's main events and delivers important messages with regard to the economic policy

Statistical Bulletin — **Frequency:** quarterly **Content:** statistics produced by the National Bank more frequently than every three months are compiled into a monthly update. The National Bank provides a wider range, with longer series, than in the Statistical bulletin free of charge on its website via 'Belgostat Online'

Statistics — **Language:** French / Dutch **Frequency:** annual **Content:** comprises overall figures, financial ratios and tables of resources

Bureau Fédéral du Plan
Federal Planning Bureau

Address: 47-49 avenue des Arts, Brussels, 1000
Telephone: +32 2 507 7311
Fax: +32 2 507 7373
Website: www.plan.be

Activity: makes studies and projections on economic, socio-economic and environmental policy issues
the FPB collects and analyses data, explores plausible evolutions, identifies alternatives, evaluates the impact of policy measures and formulates proposals

Website(s) information:
Federal Planning Bureau — **url:** www.plan.be **Description:** various bulletins, newsletters, and statistics relating to the Belgian and international economy **Coverage:** "databases" section covers input-output tables; economic forecasts, time series data on employment and National Accounts. "Forecasts" sections provides information on the consumer price index and health index used for calculating rents

Publication(s):
Euren Report — **Language:** French/Dutch **Frequency:** 2 per annum **Content:** the economic outlook in Europe analysed twice a year

Forecasts & Outlook — **Language:** French/Dutch **Frequency:** annual **Content:** macroeconomic analyses; labour market; economics; social welfare sector-based; studies, inter-industrial relations

Planning Paper — **Language:** French/Dutch **Frequency:** irregular **Content:** features different subjects such as administrative charges in Belgium for a full year, public participation in the market sector, budgetary cost of the unemployed, etc

Short Term Update - Newsletter of the Federal Planning Bureau — **Language:** English **Frequency:** quarterly **Content:** contains the main conclusions from the publications of the FPB, as well as information on new publications, together with an analysis of the most recent economic indicators

Working Papers — **Language:** French/Dutch **Frequency:** monthly **Content:** different economic articles every months such as: linking household income to macro data to project poverty indicators; fiscal councils, independent forecasts and the budgetary process; an evaluation of the risks surrounding the 2006-2012 NIME economic outlook : illustrative stochastic simulations

Institut National de Statistique
National Institute of Statistics

Address: 50 rue du progres, Brussels, 1210
Telephone: +32 2277 5504
Fax: +32 2277 5519
E-mail: info@statbel.mineco.fgov.be
Website: www.statbel.fgov.be

Guides: rapport des activités de l'Institut National de Statistique (annual; free); catalogue des Produits et Services de l'Institut National de Statistique (free; includes monthly updates). Statistics include: territory and environment; population; society; economy and finance; agriculture; industry; services, business and transport

Activity: collects data relative to Belgian society

Website(s) information:
EcoDATA — **url:** http: // ecodata.mineco.fgov.be **Description:** socio-economic statistics in Belgium **Coverage:** Belgian macro - economics data, by selection using graphs and tables

Statistics Belgium (Ministry of Economic Affairs - National Statistical Institute) — **url:** www.statbel.fgov.be **Description:** general information on the National Statistical Institute and its services; latest press releases; annual socio-economic surveys; list of major publications and studies, etc. Available in four languages **Coverage:** statistical section provides online annual data on Belgium covering different topics: territory and environment (physical and human geography, environment); population (population structure, demographic trends, households); social data (unemployment rate, general standard of living, health and education, justice and politics, etc); economy and finance (general macro-economic and financial indicators); agriculture, horticulture and fisheries; industry; services, commerce and transport

Publication(s):
Accidents de la circulation avec tués et blessés (Traffic Accidents: Mortality and Injury) — **Language:** French / Dutch **Frequency:** annual **Content:** traffic accident statistics

Annuaire de statistiques régionales (Directory of Regional Statistics) — **Language:** French / Dutch **Frequency:** annual **Content:** coded data reflecting the economic, financial and social life of various regions

Aperçu des statistiques de l'environnement (Environmental Statistics) — **Language:** French / Dutch **Frequency:** annual **Content:** environmental statistics in the form of tables, graphs and of cartogram's, and arranged by subject: air, water, waste, radioactivity, incidence of pollution on the environment, landscapes, nature, economic activities, and the right of the environment

Bulletin de statistique (Statistical Bulletin) — **Language:** French / Dutch **Frequency:** monthly **Content:** monthly publication gives an outline of socioeconomic life by presenting a series of indicators selected in most of the sectors covered by statistics. The population, agriculture, industry, foreign trade, prices, salaries, employment and the national product

Calibrage de l'enquête sur les forces de travail (Survey of the Work Force by Grade) — **Language:** French/Dutch **Content:** labour force statistics

Causes de décès (Causes of death) — **Language:** French / Dutch **Frequency:** annual **Content:** medical causes of death; diseases, accidents and murder; according to age, sex and region

Chiffres-clés (Key figures) — **Language:** French / Dutch **Frequency:** annual **Content:** statistical outline of Belgium

Communiqué hebdomadaire (Weekly Info) — **Language:** French / Dutch **Frequency:** weekly **Content:** last available statistics in the following domains: territory and environment; population; company; economy and finances; agriculture; industry; services, business and transport

Compendium commerce intérieur (Compendium of National Trade) — **Language:** French/Dutch **Frequency:** annual **Content:** data on the number of active companies in various sectors of business

Construction et logement (Construction and Housing) — **Language:** French / Dutch **Frequency:** annual **Content:** collects the data on the licences of construction granted, both for residential building and non-residential at the municipal level

Crédit à la consommation (Consumer Credit) — **Language:** French / Dutch **Frequency:** quarterly **Content:** the value and the number of contracts signed for loans or hire purchases, leases or openings of credit. Certain tables about the nature of the goods bought by means of these credits either on the duration or the value of the loans

Démographie des entreprises (Demography of companies) — **Language:** French /Dutch **Frequency:** annual **Content:** statistics of active persons liable for tax; VAT classified by province, activity according to the wordlist NACE-BEL in 2 figures, class of employment

Dépenses environnementales des entreprises en Belgique (Environmental Expenditure in Belgium) — **Language:** French/ Dutch **Content:** reports and assesses environmental investments

Emploi, chômage et grèves (Employment, Unemployment and Strikes) — **Language:** French / Dutch **Frequency:** annual **Content:** administrative data (resulting from the ONSS, from the ONEM) concerning employment, unemployment and strikes. Includes figures of unemployment in the European Union

Enquête structurelle des entreprises (Company Structure Survey) — **Language:** French / Dutch **Frequency:** annual **Content:** branches of industry: mining industries, manufacturing industry, producers and the distributors of electricity, gas and water, construction, business and the main service sectors, such as hotels and restaurants, transport, storing and communications; real-estate, rent and services companies

Enquête sur le budget des ménages (Inquiry into Household Finances) — **Language:** French / Dutch **Frequency:** annual **Content:** household finances analysis and measures the structure of Belgian household expenditure

Enquête sur l'emploi du temps (Employment Survey) — **Language:** French / Dutch **Frequency:** annual **Content:** employment, tasks, care and education of children, care staff, sleep and rest, education and training, social activities, leisure activities, movements

Enquête sur les forces de travail (Survey of the Work Force) — **Language:** French / Dutch **Frequency:** quarterly **Content:** manpower in Belgium according to various criteria: sex, age, place of residence, registry office, academic standard, sector, function, etc

Enquête voyages (Journeys Survey) — **Language:** French / Dutch **Frequency:** annual **Content:** main results of an inquiry on the behaviour of the vacationers; information on the duration and the motive for the journey, destination, type of accommodation, used means of transport and the mode of organisation for the journey; origin of the traveller

Espérance de vie en bonne santé selon le statut socio-économique en Belgique (Healthy Life Expectation by Socioeconomic Status in Belgium) — **Language:** French / Dutch **Content:** level of education and health in Belgium

Faillites (Bankruptcies) — **Language:** French / Dutch **Frequency:** monthly **Content:** contains data on bankruptcies by activity, region and duration

Hôtels, campings et locations touristiques en Belgique (Hotels, Camping and Tourist Costs in Belgium) — **Language:** French / Dutch **Frequency:** annual **Content:** contains data on the capacity of the tourism sector, arrivals, overnight stays according to the motive for the journey, the tourist region, the mode of accommodation and the country of residence of the visitors

Inégalité socio-économique et mortalité à l'âge moyen en Belgique (Socio-economic Disparity and Mortality by Average Age in Belgium) — **Language:** Dutch **Content:** contains data on mortality in Belgium, with socio-economic comparisons to other industrial nations

La conjoncture (Economic situation) — **Language:** French / Dutch **Frequency:** monthly **Content:** contains data on production, turnover and investments by production and distribution companies, prices in consumption and production, bankruptcies, employees, salaries and working hours

Les dépenses courantes de protection de l'environnement par les industries en Belgique (Running Costs of Environmental Protection by Industries in Belgium) — **Language:** French/Dutch **Content:** contains data on the environmental running costs of the Belgian industries

Mariages et divorces (Marriages and Divorce) — **Language:** French / Dutch **Frequency:** annual **Content:** contains data on marriages and divorces by nationality, previous married state, profession, social status, age, region and province

Ménages et noyaux familiaux au 1 janvier (Households on January 1st) — **Language:** Dutch/French **Frequency:** annual **Content:** contains data on private households, including number of persons in the household and number of persons with responsibility according to the age of the children

Mortalité (Mortality) — **Language:** French/Dutch **Frequency:** annual **Content:** contains data on mortality rate and number of deaths by region, province, age, gender and nationality of the deceased

Mouvement de la population et migrations (Movement of the Population and Migration) — **Language:** French / Dutch **Frequency:** annual **Content:** contains data on population, including geographic movements, changes of nationality and migratory movements

Naissances (Births) — **Language:** French / Dutch **Frequency:** annual **Content:** contains data on births by nationality, age of the mother, gender, province and region and fertility rates by age and region

Occupation du sol pour les provinces, les régions et le Royaume (Activity by Province and Region) — **Language:** French/Dutch **Frequency:** annual **Content:** contains data on land use for agricultural purposes

Population totale et belge au 1 janvier (Total Belgian Population on January 1st) — **Language:** French/Dutch **Frequency:** annual **Content:** contains data on population by sex, age and municipality and of population density by age

Prix à la consommation: indices, prix moyens et inflation (Prices: Consumer, Indicators, Averages and Inflation) — **Language:** French / Dutch **Frequency:** annual **Content:** contains data on prices by inflation, product and consumption in comparison to various countries of the European Union

Production industrielle et construction (Industrial Production and Construction) — **Language:** French / Dutch **Frequency:** monthly **Content:** contains data on the industrial production, including the building industry, construction licences, current construction, energy and recovery

Production industrielle PRODCOM et non-PRODCOM (Industrial Production with and without PRODCOM) — **Language:** French / Dutch **Frequency:** annual **Content:** contains data on the performances of big companies in various branches of industry, including deliveries and volume of employment

Recensement agricole (Agricultural Inventory) — **Language:** French / Dutch **Frequency:** annual **Content:** contains data on use of land, mode of exploitation, manpower, farm implements in use, the agricultural regions, provinces and number of animals

Santé et mortalité foeto-infantile (Health and Foetal-child Mortality) — **Frequency:** annual **Content:** contains data on health and foetal-childish mortality by place of residence, age of the mother, nationality of the mother, professional activity of the mother, social and occupational group of the father, born weight, lasted gestation and initial cause of the death

Santé publique (Public Health) — **Language:** French / Dutch **Frequency:** annual **Content:** contains data on number of doctors, hospitals, hospital beds, patients, days of hospitalization, cases of infection with HIV and AIDS and cases of tumours. Also covers household expenditure in care of health by type of expense and region

Singularité des étrangers sur le marché de l'emploi (Foreign Employment Factors) — **Language:** French / Dutch **Content:** contains data on active foreign workers on the Belgian labour market

Statistique fiscale des revenus (Fiscal Statistics of Incomes) — **Language:** French / Dutch **Frequency:** annual **Content:** contains data on income by regions, provinces and districts, distribution of the taxable net total income and its constituents

Statistique fiscale des revenus par déciles (Tax Statistics of Incomes) — **Frequency:** annual **Content:** contains data on taxable net total income and its constituents, by domestic type and age brackets

Statistiques agricoles (Agricultural Statistics) — **Language:** French / Dutch **Frequency:** quarterly **Content:** contains data on agricultural activity by production, modifications, outdoor vegetable farming, dairy farming, pig population, slaughter of animals, agricultural price indices and farm rents

Statistiques mensuelles du transport (Transport Monthly Statistics) — **Language:** French /Dutch **Frequency:** monthly **Content:** contains data on types of transport, new registrations, traffic accidents, transport of the goods by sea, waterway or by rail and travellers by plane or train

Statistiques sociales et comptes nationaux: vers une approche SAM (Labour Accounts and Social Accounting Matrices) — **Language:** French / Dutch **Content:** contains information on the manual production of SAMs per reference year

Structure and Distribution of Earnings Survey — **Language:** English **Content:** contains data on economic and financial factors and on distribution of earnings

Tourisme et hôtellerie (Tourism and Hotel Business) — **Language:** French / Dutch **Frequency:** quarterly **Content:** contains data on the hotel and catering industry, including arrivals, purpose and duration of stay and number of overnight stays by types, province and the origin of the visitors

Une analyse sur l'emploi du temps des Belges (Analysis of the timetable of Belgians) — **Language:** French / Dutch **Content:** contains data on time use of active and inactive people, including day-to-day progress, weekend activities, general activities of the population, regional differences and differences between men and women

Ventes de biens immobiliers (Sales of Real Estate) — **Language:** French / Dutch **Frequency:** annual **Content:** contains data on real estate, including number, surface, selling price and properties by district

Bosnia-Herzegovina

Agencija za bankarstvo Bosne i Hercegovine
Banking Agency of the Federation of Bosnia and Herzegovina

Address: Koševo 3, Sarajevo, 71000
Telephone: +387 33 721 400
Fax: +387 33 668 811
E-mail: agencija@fba.ba
Website: www.fba.ba

Activity: bank licensing, licensing related to changes of banks' organisational structure and payment systems, collecting, processing and recording data submitted by banks in accordance with current regulations

Website(s) information:
Agencija za bankarstvo Bosne i Hercegovine — url: www.fba.ba **Description:** reports on the banking system, financial statements and external audit of banks in the Federation of Bosnia and Herzegovina; available online in Bosnian/Croatian; links to websites of banks **Coverage:** banking system, financial statements and external audit of banks

Agencija za promociju stranih nekretnina Bosne i Hercegovine (FIPA)
Foreign Investment Promotion Agency of Bosnia and Herzegovina (FIPA)

Address: Branilaca Sarajeva 21, Sarajevo, 71000
Telephone: +387 33 278 080
Fax: +387 33 278 081
E-mail: fipa@fipa.gov.ba
Website: www.fipa.gov.ba

Activity: generating new investments; promoting foreign investments, servicing potential and existing investors, providing all information related to business environment in Bosnia and Herzegovina, analysing and promoting sectors for foreign investments, promoting investments and at the same time identifying the main legal obstacles for direct foreign investment, preparing presentations and printing promotional material, creating and maintaining database of investment projects and available locations, developing co-operation with other foreign investment agencies in the region

Website(s) information:
Agencija za promociju stranih nekretnina Bosne i Hercegovine (FIPA) — **url:** www.fipa.gov.ba **Description:** statistical information on general economic indicators available online and in English; **Coverage:** general economic indicators

Publication(s):
Investirajte u turizam (Invest in Tourism) — **Frequency:** irregular **Content:** profile report on possible investments in tourism in Bosnia and Herzegovina **Readership:** potential investors, research specialists

Sektor auto-dijelova (Auto Components Industry) — **Language:** Bosnian/Croatian/Serbian **Frequency:** irregular **Content:** profile report on auto components industry **Readership:** potential investors, reserarch specialists

Agencija za statistiku Bosne i Hercegovine
Statistical Agency of Bosnia and Herzegovina

Address: Zelenih beretki 26, Sarajevo, 71000
Telephone: +387 33 220 622
Fax: +387 33 220 622
E-mail: bhas@bhas.ba
Website: www.bhas.ba

Activity: producing and publishing statistical reports collected by the entity Institutes for Statistics related to all socio-economic sectors in accordance with internationally recognised standards, representing Bosnia and Herzegovina internationally, fostering co-operation between the two entities and their Institutes and facilitating the exchange of information between the Institutes and their branches

Website(s) information:
Agencija za statistiku Bosne i Hercegovine (Statistical Agency of Bosnia and Herzegovina) — **url:** www.bhas.ba **Description:** reports (bulletins) on economic and social situation in Bosnia and Herzegovina; narrative part of the reports are written in Bosnian/Croatian/Serbian, whilst statistical information available in English **Coverage:** socio-economic developments

Publication(s):
Bilteni (Bulletins) — **Language:** Bosnian/Croatian/Serbian/English **Frequency:** monthly **Content:** socio-economic situation/developments covering a 5-year period **Readership:** academics, statistical specialists, research specialists, governmental organisations, NGOs

Tematski bilteni (Thematic Bulletins) — **Language:** Bosnian/Croatian/Serbian and some in English **Frequency:** annual **Content:** annual overview of different industries and social indicators over a two-year period **Readership:** statistical specialists, research specialsts, academics, governmental organisations, NGOs, businesses

Centralna banka Bosne i Hercegovine
Central Bank of Bosnia and Herzegovina

Address: Marsala Tita 25, Sarajevo, 71000
Telephone: +387 33 278 100
Fax: +387 33 278 299
E-mail: contact@cbbh.ba
Website: www.cbbh.gov.ba

Activity: maintaining monetary stability, defining and controlling the implementation of monetary policy of Bosnia and Herzegovina, supporting and maintaining appropriate payment and settlement systems, co-ordinating the activities of the BH Entity Banking Agencies in charge of bank licensing and supervision

Website(s) information:
Centralna banka Bosne i Hercegovine (Central Bank of Bosnia and Herzegovina) — **url:** www.cbbh.gov.ba **Description:** offers narrative and statistical banking reports, as well as bulletins and newsletters related to socio-economic situation and developments in Bosnia and Herzegovina; documents are available in English; **Coverage:** advance release, monthly balance, financial statements, main economic indicators, governmental funds, foreign debt, financial and external sectors

Direkcija za civilnu avijaciju Bosne i Hercegovine (BHDCA)
Civil Aviation Directorate of Bosnia and Hercegovina

Address: Fehima ef. Curcica 6, Sarajevo, 71000
Telephone: +387 33 251 350
Fax: +387 33 251 351
E-mail: bhdca@bhdca.gov.ba
Website: www.bhdca.gov.ba

Activity: implementing civil aviation policy, enforcing the relevant legislation, international standards and practice, developing civil aviation strategy, representing the Directorate internationally, managing financial and other civil aviation resources

Website(s) information:
Direkcija za civilnu avijaciju Bosne i Hercegovine (BHDCA) *(Civil Aviation Directorate of Bosnia and Herzegovina)* — url: www.bhdca.gov.ba **Description:** local convergence and implementation plans, including various statistical information about the civil aviation system in BIH; available online and in Bosnian, Croatian, Serbian and English **Coverage:** civil aviation

Državna regulatorna komisija za elektricnu energiju (DERK)
State Electricity Regulatory Commission (DERK)

Address: Miška Jovanovica 4/II, Tuzla, 75000
Telephone: +387 35 302 070
Fax: +387 35 302 077
E-mail: info@derk.ba
Website: www.derk.ba

Activity: regulating electricity distribution in Bosnia and Herzegovina, distribution system operation and international trade in electricity

Website(s) information:
Državna regulatorna komisija za elektricnu energiju (DERK) — url: www.derk.ba **Description:** annual reports available online in Bosnian/Croatian/Serbian **Coverage:** energy distribution and consumption

Federalni zavod za statistiku
Federal Office for Statistics

Address: Zelenih beretki 26, Sarajevo, 71000
Telephone: +387 33 664 553
Fax: +387 33 664 553
E-mail: fedstat@fzs.ba
Website: www.fzs.ba

Guides: extensive list of publications is available on the official site
Activity: collection, processing and publication of statistical data, defining uniform statistical research methodology and standards, developing statistical information systems, developing and implementing administrative and statistical registries (population, companies, etc), exchange of statistical information with other countries and international organisations in accordance with relevant national legislation and international agreements

Website(s) information:
Federalni zavod za statistiku *(Federal Office of Statistics)* — url: www.fzs.ba **Description:** all monthly and annual data available online **Coverage:** general data: geographical, geological and census data; monthly data: industrial production, foreign trade, tourism - vital statistics, prices and cost of living. Annual data: basic information, register of business entities, industry and foreign trade, tourism, prices and cost of living, GDP, capital investment, employment/unemployment, population and wages

Publication(s):
Bilten (Bulletin) — **Language:** Bosnian/Croatian/English **Frequency:** monthly **Content:** annual publication containing detailed data related to various fields of statistical research and specific overview of each of the fields at Federal, cantonal and municipal level **Readership:** academics and research specialists

Kantoni u brojkama (Canton Statistical Report) — **Language:** Bosnian/Croatian/English **Frequency:** annual **Content:** annual publication of selected statistical information related to Federation BIH cantons **Readership:** academics and research specialists

Statisticki godišnjak/ljetopis Federacije Bosne i Hercegovine (Statistical Annual Report of the Federation of Bosnia and Herzegovina) — **Language:** Bosnian/Croatian/English **Frequency:** annual **Content:** covers detailed statistical data on population, employment/unemployment rate, annual national income, local products, agriculture, industry, transport, tourism, education, culture and social care at Federal, cantonal and municipal level **Readership:** academics and research specialists

Statisticki podaci o privrednim/gospodarskim i drugim kretanjima u Fedaraciji BIH (Statistical Data on Economic and Other Developments in Federation BIH) — **Language:** Bosnian/Croatian/English **Frequency:** monthly **Content:** contains results of monthly research of economic and other developments in Federation BIH (cantons), as well as selected annual reports **Readership:** academics and research specialists

Žene I muškarci (Gender) FBIH (Gender of the Federation BIH) — **Language:** Bosnian/Croatian/English **Frequency:** irregular **Content:** statistical data on gender in the Federation of Bosnia and Herzegovina **Readership:** academic, research specialists, NGOs

Institut za statistiku Republike Srpske
The Institute for Statistics of the Republic of Srpska

Address: Veljka Mladenovica 12d, Banja Luka, 78000
Telephone: +387 51 450 275
Fax: +387 51 450 279
E-mail: stat@rzs.rs.ba
Website: www.rzs.rs.ba

Activity: providing statistical information on all sectors in the Republic of Srpska

Website(s) information:
Institut za statistiku Republike Srpske *(Institute for Statistics of the Republic of Srpska)* — url: www.rzs.rs.ba **Description:** survey and research reports (bulletins) are available online and in English; **Coverage:** socio-economic statistics

Publication(s):
Bilteni (Bulletins) — **Language:** Bosnian/Croatian/Serbian/English **Frequency:** annual **Content:** various industries and social indicators (2004-2006) **Readership:** academics, research specialists, statistical experts, governmental organisations, NGOs, businesses

Statisticki pregled (Statistical Overview) — **Language:** Bosnian/Croatian/Serbian/English **Content:** ontly and quarterly statistical overview of socio-econoimc situation/developments **Readership:** academics, statistical specialists, research specialists, governmental organisations, NGOs, businesses

Investiciona banka Federacije Bosne i Hercegovine
Investment Bank of the Federation of Bosnia and Herzegovina

Address: Igmanska 1, Sarajevo, 71000
Telephone: +387 33 277 900
Fax: +387 33 668 952
E-mail: info@ibf-bih.com
Website: www.ibf-bih.com

Activity: investing in economic development, especially development of small and medium companies, promoting and developing commercial banks, supporting creation and development of strong national capital market, participating in restructuring and privatizing of national industry

Website(s) information:
Investiciona banka Federacije Bosne i Hercegovine *(Investment Bank of the Federation of Bosnia and Herzegovina)* — url: www.ibf-bih.com **Description:** balance sheets, income statements, profit/loss statements; available online and in English **Coverage:** assets, liabilities, interest, income, loss, expenditures

Ministarstvo finansija i trezora Bosne i Hercegovine
Ministry of Finance and Treasury of Bosnia and Hercegovina

Address: Trg BIH 1, Sarajevo, 71000
Telephone: +387 33 205 345
Fax: +387 33 219 923
E-mail: trezorbih@trezorbih.gov.ba
Website: www.trezorbih.gov.ba

Activity: developing principles of tax policy and drafting relevant legislation, establishing relations with international and national financial institutions, planning and managing the debt of Bosnia and Herzegovina, proposing policy of new indebting in country and abroad, drafting budget and final balance of accounts of the country, coordinating activities related provision of budgetary resources of the country, executing budget and financing state institutions

management of money and operating the Single Treasury Account (JRT);

establishment of accounting operations of B-H Institutions; developing and operating financial information system; developing and implementing of internal supervision of budget users;

activities on ex-SFRY succession issues;

management of property in possession of B-H Institutions; compilation, distribution and publication of consolidated Government's general fiscal data;

preparation of laws, regulations and public procurement procedures, and

management and specialist operations set forth by laws and regulations.

Website(s) information:

Ministarstvo finansija i trezora Bosne i Hercegovine *(Ministry of Finance & Treasury of Bosnia & Herzegovina)* — **url:** www.trezorbih.gov.ba **Description:** narrative and statistical report on debt of Bosnia and Herzegovina; it is available online and in Bosnian/Croatian/Serbian **Coverage:** debt related statistics

Ministarstvo komunikacija i prometa Bosne i Hercegovine
Ministry of Communications and Transport of Bosnia and Herzegovina

Address: Trg BiH 1, Sarajevo, 71000
Telephone: +387 33 284 750
Fax: +387 33 284 751
E-mail: info@mkt.gov.ba
Website: www.mkt.gov.ba

Activity: developing policies relating to and regulating common and international communication devices, international and inter-entity transport and infrastructure

producing contract, agreements and other acts relating to international and inter-entity communications and transport, maintaining relations with international organizations dealing with international and inter-entity communications and transport, drafting strategic and planning documents relating to international and inter-entity communications, transport, infrastructure and information technologies, dealing with control of unimpeded transport in international transport, civil aviation and civil transport control

Ministarstvo pravde Bosne i Hercegovine
Ministry of Justice of Bosnia and Herzegovina

Address: Trg BIH 1, Sarajevo, 71000
Telephone: +387 33 223 501
Fax: +387 33 223 504
E-mail: kontakt@mpr.gov.ba
Website: www.mpr.gov.ba

Activity: functioning as an administrative body for legal institutions, establishing and maintaining international judicial relations, drafting relevant laws, ensuring that judicial system of the country is in accordance with international agreements and acting as a central co-ordinating body to ensure approximation of the entities' legislation

Website(s) information:

Ministarstvo pravde Bosne i Hercegovine *(Ministry of Justice of Bosnia and Herzegovina)* — **url:** www.mpr.gov.ba **Description:** annual narrative reports also containing statistical information about the judicial system, including crime rates **Coverage:** crime statistics

Ministarstvo spoljne trgovine i medunarodnih odnosa Bosne i Hercegovine
Ministry of Foreign Affairs and Foreign Trade of Bosnia and Herzegovina

Address: Musala 9, Sarajevo, 71000
Telephone: +387 33 663 863
Website: www.mvteo.gov.ba

Activity: developing and implementing foreign trade and foreign investment policies, establishing and maintaining international trade relations, developing and implementing customs policy, dealing with national resources, energetics and environmental issues

Website(s) information:

Ministarstvo spoljne trgovine i medunarodnih odnosa Bosne i Hercegovine *(Ministry of Foreign Affairs and Foreign Trade of Bosnia and Herzegovina)* — **url:** www.mvteo.gov.ba **Description:** reports on direct foreign investments covering the period from 1994 to 2004 **Coverage:** direct foreign investments

OSCE misija za Bosnu i Hercegovinu
OSCE Mission to Bosnia and Hercegovina

Address: Fra Andela Zvizdovica 1A, Sarajevo, 71000
Telephone: +387 33 752 100
E-mail: press.ba@osce.org
Website: www.oscebih.org

Activity: responsibility for elections, and human rights in Bosnia and Herzegovina and regional military stabilisation, with democracy-building added subsequently; supporting the establishment of institutions and processes that will ensure Bosnia and Herzegovina's survival as an independent state

Website(s) information:

OSCE misija za Bosnu i Hercegovinu *(OSCE Mission to Bosnia and Herzegovina)* — **url:** www.oscebih.org **Description:** reports on trafficking in human beings and illegal immigration in BiH available online and in English **Coverage:** trafficking and illegal immigration, socio-political indicators

Publication(s):

Public Opinion Research - Attitudes Toward Recent Socio-political Situation in BiH — **Language:** English **Frequency:** irregular **Content:** socio-political situation **Readership:** academics, research specialists, governmental organisations, NGOs, humanitarian organisations

Report on Trafficking in Human Beings and Illegal Immigration in BiH — **Language:** English **Frequency:** irregular **Content:** rafficking and illegal immigration **Readership:** research specialists, humanitarian organisations, police

Savez poslodavaca Republike Srpske
Employers Confederation of the Republic of Srpska

Address: Mladena Stojanovica 111, Banja Luka, 51000
Telephone: +387 51 332 616
Fax: +387 51 332 616
E-mail: ecrs@blic.net
Website: www.poslodavci.rs.ba

Activity: business services, legal counselling, information sharing, organising round-table session on topics of concern to employers, representation and advocating for employers interests in the society

Website(s) information:

Savez poslodavaca Republike Srpske *(Employers Confederation of the Republic of Srpska)* — **url:** www.poslodavci.rs.ba **Description:** annual business survey reports; available online and in Serbian/English; **Coverage:** current trends and issues in business environment

Savjet/Vijece ministara
Council of Ministers

Address: Trg BIH 1, Sarajevo, 71000
Telephone: +387 33 211 581
Fax: +387 33 205 347
E-mail: cmpress@smartnet.ba
Website: www.vijeceministara.gov.ba

Activity: carrying out policies and decisions in the fields of foreign policy and foreign trade
customs, monetary issues, finances of the institutions and for the international obligations of Bosnia and Herzegovina; immigration, refugee, and asylum policy and regulation, international and inter-Entity criminal law enforcement, including relations with Interpol establishment and operation of common and international communications facilities, regulation of inter-Entity transportation, air traffic control; facilitation of inter-Entity coordination

Udruzenje/udruga poslodavaca Bosne i Hercegovine
Confederation of Employers of Bosnia and Herzegovina

Address: Zmaja od Bosne 4/XI, Sarajevo, 71000
Telephone: +387 33 264 830
Fax: +387 33 264 831
E-mail: upfbih@bih.net.ba
Website: www.upfbih.org

Activity: protecting rights of employers and entrepreneurs in the fields of labour and social legislation

Zavod za javno zdravstvo Federacije Bosne i Hercegovine
Institute for Public Health of the Federation of Bosnia and Herzegovina

Address: Maršala Tita 9, Sarajevo, 71000
Telephone: +387 33 716 600
Fax: +387 33 220 548
E-mail: zavodzz@bih.net.ba
Website: www.zzjzfbih.ba

Activity: promoting public and environmental health and illness prevention, designing and implementing health projects and conducting research in the field of public health

Bulgaria

Agency for Economic Analysis and Forecasting
Address: 31 Aksakov Street, Sofia, 1000
Telephone: +359 2 9859 5601
E-mail: aeaf@aeaf.minfin.bg
Website: www.aeaf.minfin.bg

Guides: publications in Bulgarian can be accessed free of charge; a paid subscription is required for the printed publications and for some publications in English; a full catalogue is available online
Activity: analyses the current business environment and the economic situation and elaborates assessments on the country's economic development prospects; prepares short-, medium- and long-term forecasts for Bulgaria's economic development trends under different economic policy scenarios

Website(s) information:
Agency for Economic Analysis and Forecasting — url: www.aeaf.minfin.bg
Description: files are available in PDF format, the site contains business survey series, working paper series, and information on recent developments in the Bulgarian Economy **Coverage:** detailed monthly data about the Bulgarian business climate, industrial sales and prices, CPI, PPI, unemployment, interest rates, main macroeconomic and microeconomic indicators

Publication(s):
Bulgarian Economy: Analysis and Outlook — **Language:** Bulgarian/English **Frequency:** quarterly **Content:** focuses on the latest trends in the Bulgarian economy and provides a detailed forecast for the following 12 months

Bulgarska Narodna Banka
Bulgarian National Bank

Address: 1 Alexander Battenberg Square, Sofia, 1000
Telephone: +359 2 91 459
Fax: +359 2 980 2425/980 6493
E-mail: press_office@bnbank.org
Website: www.bnb.bg

Guides: publications are available for download online - the bank maintains a free subscription policy
Activity: maintains the stability of the national currency, the Lev, through the implementation of adequate policies and of an efficient payment system; exclusive right to issue coins and banknotes in Bulgaria; regulates and supervises the banking sector aiming at the stability of the banking system; administers the Government Securities Depository and monitors the activities of the Central Depository

Website(s) information:
Bulgarian National Bank — url: www.bnb.bg **Description:** The bank maintains a free subscription policy to all its publications, covering fiscal, monetary, financial, and other matters **Coverage:** provides banking and financial statistics including: exchange rates; balance of payments; foreign trade; gross external debt; aggregated balance sheets and income statements of national commercial banks; trade rates; and monetary survey

Publication(s):
Bank Review — **Language:** English/Bulgarian **Frequency:** quarterly **Content:** contains articles covering the banking and finance sectors

Monthly Bulletin — **Language:** English/Bulgarian **Frequency:** monthly

Coordination Centre for Information, Communication, and Management Technologies
Address: 1 Dondoukov Blvd, Sofia, 1000
Telephone: +359 2 940 3643
Fax: +359 2 940 3646
E-mail: gvalchev@ccit.government.bg
Website: www.ccit.government.bg

Activity: implements information, communications and management technologies through support and coordination of state administration, the donor community and the private sector, leading to an overall improvement in the quality of the public-administrative services and the decision-making processes

Council for Electronic Media
Address: 69 Shipchenski Prohod Blvd, Sofia
Telephone: +359 2 970 8810
Fax: +359 2 973 3769
E-mail: cem@cablebg.net
Website: www.cem.bg

Guides: catalogue available online
Activity: regulation of radio and TV broadcasting in the country by registration and licensing of radio and TV operators

Durzhavna Komisija po Stokovite Borsi i Turzhishtata
State Commission on Stock Exchanges and Markets

Address: Izgrev Region, 3A 165th Street, Sofia, 1040
Telephone: +359 2 970 6037
Fax: +359 2 873 5418
E-mail: office@dksbt.bg
Website: www.dksbt.bg

Guides: available online in PDF format; in Bulgarian only
Activity: works for the creation and development of national centres for wholesale trade with food products and for the transparent functioning of stock markets in the country

Website(s) information:
State Commission on Stock Exchanges and Markets — url: www.dksbt.bg
Description: availability in PDF format - prices are presented according to product and region within Bulgaria **Coverage:** weekly and quarterly analyses of the wholesale prices of different food products

Executive Environmental Agency
Address: PO Box 251, 136 Tzar Boris III blvd, Sofia, 1618
Telephone: +359 2 955 9011
Fax: +359 2 955 9015
E-mail: ncesd@nfp-bg.eionet.eu.int
Website: nfp-bg.eionet.eu.int/ncesd/index.html

Guides: full catalogue is available online

Activity: conducts research of the main environmental indicators on the territory of Bulgaria

Website(s) information:
Executive Environmental Agency — **url:** nfp-bg.eionet.eu.int/ncesd/index.html
Description: the site provides online access to information bulletins covering environmental data; it is possible to access the online version of the "Annual State of the Environment Report" for 1998-2003 **Coverage:** data on air quality, water pollution, harmful emissions

Invest Bulgaria Agency
Address: 31 Aksakov Street, Sofia, 1000
Telephone: +359 2 985 5500
Fax: +359 2 980 1320
E-mail: iba@investbg.government.bg
Website: www.investbg.government.bg

Guides: publications are available online in PDF format in separate versions in English, Spanish, German, Italian, Japanese and Bulgarian

Activity: works with potential and existing investors in Bulgaria in order to assist and secure the successful realisation of foreign investment in Bulgaria

Website(s) information:
Invest Bulgaria Agency — **url:** www.investbg.government.bg **Description:** data is available in PDF format **Coverage:** foreign investment figures, import and export, reports on particular industries, including industries attractive for investors, macroeconomic data, country profile

Ministry of Agriculture and Forestry
Address: 55 Hristo Botev Blvd, Sofia, 1040
Telephone: +359 2 985 11255
E-mail: press@mzgar.government.bg

Guides: publications are available in PDF/zip format online

Activity: coordinates, monitors, and implements the agricultural and forestry policy of the Republic of Bulgaria

Website(s) information:
Ministry of Agriculture and Forestry — **url:** www.mzgar.government.bg
Description: the website contains PDF versions of the main publications of the Ministry - a monthly sector bulletin, an agrostatistical bulletin, and an annual industry report, available from 1998 onward; it also contains legal and policy documents and provisions **Coverage:** analyses of production and sales of staple products, livestock, etc; agrostatistical bulletin with production and structure data; annual reports on the condition of the agricultural industry, inlcuding sector specific figures on production, import and export, prices and state policy

Ministry of Economy and Energy
Address: 8 Slavianska Street, Sofia, 1052
Telephone: +359 2 940 7777
Fax: +359 2 940 7313
E-mail: callcentre@mee.government.bg
Website: www.mi.government.bg

Guides: all publications are available online

Activity: coordinates, monitors and implements the economic and energy policy of the Republic of Bulgaria

Website(s) information:
Ministry of Economy and Energy — **url:** www.mi.government.bg **Description:** the site provides information about the state of Bulgarian economy under the headings of Industry, Trade, Entrepreneurship and Eurointegration. Most reports and documents are available in both English and Bulgarian **Coverage:** covers a wide range of macroeconomic indicators in its monthly bulletin and in its issue "Basic Economic Indicators". Tourism statistics - revenue, number and percentage increase of foreign tourists by year and country of origin; international trade statistics - export figures by type of goods and destination of export; report on the condution of small and medium businesses by sector and region - production, sales, revenue; panorama report of the state of Bulgarian industry by sector - sales, production, overview and trends

Ministry of Energy and Energy Resources
Address: 8 Triadiza Street, Sofia, 1040
Telephone: +359 2 926 3636
Fax: +359 2 980 7630/988 1443
Website: www.doe.bg

Guides: full catalogue is available online; most documents are available online in PDF format

Activity: monitors energy policy in the country

Website(s) information:
Ministry of Energy and Energy Resources — **url:** www.doe.bg **Description:** reports and presentations covering the developments in the Bulgarian energy sector; most of the information is available in both English and Bulgarian; information about current projects and media coverage is also available **Coverage:** developments in the energy sector - privatisation, sector growth, investment opportunities, state of the economy by region and by energy source

Ministry of Environment and Water of Bulgaria
Address: 67 William Gladstone Steet, Sofia, 1000
Telephone: +359 2 940 6222/981 1385
Fax: +359 2 986 2533
E-mail: press@moew.government.bg
Website: www.moew.government.bg

Guides: full catalogue available online; full text available in PDF/zip format

Activity: determines and implements state environmental policy; monitors and reports on the environmental indicators in Bulgaria and elaborates guidelines for environmental protection

Publication(s):
National Catalogue of Environmental Data Sources — **Language:** Bulgarian/English **Content:** data about where and what environmental information is available in Bulgaria, in what format and access information

Ministry of Finance
Address: 102 G. S. Rakovski Street, Sofia, 1040
Telephone: +359 2 9859 2024
E-mail: feedback@minfin.bg
Website: www.minfin.government.bg

Guides: full catalogue available online; most reports and statistical information are available free of charge and can be downloaded from the website; a subscription charge applies to the monthly magazine published by the ministry "The Budget"

Activity: coordinates and implements the budgetary and tax policy of the Republic of Bulgaria

Website(s) information:
Ministry of Finance — **url:** www.minfin.government.bg **Description:** the site provides access to official reports and documents published under the heading of Statistics; the monthly bulletin on government debt management is available under the heading "Publications" **Coverage:** net cash flows to treasury single accounts, fiscal reserve account by month, data on the rebublican budget, government debt management (monthly and annual reports), tax policy and revenue breakdown

Publication(s):
Budget, The — **Language:** Bulgarian/English **Frequency:** per month **Content:** regulations and bylaws, orders, instructions, letters, comments of specialists, monthly information about the execution of the consolidated fiscal program, answers to questions in the financial sphere **Readership:** specialists in the field of finance, state and local government, tax administration, banking, statistics, accountants, students, businessmen

Ministry of Labour and Social Policy
Address: 2 Triaditsa Street, Sofia, 1052
Telephone: +359 2 811 9443
Fax: +359 2 988 4405/986 1318
E-mail: mlsp@mlsp.government.bg
Website: www.mlsp.government.bg

Guides: full catalogue is available online

Activity: determines, coordinates and implements labour and social policy of the Republic of Bulgaria; develops programmes for the reduction of unemployment; determines the minimum wage and pension

Website(s) information:
Ministry of Labour and Social Policy — url: www.mlsp.government.bg
Description: the site provides online access to various reports and programmes published by the Ministry since 2000 **Coverage:** national employment statistics by gender, age, education, and economic sector

Ministry of Transport and Communications
Address: 9 Djakon Ignatij Street, Sofia, 1000
Telephone: +359 2 987 5750
Fax: +359 2 987 1805
Website: www.mtc.government.bg

Guides: full catalogue available online
Activity: determines, coordinates and implements official policy on transport and communications

National Centre of Health Informatics
Address: 15 Academic Ivan Geshov Street, Sofia, 1431
Telephone: +359 2 951 5302/951 5303
Fax: +359 2 951 5238
Website: www.nchi.government.bg

Guides: full catalogue is available online
Activity: research in the sphere of public health and well-being indicators; works as a specialized agency of the Ministry of Healthcare and provides input for National Health Strategy

Website(s) information:
National Centre of Health Informatics — url: www.nchi.government.bg
Description: online access to the annual public health statistics publication is available in English; most data is available under the heading "health statisitcs" and "health indicators database" in Bulgarian **Coverage:** public health statistics, birth and mortality rate, morbidity indicators, trends in these indicators by region and gender; average life expectancy; health institutions' activity; economic indicators of health insitutions

National Employment Agency
Address: 3 Dondoukov Blvd, Sofia, 1000
Telephone: +359 2 980 8719
Fax: +359 986 7802
E-mail: az@az.government.bg
Website: www.nsz.government.bg

Guides: all publications are accessible online
Activity: executive agency to the Minister of Labour and Social Policy for the implementation of the government policy on employment promotion; registration of unemployed actively seeking employment and available vacancies; Implementation, of projects and programs in the field of employment, professional qualification and training, and social integration

Website(s) information:
National Employment Agency - Statistics and Analyses — url:
www.nsz.government.bg **Description:** links to monthly, periodical and annual reports on labour force dynamics in Bulgaria by region; there is a difference between the English and the Bulgarian versions of the site, the former being more informative **Coverage:** data on employment and unemployment, labour force dynamics, structure by gender, age and education, number of people attending qualification courses, etc

National Statistical Institute (NSI)
Address: 2 Panajot Volov Street, Sofia, 1038
Telephone: +359 2 985 7729/985 7457
Fax: +359 2 985 7799
E-mail: presscentre@nsi.bg
Website: www.nsi.bg

Guides: a full catalogue of printed, online, regional and library-access publications can be found online

Activity: statistical surveys and the publication and dissemination of statistical data

Website(s) information:
National Statistical Institute (NSI) — url: www.nsi.bg **Description:** available online both in Bulgarian and in English, NSI's web site provides information on the Institute's main products and services, including latest news and releases, a catalogue of available publications and access to varied online statistical data such as geographical and meteorological data, economic indicators, governmental constitution, population, employment, wages, personal consumption, GDP, money flows, agriculture, industry, communication, economic relations with foreign countries, tourism, education, culture and arts, health and pension insurance, environment **Coverage:** a wide range of socio-economic statistics are provided for both Bulgaria and other countries (Bulgaria and the World in Figures), including data collected by the NSI, as well as by major pan-regional and international official organisations (e.g. Council of Europe; ILO; etc). Data covers: population and demographics; health services; labour market; energy resources; industrial sector; agricultural sector (crops and livestock); external trade (exports and imports); and transports. There are international comparisons and year coverage varies by sector and by indicator

Publication(s):
Main Macro-economic Indicators — **Language:** Bulgarian/English **Frequency:** annual **Content:** statistical overview of the present state of Bulgaria's economy

Prices, Price Indices and Inflation — **Language:** Bulgarian **Frequency:** monthly **Content:** list of annual and monthly consumer price indices by commodities

Statistical News — **Language:** English/Bulgarian **Frequency:** monthly **Content:** monthly and quarterly updated socio-economic data, as well as statistics for all main sectors of the economy: agriculture, industry, transport, communications and trade

Statistical Yearbook of the Republic of Bulgaria — **Language:** English/Bulgarian **Frequency:** annual **Content:** compilation of annually updated statistics collected by the Institute: demographic, social, and economic indicators

United Nations Development Programme - Bulgaria
Address: Box 700, UN House in Bulgaria, 25 Khan Krum Street, Sofia, 1040
Telephone: +359 2 969 6100
Fax: +359 2 981 3184
E-mail: info@undp.bg
Website: www.undp.bg

Guides: full catalogue is available online; publications are available in English and Bulgarian in PDF format
Activity: works for poverty reduction through social inclusion and economic development; works for the improvement of quality of life through good governance for equitable regional development

Website(s) information:
International Trade Centre (UNCTAD/WTO) — url:
http://www.intracen.org/menus/countries.htm **Description:** the webiste provides country profiles of with this statistical coverage, as well as publications on Bulgaria, and a list of selected sources of information **Coverage:** trade performance index, national export performance, national import profile, trade statistics by industry sector and year (2000-2004)

Publication(s):
National Human Development Report — **Language:** English/Bulgarian **Frequency:** annual **Content:** Looks at social and economic indicators and surveys every region of Bulgaria to determine trends, developments and areas in need of reform

Croatia

Agencija za promicanje izvoza i ulaganja Hrvatske
Croatian Trade and Investment Promotion Agency
Address: Andrije Hebranga 34, Zagreb, 10000
Telephone: +385 1 486 6001
Fax: +385 1 486 6008
E-mail: zeljko.kirincic@apiu.hr
Website: www.apiu.hr

Activity: full service to investors on implementation of their investment projects, proposing measures to enhance the investment environment and promoting the country as a good investment location

Website(s) information:

Agencija za promicanje izvoza i ulaganja Hrvatske (Croatian Trade and Investment Promotion Agency) — **url:** www.apiu.hr **Description:** general socio-economic indicators and investment information available online **Coverage:** socio-economic indicators

Državni zavod za statistiku
Central Bureau of Statistics

Address: Ilica 3, Zagreb, 10000
Telephone: +385 1 480 6154
Fax: +385 1 480 6148
E-mail: stat.info@dzs.hr
Website: www.dzs.hr

Guides: calendar of statistical data issues (2005 and 2006) available on the website

Activity: collecting and publishing statistical data

Website(s) information:

Državni zavod za statistiku (Central Bureau of Statistics) — **url:** www.dzs.hr **Description:** various statistical information available online in Croatian and English including a calendar of statistical issues from 2005 and 2006 **Coverage:** geography, demography, education, general economic indicators, employment, agriculture and forestry, industry and services, transport and construction, tourism and culture

Publication(s):

Statisticke informacije (Statistical Information) — **Language:** Croatian/English **Frequency:** annual **Content:** recently introduced statistical information overview covering socio-economic indicators **Readership:** research specialists, analysts, academics, governmental and non-governmental organisations

Statisticki ljetopis (Statistical Yearbook) — **Language:** Croatian/English **Frequency:** annual **Content:** socio-economic overview **Readership:** research specialists, analysts, academics, governmental and non-governmental organisations, businesses

Ekonomski institut Zagreb
Institute of Economy Zagreb

Address: Trg J. F. Kennedyja 7, Zagreb, 10000
Telephone: +385 1 2335 700
Fax: +385 1 2335 165
E-mail: eizagreb@eizg.hr
Website: www.eizg.hr

Activity: scientific and development research in the field of economics (regional development, macro economy, innovations and technological development, company organisation and management)

Website(s) information:

Ekonomski institut Zagreb (Institute of Economy Zagreb) — **url:** www.eizg.hr **Description:** the site offers abstracts from the publications containing information about the economy of the country **Coverage:** economic indicators

Publication(s):

Croatian Economic Outlook — **Language:** English **Frequency:** quarterly **Content:** analysis of current economic trends as well as economic policies, and gives a short-term forecast of economic trends in Croatia **Readership:** economists, research specialists, analysts, governmental organisations

Privredna kretanja i privredna politka (Economic Trends and Economic Policy) — **Language:** Croatian/English (end of the year edition) **Frequency:** quarterly **Content:** economical overview **Readership:** economists, research specialists, analysts, governmental organisations

Energetski institut Hrvoje Požar
The Institute of Energy 'Hrvoje Pozar'

Address: PP 141, Savska cesta 163, Zagreb, 10001
Telephone: +385 1 632 6100
Fax: +385 1 604 0599
E-mail: eihp@eihp.hr
Website: www.eihp.hr

Activity: expert and scientific research in the field of energy for state, regional and local administration and energy companies; expertise and analyses for the Croatian Energy Regulatory Council; management of National Energy Programmes and pilot projects; organising seminars, workshops and courses; publishing editions, periodicals and other forms of communication with experts, scientists and the general public, especially via Internet

Website(s) information:

Energetski institut Hrvoje Požar (Institute for Energy 'Hrvoje Pozar') — **url:** www.eihp.hr **Description:** the site offers various statistical information related to the system of energy supply and other relevant matters in Croatian, English and German **Coverage:** energy and energy systems (gas, oil, electricity)

Financijska agencija Hrvatske (FINA)
Croatian Financial Agency (FINA)

Address: Koturaška 43, Zagreb, 10000
Telephone: +385 1 612 7111
E-mail: info@fina.hr
Website: www.fina.hr

Activity: financial mediation, business information dissemination, cash operations, e-business, archiving, electronic signature authority, payment transactions, training

Website(s) information:

Financijska agencija Hrvatske (FINA) (Croatian Financial Agency (FINA)) — **url:** www.fina.hr **Description:** various finanical and banking information available online **Coverage:** finance, banks, businesses

Publication(s):

Godišnje izviješće (Annual Report) — **Language:** Croatian/English **Frequency:** annual **Content:** basic financial indicators, business secors overview, business network, profit and loss balance, cash flow statement **Readership:** finanical experts, research specialists, analysts, governmental organisations

Hrvatska banaka za obnovu i razvitak
Croatian Bank for Reconstruction and Development

Address: Strossmayerov trg 9, Zagreb, 10000
Telephone: +385 1 459 1620
Fax: +385 1 459 1721
E-mail: info@hbor.hr
Website: www.hbor.hr

Activity: financing the reconstruction and development of the Croatian economy

Website(s) information:

Hrvatska banaka za obnovu i razvitak (Croatian Bank for Reconstruction and Development) — **url:** www.hbor.hr **Coverage:** economy and development

Publication(s):

Godišnji izvještaj (Annual Report) — **Language:** Croatian/English **Frequency:** annual **Content:** annual activities of the bank and overview of the country's economy (reports covering periods from 1998 are available online) **Readership:** financial and economic experts, research specialists, analysts, governmental organisations, investors

Institut za turizam
The Institute of Tourism

Address: Vrhovec 5, Zagreb, 10000
Telephone: +385 1 390 9666
Fax: +385 1 390 9667
E-mail: biblioteka@iztzg.hr
Website: www.iztzg.hr

Guides: publications available through library catalogue

Activity: research, information and documentation, publishing, education, planning and development

Website(s) information:

Institut za turizam — **url:** www.iztzg.hr **Description:** the site offers an online catalogue of publications, as well as magazines covering the tourism industry

Publication(s):

Casopis Turizam (Tourism Magazine) — **Language:** Croatian/English **Frequency:** quarterly **Content:** travel and tourism **Readership:** research specialists, analysts

Ministarsto vanjskih poslova i europskih integracija Hrvatske

Croatian Ministry of Foreign Affairs and European Integrations

Address: Trg N. Š. Zrinskog 7 -8, Zagreb, 10000
Telephone: +385 1 456 9964
Fax: +385 1 455 1795
E-mail: mvp@mvp.hr
Website: www.mvpei.hr

Activity: implementing national foreign affairs and international integrations policy

Website(s) information:

Mission of the Republic of Croatia to the United Nations, Ministry of Foreign Affairs and European Integrations — **url:** http://un.mfa.hr **Description:** comprehensive socio-economic overview of Croatia **Coverage:** socio-economic indicators

Ministarstvo Financija Hrvatske

Croatian Ministry of Finance

Address: Katanciceva 5, Zagreb, 10000
Telephone: +385 1 459 1333
Fax: +385 1 492 2583
E-mail: kabinet@mfin.hr
Website: www.mfin.hr

Activity: managing the financial system

Website(s) information:

Ministarstvo financija Hrvatske (Croatian Ministry of Finance) — **url:** www.mfin.hr **Description:** statistical information related to the ministry and financial system of the country **Coverage:** financial and economic indicators

Publication(s):

Financijsko izvješče javnih institucija (Financial Report on State Institutions) — **Language:** Croatian **Frequency:** quarterly **Content:** finances of public institutions (State Agency for Deposit Insurance, Croatian Development Bank, Privatisation Fund); reports cover the period of 2000 - 2005 **Readership:** research specialists, analysts, financial experts, governmental organisations

Financijsko izvješče javnih poduzeca (Financial Report on State-owned Companies) — **Language:** Croatian **Frequency:** irregular **Content:** finances of public companies (Croatia Insurance, Croatian Energy, Croatian Post Service, Croatian Forests, Croatian Oil Company, Jadrolinija, Narodne novine and Plovput); reports cover the period of 2000 - 2005 **Readership:** research specialists, analysts, governmental organisations

Godišnjak (Yearbook) — **Language:** Croatian **Frequency:** annual **Content:** overview of state finances and macroeconomic indicators from 1994 **Readership:** research specialists, analysts, governmental organisations

Statisticki prikazi (Statistical Overview) — **Language:** Croatian **Frequency:** monthly **Content:** macroeconomic indicators of the country's economy by month (1995-2006) **Readership:** research specialists, analysts, governmental organisations

Ministarstvo gospodarstva, rada i poduzetništva Hrvatske

Croatian Ministry of Economy, Labour and Entrepreneurship

Address: Ulica grada Vukovara 78, Zagreb, 10000
Telephone: +385 1 610 6111
Fax: +385 1 610 9110
E-mail: info@mingorp.hr
Website: www.mingo.hr

Activity: defining and implementing economic and labour policies

Website(s) information:

Ministarstvo gospodarstva, rada i poduzetništva Hrvatske (Croatian Ministry of Economy, Labour and Entrepreneurship) — **url:** www.mingo.hr **Description:** the site contains links to statistical economic and financial information provided by the Statistical Office and National Bank **Coverage:** economic indicators

Ministarstvo mora, turizma, prometa i razvitka Hrvatske

Croatian Ministry of the Sea, Tourism, Transport and Development

Address: Prisavlje 14, Zagreb, 10000
Telephone: +385 1 378 4520
Fax: +385 1 378 4550
E-mail: ministar@ws.mmtpr.hr
Website: www.mmtpr.hr

Activity: implementing the state policies on tourism, transport and development

Website(s) information:

Ministarstvo mora, turizma, prometa i razvitka Hrvatske (Croatian Ministry of the Sea, Tourism, Transport and Development) — **url:** www.mmtpr.hr **Coverage:** tourism related

Publication(s):

Hrvatski turizam (Croatian Tourism) — **Language:** Croatian/English **Frequency:** irregular **Content:** data on tourism in Croatia **Readership:** research specialists, analysts, toursit agencies

Turizam u brojkama (Tourism - Facts and Figures) — **Language:** Croatian/English **Frequency:** irregular **Content:** statistical reports on the tourism industry (2000 - 2005) **Readership:** research specialists, analysts, tourist organisations

Ministarstvo poljoprivrede, šumarstva i vodnoga gospodarstva Hrvatske

Croatian Ministry of Agriculture, Forestry and Water Management

Address: Ulica grada Vukovara 78, Zagreb, 10000
Telephone: +385 1 610 6600
Fax: +385 1 610 9200
E-mail: office@mps.hr
Website: www.mps.hr

Activity: defining and implementing agricultural policy

Website(s) information:

Ministarstvo poljoprivrede, šumarstva i vodnoga gospodarstva Hrvatske (Croatian Ministry of Agriculture, Forestry and Water Management) — **url:** www.mps.hr **Description:** the site offers various documents containing statistical information about the agricultural system **Coverage:** agriculture, forestry and water resources

Publication(s):

Hrvatska poljoprivreda na raskršcima (Croatian Agriculture at the Crossroads) — **Language:** Croatian/English **Frequency:** irregular **Content:** overview of the country's agricultural system **Readership:** research specialists, analysts, governmental organisations

Izvozne mogucnosti poljoprivrede, ribarstva i prehrambene industrije (Export Capacity in Agriculture, Fishery and Food Industry) — **Language:** Croatian **Frequency:** irregular **Content:** agriculture, fishery and food industry in the light of export **Readership:** analysts, research specialists, governmental institutions, agricultural specialists

Operativni program razvitka govedarske proizvodnje u Republici Hrvatskoj (Livestock Production Development Programme of the Republic of Croatia) — **Language:** Croatian **Frequency:** irregular **Content:** overview of the current livestock production and prospects for its development **Readership:** agricultural specialists, research specialists, analysts, governmental institutions

Studija o potencijalnim tržištima za certificirano drvo i drvne proizvode iz
Hrvatske (Study on Prospective Markets for Certified Wood and Forestry
Products from Croatia) — **Language:** Croatian **Frequency:**
irregular **Content:** overview of the forestry industry for potential
investors and markets **Readership:** businesses, investment
companies, research specialists, analysts

Ministarstvo pravosuda Hrvatske
Croatian Ministry of Justice

Address: Dežmanova ulica 6, Zagreb, 10000
Telephone: +385 1 371 0666
Fax: +385 1 371 0602
Website: www.pravosudje.hr

Activity: managing the legal system

Publication(s):
Statisticki pregled (Statistical Report) — **Language:** Croatian **Frequency:** annually
Content: legal system by districts and courts over the previous 5
years **Readership:** legal experts, analysts, research specialists

Narodna banka Hrvatske
Croatian National Bank

Address: Trg hrvatskih velikana 3, Zagreb, 10002
Telephone: +385 1 456 4555
Fax: +385 1 455 0726
E-mail: info@hnb.hr
Website: www.hnb.hr

Activity: formulating and executing monetary and foreign exchange policies,
holding and managing the international reserves of the Republic
of Croatia, issuing banknotes and coins, issuing and revoking
licenses for banks, supervising banks and enacting regulations on
banking operations, maintaining the accounts of banks,
performing payment transactions across these accounts, granting
loans to banks and taking deposits from banks,
regulating, improving and supervising payment system,
performing legally prescribed operations on behalf of the
Republic of Croatia, enacting regulations on operations within its
competency,
performing other operations, as stipulated by the law

Website(s) information:
Narodna Banka Hrvatske (National Bank of Croatia) — **url:** www.hnb.hr
Description: various economic and financial data and surveys
available online **Coverage:** banking sector, foreign direct
investments, economic indicators

Publication(s):
Bilten HNB (CNB Bulletin) — **Language:** Croatian/English **Frequency:** monthly
Content: monthly information on latest trends and developments in
national economy and banking system **Readership:** research
specialists, analysts, banking experts, governmental organisations,
investors

Bilten o bankama (Banks Bulletin) — **Language:** Croatian/English **Frequency:**
monthly **Content:** statistical information about banks operating in
the country **Readership:** research specialists, baking experts,
analysts

Godišnji izvještaj (Annual Report) — **Language:** Croatian/English **Frequency:**
annual **Content:** macroeconomic developments, monetary policy,
instruments and international reserves, management, banking
sector, payment operations, currency department operations,
financial statements **Readership:** banking experts, research
specialists, analysts, banks

Makrobonitetna analiza (Macroprudential Analysis) — **Language:**
Croatian/English **Frequency:** irregular **Content:** indicators of the
country's economy **Readership:** economic experts, research
specialists, analysts, banking experts, governmental and
non-governmental organisations

Monetarna politika (Monetary Policy) — **Language:** Croatian/English **Frequency:**
irregular **Content:** monetary developments, balance sheets, policy
interest rates **Readership:** research specialists, analysts, economists,
banking experts

Real Sector — **Language:** Croatian/English **Frequency:** irregular **Content:** actual
GDP growth rates, gross value added structure, inflation,
unemployment rate, nominal and real net wages, monthly labour
costs, industry **Readership:** economists, research specialists,
analysist, banking experts, governmental organisations

Sektor bankarstva (Banking Sector) — **Language:** Croatian/English **Frequency:**
irregular **Content:** statistical overview of banking system
Readership: research specialists, analysts, banks

USAID Croatia

Address: Thomas Jeffersona 2, Zagreb, 10000
Telephone: +385 1 661 2175
Fax: +385 1 661 2008
E-mail: usaid-zg@zg.htnet.hr
Website: http://zagreb.usembassy.gov

Activity: implementing a comprehensive transition program that includes
economic and fiscal reform, strengthening democratic institutions,
training activities

Publication(s):
Annual Report — **Language:** English **Frequency:** annual **Content:** Croatian
economy and society **Readership:** research specialists, analyists,
governmental and non-governmental organisations

Croatia Country Profile — **Language:** English **Frequency:** irregular **Content:**
Croatian economy **Readership:** research specialists, analysts,
governmental organisations

Vlada Republike Hrvatske
Government of the Republic of Croatia

Address: Trg Svetog Marka 2, Zagreb, 10000
Telephone: +385 1 456 9222
Fax: +385 1 630 3023
E-mail: predsjednik@vlada.hr
Website: www.vlada.hr

Activity: passes decrees, introduces legislation, proposes the state budget and
enforces laws and other regulations enacted by the Croatian Sabor

Website(s) information:
Vlada Republike Hrvatske (Government of the Republic of Croatia) — **url:**
www.vlada.hr **Description:** presentation of the country through
socio-economic indicators; site provides links to individual ministries
Coverage: socio-economic indicators

World Bank Croatia

Address: Trg. J.F. Kennedya 6b/III, Zagreb, 10000
Telephone: +385 1 235 7274
Fax: +385 1 235 7200
E-mail: mmilic@worldbank.org
Website: www.worldbank.hr

Activity: helping the country with post war reconstruction, improving people's
welfare and boosting the country's development agenda

Website(s) information:
World Bank Croatia — **url:** www.worldbank.hr **Description:** various statistical
information available online (information/ communications/
telecommunications, ICT infrastructure and access, expenditures,
and ICT business and government environment, gender, basic
demographic data, population dynamics, labour force structure,
education and health, health and nutrition, and health finance,
education statistics, investment climate indicators; the site also
offers a link to all World Bank reports since 1946 (including those on
Croatia) **Coverage:** socio-economic indicators

Publication(s):

Country Assistance Evaluation — **Language:** English **Frequency:** irregular **Content:** an assessment on the role of World Bank assistance to Croatia during 1991-2003 (accounting, adjustment lending, allocative efficiency, bank performance, bank regulation, bank restructuring, banking sector, bankruptcy, banks, bidding, budget deficits, capital flows, capital Markets, civil society, corporate governance, debt, decision making, deficits, democracy, economic assistance, education, elections, emerging markets, employment, expenditure programs, financial management, fiscal deficits, fiscal discipline, fiscal reforms, foreign exchange, foreign exchange reserves, health, health care, health indicators, health insurance, health policy, health programs, health sector, income support, incremental costs, inflation, institutional development, insurance, laws, legal framework, legislation, loan commitments, local demand, macroeconomic stabilization, negotiations, nutrition, patients, pensions, physicians, ports, primary health care, private sector, privatisation, public debt, public expenditure, public expenditure review, public expenditure reviews, public expenditures, public finance, public health, public investment, public ownership, public sector wages, public spending, real sector, reform programs, refugees, rehabilitation, roads, sanitation, savings, social issues, structural adjustment, tax, telecommunications, transport, unemployment, unemployment rate, voucher privatisation, wages, water Supply, workers) **Readership:** research specialists, analysts, governmental organisations, non-governmental organisations

Country Financial Accountability Assessment — **Language:** English **Frequency:** irregular **Content:** legal framework, institutional capacity and practices for the core financial control processes such as budgeting, treasury and cash management, accounting, financial reporting, internal control, internal audit, external audit and parliamentary oversight **Readership:** academics, finanical experts, research specialists, analysts, foreign investors

Croatia Health Study — **Language:** English **Frequency:** irregular **Content:** review of the country's health system with recommendations to budget planning and targeted social protection **Readership:** medical specialists, governmental organisations, health institutes, analysts, research specialists

Cyprus

Statistical Service of Cyprus (CYSTAT)

Address: Michalakis Karaolis Str., Nicosia, 1444
Telephone: +357 22602129
Fax: +357 22661313
E-mail: cyd.sr@cytanet.com.cy
Website:
www.mof.gov.cy/mof/cystat/statistics.nsf/index_en/index_en?OpenDocument

Guides: all publications are available for sale from the premises of the Statistical Service in Nicosia or the Government Printing Office; when available in electronic form, publications can be downloaded free of charge; the library is open 7.30- 14.30 Monday to Friday.

Activity: responsible for the compilation and the publication of most of the official statistical data in Cyprus; CYSTAT is mainly concerned with the initiation, organisation and carrying out of various censuses, surveys and statistical enquiries of an economic, social or environmental content and the publication of the results with the intention of assisting both the government and the private sector in policy-making and the planning of their activities

Website(s) information:

Statistics and Research Department, Ministry of Finance — **url:** www.pio.gov.cy/dsr/index.html **Description:** key socio-economic data available online; online database with monthly foreign trade data; available in English and Greek **Coverage:** statistical themes includes: national accounts, short-term economic indicators, agriculture, foreign trade, financial sector statistics, industry, distributive trade, energy and environment statistics, transport, community, personal, business, demographics, health and education, labour force, wages, prices

Publication(s):

Construction and Housing Statistics — **Language:** English/Greek **Frequency:** annual **Content:** data on the construction industry and housing; analysis of sector distribution of output, capital formation, value added labour costs and materials

Cyprus External Trade Statistics — **Language:** English **Frequency:** quarterly **Content:** detailed quantity and value data on imports/arrivals classified by commodity and by main trading partner

Cyprus in Figures — **Language:** English **Frequency:** annual **Content:** recent set of data on the main social and economic indicators of Cyprus

Demographic Report — **Language:** English/Greek **Frequency:** annual **Content:** population estimates by month, end of the year estimates by five-year age groups, births and fertility statistics, deaths and mortality statistics, life tables, marriages, divorces and migration; analysis of recent demographic developments

Hotels and Restaurants Statistics — **Language:** English/Greek **Frequency:** annual **Content:** data on the basic economic characteristics of the sub-sector of restaurants, hotels and other eating and drinking places, such as employment, sales costs, value added, and investments

Labour Statistics — **Language:** English/Greek **Frequency:** annual **Content:** annual statistics on employment, unemployment, vacancies, government labour force, port workers, and employment by UK Authorities, UNFICYP and NAAFI, Cypriots working temporarily abroad, industrial disputes and industrial accidents

Transport Statistics — **Language:** English/Greek **Frequency:** annual **Content:** economic accounts of the broad transport, storage and communication sector; data on the various types and categories of motor vehicles registered and licensed; accidents and casualties; shipping statistics; civil aviation, postal services and telecommunications

Wholesale and Retail Trade Statistics — **Language:** English/Greek **Frequency:** annual **Content:** annual data on the economic characteristics of all the activities classified as wholesale and retail trade; the data relates to the value of sales, current costs, value added, investments, stocks and employment

Czech Republic

Ceská národní banka
Czech National Bank

Address: Na Príkope 28, Prague 1, 115 03
Telephone: +420 2 2441 1111
Fax: +420 2 2441 2404
E-mail: info@cnb.cz
Website: www.cnb.cz

Activity: acting as a central bank of the country and the supervisor of the financial market

Website(s) information:

Ceska Narodni Banka (CNB) *(Czech National Bank)* — **url:** www.cnb.cz **Description:** the site offers various financial statistical information in both Czech and English **Coverage:** financial indicators

Publication(s):

Bankovní statistika *(Banking Statistics)* — **Language:** Czech/English **Frequency:** monthly **Content:** financial statistics **Readership:** financial experts, economists, banks, research specialists, analysts

CNB Economic Reseach Bulletin — **Language:** English **Frequency:** irregular **Content:** findings of the research and analysis of the economy and financial sector **Readership:** economists, financial experts, governmental institutions, research specialists, analysts

Prímé zahranicní investice *(Foreign Direct Investment)* — **Language:** Czech/English **Frequency:** annual **Content:** foreign investments into the country (reports cover a five year period) **Readership:** economists, investors, businesses, governmental institutions, research specialists, analysts

Výrocná správa *(Annual Report)* — **Language:** Czech/English **Frequency:** annual **Content:** economic development and monetary policy, central bank and activities, monetary stability **Readership:** economists, financial experts, bankers, research specialists, analysts

Zprává o inflaci *(Inflation Report)* — **Language:** Czech/English **Frequency:** annual **Content:** inflation - covering annual and monthly percentage changes (available reports cover the period from 2002 to 2005) **Readership:** financial experts, governmental organisations, research specialists, analysts

Zpráva o stabilite bankovního sektoru *(Banking Sector Stability Report)* — **Language:** Czech/English **Frequency:** irregular **Content:** banking sector in general, macro-economic developments, risk assessment and monitoring **Readership:** economic and financial experts, research specialists, analysts

Zpráva o výsledku hospodareni Ceské národní banky (Czech National Bank Financial Report) — **Language:** Czech **Frequency:** annual **Content:** financial indicators of the state financial system (available reports cover a period from 1999) **Readership:** financial experts, analysts, research specialists, governmental institutions

Ceský statistický úrad
Czech Statistical Office

Address: Na padesátém 81, Praha 10, 100 82
Telephone: +420 2 7405 1111
Fax: +420 2 7405 2304
E-mail: infoservis@czso.cz
Website: www.czso.cz

Activity: collecting and publishing statistical information

Website(s) information:
Ceský statistický úrad (Czech Statistical Office) — **url:** www.czso.cz **Description:** statistical information covering all socio-economic sectors; English version of the site and online catalogue of publications **Coverage:** socio-economic data

Publication(s):
Makroekonomické údaje (Macroeconomic Indicators) — **Language:** Czech/English **Frequency:** annual **Content:** macro-economy with statistics over a 10-year period **Readership:** economists, research specialists, analysts, governmental institutions, non-governmental organisations

Prumysl Ceské republiky (Industry of the Czech Republic) — **Language:** Czech/English **Frequency:** annual **Content:** industrial production figures **Readership:** investors, research specialists, analysts, businesses

Roèenka zahranièního obchodu Èeské republiky (Report on External Trade of the Czech Republic) — **Language:** Czech/English **Frequency:** monthly **Content:** external trade **Readership:** economists, businesses, investors, governmental institutions, research specialists, analysts

Spotreba paliv a energie v CR za rok (Fuel and Energy Consumption in the CR) — **Language:** Czech/English **Frequency:** annual **Content:** consumption of fuel and energy **Readership:** economists, governmental institutions, research specialists, analysts

Statistická roèenka Èeské republiky (Statistical Yearbook of the Czech Republic) — **Language:** Czech/English **Frequency:** annual **Content:** detailed socio-economic data of the country **Readership:** economists, businesses, investors, governmental institutions, non-governmental organisations, research specialists, analysts

Statistický Bulletin (Statistical Bulletin) — **Language:** Czech/English **Frequency:** quarterly **Content:** socio-economic indicators **Readership:** research specialists, analysts, governmental and non-governmental organisations

tatistický údajový mìsìèník Èeské republiky (Monthly Statistics of the Czech Republic) — **Language:** Czech/English **Frequency:** monthly **Content:** macro-economic and social indicators **Readership:** research specialists, analysts, governmental and non-governmental organisations

Tržní služby (Market Services) — **Language:** Czech/English **Frequency:** quarterly **Content:** services (market services, leisure services, real estate services, health, education, etc) **Readership:** economists, research specialists

Údaje o Ceské republice (Czech Republic in Figures) — **Language:** English **Frequency:** annual **Content:** main socio-economic indicators **Readership:** research specialists, analysts, governmental and non-governmental organisations

Vývoj ceské ekonomiky (Czech Economic Development) — **Language:** Czech/English **Frequency:** quarterly **Content:** detailed analysis of the country's economy **Readership:** economists, businesses, investors, governmental institutions, research specialists, analysts

Ministerstvo financí Ceské republiky
Ministry of Finance of the Czech Republic

Address: Letenská 15, Prague 1, 118 10
Telephone: +420 2 5704 1111
Fax: +420 2 5704 2788
E-mail: podatelna@mfcr.cz
Website: www.mfcr.cz

Activity: creating and implementing state financial policy

Website(s) information:
Ministerstvo Financi Ceske Republiky (Ministry of Finance of the Czech Republic) — **url:** www.mfcr.cz **Description:** statistical information about the financial sector in the country (only some in English) **Coverage:** financial sector

Publication(s):
Hospodareni pojištoven (Insurance Sector Development) — **Frequency:** annual **Content:** insurance sector **Readership:** financial experts, insurance sector, research specialists, analysts

Makroekonomická predikce (Macroeconomic Forecast) — **Language:** Czech/English **Frequency:** irregular **Content:** macroeconomic development and analysis **Readership:** economists, governmental institutions, research specialists, analysts

Státní dluh (State Debt) — **Language:** Czech/English **Frequency:** irregular **Content:** foreign debt of the country **Readership:** economists, governmental institutions, research specialists, analysts

Ministerstvo Promusly a obchodu Ceske Republiky
Ministry of Industry and Trade of the Czech Republic

Address: Na Frantiku 32, Prague 1, 110 15
Telephone: +420 2 2485 1111
Fax: +420 2 2481 1089
E-mail: posta@mpo.cz
Website: www.mpo.cz

Activity: central body of the government administration responsible for commodity exchange, except issues of the Ministry of Agriculture

Website(s) information:
Ministry of Industry & Trade of the Czech Republic (Ministry of Industry & Trade of the Czech Republic) — **url:** www.mpo.cz **Coverage:** coal, electricity and oil statistics, including renewables, solid fuels, electricity and heat, oil and oil products, filling station statistics. Statistical surveys available on most industries

Publication(s):
Czech Construction Industry — **Language:** English **Content:** investment development, construction industry and construction materials. Includes macroeconomic indicators: employment and wages, housing, construction, building materials **Edition:** 2006

Ústav zemedelských a potravinárských informací
Institute of Agricultural and Food Information

Address: Slezská 7, Prague 2, 120 56
Telephone: +420 2 2701 0111
Fax: +420 2 2701 0114
E-mail: info@uzpi.cz
Website: www.uzpi.cz

Activity: providing the full transfer of departmental knowledge information from the sectors of agriculture, food production, nutrition, food safety, consumer protection, forestry and environment

Website(s) information:
Ústav zemedelských a potravinárských informací (Institute of Agricultural and Food Information) — **url:** www.agronavigator.cz **Description:** agricultural web portal offers various information about agriculture and food **Coverage:** agriculture and food

Publication(s):
Napojovy prumysl (Drinks Industry) — **Language:** Czech **Frequency:** irregular **Content:** covers main news on the national and international drinks industry **Readership:** drinks manufacturers, importers, exporters, distributors, analysts, economists

Potravinarske aktuality (Food News) — **Language:** Czech **Frequency:** irregular **Content:** information on the food industry (dairy industry, bakery products, sugar, canned meals and meat production) **Readership:** food manufacturers, importers, exporters, distributors, economists, research specialists, analysts

Denmark

Danmarks Eksportråd
Danish Export Council

Address: Udenrigsministeriet, Asiatisk Plads 2, Copenhagen K, 1448
Telephone: +45 33 920 000
Fax: +45 32 540 533
E-mail: um@um.dk
Website: www.um.dk

Guides: reports on sectors and Danish companies abroad are available free online

Activity: promotes export and Danish industries abroad

Website(s) information:
Danmarks Eksportråd (Danish Export Council) — **url:** www.um.dk **Description:** provides downloadable publications on Danish export in a variety of sectors **Coverage:** contains data on turn over and production on Danish exporting companies

Danmarks Nationalbank
National Bank of Denmark

Address: Havnegade 5, Copenhagen K, 1093
Telephone: +45 3363 6363
Fax: +45 3363 7103
E-mail: info@nationalbanken.dk
Website: www.nationalbanken.dk

Guides: report and accounts available free of charge in Danish at www.nationalbanken.dk

Activity: ensure efficient and secure production and distribution of currency; contribute to efficiency and stability in the payment and clearing systems and in financial markets; act as banker to the central government; prepare reliable and relevant financial statistics; prepare and communicate credible standpoints on economic and financial issues with relation to Denmark's National bank's objectives

Website(s) information:
Danmarks Nationalbank (National Bank of Denmark) — **url:** www.nationalbanken.dk **Coverage:** includes statistical data on market rates, balance sheets, securities, banking sector, investment, direct debt, etc. Publications offered free on the web site include: Report and Accounts; Monetary Review; Financial Statistics; Working Papers

Publication(s):
Coins and Banknotes of Denmark — **Language:** English/Danish **Content:** coins and banknotes of Denmark and how the coins and banknotes are manufactured **Edition:** 2005

Danish Government Borrowing and Debt — **Language:** English **Frequency:** annual **Content:** publication describes the development during the preceding year and reports on issues of relevance to debt management

Financial Stability — **Language:** English **Frequency:** annual **Content:** Financial Stability assesses financial stability in Denmark, with emphasis on financial institutions, markets and payment systems. The report consists of two parts. The first part starts with an analysis of the development in the financial sector, with emphasis on the banking institutions. This is followed by a chapter on the development in the corporate sector and the households. Next the developments in the financial markets are reviewed and finally follow a chapter about the framework for Financial Sta

Mona — **Language:** English **Content:** Danish economy; Inflation, wages and prices; Balance of payments, foreign trade and external debt; Economic activity and employment; Public finances and fiscal policy; Models **Edition:** 2004

Monetary Policy in Denmark — **Language:** English **Frequency:** irregular **Content:** monetary and foreign-exchange policy; monetary conditions; foreign-exchange policy and cooperation; monetary policy instruments; money and currency markets **Edition:** 2003 Second Ed.

Monetary Review — **Language:** English **Frequency:** quarterly **Content:** recent economic and monetary trends

Nyt (News) — **Language:** English/Danish **Frequency:** monthly **Content:** presents key financial statistics produced by the Nationalbank

Online Statistics Database — **Language:** English **Frequency:** irregular **Content:** Danmarks Nationalbank's statistics database, which contains additional and longer time series compared to the statistics publications. You can e.g. find more detailed breakdowns by sector, instrument, country or maturity. You can search and define tables, which you can download in e.g. excel format or have shown with a graph
Tables for: Balance-sheet statistics for investment associations; External financial payments; Securities statistics; Balance and flow statistics of the consolidated MFI sector; Balance and flow statistics of mortgage-credit institutes; Balance and flow statistics of banks; Foreign direct investments
Quarterly financial accounts for Denmark; Exchange rates; Quarterly flow statistics on direct investments

Payment Systems in Denmark — **Language:** English **Content:** describes various aspects of payment systems: roles of central banks in payment systems; reviews the historical background of payment systems, including the background of the involvement of central banks; general principles and risks in various types of payment and securities settlement systems; Danish payments infrastructure and Danmarks Nationalbank's role regarding these systems **Edition:** 2005

Report and Accounts — **Language:** English **Frequency:** annual **Content:** Danmarks Nationalbank's Report and Accounts comprise a presentation and description of the bank's Accounts during the year, and the Report of the Board of Governors

Danmarks Statistik
Statistics Denmark

Address: Sejrøgade 11, Copenhagen, 2100
Telephone: +45 3917 3917
Fax: +45 3117 3999
E-mail: dst@dst.dk
Website: www.dst.dk

www.statbank.dk

Guides: publications may be purchased from Statistics Denmark or from Danish booksellers. Information about the nearest bookseller is obtainable from Statistics Denmark's Publications Service, phone + 45 3917 3020

Activity: national statistics body; produces and disseminates statistics on social and economic trends in society

Website(s) information:
StatBank Denmark (Statistics Bank of Denmark) — **url:** www.statbank.dk **Description:** information on products and services provided by Statistics Denmark: latest statistical releases; online publications and socio-economics statistics **Coverage:** socio-economic data on Denmark can be found by downloading the annual publication Statistical Yearbook, or by accessing different sections such as: Data on Denmark; key indicators; data on municipalities; key figures for transport; and main indicators (subscription required)

Publication(s):
Agriculture — **Language:** English/Danish **Frequency:** annual **Content:** agricultural and horticultural censuses, production and prices, cereal stocks, fruit and berries, feeding stuff consumption, livestock density, stocks of pigs and cattle, dairy products, commercial fertilizers, greenhouses, factor incomes, capital formation, interest payments and debts, volume and price indices and forest felling

Earnings — **Language:** English **Content:** Indices of average earnings at the level of industries in the private and public sectors; Earnings in the private sector; Earnings in the central government; Earnings in the local government; Total labour costs in the private sector

Education and Culture — **Language:** English/Danish **Content:** Cohort analysis of education; Education and employment; Adult education and continuing training; Number of students

Environment and Energy — **Language:** English **Content:** covers: environmental state of air and water, flora and fauna, environmental effects caused by agriculture, forestry, fishing, manufacturing, mining and quarrying, energy consumption, transport, waste water, refuse dumps and chemical substances. Environmental protection, municipal inspection, nature and environmental monitoring, recycling and environmental economics

External Trade — **Language:** English **Content:** total external trade - incl. latest month; Indices on total external trade - incl. latest month; Imports /exports /trade balance (SITC categories, country); Imports by end-use (BEC) and country

General Economic Statistics — **Language:** Danish/English **Content:** accounts statistics, business units registered for VAT settlement, registration of new business units, turnover in non-agricultural industries, employment in businesses and bankruptcies

Incomes, Consumption and Prices — **Language:** English/Danish **Frequency:** monthly **Content:** covers possession of consumer durables, consumption of alcoholic beverages, consumer price index, index of net retail prices, whole price index and price index for raw materials, sales of property, bankruptcies, incomes and wealth

Labour Market — **Language:** English **Content:** labour force; Labour force survey; Population by level of education and employment; Unemployment, final average figures; Unemployment, in percentage

Manufacturing Industries — **Language:** English **Content:** raw material and industrial services; Manufacturers sale divided among goods and sector of Industry; Industrial production and new orders statistics; Tendency survey for manufacturing industries; Stock changes in manufacturing industries and wholesale; Historical figures - discontinued data series

Money and Capital Market — **Language:** English **Content:** shares and bonds; Interest rates and share prices; Lending and deposits, banks and bond issuing institutions; Accounts; Non-bank consumer credit and leasing; International statistics

National Accounts and Balance of Payments — **Language:** English **Content:** balance of payments; Annual national accounts, ESA95; Quarterly national accounts; Environmental accounts

Population and Elections — **Language:** English **Content:** population size, vital statistics, foreign nationals, births, deaths, internal and external migrations, marriages, divorces, families, households, adoptions, legal abortions, mortality and occupation, fertility surveys and population forecasts

Public Finance — **Language:** English **Content:** government finances; Taxation; Financial accounts;

Retail Trade Index — **Language:** English **Content:** Retail trade index for 2000-2006 **Edition:** 2006

Services sector — **Language:** English/Danish **Content:** index of retail prices, holiday and business trips, nights spent at camping sites, hotels and youth hostels, travellers' currency, rented holiday dwellings, yachting and product statistics for the services sectors; Internet usage in the population; Public sector use of ICT

Social Conditions, Health and Justice — **Language:** English/Danish **Content:** housing benefits; Family allowance and child benefits; Hospitalizations; Justice; Social pensions; Health insurance; Payments of child maintenance

Statistical Yearbook — **Language:** English/Danish **Frequency:** annual **Content:** contains statistics and trends in Denmark, the Faroe Islands and Greenland. There is also a chapter on international statistics. Period coverage is over the previous five years.

Grønlands Statistik

Statistics Greenland

Address: PO Box 1025, Nuuk, 3900, Greenland
Telephone: +45 345 564
Fax: +45 322 954
E-mail: stat@gh.gl
Website: www.statgreen.gl

Guides: publications are available on a free database and data can be exported in several file formats

Activity: publish detailed statistical information on the Greenlandic society

Website(s) information:

Grønlands Statistiks (Statistics Greenland) — **url:** www.statgreen.gl **Description:** provides a database with socio-economic statistics and downloadable publications **Coverage:** contains data on labour market, population and housing, fishing, exports, national accounts, elections, health, tourism, crime, environment and energy

Publication(s):

Greenland in Figures — **Language:** English **Frequency:** annual **Content:** contains socio-economic data on Greenland

Statistisk Årbog (Statistical Yearbook) — **Language:** Danish/Kalaallisut **Frequency:** annual **Content:** contains socio-economic data on Greenland

Økonomiministeriet

Ministry of Economic Affairs

Address: Slotsholmsgade 10-12, Copenhagen, 1216
Telephone: +45 33 923 350
Fax: +45 33 123 778
E-mail: oem@oem.dk
Website: www.oem.dk

Guides: publications are downloadable on website

Activity: works to improve the conditions for growth in Denmark, through economic analyses and suggestions for policy initiatives in areas imperative to economic growth

Website(s) information:

Økonomiministeriet (Ministry of Economic Affairs) — **url:** www.oem.dk **Description:** provides macro-economic indicators on the Danish economy including key figures and online publications in English **Coverage:** contains macro-economic statistics, including use and supply of goods and services, key figures of the Danish economy, comparison between the present forecast and economic surveys

Estonia

Eesti Pank

Bank of Estonia

Address: Estonia pst. 13, Tallinn, 15095
Telephone: +372 668 0719
Fax: +372 668 0836
E-mail: info@epbe.ee
Website: www.eestipank.info/frontpage/en

Guides: publications catalogue available online

Activity: participating in the economic policy of Estonia via pursuing an independent monetary policy, consulting the government, and continuing international cooperation; maintaining financial stability in Estonia by shaping financial sector policy and sustaining reliable and well-functioning payment systems; arranging cash circulation in Estonia; preparing for equal partnership with the other central banks of the Euro area in developing a common economic and single monetary policy

Website(s) information:

Eesti Pank (Bank of Estonia) — **url:** www.eestipank.info/frontpage/en **Description:** access to different publications covering the latest developments and trends in Estonia's economy and financial climate. Includes access to statistics and data collected by the bank and other official organisations **Coverage:** participating in the economic policy of Estonia via pursuing an independent monetary policy, consulting the government, and continuing international cooperation; maintaining financial stability in Estonia by shaping financial sector policy and sustaining reliable and well-functioning payment systems; arranging cash circulation in Estonia; preparing for equal partnership with the other central banks of the Euro area in developing a common economic and single monetary policy

Publication(s):

Ajakiri Kroon ja Majandus — **Language:** English/Estonian **Frequency:** quarterly **Content:** quarterly newspaper; banking news; investments; etc

Eesti 2006 aasta I kvartali esialgne maksebilanss (Estonian Preliminary Balance of Payments for the First Quarter of 2006) — **Language:** English/Estonian **Frequency:** quarterly **Content:** goods; services; income; current and capital transfers; direct investment; portfolio investment; other investment; reserve assets

Eesti majanduse ülevaade Eesti Panga aastaaruandes (Estonian Economy) — **Language:** English/Estonian **Frequency:** annual **Content:** non-financial sector; Inflation; financial sector; institutional development

Eesti Panga aasta finantsaruanne (Financial Statements of Eesti Bank) — **Language:** English/Estonian **Frequency:** annual **Content:** financial statements, balance sheet, profit and loss account, statement of changes in equity and the respective appendices

Lähenemisaruanne (Convergence Report) — **Language:** English/Estonian **Frequency:** irregular **Content:** country examinations; framework for analysis; country summaries

Rahapoliitiline Ülevaade (Monetary Developments & Policy Survey) — **Language:** English/Estonian **Frequency:** annual **Content:** economic policy summary; economic developments; inflation; monetary and financial sector; economic forecast; etc

Tööturu ülevaade (Labour Market Review) — **Language:** English/Estonian
Frequency: annual **Content:** labour supply and demand;
employment; vacancies; unemployment; labour costs and price
pressures; real unit labour costs; development of labour costs by
sectors; Estonian labour market

Eesti Riiklik Autoregistrikeskus

Estonian Motor Vehicle Registration Centre

Address: Mäepealse 19, Tallinn, 12618
Telephone: +372 620 1200
Fax: +372 620 1201
E-mail: press@ark.ee
Website: www.ark.ee

Guides: publications are available free of charge
Activity: the registration of motor vehicles and their trailers, maintaining the
register and archives

Website(s) information:
Eesti Riiklik Autoregistrikeskus (Estonian Motor Vehicle Registration Centre) — **url:**
www.ark.ee **Description:** the registration of motor vehicles and
their trailers, register and archives **Coverage:** provides information
on driving licences and examinations; vehicle registration; certificate
of registration; provides overview and free publications; detailed
contacts

Publication(s):
ARK Aastaraamat (ARK Annual Report) — **Language:** English/Estonian
Frequency: annual **Content:** statistics; structure; registered cars;
motorcycles registered; classification of vehicles by administrative
territories

EV Välisministeerium

Estonian Ministry of Foreign Affairs

Address: Islandi väljak 1, Tallinn, 15049, Estonia
Telephone: +372 637 7000
Fax: +372 637 7099
E-mail: vminfo@vm.ee
Website: www.vm.ee

Guides: publications are available free online
Activity: foreign relations and diplomacy

Website(s) information:
Estonian Ministry of Foreign Affairs — **url:** www.vm.ee **Description:** access to a
series of publications covering the national economy, business
environment, political and financial structure, and trade matters
with main partners. Regularly updated titles include: "Estonian
Review" (weekly); "Estonia Today"; and the "Estonian Economy". Site
is available in Estonian, Russian, Finnish, German, Swedish, Spanish,
French, and English **Coverage:** provides up-to-date information on
foreign relations; free publications and yearbooks; available
statistics; detailed information on Estonian embassies

Publication(s):
Economy in Facts and Figures — **Language:** English **Frequency:** irregular
Content: economic activity; statistics; tables; main export and
import

Keskkonnaministeerium

Ministry of the Environment

Address: Narva mnt 7a, Tallinn, 15172
Telephone: +372 6262 802
Fax: +372 626 2801
E-mail: min@envir.ee
Website: www.envir.ee

Guides: publications are available online
Activity: to create such preconditions and conditions for preservation of natural
biodiversity and a clean environment and to ensure that natural
resources are used economically

Website(s) information:
Keskkonnaministeerium (Ministry of the Environment) — **url:** www.envir.ee
Coverage: provides statistics about environment in Estonia

Publication(s):
Aastaraamat Mets (Forestry Yearbook) — **Language:** Estonian **Content:** forest
reserves; property; deforestation

ISPA Strategy Paper for the Environmental Sector — **Language:** English
Content: water resources; water supply; wastewater; air quality;
waste management; etc

*Metsandusliku ja puidutöötlemisalase hariduse hetkeseis ja tulevik (Forest
Management and Wood Processing Industry: Education Now and the
Future)* — **Language:** Estonian **Content:** tables; overview;
statistics; etc

Konkurentsiamet

Competition Board

Address: Lõkke 4, Tallinn, 15184
Telephone: +372 680 3942
Fax: +372 680 3943
E-mail: compet@konkurentsiamet.ee
Website: www.konkurentsiamet.ee

Activity: to examine and analyse the status of competition in different markets
for goods and make recommendations for improvements

Website(s) information:
Konkurentsiamet (Competition Board) — **url:** www.konkurentsiamet.ee **Coverage:**
competition laws and analysis

Publication(s):
Aastaraamat (Annual Report) — **Language:** English/Estonian **Frequency:** annual
Content: age of employees; length of service; level of education;
waste and package sector; analysis of prices

Majandus-ja Kommunikatsiooniministeerium

Ministry of Economic Affairs and Communications

Address: Harju 11, Tallinn, 15072
Telephone: +372 625 6342
Fax: +372 631 3660
E-mail: info@mkm.ee
Website: www.mkm.ee

Guides: publications are available online
Activity: active in industry, trade, energy, housing, building, transport (including
transport infrastructure, carriage, transit, logistics and public
transport), traffic management (including traffic on railways,
highways, streets, waterways and airways), increasing road safety
and reducing environmental hazards; informatics,
telecommunications, postal service and tourism; competition
surveillance, consumer protection, export promotion and trade
safeguards

Website(s) information:
*Majandus-ja Kommunikatsiooniministeerium (Ministry of Economic Affairs and
Communications)* — **url:** www.mkm.ee **Coverage:** economic status;
transport; energy; communications; foreign trade

Publication(s):
Access of Enterprises to Venture Financing in Estonia — **Language:** English
Content: government funding; guarantee fund; expansion funds;
Investor incentives; tables; etc

Eesti Energeetika (Estonian Energy) — **Language:** English/Estonian **Frequency:**
irregular **Content:** gives a review about development of Estonian
energy during last five years; tables; statistics; etc

Turism Eestis (Tourism in Estonia) — **Language:** English **Frequency:** irregular
Content: trends; visitors; tables; statistics; etc

Põllumajandusministeerium

Ministry of Agriculture

Address: Lai 39/41, Tallinn, 15056
Telephone: +372 625 6101
Fax: +372 625 6200
E-mail: pm@agri.ee
Website: www.agri.ee

Guides: publications are available online
Activity: to provide conditions for the sustainable and diverse development of
Estonian rural development, agriculture, and fishing industry

Website(s) information:

Põllumajandusministeerium *(Ministry of Agriculture)* — **url:** www.agri.ee
Description: available in English and Estonian **Coverage:** agricultural census; results of selected agricultural holdings; trade; population; wages and salaries, all main social and economic indicators

Publication(s):

Agricultural Market and Trade — **Language:** English **Content:** export and import of agricultural products; foreign trade; tables; statistics

Agriculture and the Development of Rural Life — **Language:** English **Frequency:** irregular **Content:** meat production; alcohol production and market; agricultural research; statistics; tables

Annual report on agriculture — **Language:** English **Frequency:** annual **Content:** overview of the main trends in the agricultural sector

Eesti maaelu arengu strateegia 2007-2013 *(Estonian Agriculture Strategy Plan 2007-2013)* — **Language:** Estonian **Content:** statistics; tables; income; export; import; etc

Estonian Agriculture, Rural Economy And Food Industry — **Language:** English **Content:** economic results of agriculture; fishing; forest; statistics; tables; etc

Estonian Forestry — **Language:** English **Content:** forestry, wood processing industry, pulp and paper industry and furniture industry; tables; statistics

Estonian Rural Development Plan — **Language:** English **Content:** air pollution; animal production; statistics; tables; water; etc

Kalapüük ja varud *(Fishing and supplies)* — **Language:** Estonian **Content:** overview about Estonian fishing and supplies; statistics; tables; etc

Tööhõivest maal *(Employment in country)* — **Language:** Estonian **Content:** overview about employment in country; statistics; tables; etc

Rahandusministeerium

Ministry of Finance

Address: Suur-Ameerika 1, Tallinn, 15006
Telephone: +372 611 3558
Fax: +372 696 6810
E-mail: info@fin.ee
Website: www.fin.ee

Guides: free catalogue of publications (English and Estonian) is available from the above address
Activity: plans for and supervises the implementation of the Government's macroeconomic, fiscal and economic reform policies

Website(s) information:

Rahandusministeerium *(Ministry of Finance)* — **url:** www.fin.ee **Description:** access to online publication "Economic Review", providing a general portrait of the present socio-economic, political and business climate in Estonia. Includes analysis and data on: latest GDP growth trends; sales and real growth of the manufacturing industry; growth forecasts for Estonia's main trade partners; balance of trade and services; changes in exports and imports; private consumption; gross fixed capital formation; employment; wages and productivity; price indices; general government deficit; and forecasts for selected indicators **Coverage:** GDP; wages; productivity; forecasts

Publication(s):

2006 aasta kevadine majandusprognoos *(Macroeconomic Forecast of the Ministry of Finance of Estonia 2006)* — **Language:** English/Estonian **Frequency:** irregular **Content:** economic; unemployment rate; employment; exports and imports; government budget balance; forecast

Eesti Vabariigi Valitsuse poolt võetud laenud *(Debt Details of the Central Government of Estonia)* — **Language:** English/Estonian **Frequency:** irregular **Content:** base rates and margins; loan balance; interest rates

Estonian Economic Survey — **Language:** English/Estonian **Frequency:** monthly **Content:** external environment; prices; economic sectors; financial sector; state budget

Overview of the Financial Assets and Liabilities of the State Treasury — **Language:** English **Frequency:** irregular **Content:** financial assets, state treasury

Rahandusministeeriumi strateegiline arengukava 2006-2009 *(Ministry of Finance Strategic Development Plan 2006-2009)* — **Language:** Estonian **Frequency:** irregular **Content:** financial statistics; financial plans; bureau of customs statistics; organisation development

Rahandusministeeriumi strateegiline arengukava 2007-2010 *(Ministry of Finance Strategic Development Plan 2007-2010)* — **Language:** Estonian **Frequency:** irregular **Content:** financial statistics; financial plans; bureau of customs statistics; organization development

Tagasimakstud laenud ja riigigarantiid *(Repaid Loans and Guaranteed Debt)* — **Language:** English/Estonian **Frequency:** irregular **Content:** currency; repaid; interest and commitment paid; etc

Ravimiamet

State Agency of Medicines

Address: Nooruse 1, Tartu, 50411
Telephone: +372 737 41 40
Fax: +372 737 41 42
E-mail: sam@sam.ee
Website: www.sam.ee

Guides: publications are available free online
Activity: marketing authorisation and quality control of medicinal products including biological products, evaluation and approval of applications for clinical trials, import and export authorisation of medicinal products, control of licit use of psychotropic and narcotic substances, control over precursors, drug information, advertising and promotion control and pharmaceutical inspection

Website(s) information:

Ravimiamet *(State Agency of Medicines)* — **url:** www.sam.ee **Coverage:** provides an overview and statistics (drugs; clinical trials; etc)

Publication(s):

Eesti ravimistatistika aastaraamat *(Estonian Statistics on Medicines Yearbook)* — **Language:** English/Estonian **Content:** overview; statistics

Ravimiamet *(State Agency of Medicines)* — **Language:** Estonian **Frequency:** annual **Content:** statistics; tables; overview of the market

Sideamet

Estonian National Communications Board

Address: Ädala 2, Tallinn, 10614
Telephone: +372 693 1154
Fax: +372 693 1155
E-mail: sideamet@sa.ee/postbox@sa.ee
Website: www.sa.ee

Guides: publications are available free online
Activity: creates the necessary conditions for the development of electronic communications and postal sectors, promotion of the development of electronic communications networks, publicly available postal and communications services without giving preference to specific technologies and ensuring of the protection of the interests of users of telephone, mobile telephone, data, international telephony, cable distribution and postal services by promoting free competition, quality of service and the purposeful and fair planning, assignment and use of radio frequencies and numbering as well as exercising the supervision in all sectors of its activity

Website(s) information:

Sideamet *(Estonian National Communications Board)* — **url:** www.sa.ee **Description:** communications sector industry information also available in English **Coverage:** provides general information about communications sectors in Estonia

Publication(s):

Aastaraamat *(Annual Report)* — **Language:** English/Estonian **Frequency:** annual **Content:** wholesale market; international calls; market overview; connection fees and monthly fees; retail market overview; access to communication networks enabling broadband connection; mobile telephone numbers; overview of Estonia post cost accounting; statistics; tables

Estonian National Communications Board over 10 Years — **Language:** English **Content:** budget; salaries; travel expenses; administrative expenses; investments; etc

Siseministeerium

Ministry of Internal Affairs

Address: Pikk 61, Tallinn, 15065
Telephone: +372 612 5008
Fax: +372 612 5010
E-mail: sisemin@sisemin.gov.ee
Website: www.sisemin.gov.ee

Guides: publications are available online
Activity: internal security; population; local government and regional development

Website(s) information:

Sisministeerium (Ministry of Internal Affairs) — url: www.sisemin.gov.ee **Coverage:** provides an statistical publications (available free); information about European union; etc

Publication(s):

Analysis of the Development of Estonian Local Government — **Language:** English **Content:** population and number of municipalities; public sector in Estonia; city budgets; etc

Kohalikud Omavalitsused Eestis (Local Governments in Estonia) — **Language:** English/Estonian **Frequency:** irregular **Content:** Democracy and participation at local level; international relations in local government area; local government finances; etc

Maareform Eestis (Territorial reform in Estonia 1998) — **Language:** English/Estonian **Content:** municipal finances; municipal co-operation; overview; statistics; tables

Siseministeeriumi tutvustav brosüür (Ministry of the Interior of the Republic of Estonia) — **Language:** English **Frequency:** irregular **Content:** gives overview what is ministry internal affairs and what they do; etc

Sotsiaalministeerium

Ministry of Social Affairs

Address: Gonsiori 29, Tallinn, 15027
Telephone: +372 626 9301
Fax: +372 699 2209
E-mail: info@sm.ee
Website: www.sm.ee

Guides: publications are available online
Activity: drafting and implementation of plans to resolve state social issues; managing of public health protection and medical care, employment, the labour market and working environment, social security, social insurance and social welfare, promotion of gender equality

Website(s) information:

Sotsiaalministeerium (Ministry of Social Affairs) — url: www.sm.ee **Coverage:** provides information, statistics, overviews and publications on health; labour market; social insurance; etc

Publication(s):

Eesti täiskasvanud rahvastiku tervisekäitumise (Health Behavior among the Estonian Adult Population) — **Language:** Estonian/English **Content:** health status; smoking; dietary habits; consumption of alcohol and drugs; body mass index, physical exercise; quality of water, ambient noise; use of health services and medicines

Haigestumise majanduslikud tagajärjed Eestis (Economic Consequences of Ill-Health in Estonia) — **Language:** English **Frequency:** irregular **Content:** population structure; chronic disease prevalence; Distribution of total life years lost (DALY) by gender and diseases; tables, statistics; etc

Haigestumusinfo võrdlev uuring tervishoiu statistilise aastaaruandluse ja Eesti Haigekassa raviarvete andmebaasi põhjal (Comparative Analysis of Morbidity on the Basis of Annual Statistical Reports and the Database of Estonian Health Insurance Fund) — **Language:** English/Estonian **Content:** data collection and methods; results; statistics; tables

HIV/AIDS-i temaatikaga seotud teadmised, hoiakud ja käitumine Eesti noorte hulgas (Knowledge, Additudes and Behaviour Related to HIV/AIDS Among Estonian Youth) — **Language:** English/Estonian **Content:** socio-demographic data; overview of the implementation of the research; use of contraceptives; major risk groups; sexual activity

Impact of the European Union Common Pension Objectives on the Estonian Pension System — **Language:** English **Content:** pension overview; tables; statistics

Lapsed ja Eesti ühiskond (Children and Estonian Society) — **Language:** Estonian **Frequency:** irregular **Content:** government support; pocket money; trends; statistics; tables; etc

Nordic/Baltic Health Statistics — **Language:** English **Frequency:** irregular **Content:** statistics and tables on population and health problems

Potential of Estonia's Working Age Population to Work in the Countries of the European Union — **Language:** English **Content:** number of people wanting to work abroad; a socio-demographic picture of people wanting to work abroad; labour market situation; tables; overview; etc

Prostitutsioon - kas ühiskondlik probleem? (Prostitution - a social problem?) — **Language:** English/Estonian **Content:** criminalisation; prohibition; abolition; analysis method and samples; analysis results; statistics; tables; etc

Sotsiaalsektor arvudes (Social Sector in Figures) — **Language:** English/Estonian **Frequency:** annual **Content:** population, health care; wages and salaries; working environment; social welfare

Sotsiaaltöö ajakirjad (Social Work journals) — **Language:** Estonian **Frequency:** bi-monthly **Content:** overview on social work in Estonia; statistics; tables; articles; contact numbers

Tervishoiustatistika Aastaraamat (Health Care Statistics Yearbook) — **Language:** English/Estonian **Frequency:** annual **Content:** hospital discharges; day care; doctors' hourly wage; statistics; tables

Towards a Balanced Society-Women and Men in Estonia 2000 — **Language:** English **Frequency:** irregular **Content:** equal opportunities for men and women; health; income; gendered leisure; wage ratios; etc

Statistikaamet

Statistical Office of Estonia

Address: Endla 15, Tallinn, 15174
Telephone: +372 6259 300
Fax: +372 6259 370
E-mail: stat@stat.ee
Website: www.stat.ee

Guides: free catalogue of publications (English and Estonian) is available from the above address
Activity: collecting data; producing and publishing objective official statistics for public institutions, business and research spheres, international organisations and individuals

Website(s) information:

Statistical Office of Estonia — url: www.stat.ee **Description:** information on products and services provided by the institute, including catalogue of publications; latest releases; information service; population census; information centre, request for information, news releases, order for information, the web site, public database, ordering of foreign trade and industrial statistics and statistics on Estonia. Online databases and regional development database which includes environment, economy, population and social life **Coverage:** main socio-economic indicators including statistics on population; gross domestic product; estimated economic growth; consumer price index; producer price index; export/import price index; average monthly gross wages and salaries; environment, social life, unemployment; industrial sales; retail trade sales; trade balance

Publication(s):

Aastaaruanne (Annual Report) — **Language:** English/Estonian **Frequency:** annual **Content:** statistics on products and consumers; population; socio-economic; salaries; macroeconomic; general government and financial sector; foreign trade; enterprise; agricultural; environment and sustainable development; regional

Eesti ettevõtja ja tema sissetulek (Self-Employed in Estonia and their Income) — **Language:** English/Estonian **Frequency:** irregular **Content:** self-employed and employees by sex, main economic activities of the self-employed, self-employed and employees by region, self-employed and employees by age, self-employed and employees by type of household, self-employed and employees by income quintiles, self-employed and employees by quintiles of earned income

Eesti Põhilised Sotsiaal- ja Majandusnäitajad (Main Social and Economic Indicators of Estonia) — **Language:** English/Estonian **Frequency:** monthly **Content:** social and economic indicators

***Eesti rahvamajanduse arvepidamine** (National Accounts of Estonia)* — **Language:** English/Estonian **Frequency:** annual **Content:** contains main indicators on the national accounts of Estonia: the gross domestic product (GDP) compiled by production, expenditure and income approach, cost components of the value added of institutional sectors, gross fixed capital formation by institutional sectors and economic activity, structure of private consumption expenditure, accounts of institutional sectors

***Eesti statistika aastaraamat** (Statistical Yearbook of Estonia)* — **Language:** English/Estonian **Frequency:** annual **Content:** annual statistics on socio-economic life and environment

***Eesti Statistika Kuukiri** (Monthly Bulletin of Estonian Statistics)* — **Language:** English/Estonian **Frequency:** monthly **Content:** provides short-term statistics; environment and socio-economic

***Ehitushinnaindeks** (Construction Price Index)* — **Language:** English/Estonian **Frequency:** quarterly **Content:** buildings (detached houses, apartment buildings, industrial and office buildings) and by resources (labour force, building machines and materials); repair and reconstruction work price indices

***Energiabilanss** (Energy Balance)* — **Language:** English/Estonian **Frequency:** annual **Content:** statistics on energy production and consumption, exports and imports as well as prices for the year with comparison with previous years

Estonia, Latvia, Lithuania in Figures — **Language:** English **Frequency:** annual **Content:** statistics on economic and social conditions

***Ettevõtete majandusnäitajad** (Financial Statistics of Enterprises)* — **Language:** English/Estonian **Frequency:** annual **Content:** enterprises demography; IT use in business; research and development; enterprise groups; foreign-controlled enterprises in Estonia

***Ettevõtlus** (Business)* — **Language:** English/Estonian **Frequency:** quarterly **Content:** short-term statistics on the economic situation of enterprises

***Ettevõtlus Eestis** (Business in Estonia)* — **Language:** English/Estonian **Frequency:** irregular **Content:** pocket-sized reference book provides data on general indicators of enterprises (number of enterprises, number of persons employed, turnover, balance sheet total, investments, value added, etc

***Keskkond** (Environment)* — **Language:** English/Estonian **Frequency:** annual **Content:** analytical overview, emissions into the air, waste generation, wastewater discharge, use and emissions of chemicals and ozone depleting substances

***Keskkond arvudes** (Environment in Figures)* — **Language:** English/Estonian **Frequency:** annual **Content:** emission of pollutants, use of natural resources, etc; ph level of precipitation, pollution of air, etc; pollution prevention and control expenditures, includes tables and diagrams

***Keskkonnakaitsekulutused** (Environment Protection Expenditures)* — **Language:** English/Estonian **Frequency:** annual **Content:** public sector (Government of the Republic, municipality and city governments and Environmental Investments Centre) environmental investments, current expenditures on environment protection, expenditures on research and development and the receipts from environmental protection

***Leibkonna elujärg** (Household Living)* — **Language:** English/Estonian **Frequency:** annual **Content:** analytical overview of households, their economic situation, living conditions and expenditure in the current year and dynamics during the last ten years

***Linnad ja vallad arvudes** (Cities and Rural Municipalities in Figures)* — **Language:** English/Estonian **Frequency:** annual **Content:** includes analysis and comparisons reflecting the development of cities and rural municipalities on the basis of several indicators

***Monthly Bulletin of Estonian Statistics** (Eesti Statistika Kuukiri)* —

***Naised ja mehed** (Women and Men)* — **Language:** English/Estonian **Frequency:** irregular **Content:** demographic aspects, education, time use, income, poverty, lifestyle, labour market

***Põllumajandus** (Agriculture)* — **Language:** English/Estonian **Frequency:** annual **Content:** data on economic indicators of agriculture and supply-balance sheets of agricultural products, agricultural land use, areas under and yields of field crops, fruits and berries, number and production of livestock, use of mineral and organic fertilizers

***Põllumajandus arvudes** (Agriculture in Figures)* — **Language:** English/Estonian **Frequency:** annual **Content:** financial statistics of agriculture and supply-balance sheets of agricultural products, agricultural land use, areas under and yields of field crops, fruits and berries, number and production of livestock, use of fertilisers

***Põllumajanduslikud majapidamised** (Agricultural Holdings)* — **Language:** English/Estonian **Frequency:** annual **Content:** land use, animal husbandry, agricultural machinery and equipment, labour force and other activities of agricultural holdings

***Rahvastik** (Population)* — **Language:** English/Estonian **Frequency:** annual **Content:** population and population composition

***Sissetulek ja elamistingimused** (Income and Living Conditions)* — **Language:** English/Estonian **Frequency:** annual **Content:** living conditions of households, care of children, safety, social contacts and health of household members

***Töötasu** (Earnings)* — **Language:** English/Estonian **Frequency:** annual **Content:** full-time and part-time employees; male and female employees by group of earnings; separate part deals with hourly earnings of male and female employees by major groups of occupations and economic activities; hourly earnings of other occupational groups as a proportion of legislators', senior officials' and managers' hourly earnings and women's hourly earnings as a proportion of men's hourly earnings

***Tööturg** (Labour Market)* — **Language:** English/Estonian **Frequency:** annual **Content:** labour market by sex, age, education, place of residence and ethnic nationality

***Transport Side** (Transport Communications)* — **Language:** English/Estonian **Frequency:** annual **Content:** statistics on transport and communications; road network, vehicles, aircraft and vessels registered in registers; transport of passengers and goods carried by road, by sea, by inland waterways; railway and air transport enterprises; passenger and shipping traffic and transport of goods through ports; ship accidents, traffic accidents on public railways, road traffic accidents, persons killed and injured; the length of pipelines and the amount of gas transported via pipelines; postal and telecommunication

***Turism/Majutus** (Tourism/Accommodation)* — **Language:** English/Estonia **Frequency:** annual **Content:** foreign visitors' motivation and expenditure, tourism of Estonian population, capacity of accommodation establishments, number of tourists in accommodation establishments; sales, exports and imports of tourist services, domestic and international tourism, foreign visitors, outgoing visitors and overnight visitors served by travel agencies and tour operators, etc

***Väliskaubandus** (Foreign Trade)* — **Language:** English/Estonian **Frequency:** annual **Content:** detailed reviews of the exports and imports of agricultural products, wood and articles of wood, metal and articles of metal, machinery and equipment, transport vehicles and mineral fuels

Tervishoiuamet

Health Care Board

Address: Gonsori 29, Tallinn, 15157
Telephone: +372 650 9840
Fax: +372 650 9844
E-mail: info@tervishoiuamet.ee
Website: www.tervishoiuamet.ee

Guides: legislation; health care professionals registration documents available free; statistics available in Estonian

Activity: registration of health care professionals; issue of activity licences; exercise state supervision and apply enforcement powers of the state

Website(s) information:

***Tervishoiuamet** (Health Care Board)* — **url:** www.tervishoiuamet.ee **Coverage:** provides health overview in Estonia and free publications and online statistics

Publication(s):

***Kiirabikutsed 1998-2005** (Ambulance calls 1998-2005)* — **Language:** English/Estonian **Frequency:** irregular **Content:** tables; statistics; etc

Tööinspektsioon

Labour Inspectorate

Address: Gonsiori 29, Tallinn, 10147
Telephone: +372 626 9400
Fax: +372 626 9404
E-mail: ti@ti.ee
Website: www.ti.ee

Guides: publications are available online

Activity: investigates fatal and serious occupational accidents and diseases and analyse their causes; collects statistics on accidents in the work place

Website(s) information:

Tööinspektsioon *(Labour Inspectorate)* — **url:** www.ti.ee **Coverage:** provides statistics about accidents at work in Estonia; health problems

Publication(s):

Ametialased õnnetused ja haigused Eestis *(Occupational Accidents and Diseases in Estonia)* — **Language:** English **Frequency:** irregular **Content:** fatal accidents per 100 000 workers; occupational diseases per 100 000 workers; tables; statistics; etc

Enterprises Inspected between 1999-2002 — **Language:** English **Frequency:** irregular **Content:** tables; statistics; etc

Most recent statistical news — **Language:** English **Frequency:** irregular **Content:** economic growth; consumer price index; export and import price index; average monthly gross wages and salaries; etc

Occupational diseases by factors — **Language:** English **Frequency:** irregular **Content:** tables; statistics; etc

Population Aged 15-69 by Sex, Indicator and Year — **Language:** English **Content:** population; tables; statistics

Riik ja selle kodanikud *(The country and its people)* — **Language:** English/Estonian **Content:** demography; deaths per 1000 population; population; births per 1000 population; etc

Serious and fatal accidents by fields of activity — **Language:** English **Content:** accidents per 1000 employees; tables; field of activity; tables; statistics; etc

Tööjõud Eestis *(Labour Force in Estonia)* — **Language:** English/Estonian **Frequency:** irregular **Content:** labour force; employed persons; employees; tables; etc

Tööturuamet
Labour Market Board

Address: Gonsiori 29, Tallinn, 15156
Telephone: +372 15 501
Fax: +372 625 7702
E-mail: tta@tta.ee
Website: www.tta.ee

Guides: publications are available online
Activity: to reduce unemployment and provide assistance to those seeking work and to employers by means of an efficient labour market policy

Website(s) information:

Tööturuamet *(Labour Market Board)* — **url:** www.tta.ee **Description:** statistics available to download for the labour market for 2003 and 2004. Yearbook also available giving statistics for the period 1999-2005 **Coverage:** labour market statistics

Publication(s):

Statistics — **Language:** English **Frequency:** annual **Content:** socio-economic statistics; working age population (15-64 year-olds) by gender and status

Tööturuameti Aastaraamat *(Estonian Labour Market Board Yearbook)* — **Language:** English/Estonian **Frequency:** annual **Content:** unemployment rates; working-age population; duration of unemployment; active labour market measures; statistics; etc

Veterinaar-ja Toiduamet
Veterinary and Food Board

Address: Väike-Paala 3, Tallinn, 11415
Telephone: +372 605 1710
Fax: +372 621 1441
E-mail: vet@vet.agri.ee
Website: www.vet.agri.ee

Guides: publications are available online
Activity: to ensure the production of safe, healthy and good quality food; to prevent and eradicate infectious animal diseases

Website(s) information:

Veterinaar-ja Toiduamet *(Veterinary and Food Board)* — **url:** www.vet.agri.ee **Coverage:** animal health; animal welfare; food control; trade, import and export, organic farming

Publication(s):

Veterinaar-ja Toiduameti Aastaraamat *(Veterinary and Food Board Yearbook)* — **Language:** English/Estonian **Frequency:** annual **Content:** trade; import; export; statistics; tables; etc

Finland

Laakelaitos
National Agency for Medicines

Address: PO Box 55, Mannerheimintie 166, Helsinki, 00301
Telephone: +358 9 473 341
Fax: +358 9 714 469
E-mail: kirjaamo@nam.fi
Website: www.nam.fi

Activity: promotes the health and safety of the citizens by regulatory control of medicinal products, medical devices and blood products

Website(s) information:

Lääkelaitos Läkemedelverket *(National Agency for Medicines)* — **url:** www.nam.fi **Coverage:** prescriptions, sales and consumption of drugs

Publication(s):

Finnish Statistics on Medicines — **Language:** English/Finnish **Frequency:** annual **Content:** statistics covering drug prescriptions, drug sales, consumption, drug registration, etc

Liikenne- ja viestintäministeriö
Ministry of Transport and Communications

Address: PO Box 31, Eteläesplanadi 16-18, Helsinki, 00023
Telephone: +358 916 002
Fax: +358 9 1602 8596
E-mail: kirjaamo@mintc.fi
Website: www.mintc.fi

Guides: publications are available free
Activity: responsible for two broad government sectors: transport policy and communications policy

Website(s) information:

Liikenne- ja viestintäministeriö *(Ministry of Transport and Communications)* — **url:** www.mintc.fi **Coverage:** provides free publications and statistics data covering telecommunications, mass media, postal services and communication policy in Finland

Publication(s):

Price Level of Finnish Telecommunications Charges — **Language:** English/Finnish **Content:** call prices; long-distance calls; international calls; local calls; monthly charges; etc

Prices of Mobile Calls — **Language:** English/Finnish **Frequency:** irregular **Content:** overview of the market situation; statistics; etc

Matkailun edistämiskeskus
Finnish Tourist Board

Address: PO Box 625, Töölönkatu 11, Helsinki, 00101
Telephone: +358 10 605 8000
Fax: +358 10 605 8333
E-mail: mek@mek.fi
Website: www.mek.fi

Guides: publications are available in three languages: Finnish; English; Swedish
Activity: to promote tourism in Finland

Website(s) information:

Matkailun edistämiskeskus *(Finnish Tourist Board)* — **url:** www.mek.fi **Description:** official site of the Finnish Tourist Board. Includes statistics on the national tourism industry, including balance of payments, travel; foreign passengers visiting Finland; overnight stays in Finland; tourist attractions in Finland **Coverage:** provides online statistics and free publications; also detailed contacts about Finnish tourist board offices all over the world

Publication(s):

Annual Report — **Language:** English/Finnish **Frequency:** annual **Content:** business environment; organisation; research activity international co-operation; statistics; overview; etc

Matkailufaktat *(Travel Facts)* — **Language:** English/Finnish **Content:** statistics on the Finnish tourism sector by bookings for accommodation, etc

Matkailukohteiden Kavijamaarat (Number of Visitors to Tourist Attractions) — **Language:** English/Finnish **Content:** statistical information on visitors, basis of calculation and reliability; monthly variation in number of visitors; number of visitors to tourist attractions; current and historic numbers

Rajahaastattelututkimus: Ulkomaiset matkailijat Suomessa vuonna (Border Interview survey: Foreign Visitors in Finland) — **Language:** English/Finnish **Frequency:** annual **Content:** main reasons for visiting Finland; length of stay; main destination in Finland; outdoor activities; results by country of residence; visitors by month; age and gender

Suomen Pankki
Bank of Finland

Address: PO Box 160, Snellmaninaukio, Helsinki, 00101
Telephone: +358 10 8311
Fax: +358 9 174 872
E-mail: info@bof.fi
Website: www.bof.fi

Guides: list of publications available online
Activity: to ensure price stability and the stability and efficiency of the payment and financial system

Website(s) information:
Suomen Pankki (Bank of Finland) — **url:** www.bof.fi **Description:** economic statistics: inflation; interest rates; exchange rates; monetary aggregates; banking and finance; current account, financial account and international reserves; supply, demand and labour market; central government finances; EMU convergence criteria. Bank of Finland's balance sheet **Coverage:** statistics on Finnish, European and international interest rates, EURIBOR daily and monthly data, currency exchanges, monetary data, bonds and payments balances, public funds, and other main economic indicators

Publication(s):
Balance of Payments and International Investment Position — **Language:** English/Finnish/Swedish **Frequency:** quarterly **Content:** current account; financial account; investment position; export; import

Financial Integration — **Language:** English **Frequency:** irregular **Content:** financial integration; securities markets integration; integration of European banking and insurance; financial stability, regulation and supervision; statistics

Financial Markets (Statistical Review) — **Language:** English/Finnish/Swedish **Frequency:** monthly **Content:** daily, weekly, monthly, quarterly and annual series covering key interest rates, money market liquidity, lending, monetary aggregates and deposits, exchange rates and banks´ forex transactions, balance of payments, Bank of Finland balance sheet, and bonds

Financial Stability — **Language:** English **Frequency:** annual **Content:** international developments and provides thorough evaluations on the current state and future prospects of the financial system

Finland´s Balance of Payments — **Language:** English/Finnish **Frequency:** monthly **Content:** Includes data on main items of the balance of payments: goods and services, income, current transfers and financial accounts

Finnish Balance of Payments and International Investment Position Statistics — **Language:** English **Frequency:** irregular **Content:** external stability of the economy in real and financial transactions; financial positions; capital and financial accounts; national income; balance of savings; investments in the economy; etc

International Reserves and Foreign Currency Liquidity — **Language:** English **Frequency:** monthly **Content:** official reserve assets; predetermined short-term net drains on foreign currency assets; contingent short-term net drains on foreign currency assets

Main Indicators for the Finnish Economy — **Language:** English/Finnish **Frequency:** monthly **Content:** financial markets; statistics

Soumen Pankin Vousikertomus (Bank of Finland Annual Report) — **Language:** English/Finnish/Swedish **Frequency:** annual **Content:** monetary policy; economic policy; financial markets and statistics; maintenance of currency supply; etc

Studies in Time Series Analysis of Consumption, Asset Prices and Forecasting — **Language:** English **Frequency:** irregular **Content:** statistical models and economic analysis; economic forecasting; recent trends in applied econometrics; asset prices and co integration

Suomen joukkovelkakirjalainat (Finnish Bond Issues) — **Language:** English/Finnish/Swedish **Frequency:** annual **Content:** statistical bulletin; comprises loan-specific information on government and private sector bonds issued in Finland; etc

Tilastokeskus
Statistics Centre of Finland

Address: , , Työpajankatu 13, Helsinki, 00022
Telephone: +358 9 1734 2220
Fax: +358 9 1734 2279
E-mail: stat@stat.fi
Website: www.stat.fi

Guides: 200 different statistics and over 700 releases made annually; statistical data can be browsed by 26 topics
Activity: national statistics office

Website(s) information:
Tilastokeskus (Statistics Finland) — **url:** www.stat.fi **Description:** information on products and services provided; Statistics Finland, Eurostat and IBS News Service; and various statistical sections providing free online data on Finland and other countries **Coverage:** statistical data can be browsed by 26 topics covering socio-economic development, financial, health, labour and other sectors etc

Publication(s):
Asuntojen hinnat (House Prices) — **Language:** Finnish **Frequency:** annual **Content:** statistics on house prices; overview of changes; etc

Asuntojen hinnat neljännesvuosittain (House Prices Quarterly) — **Language:** Finnish **Frequency:** 4 per annum **Content:** statistics on quarterly changes on house prices; overview of changes; etc

Asunto-osakeyhtiöiden taloustilasto (Statistics on the Finances of Housing Corporation) — **Language:** English/Finnish **Frequency:** annual **Content:** financial statistics; overview; etc

Education in Finland — **Language:** English **Frequency:** annual **Content:** compact book in English with statistical data on education in Finland

Energiaennakko (Preliminary Energy Statistics) — **Language:** English/Finnish **Frequency:** annual **Content:** statistics on energy production in Finland

Energiatilasto (Energy Statistics) — **Language:** English/Finnish **Content:** statistical data on energy production, consumption, import and export, investment on energy, public finance of energy and emissions. National energy statistics and international review

Energy in Finland — **Language:** English **Frequency:** annual **Content:** main Finnish energy statistics, with data compiled since the 1970s

Finland in Figures — **Language:** English **Frequency:** annual **Content:** statistical overview of Finland's main socio-economic indicators

Finnish Business in Finland — **Language:** English **Frequency:** irregular **Content:** statistics and diverse information on companies operating in Finland and their development

Information Society Statistics — **Language:** English **Frequency:** annual **Content:** data on development of information society in Finland and comparisons made with the other European countries

Internet ja sähköinen kauppa yrityksissä (Internet Use and E-commerce in Enterprises) — **Language:** Finnish **Frequency:** annual **Content:** statistical data on number of internet users in Finland; development of the IT sector

Joukkoviestimet (Finnish Mass Media) — **Language:** Finnish **Frequency:** annual **Content:** statistics about Finnish mass media

Kansantalouden tilinpito (National Accounts) — **Language:** English/Finnish **Frequency:** irregular **Content:** comparisons made on changes to national accounts over a 10-year period

Kansantalouden tilinpito (National Accounts Quarterly) — **Language:** English/Finnish **Frequency:** quarterly **Content:** national accounts tables, statistics

Kansantalouden tilinpito, Ennakkotietoja (National Accounts, Preliminary Data) — **Language:** English/Finnish **Frequency:** annual **Content:** national accounts tables; domestic product at market prices; net national income

Kuluttajabarometri (Consumer Survey) — **Language:** English/Finnish **Frequency:** annual **Content:** statistical data and analysis of different surveys on consumption

Kuntasektorin palkat (Local Government Workers' Salaries) — **Language:** Finnish **Frequency:** annual **Content:** local government personnel's wage information based on area, sector, profession, education, gender and age

***Kuolemansyyt** (Causes of Death)* — **Language:** English/Finnish **Frequency:** annual **Content:** causes of death; statistics; etc

***Kymmenvuotiskatsaus** (10 Year Review)* — **Language:** Finnish **Frequency:** annual **Content:** statistical review of the development in Finland during last 10 years. Contains analysed statistical data about the development of Finnish society and economy. The key topic of the publication is business

***Liikennetilastollinen Vuosikirja** (Transport in Finland Yearbook)* — **Language:** Finnish **Frequency:** annual **Content:** data on transport statistics: road, railway, air and sea

***Luonnonvarat ja ymparisto** (Natural Resources and Environment)* — **Language:** English/Finnish/Swedish **Frequency:** annual **Content:** report on development of national resources and state of environment

***Maa-, metsä- ja kalatalous** (Agriculture, Forestry and Fishery)* — **Language:** English/Finnish/Swedish **Frequency:** annual **Content:** series of publications offering key statistics covering the agriculture, forestry and fishery industries in Finland

***Maatilatilastollinen vuosikirja** (Yearbook of Farming Statistics)* — **Language:** English/Finnish **Frequency:** annual **Content:** data on number of farms and livestock by type

***Matkailutilasto** (Tourism Statistics)* — **Language:** English/Finnish **Frequency:** annual **Content:** arrivals, departures, receipts and expenditure; business travel; length of stay; purpose of visit; etc

***Matkailutilasto kuukausittain** (Tourism Statistics Monthly)* — **Language:** English/Finnish **Content:** arrivals, departures, receipts and expenditure; business travel; length of stay; purpose of visit

***Metsätilastollinen vuosikirja** (Finnish Statistical Yearbook of Forestry)* — **Language:** English/Finnish **Frequency:** annual **Content:** data on forestry in Finland

***Moottoriajoneuvot** (Motor Vehicles in Finland)* — **Language:** English/Finnish **Frequency:** annual **Content:** statistical data on automotive sector in Finland

***Oikeustilastollinen vsk** (Annual Legal Statistics)* — **Language:** Finnish **Content:** statistics on legal environment, crime and imprisonment

***Oppilaitostilastot** (Education Statistics)* — **Content:** educational statistics from elementary schools to universities

***Päihdetilastollinen vuosikirja** (Yearbook of Alcohol and Drug Statistics)* — **Language:** English/Finnish **Frequency:** annual **Content:** statistics on drugs and alcohol use in Finland

***Perheet** (Families)* — **Language:** English/Finnish **Frequency:** annual **Content:** statistics on families; family size to education and earnings

***Sosiaali- ja terveyshuollon tilastollinen vuosikirja** (Statistical Yearbook on Social Welfare and Health Care)* — **Language:** English/Finnish **Frequency:** annual **Content:** statistical data on health care and social welfare; etc

***Suomalaisten matkailu** (Finnish Travel)* — **Language:** Finnish **Frequency:** annual **Content:** statistics and overview of Finnish tourism

***Suomen Tilastollinen Vuosikirja** (Finnish Statistical Yearbook)* — **Language:** Finnish/Swedish/English **Frequency:** annual **Content:** compilation of annual data covering a wide range of topics, including population, agriculture, fishing, forestry, industry, internal and external trade (including retailing), enterprises, banking and credit, insurance, transport and communications, state finances, income and property, national accounts, consumption and prices, labour market, wages

***Suomen tilastollinen vuosikirja** (Statistical Yearbook of Finland)* — **Language:** English/Finnish **Frequency:** annual **Content:** statistics and overview on general socio-economic indicators

***Tieto&trendit** (Information and Trends)* — **Language:** Finnish **Frequency:** 8 per annum **Content:** facts and figures, country reports, trends. Replaced former newspapers Economic Trends and Tietoaika.

***Tilastokatsaus taulukkoluettelo** (Bulletin of Statistics)* — **Language:** Finnish/English/Swedish **Frequency:** quarterly **Content:** statistical data on general socio-economic indicators

***Tukku- ja vähittäiskauppa vsk** (Wholesale and Retail Trade)* — **Language:** English/Finnish **Frequency:** irregular **Content:** statistical data on wholesale and retail trade in Finland

***Tulo-ja varallisuustilasto** (Statistics on Income and Wealth)* — **Language:** Finnish **Frequency:** annual **Content:** statistical data and comparisons on wages, wealth and taxation

***Tulonjakotilasto** (Income Distribution Statistics)* — **Language:** English/Finnish **Frequency:** annual **Content:** statistical data on incomes

***Tutkimus- ja kehittamistoiminta** (Research and Development)* — **Language:** Finnish **Content:** information on research and development activity practiced by Finnish public sector, companies and academies

***Tyotapaturmat** (Accidents at Work)* — **Language:** English/Finnish **Frequency:** irregular **Content:** statistics; overview; accident types; etc

***Työtunnin kustannus 1996-2005** (Hourly Wages 1996-2005)* — **Language:** English/Finish **Frequency:** irregular **Content:** comparisons of changes in overall cost of an hourly wage

***Työvoimatilasto** (Labour Force Statistics)* — **Language:** Finnish **Frequency:** annual **Content:** national labour force statistics

***Ulkomaalaiset ja siirtolaisuus** (Foreigners and International Migration)* — **Language:** English/Finnish **Frequency:** annual **Content:** migration statistics; tables; foreigners statistics; etc

***Ulkomaankauppa** (Foreign Trade)* — **Language:** Finnish/English **Frequency:** monthly **Content:** import and export statistics

***Väestönmuutokset** (Vital Statistics)* — **Language:** English/Finnish **Frequency:** annual **Content:** statistics; tables; vital statistics; etc

***Väestörakenne ja väestömuutokset kunnittain** (Population Structure and Vital Statistics by Municipality)* — **Language:** English/Finnish **Frequency:** annual **Content:** statistics, overview on population structure

***Valtion kuukausipalkat** (Government Workers Monthly Wages)* — **Language:** Finnish **Content:** data of government workers' wages based on age, gender, length of service, degree, region

***Vuokratilasto** (Rents)* — **Language:** English/Finnish **Frequency:** annual **Content:** statistical data on house rents in Finland

***Women and Men in Finland** — **Language:** English **Content:** statistics on equality of men and women in Finland (comparisons of the position, wages, home duties and ect.)

***Yksityisen sektorin kuukausipalkat** (Private sector monthly wages)* — **Language:** Finnish **Frequency:** annual **Content:** private sector workers' wage statistics based on profession and education

***Ympäristötilasto** (Environmental Statistics)* — **Language:** English/Finnish **Frequency:** annual **Content:** environmental statistics

Valtiovarainministerio
Ministry of Finance

Address: PO Box 28, , Helsinki, 00023,
Telephone: +358 9 160 01
Fax: +358 9 1603 4854
E-mail: valtiovarainministerio@vm.fi
Website: www.ministryoffinance.fi

Guides: publications are available free in three languages: Finnish; English; Swedish

Activity: to prepare economic and fiscal policy, drafts the annual Budget and offers experience in tax policy matters

Website(s) information:
***Valtiovarainministerio** (Ministry of Finance)* — **url:** www.vn.fi **Description:** offers information on the national economy and state finances **Coverage:** provides free graphs and statistics database of economy, budget; general government finances; etc; free publications in English, Finnish, Swedish; detailed overview about the ministry of finance and detailed contact information

Publication(s):
***Finnish Public Sector as an Employer** — **Language:** English/Finnish/Swedish **Frequency:** annual **Content:** overview of the situation of public sector as an employer in Finland; includes statistics

***Taskutilasto** (Pocket Statistics)* — **Language:** English/Finnish/Swedish **Content:** average total earnings by education; labour costs; labour costs by cost category; etc

France

Banque de France
Bank of France

Address: BP 14001, 48 rue Croix des Petit Champs, Paris, 75001
Telephone: +33 14 292 3908
Fax: +33 14 292 3940
E-mail: infos@banque-france.fr
Website: www.banque-france.fr

Guides: Catalogue des Publications available
Activity: banking and monetary policy

Website(s) information:

Banque de France *(Bank of France)* — **url:** www.banque-france.fr **Description:** information and statistics on the French banking and financial system. Data on the main economic and monetary indicators for the EU, USA and Japan, the organisation of financial activities in France, credit institutions, banking and financial regulations, payment instruments, and payment systems and securities settlement systems **Coverage:** statistics coverage include regulation, national financial accounts, statistics of the monthly digest, monetary statistics, balance of payments, international banking statistics, European sectoral references, and links to statistics pages of ESCB websites

Publication(s):

Banque de France Annual Report — **Language:** English/French **Frequency:** annual **Content:** describes the activities of the Banque de France, its balance sheet and income statements and presents the Governor's comments on the economic and monetary situation

Bulletin de la Banque de France *(Bank of France' Bulletin)* — **Language:** English/French **Frequency:** monthly **Content:** reference work on economic, monetary and financial issues

Financial Stability Review — **Language:** English/French **Frequency:** bi-monthly **Content:** provides information on financial sector players and observers, such as decision makers, academics and market participants; it reviews developments affecting financial institutions, markets and their infrastructures from a cyclical and structural perspective

French Ministry of Foreign Affairs

Address: 244 boulevard Saint-Germain, Paris, 75303
Telephone: +33 1 4317 9000
Website: www.diplomatie.gouv.fr

Guides: offers magazines covering various topics

Publication(s):

Label France — **Language:** English/French **Frequency:** quarterly **Content:** covering topics such as French cinema, tourism, business life, science and technology, humanities, international relations, and sport

Institut National de la Statistique et des Etudes Economiques (INSEE)

National Institute of Statistics and Economic Studies

Address: Tour Gamma A, 195 rue de Bercy, Paris Cédex 12, 75582
Telephone: +33 8 2588 9452
Fax: +33 1 5317 8809
E-mail: insee-contact@insee.fr
Website: www.insee.fr

Guides: annual catalogue of publications (free, available online)
Activity: collects and produces information on the French economy and society

Website(s) information:

Institut National de la Statistique et des Etudes Economiques (INSEE) *(National Institute of Statistics and Economic Studies)* — **url:** www.insee.fr **Description:** official site of INSEE, provides information on the Institute's main products and services, including list of publications and latest statistical releases; general profile of 26 French regions; access to SIRENE database (French companies database); and compilation of various online statistics **Coverage:** up-to-date statistics can be found by accessing both section "Les Grands Indicateurs" and "La France en Faits et Chiffres". Main Indicators section includes data on: consumer price index; cost-of-construction index; major economic indicators and analyses; and quarterly and annual accounts. France in Facts and Figures provides general socio-economic statistics covering: geography, population and demographics; labour force; health, education and general living standards; agriculture; industry; retailing and wholesaling; and services

Publication(s):

Annuaire Statistique de la France *(Statistical Yearbook of France)* — **Language:** French **Frequency:** annual **Content:** detailed demographic, economic and social statistics on France, with technical commentaries, notes on sources of information and bibliographic references; includes section entitled 'commerce interieur' with data on retailing establishments, by region and by type, turnover, employees, investment, etc.

Bulletin Mensuel de Statistique *(Monthly Statistical Bulletin)* — **Language:** French **Frequency:** monthly **Content:** most up-to-date information on all indices and statistical series which INSEE maintain regularly

Consommation des Menages *(Household Consumption)* — **Language:** French **Frequency:** annual **Content:** household consumption statistics covering food products, clothing, accommodation, household equipment, healthcare, transport, cultural and leisure activities and other goods and services

Courrier des Statistiques — **Language:** English/French **Frequency:** quarterly **Content:** reports on key events, developments, and debates in official French and international statistics since 1977

Daily Economic Monitor — **Language:** French **Frequency:** daily **Content:** provides information on national accounts, activity in the industrial sector, investment, employment and labour market, financing economy, foreign trade etc

Economie & Statistique — **Language:** French **Frequency:** monthly **Content:** provides information on the transition from education to employment

France in Figures — **Language:** English/French **Frequency:** every 2 years **Content:** provides information on geography, population, living standards, employment, consumer prices, business, production, external transactions, finance and budget in France

France, Social Portrait — **Language:** French **Frequency:** annual **Content:** contains detailed social data on the French population

Les Comptes de l'Agriculture *(Agriculture Accounts)* — **Language:** French **Frequency:** annual **Content:** statistical portrait of the French agricultural sector

Les Comptes du Commerce *(Retail Industry Accounts)* — **Language:** French **Frequency:** annual **Content:** results of annual survey of retail trade activities in France

Les Entreprises du Commerce *(Retailing Companies)* — **Language:** French **Frequency:** annual **Content:** results of survey of retail establishments and enterprises

Les Industries Agro-Alimentaires *(Food Industries)* — **Language:** French **Frequency:** annual **Content:** annual statistics on French agriculture and food industries

Tableaux de l'Economie Française *(French Economy Table)* — **Language:** French **Frequency:** annual **Content:** double page format of 80 tables plus commentary and explanation of technical terms, intended to make figures on the main aspects of the economy easily accessible

International Fertilizer Institute

Address: 28 rue Marbeuf, Paris, 75008
Telephone: +33 1 5393 0500
Fax: +33 1 5393 0545
E-mail: ifa@fertilizer.org
Website: www.fertilizer.org

Guides: gives access to database which contains more than 1,300 IFA publications covering all aspects of fertilizer use, manufacture and trade
Activity: main activity is to provide information about the industry worldwide, especially through conferences and meetings of various kinds in different regions, and the exchange of non-commercial information in the form of statistics and publications

Website(s) information:

International Fertilizer Institute Statistics — **url:** www.fertilizer.org **Description:** news and information on fertilisers **Coverage:** statistics on production, imports, exports and consumption of nitrogen, phosphate and potash fertilisers by country. Also includes Fertiliser Indicators, a collection of graphs and diagrams illustrating the development in different regions of the world of the capacities, production, consumption and trade of nitrogen, phosphate and potash fertilisers, and certain important intermediates and raw materials. The development of world cereal production and stocks and the crops on which fertilisers are used, is also illustrated

Publication(s):

Environmental Aspects of Phosphate and Potash Mining — **Language:** English **Content:** completes a series that looks at environmental aspects of the fertilizer industry throughout the life-cycle of mineral fertilizer products

Le ministère délégué au Tourisme
Ministry of Tourism

Address: Grande-Arche de la Défense, Paris, 92055
Telephone: +33 1 4081 2122
Fax: +33 1 4081 1178
Website: www.tourisme.gouv.fr

Guides: provides statistical data and reports on tourism in France

Activity: promotes and represents the tourism sector

Publication(s):
Tourisme et innovation- bilan et perspectives *(Tourism and Innovation- Report and Perspectives)* — **Language:** French **Content:** provides information on innovation in the tourist sector regarding new technologies

L'Institut français de l'environnement
French Institute of Environment

Address: 5 route d'Olivet, Orleans Cedex 2
Telephone: +33 2 3879 7878
Fax: +33 2 3879 7870
E-mail: ifen@ifen.fr
Website: www.ifen.fr

Activity: organises and collects data on natural risks and technological innovations; collaborates with the administration to implement necessary elements to the constitution of environmental information; implements national, European and international programmes; provides statistical data on the environment

Website(s) information:
L'Institut français de l'environnement *(French Institute of Environment)* — **url:** www.ifen.fr **Coverage:** quality of air and water, evolution of biodiversity, greenhouse gas transmissions, protection of the environment

Publication(s):
Activity Report — **Language:** French **Frequency:** annual **Content:** provides annual review from the activities of institutions, the most important environmental events and publications

Le 4 pages de l'Ifen *(The Four Pages of Ifen)* — **Language:** French **Frequency:** monthly **Content:** provides information on energy consumption and the greenhouse effect

Les dossiers de l'Ifen *(Information of Ifen)* — **Language:** French **Frequency:** monthly **Content:** analytical and technical data and news on principal environmental subjects

Ministère de l'Agriculture et de la Pêche
Ministry of Agriculture and Fisheries

Address: 78 rue de Varenne, Paris 07 SP, 75349
Telephone: +33 14 955 4955
E-mail: communication@agriculture.gouv.fr
Website: www.agriculture.gouv.fr

Guides: provides information bulletins, various reports related to the agricultural industry

Activity: monitors the quality and sanitary security of food; preservation of the environment and natural space, responsibility for agricultural teaching, economic development of agricultural sectors and agro-industrials in France and within the EU, development of employment

Website(s) information:
Ministère de l'Agriculture et de la Pêche *(Ministry of Agriculture and Fisheries)* — **url:** www.agriculture.gouv.fr **Description:** general statistics on French agricultural and fishing activities: yields and production of various sectors; livestock; labour; forestry; import and export trade figures; agricultural census; and key figures **Coverage:** provides statistical information on agricultural products

Publication(s):
La PAC : un Modèle Équilibré à Mieux Comprendre *(Understanding of Better Models)* — **Language:** French **Content:** presents nine topics related to the EU, also provides information on the French environment, and quality and security of food

Ministère de l'Économie, des Finances et de l'Industrie
Ministry of the Economy, Finances and Industry

Address: 139 rue de Bercy, Paris Cedex 12, 75572
Telephone: +33 1 4004 0404
Fax: +33 1 5318 3640
E-mail: francetresor@oat.fiances.gouv.fr
Website: www.minefi.gouv.fr

Guides: provides up-to-date information on the financial market and current events; provides reports and statistics, incorporates a Euro Info Centre

Activity: determines fiscal policy and budgetary issues

Website(s) information:
Ministère de l'Économie, des Finances et de l'Industrie *(Ministry of the Economy, Finances and Industry)* — **url:** www.minefi.gouv.fr **Coverage:** provides indexes on consumption prices, inflation

Publication(s):
Bulletin officiel de la Concurrence, de la Consommation et de la Répression des fraudes *(Official Bulletin of Competition, Consumption and the Repression of Fraud)* — **Language:** French

Georgia

Georgian - European Policy and Legal Advice Center (GEPLAC)
Address: 3a Chitadze Street, Tbilisi, 0108
Telephone: +995 32 921 371
Fax: +995 32 931 716
E-mail: office@geplac.ge
Website: www.geplac.org

Activity: to support the legal reform process and economic reform policy

Website(s) information:
Georgian - European Policy and Legal Advice Center (GEPLAC) — **url:** www.geplac.org **Coverage:** Georgian law and economic development review and legal inventory

Publication(s):
Georgian Economic Trends — **Language:** Georgian/English **Frequency:** quarterly **Content:** national accounts and main trends including agriculture & food processing, production, infrastructure, investment. Also covers government finance, money & finance, international trade, privatisation and employment **Edition:** 2006

Ministry of Economic Development of Georgia
Address: 12 Chanturia Street, Tbilisi, 0108
Telephone: +995 32 996 996
Fax: +995 32 921 845
E-mail: ministry@econom.ge
Website: www.economy.ge

Guides: data available in Georgian and English on their website

Activity: to ensure sustainable economic development based on stable macroeconomic policy and private entrepreneurship development (incorporates Department of Tourism & Resorts; Department of Highways of Georgia; Department of Statistics; State Procurement Agency; Georgian National Investment Agency; Enterprises Management Agency)

Ministry of Energy of Georgia
Address: 10 Lermontov Street, Tbilisi, 1079
Telephone: +995 32 983 194
Fax: +995 32 983 194
Website: www.minenergy.gov.ge

Activity: analyses electricity demand industrial, residential and commercial customers, to achieve economic independence and stability of the power sector and to ensure security (technical, economic and political) by means of the maximum possible utilization of the power sector resources and diversification of the import sources

Website(s) information:
Ministry of Energy of Georgia — url: www.minenergy.gov.ge **Coverage:** energy
statistics and forecasts; key players in the energy sector; energy
legislation

Publication(s):
Investment Opportunities in the Energy Sector of Georgia — **Language:** English
Content: main facts and latest developments; market structure and
legal framework; privatisation and construction **Edition:** 2006

Natural Gas Strategy for Georgia — **Language:** English **Content:** analysis and
proposals; economic and geopolitical context **Edition:** 2006

Ministry of Finance of Georgia
Address: 70 Abashidze Street, Tbilisi
Telephone: +995 32 235 013
Fax: +995 32 235 013
E-mail: finabx@mof.ge
Website: www.mof.ge

Activity: central government (state administration) institution in the field of
economic policy

Website(s) information:
Ministry of Finance of Georgia — url: www.mof.ge **Description:** provides
information on the Ministry and its working areas; publications are
available online on a free basis as well as all the current data
concerning Georgia's economic development **Coverage:** statistical
data on various economic indicators; state budget analysis

Publication(s):
Daily Bulletin — **Language:** Georgian/English **Frequency:** daily **Content:**
statistical publications on governmental finances

National Bank of Georgia
Address: 3/5 Leonidze St, Tbilisi, 380005
Telephone: +995 32 996 505
Fax: +995 32 999 885
Website: www.nbg.gov.ge

Publication(s):
Banki — **Frequency:** monthly **Content:** financial news and analysis

State Department of Statistics, Georgia
Address: 4 Gamsakhurdia Avenue, Tbilisi, 1085
Telephone: +995 32 331 450
Fax: +995 32 932 414
E-mail: info@statistics.gov.ge
Website: www.statistics.ge

Guides: collates and publish statistical information on the demographic, social
and economic status of the country
Activity: national statistics office

Website(s) information:
State Department of Statistics, Georgia — url: www.statistics.ge **Description:**
provides information about the Statistics Office and its activities;
provides access to up-to-date statistics online **Coverage:** up-to date
statistical data available online in English language on main
demographic, socio-economic, industry sector indexes

Publication(s):
Agriculture in Georgia — **Language:** Georgian **Frequency:** annual **Content:**
statistical collection contains information on rural population and its
employment, data on the share of agriculture in GDP, output of this
branch of economy, physical volume indices and other indicators,
that describe the real state of agriculture in 1985-2004

Households of Georgia — **Language:** Georgian **Frequency:** irregular **Content:**
general survey of households in Georgia

Labour Market in Georgia — **Language:** Georgian **Frequency:** irregular
Content: trends in Georgia's labour market from 2003-2005

Quarterly Statistical Bulletin — **Language:** Georgian **Frequency:** quarterly
Content: contains socio-economic and financial data

Statistical Yearbook of Georgia — **Language:** Georgian **Frequency:** annual
Content: consists of data on population, labour, income,
expenditure and consumption of households; education, science and
culture; public health and social security; natural resources and
environment; national accounts, business activities, prices

United Nations Information Centre
Address: UN House, 9 Eristavi Street, Tbilisi, 0179
Telephone: +995 32 25 1126/28/31
Fax: +995 32 25 02 71/2
E-mail: registry.ge@undp.org
Website: www.undp.org.ge

Guides: available online
Activity: UNDP along with the Georgian government has identified several areas
for targeted assistance. The projects are pro-poor, pro-women,
and environmentally sustainable

Website(s) information:
United Nations Development Programme — url: www.undp.org.ge **Coverage:**
information on human rights, labour force, social security issues

Publication(s):
Millenium Development Goals in Georgia — **Language:** English **Content:** Targets
and goals till 2015 **Edition:** 2004

National Human Development Report Georgia — **Language:** English **Frequency:**
irregular

Problems and Prospects of Agriculture and Rural Development in Georgia —
Language: English **Edition:** 1997

Germany

Bundesministerium der Finanzen (BMF)
Ministry of Finance
Address: Wilhelmstraße 97, Berlin, 11016
Telephone: +49 30 186820
Fax: +49 30 186824248
E-mail: Poststelle@bmf.bund.de
Website: www.bundesfinanzministerium.de

Guides: database of publications
Activity: shaping of financial and economic policy in Germany

Website(s) information:
Bundesministerium der Finanzen (Ministry of Finance) — url:
www.bundesfinanzministerium.de **Coverage:** research reports on
the latest trends in German public finances; overall recent economic
evolution, and outlook for the development of major economic
indicators

Publication(s):
Monatsbericht der BMF (Monthly Report of the BMF) — **Language:** German
Frequency: monthly **Content:** monthly update on new legislation
and policy

Bundesministerium für Ernährung, Landwirtschaft und Verbraucherschutz (BMELV)
Federal Ministry of Food, Agriculture and Consumer Protection
Address: Postfach 11055, Wilhelmstraße 54, Berlin, 10117
Telephone: +49 30 2006 0
Fax: +49 30 2006 4262
E-mail: poststelle@bmvel.bund.de
Website: www.bmelv.de

Guides: The Agrarpolitischer Bericht is supplemented by the
Buchführungsergebnisse der Testbetriebe in which the economic
data of over 7000 representative agricultural companies is
demonstrated.
Blickpunkt Welternährung can be downloaded from the website
whenever a report is issued. The recipients of printed versions are
issued with a report every six weeks

Website(s) information:

Bundesministerium für Ernährung, Landwirtschaft und Verbraucherschutz (BMELV) — url: www.bmelv-forschung.de **Coverage:** analysis of the implications of recent research and scientific findings on agriculture in Germany and the rest of Europe

Bundesministerium für Ernährung, Landwirtschaft und Verbraucherschutz (BMELV) (Federal Ministry of Food, Agriculture and Consumer Protection) — url: www.bmelv.de **Coverage:** statistics and analysis of the agricultural sector in Germany including data on: horticulture and viniculture national production; agricultural labour force; forestry and forestry related industries; agricultural export trade; and EU agricultural policy

Publication(s):

Agrarpolitischer Bericht (Agricultural Politics Report) — **Language:** German **Frequency:** annual **Content:** includes goals of national agricultural politics, the state of agricultural economics, agricultural and nutritional policy measures, financing of agricultural measures

Berichte über Landwirtschaft (Report on Agriculture) — **Language:** German/English **Frequency:** 3 per annum **Content:** publications on current issues of agricultural politics and science in Germany and the rest of Europe **Edition:** 83

Blickpunkt Welternährung (Focus on World Feeding) — **Language:** German **Frequency:** irregular **Content:** current topics related to international food and agricultural organisations, world feeding and sustainable development

Forschungs Report (Research Report) — **Language:** German **Frequency:** 2 per annum **Content:** reports on current issues of agricultural science which can be used as policy issues on food, agriculture and consumer protection

Statistisches Bundesamt Deutschland
Federal Statistical Office of Germany

Address: Statistisches Bundesamt, Statistischer Informationsservice, Gustav-Stresemann-Ring 11, Wiesbaden, 65189
Telephone: +49 611 752 405
Fax: +49 611 753 330
E-mail: info@destatis.de
Website: www.destatis.de

Guides: library open 9.00-15.00 Monday to Thursday and on Friday 9.00-14.00. Each region has a statistical office, and publishes results for smaller statistical units. Further details of individual titles are given in the Gesamtverzeichnis Statistischer Berichte der Statistischen Landesämter (general list of statistical reports of the regional statistical offices), available free of charge from the regional statistical offices.
The Statistical Office also publishes subject-matter related series including publications on prices, the population, energy and environment, education, the labour market, information society, culture, justice and transport in Germany

Website(s) information:

Genesis Online - Das Statistische Informationssystem (Federal Statistical Office Germany) — url: www-genesis.destatis.de **Description:** information database from all areas of official statistics. Access to Genesis-online requires registration. Registration as a guest is possible **Coverage:** focuses are on data from population statistics, employment statistics, education and transport statistics, price statistics, foreign trade statistics and national accounts

Statistisches Bundesamt Deutschland (Federal Statistical Office of Germany) — url: www.destatis.de **Description:** offers information on the Statistisches Bundesamt main products and services: list of major titles and online publications; compilation of press releases; scientific forum; and up-to-date statistical data on the country **Coverage:** includes free online statistics on Germany, covering different socio-economic and financial indicators for the last three years (period coverage may vary according to indicator/topic in question). Also offers basic key data, in the areas of: geography and climate; population and demographics; employment and salaries; finance; social security; industry and agriculture; domestic and foreign trade, etc. Tends to concentrate on data on latest economic indicators, covering: labour market; foreign trade; money and banking; national accounts; industrial production; tourism; etc

Statistisches Bundesamt Online Publications — url: www-ec.destatis.de **Description:** offers Statistisches Bundesamt publications which are downloadable online **Coverage:** offers Statistisches Bundesamt publications which are downloadable online. Data covered include: population; employment; education; environment; economy; foreign trade; prices; income and expenditure

Publication(s):

Bevölkerungsstruktur und Wirtschaftskraft der Bundesländer (Population Structure and Economic Resources of the Länder) — **Language:** German **Frequency:** biennial **Content:** publication containing selected numerical data from all spheres of official statistics. Its essential part is demographic and economic data

Datenreport (Data Report) — **Language:** German **Frequency:** biennial **Content:** publication containing a compilation of current data of official statistics and new results of survey and social research

Die Bundesländer: Strukturen und Entwicklungen (The Länder: Structures and Trends) — **Language:** German **Content:** publication presenting the economic and social situation of the Länder

Statistisches Jahrbuch für das Ausland (Statistical Yearbook for Foreign Countries) — **Language:** German **Frequency:** annual **Content:** statistical yearbook containing information on structures and trends of most countries of the world

Statistisches Jahrbuch für die Bundesrepublik Deutschland (Statistical Yearbook of Germany) — **Language:** German **Frequency:** annual **Content:** statistical yearbook giving data on latest trends in Germany's social, economic and cultural life

Wirtschaft und Statistik (Economy and Statistics) — **Language:** German **Frequency:** monthly **Content:** monthly compilation of latest national economic and social statistics

Zahlenkompass - Statistisches Taschenbuch für Deutschland (Zahlenkompass - Key Statistical Data on Germany) — **Language:** German **Frequency:** annual **Content:** handbook containing current benchmark data on all areas of German society

Greece

Bank of Greece

Address: PO Box 3105, 21 Eleftheriou Venizelos Avenue, Athens, 102 50
Telephone: +30 210 320 1111
Fax: +30 210 323 2239
E-mail: secretariat@bankofgreece.gr
Website: www.bankofgreece.gr

Guides: the bank publishes an annual report and two monetary policy reports; it also publishes economic and statistical bulletins; the special studies division publishes working papers

Activity: monitoring and analysing economic developments

Publication(s):

Annual Report — **Language:** Greek/English **Frequency:** annual **Content:** information on the Greek economy: developments, policies and prospects

Economic Bulletin — **Language:** English/Greek **Frequency:** bi-annually **Content:** specific topics on Greek economy; includes reports on external financing, growth, and capital structure of companies

Monetary Policy — **Language:** English/Greek **Frequency:** bi-annually **Content:** monetary policy and monetary policy interim reports examine the international economic environment and discuss economic developments, in the Euro area and Greece

Statistical Bulletins — **Language:** English/Greek **Content:** monthly statistical bulletin and a bulletin of regional combined indicators for Macedonia-Thrace which deal with economic indicators

General Secretariat of National Statistical Service of Greece

Address: 46 Pireos & Eponiton Street, Piraeus, 185 10
Telephone: +30 210 4852313 5
Fax: +30 210 4852819
E-mail: nfo@statistics.gr
Website: www.statistics.gr

Guides: publications can be referred to in the library, 09:00-13:00 from Monday to Friday; information on the availability of material can be accessed in the online catalogue

Activity: designs, collects and processes data from studies, censuses and statistical surveys and presents the data in statistical publications

Website(s) information:

National Statistical Service of Greece (NSSG) — **url:** www.statistics.gr **Coverage:** data on socio-economic topics covering: demography, the labour market, national accounts, trade and services, the primary and secondary (industry) sectors

Publication(s):

Concise Statistical Yearbook — **Language:** Greek/English **Frequency:** irregular **Content:** statistical publication on socio-economic indicators of Greece

Monthly Statistical Bulletin — **Language:** Greek/English **Frequency:** monthly **Content:** monthly statistical data covering a wide variety of topics, including: population; employment; labour; salaries and wages; public health; agriculture and fishing; industry; energy; trade; transports and communications; tourism; public finance; prices; and money and banking

Statistical Year Book of Greece — **Language:** Greek/English **Frequency:** annual **Content:** general demographic, economic and social statistics on Greece

---

Hellenic Marine Environment Protection Association (HELMEPA)

Address: 5, Pergamou Str., Nea Smirni, Athens, 17121
Telephone: +30 210 9343088
Fax: +30 210 9353847
E-mail: helmepa@helmepa.gr
Website: www.helmepa.gr

Guides: an annual report is available as well as information on training

Activity: to eliminate ship-generated marine pollution and enhance safety at sea

Publication(s):

Annual Report — **Language:** Greek/English **Frequency:** annual **Content:** report on the activities of the organisation as well as on education in the field

---

Hellenic Organisation for Standardisation (ELOT)

Address: Acharnon 313, Athens, 111 45
Telephone: +30 210 2120100
Fax: +30 210 228 30 34
E-mail: elotinfo@elot.gr
Website: www.elot.gr

Guides: publishes catalogues on standardisation in Greek and English

Activity: elaborates Hellenic national standards
maintains a central point for testing of materials, assesses management systems and certifies products and services, provides public or on site training and technical information

---

Ministry of Economy and Finance

Address: 5 Nikis Street, Syntagma Square, Athens, 101 80
Telephone: +30 210 3332492
Fax: +30 210 3332499
E-mail: generalsecra@mnec.gr
Website: www.mof-glk.gr

Guides: summaries of the budget, reports and studies, public debt bulletins

Activity: responsible for the budget of Greece

Publication(s):

Public Debt Bulletin — **Language:** English/Greek **Frequency:** quarterly **Content:** graphs on Greek interest rate and inflation; charts on Government securities and bonds, etc

---

National Organization for Medicines

Address: 284 Messogion Av., Athens, 155 62
Telephone: +30 210 6507200
Fax: +30 210 6545535
E-mail: relation@eof.gr
Website: www.eof.gr

Activity: ensures public health and safety with regard to medicinal products for human and veterinary use, medicated animal foods and food additives, foodstuffs intended for particular nutritional uses and food supplements, biocides, medical devices, cosmetics

---

Hungary

Gazdasagi es Kozlekedesi Miniszterium

Ministry of Economy and Transport

Address: V. Honvéd utca 13-15, Budapest, 1055
Telephone: +36 1 374 2700
E-mail: ugyfelszolgalat@gkm.gov.hu
Website: www.ikm.iif.hu

Activity: supports foreign investments, focusing on developing the transport infrastructure, facilitating the spread of information technology, encouraging research and development and strengthening micro, small and medium-sized enterprises

Website(s) information:

Gazdasagi es Kozlekedesi Miniszterium (Ministry of Economy and Transport) — **url:** http://en.gkm.gov.hu/ **Coverage:** economic policy; foreign economic affairs (foreign trade); investment promotion; retail industry and energy; infrastructure

Publication(s):

Hungarian Economy — **Language:** English **Frequency:** annual **Content:** Hungarian economic policy, economic trends, external economy, business

---

Kozponti Statisztikal Hivatal

Hungarian Central Statistical Office

Address: Keleti Károly u. 5-7, Budapest, 1024
Telephone: +36 1 345 6000
Fax: +36 1 345 6788
E-mail: erzsebet.veto@office.ksh.hu
Website: http://portal.ksh.hu/

Activity: designing and conducting surveys, recording, processing and storing data, data analyses and dissemination, protection of individual data. Provides data for the parliament and public administration, social organisations, local authorities, scientific bodies, economic organisations, the general public and the media as well as for international organisations and users abroad. Official data regarding the socio-economic situation as well as the changes in the population of the country are published by the HCSO

Website(s) information:

Kozponti Statisztikal Hivatal (Hungarian Central Statistical Office) — **url:** http://portal.ksh.hu/ **Description:** general information on library and documentation services; professional and scientific institutes; catalogue of publications; news and press releases; and access to series of databases and online statistics **Coverage:** different sections provide statistics on Hungary, including "Hungary in Figures", "Major Annual Figures" and "Agricultural Census". Major Annual Figures section provides data in more detail, covering different socio-economic topics for the last ten years (period coverage varies according to indicator/sector in question). Includes statistics on: population and labour force; earnings, household incomes, consumption and savings; health and education; culture; annual GDP by industry sector; agriculture, industry and construction; investment and finances; external trade; tourism; transports and communications; and balance of energy

Publication(s):

Cestat Statistical Bulletin — **Language:** English/Hungarian **Frequency:** quarterly **Content:** basic economic data in monthly and quarterly time series and annual national economic indicators

Change of Course in Hungary 1990-2004 — **Language:** English **Frequency:** annual **Content:** presents economic and social processes in Hungary between the change of regime and the accession to the European Union **Edition:** 2006

Consumer Price Indices — **Language:** English/Hungarian **Frequency:** annual **Content:** development of consumer prices and price levels **Edition:** 2002

Cultural Statistical Data of Hungary — **Language:** English/Hungarian **Frequency:** annual **Content:** cultural statistics from 1991. The main topics are the following: book production, libraries, cultural institutes, mass communication, theatres, museums, cinemas and film production

---

Demographic Yearbook — **Language:** English/Hungarian **Frequency:** annual **Content:** population structure and latest demographic trends in Hungary **Edition:** 2005

Environmental Statistical Yearbook of Hungary — **Language:** English/Hungarian **Frequency:** annual **Content:** analyses environmental-economic processes. The main topics are the following: land; mineral resources; energy; water resources; water uses; forestry; emissions of air pollutants; waste water discharge; waste; noise; soil, ambient air quality; water quality; wildlife; environmental health; urban (built) environment; nature conservation; environment industry; environmental protection expenditure; environmental taxes

Foreign Direct Investment in Hungary — **Language:** English/Hungarian **Frequency:** annual **Content:** foreign capital based on its originating country, sectoral and regional development

Monthly Bulletin of Statistics — **Language:** English/Hungarian **Frequency:** monthly **Content:** summarising analyses on most recent economic developments and trends evolving in the course of year concerned

National Accounts Hungary — **Language:** English/Hungarian **Frequency:** annual **Content:** macroeconomic statistics including statistical indicators. Economic cycle of production; income distribution; consumption and capital formation. Data on production and income by institutional sectors and industries; per capita GDP figures in international comparison; gross national income (GNI); income and consumption of households **Edition:** 2006

Population Trends in the East-Central-European Capitals — **Language:** English/Hungarian **Frequency:** irregular **Content:** the analysis deals primarily with the period between 1990 and 2003; main subject matters are the following: changes of the population number and their causes; fertility trends; migration trends; ageing process of the population; households and family types **Edition:** 2005

Population Trends in the East-Central-European Capitals — **Language:** English/Hungarian **Frequency:** annual **Content:** concentrates on East-Central-Europe and analyses the demographic trends of capitals. Main subject matters are: changes of the population number and their causes; fertility trends; migration trends; ageing process of the population; households and family types **Edition:** 2005

Productivity and Competitiveness of the Hungarian Economy — **Language:** English/Hungarian **Frequency:** annual **Content:** publication on productivity disseminated in recent years. Per employee GDP and per hour GDP presented as a productivity measure

Public Utilities — **Language:** English/Hungarian **Frequency:** annual **Content:** provides information on the status of energy supply; public water supply and sewerage; on municipal services (urban green areas; street cleaning; municipal solid waste and liquid waste treatment) and on the length and area of urban roads **Edition:** 2006

Regional Data of Education — **Language:** English/Hungarian **Frequency:** annual **Content:** modified regional data on education and training. Statistical data of the pre-primary level to the post secondary education are included by regions according to new methodology. English tables and summary are supplemented.

Regional Statistical Yearbook — **Language:** English/Hungarian **Frequency:** annual **Content:** data collection on the economic and social conditions in Hungary broken down by territorial units

Research and Development — **Language:** English/Hungarian **Frequency:** annual **Content:** main data of organisations having research and development activities. The number of research personnel by gender and educational attainment sum of expenditure on R&D by financial sources, separated capital expenditure in different sectors of R&D, by legal form of organizations, industries and by branch, sector of science; shows results of R&D activities; main data are detailed by regions **Edition:** 2006

Small and Medium-sized Enterprises and Entrepreneurship — **Language:** English/Hungarian **Frequency:** annual **Content:** provides a comprehensive picture on SMEs and entrepreneurship in the Hungarian economy in international perspective **Edition:** 2006

Statistical Yearbook of Agriculture — **Language:** English/ Hungarian **Frequency:** annual **Content:** status of the agricultural sector. It presents the share of this sector within the national economy and provides data on employment of the agriculture and food-industry, on production, exports, imports and consumption **Edition:** 2005

Statistical Yearbook of External Trade — **Language:** English/Hungarian **Frequency:** annual **Content:** tables demonstrate the foreign trade activity of Hungary **Edition:** 2006

Statistical Yearbook of Hungary — **Language:** English/Hungarian **Frequency:** annual **Content:** annual statistics on major socio-economic indicators **Edition:** 2004

Vineyards in Hungary — **Language:** English/Hungarian **Frequency:** annual **Content:** information on the vineyards located on the 2172 settlements in Hungary. Regional, additionally NUTS 3 and 4 level data on the distribution of the vineyards by age, varieties, size and shortage of vine-stocks

Yearbook of Household Statistics — **Language:** Hungarian/English **Frequency:** annual **Content:** a voluntary data collection based on one month diary keeping period of the responding households and an interview about their incomes and greater purchases at the end of the year **Edition:** 2006

Yearbook of Industrial and Construction Statistics — **Language:** English/Hungarian **Frequency:** annual **Content:** publishes data deriving form the industrial and construction surveys and other special statistics; contains detailed data of industrial products and services **Edition:** 2005

Yearbook of Tourism — **Language:** English/Hungarian **Frequency:** annual **Content:** statistical analysis of the tourism industry in Hungary **Edition:** 2005

Magyar Nemzeti Bank
National Bank of Hungary

Address: Szabadság tér 8/9, Budapest, 1850
Telephone: +36 1 428 2600
Fax: +36 1 428 2500
Website: www.mnb.hu

Guides: publications available online. Occasional papers available through the Library free of charge

Activity: central bank
European monetary policy; achieving financial stability; issuing of notes and coins; research library; influencing and setting exchange rates and interest rates; services to the state, financial sector and the public

Website(s) information:
Magyar Nemzeti Bank (National Bank of Hungary) — **url:** www.mnb.hu
Description: provides both information on the Bank's main activities and services, and an in-depth portrait of latest developments in the Hungarian economy and banking system. Access is provided in both English and Hungarian to the Bank's main publications, such as the "Annual Report", the "Monthly Report", and the "Quarterly Report on Inflation" **Coverage:** online titles such as the monthly updated economic reports cover a wide range of economic and financial topics, providing data on: GDP growth; consumer price index; inflation; industrial output; employment and unemployment; monthly gross earnings; monetary conditions and developments; money and capital markets; financial savings; balance of payments and external trade; and government lending and borrowing

Publication(s):
Annual Report — **Language:** English/Hungarian **Frequency:** annual **Content:** business report and financial statements of the Bank; information on the recent economic and financial developments including interest rates changes and monetary developments; financial achievements over the year **Edition:** 2006

External Accounts Statistics Hungary — **Language:** English/Hungarian **Frequency:** annual **Content:** presents country specific details of the balance of payments and international investment position

Hungarian Banking Sector — **Language:** English **Frequency:** 2 p.a. **Content:** overview of the Hungarian banking system: size and increase of the market, and changes in banking rates and bank's risks

Monetary Policy in Hungary — **Language:** English/Hungarian **Frequency:** irregular **Content:** presents an overview of the monetary policy of the National Bank of Hungary

Occasional Papers — **Language:** English or Hungarian **Frequency:** irregular **Content:** they contain the results of analysis and research work conducted at the NBH. Their purpose is to encourage readers to present their comments, which may be useful for the authors in further research.
Many issues of the NBH Working Papers are published in English/Hungarian, some of them are available only in Hungarian or in English

Report on Convergence — **Language:** English/Hungarian **Frequency:** annual **Content:** overview of the central bank's position regarding the current state of convergence and the challenges expected in the near future. Contains analysis on price stability, long-term interest rates and other factors of convergence **Edition:** 2005

Report on Financial Stability — **Language:** English/Hungarian **Frequency:** annual **Content:** it focuses on the analysis of long-term trends and the foreseeable evaluation of risks. Informs stakeholders on the topical issues related to financial stability; reviews risks which pose a threat to financial stability and identifies the components and trends which increase the vulnerability of the financial system **Edition:** 2006

Report on Inflation — **Language:** English/Hungarian **Frequency:** 2 per annum **Content:** it presents forecasts for the retail price index, underlying inflation, components of GDP and full analyses and forecasts for the financial market, and macro-economic and balance processes; twice a year partial updates of the forecasts are also prepared **Edition:** 2006

Iceland

Statistics Iceland

Address: Borgartúni 21a, Reykjavík, 150
Telephone: +354 528 1000
Fax: +354 528 1099
E-mail: information@statice.is
Website: www.statice.is

Guides: most data is downloadable from the website www.statice.is

Activity: to collect and publish socio-economic statistics on Iceland

Website(s) information:

Statistics Iceland — **url:** www.statice.is **Description:** provides a wide range of online socio-economic statistics, searchable by mulitple indicators and years **Coverage:** provides a wide range of online socio-economic statistics

Publication(s):

Agriculture — **Language:** English **Frequency:** annual **Content:** contains data on fertilisers, livestock and field crops, production and hunting

Culture — **Language:** English **Frequency:** annual **Content:** contains data on advertising, books and libraries, newspapers and periodicals, sound recordings, cinemas, videos, broadcasting, arts and museums

Education — **Language:** English **Frequency:** annual **Content:** contains data on pre-primary institutions, compulsory schools, upper secondary schools and universities

Elections — **Language:** English **Frequency:** annual **Content:** contains data on general, local government and presidential elections

Enterprises and Turnover — **Language:** English **Frequency:** annual **Content:** contains data on enterprises, insolvencies, turnover and financial accounts by industry

External Trade — **Language:** English **Frequency:** annual **Content:** contains data on balance of trade, exports and imports

Fisheries — **Language:** English **Frequency:** annual **Content:** contains data on monthly updates, catch and value, fish processing, imports and exports, fishing vessels, fish products, price indices and financial accounts for the fishing industry

Geography and Environment — **Language:** English **Frequency:** annual **Content:** contains data on geographical areas, temperature and precipitation, gas emissions and waste

Health, Social Affairs and Justice — **Language:** English **Frequency:** annual **Content:** contains data on lifestyle, health services, social protection expenditure, social insurances, municipal social services, courts, prisons and prisoners

Manufacturing and Energy — **Language:** English **Frequency:** annual **Content:** contains data on producer price index, manufacturing, construction and energy

Money and Credit — **Language:** English **Frequency:** annual **Content:** contains data on banking, currencies, stocks, loans and investment credit funds

National Accounts and Public Finance — **Language:** English **Frequency:** annual **Content:** contains data on consumption expenditure, public finances, gross fixed capital formation, production approach and short term indicators

Population — **Language:** English **Frequency:** annual **Content:** contains data on migration, municipalities, citizenship, demography, marriages and divorces, religion and names

Prices and Consumption — **Language:** English **Frequency:** annual **Content:** contains data on the consumer price index, building cost index, wage index, purchasing power parity, consumption and producer price index

Statistical Yearbook of Iceland — **Language:** English **Frequency:** annual **Content:** contains an overview of statistical information in a number of economic and social fields

Tourism, Transport and Information Technology — **Language:** English **Frequency:** annual **Content:** contains data on tourist industry, accommodations, passengers, aviation, ships, vehicles, telecommunication, postal service and IT

Wages, Income, and Labour Market — **Language:** English **Frequency:** annual **Content:** contains data on wages, income and labour market by occupation, gender, age and sector

Ireland

Central Bank of Ireland

Address: PO Box 559, Dame Street, Dublin, 2
Telephone: +353 1 434 4000/671 6666
Fax: +353 1 671 6561
E-mail: enquiries@centralbank.ie
Website: www.centralbank.ie

Guides: publishes annual reports in English and Gaelic

Activity: has responsibility for monetary policy functions, financial stability, economic analysis, currency and payment systems, investment of foreign and domestic assets and the provision of central services

Website(s) information:

Central Bank of Ireland — **url:** www.centralbank.ie **Description:** provides full information about its activities, information on the basic tasks of monetary policy and its implementation, monetary policy operations, credit institutions supervision activities and other responsibilities established by the legislation as well as information on the national macroeconomic situation, such as analysis of the developments in the national economy and financial markets, and on the financial position of the Bank; The Bank publishes annual reports, monthly and quarterly bulletins where it presents information about its activities as well as a wide range of financial and macroeconomic information **Coverage:** the "Statistics" section offers key exchange rates, euro interest rates, and the latest credit, money, and banking statistics

Publication(s):

Annual Reports — **Language:** English/Gaelic **Frequency:** annual **Content:** global economic development features review of the economy of Ireland; exchange rate and monetary policy; interest rates; foreign reserve management; cash management; payment and securities settlement systems; annual financial statements of the Bank

Financial Stability Report — **Language:** English **Frequency:** annual **Content:** involves monitoring both domestic and international financial developments and highlighting potential areas of concern relevant to the Irish financial system

Monthly Statistics — **Language:** English **Frequency:** monthly **Content:** statistical data on government finances

Quarterly Bulletin — **Language:** English **Frequency:** quarterly **Content:** quarterly analysis of latest developments in the national economy and the banking sector, supported by economic and financial statistics and data

Central Statistics Office

Address: Skehard Road, Cork
Telephone: +353 21 453 5000
Fax: +353 21 453 5555
E-mail: information@cso.ie
Website: www.cso.ie

Guides: releases more than 100 publications; all available online from the year 1993 onward

Activity: national statistics office

Website(s) information:

Central Statistics Office — **url:** www.cso.ie **Description:** provides information on Ireland's Statistics Office, its activities, surveys and mythology; provides access to all its publications and new up-dates **Coverage:** monthly, quarterly and annual statistical data covering more than 25 topics including statistics, socio-economic development, infrastructure, transport, industry

Publication(s):

Agriculture and Fishing — **Language:** English **Frequency:** monthly **Content:** consists of data on area, yield and production; agricultural labour input; livestock surveys; output, input and income in agriculture; production prices

Balance of Payments — **Frequency:** annual **Content:** consists of data on balance of international payments; external debt; foreign direct investment; service exports and imports and other related indexes

Births Deaths and Marriages — **Language:** English **Frequency:** annual **Content:** statistical data on births, deaths; marriages by age

Census of Population — **Language:** English **Frequency:** annual **Content:** includes detailed statistics covering: population classified by area; ages and marital status; household composition and family units

EU Survey on Income and Living Conditions — **Language:** English **Frequency:** quarterly **Content:** comparisons of different indexes of living conditions in EU countries

Health and Social Conditions — **Language:** English **Frequency:** annual **Content:** consists of survey on income and living conditions disability update; pensions update; module on childcare; module on health

Housing and Households — **Language:** English **Frequency:** annual **Content:** consists of module on housing; planning permissions; data on construction and building

Information Society and Telecommunications — **Language:** English **Frequency:** annual **Content:** data on development of the IT sector and information society

National Employment Survey — **Language:** English **Frequency:** annual **Content:** consists of comparisons of hourly earnings of people working in different sectors of industry

National Household Survey Module on Educational Attainment — **Language:** English **Frequency:** quarterly **Content:** comparisons of changes in educational attainment

National Income and Expenditure — **Language:** English **Frequency:** quarterly **Content:** data on income, prices of products and services, savings

Prices — **Language:** English **Frequency:** quarterly **Content:** consists of wholesale price index; consumer price index; consumer prices: average price analysis - in Dublin and outside Dublin

Quarterly National Household Survey — **Language:** English **Frequency:** quarterly **Content:** data on different household indexes

Statistical Bulletin — **Language:** English **Frequency:** quarterly **Content:** statistical data on more than 25 topics; socio-economic and industry development

Statistical Yearbook of Ireland — **Language:** English **Frequency:** annual **Content:** statistical data on more than 25 topics

Tourism and Travel — **Language:** English **Frequency:** annual **Content:** consists of data on overseas travel; tourism and travel; household travel survey

Trade Statistics — **Language:** English **Frequency:** monthly **Content:** very detailed publication, including imports and exports classified by country for current month and year-to-date

Transport — **Language:** English **Frequency:** annual **Content:** data on vehicles in the country

Department of Finance

Address: Government Buildings, Upper Merrion Street, Dublin, 2
Telephone: +353 1 676 7571
Fax: +353 1 678 9936
E-mail: webmaster@finance.gov.ie
Website: www.irlgov.ie/finance

Guides: publish statistical information and government finance information
Activity: plays a central role in implementing Government policy, in particular the Programme for Government, and in advising and supporting the Minister for Finance and the Government on the economic and financial management of the State and the overall management and development of the public sector

Website(s) information:
Department of Finance — **url:** www.irlgov.ie/finance **Description:** information on economic and business climate, providing statistical data on socio-economic, banking and finance indicators; national budget and information about taxes is provided; offers economic forecasts **Coverage:** Economic Statistics in the "Finance and Economic Information" section provides data that covers public finances, EU transfers, economic output and growth, balance of payments, external trade, production, earnings, population, prices, employment, consumption and construction

Publication(s):

Economic Bulletins — **Language:** English **Frequency:** monthly **Content:** data on economic development, government and public finances and information and data on sartorial issues like housing, tourism and agriculture

Italy

Instituto Nazionale di Statistica (ISTAT)
National Institute of Statistics

Address: Via Cesare Balbo 16, Rome, 00184
Telephone: +39 06 46731
Fax: +39 06 4673 3107
E-mail: biblio@istat.it
Website: www.istat.it

Guides: Catalogo ISTAT (annual catalogue of publications with summaries of contents)
Activity: main supplier of official statistical information in Italy; collects and produces information on Italian economy and society and makes it available for study and decision-making purposes

Website(s) information:
Istituto Nazionale di Statistica (ISTAT) *(National Institute of Statistics)* — **url:** www.istat.it **Coverage:** statistics on GDP, consumer prices, production prices, industrial production, retail trades, employment and wages

Publication(s):
Annuario Statistico Italiano *(Italian Statistical Yearbook)* — **Language:** Italian **Frequency:** annual **Content:** annual statistical review of Italy's main socioeconomic and financial indicators

Bollettino Mensile di Statistica *(Monthly Statistical Bulletin)* — **Language:** Italian **Frequency:** monthly **Content:** statistics on population and people as well as economic indicators of Italy

I viaggi in Italia e all'estero *(Travelling in Italy and Abroad)* — **Language:** Italian **Frequency:** annual **Content:** travel statistics covering the movement of Italians within the country and trips abroad

Ministero delle Politiche Agricole Alimentari e Forestali
Ministry or Agriculture and Forestry

Address: Via XX Settembre, n. 20, Rome, 00187
Telephone: +39 06 46651
Fax: +39 06 4742314
Website: www.politicheagricole.it

Guides: publications can be downloaded
Activity: is responsible for conducting policy affairs in the field of agriculture and affiliated sectors in Italy

Website(s) information:
Agricoltura Italiana Online *(Italian Agriculture)* — **url:** www.agricolturaitalianaonline.gov.it **Coverage:** information on the different sectors of agriculture; includes statistics on production, occupation, consumption, and foreign trade

Ministero delle Politiche Agricole Alimentari e Forestali *(Ministry of Agriculture and Forestry)* — **url:** www.politicheagricole.it **Coverage:** documents on the development of agriculture in Italy and Europe

Publication(s):
Parametri ex_post 2006 relativi ai prodotti primavera/estate *(Parameter of 2006 Regarding Products of Spring/Summer)* — **Language:** Italian **Content:** information on the development of the country and infrastructure

Ministero dell'Economia e delle Finanze
Ministry of Economy and Finance

Address: Via Pastrengo 22, Rome
E-mail: pubblicazione.sito@tesoro.it
Website: www.mef.gov.it

Guides: publications can be found online; all are downloadable free of charge; includes some documents in English

Activity: responsible for the economic and fiscal development of Italy; regulates policy accordingly

Website(s) information:

Ministero dell'Economia e delle Finanze *(Ministry of Economy and Finance)* — **url:** www.mef.gov.it **Coverage:** information on the development of the economy of Italy; data on public and private finance

World Food Programme (WFP)

Address: Via C G Viola 68, Parco dei Medici, Rome, 00148
Telephone: +39 6 65131
Fax: +39 6 6513 2840
E-mail: wfpinfo@wfp.org
Website: www.wfp.org

Guides: IFPRI identifies and studies policies, which help developing countries meet their food needs. Under the 'Linking Research and Action' initiative, IFPRI and WFP have joined forces to produce a series of briefs studying the linkages between food policy research and food aid programming
Activity: WFP is the food aid arm of the United Nations system

Website(s) information:

World Food Programme (WFP) — **url:** www.wfp.org **Coverage:** Lists data on its operations, including expenditures, food shipments/deliveries, resources, transport and staff. Drawing on a variety of sources, including non-governmental organisations and other UN Agencies, WFP also compiles useful facts and figures on the general state of world hunger; this data covers malnutrition, child hunger, agricultural production and global food aid

Latvia

Latvijas Banka
Bank of Latvia

Address: K. Valdemara iela 2a, Riga, LV-1050
Telephone: +371 702 2300
Fax: +371 702 2420
E-mail: info@bank.lv
Website: www.bank.lv

Guides: publishes Bank's annual reports, the quarterly monetary reviews and Latvia's balance of payments, the monthly Monetary Bulletin and Latvia's Balance of Payments and the newspaper Averss un Reverss
Activity: to regulate currency in circulation by implementing monetary policy and to maintain price stability in Latvia

Website(s) information:

Bank of Latvia — **url:** www.bank.lv **Description:** Latvian monetary system; access to wide range of general macro-economic indicators, financial data, rules and regulations; access to publications available **Coverage:** current data available on banking and monetary statistics; payment systems' statistics; balance of payment statistics; external debt statistics; interest rate statistics; securities statistics

Publication(s):

Averss un Reverss — **Language:** Latvian **Frequency:** monthly **Content:** banking news

Finansu Stabilitates Parskats *(Financial Stability Report)* — **Language:** Latvian/English **Frequency:** annual **Content:** goal of the Report is to analyse and assess the performance of the Latvian financial system, paying particular attention to the banking sector and the operation of leasing companies

Latvijas Bankas gada parskats *(Annual Reports)* — **Language:** Latvian/English **Frequency:** annual **Content:** global economic development features; review of the economy of Latvia; exchange rate and monetary policy; interest rates; foreign reserve management; cash management; payment and securities settlement systems; annual financial statements of the Bank of Lithuania

Latvijas Maksajumu Bilance *(Latvian Balance of Payments)* — **Language:** Latvian/English **Frequency:** quarterly **Content:** summarises economic transactions of Latvia's residents with the ROW; also includes Latvia's international investment position and information on foreign investment stocks in Latvia broken down by activity and country

Latvijas Maksajumu Bilance (Pamatraditaji) *(Latvia's Balance of Payments (Key Items))* — **Language:** Latvian/English **Frequency:** monthly **Content:** monetary policy and to provide a general background of money market trends

Monetarais Apskats *(Monetary Review)* — **Language:** Latvian/English **Frequency:** quarterly **Content:** discusses monetary and fiscal policies, foreign trade and developments in the national economy

Monetarais Biletens *(Monetary Bulletin)* — **Language:** Latvian/English **Frequency:** monthly **Content:** macroeconomic and monetary indicators, money market interest rates and the consolidated balance sheet of credit institutions

Latvijas Republikas Ekonomikas Ministrija
Ministry of Economy of the Republic of Latvia

Address: Brivibas iela 55, Riga, LV-1519
Telephone: +371 728 0882
Fax: +371 728 0882
E-mail: pasts@em.gov.lv
Website: www.em.gov.lv

Guides: publishes reports on the economic development and status of Latvia
Activity: central government (state administration) institution in the field of economic policy; the ministry is the head institution for the subordinated state administration institutions

Website(s) information:

Latvijas Republikas Ekonomikas Ministrija *(Ministry of Economy of the Republic of Latvia)* — **url:** www.em.gov.lv **Description:** provides information on the Ministry and its working areas: industry, tourism, foreign trade and building; publications are available online on a free basis as well as all the current data concerning Latvia's economic development; information about Latvia's EU membership is also given **Coverage:** statistical data on industries (food, wood, light, ect.), tourism, foreign trade and building in Latvia

Publication(s):

Makroekonomiskais apskats *(National Economy of Latvia: Macroeconomic Review)* — **Language:** Latvian/English **Frequency:** quarterly **Content:** review of development of the Latvian economy

Zinojums par Latvijas tautsaimniecibas attistibu *(Report on the Economic Development of Latvia)* — **Language:** Latvian/English **Frequency:** per annum 2 **Content:** evaluates the economic situation in Latvia and progress of reforms as well as offers economic development forecasts

Latvijas Republikas Finansu Ministrija
Ministry of Finance of the Republic of Latvia

Address: Smilsu iela 1, Riga, LV-1919
Telephone: +371 709 5405
Fax: +371 709 5503
E-mail: info@fm.gov.lv
Website: www.fm.gov.lv

Guides: publishes speeches, articles and interviews
Activity: ministry of finance

Website(s) information:

Latvijas Republikas Finansu Ministrija *(Ministry of Finance of the Republic of Latvia)* — **url:** www.fm.gov.lv **Description:** provides information about the Ministry, Latvian taxation and monetary systems, strategies of budget formation, international financial cooperation; information on customs; provides links to press releases, articles and commentaries; all up-to-date economic data available on free basis on-line **Coverage:** up-to-date data on state and pocket budget (monthly and annual data), data on taxes and fees, main economic indicators and forecasts

Publication(s):

Valsts Budzeta Apskats *(National Budget Explanation)* — **Language:** Latvian/English **Frequency:** annual **Content:** contains information about macroeconomic indicators in Latvia and describes its future development; analysis of the external economic environment, its development tendency and possible impact on the state national economy; information about the fiscal review, analysis of revenues, central government budget expenditure and structure of the Central Government Budget law

LR Centrala Statistikas Parvalde
Central Statistical Bureau of Latvia

Address: Lacplesa iela 1, Riga, LV-1301
Telephone: +371 7 366 6850
Fax: +371 7 830 137
E-mail: csb@csb.gov.lv
Website: www.csb.lv

Guides: statistics Latvia releases annual, bi-annual, quarterly, monthly releases on demographic, agricultural, general, industrial, foreign trade, domestic trade, as well as price and labour statistics sections

Activity: national statistical bureau

Website(s) information:
LR Centrala Statistikas Parvalde *(Central Statistical Bureau of Latvia)* — **url:** www.csb.lv **Description:** covers main products and services provided by the Central Bureau, including: a catalogue of publications (Latvian and English); press releases; population census results; and online socio-economic statistics **Coverage:** current data on macroeconomic indicators and finances; population; employment; personal income; price indices; agriculture; industry; investments and construction; transport; foreign and domestic trade; education and health; and tourism

Publication(s):
Buvnieciba Latvija *(Construction in Latvia)* — **Language:** Latvian/English **Frequency:** annual **Content:** data collection on non-financial investment, construction of objects in the social and production sector, as well as construction of private houses, the volume of construction work performed by construction enterprises, sales, exports and imports of the main construction materials, construction cost indices, labour remuneration and occupational injuries, designing, as well as construction permits issued for buildings and civil engineering

Dazada Latvija: pagasti, novadi, pilsetas, rajoni, regioni. Vertejumi, perspektivas, vizijas *(Diverse Latvia: Civil Parishes, Counties, Cities and Towns, Districts, Regions. Evaluations, Forecasts, Visions)* — **Language:** Latvian **Frequency:** irregular **Content:** socio-economic development of all administratively territorial units of Latvia between 1996 and 2003

Demografija *(Demography)* — **Language:** Latvian/English **Frequency:** annual **Content:** number and changes of population, gender, age and ethnic composition, demographic burden, registered marriages and divorces, fertility, mortality, long-term migration, citizenship, granting and loss of citizenship, asylum seekers and refugees are given in this statistical data collection

Environment Indicators in Latvia — **Language:** English **Frequency:** annual **Content:** provides information on harmful atmospheric emissions from stationary sources, water abstraction and utilisation, wastewater discharge and the operation of wastewater treatment equipment, municipal and hazardous waste, management of national parks and other reserves, forestry and hunting

Estonia, Latvia and Lithuania in Figures — **Language:** English **Frequency:** annual **Content:** essential comparable annual statistics on economic and social conditions of contemporary Estonia, Latvia and Lithuania

Estonia, Latvia and Lithuania in Figures — **Language:** English **Frequency:** quarterly **Content:** review illustrate the key principles of the country's economic policy and provide an analysis of the macroeconomic development, including forecasts of the main macroeconomic indicators

Household Budget — **Language:** English **Frequency:** annual **Content:** surveyed households, their incomes and expenditures, living conditions, self-evaluation of the living conditions of the households and other indicators of the country as a whole, in urban and rural areas, as well as in seven major cities on average and Riga separately

Housing Stock — **Language:** English **Frequency:** annual **Content:** data collection on the housing stock, provision of amenities in the country as a whole and with breakdowns by city and town, administrative district and ownership

Informacijas Sabiedriba Latvija *(Information Society in Latvia)* — **Language:** Latvian/English **Frequency:** annual **Content:** presents information on the infrastructure of information society: availability of PCs in households, enterprises, organisations and educational establishments of Latvia; use of Internet; use of information technologies for e-commercial purposes

Komercdarbibas Finansialie Pamatraditaji *(Basic Financial Indicators of Business Activity)* — **Language:** Latvian/English **Frequency:** annual **Content:** financial information on business activity within private and public sectors broken down by the main activity of the enterprise and the number employed. Indicators of financial activity are presented

Latvijas Arteja Tirdznieba *(Foreign Trade of Latvia)* — **Language:** Latvian/English **Frequency:** annual **Content:** presents aggregated data on merchandise exports and imports broken down by country and merchandise group

Latvijas Energobilance *(Energy in Latvia)* — **Language:** Latvian/English **Frequency:** annual **Content:** data collection contains statistical indicators characterising the consumption of major energy resources in Latvia, as well as breakdowns by kind of activity and information on average prices of energy resources purchased in the sector of manufacturing are provided

Latvijas Lauksaimnieciba *(Agriculture of Latvia)* — **Language:** Latvian/English **Frequency:** annual **Content:** the most important statistical indicators over the past five years characterising the situation of agriculture in total, including supply balance sheets of agricultural products, as well as main agricultural sectors; output and productivity indicators of the main agricultural products in the Baltic countries

Latvijas Makroekonomiskie Raditaji *(Macroeconomic Indicators of Latvia 2005)* — **Language:** Latvian/English **Frequency:** quarterly **Content:** the most important macroeconomic indicators such as GDP and the principal items of the balance of payments, foreign trade, government finance and banking statistics

Latvijas Regioni Skaitlos *(Latvia's Regions in Figures)* — **Language:** Latvian/English **Frequency:** annual **Content:** data collection contains information on the gross domestic product, employment and other economic indicators for the country as a whole and breakdowns by regions

Latvijas Statistikas Gadagramata *(Statistical Yearbook of Latvia)* — **Language:** Latvian/English **Frequency:** annual **Content:** statistics on Latvia's main socioeconomic indicators

Latvijas Statistikas Ikmenesa Biletens *(Monthly Bulletin of Latvian Statistics)* — **Language:** Latvian/English **Frequency:** monthly **Content:** statistical overview of the present socioeconomic environment in Latvia

Latvijas Valsts Finanses *(Public Finances of Latvia)* — **Language:** Latvian/English **Frequency:** quarterly **Content:** collection comprises data on the budget of Latvia, banking system, activities of insurance companies, financial leasing companies, Riga Stock Exchange; comparisons of the main indicators for Baltic countries are provided

Latvijas Veselibas Aprupes Statistikas Gadagramata *(Health Care Statistics in Latvia)* — **Language:** Latvian/English **Frequency:** annual **Content:** provides all-round characteristics of health and the system of health care in the country. The statistical data are compared with the data of the previous year, which are specified during the compilation of each edition. The most relevant data are compared with other countries

Paterina Cenas *(Consumer Prices)* — **Language:** Latvian/English **Frequency:** quarterly **Content:** average prices of foods and services for survey quarter in months are published

Turism Latvija *(Tourism in Latvia)* — **Language:** Latvian/English **Frequency:** annual **Content:** data collection contains information drawn from a survey of persons crossing the state border and a survey on the travelling public

Liechtenstein

Amt für Volkswirtschaft
Liechtenstein Department of Economics

Address: Giessenstrasse 3, Vaduz, 9490
Telephone: +4175 236 6876
Fax: +4175 236 6931
E-mail: info.statistik@avw.llv.li
Website: www.llv.li

Guides: data is available on website
Activity: publishes official statistics on socio-economic indicators

Website(s) information:
Amt für Volkswirtschaft *(Liechtenstein Department of Economics)* — **url:** www.llv.li **Description:** provides key statistics on Liechtenstein **Coverage:** contains data on economic indicators, population and tourism

Lithuania

Lietuvos Bankas
Bank of Lithuania

Address: Gedimino pr. 6, Vilnius, LT-01103
Telephone: +370 5 268 0029
Fax: +370 5 262 8124
E-mail: info@lb.lt
Website: www.lb.lt

Guides: the publications of the Bank of Lithuania provide information related to the activities of the Bank of Lithuania, monetary and banking policies, balance of payments and financial statistics
Activity: central bank of the Republic of Lithuania; its principal objective is to maintain price stability

Website(s) information:
Lietuvos Bankas (Bank of Lithuania) — **url:** www.lb.lt **Description:** provides full information about its activities, information on the basic tasks of monetary policy and its implementation, monetary policy operations, credit institutions supervision activities and other responsibilities established by the legislation as well as information on the national macroeconomic situation, such as analysis of the developments in the national economy and financial markets, and on the financial position of the Bank; The Bank of Lithuania publishes annual reports, monthly and quarterly bulletins where it presents information about its activities as well as a wide range of financial and macroeconomic information available from 2000; provides all the current information about adoption of the Euro in Lithuania **Coverage:** statistical data on a free basis is available on main economic and financial indicators; official exchange rate statistics; monetary policy; monetary financial institutions balance sheet and monetary statistics; monetary financial institutions interest rates on loans and deposits statistics; money, currencies and financial market statistics; balance of payments and foreign reserves statistics

Publication(s):
Banku statistikos metrastis (Banking Statistics Yearbook) — **Language:** Lithuanian/English **Frequency:** annual **Content:** provides general information about main economic indicators; detailed data on money, deposits, loans, inter-bank lending market, interest rate, foreign exchange market turnover, securities market, balance of payments **Edition:** 2006

Ketvircio biuletenis (Quarterly Bulletin) — **Language:** Lithuanian/English **Frequency:** quarterly **Content:** development of economy of Lithuania; review of Lithuanian financial markets

Lietuvos Respublikos mokejimu balansai (Balance of Payments of the Republic of Lithuania) — **Language:** Lithuanian/English **Frequency:** quarterly **Content:** balance of payments data **Edition:** 2006

Menesinis biuletenis (Monthly Bulletin) — **Language:** Lithuanian/English **Frequency:** monthly **Content:** review of general economic indicators: money, deposits, loans, interest rates on deposits and loans, money and foreign exchange markets **Edition:** 2006

Metine ataskaita (Annual Report) — **Language:** English/Lithuanian **Frequency:** annual **Content:** global economic development features review of the economy of Lithuania; exchange rate and monetary policy; interest rates; foreign reserve management; cash management; payment and securities settlement systems; annual financial statements of the Bank of Lithuania **Edition:** 2006

Metine Lietuvos Banko finansine ataskaita (Annual Financial Statements of the Bank of Lithuania) — **Language:** English/Lithuanian **Frequency:** annual **Content:** independent auditors' report; balance sheet and profit (loss) statement of the Bank of Lithuania; explanatory notes to the financial statements of the Bank of Lithuania

Lietuvos Respublikos Finansu Ministerija
Ministry of Finance of the Republic of Lithuania

Address: J Tumo-Vaizganto 8a/2, Vilnius, LT-01512
Telephone: +370 5 239 0000
Fax: +370 5 279 1481
E-mail: finmin@finmin.lt
Website: www.finmin.lt

Guides: publish statistical information on state debt and government securities
Activity: Ministry of Finance

Website(s) information:
Lietuvos Respublikos Finansu Ministerija (Ministry of Finance of the Republic of Lithuania) — **url:** www.finmin.lt **Description:** information on Lithuanian economic and business climate, providing statistical data on socio-economic, banking and finance indicators from the year of 1999; national budget and information about taxes is provided; offers economic forecast; financial aspects of Lithuania's EU membership and current information on the integration in the Euro zone **Coverage:** provides data on fiscal policies, national budget, government finance statistics, government budget deficit, state debt, taxes

Publication(s):
Bendroji valstybes skola (General Government Debt) — **Language:** Lithuanian/English **Frequency:** annual **Content:** Lithuania's economic development; credit ratings; debt level, structure, dynamics and limits; borrowing by the government

Lietuvos vyriausybes vertybiniu popieriu apzvalgos (Overview of Lithuanian Government Securities) — **Language:** Lithuanian/English **Frequency:** annual **Content:** review of Government Securities circulation

Lietuvos Respublikos Ukio Ministerija
Ministry of Economy of the Republic of Lithuania

Address: Gedimino pr 48/2, Vilnius, LT-01104
Telephone: +370 5 262 3863
Fax: +370 5 262 3974
E-mail: kanc@ukmin.lt
Website: www.ukmin.lt

Guides: publishes annual reports on development of Lithuanian economy
Activity: Ministry of Economics

Website(s) information:
Lietuvos Respublikos Ukio Ministerija (Ministry of Economy of the Republic of Lithuania) — **url:** www.ukmin.lt **Description:** provides information about the Ministry, its structure; reviews of the economic and social situation of the Republic of Lithuania, long term-development strategies and programmes; detailed information on energy sector, foreign trade, industry and business, innovation and technologies; information on European Union structural funds support to business, energy and public tourism sectors in Lithuania; provider of links to organisations that work under the Ministry of Economy of the Republic of Lithuania **Coverage:** provides all current data on development of the main economic indicators; data on energy sector, foreign trade, industry and business, innovation and technologies

Publication(s):
Energetika Lietuvoje (Energy in Lithuania) — **Language:** Lithuanian/English **Frequency:** annual **Content:** current status of the Lithuanian energy sector (power system, oil refinery, district heat and gas supply), energy balances, economical-financial indicators of the largest energy companies as well as trends of basic comparative indicators

Lietuvos ekonomines ir socialines situacijos pazvalga (Review of Economic and Social Situation of the Republic of Lithuania) — **Language:** Lithuanian/English **Frequency:** annual **Content:** short review of main data on economic development

Metine ataskaita (Annual report) — **Language:** Lithuanian/English **Frequency:** annual **Content:** covers main sectors of economy: energy, small and medium sized business and support, state property privatisation policy and management of the companies, domestic and foreign trade, tourism development; co-ordination of EU matters, management of EU structural funds

Statistikos departamentas prie Lietuvos Respublikos vyriausybes
Department of Statistics to the Government of the Republic of Lithuania

Address: Gedimino pr 29, Vilnius, LT-01500
Telephone: +370 5 236 4822
Fax: +370 5 236 4845
E-mail: statistika@stat.gov.lt
Website: www.std.lt

Guides: statistics Lithuania releases more than 100 publications, of which biggest are annual, bi-annual, quarterly, monthly and approximately 15 press releases per month

Activity: national statistics office

Website(s) information:

Statistikos Departamentas *(Department of Statistics to the Government of the Republic of Lithuania)* — **url:** www.std.lt **Description:** information is classified into 9 domains: general statistics, economy and finance, population and social statistics, business statistics, agriculture, foreign trade, transport and communication, environment and energy, science and technology, regional statistics; the majority of indicators have been produced since 1995 enables to track changes and make comparisons; registered users have an access to Statistical analytical system; the site has links to all Lithuanian public institutions, embassies, international organizations, national statistical offices **Coverage:** statistics available on a free basis provide a general socio-economic portrait of Lithuania; all information is divided into 9 main domains: general statistics, economy and finance, population and social statistics, business statistics, agriculture, foreign trade, transport and communication, environment and energy, science and technology, regional statistics

Publication(s):

Darbo jega, uzimtumas ir nedarbas *(Labour Force, Employment and Unemployment)* — **Language:** Lithuanian/English **Frequency:** annual **Content:** information on economic activity of the population based on the Labour Force Survey carried out by Statistics Lithuania; the structure of employed is given by gender, age, economic activity, occupation group and hours worked; the structure of unemployment rate is given by age, methods used for seeking work, duration of unemployment for a five-year period

Darbo jega, uzimtumas ir nedarbas *(Labour Force, Employment and Unemployment)* — **Language:** Lithuanian/English **Frequency:** quarterly **Content:** information is given on the number of employed, unemployed, unemployment rate and other indices

Darbo statistikos metrastis *(Yearbook of Labour Statistics)* — **Language:** Lithuanian/English **Frequency:** annual **Content:** data on the number of hired employees, employed, average earnings (hourly and monthly), working time, strikes, labour costs, structural indicators of tax on earnings and other labour statistics indicators of the economy of the country by economic activity, economic sector; minimum rates of earnings approved by the Government are shown

Darbo uzmokestis *(Wages and Salaries)* — **Language:** Lithuanian/English **Frequency:** quarterly **Content:** quarterly data on the number of the hired employees, average monthly earnings (gross, net, real), average hourly earnings, working time and their changes by economic activity, categories of employees (manual and non-manual) and gender in the national economy and by economic sectors (individual enterprises excluded); also, quarterly labour costs index is given

Demografinis metrastis *(Demographic Yearbook)* — **Language:** Lithuanian/English **Frequency:** annual **Content:** statistical data characterising demographic development of the country as well as comprehensive data on births, deaths and causes of deaths, marriages, divorces and migration; demographic indicators of foreign countries are presented for comparison with figures on Lithuania

Ekonominis ir socialinis vystymasis Lietuvoje *(Economic and Social Development in Lithuania)* — **Language:** Lithuanian/English **Frequency:** monthly **Content:** up-to-date information about the country's economic and social development; quarterly data in time-series for gross domestic product, direct foreign investment, budgets, households' disposable income, earnings, agriculture, construction and other indicators is presented; comparable indicators of Latvia and Estonia are published; structural indicators of the EU member states are presented

Ekonominis ir socialinis vystymasis Lietuvoje, Latvijoje ir Estijoje *(Economic and Social Development of Lithuania, Latvia and Estonia)* — **Language:** Lithuanian English **Frequency:** monthly **Content:** monthly changes in main economic and social development indicators of Lithuania, Latvia and Estonia

Finansu imoniu statistika *(Statistics of Financial Enterprises)* — **Language:** Lithuanian/English **Frequency:** annual **Content:** indicators of credit institutions, insurance companies, financial leasing companies and other financial intermediation enterprises: indicators of profit (loss) statement, balance sheet, investments

Gamtos istekliai ir aplinkosauga *(Natural Resources and Environment Protection)* — **Language:** Lithuanian/English **Frequency:** annual **Content:** data on climate, usage of natural resources, protection of atmosphere, management of waste, usage of chemical substances, expenditure related to environment protection

Gyvenamasis fondas ir statyba *(Stock of Dwellings and Construction)* — **Language:** Lithuanian/English **Frequency:** annual **Content:** data related to existing stock of dwellings and new building construction; number of dwellings, rooms, useful space, conveniences; accounting of the stock of dwellings is accomplished by type of ownership, by location; building construction consists of information on building permits granted, new residential and non-residential buildings completed

Gyventoju pajamos ir pragyvenimo lygis *(Income and Living Conditions)* — **Language:** Lithuanian/English **Frequency:** annual **Content:** data on disposable income, its structure, housing conditions, employment, health care; indicators are presented by place of residence of the household, age, sex and education of the persons

Gyvuliu skaicius *(Number of Livestock)* — **Language:** Lithuanian/English **Frequency:** annual **Content:** data on the number of livestock, poultry, beehives at the beginning of year; data on cattle are broken down by age, sex, economic purpose, data on pigs by weight, age and economic purpose

Imoniu bankrotas *(Bankruptcy of Enterprises)* — **Language:** Lithuanian/English **Frequency:** per annum 2 **Content:** presents analysis of the enterprises undergoing bankruptcy or already bankrupt in the previous year and over a five year period; information about administration of bankruptcy procedures is also included

Imoniu finansiniai rodikliai *(Financial Indicators - Enterprises)* — **Language:** Lithuanian/English **Frequency:** 2 per annum **Content:** information about quarterly financial indicators: assets, equity, liabilities, income, costs, profits

Informacija apie gamintoju parduotos pramones produkcijos kainu pokycius *(Information about Changes in Producer Prices for Industrial Production)* — **Language:** Lithuanian/English **Frequency:** monthly **Content:** brief methodology for calculation of the producer price index (PPI) and analysis of data of the reporting month as well as changes in producer prices over a month, over the period from the beginning of the year, over twelve months by main industrial grouping and by economic activity is presented in this publication; also indices in time series and weights used for the PPI calculation are shown

Informacija apie importuotu ir eksportuotu kainu pokycius *(Information about Changes in Export/Import Prices)* — **Language:** Lithuanian/English **Frequency:** monthly **Content:** short explanations of methodology on calculating export and import price indices (EPI/IPI) and analysis of statistical data of the reporting month as well as changes in export/import prices over a month, comparisons with the base year by economic activity

Informacija apie vartojimo prekiu ir paslaugu kainu pokycius *(Information on Changes in Consumer Prices for Goods and Services)* — **Language:** Lithuanian/English **Frequency:** monthly **Content:** short explanations of calculation methodologies of the consumer price index (CPI) and the harmonized CPI as well as data analysis of the reporting month are given; also, changes in prices for the group of consumer goods and services per month, period from the beginning of the year, twelve months are given; besides, average annual price changes, and indices in time series and weights used in the calculation of indices are shown; finally, the harmonized CPI of EU member states is presented

Informacines technologijos Lietuvoje *(Information Technologies in Lithuania)* — **Language:** Lithuanian/English **Frequency:** annual **Content:** statistical data on information technologies (IT) are given: the IT sector production and value added tax evaluation; IT goods production, exports and imports; a review of the information and telecommunication technologies' market; IT usage in households, enterprises, public administration, educational establishments

Ketvirtines nacionalines saskaitos *(Quarterly National Accounts)* — **Language:** Lithuanian/English **Frequency:** quarterly **Content:** quarterly macroeconomic indicators such as gross value added and gross domestic product by three approaches: production, expenditure and income; gross national income, net savings and net lending / borrowing are published; revenue and expenditure as well as financial assets and liabilities of the General Government are presented

Kuro ir energijos balansas *(Energy Balances)* — **Language:** Lithuanian/English **Frequency:** annual **Content:** annual balances of energy resources for a five-year period and other balances of fuel and energy

Lietuva Europoje *(Lithuania in Europe)* — **Language:** Lithuanian/English **Frequency:** annual **Content:** presents main economic and social indicators of Lithuania and other EU member states

Lietuva skaiciais *(Lithuania in Figures)* — **Language:** Lithuanian/English **Frequency:** annual **Content:** general information about the country, geographical and climate-related indicators, national accounts, finances, population, education, culture, science, health care, labour, industry, agriculture, construction, trade, transport and other statistics is presented in the tables and diagrams of the publication

Lietuvos apskritys (Counties of Lithuania) — **Language:** Lithuanian/English **Frequency:** annual **Content:** statistical information about the population, unemployment rate, sales of industrial production, direct foreign investment

Lietuvos apskritys (Counties of Lithuania) — **Language:** Lithuanian/English **Frequency:** annual **Content:** statistical information about economic and social development, demographic and environmental processes, industrial and commercial processes in the country, its counties and municipalities as well as definitions of the indicators are presented

Lietuvos ekonomikos apzvalga (Survey of the Lithuanian Economy) — **Language:** Lithuanian/English **Frequency:** 2 per annum **Content:** compilation of articles contains a general review of the economy; demographic situation and social status; financial market; economic relations with foreign countries; trends in industrial development; economic reforms and priorities; forecasts of macroeconomic indicators; current issues of economy, discussions

Lietuvos gyventojai pagal amziu (Lithuanian Population by Age) — **Language:** Lithuanian/English **Frequency:** annual **Content:** statistical data on population by gender and age as of 1 January are presented by county, municipality, urban and rural area

Lietuvos gyventojai: struktura ir demografine raida (Population of Lithuania: Pattern and Demographic Development) — **Language:** Lithuanian/English **Frequency:** annual **Content:** dynamics of the population, population by county and municipality, age, gender, ethnicity, religion, education, employment, marital status, structure and size of families and households, number of the children given birth, disability, migration, socio-demographic mortality differentials and innovative census-linked methodology. Publication of statistical analysis based on population censuses (1989, 2001) data

Lietuvos gyventoju mirtingumo sociodemografiniai skirtumai (Socio-demographic Mortality Differentials in Lithuania) — **Language:** Lithuanian/English **Frequency:** annual **Content:** statistical analysis on the relative cause-specific mortality ratios by socio-demographic group. Based on the census-linked methodology using socio-demographic mortality differentials. The major longevity indicators (life expectancy) are presented by urban-rural residence, education, marital status and ethnicity

Lietuvos gyventoju sveikatos tyrimu rezultatai (Health Survey Results of Lithuanian Population) — **Language:** Lithuanian/English **Frequency:** annual **Content:** information about the health status of population, chronic diseases and temporary health problems, use of health care services and use of pharmaceuticals etc. Compiled based on the results of a health population survey

Lietuvos nacionalines saskaitos (National Accounts of Lithuania) — **Language:** Lithuanian/English **Frequency:** annual **Content:** financial and non-financial national accounts are shown in series and in terms of the whole country, separately by institutional sectors and, in addition, by sub-sectors of the General Government; comparisons of GDP with other EU member states are made

Lietuvos regionu portretas (Portrait of the Regions of Lithuania) — **Language:** Lithuanian/English **Frequency:** annual **Content:** economic-social data review of the country by counties; data on: geography (including a review of the region, its advantages and disadvantages, territory and natural resources), population, employment, economy, environment, health and culture

Lietuvos statistikos darbai (Lithuanian Statistics: Articles, Reports and Studies) — **Language:** Lithuanian/English **Frequency:** irregular **Content:** economic and social articles and their abstracts

Lietuvos statistikos metrastis (Statistical Yearbook of Lithuania) — **Language:** Lithuanian/English **Frequency:** annual **Content:** detailed statistics related to different areas (country's economic and social development; demographic and environmental processes; industrial, commercial, financial, and investment activities of natural and legal persons; sustainable development and structural indicators)

Mazmenine ir didmenine prekyba (Retail and Wholesale Trade) — **Language:** Lithuanian/English **Frequency:** annual **Content:** trade and catering enterprises turnover, its changes, composition of turnover of retail trade enterprises by commodity group; turnover, number of shops, sales area in retail trade enterprises, number of seats in restaurants and other catering enterprises; basic wholesale trade indicators such as turnover, number of persons employed, and turnover by type of customer and commodity groups are also given

Metu zemes ukio strukturos tyrimo rezultatai (Results of Farm Structure Survey in Lithuania) — **Language:** Lithuanian/English **Frequency:** annual **Content:** data on the Census of Agriculture and the Farm Structure Survey on land and its usage, number of livestock by kind and age groups, tractors and other agricultural machines, farm holders and their family members, number of hired employees on the farm and duration of their working time, other non-agricultural activities

Mirties priezastys (Causes of Death) — **Language:** Lithuanian/English **Frequency:** annual **Content:** data on mortality and causes of death by age and sex; data are presented by urban and rural area, county and municipality and on national level

Mokslo darbuotojai ir ju darbai (Research Activities) — **Language:** Lithuanian/English **Frequency:** annual **Content:** data on employees engaged in research and experimental development and expenditure; personnel data; distribution of personnel by higher education, private and public sectors, field of science, sex, age

Moterys ir vyrai Lietuvoje (Women and Men in Lithuania) — **Language:** Lithuanian/English **Frequency:** annual **Content:** gender statistics: the number of men and women, family creation and its stability, education, health care and social protection, employment and unemployment, earnings, participation in public administration

Namu ukio pajamos ir islaidos (Household Income and Expenditure) — **Language:** Lithuanian/English **Frequency:** annual **Content:** statistical information about household composition, income and consumer expenditure and their structure, housing conditions, possession of consumer durables and assessment of living conditions; the indicators are presented by place of residence, socio-economic group, age, sex and education of household head as well as type of household

Nusikalstamumas ir teisesaugos instituciju veikla (Crime and the Law Enforcement Activity) — **Language:** Lithuanian/English **Frequency:** annual **Content:** information referring to crime situation, sentenced persons, incarcerated persons in imprisonment institutions, juvenile delinquency, conviction and crime prevention, as well as activity of law enforcement institutions is provided

Paslaugos (Services) — **Language:** Lithuanian/English **Frequency:** annual **Content:** short-term statistics on turnover of enterprises whose main activity is to provide services; numbers employed in the industry

Pragyvenimo lygis ir skurdas (Living Standard and Poverty) — **Language:** Lithuanian/English **Frequency:** annual **Content:** trends of changes observed in the standards of living over a three-year period; the levels of relative poverty in various household groups; indicators of social exclusion and standards of living in the households living in relative poverty

Pramones darbo rezultatai (Industrial Activity Results) — **Language:** Lithuanian/English **Frequency:** monthly **Content:** production indices of mining, quarrying, manufacturing, electricity, gas and water supply; comparisons are made to previous period, to corresponding period of previous year

Smulkiu, vidutiniu ir dideliu imoniu pagrindiniai rodikliai (Main Indicators of Small, Medium and Large Enterprises) — **Language:** Lithuanian/English **Frequency:** annual **Content:** key financial indicators according to size of enterprises: number of employees, assets, equity, costs, income, value added, debt and liquidity ratio

Socialine apsauga Lietuvoje (Social Protection in Lithuania) — **Language:** Lithuanian/English **Frequency:** annual **Content:** number of pensioners and persons entitled to benefits, support for illness, old-age, disability, unemployment and other cases, social benefits for families and children

Svietimas (Education) — **Language:** Lithuanian/English **Frequency:** annual **Content:** data on public and private educational establishments, students enrolled and teaching staff; it embraces information about pre-school establishments, general, vocational schools, colleges and universities; the number of pupils and students is shown by age, sex, educational attainment, field of study and continuation of education

Tiesiogines uzsienio investicijos Lietuvoje (Foreign Direct Investment in Lithuania) — **Language:** Lithuanian/English **Frequency:** annual **Content:** annual data on foreign direct investment (FDI) positions that reflect the real situation of FDI at the beginning of the year 2002-2006; FDI in Lithuania and Lithuanian direct investment abroad is broken down by country-investor and economic activity

Transportas ir rysiai (Transport and Communication) — **Language:** Lithuanian/English **Frequency:** annual **Content:** information about the length of roads, number of motor-vehicles, traffic of goods and passengers by all means of transport as well as about post and telecommunication services

Transporto ir rysiu imoniu rodikliai (Indicators of Transport and Communication Enterprises) — **Language:** Lithuanian/English **Frequency:** monthly **Content:** data on passengers and goods carried by road transport and railways as well as goods and passengers carried by water and air transport; information about transportation of oil and oil products by oil pipelines; review of road traffic accidents; work carried out by communication enterprises and post offices

Turizmas Lietuvoje *(Tourism in Lithuania)* — **Language:** Lithuanian/English **Frequency:** annual **Content:** data on occupation of accommodation establishments (hotels, motels, tourist camps, rest and health establishments, etc.), outgoing and incoming tourism organised by travel agencies and tour organizers as well as the survey of local and outgoing tourism

Ukio subjektai. Pagrindiniai duomenys *(Economic Entities. Main Data)* — **Language:** Lithuanian/English **Frequency:** annual **Content:** data on diverse classification of the operating economic entities from the Statistical Register of Economic entities; number of operating entities as well as small and medium sized enterprises nationwide provided by legal forms, economic activity, personnel and income by 1 January of each year

Uzsienio paskolos Lietuvai *(Foreign Loans Extended to Lithuania)* — **Language:** Lithuanian/English **Frequency:** 2 per annum **Content:** data on debt of the entities within the Government sector having the right to undertake borrowings; foreign loans, allocated to the Central Government, use, repayment and debt status by country, main financial institutions and by financing trends, are presented

Uzsienio prekyba *(Foreign Trade)* — **Language:** Lithuanian/English **Frequency:** annual **Content:** data on foreign trade balance, exports and imports by country, commodity group and commodities by country (a six-digit breakdown of the Combined Nomenclature of the European Economic Communities) are presented; also data on exported and imported commodities were grouped by the Standard International Trade Classification, Broad Economic Categories; publication deals with information about commodity distribution by main foreign trade partners, exports and imports indices, foreign trade data

Vartotoju ir gamintoju kainu indeksas *(Consumer and Producer Price Indices)* — **Language:** Lithuanian/English **Frequency:** quarterly **Content:** a short description of the calculation methodology of consumer price indices (CPI), producer price indices of manufactured goods of industry, construction input price indices, producer price indices of agricultural products also export / import price indices is given; current quarterly data are analysed; comparisons with the respective data of EU member countries are presented

Zaliavos ir medziagos *(Raw Materials)* — **Language:** Lithuanian/English **Frequency:** annual **Content:** data on main raw materials, their production, utilisation and stocks are presented; data on basic and non-ferrous scrap and secondary raw materials

Zemes ukio produkcijos supirkimas *(Purchase of Agricultural Production)* — **Language:** Lithuanian/English **Frequency:** annual **Content:** data on purchase of all types of agricultural products, by type of farm, producer prices and price indices for agricultural products

Zemes ukis Lietuvoje *(Agriculture in Lithuania)* — **Language:** Lithuanian/English **Frequency:** annual **Content:** data on total agricultural output, agricultural land area and structure, crop area, harvest and average yield, number of livestock and poultry, productivity and animal products, purchases of agricultural products

Valstybinis turizmo departamentas prie Ukio ministerijos
Lithuanian State Department of Tourism at the Ministry of Economy of the Republic of Lithuania

Address: A. Juozapaviciaus 13, Vilnius, LT-09311
Telephone: +370 5 210 8796
Fax: +370 5 210 8753
E-mail: vtd@tourism.lt
Website: www.tourism.lt

Guides: publishes information on Lithuania and its tourism opportunities
Activity: implements strategic planning of tourist activity and drafts the National Tourism Development Programme; drafts proposals to the Government on tourism policy and implementation

Website(s) information:
Lithuanian Tourism Statistics *(Lithuanian State Department of Tourism at the Ministry of Economy of the Republic of Lithuania)* — **url:** www.tourism.lt **Description:** site provides general information about the organisation, the country, tourism; Lithuanian news, formalities for foreign citizens willing to visit country, tourism statistics; has links to the Official Lithuanian Travel Guide, tourism information centres in Lithuania and abroad **Coverage:** inbound/outbound tourism, regional tourism statistics, activity of Tour operators and Travel agencies, expenditure of tourist, tourist profile; provides Lithuanian border crossing statistics; Lithuanian accommodation statistics

Publication(s):
Lietuvos turizmo statistika *(Lithuanian Tourism Statistics)* — **Language:** Lithuanian/English **Frequency:** annual **Content:** main statistical data on different aspects of tourism: inbound/outbound tourism, regional statistics, accommodation services, activity of Tour operators and Travel agencies, surveys of visitors in Lithuania, visit evaluation

Luxembourg

Service Central de la Statistique et des Etudes Economiques (STATEC)
Central Statistical and Economic Studies Service

Address: Quartier Luxembourg-Kirchberg, 13 rue Erasme, Luxembourg, L-1468
Telephone: +352 4 784 333
E-mail: info@statec.etat.lu
Website: http://www.statistiques.public.lu/fr/

Activity: provides statistical information system on the structure and the activity of the country

Website(s) information:
Service Central de la Statistique et des Etudes Economiques *(Central Statistical and Economic Studies Service (STATEC))* — **url:** statec.gouvernement.lu **Description:** offers information on products and services provided by the Service: catalogue of publications; data banks; national and international statistical programmes; international co-operation; etc **Coverage:** statistics all available online

Publication(s):
Agriculture — **Language:** French **Content:** contains data on agriculture, vine growing, forestry, hunting and fishing

Annuaire Statistique du Luxembourg *(Statistical Yearbook of Luxembourg)* — **Language:** French **Frequency:** annual **Content:** statistical overview of Luxembourg and its regions

Bulletin du Statec *(Statec Bulletin)* — **Language:** French **Frequency:** irregular **Content:** statistics and analysis of latest developments and trends in the national economy

Comptes nationaux *(National Accounts)* — **Language:** French **Content:** statistics on the national economy

Construction — **Language:** French **Content:** building costs, structure of the sector, building authorisations; turn-key projects and real property loans

Environment — **Language:** French **Content:** state of the environment and the measurements taken by the authorities to safeguard the nature and quality of life

Finances publiques *(Public Finance)* — **Language:** French **Content:** national debt; public revenue; national expenditure by government department; taxes of the State recovered during the financial year; customs duties, of excise and other receipts; treasury bills

Horeca et tourisme *(Horeca and tourism)* — **Language:** French **Content:** statistics relating to hotels and tourism

Indicateurs Rapides *(Latest Indicators)* — **Language:** French **Frequency:** monthly **Content:** statistical datasheets issued regularly to provide latest figures for consumer, construction, producer, industrial production and of construction activity; employment; new vehicle registrations; births, deaths and marriages; road traffic accidents; external trade; business prospects; and weather

Industrie *(Industry)* — **Language:** French **Content:** industry statistics including imports and exports; volumes of production and consumption, employment and prices

Le Luxembourg en Chiffres *(Luxembourg in Figures)* — **Language:** French/English/Dutch **Frequency:** annual **Content:** geographic, demographic, social and economic statistics covering Luxembourg

Population et emploi *(Population and employment)* — **Language:** French **Content:** demographic statistics and data on the evolution of employment and unemployment

Relations économiques extérieures *(Foreign Economic Relations)* — **Language:** French **Content:** trade in goods - by products and country

Santé *(Health)* — **Language:** French **Content:** includes data on hospitals, causes of death, diseases and other health statistics

Services financiers *(Financial Services)* — **Language:** French **Content:** credit institutions, Luxembourg stock exchange, undertakings for collective investment, insurances, interest rates

Territoire (Territory) — **Language:** French **Content:** provides data on the geographical situation, altitudes, hydrography and on the administrative subdivisions of the country

Transports et communications (Transport & Communications) — **Language:** French **Content:** statistical data on railroads, airports and the river ports, road transport people and goods; posts and telecommunications

Macedonia

Agency for Foreign Investments of the Republic of Macedonia

Address:	PO Box 114, 7 Nikola Vapcarov Street, Skopje, 1000
Telephone:	+389 2 311 7564
Fax:	+389 2 312 2098
E-mail:	contact@macinvest.org.mk
Website:	www.macinvest.org.mk

Guides: catalogue available online - online access

Activity: promotes economic growth in Macedonia through working to attract FDI

Website(s) information:

MacInvest — **url:** www.macinvest.org.mk **Description:** the website provides investment information - information on legal regulations, economic indicators, industry profiles; all information is available in English **Coverage:** basic economic and demographic indicators; international trade volume and structure by trading partner; business climate, industry reports; income statistics

Agency for Promotion of Entrepreneurship of the Republic of Macedonia

Address:	PO Box 657, 7 Nikola Vapcarov Street, Skopje, 1000
Telephone:	+389 2 312 0132
Fax:	+389 2 313 5494
E-mail:	apprm@apprm.org.mk
Website:	www.apprm.org.mk

Guides: catalogue available online

Activity: supports the establishment and development of small and medium enterprises in Macedonia

Publication(s):

Report of the SME Observatory — **Language:** Macedonian/English **Frequency:** annual **Content:** covers the macroeconomic framework of Macedonia; the size and structure of the SME sector, international trade, balance of trade; employment in SMEs by industry sector and region; financing SMEs - VAT, corporate tax, crediting; net profit and loss by sector

Employment Service Agency of the Republic of Macedonia

Address:	43 Vassil Gorgov Street, Skopje, 1000
Telephone:	+389 2 311 1850
Fax:	+389 2 311 1856
E-mail:	info@zvrm.gov.mk
Website:	www.zvrm.gov.mk

Activity: registers and monitors the number of unemployed persons actively seeking employment; works for the reduction of unemployment in Macedonia through projects, professional qualification programmes, maintains job centres all over the country

Website(s) information:

Employment Service Agency of the Republic of Macedonia — **url:** www.zvrm.gov.mk **Description:** the website provides access to the statistical research of the Agency; the site is available in Macedonian only **Coverage:** data on employment and unemployment figures by month; structure of the labour force - by age, gender, education; economically active population; analysis of the flow of unemployment

Ministry of Finance of the Republic of Macedonia

Address:	14 Dame Gruev Street, Skopje
Telephone:	+389 2 311 7288
Fax:	+389 2 311 7280
E-mail:	finance@finance.gov.mk
Website:	www.finance.gov.mk

Guides: all publications can be downloaded from the website

Activity: determines and coordinates the monetary and fiscal policy of FYR Macedonia

Website(s) information:

Ministry of Finance of the Republic of Macedonia — **url:** www.finance.gov.mk **Description:** the site provides access to the releases of the Bank, including monthly bulletins, brochures, financial reports, etc. Some of the information is available in Macedonian only **Coverage:** macroeconomic indicators, international debt structure and servicing, prices, international trade, short-term economic flows, budget breakdown and allocation by sector, information about ratings, prices and revenue of companies in Macedonia

Publication(s):

Annual Economic Report — **Language:** Macedonian **Frequency:** annual **Content:** surveys basic economic indicators, the real, fiscal, monetary, external and social sectors

National Bank of the Republic of Macedonia

Address:	PO Box 401, Kompleks banki b.b., Skopje, 1000
Telephone:	+389 2 310 8108
Fax:	+389 2 310 8357
E-mail:	governorsoffice@nbrm.gov.km
Website:	www.nbrm.gov.mk

Guides: full catalogue is available online - most publications can be downloaded from the Bank's website

Activity: establishes and conducts monetary policy; regulates liquidity in international payments; establishes and conducts the Denar exchange rate policy; handles and manages the foreign exchange reserves; regulates the payment system; issues banknotes and coins

Website(s) information:

National Bank of the Republic of Macedonia — **url:** www.nbrm.gov.mk **Description:** contains banking and financial information and reports on the macro-economic climate in Macedonia, accompanied by statistical data on key economic and foreign trade indicators. Free online access to some of the Bank's various publications, including: Monthly Bulletin, Quarterly Bulletin, Annual Report **Coverage:** basic economic indicators, data on economic activity, wages and employment, interest rates and deposits in banks, balance of payments, exchange rate information, data on international trade and real growth rates, public debt

Publication(s):

Annual Report — **Language:** Macedonian/English **Frequency:** monthly **Content:** the reports present data on basic economic indicators, trade, investment, information about the competitiveness and liquidity of banks, the management of government debt, etc

Bulletin — **Language:** Macedonian/English **Frequency:** quarterly

Small and Medium Enterprise Development Project at the Ministry of Economy

Address:	15 Jurij Gagarin Street, Office 17, Skopje, 1000
Telephone:	+389 2 309 3529
Fax:	+389 2 309 3530
E-mail:	smedp@economy.gov.mk
Website:	www.economy.gov.mk/smedp/mk/index.html

Guides: online catalogue available

Activity: economic analysis and problem identification; strategy and policy development; SME programme and project development; programme and project implementation and management; the monitoring and evaluation of development programmes and projects

Website(s) information:

Small and Medium Enterpise Development Project — **url:** www.economy.gov.mk/smedp/mk/index.html **Description:** online access to reports and surveys of the small and medium enterprise sector in FYR Macedonia **Coverage:** number and structure of small and medium enterprises in Macedonia, competitiveness, technological expertise, profit, trade, employees

State Statistical Office of Macedonia

Address: 4 Dame Gruev Street, Skopje, 1000
Telephone: +389 2 329 5600
Fax: +389 2 311 1336
Website: www.stat.gov.mk

Guides: annually the office releases about 30 publications and 270 releases: full catalogue available online - most publications are available in separate versions in English and Macedonian

Activity: performs regular statistical surveys and monitoring of Macedonia social, economic, and industrial indicators

Website(s) information:

Republic of Macedonia - State Statistical Office — **url:** www.stat.gov.mk
Description: the site provides links to statistical data, charts and graphs by sector and by year **Coverage:** statistical data covering population and labour figures, statistical data by sector - banking and finance, agriculture and forestry, industry and energetics, international trade, transport, tourism and other services

Publication(s):

Monthly Statistical Report — **Language:** Macedonian/English **Frequency:** monthly **Content:** conjectural data for industry, agriculture, forestry, construction, transport, turnover, prices and employment

Statistical Yearbook — **Language:** Macedonian/English **Frequency:** annual **Content:** annual data and time series for population, employment, industry, trade, gross domestic product, education

World Bank Mission in the Republic of Macedonia

Address: 34 Leninova Street, Skopje, 1000
Telephone: +389 2 311 7159
Fax: +389 2 311 7627
E-mail: dboskovski@worldbank.org
Website: www.worldbank.org.mk

Guides: catalogue available online - most publications can be read online, free of charge

Activity: works to assist economic development in Macedonia, for the promotion of civil society and economic growth

Website(s) information:

World Bank - Macedonia — **url:** www.worldbank.org.mk **Description:** the site provides access to online datasheets on Macedonia, World Bank reports on particular aspects of development and particular industries **Coverage:** macroeconomic indicators, external debt - structure and servicing; microeconomic indicators - accessibility of capital, ease of starting up business; data on indicators in particular industries (e.g. IT, energetics) and the social sphere; poverty statistics, etc

Moldova

Departamental Statisticasi Sociologie al Republicii Moldova

National Bureau of Statistics of the Republic of Moldova

Address: 106 Grenoble Street, Chisinau mun, 2019
Telephone: +373 22 40 30 00
Fax: +373 22 22 61 46
Website: www.statistica.md

Guides: e-mail: biblioteca@statistica.md
tel.: +37322 24 53 73

Activity: compiles and publishes statistical data on socio-economic indicators in Moldova

Website(s) information:

Departamental Statisticasi Sociologie al Republicii Moldova *(Department for Statistics and Sociology of the Republic of Moldova)* — **url:** www.statistica.md **Coverage:** reports on the social and economic developments in Moldova

Publication(s):

Moldova in Figures — **Language:** Moldovan (Romanian)/Russian **Frequency:** irregular **Content:** statistical information regarding the demographic, social and economic situation of the country from 2002-2005; contains data on the 2004 population census results

Prices in the Republic of Moldova — **Language:** Moldovan (Romanian)/Russian **Frequency:** irregular **Content:** statistical data that characterises the price dynamics for 2000-2005; included are analyses of monthly and annual dynamics of indices and consumer price levels for foodstuff and non-foodstuff products, services, prices of industrial products, prices of agricultural products, prices of construction works and prices for exported/imported commodities

Quarterly Statistical Bulletin — **Language:** Moldovan (Romanian)/Russian **Frequency:** quarterly **Content:** contains data on main statistical indicators which characterise the social, economic and demographic situation of the country

Netherlands

Centraal Bureau voor de Statistiek (CBS)

Statistics Netherlands

Address: Kloosterweg 1, Heerlen, 6412 CN
Telephone: +31 4557 06000
Fax: +31 4557 27440
E-mail: infoservice@cbs.nl
Website: www.cbs.nl

Guides: catalogue of publications available online

Activity: collecting, processing and publishing statistics to be used in practice, by policymakers and for scientific research; in addition to its responsibility for (official) national statistics, Statistics Netherlands also has the task of producing European (community) statistics

Website(s) information:

Centraal Bureau voor de Statistiek (CBO) *(Statistics Netherlands)* — **url:** www.cbs.nl **Description:** offers information on the Bureau's latest products and services, including catalogue of publications; access to Statline database and online publications; press releases; links to other national statistical institutes; and various online statistics **Coverage:** online statistics are available both in Dutch and English under "Listing of Key Figures" section. Different socio-economic and financial data is provided, covering the last four to five years (period coverage may vary according to indicator in question): population; standard of living; labour force; industrial resources; income, finance and expenditure; international economic relations; economic demography; prices; energy; information and automation; national accounts; culture; education, health and science; environment

StatLine — **url:** statline.cbs.nl **Coverage:** online database of statistical data drawn from Statistics Netherlands publications. Data covers both national and regional data and comes in the form of either tables or text documents

Publication(s):

Annual Report — **Language:** Dutch/English **Frequency:** annual **Content:** statistics about society, asymmetry project, media, statistics on trade and industry, economic statistics, financial statements, publications guide

Aspects of (un)Healthy Behaviour — **Language:** English/Dutch **Frequency:** irregular **Content:** trend figures on smoking, drinking wherever possible broken down by gender, type of insurance, age and highest level of education

Asylum Requests: Key Figures — **Language:** English/French **Frequency:** annual **Content:** submitted, granted asylum requests and left asylum seekers

Bankruptcies: Monthly Figures — **Language:** English/Dutch **Frequency:** monthly **Content:** pronounced bankruptcies by legal form and economic activities, debt restructuring

Births: Key Figures — **Language:** English/Dutch **Frequency:** annual **Content:** births: key figures by gender, birth order and legitimacy; including figures on stillborn children and multiple births

Business Survey: Manufacturing Industry — **Language:** English/Dutch **Frequency:** monthly **Content:** production and capacity utilisation, orders, sales prices, stocks, final products, competitive position, sales, number of employees for enterprises by activity

Consumer Confidence — **Language:** English/Dutch **Frequency:** monthly **Content:** consumer confidence, economic climate, willingness to buy, consumers' attitudes and expectations

Consumer Price Index (CPI) all Households — **Language:** English/Dutch **Frequency:** monthly **Content:** measure of the average price changes of goods and services purchased by households

Consumption — **Language:** English/Dutch **Frequency:** monthly **Content:** changes, indices, shares, value of consumption of households and of actual individual consumption of household by type of goods and services

Crime Victims by Personal Characteristics — **Language:** English/Dutch **Frequency:** annual **Content:** crime victims by background characteristics: gender, age, highest level of education, number of addresses per km2 of the place of residence, socio-economic bracket

Digital Economy — **Language:** English/Dutch **Content:** domestic ICT sector, share prices of the telecommunication companies, and investments in computers **Edition:** 5th edition

Economic Monitor — **Language:** English/Dutch **Content:** business cycle tracer, economic compass, economic situation, sentiment indicators, monthly indicators, quarterly indicators, focus and tables

Economic Totals per Region — **Language:** English/French **Frequency:** annual **Content:** GDP, GDP per capita, consistency with GDP, total value added, compensation of employees, taxes, subsidies, gross operating surplus by region, COROP area, province and groups of provinces

Emissions into the Atmosphere — **Language:** English/Dutch **Frequency:** 2 per annum **Content:** emissions by stationary and mobile sources, broken down by air polluting substance and combustion emission and other emissions

Financial institutions and markets — **Language:** Dutch/English **Content:** statistics on pension funds, security holdings, insurance companies, loans, insurers, share profits, foreign countries main financiers Dutch public sector, institutional investors, etc

Fixed Capital Formation by Region — **Language:** English/Dutch **Frequency:** annual **Content:** total fixed capital formation (gross), fixed capital formation (gross) by industry, by type of capital good by region, COROP area, province and groups of provinces

History elections: Dutch Lower House — **Language:** English/Dutch **Frequency:** every 4 years **Content:** voters, turnout, total votes, invalid votes, valid votes and distribution of seats by political party in the Dutch Lower House

Households: Key Figures — **Language:** English/Dutch **Frequency:** annual **Content:** households in the Netherlands by size and composition; persons by position in the household on 1 January

Interest Rates on the Money Market — **Language:** English/Dutch **Frequency:** irregular **Content:** official interest, rates short-term deposits unsecured and call money

Investment and Property Investment Funds — **Language:** English/Dutch **Frequency:** irregular **Content:** share index and total return index; investment- and property investment funds (average of the month)

Leisure Activities — **Language:** English/Dutch **Frequency:** annual **Content:** participation; sports, hobbies, culture, recreation, going out, use of the media and holidays by personal characteristics

Marriages: key figures — **Language:** English/Dutch **Frequency:** annual **Content:** marriages between partners of the same and opposite sex, partnership registrations and marriage partners

Monthly Statistics on Retail Trade — **Language:** English/Dutch **Frequency:** monthly **Content:** turnover, price and volume indices, increase and/or decrease in retail trade as a percentage

Mortality: key figures — **Language:** English/Dutch **Frequency:** annual **Content:** mortality: key figures by sex; including figures on infant mortality, perinatal mortality and life expectancy at birth

National Accounts of the Netherlands — **Language:** Dutch/English **Frequency:** annual **Content:** national accounts represent the official statistical review of the national economy

National Government: tax revenue accounts to the ESA — **Language:** English/Dutch **Frequency:** quarterly **Content:** tax on income and property, production and imports and death duty in terms of the ESA categories

National Statistics: Sick Leave — **Language:** English/Dutch **Frequency:** quarterly **Content:** national statistics on sick leave in % excluding pregnancy and maternity leave, by persons characteristics, region and business classification

Population: key figures — **Language:** English/Dutch **Frequency:** annual **Content:** population: key figures by gender, marital status, age, foreign background, households and population growth

Regional Economic Growth — **Language:** English/Dutch **Frequency:** annual **Content:** volume, deflation by region, COROP area, province and part of the country

Regular Educational Institutions — **Language:** English/Dutch **Frequency:** annual **Content:** number of regular educational institutions in the Netherlands; information presented by type of education, denomination and number of pupils/students per institution

Residential Buildings by Region — **Language:** English/Dutch **Frequency:** irregular **Content:** accommodation number, dwelling stock, newly built houses and other changes by region

Trends in the Use of Medical Facilities — **Language:** English/Dutch **Frequency:** annual **Content:** use of medical facilities, visit to the GP, medical specialist, dentist, physiotherapist, alternative healers, hospital admissions, medicines, contraceptive pill, health care centres

Unemployment and the Labour Force — **Language:** English/Dutch **Frequency:** monthly **Content:** employed and unemployed labour force, persons not included in the labour force, seasonally adjusted unemployment rate by gender and age

Urban Waste Water Treatment: Regions — **Language:** English/Dutch **Frequency:** annual **Content:** urban waste water treatment plants: number and capacity per type, influent and effluent; sewage sludge by destination; results by province and river basin district

Value Added Construction — **Language:** English/Dutch **Frequency:** monthly **Content:** volume changes in % compared to the same period of the previous year

Working Population by Gender — **Language:** English/Dutch **Frequency:** annual **Content:** persons employed, labour force, unemployment broken down by personal features (age, level of education, origin) and gender

De Nederlandsche Bank NV
Netherlands Bank

Address: Post Box 98, Amsterdam, 1000 AB
Telephone: +31 20 524 9111
Fax: +31 20 524 2500
E-mail: info@dnb.nl
Website: www.dnb.nl

Activity: DNB and other European central banks jointly pursue a policy designed to safeguard a stable Euro, smooth and secure payments as well as sound and reliable financial institutions

Website(s) information:
De Nederlandsche Bank NV (Netherlands Bank) — **url:** www.statistics.dnb.nl **Description:** detailed information about the bank and its publications. Monetary and financial statistical information covering key indicators; monetary and financial developments; balance of payments; capital markets; interest and exchange rates. Also has information about European Economic and Monetary Union **Coverage:** key monetary, financial and economic statistics are available; website contains monetary and financial statistics for the Netherlands compiled by the Nederlandsche Bank (time series starting in 1982) and also published in the DNB Statistical Bulletin

Publication(s):
DNB Statistisch Bulletin (DNB Statistical Bulletin) — **Language:** Dutch **Frequency:** quarterly **Content:** monetary and financial statistics

Jaarverslag DNB (Annual Report) — **Language:** Dutch **Frequency:** annual **Content:** overview of the activities, global developments, Euro area economy, Dutch economy, financial stability, payment and settlements systems, corporate governance, key economic data

Kwartaalbericht DNB (Quarterly Journal DNB) — **Language:** Dutch **Frequency:** quarterly **Content:** information concerning financial-economic developments in the Netherlands. Publishes forecasts for the Dutch economy

Overzicht Financiële Stabiliteit (Overview of Financial Stability) — **Language:** Dutch **Content:** overview of the financial system

Ministerie van Economische Zaken

Ministry of Economic Affairs

Address: Bezuidenhoutseweg 30, The Hague, 2594 AV
Telephone: +31 70 308 1986
E-mail: ezinfo@postbus51.nl
Website: www.ez.nl

Activity: stimulates sustainable economic growth; defines, implements, and regulates the enforcement of economic policy

Website(s) information:

Ministerie van Economische Zaken *(Ministry of Economic Affairs)* — **url:** www.ez.nl
Description: news and detailed data on macro-economic issues in the country such as consumer confidence, prices and business cycles **Coverage:** detailed statistics on key industries and issues including: population; labour; agriculture, forestry and fisheries; mining and manufacturing; construction; trade, hotels, restaurants, cafes and repairs; traffic, transport and communications; business and other services; income, finance and expenditure; international economic relations; prices; economic demography; energy; information and automation; national accounts; politics and government; justice and public safety; culture and recreation; education and science; health and welfare; environment

Publication(s):

Annual Report — **Language:** English/Dutch **Frequency:** annual **Content:** short, concise, and practical overview of the core activities of the Ministry of Economic Affairs; structured account of the Ministry's performance and results

Ministry of Agriculture, Nature Management and Fisheries

Address: Bezuidenhoutseweg 73, The Hague, 2594 AC
Telephone: +31 70 378 6868
Fax: +31 70 378 6100
Website: www.minlnv.nl

Website(s) information:

Ministerie von Landbauw, Natuurbeheer en Visserij *(Ministry of Agriculture, Nature Management and Fisheries)* — **url:** www.minlnv.nl **Description:** provides access to various publications on policy themes about the Dutch agricultural, livestock and fisheries sectors **Coverage:** offers statistical information on animal and crop production, nature management, forestry, trade and industry, fisheries, countryside planning and management, outdoor recreation, quality management, and agricultural research, education and extension

Publication(s):

Feiten en Cijfers van de Nederlandse Agrosector *(Facts and Figures of the Dutch Agriculture Sector)* — **Language:** Dutch **Frequency:** annual **Content:** insight in the developments of the Dutch agro sector

Jaarverslag *(Annual Report)* — **Language:** Dutch **Frequency:** annual **Content:** overview of the activities with a special theme every year, on a specific aspect of the agriculture, livestock, forestry and fishing sectors

Marktrapporten *(Market Report)* — **Language:** Dutch **Content:** market reports on agriculture

Social and Economic Council of the Netherlands

Address: Postbus 90405, Bezuidenhoutseweg 60, Den Haag, 2594 AW
Telephone: +31 70 349 9499
Fax: +31 70 383 2535
E-mail: ser.info@ser.nl
Website: www.ser.nl

Activity: main advisory body to the Dutch government and the parliament on national and international social and economic policy; has an administrative role which consists of monitoring commodity and industrial boards; helps the government to enforce the Works Councils Act, the Establishment of Businesses Act and the Insurance Agencies Act

Publication(s):

Advisory reports — **Language:** English/Dutch **Frequency:** irregular **Content:** diverse reports including co-financing of the common agricultural policy, European small claims procedure and others

Norway

Finansdepartementet

Finance Department

Address: Postboks 8008 Dep, Akersgata 40, Oslo, 0030
Telephone: +47 22 249 090
Fax: +47 22 249 510
E-mail: postmottak@fin.dep.no
Website: odin.dep.no/fin

Guides: budgetry and other information is downloadable from the website

Activity: plans and implements economic policy; co-ordinates the preparation of the budget; ensures government revenues by maintaining and developing the system of taxes and duties

Website(s) information:

Finansdepartementet — **url:** odin.dep.no/fin **Description:** comprehensive information on the Norwegian economy including government budgets; policy; projections; main indicators; government debts; taxes and financial markets

Publication(s):

Statsbudsjettet *(State Budget)* — **Language:** Norwegian **Frequency:** annual **Content:** contains information on the annual state budget

Mattilsynet

Norwegian Food Safety Authority

Address: Postboks 8187, Ullevålsveien 76, Oslo, 0454
Telephone: +47 23 216 800
Fax: +47 23 217 001
E-mail: postmottak@mattilsynet.no
Website: www.mattilsynet.no

Guides: publications are available to download free on the web site, some are available in English

Activity: responsible for food legislation and enforcement; promotes human, plant, fish and animal health, environmentally friendly production, and ethically acceptable farming of animals and fish. It performs duties relating to cosmetics and medicines, and inspects animal health personnel

Website(s) information:

Statens Naeringsmiddeltilsyn (STN) *(Norwegian Food Control Authority (SNT))* — **url:** www.snt.no **Description:** provides information on the controls put on food production and import **Coverage:** contains data on animal feed, control and health; plant health, food safety and import and export

Norges Bank

Bank of Norway

Address: Postboks 1179, Sentrum, Bankplassen 2, Oslo, 0107
Telephone: +47 22 316 000
Fax: +47 22 413 105
E-mail: central.bank@norges-bank.no
Website: www.norges-bank.no

Guides: annual reports available free of charge in Norwegian and English

Activity: works to achieve a balanced economic developments and a stable financial markets and payment systems

Website(s) information:

Norges Bank *(Bank of Norway)* — **url:** www.norges-bank.no **Description:** provides information about the bank and contains dowloadable versions of its publications **Coverage:** contains statistical information about interest rates, foreign exchange flows and foreign direct investment rates

Publication(s):

Annual Report — **Language:** Norwegian/English **Frequency:** annual **Content:** contains a summary of the international and domestic fiscal developments

Economic Bulletin — **Language:** Norwegian/English **Frequency:** quarterly **Content:** contains a review of economic trends, with data on the main economic indicators and business statistics

Financial Stability Report — **Language:** Norwegian/English **Frequency:** quarterly **Content:** contains data on developments in households, enterprises, financial institutions, international and macroeconomic

Inflation Report — **Language:** Norwegian/English **Frequency:** quarterly **Content:** contains an overview of price trends and factors which influence price and wage inflation

Investment Management — **Language:** Norwegian/English **Frequency:** quarterly **Content:** contains a review of foreign direct investments; return on the international equity portfolios; international interest rates and bond prices

Statistisk Sentralbyrå
Central Bureau of Statistics

Address: Postboks 8131 Dep, Sjøfartsbygningen, Kongens gate 6, Oslo, 0033
Telephone: +47 21 090 000
Fax: +47 21 094 973
E-mail: ssb@ssb.no
Website: www.ssb.no

Guides: publications (free; annual; contains details of main series of publications; English); Veiviser i norsk statistikk/Guide to Norwegian Statistics (free; survey of official Norwegian statistics arranged by subject in Norwegian and English); Catalogue of Norwegian Statistics and Other Publications Published by the Central Bureau of Statistics

Activity: publishes official statistics on Norway

Website(s) information:
Statistisk Sentralbyrå (Statistics Norway) — **url:** www.ssb.no **Description:** provides information on the Sentralbyrå main products and services, including catalogue of publications; Annual Report; and access to series of online publications, most of these provided both in Norwegian and in English **Coverage:** contains monthly and annual statistical data, covering a wide range of socio-economic indicators: population and the environment; health and education; personal economy and housing conditions; labour market; national economy and external trade; industrial activities and financial markets, etc. In the Statistical Yearbook, general data on other Northern European countries is also provided (covering mainly population, employment and consumer price indices)

Publication(s):
Kvinner og menn i Norge (Women and Men in Norway) — **Language:** Norwegian **Frequency:** annual **Content:** data refers to immigration, health, employment, time-use, households and crime

Naturressurser og Miljø (Natural Resources and the Environment) — **Language:** Norwegian **Frequency:** annual **Content:** data refers to growth in consumption and production and its effects on ecosystems

Økonomiske analyser (Economic Survey) — **Language:** Norwegian/English **Frequency:** quarterly **Content:** analysis of latest developments in the Norwegian and international economy, supported by statistical data on major macro-economic indicators

Olje- og gassvirksomhet (Oil and Gas Activity Quarterly) — **Language:** Norwegian **Frequency:** quarterly **Content:** data refers to production, prices, investment costs for exploration, field development, fields on stream and onshore activity

Statistisk Årbok (Statistical Yearbook of Norway) — **Language:** Norwegian/English **Frequency:** annual **Content:** annual socio-economic statistics, covering a wide range of topics, from environment and population, to labour market and financial statistics

Statistisk Månedshefte (Monthly Bulletin of Statistics) — **Language:** Norwegian/English **Frequency:** monthly **Content:** monthly highlights of major socio-economic indicators (population; health and social conditions; labour market; national economy; and public finances)

Poland

Glowny Urzad Statystyczny (GUS)
Central Statistical Office

Address: al. Niepodleglosci 208, Warsaw, 00925
Telephone: +48 22 608 3000
Fax: +48 22 608 3869
E-mail: SekretariatUSwro@stat.gov.pl, dane@stat.gov.pl
Website: www.stat.gov.pl

Guides: provides information on socio-economic, demographic, social situation in various regions

Activity: statistical service (regional data bank) and international statistics (UN, EU, OECD)

Website(s) information:
Glowny Urzad Statystyczny (GUS) (Central Statistical Office) — **url:** www.stat.gov.pl **Description:** information on the Polish economy. Statistics covering: socio-economic data; economics; infrastructure; labour and employment; trade; and industry. Only available in Polish **Coverage:** provides data and analysis on demographic, economic and marketing indicators

Publication(s):
Demographic Yearbook — **Language:** English/Polish **Frequency:** annual **Content:** statistical analysis of Poland's population structure and demographic trends

Statistical Bulletin — **Language:** Polish/English **Frequency:** monthly **Content:** monthly update of main economic indicators, covering: GDP; labour market and earnings; money and finance; agricultural and industrial production; etc

Statistical Yearbook of Foreign Trade — **Language:** Polish/English **Frequency:** annual **Content:** foreign trade statistics by country

Statistical Yearbook of Industry — **Language:** Polish/English **Frequency:** annual **Content:** statistical overview of the Polish industrial sector, covering production and manufacturing; price indices; labour costs and productivity; consumption; etc

Statistical Yearbook of Labour — **Language:** Polish/English **Frequency:** annual **Content:** structure of employment and labour market, including statistics of employment and unemployment rates; labour costs, earnings and turnover; etc

Statistical Yearbook of the Republic of Poland — **Language:** Polish/English **Frequency:** annual **Content:** main annual socio-economic statistics for Poland and international comparisons

Instytut Lacznosci
The National Institute of Telecommunications

Address: ul. Szachowa 1, Warsaw, 04894
Telephone: +48 22 512 8100
Fax: +48 22 512 8625
E-mail: info@itl.waw.pl
Website: www.nit.eu

Guides: publishes magazines and specialist scientific and technical books on telecommunications and information technology

Activity: scientific research and development, which covers all areas of telecommunications and statutory works

Website(s) information:
Instytut Lacznosci (National Institute of Telecommunications) — **url:** www.nit.eu **Coverage:** provides statistical reports on the use of computers and the internet in Poland in terms of users, purposes, locations etc

Publication(s):
Journal of Telecommunications and Information Technology — **Language:** English/Polish **Frequency:** quarterly **Content:** covers a range of topics including image coding, unequal error protection coding and data encryption, through the problems of mobile ad hoc networks, traffic management in high speed internet, to techniques enabling better bandwidth utilisation and accuracy of hardware

Ministerstwo Rolnictwa i Rozwoju Wsi
Ministry of Agriculture and Rural Development

Address: Wspólna Street No. 30, Warsaw, 00930
Telephone: +48 22 623 1000
Fax: +48 22 629 5599
E-mail: rzecznik.prasowy@minrol.gov.pl or kancelana@minrol.gov.pl
Website: www.minrol.gov.pl

Guides: developments in agriculture in 2007-2013, information on technical infrastructure, food economy in rural areas

Publication(s):
Biuletyn Informacyjny (Information Bulletin) — **Language:** Polish **Frequency:** monthly **Content:** provides current socio-economic and financing information in the agricultural market

Informacje o Rolnictwie na Swiecie (World Agricultural Information) — **Language:** Polish **Frequency:** bi-monthly **Content:** provides current socio-economic and financing information in the agricultural market provides information on organic food, investments, research

Rural Development Programme for Poland 2007-2013 — **Language:** English/Polish **Content:** agricultural policy, plant and animal production, food industry and foreign trade

Ministerstwo Srodowiska
Ministry of the Environment

Address: ul. Wawelska 52/54, Warsaw, 00922
Telephone: +48 22 579 2900
Fax: +48 22 579 2224
Website: www.mos.gov.pl

Guides: publishes documents on environmental technologies and innovations
Activity: representation, promotion and preparation of acts and documents related to the environment

Publication(s):
Enviromental Impact Assessment Procedures in Poland — **Language:** English/Polish **Content:** provides assistance in implementing a new legislation for public administration bodies responsible for carrying out EIA procedures

Roadmap for Implementation Environmental Technology Action Plan in Poland — **Language:** English/Polish **Content:** main direction-elements undertaken in Poland within the scope of environmental technologies and innovations, as well as the establishment of a framework for coordinating these activities

Ministerstwo Transportu i Budownictwa
Ministry of Transport and Construction

Address: ul. Chalubinskiego 4/6, Warsaw, 00928
Telephone: +48 22 630 1000
Fax: +48 22 630 1116
E-mail: info.fe@mtib.gov.pl
Website: www.mtib.gov.pl

Guides: provides directives, ordinances, acts related to road, air and rail transport
Activity: covers the issues related to road, rail, maritime and air transport and telecommunication; also provides development of the domestic road infrastructure network; execution of issues in the scope of construction and architecture, housing policy and management, spatial management and development support and the revitalization of cities as well as state aid in the repayment of housing credits; responsible for the issues related to the provisions of road traffic, road safety and the conditions for the execution of transport

Publication(s):
Directives and Ordinances — **Language:** English/Polish **Frequency:** irregular **Content:** provides directives and ordinances of norms, conditions, perspectives and direction of development in road, train, rail and air transport

Narodowy Bank Polandi
National Bank of Poland

Address: PO Box 1011, Information and Promotion Division, ul. Swietokrzyska 11/21, Warsaw, 00919
Telephone: +48 22 653 1000
Fax: +48 22 620 8518/263 932/269 955
E-mail: npl@nbp.pl
Website: www.nbp.pl

Guides: provides publications which contain information on overall economic and financial performance in Poland; offers various research papers, reports
Activity: maintains price stability, stabilises inflation rates, monetary policy, issue of currency banking supervision, development of payment systems, management of official reserves, education and information, services to the State Treasury

Website(s) information:
Narodowy Bank Polandi (National Bank of Poland) — **url:** www.nbp.pl
Description: offers online access to various Bank of Poland publications including: Official journal of the Bank; information bulletin; annual reports; monetary policy guidelines; inflation report **Coverage:** includes statistical reports of exchange rates; interest rates; balance of payments; loans and deposits; assets and liabilities; official reserves; external debt

Publication(s):
Inflation Report — **Language:** English/Polish **Frequency:** quarterly **Content:** inflationary trends, monetary aspects of inflation, and the non-monetary factors, external and internal, inflation

Information Bulletin — **Language:** English/Polish **Frequency:** monthly **Content:** overall economic and financial performance in Poland and on the policies of the Central Bank

Roczny Raport (Annual Report) — **Language:** English/Polish **Frequency:** annual **Content:** contains information on overall economic and financial performance in Poland and on the development of the banking sector, together with the balance sheet of the NBP and the banking system, and the balance of payments of the Republic of Poland

Portugal

Banco de Portugal - Economic Research Department
National Bank of Portugal

Address: Rua do Ouro 27, Lisbon, 1100-150
Telephone: +351 21 321 3200
Fax: +351 21 346 4843
E-mail: info@bportugal.pt
Website: www.bportugal.pt

Activity: maintaining the stability of the domestic financial system

Website(s) information:
Banco de Portugal (National Bank of Portugal) — **url:** www.bportugal.pt
Description: the section statistics includes all kind of economic and financial indicators in pdf or excel format; available in English and Portuguese **Coverage:** main economic indicators, daily reference exchange rates, reference interest rate of the Euro's area money market, monetary and financial, non financial corporation from Central Balance-Sheet database. It aslo includes a list of credit institutions and financial companies registered with the Central Bank of Portugal

Publication(s):
Boletim Económico (Economic Bulletin) — **Language:** English/Portuguese **Frequency:** quarterly **Content:** quarterly publication with papers on the policy and economic situation, as well as studies applied to the Portuguese economy

Boletim Estatístico (Statistical Bulletin) — **Language:** English/Portuguese **Frequency:** monthly **Content:** monetary and financial statistics, balance of payments and international investment position, and exchange rate statistics. Also includes chapters on main indicators, public finance and general statistics

Evolução das Economias dos PALOP e de Timor-Leste (Economic Trends of the Portuguese-Speaking African Countries and East-Timor) — **Language:** English/Portuguese **Frequency:** irregular **Content:** main economic indicators of the Portuguese-Speaking African countries: Angola, Green Cape, Guinea Bissau, Mozambique, São Tomé e Príncipe and Timor-Leste. It also includes economic and financial relations between Portugal and PALOP and East-Timor

Indicadores de Conjuntura (Monthly Economic Indicators) — **Language:** English/Portuguese **Frequency:** monthly **Content:** the main economic indicators disclosed throughout the month including tables and graphics

Inquérito aos Bancos sobre o Mercado de Crédito (Bank Lending Survey) — **Language:** English/Portuguese **Frequency:** quarterly **Content:** covers loan demands and loan supply factors. Also available from 2003

Relatório Anual (Annual Report) — **Language:** English/Portuguese **Frequency:** annual **Content:** presents an integrated analysis on the economic trend in the Euro area and in Portugal. Report and financial statements

Relatório de Estabilidade Financeira (Financial Stability Report) — **Language:** English/Portuguese **Frequency:** irregular **Content:** overall assessment, macroeconomic environment, activity, profitability and risk coverage, market Risk, liquidity risk, credit risk

Sistemas de Pagamentos em Portugal *(Payment Systems in Portugal)* —
Language: English/Portuguese **Frequency:** irregular **Content:** it
publishes regularly an extensive report on payments and securities
settlements systems (domestic and cross-border) in the European
Union Member States

Gabinete de Estratégia e Estudos (GEE)
Economic Planning Secretariat

Address: Rua José Estevão 83A, 1° Esq., Lisbon, 1169-153
Telephone: +351 21 311 0700/0770
Fax: +351 21 311 0773
Website: www.gee.min-economia.pt/site/gepe_home_pt00.asp

Activity: produces economical studies in order to help government
decision-making

Website(s) information:
Gabinete de Estrategia e Estudos *(Economic Planning Secretariat)* — **url:**
www.gee.min-economia.pt/resources/docs **Description:** Eurostat
publications available to download. Business climate indicators for
the EU **Coverage:** economic indicators

GEPE-Ministerio de Economia *(Minister of Economy)* — **url:**
www.gee.min-economia.pt **Coverage:** fact sheets, foreign trade,
energy, companies, economic indicators, balance of payments,
investment indicators, labour market, prices.

Publication(s):
Boletin Mensual de Actividad Economica *(Monthly Bulletin of Economic Activity)* —
Language: Portuguese **Frequency:** monthly **Content:** national and
international fact sheet, world economic growth forecast; statistical
index of all the economic indicators

Capital de Risco *(Risk Capital)* — **Language:** Portuguese **Frequency:** irregular
Content: current situation in Portugal, investment evolution in the
country. It also contains the investment in R&D in the EU

Dinamica Empresarial - Perspectiva Sectorial e Regional *(Dynamic Enterprises - By
Sector and Regional Perspective)* — **Language:** Portuguese
Frequency: irregular **Content:** sector industry analysis

Indicadores e Medidas *(Indicators and Measures)* — **Language:** Portuguese
Frequency: irregular **Content:** different indicators about industry,
competition, public services, labour markets

Industria de Conteudos. Uma Visao Estrategica *(Audiovisual Industry: A Strategic
Vision)* — **Language:** Portuguese **Frequency:** irregular **Content:**
contains graphics and tables about the audiovisual industry in
Portugal and also includes an analysis of the sector in Europe (GDP,
trade balance, commercial structure)

Portugal - Principales Indicadores *(Portugal - Main Indicators)* — **Language:**
English **Frequency:** irregular **Content:** main economics indicators
of Portugal for last six years. It includes trade account, structure of
international trade by group of products, trade with the countries of
the enlargement and the main origin and destiny markets of
products

Productos Industriales Transformados - Por Grau de Intensidade Tecnologica *(Final
Products - Technology Levels)* — **Language:** Portuguese **Frequency:**
irregular **Content:** exports and imports of final products (high,
medium or low technological level), balance of trade, evolution
indicators in volume and price

Projecto Competitividade *(Competition Project)* — **Language:** Portuguese
Frequency: irregular **Content:** analysis of competitive indicators in
18 sectors of foreign trade from 1998 to 2003

Sector Electrico - Comparaçoes Estatisticas entre Portugal e a Europa *(Electrical
Sector - Statistical Comparisons between Portugal and Europe)* —
Language: Portuguese **Frequency:** irregular **Content:** global
production indicators, production of electricity by country

Sector Electrico-Indicadores Comparativos Portugal e Espanha *(Electric
Sector-Comparative Indicators between Portugal and Spain)* —
Language: Portuguese **Frequency:** irregular **Content:** energy and
socio-economic indicators, main agents, production of electricity and
consumption

Instituto Nacional de Estatística (INE)
National Institute of Statistics

Address: Av. António José de Almeida, Lisbon, 1000-043
Telephone: +351 218 426 100
Fax: +351 218 426 380
E-mail: ine@ine.pt
Website: www.ine.pt

Activity: compilation of national statistics; research studies and publications

Website(s) information:
Instituto Nacional de Estatística Portugal *(National Institute of Statistics of
Portugal)* — **url:** www.ine.pt **Description:** online access to the
statistical data published by INE; database searchable by area;
geographic unit and by word; cost of the service depends on the size
of the files downloaded **Coverage:** statistics and major indicators on
consumer prices; labour; population; national economic and
financial news

Publication(s):
Anuário Estatístico de Portugal *(Statistical Yearbook of Portugal)* — **Language:**
Portuguese **Frequency:** annual **Content:** statistics and figures on
major demographic; social; economic and industrial indicators

Anuários Estatísticos Regionais *(Regional Statistical Yearbook)* — **Language:**
Portuguese **Frequency:** annual **Content:** compilation of regional
statistical publications offering a comparison among regions;
economic; social and demographic indicators

As Cidades em Números *(Cities in Figures)* — **Language:** Portuguese **Frequency:**
irregular **Content:** statistics and figures on demography;
construction and companies in 141 Portuguese cities

Boletim Mensal de Estatística *(Monthly Bulletin of Statistics)* — **Language:**
Portuguese **Frequency:** monthly **Content:** monthly update of
socio-economic indicators covering population; agriculture and
industries; internal and external commerce; services and finances

Boletim Trimestral de Estatística *(Statistical Quarterly Bulletin)* — **Language:**
Portuguese **Frequency:** quarterly **Content:** regional economic
conjuncture analysis

Estatísticas Agrícolas *(Agriculture Statistics)* — **Language:** Portuguese **Frequency:**
annual **Content:** statistics and figures on agriculture; livestock;
forestry and fishing

Estatísticas da Produção Agro-industrial *(Agro-industrial Statistics)* — **Language:**
Portuguese **Frequency:** irregular **Content:** statistics and figures on
agricultural and industrial production

Estatísticas das Comunicações *(Communications Statistics)* — **Language:**
Portuguese **Frequency:** annual **Content:** information on national
public and private postal services and telecommunications in
Portugal; financial and economic indicators

Estatísticas das Empresas *(Companies Statistics)* — **Language:** Portuguese
Frequency: annual **Content:** overview of companies' economic and
financial situation

Estatísticas do Ambiente *(Environment Statistics)* — **Language:** Portuguese
Frequency: annual **Content:** statistics and figures on the
environment

Estatísticas do Comércio Internacional *(International Trade Statistics)* —
Language: Portuguese/English **Frequency:** annual **Content:**
statistical data on imports and exports by products and by country in
Portugal; figures on external trade in Europe

Estatísticas do Turismo *(Tourism Statistics)* — **Language:** Portuguese **Frequency:**
annual **Content:** statistics and figures on domestic trade; tourism
and other services

Estatísticas dos Transportes *(Transport Statistics)* — **Language:** Portuguese
Frequency: annual **Content:** statistics and figures on maritime; air;
road and rail transport

Estatísticas Históricas Portuguesas *(Historic Portuguese Statistics)* — **Language:**
Portuguese/English **Frequency:** irregular **Content:** statistics and
figures on population; cities; national accounts; production;
currency; prices and wages; finances and foreign trade from 1994 to
2000

Gastos dos Estrangeiros não Residentes em Portugal *(Expenses of Foreigners Living
in Portugal)* — **Language:** Portuguese **Frequency:** irregular
Content: overview of cost of living in Portugal **Readership:** tourists;
future residents

Indicadores Sociais *(Social Indicators)* — **Language:** Portuguese **Frequency:**
annual **Content:** overview of general living conditions in Portugal;
covering employment; household incomes and expenditure; social
security; health and education services

Índice de Preços no Consumidor *(Consumer Prices Index)* — **Language:** Portuguese
Frequency: monthly **Content:** consumer prices indicators

O País em Números *(The Country in Figures)* — **Language:** Portuguese **Content:**
statistics and figures on economy; education; labour; tourism;
commerce; environment and other issues from 1991 to 2004; graphs
and charts

Península Ibérica em Números *(Peninsula in Figures)* — **Language:**
Portuguese/Spanish **Frequency:** annual **Content:** statistics and
figures in Portugal and Spain. Main indicators include economy;
labour; technology; transport

Retrato Territorial de Portugal (Portugal's Demographic Profile) — **Language:** Portuguese **Frequency:** annual **Content:** socio-economic description of Portugal region by region

Revista Portuguesa de Estudos Regionais (Portuguese Journal of Regional Studies) — **Language:** Portuguese **Frequency:** quarterly **Content:** statistics and research studies covering major demographic and social indicators; immigration; labour; tourism; etc

Revstat Statistical Journal — **Language:** English **Frequency:** quarterly **Content:** statistics and research studies on economy and demography

Ministério da Agricultura, do Desenvolvimento e das Pescas
Ministry of Agriculture, Rural Development and Fishing

Address: Rua Padre Antonio Vieira 1, Lisboa, 1099-073
Telephone: +351 21 346 3151
Fax: +351 21 347 3798
E-mail: geral@min-agricultura.pt
Website: www.min-agricultura.pt

Activity: responsible for agricultural and fishing policy and the rural economy

Website(s) information:
Ministério da Agricultura, do Desenvolvimento Rural e das Pescas (Ministry of Agriculture, Rural Development and Fisheries) — **url:** www.min-agricultura.pt **Description:** statistical data on agricultural production, imports and exports; forestry; fishing; and EU structural supports. National and EU legislation

Publication(s):
Agricultores, Entidades e Servicios (Farmers, Entities and Services) — **Language:** Portuguese **Frequency:** irregular **Content:** services offered in Portugal to the agricultural producers and managers

Agricultura Portuguesa Principais Indicadores (Portuguese Agriculture Main Indicators) — **Language:** English/Portuguese **Frequency:** annual **Content:** climate, Portuguese agriculture within the EU, territories, agriculture in Portugal: economy, population and employment, environment and structure

Anuario de Campanha - Principais Ajudas Directas (Campaign Yearbook - Main Benefits) — **Language:** Portuguese **Frequency:** annual **Content:** statistical analysis of the main benefits directed to the agricultural sector

Anuario Pecuario (Animal Production Yearbook) — **Language:** English/Portuguese **Frequency:** annual **Content:** cattle, pigs, sheep and goats, poultry and eggs, milk and dairy products: market overview, prices, exchange, consumer prices, foreign trade, supply balance, world market, union market, per capita consumption and degree of self sufficiency of meat and eggs in the EU. Overview of the animal mixed feed industry

Anuario Vegetal (Crop Production Yearbook) — **Language:** English/Portuguese **Frequency:** annual **Content:** fresh fruits and nuts, fresh vegetables, flowers and foliage: Production and marketing characteristics in Portugal, foreign trade, supply balances and consumer prices. Arable crops, olive oil and table olives: Production and foreign trade

Apoios a la Agricultura (Support for Agriculture) — **Language:** Portuguese **Frequency:** annual **Content:** contains tables and figures with all the support programmes available to the agricultural Industry

Envolvente Socio-Economica (Socio-Economic Indicators) — **Language:** Portuguese **Frequency:** annual **Content:** socio-economic indicators

Expectativas dos Empresarios Agricolas 2005-2007 (Farmers Expectations 2005-2007) — **Language:** Portuguese **Frequency:** irregular **Content:** result of a survey after personal interviews involving 928 farmers. Includes expectations from 2004-2006

Romania

Centrul de Informare al Organizatiei Natiunilor Unite pentru Romania
United Nations Information Centre in Romania

Address: Bulevardul Primaverii nr 48A, sector 1, Bucharest, 011975 1
Telephone: +40 21 201 7877
Fax: +40 21 201 7880
E-mail: unic@un.ro
Website: www.onuinfo.ro

Guides: publications can be viewed in the library. Opens from 8.30-13.00 and from 14.45-16.45 (Monday to Friday)
Activity: provides access to documents of the UN

Institutul National de Statistica
National Statistical Institute

Address: 16 Libertatii Avenue, district 5, Bucharest
Telephone: +40 21 318 18 50
Fax: +40 21 312 48 73
E-mail: romstat@insse.ro
Website: www.insse.ro

Activity: compiles statistics on Romania

Website(s) information:
Institutul National de Statistica (National Statistical Institute) — **url:** www.insse.ro **Description:** online information on the Institute's main products and services; includes both annual and monthly socio-economic indicators **Coverage:** main socio-economic data covering demographics and population trends; industrial production; GDP growth; foreign trade; retail trade; consumer price indices; and income and earnings

Publication(s):
Romania in Figures — **Language:** Romanian/English **Frequency:** annual **Content:** figures on population, labour force, national accounts, agriculture, industry, energy, construction, tourism and other socio-economic data

Romanian Demographic Yearbook — **Language:** Romanian/English **Frequency:** annual **Content:** data on population numbers and demographic and socio-economic structures

Romanian Foreign Trade Yearbook — **Language:** Romanian/English **Frequency:** annual **Content:** Romanian exports and imports, classified by goods

Romanian Statistical Yearbook — **Language:** Romanian/English **Frequency:** annual **Content:** compilation of a wide range of socio-economic indicators for the last five years

Romanian Tourism — **Language:** Romanian/English **Frequency:** annual **Content:** annual statistics on the tourism industry in Romania: structure of the industry; available infrastructures and resources; number of national and international tourists' arrivals; tourists by country of origin; etc

Ministerul Agriculturii, Padurilor si Dezvoltarii Rurale
Ministry of Agriculture, Forestry and Rural Development

Address: B-dul Carol I, nr. 24, sector 3, Bucharest, 020921
Telephone: +40 21 3072300
Fax: +40 21 3078685
E-mail: comunicare@maa.ro;
Website: mapam.ro

Guides: the Ministry disseminates statistics on various areas of agricultural activity in Romania
Activity: regulates policy issues regarding agriculture

Website(s) information:
Ministerul Agriculturii, Padurilor si Dezvoltarii Rurale (Ministry of Agriculture, Forestry and Rural Development) — **url:** mapam.ro **Coverage:** statistics of all the main agricultural products in Romania

Ministerul Finantelor Publice
Ministry of Public Finance

Address: 17 Apolodor Street, 5th District, Bucharest, 050741
Telephone: +40 1 4103400
Fax: +40 1 3122509
E-mail: publicinfo@mfinante.gv.ro
Website: www.mfinante.ro

Guides: access to legislation, strategic development plans, financial control and management systems, and a monthly bulletin
Activity: collects and manages public financial resources; ensures the collection of the revenues stipulated in the budget and performs treasury operations

Website(s) information:

Ministerul Finantelor Publice *(Ministry of Public Finance)* — **url:** www.mfinante.ro
Coverage: online access to various reports on strategies for growth with a focus on new markets and technologies

National Bank of Romania

Address: Strada Lipscani 25, Sector 3, Bucharest, 030031
Telephone: +40 21 3130410
E-mail: Info@bnro.ro
Website: www.bnro.ro/def_en.htm

Guides: periodicals (daily, weekly, monthly, annually) as well as publications on specific issues related to economic and financial developments; all publications can be downloaded online
Activity: the sole institution vested with the power to issue notes and coins; ensures and maintains price stability

Website(s) information:

National Bank of Romania — **url:** www.bnro.ro/def_en.htm **Coverage:** weekly and daily updates of financial development in Romania as well as specific data on foreign direct investment, financial behaviour of households and companies, gross external debt, etc

Publication(s):

Annual Reports — **Language:** Romanian/English **Frequency:** annual **Content:** overview of main economic and financial developments

Financial Stability Report — **Language:** Romanian/English **Frequency:** annual **Content:** report on the financial system and its risks

Monthly Bulletins — **Language:** English/Romanian **Frequency:** monthly **Content:** covers main monthly economic and financial developments. Includes a statistical section

Russia

Central Bank of the Russian Federation

Address: 12 Neglinnaya Street, Moscow, 107016
Telephone: +7 495 771 9100
Fax: +7 495 621 6465
Website: www.cbr.ru

Guides: catalogue available online, as well as links to PDF versions of all documents - access is free of charge
Activity: organisation of money circulation, monetary regulation, foreign economic activity and regulation of the activities of joint-stock and co-operative banks; prints banknotes and coins

Website(s) information:

Central Bank of the Russian Federation — **url:** www.cbr.ru **Description:** detailed information about the bank and the banking system in Russia. Financial market information covering inter-bank credit market; Rouble deposit rate; government securities market; foreign currency market; precious metals market; other information and analytical material. Also has daily information on foreign exchange rates, commodities rates, and Russia's financial reserve rate **Coverage:** major macroeconomic and financial data, which are disseminated by the Bank of Russia in accordance with IMF Special Data Dissemination Standard (SDDS). Monetary statistical data, balance of payment data (1994 - to date) and other types of statistical data relating to the domestic economy and financial markets

Publication(s):

Bulletin of Banking Statistics — **Language:** English/Russian **Frequency:** monthly **Content:** overview of key macroeconomic statistics; financial markets of inter-bank credits, currency exchange markets, government bonds trading, overview of the number, structure and main indicators of crediting institutions; main payments system indicators of the Russian Federation

Ministerstvo Promishlennosti i Energetiki

Ministry of Industry and Energy

Address: 7 Kitaygorodskij Proezd, Moscow, 109074
Telephone: +7 495 710 5500
Fax: +7 495 710 5722
E-mail: info@mte.gov.ru
Website: www.minprom.gov.ru

Guides: list is available online - full guide to publications and publishers details; available in Russian only
Activity: determines Government policy and designs government projects for addressing the problems of light and heavy industry and the energy industry

Website(s) information:

MinPromEnergo - Statistika *(Ministry of Industry and Energy - Statistics)* — **url:** www.minprom.gov.ru/showStatX **Description:** provides links to statistical surveys carried out by the Ministry; contains official data on government projects and policy; surveys are carried out bi-monthly and cover the main trends in the different branches of Russian industry **Coverage:** bi-monthly surveys of the state of the light and heavy industries in Russia - production and consumption figures, trade and prices

Publication(s):

Energija Promishlennogo Posta *(Energy of Industrial Growth)* — **Language:** Russian **Frequency:** monthly **Content:** mohtly overview and analyses of production figures, growth, exports and consumptions of goods in particular industries; corporate news and data about Russian companies **Readership:** businessmen, producers, government officials, investors

Ministerstvo Transporta Rossijskoj Federatsii

Ministry of Transport of the Russian Federation

Address: 1 Rozhdestvenka Street, Moscow, 109012
Telephone: +7 495 926 1000
Fax: +7 495 926 9128/926 9038
E-mail: info@mintrans.ru
Website: www.mintrans.ru

Guides: a full catalogue and publisher details are provided online
Activity: determines Government policy and the normative-legal regulatory basis for air, road, see and river transport, industrial transport and the naming of geographic sites and cartographic activity on the territory of the Russian Federation

Publication(s):

Transport Rossii *(Russia's Transport)* — **Language:** Russian **Frequency:** weekly **Content:** articles and analyses on matters in the sphere of transport - government policy, projects, economic developments and news

Ministry of Agriculture of the Russian Federation

Address: 1/11 Orlikov Pereulok, Moscow, 107139
Telephone: +7 495 207 8362
Fax: +7 495 207 8000
E-mail: info@gov.mcx.ru
Website: www.mcx.ru

Guides: available online in PDF format
Activity: determines, coordinates and implements the government's policy for the encouragement of agriculture; sets the minimum standards for agricultural production

Website(s) information:

Ministry of Agriculture of the Russian Federation — **url:** www.mcx.ru **Description:** the website provides statistsical information under the links "Analyses, Trends, Prognoses" and "Facts and Figures" (about markets of particular goods). The information is available in Russian only **Coverage:** data on the number and kind of agricultural producers by ownership type; production figures, analyses and data on mechanization and the use of artificial fertilisers and other pesticides, data on the number and structure of livestock, crops and others in the RF; financial-economic analysis of the SME sector in agriculture; figures and charts on the markets for crops, meat products, milk and dairy products, sugar, etc.

Ministry of Economic Development and Trade of the Russian Federation

Address: 1st Tverskaya-Yamskaya Street, GSP-3, A-47, Moscow, 125993
Telephone: +7 495 200 0353
Fax: +7 495 251 6965
E-mail: presscenter@economy.gov.ru
Website: www.economy.gov.ru

Guides: catalogue available online

Activity: determines, coordinates and implements the government policy and projects for the promotion of trade and economic development (regional and sectoral)

Website(s) information:

Ministry of Economic Development and Trade — **url:** www.economy.gov.ru
Description: links to statistical surveys of the economy carried out by the ministry **Coverage:** provides information about the basic macroeconomic indicators of the Russian economy - quarterly and annual information, monitoring of the average price of sugar

Ministry of Finance of the Russian Federation

Address: 9 Ilinka Street, Moscow, 103097
Telephone: +7 095 298 9101
Website: www.minfin.ru

Guides: catalogue available online - most publications are available online, free of charge

Activity: determines, coordinates and implements the fiscal and monetary policy of the Russian Federation; executes the state budget and services the national public and external debt

Website(s) information:

Special Data Dissemination Standard. National Summary Data Page — **url:** www2.minfin.ru/sdds/nsdp.htm **Description:** the website provides free access to the data produced by the Ministry of finance, Central bank and Federal State Statistics Service in accordance with the IMF's statistical standards **Coverage:** official data covering the real, fiscal, financial and external sectors and population; data on consumption, employment, investment, foreign trade - by month and year

Publication(s):

Finance — **Language:** Russian **Frequency:** monthly **Content:** banking and finance, foreign investment and Russian enterprises

Ministry of Information Technology and Communications of the Russian Federation

Address: Moscow, 125375
Telephone: +7 495 771 8100
Fax: +7 495 771 8718
Website: www.minsvyaz.ru

Guides: available online in PDF format

Activity: determines, coordinates and implements the government's policy in the sphere of IT and communications; works for the development and growth of this sector and for the implementation of unified standards of quality on the territory of the RF

Website(s) information:

Ministry of Information Technology and Communications of the Russian Federation - Statistics — **url:** www.minsvyaz.ru **Description:** the website provides links to different statistical studies, conducted by the Ministry uder the heading "Sector Statistics". The link "Library" provides access to an electronic database, which covers a wide range of topics connected to the sector, including economic information about particular branches of the sector, foreign investment in the telecommunications market and market dynamics and structure. The website provides an extensive list of IT and telecommunications companies in the RF, sorted by region, specific activity and type of ownership **Coverage:** data on basic indicators of the state of the communications and IT sector - density of services, internet users (by year and region), economic indicators - prices, profit, size of the market and growth; structure of the market and competition

Nauchno Issledovatelskij Finansovij Institut (NIFI)

Institute for Scientific Financial Research

Address: 3 Nastasinskij Pereulok, Corpus II, Moscow, 127006
Telephone: +7 495 299 7414
Fax: +7 495 299 8853
E-mail: savinskiy@nifi.ru
Website: www2.minfin.ru/nifi/index.htm

Guides: online catalogue

Activity: conducts research in the sphere of government finance, monetary and crediting policy, financial markets and other matters in the area of banking and finance

Russian Academy of Sciences, Institute of Economic Forecasting

Address: 47 Nakhimovsky Prospect, Moscow, 117418
Telephone: +7 095 129 3422/129 1800
Fax: +7 095 310 7071
E-mail: office@mail.ecfor.rssi.ru
Website: www.ecfor.rssi.ru

Guides: publishes the journal "Studies on Russian Economic Development", which covers the most important trends and developments in Russian economy and publishes the most significant statistical results of the Institute's research

Activity: carries out short-, medium- and long-term research and forecasting of macroeconomic developments and indicators in Russia

Publication(s):

Studies on Russian Economic Development — **Language:** English/Russian **Frequency:** bi-monthly **Content:** contains information on the key economic and social problems in Russia, presents the most significant results of the research at the Institute, and publishes statistics and methodological materials **Readership:** academics, students, government officials

State Committee of the Russian Federation on Statistics (GOSKOMSTAT)

Address: 39 Myasnitskaya Street, Moscow, 107450
Telephone: +7 095 207 4902
Fax: +7 095 207 4087
E-mail: stat@gks.ru
Website: www.gks.ru

Guides: full catalogue is available online; most annual publications are available in English, and others can be translated at the request of the customer; publications can be obtained in printed, CD-ROM and/or web-access format

Activity: carries out continuous statistical analysis of social and economic activity and trends in the country; the official body for gathering, analysing and disseminating statistical information and analyses on the territory of the Russian Federation

Website(s) information:

Federal Statistics Service — **url:** www.gks.ru **Description:** the official website of the Statistical Survey publishes the most important data from their statistical collections and other publications online **Coverage:** data on population, labour dynamics, economic indicators, health care and status of the population, education, GNP, industrial production, agriculture, transport, trade and services, foreign trade, finance, investment flows

Publication(s):

Agriculture in Russia — **Frequency:** annual **Content:** data on farms, livestock, crops

Demographic Yearbook — **Language:** Russian **Frequency:** annual **Content:** demographics

External Trade of the CIS Countries — **Language:** Russian **Frequency:** annual **Content:** data on foreign trade with post-soviet countries

Incomes, Expenditures and Household Consumption — **Language:** Russian **Frequency:** annual **Content:** data on wages and average expenditure on household products

Information on Socio-economic Situation in Russia — **Language:** Russian **Frequency:** monthly **Content:** monthly overview of data on main so-economic indicators and commentaries

Labour and Employment — **Language:** Russian **Frequency:** annual **Content:** data on available work force in the country and unemployment rates; data is given by regions

Population Size and Migration in Russia — **Language:** Russian **Frequency:** annual **Content:** data on the country's demographic situation

Russia in Figures — **Language:** Russian/English **Frequency:** annual **Content:** general socio-economic overview of the Russian Federation, with statistics covering: population structure and demographic trends; labour market; household expenditure; evolution of major macro-economic indicators; agricultural and industrial production; national accounts and balance of payments; etc

Statistical Insight — **Language:** Russian/English **Frequency:** quarterly **Content:** articles and commentaries on news and trends in statistical science; different types of surveys and data published

Statistical Yearbook — **Language:** Russian **Frequency:** annual **Content:** covers main socio-economic indicators

Slovakia

INFOSTAT, Inštitút informatiky a štatistiky
INFOSTAT, Institute of Information Technology and Statistics

Address: Dúbravská 3, Bratislava, 842 21
Telephone: +421 2 5937 9111
Fax: +421 2 5479 1463
E-mail: infostat@infostat.sk
Website: www.infostat.sk

Activity: developing projects relating to information technology and statistics

Website(s) information:
Inštitút Informatiky a Statistiky *(Institute of Information Technology and Statistics)* — **url:** www.infostat.sk **Description:** statistical socio-economic data **Coverage:** socio-economic indicators

Publication(s):
Makroekonomické analýzy a prognózy *(Macroeconomic Analysis and Prognosis)* — **Language:** Slovak **Frequency:** irregular **Content:** macroeconomic environment and developments in the country **Readership:** economists, research specialists, analysts

Letové prevádzkové služby Slovenskej republiky
Air Traffic Control Administration of the Slovak Republic

Address: Letisko M. R. Štefánika, Bratislava 21, 823 07
Telephone: +421 2 4857 1111
E-mail: info@lps.sk
Website: www.rlp.sk

Activity: managing air traffic and related services

Publication(s):
Výrocná správa *(Annual Report)* — **Language:** Slovak/English **Frequency:** annual **Content:** air traffic services (economic developments, audit report, balance sheet, profit and loss, cash flow) **Readership:** air traffic specialists, research specialists, analysts

Ministerstvo dopravy, pôšt a telekomunikácií SR
Ministry of Transport, Postal Services and Telecommunications of the Slovak Republic

Address: Námestie slobody c. 6, Bratislava, 810 05
Telephone: +421 2 5949 4111
Fax: +421 2 5249 4794
E-mail: info@telecom.gov.sk
Website: www.telecom.gov.sk

Activity: creating and implementing the country's policy on transport, postal services and telecommunications

Website(s) information:
Ministerstvo dopravy, pôšt a telekomunikácií SR *(Ministry of Transport, Postal Services and Telecommunications of the Slovak Republic)* — **url:** www.telecom.gov.sk **Description:** the site offers detailed statistical information about the three sectors **Coverage:** transport, postal services and telecommunications

Publication(s):
Intermodálna doprava v Slovenskey republiky *(Intermodal Transport in The Slovak Republic)* — **Language:** Slovak/English **Frequency:** annual **Content:** intermodal transport (volume of goods in tons transported by intermodal transport and development of transport in general) **Readership:** transport specialists, research specialists, analysts, governmental institutions

Štatistické údaje *(Statistical Data)* — **Language:** Slovak/English **Frequency:** irregular **Content:** infrastructure and volume of all types of transport **Readership:** transport specialists, research specialists, analysts, governmental institutions

Štatistické údaje pôšt *(Statistivcal Data on the Postal Services in SR)* — **Language:** Slovak/English **Frequency:** irregular **Content:** postal services (service indicators) **Readership:** research specialists, analysts

Vybrané štatistické údaje za odvetvie telekomunikácií v SR *(Statistic Data on Telecommunications Sector in SR)* — **Language:** Slovak/English **Frequency:** irregular **Content:** telecommunications sector (infrastracture, revenue, quality, traffic, services) **Readership:** telecommunication specialists, research specialists, analysts, governmental institutions

Výrocna správa *(Annual Report)* — **Language:** Slovak/English **Frequency:** annual **Content:** activities of the Ministry, road, rail and water transport, civil aviation, postal services, telecommunications **Readership:** transport specialists, governmental institutions, research specialists, analysts

Ministerstvo hospodárstva Slovenskej republiky
Ministry of Economy of the Slovak Republic

Address: Mierová 19, Bratislava 212, 827 15
Telephone: +421 2 4854 1111
E-mail: info@economy.gov.sk
Website: www.economy.gov.sk

Activity: central body for the industry (with the exception of food industry, construction products and manufacture of construction materials)

Website(s) information:
Ministerstvo hospodárstva Slovenskej republiky *(Ministry of Economy of the Slovak Republic)* — **url:** www.economy.gov.sk **Description:** the site offers statistical information about the country's trade and industry **Coverage:** economic indicators

Publication(s):
Statistical Data on Tourism in Slovakia — **Language:** English **Frequency:** quarterly **Content:** tourism arrivals, number of foreign tourists, departures **Readership:** research specialists, analysts

Trade Statistics — **Language:** English **Frequency:** annual **Content:** trade indicators **Readership:** economists, research specialists, analysts, governmental institutions

Ministerstvo pôdohospodárstva Slovenskey republiky
Ministry of Agriculture of the Slovak Republic

Address: Dobrovicova 12, Bratislava, 812 66
Telephone: +421 2 5926 6301
Fax: +421 2 5926 6311
E-mail: tlacove@land.gov.sk
Website: www.mpsr.sk

Activity: creating and implementing the country's agricultural policy

Website(s) information:
Ministerstvo pôdohospodárstva Slovenskey republiky *(Ministry of Agriculture of the Slovak Republic)* — **url:** www.radela.sk **Description:** presents statistical information about the development in agricultural and food sectors; it offers an extensive overview of branches within the sector **Coverage:** agriculture and food

Publication(s):
Lesné hospodárstvo *(Forestry)* — **Language:** Slovak **Frequency:** irregular **Content:** forestry industry of the country **Readership:** research specialists, analysts, governmental institutions, non-governmental organisations

Vodné hospodárstvo *(Water Industry)* — **Language:** Slovak **Frequency:** irregular **Content:** water industry data **Readership:** research specialists, analysts, governmental organisations

Zelená správa *(Green Report)* — **Language:** Slovak/English **Frequency:** annual **Content:** report on agriculture and food industry **Readership:** agricultural and food experts, governmental institutions, research specialists, analysts

Ministerstvo spravodlivosti SR
Ministry of Justice of the Slovak Republic

Address: Župné námestie 13, Bratislava, 813 11
Telephone: +421 2 5935 3111
E-mail: tlacove@justice.sk
Website: www.justice.gov.sk

Activity: creating and implementing the legal policy of the country

Website(s) information:

Ministerstvo spravodlivosti SR *(Ministry of Justice of the Slovak Republic)* — **url:** www.justice.gov.sk **Description:** the site offers information about the work of legal bodies and crime rate in the country and bay areas **Coverage:** legal system and crime

Ministerstvo zahranicných vecí SR

Ministry of Foreign Affairs of the Slovak Republic

Address: Hlboká cesta 2, Bratislava 37, 833 36
Telephone: +421 2 5978 1111
E-mail: informacie@foreign.gov.sk
Website: www.mzv.sk

Activity: creating and implementing foreign policy of the country

Website(s) information:

Ministerstvo zahranicných vecí SR *(Ministry of Foreign Affairs of the Slovak Republic)* — **url:** www.mzv.sk **Description:** the site offers social and economic indicators **Coverage:** society and economy

Publication(s):

Slovakia, Krajina v ktorej žijeme *(Slovakia, The Country Where We Live)* — **Language:** Slovakian/English/German/French/Russian **Frequency:** irregular **Content:** detailed socio-economic presentation of the country **Readership:** research specialists, analysts, governmental and non-governmental organisations

Ministerstvo zdravotníctva SR

Ministry of Health of the Slovak Republic

Address: 52, Limbová 2, Bratislava 37, 837 52
Telephone: +421 2 5937 3111
Fax: +421 2 5477 7983
E-mail: office@health.gov.sk
Website: www.health.gov.sk

Activity: making and implementing the health policy of the country

Website(s) information:

Ministerstvo zdravotníctva SR *(Ministry of Health of the Slovak Republic)* — **url:** www.health.gov.sk **Description:** the site offers statistical information about the sector **Coverage:** health system

Publication(s):

Výrocná správa Ministerstva zdravotníctva Slovenskej republiky *(Annual Report of the Ministry of Health of the Slovak Republic)* — **Language:** Slovak **Frequency:** annual **Content:** health system of the country and relevant activities of the Ministry **Readership:** health experts, governmental institutions. Research specialists, analysts

Výskyt prenosných ochorení v Slovenskej republike *(Occurrence of Infectious Diseases in the Slovak Republic)* — **Language:** Slovak/English (summary only) **Frequency:** monthly **Content:** infectious diseases data **Readership:** health experts, governmental and non-governmental organisations, research specialists, analysts

Národná banka Slovenska

National Bank of Slovakia

Address: Imricha Karvaša 1, Bratislava, 813 25
Telephone: +421 2 5787 1111
Fax: +421 2 5865 1100
E-mail: info@nbs.sk
Website: www.nbs.sk

Guides: the bank has its own library where all publications can be obtained

Activity: formulating and implementing the country's monetary policy, issuing banknotes and coins, controlling, co-ordinating and providing for the circulation of money, supervising development of the banking sector

Website(s) information:

Národná banka Slovenska *(National Bank of Slovakia)* — **url:** www.nbs.sk **Description:** the site offers detailed information about the country's banking system **Coverage:** facts and figures about the country's banking system

Publication(s):

Analýza bankového sektora *(Analysis of Banking Sector)* — **Language:** Slovak **Frequency:** irregular **Content:** banking sector **Readership:** bankers, investment banks, research specialists, analysts

BIATEC- odborný bankový casopis *(BIATEC - Banking Journal)* — **Language:** Slovenian **Frequency:** irregular **Content:** news from and development of the country's financial system **Readership:** bankers, financial experts, analysts, research specialists

Menový prehlad *(Monetary Survey)* — **Language:** Slovak/English **Frequency:** monthly **Content:** review of economic and financial trends with statistical data covering key economic and financial indicators **Readership:** finanical experts, bankers, governmental institutions, research specialists, analysts

Výrocná správa *(Report on Monetary Development)* — **Language:** Slovenian/English **Frequency:** annual **Content:** monetary system and its development **Readership:** financial experts, bankers, research specialists, analysts

Slovenská agentúra životného prostredia

Slovak Environmental Agency

Address: Tajovskeho 28, Banská Bystrica, 975 90
Telephone: +421 48 437 4111
Fax: +421 48 423 0409
E-mail: sazp@sazp.sk
Website: www.sazp.sk

Activity: ensuring that international requirements regarding environmental protection are complied with, conducting monitoring, implementing waste management policy, assessing risks, implementing project relating to environmental protection

Website(s) information:

Slovenská agentúra životného prostredia *(Slovak Environmental Agency)* — **url:** www.sazp.sk **Coverage:** pollution and waste management

Štatistický úrad SR

Statistical Office of the Slovak Republic

Address: Mileticova 3, Bratislava, 824 67
Telephone: +421 2 5023 6335
Fax: +421 2 5556 1361
Website: www.statistics.sk

Activity: collation and publishing of official statistics

Website(s) information:

Štatistický úrad SR *(Statistical Office of the Slovak Republic)* — **url:** www.statistics.sk **Description:** the site offers the information about products and services, including publications catalogue **Coverage:** detailed socio-economic statistical information

Publication(s):

Aktualizovaná prognóza vývoja vybraných ukazovatelov na rok *(Revised Development Prognosis by Selected Indicators)* — **Language:** Slovak/English **Frequency:** annual **Content:** development trends (findings of a survey on the sectors of industry, construction, trade and market services) **Readership:** economists, research specialists, analysts, governmental organisations, investors

Bulletin SÚ SR *(Bulletin of the Statistical Office of the Slovak Republic)* — **Language:** Slovak/English **Frequency:** monthly **Content:** statistical and narrative report on the latest developments in the Slovak national economy and society **Readership:** economists, research specialists, analysts, governmental organisations, non-governmental organisations

Hospodársky ukazovatel *(Monitor of the Economy)* — **Language:** Slovak/English **Frequency:** monthly **Content:** compilation of monthly and quarterly statistics of the country's economy **Readership:** economists, research specialists, analysts, businesses, governmental institutions

Priemyselná produkcia *(Industrial Production)* — **Language:** Slovak/English **Frequency:** monthly **Content:** industrial production figures **Readership:** statistical and research specialist, analysts, governmental institutions, industrial sector

Rocenka zahranicného obchodu *(Yearbook of Foreign Trade of the Slovak Republic)* — **Language:** Slovak/English **Frequency:** annual **Content:** annual statistical report on the country's foreign trade **Readership:** economists, research specialists, analysts, investors, businessmen

Sociálny vývoj (Social Development Trends in the Slovak Republic) — **Language:** Slovak/English **Frequency:** irregular **Content:** indicators of the country's social development **Readership:** research specialists, analysts, governmental institutions and non-governmental organisations

Statistická rocenka SR (Statistical Yearbook of the Slovak Republic) — **Language:** Slovak/English **Frequency:** annual **Content:** a wide range of detailed socio-economic statistics **Readership:** economists, research specialists, analysts, governmental institutions, non-governmental organisations

Štatistický prehlad o SR (Statistical Review of the Slovak Republic) — **Language:** Slovak/English **Frequency:** quarterly **Content:** latest macro-economic indicators and findings of the most recent surveys and analyses **Readership:** research specialists, analysts, governmental and non-governmental organisations, business and industrial sector

Stavebná produkcia (Construction Industry) — **Language:** Slovak/English **Frequency:** monthly **Content:** construction industry **Readership:** civil engineers, construction industry, research specialists, analysts, investors

Štrukturálny census fariem (Structural Farm Analysis) — **Language:** Slovak/English **Frequency:** irregular **Content:** farming in light of accession to the EU **Readership:** agricultural experts, research specialists, relevant governmental institutions

Vývoj harmonizovaných indexov spotrebitelských cien (Consumer Price Indices) — **Language:** Slovak/English **Frequency:** monthly **Content:** prices and consumers' habits covering certain period and comparison with the previous **Readership:** consumer experts, research specialists, analysts, consumer organisations, businesses

Zamestnanost a priemerná mesacná mzda vo vybraných odvetviach (Employment and Average Monthly Wages by Industries) — **Language:** Slovak/English **Frequency:** monthly **Content:** employment and wages by industries **Readership:** economists, businesses, research specialists, analysts

Výskumné demografické centrum INFOSTAT
Demographic Research Centre INFOSTAT

Address: Dúbravská 3, Bratislava 45, 845 24
Telephone: +421 2 5937 9245
Fax: +421 2 5479 1463
E-mail: vdc@infostat.sk
Website: www.infostat.sk/vdc

Activity: conducting and co-ordinating demographic research in the Slovak Republic

Website(s) information:
Výskumné demografické centrum INFOSTAT (Demographic Research Centre INFOSTAT) — url: www.infostat.sk/vdc **Description:** the site offers detailed statistical information about the demographic trends and situation in the country **Coverage:** demographics

Publication(s):
Populacný vývoj v Slovenskej republike (Population in Slovakia) — **Language:** Slovak/English **Frequency:** annual **Content:** demographic indicators **Readership:** research specialists, analysts, governmental and non-governmental organisations

Prognóza vývoja obyvatelov v okresoch SR do roku 2025 (Population Projection of Districts in Slovakia until 2025) — **Language:** Slovak/English **Frequency:** irregular **Content:** analysis of the current and prognosis of the future demographic developments **Readership:** research specialists, analysts, governmental and non-governmental organisations

Reprodukcné správanie obyvatelstva v obciach s nízkym životným štandardom (The Reproductive Behaviour in Municipalities with Low Living Standard) — **Language:** Slovak/English **Frequency:** irregular **Content:** general birth rate and trends in the areas with low living standards **Readership:** research specialists, analysts, governmental and non-governmental organisations

Výskumný ústav dopravný
Transport Research Institute

Address: Velký Diel 3323, Žilina, 010 08
Telephone: +421 41 565 2819
Fax: +421 41 565 2883
E-mail: info@vud.sk
Website: www.vud.sk

Activity: advising on national transport policy making and implementation, conducting research in the fields of engineering and technology, operation, economy, legislation, management and organisation, informatics and automation, ecology, power system, transport infrastructure safety and quality, transport services and tourism management, transport policy, certification and testing in transport

Publication(s):
Horizonty dopravy (Transport Horizons) — **Language:** Slovak **Frequency:** quarterly **Content:** developments in the transport sector **Readership:** transport specialists, analysts, governmental institutions

Výrocná správa za rok (Annual Report) — **Language:** Slovak/English **Frequency:** annual **Content:** information about implemented transport projects and their impact **Readership:** economists, research specialists, analysts

Výskumný ústav ekonomiky polnohospodárstva a potravinárstva
Research Institute of Agricultural and Food Economics

Address: Trencianska 55, Bratislava 3, 821 80
Telephone: +421 2 5341 7428
Fax: +421 2 5341 6408
E-mail: vuz@vuz.sk
Website: www.vuepp.sk

Guides: publications can be obtained from the Institute's library
Activity: conducting research in the fields of agriculture and food (economic analysis, structural development)

Publication(s):
Ekonomický polnohospodársky úcet SR (Economical Overview of Slovak Agriculture) — **Language:** Slovak **Frequency:** irregular **Content:** economic aspect of the agricultural sector **Readership:** agricultural experts, economists, governmental institutions, research specialists, analysts

Slovenské polnohospodárstvo v rokoch 2001-2005 (Slovak Agriculture 2001-2005) — **Language:** Slovak **Frequency:** irregular **Content:** development of agricultural sector of the country **Readership:** agricultural experts, governmental and non-governmental organisations, research specialists, analysts

Vedecký casopis - Ekonomika polnohospodárstva (Economy in Agriculture - Magazine) — **Language:** Slovak **Frequency:** quarterly **Content:** agriculture and economy in the sector **Readership:** agricultural experts, farmers, research specialists, analysts

Slovenia

Agencija Republike Slovenije za kmetijske trge in razvoj podeželja (ARSKTRP)
Agency of the Republic of Slovenia for Agricultural Markets and Rural Development

Address: Dunajska 160, Ljubljana, 1000
Telephone: +386 1 580 7660
Fax: +386 1 478 9206
E-mail: aktrp@gov.si
Website: www.arsktrp.gov.si

Activity: technical implementation of agricultural policy measures; promoting the maintenance and development of Slovenian rural areas and strengthening of agricultural markets

Website(s) information:
Agencija Republike Slovenije za kmetijske trge in razvoj podeželja (ARSKTRP) (Agency of the Republic of Slovenia for Agricultural Markets and Rural Development) — url: www.arsktrp.gov.si **Description:** the site offers information about agricultural system **Coverage:** agriculture

Agencija za zavarovalni nadzor Slovenije
Insurance Supervision Agency of Slovenia

Address: Trg republike 3, Ljubljana, 1000
Telephone: +386 1 252 8600
Fax: +386 1 252 8630
E-mail: agencija@a-zn.si
Website: www.a-zn.si

Activity: supervising the country's insurance sector

Website(s) information:

Agencija za zavarovalni nadzor Slovenije *(Insurance Supervision Agency of Slovenia)* — **url:** www.a-zn.si **Description:** the site offers various information about the insurance industry **Coverage:** insurance

Publication(s):

Letno porocilo *(Annual Report)* — **Language:** Slovenian/English **Frequency:** annual **Content:** developments in the insurance sector and the achievements of the agency itself **Readership:** financial experts, research specialists, analysts

Porocilo o stanju na podrocju zavarovalništva *(Report on Business Performance of the Insurance Industry)* — **Language:** Slovenian/English **Frequency:** annual **Content:** developments in the insurance sector, structure of the insurance market and performance indicators (reports cover period from 2000 to 2004) **Readership:** financial experts, research specialists, analysts

Register zavarovalnih zastopniških in posredniških družb *(Directory of Insurance Agencies and Insurance Brokerage Companies)* — **Language:** Slovenian **Frequency:** irregular **Content:** insurance companies operating in the country **Readership:** businessmen, investors, research specialists

Banka Slovenije
The Bank of Slovenia

Address: Slovenska 35, Ljubljana, 1505
Telephone: +386 1 471 9000
Fax: +386 1 251 5516
E-mail: bsl@bsi.si
Website: www.bsi.si

Guides: all publications can be obtained in the library of the bank
Activity: the bank of issue and the central bank of the Republic of Slovenia

Website(s) information:

Banka Slovenije *(Bank of Slovenia)* — **url:** www.bsi.si **Description:** various statistical information about the bank's operation and national monetary and banking system available online **Coverage:** monetary and banking sector

Publication(s):

Bilten Banke Slovenije *(Monthly Bulletin)* — **Language:** Slovenian/English (summary only) **Frequency:** monthly **Content:** monetary and banking system **Readership:** financial experts, research specialists, analysts, academics, governmental institutions

Denarni pregled *(Monetary Review)* — **Language:** Slovenian/English (summary only) **Frequency:** monthly **Content:** monetary system information **Readership:** financial and monetary experts, research specialists, analysts, governmental institutions

Ekonomski indikatorji mednarodnega okolja *(Evaluation of Economic Trends)* — **Language:** Slovenian/English **Frequency:** monthly **Content:** real sector, public sector, inflation, balance of payments, international financial transactions, monetary overview and policy, exchange and interest rates **Readership:** economic and finanical experts, research specialists, analysts, investors, banks

Letno porocilo *(Annual Report)* — **Language:** Slovenian/English **Frequency:** annual **Content:** economic indicators, monetary policy, banking system, financial statements **Readership:** financial experts, research specilists, analysts, governmental organisations, investors

Porocilo o naložbah *(Investment Report)* — **Language:** Slovenian/English (summary only) **Frequency:** irregular **Content:** investments (reports cover the period from 1994 to 2004) **Readership:** financial experts, research specialists, analysts, investors, governmental institutions

Inštitut za ekonomska raziskovanja Slovenije
Slovenian Institute for Economic Research

Address: Kardeljeva plo?cad 17, Ljubljana, 1000
Telephone: +386 1 530 3800
Fax: +386 1 530 3874
E-mail: ier@ier.si
Website: www.ier.si

Guides: publications can be ordered through the library
Activity: conducting macroeconomic and microeconomic research and analysis

Website(s) information:

Inštitut za ekonomska raziskovanja Slovenije *(Slovenian Institute for Economic Research)* — **url:** www.ier.si **Description:** the site offers summaries of various publications; the catalogue of all publications can be accessed via the Co-operative Online Bibliographic System & Services (COBISS) at www.izum.si **Coverage:** economy

Publication(s):

An Analysis of the Slovenian Economy with a Quarterly Econometric Model — **Language:** English **Frequency:** irregular **Content:** overview of the economy **Readership:** analysts, research specialists, economists, governmental organisations, trade development bodies

Analysis of Slovenian Households (Income and Quality of Living) — **Language:** English **Frequency:** irregular **Content:** homes and households in the country, standards of living **Readership:** research specialists, analysts

Emerging Economic Geography in Slovenia — **Language:** English **Frequency:** irregular **Content:** economic growth by geographical areas **Readership:** research specialists, analysts, investors

Sector Performance in the Slovene Economy: Winners and Losers of the EU Integrations — **Language:** English **Frequency:** irregular **Content:** economy by sectors with a view to the country's integration in the EU **Readership:** economists, research specialists, analysts, investors

Javna agencija Republike Slovenije za energijo
Energy Agency of the Republic of Slovenia

Address: PO Box 1579, Strossmayerjeva ulica 30, Maribor, 2000
Telephone: +386 2 234 03 00
Fax: +386 2 234 03 20
E-mail: info@agen-rs.si
Website: www.agen-rs.si

Activity: performing regulatory, development and expert tasks in the energy area with the purpose of ensuring transparent and non-discriminatory operation of the energy markets

Website(s) information:

Javna agencija Republike Slovenije za energijo *(Energy Agency of the Republic of Slovenia)* — **url:** www.agen-rs.si **Description:** the site offers various information about the energy supply and market in the country **Coverage:** energy

Publication(s):

Letno porocilo Javne agencije RS za energijo *(Report on the Energy Sector in Slovenia)* — **Language:** Slovenian/English **Frequency:** annual **Content:** performance of the agency, energy sector and relevant legislation **Readership:** economists, research specialists, analysts, governmental organisations

Porocilo o morebitnem prevladujocem položaju na trgu z elektricno energijo, okoriščanju in zatiranju *(Report on Market Dominance, Predatory and Anti-competitive Behaviour)* — **Language:** Slovenian **Frequency:** annual **Content:** energy market data, companies operating in the market, energy production **Readership:** research specialists, analysts, governmental institutions

Porocilo o stanju na podrocju energetike *(Report on the Energy Sector)* — **Language:** Slovenian/English **Frequency:** annual **Content:** all available sources of energy in the country **Readership:** research specialists, analysts, governmental institutions

Javna agencija Republike Slovenije za podjetništvo in tuje investicije (JAPTI)
Public Agency of the Republic of Slovenia for Entrepreneurship and Foreign Investments

Address: Dunajska 156, Ljubljana, 1000
Telephone: +386 1 589 1870
Fax: +386 1 589 1877
E-mail: japti@japti.si
Website: www.japti.si

Activity: supporting development of entrepreneurship and promoting the country for foreign investments

Website(s) information:
Javna agencija Republike Slovenije za podjetništvo in tuje investicije (JAPTI)
(Public Agency of the Republic of Slovenia for Entrepreneurship and Foreign Investments) — **url:** www.japti.si **Description:** the site offers numerous information about small and medium entrepreneurship sector and economy **Coverage:** business sector and economy in general

Publication(s):
Business Offer from Slovenia — **Language:** Slovenian/English **Frequency:** irregular **Content:** list of companies with a short description of their business and products they offer to potential international partners **Readership:** businessmen, investors, analysts

Slovenian Country Profile — **Language:** English **Frequency:** irregular **Content:** general socio-economic indicators **Readership:** research specialists, analysts, governmental and non-governmental organisations

Javna agencija za raziskovalno dejavnost RS
Slovenian Research Agency

Address: Tivolska cesta 30, Ljubljana, 1000
Telephone: +386 1 400 5910
Fax: +386 1 400 5957
E-mail: info@arrs.si
Website: www.arrs.gov.si

Activity: selecting and financing research and infrastructure development programmes
managing research projects and other projects assigned to the Agency as part of the National Research and Development Programme and the annual plan of the ministry responsible for science; monitoring the performance, innovation, efficiency, quality, competitiveness and professionalism of funded research organisations; promoting international cooperation ensuring the acquisition of the additional funding for the National Research and Development Programme;
evaluating and analysing the implementation of research and development work; participating in national research and development policy making

Publication(s):
Letna porocilo o financiranju raziskovalne dejavnosti *(Annual Report on Research Programme Funding)* — **Language:** Slovenian **Frequency:** annually **Content:** research programmes in the country and funding **Readership:** research specialists, analysts

Kmetijski inštitut Slovenije
Agricultural Institute of Slovenia

Address: Hacquetova 17, Ljubljana, 1000
Telephone: +386 1 280 5262
Fax: +386 1 280 5255
E-mail: info@kis.si
Website: www.kis.si

Guides: all publications can be obtained in the Institute's library; in addition to numerous publications relating to agriculture, the library also contains a great number of local and international agricultural journals

Activity: conducting basic and applied research in the field of agriculture; supervising and verification of quality of agricultural products

Website(s) information:
Biotehniška fakulteta, Ljubljana *(Biotechnical Faculty, Ljubljana)* — **url:** www.agroweb.bf.uni-lj.si **Description:** the site offers numerous information starting from country's profile to detailed agricultural sector overview **Coverage:** agriculture

Kmetijski inštitut Slovenije *(Agricultural Institute of Slovenia)* — **url:** www.kis.si **Description:** the site offers information about the country's agriculture **Coverage:** agricultural production and sector in general

Mednarodni inštitut za turizem Slovenije
International Tourism Institute Slovenia

Address: Vošnjakova 5, Ljubljana, 1000
Telephone: +386 1 433 9440
Fax: +386 1 433 8659
E-mail: info@turizem-institut.si
Website: www.turizem-institut.si

Activity: research short-term forecasts, implementing educational and training seminars in the field of tourism, designing tourist development and marketing strategies, qualitative research regarding the development of high-quality tourist trademarks

Website(s) information:
Mednarodni inštitut za turizem Slovenije *(International Tourism Institute Slovenia)* — **url:** www.turizem-institut.si **Description:** the site offers general information about travel and tourism; publications can be ordered via the site **Coverage:** tourism

Ministrstvo za finance RS
Slovenian Ministry of Finance

Address: Županciceva 3, Ljubljana, 1502
Telephone: +386 1 369 5200
Fax: +386 1 369 6659
E-mail: gp.mf@gov.si
Website: www.gov.si/mf

Activity: developing and implementing the country's financial policy

Website(s) information:
Ministrstvo za finance RS *(Slovenian Ministry of Finance)* — **url:** www.gov.si/mf **Description:** offers numerous documents relating to the state budget and finance **Coverage:** economic and financial indicators

Publication(s):
Bilten javnih financ *(Public Finance Bulletin)* — **Language:** Slovenian **Frequency:** monthly **Content:** public finance **Readership:** financial experts, research specialists, analysts, governmental organisations

Konvergencni program *(Convergence Programme)* — **Language:** Slovenian/English **Frequency:** annual **Content:** economic outlook, general government balance and debt, analysis and comparison of the previous and current economic developments and budgetary projections (reports covering the period 2001-2005 available) **Readership:** research specialists, analysts, financial experts, governmental institutions

Porocilo o primanjkljaju in dolgu sektorja država *(Report on Deficit and Debts)* — **Language:** Slovenian/English **Frequency:** irregular **Content:** deficit and debt **Readership:** financial experts, governmental organisations, research specialists, analysts

Ministrstvo za gospodarstvo Republike Slovenije
Ministry of Economy of the Republic of Slovenia

Address: Kotnikova 5, Ljubljana, 1000
Telephone: +386 1 478 3311
Fax: +386 1 433 1031
E-mail: gp.mg@gov.si
Website: www.mg.gov.si

Activity: supporting further strengthening of international competitiveness of Slovenian companies and the adjustment of the structure of Slovenia's economy

Website(s) information:
Ministrstvo za gospodarstvo Republike Slovenije *(Ministry of Economy of the Republic of Slovenia)* — **url:** www.mg.gov.si **Description:** various statistical information about the economy in general and by sectors available online **Coverage:** economic indicators

Publication(s):
Analiza programa za pospeševanje razvoja podjetniškega sektora in konkurencnosti *(Analysis of the Entrepreneurship and Concurrency Development Programme)* — **Language:** Slovenian **Frequency:** irregular **Content:** analysis of various economic programmes by sectors based on the allocated funding **Readership:** economists, financial experts, research specialists, analysts

Energetska bilanca RS *(Report on Energy in the Republic of Slovenia)* — **Language:** Slovenian **Frequency:** annual **Content:** production, import and consumption of sources of energy **Readership:** research specialists, analysts

Ministrstvo za kmetijstvo, gozdarstvo in prehrano RS
Ministry of Agriculture, Forestry and Food of the Republic of Slovenia

Address: Dunajska 58, Ljubljana, 1000
Telephone: +386 1 478 9000
Fax: +386 1 478 9021
E-mail: gp.mkgp@gov.si
Website: www.mkgp.gov.si

Activity: developing and implementing agricultural and food policy

Website(s) information:
Ministrstvo za kmetijstvo, gozdarstvo in prehrano RS *(Ministry of Agriculture, Forestry and Food of the Republic of Slovenia)* — **url:** www.mkgp.gov.si **Description:** the site offers general information about agriculture, forestry and food **Coverage:** agriculture, forestry and food

Publication(s):
Reforma skupne kmetijske politike EU *(EU Agricultural Reform)* — **Language:** Slovenian **Frequency:** irregular **Content:** Slovenian agriculture with a view to the general reform of EU agriculture **Readership:** agricultural experts, governmental organisations, research specialists, analysts

Ministrstvo za okolje, prostor in energijo Republike Slovenije
Ministry of Environment, Spatial Planning and Energy of the Republic of Slovenia

Address: PO Box 653, Dunajska c. 48, Ljubljana, 1000
Telephone: +386 1 478 7300
Fax: +386 1 478 7427
E-mail: gp.mop@gov.si
Website: www.sigov.si/mop

Activity: ensuring a healthy living environment for all the inhabitants of Slovenia and encouraging and co-ordinating efforts towards a sustainable development base

Website(s) information:
Ministrstvo za okolje, prostor in energijo Republike Slovenije *(Ministry of Environment, Spatial Planning and Energy of the Republic of Slovenia)* — **url:** www.sigov.si/mop **Coverage:** environmental issues, water and energy resources

Publication(s):
Bilten Okolje in prostor *(Environment and Planning Information Bulletin)* — **Language:** Slovenian/English **Frequency:** monthly **Content:** general information on environment, spatial planning and natural resources **Readership:** environmental experts, research specialists, analysts, governmental organisations

Kazalci okolja *(Environmental Indicators)* — **Language:** Slovenian/English **Frequency:** annual **Content:** environmental indicators in respect of agriculture, air, climate change, energy, nature and land use, tourism and transport **Readership:** environmental experts, research specialists, analysts, governmental and non-governmental organisations

Vodni svet Slovenije *(Slovenian Waters)* — **Language:** Slovenian **Frequency:** irregular **Content:** water resources in Slovenia **Readership:** environmental experts, research specialists, analysts, governmental and non-governmental organisations **Edition:** 2004

Ministrstvo za promet Republike Slovenije
Ministry of Transport of the Republic of Slovenia

Address: Langusova 4, Ljubljana, 1000
Telephone: +386 1 478 8000
Fax: +386 1 478 8139
E-mail: gp.mzp@gov.si
Website: www.mzp.gov.si

Activity: performing tasks in the field of railway transport, air transport, maritime and inland waterway transport and road transport (with the exception of road transport safety control), as well as tasks in the field of transport infrastructure and cableway installations

Website(s) information:
Ministrstvo za promet Republike Slovenije *(Ministry of Transport of the Republic of Slovenia)* — **url:** www.mzp.gov.si **Description:** the site offers information about the road transport system **Coverage:** road transport

Ministrstvo za zdravje Republike Slovenije
Ministry of Health of the Republic of Slovenia

Address: Štefanova 5, Ljubljana, 1000
Telephone: +386 1 478 6001
Fax: +386 1 478 6058
E-mail: gp.mz@gov.si
Website: www.mz.gov.si

Activity: creating and implementing the country's health policy

Website(s) information:
Ministrstvo za zdravje Republike Slovenije *(Ministry of Health of the Republic of Slovenia)* — **url:** www.mz.gov.si **Description:** the site offers general information about the health care system of the country **Coverage:** health care

Statisticni urad Republike Slovenije
Statistical Office of the Republic of Slovenia

Address: Vožarski pot 12, Ljubljana, 1000
Telephone: +386 1 241 5104
Fax: +386 1 241 5344
E-mail: info.stat@gov.si
Website: www.stat.si

Activity: collecting and publishing statistical information

Website(s) information:
Statisticni urad Republike Slovenije *(Statistical Office of the Republic of Slovenia)* — **url:** www.sigov.si/zrs/ **Description:** various statistical information and reports available online **Coverage:** demography and social statistics, economy, environment and natural resources, general

Publication(s):
Mesecni statisticni pregled Republike Slovenije *(Monthly Statistical Review of the Republic of Slovenia)* — **Language:** Slovenian **Frequency:** monthly **Content:** monthly and quarterly updated statistics on main socio-economic indicators **Readership:** research specialists, analysts, governmental and non-governmental organisations

Pomembnejši statisticni podatki o Sloveniji *(Some Important Statistics on Slovenia)* — **Language:** Slovenian/English **Frequency:** monthly **Content:** designed for users who want to obtain the annual (for the last five years), quarterly (for the last eight quarters) or monthly (for the last twelve months) series of statistics regarding different fields; the data about a particular statistical field are selected according to the demand of the users (e.g. consumer price indices, gross and net earnings by activity, natural and migration changes) **Readership:** research specialists, analysts

Slovenija v številkah *(Slovenia in Figures)* — **Language:** Slovenian/English **Frequency:** annual **Content:** socio-economic indicators **Readership:** research specialists, analysts, governmental and non-governmental organisations, academics

Statisticni letopis *(Statistical Yearbook)* — **Language:** Slovenian/English **Frequency:** annual **Content:** socio-economic structure (covering a wide range of topics, such as population, labour market, agricultural and industrial sectors, national accounts, foreign trade, etc. The data provided cover both national and regional level and are compared against international trends) **Readership:** research specialists, analysts, governmental and non-governmental institutions, investors, businesses

Statisticni portret Slovenije v Evropski Uniji *(Statistical Portrait of Slovenia in the EU)* — **Language:** Slovenian/English **Frequency:** irregular **Content:** socio-economic overview of the country comparing to the EU **Readership:** research specialists, analysts, governmental and non-governmental organisations

Svet za varstvo okolja
The Council for Environmental Protection

Address: Slovenska cesta 56, Ljubljana, 1000
Telephone: +386 1 430 60 70
Fax: +386 1 430 60 75
E-mail: svo@svo-rs.si
Website: www.gov.si/svo

Activity: monitoring the quality and the protection of the environment in Slovenia

Website(s) information:
Svet za varstvo okolja (Council for Environmental Protection) — **url:** www.gov.si/svo
Description: the site offers various information about the environment in Slovenian and English **Coverage:** environmental data

Publication(s):
Okolje in uravnoteženi razvoj Slovenije (Environment and Sustainable Development of Slovenia) — **Language:** Slovenian **Frequency:** irregular **Content:** environmental issues in light of technological development of the country **Readership:** ecologists, research specialists, analysts, governmental institutions, non-governmental organisations

Promet in okolje (Traffic and Environment) — **Language:** Slovenian **Frequency:** irregular **Content:** traffic in Slovenia and its influence on the environment **Readership:** ecologists, research specialists, analysts, governmental institutions, non-governmental organisations

Turizem in okolje (Tourism and Environment) — **Language:** Slovenian **Frequency:** irregular **Content:** report on the impact of tourism on the environment **Readership:** ecologists, research specialists, analysts, governmental institutions, non-governmental organisations

Uprava Republike Slovenije za civilno letalstvo
Civil Aviation Authority of the Republic of Slovenia

Address: Kotnikova 19a, Ljubljana, 1000
Telephone: +386 1 473 4600
Fax: +386 1 431 6035
E-mail: urscl@caa-rs.si
Website: www.caa-rs.si

Activity: maintaining a safe environment for air traffic

Website(s) information:
Uprava Republike Slovenije za civilno letalstvo (Civil Aviation Authority of the Republic of Slovenia) — **url:** www.caa-rs.si **Description:** statistics on civil aviation **Coverage:** civil aviation

Urad Vlade za informiranje
Slovenian Government Public Information and Media Office

Address: Gregorciceva 25, Ljubljana, 1000
Telephone: +386 1 478 2600
Fax: +386 1 251 2312
Website: www.uvi.gov.si

Activity: providing assistance to foreign media in carrying out their work

Website(s) information:
Slovenia.si - Your Gateway to Information on Slovenia — **url:** www.slovenia.si **Description:** the site is intended to present Slovenia through various socio-economic statistical and other types of information **Coverage:** socio-economic

Urad Vlade za informiranje (Slovenian Government Public Information and Media Office) — **url:** www.uvi.gov.si **Description:** the site offers various statistical and other types of information about the country, developments and events **Coverage:** socio-economic indicators

Publication(s):
Facts about Slovenia — **Language:** English **Frequency:** irregular **Content:** short and concise 4-page fact-sheets (general information, international relations, tourism, agriculture and forestry, food, sports) **Readership:** research specialists, analysts, governmental and non-governmental organisations, investors, businessmen, tourists

Facts about Slovenia - Booklet — **Language:** English/German/Russian **Frequency:** irregular **Content:** introduction to the country's social and economic indicators (116 pages **Readership:** analysts, research specialists, governmental and non-governmental organisations, economists, businessmen

Sinfo (Sinfo - Promotional Monthly Magazine on Slovenia) — **Language:** English **Frequency:** monthly **Content:** news on politics, environment, culture, business and sports **Readership:** analysts, research specialists, governmental and non-governmental organisations, economists, businessmen

Slovenia in Brief — **Language:** English **Frequency:** irregular **Content:** culture, economy, education and science, geography, social and health care, history, holidays, media, country and people, sport, state, tourism and international relations **Readership:** research specialists, analysts, governmental and non-governmental organisations

Slovenia News — **Language:** English **Frequency:** weekly **Content:** weekly newsletter on politics, environment, culture, business, science, sports **Readership:** governmental and non-governmental organisations, research specialists, analysts, businessmen, investors, economists

Urad za makroekonomske analize in razvoj Slovenije
Slovenian Office for Macroeconomic Analysis and Development

Address: Gregorciceva 27, Ljubljana, 1000
Telephone: +386 1 478 1012
Fax: +386 1 478 1070
E-mail: gp.umar@gov.si
Website: www.sigov.si/zmar

Activity: monitoring, analysing and forecasting economic developments, participating in drawing up main strategic documents and formulating government policies, research and international co-operation

Website(s) information:
Urad za makroekonomske analize in razvoj Slovenije (Slovenian Office for Macroeconomic Analysis and Development) — **url:** www.sigov.si/zmar **Description:** the site offers various documents containing statistical information about the country's economy and developments **Coverage:** economy and development

Publication(s):
Ekonomsko ogledalo (Slovenian Economic Mirror) — **Language:** Slovenian/English **Frequency:** monthly **Content:** indicators of the country's economy by sectors and topics **Readership:** economists, research specialists, analysts, investors, governmental and non-governmental organisations

Pomladanska napoved gospodarskih gibanj (Spring Forecasts of Economic Trends) — **Language:** Slovenian/English **Frequency:** irregular **Content:** economic developments and trends **Readership:** research specialists, analysts, economists, investors, governmental organisations

Pomladansko porocilo (Autumn Report) — **Language:** Slovenian/English **Frequency:** annual **Content:** autumn economic forecast including the scenario of economic trends beyond 2007 **Readership:** research specialists, analysts, economists, governmental organisations

Slovenija: Porocilo o razvoju (Slovenia: Development Report) — **Language:** Slovenian/English **Frequency:** annual **Content:** economic development in association with EU and international agreements **Readership:** research specialists, analysts, governmental organisations

Vlada Republike Slovenije
Government of the Republic of Slovenia

Address: Slovenska cesta 29, Ljubljana, 1000
Telephone: +386 1 478 2600
Fax: +386 1 251 2312
Website: www.vlada.si

Activity: implementing state policy

Website(s) information:
Vlada Republike Slovenije, Urad za informiranje (Government of the Republic of Slovenia, Public Relations and Media Office) — **url:** www.uvi.si **Description:** the site offers general socio-economic information in a form of presentation available in English; the site also provides links to economic periodicals published by the Chamber of Commerce and other trade development bodies **Coverage:** culture, economy, education and science, geography, social security and health care, history, holidays, media, people, sport, state, tourism

World Bank Group Slovenia

Address: Ljubljana
Website: www.worldbank.org/si

Activity: helping developing countries and their people alleviate poverty, building the climate for investment, jobs and sustainable growth, investing in and empowering poor people to participate in development

Website(s) information:
World Bank Group Slovenia — **url:** www.worldbank.org/si **Description:** the site offers extensive statistical and other types of information about the country **Coverage:** economic indicators

Publication(s):
Gender Statistics — **Language:** English **Frequency:** irregular **Content:** gender indicators, basic demographic data, population dynamics, labour force structure, and education and health statistics **Readership:** research specialists, analysts, governmental institutions and non-governmental organisations

Governance Indicators — **Language:** English **Frequency:** irregular **Content:** indicators of the cost of doing business by identifying specific regulations that enhance or constrain the business investment, productivity, and growth **Readership:** businessmen, investors, research specialists, analysts, governmental institutions

Health Nutrition Population Statistics — **Language:** English **Frequency:** irregular **Content:** summary indicators for health status, health determinants and health finance **Readership:** health experts, research specialists, analysts, governmental institutions and non-governmental organisations

Information/ Communications/ Telecommunications — **Language:** English **Frequency:** irregular **Content:** ICT infrastructure and access, computers and the internet, ICT expenditures, and ICT business and government environment **Readership:** ICT specialists, research specialists, analysts

Slovenia Country Data Profile — **Language:** English **Frequency:** irregular **Content:** socio-economic profile of the country **Readership:** research specialists, analysts, governmental institutions

Spain

Banco de España
Bank of Spain

Address: Alcalá, 48, Madrid, 28014
Telephone: +34 91 338 50 00
Fax: +34 91 531 00 59
E-mail: be-estad@bde.es
Website: www.bde.es

Website(s) information:
Banco de España *(Bank of Spain)* — **url:** www.bde.es **Description:** provides access to statistical publications **Coverage:** data on various socio-economic and financial issues

Publication(s):
Boletín de Operaciones *(Operations Bulletin)* — **Language:** Spanish **Frequency:** daily **Content:** exchange rates; interbank deposits and issues of public debt

Boletín del Mercado de Deuda Pública *(Public Debt Market Bulletin)* — **Language:** Spanish **Frequency:** daily **Content:** data on government and public debt

Boletín Económico *(Economic Bulletin)* — **Language:** Spanish/English **Frequency:** monthly **Content:** data on the Spanish economy with economic indicators; financial regulation and non-financial corporations

Boletín Estadístico *(Statistical Bulletin)* — **Language:** Spanish/English **Frequency:** irregular **Content:** data on credit system; other financial systems; financial markets; general government agencies and balance of payments

Indicadores Económicos *(Economic Indicators)* — **Language:** Spanish/English **Content:** data on national demand and activity; prices; general government; labour market; balance of payments and financial variables

Informe de Estabilidad Financiera *(Financial Stability Report)* — **Language:** Spanish/English **Frequency:** half-yearly **Content:** financial data on credit and market risks

Tipos de Cambio *(Exchange Rates)* — **Language:** Spanish/English **Frequency:** daily/monthly **Content:** data on exchange rates on the Euro

Tipos de Interés *(Interest Rates)* — **Language:** Spanish/English **Frequency:** daily **Content:** data on Eurosystem monetary operations; interests rates; stock exchange and debt return indexes

Empresa Nacional Mercasa

Address: Paseo de la Habana 180, Madrid, 28036
Telephone: +34 91 350 0609
Fax: +34 91 350 4304
E-mail: mercasa@mercasa.es
Website: www.mercasa.es

Activity: promotes and operates the distribution network Mercasa, comprising 23 wholesale distribution units and logistic services for the food industry in Spain; provides statistics and publications

Website(s) information:
MERCASA — **url:** www.mercasa.es **Description:** provides access to publications **Coverage:** data on production, distribution and food consumption

Publication(s):
Alimentación en España *(Food in Spain)* — **Language:** Spanish **Frequency:** annual **Content:** statistics and reports on production; industry; distribution and food consumption

Distribución y Consumo *(Distribution and Consumption)* — **Language:** Spanish **Frequency:** bi-monthly **Content:** analysis and forecast, evolution of the consumption sectors: food, toiletries, furniture, DIY and textiles

Instituto Nacional de Estadística (INE)
National Institute of Statistics

Address: Paseo de la Castellana 183, Madrid, 28071
Telephone: +34 91 583 9100
Fax: +34 91 583 9158
E-mail: indice@ine.es
Website: www.ine.es

Guides: Catálogo de Publicaciones - INE (Publications Catalogue)
Activity: national statistic office

Website(s) information:
Instituto Nacional de Estadística (INE) *(National Institute of Statistics (INE))* — **url:** www.ine.es **Description:** provides free access to statistics, surveys and reports **Coverage:** statistics on main socio-economic indicators such as geography and population; labour market and wages; prices; health and education services; agriculture; transport and communications; tourism; and national accounts

Publication(s):
Anuario Estadístico de España *(Statistical Yearbook of Spain)* — **Language:** Spanish **Frequency:** annual **Content:** annual socio-economic portrait of Spain, covering demography; agriculture; forestry; fishing; industry; production; transport and communications; retailing and distribution; external trade; balance of payments; employment and tourism

Boletín Mensual de Estadística *(Monthly Statistical Bulletin)* — **Language:** Spanish **Frequency:** monthly **Content:** data on a range of socio-economic indicators

Cifras de Poblacion *(Population Figures)* — **Language:** Spanish **Content:** population figures of every municipality grouped by provinces and summaries for autonomous communities; provinces; capitals of provinces and islands

Educacion y Cultura *(Education and Culture)* — **Language:** Spanish **Content:** data on public and private educational institutions; libraries and universities

Encuesta Continua de Presupuestos Familiares *(Household Budget Survey)* — **Language:** Spanish **Frequency:** annual **Content:** data on household expenditure by various socio-demographic characteristics

Encuesta de Servicios *(Services Survey)* — **Language:** Spanish **Frequency:** annual **Content:** data on activities relating to tourism; transport; information; society; real estate and rent; corporate services; recreational, cultural and sports activities and personal services

Encuesta Industrial de Empresas *(Industrial Survey of Companies)* — **Language:** Spanish **Content:** statistics on the industrial sector

Encuesta Industrial de Productos *(Industrial Survey of Products)* — **Language:** Spanish **Frequency:** annual **Content:** data on the value of principal Spanish industrial products

Estadística de Hipotecas (Mortgage Statistics) — **Language:** Spanish **Frequency:** monthly **Content:** statistics of mortgaged goods and total quantity of loans

Indicadores de Ciencia y Tecnología (Indicators of Science and Technology) — **Language:** Spanish **Content:** information on technological innovation and high technology products

Indicadores Sociales (Social Statistics) — **Language:** Spanish **Frequency:** annual **Content:** data on the aging population; pensions; poverty; science and technology

Medio Ambiente (Environment) — **Language:** Spanish **Content:** statistics on water; waste; recycling and treatment

Salud y Servicios Sanitarios (Health and Health Care Services) — **Language:** Spanish **Content:** data on the national health; hospital indicators; causes of death; surveys on disabilities, impairments and health status

Spain in Figures — **Language:** English/Spanish **Frequency:** annual **Content:** data on the demographic, social and economic environment of Spain

Ministerio de Agricultura, Pesca y Alimentación (MAPA)
Ministry of Agriculture, Fisheries and Food

Address: Paseo de la Infanta Isabel 1, Madrid, 28014
Telephone: +34 91 347 55 51
Fax: +34 91 347 57 22
E-mail: mllopisj@mapya.es
Website: www.mapa.es

Activity: publishes statistics on the agriculture and fishing industry

Website(s) information:
Ministerio de Agricultura, Pesca y Alimentación (Ministry of Agriculture, Fisheries and Food) — **url:** www.mapa.es **Description:** provides access to a wide range of information on agriculture, farming, rural development, fishing and food and information on EU legislation and the Common Agricultural Policy **Coverage:** data on the Spanish agricultural, farming and fishing industry, including: annual production; exports and imports; number of livestock and meat production; organic farming; agricultural area and production; socio-economic structure of rural areas; food consumption patterns and food trends

Publication(s):
Anuario de Estadística Agroalimentaria (Agricultural and Food Statistics Yearbook) — **Language:** Spanish **Frequency:** annual **Content:** general agricultural and food statistics

Boletín de Estadística (Bulletin of Statistics) — **Language:** Spanish **Frequency:** monthly **Content:** information on agricultural and cattle sector; production and agrarian economy

Estadística láctea (Lacteal statistics) — **Language:** Spanish **Frequency:** monthly/annual **Content:** statistics on the dairy industry

Estadísticas de Ganadería (Cattle Statistics) — **Language:** Spanish **Content:** data on cattle production and population

Fishing in Spain — **Language:** English **Content:** information about fisheries, fishing fleets and fishing trade

Indicadores de precios y salarios agrarios (Agrarian Price and Salary Indicators) — **Language:** Spanish **Frequency:** monthly **Content:** agrarian salaries and prices paid by the farmers

Informe Semanal de Coyuntura (Weekly Status Report) — **Language:** Spanish **Frequency:** weekly **Content:** information on national food prices including wines; rice; meat; cereals and olive oil

Maquinaria agrícola (Agricultural Machinery) — **Language:** Spanish **Frequency:** monthly **Content:** index of agricultural machinery

Precios de la tierra (Land Prices) — **Language:** Spanish **Frequency:** annual **Content:** growth of average prices of agricultural land

Ministerio de Economía
Ministry of Economy

Address: Subsecretaría de Economía, Alcalá, 5 - 2ª Planta, Madrid, 28071
Telephone: +34 91 595 8000
Fax: +34 91 595 84 77
E-mail: informacion.alcala@meh.es
Website: www.mineco.es

Activity: government ministry

Website(s) information:
Ministerio de Economía (Ministry of Economy) — **url:** www.mineco.es **Description:** provides access to statistical publications **Coverage:** statistics on major socio-economic indicators, with monthly updated analysis on GDP evolution, inflation rates, industrial production indices, consumer price indices and external trade

Publication(s):
Estadísticas Territoriales (Territorial Funding Statistics) — **Language:** Spanish **Frequency:** annual **Content:** data on budgets and liquidation of budgets

Fondos Europeos (European Funds) — **Language:** Spanish **Frequency:** irregular **Content:** data on European funds

Impuestos (Taxes) — **Language:** Spanish **Frequency:** annual **Content:** data on taxes collection and information about VAT; economic results

Indicadores Económicos (Economic Indicators) — **Frequency:** monthly **Content:** data on the Spanish economy, macro-economic forecasts and principal economic indicators

Juegos y Apuestas del Estado (State Lotteries and Gaming) — **Language:** Spanish **Frequency:** weekly **Content:** data on sales of state lotteries and gaming

Presupuesto y Cuentas Públicas (Budget and Public Expenditure) — **Language:** Spanish **Frequency:** annual **Content:** statistical information about the budgets

Tabaco (Tobacco) — **Language:** Spanish **Frequency:** annual **Content:** figures and information about the tobacco market

Tesoro (Treasury) — **Language:** Spanish/English **Frequency:** monthly **Content:** statistics about central government outstanding debt and financing

Ministerio de Educación y Ciencia
Ministry of Education and Science

Address: , Alcalá 36, Madrid, 28071
Telephone: +34 91 701 80 00
E-mail: informacion@mec.es
Website: www.mec.es

Website(s) information:
Ministerio de Educación, Cultura y Deporte (Ministry of Education, Culture and Sport) — **url:** www.mec.es **Description:** provides access to publications catalogue, press release archive and statistical data on education **Coverage:** statistical indicators on education in Spain, including primary and secondary education, university education and government expenditure on education. Data available for 1991-2001

Publication(s):
Estadística Universitaria (University Statistics) — **Language:** Spanish **Frequency:** irregular **Content:** information and figures of the university system; university surveys and reports

Estadísticas Deportivas (Sports Statistics) — **Frequency:** irregular **Content:** statistics of federated sport; public sports installations and doping controls

Estadísticas e Indicadores de Ciencia y Tecnología (Science and Technology Statistics and Indicators) — **Frequency:** annual **Content:** statistics on budgetary public credits; science and technology indicators

Estadísticas Educativas (Educational Statistics) — **Language:** Spanish **Content:** statistics on public expenditure in education and scholarships

Ministerio de Fomento
Ministry of Economic and Industrial Development

Address: Paseo de la Castellana 67, Madrid, 28071
Telephone: +34 91 597 87 87
Fax: +34 91 597 85 73
E-mail: atencionciudadano@fomento.es; portal@administracion.es
Website: www.mfom.es

Website(s) information:

Ministerio de Fomento *(Ministry of Economic and Industrial Development)* — **url:** www.mfom.es **Description:** provides access to press release archive, publication catalogue and statistical information on population, housing and information on budget and investment, grouped by geographical area **Coverage:** socio-economic and housing indicators, with data on population trends, population by age groups, number of households grouped by number of occupants, number of occupants per household, population density, number and distribution of buildings by type of owner and type of building, and dwellings by number of rooms and liveable area

Publication(s):

Anuario Estadístico *(Statistical Yearbook)* — **Language:** Spanish **Frequency:** annual **Content:** statistical information at national; regional and provincial level on liquidation of the ministry budget, transport and communications

Boletín Estadístico *(Statistical Bulletin)* — **Language:** Spanish **Frequency:** monthly **Content:** information referring to construction and housing; transport; communications and ministerial management

Cifras *(Figures)* — **Language:** Spanish **Frequency:** annual **Content:** data on construction and housing; transport; communications and economic management of the department

Estructura Coyuntural de la Construcción *(Construction Structure)* — **Language:** Spanish **Frequency:** annual **Content:** key information and indicators of the construction sector

Indice de Precios de la Vivienda *(Index of Housing Prices)* — **Language:** Spanish **Frequency:** irregular **Content:** statistics of housing prices

Sweden

Konjunkturinstitutet

National Institute of Economic Research

Address: PO Box 3116, Kungsgatan 12-14, 6th floor, Stockholm, 10362
Telephone: +46 8 453 5900
Fax: +46 8 453 5980
E-mail: ki@konj.se
Website: www.konj.se

Guides: reports are published in their entirety on the website and some are available in print
Activity: performs analyses and forecasts of the Swedish and international economy and conducts related research

Website(s) information:

Konjunkturinstitutet *(National Institute of Economic Research)* — **url:** www.konj.se **Description:** detailed information about the institute and its publications. Latest economic forecast; business tendency survey; main economic indicators; forecast comparisons; press releases **Coverage:** economic analyses and forecasts covers wages; supply and demand; public finance; profits, cost of output and prices; public consumption; foreign trade; international economy. Business tendency survey includes data about manufacturing, durables and non-durables goods trade, and construction

Publication(s):

Hushållens Inköpsplaner *(Household Consumer Survey)* — **Language:** Swedish/English **Frequency:** monthly **Content:** data refers to household expectations about the Swedish economy, unemployment and personal finances

Konjunkturbarometern *(Business Tendency Survey)* — **Language:** Swedish/English **Frequency:** monthly **Content:** performs analyses and forecasts on the outcomes and expectations of firms in manufacturing; construction; retail trade; and the private service sector

Konjunkturläget *(Swedish Economy)* — **Language:** Swedish/English **Frequency:** quarterly **Content:** report provides forecasts and analyses on the Swedish and international economy; financial markets, household and government consumption; foreign trade; labour market; and public finances

Lönebildningsrapport *(Wage Formation)* — **Language:** Swedish/English **Frequency:** annual **Content:** analyses the labour market; wage forming and negotiations

Regeringskansliet-Finansdepartementet

Ministry of Finance

Address: Drottninggatan 21, Stockholm, 10333
Telephone: +46 8 405 10 00
Fax: +46 8 21 73 86
E-mail: registrator@finance.ministry.se
Website: finans.regeringen.se

Activity: work to fulfil the economic political goals of the government

Website(s) information:

Regeringskansliet-Finansdepartementet *(Ministry of Finance)* — **url:** finans.regeringen.se **Description:** updates and releases on monetary, budget and macro-economic issues **Coverage:** the Swedish Money Report provides statistics on: GDP, central government debt, expenditure areas, public sector expenditure (available online)

Publication(s):

Internationella Kasinon i Sverige *(International Casinos in Sweden)* — **Language:** Swedish **Frequency:** irregular **Content:** analyses the turnover and the development in international casino activity in Sweden

Sociala broar - Att möta globaliseringens utmaningar *(Social Bridges - Meeting the Challenges of Globalisation)* — **Language:** Swedish/English **Frequency:** irregular **Content:** analyses the economic trends of globalisation and the suggests policies that can reinforce the strength of the global market of goods, services and investments

Svenska vindkraftspolitik *(Swedish Wind Power Politics)* — **Language:** Swedish **Frequency:** irregular **Content:** rapport analyses socio-economical and energy political trends in relation to wind power

Sveriges handlingsplan för sysselsättning *(Sweden's Action Plan for Employment)* — **Language:** Swedish/English **Frequency:** irregular **Content:** analysis and forecasts of employment and unemployment trends; actions to promote employment growth in Sweden; analysis of the labour market in the EU

Statistiska Centralbyrån

Statistics Sweden

Address: SCB Box 24 300, Karlavägen 100, Stockholm, 10451
Telephone: +46 8 5069 4000
Fax: +46 8 661 5261
E-mail: swestat@scb.se
Website: www.scb.se

Guides: catalogue available on website
Activity: produces, supports and coordinates the Swedish system for official statistics

Website(s) information:

Statistiska Centralbyrån *(Statistics Sweden)* — **url:** www.scb.se **Description:** offers information on products and services provided by Statistics Sweden. Includes major publications; statistical databases; latest press releases; and various online statistics, both in Swedish and English **Coverage:** data can be accessed by downloading publications, or by accessing the databases (where registration is required when requesting more than 1000 data cells). National socio-economic statistics on population; housing; labour market; trade; national accounts; education etc are presented in annual publications. In addition, miscellaneous data exists for citizen political and social influence; juridical system; social insurance and service; transport etc

Publication(s):

Arbetskraftsundersökningen *(Labour Force Survey)* — **Language:** Swedish/English **Frequency:** quarterly **Content:** data refers to employment and unemployment rates by gender, age, main activity, sector and by birth country. Aspects of the data are available in English and is also available monthly and annually

Befolkningsstatistik *(Population Statistics)* — **Language:** Swedish/English **Frequency:** annual **Content:** data refers to the population by gender, age, civil status, country of birth and residency in different Swedish regions. The publication also includes data on the changes in population by births, deaths, immigration, migration, marriages, divorces, registered partnership, residency transfers and adoptions. Aspects of the data are available in English

Bostads- och Byggnadsstatistisk Årsbok *(Housing and Building Statistical Yearbook)* — **Language:** Swedish/English **Frequency:** annual **Content:** data refers to housing, building, housing stock, heating and energy usage

Finansiella Företag (Financial Enterprises) — **Language:** Swedish/English **Frequency:** annual **Content:** data refers to industry turnover and performance of banks and other financial institutes and investments enterprises. The data does not include insurance companies for which separate data can be found on the website. Some aspects of the data are available in English

Hushållens utgifter (Household Budget Survey) — **Language:** Swedish/English **Frequency:** annual **Content:** data refers to expenditure on goods and services in households where at least one of the members is aged 0-79. The data also contains expenditure by gender. Aspects of the data are available in English

Jordbruksekonomiska undersökningen (Farm Economic Survey) — **Language:** Swedish/English **Frequency:** annual **Content:** data refers to agricultural income and expenditure, by type of production and size. Aspects of the data are available in English

Konsumentprisindex (Consumer Price Index) — **Language:** Swedish/English **Frequency:** monthly **Content:** data refers to the consumption of the entire population of the country. Prices used in the index are regular prices paid by the public. Aspects of the data are available in English

Miljöskyddskostnader i Industrin (Environmental Protection Expenditure in Industry) — **Language:** Swedish/English **Frequency:** annual **Content:** data refers to investments and expenditure in environmental protection by types of costs, environmental domains, industry activities, and numbers of employees

På tal om Kvinnor och Män (Men and Women in Sweden) — **Language:** Swedish/English **Frequency:** annual **Content:** data refers to education, health, employment, time use, child care, crime and political influence in relation to gender

Privatpersoners Användning av Datorer och Internet (Use of Computers and the Internet by the Private Sector) — **Language:** Swedish/English **Frequency:** annual **Content:** data refers to how often and in what way households are using computers and the internet. It also contains information about IT literacy and access to IT equipment

Statistisk årsbok för Sverige (Statistical Yearbook of Sweden) — **Language:** Swedish/English **Frequency:** annual **Content:** compilation of socio-economic statistics. Aspects of the data are available in English

Sveriges Ekonomi - Statistiskt Perspektiv (Swedish Economy - Statistical Perspective) — **Language:** Swedish/English **Frequency:** quarterly **Content:** data refers to social and economic indicators with emphasis on economic changes and the consistency and inconsistency between different statistical outcomes

Utbildningsstatistisk Årsbok (Statistical Yearbook for Education) — **Language:** Swedish/English **Frequency:** annual **Content:** data refers to all levels of education, including Swedish education abroad, adult education for people with learning difficulties and Swedish for immigrants, by age and gender

Utrikeshandel med varor (Foreign Trade in Goods) — **Language:** Swedish/English **Frequency:** monthly **Content:** data is reported in tables with monthly figures (quarterly data for volume indexes) and annual figures. Collected data on goods, countries and the combination of goods/countries; selected data available in English

Sveriges Riksbank
Swedish Central Bank

Address: Brunkebergstorg 11, Stockholm, 10337
Telephone: +46 8 787 0000
Fax: +46 8 210 531
E-mail: registratorn@riksbank.se or info@riksbank.se
Website: www.riksbank.se

Guides: Riksbank publications information online
Activity: to maintain price stability, with low stable inflation, promote a safe and efficient payment system, where the consumer price index, CPI, aimed to be maintained at around 2 per cent

Website(s) information:
Sveriges Riksbank (Swedish Central Bank) — **url:** www.riksbank.se **Description:** detailed information about the bank, its policies and its publications. Weekly statistical report covering balance of payments; interest rates; exchange rates **Coverage:** provides downloadable statistics on interest rates; currencies; national, private and public finances etc. in the real; fiscal; financial; and external sector. The website also provides links to relevant statistics at other organisations

Publication(s):
Årsredovisning (Annual Report) —

Direktinvesteringar (Direct Investment) — **Language:** Swedish/English **Frequency:** annual **Content:** data refers to direct investments in and outside Sweden, by country, business activity and geographical zones

Finansiell stabilitet Rapport (Financial Stability Report) — **Language:** Swedish/English **Frequency:** 2 per annum **Content:** contains the Riksbank's analyses and assessments of the stability of the financial system in Sweden, as well as articles discussing particular fields or the Riksbank's policy on financial stability

Inflationsrapport (Inflation Report) — **Language:** Swedish/English **Frequency:** annual **Content:** the report aims to provide background material for monetary policy decisions and spread knowledge about the Riksbank's assessments. It also contains a three year forecast and a risk assessment

Penning- och Oligationsmarknadens Omsättningen (Money and Bond Markets' Turnover) — **Language:** Swedish/English **Frequency:** monthly **Content:** data refers to turnover in the Swedish government and mortgage securities market, by bonds, consumer, broker and market

Penning- och valutapolitik (Economic Review) — **Language:** Swedish/English **Frequency:** quarterly **Content:** report contains articles on topics relevant to the Riksbank's field of operation, as well as a monetary and exchange rate calendar, tables and diagrams depicting statistics concerning central banks and financial markets balances of payment

Svenska Finansmarknaden (Swedish Financial Market) — **Language:** Swedish/English **Frequency:** annual **Content:** the report contains a description of the financial market in Sweden and presents statistics on the financial sector's different components, and aims to explain how these markets, institutions and systems work and what their main functions are in the economy

Tillgångar och Skulder (Assets and Liabilities) —

Switzerland

Banque Nationale Suisse
Swiss National Bank

Address: Börsenstraße 15, Zurich, 8022
Telephone: +41 631 3111
Fax: +41 631 3911
E-mail: snb@snb.ch
Website: www.snb.ch

Guides: list of publications obtainable online; publications are on price stability, foreign investments, monetary policy of Switzerland
Activity: marshals the money and currency policy in Switzerland; it's primary duty is to guarantee price stability with regard to the economic cycle

Website(s) information:
Banque Nationale Suisse (Swiss National Bank) — **url:** www.snb.ch **Description:** contains economic information on monetary policy concepts, press releases, federal bond issues and debt register claims, current interest rates and exchange rates **Coverage:** various economic, banking and monetary statistics

Publication(s):
Bankenstatistisches Monatsheft (Monthly Booklet on Bank Statistics) — **Language:** German/French/English **Frequency:** monthly **Content:** bank statistics; includes data on credit volume, dividends, trust transactions, etc.

Die Banken in der Schweiz (Banks in Switzerland) — **Language:** German/French **Frequency:** annual **Content:** commented statistics on the development of the banking sector in Switzerland

Statistisches Monatsheft — **Language:** German/French/English **Frequency:** monthly **Content:** key data on Swiss and international economies **Edition:** 81

Bundesamt für Landwirtschaft (BLW)
Swiss Federal Office for Agriculture

Address: Mattenhofstraße 5, Bern, 3003
Telephone: +41 31 322 2511
Fax: +41 31 322 2634
E-mail: info@blw.admin.ch
Website: www.blw.admin.ch

Guides: periodically publishes market reports

Activity: responsible for legislation in the field of agriculture as well as various aspects of policy concerning trade in agricultural products and rural development

Website(s) information:
Bundesamt für Landwirtschaft *(Swiss Federal Office for Agriculture)* — **url:** www.blw.admin.ch **Coverage:** market reports (regarding prices, turnover, etc) on fruit and vegetables, meat, milk, cereals and eggs, retailers and markets; forecasts of the agricultural sector; imports and exports

Publication(s):
Agrarbeircht *(Agricultural Report)* — **Language:** German/French/English/Italian **Frequency:** annual **Content:** annual survey of the agricultural market in Switzerland; includes general state of agriculture, policy measures and international aspects

---

Bundesamt für Statistik/Office Fédéral de la Statistique
Swiss Federal Statistical Office

Address: Information Service, 10, Espace de l'Europe, Neuchâtel, 2010
Telephone: +41 32 713 6011
Fax: +41 32 713 6012
E-mail: info@bfs.admin.ch
Website: www.statistik.admin.ch

Guides: the website provides a databank of publications
Activity: provides statistics on population and people, the environment, the economy, prices, industry and services, tourism, transport

Website(s) information:
Bundesamt für Statistik/Office Fédéral de la Statistique *(Statistics Switzerland)* — **url:** www.statistik.admin.ch **Description:** general information on the Institutes' main products and services, including latest press releases and news and series of socio-economic online statistics. Also includes news on events, admission, official notices and press releases **Coverage:** statistical data is provided under different sections, covering socio-economic indicators at both national and regional (Cantons) levels. "Key Data for the Whole of Switzerland" provides annual figures for: national consumer price index; index of producer and import prices; industry - production and sales; retail trade; labour market; and GDP growth rates. "Economic and Financial Data for Switzerland" covers the real sector; fiscal and financial sector; external sector; and population

Publication(s):
Arbeitsmarkt Indikatoren *(Employment Market Indicators)* — **Language:** French/German **Frequency:** annual **Content:** labour market structure and unemployment rates statistics

Demos. Informationen aus der Demografie *(Demos. Information of Demography)* — **Language:** German **Frequency:** quarterly **Content:** population statistics; concentrates on one issue related to demography

Landesindex der Konsumentenpreise/L'indice suisse des prix à la consommation *(Consumer Price Index)* — **Language:** German/French **Frequency:** monthly **Content:** average prices of products and services, analyses the prices of essential products and determines the state of the Swiss economy

Mémento statistique de la Suisse/Taschenstatistik der Schweiz/Prontuario statistico della Svizzera/Survista statistica da la Svizra *(Statistical Data on Switzerland 2006)* — **Language:** German/French/Italian/English **Frequency:** annual **Content:** statistics on every stage in a Swiss national's life, from birth rates to education, careers and pensions

Schweizer Tourismus in Zahlen *(Swiss Tourism in Figures)* — **Language:** German/French **Frequency:** annual **Content:** figures on Swiss tourism such as the number of people travelling to and from Switzerland, preferred destinations

Statistisches Jahrbuch der Schweiz/Annuaire Statistique de la Suisse *(Swiss Statistical Yearbook)* — **Language:** French/German **Frequency:** annual **Content:** data covering demographic, economic, social, cultural and political aspects of Swiss life; sections in Italian and English

Eidgenössische Finanzdepartement (EFV)
Federal Department of Finance

Address: Bundesgasse 3, Bern, 3003
Telephone: +41 31 322 21 11
Fax: +41 31 323 3852
E-mail: info@gs-efd.admin.ch
Website: www.efd.admin.ch

Guides: publishes information on financial policy, taxes, economy and currency, management, excise and customs
Activity: the EFV plans and decides on the allocation of resources within the State regarding finances, construction, human resources, and IT

Website(s) information:
Eidg. Finanzverwaltung (EFV) *(Federal Department of Finance)* — **url:** www.efd.admin.ch **Description:** news, press releases and reports concerning all aspects of governmental finances such as budget and public expenditure; information available in English, French, Italian, and German **Coverage:** statistics regarding Swiss public financing; includes an international comparison

Publication(s):
Öffentliche Finanzen *(Public Finance)* — **Language:** German/French **Frequency:** annual **Content:** overview of the financial policy of the government, as well as balances of regional entities

---

Staatssekretariat für Wirtschaft/Secrétariat d'Etat á l'économie
State Secretariat for Economic Affairs (SECO)

Address: Effingerstrasse 1, Bern, 3003
Telephone: +41 31 322 56 56
Fax: +41 31 322 56 00
E-mail: biblio@seco.admin.ch
Website: www.seco-admin.ch

Guides: publications on various economic indicators, can be obtained it German, French, English, and Italian
Activity: official organisation for economic policy issues; object of the organisation is to create a common standard for economic policy issues for the purpose of promoting the development of the general economy; prevents and fights unemployment

Website(s) information:
Staatssekretariat für Wirtschaft/Secrétariat d'Etat á l'économie *(State Secretariat for Economic Affairs)* — **url:** www.seco-admin.ch **Coverage:** data on economic development and forecasts, quarterly estimated GDP, figures on unemployment, consumer moods, economic cycle policy instruments, and economic growth

Publication(s):
Die Lage auf dem Arbeitsmarkt *(The State of the Labour Market)* — **Language:** German/French/Italian **Frequency:** monthly **Content:** reports and statistics on the development of the Swiss labour market

Die Volkswirtschaft *(The Economy)* — **Language:** German/French **Frequency:** 10 per annum **Content:** reports and statistical data covering specific issues related to the Swiss economy **Edition:** 78

Prognosen für den Schweizer Tourismus *(Prognoses of Swiss Tourism)* — **Language:** German/French **Frequency:** biannually **Content:** forecasts regarding the tourism industry in Switzerland as well as reports on industry developments such as the number of Swiss nationals and foreign nationals in comparison, the number of beds occupied in hotels, etc

---

Turkey

Basin Yayin ve Enformasyon Genel Mudurlugu
Directorate General of Press and Information

Address: 203 Ataturk Bulvari, Kavaklidere, Ankara, 06688
Telephone: +90 312 455 9000
Fax: +90 312 426 6617
E-mail: newspot@byegm.gov.tr, webadmin@byegm.gov.tr
Website: www.byegm.gov.tr

Activity: contribute to the promotion policy of the state and to the strategies implemented by the government

Website(s) information:

Turk Basini *(Turkish Press)* — **url:**
www.byegm.gov.tr/turkbasini/turkbasini/internetbasini.htm
Coverage: directory of all media types (paper, online, radio and television)

Publication(s):

NewSpot — **Language:** English/French/German **Frequency:** 2 per month
Content: political and economic news

Turkey — **Language:** Turkish/English/French/German/Russian **Frequency:** irregular **Content:** country and people; geographical regions; history; state order, constitution, legal system; developments in the economic sector; macroeconomic developments; work life and social policies; education and science; life in society; cultural life

Baskanlik Dis Ticaret Mustesarligi
Under secretariat of Prime Ministry for Foreign Trade

Address: Inönü Bulvari No 36, Emek, Ankara, 06510
Telephone: +90 312 204 7500
Fax: +90 312 212 3784
E-mail: www@foreigntrade.gov.tr
Website: www.foreigntrade.gov.tr

Website(s) information:

Undersecretariat of Foreign Trade — **url:** www.foreigntrade.gov.tr **Description:** information on the Turkish economy and foreign trade matters. Access to database of Turkish exporters, searchable by exporter's name, product type, or country of destination. Provides various statistics on Turkey's economy and trade **Coverage:** statistics on macro-economic indicators; public sector; monetary developments; and balance of payments. Statistics on foreign trade are included, providing data on US$ value exports and imports by month for each year, as well as ranking of countries of origin and destination

Publication(s):

Export Regime of Turkey — **Language:** English **Content:** objectives, recent developments/strategy

Foreign Investment in Turkey — **Language:** English **Content:** reports; foreign investment legislation; foreign investment statistics; investment in Turkey and improving the investment climate

Free Trade Zones in Turkey — **Language:** English **Content:** Turkish free trade zones (statistics, bulletins, incentives, international membership)

Trade Policies and Measures — **Language:** English **Content:** imports, exports, technical regulations and standardisation for Foreign Trade

Turkey - European Union Relations — **Language:** English **Content:** Turkey-EU customs union; recent developments in Turkey-EU relations; Turkey-EU trade statistics; Turkey-EU financial cooperation

Turkish Economy — **Language:** English **Content:** economic and social indicators of Turkey; foreign trade (1990-2004); foreign trade statistics

Ministry of Foreign Affairs

Address: Disisleri Bakanligi, Balgat, Ankara, 06100
Telephone: +90 312 292 1000
E-mail: webmaster@mfa.gov.tr
Website: www.mfa.gov.tr

Activity: conducts and further promotes international political, economic and cultural relations in the bilateral and multilateral context as well as to contribute to peace, stability and prosperity

Website(s) information:

Ministry of Foreign Affairs — **url:** www.mfa.gov.tr **Description:** general historic and socio-geographic portrait of Turkey, accompanied by an overview of the present state of the economy and latest developments in the national business and financial climate. Includes latest annual data on foreign trade and other selected economic indicators

Publication(s):

Perceptions - Journal of International Affairs — **Language:** English **Frequency:** quarterly **Content:** review of international affairs with Turkey and beyond

T.C. Baskanlik Hazine Mustesarligi
Ministry of Treasury of Turkey

Address: Inönü Bulvari No:36, Emek, Ankara, 06510
Telephone: +90 312 204 6000
Fax: +90 312 212 8764
E-mail: bilgiedinme@hazine.gov.tr
Website: www.hazine.gov.tr

Activity: government treasury body

Website(s) information:

T.C. Baskanlik Hazine Mustesarligi *(Ministry of the Treasury)* — **url:** www.hazine.gov.tr **Coverage:** statistical publications, monthly bulletins and annual reports on foreign direct investment, economic development, insurance

Publication(s):

Dogrudan Yabanci Yatirim Verileri Bülteni *(Foreign Direct Investment Information Bulletin)* — **Language:** English/Turkish **Frequency:** monthly **Content:** number of companies with foreign captial; breakdown of companies with foreign capital by type of establishment, by sector, and by amount of equity

Economic Indicators Bulletin — **Language:** Turkish/English **Frequency:** monthly **Content:** production, investment, employment, productivity and wages; expectations; foreign trade and balance of payments; public finance; prices and financial markets

Hazine Istatistikleri 1980-2003 *(Treasury Statistics 1980-2003)* — **Language:** Turkish/English **Content:** results of main economic policy implementations

Türkiye Cumhuriyet Merkez Bankasi
Central Bank of the Republic of Turkey

Address: Istiklal Caddesi 10 Ulus, Ankara, 06100
Telephone: +90 312 310 3646
Fax: +90 312 310 7434
E-mail: info@tcmb.gov.tr or iletisimbilgi@tcmb.gov.tr
Website: www.tcmb.gov.tr

Activity: carry out open market operations; take necessary measures in order to protect the domestic and international value of Turkish Lira and to establish the exchange rate policy in determining the parity of Turkish Lira against gold and foreign currencies

Website(s) information:

Central Bank of the Republic of Turkey — **url:** www.tcmb.gov.tr **Description:** all main national economic and financial indicators. Also includes weekly, monthly and quarterly bulletins, publications, central bank data, link to other banks in Turkey, and information about the departments within the bank **Coverage:** statistics and data exists on the following subjects: exchange rates, Fixed Bank deposits, financial markets and other types of banking data in a time series format

Publication(s):

Annual Report — **Language:** English **Frequency:** annual **Content:** main macro economic indicators; monetary policy and markets, financial markets, central bank balance sheet

Balance of Payments Report — **Language:** English **Frequency:** quarterly **Content:** external economic developments; goods exports and imports; trade and current account; capital movements

Banks' Loans Tendency Survey — **Language:** English **Frequency:** quarterly **Content:** monitor changes which have already been observed in the supply of loans, as well as those foreseen in the future; identify the factors that are believed to be effective on these changes, and demand for credit

Business Tendency Survey and Real Sector Confidence Index — **Language:** English **Content:** results of a survey conducted with private sector enterprises that are ranked among the "First 500 Industrial Enterprises of Turkey" and the "Next 500 Major Industrial Enterprises of Turkey" lists prepared by the Istanbul Industrial Chamber. BTS aims to find out the senior managers' tendencies and expectations

CBRT Quarterly Bulletin — **Language:** Turkish/English **Frequency:** quarterly **Content:** statistics on economic and business trends in Turkey with data for the latest quarter and some previous quarters **Edition:** 2006

Financial Stability Report — **Language:** Turkish/English **Frequency:** annual **Content:** developments related to banking, public finance, households, corporate and the external sector are discussed. Additionally, the implications of these developments on the financial system and the resilience of the system against shocks are assessed.

Independent Audit Report for Year — **Language:** Turkish/English **Frequency:** annual **Content:** financial report

Türkiye Istatistik Kurumu
State Institute of Statistics

Address: Necatibey Caddesi No 114, Bakanliklar, Ankara, 06100
Telephone: +90 312 410 0410
Fax: +90 312 425 3387
E-mail: bilgi@tuik.gov.tr
Website: www.tuik.gov.tr

Activity: state statistics committee

Website(s) information:
Latest Figures — **url:** www.die.gov.tr/english/SONIST/sonist.html **Description:** statistical information database **Coverage:** statistics covering major industry, economy, and social indicators

SDDS - TURKEY, National Summary Data Page — **url:** www.tuik.gov.tr/english/turcat/turcat.html **Coverage:** economic and financial data

SIS World Wide Web Service — **url:** www.turkstat.gov.tr **Coverage:** recent releases of statistical information on major industrial/social/economic sector

Publication(s):
Agricultural Structure; Production, Price and Value — **Language:** English/Turkish **Frequency:** annual **Content:** includes statistical data on field crops, fruits, vegetables, agricultural equipment and machinery, number of livestock, animal products, poultry, apiculture, sericulture, prices and the marketing ratios of agricultural products

Fishery Statistics — **Language:** English/Turkish **Frequency:** annually **Content:** includes Turkey and region information on fisheries. Breeding information on culture and freshwater fish are included on the basis of provinces **Edition:** 2003

Foreign Trade Statistics — **Language:** Turkish/English **Frequency:** annual **Content:** detailed statistics on Turkish foreign trade activities: imports and exports by commodity, sector and country of origin and destination (accompanied by Excel spreadsheets) **Edition:** 2006

Labour Force — **Language:** Turkish/English **Content:** data represented in excel spreadsheet **Edition:** 2006

Statistical Indicators — **Content:** provides historical perspective on a number of key statistical indicators, including population, demography, health, education, culture, social security and public assistance, agriculture, mining, energy and power, manufacturing, construction, transportation, communication, tourism, domestic and foreign trade, prices and indexes, money and banking, finance, and national accounts. Data from 1923

Statistical Yearbook of Turkey — **Language:** Turkish/English **Frequency:** annual **Content:** annual geographical, socio-economic, and financial statistical portrait of Turkey **Edition:** 2005

Ukraine

National Bank of the Ukraine
Address: 9 Institutska Street, Kyiv, 01601
Telephone: +380 44 253 0180
Fax: +380 44 230 2033/253 7750
E-mail: info@bank.gov.ua
Website: www.bank.gov.ua

Activity: determine and pursue monetary policy in accordance with the general principles developed by the Council of the National Bank of Ukraine

Website(s) information:
National Bank of Ukraine — **url:** www.bank.gov.ua **Description:** detailed economic and financial statistics including: balance sheet of National Bank of Ukraine; interest rates; credit and deposit statistics; GDP; industrial production; consumer goods production; retail turnover; employment; wages; consumer expenditure; imports and exports. Free publications include: Bulletin and Visnyk of the National Bank of Ukraine **Coverage:** statistical data on a free basis is available on main economic and financial indicators; official exchange rate statistics; monetary policy; monetary financial institutions balance sheet and monetary statistics; monetary financial institutions interest rates on loans and deposits statistics; money, currencies and financial market statistics; balance of payments and foreign reserves statistics

Publication(s):
Annual Report of the National Bank of Ukraine — **Language:** English/Russian/Ukrainian **Frequency:** annual **Content:** financial economic indicators for the year

Balance of Payments — **Language:** English/Russian/Ukrainian **Frequency:** quarterly **Content:** general current balance of payments, current account, capital and financial transactions account; balance of payments and trends in Ukrainian balance of payments, trade structure of export and import of goods

Monthly Bulletin of the National Bank of Ukraine — **Language:** English/Russian/Ukrainian **Frequency:** monthly **Content:** general economic, analytical and statistical data; banking and development of banking system (money supply, crediting of economy, refinancing of commercial banks, interest rates, foreign exchange market, government securities market)

National Institute for Strategic Studies
Address: 7A Pirogova Street, Kyiv, 010010
Telephone: +380 44 234 5007
Fax: +380 44 235 2060
Website: www.niss.gov.ua

Activity: divisions of the institution: political strategies; humanitarian policy; social relations and civic community; economic and social strategy; military policy; strategic prognostication; regional policy; sociological studies

Publication(s):
Competitive Economy of the Ukraine under the Conditions of Globalization — **Language:** Ukrainian **Content:** competition and national economy of the Ukraine **Edition:** 2005

Regions of Ukraine: Problem & Priorities of Social & Economic Development — **Language:** Ukrainian **Frequency:** irregular **Content:** contemporary state and trends of economic and social development in the Ukraine

Strategic Panorama — **Language:** Ukrainian/Russian **Frequency:** quarterly **Content:** articles on national security and defence, problems of the national and global safety, regional-economic policy, humanitarian problems, information -communication technologies

State Committee of Statistics of Ukraine
Address: 3 Shota Rustavely street, Kiev, 01023
Telephone: +380 44 287 2433
Fax: +380 44 235 3739
E-mail: office@ukrstat.gov.ua
Website: www.ukrstat.gov.ua

Activity: government statistics committee

Website(s) information:
State Committee of Statistics of Ukraine — **url:** www.ukrstat.gov.ua **Description:** Government statistics department **Coverage:** consolidated statistical analysis, National accounts, finance statistics, industrial statistics, investment and construction statistics, agriculture and environment statistics, transport and communications statistics, Population statistics, Science and innovation statistics

Publication(s):
Agriculture of Ukraine — **Language:** Ukrainian/English **Frequency:** regular **Content:** presents key data on the social and economic development of agriculture in Ukraine and its regions from 1990 up to the current year. It also includes data on share of agriculture in the total country's output, number of employees at agricultural enterprises, value of fixed assets, amounts of domestic and foreign investment. Statistics on resource capacities of agriculture, amounts of output, sales and consumption of agricultural products

Capital Investment in Ukraine — **Language:** Ukrainian/English **Content:** contains information about the implemented capital investment and investment into fixed capital (capital formation). Data are given by region, economic activity, technological structure and sources for financing

Consumer Price Indices — **Language:** Ukrainian/English **Frequency:** annual **Content:** contains information about producer price indices for industrial output, construction and assembly operations; indices of tariffs for communication services for enterprises, departments, organizations; indices of tariffs for shipment of cargo by rail and pipeline, international comparisons, methodological explanations

Household Expenditures and Resources in Ukraine — **Language:** Ukrainian/English **Frequency:** annual **Content:** publication provides analysis of annual data from household living condition survey. It reports information about subsistence level of the population, its characteristics by structure of income, expenditures and resources; consumption of foodstuffs and durables and services by households depending on level of well-being; composition of household by number of children and employees, by sex and age of the head of household, etc

Industry of Ukraine — **Language:** Ukrainian/Russian **Frequency:** annual **Content:** publication provides data that characterize the development of industrial production over the last five years; it has information about structural changes, investment, labour and prices in industry, innovation activity of enterprises, and international comparisons. For most indicators, information is broken down by basic economic activity and regions of Ukraine

Investment of Foreign Trade Activities — **Language:** Ukrainian/English **Frequency:** annual **Content:** contains information about the direct and portfolio investment that had been invested into the Ukraine's economy and abroad, by country, type of economic activity, region, type of currency for the last ten years

Key Financial Indicators of Enterprises of Different Forms of Ownership, by Selected Type of Activity — **Language:** Ukrainian/English **Frequency:** quarterly **Content:** the bulletin gives statistical indicators that characterize financial and economic activity of enterprises. Indicators are presented by type of ownership, region and type of economic activity (960 pages)

National Accounts of Ukraine — **Language:** Ukrainian/English **Frequency:** annual **Content:** contains final data on volumes and changes in GDP, basic accounts of the country's economic activity and Input/Output Table which give the general characteristics of the processes that took place in the country's economy

Population of Ukraine — **Language:** Ukrainian/English **Frequency:** annual **Content:** provides population statistics by region, urban and rural areas; sex and age composition of the population, its distribution within the country's area. It also shows data on births by sex and age of mother; deaths by cause of death; marriages by length of marriage and divorces by duration of marriage; annual migration and international comparisons

Statistical Yearbook of the Ukraine — **Language:** Ukrainian/English **Frequency:** annual **Content:** reports wide range of data on social and economic situation in Ukraine. The publication is compiled by the following sections: prices and tariffs, business register, industry, agriculture, hunting, forestry and fishery, investment and construction, transport and communications, external economic activity, wholesale and retail trade, restaurants, services, science, innovations and information, population, employment, population income, expenditure and housing conditions, education, health care, social assi

Statistics of the Ukraine — **Language:** Ukrainian **Frequency:** quarterly **Content:** analysis and statistical publication of issues of social-economic development of the country

Ukraine in Figures — **Language:** Ukrainian/English **Frequency:** annual **Content:** provides a wide range of statistics highlighting social and economic situation in Ukraine for the past year with comparative data. Statistics are compiled according to types of economic or industrial activity, some indicators are presented by region. The sections of the publication cover such topics as national accounts, prices, Unified State Register of Enterprises and Organizations of Ukraine (Business register), industry, agriculture, hunting, forestry and fishery, investment and construction activity,

United Kingdom

Bank of England
Address: Threadneedle Street, London, EC2R 8AH
Telephone: +44 20 7601 4878
Fax: +44 20 7601 5460
E-mail: enquiries@bankofengland.co.uk
Website: www.bankofengland.co.uk

Guides: online catalogue of past and current publications
Activity: determines the monetary policy of the UK, with the core purposes of maintaining monetary and financial stability

Website(s) information:
Bank of England — **url:** www.bankofengland.co.uk **Description:** complete document or a summary of the contents of all the publications of the bank. Searchable by subject (general; monetary analyses and policy; supervision; markets; small business; European Matters) or by format (regular and ad-hoc reports; speeches; fact sheets; press releases; Monetary Policy committee minutes; working papers; consultative papers; CCBS Training Handbooks). Recent highlights such as current inflation reports are also available. Financial markets information is accessible in under the following headings: Open Market Operations, Foreign Exchange Market, Payment and Settlement Systems, Relevant Material, Relevant News Releases, Registrars Brokerage Service, Registrars Main Page, Bank of England Legislation **Coverage:** the statistical section of the web site contains statistical series and supporting material compiled and produced by the Bank of England, consisting mainly of the Bank of England's monetary and financial statistics. Also includes the Bank of England/NOP Inflation Attitudes Survey

Publication(s):
Financial Stability Report — **Language:** English **Frequency:** 2 per annum **Content:** shocks to the UK financial system - assessing how macroeconomic and financial developments over the past six months have affected risks to the UK financial system; structure of the UK financial system - looks at changes in the structure of the system over this period; prospects for the UK financial system - provides the Bank's assessment of key vulnerabilities in the light of those developments;
mitigating risks to the UK financial system - links this risk assessment to the mitigating actions that might be undertaken **Readership:** professionals and managers in the financial sector, government officials

Inflation Report — **Language:** English **Frequency:** quarterly **Content:** sets out the detailed economic analysis and inflation projections on which the Bank's Monetary Policy Committee bases its interest rate decisions, and presents an assessment of the prospects for UK inflation over the following two years; contains analysis of money and asset prices; analysis of demand; analysis of output and supply; analysis of costs and prices; assessment of the medium-term inflation prospects and risks

Monetary and Financial Statistics — **Language:** English **Frequency:** monthly **Content:** statistical publication which contains data on money and lending; monetary financial institutions' balance sheets; further analyses of deposits and lending; external business of banks operating in the UK, public sector debt and the money markets (including gilt repo and stock lending); sterling commercial paper, other debt securities, capital issues; financial derivatives, interest and exchange rates and occasional background articles.

Quarterly Bulletin — **Language:** English **Frequency:** quarterly **Content:** provides regular commentary on market developments and UK monetary policy operations; contains research and analysis and reports on a wide range of topical economic and financial issues, both domestic and international **Readership:** profesionals and executives in the financial services sector

Department for Environment, Food & Rural Affairs (Defra)
Address: Nobel House, 17 Smith Square, London, SW1P 3JR
Telephone: +44 8459 335 577
Fax: +44 20 7238 2188
E-mail: helpline@defra.gsi.goc.uk
Website: www.defra.gov.uk

Guides: online catalogue
Activity: works for sustainable development in the UK; develops environmental projects and programmes and works for the implementation of sustainable energy, agricultural and food policies

Website(s) information:

Department for Environment, Food and Rural Affairs — **url:** statistics.defra.gov.uk/esg **Description:** all statistical releases of DEFRA are made available on this site concerning the status and developments in the agricultural sector **Coverage:** broad statistical coverage including: farming and food; environmental matters and latest development (greenhouse); beverages; fisheries; development indicators; external trade; rural statistics; price indices of agricultural production; agricultural census data

Publication(s):

UK Agricultural Statistics — **Language:** English **Frequency:** annual **Content:** a statistical publication which contains data on key indicators in the agricultural sector such as production, export, import, use of fertilizers, share of organic production, price indices, regional data

Food Standards Agency

Address: Aviation House, 125 Kingsway, London, WC2B 6NH
Telephone: +44 20 7276 8000
E-mail: paul.boyle@foodstandards.gsi.gov.uk
Website: www.foodstandards.gov.uk

Guides: list of available publications is available online
Activity: sets and monitors food quality standards in the UK

Website(s) information:

Food Standards Agency — **url:** www.foodstandards.gov.uk **Description:** offers press releases, news and regulations information on the food industry. It also provides summaries of market and scientific research projects **Coverage:** statistics on number and type of inspections carried out and infringements established and results of the inspections searchable by region

Publication(s):

Annual Consumer Survey — **Language:** English **Frequency:** annual **Content:** annual investigation into consumer attitudes to food, covering issues such as safety and hygiene, nutrition, diet and shopping

HM Treasury

Address: 1 Horse Guards Road, London, SW1A 2HQ
Telephone: +44 20 7270 4558
Fax: +44 20 7270 4861
E-mail: public.enquiries@hm-treasury.gsi.gov.uk
Website: www.hm-treasury.gov.uk

Guides: available online, free of charge; publications can be found under the relevant headings of different policy areas
Activity: responsible for formulating and implementing the Government's financial and economic policy

Website(s) information:

HM Treasury — **url:** www.hm-treasury.gov.uk **Description:** monthly economic forecasts for the UK economy; debt management reports; report on the overall economic strategy; recent economic developments report; economic indicators; archive of previous economic indicators; latest press releases **Coverage:** data covers a wide range of macroeconomic statistics and the results of various policies, undertaken by the Treasury

Publication(s):

Annual Budget — **Language:** English **Frequency:** annual **Content:** contains an economic and fiscal strategy report and the financial statement and budget report; surveys the macroeconomic situation in the country, trends in productivity, employment and job creation

National Assembly of Wales

Address: Cardiff Bay, Cardiff, CF99 1NA
Telephone: +44 29 2089 8200
E-mail: assembly.info@wales.gsi.gov.uk
Website: www.wales.gov.uk

Guides: full list available online; publications are available in both English and Welsh, and sometimes in minority languages
Activity: allocates funds made available to it by the UK treasury; develops projects and approves legislation that benefit the population of Wales

Website(s) information:

National Assembly of Wales — **url:** www.wales.gov.uk **Description:** some of the publications released by the Assembly can be downloaded directly from the webpage; publications cover a wide range of socio-economic issues and provide comprehensive statistical and legal data on the region **Coverage:** varies in different publications

Publication(s):

Annual Population Survey — **Language:** English **Frequency:** annual **Content:** surveys labour markets in Wales and presents statistical data on the characteristics of the labour force

Index of Production and Index of Construction for Wales — **Language:** English/Welsh **Frequency:** quarterly **Content:** statistical information about production in key industry sectors, monitoring of production figures, construction indicators

Welsh Exports — **Language:** English/Welsh **Frequency:** quarterly **Content:** statistical data covering the volume and value of Welsh and UK exports; exports by destination and product type, top export destinations

Welsh Transport Statistics — **Language:** English **Frequency:** annual **Content:** covers a wide range of statistical data, regarding road length and quality, licensing and vehicle ownership, road safety, road traffic, sea, air and river transport, motoring offences

Office for National Statistics (ONS)

Address: Cardiff Road, Newport, NP10 8XG
Telephone: +44 845 601 3034
Fax: +44 1633 652 747
E-mail: info@statistics.gov.uk
Website: www.statistics.gov.uk

Guides: publications are sorted by subject area and can be viewed online free of charge
Activity: the government department that provides UK statistical and registration services. Provides a wide range of economic and social statistics for the use of the government and public, business statistics for corporate users

Website(s) information:

Statistics — **url:** www.statistics.gov.uk **Description:** The datasets cover most macro-economic time series data compiled by the Office for National Statistics, other government departments and the Bank of England. Monthly datasets include: index of production; financial statistics; producer price indices; retail prices indices; retail sales; labour market; monthly digest of statistics; employment and earnings; economic trends; consumer price indices; retail sales indices. Quarterly datasets include: mergers and acquisitions; UK output, income and expenditure; trade by industry; GDP; consumer trends; economic accounts; public sector accounts. Annual datasets include: balance of payments; UK national accounts; economic trends annual supplement **Coverage:** access to statistical surveys carried out by the Office and grouped in categories covering economics, population, agriculture, consumer trends, etc.

Publication(s):

Agriculture in the United Kingdom — **Language:** English **Frequency:** annual **Content:** general overview of the national agricultural sector. Includes agricultural statistics; information on the impact of agriculture and the food industry in the national economy; structure of the sector and its present economic conditions; output prices and input costs; commodities; incomes; rent; land prices; etc

Consumer Price Indices — **Language:** English **Frequency:** monthly **Content:** information on price indices, including historical series and international indices, as well as average prices of selected products

Consumer Trends — **Language:** English **Frequency:** quarterly **Content:** consumers' expenditure data with description and analysis of underlying factors affecting household consumption trends

Economic Trends — **Language:** English **Frequency:** monthly **Content:** latest statistics on major economic indicators. Includes data for the last five years for national economic accounts; prices, labour market, output and demand, etc. Data is often accompanied by a commentary and analysis of recent developments in the regional, national and international economy

Family Spending — **Language:** English **Frequency:** annual **Content:** analysis of household expenditure and income in the UK. Includes data and information on expenditure on goods and services by household income, structure and location

Key Population and Vital Statistics — **Language:** English **Frequency:** annual **Content:** statistical data on population and demographic trends by health areas in the United Kingdom. Includes data on population estimates; birth and death rates; and internal movements

Labour Market Trends — **Language:** English **Frequency:** annual **Content:** monthly analysis of the UK labour market, providing statistics and information on employment and unemployment rates; training opportunities; vacancies; etc

Living in Britain: Results from the General Household Survey — **Language:** English **Frequency:** annual **Content:** annual statistics compiled from the General Household Survey. The survey covers the following topics; demography, household accommodation, consumer durables, employment, pensions, education, health, smoking, drinking, income

Monthly Digest of Statistics — **Language:** English **Frequency:** monthly **Content:** monthly and quarterly statistics on different social, economic and financial topics

Motor Vehicle Production and New Registrations — **Language:** English **Frequency:** monthly **Content:** monthly statistical data on national vehicle production and registrations, and export production of commercial vehicles by vehicle type and cylinder capacity size

National Food Survey — **Language:** English **Frequency:** annual **Content:** annual report covering household food expenditure, consumption and nutrient intakes. Contains data for the preceding ten years

Overseas Trade Statistics — **Language:** English **Frequency:** annual **Content:** series of five different titles providing data on Great Britain's international trade activities. Data covered includes figures on the UK trade with the EU, with non-EU countries, and the whole world

Social Trends — **Language:** English **Frequency:** annual **Content:** compilation of data and information collected and produced by different official organisations and bodies, providing a general portrait of the present British society and lifestyles in the United Kingdom

Transport Statistics Great Britain — **Language:** English **Frequency:** annual **Content:** annual statistics on the UK's transports' sector, covering road, rail and air travel

Travel Trends - A Report on the International Passenger Survey — **Language:** English **Frequency:** annual **Content:** information and data on patterns of travel to and from the United Kingdom - number of travellers; transports used; accommodation and expenditure; etc

United Kingdom in Figures — **Language:** English **Frequency:** annual **Content:** general overview of a wide range of social and economic topics in the UK

United Kingdom National Accounts: The Blue Book — **Language:** English **Frequency:** annual **Content:** contains estimates of the domestic and national product, income and expenditure. Includes figures for the last 18 years

OSPAR Commission for the Protection of the Marine Environment of the North-East Atlantic

Address: New Court, 48 Carey Street, London, WC2A 2JQ
Telephone: +44 20 7430 5200
Fax: +44 20 7430 5225
E-mail: secretariat@ospar.org
Website: www.ospar.org

Guides: online catalogue with publications covering biological diversity and ecosystems, hazardous substances, offshore oil and gas industry, radioactive substances, monitoring and assessment, available to download

Activity: protection of the marine environment of the North-East Atlantic

Index

Y